Tax Formula for Corporate Taxpayers

Income *(from whatever source)*	$xxx,xxx
Less: Exclusions from gross income	– xx,xxx
Gross Income	$xxx,xxx
Less: Deductions	– xx,xxx
Taxable Income	$xxx,xxx
Applicable tax rates	× xx%
Gross Tax	$ xx,xxx
Less: Tax credits and prepayments	– x,xxx
Tax Due *(or refund)*	$ xx,xxx

SOUTH-WESTERN
FEDERAL TAXATION

CORPORATIONS, PARTNERSHIPS, ESTATES & TRUSTS 2012 EDITION

GENERAL EDITORS

William H. Hoffman, Jr.
J.D., Ph.D., CPA

William A. Raabe
Ph.D., CPA

James E. Smith
Ph.D., CPA

David M. Maloney
Ph.D., CPA

CONTRIBUTING AUTHORS

James H. Boyd
Ph.D., CPA
Arizona State University

D. Larry Crumbley
Ph.D., CPA
Louisiana State University

Jon S. Davis
Ph.D., CPA
University of Wisconsin–Madison

Steven C. Dilley
J.D., Ph.D., CPA
Michigan State University

William H. Hoffman, Jr.
J.D., Ph.D., CPA
University of Houston

David M. Maloney
Ph.D., CPA
University of Virginia

Gary A. McGill
Ph.D., CPA
University of Florida

Mark B. Persellin
Ph.D., CPA, CFP®
St. Mary's University

William A. Raabe
Ph.D., CPA
The Ohio State University

Boyd C. Randall
J.D., Ph.D.
Brigham Young University

Debra L. Sanders
Ph.D., CPA
Washington State University, Vancouver

W. Eugene Seago
J.D., Ph.D., CPA
Virginia Polytechnic
Institute and State University

James E. Smith
Ph.D., CPA
College of William and Mary

Australia • Brazil • Japan • Korea • Mexico • Singapore • Spain • United Kingdom • United States

South-Western Federal Taxation: Corporations, Partnerships, Estates & Trusts, 2012 Edition

William H. Hoffman, Jr., William A. Raabe, James E. Smith, David M. Maloney

Vice President of Editorial, Business: Jack W. Calhoun

Editor-in-Chief: Rob Dewey

Senior Acquisitions Editor: Mike Schenk

Senior Developmental Editor: Craig Avery

Editorial Assistant: Ann Mazzaro

Marketing Manager: Natalie Livingston

Senior Content Project Manager: Colleen A. Farmer

Media Editor: Chris Valentine

Senior Frontlist Buyer, Manufacturing: Doug Wilke

Marketing Communications Manager: Libby Shipp

Production Service: Cadmus Communications

Senior Art Director: Michelle Kunkler

Internal and Cover Designer: Chris Miller

Cover Image: ©iolo72/Shutterstock

Rights Acquisitions Specialist – Text: John Hill

Student Edition ISBN 13: 978-1-111-22169-0
Student Edition ISBN 10: 1-111-22169-3
Student Edition with CD ISBN 13: 978-1-111-22172-0
Student Edition with CD ISBN 10: 1-111-22172-3

ISSN: 0270-5265
2012 Annual Edition

South-Western
5191 Natorp Boulevard
Mason, OH 45040
USA

Cengage Learning products are represented in Canada by Nelson Education, Ltd.

For your course and learning solutions, visit **www.cengage.com**
Purchase any of our products at your local college store or at our preferred online store **www.cengagebrain.com**

Printed in the United States of America
1 2 3 4 5 6 7 15 14 13 12 11

Preface

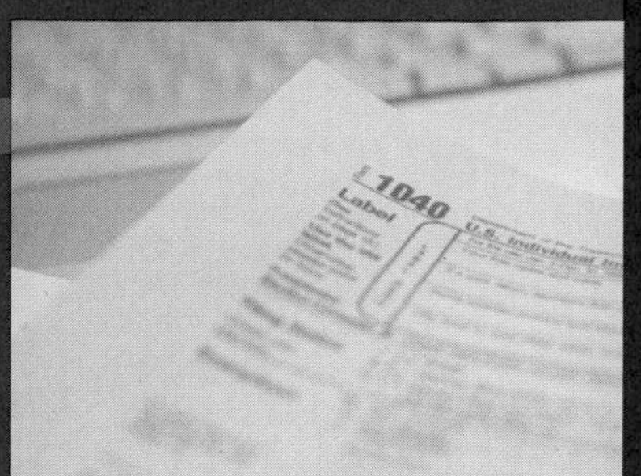

To The Student

THE LEADERSHIP YOU TRUST.
THE INNOVATION YOU EXPECT.
THE SERVICE YOU DESERVE.

South-Western Federal Taxation is the most trusted and best-selling series in college taxation. We are focused exclusively on providing the most useful, comprehensive, and up-to-date tax texts, online study aids, tax preparation tools, and printed study guides to help you succeed in your tax courses and beyond.

Studying Is Easier with the Right Tools. ***Corporations, Partnerships, Estates & Trusts, 2012 Edition*** provides a dynamic learning experience inside and outside of the classroom. Built with resources and tools that students have identified as the most important, our complete study system provides options for the way you learn.

Here's how ***Corporations, Partnerships, Estates & Trusts, 2012 Edition*** is designed to help you learn!

PRACTICAL TAX SCENARIOS AT THE START OF EVERY CHAPTER...

The Big Picture: Tax Solutions for the Real World. Taxation comes alive at the start of each chapter. **The Big Picture** is a glimpse into the lives, families, careers, and tax situations of typical filers. Each **Big Picture** case asks you to apply what you will learn in the upcoming chapter to develop the best tax solution to these real-life dilemmas.

THE BIG PICTURE **Tax Solutions for the Real World**

A CORPORATION CONTEMPLATES A MERGER

Alexander Corporation has had a long-term association with one of its suppliers, Hamilton Corporation. In the past, Hamilton was a highly profitable operation and was even able to make loans to Alexander to cover short-term working capital needs. Recently, however, Hamilton has been consistently late in meeting current obligations. Alexander has had to grant extensions of up to nine months on Hamilton's payables. Several vendors have even ceased doing business with Hamilton. Nevertheless, Alexander feels confident that Hamilton's fortunes will improve. If this financial turnaround occurs, Alexander will continue dealing with Hamilton in the same manner as in the past.

But Alexander's tax advisers have suggested another alternative. They say that Alexander should consider acquiring Hamilton in a merger or other takeover that qualifies as a tax-favored reorganization (see Chapter 7), so as to avoid any immediate Federal income tax liability. Hamilton's downturn has left it with sizable net operating losses that would be attractive to Alexander for use on future joint tax returns. Since Hamilton's name, reputation, and location still have value in the marketplace, it could continue as a separate division or subsidiary of Alexander. Furthermore, the takeover would give other businesses greater assurance of Hamilton's financial viability. Lastly, there could be tax advantages to Alexander, the new parent of a two-corporation group.

Evaluate this and other viable alternatives for Alexander taking into account various possible outcomes (e.g., the success or failure of Hamilton's business). **Read the chapter and formulate your response.**

. . . BIG PICTURE EXAMPLES TO HELP YOU FOLLOW CLIENTS THROUGH THE CHAPTER . . .

Among the many examples in every chapter are an average of almost four examples per chapter based on the **Big Picture** tax situation that opens the text. That means less confusion understanding new topics, a more consistent application of data for you to learn, and practical tax stories that span the whole chapter.

EXAMPLE 18
THE BIG PICTURE

Return to the facts of *The Big Picture* on p. 8-2. Assume that Alexander acquired all of the outstanding Hamilton stock on January 1, 2010, for $1 million. The parties immediately elected to file consolidated Federal income tax returns. Hamilton reported a 2010 taxable loss of $100,000, but it generated $40,000 taxable income in 2011 and $65,000 in 2012. Hamilton paid a $10,000 dividend to Alexander in mid-2012.

Alexander holds the following stock bases in Hamilton on the last day of each of the indicated tax years.

2010	$900,000	2011	$940,000	2012	$995,000 ∎

. . .AND PRACTICAL CONCLUSIONS TO THOSE TAX SCENARIOS

Refocus on the Big Picture. Returning to the client situations introduced in the chapter-opening **Big Picture**, these end-of-chapter summaries and tax planning scenarios apply concepts and topics from the chapter in a reasonable and professional solution. A **What If?** section then demonstrates how tax treatments might change as a result of potential changes in the filer's situation—making **What If?** a valuable consideration in tax planning.

What If? adds realistic options that will spur you to think about how changes in taxpayers' situations affect how they would file their returns.

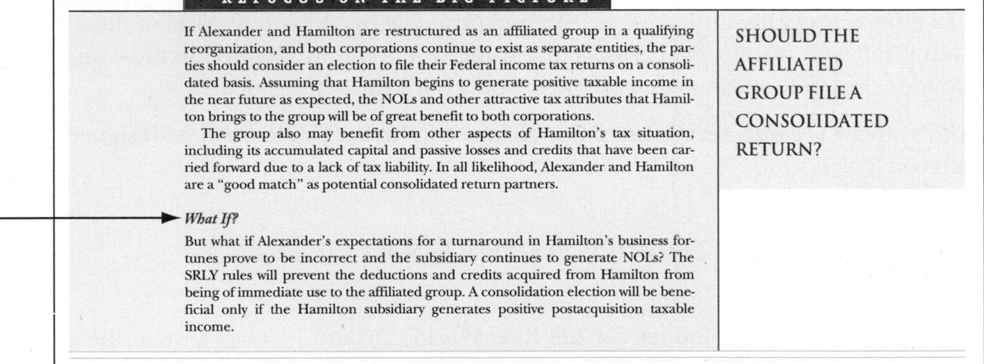
REFOCUS ON THE BIG PICTURE

SHOULD THE AFFILIATED GROUP FILE A CONSOLIDATED RETURN?

If Alexander and Hamilton are restructured as an affiliated group in a qualifying reorganization, and both corporations continue to exist as separate entities, the parties should consider an election to file their Federal income tax returns on a consolidated basis. Assuming that Hamilton begins to generate positive taxable income in the near future as expected, the NOLs and other attractive tax attributes that Hamilton brings to the group will be of great benefit to both corporations.

The group also may benefit from other aspects of Hamilton's tax situation, including its accumulated capital and passive losses and credits that have been carried forward due to a lack of tax liability. In all likelihood, Alexander and Hamilton are a "good match" as potential consolidated return partners.

What If?

But what if Alexander's expectations for a turnaround in Hamilton's business fortunes prove to be incorrect and the subsidiary continues to generate NOLs? The SRLY rules will prevent the deductions and credits acquired from Hamilton from being of immediate use to the affiliated group. A consolidation election will be beneficial only if the Hamilton subsidiary generates positive postacquisition taxable income.

NEW FINANCIAL DISCLOSURE INSIGHTS

Increasingly, tax professionals need to understand how taxes affect the income statement and balance sheet. These features, appearing throughout the text, use current data about existing taxpayers to highlight book-tax reporting differences, effective tax rates, and trends in reporting conventions. **Financial Disclosure Insights** help you integrate financial knowledge with the results of state and Federal tax law. **SWFT's coverage of the role of tax data on the financial statements far exceeds that of any other tax text.**

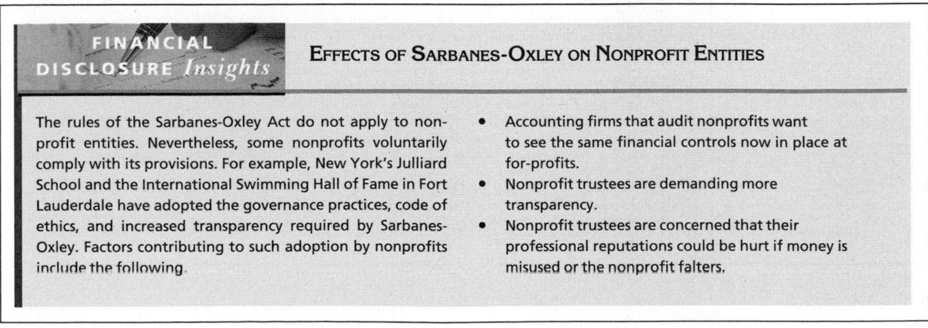
FINANCIAL DISCLOSURE *Insights*

EFFECTS OF SARBANES-OXLEY ON NONPROFIT ENTITIES

The rules of the Sarbanes-Oxley Act do not apply to nonprofit entities. Nevertheless, some nonprofits voluntarily comply with its provisions. For example, New York's Julliard School and the International Swimming Hall of Fame in Fort Lauderdale have adopted the governance practices, code of ethics, and increased transparency required by Sarbanes-Oxley. Factors contributing to such adoption by nonprofits include the following.

- Accounting firms that audit nonprofits want to see the same financial controls now in place at for-profits.
- Nonprofit trustees are demanding more transparency.
- Nonprofit trustees are concerned that their professional reputations could be hurt if money is misused or the nonprofit falters.

EXAMPLES AND LEARNING OBJECTIVES TO HELP YOU STUDY AND EXCEL AT HOMEWORK

Examples You'll Use in Every Chapter. An **average of 38 examples in each chapter** use realistic situations to illustrate the complexities of the tax law and demonstrate concepts.

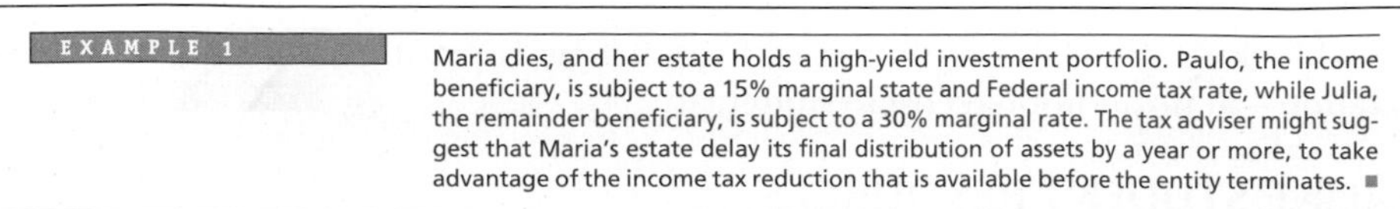
EXAMPLE 1

Maria dies, and her estate holds a high-yield investment portfolio. Paulo, the income beneficiary, is subject to a 15% marginal state and Federal income tax rate, while Julia, the remainder beneficiary, is subject to a 30% marginal rate. The tax adviser might suggest that Maria's estate delay its final distribution of assets by a year or more, to take advantage of the income tax reduction that is available before the entity terminates. ■

Homework Linked to Chapter Learning Objectives. Students tell us that for maximum learning value, homework assignments should refer back to specific chapter topics and sections. Each end-of-chapter Question and Problem is labeled with the Learning Objective(s) that appear beside key topics in the text margins. **It is easier to go back to the section of the text where the concept in the homework item is covered—saving you time, better organizing your study, and increasing your confidence in earning a better grade.**

27. **LO.6, 8, 9** Betty is a shareholder in a calendar year S corporation. At the beginning of the year, her stock basis is $10,000, her share of AAA is $2,000, and her share of corporate AEP is $6,000. She receives a $6,000 distribution, and her share of S corporation items includes a $2,000 long-term capital gain and a $9,000 ordinary loss. Determine the effects of these events on AAA, stock basis, and AEP.

ONLINE RESOURCES AND STUDY TOOLS

Aplia™ is an online interactive homework solution that improves learning by increasing student effort and engagement. Aplia for tax ensures that you stay on top of your coursework with regularly scheduled homework assignments. The Aplia assignments are derived from select end-of-chapter problems from the textbook, allowing you to apply what you learn. To explore the benefits Aplia offers, ask your instructor or visit **www.aplia.com/tax**.

CHECKPOINT® STUDENT EDITION

Checkpoint® Student Edition from Thomson Reuters comes with every new copy of this textbook to help you succeed in the tax research portion of your studies.*

3 Simple Ways Checkpoint® Helps You Make Sense of All Those Taxes:

- Intuitive web-based design makes it fast and simple to find what you need.
- A comprehensive collection of primary tax law, cases, and rulings along with analytical insight you simply can't find anywhere else.
- Checkpoint® has built-in productivity tools such as calculators to make research more efficient—a resource more tax pros use than any other.

CPAexcel CPA EXAM REVIEW

With your purchase of a new copy of ***Corporations, Partnerships, Estates & Trusts****, you have a 6-month access to CPAexcel content, the best CPA review course for busy students! With CPA exam content matched to your taxation course, you will have access to:

- Online exam review that may be accessed anytime, anywhere.
- Over 800 past exam and proficiency questions.
- Exam-identical simulations and comprehensive diagnostics.

*Not available with the Professional Editions of *South-Western Federal Taxation*.

H&R BLOCK AT HOME™

More than software: Put the experience of H&R Block tax professionals on your side.

- A step-by-step interview guides you through a customized process.
- Accurate calculations and 100% satisfaction—guaranteed.
- Worry-free Audit Support™ and tax advice from an H&R Block tax professional.

H&R Block At Home™ is offered with each new copy of **South-Western Federal Taxation**—at no additional cost to students!

CENGAGEbrain.com

ONLINE STUDENT RESOURCES

Go to **www.cengagebrain.com** for free resources to help you study as well as the opportunity to purchase additional study aids. These valuable free study resources will help you earn a better grade:

- **Interactive quizzes** are short and auto-graded to help you brush up on important chapter topics.
- **Flashcards** use chapter terms and definitions to aid you in learning tax terminology for each chapter.
- **Online glossary** for each chapter provides terms and definitions from the text in alphabetical order for easy reference.
- **Learning objectives** can be downloaded for each chapter to help keep you on track.
- **Tax Tips for the Recent Graduate** introduce the college graduate to some common tax considerations that could be beneficial in reducing the dreaded "tax bite."
- **Tax Updates** provide the most recent tax information and major changes to the tax law.
- **Tax tables** used in the textbook are downloadable for reference.

ADDITIONAL STUDENT RESOURCES

Study Guide, ISBN 1-111-82468-1
Do you need more help studying for your taxation class? Order the study guide to receive:

- **Study Highlights**—an outline of key topics for each chapter.
- **Key Terms** used in the chapter.
- **Self-Quizzing** with helpful, annotated answers that are keyed to pages in the 2012 Edition.

Check with your bookstore or order on **CengageBrain.com**.

Corporations, S Corporations, and Partnerships Practice Sets, ISBN 1-111-82475-4
Ask your instructor about assigning these practice sets.

Written specifically for ***Corporations, Partnerships, Estates & Trusts, 2012 Edition***, these practice sets are comprehensive and designed to be completed near the end of the course using tax preparation software such as H&R Block at Home™.

Check with your instructor before ordering practice sets. Solutions are available to instructors only.

For over 35 years, the **South-Western Federal Taxation** Series has guided more than 1.5 million students through the ever-changing field of Federal taxation.

With our promise of leadership, innovation, and service, we are committed to your success both now and in the future.

About the Editors

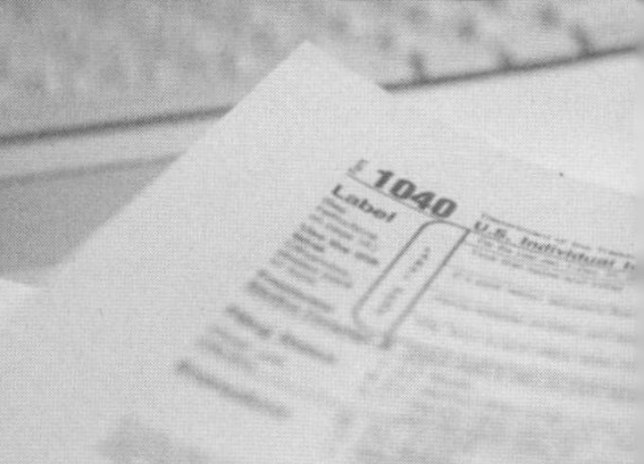

WILLIAM H. HOFFMAN JR. earned B.A. and J.D. degrees from the University of Michigan and M.B.A. and Ph.D. degrees from The University of Texas. He is a licensed CPA and attorney in Texas. His teaching experience includes The University of Texas (1957–1961), Louisiana State University (1961–1967), and the University of Houston (1967–1999). Professor Hoffman has addressed many tax institutes and conferences and has published extensively in academic and professional journals. His articles appear in *The Journal of Taxation, The Tax Adviser, Taxes—The Tax Magazine, The Journal of Accountancy, The Accounting Review,* and *Taxation for Accountants.*

WILLIAM A. RAABE teaches tax courses in the Fisher College of Business at The Ohio State University. A graduate of Carroll University (Wisconsin) and the University of Illinois, Dr. Raabe's teaching and research interests include international and multistate taxation, technology in tax education, personal financial planning, and the economic impact of sports teams and fine arts groups. Professor Raabe also writes *Federal Tax Research* and the PricewaterhouseCoopers Tax Case Studies. He has written extensively about book-tax differences in financial reporting, including a book about the corporate Schedule M–3 and articles and cases addressing FIN 48 issues. Dr. Raabe has been a visiting tax faculty member for a number of public accounting firms, bar associations, and CPA societies. He has received numerous teaching awards, including the Accounting Educator of the Year award from the Wisconsin Institute of CPAs. He has been the faculty adviser for student teams in the Deloitte Tax Case Competition (national finalists at three different schools) and the PricewaterhouseCoopers Extreme Tax policy competition (national finalist). For more information about Dr. Raabe, visit http://fisher.osu.edu/~raabe_12/.

JAMES E. SMITH is the John S. Quinn Professor of Accounting at the College of William and Mary. He has been a member of the Accounting Faculty for over 30 years. He received his Ph.D. degree from the University of Arizona. Professor Smith has served as a discussion leader for Continuing Professional Education programs for the AICPA, Federal Tax Workshops, and various state CPA societies. He has conducted programs in more than 40 states for approximately 25,000 CPAs. He has been the recipient of the AICPA's Outstanding Discussion Leader Award and the American Taxation Association/Arthur Andersen Teaching Innovation Award. Among his other awards are the Virginia Society of CPAs' Outstanding Accounting Educator Award and the James Madison University's Outstanding Accounting Educator Award. He was the President of the Administrators of Accounting Programs Group (AAPG) in 1991–1992. He was the faculty adviser for the William and Mary teams that received first place in the Andersen Tax Challenge in 1994, 1995, 1997, 2000, and 2001 and in the Deloitte Tax Case Study Competition in 2002, 2004, 2005, 2006, and 2008.

DAVID M. MALONEY, Ph.D., CPA, is the Carman G. Blough Professor of Accounting at the University of Virginia's McIntire School of Commerce. He completed his undergraduate work at the University of Richmond and his graduate work at the University of Illinois at Urbana-Champaign. Since joining the Virginia faculty in January 1984, Professor Maloney has taught Federal taxation in the graduate and undergraduate programs and has received major research grants from the Ernst & Young and KPMG Foundations. In addition, his work has been published in numerous professional journals, including *Journal of Taxation, The Tax Adviser, Tax Notes, Corporate Taxation, Accounting Horizons, Journal of Taxation of Investments,* and *Journal of Accountancy.* He is a member of several professional organizations, including the American Accounting Association and the American Taxation Association.

Brief Contents

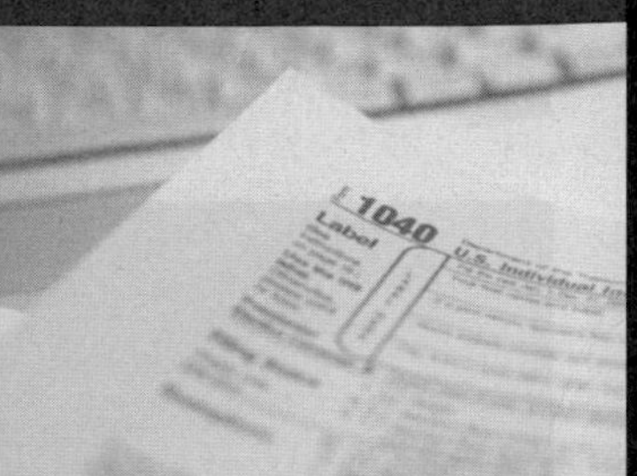

PART 1: INTRODUCTION

PART 2: CORPORATIONS

PART 3: FLOW-THROUGH ENTITIES

PART 4: ADVANCED TAX PRACTICE CONSIDERATIONS

PART 5: FAMILY TAX PLANNING

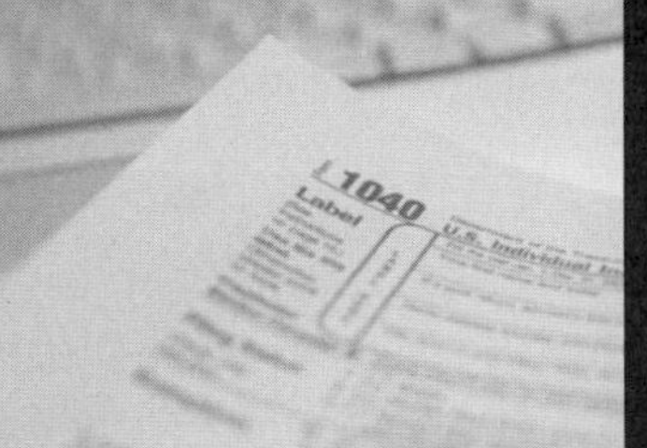

Contents

PART 1: Introduction

PART 2: Corporations

APPENDIXES

Part 1

Introduction

The Federal law is an unbelievably complex set of rules. In working with these rules, however, it is helpful to understand why they came about. Also necessary is the ability to locate the sources of these rules. Part 1, therefore, is devoted to the "whys" of the tax law and the applications of the tax research process.

Understanding and Working with the Federal Tax Law

CHAPTER 1

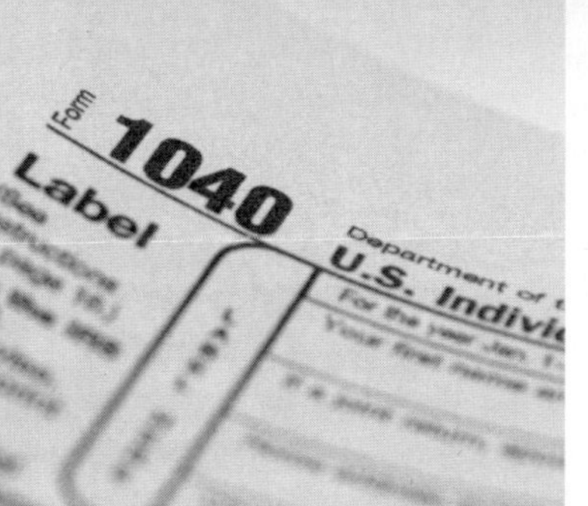

LEARNING OBJECTIVES

After completing Chapter 1, you should be able to:

LO.1 Discuss the importance of revenue needs as an objective of Federal tax law.

LO.2 Demonstrate the influence of economic, social, equity, and political considerations on the development of the tax law.

LO.3 Explain how the IRS, as the protector of the revenue, has affected tax law.

LO.4 Recognize the role of the courts in interpreting and shaping tax law.

LO.5 Identify tax law sources—statutory, administrative, and judicial.

LO.6 List and assess tax law sources.

LO.7 Demonstrate tax research.

LO.8 Assess the validity and weight of tax law sources.

LO.9 Describe various tax planning procedures.

LO.10 Discuss the role of taxation on the CPA examination.

OUTLINE

For the latest in changes to tax legislation, visit **www.cengage.com/taxation/swft.**

1.1 The Whys of the Tax Law

The Federal tax law is a mixture of statutory provisions, administrative pronouncements, and court decisions. Anyone who has attempted to work with this body of knowledge is familiar with its complexity. Commenting on his 48-page tax return, author James Michener said, "It is unimaginable in that I graduated from one of America's better colleges, yet I am totally incapable of understanding tax returns." For the person who has to wade through rule upon rule to find the solution to a tax problem, it may be of some consolation to know that the law's complexity can be explained. There is a reason for the formulation of every rule. Knowing these reasons, therefore, is a considerable step toward understanding the Federal tax law.

The major objective of the Federal tax law is the raising of revenue. Despite the importance of the fiscal needs of the government, however, other considerations explain certain portions of the law. In particular, economic, social, equity, and political factors play a significant role. Added to these factors is the marked impact the Internal Revenue Service (IRS) and the courts have had and will continue to have on the evolution of Federal tax law. These matters are treated in the first part of this chapter. Wherever appropriate, the discussion is related to subjects covered later in the text.

LO.1

Discuss the importance of revenue needs as an objective of Federal tax law.

REVENUE NEEDS

The foundation of any tax system has to be the raising of revenue to absorb the cost of government operations. Ideally, annual outlays should not exceed anticipated revenues. This situation leads to a balanced budget with no deficit. Many states have achieved this objective by passing laws or constitutional amendments precluding deficit spending. Unfortunately, the Federal government has no such prohibition, and the national debt is heading off the charts, reaching more than $13.5 trillion, or more than $43,500 per citizen, in early October 2010. According to the U.S. National Debt Clock, the national debt has increased an average of $4.14 billion per day since September 28, 2007.

When enacting tax legislation, Congress often is guided by the concept of **revenue neutrality** so that any changes neither increase nor decrease the net revenues raised under the prior rules. Revenue neutrality does not mean that any one taxpayer's tax liability remains the same. Since this liability depends upon the circumstances involved, one taxpayer's increased tax liability could be another's tax saving. Revenue-neutral tax reform does not reduce deficits, but at least it does not aggravate the problem.

LO.2

Demonstrate the influence of economic, social, equity, and political considerations on the development of the tax law.

ECONOMIC CONSIDERATIONS

Using the tax system to attempt to accomplish economic objectives has become increasingly popular in recent years. Generally, this process involves amending the Internal Revenue Code[1] through tax legislation and emphasizes measures designed to help control the economy or encourage certain activities and businesses.

Control of the Economy

Congress has made use of depreciation write-offs as a means of controlling the economy. Theoretically, shorter asset lives and accelerated methods should encourage additional investments in depreciable property acquired for business use. Conversely, longer class lives and the required use of the straight-line method of depreciation dampen the tax incentive for capital outlays.

[1] The Internal Revenue Code is a compilation of Federal tax legislation that appears in Title 26 of the U.S. Code.

TAX *in* the *NEWS*

STIMULATING THE ECONOMY

During the current economic downturn, there has been considerable discussion about what the government should do. There are two primary ways to stabilize an economy through government policy: fiscal policy and monetary policy. Fiscal policy involves spending and taxation.

There are two forms of fiscal policy: discretionary and automatic. President Obama's stimulus package, which provided various tax cuts and incentives and increased government spending by statute, also thereby increasing government deficits, is an example of discretionary fiscal policy. Income tax is an example of an automatic fiscal stabilizer—it is automatic because as incomes decline during a recession, taxes owed also decline. In general, in recent years changes in the Internal Revenue Code have become less important than government spending programs as a way to stimulate the economy.

Source: Adapted from Yair Listokin, "Stabilizing the Economy through the Income Tax Code," *Tax Notes*, June 29, 2009, pp. 1575–1577.

Another approach that utilizes depreciation as a means of controlling capital investment is the amount of write-off allowed upon the acquisition of assets. This approach is followed by the § 179 election to immediately expense assets up to a certain amount. It also was the approach used by Congress in various provisions that permitted up to 50 percent additional first-year depreciation.

A change in the tax rate structure has a more immediate impact on the economy. When tax rates are lowered, taxpayers are able to obtain additional spendable funds. In the interest of revenue neutrality, however, rate decreases may be accompanied by a reduction or elimination of deductions or credits. Thus, lower rates do not always mean lower taxes.

Encouragement of Certain Activities

Without passing judgment on the wisdom of any such choices, it is quite clear that the tax law does encourage certain types of economic activity or segments of the economy. For example, the desire to foster technological progress helps explain the favorable treatment accorded to research and development expenditures. Under the tax law, such expenditures can be deducted in the year incurred or, alternatively, capitalized and amortized over a period of 60 months or more. In terms of timing the tax saving, such options usually are preferable to a capitalization of the cost with a write-off over the estimated useful life of the asset created.[2]

The encouragement of technological progress can also explain why the tax law places the inventor in a special position. Not only can patents qualify as capital assets, but under certain conditions their disposition automatically carries long-term capital gain treatment.[3]

Are ecological considerations a desirable objective? If they are, it explains why the tax law permits a 60-month amortization period for costs incurred in the installation of pollution control facilities.

With a view toward conserving and developing national energy resources, in 2005 and 2008 Congress enacted legislation that provides tax incentives to encourage certain activities. Not only are various tax credits made available for home energy conservation expenditures but favorable tax treatment is extended to the purchase of "clean fuel" vehicles. Further, the law provides significant tax incentives to encourage the development of more efficient and reliable energy infrastructure (i.e., power grids).

Does stimulating the development and rehabilitation of low-income rental housing benefit the economy? The tax law definitely favors these activities by allowing generous tax credits to taxpayers incurring such costs.

Is saving desirable for the economy? Saving leads to capital formation and thus makes funds available to finance home construction and industrial expansion. The

[2] If the asset developed has no estimated useful life, no write-off would be available without the two options allowed by the tax law.

[3] A long-term capital gain has a favorable tax advantage for individuals.

tax law provides incentives to encourage saving by giving private retirement plans preferential treatment. Not only are contributions to Keogh (H.R. 10) plans and certain Individual Retirement Accounts (IRAs) deductible, but income from such contributions accumulates on a tax-free basis. As noted in a following section, the encouragement of private-sector pension plans can be justified under social considerations as well.

Encouragement of Certain Industries

Who can question the proposition that a sound agricultural base is necessary for a well-balanced national economy? Undoubtedly, this belief can explain why farmers are accorded special treatment under the Federal tax system. Among the benefits are the election to expense rather than capitalize certain expenditures for soil and water conservation and fertilizers and the election to defer the recognition of gain on the receipt of crop insurance proceeds.

The tax law favors the development of natural resources by permitting the use of percentage depletion on the extraction and sale of oil and gas and specified mineral deposits and a write-off (rather than a capitalization) of certain exploration costs. The railroad and banking industries also receive special tax treatment. All of these provisions can be explained, in whole or in part, by economic considerations.

A well-balanced economy should also include a vigorous and dynamic manufacturing industry. To encourage this sector, Congress has enacted a tax incentive based on profits from manufacturing. Known as the domestic production activities deduction, the benefit is structured in such a manner as to stimulate the creation of jobs.

Encouragement of Small Business

At least in the United States, a consensus exists that what is good for small business is good for the economy as a whole. This assumption has led to a definite bias in the tax law favoring small business.

In the corporate tax area, several provisions can be explained by the desire to benefit small business. One provision enables a shareholder in a small business corporation to obtain an ordinary deduction for any loss recognized on a stock investment. Normally, such a loss would receive the less attractive capital loss treatment. The point of this favoritism is to encourage additional equity investments in small business corporations.[4] Another provision permits the shareholders of a small business corporation to make a special election that generally will avoid the imposition of the corporate income tax.[5] Furthermore, such an election enables the corporation to pass through to its shareholders any of its operating losses.[6]

The tax rates applicable to corporations tend to favor small business in that size is relative to the amount of taxable income generated in any one year. Since a corporate tax rate of 34 percent applies only to taxable income in excess of $75,000, corporations that stay within this limit are subject to lower average tax rates.

EXAMPLE 1

For calendar year 2011, Brown Corporation has taxable income of $75,000, and Red Corporation has taxable income of $100,000. Based on this information, the corporate income tax is $13,750 for Brown Corporation and $22,250 for Red Corporation (see Chapter 2). Brown Corporation is subject to an average tax rate of 18.33% ($13,750/ $75,000), while Red Corporation is subject to an average rate of 22.25% ($22,250/ $100,000). ■

If a corporation has taxable income in excess of $100,000, the benefits of the lower brackets are phased out until all income is taxed at the maximum rate of 34 percent. Once taxable income reaches $10 million, the rate becomes 35 percent.

[4] Known as Section 1244 stock, this subject is covered in Chapter 4.

[5] Known as the S corporation election, the subject is discussed extensively in Chapter 12.

[6] In general, an operating loss can benefit only the corporation incurring the loss through a carryback or carryover to profitable years. Consequently, the shareholders of the corporation usually cannot take advantage of any such loss.

TAX in the NEWS

Did Rome Fall because of Taxation?

Some scholars believe that crippling taxation contributed to the fall of the Roman Empire. In 1966, classicist M. I. Finley said that "the army could not be enlarged because the land could not stand further depletion of manpower; the situation of the land had deteriorated because taxes were too high."

The real problem, however, may have been tax evasion. Large landowners evaded their taxes through a variety of legal and illegal means. Bribery was used to obtain low assessments, and the large landowners would stall the tax collectors and use their influence to obtain amnesties. As the U.S. tax system becomes more and more progressive, with taxes being paid mostly by the wealthy, will taxation—and tax evasion—lead to the fall of the United States?

Source: Adapted from Charles Adams, "*Fight, Flight, Fraud: The Story of Taxation,*" (Buffalo:Euro-Dutch Publishers, 1982), p. 95.

One of the justifications for the enactment of the tax law governing corporate reorganizations (see Chapter 7) was the economic benefit it would provide for small businesses. By allowing corporations to combine without adverse tax consequences, small corporations would be in a position to compete more effectively with larger concerns.

SOCIAL CONSIDERATIONS

Some of the tax laws, especially those related to the Federal income tax of individuals, can be explained by social considerations. Rather than using loans, grants, and other programs to reach desired goals, Congress often uses the Tax Code to provide incentives and benefits (e.g., the higher education incentives). The following are some notable examples:

- The refundable earned income tax credit. As Congress has deemed it socially desirable to reduce the number of people on the welfare rolls and to cut funding for welfare programs, this credit has come to replace some welfare programs.
- The nontaxability of certain benefits provided to employees through accident and health plans financed by employers. It is socially desirable to encourage such plans, since they provide medical benefits in the event of an employee's illness or injury.
- The nontaxability to the employee of some of the premiums paid by an employer for group term insurance covering the life of the employee. These arrangements can be justified in that they provide funds to help the family unit adjust to the loss of wages caused by the employee's death.
- The tax treatment to the employee of contributions made by an employer to qualified pension or profit sharing plans. The contribution and any income it earns are not taxed to the employee until the funds are distributed. Private retirement plans are encouraged because they supplement the subsistence income level the employee would otherwise have under the Social Security system.[7]
- The deduction allowed for contributions to qualified charitable organizations. The deduction attempts to shift some of the financial and administrative burden of socially desirable programs from the public (the government) to the private (the citizens) sector.
- Various tax credits, deductions, and exclusions that are designed to encourage taxpayers to obtain additional education (e.g., American Opportunity

[7]The same rationale explains the availability of similar arrangements for self-employed persons (the H.R. 10 or Keogh plan).

tax credit, lifetime learning credit, and the Coverdell Education Savings Account).[8]

- The credit allowed for amounts spent to furnish care for certain minor or disabled dependents to enable the taxpayer to seek or maintain gainful employment. Who could deny the social desirability of encouraging taxpayers to provide care for their children while they work?
- The disallowance of a tax deduction for certain expenditures that are deemed to be contrary to public policy. This disallowance extends to such items as fines, penalties, illegal kickbacks, and bribes to government officials. Public policy considerations also have been used to disallow gambling losses in excess of gambling gains and political campaign expenditures in excess of campaign contributions. Social considerations dictate that the tax law should not encourage these activities by permitting a deduction.
- The adoption tax credit to cover some (or all) of the expenses incurred by individuals who adopt or attempt to adopt a child.

Many other examples could be included, but the conclusion would be unchanged: social considerations do explain a significant part of the Federal tax law.

EQUITY CONSIDERATIONS

The concept of equity is relative. Reasonable persons can, and often do, disagree about what is fair or unfair. In the tax area, moreover, equity is generally tied to a particular taxpayer's personal situation. To illustrate, Ms. Jones may have difficulty understanding why none of the rent she pays on her apartment is deductible, while her brother, Mr. Jones, is able to deduct a large portion of the monthly payments he makes on his personal residence in the form of interest and taxes.[9]

In the same vein, compare the tax treatment of a corporation with that of a partnership. Two businesses may be of equal size, similarly situated, and competitors in the production of goods or services, but they are not comparably treated under the tax law. The corporation is subject to a separate Federal income tax; the partnership is not. Whether the differences in tax treatment can be logically justified in terms of equity is beside the point. The tax law can and does make a distinction between these business forms.

Equity, then, is not what appears fair or unfair to any one taxpayer or group of taxpayers. It is, instead, what the tax law recognizes. Some recognition of equity does exist, however, and explains part of the law. The concept of equity appears in tax provisions that alleviate the effect of multiple taxation and postpone the recognition of gain when the taxpayer lacks the ability or wherewithal to pay the tax. Equity also helps mitigate the effect of the application of the annual accounting period concept and helps taxpayers cope with the eroding result of inflation.

Alleviating the Effect of Multiple Taxation

The same income earned by a taxpayer may be subject to taxes imposed by different taxing authorities. If, for example, the taxpayer is a resident of New York City, income might generate Federal, New York State, and New York City income taxes. To compensate for this inequity, the Federal tax law allows a taxpayer to claim a deduction for state and local income taxes. The deduction, however, does not neutralize the effect of multiple taxation since the benefit derived depends on the taxpayer's Federal income tax rate.[10]

[8]These provisions can also be justified under the category of economic considerations. No one can take issue with the conclusion that a better educated workforce carries a positive economic impact.

[9]The encouragement of home ownership can be justified on both economic and social grounds. In this regard, it is interesting to note that some state income tax laws allow a form of relief (e.g., tax credit) to the taxpayer who rents his or her personal residence.

[10]A tax credit, rather than a deduction, would eliminate the effects of multiple taxation on the same income.

Treating Everyone the Same

The justification for allowing a Federal income tax deduction for state and local income taxes paid is to mitigate the effect of having the same income be taxed twice. But what if instead of imposing an income tax a state derives comparable amounts of revenue from a general sales tax? Is it fair to deny a deduction to taxpayers in that state just because the tax the state levies is imposed on sales rather than on income?

Congress, in the American Jobs Creation Act of 2004, resolved this purported inequity by allowing a Federal income tax deduction for state and local general sales taxes. However, a taxpayer who is subject to both state income and sales taxes must make a choice. One or the other, but not both, can be claimed as a deduction.

Comment on the equity of a tax system that requires this choice.

Equity considerations can explain the Federal tax treatment of certain income from foreign sources. Since double taxation results when the same income is subject to both foreign and U.S. income taxes, the tax law permits the taxpayer to choose either a credit or a deduction for the foreign taxes paid.

The imposition of a separate income tax on corporations leads to multiple taxation of the same income.

EXAMPLE 2

During the current year, Gray Corporation has net income of $100,000, of which $5,000 was received as dividends from stock it owns in IBM Corporation. Assume Gray Corporation distributes the after-tax income to its shareholders (all individuals). At a minimum, the distribution received by the shareholders will be subject to two income taxes: the corporate income tax when the income is earned by Gray Corporation and the individual income tax when the balance is distributed to the shareholders as a dividend. The $5,000 Gray receives from IBM Corporation fares even worse. Because it is paid from income earned by IBM, it has been subjected to a third income tax (the corporate income tax imposed on IBM).[11] ■

For corporate shareholders, for whom triple taxation is possible, the law provides a deduction for dividends received from certain domestic corporations. The deduction, usually 70 percent of the dividends, would be allowed to Gray Corporation for the $5,000 it received from IBM Corporation. (See the discussion in Chapter 2.) For the individual shareholder, legislation has reduced the tax on qualified dividends to 15 percent (0 percent for lower-bracket shareholders). By allowing a preferential lower tax rate, the approach is to *mitigate* (not *eliminate*) the effect of multiple taxation. (See the discussion in Chapter 5.)

In the area of the Federal estate tax, several provisions reflect attempts to mitigate the effect of multiple taxation. Some degree of equity is achieved, for example, by allowing a limited credit against the estate tax for foreign death taxes imposed on the same transfer. Other estate tax credits are available and can be explained on the same grounds.[12]

The Wherewithal to Pay Concept

The **wherewithal to pay** concept recognizes the inequity of taxing a transaction when the taxpayer lacks the means with which to pay the tax. It is particularly suited to situations when the taxpayer's economic position has not changed significantly as a result of a transaction.

[11]This result materializes because under the tax law a corporation is not allowed a deduction for the dividend distributions it makes.

[12]See Chapter 18.

EXAMPLE 3

White Corporation holds unimproved land as an investment. The land has a basis to White of $60,000 and a fair market value of $100,000. The land is exchanged for a building (worth $100,000) that White will use in its business.[13] ■

EXAMPLE 4

White Corporation owns a warehouse that it uses in its business. At a time when the warehouse has an adjusted basis of $60,000, it is destroyed by fire. White collects the insurance proceeds of $100,000 and, within two years of the end of the year in which the fire occurred, uses all of the proceeds to purchase a new warehouse.[14] ■

EXAMPLE 5

Tom, a sole proprietor, decides to incorporate his business. In exchange for the business's assets (adjusted basis of $60,000 and a fair market value of $100,000), Tom receives all of the stock of Azure Corporation, a newly created corporation.[15] The Azure stock is worth $100,000. ■

EXAMPLE 6

Rose, Sam, and Tom want to develop unimproved land owned by Tom. The land has a basis to Tom of $60,000 and a fair market value of $100,000. The RST Partnership is formed with the following investments: land worth $100,000 transferred by Tom, $100,000 cash by Rose, and $100,000 cash by Sam. Each party receives a one-third interest in the RST Partnership.[16] ■

EXAMPLE 7

Amber Corporation and Crimson Corporation decide to consolidate to form Aqua Corporation.[17] Pursuant to the plan of reorganization, Tera exchanges her stock in Amber Corporation (basis of $60,000 and fair market value of $100,000) for stock in Aqua Corporation worth $100,000. ■

In all of the preceding examples, White Corporation, Tom, or Tera had a realized gain of $40,000 [$100,000 (fair market value of the property received) – $60,000 (basis of the property given up)].[18] It seems inequitable to force the taxpayer to recognize any of this gain for two reasons. First, without disposing of the property or interest acquired, the taxpayer would be hard-pressed to pay the tax.[19] Second, the taxpayer's economic situation has not changed significantly. To illustrate by referring to Example 5, can it be said that Tom's position as sole shareholder of Azure Corporation is much different from his prior status as owner of a sole proprietorship?

Several warnings are in order concerning the application of the wherewithal to pay concept. Recognized gain is merely postponed and not necessarily avoided. Because of the basis carryover to the new property or interest acquired in these nontaxable transactions, the gain element is still present and might be recognized upon a subsequent taxable disposition. Referring to Example 5, suppose Tom later sold the stock in Azure Corporation for $100,000. Tom's basis in the stock is $60,000 (the same basis as in the assets transferred), and the sale results in a recognized gain of $40,000. Also, many of the provisions previously illustrated prevent the recognition of realized losses. Since such provisions are automatic in application (not elective with the taxpayer), they could operate to the detriment of a taxpayer who wishes to obtain a deduction for a loss. The notable exception involves involuntary conversions (Example 4). Here, nonrecognition treatment is elective with the taxpayer and will not apply to a realized loss if it is otherwise deductible.

[13]The nontaxability of like-kind exchanges applies to the exchange of property held for investment or used in a trade or business for property to be similarly held or used.

[14]The nontaxability of gains realized from involuntary conversions applies when the proceeds received by the taxpayer are reinvested within a prescribed period of time in property similar or related in service or use to that converted. Involuntary conversions take place as a result of casualty losses, theft losses, and condemnations by a public authority.

[15]Transfers of property to controlled corporations are discussed in Chapter 4.

[16]The formation of a partnership is discussed in Chapter 10.

[17]Corporate reorganizations are discussed in Chapter 7.

[18]Realized gain can be likened to economic gain. However, the Federal income tax is imposed only on that portion of realized gain considered to be recognized under the law. Generally, recognized (or taxable) gain can never exceed realized gain.

[19]If the taxpayer ends up with other property (boot) as part of the transfer, gain may be recognized to this extent. The presence of boot, however, helps solve the wherewithal to pay problem, since it provides property (other than the property or interest central to the transaction) with which to pay the tax.

The wherewithal to pay concept has definitely served as a guideline in shaping part of the tax law. Nevertheless, it is not a hard and fast principle that is followed in every case. Only when the tax law specifically provides for no tax consequences will this result materialize.

EXAMPLE 8

Mary Jo exchanges stock in Green Corporation (basis of $60,000 and fair market value of $100,000) for stock in Purple Corporation (fair market value of $100,000). The exchange is not pursuant to a reorganization. Under these circumstances, Mary Jo's realized gain of $40,000 is recognized for Federal income tax purposes.[20] ■

The result reached in Example 8 seems harsh in that the exchange does not place Mary Jo in a position to pay the tax on the $40,000 gain. How can this result be reconciled with that reached in Example 7 when the exchange was nontaxable? In other words, why does the tax law apply the wherewithal to pay concept to the exchange of stock pursuant to a corporate reorganization (Example 7) but not to certain other stock exchanges (Example 8)?

Recall that the wherewithal to pay concept is particularly suited to situations in which the taxpayer's economic position has not changed significantly as a result of a transaction. In Example 7, Tera's stock investment in Amber Corporation really continues in the form of the Aqua Corporation stock since Aqua was formed through a consolidation of Amber and Crimson Corporations.[21] In Example 8, however, the investment has not continued. Here Mary Jo's ownership in Green Corporation has ceased, and an investment in an entirely different corporation has been substituted.

Mitigating the Effect of the Annual Accounting Period Concept

For purposes of effective administration of the tax law, all taxpayers must report to and settle with the Federal government at periodic intervals. Otherwise, taxpayers would remain uncertain as to their tax liabilities, and the government would have difficulty judging revenues and budgeting expenditures. The period selected for final settlement of most tax liabilities is one year. At the close of each year, a taxpayer's position becomes complete for that particular year. Referred to as the annual accounting period concept, the effect is to divide each taxpayer's life into equal annual intervals for tax purposes.

The finality of the annual accounting period concept can lead to dissimilar tax treatment for taxpayers who are, from a long-range standpoint, in the same economic position.

EXAMPLE 9

Rena and Samuel are both sole proprietors and have experienced the following results during the past three years:

	Profit (or Loss)	
Year	**Rena**	**Samuel**
2009	$50,000	$150,000
2010	60,000	60,000
2011	60,000	(40,000)

Although Rena and Samuel have the same profit of $170,000 over the period 2009–2011, the finality of the annual accounting period concept places Samuel at a definite disadvantage for tax purposes. The net operating loss procedure offers Samuel some relief by allowing him to apply some or all of his 2011 loss to the earliest profitable years (in this case 2009). Thus, Samuel, with a net operating loss carryback, is placed

[20] The exchange of stock does not qualify for nontaxable treatment as a like-kind exchange (refer to Example 3).

[21] This continuation is known as the continuity of interest concept, which forms the foundation for all nontaxable corporate reorganizations. The concept is discussed at length in Chapter 7.

in a position to obtain a refund for some of the taxes he paid on the $150,000 profit reported for 2009. ■

The same reasoning used to support the deduction of net operating losses can be applied to explain the special treatment excess capital losses and excess charitable contributions receive. Carryback and carryover procedures help mitigate the effect of limiting a loss or a deduction to the accounting period in which it is realized. With such procedures, a taxpayer may be able to salvage a loss or a deduction that might otherwise be wasted.

The installment method of recognizing gain on the sale of property allows a taxpayer to spread tax consequences over the payout period.[22] The harsh effect of taxing all the gain in the year of sale is avoided. The installment method can also be explained by the wherewithal to pay concept since recognition of gain is tied to the collection of the installment notes received from the sale of the property. Tax consequences tend to correspond to the seller's ability to pay the tax.

EXAMPLE 10

In 2009, Tim sold unimproved real estate (cost of $40,000) for $100,000. Under the terms of the sale, Tim receives two notes from the purchaser, each for $50,000 (plus interest). One note is payable in 2010 and the other note in 2011. Without the installment method, Tim would have to recognize and pay a tax on the gain of $60,000 for the year of the sale (2009). This result is harsh, since none of the sale proceeds will be received until 2010 and 2011. With the installment method, and presuming the notes are paid when each comes due, Tim recognizes half of the gain ($30,000) in 2010 and the remaining half in 2011. ■

The annual accounting period concept has been modified to apply to situations in which taxpayers may have difficulty accurately assessing their tax positions by year-end. In many such cases, the law permits taxpayers to treat transactions taking place in the next year as having occurred in the prior year.

EXAMPLE 11

Monica, a calendar year taxpayer, is a participant in an H.R. 10(Keogh) retirement plan. (See Appendix C for a definition of a Keogh plan.) Under the plan, Monica contributes 20% of her net self-employment income, such amount being deductible for Federal income tax purposes. On April 9, 2011, Monica determines that her net self-employment income for calendar year 2010 was $80,000. Consequently, she contributes $16,000 (20% × $80,000) to the plan. Even though the $16,000 contribution was made in 2011, the law permits Monica to claim it as a deduction for tax year 2010. Requiring Monica to make the contribution by December 31, 2010, in order to obtain the deduction for that year would force her to arrive at an accurate determination of net self-employment income long before her income tax return must be prepared and filed. ■

Similar exceptions to the annual accounting period concept cover certain charitable contributions by accrual basis corporations (Chapter 2), and the dividend distributions by S corporations (Chapter 12).

Coping with Inflation

During periods of inflation, bracket creep has plagued the working person. Because of the progressive nature of the income tax, any wage adjustment to compensate for inflation can increase the income tax bracket of the recipient. The overall impact is an erosion of purchasing power. Congress recognized this problem and began to adjust various income tax components (the **indexation** procedure) in 1985, based upon the rise in the consumer price index over the prior year. For example, due to the inflation factor, the amount of a personal and dependency exemption has been

[22]Under the installment method, each payment received by the seller represents a return of basis (the nontaxable portion) and profit from the sale (the taxable portion).

increased over the years. Indexation also applies to dollar amounts of other components, including the tax brackets and the standard deduction.

POLITICAL CONSIDERATIONS

A large segment of the Federal tax law is made up of statutory provisions. Since these statutes are enacted by Congress, is it any surprise that political considerations influence tax law? For purposes of discussion, the effect of political considerations on the tax law is divided into the following topics: special interest legislation, political expediency, and state and local influences.

Special Interest Legislation

Unquestionably, certain provisions of the tax law can be explained largely by looking to the political influence some pressure groups have exerted on Congress. For example, is there any other reason why prepaid subscription and dues income is not taxed until earned while prepaid rents are taxed to the landlord in the year received? These exceptions came about because certain organizations (e.g., the American Automobile Association) convinced Congress that special tax treatment was needed to cover income received from multiyear dues and subscriptions.

Special interest legislation is not necessarily to be condemned if it can be justified on economic or social grounds. At any rate, it is an inevitable product of our political system.

Political Expediency

Various tax reform proposals rise and fall in favor, depending upon the shifting moods of the American public. That Congress is sensitive to popular feeling is an accepted fact. Therefore, certain provisions of the tax law can be explained on the basis of the political climate at the time of enactment. Once the general public became aware that certain large and profitable corporations were able to avoid the corporate income tax, Congress responded with an alternative minimum tax. Since a portion of a corporation's adjusted current earnings has been made a tax preference item, many large corporations no longer escape taxation (see Chapter 3).

Measures that deter more affluent taxpayers from obtaining so-called preferential tax treatment have always had popular appeal and, consequently, the support of Congress. Provisions such as the alternative minimum tax, the imputed interest rules, and the limitation on the deductibility of interest on investment indebtedness can be explained on this basis. In the same vein are the provisions imposing penalty taxes on corporations that unreasonably accumulate earnings or are classified as personal holding companies (see Chapter 3).

The provisions raising income tax rates on more affluent taxpayers and increasing the amount of the earned income credit are also at least partially attributable to political expediency.

State and Local Influences

Political considerations have played a major role in the exclusion from gross income of interest received on state and local obligations. In view of the furor that has been raised by state and local political figures every time repeal of this tax provision has been proposed, one might well regard it as sacred.

Somewhat less apparent has been the influence state law has had in shaping our present Federal tax law. Of prime importance in this regard has been the effect of the community property system employed in some states.[23] At one time, the tax

[23]The states with community property systems are Louisiana, Texas, New Mexico, Arizona, California, Washington, Idaho, Nevada, Wisconsin, and (if elected by the spouses) Alaska. The rest of the states are classified as common law jurisdictions. The difference between common law and community property systems centers around the property rights possessed by married persons. In a common law system, each spouse owns whatever he or she earns. Under a community property system, one-half of the earnings of each spouse is considered owned by the other spouse. Assume, for example, Harold and Ruth are husband and wife, and their only income is the $80,000 annual salary Harold receives. If they live in New York (a common law state), the $80,000 salary belongs to Harold. If, however, they live in Texas (a community property state), the $80,000 salary is divided equally, in terms of ownership, between Harold and Ruth.

position of the residents of these states was so advantageous that many common law states actually adopted community property systems.[24] The political pressure placed on Congress to correct the disparity in tax treatment was considerable. To a large extent, this was accomplished in the Revenue Act of 1948, which extended many of the community property tax advantages to residents of common law jurisdictions.[25] Thus, common law states avoided the trauma of discarding the time-honored legal system familiar to everyone. The impact of community property law on the Federal estate and gift taxes is further explored in Chapters 18 and 19.

LO.3

Explain how the IRS, as the protector of the revenue, has affected tax law.

INFLUENCE OF THE INTERNAL REVENUE SERVICE

The IRS has been influential in many areas beyond its role in issuing administrative pronouncements. In its capacity as the protector of the national revenue, the IRS has been instrumental in securing the passage of much legislation designed to curtail the most flagrant tax avoidance practices (closing tax loopholes). In its capacity as the administrator of the tax laws, the IRS has sought and obtained legislation to make its job easier (administrative feasibility).

The IRS as Protector of the Revenue

Innumerable examples can be given of provisions in the tax law that have stemmed from the direct efforts of the IRS to prevent taxpayers from exploiting a loophole. Working within the letter of existing law, ingenious taxpayers and their advisers devise techniques that accomplish indirectly what cannot be accomplished directly. As a consequence, legislation is enacted to close the loophole that taxpayers have located and exploited. The following examples can be explained in this fashion and are discussed in more detail in the chapters to follow:

- The use of a fiscal year by personal service corporations, partnerships, S corporations, and trusts to defer income recognition to the owners (see Chapters 2, 10, 12, and 20).
- The use of the cash basis method of accounting by certain large corporations (see Chapter 2).
- The deduction of passive investment losses and expenses against other income (see Chapters 2 and 10).
- The shifting of income to lower-bracket taxpayers through the use of reversionary trusts (see Chapter 20).

In addition, the IRS has secured from Congress legislation of a more general nature that enables it to make adjustments based upon the substance, rather than the formal construction, of what a taxpayer has done. One provision, for example, authorizes the IRS to establish guidelines on the thin capitalization issue. This question involves when corporate debt will be recognized as debt for tax purposes and when it will be reclassified as equity or stock (see the discussion of thin capitalization in Chapter 4). Another provision permits the IRS to make adjustments to a taxpayer's method of accounting when the method used by the taxpayer does not clearly reflect income. The IRS has also been granted the authority to allocate income and deductions among businesses owned or controlled by the same interests when the allocation is necessary to prevent the evasion of taxes or to reflect the income of each business clearly.

EXAMPLE 12

Gold Corporation and Silver Corporation are brother-sister corporations (the stock of each is owned by the same shareholders), and both use the calendar year for tax purposes. For the current tax year, each has taxable income as follows: $335,000 for Gold

[24]Such states included Michigan, Oklahoma, and Pennsylvania.

[25]The major advantage extended was the provision allowing married taxpayers to file joint returns and compute the tax liability as if the income had been earned one-half by each spouse. This result is automatic in a community property state since half of the income earned by one spouse belongs to the other spouse. The income-splitting benefits of a joint return are now incorporated as part of the tax rates applicable to married taxpayers.

Corporation and $50,000 for Silver Corporation. Not included in Gold Corporation's taxable income, however, is $10,000 of rent income usually charged Silver Corporation for the use of some property owned by Gold. Since the parties have not clearly reflected the taxable income of each business, the IRS can allocate $10,000 of rent income to Gold Corporation. After the allocation, Gold Corporation has taxable income of $345,000, and Silver Corporation has taxable income of $40,000.[26] ■

Also of a general nature is the authority Congress has given the IRS to prevent taxpayers from acquiring corporations to obtain a tax advantage when the principal purpose of the acquisition is the evasion or avoidance of the Federal income tax. The provision of the tax law that provides this authority is discussed briefly in Chapter 7.

Administrative Feasibility

Some of the tax law is justified on the grounds that it simplifies the task of the IRS in collecting the revenue and administering the law. With regard to collecting the revenue, the IRS long ago realized the importance of placing taxpayers on a pay-as-you-go basis. Elaborate withholding procedures apply to wages, while the tax on other types of income may have to be paid at periodic intervals throughout the year. The IRS has been instrumental in convincing the courts that accrual basis taxpayers should pay taxes on prepaid income in the year received and not when earned. This approach may be contrary to generally accepted accounting principles, but it is consistent with the wherewithal to pay concept.

Of considerable aid to the IRS in collecting revenue are the numerous provisions that impose interest and penalties on taxpayers for noncompliance with the tax law. These provisions include penalties for failure to pay a tax or to file a return that is due and the negligence penalty for intentional disregard of rules and regulations. Various penalties for civil and criminal fraud also serve as deterrents to taxpayer noncompliance. This aspect of the tax law is discussed in Chapter 17.

One of the keys to the effective administration of our tax system is the audit process conducted by the IRS. To carry out this function, the IRS is aided by provisions that reduce the chance of taxpayer error or manipulation and therefore simplify the audit effort that is necessary. An increase in the amount of the standard deduction reduces the number of individual taxpayers who will be in a position to claim itemized deductions. With fewer deductions to check, the audit function is simplified.[27] The same objective can be used to explain the $13,000 annual gift tax exclusion (see Chapter 18). This provision decreases the number of tax returns that must be filed (as well as reduces the taxes paid) and thereby saves audit effort.[28]

INFLUENCE OF THE COURTS

LO.4

Recognize the role of the courts in interpreting and shaping tax law.

In addition to interpreting statutory provisions and the administrative pronouncements issued by the IRS, the Federal courts have influenced tax law in two other respects.[29] First, the courts have formulated certain judicial concepts that serve as guides in the application of various tax provisions. Second, certain key decisions have led to changes in the Internal Revenue Code. Understanding this influence helps explain some of our tax laws.

[26]By shifting $10,000 of income to Gold Corporation (which is in the 34% bracket), the IRS gains $3,400 in taxes. Allowing the $10,000 deduction to Silver Corporation (which is in the 15% bracket) costs the IRS only $1,500. See Chapter 2 for a further discussion of the income tax rates applicable to corporations.

[27]The IRS gave the same justification when it proposed to Congress the $100 per event limitation on personal casualty and theft losses. Imposition of the limitation eliminated many casualty and theft loss deductions and, as a consequence, saved the IRS considerable audit time. Also, an additional limitation equal to 10% of adjusted gross income applies to the total of nonbusiness losses after reduction by the floor of $100 for each loss.

[28]Particularly in the case of nominal gifts among family members, taxpayer compliance in reporting and paying a tax on such transfers would be questionable. The absence of the $13,000 gift tax exclusion would create a serious enforcement problem for the IRS.

[29]A great deal of case law is devoted to ascertaining congressional intent. The courts, in effect, ask: What did Congress have in mind when it enacted a particular tax provision?

Judicial Concepts Relating to Tax Law

Although ranking the tax concepts developed by the courts in order of importance is difficult, the concept of substance over form would almost certainly be near the top of any list. Variously described as the "telescoping" or "collapsing" process or the "step transaction approach," it involves determining the true substance of what occurred. In a transaction involving many steps, any one step may be collapsed (or disregarded) to arrive directly at the result reached.

EXAMPLE 13

In 2011, Mrs. Greer, a widow, wants to give $26,000 to Jean without incurring any gift tax liability.[30] She knows that the law permits her to give up to $13,000 each year per person without any tax consequences (the annual exclusion). With this in mind, the following steps are taken: a gift by Mrs. Greer to Jean of $13,000 (nontaxable because of the $13,000 annual exclusion), a gift by Mrs. Greer to Ben of $13,000 (also nontaxable), and a gift by Ben to Jean of $13,000 (nontaxable because of Ben's annual exclusion). Considering only the form of what Mrs. Greer and Ben have done, all appears well from a tax standpoint. In substance, however, what has happened? By collapsing the steps involving Ben, it is apparent that Mrs. Greer has made a gift of $26,000 to Jean and therefore has not avoided the Federal gift tax. ■

The substance over form concept plays an important role in transactions involving corporations.

Another leading tax concept developed by the courts deals with the interpretation of statutory tax provisions that operate to benefit taxpayers. The courts have established the rule that these relief provisions are to be narrowly construed against taxpayers if there is any doubt about their application. Suppose, for example, Beige Corporation wants to be treated as an S corporation (see Chapter 12) but has not satisfied the statutory requirements for making the required election. Because S corporation status is a relief provision favoring taxpayers, chances are the courts will deny Beige Corporation this treatment.

Important in the area of corporate-shareholder dealings (see the discussion of constructive dividends in Chapter 5) and in the resolution of valuation problems for estate and gift tax purposes (see Chapters 18 and 19) is the **arm's length concept**. Particularly in dealings between related parties, transactions can be tested by questioning whether the taxpayers acted in an "arm's length" manner. The question to be asked is: Would unrelated parties have handled the transaction in the same way?

EXAMPLE 14

The sole shareholder of a corporation leases property to the corporation for a monthly rental of $50,000. To test whether the corporation should be allowed a rent deduction for this amount, the IRS and the courts will apply the arm's length concept. Would the corporation have paid $50,000 a month in rent if the same property had been leased from an unrelated party (rather than from the sole shareholder)? ■

The **continuity of interest concept** originated with the courts but has, in many situations, been incorporated into statutory provisions of the tax law. Primarily concerned with business readjustments, the concept permits tax-free treatment only if the taxpayer retains a substantial continuing interest in the property transferred to the new business. Due to the continuing interest retained, the transfer should not have tax consequences because the position of the taxpayer has not changed. This concept applies to transfers to controlled corporations (Chapter 4), corporate reorganizations (Chapter 7), and transfers to partnerships (Chapter 10). The continuity

[30] The example assumes that Mrs. Greer has exhausted her unified tax credit. See Chapter 18.

of interest concept helps explain the results reached in Examples 5 through 7 of this chapter. This concept is further discussed in Chapter 7.

Also developed by the courts, the **business purpose concept** principally applies to transactions involving corporations. Under this concept, some sound business reason that motivates the transaction must be present in order for the prescribed tax treatment to result. The avoidance of taxation is not considered to be a sound business purpose.

EXAMPLE 15

Beth and Charles are equal shareholders in Brown Corporation. They have recently disagreed about the company's operations and are at an impasse about the future of Brown Corporation. This shareholder disagreement on corporate policy constitutes a sound business purpose and would justify a division of Brown Corporation that will permit Beth and Charles to go their separate ways. Whether the division of Brown would be nontaxable to the parties depends on their compliance with the statutory provisions dealing with corporate reorganizations. The point is, however, that compliance with statutory provisions would not be enough to ensure nontaxability without a business purpose for the transaction. ■

The business purpose concept is discussed further in Chapter 7.

Judicial Influence on Statutory Provisions

Some court decisions have been of such consequence that Congress has incorporated them into statutory tax law. An illustration of this influence appears in Example 16.

EXAMPLE 16

In 1983, Brad claimed a capital loss of $100,000 for Tan Corporation stock that had become worthless during the year. In the absence of any offsetting gains, the capital loss deduction produced no income tax savings for Brad either in 1983 or in future years. In 1986, Brad institutes a lawsuit against the former officers of Tan Corporation for their misconduct that resulted in the corporation's failure and thereby led to Brad's $100,000 loss. In settlement of the suit, the officers pay $50,000 to Brad. The IRS argued that the full $50,000 should be taxed as gain to Brad. The Tan stock was written off in 1983 and had a zero basis for tax purposes. The $50,000 recovery Brad received on the stock was, therefore, all gain. The IRS's position was logical, but not equitable. The court stated that Brad should not be taxed on the recovery of an amount previously deducted unless the deduction produced a tax savings. Since the $100,000 capital loss deduction in 1983 produced no tax benefit, none of the $50,000 received in 1986 results in gain. ■

The decision reached by the courts in Example 16, known as the **tax benefit rule**, is part of the statutory tax law.

Court decisions sometimes create uncertainty about the tax law. Such decisions may reach the right result but do not produce the guidelines necessary to enable taxpayers to comply. In many situations, Congress may be compelled to add certainty to the law by enacting statutory provisions specifying when a particular tax consequence will or will not materialize. The following are examples of this type of judicial "cause" and the statutory "effect":

- When a stock redemption will be treated as an exchange or as a dividend (see Chapter 6).
- What basis a parent corporation will have in the assets received from a subsidiary that is liquidated shortly after its acquisition (see Chapter 6).

Some of the statutory provisions can be explained by a negative reaction by Congress to a particular court decision. One decision, for example, held that the transfer of a liability to a controlled corporation should be treated as boot received by the transferor (see Chapter 4). Congress apparently disagreed with this treatment and promptly enacted legislation to change the result.

1.2 Summary

In addition to its revenue-raising objective, the Federal tax law has developed in response to several other factors:

- *Economic considerations.* Here, the emphasis is on tax provisions that help regulate the economy and encourage certain activities and types of businesses.
- *Social considerations.* Some tax provisions are designed to encourage or discourage certain socially desirable or undesirable practices.
- *Equity considerations.* Of principal concern in this area are tax provisions that alleviate the effect of multiple taxation, recognize the wherewithal to pay concept, mitigate the effect of the annual accounting period concept, and recognize the eroding effect of inflation.
- *Political considerations.* Of significance in this regard are tax provisions that represent special interest legislation, reflect political expediency, and illustrate the effect of state law.
- *Influence of the IRS.* Many tax provisions are intended to aid the IRS in collecting revenue and administering the tax law.
- *Influence of the courts.* Court decisions have established a body of judicial concepts relating to tax law and have, on occasion, led Congress to enact statutory provisions that either clarify or negate their effect.

These factors explain various tax provisions and thereby help in understanding why the tax law developed to its present state. The next step involves learning to work with the tax law.

1.3 Reconciling Accounting Concepts

The vast majority of an entity's business transactions receive the same treatment for financial accounting purposes as under Federal and state tax law. But "book-tax differences" exist. When variances between **Generally Accepted Accounting Principles (GAAP)** or **International Financial Reporting Standards (IFRS)** and tax rules do arise, these are highlighted and discussed in a special feature, titled *Financial Disclosure Insights.*

1.4 Working with the Tax Law— Tax Sources

Understanding taxation requires a mastery of the sources of tax law. These sources include not only the legislative provisions in the Internal Revenue Code, but also congressional Committee Reports, Regulations, Treasury Department pronouncements, and court decisions. Thus, the primary sources of tax information are the pronouncements of the three branches of government: legislative, executive, and judicial.

The law is of little significance, however, until it is applied to a set of facts and circumstances. A tax researcher must not only be able to read and interpret the sources of the law but must also understand the relative weight of authority within the rules of law. Learning to work with the tax law involves three basic steps:

1. Familiarity with the sources of the law.
2. Application of research techniques.
3. Effective use of planning procedures.

The remainder of this chapter introduces the sources of tax law and explains how the law is applied to problems and conditions of individual and business transactions. Statutory, administrative, and judicial sources of the tax law are considered first.

TAX in the NEWS

The 67,204-Page Gorilla

Few will dispute that our tax laws are extremely complex. Albert Einstein reportedly said that "the hardest thing in the world to understand is the income tax." Almost 60 percent of tax filers pay a professional to calculate their taxes, and individuals and businesses paid $368.4 billion in Federal income tax preparation costs in 2010, according to the Tax Foundation. That's a 24 percent surcharge on top of the more than $1.5 trillion in taxes actually paid.

Even tax professionals cannot agree on the taxes owed by a typical taxpayer with a complex tax return. Of course, much of the problem is the tangle of deductions, credits, and exceptions that are found in the approximately 67,204-page Internal Revenue Code. Since simplification would require taking away many tax breaks, do not expect the 67,204-page gorilla to go away.

STATUTORY SOURCES OF THE TAX LAW

LO.5

Identify tax law sources—statutory, administrative, and judicial.

Origin of the Internal Revenue Code

Before 1939, the statutory provisions relating to taxation were contained in the individual revenue acts enacted by Congress. The inconvenience and confusion that resulted from dealing with many separate acts led Congress to codify all of the Federal tax laws. Known as the Internal Revenue Code of 1939, the codification arranged all Federal tax provisions in a logical sequence and placed them in a separate part of the Federal statutes. A further rearrangement took place in 1954 and resulted in the Internal Revenue Code of 1954.

Perhaps to emphasize the magnitude of the changes made by the Tax Reform Act (TRA) of 1986, Congress redesignated the Internal Revenue Code of 1954 as the Internal Revenue Code of 1986. This change is somewhat deceiving since the tax law was not recodified in 1986, as it had been in 1954. TRA of 1986 merely amended, deleted, or added provisions to the Internal Revenue Code of 1954. For example, before TRA of 1986, § 336 provided the general rule that no gain or loss would be recognized by a corporation when it distributed assets in kind to its shareholders in complete liquidation. After the effective date of TRA of 1986, § 336 provides that gain or loss will be recognized upon the same distributions (see Chapter 6).

The following observations will help clarify the significance of the three Codes:

- Neither the 1939, the 1954, nor the 1986 Code changed all of the tax law existing on the date of enactment. Much of the 1939 Code, for example, was incorporated into the 1954 Code. The same can be said for the transition from the 1954 to the 1986 Code. This point is important in assessing judicial and administrative decisions interpreting provisions under prior Codes. For example, a decision interpreting § 61 of the Internal Revenue Code of 1954 will have continuing validity since this provision carried over unchanged to the Internal Revenue Code of 1986.
- Statutory amendments to the tax law are integrated into the existing Code. Thus, the tax provisions of the American Recovery and Reinvestment Tax Act of 2009 became part of the Internal Revenue Code of 1986.

Do not conclude, however, that the codification and recodification process has made the Internal Revenue Code a simplistic body of laws. To a large extent, the complexity of our current Code can be attributed to its growth.

The Legislative Process

Federal tax legislation generally originates in the House of Representatives, where it is first considered by the House Ways and Means Committee. Tax bills originate in the Senate when they are attached as riders to other legislative proposals.[31] If

[31]The Tax Equity and Fiscal Responsibility Act of 1982 originated in the Senate; its constitutionality was unsuccessfully challenged in the courts. The Senate version of the Deficit Reduction Act of 1984 was attached as an amendment to the Federal Boat Safety Act.

acceptable to the House Ways and Means Committee, the proposed bill is referred to the entire House of Representatives for approval or disapproval. Approved bills are sent to the Senate, where they are referred to the Senate Finance Committee for further consideration.

In the next step, the bill is referred from the Senate Finance Committee to the whole Senate. Assuming no disagreement between the House and the Senate, a bill passed by the Senate is referred to the President for approval or veto. If the bill is approved or if the President's veto is overridden by a two-thirds vote, the bill becomes law and part of the Internal Revenue Code.

When the Senate version of the bill differs from that passed by the House, the Joint Conference Committee resolves these differences. The Joint Conference Committee includes members of the House Ways and Means Committee and the Senate Finance Committee.

Referrals from the House Ways and Means Committee, the Senate Finance Committee, and the Joint Conference Committee are usually accompanied by Committee Reports. These Committee Reports often explain the provisions of the proposed legislation and are therefore a valuable source in ascertaining the *intent* of Congress. What Congress has in mind when it considers and enacts tax legislation is, of course, the key to interpreting that legislation. Since Regulations normally are not issued immediately after a statute is enacted, taxpayers often look to Committee Reports to ascertain congressional intent.

The typical legislative process dealing with tax bills can be summarized as follows:

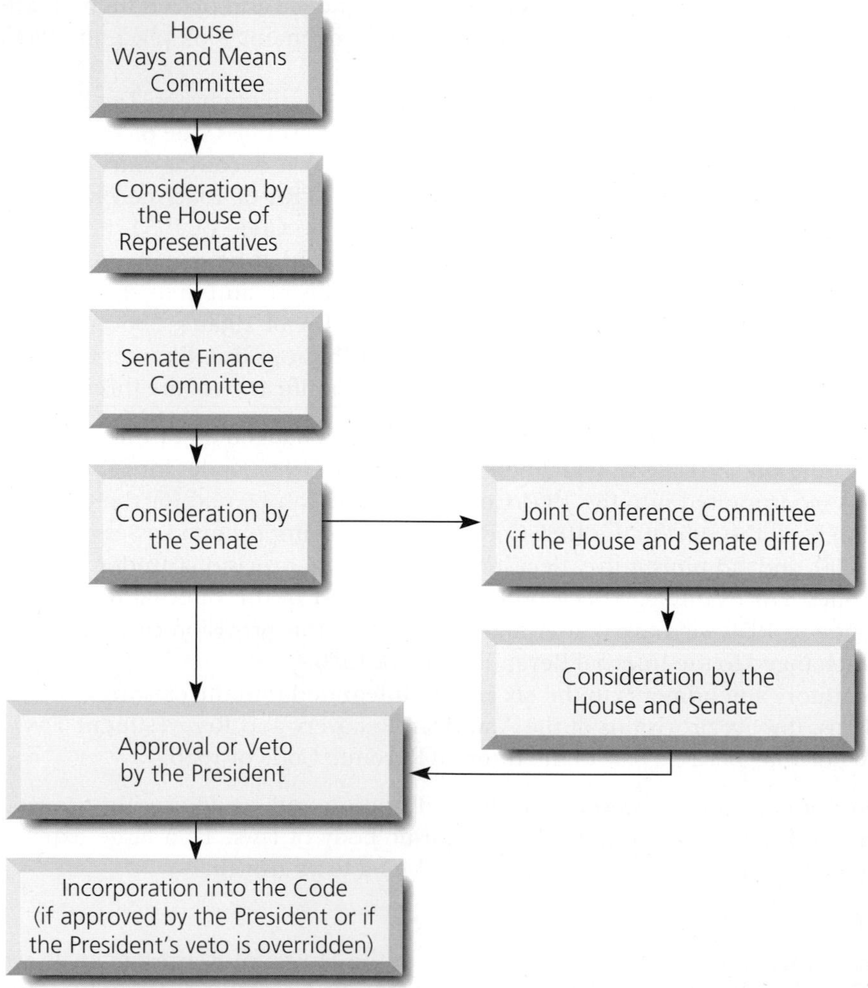

The role of the Joint Conference Committee indicates the importance of compromise in the legislative process. The practical effect of the compromise process can be illustrated by reviewing what happened in the Hiring Incentives to Restore Employment Act of 2010 regarding a new credit.

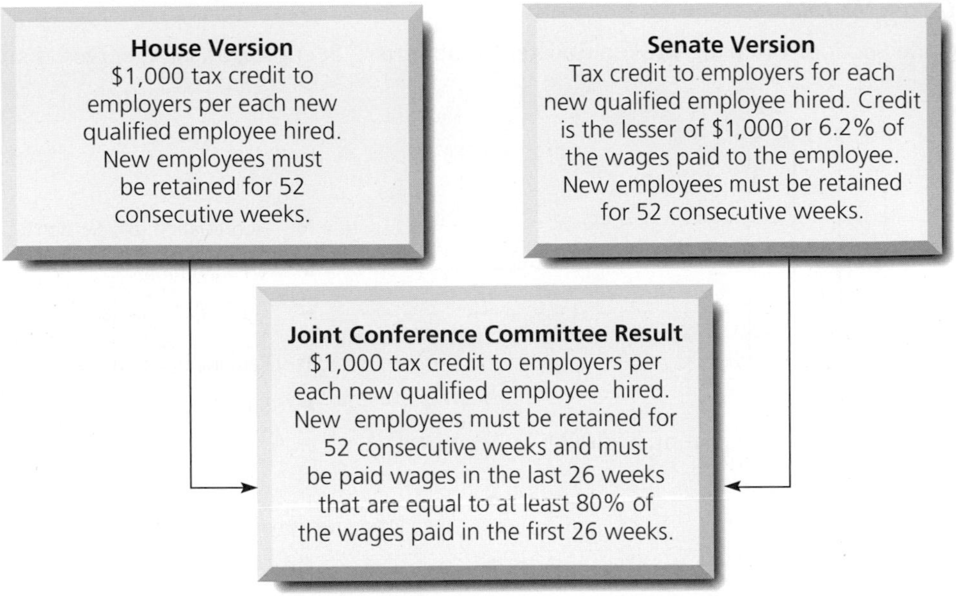

House Version
$1,000 tax credit to employers per each new qualified employee hired. New employees must be retained for 52 consecutive weeks.

Senate Version
Tax credit to employers for each new qualified employee hired. Credit is the lesser of $1,000 or 6.2% of the wages paid to the employee. New employees must be retained for 52 consecutive weeks.

Joint Conference Committee Result
$1,000 tax credit to employers per each new qualified employee hired. New employees must be retained for 52 consecutive weeks and must be paid wages in the last 26 weeks that are equal to at least 80% of the wages paid in the first 26 weeks.

Some tax provisions are commonly referred to by the number the bill received in the House when first proposed or by the name of the member of Congress sponsoring the legislation. For example, the Self-Employed Individuals Tax Retirement Act of 1962 is popularly known as H.R. 10 (the House of Representatives Bill No. 10) or as the Keogh Act (Keogh being one of the members of Congress sponsoring the bill).

Arrangement of the Code

In working with the Code, it helps to understand the format. Note the following partial table of contents:

Subtitle A. Income Taxes
  Chapter 1. Normal Taxes and Surtaxes
    Subchapter A. Determination of Tax Liability
      Part I. Tax on Individuals
        Sections 1–5
      Part II. Tax on Corporations
        Sections 11–12

* * *

In referring to a provision of the Code, the *key* is usually the Section number. In citing Section 2(a) (dealing with the status of a surviving spouse), for example, it is unnecessary to include Subtitle A, Chapter 1, Subchapter A, Part I. Merely mentioning Section 2(a) will suffice since the Section numbers run consecutively and do not begin again with each new Subtitle, Chapter, Subchapter, or Part. Not all Code Section numbers are used, however. Note that Part I ends with Section 5 and Part II starts with Section 11 (at present there are no Sections 6, 7, 8, 9, and 10).[32]

Tax practitioners commonly refer to a specific area of income taxation by Subchapter designation. Some of the more common Subchapter designations include Subchapter C (Corporate Distributions and Adjustments), Subchapter K (Partners and Partnerships), and Subchapter S (Tax Treatment of S Corporations and Their Shareholders). Particularly in the last situation, it is much more convenient to describe the subject of the applicable Code provisions (Sections 1361 through 1379) as S corporation status rather than as the "Tax Treatment of S Corporations and Their Shareholders."

[32]When the 1954 Code was drafted, Section numbers were intentionally omitted. This omission provided flexibility to incorporate later changes into the Code without disrupting its organization. When Congress does not leave enough space, subsequent Code Sections are given A, B, C, etc., designations. A good example is the treatment of §§ 280A through 280H.

Citing the Code

Code Sections often are broken down into subparts.[33] Section 2(a)(1)(A) serves as an example.

Broken down as to content, § 2(a)(1)(A) becomes:

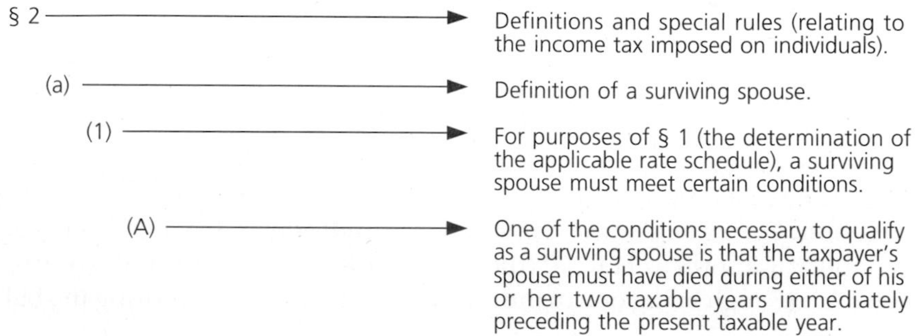

§ 2
Definitions and special rules (relating to the income tax imposed on individuals).
(a)
Definition of a surviving spouse.
(1)
For purposes of § 1 (the determination of the applicable rate schedule), a surviving spouse must meet certain conditions.
(A)
One of the conditions necessary to qualify as a surviving spouse is that the taxpayer's spouse must have died during either of his or her two taxable years immediately preceding the present taxable year.

Throughout this text, references to Code Sections are in the form just given. The symbols "§" and "§§" are used in place of "Section" and "Sections." Unless otherwise stated, all Code references are to the Internal Revenue Code of 1986. The format followed in the remainder of the text is summarized as follows:

Complete Reference	Text Reference
Section 2(a)(1)(A) of the Internal Revenue Code of 1986	§ 2(a)(1)(A)
Sections 1 and 2 of the Internal Revenue Code of 1986	§§ 1 and 2
Section 2 of the Internal Revenue Code of 1954	§ 2 of the Internal Revenue Code of 1954
Section 12(d) of the Internal Revenue Code of 1939[35]	§ 12(d) of the Internal Revenue Code of 1939

ADMINISTRATIVE SOURCES OF THE TAX LAW

The administrative sources of the Federal tax law can be grouped as follows: Treasury Department Regulations, Revenue Rulings and Procedures, and various other administrative pronouncements. All are issued either by the U.S. Treasury Department or the IRS. The role played by the IRS in this process is considered in greater depth in Chapter 17.

Treasury Department Regulations

Regulations are issued by the U.S. Treasury Department under authority granted by Congress. Interpretative by nature, they provide taxpayers with considerable guidance on the meaning and application of the Code. Although not issued by Congress,

[33] Some Code Sections do not have subparts. See, for example, § 482.

[34] Some Code Sections omit the subsection designation and use, instead, the paragraph designation as the first subpart. See, for example, §§ 212(1) and 1222(1).

[35] Section 12(d) of the Internal Revenue Code of 1939 is the predecessor to § 2 of the Internal Revenue Code of 1954. Keep in mind that the 1954 Code superseded the 1939 Code.

Regulations do carry considerable weight. They are an important factor to consider in complying with the tax law. Anyone taking a position contrary to a finalized Regulation must disclose that fact on Form 8275 or Form 8275–R in order to avoid costly penalties.

Since Regulations interpret the Code, they are arranged in the same sequence. Regulations are, however, prefixed by a number that indicates the type of tax or administrative, procedural, or definitional matter to which they relate. For example, the prefix 1 designates the Regulations under the income tax law. Thus, the Regulations under Code § 2 would be cited as Reg. § 1.2, with subparts added for further identification. The numbering of these subparts often has no correlation with the Code subsections. The prefix 20 designates estate tax Regulations; 25 covers gift tax Regulations; 31 relates to employment taxes; and 301 refers to Regulations dealing with procedure and administration. This listing is not all-inclusive.

New Regulations and changes in existing Regulations usually are issued in proposed form before they are finalized. The time interval between the proposal of a Regulation and its finalization permits taxpayers and other interested parties to comment on the propriety of the proposal. **Proposed Regulations** under Code § 2, for example, would be cited as Prop.Reg. § 1.2.

Sometimes the Treasury Department issues **Temporary Regulations** relating to elections and other matters where immediate guidance is critical. Temporary Regulations often are needed for recent legislation that takes effect immediately. Temporary Regulations have the same authoritative value as final Regulations and may be cited as precedent for three years. Temporary Regulations also are issued as Proposed Regulations and automatically expire within three years after the date of issuance. Temporary Regulations and the simultaneously issued Proposed Regulations carry more weight than traditional Proposed Regulations. An example of a Temporary Regulation is Temp.Reg. § 1.428–7T(b)(4), which provides guidance for both prior and new cost sharing arrangements.

Proposed, final, and Temporary Regulations are published in the *Federal Register* (now online) and are reproduced in major tax services. Final Regulations are issued as Treasury Decisions (TDs).

Revenue Rulings and Revenue Procedures

Revenue Rulings are official pronouncements of the National Office of the IRS. Like Regulations, Revenue Rulings are designed to provide interpretation of the tax law. However, they do not carry the same legal force and effect as Regulations and usually deal with more restricted problems.

A Revenue Ruling often results from a specific taxpayer's request for a letter ruling (as discussed below). If the IRS believes that a taxpayer's request for a letter ruling deserves official publication due to its widespread impact, the holding will be converted into a Revenue Ruling. In making this conversion, names, identifying facts, and money amounts are changed to disguise the identity of the requesting taxpayer. The IRS then issues what would have been a letter ruling as a Revenue Ruling.

Revenue Procedures are issued in the same manner as Revenue Rulings, but deal with the internal management practices and procedures of the IRS. Familiarity with these procedures increases taxpayer compliance and helps make the administration of the tax laws more efficient. Revenue Procedures often involve mechanical rules, but sometimes substantive positions are embedded in them as well. Revenue Rulings and Revenue Procedures serve an important function in that they provide guidance to both IRS personnel and taxpayers in handling routine tax matters.

Both Revenue Rulings and Revenue Procedures are published weekly by the U.S. Government in the *Internal Revenue Bulletin* (I.R.B.). Semiannually, the bulletins for a six-month period are gathered together and published in a bound volume called the *Cumulative Bulletin* (C.B.).[36] The proper form for citing Rulings and Procedures

[36]Generally, only two volumes of the *Cumulative Bulletin* are published each year. The I.R.B.'s are available at **www.irs.gov**. Another excellent online source for finding the I.R.B.'s is Tax Almanac (**www.taxalmanac.org**).

depends on whether the item has been published in the *Cumulative Bulletin* or is available in I.R.B. form. Consider, for example, the following transition:

Temporary Citation { Rev.Rul. 2010–19, I.R.B. No. 31, 174.
Explanation: Revenue Ruling Number 19, appearing on page 174 of the 31st weekly issue of the *Internal Revenue Bulletin* for 2010.

Permanent Citation { Rev.Rul. 2010–19, 2010–2 C.B. 174.
Explanation: Revenue Ruling Number 19, appearing on page 174 of volume 2 of the *Cumulative Bulletin* for 2010.

Note that the page reference of 174 is the same for both the I.R.B. (temporary) and the C.B. (permanent) versions of the Ruling. The IRS numbers the pages of the I.R.B.'s consecutively for each six-month period to facilitate their conversion to C.B. form.

Revenue Procedures are cited in the same manner, except that "Rev.Proc." is substituted for "Rev.Rul." Procedures, like Rulings, are published in the *Internal Revenue Bulletin* (the temporary source) and later transferred to the *Cumulative Bulletin* (the permanent source).

Other Administrative Pronouncements

Treasury Decisions (TDs) are issued by the Treasury Department to promulgate new Regulations, to amend or otherwise change existing Regulations, or to announce the position of the Government on selected court decisions. Like Revenue Rulings and Revenue Procedures, TDs are published in the *Internal Revenue Bulletin* and subsequently transferred to the *Cumulative Bulletin*.

Technical Information Releases (TIRs) are usually issued to announce the publication of various IRS pronouncements (e.g., Revenue Rulings, Revenue Procedures).

Letter rulings are issued for a fee by the National Office of the IRS upon a taxpayer's request and describe how the IRS will treat a proposed transaction for tax purposes. In general, they apply only to the taxpayer who asks for and obtains the ruling, but post-1984 rulings may be substantial authority for purposes of avoiding the accuracy-related penalties.[37] Although this procedure may sound like the only real way to carry out effective tax planning, the IRS limits the issuance of letter rulings to restricted, preannounced areas of taxation. Thus, a ruling may not be obtained on many of the problems that are particularly troublesome for taxpayers.[38] For example, the IRS will not issue a ruling as to whether compensation paid to shareholder-employees is reasonable (see Chapter 5) or whether § 269 applies (the acquisition of a corporation to evade or avoid income tax [see Chapter 7]). The main reason the IRS will not rule on such matters is that they involve fact-oriented situations.

The IRS must make letter rulings available for public inspection after identifying details are deleted. Published digests of private letter rulings can be found in *Private Letter Rulings* (published by Research Institute of America), BNA *Daily Tax Reports*, and Tax Analysts *Tax Notes*. In addition, computerized databases of letter rulings are available through several private publishers.

Around 2,000 letter rulings are issued annually. In contrast, Revenue Rulings have declined from a high of 128 in 2003 to 40 in 2009.

The National Office of the IRS releases technical advice memoranda (TAMs) weekly. TAMs resemble letter rulings in that they give the IRS's determination of an issue. Letter rulings, however, are responses to requests by taxpayers, whereas TAMs are issued by the National Office of the IRS in response to questions raised by taxpayers or IRS field personnel during audits. TAMs deal with completed rather than proposed transactions and are often requested for questions relating to exempt organizations and employee plans. Post-1984 TAMs may be substantial authority for

[37]Notice 90–20, 1990–1 C.B. 328, part V (A).

[38]Rev.Proc. 2011–3, I.R.B. No. 1, 111, contains a list of areas in which the IRS will not issue advance rulings. From time to time, subsequent Revenue Procedures are issued that modify or amplify Rev.Proc. 2011–3.

purposes of the accuracy-related penalties. See Chapter 17 for a discussion of these penalties.

Both letter rulings and TAMs are issued with multidigit file numbers. Consider, for example, Ltr.Rul. 201031004, which requests an extension of time to make an election for an association to be taxed as a corporation. Broken down by digits, the file number reveals the following information:

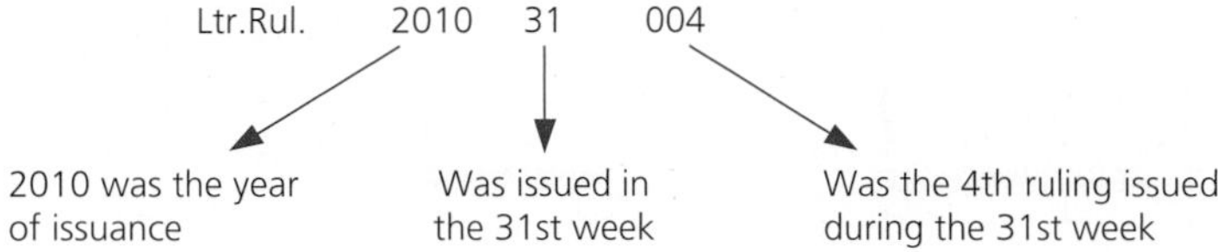

Letter rulings and TAMs issued before 2000 are often cited with only two-digit years (e.g., Ltr.Rul. 9933108).

Like letter rulings, **determination letters** are issued at the request of taxpayers and provide guidance concerning the application of the tax law. They differ from individual rulings in that the issuing source is the Area Director rather than the National Office of the IRS. Also, determination letters usually involve completed (as opposed to proposed) transactions. Determination letters are not published and are made known only to the party making the request.

The following examples illustrate the distinction between individual rulings and determination letters:

EXAMPLE 17

The shareholders of Black Corporation and White Corporation want assurance that the consolidation of the corporations into Gray Corporation will be a nontaxable reorganization (see Chapter 7). The proper approach is to request from the National Office of the IRS an individual ruling concerning the income tax effect of the proposed transaction. ■

EXAMPLE 18

Gilbert operates a barber shop in which he employs eight barbers. To comply with the rules governing income tax and payroll tax withholdings, Gilbert wants to know whether the barbers working for him are employees or independent contractors. The proper procedure is to request a determination letter on the status of the barbers from the Area Director in Holtsville, New York, or Newport, Vermont, depending on the location of the requesting firm. ■

JUDICIAL SOURCES OF THE TAX LAW

The Judicial Process in General

After a taxpayer has exhausted some or all of the remedies available within the IRS (no satisfactory settlement has been reached at the agent or at the conference level discussed in Chapter 17), the dispute can be taken to the Federal courts. The dispute is first considered by a court of original jurisdiction (known as a trial court) with any appeal (either by the taxpayer or the IRS) taken to the appropriate appellate court. In most situations, the taxpayer has a choice of any of four trial courts: a Federal District Court, the U.S. Court of Federal Claims, the Tax Court, or the Small Cases Division of the Tax Court. The trial and appellate court system for Federal tax litigation is illustrated in Figure 1.1.

The broken line between the Tax Court and the Small Cases Division indicates that there is no appeal from the Small Cases Division. Currently, the jurisdiction of the Small Cases Division of the Tax Court is limited to $50,000 or less. The proceedings of the Small Cases Division are informal, and its decisions are not precedents for any other court decision and are not reviewable by any higher court. Proceedings can be more timely and less expensive in the Small Cases Division. Some of these cases can now be found on the U.S. Tax Court Internet site.

FIGURE 1.1 Federal Judicial Tax Process

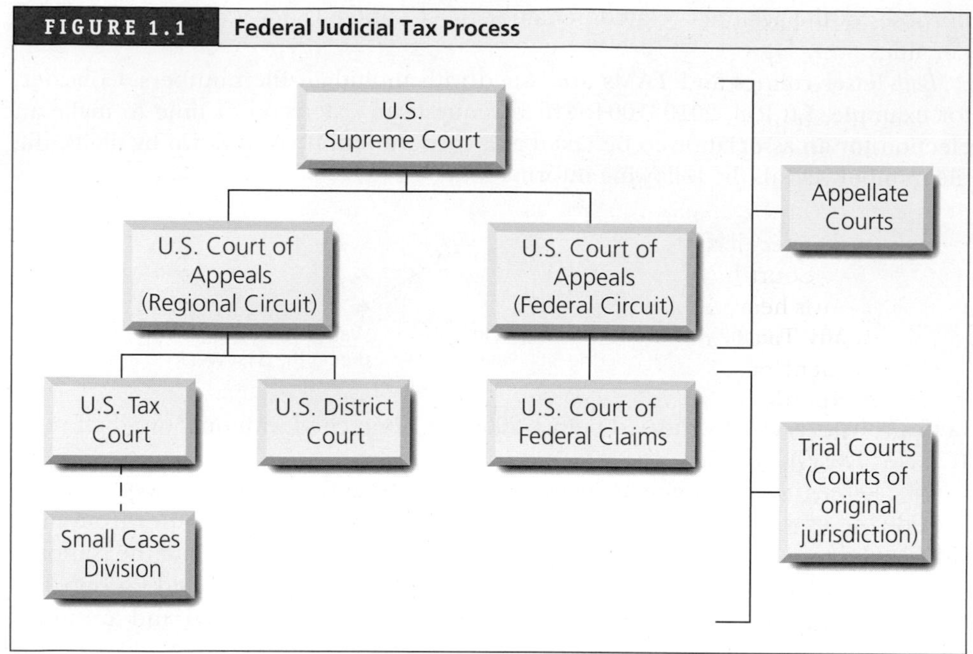

American law, following English law, is frequently *made* by judicial decisions. Under the doctrine of *stare decisis*, each case (except in the Small Cases Division) has precedential value for future cases with the same controlling set of facts.

Judges are not required to follow judicial precedent beyond their own jurisdiction. For example, the decisions of an appellate court are binding only on the trial courts within its jurisdiction and not on other trial courts. Different appellate courts may reach different opinions about the same issue. Further, the doctrine of precedential authority requires a court to follow prior cases only where the issues and material facts of the current case are essentially the same as those involved in the prior decisions.

Most Federal and state appellate court decisions and some decisions of trial courts are published. Published court decisions are organized by jurisdiction (Federal or state) and level of court (appellate or trial).

Trial Courts

The differences between the various trial courts (courts of original jurisdiction) can be summarized as follows:

- There is only one Court of Federal Claims and only one Tax Court, but there are many Federal District Courts. The taxpayer does not select the District Court that will hear the dispute but must sue in the one that has jurisdiction.
- The U.S. Court of Federal Claims has jurisdiction over any claim against the United States that is based on the Constitution, any Act of Congress, or any regulation of an executive department.
- Each of the 94 District Courts has only one judge, the Court of Federal Claims has 16 judges, and the Tax Court has 19 regular judges. In the case of the Tax Court, the whole court will review a case (the case is sent to court conference) only when more important or novel tax issues are involved. Many cases will be heard and decided by one of the 19 regular judges. If a case is reviewed by the full Tax Court, such an *en banc* decision has compelling authority.
- The Court of Federal Claims meets most often in Washington, D.C., while a District Court meets at a prescribed seat for the particular district. Since

each state has at least one District Court and many of the populous states have more, the inconvenience and expense of traveling for the taxpayer and counsel (present with many suits in the Court of Federal Claims) are largely eliminated. The Tax Court is officially based in Washington, D.C., but the various judges travel to different parts of the country and hear cases at predetermined locations and dates. This procedure eases the distance problem for the taxpayer, but it can mean a delay before the case comes to trial and is decided.

- The Tax Court hears only tax cases; the Court of Federal Claims and District Courts hear nontax litigation as well. This difference, as well as the fact that many Tax Court justices have been appointed from IRS or Treasury Department positions, has led some to conclude that the Tax Court has more expertise in tax matters.
- The only court in which a taxpayer can obtain a jury trial is a District Court. Juries can decide only questions of fact and not questions of law, however. Therefore, taxpayers who choose the District Court route often do not request a jury trial. In this event, the judge will decide all issues. Note that a District Court decision is controlling only in the district in which the court has jurisdiction.
- Before the Court of Federal Claims or a District Court can have jurisdiction, the taxpayer must pay the tax deficiency assessed by the IRS and then sue for a refund. If the taxpayer wins (assuming no successful appeal by the IRS), the tax paid plus appropriate interest will be recovered. Jurisdiction in the Tax Court, however, is usually obtained without first paying the assessed tax deficiency. In the event the taxpayer loses in the Tax Court (and no appeal is taken or any appeal is unsuccessful), the deficiency must be paid with accrued interest.
- Appeals from a District Court or a Tax Court decision are to the appropriate U.S. Court of Appeals. Appeals from the Court of Federal Claims go to the Court of Appeals for the Federal Circuit.
- Special trial judges hear small tax cases and write summary opinions. The IRS's deficiency recovery rate is higher here than in regular Tax Court decisions. Beginning in 2001, these summary opinions are now posted on the U.S. Tax Court's Internet site; regular decisions have been posted there since 1995.
- Since there are "gray areas" in the tax laws, courts may disagree as to the proper tax treatment of a dispute. With these splits in judicial authority, a taxpayer may have some flexibility to "forum shop"—choose the most favorable route to bring a lawsuit.

Some of the characteristics of the judicial system described above are summarized in Concept Summary 1.1.

Appellate Courts

An appeal from a trial court goes to the U.S. Court of Appeals of appropriate jurisdiction. Generally, a three-judge panel hears a Court of Appeals case, but occasionally the *full* court will decide more controversial conflicts. A jury trial is not available.

Figure 1.2 shows the geographic area within the jurisdiction of each Federal Court of Appeals.

If the IRS loses at the trial court level (District Court, Tax Court, or Court of Federal Claims), it need not (and frequently does not) appeal. The fact that an appeal is not made, however, does not indicate that the IRS agrees with the result and will not litigate similar issues in the future.

The IRS may decide not to appeal for a number of reasons. First, the current litigation load may be heavy. As a consequence, the IRS may decide that available personnel should be assigned to other, more important cases. Second, the IRS may determine that this is not a good case to appeal. For example, the taxpayer may be in

CONCEPT SUMMARY 1.1

Federal Judicial System

Issue	U.S. Tax Court	U.S. District Court	U.S. Court of Federal Claims
Number of judges per court	19*	1	16
Payment of deficiency before trial	No	Yes	Yes
Jury trial available	No	Yes	No
Types of disputes	Tax cases only	Most criminal/civil cases	Claims against the United States
Jurisdiction	Nationwide	Location of taxpayer	Nationwide
Appeal route	U.S. Court of Appeals	U.S. Court of Appeals	U.S. Court of Appeals for the Federal Circuit

*There are also 14 special trial judges and 9 senior judges.

a sympathetic position, or the facts may be particularly strong in his or her favor. In such event, the IRS may wait to test the legal issues involved with a taxpayer who has a much weaker case. Third, if the appeal is from a District Court or the Tax Court, the Court of Appeals of jurisdiction could have some bearing on whether the IRS decides to pursue an appeal. Based on past experience and precedent, the IRS may conclude that the chance for success on a particular issue might be more promising in another Court of Appeals. The IRS will wait for a similar case to arise in a different jurisdiction.

CHOOSING CASES FOR APPEAL

The IRS loses a tax case against a prominent citizen in the U.S. District Court of Iowa. The taxpayer, a minister, had set up three separate trusts for each of his three children (i.e., a total of nine trusts). The IRS argued that under Reg. § 1.641(a)–0(c) these trusts should be consolidated and treated as three trusts to stop the taxpayer from mitigating the progressive tax structure (e.g., the 35 percent top tax bracket).

The IRS has decided to appeal a case in the multiple trust area. As one of the IRS's attorneys, you must choose between the Iowa case and a similar multiple trust conflict in the U.S. District Court of Virginia. Here the taxpayer is a CPA who has established two different trusts for her two children (i.e., a total of four trusts). [See *Estelle Morris Trusts*, 51 T.C. 20 (1968).] In making your decision, you note that potentially more sympathy may be associated with the minister's profession than with the CPA's. Other considerations are the facts indicating that the attempt at tax avoidance is more egregious in the Iowa case and a colleague's opinion that the Virginia case is winnable. Which case will you select? Comment on whether it is fair for the IRS to select a case to appeal in this fashion.

District Courts, the Tax Court, and the Court of Federal Claims must abide by the precedents set by the Court of Appeals of jurisdiction. A particular Court of Appeals need not follow the decisions of another Court of Appeals. All courts, however, must follow the decisions of the U.S. Supreme Court.

The role of appellate courts is limited to a review of the trial record compiled by the trial courts. Thus, the appellate process usually involves a determination of whether the trial court applied the proper law in arriving at its decision. Usually, an appellate court will not dispute a lower court's fact-finding determination.

An appeal can have any of a number of possible outcomes. The appellate court may approve (affirm) or disapprove (reverse) the lower court's finding, and it may also send the case back for further consideration (remand). When many issues are

FIGURE 1.2 **The Federal Courts of Appeals**

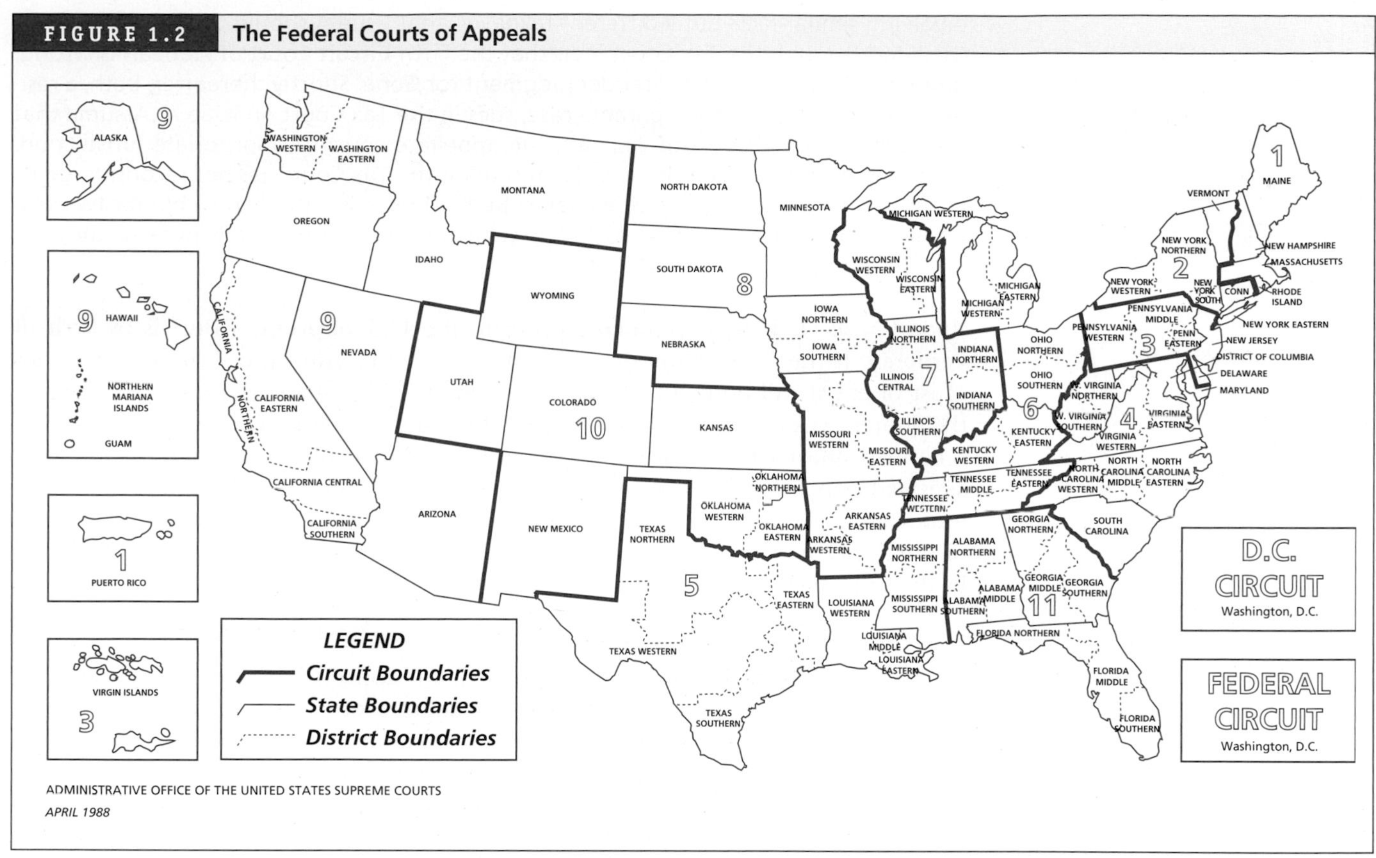

involved, it is not unusual to encounter a mixed result. Thus, the lower court may be affirmed (*aff'd*) on Issue A and reversed (*rev'd*) on Issue B, while Issue C is remanded (*rem'd*) for additional fact finding.

When more than one judge is involved in the decision-making process, disagreement is not uncommon. In addition to the majority view, one or more judges may concur (agree with the result reached but not with some or all of the reasoning) or dissent (disagree with the result). In any one case, the majority view controls. But concurring and dissenting views can have influence on other courts or, at some subsequent date when the composition of the court has changed, even on the same court.

Appealing from the Tax Court The Tax Court is a national court, meaning that it hears and decides cases from all parts of the country. For many years, the Tax Court followed a policy of deciding cases based on what it thought the result should be, even when its decision might be appealed to a Court of Appeals that had previously decided a similar case differently.

Some years ago, this policy was changed. Now the Tax Court will still decide a case as it feels the law should be applied *only* if the Court of Appeals of appropriate jurisdiction has not yet ruled on the issue or has previously decided a similar case in accordance with the Tax Court's decision. If the Court of Appeals of appropriate jurisdiction has previously held squarely on point otherwise, the Tax Court will conform even though it disagrees with the holding.[39] This policy is known as the *Golsen* rule.

EXAMPLE 19

Gene lives in Texas and sues in the Tax Court on Issue A. The Fifth Circuit Court of Appeals, the appellate court of appropriate jurisdiction, has already decided, in a case

[39] *Jack E. Golsen*, 54 T.C. 742 (1970); see also *John A. Lardas*, 99 T.C. 490 (1992).

involving similar facts but a different taxpayer, that Issue A should be resolved against the IRS. Although the Tax Court feels that the Fifth Circuit Court of Appeals is wrong, under the *Golsen* rule, it will render judgment for Gene. Shortly thereafter, Beth, a resident of New York, in a comparable case, sues in the Tax Court on Issue A. Assume that the Second Circuit Court of Appeals, the appellate court of appropriate jurisdiction, has never expressed itself on Issue A. Presuming the Tax Court has not reconsidered its position on Issue A, it will decide against Beth. Thus, it is entirely possible for two taxpayers suing in the same court to end up with opposite results merely because they live in different parts of the country. ■

Appeal to the U.S. Supreme Court Appeal to the U.S. Supreme Court is by Writ of **Certiorari**. If the Court agrees to hear the case, it will grant the Writ (*cert. granted*). Most often, it will deny jurisdiction (*cert. denied*). For whatever reason or reasons, the Supreme Court rarely hears tax cases. The Court usually grants certiorari to resolve a conflict among the Courts of Appeals (e.g., two or more appellate courts have assumed opposing positions on a particular issue) or when the tax issue is extremely important. The granting of a Writ of Certiorari indicates that at least four members of the Supreme Court believe that the issue is of sufficient importance to be heard by the full Court.

Judicial Citations

Having briefly described the judicial process, it is appropriate to consider the more practical problem of the relationship of case law to tax research. As previously noted, court decisions are an important source of tax law. The ability to cite a case and to locate it is therefore a must in working with the tax law. The usual pattern for a judicial citation is as follows: case name, volume number, reporter series, page or paragraph number, and court (where necessary).

Judicial Citations—The U.S. Tax Court A good starting point is the U.S. Tax Court. The Tax Court issues three types of decisions: Regular decisions, Memorandum decisions, and summary opinions. They differ in both substance and form. In terms of substance, Memorandum decisions deal with situations necessitating only the application of already established principles of law. Regular decisions involve novel issues not previously resolved by the Tax Court. In actual practice, this distinction is not always preserved. Not infrequently, Memorandum decisions will be encountered that appear to warrant Regular status and vice versa. At any rate, do not conclude that Memorandum decisions possess no value as precedents. Both Memorandum and Regular decisions represent the position of the Tax Court and, as such, can be relied upon. Summary opinions, on the other hand, are issued in small tax cases and may not be used as precedent in any other case.

Regular decisions are published by the U.S. Government in a series called *Tax Court of the United States Reports* (T.C.). Each volume of these reports covers a six-month period (January 1 through June 30 and July 1 through December 31) and is given a succeeding volume number. But, there is usually a time lag between the date a decision is rendered and the date it appears in bound form. A temporary citation may be necessary to help the researcher locate a recent Regular decision. Consider, for example, the temporary and permanent citations for *Morton L. Ginsberg*, a decision filed on April 28, 2008:

Temporary Citation	*Morton L. Ginsberg*, 130 T.C. ___, No. 7 (2008). *Explanation:* Page number left blank because not yet known.
Permanent Citation	*Morton L. Ginsberg*, 130 T.C. 88 (2008). *Explanation:* Page number now available.

Both citations tell us that the case ultimately will appear in Volume 130 of the *Tax Court of the United States Reports*. But until this volume is bound and made available to the general public, the page number must be left blank. Instead, the temporary citation identifies the case as being the 7th Regular decision issued by the

Tax Court since Volume 129 ended. With this information, the decision can be easily located in either of the special Tax Court services published by Commerce Clearing House (CCH) and by Research Institute of America (RIA—formerly by Prentice-Hall [P-H]). Once Volume 130 is released, the permanent citation can be substituted and the number of the case dropped. Starting in 1995, both Regular and Memorandum decisions are issued on the U.S. Tax Court website (**www.ustaxcourt.gov**).

Before 1943, the Tax Court was called the Board of Tax Appeals, and its decisions were published as the *United States Board of Tax Appeals Reports* (B.T.A.). These 47 volumes cover the period from 1924 to 1942. For example, the citation *Karl Pauli* 11 B.T.A. 784 (1928) refers to the 11th volume of the *Board of Tax Appeals Reports*, page 784, issued in 1928.

Memorandum decisions are published by CCH and by RIA (formerly by P-H). Consider for example, the three different ways that *Nick R. Hughes* can be cited:

> *Nick R. Hughes*, T.C.Memo. 2009–94
> The 94th Memorandum decision issued by the Tax Court in 2009.
>
> *Nick R. Hughes*, 97 TCM 1488
> Page 1488 of Vol. 97 of the CCH *Tax Court Memorandum Decisions.*
>
> *Nick R. Hughes*, 2009 RIA T.C. Memo. ¶2009,094
> Paragraph 2009,094 of the RIA *T.C. Memorandum Decisions.*

Note that the third citation contains the same information as the first. Thus ¶2009,094 indicates the following information about the case: year 2009, 94th T.C.Memo. decision. Before the Prentice-Hall Service division was incorporated into the Research Institute of America, "P-H" was used in the third citation instead of "RIA."[40]

Summary opinions are cited as in the following example for *John H. Wong*, filed on October 5, 2009.

> *John H. Wong*, T.C. Summary Opinion 2009–152.

Starting in 2001, summary opinions are reported on the U.S. Tax Court website.

Judicial Citations—The U.S. District Courts, Claims Court, and Courts of Appeals District Court, Claims Court (now Court of Federal Claims), Court of Appeals, and Supreme Court decisions dealing with Federal tax matters are reported in both the CCH *U.S. Tax Cases* (USTC) and the RIA (formerly P-H) *American Federal Tax Reports* (AFTR) series.

Federal District Court decisions, dealing with *both* tax and nontax issues, are also published by West (owned by Thomson Reuters) in its *Federal Supplement* (F.Supp.) series. The following examples illustrate how a District Court case can be cited in three different forms:

> *Turner v. U.S.*, 2004–1 USTC ¶60,478 (D.Ct. Tex., 2004).
> *Explanation:* Reported in the first volume of the *U.S. Tax Cases* published by Commerce Clearing House for calendar year 2004 (2004–1) and located at paragraph 60,478 (¶ 60,478).
>
> *Turner v. U.S.*, 93 AFTR 2d 2004–686 (D.Ct. Tex., 2004).
> *Explanation:* Reported in the 93rd volume of the second series of the *American Federal Tax Reports* (AFTR 2d) published by Prentice-Hall and beginning on page 686.
>
> *Turner v. U.S.*, 306 F.Supp.2d 668 (D.Ct. Tex., 2004).
> *Explanation:* Reported in the 306th volume of the second series of the *Federal Supplement* (F.Supp.2d) published by West and beginning on page 668.

[40]In this text, the Research Institute of America (RIA) citation for Memorandum decisions of the U.S. Tax Court is omitted. Thus, *Nick R. Hughes* will be cited as 97 TCM 1488, T.C.Memo. 2009–94.

In all of the preceding citations, note that the name of the case is the same (Turner being the taxpayer), as is the reference to the Federal District Court of Texas (D.Ct. Tex.) and the year the decision was rendered (2004).[41]

Beginning in October of 1982, decisions of the Claims Court are reported by West in a series designated *Federal Claims Reporter*. Thus, the Claims Court decision in *Recchie v. U.S.* appears as follows:

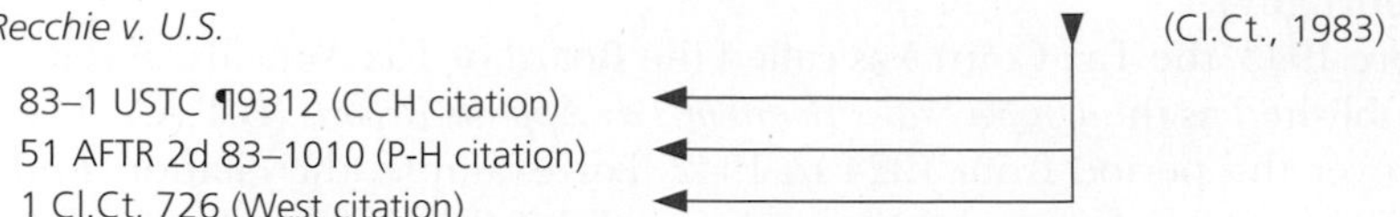

Beginning on October 30, 1992, the Claims Court underwent a further name change. The new designation, U.S. Court of Federal Claims, began with Volume 27 of the former Cl.Ct. (West citation), now abbreviated as Fed.Cl.

Decisions of the Courts of Appeals are published in a West reporter designated as the *Federal Third* (F.3d) series, which began in October 1993, at the conclusion of the *Federal Second* (F.2d) series. Illustrations of the different forms follow:

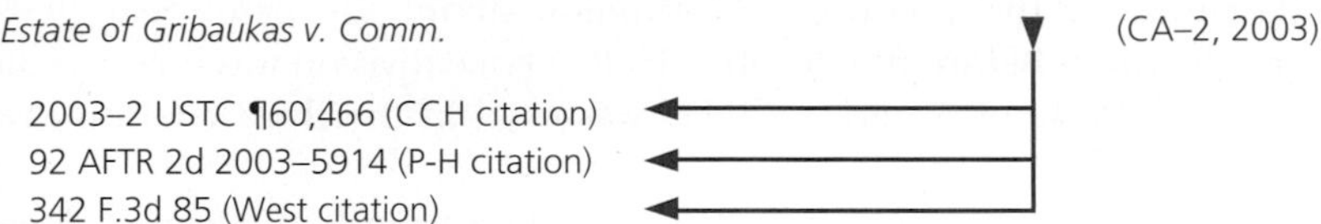

Note that *Estate of Gribaukas v. Comm.* is a decision rendered by the Second Circuit Court of Appeals in 2003 (CA–2, 2003).

If the IRS loses in a decision, it may indicate whether it agrees or disagrees with the results reached by the court by publishing an **acquiescence** ("A" or "*Acq.*") or **nonacquiescence** ("NA" or "*Nonacq.*"), respectively. The acquiescence or nonacquiescence is published in the *Internal Revenue Bulletin* and the *Cumulative Bulletin* as an *Action on Decision.* The IRS can retroactively revoke an acquiescence or nonacquiescence. Originally, acquiescences and nonacquiescences were published only for Regular U.S. Tax Court decisions, but since 1991 the IRS has expanded its acquiescence program to include other civil tax cases where guidance is helpful.

Judicial Citations—The U.S. Supreme Court Like all other Federal tax cases (except those rendered by the U.S. Tax Court), Supreme Court decisions are published by Commerce Clearing House in the USTCs and by Research Institute of America in the AFTRs. The U.S. Government Printing Office also publishes these decisions in the *United States Supreme Court Reports* (U.S.) as does West in its *Supreme Court Reporter* (S.Ct.) and the Lawyer's Co-operative Publishing Company in its *United States Reports, Lawyer's Edition* (L.Ed.). The following illustrates the different ways the same decision can be cited:

[41]In the text, the case will be cited in the following form: *Turner v. U.S.*, 2004–1 USTC ¶60,478, 93 AFTR 2d 2004 686, 306 F.Supp.2d 668 (D.Ct 2004).

GLOBAL *Tax Issues*

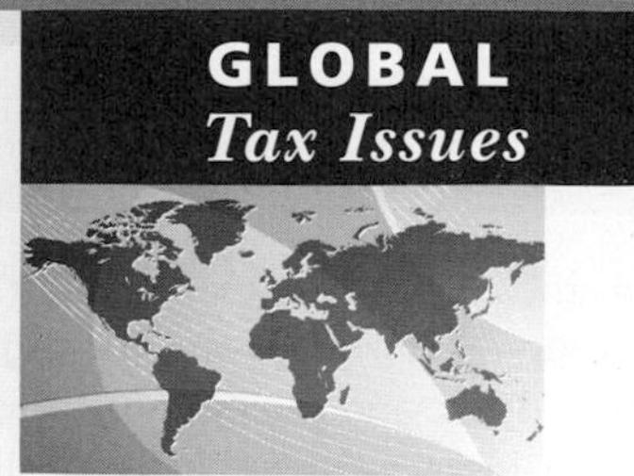

Rolling Stones Gather Little Taxes

The Rolling Stones—Sir Mick Jagger, Charlie Watts, and Keith Richards—paid tax of only 1.6 percent on their earnings of approximately $455 million over the past 20 years. Not only did they use offshore trusts and companies to obtain tax breaks, but more importantly, they became tax exiles from Great Britain, moving to the Netherlands in 1972. There is no direct tax on royalties under Dutch law. Sir Mick Jagger's fortune is estimated to be approximately $385 million. International tax planning does help a poor soul.

The parenthetical reference (USSC, 1969) identifies the decision as having been rendered by the U.S. Supreme Court in 1969. The citations given in this text for Supreme Court decisions will be limited to the CCH (USTC), the RIA or P-H for older volumes (AFTR), and the West (S.Ct.) versions.

OTHER SOURCES OF THE TAX LAW

Other sources of the tax law include tax treaties and tax periodicals.

Effect of Treaties

The United States signs certain tax treaties (sometimes called tax conventions) with foreign countries to render mutual assistance in tax enforcement and to avoid double taxation. The Technical and Miscellaneous Revenue Act of 1988 provided that neither a tax law nor a tax treaty takes general precedence. Thus, when there is a direct conflict, the most recent item will take precedence. More than 34 Sections of the Code contain direct references to treaties [e.g., § 245(a)(10)].

Tax Periodicals

The use of tax periodicals can often shorten the research time needed to resolve a tax problem. If the article is relevant to the issue at hand, it may provide the references needed to locate the primary sources of the tax that apply (e.g., citations to judicial decisions, Regulations, and other IRS pronouncements). Thus, the researcher obtains a "running start" in arriving at a solution to the problem.

Among the many indexes available for locating tax articles are *Federal Tax Articles* (published by CCH) and *Index to Federal Tax Articles* (published by Warren, Gorham and Lamont). These indexes are updated periodically but are available only in print form.

The following are some of the more useful tax periodicals with their online addresses (usually preceded by **http://**):

Journal of Taxation
Journal of International Taxation
Practical Tax Strategies
Estate Planning
Corporate Taxation
Business Entities
ria.thomsonreuters.com/Journals

The Tax Executive
www.tei.org

The Tax Adviser
aicpa.org/pubs/taxadv

Tax Law Review
www.law.nyu.edu/llmjsd/tax/taxlawreview/ECM_DLV_005627

Journal of the American Taxation Association
aaahq.org/ata/_ATAMenu/ATAPubJATA.html

The ATA Journal of Legal Tax Research
aaahq.org/ata/_ATAMenu/ATAPubJLTR.html

Oil, Gas & Energy Quarterly
www.bus.lsu.edu/accounting/faculty/lcrumbley/oilgas.html

Trusts and Estates
trustsandestates.com

Journal of Passthrough Entities
TAXES—The Tax Magazine
tax.cchgroup.com/Books

Tax Notes
www.taxanalysts.com

FINANCIAL DISCLOSURE *Insights* — WHERE DOES GAAP COME FROM?

As this chapter has explained, the tax law has many sources including Congress and the legislators of other countries, the courts, and the IRS. Similarly, accounting principles also have many sources. In reconciling the tax and financial accounting reporting of a transaction, the tax professional may need to know the hierarchy of authority of accounting principles so that the proper level of importance can be assigned to a specific GAAP document. The diagram shown below presents the sources of GAAP, listed in general order of authority, from highest to lowest.

Professional research is conducted to find and analyze the sources of accounting reporting standards, in much the same way that tax professionals conduct research into open tax questions. In fact, many of the publishers that provide tax research materials also can be used to find GAAP and IFRS documents. These include the Research Institute of America (RIA) and Commerce Clearing House (CCH). The Financial Accounting Standards Board (FASB) also makes its standards and interpretations available by subscription.

Highest Authority

- Financial Accounting Standards and Interpretations of the FASB.
- Pronouncements of bodies that preceded the FASB, such as the Accounting Principles Board (APB).

- FASB Technical Bulletins.
- Audit and Accounting Guides, prepared by the American Institute of CPAs (AICPA) and cleared by the FASB.
- Practice Bulletins, prepared by the AICPA and cleared by the FASB.

- Interpretation Guides of the FASB Staff.
- Accounting Interpretations of the AICPA.
- IASB Accounting Standards.
- FASB Concepts Statements.
- Widely accepted accounting practices, professional journals, accounting textbooks, and treatises.

1.5 Working With the Tax Law—Locating and Using Tax Sources

LO.6

List and assess tax law sources.

Tax law consists of a body of legislative (e.g., Code Sections, tax treaties), administrative (e.g., Regulations, Rulings), and judicial (e.g., court cases) pronouncements. Working with the tax law, moreover, requires being able to locate and effectively use these sources. A key consideration is the time required to carry out this search and find activity.

Unless the problem is simple (e.g., the Code Section is known and there is a Regulation on point), the research process will begin with a tax service.

COMMERCIAL TAX SERVICES

Due to various changes, categorizing tax services has become an almost impossible task. The old classification of *annotated* (i.e., organized by Internal Revenue Code) or *topical* (i.e., organized by major topics) no longer is appropriate for many services as their format has been modified. Often the change is due to the acquisition of a competing service. For example, the *United States Tax Reporter* (annotated) now has a version containing the *Federal Tax Coordinator 2d* (topical).

In addition, services can no longer be distinguished based on whether they are available in hard copy or online versions. *Tax Management Portfolios,* for example, was previously solely a print publication. Now, like most other services, it is also accessible online.

The list of publishers producing the tax services has also changed. Not only have ownership changes occurred (e.g., Research Institute of America [RIA] now owns Prentice-Hall [P-H]), but new players have arrived. LexisNexis, for example, through *Tax Center,* now offers primary tax services such as the Code and Regulations as well as material obtained from the Matthew Bender and Kleinrock services. Due to the common ownership by Thomson Reuters, Westlaw offers the RIA products and also the Mertens service.

Like automobiles, many new services are available in standard models or with extra features, depending on the practitioner's needs and financial resources. Thus, a practitioner with minimal tax research needs can select an abbreviated version of the regular ("standard") service (e.g., CCH and its two-volume *Federal Tax Guide*), while another chooses a product with "extras" (e.g., CCH and its *Federal Excise Tax Reporter*).

A partial list of the available commercial services includes the following:

- *Standard Federal Tax Reporter,* Commerce Clearing House.
- *Tax Research NetWork,* Commerce Clearing House Internet service.
- *United States Tax Reporter,* Research Institute of America.
- *RIA Checkpoint,* Research Institute of America. This is the online version of *United States Tax Reporter* and can also include the *Federal Tax Coordinator.*
- ATX/Kleinrock *Tax Expert,* CCH/Wolters Kluwer Business Services.
- *Tax Management Portfolios,* Bureau of National Affairs.
- *Mertens Law of Federal Income Taxation,* West Group.
- Westlaw services—compilations include access to *Tax Management Portfolios, Federal Tax Coordinator 2d,* and *Mertens.*
- *Tax Center,* LexisNexis compilation of primary sources and various materials taken from CCH, Matthew Bender, Kleinrock, and Bureau of National Affairs.
- *Federal Research Library,* Tax Analysts (a nonprofit organization) databases dealing with explanations and commentaries on primary source materials.

USING ONLINE SERVICES

Instructions on how to use a tax service are not particularly worthwhile unless a specific service is involved. Even then, instructions need to be followed by hands-on experience. Following certain procedures, however, can simplify the process of using an online version of a tax service. Since a practitioner's time is valuable and various research services base usage charges on time spent, time is of the essence.

Given this emphasis on time, every shortcut helps. Some suggestions (most of which are familiar to any user of the Internet) follow.[42]

- Take care in choosing keywords for the search. Words with a broad usage, such as *income,* are worthless when standing alone. If the researcher is interested in qualified dividend income, even *dividend income* is too broad as it will call up a variety of subjects such as stock dividends, constructive dividends, and liquidating dividends. By using *qualified dividend income* at the outset, the search is considerably narrowed. In RIA *Checkpoint,* for example, these two modifications narrowed the search from 10,000 items to 3,824 and finally to 884. Obviously, further contraction will be needed, but at least the researcher is starting with a considerably narrower field.
- Take advantage of *connectors* to place parameters on the search and further restrict the output. Although each service has its own set of connectors, many are common as to usage. Thus, enclosing words in quotation marks (e.g., "personal service corporation") means *exact phrase* in both RIA *Checkpoint* and CCH *NetWork.*

[42]For a more complete discussion of the use of RIA *Checkpoint* and CCH *Tax Research NetWork,* as well as Internet research in taxation in general, see William A. Raabe, Gerald E. Whittenburg, and Debra L. Sanders, *Federal Tax Research,* 9th ed. (Cincinnati, OH: South-Western Cengage Learning, 2011), Chapters 6 and 7.

- Be selective in choosing a database. For example, if the research project will not involve case law, there is no point in including judicial decisions in the search database. Doing so just adds to the output and will necessitate further screening through a search modification.
- Although the keyword approach is most frequently used, consider using the table of contents or index, or searching by citation. The first two of these methods are the usual approach with print versions of a tax service. Citations may be used to search for statutory (e.g., Code Section), administrative (e.g., Rev.Rul.), or judicial (e.g., Tax Court) sources, depending on the service. When a judicial citation is wanted and only the taxpayer's last name is known, however, problems can arise. For example, how many responses would a taxpayer named Smith yield? Likewise, before a Code Section is used, consider its scope. How many items would § 162 retrieve? Nevertheless, the use of content, index, or citation can be a valuable time-saver under the right circumstances.

NONCOMMERCIAL ONLINE SOURCES

The Internet provides a wealth of tax information in several popular forms, sometimes at no direct cost to the researcher. Using so-called browser software that often is distributed with new computer systems and their communication devices, the tax professional can access information provided around the world that can aid the research process.

- *Home pages (sites) on the Web* are provided by accounting and consulting firms, publishers, tax academics and libraries, and governmental bodies as a means of making information widely available or of soliciting subscriptions or consulting engagements. The best sites offer links to other sites and direct contact to the site providers. One of the best sites available to the tax practitioner is the Internal Revenue Service's home page, illustrated in Exhibit 1.1. This site offers downloadable forms and instructions, "plain English" versions of Regulations, and news update items. Exhibit 1.2 lists some of the websites that may be most useful to tax researchers and their Internet addresses as of press date. Particularly useful is the directory at **http://taxsites.com**, which provides links to accounting and tax sources (includes international as well as payroll).
- *Newsgroups* provide a means by which information related to the tax law can be exchanged among taxpayers, tax professionals, and others who subscribe to the group's services. Newsgroup members can read the exchanges among other members and offer replies and suggestions to inquiries as desired. Discussions address the interpretation and application of existing law, analysis of proposals and new pronouncements, and reviews of tax software.

1.6 Working with the Tax Law—Tax Research

LO.7
Demonstrate tax research.

Tax research is the method used to determine the best available solution to a situation that possesses tax consequences. In other words, it is the process of finding a competent and professional conclusion to a tax problem. The problem may originate from either completed or proposed transactions. In the case of a completed transaction, the objective of the research is to determine the tax result of what has already taken place. For example, is the expenditure incurred by the taxpayer deductible or not deductible for tax purposes? When dealing with proposed transactions, the tax research process is concerned with the determination of possible alternative tax consequences. To the extent that tax research leads to a choice of alternatives or otherwise influences the future actions of the taxpayer, it becomes the key to effective tax planning.

EXHIBIT 1.1 **The IRS's Home Page**

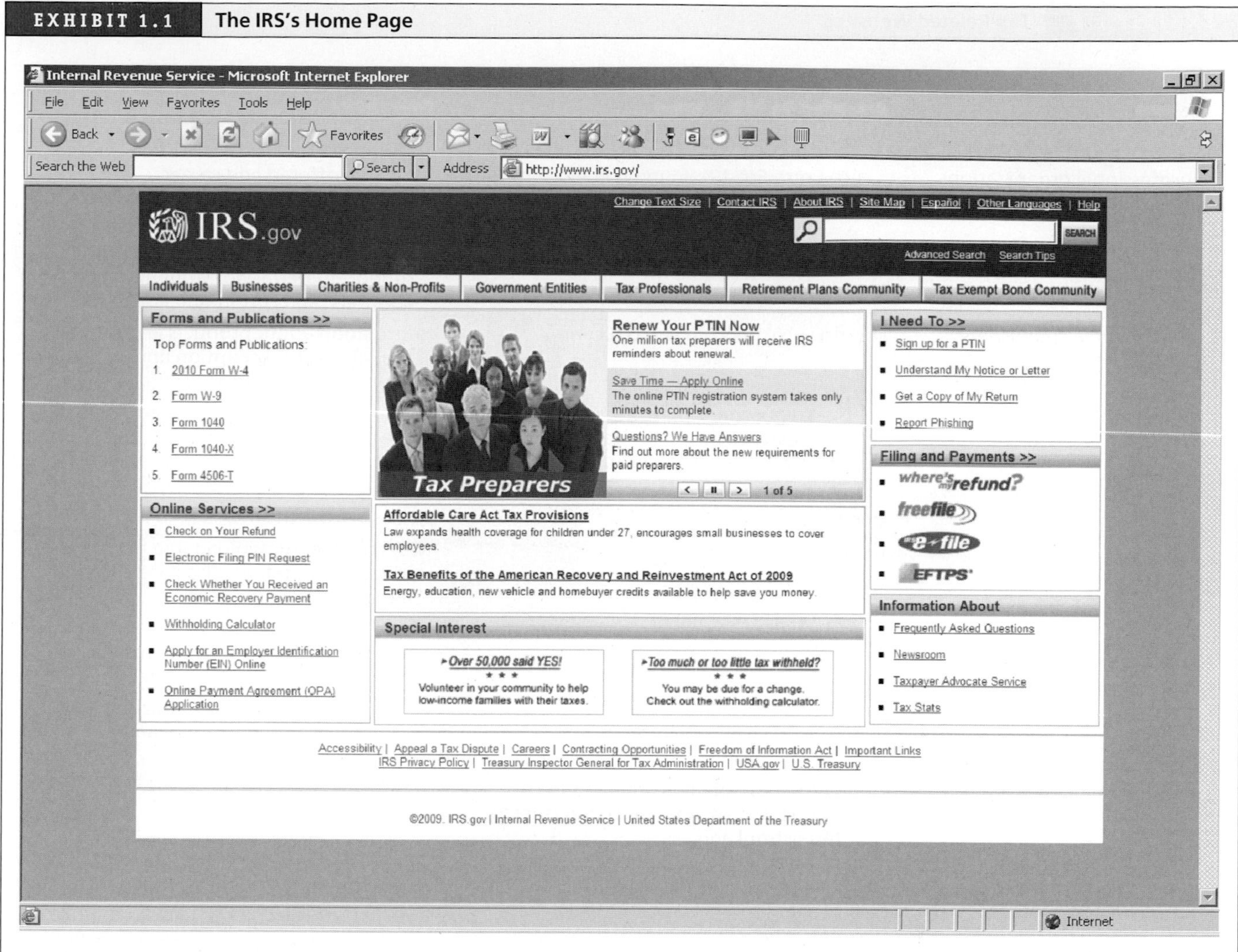

Tax research involves the following procedures:

- Identifying and refining the problem.
- Locating the appropriate tax law sources.
- Assessing the validity of the tax law sources.
- Arriving at the solution or at alternative solutions while giving due consideration to nontax factors.
- Effectively communicating the solution to the taxpayer or the taxpayer's representative.
- Following up on the solution (where appropriate) in light of new developments.

This process is depicted schematically in Figure 1.3. The broken lines indicate steps of particular interest when tax research is directed toward proposed, rather than completed, transactions.

IDENTIFYING THE PROBLEM

Problem identification starts with a compilation of the relevant facts involved. In this regard, *all* of the facts that might have a bearing on the problem must be gathered as any omission could modify the solution reached. To illustrate, consider what appears to be a very simple problem.

EXHIBIT 1.2 **Tax-Related Websites**

Website	WWW Address at Press Date (Usually preceded by http://www.)	Description
Accounting firms and professional organizations	For instance, the AICPA's page is at **aicpa.org**, Ernst & Young is at **ey.com**, and KPMG is at **kpmg.com**	Tax planning newsletters, descriptions of services offered and career opportunities, and exchange of data with clients and subscribers
Cengage Learning South-Western	**cengage.com/taxation/swft**	Informational updates, newsletters, support materials for students and adopters, and continuing education
Commercial tax publishers	For instance, **tax.com** and **cch.com**	Information about products and services available for subscription and newsletter excerpts
Court opinions	The site at **lexisone.com/lx1/caselaw/freecaselaw** covers some state, Federal circuit (last 10 years), and Supreme Court (all years) decisions but not Tax Court	Provides a synopsis of result reached by the court
Federal Register	**gpoaccess.gov/fr**	Releases from the IRS, such as Regulations
Internal Revenue Service	**irs.gov**	News releases, downloadable forms and instructions, tables, Circular 230, and e-mail
Tax Analysts	**taxanalysts.com**	Policy-oriented readings on the tax law and proposals to change it, moderated bulletins on various tax subjects
Tax Foundation	**taxfoundation.org**	Nonprofit educational organization that promotes sound tax policy and measures tax burdens
Tax laws online	Regulations are at **law.cornell.edu/cfr** and the Code is at **uscode.house.gov/search/criteria.shtml** and **www4.law.cornell.edu/uscode**	
Tax Sites Directory	**taxsites.com**	References and links to tax sites on the Internet, including state and Federal tax sites, academic and professional pages, tax forms, and software
U.S. Tax Court decisions	**ustaxcourt.gov**	Recent U.S. Tax Court decisions

NOTE: Caution: addresses change frequently.

EXAMPLE 20

Dana Pehrson advances $92,000 to her nephew in 2004 to enable him to attend a private college. Seven years later, she claims a bad debt deduction for $77,000 that the nephew has not repaid. The problem: Is Dana entitled to a bad debt deduction? ■

Refining the Problem

Before a bad debt deduction can arise, it must be established that a debt really existed. In a related-party setting (e.g., aunt and nephew), the IRS may contend that the original advance was not a loan but was, in reality, a gift. Of key significance in this regard would be whether the lender (the aunt) had an honest and real expectation of payment by the borrower (the nephew).[43] Indicative of this repayment expectation is whether the parties preserved the formalities of a loan, including the following:

- The borrower issued a written instrument evidencing the obligation.
- The loan arrangement provided for interest.

[43] *William F. Mercil*, 24 T.C. 1150 (1955), and *Evans Clark*, 18 T.C. 780 (1952), *aff'd* 53–2 USTC ¶9452, 44 AFTR 70, 205 F.2d 353 (CA–2, 1953).

FIGURE 1.3 Tax Research Process

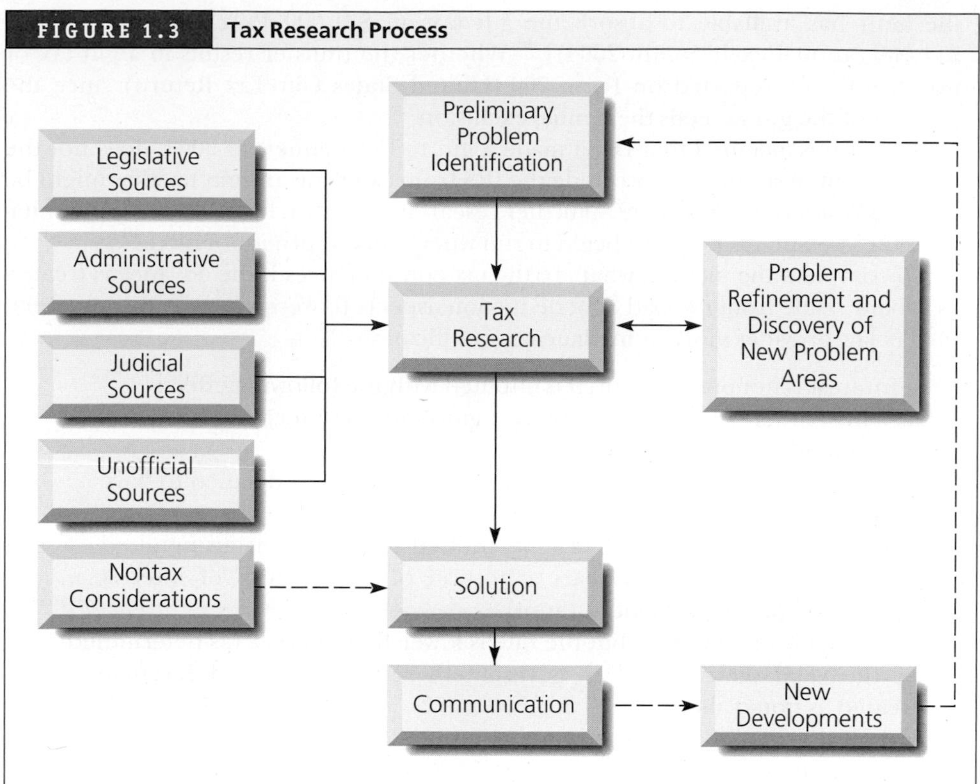

- The note specified a set due date.
- Collateral was available to the lender in the event of default by the borrower.[44]

The presence of some or all of these formalities does not, however, guarantee that a bona fide loan will be found. By the same token, the absence of some or all of the formalities does not make the advance a gift. Applying the formalities criteria to Example 20 is not possible since key facts (e.g., the presence or absence of a written note) are not given. Nevertheless, several inferences might be made that lead to a loan interpretation:

- It appears that the nephew has repaid at least $15,000 of the $92,000 that he borrowed. If the parties intended a gift of the full amount of the loan, why was partial repayment made?
- Although one would not expect a nephew on his way to college to have assets to serve as collateral for a loan, the fact that he was obtaining additional education could reinforce any expectation of repayment. In most situations, a person with a college education will possess a higher earning potential than one without such education. This education would improve the nephew's financial ability to repay the loan.

Further Refinement of the Problem

It may be impossible to determine whether the advance constitutes a loan or a gift with any degree of certainty. In either event, however, the tax consequences of each possibility must be ascertained.

If the advance is determined to be a gift, it is subject to the Federal gift tax.[45] Whether or not a gift tax results depends upon how much of the unified tax credit

[44] *Arthur T. Davidson*, 37 TCM 725, T.C.Memo. 1978–167.

[45] The transfer does not come within the unlimited gift tax exclusion of § 2503(e)(2)(A) since the aunt did not pay the amount directly to an educational institution. Besides, the exclusion covers only tuition payments and not other costs attendant on going to college (e.g., room and board).

the aunt has available to absorb the gift tax on $81,000 [$92,000 (total gift) – $11,000 (annual exclusion in 2004)].[46] Whether the transfer results in a gift tax or not, it must be reported on Form 709 (United States Gift Tax Return) since the amount of the gift exceeds the annual exclusion.

Even if it is assumed that Dana made a gift to her nephew in 2004, does not the intervention of seven years preclude the IRS from assessing any gift tax that might be due as a result of the transfer?[47] Further research indicates that the statute of limitations on assessments does not begin to run when a tax return is not filed.[48]

To complete the picture, what are the tax consequences if the advance is treated as a loan? Aside from the bad debt deduction aspects (covered later in the chapter), the tax law provides more immediate tax ramifications:[49]

- If interest is not provided for, it is imputed with the following effect:
  a. The lender (the aunt) must recognize interest income as to the imputed value.
  b. Since the lender has not received the interest, she is deemed to have made a gift of the interest to the borrower.
  c. The borrower (nephew) may be entitled to deduct (as an itemized expense) in some tax years a portion of the amount of interest deemed paid to the lender (aunt).
- If interest is provided for but the rate is lower than market (as determined by the yield on certain U.S. government securities), the differential is treated as noted above.
- For gift loans of $100,000 or less, the imputed element cannot exceed the net investment income of the borrower.

LOCATING THE APPROPRIATE TAX LAW SOURCES

Once the problem is clearly defined, what is the next step? Although the next step is a matter of individual judgment, most tax research begins with the index volume of a hard copy tax service or a keyword search on an online tax service (see the earlier discussion). If the problem is not complex, the researcher may bypass the tax service and turn directly to the Internal Revenue Code and the Treasury Regulations. For the beginner, this latter procedure saves time and will solve many of the more basic problems. If the researcher does not have a personal copy of the Code or Regulations, resorting to the appropriate volume(s) of a tax service may be necessary. Several of the major tax services publish paperback editions of the Code and Treasury Regulations that can be purchased at modest prices. These editions are usually revised twice each year.

LO.8

Assess the validity and weight of tax law sources.

ASSESSING THE VALIDITY OF TAX LAW SOURCES

After a source has been located, the next step is to assess the source in light of the problem at hand. Proper assessment involves careful interpretation of the tax law and consideration of the law's relevance and validity.

Interpreting the Internal Revenue Code

The language of the Code often is extremely difficult to comprehend. For example, a former subsection [§ 341(e)] relating to collapsible corporations contained *one* sentence of more than 450 words (twice as many as in the Gettysburg Address). Within this same subsection was another sentence of 300 words.

The Code must be read carefully for restrictive language such as "*at least* 80 percent" and "*more than* 80 percent" or "*less than* 50 percent" and "*exceeds* 50 percent."

[46]The tax, in turn, depends upon the amount of taxable gifts the aunt has made in the past. For a discussion of the mechanics of the Federal gift tax, see Chapter 18.

[47]Throughout the discussion of Example 20, the assumption has been made that if a gift occurred, it took place in 2004. That assumption need not be the case. Depending upon the aunt's intent, she could have decided to make a gift of the unpaid balance anytime after the loan was made (e.g., 2005, 2006, etc.).

[48]See § 6501(c)(3) and the discussion of the statute of limitations in Chapter 17.

[49]§ 7872.

It also makes a great deal of difference, for example, whether two or more clauses are connected by "*or*" or by "*and*."

If an answer is not in the Code, it may be necessary to resort to the Regulations and judicial decisions. In 1969, Congress directed the Treasury Department to promulgate Regulations under § 385 to distinguish corporate debt from corporate equity. As of yet, there are no Regulations under § 385. The researcher, therefore, must resort to past judicial decisions for a definition of debt.

Sometimes the Code directs the researcher elsewhere for the answer. For example, § 162(c) refers to the Foreign Corrupt Practices Act for purposes of determining when payments to foreign officials are deductible.

Cross-referencing between Code Sections is often poor or nonexistent. Code Sections are enacted at different times by Congresses that are operating under stringent deadlines. Consequently, a certain lack of integration within the Code is frequently apparent.

Definitions vary from one Code Section to another. For example, § 267 disallows losses between related parties and includes brothers and sisters in the definition of related parties. Not so with § 318, which deals with the definition of related parties as to certain stock redemptions.

Assessing the Validity of a Treasury Regulation

Treasury Regulations are often said to have the force and effect of law. This statement is certainly true for most Regulations, but some judicial decisions have held a Regulation or a portion thereof invalid. Usually, this is done on the grounds that the Regulation is contrary to the intent of Congress.

Keep the following observations in mind when assessing the validity of a Regulation:

- In a challenge, the burden of proof is on the taxpayer to show that the Regulation is wrong. However, a court may invalidate a Regulation that varies from the language of the statute and has no support in the Committee Reports.
- If the taxpayer loses the challenge, the negligence penalty may be imposed. This accuracy-related provision deals with the "intentional disregard of rules and regulations" on the part of the taxpayer and is explained further in Chapter 17.
- Some Regulations merely reprint or rephrase what Congress has stated in its Committee Reports issued in connection with the enactment of tax legislation. Such Regulations are "hard and solid" and almost impossible to overturn because they clearly reflect the intent of Congress.
- In some Code Sections, Congress has given to the "Secretary or his delegate" the authority to prescribe Regulations to carry out the details of administration or to otherwise complete the operating rules. Under such circumstances, it could almost be said that Congress is delegating its legislative powers to the Treasury Department. The Congressional Research Service found that Congress delegated regulatory authority to the Treasury on more than 240 occasions from 1992 through 2000, an average of more than 26 delegations per year. Regulations issued pursuant to this type of authority truly possess the force and effect of law and are often called "legislative" Regulations. They are to be distinguished from "interpretative" Regulations, which purport to explain the meaning of a particular Code Section. Examples of legislative Regulations are those dealing with consolidated returns issued under §§ 1501 through 1505. As a further example, note the authority granted to the Treasury Department by § 385 to issue Regulations setting forth guidelines on when corporate debt can be reclassified as equity (see Chapter 4).

Assessing the Validity of Other Administrative Sources of the Tax Law

Revenue Rulings issued by the IRS carry less weight than Treasury Department Regulations. Rulings are important, however, in that they reflect the position of the IRS on tax matters. In any dispute with the IRS on the interpretation of tax law, taxpayers should expect agents to follow the results reached in any applicable rulings.

Actions on Decisions further tell the taxpayer the IRS's reaction to certain court decisions. Recall that the IRS follows a practice of either acquiescing (agreeing) or nonacquiescing (not agreeing) with court decisions where guidance may be helpful. This practice does not mean that a particular decision has no value if the IRS has nonacquiesced in the result. It does, however, indicate that the IRS will continue to litigate the issue involved.

The validity of individual letter rulings issued by the IRS is discussed in Chapter 17.

Assessing the Validity of Judicial Sources of the Tax Law

The judicial process as it relates to the formulation of tax law has been described. How much reliance can be placed on a particular decision depends upon the following variables:

- The level of the court. A decision rendered by a trial court (e.g., a Federal District Court) carries less weight than one issued by an appellate court (e.g., the Fifth Circuit Court of Appeals). Unless Congress changes the Code, decisions by the U.S. Supreme Court represent the last word on any tax issue.
- The legal residence of the taxpayer. If, for example, a taxpayer lives in Texas, a decision of the Fifth Circuit Court of Appeals means more than one rendered by the Second Circuit Court of Appeals. This is true because any appeal from a U.S. District Court or the U.S. Tax Court would be to the Fifth Circuit Court of Appeals and not to the Second Circuit Court of Appeals.
- Whether the decision represents the weight of authority on the issue. In other words, is it supported by the results reached by other courts?
- The outcome or status of the decision on appeal. For example, was the decision appealed and, if so, with what result?

In connection with the last two variables, the use of a manual citator or a computer search is invaluable to tax research. A citator provides the history of a case including the authority relied on (e.g., other judicial decisions) in reaching the result. Reviewing the references listed in the citator discloses whether the decision was appealed and, if so, with what result (e.g., affirmed, reversed, remanded). It also reveals other cases with the same or similar issues and how they were decided. Thus, a citator reflects on the validity of a case and may lead to other relevant judicial material.[50]

Assessing the Validity of Other Sources

Primary sources of tax law include the Constitution, legislative history materials, statutes, treaties, Treasury Regulations, IRS pronouncements, and judicial decisions. The IRS regards only primary sources as substantial authority. However, reference to secondary materials such as legal periodicals, treatises, legal opinions, general counsel memoranda, technical advice memoranda, and written determinations can be useful. In general, secondary sources are not authority.

Although the statement that the IRS regards only primary sources as substantial authority is generally true, there is one exception. For purposes of the accuracy-related penalty in § 6662, the IRS has expanded the list of substantial authority to include a number of secondary materials (e.g., letter rulings, general counsel and technical advice memoranda, and the "Blue Book").[51] The "Blue Book" is the

[50]The major manual citators are published by Commerce Clearing House, RIA, and Shepard's Citations, Inc. The CCH and RIA versions are available online through the CCH *Network* service and RIA's *Checkpoint*, respectively. Shepard's Internet version is part of LexisNexis.

[51]Notice 90–20, 1990–1 C.B. 328, part V (A).

general explanation of tax legislation prepared by the Joint Committee on Taxation of the U.S. Congress.

As under former § 6661, "authority" does not include conclusions reached in treatises, legal periodicals, and opinions rendered by tax professionals.

ARRIVING AT THE SOLUTION OR AT ALTERNATIVE SOLUTIONS

Returning to Example 20, assume the parties decide that the loan approach can be justified from the factual situation involved. Does this assumption lead to a bad debt deduction for the aunt? Before this question can be resolved, the loan needs to be classified as either a business or a nonbusiness debt. One of the reasons the classification is important is that a nonbusiness bad debt cannot be deducted until it becomes entirely worthless. Unlike a business debt, no deduction for partial worthlessness is allowed.[52]

It is very likely that the loan the aunt made in 2004 falls into the nonbusiness category. Unless exceptional circumstances exist (e.g., the lender was in the trade or business of lending money), loans in a related-party setting are treated as nonbusiness. The probability is high that the aunt would be relegated to nonbusiness bad debt status.

The aunt has the burden of proving that the remaining unpaid balance of $77,000 is *entirely* worthless.[53] In this connection, what collection effort, if any, has the aunt made? But would any such collection effort be fruitless? Perhaps the nephew is insolvent, ill, or unemployed, or has departed for parts unknown.

Even if the debt is entirely worthless, one further issue remains to be resolved. In what year did the worthlessness occur? It could be, for example, that worthlessness took place in a year before it was claimed.[54]

A clear-cut answer may not be possible as to a bad debt deduction for the aunt in year 2011 (seven years after the advance was made). This uncertainty does not detract from the value of the research. Often a guarded judgment is the best possible solution to a tax problem.

COMMUNICATING TAX RESEARCH

Once the problem has been researched adequately, a memo, letter, or spoken presentation setting forth the result may be required. The form such a communication takes could depend on a number of considerations. For example, is any particular procedure or format for communicating tax research recommended by either an employer or an instructor? Are the research results to be given directly to the client, or will they first pass to the preparer's employer? If an oral presentation is required, who will be the audience? How long should you talk?[55] Whatever form it takes, a good tax research communication should contain the following elements:

- A clear statement of the issue.
- In more complex situations, a short review of the factual pattern that raises the issue.
- A review of the pertinent tax law sources (e.g., Code, Regulations, rulings, judicial authority).
- Any assumptions made in arriving at the solution.
- The solution recommended and the logic or reasoning in its support.
- The references consulted in the research process.

Figures 1.4, 1.5, and 1.6 present a sample client letter and memoranda for the tax files.

[52]See § 166 and the discussion of Investor Losses in Chapter 4.

[53]Compare *John K. Sexton*, 48 TCM 512, T.C.Memo. 1984–360, with *Stewart T. Oatman*, 45 TCM 214, T.C.Memo. 1982–684.

[54]*Ruth Wertheim Smith*, 34 TCM 1474, T.C.Memo. 1975–339.

[55]For more on crafting oral presentations, see W. A. Raabe and G. E. Whittenburg, "Talking Tax: How to Make a Tax Presentation," *Tax Adviser*, March 1997, pp. 179–182.

FIGURE 1.4 Client Letter

Hoffman, Raabe, Smith, & Maloney, CPAs
5191 Natorp Boulevard
Mason, OH 45040

August 25, 2011

Dana Pehrson
111 Avenue G
Lakeway, OH 45232

Dear Ms. Pehrson:

This letter is in response to your question with respect to your $92,000 advance to your nephew in 2004. I need some additional information.

1. Is there a written instrument evidencing this obligation, and is an interest rate specified?
2. When and how much has your nephew paid on the loan?
3. What factors exist to indicate whether the remaining debt will or will not be repaid?
4. What collection efforts, if any, have you made to collect the remaining $77,000?

Any other information or material that you can provide would be greatly appreciated.

Sincerely,

James Hicks, CPA
Partner

FIGURE 1.5 Tax File Memorandum

August 18, 2011

TAX FILE MEMORANDUM

FROM: James Hicks

SUBJECT: Dana Pehrson
Engagement Issues

Today, I talked to Dana Pehrson with regard to her letter of August 14, 2011.

Dana Pehrson advanced $92,000 to her nephew in 2004 to enable him to attend a private college. Seven years later, she claims a bad debt deduction for $77,000 that the nephew has not repaid.

ISSUE: Is Dana entitled to a bad debt deduction?

FIGURE 1.6 Tax File Memorandum

August 26, 2011

TAX FILE MEMORANDUM

FROM: James Hicks

SUBJECT: Dana Pehrson
Tentative Conclusions

The initial advance could have been a gift rather than a loan and possibly subject to the gift tax. In any case, if the advance was a gift, it should have been reported on Form 709. Further, the statute of limitations does not begin to run when a tax return is not filed.

If the advance is treated as a loan, the probability is high that the aunt would receive nonbusiness bad debt status. This classification means that Ms. Pehrson has the burden of proving that the $77,000 unpaid balance is entirely worthless.

1.7 Working with the Tax Law—Tax Planning

LO.9

Describe various tax planning procedures.

Tax research and tax planning are inseparable. The main purpose of effective tax planning is to reduce the taxpayer's total tax bill. This reduction does not mean that the course of action selected must produce the lowest possible tax under the circumstances. The minimization of tax payments must be considered in the context of the legitimate business goals of the taxpayer.

NONTAX CONSIDERATIONS

There is a danger that tax motivations may take on a significance that does not conform to the true values involved. In other words, tax considerations can operate to impair the exercise of sound business judgment. Thus, the tax planning process can lead to ends that are socially and economically objectionable. Unfortunately, a tendency exists for planning to move toward the opposing extremes of either not enough or too much emphasis on tax considerations. The happy medium is a balance that recognizes the significance of taxes, but not beyond the point at which planning detracts from the exercise of good business judgment.

The remark is often made that a good rule to follow is to refrain from pursuing any course of action that would not be followed were it not for certain tax considerations. This statement is not entirely correct, but it does illustrate the desirability of preventing business logic from being "sacrificed at the altar of tax planning."

COMPONENTS OF TAX PLANNING

Popular perception of tax planning often is restricted to the adage "defer income and accelerate deductions." Although this timing approach does hold true and is important, meaningful tax planning involves considerably more.

Preferable to deferring income is complete *avoidance*. Consider, for example, the corporate employee who chooses nontaxable fringe benefits over a fully taxable future pay increase.[56] Complete avoidance of gain recognition also occurs when the owner of appreciated property transfers it by death. Presuming a step-up in basis occurs, the built-in appreciation forever escapes the income tax.[57]

If the recognition of income cannot be avoided, its deferral will postpone income tax consequences. A tax paid in the future costs less than a tax paid today because of the time value of money. *Deferral* of income can take many forms. Besides like-kind exchanges and involuntary conversions, most retirement plans put off income tax consequences until the payout period. Deferral of gain recognition can also occur when appreciated property is transferred to a newly formed corporation or partnership.[58]

A corollary to the deferral of income is the acceleration of deductions. For example, an accrual basis, calendar year corporation desires an additional charitable deduction for 2011 but has a cash-flow problem. If the corporation authorizes the contribution in 2011 and pays it on or before March 15, 2012, the deduction can be claimed for 2011.[59] Taxes can be saved by *shifting* income to lower-bracket taxpayers. Gifts of appreciated property to lower-bracket family members can reduce the applicable capital gain rate on a later sale by 15 percentage points (from 15 percent to 0 percent).[60]

If income cannot be avoided, deferred, or shifted, the nature of the gain can be *converted*. By changing the classification of property, income taxes can be reduced. Thus, the taxpayer who transfers appreciated inventory to a controlled corporation

[56]See Example 10 in Chapter 13.

[57]See Example 19 in Chapter 19.

[58]See Example 1 in Chapter 4 and Example 8 in Chapter 10.

[59]See Example 17 in Chapter 2.

[60]See Example 34 in Chapter 19.

TAX in the NEWS — Tax Avoidance and Tax Evasion

There is a fine line between legal tax planning and illegal tax planning—**tax avoidance** versus **tax evasion**. Though both aim to eliminate or reduce taxes, tax evasion implies the use of subterfuge and fraud as a means to this end. The IRS believes that through tax evasion taxpayers short-changed the government by a staggering $345 billion in a recent year. This gross tax gap is the annual difference between Federal taxes owed and those timely paid.

Tax avoidance, however, is merely tax minimization through legal techniques. In this sense, tax avoidance becomes the proper objective of all tax planning. Perhaps because common goals are involved, popular usage has blurred the distinction between tax avoidance and tax evasion. Consequently, the association of the two concepts has kept some taxpayers from properly taking advantage of planning possibilities. The now-classic words of Judge Learned Hand in *Commissioner v. Newman** reflect the true values a taxpayer should have:

> Over and over again courts have said that there is nothing sinister in so arranging one's affairs as to keep taxes as low as possible. Everybody does so, rich or poor; and all do right, for nobody owes any public duty to pay more than the law demands: taxes are enforced extractions, not voluntary contributions. To demand more in the name of morals is mere cant.

*47-1 USTC ¶9175, 35 AFTR 857, 159 F.2d 848(CA-2, 1947).

has converted ordinary income property to a capital asset. When the stock is later sold, preferential capital gain rates apply.[61]

The conversion approach can also work in tax planning for losses. Properly structured, a loan to a corporation that becomes worthless can be an ordinary loss rather than the less desirable capital loss. Likewise, planning with § 1244 permits an investor in qualified small business stock to convert what would be a capital loss into an ordinary loss.[62]

Effective tax planning requires that careful consideration be given to the *choice of entity* used for conducting a business. The corporate form results in double taxation but permits shareholder-employees to be covered by fringe benefit programs. Partnerships and S corporations allow a pass-through of losses and other tax attributes, but transferring ownership interests as gifts to family members may be difficult.[63]

Although the substance of a transaction, rather than its form, generally controls, this rule is not always the case with tax planning. *Preserving formalities* often is crucial to the result. Is an advance to a corporation a loan or a contribution to capital? The answer may well depend on the existence of a note. Along with preserving formalities, the taxpayer should keep records that support a transaction. Returning to the issue of loan versus contribution to capital, how is the advance listed on the books of the borrower? What do the corporate minutes say about the advance?

Lastly, effective tax planning requires *consistency* on the part of taxpayers. A shareholder who treats a corporate distribution as a return of capital cannot later avoid a stock basis adjustment by contending that the distribution was really a dividend.

In summary, the key components of tax planning include the following:

- *Avoid* the recognition of income (usually by resorting to a nontaxable source or nontaxable event).
- *Defer* the recognition of income (or accelerate deductions).
- *Convert* the classification of income (or deductions) to a more advantageous form (e.g., ordinary income into capital gain).
- *Choose* the business *entity* with the desired tax attributes.

[61] See Concept Summary 13.1 in Chapter 13.

[62] See Examples 30 and 31 in Chapter 4.

[63] See Example 43 in Chapter 11 and Example 45 in Chapter 12.

Australia Holds Crocodile Dundee Hostage for Tax Sham

Actor Paul Hogan, star of the "Crocodile Dundee" movies, went to Australia to attend his 101-year-old mother's funeral. While he was there, the Australian Taxation Office served him with a departure-prohibition order that stranded him Down Under.

The Australian Taxation Office accused Hogan of misrepresenting his tax residency status to the United States and Australia between 2002 and 2005 in order to dodge taxes. The result is a $34 million tax deficiency.

The Golden Globe–winning actor and his tax adviser, Tony Stewart, allegedly engaged in a "scheme or conspiracy" to allow money to be paid to Hogan when he "was not a tax resident of any country and therefore the payment was free of tax." So an actor may avoid the strong jaws of a crocodile, but cannot escape the strong arms of international tax laws. Does Hogan owe the U.S. government any taxes?

Sources: Adapted from "Stranded Actor Paul Hogan in Australia Tax Deal," Yahoo! News, September 3, 2010; D. Snow and E. Sexton, "Crime Body Suspects Hogan of Travel Sham," **theage.com.au**, August 22, 2008.

- Preserve *formalities* by generating and maintaining supporting documentation.
- Act in a manner *consistent* with the intended objective.

TAX PLANNING—A PRACTICAL APPLICATION

Returning to the facts in Example 20, what should be done to help protect the aunt's bad debt deduction?

- All formalities of a loan should be present (e.g., written instrument, definite and realistic due date).
- Upon default, the lender (aunt) should make a reasonable effort to collect from the borrower (nephew). If not, the aunt should be in a position to explain why any such effort would be to no avail.
- If interest is provided for, it should be paid.
- Any interest paid (or imputed under § 7872) should be recognized as income by the aunt.
- Because of the annual exclusion of $11,000 in 2004 (now $13,000), it appears doubtful that actual (or imputed) interest would necessitate the filing of a Federal gift tax return by the aunt. But should one be due, it should be filed.
- If § 7872 applies (not enough or no interest is provided for), the nephew should keep track of his net investment income. This record keeping is important since the income the aunt must recognize may be limited by this amount.

In terms of the components of tax planning (see prior discussion beginning on p. 1–43), what do these suggestions entail? Note the emphasis on the formalities—written instrument, definite and realistic due date. Also, much is done to provide the needed documentation—gift tax returns, if necessary, are filed, and the nephew keeps track of his investment income. Most important, however, is that the aunt will have been *consistent* in her actions—recognizing actual (or imputed) interest income and making a reasonable effort to collect on the loan.

Throughout this text, each chapter concludes with observations on Tax Planning. Such observations are not all-inclusive but are intended to illustrate some of the ways in which the material in the chapter can be effectively used to minimize taxes.

FOLLOW-UP PROCEDURES

Tax planning usually involves a proposed (as opposed to a completed) transaction and is based upon the continuing validity of the advice resulting from tax research. A change in the tax law (either legislative, administrative, or judicial) could alter the original conclusion. Additional research may be necessary to test the solution in light of current developments.

Under what circumstances does a tax practitioner have an obligation to inform a client as to changes in the tax law? The legal and ethical aspects of this question are discussed in Chapter 17.

1.8 Taxation on the CPA Examination

LO.10

Discuss the role of taxation on the CPA examination.

The CPA examination has changed from a paper-and-pencil exam to a computer-based exam with increased emphasis on information technology and general business knowledge. The 14-hour exam has four sections, and taxation is included in the 3-hour Regulation section.

As of January 1, 2011, the CPA examination has been reorganized, with all written communication tasks now concentrated in the Business Environment & Concepts section. Shorter simulations are replacing the longer simulations.

Each exam section includes multiple-choice questions, and the Regulation section and two other sections will also have short task-based simulation (TBS) questions. The Regulation section is 60 percent Taxation and 40 percent Law & Professional Responsibilities (all areas other than Business Structure). The Regulation section has a new format:

- Three multiple-choice question (MCQ) testlets consisting of 72 questions.
- One testlet containing six short task-based simulations with the research question in a new format.

A candidate may review and change answers within each testlet but cannot go back after exiting a testlet. Candidates take different, but equivalent exams.

Simulations are small case studies designed to test a candidate's tax knowledge and skills using real-life work-related situations. Simulations include a four-function pop-up calculator, a blank spreadsheet with some elementary functionality, and authoritative literature appropriate to the subject matter. The taxation database includes authoritative excerpts (e.g., Internal Revenue Code and Regulations, IRS publications, Federal tax forms) that are necessary to complete the tax case study simulations. Examples of the simulations follow.

EXAMPLE 21

The *tax citation type* simulation requires the candidate to research the Internal Revenue Code and enter a Code Section and subsection. For example, Amber Company is considering using the simplified dollar-value method of pricing its inventory for purposes of the LIFO method that is available to certain small businesses. What Code Section is the relevant authority in the Internal Revenue Code to which you should turn to determine whether the taxpayer is eligible to use this method? To be successful, the candidate needs to find § 474. ■

EXAMPLE 22

A *tax form completion* simulation requires the candidate to fill out a portion of a tax form. For example, Blue Company is a limited liability company (LLC) for tax purposes. Complete the income section of the 2010 IRS Form 1065 for Blue Company using the values found and calculated on previous tabs along with the following data:

Ordinary income from other partnerships	$ 5,200
Net gain (loss) from Form 4797	2,400
Management fee income	12,000

The candidate is provided with page 1 of Form 1065 on which to record the appropriate amounts. Any field that requires an entry is a shaded rectangular cell. Some white rectangular cells will automatically calculate based on the entries in the shaded cell. ■

Candidates can learn more about the CPA examination at **www.cpa-exam.org**. This online tutorial site's topics include the following:

- Common tools.
- Navigation.
- Forms completion.
- Numeric entry.
- Research questions.
- Authoritative literature search.
- Written communication.

The common tools are a calculator, a spreadsheet, reminder flags, and an examination clock. A 30- to 60-minute sample examination will familiarize a candidate with the type of questions on the exam.

KEY TERMS

Acquiescence, 1–30
Arm's length concept, 1–14
Business purpose concept, 1–15
Certiorari, 1–28
Continuity of interest concept, 1–14
Determination letters, 1–23
Generally Accepted Accounting Principles (GAAP), 1–16
Indexation, 1–10
International Financial Reporting Standards (IFRS), 1–16
Letter rulings, 1–22
Nonacquiescence, 1–30
Proposed Regulations, 1–21
Revenue neutrality, 1–2
Revenue Procedures, 1–21
Revenue Rulings, 1–21
Tax avoidance, 1–44
Tax benefit rule, 1–15
Tax evasion, 1–44
Temporary Regulations, 1–21
Wherewithal to pay, 1–7

DISCUSSION QUESTIONS

1. **LO.1** What is meant by *revenue neutrality?*
2. **LO.2** In terms of asset acquisitions, what tax provisions can Congress use to control the economy?
3. **LO.2** List some tax provisions that encourage particular industries.
4. **LO.2** What economic objective is encouraged by favorable tax treatment of research and development expenditures?
5. **LO.2** List three tax provisions that can be justified by social considerations.
6. **LO.2** What purpose is served by the refundable earned income credit?
7. **LO.2** What purpose is served by allowing a deduction for charitable contributions?
8. **LO.2** What is the reason for the disallowance of certain fines and penalties?
9. **LO.2** What is the justification for the favorable treatment of home ownership?
10. **LO.2** What is the justification for the various credits, deductions, and exclusions that are designed to encourage taxpayers to obtain additional education?
11. **LO.2** In mitigating the effect of the double taxation of income at the Federal level, what relief does a deduction for state income taxes paid provide? Would a credit be preferable?

12. **LO.2** Some states that impose a state income tax allow the taxpayer a deduction for any Federal income taxes paid. What is the justification for such an approach?

ISSUE ID

13. **LO.2** A provision of the Code allows a taxpayer a deduction for Federal income tax purposes for state and local income taxes paid. Does this provision eliminate the effect of multiple taxation of the same income? Why or why not? In this connection, consider the following:
    a. Taxpayer, an individual, has itemized deductions that are less than the standard deduction.
    b. Taxpayer is in the 10% tax bracket for Federal income tax purposes. The 33% tax bracket.

14. **LO.2** Stacey and her partners operate a profitable partnership. Because the business is expanding, the partners would like to transfer it to a newly created corporation. Stacey is concerned, however, over the possible tax consequences that would result from incorporating. Please comment.

ISSUE ID

15. **LO.2** Assume the same facts as in Question 14. Stacey is also worried that once the partnership incorporates, the business will be subject to the Federal corporate income tax. Any suggestions?

16. **LO.2** Give some examples of the wherewithal to pay concept.

17. **LO.2** Can recognized gain exceed the realized gain?

18. **LO.2** In a like-kind exchange, recognized gain is postponed and not avoided. Explain.

19. **LO.2** Under the annual accounting period concept, what time period is normally selected for final settlement of most tax liabilities?

20. **LO.2** How does the installment method overcome the harsh treatment of the annual accounting treatment concept?

21. **LO.2** Why is there a grace period for contributions to a Keogh retirement plan?

22. **LO.2** What is "bracket creep"?

23. **LO.2** List the community property states.

24. **LO.2** Contrast the tax treatment between a community property state and a common law state.

25. **LO.2** List some tax provisions used to deter affluent taxpayers from obtaining preferential tax treatment.

26. **LO.3** How does the $13,000 annual gift tax exclusion help the IRS?

27. **LO.4** Explain the continuity of interest concept.

ISSUE ID

28. **LO.3** Black Corporation lends $205,000 to Red Corporation with no provision for interest. Black Corporation and Red Corporation are owned by the same shareholders. How might the IRS restructure this transaction with adverse tax consequences?

29. **LO.5** What are the primary sources of tax laws?

30. **LO.5** To what factor can the complexity of the current tax Code be attributed?

31. **LO.5** Presuming IRS Regulations have not yet been issued, what do practitioners and taxpayers look to in order to ascertain congressional intent?

32. **LO.5** Give an example of a tax provision that was named after a member of Congress.

33. **LO.5** Determine the subparts of § 166(d)(1)(B).

34. **LO.5** Is § 212(1) a proper Code Section citation?

35. **LO.5** Why are certain Code Section numbers missing from the Internal Revenue Code (e.g., §§ 6, 7, 8, 9, 10)?

36. **LO.6** Where can a researcher find newly issued Proposed, final, and Temporary Regulations?

37. **LO.6** Interpret each of the following citations:
    a. Prop.Reg. § 1.381(b)–1(a).
    b. Rev.Rul. 72–171, 1972–1 C.B. 208.
    c. TAM 200803017.

38. **LO.5** Sammy Young calls you requesting an explanation of the fact-finding determination of a Federal Court of Appeals. Prepare a letter to be sent to Sammy answering this query. His address is 1072 Richmond Lane, Keene, NH 01720. **COMMUNICATIONS**

39. **LO.5** Cody Pappas calls you with respect to a tax issue. He has found a tax case in the U.S. District Court of South Carolina that is in favor of his position. The IRS lost and did not appeal the case. Over the phone, you explain to Cody the significance of the failure to appeal. Prepare a tax file memorandum outlining your remarks to Cody. **COMMUNICATIONS**

40. **LO.5, 8** In assessing the validity of a court decision, discuss the significance of the following:
    a. The decision was rendered by the U.S. District Court of Wyoming. Taxpayer lives in Wyoming.
    b. The decision was rendered by the U.S. Court of Federal Claims. Taxpayer lives in Wyoming.
    c. The decision was rendered by the Second Circuit Court of Appeals. Taxpayer lives in California.
    d. The decision was rendered by the U.S. Supreme Court.
    e. The decision was rendered by the U.S. Tax Court. The IRS has acquiesced in the result.
    f. Same as (e) except that the IRS has issued a nonacquiescence as to the result.

41. **LO.5** Referring to the citations only, determine which court issued these decisions.
    a. *Burton-Sutton Oil Co., Inc.*, 328 U.S. 25 (1946).
    b. *Rite Aid Corp.*, 85 AFTR 2d 2000–1439 (Fed.Cl., 2000) *rev'd* 255 F.3d 1357, 88 AFTR 2d 2001–5058 (CA–Fed.Cir., 2001).
    c. *Herbert C. Hayes, Inc.*, T.C.Memo. 2004–185.
    d. *In re Continental Airlines*, 125 F.3d 120 (CA–3, 1997).
    e. *O'Neil v. Sears, Roebuck & Co.*, 108 F.Supp.2d 443 (D.Ct. Pa., 2000).
    f. Rev.Rul., 72–171, 1972–1 C.B. 208.

42. **LO.6** Bill Rogers needs to learn quickly about stock redemptions. How should Bill approach his research? **DECISION MAKING**

43. **LO.8** Determine whether the following items are primary sources or secondary sources for the purpose of substantial authority.
    a. Revenue Procedure.
    b. Article written by a judge in *Journal of Taxation.*
    c. U.S. Tax Court Memorandum decision.
    d. The "Blue Book."
    e. A general counsel memorandum.

44. **LO.9** What elements should a good tax research communication contain?

PROBLEMS

45. **LO.4** Thelma owns some real estate (basis of $120,000 and fair market value of $65,000) that she would like to sell to her son, Sandy, for $65,000. Thelma is aware, however, that losses on sales between certain related parties are disallowed for Federal income tax purposes [§ 267(a)(1)]. Thelma therefore sells the property to Paul (an unrelated party) for $65,000. On the next day, Paul sells the property to Sandy for the same amount. Is Thelma's realized loss of $55,000 deductible? Explain.

46. **LO.2** Bart exchanges some real estate (basis of $800,000 and fair market value of $1 million) for other real estate owned by Roland (basis of $1.2 million and fair market value of $900,000) and $100,000 in cash. The real estate involved is unimproved and is held by Bart and Roland, before and after the exchange, as investment property.
    a. What is Bart's realized gain on the exchange? Recognized gain?
    b. What is Roland's realized loss? Recognized loss?
    c. Support your results to (a) and (b) under the wherewithal to pay concept as applied to like-kind exchanges (§ 1031).

47. **LO.2, 3** Using the legend provided, classify the overall objective of the particular tax provision:

Legend	
CE = Control of the economy	W = Wherewithal to pay concept
EA = Encouragement of certain activities	AF = Administrative feasibility
EI = Encouragement of certain industries	ESB = Encouragement of small business
SC = Social considerations	

a. Like-kind exchange treatment.
b. An increase in the individual tax rate.
c. The S corporation election.
d. Adoption expense credit.
e. Percentage depletion.
f. Unified estate tax credit.
g. Charitable contribution deduction.

48. **LO.2** Determine whether the following states are community property or common law states:
a. Louisiana.
b. Utah.
c. Arizona.
d. North Carolina.
e. Alaska.
f. Washington.

49. **LO.4** Roy sells property (basis of $30,000) to Beige Corporation for $60,000. Based on the following conditions, how could the IRS challenge this transaction?
a. Roy is the sole shareholder of Beige Corporation.
b. Roy is the son of the sole shareholder of Beige Corporation.
c. Roy is neither a shareholder in Beige Corporation nor related to any of Beige's shareholders.

50. **LO.5** Answer the following questions:
a. What are letter rulings?
b. What are technical advice memoranda (TAMs)?

51. **LO.5** Explain what is meant by the following citations:
a. Rev.Proc. 2001–10, 2001–1 C.B. 272.
b. Rev.Rul. 93–86, 1993–2 C.B. 71.
c. Notice 2001–76, 2001–2 C.B. 613.

52. **LO.6** Using the legend provided, classify each of the following citations as to the location. There may be more than one answer for a citation.

Legend	
IRC = Internal Revenue Code	FR = *Federal Register*
IRB = *Internal Revenue Bulletin*	NA = Not applicable
CB = *Cumulative Bulletin*	

a. Rev.Rul. 64–56, 1964–1 C.B. 133.
b. § 6110(j).
c. *Jack L. Easson*, 33 T.C. 963 (1960).
d. TD 8875.
e. Reg. § 1.453–9(c).
f. Ltr.Rul. 200041022.
g. Temp.Reg. § 1.404(b)–1T.

53. **LO.5** To which U.S. Court of Appeals would a person living in each of the following states appeal from the U.S. Tax Court?
a. Texas.
b. Kansas.
c. Georgia.
d. Oregon.
e. New York.

54. **LO.5** Using the legend provided, classify each of the following citations as to the court:

Legend	
T = U.S. Tax Court	D = U.S. District Court
C = U.S. Court of Federal Claims	A = U.S. Court of Appeals
U = U.S. Supreme Court	N = None of the above

a. 2001–43, 2001–2 C.B. 191.
b. 379 F.Supp. 227 (D.Ct. N.Y., 1974).
c. 4 T.C. 600 (1945).
d. 27 B.T.A. 837 (1933).
e. T.C.Memo. 1975–245.
f. 1 Cl.Ct. 726 (Cl.Ct., 1983).
g. 310 U.S. 404 (1940).
h. 70 F.2d 720 (CA–2, 1934).

55. **LO.6** Locate the following tax services in your library and indicate the name of the publisher:
a. *United States Tax Reporter.*
b. *Standard Federal Tax Reporter.*
c. *Federal Tax Coordinator 2d.*
d. *Mertens Law of Federal Income Taxation.*
e. *Tax Management Portfolios.*
f. *CCH's Tax Research Consultant.*

56. **LO.5, 8** Using the legend provided, classify each of the following tax sources:

Legend	
P = Primary tax source	B = Both
S = Secondary tax source	N = Neither

a. Sixteenth Amendment to the Constitution.
b. Tax treaty between the United States and Russia.
c. Temporary Regulations.
d. Revenue Ruling.
e. General counsel memoranda (1988).
f. Tax Court Memorandum decision.
g. *Journal of Taxation* article.
h. Legislative Regulations.
i. Letter ruling (before 1985).
j. District Court decision.
k. Small Cases Division of U.S. Tax Court decision.
l. House Ways and Means Committee Report.
m. Technical advice memorandum (1991).
n. Proposed Regulations.

57. **LO.5** Interpret each of the following citations:
a. 54 T.C. 1514 (1970).
b. 408 F.2d 1117 (CA–2, 1969).
c. 69–1 USTC ¶ 9319 (CA–2, 1969).
d. 23 AFTR 2d 69–1090 (CA–2, 1969).
e. 293 F.Supp. 1129 (D.Ct. Miss., 1967).
f. 67–1 USTC ¶ 9253 (D.Ct. Miss., 1967).
g. 19 AFTR 2d 647 (D.Ct. Miss., 1967).
h. 56 S.Ct. 289 (USSC, 1935).
i. 36–1 USTC ¶ 9020 (USSC, 1935).
j. 16 AFTR 1274 (USSC, 1935).
k. 422 F.2d 1336 (Ct.Cl., 1970).

RESEARCH PROBLEMS

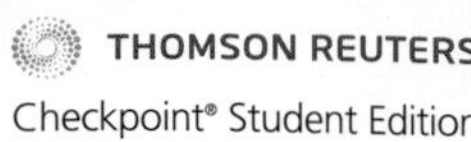

Checkpoint® Student Edition

Note: Solutions to Research Problems can be prepared by using the **Checkpoint® Student Edition** online research product, which is available to accompany this text. It is also possible to prepare solutions to the Research Problems by using tax research materials found in a standard tax library.

Research Problem 1. Find the Aerospace Industry—Audit Technique Guide—January 2005.

a. Is the document a legal precedent?
b. How many chapters does the ATG have?
c. What is the focus of the document?
d. In which chapter is the "Flow Chart of Audit Tasks"?

Research Problem 2. Find the *SOI Bulletin,* Summer 2010.

a. For tax year 2008, how many individuals reported nonfarm sole proprietorship activity?
b. Which sector had the largest profit?
c. What percentage of all U.S. corporate income tax returns did foreign-controlled domestic corporations account for in 2007?

Research Problem 3. Are Technical Expedited Advice Memoranda (TEAMs) still being issued?

Research Problem 4. The TV show TMZ spoke with Larry Edema from Michigan, who was selected to be in the audience for Oprah's big giveaway: a free trip to Australia! Supposedly, Winfrey had a certified public accountant on hand to address the tax issue right after the taping. Edema says the CPA assured the group that all taxes associated with the trip would be "handled by the Oprah show," so the trip would truly be 100% free. The CPA also explained that Oprah would cover all sightseeing costs and travel-related expenses, including passport costs for people who cannot afford them. It's a big change from Oprah's 2004 controversy when she famously gave away brand-new cars, but saddled audience members with as much as $7,000 in income taxes.

Discuss any tax aspects or problems with this statement.

Use the tax resources of the Internet to address the following questions. Do not restrict your search to the Web, but include a review of newsgroups and general reference materials, practitioner sites and resources, primary sources of the tax law, chat rooms and discussion groups, and other opportunities.

Research Problem 5. Go to each of the following Internet locations:

a. Several primary sources of the tax law, including the U.S. Supreme Court, a Court of Appeals, the Internal Revenue Service, the U.S. Tax Court, and final Regulations.
b. Sources of proposed Federal tax legislation.
c. A collection of tax rules for your state.

Research Problem 6. Using the Internet, obtain definitions of these terms:

a. Rule 155.
b. *En banc.*
c. *Pro se.*
d. Dicta.
e. Parallel cite.
f. Sunset provisions.
g. Work product.

Part 2

Corporations

Corporations are separate entities for Federal income tax purposes. Subchapter C of the Code is devoted to the tax treatment of regular corporations. Part 2 deals mainly with the operating rules contained in Subchapter C that apply to regular corporations and with the effects of various capital transactions on the C corporation and its shareholders.

CHAPTER

2

Corporations: Introduction and Operating Rules

LEARNING OBJECTIVES

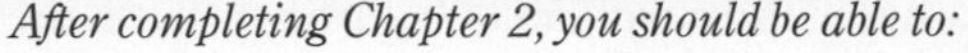

After completing Chapter 2, you should be able to:

LO.1

Summarize the tax treatment of various forms of conducting a business.

LO.2

Compare the taxation of individuals and corporations.

LO.3

Discuss the tax rules unique to corporations.

LO.4

Compute the corporate income tax.

LO.5

Explain the rules unique to computing the tax of related corporations.

LO.6

Describe and illustrate the reporting process for corporations.

LO.7

Evaluate corporations as an entity form for conducting a business.

OUTLINE

For the latest in changes to tax legislation, visit **www.cengage.com/taxation/swft.**

THE BIG PICTURE **Tax Solutions for the Real World**

A HALF-BAKED IDEA?

Samantha Johnson owns Skylark Bakery. Currently, the bakery is operated as a sole proprietorship and generates an annual operating profit of $100,000. In addition, the bakery earns annual dividends of $5,000 from investing excess working capital in the stock of publicly traded corporations. These stock investments typically are held for a minimum of three to four months before funds are required for the business. As a result of income from other business ventures and investments, Samantha is in the 35 percent marginal tax rate bracket irrespective of the bakery. In the past, Samantha has withdrawn $50,000 annually from the bakery, which she regards as reasonable payment for her services.

Samantha has asked you about the tax consequences of conducting the business as a regular (C) corporation. Based on the given information, what would be the annual income tax savings (or cost) of operating the bakery as a corporation? For purposes of this analysis, use the 2011 tax rates and ignore any employment tax or state tax considerations. **Read the chapter and formulate your response.**

2.1 Tax Treatment of Various Business Forms

LO.1

Summarize the tax treatment of various forms of conducting a business.

Business operations can be conducted in a number of different forms. Among the various possibilities are the following:

- Sole proprietorships.
- Partnerships.
- Trusts and estates.
- S corporations (also called Subchapter S corporations).
- Regular corporations (also called Subchapter C or C corporations).
- Limited liability companies.

For Federal income tax purposes, the distinctions among these forms of business organization are very important. The following discussion of the tax treatment of sole proprietorships, partnerships, and regular corporations highlights these distinctions. Limited liability companies, which are taxed as one of the three preceding entity forms, are also discussed. Trusts and estates are covered in Chapter 20, and S corporations are discussed in Chapter 12.

SOLE PROPRIETORSHIPS

A sole proprietorship is not a taxable entity separate from the individual who owns the proprietorship. The owner of a sole proprietorship reports all business income and expenses of the proprietorship on Schedule C of Form 1040. The net profit or loss from the proprietorship is then transferred from Schedule C to Form 1040, which is used by the taxpayer to report taxable income. The proprietor reports all of the net profit from the business, regardless of the amount actually withdrawn during the year.

Income and expenses of the proprietorship retain their character when reported by the proprietor. For example, ordinary income of the proprietorship is treated as ordinary income when reported by the proprietor, and capital gain is treated as capital gain.

EXAMPLE 1
THE BIG PICTURE

Return to the facts of *The Big Picture* on p. 2-2. Samantha, the sole proprietor of Skylark Bakery, reports the $100,000 net profit (ordinary income) from the business on Schedule C of her individual tax return. Even though she withdrew only $50,000, Samantha reports all of the $100,000 net profit from the business on Form 1040, where she computes taxable income for the year. She also reports dividend income of $5,000 on Schedule B of Form 1040. ■

PARTNERSHIPS

Partnerships are not subject to a Federal income tax. However, a partnership is required to file Form 1065, which reports the results of the partnership's business activities. Most income and expense items are aggregated in computing the net profit or loss of the partnership on Form 1065. Any income and expense items that are not aggregated in computing the partnership's net profit (loss) are reported separately to the partners. Some examples of separately reported income items are interest income, dividend income, and long-term capital gain. Examples of separately reported expenses include charitable contributions and expenses related to investment income. Partnership reporting is discussed in detail in Chapter 10.

The partnership net profit (loss) and the separately reported items are allocated to the partners according to the partnership's profit and loss sharing agreement. Each partner receives a Schedule K–1 that reports the partner's share of the partnership net profit (loss) and separately reported income and expense items. Each partner reports these items on his or her own tax return.

EXAMPLE 2

Jim and Bob are equal partners in Canary Enterprises, a calendar year partnership. During the year, Canary Enterprises had $500,000 gross income and $350,000 operating expenses. In addition, the partnership sold land that had been held for investment purposes for a long-term capital gain of $60,000. During the year, Jim withdrew $40,000 from the partnership, and Bob withdrew $45,000. The partnership's Form 1065 reports net profit of $150,000 ($500,000 income − $350,000 expenses). The partnership also reports the $60,000 long-term capital gain as a separately stated item on Form 1065. Jim and Bob each receive a Schedule K–1 reporting net profit of $75,000 and separately stated long-term capital gain of $30,000. Each partner reports net profit of $75,000 and long-term capital gain of $30,000 on his own return. ■

CORPORATIONS

Corporations are governed by Subchapter C or Subchapter S of the Internal Revenue Code. Those governed by Subchapter C are referred to as **C corporations** or **regular corporations.** Corporations governed by Subchapter S are referred to as **S corporations.**

S corporations, which generally do not pay Federal income tax, are similar to partnerships in that net profit or loss flows through to the shareholders to be reported on their separate returns. Also like partnerships, S corporations do not aggregate all income and expense items in computing net profit or loss. Certain items flow through to the shareholders and retain their separate character when reported on the shareholders' returns. The S corporation net profit (loss) and the separately reported items are allocated to the shareholders according to their stock ownership interests. See Chapter 12 for detailed coverage of S corporations.

Unlike proprietorships, partnerships, and S corporations, C corporations are subject to an entity-level Federal income tax. This results in what is known as a *double taxation* effect. A C corporation reports its income and expenses on Form 1120. The corporation computes tax on the taxable income reported on the Form 1120 using the rate schedule applicable to corporations (see Exhibit 2.1 later in this section). When a corporation distributes its income, the corporation's shareholders report dividend income on their own tax returns. Thus, income that has already been taxed at the corporate level is also taxed at the shareholder level. The effects of double taxation are illustrated in Examples 3 and 4.

EXAMPLE 3

Lavender Corporation has taxable income of $100,000 in 2011. It pays corporate tax of $22,250 (refer to Exhibit 2.1 on p. 2-5). This leaves $77,750, all of which is distributed as a dividend to Mike, a 43-year-old single individual and the corporation's sole shareholder. Mike has no income sources other than Lavender Corporation. Mike has taxable income of $68,250 ($77,750 – $5,800 standard deduction – $3,700 personal exemption). He pays tax at the preferential rate applicable to dividends received by individuals. His tax is $5,063 [($34,500 × 0%) + ($33,750 × 15%)]. The combined tax on the corporation's net profit is $27,313 ($22,250 paid by the corporation + $5,063 paid by the shareholder). ■

EXAMPLE 4

Assume the same facts as in Example 3, except that the business is organized as a sole proprietorship. Mike reports the $100,000 profit from the business on his tax return. He has taxable income of $90,500 ($100,000 – $5,800 standard deduction – $3,700 personal exemption) and pays tax of $18,957. Therefore, operating the business as a sole proprietorship results in a tax *savings* of $8,356 in 2011 ($27,313 from Example 3 – $18,957). ■

In many cases, the tax burden will be greater if the business is operated as a corporation (as in Example 3), but sometimes operating as a corporation can result in tax savings, as illustrated in Examples 5 and 6.

EXAMPLE 5

In 2011, Tan Corporation files Form 1120 reporting taxable income of $100,000. The corporation pays tax of $22,250 and distributes the remaining $77,750 as a dividend to Carla, the sole shareholder of the corporation. Carla has income from other sources and is in the top individual tax bracket of 35% in 2011. As a result, she pays tax of $11,663 ($77,750 × 15% rate on dividends) on the distribution. The combined tax on the corporation's earnings is $33,913 ($22,250 paid by the corporation + $11,663 paid by the shareholder). ■

EXAMPLE 6

Assume the same facts as in Example 5, except that the business is a sole proprietorship. Carla reports the $100,000 profit from the business on her tax return and pays tax of $35,000 ($100,000 × 35% marginal rate). Therefore, operating the business as a sole proprietorship results in a tax *cost* of $1,087 in 2011 ($35,000 – $33,913 tax from Example 5). ■

The conclusions reached in these examples cannot be extended to all decisions about a form of business organization, as each specific set of facts and circumstances requires a thorough analysis of the tax factors. Further, the effect of other taxes (e.g., payroll and self-employment taxes, state income and franchise taxes) must be considered in such an analysis.

Taxation of Dividends

As noted earlier, the income of a C corporation is subject to double taxation—once at the corporate level when it is earned and again at the shareholder level when it is distributed as dividends. Double taxation stems, in part, from the fact that dividend distributions are not deductible by the corporation. Shareholders of closely held corporations frequently attempt to circumvent this disallowance by disguising a dividend distribution as some other purported transaction. One of the more common ways of disguising dividend distributions is to pay excessive compensation to shareholder-employees of a closely held corporation. The IRS scrutinizes compensation and other economic transactions (e.g., loans, leases, sales) between shareholders and closely held corporations to ensure that payments are reasonable in amount. (See Chapter 5 for more discussion on constructive dividends.)

Double taxation also stems from the fact that dividend distributions are taxable to the shareholders. Historically, dividend income has been taxed at the same rates as ordinary income. However, to alleviate some of the double taxation effect, Congress reduced the tax rate applicable to dividend income of individuals for years after 2002. Qualified dividend income is currently taxed at the same preferential rate as long-term capital gains—15 percent (0 percent for

EXHIBIT 2.1 Corporate Income Tax Rates

Taxable Income		Tax Is:	
Over—	**But Not Over—**		**Of the Amount Over—**
$ 0	$ 50,000	15%	$ 0
50,000	75,000	$ 7,500 + 25%	50,000
75,000	100,000	13,750 + 34%	75,000
100,000	335,000	22,250 + 39%	100,000
335,000	10,000,000	113,900 + 34%	335,000
10,000,000	15,000,000	3,400,000 + 35%	10,000,000
15,000,000	18,333,333	5,150,000 + 38%	15,000,000
18,333,333	—	35%	0

taxpayers in the bottom two tax brackets). The preferential rate on dividend income is set to expire for years after 2012.

Comparison of Corporations and Other Forms of Doing Business

Chapter 13 presents a detailed comparison of sole proprietorships, partnerships, S corporations, and C corporations as forms of doing business. However, it is appropriate at this point to consider some of the tax and nontax factors that favor corporations over proprietorships.

Consideration of tax factors requires an examination of the corporate rate structure. The income tax rate schedule applicable to corporations is reproduced in Exhibit 2.1. As this schedule shows, the marginal rates for corporations range from 15 percent to 39 percent. In comparison, the marginal rates for individuals range from 10 percent to 35 percent. The corporate form of doing business presents tax savings opportunities when the applicable corporate marginal rate is lower than the applicable individual marginal rate.

EXAMPLE 7

Susanna, an individual taxpayer in the 35% marginal tax rate bracket, can generate $100,000 of additional taxable income in the current year. If the income is taxed to Susanna, the associated tax is $35,000 ($100,000 × 35%). If, however, Susanna is able to shift the income to a newly created corporation, the corporate tax is $22,250 (see Exhibit 2.1). Thus, by taking advantage of the lower corporate marginal tax rates, a tax *savings* of $12,750 ($35,000 – $22,250) is achieved. ■

Any attempt to arbitrage the difference between the corporate and individual marginal tax rates also must consider the double taxation effect. When the preferential rate for dividend income is considered, however, tax savings opportunities still exist.

EXAMPLE 8

Assume in Example 7 that the corporation distributes all of its after-tax earnings to Susanna as a dividend. The dividend results in tax of $11,663 [($100,000 – $22,250) × 15%] to Susanna. Thus, even when the double taxation effect is considered, the combined tax burden of $33,913 ($22,250 paid by the corporation + $11,663 paid by the shareholder) represents a tax *savings* of $1,087 when compared to the $35,000 of tax that results when the $100,000 of income is subject to Susanna's 35% marginal rate. ■

TAX *in the NEWS* U.S. Corporate Tax Rate Second Highest among OECD Countries

According to the Organization for Economic Cooperation and Development (OECD), the U.S. corporate income tax rate is the second highest among member states. Only Japan has a higher corporate tax rate than the United States, and Japan's new prime minister has vowed to reduce his country's corporate tax burden. The effective tax rate that most corporations pay in the United States is substantially less than the top statutory rate, however, as taxpayers reduce their exposure to the corporate tax through the use of exclusions, deductions, credits, and deferral provisions. Still, the relatively high corporate tax rate puts the United States at a competitive disadvantage in attracting capital investment, and it encourages U.S. corporations to utilize foreign entities to shelter income from U.S. taxation. Many economists argue that a reduced corporate tax rate would improve the United States' competitive economic position in the world. Any reduction in the corporate tax rates, however, likely will be paired with a broadening of the corporate tax base (e.g., the elimination or reduction of some corporate deductions). Recent legislative proposals to reduce the corporate tax rate have included provisions designed to broaden the corporate tax base. (See, e.g., H.R. 3970, introduced by Representative Charles Rangel in the 110th Congress, and S. 3018, introduced by Senators Ron Wyden and Judd Gregg in the 111th Congress.)

Source: www.oecd.org/ctp/taxdatabase.

Examples 7 and 8 ignore other tax considerations that also must be considered in selecting the proper form of doing business, but they illustrate the tax savings that can be achieved by taking advantage of rate differentials. Some of the other tax considerations that could affect the selection of a business form include the character of business income, the expectation of business losses, payroll taxes, and state taxes.

All income and expense items of a proprietorship retain their character when reported on the proprietor's tax return. In the case of a partnership or S corporation, separately reported items (e.g., charitable contributions and long-term capital gains) retain their character when passed through to the partners or shareholders, respectively. However, the tax attributes of income and expense items of a C corporation do not pass through the corporate entity to the shareholders. As a result, if the business is expected to generate tax-favored income (e.g., tax-exempt income or long-term capital gains), one of the other (non-C corporation) forms of business may be desirable.

Losses of a C corporation are treated differently than losses of a proprietorship, partnership, or S corporation. A loss incurred by a proprietorship may be deductible by the owner, because all income and expense items are reported by the proprietor. Partnership losses are passed through the partnership entity and may be deductible by the partners, and S corporation losses are passed through to the shareholders. C corporation losses, however, have no effect on the taxable income of the shareholders. Therefore, one of the non-C corporation forms of business may be desirable if business losses are anticipated.

EXAMPLE 9

Franco plans to start a business this year. He expects the business will incur operating losses for the first three years and then become highly profitable. Franco decides to operate as an S corporation during the loss period, because the losses will flow through and be deductible on his personal return. When the business becomes profitable, he intends to switch to C corporation status. ■

Employment taxes must be factored into any analysis of a business form. The net income of a proprietorship is subject to the self-employment tax, as are some partnership allocations of income to partners. In the alternative, wages paid to a shareholder-employee of a corporation (C or S) are subject to payroll taxes. The combined corporation-employee payroll tax burden should be compared with the self-employment tax associated with the proprietorship and partnership forms of business. This analysis should include the benefit of the deduction available to a corporation for payroll taxes paid, as well as the deduction available to an individual for one-half of self-employment taxes paid.

State taxation also must be considered in the selection of a business form. At the entity level, state corporate income taxes and/or franchise taxes are applicable for businesses formed as corporations. Although no entity-level Federal income tax is typically assessed on S corporations, limited liability companies (LLCs), or partnerships, a few states impose a corporate income tax or franchise tax on such business forms. Consideration of state taxation when selecting a business form is particularly relevant for businesses that operate in more than one state. (See Chapter 16 for a discussion of the taxation of multistate corporations.) At the owner level, the income of sole proprietorships, S corporations, and partnerships (including most LLCs) is subject to state individual income taxation. Similarly, dividend income from corporate distributions is subject to state income taxation and without any rate preference for such income.

Nontax Considerations

Nontax considerations will sometimes override tax considerations and lead to the conclusion that a business should be operated as a corporation. The following are some of the more important nontax considerations:

- Sole proprietors and general partners in partnerships face the danger of *unlimited liability.* That is, creditors of the business may file claims not only against the assets of the business but also against the personal assets of proprietors or general partners. State corporate law protects shareholders from claims against their personal assets for corporate debts.
- The corporate form of business can provide a vehicle for raising large amounts of capital through widespread stock ownership. Most major businesses in the United States are operated as corporations.
- Shares of stock in a corporation are freely transferable, whereas a partner's sale of his or her partnership interest is subject to approval by the other partners.
- Shareholders may come and go, but a corporation can continue to exist. Death or withdrawal of a partner, on the other hand, may terminate the existing partnership and cause financial difficulties that result in dissolution of the entity. This *continuity of life* is a distinct advantage of the corporate form of doing business.
- Corporations have *centralized management.* All management responsibility is assigned to a board of directors, who appoint officers to carry out the corporation's business. Partnerships, by contrast, may have decentralized management, in which every partner has a right to participate in the organization's business decisions. **Limited partnerships**, though, may have centralized management. Centralized management is essential for the smooth operation of a widely held business.

LIMITED LIABILITY COMPANIES

The **limited liability company (LLC)** has proliferated greatly in recent years, particularly since 1988 when the IRS first ruled that it would treat qualifying LLCs as partnerships for tax purposes. All 50 states and the District of Columbia have passed laws that allow LLCs, and thousands of companies have chosen LLC status. As with a corporation, operating as an LLC allows its owners to avoid unlimited liability, which is a primary *nontax* consideration in choosing the form of business organization. The tax advantage of LLCs is that qualifying businesses may be treated as proprietorships or partnerships for tax purposes, thereby avoiding the problem of double taxation associated with regular corporations.

Some states allow an LLC to have centralized management, but not continuity of life or free transferability of interests. Other states allow LLCs to adopt any or all of the corporate characteristics of centralized management, continuity of life, and free transferability of interests. The comparison of business entities in Chapter 13 includes a discussion of LLCs.

Entity Classification

Can an organization not qualifying as a corporation under state law still be treated as such for Federal income tax purposes? The tax law defines a corporation as including "associations, joint stock companies, and insurance companies."[1] Unfortunately, the Code contains no definition of what constitutes an *association*, and the issue became the subject of frequent litigation.

It was finally determined that an entity would be treated as a corporation if it had a majority of characteristics common to corporations. For this purpose, relevant characteristics are:

- Continuity of life.
- Centralized management.
- Limited liability.
- Free transferability of interests.

These criteria did not resolve all of the problems that continued to arise over corporate classification. When a new type of business entity—the limited liability company—was developed, the IRS was deluged with inquiries regarding its tax status. As LLCs became increasingly popular with professional groups, all states enacted statutes allowing some form of this entity. Invariably, the statutes permitted the corporate characteristic of limited liability and, often, that of centralized management. Because continuity of life and free transferability of interests are absent, partnership classification was hoped for. This treatment avoided the double taxation inherent in the corporate form.

In 1996, the IRS eased the entity classification problem by issuing the **check-the-box Regulations.**[2] The Regulations enable taxpayers to choose the tax status of a business entity without regard to its corporate (or noncorporate) characteristics. These rules simplified tax administration considerably and eliminated much of the litigation that arose with regard to the association (i.e., corporation) status.

Under the check-the-box rules, entities with more than one owner can elect to be classified as either a partnership or a corporation. An entity with only one owner can elect to be classified as a corporation or as a sole proprietorship. Eligible entities make the election as to tax status by filing Form 8832 (Entity Classification Election). In the event of default (i.e., no election is made), multi-owner entities are classified as partnerships and single-person businesses as sole proprietorships.

The election is not available to entities that are actually incorporated under state law or to entities that are required to be taxed as corporations under Federal law (e.g., certain publicly traded partnerships). Otherwise, LLCs are not treated as being incorporated under state law. Although LLCs are generally disregarded entities for income tax purposes, they are obligated to report and pay employment and excise taxes.

2.2 An Introduction to the Income Taxation of Corporations

LO.2

Compare the taxation of individuals and corporations.

AN OVERVIEW OF CORPORATE VERSUS INDIVIDUAL INCOME TAX TREATMENT

When examining how corporations are treated under the Federal income tax, a useful approach is to compare their treatment with that applicable to individual taxpayers. The tax formula for computing the Federal income tax for a corporation is compared with that of an individual taxpayer in Figure 2.1, and the following discussion highlights similarities and differences between the two formulas.

[1] § 7701(a)(3).

[2] Reg. §§ 301.7701-1 through -4, and -7.

FIGURE 2.1 Tax Formulas

Corporations	Individuals
Income (broadly conceived)	Income (broadly conceived)
(Exclusions)	(Exclusions)
Gross income	Gross income
(Deductions except for NOL and DRD*)	(Deductions for AGI**)
Taxable income before NOL and DRD	Adjusted gross income
(Net operating loss deduction)	(Greater of itemized or standard deductions)
(Dividends received deduction)	(Personal and dependency exemptions)
Taxable income	Taxable income
Tax on taxable income	Tax on taxable income
(Tax credits)	(Tax credits)
Tax due (or refund)	Tax due (or refund)

*NOL = net operating loss; DRD = dividends received deduction.
**AGI = adjusted gross income.

Similarities

Gross income of a corporation is determined in much the same manner as it is for individuals. Thus, gross income includes compensation for services rendered, income derived from a business, gains from dealings in property, interest, rents, royalties, dividends—to name only a few items. Both individuals and corporations are entitled to exclusions from gross income. However, corporate taxpayers are allowed fewer exclusions. Interest on municipal bonds and life insurance proceeds are two exclusions that are applicable to both individual and corporate taxpayers.

Gains and losses from property transactions are handled similarly. For example, whether a gain or loss is capital or ordinary depends upon the nature of the asset in the hands of the taxpayer making the taxable disposition. In defining what is not a capital asset, § 1221 makes no distinction between corporate and noncorporate taxpayers.

In the area of nontaxable exchanges, corporations are like individuals in that they do not recognize gain or loss on a like-kind exchange and may defer recognized gain on an involuntary conversion of property. The exclusion of gain from the sale of a personal residence does not apply to corporations. The disallowance of losses on sales of property to related parties and on wash sales of securities applies equally to individual and corporate taxpayers.

The business deductions of corporations also parallel those available to individuals. Deductions are allowed for all ordinary and necessary expenses paid or incurred in carrying on a trade or business. Specific provision is made for the deductibility of interest, certain taxes, losses, bad debts, accelerated cost recovery, charitable contributions, net operating losses, research and experimental expenditures, and other less common deductions. There is no distinction between business and nonbusiness interest or business and nonbusiness bad debts for corporations. Thus, these amounts are deductible in full as ordinary deductions by corporations. Like individuals, corporations are not allowed a deduction for interest paid or incurred on amounts borrowed to purchase or carry tax-exempt securities. The same holds true for expenses contrary to public policy and certain unpaid expenses and interest between related parties.

Some of the tax credits available to individuals, such as the foreign tax credit, can also be claimed by corporations. Not available to corporations are certain credits that are personal in nature, such as the child tax credit, the credit for elderly or disabled taxpayers, and the earned income credit.

Dissimilarities

The income taxation of corporations and individuals also differs significantly. As noted earlier, different tax rates apply to corporations and to individuals. Corporate tax rates are discussed in more detail later in the chapter (see Examples 29 and 30).

All allowable corporate deductions are treated as business deductions. Thus, the determination of adjusted gross income (AGI), so essential for individual taxpayers, has no relevance to corporations. Taxable income is computed simply by subtracting from gross income all allowable deductions and losses. Itemized deductions, the standard deduction, and the deduction for personal and dependency exemptions do not apply to corporations. The $100 floor and 10 percent-of-AGI limitations on the deductible portion of personal casualty and theft losses applicable to individuals do not apply to corporations.

SPECIFIC PROVISIONS COMPARED

A comparison of the income taxation of individuals and corporations appears in Concept Summary 2.1 located at the end of this chapter. In making this comparison, the following areas warrant special discussion:

- Accounting periods and methods.
- Capital gains and losses.
- Recapture of depreciation.
- Passive losses.
- Charitable contributions.
- Domestic production activities deduction.
- Net operating losses.
- Special deductions available only to corporations.

ACCOUNTING PERIODS AND METHODS

Accounting Periods

Corporations generally have the same choices of accounting periods as do individual taxpayers. Like an individual, a corporation may choose a calendar year or a fiscal year for reporting purposes. Corporations usually can have different tax years from those of their shareholders. Also, newly formed corporations (as new taxpayers) usually have a choice of any approved accounting period without having to obtain the consent of the IRS. **Personal service corporations (PSCs)** and S corporations, however, are subject to severe restrictions in the use of a fiscal year. The rules applicable to S corporations are discussed in Chapter 12.

A PSC has as its principal activity the performance of personal services, and such services are substantially performed by shareholder-employees. The performance of services must be in the fields of health, law, engineering, architecture, accounting, actuarial science, performing arts, or consulting.[3] To limit the deferral of income possible when a PSC has a tax year different from that of its calendar year shareholder-employees, a PSC must generally use a calendar year.[4] However, a PSC can *elect* a fiscal year under any of the following conditions:

- A business purpose for the year can be demonstrated.
- The PSC year results in a deferral of not more than three months' income. An election under § 444 is required, and the PSC will be subject to the deduction limitations of § 280H. Under the latter provision, a PSC's deduction for shareholder-employee salaries will be limited if payment of those salaries is disproportionately postponed beyond December 31 (see Example 11).
- The PSC retained the same year that was used for its fiscal year ending 1987, provided an election was made under § 444 and subject to the deduction limitations of § 280H.

[3] § 448(d)(2)(A).

[4] § 441(i).

EXAMPLE 10

Valdez & Vance is a professional association of public accountants that receives over 40% of its gross receipts in March and April of each year from the preparation of tax returns. Valdez & Vance may be able to qualify for a May 1 to April 30 fiscal year. Under these circumstances, the IRS might permit Valdez & Vance to use the fiscal year chosen since it reflects a natural business cycle (the end of the tax season). Valdez & Vance has a business purpose for using a fiscal year. ■

EXAMPLE 11

Beige Corporation, a PSC, has made an election under § 444 to use a fiscal year ending September 30. For its fiscal year ending September 30, 2011, Beige paid Burke, its sole shareholder, $120,000 in salary. Under § 280H, Burke must receive at least $30,000 [(3 months ÷ 12 months) × $120,000] as salary during the period October 1 through December 31, 2011. ■

Accounting Methods

As a general rule, the cash method of accounting is unavailable to corporations.[5] However, several important exceptions apply in the case of the following types of corporations:

- S corporations.
- Corporations engaged in the trade or business of farming and timber.
- Qualified PSCs.
- Corporations with average annual gross receipts of $5 million or less for the most recent three-year period.

Most individuals and corporations that maintain inventory for sale to customers are required to use the accrual method of accounting for determining sales and cost of goods sold. However, as a matter of administrative convenience, the IRS will permit any entity with average annual gross receipts of not more than $1 million for the most recent three-year period to use the cash method. This applies even if the taxpayer is buying and selling inventory. Also as a matter of administrative convenience, the IRS will permit certain entities with average annual gross receipts greater than $1 million but not more than $10 million for the most recent three-year period to use the cash method.[6]

A corporation that uses the accrual method of accounting must observe a special rule in dealing with cash basis related parties. If the corporation has an accrual outstanding at the end of any taxable year with respect to such a related party, it cannot claim a deduction until the recipient reports the amount as income.[7] This rule is most often encountered when a corporation deals with an individual who owns more than 50 percent of the corporation's stock.

EXAMPLE 12
THE BIG PICTURE

Return to the facts of *The Big Picture* on p. 2-2. Assume that Samantha incorporates her business as Skylark Bakery, Inc., a calendar year, accrual method C corporation. Samantha, a cash method taxpayer, owns 100% of the corporation's stock at the end of 2011. On December 31, 2011, Skylark Bakery has accrued a $10,000 bonus to Samantha. Samantha receives the bonus in 2012 and reports it on her 2012 tax return. Skylark Bakery cannot claim a deduction for the $10,000 until 2012. ■

CAPITAL GAINS AND LOSSES

Capital gains and losses result from the taxable sales or exchanges of capital assets.[8] Whether these gains and losses are long term or short term depends upon the holding

[5] § 448.

[6] Rev.Proc. 2001–10, 2001–1 C.B. 272, and Rev.Proc. 2002–28, 2002–1 C.B. 815.

[7] § 267(a)(2).

[8] See Chapter 16 of *South-Western Federal Taxation: Individual Income Taxes* (2012 Edition) for a detailed discussion of capital gains and losses.

GLOBAL *Tax Issues*

The Matching Principle Applies When a Related Party Is a Foreign Taxpayer

Under § 267, an accrual method corporation cannot deduct an accrued expense attributable to a related-party cash basis taxpayer until the recipient includes such amount in gross income. This matching principle is applicable even if the related party is a foreign taxpayer. For example, cash basis, calendar year Foreign Parent loans funds to its accrual method, calendar year U.S. Subsidiary. At the end of the tax year, U.S. Subsidiary accrues interest expense on the Foreign Parent loan, but does not pay the interest in the current year. Section 267 denies U.S. Subsidiary a deduction for the accrued interest until that interest is included in Foreign Parent's gross income (i.e., the year of payment).

Sources: Reg. § 1.267–3(a). See also FAA 20090801F.

period of the assets sold or exchanged. Each year, a taxpayer's short-term gains and losses are combined, and long-term gains and losses are combined. The result is a net short-term capital gain or loss and a net long-term capital gain or loss. If gains *and* losses result (e.g., net short-term capital gain and net long-term capital loss), such amounts are further netted against each other. If instead the results are *all* gains or *all* losses (e.g., net short-term capital loss and net long-term capital loss), no further combination is necessary.

Capital Gains

Individuals generally pay a preferential tax rate of 15 percent on net capital gains (i.e., excess of net long-term capital gain over net short-term capital loss).[9] Corporations, however, receive no favorable tax rate on long-term capital gains, and such income is taxed at the normal corporate tax rates.

Capital Losses

Net capital losses of corporate and individual taxpayers receive different income tax treatment. Generally, individual taxpayers can deduct up to $3,000 of such net losses against other income. Any remaining capital losses can be carried forward to future years until absorbed by capital gains or by the $3,000 deduction.[10] Loss carryovers retain their identity as either long term or short term.

EXAMPLE 13

Robin, an individual, incurs a net long-term capital loss of $7,500 for calendar year 2011. Assuming adequate taxable income, Robin may deduct $3,000 of this loss on his 2011 return. The remaining $4,500 ($7,500 – $3,000) of the loss is carried to 2012 and years thereafter until completely deducted. The $4,500 will be carried forward as a long-term capital loss. ■

Unlike individuals, corporate taxpayers are not permitted to claim any net capital losses as a deduction against ordinary income. Capital losses, therefore, can be used only as an offset against capital gains. Corporations may, however, carry back net capital losses to three preceding years, applying them first to the earliest year in point of time. Carryforwards are allowed for a period of five years from the year of the loss. When carried back or forward, a long-term capital loss is treated as a short-term capital loss.

EXAMPLE 14

Assume the same facts as in Example 13, except that Robin is a corporation. None of the $7,500 long-term capital loss incurred in 2011 can be deducted in that year. Robin Corporation may, however, carry back the loss to years 2008, 2009, and 2010 (in this order) and offset it against any capital gains recognized in these years. If the

[9] A 0% rate applies to individual taxpayers in the 10% and 15% brackets.

[10] § 1212.

carryback does not exhaust the loss, it may be carried forward to calendar years 2012, 2013, 2014, 2015, and 2016 (in this order). The long-term capital loss is treated as short term in any carryover year. ■

TIMING IS EVERYTHING!

During 2011, Harrier Corporation, a calendar year C corporation, has a $100,000 gain from the sale of real estate. The real estate was unimproved land that had been owned by Harrier for many years as an investment. Concerned about its tax situation, in December Harrier sells stock in Falcon Corporation (also held as an investment) for a loss of $103,000. Because Falcon has significant growth potential, Harrier repurchases the stock in 2012. On its 2011 corporate income tax return, Harrier plans to deduct a net capital loss of $3,000. Evaluate the propriety of Harrier's plans.

RECAPTURE OF DEPRECIATION

In general, the recapture rules under §§ 1245 and 1250 are equally applicable to both individual and corporate taxpayers. However, corporations may have more depreciation recapture (ordinary income) on the disposition of § 1250 property than individuals. Under § 291, a corporation will have additional ordinary income equal to 20 percent of the excess of the amount of depreciation recapture that would arise if the property was § 1245 property over the amount of depreciation recapture computed under § 1250 (without regard to § 291). As a result, the § 1231 portion of the corporation's gain on the disposition is correspondingly reduced by the additional recapture.

Under § 1250, recapture is limited to the excess of accelerated depreciation over straight-line depreciation. In general, only straight-line depreciation is allowed for real property placed in service after 1986; thus, there will usually be no depreciation recapture on the disposition of § 1250 property (without regard to § 291). In contrast, all depreciation taken on § 1245 property is subject to recapture under that provision.

EXAMPLE 15

Red Corporation purchases nonresidential real property on May 3, 1996, for $800,000. Straight-line depreciation is taken in the amount of $316,239 before the property is sold on October 8, 2011, for $1.2 million.

First, determine the recognized gain:

Sales price		$1,200,000
Less: Adjusted basis:		
Cost of property	$ 800,000	
Less: Cost recovery	(316,239)	(483,761)
Recognized gain		$ 716,239

Second, determine the § 1245 recapture potential. This is the lesser of $716,239 (recognized gain) or $316,239 (cost recovery claimed).

Third, determine the normal § 1250 recapture amount:

Cost recovery taken	$ 316,239
Less: Straight-line cost recovery	(316,239)
§ 1250 ordinary income	$ –0–

Fourth, because the taxpayer is a corporation, determine the additional § 291 amount:

§ 1245 recapture potential	$316,239
Less: § 1250 recapture amount	(–0–)
Excess § 1245 recapture potential	$316,239
Apply § 291 percentage	20%
Additional ordinary income under § 291	$ 63,248

Red Corporation's recognized gain of $716,239 is accounted for as follows:

Ordinary income under § 1250	$ –0–
Ordinary income under § 291	63,248
§ 1231 gain	652,991
Total recognized gain	$716,239

■

PASSIVE LOSSES

The **passive loss** rules apply to individual taxpayers and to closely held C corporations and personal service corporations (PSCs).[11] For S corporations and partnerships, passive income or loss flows through to the owners, and the passive loss rules are applied at the owner level. The passive loss rules are applied to closely held C corporations and to PSCs to prevent taxpayers from incorporating to avoid the passive loss limitation.

A corporation is closely held if, at any time during the taxable year, more than 50 percent of the value of the corporation's outstanding stock is owned, directly or indirectly, by or for not more than five individuals. A corporation is classified as a PSC if it meets the following requirements:

- The principal activity of the corporation is the performance of personal services.
- The services are substantially performed by shareholder-employees.
- More than 10 percent of the stock (in value) is held by shareholder-employees. *Any* stock held by an employee on *any* one day causes the employee to be a shareholder-employee.

The general passive loss rules apply to PSCs. Passive losses cannot be offset against either active income or portfolio income. The application of the passive loss rules is not as harsh for closely held C corporations. They may offset passive losses against active income, but not against portfolio income.

EXAMPLE 16

Brown, a closely held C corporation that is not a PSC, has $300,000 of passive losses from a rental activity, $200,000 of active business income, and $100,000 of portfolio income. The corporation may offset $200,000 of the $300,000 passive loss against the $200,000 active business income, but may not offset the remainder against the $100,000 of portfolio income. If Brown is a PSC, then none of the $300,000 of passive losses is deductible in the current year. ■

Subject to certain exceptions, individual taxpayers are not allowed to offset passive losses against *either* active or portfolio income.

CHARITABLE CONTRIBUTIONS

Both corporate and individual taxpayers may deduct charitable contributions if the recipient is a qualified charitable organization. Generally, a deduction will be allowed only for the year in which the payment is made. However, an important exception is made for *accrual basis corporations.* They may claim the deduction in the year preceding payment if two requirements are met. First, the contribution must be authorized by the board of directors by the end of that year. Second, it must be paid on or before the fifteenth day of the third month of the next year.

EXAMPLE 17

On December 29, 2011, Blue Company, a calendar year, accrual basis taxpayer, authorizes a $5,000 donation to the Atlanta Symphony Association (a qualified charitable organization). The donation is made on March 12, 2012. If Blue Company is a partnership, the contribution can be deducted only in 2012.[12] However, if Blue Company is a

[11] § 469(a).

[12] Each calendar year partner will report an allocable portion of the charitable contribution deduction as of December 31, 2012 (the end of the partnership's tax year). See Chapter 10.

corporation and the December 29, 2011 authorization was made by its board of directors, Blue may claim the $5,000 donation as a deduction for calendar year 2011. ■

Property Contributions

The amount that can be deducted for a noncash charitable contribution depends on the type of property contributed. Property must be identified as capital gain property or ordinary income property. *Capital gain property* is property that, if sold, would result in long-term capital gain or § 1231 gain for the taxpayer. Such property generally must be a capital asset and must be held for the long-term holding period (more than 12 months).

The deduction for a charitable contribution of capital gain property is generally measured by the property's fair market value.

EXAMPLE 18

During the current year, Mallard Corporation donates a parcel of land (a capital asset) to Oakland Community College. Mallard acquired the land in 1988 for $60,000, and the fair market value on the date of the contribution is $100,000. The corporation's charitable contribution deduction (subject to a percentage limitation discussed later) is measured by the asset's fair market value of $100,000, even though the $40,000 appreciation on the land has never been included in income. ■

In two situations, a charitable contribution of capital gain property is measured by the basis of the property, rather than fair market value. If the corporation contributes *tangible personal property* and the charitable organization puts the property to an unrelated use, the appreciation on the property is not deductible. Unrelated use is defined as use that is not related to the purpose or function that qualifies the organization for exempt status.

EXAMPLE 19

White Corporation donates a painting worth $200,000 to Western States Art Museum (a qualified organization), which exhibits the painting. White had acquired the painting in 1980 for $90,000. Because the museum put the painting to a related use, White is allowed to deduct $200,000, the fair market value of the painting. ■

EXAMPLE 20

Assume the same facts as in the previous example, except that White Corporation donates the painting to the American Cancer Society, which sells the painting and deposits the $200,000 proceeds in the organization's general fund. White's deduction is limited to the $90,000 basis because it contributed tangible personal property that was put to an unrelated use by the charitable organization. ■

The deduction for charitable contributions of capital gain property to certain private nonoperating foundations is also limited to the basis of the property.

Ordinary income property is property that, if sold, would *not* result in long-term capital gain or § 1231 gain for the taxpayer. Examples of ordinary income property include inventory and capital assets that have not been held more than 12 months. In addition, § 1231 property (depreciable property used in a trade or business) is treated as ordinary income property to the extent of any depreciation recaptured under § 1245 or § 1250 (as adjusted under § 291). As a general rule, the deduction for a contribution of ordinary income property is limited to the basis of the property. On certain contributions of inventory by *corporations*, however, the amount of the deduction is equal to the lesser of (1) the sum of the property's basis plus 50 percent of the appreciation on the property or (2) twice the property's basis. The following contributions of inventory qualify for this increased contribution amount.

- A contribution of property to a charitable organization for use that is related to the organization's exempt function and such use is solely for the care of the ill, needy, or infants. (Individual taxpayers also qualify for this exception if the property is "wholesome food.")
- A contribution of books to a public school (K through 12) that uses the books in its educational programs.

- A contribution of tangible personal research property constructed by the corporation to a qualified educational or scientific organization that uses the property for research or experimentation, or research training. (The property must be contributed within two years from the date of its construction by the donor, and its original use must begin with the donee.)
- A contribution of computer equipment and software to a qualified educational organization or public library that uses the property for educational purposes. (The property must be contributed within three years from the date of its acquisition or construction by the donor, and its original use must begin with the donor or donee.)[13]

EXAMPLE 21

Lark Corporation, a clothing retailer, donates children's clothing to the Salvation Army to be used to attire homeless children. Lark's basis in the clothes is $2,000, and the fair market value is $3,000. Lark's deduction is $2,500 [$2,000 basis + 50%($3,000 – $2,000)]. If, instead, the fair market value is $7,000, Lark's deduction is $4,000 (2 × $2,000 basis). ■

ART IS IN THE EYE OF THE BEHOLDER!

Snipe Corporation, your client, donated a painting to the Lexington Museum of Art. The painting, which had been displayed in the corporate offices for several years, had a fair market value of $150,000 at the time of the donation (basis of $60,000). Snipe deducted a charitable contribution of $150,000 for the gift. You have learned that the museum, also a client of yours, did not display the painting because it did not fit well with the museum's collection. Instead, the museum sold the painting for $150,000 and placed the funds in its operating budget. What action, if any, should you take?

Limitations Imposed on Charitable Contribution Deductions

Like individuals, corporations are subject to percentage limits on the charitable contribution deduction.[14] For any tax year, a corporate taxpayer's contribution deduction is limited to 10 percent of taxable income. For this purpose, taxable income is computed without regard to the charitable contribution deduction, any net operating loss carryback or capital loss carryback, dividends received deduction, and domestic production activities deduction. Any contributions in excess of the 10 percent limitation may be carried forward to the five succeeding tax years. Any carryforward must be added to subsequent contributions and will be subject to the 10 percent limitation. In applying this limitation, the current year's contributions must be deducted first, with carryover amounts from previous years deducted in order of time.[15]

EXAMPLE 22

During 2011, Orange Corporation (a calendar year taxpayer) had the following income and expenses:

Income from operations	$140,000
Expenses from operations	110,000
Dividends received	10,000
Charitable contributions made in May 2011	6,000

For purposes of the 10% limitation *only*, Orange Corporation's taxable income is $40,000 ($140,000 – $110,000 + $10,000). Consequently, the allowable charitable deduction for 2011 is $4,000 (10% × $40,000). The $2,000 unused portion of the contribution can be carried forward to 2012, 2013, 2014, 2015, and 2016 (in that order) until exhausted. ■

[13]These conditions are set forth in §§ 170(e)(3), (4), and (6). The enhanced deduction associated with the contribution of food, book, and computer equipment inventory is available only for contributions made by December 31, 2011.

[14]The percentage limitations applicable to individuals and corporations are set forth in § 170(b).

[15]The carryover rules relating to all taxpayers are in § 170(d).

EXAMPLE 23

Assume the same facts as in Example 22. In 2012, Orange Corporation has taxable income (for purposes of the 10% limitation) of $50,000 and makes a charitable contribution of $4,500. The maximum deduction allowed for 2012 is $5,000 (10% × $50,000). The first $4,500 of the allowed deduction must be allocated to the contribution made in 2012, and the $500 balance is carried over from 2011. The remaining $1,500 of the 2011 contribution may be carried over to 2013, etc. ■

DOMESTIC PRODUCTION ACTIVITIES DEDUCTION

One important purpose of the American Jobs Creation Act of 2004 was to replace certain tax provisions that our world trading partners regarded as allowing unfair advantage to U.S. exports. Among other changes, the Act created a deduction based on the income from manufacturing activities (designated as *domestic production activities*). For 2011, the **domestic production activities deduction (DPAD)** is 9 percent of the lower of:

- Qualified production activities income, or
- Taxable income (computed without regard to the DPAD).[16]

For individuals, adjusted gross income is substituted for "taxable income." The DPAD cannot exceed 50 percent of an employer's W–2 wages related to qualified production activities income.

EXAMPLE 24

Elk Corporation, a calendar year taxpayer, manufactures golf equipment. For 2011, Elk had taxable income of $360,000 (before considering the DPAD) and qualified production activities income of $380,000. Elk's deduction is $32,400 [9% × $360,000 (the lesser of $380,000 or $360,000)]. Elk's W–2 wages related to qualified production activities income were $70,000, so the W–2 wage limitation ($70,000 × 50% = $35,000) does not apply. ■

See Chapter 3 for a detailed discussion of the domestic production activities deduction.

NET OPERATING LOSSES

Like the net operating loss (NOL) of an individual, the NOL of a corporation may be carried back 2 years and forward 20 to offset taxable income for those years. Similarly, corporations also may elect to forgo the carryback period and just carry forward an NOL. Unlike individual taxpayers, however, a corporation does not adjust its tax loss for the year for capital losses, because a corporation is not permitted a deduction for net capital losses. Nor does a corporation make adjustments for any nonbusiness deductions as individual taxpayers do. Further, a corporation is allowed to include the dividends received deduction (discussed below) in computing its NOL.[17]

EXAMPLE 25

In 2011, Green Corporation has gross income (including dividends) of $200,000 and deductions of $300,000 excluding the dividends received deduction. Green Corporation had received $100,000 of dividends from Fox, Inc., in which Green holds a 5% stock interest. Green has an NOL computed as follows:

Gross income (including dividends)		$ 200,000
Less:		
Business deductions	$300,000	
Dividends received deduction (70% of $100,000)	70,000	(370,000)
Taxable income (or loss)		($ 170,000)

The NOL is carried back two years to 2009. (Green Corporation may forgo the carryback option and elect instead to carry forward the loss.) Assume Green had taxable income of $40,000 in 2009. The carryover to 2010 is computed as follows:

[16] § 199.

[17] The modifications required to arrive at the amount of NOL that can be carried back or forward are in § 172(d).

TAX *in* the NEWS

The President's Economic Recovery Advisory Board Offers Options for Corporate Tax Reform

In February 2009, President Obama established the President's Economic Recovery Advisory Board (PERAB). Chaired by Paul Volcker (former chair of the Federal Reserve), PERAB was charged, in part, with providing the President with options for reforming the corporate tax system. On August 27, 2010, PERAB released "The Report on Tax Reform Options: Simplification, Compliance, and Corporate Taxation." With a view toward reducing economic distortions associated with the current corporate tax system, PERAB's emphasis was on a broader corporate tax base and a lower corporate tax rate. The report offers several options for corporate tax reform, including the following:

- Reduce the corporate tax rate.
- Allow immediate expensing of new investments in business assets.
- Limit deductibility of interest expense.
- Impose the corporate tax on unincorporated businesses possessing certain corporate characteristics.
- Eliminate or reduce certain tax benefits (e.g., the domestic production activities deduction).

PERAB's report could serve as a blueprint for any future attempts at comprehensive corporate tax reform.

Taxable income for 2009	$ 40,000
Less: NOL carryback	(170,000)
Taxable income for 2009 after NOL carryback (carryover to 2010)	($ 130,000)

■

LO.3

Discuss the tax rules unique to corporations.

DEDUCTIONS AVAILABLE ONLY TO CORPORATIONS

Dividends Received Deduction

The purpose of the **dividends received deduction** is to mitigate multiple taxation of corporate income. Without the deduction, income paid to a corporation in the form of a dividend would be taxed to the recipient corporation with no corresponding deduction to the distributing corporation. Later, when the recipient corporation paid the income to its shareholders, the income would again be subject to taxation with no corresponding deduction to the corporation. The dividends received deduction alleviates this inequity by causing only some or none of the dividend income to be taxable to the recipient corporation.

As the following table illustrates, the amount of the dividends received deduction depends upon the percentage of ownership (voting power and value) the recipient corporate shareholder holds in a *domestic corporation* making the dividend distribution.[18]

Percentage of Ownership by Corporate Shareholder	Deduction Percentage
Less than 20%	70%
20% or more (but less than 80%)	80%
80% or more*	100%

*The payor corporation must be a member of an affiliated group with the recipient corporation.

The dividends received deduction is limited to a percentage of the taxable income of a corporation. For this purpose, taxable income is computed without regard to the NOL deduction, the domestic production activities deduction, the dividends received deduction, and any capital loss carryback to the current tax year. The percentage of taxable income limitation corresponds to the deduction

[18] § 243(a). Dividends from foreign corporations generally do not qualify for a dividends received deduction. But see § 245.

percentage. Thus, if a corporate shareholder owns less than 20 percent of the stock in the distributing corporation, the dividends received deduction is limited to 70 percent of taxable income. However, the taxable income limitation does not apply if the corporation has an NOL for the current taxable year.[19]

The following steps are useful in applying these rules.

1. Multiply the dividends received by the deduction percentage.
2. Multiply the taxable income by the deduction percentage.
3. The deduction is limited to the lesser of Step 1 or Step 2, unless deducting the amount derived in Step 1 results in an NOL. If so, the amount derived in Step 1 should be used. This is referred to as the NOL rule.

EXAMPLE 26

Red, White, and Blue Corporations, three unrelated calendar year corporations, have the following information for the year:

	Red Corporation	White Corporation	Blue Corporation
Gross income from operations	$ 400,000	$ 320,000	$ 260,000
Expenses from operations	(340,000)	(340,000)	(340,000)
Dividends received from domestic corporations (less than 20% ownership)	200,000	200,000	200,000
Taxable income before the dividends received deduction	$ 260,000	$ 180,000	$ 120,000

In determining the dividends received deduction, use the three-step procedure described above:

Step 1 (70% × $200,000)	$140,000	$140,000	$140,000
Step 2			
70% × $260,000 (taxable income)	$182,000		
70% × $180,000 (taxable income)		$126,000	
70% × $120,000 (taxable income)			$84,000
Step 3			
Lesser of Step 1 or Step 2	$140,000	$126,000	
Deduction results in an NOL			$140,000

■

White Corporation is subject to the 70 percent of taxable income limitation. It does not qualify for NOL rule treatment since subtracting $140,000 (Step 1) from $180,000 (taxable income before the DRD) does not yield a negative figure. Blue Corporation does qualify for NOL rule treatment because subtracting $140,000 (Step 1) from $120,000 (taxable income before the DRD) yields a negative figure. In summary, each corporation has a dividends received deduction for the year as follows: $140,000 for Red Corporation, $126,000 for White Corporation, and $140,000 for Blue Corporation.

No dividends received deduction is allowed unless the corporation has held the stock for more than 45 days.[20] This restriction was enacted to close a tax loophole involving dividends on stock that is held only transitorily. When stock is purchased shortly before a dividend record date and soon thereafter sold ex-dividend, a capital loss corresponding to the amount of the dividend often results (ignoring other market valuation changes). If the dividends received deduction was allowed in such cases, the capital loss resulting from the stock sale would exceed the taxable portion of the related dividend income.

[19]Further, the limitation does not apply in the case of the 100% deduction available to members of an affiliated group. § 246(b).

[20]The stock must be held more than 45 days during the 91-day period beginning on the date that is 45 days before the ex-dividend date (or, in the case of preferred stock, more than 90 days during the 181-day period beginning on the date that is 90 days before the ex-dividend date). § 246(c).

EXAMPLE 27

On October 3, 2011, Pink Corporation (5 million shares outstanding) declares a $1 per share dividend for shareholders of record as of November 1, 2011, and payable on December 1, 2011. Black Corporation purchases 10,000 shares of Pink stock on October 28, 2011, for $25,000, and sells those 10,000 shares ex-dividend on November 5, 2011, for $15,000. (It is assumed that there is no fluctuation in the market price of the Pink stock other than the dividend element.) The sale results in a short-term capital loss of $10,000 ($15,000 amount realized − $25,000 basis). On December 1, Black receives a $10,000 dividend from Pink. Without the holding period restriction, Black Corporation would recognize a $10,000 deduction (subject to the capital loss limitation) but only $3,000 of income [$10,000 dividend − $7,000 dividends received deduction ($10,000 × 70%)], or a $7,000 net loss. However, since Black did not hold the Pink stock for more than 45 days, no dividends received deduction is allowed. ■

Another restriction applies to the dividends received deduction when the underlying stock is debt financed. Like the holding period restriction, this provision also was enacted to close a tax loophole. A corporation that finances the purchase of dividend-paying stock receives an interest expense deduction from such financing, but would report only a small amount of the related income if the dividends received deduction was allowed unabated. In general, the debt-financed stock restriction reduces the dividends received deduction with respect to any dividend-paying stock by the percentage of the investment in the stock that is debt financed.[21] For instance, if a stock purchase is financed 50 percent by debt, the dividends received deduction for dividends on such stock is reduced by 50 percent. However, the reduction in the dividends received deduction cannot exceed the amount of the interest deduction allocable to the dividend.

Organizational Expenditures Deduction

Expenses incurred in connection with the organization of a corporation normally are chargeable to a capital account. That they benefit the corporation during its existence seems clear. But how can they be amortized when most corporations possess unlimited life? The lack of a determinable and limited estimated useful life would therefore preclude any tax write-off. Section 248 was enacted to solve this problem.

Under § 248, a corporation may elect to amortize **organizational expenditures** over the 180-month period beginning with the month in which the corporation begins business.[22] Organizational expenditures include the following:

- Legal services incident to organization (e.g., drafting the corporate charter, bylaws, minutes of organizational meetings, terms of original stock certificates).
- Necessary accounting services.
- Expenses of temporary directors and of organizational meetings of directors or shareholders.
- Fees paid to the state of incorporation.

Expenditures that *do not qualify* as organizational expenditures include those connected with issuing or selling shares of stock or other securities (e.g., commissions, professional fees, and printing costs) or with the transfer of assets to a corporation. These expenditures reduce the amount of capital raised and are not deductible at all.

The first $5,000 of organizational costs can be immediately expensed, with any remaining amount of organizational costs amortized over a 180-month period. However, this $5,000 expensing amount is phased out on a dollar-for-dollar basis when these costs exceed $50,000. For example, a corporation with $52,000 of organizational costs would expense $3,000 [$5,000 − ($52,000 − $50,000)] of this amount and amortize the $49,000 balance ($52,000 − $3,000) over 180 months.

To qualify for the election, the expenditure must be *incurred* before the end of the taxable year in which the corporation begins business. In this regard, the

[21] § 246A.

[22] The month in which a corporation begins business may not be immediately apparent. Ordinarily, a corporation begins business when it starts the business operations for which it was organized. Reg. § 1.248–1T(d). For a similar problem in the Subchapter S area, see Chapter 12.

corporation's method of accounting is of no consequence. Thus, an expense incurred by a cash basis corporation in its first tax year qualifies even though the expense is not paid until a subsequent year.

A corporation is deemed to have made the election to amortize organizational expenditures for the taxable year in which it begins business. No separate statement or specific identification of the deducted amount as organizational expenditures is required. A corporation can elect to forgo the deemed election by clearly electing to capitalize organizational expenditures on a timely filed return for its first taxable year. In that case, the capitalized amount will be deductible by the corporation at such time as it ceases to do business and liquidates.

EXAMPLE 28

Black Corporation, an accrual basis taxpayer, was formed and began operations on April 1, 2011. The following expenses were incurred during its first year of operations (April 1–December 31, 2011):

Expenses of temporary directors and of organizational meetings	$15,500
Fee paid to the state of incorporation	2,000
Accounting services incident to organization	18,000
Legal services for drafting the corporate charter and bylaws	32,000
Expenses incident to the printing and sale of stock certificates	48,000

Black Corporation elects to amortize organizational costs under § 248. Because of the dollar cap (i.e., dollar-for-dollar reduction for amounts in excess of $50,000), no immediate expensing under the $5,000 rule is available. The monthly amortization is $375 [($15,500 + $2,000 + $18,000 + $32,000) ÷ 180 months], and $3,375 ($375 × 9 months) is deductible for tax year 2011. Note that the $48,000 of expenses incident to the printing and sale of stock certificates does not qualify for the election. These expenses cannot be deducted at all but reduce the amount of the capital realized from the sale of stock. ■

Organizational expenditures are distinguished from *startup expenditures.*[23] Startup expenditures include various investigation expenses involved in entering a new business, whether incurred by a corporate or an individual taxpayer. Startup expenses also include operating expenses, such as rent and payroll, that are incurred by a corporation before it actually begins to produce any gross income. At the election of the taxpayer, such expenditures (e.g., travel, market surveys, financial audits, legal fees) are deductible in the same manner as organizational expenditures. Thus, up to $5,000 can be immediately expensed (subject to the phaseout) and any remaining amounts amortized over a period of 180 months. (For tax years beginning *only* in 2010, the immediate expensing amount for startup expenditures is increased to $10,000, and the phaseout of such amount begins at $60,000 of expenditures.) The same rules that apply to the deemed election (and election to forgo the deemed election) for organizational expenditures also apply to startup expenditures.

2.3 Determining the Corporate Income Tax Liability

CORPORATE INCOME TAX RATES

LO.4

Compute the corporate income tax.

Corporate income tax rates have fluctuated widely over the years, with the current rate structure reflecting a significant reduction that occurred in the Tax Reform Act of 1986. Refer to Exhibit 2.1 for a schedule of current corporate income tax rates. Unlike the individual income tax rate brackets, the corporate income tax rate brackets are not indexed for inflation.

[23] § 195.

EXAMPLE 29
THE BIG PICTURE

Return to the facts of *The Big Picture* on p. 2-2. Assume that Samantha incorporates her business as Skylark Bakery, Inc., a calendar year C corporation. The corporation pays Samantha a salary of $50,000 for the current year. For 2011, Skylark Bakery has taxable income of $51,500 [$100,000 operating profit + $5,000 dividends − $50,000 salary expense − $3,500 dividends received deduction ($5,000 × 70%)]. Its income tax liability is $7,875, determined as follows:

Tax on $50,000 at 15%	$7,500
Tax on $1,500 at 25%	375
Tax liability	$7,875

■

For taxable income in excess of $100,000 for any tax year, the amount of the tax is increased by the lesser of (1) 5 percent of the excess or (2) $11,750. In effect, the additional tax means a 39 percent rate for every dollar of taxable income from $100,000 to $335,000.

EXAMPLE 30

Silver Corporation, a calendar year taxpayer, has taxable income of $335,000 for 2011. Its income tax liability is $113,900, determined as follows:

Tax on $100,000	$ 22,250
Tax on $235,000 × 39%	91,650
Tax liability	$113,900

Note that the tax liability of $113,900 is 34% of $335,000. Thus, due to the 39% rate (34% normal rate + 5% additional tax on taxable income between $100,000 and $335,000), the benefit of the lower rates on the first $75,000 of taxable income completely phases out at $335,000. The tax rate drops back to 34% on taxable income between $335,000 and $10 million. ■

Under § 11(b)(2), personal service corporations are taxed at a flat 35 percent rate on all taxable income. Thus, PSCs do not enjoy the tax savings of the 15 to 34 percent brackets applicable to other corporations. For this purpose, a PSC is a corporation that is substantially employee owned. Also, it must engage in one of the following activities: health, law, engineering, architecture, accounting, actuarial science, performing arts, or consulting.

ALTERNATIVE MINIMUM TAX

Corporations are subject to an alternative minimum tax (AMT) that is similar to the AMT applicable to individuals, both in objective and in application.[24] The AMT for corporations, as for individuals, involves a broader tax base than does the regular tax. Like an individual, a corporation is required to apply a minimum tax rate to the expanded base and pay an AMT equal to the difference between the tentative AMT and the regular tax. Many of the adjustments and tax preference items necessary to arrive at alternative minimum taxable income (AMTI) are the same for individuals and corporations. The AMT rate and exemption amount for corporations are different from those applicable to individuals, however. Computation of the AMT for corporations is discussed in Chapter 3.

TAX LIABILITY OF RELATED CORPORATIONS

LO.5

Explain the rules unique to computing the tax of related corporations.

Members of a controlled group of corporations (**related corporations**) are subject to special rules for computing the income tax, the accumulated earnings credit, and the AMT exemption.[25] If these restrictions did not exist, the shareholders of a corporation could gain significant tax advantages by splitting a single corporation into *multiple* corporations. The next two examples illustrate the potential *income tax* advantage of multiple corporations.

[24]Small corporations are not subject to the alternative minimum tax.

[25]§ 1561(a).

EXAMPLE 31

Gray Corporation annually yields taxable income of $300,000. The corporate tax on $300,000 is $100,250, computed as follows:

Tax on $100,000	$ 22,250
Tax on $200,000 × 39%	78,000
Tax liability	$100,250

■

EXAMPLE 32

Assume that Gray Corporation in the previous example is divided equally into four corporations. Each corporation would have taxable income of $75,000, and the tax for each (absent the special provisions for related corporations) would be computed as follows:

Tax on $50,000	$ 7,500
Tax on $25,000 × 25%	6,250
Tax liability	$13,750

The total liability for the four corporations would be $55,000 ($13,750 × 4). The savings would be $45,250 ($100,250 – $55,000). ■

A comparison of Examples 31 and 32 reveals that the income tax savings that could be achieved by using multiple corporations result from having more of the total taxable income taxed at lower rates. To close this loophole, the law limits a controlled group's taxable income in the tax brackets below 35 percent to the amount the corporations in the group would have if they were one corporation. Thus, in Example 32, under the controlled corporation rules, only $12,500 (one-fourth of the first $50,000 of taxable income) for each of the four related corporations would be taxed at the 15 percent rate. The 25 percent rate would apply to the next $6,250 (one-fourth of the next $25,000) of taxable income of each corporation. This equal allocation of the $50,000 and $25,000 amounts is required unless all members of the controlled group consent to an apportionment plan providing for an unequal allocation. Controlled groups include parent-subsidiary groups, brother-sister groups, combined groups, and certain insurance companies.

Similar limitations apply to controlled groups with respect to the $250,000 accumulated earnings credit and the $40,000 AMT exemption amount. Both the accumulated earnings tax and the AMT are discussed in Chapter 3. Controlled groups are discussed in detail in Chapter 8.

2.4 Procedural Matters

FILING REQUIREMENTS FOR CORPORATIONS

LO.6

Describe and illustrate the reporting process for corporations.

A corporation must file a Federal income tax return whether or not it has taxable income.[26] A corporation that was not in existence throughout an entire annual accounting period is required to file a return for the portion of the year during which it was in existence. In addition, a corporation must file a return even though it has ceased to do business if it has valuable claims for which it will bring suit. A corporation is relieved of filing income tax returns only when it ceases to do business and retains no assets.

The corporate return is filed on Form 1120. Corporations electing under Subchapter S (see Chapter 12) file on Form 1120S. Forms 1120 and 1120S are reproduced in Appendix B. Corporations with assets of $10 million or more generally are required to file returns electronically.

The return must be filed on or before the fifteenth day of the third month following the close of a corporation's tax year. As noted previously, a regular corporation, other than a PSC, can use either a calendar year or a fiscal year to report its taxable income. The tax year of the shareholders has no effect on the corporation's tax year.

Corporations can receive an automatic extension of six months for filing the corporate return by filing Form 7004 by the due date for the return. However, the IRS

[26] § 6012(a)(2).

may terminate the extension by mailing a 10-day notice to the corporation. A Form 7004 must be accompanied by the corporation's estimated tax liability.[27]

ESTIMATED TAX PAYMENTS

A corporation must make payments of estimated tax unless its tax liability can reasonably be expected to be less than $500. The required annual payment (which includes any estimated AMT liability) is the *lesser* of (1) 100 percent of the corporation's tax for the current year or (2) 100 percent of the tax for the preceding year (if that was a 12-month tax year and the return filed showed a tax liability).[28] Estimated payments can be made in four installments due on or before the fifteenth day of the fourth month, the sixth month, the ninth month, and the twelfth month of the corporate taxable year. The full amount of the unpaid tax is due on the due date of the return. For a calendar year corporation, the payment dates are as follows:

April 15
June 15
September 15
December 15

A corporation failing to pay its required estimated tax payments will be subjected to a nondeductible penalty on the amount by which the installments are less than the tax due. However, the underpayment penalty will not be imposed if the estimated payments are timely and are equal to the tax liability of the corporation for the prior year or equal to the tax due computed on an annualized basis. If the annualized method is used for one installment and the corporation does not use this method for a subsequent installment, any shortfall from using the annualized method for a prior payment(s) must be made up in the subsequent installment payment. The penalty is imposed on each installment; that is, a corporation must pay one-fourth of its required annual payment by the due date of each installment.

A *large* corporation cannot base its installment payments on its previous year's tax liability except for its first installment payment. A corporation is considered large if it had taxable income of $1 million or more in any of its three preceding years.

EXAMPLE 33

Condor Corporation, a calendar year C corporation, has taxable income of $1.5 million and $2 million for 2010 and 2011, respectively. The required 2011 estimated tax installment payments for Condor, a "large corporation," are computed as follows:

Payment	Amount
April 15, 2011	$127,500*
June 15, 2011	212,500**
September 15, 2011	170,000
December 15, 2011	170,000
Total	$680,000

* Based on preceding year's tax, for first installment only: [$1.5 million taxable income × 34% (see Exhibit 2.1)] = $510,000 ÷ 4 = $127,500.

** Based on current year's tax, for remaining installments: [$2 million taxable income × 34% (see Exhibit 2.1)] = $680,000 ÷ 4 = $170,000. Second installment must include shortfall from first installment: [$170,000 + ($170,000 – $127,500)] = $212,500. ■

SCHEDULE M–1—RECONCILIATION OF TAXABLE INCOME AND FINANCIAL NET INCOME

Schedule M–1 of Form 1120 is used to *reconcile* net income as computed for financial accounting purposes with taxable income reported on the corporation's income tax

[27] Reg. § 1.6081–3.

[28] §§ 6655(d) and (e).

return (commonly referred to as book-tax differences). Schedule M–1 is required of corporations with less than $10 million of total assets.

The starting point on Schedule M–1 is net income (loss) per books. Additions and subtractions are entered for items that affect financial accounting net income and taxable income differently. The following items are entered as additions (see lines 2 through 5 of Schedule M–1):

- Federal income tax per books (deducted in computing net income per books but not deductible in computing taxable income).
- The excess of capital losses over capital gains (deducted for financial accounting purposes but not deductible by corporations for income tax purposes).
- Income that is reported in the current year for tax purposes but is not reported in computing net income per books (e.g., prepaid income).
- Various expenses that are deducted in computing net income per books but are not allowed in computing taxable income (e.g., charitable contributions in excess of the 10 percent ceiling applicable to corporations).

The following subtractions are entered on lines 7 and 8 of Schedule M–1:

- Income reported for financial accounting purposes but not included in taxable income (e.g., tax-exempt interest).
- Deductions taken on the tax return but not expensed in computing net income per books (e.g., domestic production activities deduction).

The result is taxable income (before the NOL deduction and the dividends received deduction).

EXAMPLE 34

During the current year, Tern Corporation had the following transactions:

Net income per books (after tax)	$92,400
Taxable income	50,000
Federal income tax per books (15% × $50,000)	7,500
Interest income from tax-exempt bonds	5,000
Interest paid on loan, the proceeds of which were used to purchase the tax-exempt bonds	500
Life insurance proceeds received as a result of the death of a key employee	50,000
Premiums paid on key employee life insurance policy	2,600
Excess of capital losses over capital gains	2,000

For book and tax purposes, Tern Corporation determines depreciation under the straight-line method. Tern's Schedule M–1 for the current year is as follows:

Schedule M-1 **Reconciliation of Income (Loss) per Books With Income per Return**
Note: Schedule M-3 required instead of Schedule M-1 if total assets are $10 million or more—see instructions

1	Net income (loss) per books	*92,400*	7	Income recorded on books this year not included on this return (itemize): Tax-exempt interest $ *5,000* *Life insurance proceeds 50,000*	*55,000*
2	Federal income tax per books	*7,500*			
3	Excess of capital losses over capital gains	*2,000*			
4	Income subject to tax not recorded on books this year (itemize):		8	Deductions on this return not charged against book income this year (itemize):	
5	Expenses recorded on books this year not deducted on this return (itemize):		a	Depreciation $	
a	Depreciation $		b	Charitable contributions $	
b	Charitable contributions $				
c	Travel and entertainment $				
	Prem.–life ins. $2,600; Int.– state bonds $500	*3,100*	9	Add lines 7 and 8	*55,000*
6	Add lines 1 through 5	*105,000*	10	Income (page 1, line 28)—line 6 less line 9	*50,000*

Schedule M–2 reconciles unappropriated retained earnings at the beginning of the year with unappropriated retained earnings at year-end. Beginning balance plus net income per books, as entered on line 1 of Schedule M–1, less dividend distributions during the year equals ending retained earnings. Other sources of increases or decreases in retained earnings are also listed on Schedule M–2.

EXAMPLE 35

Assume the same facts as in Example 34. Tern Corporation's beginning balance in unappropriated retained earnings is $125,000. During the year, Tern distributed a cash dividend of $30,000 to its shareholders. Based on these further assumptions, Tern's Schedule M–2 for the current year is as follows:

Schedule M-2 **Analysis of Unappropriated Retained Earnings per Books (Line 25, Schedule L)**

1	Balance at beginning of year	125,000	5	Distributions: a Cash	30,000
2	Net income (loss) per books	92,400		b Stock	
3	Other increases (itemize):			c Property	
			6	Other decreases (itemize):	
			7	Add lines 5 and 6	30,000
4	Add lines 1, 2, and 3	217,400	8	Balance at end of year (line 4 less line 7)	187,400

Form **1120** (2010) ■

Corporations with less than $250,000 of gross receipts and less than $250,000 in assets do not have to complete Schedule L (balance sheet) and Schedules M–1 and M–2 of Form 1120. Similar rules apply to Form 1120S. These rules are intended to ease the compliance burden on small business.

SCHEDULE M–3—NET INCOME (LOSS) RECONCILIATION FOR CORPORATIONS WITH TOTAL ASSETS OF $10 MILLION OR MORE

Corporate taxpayers with total assets of $10 million or more are required to report much greater detail relative to differences between income (loss) reported for financial purposes and income (loss) reported for tax purposes. This expanded reconciliation of book and taxable income (loss) is reported on **Schedule M–3**. Corporations that are not required to file Schedule M–3 may do so voluntarily. Any corporation that files Schedule M–3 is not allowed to file Schedule M–1. Comparison of Schedule M–3 with Schedule M–1 (illustrated in Example 34) reveals the significantly greater disclosure requirements. Schedule M–3 is reproduced in Appendix B of this text.

Schedule M–3 is a response, at least in part, to financial reporting scandals, such as Enron and WorldCom. One objective of Schedule M–3 is to create greater transparency between corporate financial statements and tax returns. Another objective is to identify corporations that engage in aggressive tax practices by requiring that transactions that create book/tax differences be disclosed on corporate tax returns. The increase in transparency and disclosure comes at a cost, however, as the IRS estimates that, on average, almost 89 hours are needed to comply with the requirements of Schedule M–3, and many tax professionals believe that estimate is too low.

Total assets for purposes of the $10 million test and the income and expense amounts required by Schedule M–3 are determined from the taxpayer's financial reports. If the taxpayer files Form 10–K with the Securities and Exchange Commission (SEC), that statement is used. If no 10–K is filed, information from another financial source is used, in the following order: certified financial statements, prepared income statements, or the taxpayer's books and records.

Part I—Financial Information and Net Income (Loss) Reconciliation

Part I requires the following financial information about the corporation.

- The source of the financial net income (loss) amount used in the reconciliation—SEC Form 10–K, audited financial statements, prepared financial statements, or the corporation's books and records.
- Any restatements of the corporation's income statement for the filing period, as well as any restatements for the past five filing periods.
- Any required adjustments to the net income (loss) amount referred to above (see Part I, lines 5 through 10).

The adjusted net income (loss) amount must be reconciled with the amount of taxable income reported on the corporation's Form 1120.

Because of Schedule M–3's complexity, the coverage in this chapter will be limited to some of the more important concepts underlying the schedule. A series of examples adapted from the instructions for Schedule M–3 will be used to illustrate these concepts.

FINANCIAL DISCLOSURE *Insights*

Processing the Corporate Income Tax Return

Seldom is a Form 1120 prepared by itself. In almost every case, the taxpayer and its tax advisers start with the financial accounting records; then they modify book income directly with the book-tax differences that are known by the financial accountants and independent auditors. The tax professionals take these computations, adjust them for tax law changes, and clarify items that require detailed tax research. As the figure illustrates, taxable income for the Form 1120 results from this process.

Notice that this process mirrors that of the preparation of Schedule M–1 or M–3. In preparing these schedules, book income is modified to account for various temporary and permanent book-tax differences as specified by the layout the of forms, resulting in the taxable income amount that is used on page 1 of Form 1120. Some tax professionals maintain that, given the detail required to complete Schedule M–3, the traditional structure of Form 1120 is redundant for large entities. In this regard, page 1 of Form 1120 could be eliminated—taxable income could be computed using Schedule M–3 alone.

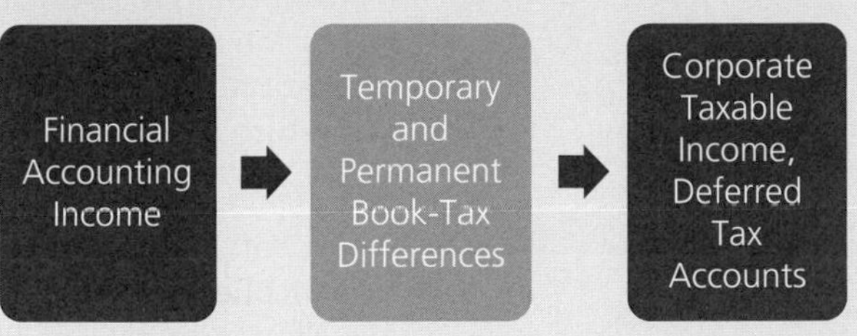

EXAMPLE 36

Southwest Sportsman's Corporation (SSC) sells hunting and fishing equipment to sportsmen. SSC has several stores in Texas, New Mexico, and Arizona. It also has a subsidiary in Mexico, which is organized as a Mexican corporation. SSC, which does not file a Form 10–K with the SEC, reports income from its Mexican subsidiary on its audited financial statements, which show net income of $45 million in 2011. The Mexican corporation, which is not consolidated by SSC for tax purposes and is therefore not an includible corporation, had net income of $7 million. SSC must enter $7 million on Part I, line 5a of Schedule M–3, resulting in net income per income statement of includible corporations of $38 million. ■

A situation similar to that described in Example 36 could result in additional entries in Part I of Schedule M–3. For example, if SSC engaged in transactions with its nonincludible Mexican subsidiary, an entry would be required on line 8 (adjustment to eliminations of transactions between includible corporations and nonincludible entities).

Part II—Reconciliation of Net Income (Loss) per Income Statement of Includible Corporations with Taxable Income per Return

Part II reconciles income and loss items of includible corporations, while Part III reconciles expenses and deductions. As indicated in Example 36, corporations included in a financial reporting group may differ from corporations in a tax reporting group. Corporations may also be partners in a partnership, which is a flow-through entity. The following example illustrates the adjustments that are required in this situation.

EXAMPLE 37

Southwest Sportsman's Corporation also owns an interest in a U.S. partnership, Southwest Hunting Lodges (SHL). On its audited financial statements, SSC reported net income of $10 million as its distributive share from SHL. SSC's Schedule K–1 from SHL reports the following amounts:

Ordinary income	$5,000,000
Long-term capital gain	7,000,000
Charitable contributions	4,000,000
Section 179 expense	100,000

In order to adjust for the flow-through items from the partnership, SSC must report these items on Schedule M–3, Part II, line 9 [Income (loss) from U.S. partnerships]. The corporation reports $10 million (book income) on line 9, column (a). SSC reports income per tax return of $7.9 million ($5,000,000 + $7,000,000 – $4,000,000 – $100,000) in column (d) of line 9, and a permanent difference of $2.1 million in column (c). ■

Part III—Reconciliation of Expense/Deduction Items

Part III lists 36 reconciling items relating to expenses and deductions. For these items, taxpayers must reconcile differences between income statement amounts (column a) and tax return amounts (column d), then classify these differences as temporary (column b) or permanent (column c) differences. The totals of the reconciling items from Part III are transferred to Part II, line 27, and are included with other items required to reconcile financial statement net income (loss) to tax return net income (loss).

EXAMPLE 38

Southwest Sportsman's Corporation acquired intellectual property in 2011 and deducted amortization of $20,000 on its financial statements, which were prepared according to GAAP. For Federal income tax purposes, SSC deducted $30,000. The corporation must report the amortization on line 28, Part III as follows: $20,000 book amortization in column (a), $10,000 temporary difference in column (b), and $30,000 tax return amortization in column (d). ■

EXAMPLE 39

In January 2011, Southwest Sportsman's Corporation established an allowance for uncollectible accounts (bad debt reserve) of $35,000 on its books and increased the allowance by $65,000 during the year. As a result of a client's bankruptcy, SSC decreased the allowance by $25,000 in November 2011. The corporation deducted the $100,000 of increases to the allowance on its 2011 income statement but was not allowed to deduct that amount on its tax return. On its 2011 tax return, the corporation was allowed to deduct the $25,000 actual loss sustained because of its client's bankruptcy. These amounts must be reported on line 32, Part III as follows: $100,000 book bad debt expense in column (a), $75,000 temporary difference in column (b), and $25,000 tax return bad debt expense in column (d). ■

Example 38 illustrates the Schedule M–3 reporting when book expenses are less than tax return deductions. Example 39 illustrates reporting procedures when book expenses are greater than tax return deductions. Both examples illustrate the reporting of temporary differences. The amounts from both examples are included in the totals derived in Part III and are carried to Part II, line 27. The reconciliation of book income and taxable income occurs in lines 26 through 30. The reconciled amount on Part II, line 30, column (a) must be equal to the net income per income statement of includible corporations on Part I, line 11. The reconciled amount on Part II, line 30, column (d) must be equal to the taxable income reported on Form 1120.

EFFECT OF TAXES ON THE FINANCIAL STATEMENTS

Because differences exist between taxable income and net income per books, what effect do these differences have on an entity's financial statements? How are income tax accruals arrived at and reported for accounting purposes? What other types of disclosures regarding present and potential tax liabilities are required to satisfy accounting standards? These and other questions are answered and discussed at length in Chapter 14.

For 2010 tax returns, a corporation with total assets of $100 million or more must file new Schedule UTP (Uncertain Tax Position Statement) with its Form 1120. A lower filing requirement of $10 million or more of assets will be fully phased in for 2014 returns. In general, a corporation is required to report tax positions taken on a current or prior year's Federal income tax return and for which the corporation recorded a reserve for Federal income tax in its audited financial statements (or for which no reserve was recorded because of an expectation to litigate). Financial reporting of tax positions is discussed in Chapter 14.

FORM 1120 ILLUSTRATED

To provide an example on the use of the corporate income tax return, a Form 1120 has been completed for Swift Corporation (see below). Due to the $10 million test, Swift Corporation does not require the use of Schedule M–3.

Swift Corporation was formed on January 10, 1985, by James Brown and Martha Swift to sell men's clothing. Pertinent information regarding Swift is summarized as follows:

- The business address is 6210 Norman Street, Buffalo, TX 79330.
- The employer identification number is 11–1111111; the principal business activity code is 448110.
- James Brown and Martha Swift each own one-half of the outstanding common stock; no other class of stock is authorized. James Brown is president of the company, and Martha Swift is secretary-treasurer. Both are full-time employees of the corporation, and each receives a salary of $70,000. James's Social Security number is 123-45-6789; Martha's Social Security number is 987-65-4321.
- The corporation uses the accrual method of accounting and reports on a calendar basis. The specific chargeoff method is used in handling bad debt losses, and inventories are determined using the lower of cost or market method. For book and tax purposes, the straight-line method of depreciation is used.
- During 2010, the corporation distributed a cash dividend of $35,000. Selected portions of Swift's profit and loss statement reflect the following debits and credits:

Account		Debit	Credit
Gross sales			$1,040,000
Sales returns and allowances		$ 50,000	
Purchases		506,000	
Dividends received from stock investments in less-than-20%-owned U.S. corporations			60,000
Interest income			
State bonds	$ 9,000		
Certificates of deposit	11,000		20,000
Premiums on term life insurance policies on the lives of James Brown and Martha Swift; Swift Corporation is the designated beneficiary		8,000	
Salaries—officers		140,000	
Salaries—clerical and sales		100,000	
Taxes (state, local, and payroll)		35,000	
Repairs		20,000	
Interest expense			
Loan to purchase state bonds	$ 4,000		
Other business loans	10,000	14,000	
Advertising		8,000	
Rental expense		24,000	
Depreciation		16,000	
Other deductions		21,000	

A comparative balance sheet for Swift Corporation reveals the following information:

Assets	January 1, 2010	December 31, 2010
Cash	$ 240,000	$ 163,850
Trade notes and accounts receivable	104,200	142,300
Inventories	300,000	356,000
Federal bonds	50,000	50,000
State bonds	100,000	100,000
Prepaid Federal tax	—	1,700
Stock investment	300,000	400,000
Buildings and other depreciable assets	120,000	120,000
Accumulated depreciation	(44,400)	(60,400)
Land	10,000	10,000
Other assets	1,800	1,000
Total assets	$1,181,600	$1,284,450

Liabilities and Equity		
Accounts payable	$ 150,000	$ 125,000
Other current liabilities	40,150	33,300
Mortgages	105,000	100,000
Capital stock	250,000	250,000
Retained earnings	636,450	776,150
Total liabilities and equity	$1,181,600	$1,284,450

Net income per books (before any income tax accrual) is $234,000. During 2010, Swift Corporation made estimated tax payments to the IRS of $61,000. Swift Corporation's Form 1120 for 2010 is reproduced on the following pages.

Although most of the entries on Form 1120 for Swift Corporation are self-explanatory, the following comments may be helpful:

- In order to arrive at the cost of goods sold amount (line 2 on page 1), Schedule A (page 2) must be completed.
- Reporting of dividends requires the completion of Schedule C (page 2). Gross dividends are shown on line 4 (page 1), and the dividends received deduction appears on line 29b (page 1). Separating the dividend from the deduction facilitates the application of the taxable income limitation (which did not apply in Swift's case).
- Income tax liability is $59,300, computed as follows:

Tax on $100,000	$22,250
Tax on $95,000 at 39%	37,050
	$59,300

The result is transferred to line 2 of Schedule J and ultimately is listed on line 31 (page 1). Because the estimated tax payment of $61,000 is more than the tax liability of $59,300, Swift will receive a tax refund of $1,700.

- In completing Schedule M–1 (page 5), the net income per books (line 1) is net of the Federal income tax ($234,000 – $59,300). The left side of Schedule M–1 (lines 2–5) represents positive adjustments to net income per books. After the negative adjustments are made (line 9), the result is taxable income before NOLs and special deductions (line 28, page 1).
- In completing Schedule M–2 (page 5), the beginning retained earnings figure of $636,450 is added to the net income per books as entered on Schedule M–1 (line 1). The dividends distributed in the amount of $35,000 are entered on line 5 and subtracted to arrive at the ending balance in unappropriated retained earnings of $776,150.
- Because this example lacks certain details, supporting schedules that would be attached to Form 1120 have not been included. For example, a Form 4562 would be included to verify the depreciation deduction (line 20, page 1), and other deductions (line 26, page 1) would be supported by a schedule.

CONSOLIDATED RETURNS

Corporations that are members of a parent-subsidiary affiliated group may be able to file a consolidated income tax return for a taxable year. Consolidated returns are discussed in Chapter 8.

Form **1120** Department of the Treasury Internal Revenue Service

U.S. Corporation Income Tax Return

For calendar year 2010 or tax year beginning ________, 2010, ending ________, 20 ____

▶ See separate instructions.

OMB No. 1545-0123 **2010**

A Check if:
1a Consolidated return (attach Form 851) ☐
b Life/nonlife consolidated return ☐
2 Personal holding co. (attach Sch. PH) ☐
3 Personal service corp. (see instructions) ☐
4 Schedule M-3 attached ☐

Print or type

Name: *Swift Corporation*

Number, street, and room or suite no. If a P.O. box, see instructions.: *6210 Norman Street*

City or town, state, and ZIP code: *Buffalo, TX 79330*

B Employer identification number *11–1111111*

C Date incorporated *1-10-85*

D Total assets (see instructions) $ *1,284,450* | *00*

E Check if: (1) ☐ Initial return (2) ☐ Final return (3) ☐ Name change (4) ☐ Address change

Income	1a	Gross receipts or sales *1,040,000 00*	b Less returns and allowances *50,000.00 00*	c Bal ▶	1c	*990,000 00*
	2	Cost of goods sold (Schedule A, line 8)			2	*450,000 00*
	3	Gross profit. Subtract line 2 from line 1c			3	*540,000 00*
	4	Dividends (Schedule C, line 19)			4	*60,000 00*
	5	Interest			5	*11,000 00*
	6	Gross rents			6	
	7	Gross royalties			7	
	8	Capital gain net income (attach Schedule D (Form 1120))			8	
	9	Net gain or (loss) from Form 4797, Part II, line 17 (attach Form 4797)			9	
	10	Other income (see instructions—attach schedule)			10	
	11	**Total income.** Add lines 3 through 10 ▶			11	*611,000 00*
Deductions (See instructions for limitations on deductions.)	12	Compensation of officers (Schedule E, line 4) ▶			12	*140,000 00*
	13	Salaries and wages (less employment credits)			13	*100,000 00*
	14	Repairs and maintenance			14	*20,000 00*
	15	Bad debts			15	
	16	Rents			16	*24,000 00*
	17	Taxes and licenses			17	*35,000 00*
	18	Interest			18	*10,000 00*
	19	Charitable contributions			19	
	20	Depreciation from Form 4562 not claimed on Schedule A or elsewhere on return (attach Form 4562)			20	*16,000 00*
	21	Depletion			21	
	22	Advertising			22	*8,000 00*
	23	Pension, profit-sharing, etc., plans			23	
	24	Employee benefit programs			24	
	25	Domestic production activities deduction (attach Form 8903)			25	
	26	Other deductions (attach schedule)			26	*21,000 00*
	27	**Total deductions.** Add lines 12 through 26 ▶			27	*374,000 00*
	28	Taxable income before net operating loss deduction and special deductions. Subtract line 27 from line 11			28	*237,000 00*
	29	**Less: a** Net operating loss deduction (see instructions)	29a			
		b Special deductions (Schedule C, line 20)	29b	*42,000 00*	29c	*42,000 00*
Tax, Refundable Credits, and Payments	30	**Taxable income.** Subtract line 29c from line 28 (see instructions)			30	*195,000 00*
	31	**Total tax** (Schedule J, line 10)			31	*59,300 00*
	32a	2009 overpayment credited to 2010	32a			
	b	2010 estimated tax payments	32b	*61,000 00*		
	c	2010 refund applied for on Form 4466	32c ( )	d Bal ▶ 32d *61,000 00*		
	e	Tax deposited with Form 7004	32e			
	f	Credits: (1) Form 2439 ____ (2) Form 4136 ____	32f			
	g	Refundable credits from Form 3800, line 19c, and Form 8827, line 8c	32g		32h	*61,000 00*
	33	Estimated tax penalty (see instructions). Check if Form 2220 is attached ▶ ☐			33	
	34	**Amount owed.** If line 32h is smaller than the total of lines 31 and 33, enter amount owed			34	
	35	**Overpayment.** If line 32h is larger than the total of lines 31 and 33, enter amount overpaid			35	*1,700 00*
	36	Enter amount from line 35 you want: **Credited to 2011 estimated tax ▶**		Refunded ▶	36	*1,700 00*

Sign Here

Under penalties of perjury, I declare that I have examined this return, including accompanying schedules and statements, and to the best of my knowledge and belief, it is true, correct, and complete. Declaration of preparer (other than taxpayer) is based on all information of which preparer has any knowledge.

▶ Signature of officer ____ Date ____ ▶ Title ____

May the IRS discuss this return with the preparer shown below (see instructions)? ☐ Yes ☐ No

Paid Preparer Use Only

Print/Type preparer's name	Preparer's signature	Date	Check ☐ if self-employed	PTIN
Firm's name ▶			Firm's EIN ▶	
Firm's address ▶			Phone no.	

For Paperwork Reduction Act Notice, see separate instructions. Cat. No. 11450Q Form **1120** (2010)

Form 1120 (2010) Page **2**

Schedule A Cost of Goods Sold (see instructions)

1	Inventory at beginning of year	1	*300,000*
2	Purchases	2	*506,000*
3	Cost of labor	3	
4	Additional section 263A costs (attach schedule)	4	
5	Other costs (attach schedule)	5	
6	**Total.** Add lines 1 through 5	6	*806,000*
7	Inventory at end of year	7	*356,000*
8	**Cost of goods sold.** Subtract line 7 from line 6. Enter here and on page 1, line 2	8	*450,000*

9a Check all methods used for valuing closing inventory:

(i) ☐ Cost

(ii) ☒ Lower of cost or market

(iii) ☐ Other (Specify method used and attach explanation.) ▶

b Check if there was a writedown of subnormal goods ▶ ☐

c Check if the LIFO inventory method was adopted this tax year for any goods (if checked, attach Form 970) ▶ ☐

d If the LIFO inventory method was used for this tax year, enter percentage (or amounts) of closing inventory computed under LIFO **9d**

e If property is produced or acquired for resale, do the rules of section 263A apply to the corporation? ☐ Yes ☒ No

f Was there any change in determining quantities, cost, or valuations between opening and closing inventory? If "Yes," attach explanation ☐ Yes ☒ No

Schedule C Dividends and Special Deductions (see instructions)

		(a) Dividends received	(b) %	(c) Special deductions (a) × (b)
1	Dividends from less-than-20%-owned domestic corporations (other than debt-financed stock)	*60,000*	70	*42,000*
2	Dividends from 20%-or-more-owned domestic corporations (other than debt-financed stock)		80	
3	Dividends on debt-financed stock of domestic and foreign corporations		see instructions	
4	Dividends on certain preferred stock of less-than-20%-owned public utilities		42	
5	Dividends on certain preferred stock of 20%-or-more-owned public utilities		48	
6	Dividends from less-than-20%-owned foreign corporations and certain FSCs		70	
7	Dividends from 20%-or-more-owned foreign corporations and certain FSCs		80	
8	Dividends from wholly owned foreign subsidiaries		100	
9	**Total.** Add lines 1 through 8. See instructions for limitation			*42,000*
10	Dividends from domestic corporations received by a small business investment company operating under the Small Business Investment Act of 1958		100	
11	Dividends from affiliated group members		100	
12	Dividends from certain FSCs		100	
13	Dividends from foreign corporations not included on lines 3, 6, 7, 8, 11, or 12			
14	Income from controlled foreign corporations under subpart F (attach Form(s) 5471)			
15	Foreign dividend gross-up			
16	IC-DISC and former DISC dividends not included on lines 1, 2, or 3			
17	Other dividends			
18	Deduction for dividends paid on certain preferred stock of public utilities			
19	**Total dividends.** Add lines 1 through 17. Enter here and on page 1, line 4 ▶	*60,000*		
20	**Total special deductions.** Add lines 9, 10, 11, 12, and 18. Enter here and on page 1, line 29b ▶			*42,000*

Schedule E Compensation of Officers (see instructions for page 1, line 12)

Note: *Complete Schedule E only if total receipts (line 1a plus lines 4 through 10 on page 1) are $500,000 or more.*

	(a) Name of officer	(b) Social security number	(c) Percent of time devoted to business	Percent of corporation stock owned (d) Common	(e) Preferred	(f) Amount of compensation
1	*James Brown*	*123-45-6789*	*100* %	*50* %	%	*70,000*
	Martha Swift	*987-65-4321*	*100* %	*50* %	%	*70,000*
			%	%	%	
			%	%	%	
			%	%	%	

2	Total compensation of officers	*140,000*
3	Compensation of officers claimed on Schedule A and elsewhere on return	
4	Subtract line 3 from line 2. Enter the result here and on page 1, line 12	*140,000*

Form **1120** (2010)

Form 1120 (2010) Page 3

Schedule J Tax Computation (see instructions)

Line	Description			Ref	Amount	Cents
1	Check if the corporation is a member of a controlled group (attach Schedule O (Form 1120)) ▶ ☐					
2	Income tax. Check if a qualified personal service corporation (see instructions) ▶ ☐			2	59,300	00
3	Alternative minimum tax (attach Form 4626)			3		
4	Add lines 2 and 3			4	59,300	00
5a	Foreign tax credit (attach Form 1118)	5a				
b	Credit from Form 8834, line 29	5b				
c	General business credit (attach Form 3800)	5c				
d	Credit for prior year minimum tax (attach Form 8827)	5d				
e	Bond credits from Form 8912	5e				
6	**Total credits.** Add lines 5a through 5e			6		
7	Subtract line 6 from line 4			7	59,300	00
8	Personal holding company tax (attach Schedule PH (Form 1120))			8		
9	Other taxes. Check if from: ☐ Form 4255 ☐ Form 8611 ☐ Form 8697 ☐ Form 8866 ☐ Form 8902 ☐ Other (attach schedule)			9		
10	**Total tax.** Add lines 7 through 9. Enter here and on page 1, line 31			10	59,300	00

Schedule K Other Information (see instructions)

		Yes	No
1	Check accounting method: **a** ☐ Cash **b** ☒ Accrual **c** ☐ Other (specify) ▶		
2	See the instructions and enter the:		
a	Business activity code no. ▶ *448110*		
b	Business activity ▶ *Retail sales*		
c	Product or service ▶ *Men's clothing*		
3	Is the corporation a subsidiary in an affiliated group or a parent-subsidiary controlled group? If "Yes," enter name and EIN of the parent corporation ▶		X
4	At the end of the tax year:		
a	Did any foreign or domestic corporation, partnership (including any entity treated as a partnership), trust, or tax-exempt organization own directly 20% or more, or own, directly or indirectly, 50% or more of the total voting power of all classes of the corporation's stock entitled to vote? If "Yes," complete Part I of Schedule G (Form 1120) (attach Schedule G)		X
b	Did any individual or estate own directly 20% or more, or own, directly or indirectly, 50% or more of the total voting power of all classes of the corporation's stock entitled to vote? If "Yes," complete Part II of Schedule G (Form 1120) (attach Schedule G)	X	
5	At the end of the tax year, did the corporation:		
a	Own directly 20% or more, or own, directly or indirectly, 50% or more of the total voting power of all classes of stock entitled to vote of any foreign or domestic corporation not included on **Form 851,** Affiliations Schedule? For rules of constructive ownership, see instructions If "Yes," complete (i) through (iv).		X

(i) Name of Corporation	**(ii)** Employer Identification Number (if any)	**(iii)** Country of Incorporation	**(iv)** Percentage Owned in Voting Stock

Form **1120** (2010)

Form 1120 (2010) Page 4

Schedule K *Continued*

	Yes	No
b Own directly an interest of 20% or more, or own, directly or indirectly, an interest of 50% or more in any foreign or domestic partnership (including an entity treated as a partnership) or in the beneficial interest of a trust? For rules of constructive ownership, see instructions. If "Yes," complete (i) through (iv).		X

(i) Name of Entity	**(ii)** Employer Identification Number (if any)	**(iii)** Country of Organization	**(iv)** Maximum Percentage Owned in Profit, Loss, or Capital

	Yes	No
6 During this tax year, did the corporation pay dividends (other than stock dividends and distributions in exchange for stock) in excess of the corporation's current and accumulated earnings and profits? (See sections 301 and 316.)		X
If "Yes," file **Form 5452,** Corporate Report of Nondividend Distributions. If this is a consolidated return, answer here for the parent corporation and on Form 851 for each subsidiary.		
7 At any time during the tax year, did one foreign person own, directly or indirectly, at least 25% of **(a)** the total voting power of all classes of the corporation's stock entitled to vote or **(b)** the total value of all classes of the corporation's stock?		X
For rules of attribution, see section 318. If "Yes," enter: **(i)** Percentage owned ▶ ______ and **(ii)** Owner's country ▶ ______ **(c)** The corporation may have to file **Form 5472,** Information Return of a 25% Foreign-Owned U.S. Corporation or a Foreign Corporation Engaged in a U.S. Trade or Business. Enter the number of Forms 5472 attached ▶ ______		
8 Check this box if the corporation issued publicly offered debt instruments with original issue discount ▶ ☐ If checked, the corporation may have to file **Form 8281,** Information Return for Publicly Offered Original Issue Discount Instruments.		
9 Enter the amount of tax-exempt interest received or accrued during the tax year ▶ $ *9,000*		
10 Enter the number of shareholders at the end of the tax year (if 100 or fewer) ▶ *2*		
11 If the corporation has an NOL for the tax year and is electing to forego the carryback period, check here ▶ ☐ If the corporation is filing a consolidated return, the statement required by Regulations section 1.1502-21(b)(3) must be attached or the election will not be valid.		
12 Enter the available NOL carryover from prior tax years (do not reduce it by any deduction on line 29a.) ▶ $ ______		
13 Are the corporation's total receipts (line 1a plus lines 4 through 10 on page 1) for the tax year **and** its total assets at the end of the tax year less than $250,000?		X
If "Yes," the corporation is not required to complete Schedules L, M-1, and M-2 on page 5. Instead, enter the total amount of cash distributions and the book value of property distributions (other than cash) made during the tax year. ▶ $ ______		
14 Is the corporation required to file Schedule UTP (Form 1120), Uncertain Tax Position Statement (see instructions)?		X
If "Yes," complete and attach Schedule UTP.		

Form **1120** (2010)

Form 1120 (2010) Page **5**

Schedule L **Balance Sheets per Books**

Assets	Beginning of tax year (a)	(b)	End of tax year (c)	(d)
1 Cash		240,000		163,850
2a Trade notes and accounts receivable	104,200		142,300	
b Less allowance for bad debts	( )	104,200	( )	142,300
3 Inventories		300,000		356,000
4 U.S. government obligations		50,000		50,000
5 Tax-exempt securities (see instructions)		100,000		100,000
6 Other current assets (attach schedule)				1,700
7 Loans to shareholders				
8 Mortgage and real estate loans				
9 Other investments (attach schedule)		300,000		400,000
10a Buildings and other depreciable assets	120,000		120,000	
b Less accumulated depreciation	(44,400)	75,600	(60,400)	59,600
11a Depletable assets				
b Less accumulated depletion	( )		( )	
12 Land (net of any amortization)		10,000		10,000
13a Intangible assets (amortizable only)				
b Less accumulated amortization	( )		( )	
14 Other assets (attach schedule)		1,800		1,000
15 Total assets		1,181,600		1,284,450
Liabilities and Shareholders' Equity				
16 Accounts payable		150,000		125,000
17 Mortgages, notes, bonds payable in less than 1 year				
18 Other current liabilities (attach schedule)		40,150		33,300
19 Loans from shareholders				
20 Mortgages, notes, bonds payable in 1 year or more		105,000		100,000
21 Other liabilities (attach schedule)				
22 Capital stock: **a** Preferred stock				
b Common stock	250,000	250,000	250,000	250,000
23 Additional paid-in capital				
24 Retained earnings—Appropriated (attach schedule)				
25 Retained earnings—Unappropriated		636,450		776,150
26 Adjustments to shareholders' equity (attach schedule)				
27 Less cost of treasury stock		( )		( )
28 Total liabilities and shareholders' equity		1,181,600		1,284,450

Schedule M-1 **Reconciliation of Income (Loss) per Books With Income per Return**

Note: Schedule M-3 required instead of Schedule M-1 if total assets are $10 million or more—see instructions

1 Net income (loss) per books	174,700	7 Income recorded on books this year not included on this return (itemize): Tax-exempt interest $ 9,000	9,000
2 Federal income tax per books	59,300		
3 Excess of capital losses over capital gains			
4 Income subject to tax not recorded on books this year (itemize):			
5 Expenses recorded on books this year not deducted on this return (itemize):		8 Deductions on this return not charged against book income this year (itemize):	
a Depreciation $		a Depreciation $	
b Charitable contributions $		b Charitable contributions $	
c Travel and entertainment $			
Prem.–life ins. $8,000; Int.– state bonds $4,000	12,000	9 Add lines 7 and 8	9,000
6 Add lines 1 through 5	246,000	10 Income (page 1, line 28)—line 6 less line 9	237,000

Schedule M-2 **Analysis of Unappropriated Retained Earnings per Books (Line 25, Schedule L)**

1 Balance at beginning of year	636,450	5 Distributions: **a** Cash	35,000
2 Net income (loss) per books	174,700	**b** Stock	
3 Other increases (itemize):		**c** Property	
		6 Other decreases (itemize):	
		7 Add lines 5 and 6	35,000
4 Add lines 1, 2, and 3	811,150	8 Balance at end of year (line 4 less line 7)	776,150

Form **1120** (2010)

SCHEDULE G (Form 1120)

Department of the Treasury
Internal Revenue Service

Information on Certain Persons Owning the Corporation's Voting Stock

▶ Attach to Form 1120.

▶ See instructions on page 2.

OMB No. 1545-0123

2010

Name	Employer identification number (EIN)
Swift Corporation	*11-1111111*

Part I **Certain Entities Owning the Corporation's Voting Stock.** (Form 1120, Schedule K, Question 4a). Complete columns (i) through (v) below for any foreign or domestic corporation, partnership (including any entity treated as a partnership), trust, or tax-exempt organization that owns directly 20% or more, or owns, directly or indirectly, 50% or more of the total voting power of all classes of the corporation's stock entitled to vote (see instructions).

(i) Name of Entity	(ii) Employer Identification Number (if any)	(iii) Type of Entity	(iv) Country of Organization	(v) Percentage Owned in Voting Stock

Part II **Certain Individuals and Estates Owning the Corporation's Voting Stock.** (Form 1120, Schedule K, Question 4b). Complete columns (i) through (iv) below for any individual or estate that owns directly 20% or more, or owns, directly or indirectly, 50% or more of the total voting power of all classes of the corporation's stock entitled to vote (see instructions).

(i) Name of Individual or Estate	(ii) Identifying Number (if any)	(iii) Country of Citizenship (see instructions)	(iv) Percentage Owned in Voting Stock
James Brown	*123-45-6789*	*United States*	*50.000%*
Martha Swift	*987-65-4321*	*United States*	*50.000%*

For Paperwork Reduction Act Notice, see the Instructions for Form 1120. Cat. No. 52684S **Schedule G (Form 1120) 2010**

FINANCIAL DISCLOSURE *Insights*

DEFERRED TAXES ON THE BALANCE SHEET

A business entity that follows GAAP, whether it is incorporated or not, typically records deferred tax assets and liabilities on its Statement of Financial Position (the "balance sheet"). These differences between the entity's total tax expense and its current tax expense can represent sizable amounts on the balance sheet. Because certain transactions result in deferred tax assets, and others in deferred tax liabilities, many balance sheets include dollar amounts for both accounts, as indicated by the following estimates from recent financial reports.

	Deferred Tax Liabilities ($000)	**Deferred Tax Assets ($000)**
General Electric	34,200	22,000
ExxonMobil	30,200	11,200
Berkshire Hathaway	22,500	4,300
Ford Motor	14,500	15,000

As deferred tax amounts "reverse" themselves into the Statement of Earnings and Comprehensive Income (the "income statement"), shareholders and investment analysts must determine whether and how the tax deferrals indicate the current and future profitability of the entity. This becomes especially difficult when any of the following occur:

- The taxpayer wins or loses an audit or other appeal with a taxing jurisdiction, creating an unusual amount due or refund.
- Tax rates change and the amounts of the tax deferrals change accordingly.
- A multinational entity deals with countries outside the United States that apply a different mix of taxes and rates.

Much of the public information regarding tax deferrals is found in the footnotes to the entity's financial statements, but these data can be difficult to interpret for large businesses with complex legal structures.

TAX PLANNING:

2.5 CORPORATE VERSUS NONCORPORATE FORMS OF BUSINESS ORGANIZATION

LO.7

Evaluate corporations as an entity form for conducting a business.

The decision to use the corporate form in conducting a trade or business must be weighed carefully. Besides the nontax considerations of the corporate form (limited liability, continuity of life, free transferability of interests, and centralized management), tax ramifications will play an important role in any such decision. Close attention should be paid to the following:

1. Operating as a regular corporate entity (C corporation) results in the imposition of the corporate income tax. Corporate taxable income will be taxed twice—once as earned by the corporation and again when distributed to the shareholders. Since dividends are not deductible, a closely held corporation may have a strong incentive to structure corporate distributions in a deductible form. Before legislation in 2003 lowered the rate on qualified dividends to 15 percent, shareholders had a tax incentive to bail out profits in the form of salaries, interest, or rent.[29] With the 15 percent rate on qualified dividends, shareholders may save taxes by having the corporation pay dividends rather than salaries, rent, or interest, which could be taxed at an individual marginal rate as high as 35 percent. The decision should be made only after comparing the tax cost of the two alternatives. The window of opportunity for reaping the benefit of the preferential tax rate on dividend

[29]Such procedures lead to a multitude of problems, one of which, the reclassification of debt as equity, is discussed in Chapter 4. The problems of unreasonable salaries and rents are covered in Chapter 5 in the discussion of constructive dividends.

income is set to close by 2013, however, and this must be considered in the analysis.

2. The differences in Federal tax brackets between an individual and a corporation may not be substantial. Furthermore, several state and local governments impose higher taxes on corporations than on individuals. In these jurisdictions, the combined Federal, state, and local tax rates on the two types of taxpayers are practically identical. Consequently, the tax ramifications of incorporating can be determined *only* on a case-by-case basis.
3. Corporate-source income loses its identity as it passes through the corporation to the shareholders. Thus, items that normally receive preferential tax treatment (e.g., interest on municipal bonds) are not taxed as such to the shareholders.
4. As noted in Chapter 5, it may be difficult for shareholders to recover some or all of their investment in the corporation without an ordinary income result. Most corporate distributions are treated as dividends to the extent of the corporation's earnings and profits. However, with the 15 percent rate on qualified dividends, dividends are taxed at the same rate as net capital gains.
5. Corporate losses cannot be passed through to the shareholders.[30]
6. The liquidation of a corporation will normally generate tax consequences to both the corporation and its shareholders (see Chapter 6).
7. The corporate form provides shareholders with the opportunity to be treated as employees for tax purposes if the shareholders render services to the corporation. Such status makes a number of attractive tax-sheltered fringe benefits available. They include, but are not limited to, group term life insurance and excludible meals and lodging. One of the most attractive benefits of incorporation is the ability of the business to provide accident and health insurance to its employees, including shareholder-employees. Such benefits are not included in the employee's gross income. Similar rules apply to other medical costs paid by the employer. These benefits are not available to partners, sole proprietors, and more-than-2 percent shareholder-employees of S corporations.

2.6 Operating the Corporation

Tax planning to reduce corporate income taxes should occur before the end of the tax year. Effective planning can cause income to be shifted to the next tax year and can produce large deductions by incurring expenses before year-end. Particular attention should be focused on the following.

CHARITABLE CONTRIBUTIONS

Recall that accrual basis corporations may claim a deduction for charitable contributions in the year preceding payment. The contribution must be authorized by the board of directors by the end of the tax year and paid on or before the fifteenth day of the third month of the following year. It might be useful to authorize a contribution even though it may not ultimately be made. A deduction cannot be thrown back to the previous year (even if paid within the two and one-half months) if it has not been authorized.

[30] Points 1, 2, and 5 could be resolved through a Subchapter S election (see Chapter 12), assuming the corporation qualifies for such an election. In part, the same can be said for point 3.

The enhanced deduction amount for contributions of qualified inventory can produce significant tax savings. Gifts of inventory should be designed to take advantage of this provision whenever feasible. Effort should be taken to properly document the type of inventory donated and each recipient charitable organization, as the statutory provisions that allow for an enhanced deduction have very specific requirements for qualification. Further, a corporation's cost of goods sold must be reduced to reflect any charitable contribution of inventory.

The five-year carryover period for excess charitable contributions, coupled with the requirement that a current year's contribution be applied against the 10 percent-of-taxable-income limitation before the utilization of any carryover amount, may require some tax planning. Under these rules, a charitable contribution in the current year could preclude any deduction for an amount in its fifth year of the carryover period. For a corporation with an annual gift-giving plan, this dilemma may require the deferral of a current year's contribution in order to obtain a deduction for the expiring carryover amount.

TIMING OF CAPITAL GAINS AND LOSSES

A corporation should consider offsetting profits on the sale of capital assets by selling some of the depreciated securities in the corporate portfolio. (See the "Ethics & Equity" feature on p. 2-13.) In addition, any already realized capital losses should be carefully monitored. Recall that corporate taxpayers are not permitted to claim any net capital losses as deductions against ordinary income. Capital losses can be used only as an offset against capital gains. Further, net capital losses can only be carried back three years and forward five. Gains from the sales of capital assets should be timed to offset any capital losses. The expiration of the carryover period for any net capital losses should be watched carefully so that sales of appreciated capital assets occur before that date.

NET OPERATING LOSSES

In some situations, electing to forgo an NOL carryback and utilizing the carryforward option may generate greater tax savings.

EXAMPLE 40

Ruby Corporation incurred a $50,000 NOL in 2011. Ruby, which was in the 15% bracket in 2009 and 2010, has developed a new product that management predicts will push the corporation into the 34% bracket in 2012. If Ruby carries the NOL back, the tax savings will be $7,500 ($50,000 × 15%). However, if Ruby elects to carry the NOL forward, assuming management's prediction is accurate, the tax savings will be $17,000 ($50,000 × 34%). ■

When deciding whether to forgo the carryback option, several factors should be considered. First, the time value of the tax refund that is lost by not using the carryback procedure should be calculated. Second, the election to forgo an NOL carryback is irrevocable. Thus, one cannot later choose to change if the predicted high profits do not materialize. Third, consider the future increases (or decreases) in corporate income tax rates that can reasonably be anticipated. This last consideration is the most difficult to work with. Although corporate tax rates have remained relatively stable in recent years, taxpayers have little assurance that future rates will remain constant.

DIVIDENDS RECEIVED DEDUCTION

In those cases where the taxable income limitation is applicable to a corporation's dividends received deduction, consideration should be given to the proper timing of income and deductions so as to bring the NOL rule into play. The NOL rule, the exception to the taxable income limitation, can result in a significant increase in the amount of a corporation's dividends received deduction.

EXAMPLE 41

Pearl Corporation, a calendar year C corporation, has the following information for the year:

Gross income from operations	$ 200,000
Expenses from operations	(225,000)
Dividends received from domestic corporations (less than 20% ownership)	100,000
Taxable income before dividends received deduction	$ 75,000

Pearl's dividends received deduction is $52,500 [70% × $75,000 (taxable income limitation)]. If, however, Pearl incurs additional expenses of $5,001 (or defers $5,001 of income), then the NOL rule applies, and Pearl's dividends received deduction is $70,000 [70% × $100,000 (dividends received)]. ■

The other two limitations applicable to the dividends received deduction can be avoided with some basic planning tenets. First, the holding period requirement is satisfied by holding stock for at least 46 days. Second, the debt-financed stock restriction is avoided if indebtedness is not directly attributable to an investment in stock. Clearly, indebtedness incurred specifically to acquire stock should be avoided. However, the use of stock as security for a loan should also be avoided, as the debt-financed restriction can apply in such cases.

ORGANIZATIONAL EXPENDITURES

To qualify for the 180-month amortization procedure of § 248, only organizational expenditures incurred in the first taxable year of the corporation can be considered. This rule could prove to be an unfortunate trap for corporations formed late in the year.

EXAMPLE 42

Thrush Corporation is formed in December 2011. Qualified organizational expenditures are incurred as follows: $62,000 in December 2011 and $30,000 in January 2012. If Thrush uses the calendar year for tax purposes, only $62,000 of the organizational expenditures can be written off over a period of 180 months. ■

The solution to the problem posed by Example 42 is for Thrush Corporation to adopt a fiscal year that ends on or beyond January 31. All organizational expenditures will then have been incurred before the close of the first taxable year.

SHAREHOLDER-EMPLOYEE PAYMENT OF CORPORATE EXPENSES

In a closely held corporate setting, shareholder-employees often pay corporate expenses (e.g., travel and entertainment) for which they are not reimbursed by the corporation. The IRS often disallows the deduction of these expenses by the shareholder-employee, since the payments are voluntary on his or her part. If the deduction is more beneficial at the shareholder-employee level, a corporate policy against reimbursement of such expenses should be established. Proper planning in this regard would be to decide before the beginning of each tax year where the deduction would do the most good. Corporate policy on reimbursement of such expenses could be modified on a year-to-year basis depending upon the circumstances.

In deciding whether corporate expenses should be kept at the corporate level or shifted to the shareholder-employee, the treatment of unreimbursed employee expenses must be considered. First, since employee expenses are itemized deductions, they will be of no benefit to the taxpayer who chooses the standard deduction option. Second, these expenses will be subject to the 2 percent-of-AGI floor. No such limitation will be imposed if the corporation claims the expenses.

CONCEPT SUMMARY 2.1

Income Taxation of Individuals and Corporations Compared

	Individuals	Corporations
Computation of gross income	§ 61.	§ 61.
Computation of taxable income	§§ 62, 63(b) through (h).	§ 63(a). Concept of AGI has no relevance.
Deductions	Trade or business (§ 162); nonbusiness (§ 212); some personal and employee expenses (generally deductible as itemized deductions).	Trade or business (§ 162).
Charitable contributions	Limited in any tax year to 50% of AGI; 30% for capital gain property unless election is made to reduce fair market value of gift.	Limited in any tax year to 10% of taxable income computed without regard to the charitable contribution deduction, NOL carryback, capital loss carryback, dividends received deduction, and domestic production activities deduction.
	Excess charitable contributions carried over for five years.	Same as for individuals.
	Amount of contribution is the fair market value of capital gain property; ordinary income property is limited to adjusted basis; capital gain property is treated as ordinary income property if certain tangible personalty is donated to a nonuse charity or a private nonoperating foundation is the donee.	Same as for individuals, but exceptions allowed for certain inventory and for scientific property where one-half of the appreciation is allowed as a deduction.
	Time of deduction—year in which payment is made.	Time of deduction—year in which payment is made unless accrual basis taxpayer. Accrual basis corporation can take deduction in year preceding payment if contribution was authorized by board of directors by end of year and contribution is paid by fifteenth day of third month of following year.
Casualty losses	$100 floor on personal casualty and theft losses; personal casualty losses deductible only to extent losses exceed 10% of AGI.	Deductible in full.
Net operating loss	Adjusted for several items, including nonbusiness deductions over nonbusiness income and personal exemptions.	Generally no adjustments.
	Carryback period is 2 years while carryforward period is 20 years.	Same as for individuals.
Dividends received deduction	None.	70%, 80%, or 100% of dividends received depending on percentage of ownership by corporate shareholder.
Net capital gains	Taxed in full. Tax rate generally cannot exceed 15% on net long-term capital gains.	Taxed in full.
Capital losses	Only $3,000 of capital loss per year can offset ordinary income; unused loss is carried forward indefinitely to offset capital gains or ordinary income up to $3,000; short-term and long-term carryovers retain their character.	Can offset only capital gains; unused loss is carried back three years and forward five; carryovers and carrybacks are characterized as short-term losses.
Passive losses	In general, passive losses cannot offset either active income or portfolio income.	Passive loss rules apply to closely held C corporations and personal service corporations.
		For personal service corporations, passive losses cannot offset either active income or portfolio income.
		For closely held C corporations, passive losses may offset active income but not portfolio income.

Income Taxation of Individuals and Corporations Compared—Continued

	Individuals	Corporations
Domestic production activities deduction	Based on 9% of the lesser of qualified production activities income (QPAI) *or* modified AGI.	Based on 9% of the lesser of qualified production activities income (QPAI) *or* taxable income.
Tax rates	Progressive with six rates (10%, 15%, 25%, 28%, 33%, 35%).	Progressive with four rates (15%, 25%, 34%, 35%). Two lowest brackets phased out between $100,000 and $335,000 of taxable income, and additional tax imposed between $15,000,000 and $18,333,333 of taxable income.
Alternative minimum tax	Applied at a graduated rate schedule of 26% and 28%. Exemption allowed depending on filing status (e.g., $74,450 in 2011 for married filing jointly); phaseout begins when AMTI reaches a certain amount (e.g., $150,000 for married filing jointly).	Applied at a 20% rate on AMTI less exemption; $40,000 exemption allowed but phaseout begins when AMTI reaches $150,000; adjustments and tax preference items are similar to those applicable to individuals but also include 75% adjusted current earnings. Small corporations (gross receipts of $5 million or less) are not subject to AMT.

REFOCUS ON THE BIG PICTURE

COOKED TO PERFECTION

Conducting Skylark Bakery as a corporation would save Samantha $10,375 in income taxes annually, computed as follows:

Bakery Operated as Sole Proprietorship

Operating profit of $100,000:	
Tax on $100,000 @ 35%	$35,000
Dividends of $5,000:	
Tax on $5,000 @ 15%	750
Withdrawals of $50,000:	
No tax	–0–
Total income tax when operated as sole proprietorship	$35,750

Bakery Operated as Regular Corporation

Corporate taxable income of $51,500* (see below):	
Tax on $50,000 @ 15%	$ 7,500
Tax on $1,500 @ 25%	375
Total corporate income tax	$ 7,875
Samantha's salary of $50,000:	
Tax on $50,000 @ 35%	17,500
Total income tax when operated as C corporation	$ 25,375

*Computation of corporate taxable income:

Operating profit	$100,000
Dividends	5,000
Less: Salary to Samantha	(50,000)
Dividends received deduction (70%)	(3,500)
Taxable income	$ 51,500

The example illustrates the tax savings available when a high-income individual taxpayer takes advantage of the lower marginal tax rates of corporations. However,

CONTINUED

other issues, such as employment tax considerations and the planned expiration of the preferential tax rate on dividend income, also should be considered. Further, other potential entity options, such as the LLC and S corporation, also should be evaluated.

What If?

What if the bakery in the first year it becomes a corporation generates a $10,000 short-term capital loss (STCL) on the disposition of some of its stock investments? Regular corporations can only deduct capital losses against capital gains; thus, the $10,000 STCL would not be deductible currently by the corporation and, instead, would be carried forward for up to five years. If the bakery is operated as a sole proprietorship, Samantha would report the capital loss on her individual return. She could use the $10,000 STCL to offset any capital gains she may have, and deduct up to $3,000 of the loss against ordinary income.

KEY TERMS

C corporations, 2–3
Check-the-box Regulations, 2–8
Dividends received deduction, 2–18
Domestic production activities deduction (DPAD), 2–17
Limited liability company (LLC), 2–7
Limited partnerships, 2–7
Organizational expenditures, 2–20
Passive loss, 2–14
Personal service corporations (PSCs), 2–10
Regular corporations, 2–3
Related corporations, 2–22
S corporations, 2–3
Schedule M–1, 2–24
Schedule M–3, 2–26

DISCUSSION QUESTIONS

1. **LO.1** Jennifer and Jamie are starting a business and have asked you for advice about whether they should form a partnership, a corporation, or some other type of entity. Prepare a list of questions you would ask in helping them decide which type of entity they should choose. Explain your reasons for asking each of the questions.

2. **LO.1** Dwayne owns 50% of the stock of Tangerine Corporation (a C corporation) and 50% of the stock of Heron Corporation (an S corporation), each of which incurs an operating loss of $80,000 during 2011. Neither corporation pays any dividends during the year. Discuss Dwayne's tax consequences.

3. **LO.1, 7** Art, an executive with Azure Corporation, plans to start a part-time business selling products on the Internet. He will devote about 15 hours each week to running the business. Art's salary from Azure places him in the 35% tax bracket. He projects substantial losses from the new business in each of the first three years and expects sizable profits thereafter. Art plans to leave the profits in the business for several years, sell the business, and retire. Would you advise Art to incorporate the business or operate it as a sole proprietorship? **DECISION MAKING**

4. **LO.1, 2** In 2011, Plover Corporation, a C corporation with four equal shareholders, had an operating loss of $80,000 and a long-term capital gain of $20,000. Also in 2011, Vireo Partnership, with four equal partners, had an operating loss of $80,000 and a long-term capital gain of $20,000. Plover did not pay any dividends, and Vireo's partners did not make any withdrawals. Contrast the tax treatment of the entities and their owners.

5. **LO.1, 2** Samantha is the sole owner of Blue Company. In 2011, Blue had operating income of $200,000, a short-term capital loss of $10,000, and tax- exempt interest income of $3,000. Samantha withdrew $50,000 of profit from Blue. How should Samantha report this information on her individual tax return for 2011 if Blue Company is:
   a. An LLC?
   b. An S corporation?
   c. A C corporation?

ISSUE ID

6. **LO.1, 7** Shareholders of closely held corporations frequently engage in dealings with such corporations. These dealings provide an opportunity to extract earnings out of a corporate entity in some form other than a nondeductible dividend distribution. Provide several examples of shareholder-corporation transactions and, for each example, briefly note the requirement that would need to be satisfied to avoid recharacterization by the IRS as a disguised dividend distribution.

7. **LO.1** Contrast the marginal tax rates of C corporations with those of individuals.

8. **LO.1** Briefly describe how LLCs are treated for Federal income tax purposes.

9. **LO.1** In the current year, Shauna formed a single-member LLC and did not file Form 8832 (Entity Classification Election). As a result, the LLC will be treated as a corporation for Federal tax purposes. Assess the validity of this statement.

10. **LO.2** Briefly describe several similarities and differences in the Federal taxation of individual and corporate taxpayers.

11. **LO.2** What is a personal service corporation (PSC)? When can a PSC select an accounting period other than a calendar year?

12. **LO.2** Which of the following C corporations will be allowed to use the cash method of accounting in 2011? Explain your answers.
    a. Red Corporation, which had gross receipts of $4.3 million in 2008, $6.1 million in 2009, and $4.9 million in 2010.
    b. White Corporation, which had gross receipts of $4.8 million in 2008, $5.2 million in 2009, and $4.1 million in 2010.

13. **LO.2** Wang, a cash basis taxpayer, owns 65% of the stock of Pink, Inc., a calendar year, accrual basis C corporation. On January 1, 2011, Wang loaned Pink a substantial amount of money. On December 31, 2011, Pink, Inc., accrued $35,000 of interest expense on the loan but does not pay the interest to Wang until February 1, 2012. In which year can Pink deduct the interest? When must Wang report the interest income?

14. **LO.2** In 2011, Jeanette, an individual in the 35% marginal tax bracket, recognized a $50,000 long-term capital gain. Also in 2011, Parrot Corporation, a C corporation in the 35% marginal tax bracket, recognized a $50,000 long-term capital gain. Neither taxpayer had any other property transactions in the year. What tax rates are applicable to these capital gains?

15. **LO.2** John (a sole proprietor) and Eagle Corporation (a C corporation) each recognize a short-term capital gain of $6,000 and a long-term capital loss of $8,000 on the sale of capital assets. Neither taxpayer had any other property transactions during the year. Describe the tax consequences of these gains and losses for John and for Eagle.

16. **LO.2** In the current year, Erica recognized a gain on the sale of a warehouse that she had used in her sole proprietorship. Erica had purchased the warehouse in 2002, and straight-line depreciation was properly claimed with respect to the realty. Also in the current year, Brown Corporation, a C corporation, recognized a gain on the sale of a warehouse that it had used in its business. Brown had purchased the warehouse in 2002, and straight-line depreciation was properly claimed with respect to the realty. The gains recognized by Erica and by Brown Corporation are treated entirely as § 1231 gains. Assess the validity of this statement.

17. **LO.2** Osprey Corporation, a closely held corporation, has $75,000 of active income, $25,000 of portfolio income, and a $60,000 loss from a passive activity.
    a. How much of the passive loss can Osprey deduct in the current year if it is a PSC?
    b. If it is not a PSC?

18. **LO.2** Hummingbird Corporation, a closely held corporation that is not a PSC, has $50,000 of active income, $30,000 of portfolio income, and a $75,000 loss from a passive activity. What is Hummingbird's taxable income for the year?

19. **LO.2** On December 20, 2011, the directors of Partridge Corporation, an accrual basis calendar year taxpayer, authorized a cash contribution of $25,000 to the American Cancer Association. The payment is made on February 14, 2012. Can Partridge deduct the charitable contribution in 2011?

20. **LO.2** Describe the rules regarding a charitable deduction for a contribution of inventory by a corporate taxpayer. (Ignore the taxable income limitation.)

21. **LO.2, 7** The board of directors of Orange Corporation, a calendar year taxpayer, is holding its year-end meeting on December 28, 2011. One topic on the board's agenda is the approval of a $25,000 gift to a qualified charitable organization. Orange has a $20,000 charitable contribution carryover to 2011 from a prior year. Identify the tax issues the board should consider regarding the proposed contribution.

22. **LO.2** Briefly describe the calculation of the domestic production activities deduction for a corporate taxpayer.

23. **LO.2, 3, 7** Gold Corporation, a calendar year C corporation, was formed in 2005 and has been profitable until the current year. In 2011, Gold incurs a net operating loss. Identify the issues Gold Corporation should consider regarding its NOL carryback and carryover options.

24. **LO.1, 3** Marmot Corporation pays a dividend of $400,000 in 2011. Otter Corporation, which is in the 35% marginal bracket, owns 25% of Marmot's stock. Gerald, an individual taxpayer in the 35% marginal bracket, also owns 25% of Marmot's stock. Compare and contrast the treatment of the dividend by Otter Corporation and Gerald.

25. **LO.3** Mauve Corporation (a C corporation) owns 85% of the stock of Lavender Corporation (a C corporation), which pays Mauve a substantial dividend each year. Mauve Corporation plans on selling half of its stock in Lavender Corporation. How will this stock disposition affect the amount of Mauve's dividends received deduction?

26. **LO.3** What are the debt-financed stock restrictions applicable to the dividends received deduction?

27. **LO.3** Determine whether the following expenditures by Cuckoo Corporation are organizational expenditures, startup expenditures, or neither.
    a. Legal expenses incurred for drafting the corporate charter and bylaws.
    b. Expenses incurred in printing stock certificates.
    c. Expenses of temporary board of directors' organizational meetings.
    d. Employee salaries incurred during the training period before opening for business.
    e. State incorporation fee.

28. **LO.4** The highest marginal tax rate for a C corporation is 35%. Assess the validity of this statement.

29. **LO.5** How does the tax law prevent a corporation from splitting into multiple corporations in order to spread income and reduce Federal income tax?

30. **LO.6** When are C corporations required to make estimated tax payments? How are these payments calculated?

31. **LO.6** Schedule M–1 of Form 1120 is used to reconcile financial net income with taxable income reported on the corporation's income tax return as follows: net income per books + additions − subtractions = taxable income. Classify the following items as additions or subtractions in the Schedule M–1 reconciliation.
    a. Nondeductible portion of meals and entertainment.
    b. Tax depreciation in excess of book depreciation.
    c. Federal income tax per books.
    d. Capital loss in excess of capital gain.
    e. Charitable contributions in excess of taxable income limitation.
    f. Tax-exempt interest income.
    g. Domestic production activities deduction.

32. **LO.6** In 2011, Woodpecker, Inc., a C corporation with $13.5 million in assets, deducted amortization of $40,000 on its financial statements and $55,000 on its Federal tax return. Is Woodpecker required to file Schedule M–3? If so, how is the difference in amortization amounts treated on that schedule?

PROBLEMS

33. **LO.1** In 2011, Osprey Company had operating income of $320,000, operating expenses of $270,000, and a long-term capital gain of $20,000. How does Juanita, the sole owner of Osprey Company, report this information on her individual tax return under the following assumptions?

a. Osprey Company is a proprietorship, and Juanita did not make any withdrawals from the business during the year.
b. Osprey Company is a C corporation and pays no dividends during the year.

34. **LO.1** Ellie and Linda are equal owners in Otter Enterprises, a calendar year business. During the year, Otter Enterprises has $320,000 of gross income and $210,000 of operating expenses. In addition, Otter has a short-term capital loss of $15,000 and makes distributions to Ellie and Linda of $25,000 each. Discuss the impact of this information on the taxable income of Otter, Ellie, and Linda if Otter is:
    a. A partnership.
    b. An S corporation.
    c. A C corporation.

35. **LO.1, 2** In the current year, Azure Company has $500,000 of net operating income before deducting any compensation or other payment to its sole owner, Sasha. In addition, Azure has a long-term capital gain of $50,000. Sasha has significant income from other sources and is in the 35% marginal tax bracket. Based on this information, determine the income tax consequences to Azure Company and to Sasha during the year for each of the following independent situations.
    a. Azure is a C corporation and pays no dividends or salary to Sasha.
    b. Azure is a C corporation and distributes $100,000 of dividends to Sasha.
    c. Azure is a C corporation and pays $100,000 of salary to Sasha.
    d. Azure is a sole proprietorship and Sasha withdraws $0.
    e. Azure is a sole proprietorship and Sasha withdraws $100,000.

36. **LO.1, 2** Chris owns 100% of Orange Company, which had an NOL of $220,000 ($190,000 operating income − $410,000 operating expenses) in 2011. Chris was a material participant in the activities of the business during the year. Orange Company also had a long-term capital loss of $35,000. Chris has sufficient income from other activities to be in the 35% marginal tax bracket without regard to results from Orange Company. He has no recognized capital gains in 2011. Explain the tax treatment if Orange Company is:
    a. A corporation.
    b. An LLC.

37. **LO.1** Purple Company has $200,000 in net income for 2011 before deducting any compensation or other payment to its sole owner, Kirsten. Kirsten is single and has no dependents. She claims the $5,800 standard deduction, and her personal exemption is $3,700 for 2011. Purple Company is Kirsten's only source of income. Ignoring any employment tax considerations, compute Kirsten's after-tax income if:
    a. Purple Company is a proprietorship, and Kirsten withdraws $50,000 from the business during the year.
    b. Purple Company is a C corporation, and the corporation pays out all of its after-tax income as a dividend to Kirsten.
    c. Purple Company is a C corporation, and the corporation pays Kirsten a salary of $138,750.

38. **LO.2** In 2011, Wilson Enterprises, a calendar year taxpayer, suffers a casualty loss of $60,000. How much of the casualty loss will be deductible by Wilson under the following circumstances?
    a. Wilson is an individual proprietor and has AGI of $150,000. The casualty loss was a personal loss, and the insurance recovered was $40,000.
    b. Wilson is a corporation, and the insurance recovered was $40,000.

DECISION MAKING

COMMUNICATIONS

39. **LO.1, 4, 7** Benton Company (BC) has one owner, who is in the 35% Federal income tax bracket. BC's gross income is $295,000, and its ordinary trade or business deductions are $135,000. Compute the tax liability on BC's income for 2011 under the following assumptions:
    a. BC is operated as a proprietorship, and the owner withdraws $70,000 for personal use.
    b. BC is operated as a corporation, pays out $70,000 as salary, and pays no dividends to its shareholder.
    c. BC is operated as a corporation and pays out no salary or dividends to its shareholder.
    d. BC is operated as a corporation, pays out $70,000 as salary, and pays out the remainder of its earnings as dividends.

e. Assume Robert Benton of 1121 Monroe Street, Ironton, OH 45638 is the owner of BC, which was operated as a proprietorship in 2011. Robert is thinking about incorporating the business in 2012 and asks your advice. He expects about the same amounts of income and expenses in 2012 and plans to take $70,000 per year out of the company whether he incorporates or not. Write a letter to Robert [based on your analysis in (a) and (b) above] containing your recommendations.

40. **LO.2, 4** Chastity, an architect, is the sole shareholder of Orange Corporation, a professional association. Orange paid Chastity a salary of $180,000 during its fiscal year ending October 31, 2011.
    a. How much salary must Orange Corporation pay Chastity during the period November 1 through December 31, 2011, to permit the corporation to continue to use its fiscal year without negative tax effects?
    b. Orange Corporation had taxable income of $50,000 for the year ending October 31, 2011. Compute the corporation's tax liability for the year.

41. **LO.2** Pelican Corporation, a calendar year taxpayer, has two unrelated, cash method shareholders: Charles owns 40% of the stock, and Lucinda owns the remaining 60%. As executives of Pelican, Charles and Lucinda each receive a year-end bonus that is based on the profitability of the corporation. The bonuses for 2011 amount to $75,000 for Charles and $90,000 for Lucinda. The bonuses are paid to both individuals on January 27, 2012. How much of the $165,000 of bonuses is deductible by Pelican in 2011 if the corporation is:
    a. A cash method taxpayer?
    b. An accrual method taxpayer?

42. **LO.2, 4** Ramona owns 100% of Violet Company. In 2011, Violet recognizes a long-term capital gain of $85,000 and no other income (or loss). Ramona is in the 35% tax bracket and has no recognized capital gains (or losses) before considering her ownership interest in Violet. How much income tax results from the $85,000 long-term capital gain if Violet is:
    a. A C corporation?
    b. A proprietorship?

43. **LO.2** In the current year, Sandpiper Corporation (a C corporation) had operating income of $215,000 and operating expenses of $155,000. In addition, Sandpiper had a long-term capital gain of $12,000 and a short-term capital loss of $27,000.
    a. Compute Sandpiper's taxable income and tax for the year.
    b. Assume the same facts except that Sandpiper's long-term capital gain was $35,000. Compute Sandpiper's taxable income and tax for the year.

44. **LO.2** In 2011, Bronze Company had operating profit of $75,000 ($125,000 operating income – $50,000 operating expenses). In addition, Bronze had a short-term capital gain of $16,000 and a long-term capital loss of $31,000. How much of the long-term capital loss may be deducted in 2011, and how much is carried back or forward under the following circumstances?
    a. Bronze Company is a proprietorship owned by Kenneth, and he had no other property transactions in 2011.
    b. Bronze Company is a C corporation.

45. **LO.2** During 2011, Gorilla Corporation has net short-term capital gains of $70,000, net long-term capital losses of $195,000, and taxable income from other sources of $620,000. Prior years' transactions included the following:

2007 net short-term capital gains	$30,000
2008 net long-term capital gains	55,000
2009 net short-term capital gains	15,000
2010 net long-term capital gains	40,000

    a. How are the capital gains and losses treated on Gorilla's 2011 tax return?
    b. Determine the amount of the 2011 capital loss that is carried back to each of the previous years.
    c. Compute the amount of capital loss carryover, if any, and indicate the years to which the loss may be carried.
    d. If Gorilla is a sole proprietorship, rather than a corporation, how would the owner report these transactions on her 2011 tax return?

46. **LO.2** Heron Company purchases commercial realty on November 13, 1998, for $650,000. Straight-line depreciation of $204,167 is claimed before the property is sold on February 22, 2011, for $920,000. What are the tax consequences of the sale of realty if Heron is:
    a. A C corporation?
    b. A sole proprietorship?

47. **LO.2** In 2011, Condor Corporation, a closely held C corporation that is not a PSC, has $225,000 of active business income, $35,000 of portfolio income, and a $300,000 passive loss from a rental activity. How much of the passive loss can Condor deduct in 2011? Would your answer differ if Condor were a PSC?

48. **LO.2** In the current year, Robin Corporation, a computer manufacturer, contributes 100 laptop computers (fair market value of $115,000) to a qualified charitable organization. The computers were manufactured earlier this year by Robin at a cost of $45,000. Determine the amount of Robin Corporation's charitable deduction for each of the following situations. (Ignore the taxable income limitation.)
    a. The qualified organization is a local church that will sell the computers and use the proceeds for an addition to its day care facility.
    b. The qualified organization is a local university that will use the computers in its student computer lab.
    c. Assume the same facts as in (b), except that the computers are worth $155,000 on the date of the contribution.

DECISION MAKING

COMMUNICATIONS

49. **LO.2, 7** Joseph Thompson is president and sole shareholder of Jay Corporation. In December 2011, Joe asks your advice regarding a charitable contribution he plans to have the corporation make to the University of Maine, a qualified public charity. Joe is considering the following alternatives as charitable contributions in December 2011:

	Fair Market Value
(1) Cash donation	$200,000
(2) Unimproved land held for six years ($310,000 basis)	200,000
(3) Maize Corporation stock held for eight years ($120,000 basis)	200,000
(4) Brown Corporation stock held for nine months ($70,000 basis)	200,000

Joe has asked you to help him decide which of these potential contributions will be most advantageous taxwise. Jay's taxable income is $3.5 million before considering the contribution. Rank the four alternatives and write a letter to Joe communicating your advice. The corporation's address is 1442 Main Street, Freeport, ME 04032.

DECISION MAKING

50. **LO.2, 7** In 2011, Gray Corporation, a calendar year C corporation, has a $75,000 charitable contribution carryover from a gift made in 2006. Gray is contemplating a gift of land to a qualified charity in either 2011 or 2012. Gray purchased the land as an investment five years ago for $100,000 (current fair market value is $250,000). Before considering any charitable deduction, Gray projects taxable income of $1 million for 2011 and $1.2 million for 2012. Should Gray make the gift of the land to charity in 2011 or in 2012? Provide support for your answer.

DECISION MAKING

COMMUNICATIONS

51. **LO.2, 7** Dan Simms is the president and sole shareholder of Simms Corporation, 1121 Madison Street, Seattle, WA 98121. Dan plans for the corporation to make a charitable contribution to the University of Washington, a qualified public charity. He will have the corporation donate Jaybird Corporation stock, held for five years, with a basis of $11,000 and a fair market value of $25,000. Dan projects a $310,000 net profit for Simms Corporation in 2011 and a $100,000 net profit in 2012. Dan calls you on December 13, 2011, and asks whether he should make the contribution in 2011 or 2012. Write a letter advising Dan about the timing of the contribution.

52. **LO.2** Flamingo Corporation, a calendar year C corporation, manufactures appliances in the United States. For 2011, Flamingo has taxable income (before the domestic productions activity deduction [DPAD]) of $850,000, qualified production activities income (QPAI) of $740,000, and W–2 wages attributable to QPAI of $150,000.
    a. How much is Flamingo's DPAD for 2011?
    b. Assume, instead, that W–2 wages attributable to QPAI are $120,000. How much is Flamingo's DPAD for 2011?

53. **LO.2, 7** During the year, Ruby Corporation, a calendar year taxpayer, has the following transactions:

Income from operations	$300,000
Expenses from operations	375,000
Dividends (less than 20% ownership)	150,000

a. Determine Ruby's NOL for the year.
b. What are Ruby's options as to the carryover of the NOL?

54. **LO.3** In each of the following independent situations, determine the dividends received deduction. Assume that none of the corporate shareholders owns 20% or more of the stock in the corporations paying the dividends.

	Green Corporation	Orange Corporation	Yellow Corporation
Income from operations	$ 700,000	$ 700,000	$ 700,000
Expenses from operation	(650,000)	(750,000)	(850,000)
Qualifying dividends	200,000	200,000	200,000

55. **LO.3** Gull Corporation, a cash method, calendar year C corporation, was formed and began business on July 1, 2011. Gull incurred the following expenses during its first year of operations (July 1, 2011–December 31, 2011):

Expenses of temporary directors and organizational meetings	$17,000
Fee paid to state of incorporation	2,500
Expenses for printing and sale of stock certificates	8,000
Legal services for drafting the corporate charter and bylaws (not paid until January 2012)	25,000

a. Assuming that Gull Corporation elects under § 248 to expense and amortize organizational expenditures, what amount may be deducted in 2011?
b. Assume the same facts as above, except that the amount paid for the legal services was $35,000 (instead of $25,000). What amount may be deducted as organizational expenditures in 2011?

56. **LO.3** Egret Corporation, a calendar year C corporation, was formed on June 7, 2011, and opened for business on September 1, 2011. After its formation but prior to opening for business, Egret incurred the following expenditures:

Accounting	$ 4,000
Advertising	9,500
Employee payroll	12,000
Rent	9,000
Utilities	2,000

What is the maximum amount of these expenditures that Egret can deduct in 2011?

57. **LO.4** In each of the following independent situations, determine the corporation's income tax liability. Assume that all corporations use a calendar year for tax purposes and that the tax year involved is 2011.

	Taxable Income
Purple Corporation	$ 45,000
Azul Corporation	310,000
Pink Corporation	2,350,000
Turquoise Corporation	21,000,000
Teal Corporation (a personal service corporation)	80,000

58. **LO.5** Red Corporation and White Corporation, both calendar year C corporations, are members of a controlled group of corporations. For 2011, Red has taxable income of $80,000, and White has taxable income of $150,000. Assuming the controlled group does

not make an election regarding the apportionment of the marginal tax brackets, what is the income tax liability for each of the corporations?

59. **LO.6** Pelican Corporation, a calendar year C corporation, has taxable income of $3 million for 2011. In 2010, the first year of operations, it had taxable income of $1.8 million. What are Pelican's minimum required estimated tax payments for 2011?

60. **LO.6** Eagle Corporation, a calendar year and accrual method taxpayer, provides the following information and asks you to prepare Schedule M–1 for 2011:

Net income per books (after-tax)	$386,250
Federal income tax per books	30,050
Tax-exempt interest income	5,000
Life insurance proceeds received as a result of death of corporate president	300,000
Nondeductible penalties	2,500
Interest on loan to purchase tax-exempt bonds	1,700
Excess of capital loss over capital gains	5,300
Premiums paid on life insurance policy on life of Eagle's president	4,200
Domestic production activities deduction	2,000
Excess of tax depreciation over book depreciation	3,000

61. **LO.6** The following information for 2011 relates to Sparrow Corporation, a calendar year, accrual method taxpayer.

Net income per books (after-tax)	$119,738
Federal income tax per books	49,862
Tax-exempt interest income	7,500
MACRS depreciation in excess of straight-line depreciation used for financial purposes	10,000
Charitable contribution in excess of taxable income limitation	8,750
Premiums paid on life insurance policy on the president (Sparrow is beneficiary of policy)	6,250
Interest on loan to purchase tax-exempt bonds	3,700

Based on the above information, use Schedule M–1 of Form 1120, which is available on the IRS website, to determine Sparrow's taxable income for 2011.

62. **LO.6** Swan Corporation, a calendar year C corporation, had the following information for 2011:

Net income per books (after-tax)	$174,700
Taxable income	195,000
Federal income tax per books	59,300
Cash dividend distributions	35,000
Unappropriated retained earnings, as of January 1, 2011	636,450

Based on the above, use Schedule M–2 of Form 1120 (see Example 35 in the text) to determine Swan's unappropriated retained earnings balance as of December 31, 2011.

63. **LO.6** In the current year, Pelican, Inc., incurs $10,000 of meals and entertainment expenses that it deducts in computing net income per the corporation's financial statements. All of the meals and entertainment expenditures are subject to the 50% cutback rule applicable to such expenditures. How is this information reported on Schedule M–3?

64. **LO.6** In the current year, Pelican, Inc., incurs $50,000 of nondeductible fines and penalties. Its depreciation expense is $245,000 for financial statement purposes and $310,000 for tax purposes. How is this information reported on Schedule M–3?

65. **LO.6** In January 2011, Pelican, Inc., established an allowance for uncollectible accounts (bad debt reserve) of $110,000 on its books and increased the allowance by $160,000 during the year. As a result of a client's bankruptcy, Pelican, Inc., decreased the allowance by $90,000 in November 2011. Pelican, Inc., deducted the $270,000 of increases to the allowance on its 2011 income statement but was not allowed to deduct

that amount on its tax return. On its 2011 tax return, the corporation was allowed to deduct the $90,000 actual loss sustained because of its client's bankruptcy. On its financial statements, Pelican, Inc., treated the $270,000 increase in the bad debt reserve as an expense that gave rise to a temporary difference. On its 2011 tax return, Pelican, Inc., took a $90,000 deduction for bad debt expense. How is this information reported on Schedule M–3?

66. **LO.2, 3, 7** In January, Don and Steve each invested $100,000 cash to form a corporation to conduct business as a retail golf equipment store. On January 5, they paid Bill, an attorney, to draft the corporate charter, file the necessary forms with the state, and write the bylaws. They leased a store building and began to acquire inventory, furniture, display equipment, and office equipment in February. They hired a sales staff and clerical personnel in March and conducted training sessions during the month. They had a successful opening on April 1, and sales increased steadily throughout the summer. The weather turned cold in October, and all local golf courses closed by October 15, which resulted in a drastic decline in sales. Don and Steve expect business to be very good during the Christmas season and then to taper off significantly from January 1 through the end of February. The corporation accrued bonuses to Don and Steve on December 31, payable on April 15 of the following year. The corporation made timely estimated tax payments throughout the year. The corporation hired a bookkeeper in February, but he does not know much about taxation. Don and Steve have retained you as a tax consultant and have asked you to identify the tax issues that they should consider. **ISSUE ID**

TAX RETURN PROBLEMS

1. On November 1, 2005, Janet Morton and Kim Wong formed Pet Kingdom, Inc., to sell pets and pet supplies. Pertinent information regarding Pet Kingdom is summarized as follows:
   - Pet Kingdom's business address is 1010 Northwest Parkway, Dallas, TX 75225; its telephone number is (214) 555-2211; and its e-mail address is petkingdom@pki.com.
   - The employer identification number is 11–1111111, and the principal business activity code is 453910.
   - Janet and Kim each own 50% of the common stock; Janet is president and Kim is vice president of the company. No other class of stock is authorized.
   - Both Janet and Kim are full-time employees of Pet Kingdom. Janet's Social Security number is 123–45–6789, and Kim's Social Security number is 987–65–4321.
   - Pet Kingdom is an accrual method, calendar year taxpayer. Inventories are determined using FIFO and the lower of cost or market method. Pet Kingdom uses the straight-line method of depreciation for book purposes and accelerated depreciation (MACRS) for tax purposes.
   - During 2010, the corporation distributed cash dividends of $200,000.

   Pet Kingdom's financial statements for 2010 are shown below.

Income Statement

Income		
Gross sales		$4,600,000
Sales returns and allowances		(160,000)
Net sales		$4,440,000
Cost of goods sold		(1,840,000)
Gross profit		$2,600,000
Dividends received from stock investments in less-than-20%-owned U.S. corporations		35,000
Interest income:		
State bonds	$12,000	
Certificates of deposit	16,000	28,000
Total income		$2,663,000

Expenses			
Salaries—officers			
Janet Morton	$210,000		
Kim Wong	210,000	$420,000	
Salaries—clerical and sales		580,000	
Taxes (state, local, and payroll)		190,000	
Repairs and maintenance		112,000	
Interest expense:			
Loan to purchase state bonds	$ 7,000		
Other business loans	174,000	181,000	
Advertising		46,000	
Rental expense		86,000	
Depreciation*		80,000	
Charitable contributions		30,000	
Employee benefit programs		48,000	
Premiums on term life insurance policies on lives of Janet and Kim; Pet Kingdom is the designated beneficiary		32,000	
Total expenses			(1,805,000)
Net income before taxes			$ 858,000
Federal income tax			(282,370)
Net income per books			$ 575,630

*Depreciation for tax purposes is $110,000. You are not provided enough detailed data to complete a Form 4562 (depreciation). If you solve this problem using H&R BLOCK At Home, enter the amount of depreciation on line 20 of Form 1120.

Balance Sheet

Assets	January 1, 2010	December 31, 2010
Cash	$ 960,000	$ 680,000
Trade notes and accounts receivable	1,650,000	1,838,000
Inventories	2,200,000	2,424,000
Stock investment	900,000	900,000
State bonds	300,000	300,000
Certificates of deposit	350,000	350,000
Prepaid Federal tax	—	3,630
Buildings and other depreciable assets	4,365,000	4,365,000
Accumulated depreciation	(485,000)	(565,000)
Land	650,000	650,000
Other assets	112,000	102,800
Total assets	$11,002,000	$11,048,430

Liabilities and Equity	January 1, 2010	December 31, 2010
Accounts payable	$ 1,850,000	$ 1,579,800
Other current liabilities	142,000	123,000
Mortgages	3,700,000	3,660,000
Capital stock	2,000,000	2,000,000
Retained earnings	3,310,000	3,685,630
Total liabilities and equity	$11,002,000	$11,048,430

During 2010, Pet Kingdom made estimated tax payments of $71,500 each quarter to the IRS. Prepare a Form 1120 for Pet Kingdom for tax year 2010. Suggested software: H&R BLOCK At Home.

H&R BLOCK At Home

2. Belinda Jackson and Ahmad Sharma each own 50% of the common stock of By the Numbers, Inc. (BNI). No other class of stock is authorized. On August 8, 2005, they

formed BNI to provide actuarial services. Pertinent information regarding BNI is summarized as follows:

- BNI's business address is 1001 N. Main Street, Los Angeles, CA 90012; its telephone number is (575) 541-1122; and its e-mail address is BNI@BNI.com.
- The employer identification number is 11–1111111, and the principal business activity code is 541990.
- Belinda is president of the company, and Ahmad is vice president.
- Belinda and Ahmad are the only full-time actuaries employed by BNI, and they perform all of the professional actuarial services of the corporation. Belinda's Social Security number is 123–45–6789, and Ahmad's Social Security number is 987–65–4321.
- BNI is a cash method, calendar year taxpayer. BNI uses the straight-line method of depreciation for both book and tax purposes. The corporation does not maintain any inventory.
- During 2010, the corporation distributed cash dividends of $20,000.

BNI's financial statements for 2010 are shown below.

Income Statement

Income			
Professional fees			$530,000
Interest income (state bonds)			3,000
Total income			$533,000
Expenses			
Salaries—officers:			
Belinda Jackson	$125,000		
Ahmed Sharma	125,000	$250,000	
Salaries—clerical		55,000	
Taxes:			
Property	$ 21,500		
Payroll	20,020		
State income	2,250		
Other miscellaneous	1,700	45,470	
Repairs and maintenance		8,500	
Meals and entertainment		7,600	
Travel		6,300	
Charitable contributions		2,000	
Interest expense on business loans		12,800	
Advertising		19,300	
Rental expense		4,100	
Depreciation*		22,400	
Contributions to pension plans		25,000	
Employee benefit programs		16,900	
Accounting services		7,300	
Dues and subscriptions		4,900	
Insurance		15,000	
Legal and professional services		12,500	
Miscellaneous expenses		3,000	
Telephone		2,400	
Total expenses			(520,470)
Net income before taxes			$ 12,530
Federal income tax			(4,666)
Net income per books			$ 7,864

*You are not provided enough detailed data to complete a Form 4562 (depreciation). If you solve this problem using H&R BLOCK At Home, enter the amount of depreciation on line 20 of Form 1120.

Balance Sheet

Assets	January 1, 2010	December 31, 2010
Cash	$ 23,220	$ 26,300
Trade notes and accounts receivable	35,850	32,100
State bonds	75,000	75,000
Buildings and other depreciable assets	295,600	311,700
Accumulated depreciation	(63,500)	(85,900)
Land	35,000	35,000
Other assets	2,980	2,110
Total assets	$404,150	$396,310

Liabilities and Equity	January 1, 2010	December 31, 2010
Accounts payable	$ 34,800	$ 35,596
Other current liabilities	9,350	18,250
Mortgages	114,000	108,600
Capital stock	200,000	200,000
Retained earnings	46,000	33,864
Total liabilities and equity	$404,150	$396,310

During 2010, BNI made estimated tax payments of $1,250 each quarter to the IRS. Prepare a Form 1120 for BNI for tax year 2010. Suggested software: H&R BLOCK At Home.

RESEARCH PROBLEMS

THOMSON REUTERS
Checkpoint® Student Edition

Note: Solutions to Research Problems can be prepared by using the **Checkpoint® Student Edition** online research product, which is available to accompany this text. It is also possible to prepare solutions to the Research Problems by using tax research materials found in a standard tax library.

COMMUNICATIONS

Research Problem 1. A new client, Southwest Grocers, is a calendar year C corporation that owns and operates a chain of grocery stores. Southwest Grocers is interested in donating food inventory to one or more charitable organizations. In some cases, the donated items would consist of dented canned food and fungible food items (e.g., baked goods) nearing their freshness expiration dates. Inedible food or food past its expiration date would not be included in any donation. Prepare an outline detailing the information you would provide to Southwest Grocers regarding charitable contributions of food inventory. Be sure to include support for the content of your outline.

COMMUNICATIONS

Research Problem 2. Tern Corporation, a calendar year C corporation, is solely owned by Jessica Ramirez. Tern's only business since its incorporation in 2008 has been land surveying services. In Tern's state of incorporation, land surveying can be performed only by a licensed surveyor. Jessica, Tern's only employee, is a licensed surveyor but is not a licensed engineer. Upon audit of Tern's 2008 and 2009 tax returns, the IRS assessed tax deficiencies stemming from its conclusion that the corporation was a personal service corporation subject to the flat tax rate of 35%. Jessica believes that the IRS's determination is incorrect, and she has asked you for advice on how to proceed. Evaluate the IRS's position regarding the treatment of Tern Corporation as a personal service corporation, and prepare a memo for the client files describing the results of your research.

COMMUNICATIONS

Research Problem 3. Cynthia Thomas is the president and sole shareholder of Violet Corporation, a calendar year taxpayer. In 2009, Cynthia incurred $9,500 of business expenditures for travel, entertainment, and promotion on behalf of Violet. Because Violet was in a precarious financial condition, Cynthia decided not to seek reimbursement for these expenditures. Instead, she deducted them on her own tax return (Form 1040). Upon audit of Cynthia's 2009 return, the IRS disallowed the deduction of the expenditures. Evaluate the merits of the position of the IRS and prepare a memo for the client files describing the results of your research.

Partial list of research aids:
Rev.Rul. 57–502, 1957–2 C.B. 118.
Roy. L. Harding, 29 TCM 789, T.C.Memo. 1970–179.

Use the tax resources of the Internet to address the following questions. Do not restrict your search to the Web, but include a review of newsgroups and general reference materials, practitioner sites and resources, primary sources of the tax law, chat rooms and discussion groups, and other opportunities.

COMMUNICATIONS

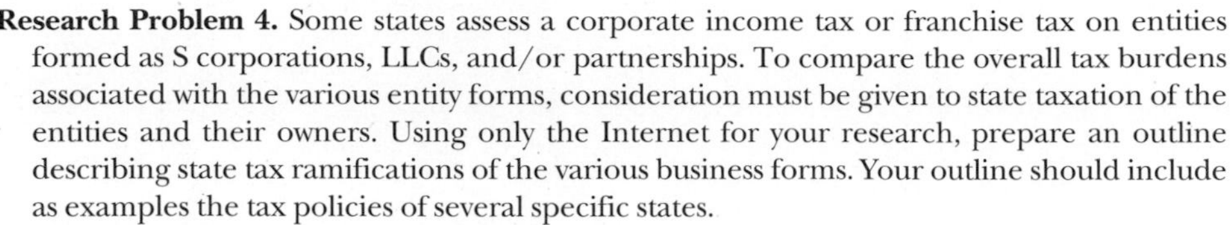

Research Problem 4. Some states assess a corporate income tax or franchise tax on entities formed as S corporations, LLCs, and/or partnerships. To compare the overall tax burdens associated with the various entity forms, consideration must be given to state taxation of the entities and their owners. Using only the Internet for your research, prepare an outline describing state tax ramifications of the various business forms. Your outline should include as examples the tax policies of several specific states.

COMMUNICATIONS

Research Problem 5. In recent years, there has been much discussion of U.S. corporate taxation and its effect on the country's global competitiveness. Using the Internet as your sole research source, prepare an outline comparing U.S. corporate taxation with that of other industrialized countries. In addition to comparing corporate income tax rates, your outline should also address the effective corporate tax rates of these countries.

Research Problem 6. Download Schedule M–3 and the accompanying instructions from the IRS website. The instructions provide several examples of adjustments that are reported on Schedule M–3. Select three of these examples and make the required entries on the appropriate parts and lines of Schedule M–3.

CHAPTER

3

Corporations: Special Situations

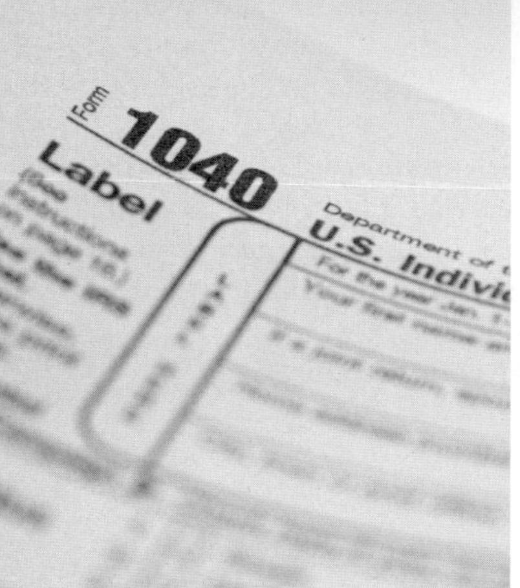

LEARNING OBJECTIVES

After completing Chapter 3, you should be able to:

LO.1 Explain the reasons for the domestic production activities deduction (DPAD).

LO.2 Identify the components of the domestic production activities deduction (DPAD).

LO.3 Recognize and work with the different types of domestic production gross receipts (DPGR).

LO.4 Describe the necessary adjustments to DPGR to arrive at qualified production activities income (QPAI).

LO.5 List the collateral problems associated with the domestic production activities deduction (DPAD).

LO.6 Explain the reason for the alternative minimum tax.

LO.7 Calculate the alternative minimum tax applicable to corporations.

LO.8 Discuss the function of adjusted current earnings (ACE).

LO.9 Evaluate the current status of the penalty taxes on corporate accumulations.

LO.10 Demonstrate the accumulated earnings and personal holding company taxes.

LO.11 Apply various tax planning procedures to maximize the domestic production activities deduction (DPAD) and to minimize the imposition of the AMT.

OUTLINE

For the latest in changes to tax legislation, visit **www.cengage.com/taxation/swft.**

THE BIG PICTURE Tax Solutions for the Real World

DEALING WITH THE DPAD AND THE AMT

Determining DPGR for the Domestic Production Activities Deduction

Mocha, Inc., produces ice cream at various manufacturing facilities throughout the South and sells it to food stores and restaurants. Mocha also operates snack shops next to its facilities where it sells ice cream, coffee, and other snacks to the general public.

Mocha has gross receipts of $42 million from the wholesale sale of its ice cream and $5 million from the operation of the snack shops. What receipts are considered to be domestic production gross receipts (DPGR) for the domestic production activities deduction (DPAD)? What planning tip might you give to Mocha? **Read the chapter and formulate your response.**

Who Pays the AMT?

Carmine, Inc., has a tentative minimum tax base of $7 million and *average* gross receipts for this year and the prior three years of less than $7.5 million.

Taupe, Inc., has a tentative minimum tax base of $7.1 million and *average* gross receipts for this year and the prior three years of less than $7.5 million. Carmine is not subject to the *alternative minimum tax (AMT),* but Taupe is.

How can this happen? **Read the chapter and formulate your response.**

When a business is operated as a C corporation, situations are encountered that require the application of specialized tax rules. This chapter discusses these situations, which involve the following provisions of the tax law:

- The domestic production activities deduction (DPAD) of § 199.
- The alternative minimum tax (AMT) of § 55.
- The penalty taxes of § 531 and § 541.

The DPAD (also known as the "manufacturers' deduction") is not limited to C corporations and is available to other types of entities as well. Nevertheless, the DPAD is more apt to be found among corporations (either C or S types) than among individuals. The reason is that manufacturing activities require capital, which is easily raised through the use of a corporate entity. Moreover, the DPAD presents unique problems for C corporations, particularly when extended affiliated group members are involved.

Like the DPAD, the AMT is not limited to C corporations and applies to other types of entities as well. Fewer corporations may be subject to the AMT than to the DPAD, however, due to the exemption for small corporations. An ACE adjustment relates only to certain corporations and is not required of other taxpayers.

The penalty taxes of § 531 and § 541 are unique to C corporations. The taxes are characteristically imposed on closely held corporations that accumulate profits to avoid dividend distributions. Since dividends may be taxed as ordinary income after 2012, steps should be taken to avoid these penalty taxes. Awareness of the potential danger is necessary to preclude a punitive tax. This awareness is particularly needed with the tax on personal holding companies (i.e., § 541), since its imposition is not dependent on the existence of a tax avoidance motive.

Congress Works in Strange Ways

To improve the balance of trade and mitigate the effect of its relatively high corporate tax rates, the United States has had a number of export incentives—the last of which was the extraterritorial income (ETI) regime. The ETI regime provided the benefit of an exclusion from income for certain foreign sales. Consequently, it is not surprising that the World Trade Organization found the ETI provisions to be an illegal export subsidy.

The American Jobs Creation Act of 2004 repealed the ETI exclusion but did not replace it with a comparable tax benefit for U.S. exporters. Instead, a new broad-based "domestic production activities deduction" for U.S. manufacturers was enacted.* Certain domestic producers can claim a deduction equal to 9 percent of qualified production activities income subject to several limitations. To curtail revenue loss, the deduction was phased in as follows: 3 percent for tax years beginning in 2005 or 2006, 6 percent for tax years beginning in 2007 to 2009, and 9 percent for tax years thereafter.**

The domestic production activities deduction, as a replacement for ETI, no longer presents an "international tax" issue—the deduction does not require exporting or any other activity outside the United States. Also, the deduction is not limited to the taxpayers that benefited from the ETI provisions and provides benefits to more businesses than just those considered manufacturers. Thus, Congress tried to solve an international export subsidy and ended up encouraging domestic manufacturing.

*Section 101 of the American Jobs Creation Act of 2004, as modified by § 513(b) of the Tax Increase Prevention and Reconciliation Act of 2005 (TIPRA).
**§ 199(a)(2).

3.1 Domestic Production Activities Deduction

LO.1

Explain the reasons for the domestic production activities deduction (DPAD).

The **domestic production activities deduction (DPAD)** is a special deduction that is available for organizations with domestic production activities, including those in manufacturing, film production, construction, print media, engineering, and power generation. The deduction, which was fully phased in at 9 percent by 2010, reduces the corporate tax rates by about 3 percentage points.

There is an important limitation on the amount of the deduction. The DPAD cannot exceed 50 percent of the **W–2 wages** paid by the taxpayer during the tax year. The purpose of this limitation is to preserve U.S. manufacturing jobs and discourage their outsourcing.

The deduction is available to a variety of taxpayers including individuals, partnerships, S corporations, cooperatives, estates, and trusts. For a pass-through entity (e.g., partnerships, S corporations), the deduction flows through to the individual owners. In the case of a sole proprietor, a deduction *for* adjusted gross income (AGI) results and is claimed on Form 1040, line 35, page 1. A Form 8903 must be attached to support the deduction. The Joint Committee on Taxation estimates that about 25 percent of the total benefit will accrue to 45,000 S corporations, 15,000 partnerships, and 50,000 sole proprietorships. Table 3.1 reflects the present savings that this provision will offer for C corporations.

EXAMPLE 1

The DPAD applies to more companies than just the typical manufacturer. The tax benefit is available to farmers, fishermen, miners, and the construction industry. Businesses involved in painting, drywalling, and landscaping qualify. Engineering and architectural firms qualify as long as their services relate to construction, even if no actual construction takes place. Businesses conducting feasibility and environmental impact studies also qualify for the deduction. ■

TABLE 3.1 Maximum DPAD Savings for C Corporations (Years after 2009)

Taxable Income Range	Marginal Tax Rate*	Maximum Tax Savings**
$1–$50,000	15%	$675
$50,001–$75,000	25%	$1,688
$75,001–$100,000	35%	$3,150
$100,001–$335,000	39%	$11,758
$335,001–$10,000,000	34%	$306,000
$10,000,001–$15,000,000	35%	$472,500
$15,000,001–$18,333,333	35%	$577,500
>$18,333,333	35%	>$577,500

*Assumptions: corporate tax rates remain the same for 2011 as in 2009, and the § 199 deduction does not reduce taxable income sufficiently to reduce the marginal tax rate.

**Taxable income × 0.09 × marginal tax rate.

Source: Adapted from S. C. Dilley and Fred Jacobs, "The Qualified Production Activities Deduction: Some Planning Tools," *Tax Notes*, July 4, 2005, p. 95.

The DPAD is designed to provide a tax benefit in a somewhat unique manner. Unlike other deductions, the DPAD does not result from a direct expenditure or other outlay. Instead, it is a deduction based on the net income earned from a specified source. A manufacturing concern, therefore, will determine its DPAD on the profit from the sale of the item produced, not on the cost of production. Thus, the DPAD is a deduction based on income!

Since the DPAD requires no additional outlay, the overall tax effect is similar to that of a rate reduction or a tax credit. The DPAD should not directly reduce earnings and profits, and FASB requires this benefit to be reported as a special charge (e.g., similar to a tax credit).[1]

The DPAD rules introduce a number of terms and related acronyms. To help clarify the discussion that follows, Exhibit 3.1 lists some of the more common acronyms found in § 199.

LO.2

Identify the components of the domestic production activities deduction (DPAD).

COMPONENTS OF THE DEDUCTION

The domestic production activities deduction (DPAD) is based on the following formula after 2009.[2]

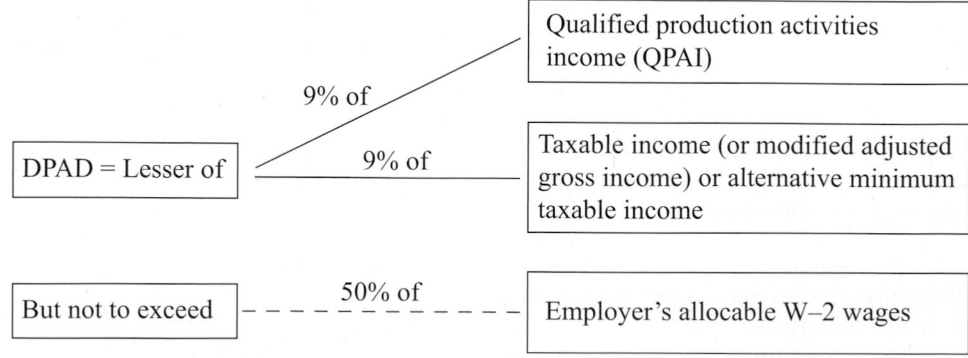

[1]FASB Staff Position No. FAS 109-1. **http://72.3.243.42/pdf/fsp_fas109-1.pdf**.

[2]A 6% rate applied to 2008–2009.

EXHIBIT 3.1 Some Common § 199 Acronyms

CGS = cost of goods sold
DPAD = domestic production activities deduction
DPGR = domestic production gross receipts
EAG = expanded affiliated group
MPGE = manufactured, produced, grown, or extracted
QPAI = qualified production activities income
QPP = qualified production property
TPP = tangible personal property

Taxable income is determined without regard to the DPAD. In the case of an individual (sole proprietor or an owner of a flow-through entity), modified AGI is substituted for taxable income.[3]

The taxable income limitation is determined after the application of any net operating loss (NOL) deduction for the tax year. Thus, a company with an NOL carryforward for a tax year is ineligible for the DPAD if such carryforward eliminates current taxable income. Further, a taxpayer may lose part or all of the DPAD benefit if there is an NOL carryback for that year. As taxable income is reduced by the NOL carryback, there is a corresponding reduction in the DPAD. If **qualified production activities income (QPAI)** cannot be used in a particular year due to the taxable income limitation (see the formula on the previous page), it is lost forever.

EXAMPLE 2

Opal, Inc., manufactures and sells costume jewelry. It also sells costume jewelry purchased from other manufacturers. During 2011, Opal had a *profit* of $200,000 (QPAI) from the sale of its own manufactured jewelry and a *loss* of $50,000 from the sale of the purchased jewelry. Based on this information, Opal's QPAI is $200,000, and its taxable income (TI) is $150,000 ($200,000 – $50,000). Opal's DPAD becomes $13,500 [9% of the lesser of $200,000 (QPAI) or $150,000 (TI)]. ■

EXAMPLE 3

Assume the same facts as in Example 2, except that Opal also has an NOL carryover of $300,000 from 2010. As taxable income for 2011 is zero ($200,000 – $50,000 – $300,000), there is no DPAD. ■

The DPAD is further limited by 50 percent of the W–2 wages paid by the taxpayer that are allocable to domestic production gross receipts (DPGR), including the sum of the aggregate amount of wages and elective deferrals, required to be included on the W–2 wage statement for the employees during the employer's taxable year. Thus, the lower a taxpayer's W–2 wages, the less the potential deduction. If an employer has employees whose activities are applicable to providing services or other activities that do not create DPGR or QPAI, such W–2 wages are not included in the favorable category.[4]

EXAMPLE 4

In 2011, Red, Inc., has QPAI of $2 million and taxable income of $2.1 million. Since Red outsources much of its work to independent contractors, its W–2 wage base that relates entirely to domestic production activities is $80,000. Although Red's DPAD normally would be $180,000 [9% of the lesser of $2 million (QPAI) or $2.1 million (TI)], it is limited to $40,000 [50% of $80,000 (W–2 wages)]. ■

[3]§ 199(d)(2). Modified AGI means AGI without any DPAD allowance and determined in accordance with the instructions to Form 8903.

[4]§§ 199(b)(2)(B) and (C); Reg. § 1.199–2 T. W–2 wages do not include any amount that is not properly included in a return filed with the Social Security Administration on or before the sixtieth day after the due date (including extensions) for such return.

GLOBAL *Tax Issues*

THE UNITED STATES CAN LEARN FROM OTHERS!

Although a producers' deduction is new to the United States, it is not a stranger elsewhere. Canada wrestled with a similar provision for more than two decades and recently scrapped it as being too controversial. During its existence, taxpayers' efforts to qualify for the deduction led to some bizarre situations. A ski resort claimed that it qualified because it manufactured artificial snow when the weather failed to cooperate. A radiologist claimed he was "processing" X-rays in reaching a diagnosis. The *coup de grâce* came when Burger King successfully contended that the assembling of salads and the broiling of burgers constituted "manufacturing."

Although our DPAD has shortcomings, we have profited from Canada's mistakes and avoided many of its problems.

The IRS provides various alternative methods for calculating the W–2 wage amount. There are two safe harbors for calculating the W–2 wage amount:

1. With a wage-expense method, the employer multiplies the W–2 wages by the ratio of the wage expenses used to determine QPAI to the total wage expenses used to determine taxable income for the tax year.
2. Under a small business simplified overall method, W–2 wages are charged against DPGR in the same proportion as DPGR bears to total gross receipts.

Presuming the taxable income and W–2 wage limitations are not applicable, the DPAD is a percentage of qualified production activities income (QPAI). QPAI is the excess of **domestic production gross receipts (DPGR)** over the sum of cost of goods sold (CGS) and other deductions and a ratable portion of deductions not directly allocable to such receipts.[5]

A PROPER ALLOCATION FOR W–2 WAGES PURPOSES?

Egret, a closely held C corporation, owns and operates a factory and a repair shop in southwest Texas. At its factory, it manufactures components for RVs, while at the repair shop it repairs RVs of those traveling south for the winter (i.e., "snowbirds"). Egret's labor force consists of independent contractors, workers *with* Social Security numbers (i.e., W–2 wage earners), and those who have "lost" their Social Security numbers. In arriving at the QPAI for the manufacturing activity, Egret reduces the DPGR only by the W–2 wages. All other wage and labor payments are assigned to the repair activity (i.e., non-DPGR). Egret claims a DPAD based on QPAI from the manufacturing operation. Comment on the propriety of Egret's actions.

LO.3

Recognize and work with the different types of domestic production gross receipts (DPGR).

DOMESTIC PRODUCTION GROSS RECEIPTS

These five specific categories of DPGR qualify for the DPAD:

- Lease, rental, license, sale, exchange, or other disposition of qualified production property (QPP) that was manufactured, produced, grown, or extracted (MPGE) in the United States.
- Qualified films largely created in the United States.
- Production of electricity, natural gas, or potable water.

[5]§ 199(c); Notice 2004–14, 2005–1 C.B. 498.

TAX *in the NEWS*

STATISTICAL SAMPLING TO THE RESCUE?

Although the full 9 percent deduction beginning in 2010 presents greater opportunities for companies to maximize their DPAD, there is also increased compliance risk. Calculating DPGR can present difficulties for companies that produce products that include components of DPGR and non-DPGR. Statistical sampling may come to the rescue.

A company can sample a portion of a body or population of data and extrapolate the results of the sample to the entire data population, thereby substantially reducing the time and cost of complying with the necessary allocations. Statistical sampling may be used in these situations:

- Allocating gross receipts between DPGR and non-DPGR.
- Determining whether gross receipts qualify as DPGR on an item-by-item basis.
- Allocating cost of goods sold between DPGR and non-DPGR.
- Allocating deductions that are properly allocable to DPGR or gross income attributable to DPGR.

Sources: Rev.Rul. 2007–35, 2007–1 C.B. 1345; Andy Zaleski, "Using Statistical Sampling to Support the Sec. 199 Deduction," *The Tax Adviser*, May 2009, pp. 280–282.

- Construction (but not self-construction) performed in the United States.
- Engineering and architectural services for domestic construction.

The operation of these categories is illustrated in Figure 3.1. In general, DPGR does not include any gross receipts derived from property leased, licensed, or rented for use by a related person.

The sale of food and beverages prepared by a taxpayer at a retail establishment and the transmission or distribution of electricity, natural gas, or potable water are specifically excluded from the definition of DPGR.

Gross Receipts That Qualify

In many cases, a taxpayer must determine the portion of its total gross receipts that is DPGR. For example, suppose a taxpayer produces a product in the United States that qualifies for the deduction and also produces the same product at a facility outside the United States. Does the taxpayer's accounting system reflect the portion of the gross receipts that is attributable to the U.S. production and the portion attributable to production outside the United States? In order to determine DPGR, an apportionment will be necessary. The IRS indicates that a taxpayer must use a reasonable method that accurately identifies DPGR and non-DPGR based on all of the information available.[6] If a taxpayer uses a specific identification method (e.g., specifically identifies where the product was MPGE) for any other purpose, the same method must be used to determine DPGR.

An overall *de minimis* safe-harbor test is applicable when small amounts of non-DPGR are present. A taxpayer with less than 5 percent of total gross receipts from non-DPGR may treat all gross receipts as DPGR and is not required to allocate.

EXAMPLE 5

Orange, Inc., produces a product in both the United States and Mexico. Gross receipts derived are $2.2 million for the United States and $900,000 for Mexico. Only the $2.2 million qualifies as DPGR. ■

EXAMPLE 6

Assume the same facts as in Example 5, except that the production in Mexico yields only $100,000 (rather than $900,000) in gross receipts. Now, the safe-harbor test is met since 4.3% ($100,000/$2,300,000) is less than 5%. Consequently, the full $2.3 million ($2.2 million + $100,000) is DPGR. ■

[6] Reg. § 1.199–1(d)(2) and Notice 2005–14. The Notice also mentions the factors the IRS will consider in determining if the taxpayer's allocation method is reasonable.

FIGURE 3.1 Scheme of the § 199 Domestic Production Activities Deduction (DPAD)

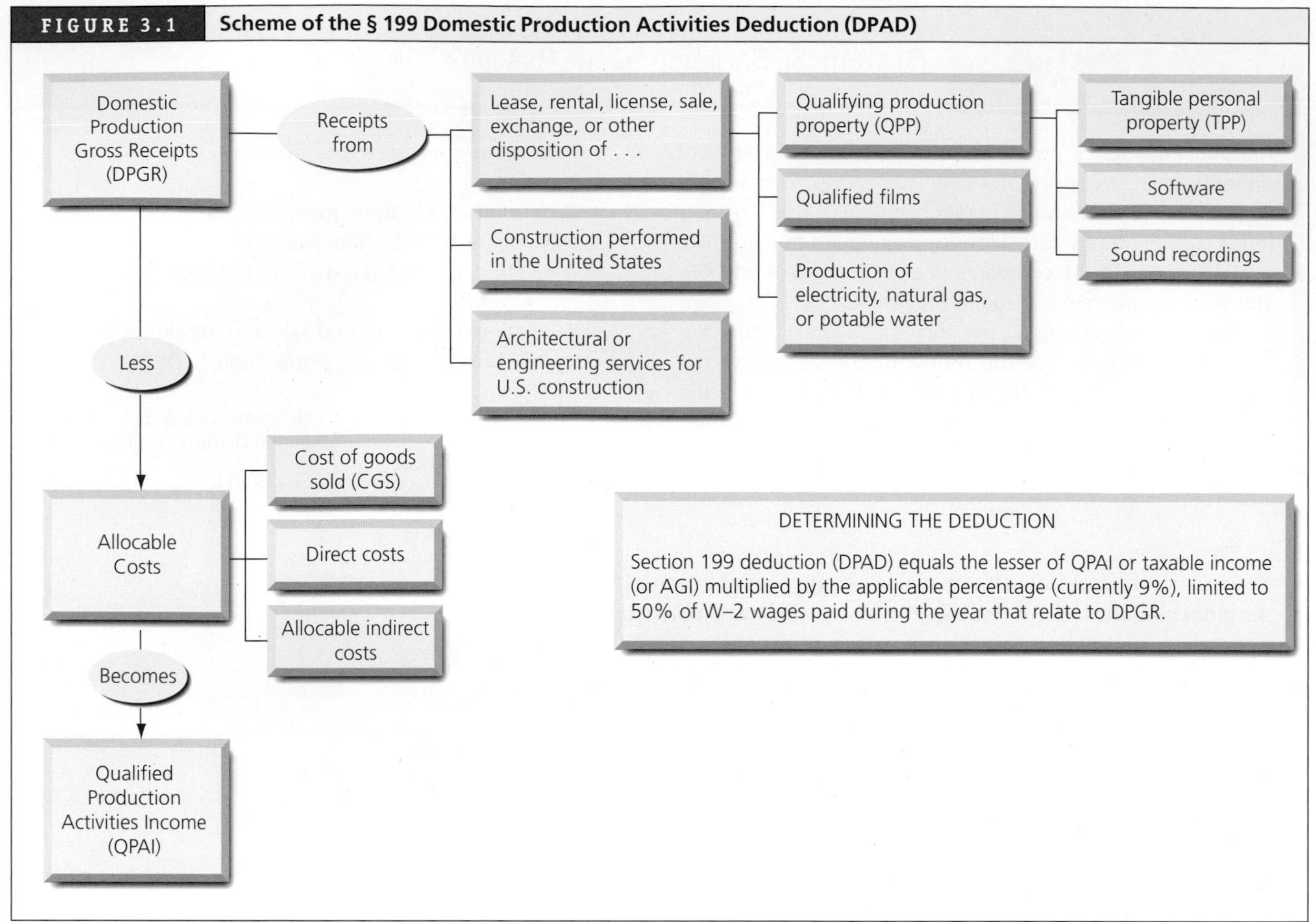

For some taxpayers, the benefits to be derived from § 199 are so minimal that the costs of compliance are not worth the tax saving that will result. For such cases, a reverse *de minimis* safe harbor exists. Under this provision, a taxpayer can treat all of its receipts as non-DPGR if less than 5 percent of the total are DPGR.[7]

EXAMPLE 7

Garnet Corporation refines and sells gasoline in the United States. Of the gasoline it sells, 4% is refined in Texas, and 96% is purchased from a nonrelated source in Kuwait. Garnet can treat all of its receipts as non-DPGR and thereby avoid the application of § 199. ■

Gross receipts for the tax year are those that are properly recognized under the taxpayer's method of accounting utilized for Federal tax purposes. Gross receipts include total sales (net of returns and allowances), amounts received from services, and income from investments such as dividends, rents, interest, royalties, and annuities. Items that *do not qualify* as gross receipts include repayment of loans, nonrecognition transactions, and sales taxes collected and remitted.

Gross receipts derived from the performance of services do not qualify as DPGR. Thus, the lease, rental, license, sale, exchange, or other disposition of property that contains an "embedded service" requires an allocation of the gross receipts

[7]Reg. §§ 1.199(d)(3)(ii) and (d)(4).

and costs attributable to the embedded services. Net receipts allocated to the embedded service are not DPGR. A service is treated as embedded when the price of the service is included in the amount charged by the taxpayer for the property.

Examples of embedded services include product warranties, maintenance agreements, training in product use, and customer call-in help assistance. DPGR is created, though, from payments for embedded services related to most warranty contracts, where the warranty price is not stated separately and the customer is not offered the option of purchasing the warranty separately from the underlying product. Similar rules create DPGR for installation, delivery, and software update services.

DPGR also is created when the service component meets a 5 percent *de minimis* test (i.e., it is worth less than 5 percent of the selling price of the product). The embedded service must not be priced or offered separately from the underlying product, if this rule is to apply.[8]

EXAMPLE 8

Amber Company manufactures and sells high-definition (HD) televisions. The sales price of every set includes a "free annual check-up" of the HD settings so that the television's picture stays at an optimal level. If the allocated cost of the check-up services constitutes 4% of the total price of the television, the services constitute DPGR, under the *de minimis* rule. No DPGR is created for the check-up services, though, if the allocated cost of the check-up is 5% or more of the sales price. ■

Qualified Production Property

One of the components of DPGR is the lease, rental, license, sale, exchange, or other disposition of qualified production property. Qualified production property (QPP) includes tangible personal property (TPP), computer software, and sound recordings (see Figure 3.1). Local law is not controlling for purposes of determining whether property is considered tangible personal property. Tangible personal property does not include land, buildings, structural components of buildings, or intangible property such as patents, copyrights, and subscription lists. Tangible personal property does include such items as automobiles, books, food, clothing, display racks and shelves, and grocery counters.

Machinery and equipment that are not inherently permanent structures are also tangible personal property. An inherently permanent structural component of a building is real property. Real property also includes swimming pools, paved parking lots, water systems, railroad spurs, communication facilities, sewers, sidewalks, walls, doors, plumbing, pipes and ducts, elevators and escalators, central air-conditioning and heating systems, oil and gas wells, cable, wiring, and inherently permanent oil and gas platforms.[9]

In order to qualify as DPGR, QPP must be manufactured, produced, grown, or extracted (MPGE) *in whole or in significant part* within the United States. Included in this MPGE definition is the making of QPP out of salvage, scrap, or junk materials, or by the use of new or raw materials. "Making" can involve processing, manipulating, refining, or changing the form of an article or combining or assembling two or more articles. Cultivating soil, raising livestock, fishing, and mining minerals fall under MPGE.

The "in whole or in significant part" requirement is satisfied if the employer's MPGE activity is substantial in nature. The substantial in nature requirement is relevant in deciding whether the MPGE activity (already determined to have occurred) was performed in whole or in significant part by the taxpayer in the United States. The requirement is applied by taking into account all of the facts and circumstances. This substantial in nature test is a facts and circumstances test, and a taxpayer cannot use the analogous authorities under the Subpart F Regulations

[8]Reg. § 1.199–3(i)(4)(i).

[9]Reg. § 1.48–1(c); Notice 2005–14, § 3.04(11)(c).

(dealing with controlled foreign corporations—see Chapter 9) in applying this standard. There is a safe harbor if an employer incurs conversion costs (direct labor and related factory burden) related to MPGE of the property within the United States and the costs account for 20 percent or more of the property's cost of goods sold.[10]

EXAMPLE 9

Ecru, Inc., pays $75 to purchase a small motor and other parts and materials from related suppliers in Mexico. Ecru incurs $25 in labor costs at its factory in the United States to fabricate a plastic tank body from the materials and to assemble a toy tank. The company also incurs packaging, selling, and other costs of $2 and sells the toy tank for $112.

The toy tank will be treated as manufactured by the employer "in significant part" because Ecru's labor costs are substantial—they are more than 20% of the taxpayer's total cost for the toy tank [$25/($25 + $75) = 25%]. As a result, Ecru's DPGR is $112, and the full $10 in profit ($112 – $75 – $25 – $2) is QPAI. ■

EXAMPLE 10

Assume the same facts as in Example 9, except that Ecru incurred only $15 (instead of $25) in labor costs. Now, the "significant part" requirement is not met because Ecru's MPGE activity is not substantial under the safe-harbor provision: 16.7% [$15/($15 + $75)] is less than 20%. Therefore, none of the profit is DPGR, and there is no producers' deduction (DPAD). ■

Only one producer may claim the DPAD. The taxpayer that has the benefits and burdens of ownership under the Federal income tax system during the period the qualifying activity occurs may claim the deduction.

EXAMPLE 11

Crimson, Inc., enters into an agreement to have an unrelated supplier, Gray, Inc., manufacture items for Crimson. Only one of the taxpayers is treated as having MPGE the items for purposes of the DPAD. Crimson may obtain the deduction only if it bears the benefits and burdens of ownership.[11] ■

Barring a special agreement establishing ownership, the result in Example 11 will usually favor Gray, Inc. Most often the party providing the manufacturing facility will have title to the goods being manufactured. In many situations, moreover, title may change as a product moves through the manufacturing process.

EXAMPLE 12

Crimson manufactures and sells lawn mowers. The lawn mowers are powered by motors that Crimson purchases from Gray, an unrelated domestic producer. Assuming no arrangement to the contrary, Gray has DPGR from the sale of the motors, while Crimson has DPGR from the sale of the lawn mowers. Gray has title to the motors while they are being manufactured, and Crimson owns the rest of the mower it produces. Crimson will not have a double DPAD because it will have to deduct what it paid for the motors (part of cost of goods sold) in arriving at QPAI (see Figure 3.1). ■

Qualified Films

A qualified film includes any motion picture film or videotape, as well as live or delayed television programming, if not less than 50 percent of the total compensation relating to the production of the property is compensation for services performed in the United States by actors, production personnel, directors, and

[10]Reg. § 1.199–3(g)(3).

[11]There is much dissatisfaction with this "one owner" rule as to contract manufacturing, which often takes place on a consignment basis.

producers. A taxpayer that MPGE a qualified film may treat the tangible medium to which the qualified film is affixed (e.g., DVD and Blu-ray Disc) as part of the qualified film, even if the taxpayer purchased the tangible medium. A taxpayer may subcontract the affixing of the film onto a tangible medium. Ticket sales for viewing qualified films do not constitute DPGR. Merely writing a screenplay or other similar material does not result in qualified gross receipts.

EXAMPLE 13

Maize, Inc., produces a qualified film and contracts with Magenta, Inc., an unrelated party, to duplicate the film onto DVDs. Magenta manufactures blank DVDs and duplicates Maize's film onto the DVDs within the United States. It sells the DVDs with the qualified film to Maize, which then sells them to customers. Magenta's gross receipts from manufacturing the DVDs and duplicating the film onto the DVDs are DPGR (assuming all the other requirements are met). Maize's gross receipts from the sale of the DVDs to customers are DPGR (assuming all the other requirements are met). ■

Construction Projects

The DPAD is available to a taxpayer who is involved in the trade or business of construction and performs a qualifying construction activity with respect to U.S. real property. The deduction is not available for taxpayers who self-construct real property. The term "construction" includes most activities that are typically performed in connection with the erection or substantial renovation of real property.

Real property includes residential and commercial buildings (including structural components), inherently permanent structures (but not machinery), and inherently permanent land improvements and infrastructure. Appliances, furniture, and fixtures sold as part of a construction site are not considered to be real property. If, however, more than 95 percent of the total gross receipts derived by a taxpayer from a construction project are attributable to real property, the total gross receipts are DPGR from construction.

Tangential services such as the hauling of trash and debris and the delivery of materials are excluded from DPGR, unless the taxpayer is performing such services in connection with a construction project. Also, proceeds attributable to the disposition of land are not considered gross receipts derived from construction. Further, DPGR does not include gross receipts from the lease or rental of constructed real property.

With respect to land, there is a safe harbor for allocating gross receipts between the proceeds from the sale, exchange, or other disposition of real property constructed by the taxpayer, which qualify for DPGR, and the gross receipts attributable to the sale, exchange, or other disposition of land (which do not qualify). The taxpayer is able to reduce its DPGR costs by certain land costs plus a percentage based on the number of months that lapse between the date the taxpayer acquires the land and the date the taxpayer sells each item of rental property on the land (e.g., 5 percent for land held not more than 60 months).[12]

Gross receipts attributable to the sale or other disposition of land (including zoning, planning, and entitlement costs) are considered gross receipts attributable to the land, and not to a qualifying construction activity, and therefore are non-DPGR. Costs incurred for cleaning, grading, and demolition in connection with a construction project are now construction activities under the Final Regulations. Any income stream (e.g., rent) from renting apartments in a building prior to its sale is not DPGR.

[12]Reg. § 1.199–3(m)(6)(iv)(A). The percentage is 10% for land held more than 60 months but not more than 120 months; it is 15% for land held more than 120 months but not more than 180 months. Land held more than 180 months is not eligible.

EXAMPLE 14

Gold Construction Company purchases five residential lots in a new subdivision for $500,000. On these lots it builds five residences that it sells for $4 million. Because the proceeds attributable to the sale of the land cannot qualify, Gold has DPGR of only $3.5 million ($4,000,000 – $500,000). ■

EXAMPLE 15

A business owner (not engaged in construction activities) retains a general contractor to oversee a substantial renovation of a building, and the general contractor hires a subcontractor to install an electrical system as part of the substantial renovation. Here, both the amount the general contractor receives from the building owner and the amount the subcontractor receives from the general contractor qualify as DPGR from construction. However, the amount that the building owner receives from the sale upon the disposition of the building does not qualify as DPGR because the owner was not involved in qualified construction activity with respect to the building.[13] ■

Construction activities need not satisfy the legal title restrictions that are applicable under the QPP rules to the manufacture of tangible personal property (see the discussion in connection with Examples 11 and 12 above). In Example 15, for instance, note that neither the general contractor nor the subcontractor owned the building they were working on, yet their income qualified for DPGR treatment.

Substantial renovation refers to the renovation of a major component or substantial structural part of real property that materially increases the value of the property, substantially prolongs the useful life of the property, or adapts the property to a new or different use. Thus, cosmetic changes such as painting and replacing shingles would not qualify.

Production of Electricity, Natural Gas, and Potable Water

DPGR includes gross receipts derived from any lease, rental, license, sale, exchange, or other disposition of electricity, natural gas, or potable water produced in the United States (see Figure 3.1). It does not include those receipts derived from the transmission or distribution of these items to final customers. An integrated taxpayer that carries out all of these functions must allocate the gross receipts among production, transmission, and delivery.

EXAMPLE 16

PowerCo generates electricity that it sells to TransmissionCo. TransmissionCo sells the electricity to ElectricCo, which, in turn, retails it to user-customers. Only PowerCo's gross receipts qualify as DPGR. ■

EXAMPLE 17

Assume the same facts as in Example 16, except that PowerCo is an integrated producer that generates electricity and delivers it to end users. The gross receipts attributable to the transmission of electricity from the generating facility to a point of local distribution and any gross receipts attributable to the distribution of electricity to final customers are not qualified DPGR. ■

The term "natural gas" includes only natural gas extracted from a natural deposit, not methane gas extracted from a landfill. Natural gas production includes all activities involved in extracting natural gas from the ground and processing the gas into pipeline-quality gas. Gross receipts from the transmission of pipeline-quality gas from a natural gas field or plant to a local distribution company are not DPGR. Further, gross receipts from the transmission from the local gas distribution company to local customers do not qualify.

Production activities with respect to potable water include the acquisition, collection, and storage of untreated water; transportation of such water to a water treatment facility; and treatment of untreated water at such a facility. Potable water refers to

[13] Reg. § 1.199–3(m).

TAX *in the NEWS*

ARE YOUR PROFITS TOO HIGH?

Some members of Congress were disturbed by the record profits reported by some of the major oil companies in recent years. Two of the more favorable tax-saving provisions for oil and gas companies are the DPAD and FIFO. Although proposals were advanced that would have imposed a special excess profits tax on such earnings, Congress settled on a less direct approach, at least through 2010. Under the Emergency Economic Stabilization Act of 2008, oil and gas companies were denied the increase to 9 percent of QPAI for purposes of the DPAD. In other words, the allowance is frozen at 6 percent for all taxpayers with QPAI that is oil and gas related.

unbottled drinking water. DPGR does not include gross receipts derived from the storage of potable water (after completion of treatment) or the delivery of potable water to customers. The IRS believes this provision applies to water utilities and not to taxpayers engaged in the trade or business of producing bottled water. Thus, bottled water companies are to be treated as the producers of tangible personal property.

ADJUSTMENTS IN ARRIVING AT QPAI

LO.4

Describe the necessary adjustments to DPGR to arrive at qualified production activities income (QPAI).

Once DPGR is determined, certain adjustments must be made to arrive at qualified production activities income (QPAI). Recall that it is usually 9 percent of QPAI that yields the DPAD. The adjustments that are necessary are listed in Figure 3.1 and include the following:

1. Cost of goods sold (CGS)
2. Direct costs
3. Allocable indirect costs

CGS is equal to beginning inventory plus purchases and production costs and less ending inventory. If a taxpayer can identify from its books and records the CGS allocable to DPGR, that amount is allocable to DPGR. If identification is not possible, a taxpayer must use a reasonable method, but it may not use a different allocation method than it used to allocate gross receipts between DPGR and non-DPGR. Reasonable methods may include those based on gross receipts, number of units sold, number of units produced, or total production costs.

The second category of expenses (direct costs) includes selling and marketing expenses. The third category (allocable indirect costs) is further removed and includes, for example, general and administrative expenses attributable to the selling and marketing expenses.

The second and third categories of expenses (i.e., direct allocable and indirect allocable) may be allocated by one of three methods:

- The *§ 861 Regulation method* may be used by *all* taxpayers but *must* be used by those taxpayers with average annual gross receipts of more than $100 million. Essentially, certain deductions incurred by a U.S. taxpayer must be allocated to various classes of gross income and apportioned between foreign sources and domestic sources. Although time-consuming, the § 861 Regulation method is the most accurate. Unfortunately, for those concerns without international operations, the use of this method will necessitate a resort to unfamiliar rules. The mechanics of the § 861 Regulations are explained and illustrated in Chapter 9 under the heading Allocation and Apportionment of Deductions.
- For employers with average annual gross receipts of $100 million or less or total assets at the end of the taxable year of $10 million or less, a *simplified deduction method* based on relative gross receipts is available. The deductions are apportioned to DPGR in the same proportion as DPGR bears to total gross receipts.

TAX in the NEWS

States Are Decoupling from the DPAD

Most states impose an income tax on corporations. Unless otherwise provided, these state income taxes generally use as a tax base the taxable income as determined for Federal income tax purposes. Thus, a DPAD claimed on Form 1120 reduces not only Federal income taxes, but also state income taxes.

With many states facing budget shortfalls and with the DPAD percentage now at 9 percent, more than 20 states have eliminated the deduction. In decoupling from the DPAD, these states require that any DPAD be added back to taxable income for state income tax purposes. Thus, the DPAD is allowed for Federal, but not state, income tax purposes.

Unless economic conditions substantially improve, the number of states decoupling from the DPAD probably will increase. One report indicates that 27 states can reduce revenue losses by decoupling from § 199.

Source: Jason Levitis, Nicholas Johnson, and Katherine Lira, "States Can Opt Out of the Costly and Ineffective Domestic Production Deduction Corporate Tax Break," Center on Budget and Policy Priorities, July 29, 2009.

- For taxpayers that have average gross receipts of $5 million or less or are eligible to use the cash method, a *small business simplified overall method* is available. This method is the same as the previous method except that it can also be used to arrive at CGS.

EXAMPLE 18

Brown, Inc., a qualifying small taxpayer,[14] has total gross receipts of $4.3 million, DPGR of $3.1 million, CGS of $1.3 million, and advertising, selling, and administrative expenses of $500,000. Under the small business simplified overall method, CGS and deductions are apportioned to DPGR in the same proportion as DPGR bears to total gross receipts.

Thus, Brown's QPAI is computed as follows:

DPGR	$3,100,000
Less allowable CGS:	
[($3.1 million/$4.3 million) × $1.3 million]	(937,209)
Less allocable expenses:	
[($3.1 million/$4.3 million) × $500,000]	(360,465)
QPAI	$1,802,326

Presuming the taxable income and W–2 wage limitations do not intervene, Brown's DPAD for 2011 is $162,209 (9% × $1,802,326). ■

To determine if one of the simplified methods may be used, the average annual gross receipts must be determined at the expanded affiliated group level (discussed later). Also, a member of the expanded affiliated group that qualifies to use one of the simplified methods may do so only if all members of the group elect to use that method.

LO.5

List the collateral problems associated with the domestic production activities deduction (DPAD).

COLLATERAL PROBLEMS

Disallowed Production Activities—Preparation of Food and Beverages

DPGR does not include gross receipts from the sale of food and beverages prepared by a taxpayer at a retail establishment.[15] A retail establishment includes real property leased, occupied, or otherwise used by a taxpayer in its trade or business of selling food or beverages to the public and at which the taxpayer makes retail sales. A facility

[14] As defined in Reg. § 1.199–4(f)(2).

[15] § 199(c)(4)(B)(i).

is not a retail establishment if the employer uses the facility only to prepare food or beverages for wholesale sale. There is a 5 percent *de minimis* safe harbor.

EXAMPLE 19

Silver Company buys coffee beans that it roasts and packages at a special facility. The company sells the roasted coffee through a variety of unrelated third-party vendors and also sells roasted coffee at its own retail establishments. These receipts are qualified DPGR.

At Silver's retail establishments, it prepares and sells brewed coffee and food. These receipts are not DPGR. Nevertheless, part of the receipts from the sale of the brewed coffee may be allocated to DPGR to the extent of the value of the roasted beans used to brew the coffee. The amount to be allocated is determined by the price Silver receives from the sale of the roasted beans. ■

EXAMPLE 20
THE BIG PICTURE

Return to the facts of *The Big Picture* on p. 3–2. Suppose that Mocha has $42 million from the wholesale sale of its ice cream and only $2 million from the operation of the snack shops next to its facilities where it sells ice cream to the general public. The full $44 million is DPGR because the $2 million falls under the *de minimis* safe-harbor exception [$2 million is less than 5% of $44 million ($42 million + $2 million)]. ■

The prohibition against the retail sale of prepared food cannot be avoided by restricting sales to take-out orders. The prohibition does not, however, apply to the sale of prepared meals to others for resale.

EXAMPLE 21

Beige Brothers operates a food service business that prepares meals. Some of the meals are served to diners at a café it owns adjacent to the plant, some are sold to customers on a take-out basis, and some are frozen and sold to supermarkets for resale. Only the proceeds from the latter operation will qualify as DPGR. ■

The prepared food restrictions may have been motivated by the trauma experienced by Canada before it rescinded its producers' deduction—see the discussion in the "Global Tax Issues" earlier in this chapter. As a result, the broiling and assembly of hamburgers and salads by Burger King will not qualify under the U.S. version of the producers' deduction.

Expanded Affiliated Group Rules

Special rules apply to corporations that are members of an **expanded affiliated group (EAG)**. An EAG is an affiliated group as defined for purposes of the consolidated return rules, except that the stock ownership requirement is reduced to more than 50 percent (from 80 percent) and insurance companies and possession credit corporations are not excluded from the group.[16]

In the case of corporations that are members of an EAG, the DPAD is determined by treating the group as a single taxpayer. In effect, therefore, each member of the group is treated as being engaged in the same activities as every other member. The deduction is then allocated among the members in proportion to each member's respective amount of QPAI.

EXAMPLE 22

Red Corporation and Blue Corporation are members of an EAG but do not file a consolidated return. Red manufactures a machine at a cost of $3,000, which it then sells to Blue for $5,000. Blue incurs additional costs of $1,000 on marketing, then sells the machine to an unrelated customer for $7,000. QPAI is $3,000 ($7,000 – $3,000 – $1,000) even though Blue did not perform any manufacturing. Note that this is the same result

[16] § 199(d)(4).

that would be reached if Blue had not been involved and Red had conducted its own marketing function. ■

EXAMPLE 23

Assume the same facts as in Example 22, except that the parties are not related. Under these circumstances, Red Corporation has QPAI of $2,000 ($5,000 – $3,000), and Blue Corporation has none. Blue's activities when considered alone are not QPAI since they involve marketing and not production. ■

If all of the members of an EAG are members of the same consolidated group, the consolidated group's DPAD is calculated based on the group's consolidated taxable income or loss, and not the separate taxable income or loss of its members. The DPAD of a consolidated group must be allocated to the group's members in proportion to each member's QPAI (if any), regardless of whether the member has separate taxable income or loss for the tax year and whether the member has W–2 wages for the tax year.

Pass-Through Entities Provisions

In the case of pass-through entities (i.e., partnerships, S corporations, trusts, and estates), special rules apply for handling DPADs. Because the deduction is determined at the owner level, each partner or shareholder must make the computation separately.[17] Consequently, the entity allocates to each owner his or her share of QPAI. The QPAI allocated is then combined with the domestic production activities the owner may have from other sources (e.g., a partner also conducts a manufacturing activity of his or her own).

In working with the wage limitation in a pass-through setting, an allocable portion of W–2 wages of the pass-through entity is passed through to the owner, but only those wages properly allocable to DPGR. The partner or shareholder, however, may add any wages separately paid to the amount allocated from the entity. In the case of a partnership, guaranteed payments are not regarded as W–2 wages. Also, if QPAI (computed taking into account only partnership items allocated to the partner for the tax year) is not greater than zero, a partner cannot use any partnership W–2 wages in calculating the DPAD.[18] The wage limitation applies to non-grantor trusts and estates in the same way it applies to partnerships and S corporations.

Generally, the DPAD is determined at the owner level in a pass-through entity situation. In some instances, however, the pass-through of the data needed to make this determination can be cumbersome and burdensome. To simplify matters, therefore, the IRS allows eligible partnerships and S corporations to calculate QPAI and W–2 wages for some or all of the owners at the entity level.[19]

The DPAD has no effect on an S shareholder's stock basis because the deduction is not listed in § 1367(a). Further, an S corporation or partnership that is a qualified small taxpayer may use the small business simplified overall method to apportion cost of goods sold and deductions between DPGR and non-DPGR at the entity level. Also, the IRS may permit a partnership or an S corporation to calculate a shareholder's share of QPAI at the entity level, which is then combined with the shareholder's QPAI.[20] The owner is not allowed to use another cost allocation method to reallocate the costs of the pass-through entity regardless of the method used by the owner to allocate or apportion costs.

The pass-through information is reported by the entity on its Schedule K–1 of Form 1065 (partnership) or Form 1120S (S corporation). Owners include their share of QPAI and W–2 wages on Lines 7 and 17 of Form 8903 (Domestic Production Activities Deduction).

[17] § 199(d)(1)(A).

[18] Reg. § 1.199–9(b)(3).

[19] Rev.Proc. 2007–34, 2007–1 C.B. 1345.

[20] Reg. §§ 1.199–9(b)(1)(ii) and 1.199–9(c)(1)(ii).

When an entity uses a different tax year than its owners, the pass-through of DPAD attributes may be delayed. As § 199 took effect for tax years beginning after December 31, 2004, coverage for a fiscal year entity could begin only in 2005.

EXAMPLE 24

John, a calendar year taxpayer, is a partner in Crimson Partnership, which uses a July 1–June 30 fiscal year. John will not be able to pick up any of the partnership's 2010–2011 QPAI until his 2011 individual return (the June 30, 2011 pass-through on Crimson's 2010–2011 fiscal year), which he will file in 2012! ■

Coordination with the AMT

The DPAD is allowed for purposes of the alternative minimum tax (AMT), except that after 2009 the deduction is equal to 9 percent of the smaller of (1) QPAI or (2) alternative minimum taxable income (without considering the DPAD) for the tax year. In the case of an individual, modified AGI (ignoring the DPAD) is substituted for AMTI.[21]

3.2 Alternative Minimum Tax

LO.6

Explain the reason for the alternative minimum tax.

The perception that many large corporations were not paying their fair share of Federal income tax was especially widespread in the early 1980s. A study released in 1986 reported that 130 of the 250 largest corporations in the United States paid zero or less in Federal taxes in at least one year between 1981 and 1985 (e.g., Reynolds Metals, General Dynamics, Georgia Pacific, and Texas Commerce Bankshares).

Political pressure subsequently led to the adoption of an alternative minimum tax to ensure that corporations with substantial economic income pay a minimum amount of Federal taxes. Corporations are now less able to use exclusions, deductions, and credits available under the law to pay no taxes. A separate tax system with a quasi-flat tax rate is applied each year to a corporation's economic income. If the tentative alternative minimum tax is greater than the regular corporate income tax under § 11, then the corporation must pay the regular tax plus this excess, the **alternative minimum tax (AMT)**.

In general, a corporation is likely to pay an AMT for one or more of three reasons:

- A high level of investment in assets such as equipment and structures.
- Low taxable income due to a cyclical downturn, strong international competition, a low-margin industry, or other factors.
- Investment at low real interest rates, which increases the company's deductions for depreciation relative to those for interest payments.

The 20 percent AMT applicable to many regular corporations is similar to the AMT applicable to individuals.[22] Many of the adjustments and tax preference items necessary to arrive at **alternative minimum taxable income (AMTI)** are the same. The rates and exemptions are different, but the objective is identical—to force taxpayers that are more profitable than their taxable income reflects to pay additional income taxes.

As the AMT is in addition to the regular corporate tax, it is computed somewhat differently. Separate and independent calculations of the amount and character of all items affecting the computation of the AMT are required. The Code itself mandates the treatment of many items affecting the computation of the AMT. Regulations provide broad rules governing the treatment of other items for AMT purposes. However, the Code and Regulations do not provide guidance for many items.

[21] § 199(d)(6).

[22] The AMT provisions for both corporate and noncorporate taxpayers are contained in §§ 55 through 59. The individual AMT rates are 26%/28%.

FIGURE 3.2 AMT Formula for Corporations

Regular taxable income before NOL deduction	
Plus/minus:	AMT adjustments (except ACE adjustment)
Plus:	Tax preferences
Equals:	AMTI before AMT NOL deduction and ACE adjustment
Plus/minus:	ACE adjustment
Equals:	AMTI before AMT NOL deduction
Minus:	AMT NOL deduction (limited to 90%)
Equals:	Alternative minimum taxable income (AMTI)
Minus:	Exemption
Equals:	Tentative minimum tax base
Times:	20% rate
Equals:	Tentative minimum tax before AMT foreign tax credit
Minus:	AMT foreign tax credit
Equals:	Tentative minimum tax
Minus:	Regular tax liability before credits minus regular foreign tax credit
Equals:	Alternative minimum tax (AMT)

The formula for determining the AMT liability of corporate taxpayers appears in Figure 3.2 and follows the format of Form 4626 (Alternative Minimum Tax—Corporations).

SMALL CORPORATION EXEMPTION

For tax years beginning after December 31, 1997, many smaller corporations are not subject to the AMT. Certain corporations that meet several gross receipts tests are exempted from the AMT as long as they remain "small corporations." A corporation initially qualifies as a "small corporation" if it had *average* gross receipts of $5 million or less in the preceding three-year period. If a corporation is not in existence for the entire three-year period, the $5 million test is applied on the basis of the period during which the corporation is in existence.[23]

EXAMPLE 25
THE BIG PICTURE

Return to the facts of *The Big Picture* on p. 3-2. Suppose that Carmine, Inc., had gross receipts of $3.7 million, $4.8 million, and $4.6 million for tax years 2008, 2009, and 2010, respectively, for an average of $4.37 million. For 2011 AMT purposes, Carmine is considered to be a small corporation. ■

A corporation that passes the $5 million average gross receipts test will continue to be treated as a small corporation as long as its *average* gross receipts for the three-year period preceding the taxable year do not exceed $7.5 million. For both the $7.5 million and the $5 million test, certain aggregating rules apply to related taxpayers. Once a corporation loses its small corporation protection, the corporation is then liable for the AMT for that year and future years. However, many of the AMT and adjusted current earnings adjustments are modified so that they pertain only to transactions and investments that were entered into *after* the corporation lost its small corporation status (e.g., property placed into service in or after the change year).

These calculations are based on gross receipts and not gross income or net income. Once a company fails the small corporation exemption, the meager $40,000 statutory exemption is available. A corporation is treated as a small business corporation in its first tax year regardless of its gross receipts for the year.

[23] § 55(e).

EXAMPLE 26

Vorhies, Inc., a calendar year corporation that was created in January 2007, has gross receipts as follows:

Year	Gross Receipts
2007	$3,250,000
2008	3,700,000
2009	4,950,000
2010	7,800,000
2011	9,200,000

Since Vorhies was a new corporation in 2007, the company was automatically exempt from the corporate AMT for that year under the small corporation exception regardless of gross receipts.

In subsequent tax years, Vorhies calculates average gross receipts as follows to determine whether the small business exemption is available.

2007–2008:	$3,475,000	[($3,250,000 + $3,700,000) ÷ 2]
2007–2009:	$3,966,667	[($3,250,000 + $3,700,000 + $4,950,000) ÷ 3]
2008–2010:	$5,483,333	[($3,700,000 + $4,950,000 + $7,800,000) ÷ 3]
2009–2011:	$7,316,667	[($4,950,000 + $7,800,000 + $9,200,000) ÷ 3]

Vorhies qualified for the exemption in 2009, since the average gross receipts for 2007–2008 did not exceed $5 million. Likewise, Vorhies continues to qualify for the exemption in 2010, 2011, and 2012 since the average gross receipts for each preceding three-year period (2007–2009, 2008–2010, and 2009–2011, respectively) do not exceed the $7.5 million exemption.

Even if Vorhies's gross receipts decrease to $8.6 million for 2012, the corporation will fail the gross receipts test in 2013 because its average gross receipts will be $8,533,333 [($7,800,000 + $9,200,000 + $8,600,000) ÷ 3]. ■

AMT ADJUSTMENTS

LO.7

Calculate the alternative minimum tax applicable to corporations.

As Figure 3.2 indicates, the starting point for computing AMTI is the taxable income of the corporation before any NOL deduction. Certain adjustments must be made to this amount. Unlike tax preference items, which are always additions, **AMT adjustments** may either increase or decrease taxable income. For example, the deduction for domestic manufacturing activities (DPAD) is available for purposes of computing minimum taxable income (as well as adjusted current earnings). However, the deduction is limited to the smaller of the qualified production income as determined for the § 11 tax (the regular corporate income tax) or the AMTI without regard to the manufacturing deduction.

The positive adjustments arise as a result of timing differences and are added back to the taxable income in computing AMTI. Since most adjustments only defer taxes, a corporation may recoup AMT paid on these adjustments when the deferral of regular tax created by the adjustment is reversed and the regular tax is due. Once AMT adjustments reverse themselves, they are deducted from taxable income to arrive at AMTI. This mechanism is called the *netting process.*

Although NOLs are separately stated in Figure 3.2, they are actually negative adjustments. They are separately stated in Figure 3.2 and on Form 4626 because they may not exceed 90 percent of AMTI. Thus, such adjustments cannot be determined until all other adjustments and tax preference items are considered.

Other adjustments to regular taxable income include the following:

- A portion of depreciation on property placed in service after 1986. Depreciation allowances for purposes of the AMT are generally much less favorable than for the regular corporate income tax. For property placed into service after 1998, this adjustment applies only to MACRS 3-, 5-, 7-, and 10-year property that is depreciated using the 200 percent declining-balance method. The adjustment is the difference between the depreciation claimed for regular tax purposes and the depreciation using the 150 percent declining-balance method over the property's shorter regular MACRS recovery period.

EXAMPLE 27

Purple Corporation placed an asset costing $10,000 in service on March 15, 2010. Based upon a three-year recovery class life, this personalty has the following effect upon AMTI:

Year	Tax Deduction 200%	AMT Deduction 150%	Increase or (Decrease) AMT Adjustment
2010	$3,333	$2,500	$ 833
2011	4,445	3,750	695
2012	1,481	2,500	(1,019)
2013	741	1,250	(509)

■

- Since different depreciation methods may be used for AMT and regular tax purposes, the adjusted bases for these depreciable assets are affected. When the bases are different and the asset is disposed of, a basis adjustment is necessary to reflect the difference in the AMT gain or loss *and* the regular tax gain or loss.

EXAMPLE 28

Assume the same facts as in Example 27, except that the asset is sold at the end of the second year for $4,000. For regular tax purposes, the basis is $2,222 ($10,000 – $3,333 – $4,445), and the basis for AMT purposes is $3,750 ($10,000 – $2,500 – $3,750). Thus, the regular tax gain is $1,778($4,000 – $2,222), and the AMT gain is $250 ($4,000 – $3,750). Consequently, a $1,528 negative basis adjustment is required when computing AMT ($250 – $1,778). ■

- Passive activity losses of certain closely held corporations and personal service corporations.
- The excess of mining exploration and development costs deducted over what would have resulted if the costs had been capitalized and written off over 10 years.
- The difference between completed contract and percentage of completion reporting on long-term construction contracts, for some contracts reported under the completed contract method.
- Amortization claimed on certified pollution control facilities.
- The difference between installment and total gain, for dealers using the installment method to account for sales. The installment method is not allowed for AMTI purposes.
- A portion of the difference between adjusted current earnings (ACE) and unadjusted AMTI (post-1989)—see below.

TAX PREFERENCES

AMTI includes designated **tax preference items**. In many cases, this inclusion has the effect of subjecting nontaxable income to the AMT. Some of the most common tax preferences include the following:

- Accelerated depreciation on real property in excess of straight-line (placed in service before 1987).
- Tax-exempt interest on state and local bonds where the generated funds are not used for an essential function of the government (but not for bonds issued in 2009 and 2010).
- Percentage depletion claimed in excess of the adjusted basis of property.

CONCEPT SUMMARY 3.1

AMT Adjustments and Preferences for Corporations

Adjustments	**Positive**	**Negative**	**Either**[1]
Depreciation of post-1986 real property			X
Depreciation of post-1986 personal property			X
Pollution control facilities			X
Mining exploration and development costs			X
Circulation expenditures[2]			X
Completed contract method			X
Adjusted gain or loss			X
Passive activity losses[2,3]			X
Alternative minimum tax NOL deduction		X	
Loss limitation			X
Nondealer installment sales			X
Adjusted current earnings adjustment			X
Domestic production activities deduction			X
Preferences			
Percentage depletion in excess of adjusted basis	X		
Accelerated depreciation on pre-1987 real property	X		
Intangible drilling costs[4]	X		
Private activity bond interest income[5]	X		

[1]Timing difference.
[2]Personal service corporations.
[3]Closely held corporations.
[4]Integrated oil companies only.
[5]Not for bonds issued in 2009 and 2010.

- For integrated oil companies (ExxonMobil, Chevron), the excess of intangible drilling costs over 10-year amortization if in excess of 65 percent of net oil and gas income. This item is not a tax preference for independent oil and gas producers and royalty owners.

COMPUTING ALTERNATIVE MINIMUM TAXABLE INCOME

The various modifications needed to arrive at the AMTI of a corporation are set forth in Concept Summary 3.1. The Concept Summary shows the effect of the different adjustments and preferences as applied to the taxable income of a C corporation. Some of the items included in the Concept Summary are not discussed in the text. Refer to the instructions to Form 4626 for further coverage of these items.

The following example illustrates the effect of tax preferences and adjustments in arriving at AMTI.

EXAMPLE 29

For 2011, Tan Corporation (a calendar year, integrated oil company) had the following transactions:

Taxable income	$6,000,000
Mining exploration costs	500,000
Percentage depletion claimed (the property has a zero adjusted basis)	700,000
Donation of land held since 1980 as an investment (basis of $400,000 and fair market value of $500,000) to a qualified charity	500,000
Excess intangible drilling costs	300,000

FIGURE 3.3 Determining the ACE Adjustment

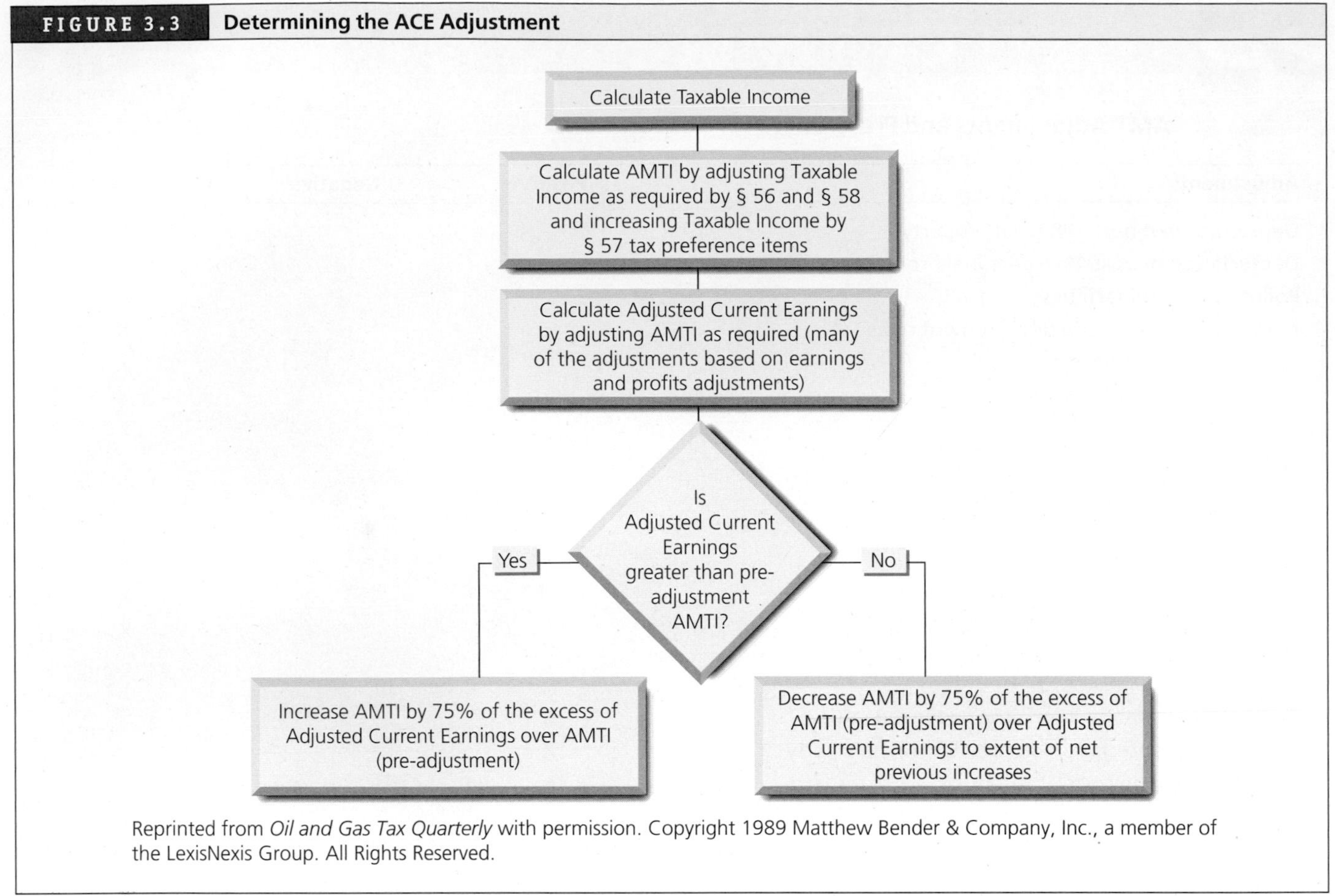

Tan Corporation's AMTI for 2011 is determined as follows:

Taxable income		$6,000,000
Adjustments:		
Excess mining exploration costs [$500,000 (amount expensed) – $50,000 (amount allowed over a 10-year amortization period)]		450,000
Tax preferences:		
Excess depletion	$700,000	
Excess intangible drilling costs	300,000	1,000,000
AMTI		$7,450,000

■

LO.8

Discuss the function of adjusted current earnings (ACE).

ADJUSTED CURRENT EARNINGS (ACE)

The purpose of **adjusted current earnings (ACE)** is to ensure that the mismatching of earnings and profits (E & P) and taxable income will not produce inequitable results. The calculation of ACE is similar to the calculation of E & P (which is similar to the economic concept of income). S corporations, real estate investment trusts, regulated investment companies, and real estate mortgage investment conduits are not subject to the ACE provisions.

The ACE adjustment is tax-based and can be a negative amount. AMTI is increased by 75 percent of the excess of ACE over unadjusted AMTI. Or AMTI is reduced by 75 percent of the excess of unadjusted AMTI over ACE. This negative adjustment is limited to the aggregate of the positive adjustments under ACE for prior years reduced by the previously claimed negative adjustments (see Figure 3.3). Thus, the ordering of

CONCEPT SUMMARY 3.2

Impact of Various Transactions on ACE

	Effect on Unadjusted AMTI in Arriving at ACE
Tax-exempt income (net of expenses)	Add
Federal income tax	No effect
Dividends received deduction (80% and 100% rules)	No effect
Dividends received deduction (70% rule)	Add
Exemption amount of $40,000	No effect
Excess charitable contribution	No effect
Excess capital losses	No effect
Disallowed travel and entertainment expenses	No effect
Penalties and fines	No effect
Intangible drilling costs deducted currently	Add
Deferred gain on installment sales	Add
Realized (not recognized) gain (e.g., involuntary conversion, like-kind exchanges)	No effect
Loss on sale between related parties	No effect
Key employee insurance proceeds	Add
Premiums paid on key employee insurance	Subtract
Net buildup on life insurance policy	Add

the timing differences is crucial because any unused negative adjustment is lost forever. Unadjusted AMTI is AMTI without the ACE adjustment or the AMT NOL.

EXAMPLE 30

A calendar year corporation has the following data:

	2010	2011	2012
Unadjusted AMTI	$6,000,000	$6,000,000	$6,100,000
Adjusted current earnings	7,000,000	6,000,000	5,000,000

In 2010, since ACE exceeds unadjusted AMTI by $1 million, $750,000 (75% × $1,000,000) is included as a positive adjustment to AMTI. No adjustment is necessary for 2011. Unadjusted AMTI exceeds ACE by $1.1 million in 2012, so there is a potential negative adjustment to AMTI of $825,000. Since the total increases to AMTI for prior years equal $750,000 (and there are no negative adjustments), only $750,000 of the potential negative adjustment will reduce AMTI for 2012. Further, $75,000 of the negative amount is lost forever ($825,000 – $750,000). Prior book income adjustments are ignored for limitation purposes. ■

ACE should not be confused with current E & P. Many items are treated in the same manner, but certain items that are deductible in computing E & P (but are not deductible in calculating taxable income) generally are not deductible in computing ACE (e.g., Federal income taxes). Concept Summary 3.2 shows the impact of various transactions on ACE, while the rules relating to E & P and its determination are discussed at length in Chapter 5.

The starting point for computing ACE is unadjusted AMTI (as specially computed for purposes of computing ACE). This specially computed AMTI is the corporation's regular taxable income after all the normal AMT adjustments other than the ACE adjustment and the AMT NOL adjustment and after tax preferences.[24] Essentially, a corporation must keep at least three sets of books to calculate its Federal tax burden: one for the regular tax, one for the AMTI, and a third for the ACE adjustments. The resulting figure is adjusted for the following items in order to determine ACE:

- *Exclusion items.* These are income items (net of related expenses) that will never be included in regular taxable income or AMTI (except on liquidation or disposal of a business). In essence, items that are permanently excluded from unadjusted AMTI are therefore included in ACE (e.g., life insurance proceeds, interest on tax-exempt bonds, and tax benefit rule exclusions).
- *Disallowed items.* Since the starting point for ACE is AMTI before the NOL, no adjustment is necessary for the NOL. A deduction *is not allowed* for the dividends received deduction of 70 percent (less than 20 percent ownership). But a deduction *is allowed* for the dividends received deduction of 80 percent (20 percent but less than 80 percent ownership) and 100 percent (80 percent or more ownership).
- *Other adjustments.* Adjustments for the following items are necessary: intangible drilling costs, circulation expenditures, organization expense amortization, and installment sales deferrals.
- *Both AMTI and ACE.* Certain deductible items do not reduce ACE: excess charitable contributions, excess capital losses, disallowed travel and entertainment expenses, penalties, fines, bribes, and golden parachute payments.
- *Lessee improvements.* The value of improvements made by a lessee to a lessor's property that is excluded from the lessor's income is excluded from both unadjusted AMTI and ACE.
- *LIFO recapture adjustments.* An increase or decrease in the LIFO recapture amount will result in a corresponding increase or decrease in ACE.

EXAMPLE 31

Crimson Corporation makes the ACE adjustment calculation as follows:

AMTI		$5,780,000
Plus:		
Municipal bond interest	$210,000	
Installment gain	140,000	
70% dividends received deduction	300,000	
Income element in cash surrender life insurance	60,000	
Organization expense amortization	70,000	780,000
		$6,560,000
Less:		
Decreases in LIFO recapture amount	$230,000	
Life insurance premiums paid on key employee policy	10,000	240,000
Adjusted current earnings		$6,320,000
AMTI		–5,780,000
Difference		$ 540,000
Times		.75
ACE adjustment (positive)		$ 405,000

■

EXEMPTION

The AMT is 20 percent of AMTI that exceeds the exemption amount. The exemption amount for a corporation is $40,000 reduced by 25 percent of the amount by which AMTI exceeds $150,000.[25]

EXAMPLE 32

Beige Corporation has lost its small corporation status and has AMTI of $180,000. Since the exemption amount is reduced by $7,500 [25% × ($180,000 – $150,000)], the

[24] The tax rules pertaining to the ACE adjustment are contained in § 56(g).

[25] § 55(d)(2).

FINANCIAL DISCLOSURE *Insights*

THE ALTERNATIVE MINIMUM TAX AS PREPAYMENT

Tax professionals often describe the alternative minimum tax (AMT) as a "mere prepayment device," in that by applying the minimum tax credit, the entity recovers its payment for the AMT in a later tax year when it returns to regular tax status. Critics observe that this statement is misleading for several important reasons.

- Due to the makeup of their assets or income sources, many businesses are subject to the AMT every year. Thus, the minimum tax credit never will be available as there will not be another regular tax year in the foreseeable future.
- Any prepayment of tax reduces the present value of the credit that is claimed in a future tax year. Consequently, the AMT generates a permanent loss of funds to the taxpayer. For example, if the after-tax rate of return for the entity is 6 percent, a $1 million minimum tax credit that is claimed five years after the AMT is paid is worth only about $750,000 (Tables 7.1 and 7.2 in Chapter 7 can be used to make these analyses).

If the minimum tax credit is to be claimed in future years, a deferred tax asset is created on the taxpayer's GAAP balance sheet. This deferred tax asset might also address the basis differences for assets that are depreciated under MACRS for regular tax purposes and ADS in computing the AMT. In a recent year, the trucking firm Ryder Systems reported a deferred tax asset of approximately $10 million relating to the application of the AMT for the year. For the prior year, the Ryder deferred tax asset for the AMT had been approximately $12.5 million, so one can infer that some of the minimum tax credit had been claimed at least for that tax year.

amount remaining is $32,500 ($40,000 – $7,500). Thus, Beige Corporation's alternative minimum tax base (refer to Figure 3.2) is $147,500 ($180,000 – $32,500). ■

Note that the exemption phases out entirely when AMTI reaches $310,000. With the $5 million small corporation exception, this exemption is less important to profitable corporations.

MINIMUM TAX CREDIT

The AMT is a separate tax system that is computed side-by-side with the regular tax. Along with the "netting concept," a **minimum tax credit** is available to eliminate the possibility of double taxation.[26] Essentially, the AMT paid in one tax year may be carried forward indefinitely and used as a credit against the corporation's future *regular* tax liability that exceeds its tentative minimum tax. The minimum tax credit may not be carried back and may not be offset against any future *minimum* tax liability. The credit can be used to reduce regular tax liability in future years (but not below the tentative AMT).

Unfortunately, the law does not cover the reverse situation (a preference item generates a regular tax in one year and results in an AMT in a later year). An example could be unearned income that is taxed in the year of receipt but is not recognized for book income purposes until the year earned. Consequently, it is entirely possible that the same income could be taxed twice.

EXAMPLE 33

Returning to the facts of Example 29, Tan Corporation's AMTI exceeds $310,000, so there is no exemption amount. The tentative minimum tax is $1,490,000 (20% of $7,450,000). Assuming the regular tax liability in 2011 is $1,400,000, the AMT liability is $90,000 ($1,490,000 – $1,400,000). The amount of the minimum tax credit carryover is $90,000, which is all of the current year's AMT. ■

[26] § 53.

Since the tentative minimum tax of a small corporation will be zero, a small corporation with unused minimum tax credits after 1997 may use them up to the amount of the corporation's regular tax liability (after other credits) *less* 25 percent of the excess, if any, of the regular tax liability over $25,000. This will accelerate a small corporation's ability to use any available tax credits.

EXAMPLE 34

Purple Corporation, a small company, has a significant amount of minimum tax credits, but no AMT liability in 2011. The corporation's regular tax liability (less other credits) for 2011 is $75,000. Purple's allowable minimum tax credit for 2011 is limited to $62,500 [$75,000 – .25($75,000 – $25,000)]. ■

OTHER ASPECTS OF THE AMT

In addition to paying their regular tax liability, corporations have to make estimated tax payments of the AMT liability. Even corporations that prepare quarterly financial statements may find this requirement adds to compliance costs. Unfortunately, the estimated tax payment dates will not coincide with the dates of the financial statements. Accordingly, estimating book income accurately for AMT purposes from the information usually available may be difficult.

The only credit that can be used to offset the AMT is the foreign tax credit (FTC). The general business credit and other credits are unavailable in AMT years.

FORM 4626 ILLUSTRATED

Form 4626 is used to compute the alternative minimum tax for a corporation that is not exempt from the AMT. For an affiliated group filing a consolidated tax return, the AMT must be computed on a consolidated basis.

A corporation must file Form 4626 if any of the following apply:

- The corporation is not a "small corporation" exempt from the AMT.
- The corporation's taxable income or loss before the NOL deduction plus its adjustments and preferences totals more than $40,000 or, if smaller, its allowable exemption amount.
- The corporation claims any general business credit, any qualified electric vehicle passive activity credit from prior years, or the credit for prior year minimum tax.

EXAMPLE 35

The following facts apply to a calendar year corporation in 2011 that is not a small corporation:

Taxable income before NOL	$3,417,640
Domestic production activities deduction	(18,222)
Tax-exempt interest from specified private activity bonds	11,021
Adjusted loss	(33,014)
Amortization of mining exploration and development costs	(19,421)
Amortization of certified pollution control facilities	53,013
Depreciation of post-1986 property	476,557
ACE from line 10 of worksheet	5,100,460
Line 4d	244,225

Review Form 4626 on the next page to see how the corporation arrived at no AMT. ■

Form **4626**

Department of the Treasury
Internal Revenue Service

Alternative Minimum Tax—Corporations

▶ See separate instructions.
▶ Attach to the corporation's tax return.

OMB No. 1545-0175

2010

Name | Employer identification number

Note: *See the instructions to find out if the corporation is a small corporation exempt from the alternative minimum tax (AMT) under section 55(e).*

				Line	Amount
1	Taxable income or (loss) before net operating loss deduction			1	3,417,640
2	**Adjustments and preferences:**				
a	Depreciation of post-1986 property			2a	476,557
b	Amortization of certified pollution control facilities			2b	53,013
c	Amortization of mining exploration and development costs			2c	(19,421)
d	Amortization of circulation expenditures (personal holding companies only)			2d	
e	Adjusted gain or loss			2e	(33,014)
f	Long-term contracts			2f	
g	Merchant marine capital construction funds			2g	
h	Section 833(b) deduction (Blue Cross, Blue Shield, and similar type organizations only)			2h	
i	Tax shelter farm activities (personal service corporations only)			2i	
j	Passive activities (closely held corporations and personal service corporations only)			2j	
k	Loss limitations			2k	
l	Depletion			2l	
m	Tax-exempt interest income from specified private activity bonds			2m	11,021
n	Intangible drilling costs			2n	
o	Other adjustments and preferences			2o	(18,222)
3	Pre-adjustment alternative minimum taxable income (AMTI). Combine lines 1 through 2o			3	3,887,574
4	**Adjusted current earnings (ACE) adjustment:**				
a	ACE from line 10 of the ACE worksheet in the instructions	4a	5,100,460		
b	Subtract line 3 from line 4a. If line 3 exceeds line 4a, enter the difference as a negative amount (see instructions)	4b	1,212,886		
c	Multiply line 4b by 75% (.75). Enter the result as a positive amount	4c	909,664		
d	Enter the excess, if any, of the corporation's total increases in AMTI from prior year ACE adjustments over its total reductions in AMTI from prior year ACE adjustments (see instructions). **Note:** *You* ***must*** *enter an amount on line 4d (even if line 4b is positive)*	4d	244,225		
e	ACE adjustment. • If line 4b is zero or more, enter the amount from line 4c • If line 4b is less than zero, enter the **smaller** of line 4c or line 4d as a negative amount			4e	909,664
5	Combine lines 3 and 4e. If zero or less, stop here; the corporation does not owe any AMT			5	4,797,238
6	Alternative tax net operating loss deduction (see instructions)			6	0
7	**Alternative minimum taxable income.** Subtract line 6 from line 5. If the corporation held a residual interest in a REMIC, see instructions			7	
8	**Exemption phase-out** (if line 7 is $310,000 or more, skip lines 8a and 8b and enter -0- on line 8c):				
a	Subtract $150,000 from line 7 (if completing this line for a member of a controlled group, see instructions). If zero or less, enter -0-	8a			
b	Multiply line 8a by 25% (.25)	8b			
c	Exemption. Subtract line 8b from $40,000 (if completing this line for a member of a controlled group, see instructions). If zero or less, enter -0-			8c	0
9	Subtract line 8c from line 7. If zero or less, enter -0-			9	4,797,238
10	Multiply line 9 by 20% (.20)			10	959,448
11	Alternative minimum tax foreign tax credit (AMTFTC) (see instructions)			11	-
12	Tentative minimum tax. Subtract line 11 from line 10			12	959,448
13	Regular tax liability before applying all credits except the foreign tax credit			13	1,161,997
14	**Alternative minimum tax.** Subtract line 13 from line 12. If zero or less, enter -0-. Enter here and on Form 1120, Schedule J, line 3, or the appropriate line of the corporation's income tax return			14	0

For Paperwork Reduction Act Notice, see the instructions. Cat. No. 12955I Form **4626** (2010)

3.3 Penalty Taxes on Corporate Accumulations

LO.9

Evaluate the current status of the penalty taxes on corporate accumulations.

When dividends were taxed as ordinary income, avoiding corporate distributions often proved desirable. In closely held settings where a few high-bracket shareholders controlled corporate policy, the following approach would be taken:

- Accumulate earnings within the corporation. Distribute dividends, if at all, only when the shareholders are in a favorable tax position (e.g., are in low brackets or have offsetting losses).
- The accumulations will cause the stock to appreciate in value.
- The shareholders ultimately can recognize this appreciation in value at favorable capital gain rates by selling the stock. Or, if the stock is transferred by death, no gain is ever recognized due to the step-up in basis under § 1014 (see Chapter 19).

Consequently, by not paying dividends, a tax rate of 15 percent (i.e., maximum rate on capital gains) has been substituted for 35 percent (i.e., maximum rate on ordinary income). Equally beneficial, recognition of gain has been deferred (to the date of sale) or completely avoided (transfer by death).

Due to the tax avoidance that was occurring through corporate accumulations, the penalty taxes of § 531 (**accumulated earnings tax**) and § 541 (**personal holding company tax**) were enacted. These provisions imposed a penalty tax equal to the highest rate applicable to individuals on corporations used to avoid taxes on shareholders. Prior to the Jobs and Growth Tax Relief Reconciliation Act (JGTRRA) of 2003, the penalty tax rate was 39.6 percent. The penalty tax was imposed in addition to the regular corporate income tax of § 11.

JGTRRA of 2003 temporarily reduced the motivation to accumulate at the corporate level with two changes. First, dividends are no longer taxed as ordinary income but are subject to a top rate of 15 percent (before 2013). Second, the penalty tax rate under § 531 and § 541 was reduced to 15 percent (before 2013).

Beginning in 2013, however, dividends may be taxed at the highest individual tax rate (39.6 percent), which increases the motivation to accumulate earnings. Likewise, beginning in 2013, both of the penalty tax rates become the highest individual tax rate (e.g., 39.6 percent), causing both taxes to again be punitive. For example, a personal holding company with $2.2 million undistributed after-tax income would owe $871,200 of personal holding company tax in 2013 ($2,200,000 × 39.6%), above and beyond corporate income taxes.

LO.10

Demonstrate the accumulated earnings and personal holding company taxes.

ACCUMULATED EARNINGS TAX (§§ 531–537)

The § 531 tax of 15 percent (before 2013) is imposed on **accumulated taxable income (ATI)**, determined as follows:[27]

$$\text{ATI} = \text{Taxable income} \pm \text{Adjustments} - \text{Dividends paid}$$
$$- \text{Accumulated earnings credit}$$

Taxable income is determined in the same manner as in the case of the regular corporate income tax. The adjustments to taxable income generally pertain to a corporation's ability to pay a dividend. Thus, deductions include the corporate income tax, excess charitable contributions, and long-term capital gains (net of tax), while additions include the NOL and dividends received deductions.

The **accumulated earnings credit** is the greater of the minimum credit of $250,000 ($150,000 for personal service corporations) or the current E & P for the year needed to meet the **reasonable needs of the business**. In determining the minimum credit or the current E & P required to meet the reasonable needs of the business,

[27] § 535.

the balance of past (i.e., accumulated) E & P must be considered. This balance, once it reaches $250,000, also eliminates the use of the minimum credit.

EXAMPLE 36

Hazel, a calendar year C corporation, has accumulated E & P of $3.1 million as of January 1, 2011. Its current E & P for 2011 is $500,000, and it has reasonable business needs of $3.5 million. Hazel Corporation's accumulated earnings credit is $400,000 [$3.5 million (reasonable needs) – $3.1 million (accumulated E & P)]. Presuming that Hazel Corporation's current E & P is the same as taxable income as adjusted (see above formula), its ATI for 2011 is $100,000 [$500,000 (taxable income as adjusted) – $400,000 (accumulated earnings credit)]. ■

EXAMPLE 37

Assume the same facts as in Example 36, except that Hazel Corporation distributes a cash dividend of $100,000 to its shareholders during 2011. Hazel's ATI for 2011 now becomes $0 [$500,000 (taxable income as adjusted) – $400,000 (accumulated earnings credit) – $100,000 (dividends paid)]. ■

In most cases, ATI and vulnerability to the § 531 penalty tax are avoided by resorting to the accumulated earnings credit. Hence, it is important to recognize what constitutes the reasonable needs of the business. These include expansion of the business, replacement of plant and equipment, working capital needs, product liability losses, debt retirement, self-insurance, and loans to suppliers and customers.[28] Reasonable needs do not include loans to shareholders, investments in unrelated properties or businesses, and unrealistic hazards and contingencies.[29] Finally, if the accumulated earnings credit does not suffice, dividend payments will reduce or eliminate ATI (see Example 37 above).

PERSONAL HOLDING COMPANY TAX (§§ 541–547)

Often referred to as the tax on "incorporated pocketbooks," the § 541 tax is aimed at the use of the corporate form to shelter investment income. As was true of the § 531 tax, the assumption is that the income will be taxed, if at all,[30] at a lower rate in the hands of a corporate investor than in the case of an individual.

Before the § 541 tax can apply, the corporation must be a personal holding company (PHC). To be a PHC, both the stock ownership and the gross income tests must be satisfied.[31] Under the stock ownership test, more than 50 percent of the value of the outstanding stock must be owned by five or fewer individuals at any time during the last half of the taxable year. Under the gross income test, 60 percent or more of gross income (as adjusted) must consist of personal holding company income (PHCI).

Under the stock ownership test, constructive ownership is taken into account to cover indirect interests. Broad stock attribution rules apply for both family and entity ownership.[32] Closely held family corporations will find the stock ownership test difficult to avoid.

Regarding the gross income test, gross income is adjusted by subtracting capital and § 1231 gains and certain other expenses.[33] PHCI consists of passive types of income such as dividends, interest, rents, and royalties. Rents *or* royalties may be excluded if they are significant in amount (i.e., comprise more than 50 percent of the adjusted gross income). In limited situations, income from personal service contracts performed by a shareholder-employee may be PHCI.[34]

If the PHC definition is satisfied, the penalty tax of 15 percent (before 2013) is imposed on **undistributed PHCI**.[35] Undistributed PHCI is taxable income plus or

[28] § 537 and Reg. § 1.537–1.

[29] Reg. § 1.537–2(c).

[30] Although capital gains are subject to the corporate income tax, they are not taxed under either the § 531 or § 541 penalty taxes.

[31] § 542(a).

[32] § 544.

[33] As prescribed by § 543(b)(2).

[34] § 543(a).

[35] § 541.

minus various adjustments and less the dividends paid deduction.[36] The adjustments are similar to those made in arriving at ATI (for purposes of the § 531 tax) and largely reflect the corporation's financial capacity to pay dividends. Thus, the dividends received and NOL deductions are added back, and the corporate income tax, excess charitable contributions (i.e., in excess of the 10 percent limitation), and long-term capital gain (net of tax) are subtracted.

Note that taxable dividend payments *reduce* both ATI and undistributed PHCI. As these are the bases on which the § 531 tax or the § 541 tax is imposed, either tax can be completely avoided by paying sufficient dividends. This escape hatch is consistent with the reason for these penalty taxes—to punish the use of corporations that improperly accumulate surplus (by not paying dividends).

Both the § 531 tax and the § 541 tax cannot be imposed in the same situation. If a corporation could be subject to both taxes, the § 541 tax predominates.[37] A corporation that qualifies as a PHC is required to attach a Schedule PH calculating the PHC tax to its annual Form 1120.

TAX PLANNING:

3.4 Domestic Production Activities Deduction

LO.11

Apply various tax planning procedures to maximize the domestic production activities deduction (DPAD) and to minimize the imposition of the AMT.

In most states, one problem to be faced with the producers' deduction is its status under local law. Even in those states that do not impose an income tax on individuals, an income tax on corporations may exist. Also, the franchise tax levied on corporations may possess some of the characteristics of an income tax. Do these state taxes allow the DPAD? As described in the "Tax in the News" earlier in this chapter, many states are decoupling from the Federal rules and are not permitting the deduction for state income tax purposes—a trend that has become more pronounced since the DPAD rate increased to 9 percent in 2010. Any decoupling from the DPAD adds to the discrepancy that exists between the Federal and state tax treatment of income and deductions. For taxpayers with multistate operations, however, it could mean a shifting of some operations to the more tax-friendly jurisdictions (see Tax Planning in Chapter 16).

The DPAD will compel taxpayers to use extreme care in structuring business transactions. As an illustration, how should the cost of embedded services be treated? Should the cost of a warranty be included as part of the price of the product, or should it be accounted for separately? The answer may depend on what the taxpayer does in the normal course of business. If the warranty is not separately bargained for and is customarily included in the price of the product, then the embedded service qualifies for the DPAD and requires no unbundling (i.e., separation). Also, the *de minimis* rule can avoid the embedded service hurdle if properly used (see Example 8 in this chapter).

When contract manufacturing is involved, the key to the availability of the DPAD depends on the incidents of ownership. Here, advance planning becomes crucial. The parties should decide beforehand who is to receive the deduction. Legal title to the property being produced should then be placed in conformance with this decision (see Examples 11 and 12 in this chapter). But see the discussion of the W–2 wage hurdle in the "Tax in the News" on p. 3–31.

If the production process includes offshore activity, recall that § 199 requires that a "significant part" be performed in the United States. According to the IRS, "significant" means "substantial," and this condition can be satisfied by meeting a 20 percent safe-harbor rule (see Examples 9 and 10 in this chapter). In cases where compliance with this safe-harbor rule is questionable, a ready solution would be to shift some of the offshore production to the United States.

[36] § 545.

[37] § 532(b)(1).

TAX *in the NEWS*

W–2 Limitations May Restrict Manufacturers' Deduction

Since only one party may claim the DPAD with respect to the same function performed, taxpayers must maintain the benefits and burdens of ownership while the qualified production activity takes place. But these taxpayers must incur their own W–2 wages in performing the qualified production activities. For certain industries, these overlapping requirements could jeopardize the deduction. For example, if a contract manufacturer's labor and overhead are attributed to a contractor with the ownership of the property, there may be no attribution regarding W–2 wages paid by the contract manufacturer. Furthermore, even if a contract manufacturer retains ownership, the deduction is lost if the taxpayer has no common law employees engaged in the qualified production activities.

Particularly with a DPAD rate of 9 percent of QPAI, many shareholders of C corporations may prefer a pass-through of the deduction. In such cases, making an S election becomes a viable course of action.

Pass-through entities should consider these approaches:

- An S corporation or partnership that is a qualified small taxpayer may use the small business simplified method to apportion CGS and deductions between DPGR and non-DPGR at the entity level.
- The IRS permits a partnership or an S corporation to calculate the pass-through portions of QPAI at the entity level, which then can be combined with the owner's QPAI.

In order to avoid the W–2 wage limitation imposed on the DPAD, the following observations should be considered:

- For sole proprietors, the self-employment tax does not qualify. In some cases, family members may need to be placed on the payroll to meet the W–2 wage limitation.
- Wages paid and not reported cannot be counted.
- Amounts paid to independent contractors do not qualify.
- Guaranteed payments made to a partner do not qualify.
- Taxpayers that have both qualifying and nonqualifying sales must keep careful records to allocate their W–2 wages.
- A taxpayer's payments to employees for domestic services in a private home are not included in W–2 wages for purposes of the DPAD.
- An individual filing as part of a joint return may take into account wages paid to employees of his or her spouse, provided that the wages are paid in a trade or business (and other requirements are met). This is not true if a taxpayer and spouse file separate returns.

If the taxpayer wants to avoid the allocation and apportionment procedures prescribed by the IRS, complete accounting records that identify the relevant receipts and expenses are essential. For example, the records should reflect what portion of gross receipts qualifies as DPGR and what part does not. In arriving at QPAI, what expenses (including CGS) should be allocated to DPGR and which should not? When based on specific identification, the results reached by a taxpayer should weather any IRS challenge. This type of sophisticated accounting system, however, will generate considerable compliance costs for many taxpayers.

3.5 Alternative Minimum Tax

Planning for the AMT is complicated by the fact that many of the procedures recommended run counter to what is done to reduce the regular corporate income tax.

Further, the AMT has the perverse effect of increasing a company's effective tax rate during economic slowdowns.

AVOIDING PREFERENCES AND ADJUSTMENTS

Investments in state and local bonds are attractive for income tax purposes because the interest is not included in gross income. Some of these bonds are issued to generate funds that are not used for an essential function of the government. The interest on such bonds could be a tax preference item and could lead to the imposition of the AMT. When the AMT applies, an investment in regular tax-exempt bonds or even fully taxed private-sector bonds might yield a higher after-tax rate of return.

For a corporation anticipating AMT problems, capitalizing rather than expensing certain costs can avoid generating preferences and adjustments. The decision should be based on the present discounted value of after-tax cash flows under the available alternatives. Costs that may be capitalized and amortized, rather than expensed, include circulation expenditures, mining exploration and development costs, and research and experimentation expenditures.

CONTROLLING THE TIMING OF PREFERENCES AND ADJUSTMENTS

In many situations, smaller corporations may be able to avoid the AMT by making use of the exemption. To maximize the exemption, taxpayers should attempt to avoid bunching positive adjustments and tax preferences in any one year. When the expenditure is largely within the control of the taxpayer, timing to avoid bunching is more easily accomplished.

OPTIMUM USE OF THE AMT AND REGULAR CORPORATE INCOME TAX RATE DIFFERENCE

A corporation that cannot avoid the AMT in a particular year can often save taxes by taking advantage of the difference between the AMT and the regular tax rates. In general, a corporation that expects to be subject to the AMT should accelerate income and defer deductions for the remainder of the year. Since the difference between the regular tax and the AMT may be as much as 14 or 15 percentage points, this strategy results in the income being taxed at less than it would be if reported in the next year. There is always the risk that the regular corporate rates may increase in future years. If the same corporation expects to be subject to the AMT for the next year (or years), this technique must be reversed. The corporation should defer income and accelerate deductions. The strategy delays the date the corporation has to pay the tax.

EXAMPLE 38

Falcon Corporation expects to be in the 34% tax bracket in 2012 but is subject to the AMT in 2011. In late 2011, Falcon is contemplating selling a tract of unimproved land (basis of $200,000 and fair market value of $1 million). Under these circumstances, it is preferable to sell the land in 2011. The gain of $800,000 ($1,000,000 − $200,000) generates a tax of $160,000 [$800,000 (recognized gain) × 20% (AMT rate)]. However, if the land is sold in 2012, the resulting tax is $272,000 [$800,000 (recognized gain) × 34% (regular corporate income tax rate)]. A savings of $112,000 ($272,000 − $160,000) materializes by making the sale in 2011. ■

THE S CORPORATION OPTION

Corporations that make the S election will not be subject to the corporate AMT. As noted in Chapter 12, however, various AMT adjustments and preferences pass through to the individual shareholders. But one troublesome adjustment, the one involving the ACE adjustment, is eliminated since it does not apply to individual taxpayers. Similarly, the accumulated earnings and personal holding company taxes cannot be imposed on an S corporation.

REFOCUS ON THE BIG PICTURE

DEALING WITH THE DPAD AND THE AMT

Determining DPGR for the DPAD

The $42 million gross receipts from the wholesale sale of Mocha's ice cream are considered DPGR. However, the *de minimis* safe-harbor 5 percent exception does not apply to include the gross receipts from the sale of the ice cream and coffee at the snack shops ($5 million divided by $47 million = 10.6%). The sales from the snack shops could qualify as DPGR if Mocha were to restrict sales somewhat to take advantage of the 5 percent *de minimis* exception. For example, keeping snack sales at around $2.2 million would satisfy the 5 percent exception. Thus, Mocha will have to decide whether the 9 percent DPAD is worth forgoing the profit on the snack sales. Keep in mind that the DPAD is allowed for the AMT.

Who Pays the AMT?

Carmine, Inc., has met the several gross receipts tests, including initially qualifying as a "small corporation." To qualify as a "small corporation," the business must have had average gross receipts of $5 million or less in the preceding three years. Once Carmine passed the $5 million average gross receipts test, it will continue to be treated as a "small corporation" and be exempt from the AMT for as long as its average gross receipts for the three-year period preceding the taxable year do not exceed $7.5 million.

Unfortunately, Taupe, Inc., did not meet the initial $5 million test, so it does not fall within the $7.5 million exemption.

KEY TERMS

Accumulated earnings credit, 3–28
Accumulated earnings tax, 3–28
Accumulated taxable income (ATI), 3–28
Adjusted current earnings (ACE), 3-22
Alternative minimum tax (AMT), 3–17
Alternative minimum taxable income (AMTI), 3–17
AMT adjustments, 3-19
Domestic production activities deduction (DPAD), 3–3
Domestic production gross receipts (DPGR), 3–6
Expanded affiliated group (EAG), 3–15
Minimum tax credit, 3–25
Personal holding company tax, 3–28
Qualified production activities income (QPAI), 3–5
Reasonable needs of the business, 3–28
Tax preference items, 3–20
Undistributed PHCI, 3–29
W–2 wages, 3–3

DISCUSSION QUESTIONS

1. **LO.1** Who can claim the DPAD? Which taxpayers are more likely to use it?
2. **LO.1** Unlike other deductions, the DPAD is based on income, not costs. Explain.
3. **LO.1, 2, 3, 4, 5** Explain the relationship between the following items:
   a. DPAD and W–2 wages.
   b. DPAD and QPAI.
   c. DPAD and TI.
   d. DPGR and QPAI.
   e. DPAD and AMT.
   f. EAG and DPAD.
4. **LO.2** What effect, if any, do NOLs have on the DPAD?

5. **LO.2** For purposes of the limitation on the DPAD, what is included in W–2 wages?

ISSUE ID

6. **LO.1, 5** Scott is independently wealthy and does not work. Except for household servants, he has no employees. Due to the phaseout of itemized deductions, Scott claims the standard deduction when he files his Form 1040. Is it possible that Scott might be able to claim a DPAD? Explain.

7. **LO.3** In what manner can statistical sampling be helpful in arriving at the DPAD?

8. **LO.3** Citron Corporation has some domestic production gross receipts (DPGR) that qualify for the DPAD and some that do not qualify.
   a. Is there a safe harbor that allows non-DPGR to be included in DPGR?
   b. Would Citron ever want to treat DPGR as non-DPGR? Why or why not?
   c. Continuing with part (b), when can this be done?

9. **LO.3, 11** Gold Company manufactures a product and sells it with an embedded service.
   a. What does this mean?
   b. Give some examples of embedded services.
   c. Under what circumstances can the amount attributable to an embedded service be part of DPGR?

10. **LO.3, 11** In order to qualify as DPGR, QPP must be MPGE in whole or in significant part within the United States.
   a. Interpret this statement.
   b. What does "significant" mean?
   c. In what context does this problem arise?

11. **LO.3, 11** Only one producer may claim the DPAD. Explain.
   a. Why is this rule important in the area of contract manufacturing?
   b. Does the rule present any planning opportunities?

12. **LO.4** Once DPGR is determined, what adjustments are necessary to arrive at QPAI?

13. **LO.3, 5** Erica operates a chain of Tex-Mex fast-food outlets. She also wholesales frozen prepared meals to grocery stores.
   a. Can Erica claim a DPAD? Explain.
   b. Would it matter if all of the fast-food sales are on a take-out basis as the retail outlets have no dining facilities?

ISSUE ID

14. **LO.3, 5** MASH, Inc., produces two live television programs and licenses the first program to Clear, Inc., a television station. MASH licenses the second television program to Zebra's television station, which broadcasts the program on its channel. Both programs contain product placements and advertising for which MASH receives compensation. MASH and Clear are unrelated parties and are not members of an EAG. Discuss the DPGR tax result.

ISSUE ID

15. **LO.2, 5** Justin and Kathleen are equal partners in Blue Partnership. For the year, they receive a pass-through of the same amount of QPAI and W–2 wages from Blue. Justin, however, is able to claim a larger DPAD on his income tax return than Kathleen. Why?

16. **LO.5** Is the DPAD available for purposes of the alternative minimum tax (AMT)?

17. **LO.6** If the AMT is greater than the regular corporate tax, the corporation must pay the greater AMT. Discuss.

18. **LO.6** What is the small corporation exemption from the AMT? When is it available and not available?

19. **LO.6, 7** Since tax preference items are merely timing differences, they may be positive or negative. Assess the validity of this statement.

20. **LO.7** Is the excess of intangible drilling costs over 10-year amortization always a tax preference item?

21. **LO.6, 7** In arriving at AMTI, why are NOLs stated separately instead of being included with other adjustments?

22. **LO.7, 8** Using the legend provided, classify the impact each of the following items has upon unadjusted AMTI in arriving at ACE:

Legend
I = Increase in AMTI
D = Decrease in AMTI
E = Either an increase or a decrease in AMTI
N = No impact

a. Currently deducted intangible drilling costs.
b. Loss on sale of a piece of equipment to a related party.
c. Purchase of raw materials.
d. Nondeductible transportation fines.
e. Dividends received deduction for a 15%-owned business.
f. Proceeds from a key employee insurance policy.
g. Tax-exempt interest.

23. **LO.6, 7, 8** Using the legend provided, classify the impact each of the following items has upon taxable income or loss for purposes of determining AMTI:

Legend
I = Increase in taxable income
D = Decrease in taxable income
E = Either an increase or a decrease in taxable income
N = No impact

a. Amortization claimed on certified pollution control facilities.
b. Adjusted current earnings (ACE) adjustment.
c. AMT net operating loss deduction.
d. Excess mining exploration and development costs.
e. Statutory AMT exemption.
f. Accelerated depreciation on post-1986 property acquisitions.
g. Tax-exempt interest on general purpose municipal bonds.
h. LIFO inventory recapture amount.
i. Excess percentage depletion of an integrated oil company.

24. **LO.8** Alice Tiras, an auditor on your staff, calls you to ask what impact current E & P has on ACE. She wants to know if ACE is the same as current E & P. Prepare a tax file memo indicating what you told Ms. Tiras. **COMMUNICATIONS**

25. **LO.8** What is the effect of the following on unadjusted AMTI in arriving at ACE?
a. Proceeds from life insurance on key employee.
b. Tax-exempt income (net of expenses).
c. Exemption amount of $40,000.
d. IDC deducted currently.
e. Excess capital loss.
f. Deferred gain on installment sales.
g. Excess charitable contributions.
h. Premiums paid on key employee insurance policy.

26. **LO.8** Which of the following credits may be used to offset the AMT?
a. General business credit.
b. Federal solar credit.
c. Foreign tax credit.
d. Qualified electric vehicle.

27. **LO.8** Explain how the AMT exemption amount is calculated.

28. **LO.10** In making the "adjustments" necessary to arrive at accumulated taxable income, which of the following items should be added (+), subtracted (−), or have no effect (*NE*) on taxable income?
a. Corporate income tax incurred and paid.
b. A nontaxable stock dividend distributed by the corporation to its shareholders.

c. Charitable contributions paid in the amount of 10% of taxable income.
d. The dividends received deduction.
e. Deduction of an NOL carried over from a prior year.

29. **LO.10** ATI = Taxable income ± Adjustments + Dividends received − Accumulated earnings credit. Comment on the validity of this formula.

COMMUNICATIONS

30. **LO.6, 7, 8, 11** A regular corporation anticipates AMT problems during 2011. Prepare PowerPoint slides for a technical presentation to the audit staff pointing out some strategies available to avoid or minimize the AMT.

31. **LO.10** Ashley McQuiston calls you to ask about the impact that future tax rates on dividends and capital gains will have on his closely held corporation. He is worried about the accumulated earnings tax. What will you tell him?

PROBLEMS

32. **LO.1** Tiger, Inc., has $11 million of taxable income. What is the tax savings from Tiger's maximum DPAD in 2011?

33. **LO.2** In each of the following *independent* situations, determine the DPAD for 2011 for the corporation involved.

	Taxpayer	QPAI	TI	W–2 Wages
a.	Green	$800,000	$600,000	$120,000
b.	Red	400,000	500,000	20,000
c.	Ecru	900,000	900,000*	300,000
d.	Blue	700,000	900,000	200,000
e.	Orange	900,000	900,000	200,000**

*Does not include a $100,000 NOL carryover from the previous year.
**Only $50,000 relates directly to manufacturing activities.

34. **LO.3** Tern Corporation produces and sells refrigerators for outdoor use (e.g., patios, porches, verandas). Its major manufacturing facility is in Georgia, but it also has a smaller plant in Nicaragua. Gross receipts for the current year are derived as follows: $8.2 million from Georgia and $2 million from Nicaragua.
   a. What is Tern's DPGR for the current year?
   b. What if the gross receipts from the Nicaragua plant are only $400,000 (not $2 million)?

35. **LO.3** Cowbird, Inc., refines and sells gasoline in the United States. Of the gasoline it sells, about 4% is refined in Louisiana, and the remaining 96% is purchased from a nonrelated source in the Middle East. Suppose that currently the benefits of § 199 to Cowbird are so minimal that the tax savings are not worth the costs of compliance. Is there anything that Cowbird can do?

36. **LO.3** Dove Corporation manufactures and sells climate-controlled wine cabinets. Its most popular model sells for $3,000 and comes with a basic 90-day warranty. For an extra $150, this warranty is extended to 3 years, and for $300 the warranty is extended to 10 years.
   a. If a customer buys a wine cabinet with the basic warranty, how much of the $3,000 paid represents DPGR to Dove?
   b. Assume a customer pays $3,150 to include the extended 3-year warranty. How much of this amount is DPGR?
   c. Assume $3,300 is paid to include the extended 10-year warranty. How much is DPGR?
   d. Could the sales agreement be modified so as to increase the amount qualifying as DPGR? Explain.

37. **LO.3, 4** Finch Corporation sells portable air filtration systems by means of the Internet and direct mail orders. Most of the components are purchased from foreign suppliers at a cost of $1,600. Finch supplies the remaining components and assembles the final

product at a cost of $400. Finch's marketing, packaging, and shipping expenses total $40 per unit. Each unit is sold for $2,800.

a. What is Finch's DPGR per unit?
b. Its QPAI?

38. **LO.3, 4** Assume the same facts as in Problem 37, except that Finch incurred only $340 (not $400) in production costs.
    a. What is Finch's DPGR per unit? Its QPAI?
    b. How could this result have been avoided?

39. **LO.3** Don is the owner of a large apartment complex that was built 30 years ago. As the complex is in serious need of renovation, Don pays Cardinal Construction Corporation $2.8 million to do the work. Don also pays an architect $400,000 to draw up plans for the project. Because the rewiring requirements are so extensive, Cardinal pays Dove Electric Company $500,000 to handle this part of the renovation. At all times title to the apartment complex remains with Don. Who has DPGR and in what amount?

ISSUE ID

40. **LO.2, 3, 4** Danping Corporation, a calendar year taxpayer, sells lawn furniture through big box stores. It manufactures some of the furniture and imports some from unrelated foreign producers. For tax year 2011, Danping's records reveal the following information:

	Furniture Sold	
	Manufactured	**Imported**
Gross receipts	$2,600,000	$1,600,000
CGS	1,100,000	850,000

Danping also has selling and marketing expenses of $700,000 and administrative expenses of $300,000. Under the simplified deduction method, what is Danping's:

a. DPGR?
b. QPAI?
c. DPAD?

41. **LO.2, 3, 4** Assume the same facts as in Problem 40, except that Danping's records do not identify its CGS (as between manufactured and imported furniture) but reflect an unallocated amount of $1,950,000. Further assume that Danping is qualified to (and does) use the small business simplified method of allocating CGS and other expenses. What is Danping's:
    a. QPAI?
    b. DPAD?

42. **LO.5** Flicker Corporation, a calendar year taxpayer, manufactures yogurt that it wholesales to grocery stores and other food outlets. It also operates a yogurt shop near its factory where it sells directly to the general public. For tax years 2010 and 2011, gross receipts are as follows:

	Gross Receipts	
	Wholesale	**Snack Shop**
2010	$2,000,000	$110,000
2011	2,500,000	130,000

What is Flicker's DPGR for:

a. 2010?
b. 2011?

43. **LO.2, 3, 4, 5** Purple Corporation manufactures an exercise machine at a cost of $800 and sells the machine to Scarlet Corporation for $1,200 in 2011. Scarlet incurs TV advertising expenses of $300 and sells the machine by phone order for $1,600. If Purple and Scarlet are not related parties, determine their:
    a. DPGR.
    b. QPAI.
    c. DPAD.

44. **LO.2, 3, 4, 5** Assume the same facts as in Problem 43, except that Purple Corporation and Scarlet Corporation are members of an EAG. Determine their:
    a. DPGR.
    b. QPAI.
    c. DPAD.

45. **LO.1, 2, 5** The Ryan Partnership has two equal partners in the 35% marginal tax bracket. If the partnership has QPAI of $13 million in 2010 and $11 million in 2011, what would be the maximum tax savings for this partnership and its partners?

46. **LO.6** Campbell, Inc., a calendar year corporation that was created in February 2007, has gross receipts as follows:

Year	Gross Receipts
2007	$2,990,220
2008	3,310,763
2009	4,885,027
2010	7,626,681
2011	9,120,132

Does Campbell qualify for the small corporation exemption for each year?

47. **LO.6, 7** For 2011, Apple Corporation (a calendar year integrated oil company) had the following transactions:

Taxable income	$4,000,000
Regular tax depreciation on realty in excess of ADS (placed in service in 1989)	1,700,000
Excess intangible drilling costs	500,000
Percentage depletion in excess of the property's adjusted basis	700,000

Assume no ACE adjustment.
    a. Determine Apple Corporation's AMTI for 2011.
    b. Determine the tentative minimum tax base (refer to Figure 3.2).
    c. Determine the tentative minimum tax.
    d. What is the amount of the AMT?

48. **LO.6, 7** For 2011, Gold Corporation (a calendar year business) had the following transactions:

Taxable income	$4,200,000
Accelerated depreciation on pre-1987 real property (in excess of straight-line depreciation)	1,500,500
Excess intangible drilling costs	575,250
AMT NOL deduction	989,570

Assume no ACE adjustment.
    a. Determine Gold Corporation's AMTI for 2011.
    b. Determine the tentative minimum tax base (refer to Figure 3.2).
    c. Determine the tentative minimum tax.
    d. What is the amount of the AMT, if any?

49. **LO.8** Brown Corporation, a calendar year taxpayer, began operations in 2008. It reports the following pre-adjusted AMTI and ACE for 2008 through 2011:

	Pre-adjusted AMTI	ACE
2008	$80,000,000	$70,000,000
2009	60,000,000	90,000,000
2010	50,000,000	40,000,000
2011	55,000,000	20,000,000

Calculate Brown's positive and negative adjustments, if any, for ACE.

50. **LO.8** Based upon the following facts of Fred, Inc., calculate adjusted current earnings (ACE):

Alternative minimum taxable income (AMTI)	$7,220,000
Municipal bond interest	630,000
Expenses related to municipal bonds	61,000
Key employee life insurance proceeds in excess of cash surrender value	2,000,000
Increase in LIFO recapture amount	170,000
Organization expense amortization	200,000
Cost of goods sold	4,922,000
Advertising expenses	631,000
Loss between related parties	230,000
Life insurance premiums paid on key person policy	310,000
Administrative expenses	521,014

51. **LO.6, 7** In each of the following independent situations, determine the tentative minimum tax (assume the companies are not in small corporation status):

	AMTI (before the Exemption Amount)
Brant Corporation	$170,000
Tern Corporation	190,000
Snipe Corporation	325,000

52. **LO.10** In each of the following *independent* situations relating to the penalty tax under § 531, determine the dividend that the corporation would have to pay to make its ATI (accumulated taxable income) be $0.

	Corporation	Beginning Balance in Accumulated E & P	Taxable Income (as Adjusted)	Reasonable Needs of the Business
a.	Oriole	$3,000,000	$200,000	$3,100,000
b.	Teal	3,900,000	300,000	4,000,000
c.	Wren	4,000,000	300,000	4,400,000
d.	Stork	5,000,000	500,000	5,000,000

53. **LO.10** A company is facing a possible accumulated earnings tax or the personal holding company tax in 2011. What is the total tax due, and what is the effective tax rate for this company based upon these facts?

Taxable income	$522,000
Dividends received deduction	47,000
Accumulated earnings credit	36,100
Excess charitable contributions	23,400
Dividends paid	38,000
Federal income taxes	177,480

RESEARCH PROBLEMS

Note: Solutions to Research Problems can be prepared by using the **Checkpoint® Student Edition** online research product, which is available to accompany this text. It is also possible to prepare solutions to the Research Problems by using tax research materials found in a standard tax library.

THOMSON REUTERS
Checkpoint® Student Edition

Research Problem 1. Orange Corporation enters into a lump-sum priced contract with Swift Company whereby it will produce and sell machines to Swift. As part of the arrangement:

- The machines will be delivered to Swift.
- A one-year warranty will be provided.
- Operating and maintenance manuals will be provided with the machines.
- Orange will offer Swift employees 100 hours of training and furnish training manuals.
- Spare parts will be available at a discount.
- A three-year service agreement for the machines is included.

None of the above services or property extras are separately offered or bargained for by Orange in selling its products. According to the pronouncements issued by the IRS, which of the above items will generate DPGR?

Research Problem 2. Two members of an expanded affiliated group (EAG), which do not file a consolidated Federal tax return, have positive QPAI. Dane, Inc., has taxable income, but Sloane, Inc., has a $230,000 net operating loss that offsets Dane's taxable income (and reduces any DPAD). However, the NOL could be carried back or forward to another tax year and then reduce the EAG member's QPAI again, thus reducing the EAG's taxable income a second time. Advise the CFO of Dane as to this problem.

Research Problem 3. How does the IRS suggest that corporate taxpayers apportion prior-period compensation expenses that are not part of cost of goods sold? See Industry Director Directive (LMSB 04-0209-004), March 2009.

COMMUNICATIONS

Research Problem 4. Owl, Inc., was owned entirely by Jeri Bell and Jerry Gore, each owning 620,000 of the 1,240,000 shares of common stock outstanding. On January 1, 2011, Owl established an employee stock ownership plan (ESOP) that later received a favorable determination letter from the IRS.

On February 1, 2011, Bell and Gore each sold 500,000 of their shares to the ESOP, each receiving $2.5 million. To facilitate the transaction, the ESOP borrowed $5 million from a local bank; the loan was guaranteed by Owl. During the year, Owl paid $1.4 million in cash dividends to the ESOP with respect to its stock. The ESOP transferred the cash to the bank as payment of principal and interest under the note.

Jeri Bell calls you and asks if Owl may claim a deduction under § 404(k) for the $1.4 million cash dividends. Does Owl have to include the dividends in its computation of ACE, thus avoiding any AMT? Write a memo for the tax files in response to Ms. Bell.

Research Problem 5. The excess of the depletion deduction allowable under § 611 over the "adjusted basis of the property" at the end of the tax year (determined without regard to the depletion deduction for the tax year) is an item of tax preference.

a. Should a taxpayer include in the basis of a § 614 property any unamortized basis under § 56(a)(2)?
b. Should the basis used for this purpose be the property's AMT basis or its regular income tax basis?

Use the tax resources of the Internet to address the following questions. Do not restrict your search to the Web, but include a review of newsgroups and general reference materials, practitioner sites and resources, primary sources of the tax law, chat rooms and discussion groups, and other opportunities.

COMMUNICATIONS

Research Problem 6. Locate the following article: T. R. Chorvat and M. S. Knoll, "The Economic and Policy Implications of Repealing the Corporate AMT," *Tax Foundation*, February 2002, Number 40. Prepare PowerPoint slides outlining how the AMT negatively affects firms' behavior.

Research Problem 7. In 2013, dividends become taxable as ordinary income, and the accumulated earnings and personal holding company rates move to 39.6%. What impact will these changes have on closely held corporations?

CHAPTER

4

Corporations: Organization and Capital Structure

LEARNING OBJECTIVES

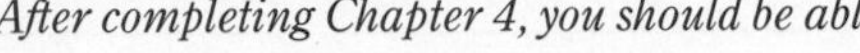

After completing Chapter 4, you should be able to:

LO.1

Identify the tax consequences of incorporating a business.

LO.2

Understand the special rules that apply when liabilities are assumed by a corporation.

LO.3

Recognize the basis issues relevant to the shareholder and the corporation.

LO.4

Appreciate the tax aspects of the capital structure of a corporation.

LO.5

Recognize the tax differences between debt and equity investments.

LO.6

Handle the tax treatment of shareholder debt and stock losses.

LO.7

Identify tax planning opportunities associated with organizing and financing a corporation.

OUTLINE

For the latest in changes to tax legislation, visit **www.cengage.com/taxation/swft.**

THE BIG PICTURE **Tax Solutions for the Real World**

TAX ISSUES ASSOCIATED WITH GROWING INTO THE CORPORATE FORM

Emily has operated her business as a sole proprietorship since it was formed 10 years ago. Now, however, she has decided to incorporate the business because the corporate form offers several important nontax advantages (e.g., limited liability). Also, the incorporation would enable her husband, David, to become a part owner in the business. Emily expects to transfer her business assets in exchange for her corporate interest, while David will provide services for his interest. Emily's sole proprietorship assets available for transfer to the new corporation are:

	Adjusted Basis	Fair Market Value
Accounts receivable	$ –0–	$ 25,000
Building	50,000	200,000
Other assets	150,000	275,000
	$200,000	$500,000

Aware of the problem of double taxation associated with operating as a regular corporation, Emily is considering receiving some corporate debt at the time of incorporation. The interest expense on the debt will then provide a deduction for the corporation. Emily's main concern, however, is that the incorporation will be a taxable transaction. Can her fears be allayed? **Read the chapter and formulate your response.**

Chapters 2 and 3 dealt with four principal areas fundamental to working with corporations: (1) determination of whether an entity is a corporation for Federal income tax purposes, (2) tax rules applicable to the day-to-day operation of a corporation, (3) filing and reporting procedures, and (4) special situations involving corporations.

Chapter 4 addresses more sophisticated issues involving corporations:

- The tax consequences to the shareholders and the corporation upon the organization of and original transfer of property to the corporation.
- The tax result that ensues when shareholders make transfers of property to a corporation after organization.
- The capital structure of a corporation, including equity and debt financing.
- The tax treatment of investor losses.

4.1 Organization of and Transfers to Controlled Corporations

LO.1

Identify the tax consequences of incorporating a business.

IN GENERAL

Property transactions normally produce tax consequences if a gain or loss is realized. As a result, unless an exception in the Code applies, a transfer of property to a corporation in exchange for stock constitutes a taxable sale or exchange of property. The amount of gain or loss is measured by the difference between the value of the stock received and the tax basis of the property transferred.

When a taxpayer's economic status has not changed and the wherewithal to pay is lacking, however, the Code provides special exceptions to the requirement that realized gain or loss be recognized. One such exception pertains to like-kind exchanges. When a taxpayer exchanges property for other property of a like kind, § 1031 provides that gain (or loss) on the exchange is not recognized because a substantive change in the taxpayer's investment has not occurred. Section 1031 is merely a deferral mechanism and does not authorize the permanent nonrecognition of gain or loss. The deferral mechanism is accomplished by calculating a substituted basis for the like-kind property received. With this substituted basis, the realized gain or loss associated with the property given up is ultimately recognized when the property received in the exchange is sold.

Another exception to the general rule deals with transfers to controlled corporations. Section 351 provides that gain or loss is not recognized upon the transfer of property to a corporation when certain conditions are met. This provision reflects the principle that gain should not be recognized when a taxpayer's investment has not substantively changed. For example, when a business is incorporated, the owner's economic status remains the same; only the *form* of the investment has changed. The investment in the business assets carries over to the investment in corporate stock. Further, if only stock in the corporation is received, the taxpayer is hardly in a position to pay a tax on any realized gain. Thus, this approach also is justified under the wherewithal to pay concept discussed in Chapter 1. As noted later, however, if the taxpayer receives property other than stock (i.e., cash or other "boot") from the corporation, realized gain is recognized.

Finally, § 351 exists because Congress believes that tax rules should not impede the exercise of sound business judgment (e.g., choice of the corporate form of doing business). For example, a taxpayer would think twice about forming a corporation if gain recognition (and the payment of a tax) would always be a consequence.

Therefore, the same principles govern the nonrecognition of gain or loss under § 1031 and § 351. With both provisions, gain or loss is postponed until a substantive change in the taxpayer's investment occurs (e.g., a sale to outsiders).

EXAMPLE 1

Ron is considering incorporating his sole proprietorship in order to obtain the limited liability of the corporate form. Ron realizes that if he incorporates, he will be personally liable only for the debts of the business that he has guaranteed. If Ron incorporates his business, the following assets will be transferred to the corporation:

	Tax Basis	Fair Market Value
Cash	$ 10,000	$ 10,000
Furniture and fixtures	20,000	60,000
Land and building	240,000	300,000
	$270,000	$370,000

In this change of business form, Ron will receive the corporation's stock worth $370,000 in exchange for the assets he transfers. Without the nonrecognition provisions of § 351, Ron would recognize a taxable gain of $100,000 on the transfer ($370,000 value of the stock received – $270,000 basis of the assets transferred). Under § 351, however, Ron does not recognize any gain because his economic status has not really changed. Ron's investment in the assets of his sole proprietorship is now represented by his ownership of stock in the corporation. Thus, § 351 provides for tax neutrality on the incorporation decision. ■

In a like-kind exchange, the recognition of gain is avoided only to the extent that the taxpayer receives like-kind property. However, the taxpayer must recognize some or all of the realized gain when receiving "boot" (i.e., property of an unlike kind, such as cash). For example, if a taxpayer exchanges a truck used in a business for another truck to be used in the business and also receives cash, the taxpayer has the wherewithal to pay an income tax on the cash involved. Further, the taxpayer's economic status has changed to the extent that cash is received. Thus, realized gain on the exchange is recognized to the extent of the cash received. In like manner, if a taxpayer transfers property to a corporation and receives cash or property other

CHOICE OF ORGANIZATIONAL FORM WHEN OPERATING OVERSEAS

When the management of a corporation decides to expand its business by establishing a presence in a foreign market, the new business venture may take one of several organizational forms. As each form comes with its respective advantages and disadvantages, making the best choice can be difficult.

One common approach is to conduct the foreign activity as a *branch* operation of the U.S. corporation. The foreign branch is not a separate legal entity, but a division of the U.S. corporation established overseas. As a result, any gains and losses produced by the foreign unit are included in the corporation's overall financial results.

Another possibility is to organize the foreign operations as a *subsidiary* of the U.S. parent corporation. If this route is chosen, the subsidiary may be either a *domestic* subsidiary (i.e., organized in the United States) or a *foreign* subsidiary (organized under the laws of a foreign country).

One fundamental tax difference between these two approaches is that the gains and losses of a domestic subsidiary may be consolidated with the operations of the U.S. parent, while the operations of a foreign subsidiary cannot. Thus, the use of a domestic subsidiary to conduct foreign operations will generally yield the same final result as the use of a branch. With both approaches, the financial statements of the U.S. parent reflect the results of its worldwide operations.

than stock, gain (but not loss) is recognized to the extent of the lesser of the gain realized or the boot received (i.e., the amount of cash and the fair market value of other property received). Any gain recognized is classified (e.g., ordinary, capital) according to the type of assets transferred.[1] As discussed later, the nonrecognition of gain or loss is accompanied by a substituted basis in the shareholder's stock.[2]

EXAMPLE 2

Amanda and Calvin form Quail Corporation. Amanda transfers property with an adjusted basis of $30,000, fair market value of $60,000, for 50% of the stock, worth $60,000. Calvin transfers property with an adjusted basis of $70,000, fair market value of $60,000, for the remaining 50% of the stock. The transfers qualify under § 351. Amanda has an unrecognized gain of $30,000, and Calvin has an unrecognized loss of $10,000. Both have a substituted basis in the stock in Quail Corporation. Amanda has a basis of $30,000 in her stock, and Calvin has a basis of $70,000 in his stock. Therefore, if either Amanda or Calvin later disposes of the Quail stock in a taxable transaction (e.g., a sale), this deferred gain/loss will then be fully recognized—a $30,000 gain to Amanda and a $10,000 loss to Calvin. ■

Section 351 is *mandatory* if a transaction satisfies the provision's requirements. The three requirements for nonrecognition of gain or loss under § 351 are that (1) *property* is transferred (2) in exchange for *stock* and (3) the property transferors are in *control* of the corporation after the exchange. Therefore, if recognition of gain or loss is *desired*, the taxpayer must plan to fail to meet at least one of these requirements.

PROPERTY DEFINED

Questions have arisen concerning what constitutes **property** for purposes of § 351. In general, the definition of property is comprehensive. For example, along with plant and equipment, unrealized receivables of a cash basis taxpayer and installment obligations are considered property.[3] Although the disposition of an installment note receivable normally triggers deferred gain, its transfer under § 351 is not treated as a disposition. Thus, gain is not recognized to the transferor. Secret processes and

[1] § 351(b) and Rev.Rul. 68–55, 1968–1 C.B. 140.

[2] § 358(a). See the discussion preceding Example 20.

[3] *Hempt Brothers, Inc. v. U.S.*, 74–1 USTC ¶9188, 33 AFTR 2d 74–570, 490 F.2d 1172 (CA–3, 1974), and Reg. § 1.453–9(c)(2).

formulas, as well as secret information in the general nature of a patentable invention, also qualify as property under § 351.[4]

However, the Code specifically excludes services rendered from the definition of property. Services are not considered to be property under § 351 for a critical reason. A taxpayer must report as income the fair market value of any consideration received as compensation for services rendered.[5] Consequently, when a taxpayer receives stock in a corporation as consideration for rendering services to the corporation, taxable income results. In this case, the amount of income recognized by the taxpayer is equal to the fair market value of the stock received. The taxpayer's basis in the stock received is its fair market value.

EXAMPLE 3

Ann and Bob form Olive Corporation with the transfer of the following consideration:

	Consideration Transferred		
	Basis to Transferor	Fair Market Value	Number of Shares Issued
From Ann:			
Personal services rendered to Olive Corporation	$ –0–	$20,000	200
From Bob:			
Installment obligation	5,000	40,000	
Inventory	10,000	30,000	800
Secret process	–0–	10,000	

The value of each share in Olive Corporation is $100.[6] Ann has income of $20,000 on the transfer because services do not qualify as "property." She has a basis of $20,000 in her 200 shares of Olive (i.e., Ann is treated as having bought some of the Olive stock by rendering services). Bob has no recognized gain on the receipt of stock because all of the consideration he transfers to Olive qualifies as "property" and he has "control" of Olive after the transfer; see the discussion concerning control that follows. Bob has a substituted basis of $15,000 in the Olive stock. ■

STOCK TRANSFERRED

Nonrecognition of gain occurs only when the shareholder receives stock. Stock includes both common and most preferred. However, it does not include "nonqualified preferred stock," which possesses many of the attributes of debt. In addition, the Regulations state that the term "stock" does not include stock rights and stock warrants. Otherwise, the term "stock" generally needs no clarification.[7]

Thus, any corporate debt or **securities** (e.g., long-term debt such as bonds) received are treated as boot because they do not qualify as stock. Therefore, the receipt of debt in exchange for the transfer of appreciated property to a controlled corporation causes recognition of gain.

EXAMPLE 4
THE BIG PICTURE

Return to the facts of *The Big Picture* on p. 4-2. Assume the proposed transaction qualifies under § 351 (i.e., the transfer of *property* in exchange for *stock* meets the *control* test), but Emily decides to receive some corporate debt along with the stock. If she receives stock worth $450,000 and corporate debt of $50,000 in exchange for the property transferred, Emily realizes gain of $300,000 [$500,000 (value of consideration

[4]Rev.Rul. 64–56, 1964–1 C.B. 133; Rev.Rul. 71–564, 1971–2 C.B. 179.

[5]§§ 61 and 83.

[6]The value of closely held stock normally is presumed to be equal to the value of the property transferred.

[7]§ 351(g). Examples of nonqualified preferred stock include preferred stock that is redeemable within 20 years of issuance and whose dividend rate is based on factors other than corporate performance. Therefore, gain is recognized up to the fair market value of the nonqualified preferred stock received. Loss may be recognized when the transferor receives *only* nonqualified preferred stock (or nonqualified preferred stock and other boot) in exchange for property. See also Reg. § 1.351–1(a)(1)(ii).

received) – $200,000 (basis in the transferred property)]. However, because the transaction qualifies under § 351, only $50,000 of gain is recognized—the $50,000 of corporate debt is treated as boot. The remaining realized gain of $250,000 is deferred. ■

CONTROL OF THE CORPORATION

For the transaction to qualify as nontaxable under § 351, the property transferors must be in **control** of the corporation immediately after the exchange. Control means that the person or persons transferring the property must have at least an 80 percent stock ownership in the corporation. More specifically, the property transferors must own stock possessing at least 80 percent of the total combined *voting power* of all classes of stock entitled to vote *and* at least 80 percent of the total *number of shares* of all other classes of stock.[8]

Control Immediately after the Transfer

Immediately after the exchange, the property transferors must control the corporation. Control can apply to a single person or to several taxpayers if they are all parties to an integrated transaction. When more than one person is involved, the exchange does not necessarily require simultaneous exchanges by those persons. However, the rights of those transferring property to the corporation must be previously set out and determined. Also, the agreement to transfer property should be executed "with an expedition consistent with orderly procedure."[9] Therefore, if two or more persons transfer property to a corporation for stock and want to defer gain, it is helpful if the transfers occur close together in time and are made in accordance with an agreement among the parties.

EXAMPLE 5

Jack exchanges property, basis of $60,000 and fair market value of $100,000, for 70% of the stock of Gray Corporation. The other 30% of the stock is owned by Jane, who acquired it several years ago. The fair market value of Jack's stock is $100,000. Jack recognizes a taxable gain of $40,000 on the transfer because he does not have control of the corporation after his transfer and his transaction cannot be integrated with Jane's for purposes of the control requirement. ■

EXAMPLE 6

Rebecca, Daryl, and Paige incorporate their businesses by forming Green Corporation. Rebecca exchanges her property for 300 shares in Green on January 7, 2011. Daryl exchanges his property for 400 shares of Green Corporation stock on January 14, 2011, and Paige exchanges her property for 300 shares in Green on March 4, 2011. Because the three exchanges are part of a prearranged plan and the control test is met, the nonrecognition provisions of § 351 apply to all of the exchanges. ■

Stock need not be issued to the property transferors in the same proportion as the relative value of the property transferred by each. However, when stock received is not proportionate to the value of the property transferred, the actual effect of the transactions must be properly characterized. For example, in such situations one transferor may actually be making a gift of valuable consideration to another transferor.

EXAMPLE 7

Ron and Shelia, father and daughter, form Oak Corporation. Ron transfers property worth $50,000 in exchange for 100 shares of stock, while Shelia transfers property worth $50,000 for 400 shares of stock. The transfers qualify under § 351 because Ron and Shelia have control of the Oak stock immediately after the transfers of property. However, the implicit gift by Ron to Shelia must be recognized and appropriately characterized. As such, the value of the gift might be subject to the gift tax (see Chapter 18). ■

[8] § 368(c). Nonqualified preferred stock is treated as stock, and not boot, for purposes of this control test.

[9] Reg. § 1.351–1(a)(1).

A Professional-Free Incorporation

Allen and Beth agree to form Jay Corporation. Allen, who has a reputation for being extremely frugal, decides to follow instructions for incorporating a business that he has found on a free Internet site. Based on his plan, Allen transfers appreciated property to Jay Corporation in exchange for 75 percent of its stock. Beth agrees to provide services to the business for 25 percent of the stock.

Several months later, Allen learns that he has made a terrible blunder. To avoid paying tax on the transfer of his appreciated property, he should have received 80 percent, not 75 percent, of the stock. To correct the problem, Allen persuades Beth to transfer to him 5 percent of the corporation's stock. In return, Allen will give Beth some antiques he has collected. Allen tells Beth that this is a better deal for her because now she will have to report the value of only 20 percent of the corporation's stock as income (instead of 25 percent). Further, she receives the antiques as a tax-free gift.

How do you react to Allen's actions?

Once control has been achieved, it is not necessarily lost if stock received by shareholders is sold or given to persons who are not parties to the exchange shortly after the transaction. However, a different result might materialize if a *plan* for the ultimate disposition of the stock existed *before* the exchange.[10]

EXAMPLE 8

Naomi and Eric form Eagle Corporation. They transfer appreciated property to the corporation with each receiving 50 shares of the stock. Shortly after the formation, Naomi gives 25 shares to her son. Because Naomi was not committed to make the gift, she is considered to own her original shares of Eagle Corporation stock and, along with Eric, to control Eagle "immediately after the exchange." Therefore, the requirements of § 351 are met, and neither Naomi nor Eric is taxed on the exchange. Alternatively, had Naomi immediately given 25 shares to a business associate pursuant to a plan to satisfy an outstanding obligation, the formation of Eagle would be taxable to Naomi and Eric because of their lack of control (i.e., Naomi and Eric, the property transferors, would own only 75% of the stock). ■

Transfers for Property and Services

Nonrecognition treatment for the property transferors may be lost if "too much" stock is transferred to persons who did not contribute property.

EXAMPLE 9
THE BIG PICTURE

Return to the facts of *The Big Picture* on p. 4-2. Assume Emily transfers her $500,000 of property to the new corporation and receives 50% of its stock. David receives the other 50% of the stock for services rendered (worth $500,000). Both Emily and David have tax consequences from the transfers. David has ordinary income of $500,000 because he does not exchange property for stock. Emily has a taxable gain of $300,000 [$500,000 (fair market value of the stock in the new corporation) – $200,000 (basis in the transferred property)]. As the sole transferor of property, she receives only 50% of the corporation's stock. ■

A person who receives stock both in exchange for services and for property transferred may be treated as a member of the transferring group for purposes of the control test. When this is the case, the person is taxed on the value of the stock issued for services but not on the stock issued for property, assuming the property transferors control the corporation. In this case, all the stock received by the person transferring both property and services is counted in determining whether the transferors acquired control of the corporation.[11]

[10] *Wilgard Realty Co. v. Comm.*, 42–1 USTC ¶9452, 29 AFTR 325, 127 F.2d 514 (CA–2, 1942).

[11] Reg. § 1.351–1(a)(2), Ex. 3.

EXAMPLE 10
THE BIG PICTURE

Assume the same facts as in Example 9 except that David transfers property worth $400,000 (basis of $130,000) in addition to services rendered to the corporation (valued at $100,000). Now David becomes a part of the control group. Emily and David, as property transferors, together receive 100% of the corporation's stock. Consequently, § 351 is applicable to the exchanges. As a result, Emily has no recognized gain. David does not recognize gain on the transfer of the property, but he recognizes ordinary income to the extent of the value of the shares issued for services rendered. David has current taxable income of $100,000. ■

Transfers for Services and Nominal Property

To be a member of the group and aid in qualifying all transferors under the 80 percent control test, the person contributing services must transfer property having more than a "relatively small value" compared to the services performed. The Regulations provide that stock issued for property whose value is relatively small compared to the value of the stock already owned (or to be received for services rendered) will not be treated as issued in return for property. This will be the result when the primary purpose of the transfer is to qualify the transaction under § 351 for concurrent transferors.[12]

EXAMPLE 11

Rosalyn and Mark transfer property to Redbird Corporation, each in exchange for one-third of the stock. Reed receives the other one-third of the stock for services rendered. The transaction does not qualify under § 351 because Reed is not a member of the group transferring property and Rosalyn and Mark, as the sole property transferors, together receive only $66\frac{2}{3}$% of the stock. As a result, the post-transfer control requirement is not met.

Assume instead that Reed also transfers a substantial amount of property. Then he is a member of the group, and the transaction qualifies under § 351. Reed is taxed on the value of the stock issued for services, but the remainder of the transaction does not trigger gain or loss recognition. However, if the property transferred by Reed is of a relatively small value in comparison to the stock he receives for his services, and the primary purpose for transferring the property is to cause the transaction to be tax-free for Rosalyn and Mark, the exchange does not qualify under § 351 for any of the taxpayers. ■

Exactly when a taxpayer who renders services and transfers property is included in the control group is often subject to question. However, the IRS has stated that such a transferor can be included in the control group if the value of the property transferred is at least 10 percent of the value of the services provided.[13] If the value of the property transferred is less than this amount, the IRS will not issue an advance ruling that the exchange meets the requirements of § 351.

EXAMPLE 12

Sara and Rick form Grouse Corporation. Sara transfers land (worth $100,000, basis of $20,000) for 50% of the stock in Grouse. Rick transfers equipment (worth $50,000, adjusted basis of $10,000) and provides services worth $50,000 for 50% of the stock. Because the value of the property Rick transfers is not small relative to the value of the services he renders, his stock in Grouse Corporation is counted in determining control for purposes of § 351; thus, the transferors own 100% of the stock in Grouse. In addition, all of Rick's stock, not just the shares received for the equipment, is counted in determining control. As a result, Sara does not recognize gain on the transfer of the land. Rick, however, must recognize income of $50,000 on the transfer of services. Even though the transfer of the equipment qualifies under § 351, his transfer of services for stock does not.

Alternatively, had the value of Rick's property been small relative to the value of his services, the transaction would be fully taxable to both Sara and Rick. In that situation, Sara, the sole property transferor, would not have at least 80% control of Grouse Corporation following the transfer. As a result, she would fully recognize her realized

[12] Reg. § 1.351–1(a)(1)(ii).

[13] Rev.Proc. 77–37, 1977–2 C.B. 568.

gain. Further, because Rick would not be treated as having transferred property, the § 351 deferral would not be available to him either. ■

Transfers to Existing Corporations

Once a corporation is in operation, § 351 also applies to any later transfers of property for stock by either new or existing shareholders.

EXAMPLE 13

Tyrone and Seth formed Blue Corporation three years ago. Both Tyrone and Seth transferred appreciated property to Blue in exchange for 50 shares each in the corporation. The original transfers qualified under § 351, and neither Tyrone nor Seth was taxed on the exchange. In the current year, Tyrone transfers property (worth $90,000, adjusted basis of $5,000) for 50 additional Blue shares. Tyrone has a taxable gain of $85,000 on the transfer. The exchange does not qualify under § 351 because Tyrone does not have 80% control of Blue Corporation immediately after the transfer—he owns 100 shares of the 150 shares outstanding, or a $66^2/_3$% interest. ■

See the Tax Planning portion of this chapter for additional discussion of this issue.

ASSUMPTION OF LIABILITIES—§ 357

LO.2

Understand the special rules that apply when liabilities are assumed by a corporation.

Without a provision to the contrary, the transfer of mortgaged property to a controlled corporation could trigger gain to the property transferor if the corporation took over the mortgage. This would be consistent with the treatment given in like-kind exchanges under § 1031. Generally, when liabilities are assumed by another party, the party who is relieved of the debt is treated as having received cash or boot. Section 357(a) provides, however, that when the acquiring corporation assumes a liability in a § 351 transaction, the liability is not treated as boot received for gain recognition purposes. Nevertheless, liabilities assumed by the transferee corporation are treated as boot in determining the basis of the stock received by the shareholder. As a result, the basis of the stock received is reduced by the amount of the liabilities assumed by the corporation. See the more complete discussion of basis computations later.

EXAMPLE 14

Vera transfers property with an adjusted basis of $60,000, fair market value of $100,000, to Oriole Corporation for 100% of the stock in Oriole. The property is subject to a liability of $25,000 that Oriole Corporation assumes. The exchange is tax-free under § 351 because the release of a liability is not treated as boot under § 357(a). However, the basis to Vera of the Oriole stock is $35,000 [$60,000 (basis of property transferred) – $25,000 (amount of the liability assumed by Oriole)]. ■

The general rule of § 357(a) has two exceptions: (1) § 357(b) provides that if the principal purpose of the assumption of the liabilities is to avoid tax *or* if there is no bona fide business purpose behind the exchange, the liabilities are treated as boot; and (2) § 357(c) provides that if the sum of the liabilities exceeds the adjusted basis of the properties transferred, the excess is taxable gain.

Exception (1): Tax Avoidance or No Bona Fide Business Purpose

Unless liabilities are incurred shortly before incorporation, § 357(b) generally poses few problems. A tax avoidance purpose for transferring liabilities to a controlled corporation normally is not a concern in view of the basis adjustment as noted above. Since the liabilities transferred reduce the basis of the stock received, any realized gain merely is deferred and not completely eliminated. Any postponed gain is recognized when and if the stock is disposed of in a taxable sale or exchange.

Satisfying the bona fide business purpose requirement is not difficult if the liabilities were incurred in connection with the transferor's normal course of conducting a trade or business. But this requirement can cause difficulty if the liability is taken out shortly before the property is transferred and the proceeds are utilized for personal purposes.[14] This type of situation is analogous to a cash distribution by the corporation to the shareholder, which is taxed as boot.

EXAMPLE 15

Dan transfers real estate (basis of $40,000 and fair market value of $90,000) to a controlled corporation in return for stock in the corporation. However, shortly before the transfer, Dan mortgages the real estate and uses the $20,000 proceeds to meet personal obligations. Thus, along with the real estate, the mortgage is transferred to the corporation. In this case, the assumption of the mortgage lacks a bona fide business purpose. Consequently, the release of the liability is treated as boot received, and Dan has a taxable gain on the transfer of $20,000.[15]

Amount realized:	
Stock	$ 70,000
Release of liability—treated as boot	20,000
Total amount realized	$ 90,000
Less: Basis of real estate	(40,000)
Realized gain	$ 50,000
Recognized gain	$ 20,000

■

The effect of the application of § 357(b) is to taint *all* liabilities transferred even if some are supported by a bona fide business purpose.

EXAMPLE 16

Tim, an accrual basis taxpayer, incorporates his sole proprietorship. Among the liabilities transferred to the new corporation are trade accounts payable of $100,000 and a credit card bill of $5,000. Tim had used the credit card to purchase a wedding anniversary gift for his wife. Under these circumstances, *all* of the $105,000 liabilities are treated as boot and trigger the recognition of gain to the extent gain is realized. ■

Exception (2): Liabilities in Excess of Basis

The second exception, § 357(c), provides that if the amount of the liabilities assumed exceeds the total of the adjusted bases of the properties transferred, the excess is taxable gain. Without this provision, when **liabilities exceed the basis** in property exchanged, a taxpayer would have a negative basis in the stock received in the controlled corporation.[16] Section 357(c) precludes the negative basis possibility by treating the excess over basis as gain to the transferor.

EXAMPLE 17

Andre transfers land and equipment with adjusted bases of $35,000 and $5,000, respectively, to a newly formed corporation in exchange for 100% of the stock. The corporation assumes the liability on the transferred land in the amount of $50,000. Without § 357(c), Andre's basis in the stock of the new corporation would be a negative $10,000 [$40,000 (bases of properties transferred) + $0 (gain recognized) – $0 (boot received) – $50,000 (liability assumed)]. Section 357(c), however, requires Andre to recognize a gain of $10,000 ($50,000 liability assumed – $40,000 bases of assets transferred). As a result, the stock has a zero basis in Andre's hands, determined as follows:

Bases in the properties transferred ($35,000 + $5,000)	$ 40,000
Plus: Gain recognized	10,000
Less: Boot received	–0–
Less: Liability assumed	(50,000)
Basis in the stock received	$ –0–

Thus, Andre recognizes $10,000 of gain, and a negative stock basis is avoided. ■

[14] See, for example, *Campbell, Jr. v. Wheeler*, 65–1 USTC ¶9294, 15 AFTR 2d 578, 342 F.2d 837 (CA–5, 1965).

[15] § 351(b).

[16] *Jack L. Easson*, 33 T.C. 963 (1960), *rev'd* in 61–2 USTC ¶9654, 8 AFTR 2d 5448, 294 F.2d 653 (CA–9, 1961).

The definition of liabilities under § 357(c) excludes obligations that would have been deductible to the transferor had those obligations been paid before the transfer. Therefore, accounts payable of a cash basis taxpayer are not considered to be liabilities for purposes of § 357(c). In addition, they are not considered in the computation of the shareholder's stock basis.

EXAMPLE 18

Tina, a cash basis taxpayer, incorporates her sole proprietorship. In return for all of the stock of the new corporation, she transfers the following items:

	Adjusted Basis	Fair Market Value
Cash	$10,000	$10,000
Unrealized accounts receivable (amounts due to Tina but not yet received by her)	–0–	40,000
Trade accounts payable	–0–	30,000
Note payable	5,000	5,000

Because the unrealized accounts receivable and trade accounts payable have a zero basis under the cash method of accounting, no income is recognized until the receivables are collected, and no deduction materializes until the payables are satisfied. The note payable has a basis because it was issued for consideration received.

In this situation, the trade accounts payable are disregarded for gain recognition purposes and in determining Tina's stock basis. Thus, for purposes of § 357(c), because the balance of the note payable does not exceed the basis of the assets transferred, Tina does not have a problem of liabilities in excess of basis (i.e., the note payable of $5,000 does not exceed the aggregate basis in the cash and accounts receivable of $10,000). ■

Conceivably, a situation could arise where both §§ 357(b) and (c) apply in the same transfer. In such a situation, § 357(b) predominates.[17] This could be significant because § 357(b) does not create gain on the transfer, as does § 357(c), but merely converts the liability to boot. Thus, the realized gain limitation continues to apply to § 357(b) transactions.

EXAMPLE 19

Chris forms Robin Corporation by transferring land with a basis of $100,000, fair market value of $1 million. The land is subject to a mortgage of $300,000. One month prior to incorporating Robin, Chris borrows $200,000 for personal purposes and gives the lender a second mortgage on the land. Therefore, on the incorporation, Robin issues stock worth $500,000 to Chris and assumes the two mortgages on the land. Section 357(c) seems to apply to the transfer, given that the mortgages on the property ($500,000) exceed the basis of the property ($100,000). Thus, Chris would have a gain of $400,000 under § 357(c). Section 357(b), however, also applies to the transfer because Chris borrowed $200,000 just prior to the transfer and used the loan proceeds for personal purposes. Thus, under § 357(b), Chris has boot of $500,000 in the amount of the liabilities. Note that *all* of the liabilities are treated as boot, not just the tainted $200,000 liability. Consequently, he has realized gain of $900,000 [$1,000,000 (stock of $500,000 and assumption of liabilities of $500,000) – $100,000 (basis in the land)], and gain is recognized to the extent of the boot received of $500,000. Unfortunately for Chris, the relatively more onerous rule of § 357(b) predominates over § 357(c) ■

BASIS DETERMINATION AND RELATED ISSUES

LO.3

Recognize the basis issues relevant to the shareholder and the corporation.

Recall that § 351(a) postpones gain or loss until the transferor-shareholder disposes of the stock in a taxable transaction. The postponement of shareholder gain or loss has a corollary effect on the basis of the stock received by the shareholder and the

[17] § 357(c)(2)(A).

FIGURE 4.1	Shareholder's Basis of Stock Received in Exchange for Property
Adjusted basis of property transferred	$xx,xxx
Plus: Gain recognized	xxx
Minus: Boot received (including any liabilities transferred)	(xxx)
Minus: Adjustment for loss property (if elected)	(xxx)
Equals: Basis of stock received	$xx,xxx

basis of the property received by the corporation. This procedure ensures that any gain or loss postponed under § 351 ultimately will be recognized when the affected asset is disposed of in a taxable transaction.

Basis of Stock to Shareholder

For a taxpayer transferring property to a corporation in a § 351 transaction, the *stock* received in the transaction is given a substituted basis. Essentially, the stock's basis is the same as the basis the taxpayer had in the property transferred, increased by any gain recognized on the exchange of property and decreased by boot received. Recall that for basis purposes, boot received includes liabilities transferred by the shareholder to the corporation. Also note that if the shareholder receives *other property* (i.e., boot) along with the stock, it takes a basis equal to its fair market value.[18] In Figure 4.1, the reference to gain recognized does not consider any income resulting from the performance of personal services. (Recall from earlier discussions that the basis of stock received for services rendered equals its fair market value.) See the discussion that follows relating to an elective stock basis reduction that may be made when a shareholder contributes property with a net built-in loss.

Basis of Property to Corporation

The basis of *property* received by the corporation generally is determined under a carryover basis rule. This rule provides that the property's basis to the corporation is equal to the basis in the hands of the transferor increased by the amount of any gain recognized on the transfer by the transferor-shareholder.[19]

These basis rules are illustrated in Examples 20 and 21.

EXAMPLE 20

Kesha and Ned form Brown Corporation. Kesha transfers land (basis of $30,000 and fair market value of $70,000); Ned invests cash ($60,000). They each receive 50 shares in Brown Corporation, worth $60,000, but Kesha also receives $10,000 in cash from Brown. The transfers of property, the realized and recognized gain on the transfers, and the basis of the stock in Brown Corporation to Kesha and Ned are as follows:

	A	B	C	D	E	F
	Basis of Property Transferred	FMV of Stock Received	Boot Received	Realized Gain (B + C – A)	Recognized Gain (Lesser of C or D)	Basis of Stock in Brown (A – C + E)
From Kesha:						
Land	$30,000	$60,000	$10,000	$40,000	$10,000	$30,000
From Ned:						
Cash	60,000	60,000	–0–	–0–	–0–	60,000

Brown Corporation has a basis of $40,000 in the land (Kesha's basis of $30,000 plus her recognized gain of $10,000). ■

[18] § 358(a).

[19] § 362(a).

FIGURE 4.2 **Corporation's Basis in Property Received**

Adjusted basis of property transferred	$xx,xxx
Plus: Gain recognized by transferor-shareholder	xxx
Minus: Adjustment for loss property (if required)	(xxx)
Equals: Basis of property to corporation	$xx,xxx

EXAMPLE 21

Assume the same facts as in Example 20 except that Kesha's basis in the land is $68,000 (instead of $30,000). Because recognized gain cannot exceed realized gain, the transfer generates only $2,000 of gain to Kesha. The realized and recognized gain and the basis of the stock in Brown Corporation to Kesha are as follows:

	A	B	C	D	E	F
	Basis of Property Transferred	**FMV of Stock Received**	**Boot Received**	**Realized Gain (B + C – A)**	**Recognized Gain (Lesser of C or D)**	**Basis of Stock in Brown (A – C + E)**
Land	$68,000	$60,000	$10,000	$2,000	$2,000	$60,000

Brown's basis in the land is $70,000 ($68,000 basis to Kesha + $2,000 gain recognized by Kesha). ■

Figure 4.2 summarizes the basis calculation for property received by a corporation. Concept Summary 4.1 shows the shareholder and corporate consequences of a transfer of property to a corporation for stock, with and without the application of § 351. The facts applicable to shareholder Kesha's transfer in Example 20 are used to illustrate the differences between the transaction being tax deferred and taxable.

Basis Adjustment for Loss Property

As noted above, when a corporation receives property in a § 351 transaction, the basis for that property is carried over from the shareholder. As a result, the corporation's basis for the property has no correlation to its fair market value. However, in certain situations when **built-in loss property** is contributed to a corporation, its aggregate basis in the property may have to be stepped down so that the basis does not exceed the fair market value of the property transferred. This basis adjustment is necessary to prevent the parties from obtaining a double benefit from the losses involved.

The anti-loss duplication rule applies when the aggregate basis of the assets transferred by a shareholder exceeds their fair market value. When this built-in loss situation exists, the basis in the loss properties is stepped down. The step-down in basis is allocated proportionately among the assets with the built-in loss.[20]

EXAMPLE 22

In a transaction qualifying under § 351, Charles transfers the following assets to Gold Corporation in exchange for all of its stock:

	Tax Basis	Fair Market Value	Built-in Gain/ (Loss)
Equipment	$100,000	$ 90,000	($ 10,000)
Land	200,000	230,000	30,000
Building	150,000	100,000	(50,000)
	$450,000	$420,000	($ 30,000)

[20] § 362(e)(2). This adjustment is determined separately with respect to each property transferor. In addition, this adjustment also is required in the case of a contribution to capital by a shareholder.

CONCEPT SUMMARY 4.1

Tax Consequences to the Shareholders and Corporation: With and Without the Application of § 351 (Based on the Facts of Example 20)

	With § 351			Without § 351		
Shareholder	Gain/Loss Recognized	Stock Basis	Other Property Basis	Gain/Loss Recognized	Stock Basis	Other Property Basis
Kesha	Realized gain recognized to extent of boot received; loss not recognized.	Substituted (see Figure 4.1).	FMV	All realized gain or loss recognized.	FMV	FMV
	$10,000	$30,000	$10,000	$40,000	$60,000	$10,000

	With § 351		Without § 351	
Corporation	Gain/Loss Recognized	Property Basis	Gain/Loss Recognized	Property Basis
Brown	No gain or loss recognized on the transfer of corporate stock for property.	Carryover (see Figure 4.2).	No gain or loss recognized on the transfer of corporate stock for property.	FMV
	$0	$40,000	$0	$70,000

Note that the benefit to Kesha of deferring $30,000 of gain under § 351 comes with a cost: her stock basis is $30,000 (rather than $60,000), and the corporation's basis in the property received is $40,000 (rather than $70,000).

Charles's stock basis is $450,000 [$450,000 (basis of the property transferred) + $0 (gain recognized) − $0 (boot received)]. However, Gold's basis for the loss assets transferred must be reduced by the amount of the net built-in loss ($30,000) in proportion to each asset's share of the loss.

	Unadjusted Tax Basis	Adjustment	Adjusted Tax Basis
Equipment	$100,000	($ 5,000)*	$ 95,000
Land	200,000		200,000
Building	150,000	(25,000)**	125,000
	$450,000	($ 30,000)	$420,000

$$\frac{\text{*\$10,000 (loss attributable to equipment)}}{\text{\$60,000 (\textit{total} built-in loss)}} \times \text{\$30,000 (\textit{net} built-in loss)}$$

= $5,000 (adjustment to basis in equipment).

$$\frac{\text{**\$50,000 (loss attributable to building)}}{\text{\$60,000 (\textit{total} built-in loss)}} \times \text{\$30,000 (\textit{net} built-in loss)}$$

= $25,000 (adjustment to basis in building). ■

Note the end result of Example 22:

- Charles still has a built-in loss in his stock basis. Thus, if he sells the Gold Corporation stock, he will recognize a loss of $30,000 [$420,000 (selling price based on presumed value of the stock) − $450,000 (basis in the stock)].

- Gold Corporation can no longer recognize any loss on the sale of *all* of its assets [$420,000 (selling price based on value of assets) – $420,000 (adjusted basis in assets) = $0 (gain or loss)].

In the event a corporation is subject to the built-in loss adjustment, an alternative approach is available. If the shareholder and the corporation both elect, the basis reduction can be made to the shareholder's stock rather than to the corporation's property.

EXAMPLE 23

Assume the same facts as in the previous example. If Charles and Gold elect, Charles can reduce his stock basis to $420,000 ($450,000 – $30,000). As a result, Gold's aggregate basis in the assets it receives is $450,000. If Charles has no intention of selling his stock, this election could be desirable as it benefits Gold by giving the corporation a higher depreciable basis in the equipment and building. ■

Note the end result of Example 23:

- Charles has no built-in loss. Thus, if he sells the Gold Corporation stock, he will recognize no gain or loss [$420,000 (presumed value of the stock) – $420,000 (basis in the stock)].
- Gold Corporation has a built-in loss. Thus, if it sells *all* of its assets [$420,000 (selling price based on value of assets) – $450,000 (basis in assets)], it recognizes a loss of $30,000.

Consequently, the built-in loss adjustment places the loss with either the shareholder or the corporation but not both (compare Examples 22 and 23).

Stock Issued for Services Rendered

A transfer of stock for services is not a taxable transaction to a corporation.[21] But another issue arises: Can a corporation deduct the fair market value of the stock it issues in consideration of services as a business expense? Yes, unless the services are such that the payment is characterized as a capital expenditure.[22]

EXAMPLE 24

Esther and Carl form White Corporation. Esther transfers cash of $500,000 for 100 shares of White Corporation stock. Carl transfers property worth $400,000 (basis of $90,000) and agrees to serve as manager of the corporation for one year; in return, Carl receives 100 shares of stock in White. The value of Carl's services to White Corporation is $100,000. Esther's and Carl's transfers qualify under § 351. Neither Esther nor Carl is taxed on the transfer of their property. However, Carl has income of $100,000, the value of the stock received for the services he will render to White Corporation. White has a basis of $90,000 in the property it acquired from Carl, and it may claim a compensation expense deduction under § 162 for $100,000. Carl's stock basis is $190,000 [$90,000 (basis of property transferred) + $100,000 (income recognized for services rendered)]. ■

EXAMPLE 25

Assume the same facts as in Example 24 except that Carl provides legal services (instead of management services) in organizing the corporation. The value of Carl's legal services is $100,000. Carl has no gain on the transfer of the property but has income of $100,000 for the value of the stock received for the services rendered. White Corporation has a basis of $90,000 in the property it acquired from Carl and must capitalize the $100,000 as an organizational expenditure. Carl's stock basis is $190,000 [$90,000 (basis of property transferred) + $100,000 (income recognized for services rendered)]. ■

[21] Reg. § 1.1032–1(a).

[22] Rev.Rul. 62–217, 1962–2 C.B. 59, modified by Rev.Rul. 74–503, 1974–2 C.B. 117.

GLOBAL *Tax Issues*

Does § 351 Cover the Incorporation of a Foreign Business?

When a taxpayer wishes to incorporate a business overseas by moving assets across U.S. borders, the deferral mechanism of § 351 applies in certain situations, but not in others. In general, § 351 is available to defer gain recognition when starting up a new corporation outside the United States unless so-called tainted assets are involved. Under § 367, tainted assets, which include assets such as inventory and accounts receivable, are treated as having been sold by the taxpayer prior to the corporate formation; therefore, their transfer results in the current recognition of gain. The presence of tainted assets triggers gain because Congress does not want taxpayers to be able to shift the gain outside the U.S. jurisdiction. The gain recognized is ordinary or capital, depending on the nature of the asset involved.

Holding Period for Shareholder and Transferee Corporation

In a § 351 transfer, the shareholder's holding period for stock received in exchange for a capital asset or § 1231 property includes the holding period of the property transferred to the corporation. That is, the holding period of the property is "tacked on" to the holding period of the stock. The holding period for stock received for any other property (e.g., inventory) begins on the day after the exchange. The corporation's holding period for property acquired in a § 351 transfer is the holding period of the transferor-shareholder, regardless of the character of the property in the transferor's hands.[23]

Recapture Considerations

In a § 351(a) transfer where no gain is recognized, the depreciation recapture rules do not apply.[24] However, any recapture potential associated with the property carries over to the corporation as it steps into the shoes of the transferor-shareholder for purposes of basis determination.

EXAMPLE 26

Paul transfers equipment (adjusted basis of $30,000, original cost of $120,000, and fair market value of $100,000) to a controlled corporation in return for stock. If Paul had sold the equipment, it would have yielded a gain of $70,000, all of which would be recaptured as ordinary income under § 1245. Because the transfer comes within § 351(a), Paul has no recognized gain and no depreciation to recapture. However, if the corporation later disposes of the equipment in a taxable transaction, it must take into account the § 1245 recapture potential originating with Paul. ■

4.2 Capital Structure of a Corporation

LO.4

Appreciate the tax aspects of the capital structure of a corporation.

CAPITAL CONTRIBUTIONS

When a corporation receives money or property in exchange for capital stock (including treasury stock), neither gain nor loss is recognized by the corporation.[25] Nor does a corporation's gross income include shareholders' contributions of money or property to the capital of the corporation. Moreover, additional money or property received from shareholders through voluntary pro rata transfers also is not income to the corporation. This is the case even though there is no increase in the

[23] §§ 1223(1) and (2).

[24] §§ 1245(b)(3) and 1250(d)(3).

[25] § 1032.

TAX *in* the NEWS

During Both Good and Bad Times, Local and State Governments Compete

As a business seeks to grow and strategies shift, managers must be on the lookout for locations that will best suit their needs. Among the factors that can make a critical difference in an expansion or relocation decision is the availability of tax incentives offered by state and local governments as inducements.

As an example, Northrop Grumman, a leading global security company, recently decided to move its headquarters from Los Angeles to the Washington, D.C. area to be closer to its largest client, the Federal government. As part of the process of choosing the particular location, the company negotiated with government officials in Washington, D.C., Maryland, and Virginia. In the end, Northrop Grumman chose Fairfax County, Virginia, because of the incentive package pieced together by the state and local governments. In return, Northrop Grumman is expected to make a $24 million investment at its new facility and create 300 new jobs with average annual salaries of $200,000.

outstanding shares of stock of the corporation. The contributions represent an additional price paid for the shares held by the shareholders and are treated as additions to the operating capital of the corporation.[26]

Contributions by nonshareholders, such as land contributed to a corporation by a civic group or a governmental group to induce the corporation to locate in a particular community, are also excluded from the gross income of a corporation.[27] However, if the property is transferred to a corporation by a nonshareholder in exchange for goods or services, then the corporation must recognize income.[28]

EXAMPLE 27

A cable television company charges its customers an initial fee to hook up to a new cable system installed in the area. These payments are used to finance the total cost of constructing the cable facilities. In addition, the customers will make monthly payments for the cable service. The initial payments are used for capital expenditures, but they represent payments for services to be rendered by the cable company. As such, they are taxable income to the cable company and not contributions to capital by nonshareholders. ■

The basis of property received by a corporation from a shareholder as a **capital contribution** is equal to the basis of the property in the hands of the shareholder, although the basis is subject to a downward adjustment when loss property is contributed. The basis of property transferred to a corporation by a nonshareholder as a contribution to capital is zero.

If a corporation receives *money* as a contribution to capital from a nonshareholder, a special rule applies. The basis of any property acquired with the money during a 12-month period beginning on the day the contribution was received is reduced by the amount of the contribution. The excess of money received over the cost of new property reduces the basis of other property held by the corporation and is applied in the following order:

- Depreciable property.
- Property subject to amortization.
- Property subject to depletion.
- All other remaining properties.

---

[26]§ 118 and Reg. § 1.118–1.

[27]See *Edwards v. Cuba Railroad Co.*, 1 USTC ¶139, 5 AFTR 5398, 45 S.Ct. 614 (USSC, 1925).

[28]Reg. § 1.118–1. See also *Teleservice Co. of Wyoming Valley*, 27 T.C. 722 (1957), *aff'd* in 58–1 USTC ¶9383, 1 AFTR 2d 1249, 254 F.2d 105 (CA–3, 1958), *cert. den.* 78 S.Ct. 1360 (USSC, 1958).

The basis of property within each category is reduced in proportion to the relative bases of the properties.[29]

EXAMPLE 28

A city donates land worth $400,000 to Teal Corporation as an inducement for Teal to locate in the city. The receipt of the land produces no taxable income to Teal, and the land's basis to the corporation is zero. If, in addition, the city gives the corporation $100,000 in cash, the money is not taxable income to the corporation. However, if the corporation purchases property with the $100,000 cash within the next 12 months, the basis of the acquired property is reduced by $100,000. Any excess cash retained by Teal is handled according to the ordering rules noted above. ■

LO.5

Recognize the tax differences between debt and equity investments.

DEBT IN THE CAPITAL STRUCTURE

Advantages of Debt

Significant tax differences exist between debt and equity in the capital structure. The advantages of issuing long-term debt instead of stock are numerous. Interest on debt is deductible by the corporation, while dividend payments are not. Further, loan repayments are not taxable to investors unless the repayments exceed basis. A shareholder's receipt of property from a corporation, however, cannot be tax-free as long as the corporation has earnings and profits (see Chapter 5). Such distributions will be taxed as dividends to the extent of earnings and profits of the distributing corporation.

Currently, another distinction between debt and equity relates to the taxation of dividend and interest income. Dividend income on equity holdings is taxed to individual investors at low capital gains rates, while interest income on debt is taxed at higher ordinary income rates.

EXAMPLE 29

Wade transfers cash of $100,000 to a newly formed corporation for 100% of the stock. In its initial year, the corporation has net income of $40,000. The income is credited to the earnings and profits account of the corporation. If the corporation distributes $9,500 to Wade, the distribution is a taxable dividend to Wade with no corresponding deduction to the corporation. Assume, instead, that Wade transfers to the corporation cash of $50,000 for stock and cash of $50,000 for a note of the same amount. The note is payable in equal annual installments of $5,000 and bears interest at the rate of 9%. At the end of the year, the corporation pays Wade interest of $4,500 ($50,000 × 9%) and a note repayment of $5,000. The interest payment is deductible to the corporation and taxable to Wade. The $5,000 principal repayment on the note is neither deducted by the corporation nor taxed to Wade. The after-tax impact to Wade and the corporation under each alternative is illustrated below.

	If the Distribution Is	
	$9,500 Dividend	**$5,000 Note Repayment and $4,500 Interest**
*After-tax benefit to Wade**		
[$9,500 × (1 – 15%)]	$8,075	
{$5,000 + [$4,500 × (1 – 35%)]}		$7,925
*After-tax cost to corporation***		
No deduction to corporation	9,500	
{$5,000 + [$4,500 × (1 – 35%)]}		7,925

*Assumes Wade's dividend income is taxed at the 15% capital gains rate and his interest income is taxed at the 35% ordinary income rate.
**Assumes the corporation is in the 35% marginal tax bracket. ■

[29] § 362(a) and Reg. § 1.362–2(b).

TAX *in* the NEWS

Debt That Cannot Be Fully Repaid

Having debt in the capital structure of a corporation can carry many tax advantages to the parties involved. Problems arise, however, when such debt becomes due and cannot be fully repaid by the corporate debtor. In the case of outside creditors (i.e., nonshareholders), the options are twofold: declare bankruptcy or restructure the terms of the debt. The latter option entails reducing the amount of the debt or allowing the debtor to repurchase the debt instruments (e.g., notes, bonds) at a discount. Either way generates income to the debtor under the discharge of indebtedness provision of § 108. Because the results are less drastic to the parties involved (i.e., creditor/debtor) and less disruptive in economic effect, Congress has attempted to encourage the use of the restructuring option.

Under the American Recovery and Reinvestment Tax Act of 2009, the income from the repurchase of business debt at a discount can be deferred until 2014 and can be spread over the next five years. These income deferral rules apply to repurchase situations occurring after December 31, 2008, and before January 1, 2011. The "buyback" rules will be of particular benefit in helping many private equity firms avoid bankruptcy due to their troubled debt.

Reclassification of Debt as Equity (Thin Capitalization Problem)

In situations where the corporation is said to be thinly capitalized, the IRS contends that debt is really an equity interest and denies the corporation the tax advantages of debt financing. If the debt instrument has too many features of stock, it may be treated for tax purposes as stock. In that case, the principal and interest payments are considered dividends. In the current environment, however, the IRS may be less inclined to raise the thin capitalization issue because the conversion of interest income to dividend income would produce a tax benefit to individual investors.

Section 385 lists several factors that *may* be used to determine whether a debtor-creditor relationship or a shareholder-corporation relationship exists. The section authorizes the Treasury to prescribe Regulations that provide more definitive guidelines. To date, the Treasury has not drafted acceptable Regulations. Consequently, taxpayers must rely on judicial decisions to determine whether a true debtor-creditor relationship exists.

For the most part, the principles used to classify debt as equity developed in connection with closely held corporations. Here, the holders of the debt are also shareholders. Consequently, the rules have often proved inadequate for dealing with such problems in large, publicly traded corporations.

Together, Congress, through § 385, and the courts have identified the following factors to be considered in resolving the **thin capitalization** issue:

- Whether the debt instrument is in proper form. An open account advance is more easily characterized as a contribution to capital than a loan evidenced by a properly written note.[30]
- Whether the debt instrument bears a reasonable rate of interest and has a definite maturity date. When a shareholder advance does not provide for interest, the return expected may appear to be a share of the profits or an increase in the value of the shares.[31] Likewise, a lender unrelated to the corporation will usually be unwilling to commit funds to the corporation without a definite due date.

[30] *Estate of Mixon, Jr. v. U.S.*, 72–2 USTC ¶9537, 30 AFTR 2d 72–5094, 464 F.2d 394 (CA–5, 1972).

[31] *Slappey Drive Industrial Park v. U.S.*, 77–2 USTC ¶9696, 40 AFTR 2d 77–5940, 561 F.2d 572 (CA–5, 1977).

- Whether the debt is paid on a timely basis. A lender's failure to insist upon timely repayment or satisfactory renegotiation indicates that the return sought does not depend upon interest income and the repayment of principal.
- Whether payment is contingent upon earnings. A lender ordinarily will not advance funds that are likely to be repaid only if the venture is successful.
- Whether the debt is subordinated to other liabilities. Subordination tends to eliminate a significant characteristic of the creditor-debtor relationship. Creditors should have the right to share with other general creditors in the event of the corporation's dissolution or liquidation. Subordination also destroys another basic attribute of creditor status—the power to demand payment at a fixed maturity date.[32]
- Whether holdings of debt and stock are proportionate (e.g., each shareholder owns the same percentage of debt as stock). When debt and equity obligations are held in the same proportion, shareholders are, apart from tax considerations, indifferent as to whether corporate distributions are in the form of interest or dividends.
- Whether funds loaned to the corporation are used to finance initial operations or capital asset acquisitions. Funds used to finance initial operations or to acquire capital assets the corporation needs are generally obtained through equity investments.
- Whether the corporation has a high ratio of shareholder debt to shareholder equity. Thin capitalization occurs when shareholder debt is high relative to shareholder equity. This indicates the corporation lacks reserves to pay interest and principal on debt when corporate income is insufficient to meet current needs.[33] In determining a corporation's debt-equity ratio, courts look at the relation of the debt both to the book value of the corporation's assets and to their actual fair market value.[34]

Under § 385, the IRS also has the authority to classify an instrument either as *wholly* debt or equity or as *part* debt and *part* equity. This flexible approach is important because some instruments cannot readily be classified either wholly as stock or wholly as debt. It may also provide an avenue for the IRS to address problems in publicly traded corporations.

4.3 Investor Losses

LO.6

Handle the tax treatment of shareholder debt and stock losses.

The difference between equity and debt financing involves a consideration of the tax treatment of worthless stock and securities versus that applicable to bad debts.

STOCK AND SECURITY LOSSES

If stocks and bonds are capital assets in their owner's hands, losses from their worthlessness are governed by § 165(g)(1). Under this provision, a capital loss materializes as of the last day of the taxable year in which the stocks or bonds become worthless. No deduction is allowed for a mere decline in value. The burden of proving complete worthlessness is on the taxpayer claiming the loss. One way to recognize partial worthlessness is to dispose of the stocks or bonds in a taxable sale or exchange.[35] But even then, the **investor loss** is disallowed if the sale or exchange is to a related party

[32] *Fin Hay Realty Co. v. U.S.*, 68–2 USTC ¶9438, 22 AFTR 2d 5004, 398 F.2d 694 (CA–3, 1968).

[33] A court held that a debt-equity ratio of approximately 14.6:1 was not excessive. See *Tomlinson v. 1661 Corp.*, 67–1 USTC ¶9438, 19 AFTR 2d 1413, 377 F.2d 291 (CA–5, 1967). A 26:1 ratio was found acceptable in *Delta Plastics, Inc.*, 85 TCM 940, T.C.Memo. 2003–54.

[34] In *Bauer v. Comm.*, 84–2 USTC ¶9996, 55 AFTR 2d 85–433, 748 F.2d 1365 (CA–9, 1984), a debt-equity ratio of 92:1 resulted when book value was used. But the ratio ranged from 2:1 to 8:1 when equity included both paid-in capital and accumulated earnings.

[35] Reg. § 1.165–4(a).

as defined under § 267(b) (e.g., parents and children are related, but aunts, uncles, and cousins are not considered related).

When the stocks or bonds are not capital assets, worthlessness yields an ordinary loss.[36] For example, if the stocks or bonds are held by a broker for resale to customers in the normal course of business, they are not capital assets. Usually, however, stocks and bonds are held as investments and, as a result, are capital assets.

Under certain circumstances involving stocks and bonds of affiliated corporations, an ordinary loss is allowed upon worthlessness.[37] A corporation is an affiliate of another corporation if the corporate shareholder owns at least 80 percent of the voting power of all classes of stock entitled to vote and 80 percent of each class of nonvoting stock. Further, to be considered affiliated, the corporation must have derived more than 90 percent of its aggregate gross receipts for all taxable years from sources other than passive income. Passive income for this purpose includes such items as rents, royalties, dividends, and interest.

BUSINESS VERSUS NONBUSINESS BAD DEBTS

In addition to worthlessness of stocks and bonds, the financial demise of a corporation can result in bad debt deductions to those who have extended credit to the corporation. These deductions can be either business bad debts or **nonbusiness bad debts**. The distinction between the two types of deductions is important for tax purposes in the following respects:

- Business bad debts are deducted as ordinary losses while nonbusiness bad debts are treated as short-term capital losses.[38] A business bad debt can generate a net operating loss, but a nonbusiness bad debt cannot.[39]
- A deduction is allowed for the partial worthlessness of a business debt, but nonbusiness debts can be written off only when they become entirely worthless.[40]
- Nonbusiness bad debt treatment is limited to noncorporate taxpayers. However, all of the bad debts of a corporation qualify as business bad debts.[41]

When is a debt business or nonbusiness? Unfortunately, since the Code sheds little light on the matter, the distinction has been left to the courts.[42] In a leading decision, the Supreme Court somewhat clarified the picture when it held that if individual shareholders lend money to a corporation in their capacity as investors, any resulting bad debt is classified as nonbusiness.[43] Nevertheless, the Court did not preclude the possibility of a shareholder-creditor incurring a business bad debt.

If a loan is made in some capacity that qualifies as a trade or business, nonbusiness bad debt treatment is avoided. For example, if an employee, who is also a shareholder, makes a loan to preserve employment status, the loan qualifies for business bad debt treatment.[44] Shareholders also receive business bad debt treatment if they are in the trade or business of lending money or of buying, promoting, and selling corporations. If the shareholder has multiple motives for making the loan, according to the Supreme Court, the "dominant" or "primary" motive for making the loan controls the classification of the loss.[45]

[36] § 165(a) and Reg. § 1.165–5(b).
[37] § 165(g)(3).
[38] Compare § 166(a) with § 166(d)(1)(B).
[39] Note the modification required by § 172(d)(2).
[40] Compare § 166(a)(2) with § 166(d)(1)(A).
[41] § 166(d)(1).
[42] For definitional purposes, § 166(d)(2) is almost as worthless as the debt it purports to describe.
[43] *Whipple v. Comm.*, 63–1 USTC ¶9466, 11 AFTR 2d 1454, 83 S.Ct. 1168 (USSC, 1963).
[44] *Trent v. Comm.*, 61–2 USTC ¶9506, 7 AFTR 2d 1599, 291 F.2d 669 (CA–2, 1961).
[45] *U.S. v. Generes*, 72–1 USTC ¶9259, 29 AFTR 2d 72–609, 92 S.Ct. 827 (USSC, 1972).

TAX *in* the NEWS — Losses Arising from Stock Market Investments: Capital Losses or Theft Losses?

Losses incurred by individuals from poor performing stocks and securities, whether from actual sales or due to worthlessness, receive capital loss treatment. Thus, the losses can offset any capital gains, and if a net loss results, a deduction of up to $3,000 may be taken for the year. If the net loss exceeds $3,000, the excess may be carried over to future years. However, many years may have to pass before a large net capital loss is fully deductible.

As an alternative, if the loss on the security is due to theft, it is not subject to the capital loss limitation. Instead, the theft loss is ordinary and could totally wipe out a taxpayer's income, and in some cases, it could be carried back or forward as a net operating loss deduction. Among the taxpayers who can utilize theft loss treatment are the unfortunate investors who lost billions of dollars in the well-publicized Madoff scam. Revenue Ruling 2009–9 (2009-1 C.B. 735) provides theft loss treatment for investors who paid money to investment advisers, such as Bernard Madoff, who later were discovered to have used the funds in a Ponzi-style scheme. Further, because the taxpayers originally engaged in such "investments" with an expectation of generating profits, the deductions *are not* subject to the restrictions applicable to personal casualty and theft loss (e.g., the 10 percent-of-AGI floor). Thus, these unhappy fraud victims may find some solace in the favorable tax treatment that provides an immediate and full deduction for the losses sustained.

EXAMPLE 30

Norman owns 48% of the stock of Lark Corporation, which he acquired several years ago at a cost of $600,000. Norman is also employed by the corporation at an annual salary of $240,000. At a time when Lark Corporation is experiencing financial problems, Norman lends it $300,000. Subsequently, the corporation becomes bankrupt, and both Norman's stock investment and his loan become worthless. ■

Norman's stock investment is treated as a long-term capital loss (assuming § 1244 does not apply, as discussed below). But how is the bad debt classified? If Norman can prove that his dominant or primary reason for making the loan was to protect his salary, a business bad debt deduction results. If not, it is assumed that Norman was trying to protect his stock investment, and nonbusiness bad debt treatment results. Factors to be considered in resolving this matter include the following:

- A comparison of the amount of the stock investment with the trade or business benefit derived. In Example 30, the stock investment of $600,000 is compared with the annual salary of $240,000. In this regard, the salary should be considered as a recurring item and not viewed in isolation. A salary of $240,000 each year means a great deal to a person who has no other means of support and may have difficulty obtaining similar employment elsewhere.
- A comparison of the amount of the loan with the stock investment and the trade or business benefit derived.
- The percentage of ownership held by the shareholder. A minority shareholder, for example, is under more compulsion to lend the corporation money to protect a job than one who is in control of corporate policy.

In summary, it is impossible to conclude whether Norman in Example 30 suffered a business or nonbusiness bad debt without additional facts. Even with such facts, the guidelines are vague. Recall that a taxpayer's intent or motivation is at issue. For this reason, the problem is frequently the subject of litigation.[46]

[46]See, for example, *Kelson v. U.S.*, 74–2 USTC ¶9714, 34 AFTR 2d 74–6007, 503 F.2d 1291 (CA–10, 1974) and *Kenneth W. Graves*, 87 TCM 1409, T.C.Memo. 2004–140.

SECTION 1244 STOCK

In an exception to the capital treatment that generally results, § 1244 permits ordinary loss treatment for losses on the sale or worthlessness of stock of so-called small business corporations. By placing shareholders on a more nearly equal basis with proprietors and partners in terms of the tax treatment of losses, the provision encourages investment of capital in small corporations. Gain on the sale of § 1244 stock remains capital. Consequently, the shareholder has nothing to lose and everything to gain by complying with § 1244.

Qualification for § 1244

The ordinary loss treatment for **§ 1244 stock** applies to the first $1 million of capitalized value of the corporation's stock. If more than $1 million of the corporation's stock is issued, the entity designates which of the shares qualify for § 1244 treatment.[47] In measuring the capitalization of the newly issued stock, property received in exchange for stock is valued at its adjusted basis, reduced by any liabilities assumed by the corporation or to which the property is subject. The fair market value of the property is not considered. The $1 million limitation is determined on the date the stock is issued. Consequently, even though a corporation fails to meet these requirements when the stock later is disposed of by the shareholder, the stock can still qualify as § 1244 stock if the requirements were met on the date the stock was issued.

Mechanics of the Loss Deduction

The amount of ordinary loss deductible in any one year from the disposition of § 1244 stock is limited to $50,000 (or $100,000 for spouses filing a joint return). If the amount of the loss sustained in the taxable year exceeds these amounts, the remainder is considered a capital loss.

EXAMPLE 31

Harvey acquires § 1244 stock at a cost of $100,000. He sells the stock for $10,000 in the current year. He has an ordinary loss of $50,000 and a capital loss of $40,000. Alternatively, on a joint return, the entire $90,000 loss is ordinary. ■

Only the original holder of § 1244 stock, whether an individual or a partnership, qualifies for ordinary loss treatment. If the stock is sold or donated, it loses its § 1244 status.

Special treatment applies if § 1244 stock is issued by a corporation in exchange for property that has an adjusted basis above its fair market value immediately before the exchange. For purposes of determining ordinary loss upon a subsequent sale, the stock basis is reduced to the fair market value of the property on the date of the exchange.

EXAMPLE 32

Dana transfers property with a basis of $10,000 and a fair market value of $5,000 to a corporation in exchange for shares of § 1244 stock. Assuming the transfer qualifies under § 351, the basis of the stock under the general rule is $10,000, the same as Dana's basis in the property. However, for purposes of § 1244 and measuring the amount of ordinary loss, the stock basis is only $5,000. If the stock is later sold for $3,000, the total loss sustained is $7,000 ($3,000 – $10,000); however, only $2,000 of the loss is ordinary ($3,000 – $5,000). The remaining portion of the loss, $5,000, is a capital loss. ■

Recall the advantages of issuing some debt to shareholders in exchange for cash contributions to a corporation. A disadvantage of issuing debt is that it does not qualify under § 1244. Should the debt become worthless, the taxpayer generally has a short-term capital loss rather than the ordinary loss for § 1244 stock.

[47] Reg. § 1.1244(c)–2(b)(2).

4.4 Gain from Qualified Small Business Stock

Shareholders are given special tax relief for gains recognized on the sale or exchange of stock acquired in a **qualified small business corporation**. The holder of **qualified small business stock** may exclude 50 percent of any gain from the sale or exchange of such stock. However, under the American Recovery and Reinvestment Tax Act of 2009, the exclusion increases to 75 percent for qualified small business stock acquired after February 17, 2009, and from legislation in 2010, the exclusion increases to 100 percent for qualified stock acquired after September 27, 2010, and before 2012.[48] To qualify for the exclusion, the taxpayer must have held the stock for more than five years and must have acquired the stock as part of an original issue.[49] Only noncorporate shareholders qualify for the exclusion.

A qualified small business corporation is a C corporation whose aggregate gross assets did not exceed $50 million on the date the stock was issued.[50] The corporation must be actively involved in a trade or business. This means that at least 80 percent of the corporation's assets must be used in the active conduct of one or more qualified trades or businesses.

A shareholder can apply the exclusion to the greater of (1) $10 million or (2) 10 times the shareholder's aggregate adjusted basis in the qualified stock disposed of during a taxable year.[51]

TAX PLANNING:

4.5 Working with § 351

LO.7

Identify tax planning opportunities associated with organizing and financing a corporation.

Effective tax planning with transfers of property to corporations requires a clear understanding of § 351 and its related Code provisions. The most important question in planning is simply: Does the desired tax result come from complying with § 351 or from avoiding it?

UTILIZING § 351

If the tax-free treatment of § 351 is desired, ensure that the parties transferring property (which includes cash) receive control of the corporation. Simultaneous transfers are not necessary, but a long period of time between transfers could be disastrous if the transfers are not properly documented as part of a single plan. The parties should document and preserve evidence of their intentions. Also, it is helpful to have some reasonable explanation for any delay in the transfers.

To meet the requirements of § 351, mere momentary control on the part of the transferor may not suffice if loss of control is compelled by a prearranged agreement.[52]

EXAMPLE 33

For many years, Paula operated a business as a sole proprietor employing Brooke as manager. To dissuade Brooke from quitting and going out on her own, Paula promised her a 30% interest in the business. To fulfill this promise, Paula transfers the business to newly formed Green Corporation in return for all its stock. Immediately thereafter, Paula transfers 30% of the stock to Brooke. Section 351 probably does not apply to Paula's transfer to Green Corporation because it appears that Paula was under an obligation to relinquish control. If this preexisting obligation exists, § 351 will not be available to Paula because, as the sole property transferor, she does not have control of

[48] § 1202. The 0% and 15% capital gains rates do not apply. Thus, the maximum effective tax rate on the sale of qualified small business stock is 14% (28% × 50%), 7% (28% × 25%), or 0% (28% × 0%).

[49] The stock must have been issued after August 10, 1993, which is the effective date of § 1202 as originally enacted.

[50] § 1202(d). Its aggregate assets may not exceed this amount at any time between August 10, 1993, and the date the stock was issued.

[51] § 1202(b). The amount is $5 million for married taxpayers filing separately.

[52] Rev.Rul. 54–96, 1954–1 C.B. 111.

Green Corporation. However, if there is no obligation and the loss of control was voluntary on Paula's part, momentary control would suffice.[53] ■

Be sure that later transfers of property to an existing corporation satisfy the control requirement if recognition of gain is to be avoided. In this connection, another transferor's interest cannot be counted if the value of stock received is relatively small compared with the value of stock already owned and the primary purpose of the transfer is to qualify other transferors for § 351 treatment.[54]

AVOIDING § 351

Because § 351 provides for the nonrecognition of gain on transfers to controlled corporations, it is often regarded as a favorable relief provision. In some situations, however, avoiding § 351 may produce a more advantageous tax result. The transferors might prefer to recognize gain on the transfer of property if they cannot be particularly harmed by the gain. For example, they may be in low tax brackets, or the gain may be a capital gain from which substantial capital losses can be offset. The corporation will then have a stepped-up basis in the transferred property.

A transferor might also prefer to avoid § 351 to allow for immediate recognition of a loss. Recall that § 351 provides for the nonrecognition of both gains and losses. A transferor who wishes to recognize loss has several alternatives:

- Sell the property to the corporation for its stock. The IRS could attempt to collapse the "sale," however, by taking the approach that the transfer really falls under § 351.[55] If the sale is disregarded, the transferor ends up with a realized, but unrecognized, loss.
- Sell the property to the corporation for other property or boot. Because the transferor receives no stock, § 351 is inapplicable.
- Transfer the property to the corporation in return for securities or nonqualified preferred stock. Recall that § 351 does not apply to a transferor who receives securities or nonqualified preferred stock. In both this and the previous alternatives, watch for the possible disallowance of the loss under the related-party rules.

WILL THE SALE BE RECOGNIZED?

Early in the year, Charles, Lane, and Tami form the Harrier Corporation for the express purpose of developing a shopping center. All parties are experienced contractors, and they transfer various business assets (e.g., building materials, land) to Harrier in exchange for all of its stock. Three months after it is formed, Harrier purchases two cranes from Lane for their fair market value of $400,000 by issuing four annual installment notes of $100,000 each. Since the adjusted basis of the cranes is $550,000, Lane plans to recognize a § 1231 loss of $150,000 in the year of the sale. Does Lane have any potential income tax problem with this plan?

Suppose the loss property is to be transferred to the corporation and no loss is recognized by the transferor due to § 351. This could present an interesting problem in terms of assessing the economic realities involved.

EXAMPLE 34

Iris and Lamont form Wren Corporation with the following investments: property by Iris (basis of $40,000 and fair market value of $50,000) and property by Lamont (basis of $60,000 and fair market value of $50,000). Each receives 50% of the Wren stock. Has

[53]Compare *Fahs v. Florida Machine and Foundry Co.*, 48–2 USTC ¶9329, 36 AFTR 1161, 168 F.2d 957 (CA–5, 1948), with *John C. O'Connor*, 16 TCM 213, T.C.Memo. 1957–50, *aff'd* in 58–2 USTC ¶9913, 2 AFTR 2d 6011, 260 F.2d 358 (CA–6, 1958).

[54]Reg. § 1.351–1(a)(1)(ii).

[55]*U.S. v. Hertwig*, 68–2 USTC ¶9495, 22 AFTR 2d 5249, 398 F.2d 452 (CA–5, 1968).

Lamont acted wisely in settling for only 50% of the stock? At first, it would appear so, since Iris and Lamont each invested property of the same value ($50,000). But what about tax considerations? By applying the general carryover basis rules, the corporation now has a basis of $40,000 in Iris's property and $60,000 in Lamont's property. In essence, Iris has shifted a possible $10,000 gain to the corporation while Lamont has transferred a $10,000 potential loss. With this in mind, an equitable allocation of the Wren stock would call for Lamont to receive a greater percentage interest than Iris. This issue is further complicated by the special basis adjustment required when a shareholder, such as Lamont, contributes property with a built-in loss to a corporation. In this situation, if Wren is to take a carryover basis in Lamont's property, Lamont must reduce his stock basis by the $10,000 built-in loss. This reduced stock basis, of course, could lead to a greater tax burden on Lamont when he sells the Wren stock. This may suggest additional support for Lamont having a greater percentage interest than Iris. ■

4.6 Selecting Assets to Transfer

When a business is incorporated, the organizers must determine which assets and liabilities should be transferred to the corporation. A transfer of assets that produce passive income (rents, royalties, dividends, and interest) can cause the corporation to be a personal holding company in a tax year when operating income is low. Thus, the corporation could be subject to the personal holding company penalty tax (see the discussion in Chapter 3) in addition to the regular income tax.

Leasing property to the corporation may be a more attractive alternative than transferring ownership. Leasing provides the taxpayer with the opportunity to withdraw money from the corporation in a deductible form without the payment being characterized as a nondeductible dividend. If the property is given to a family member in a lower tax bracket, the lease income can be shifted as well. If the depreciation and other deductions available in connection with the property are larger than the lease income, the taxpayer would retain the property until the income exceeds the deductions.

When an existing cash basis business is incorporated, an important issue to consider is whether the business's accounts receivable and accounts payable will be transferred to the new corporation or be retained by the owner of the unincorporated business. Depending on the approach taken, either the new corporation or the owner of the old unincorporated business will recognize the income associated with the cash basis receivables when they are collected. The cash basis accounts payable raise the corresponding issue of who will claim the deduction.

EXAMPLE 35
THE BIG PICTURE

Return to the facts of *The Big Picture* on p. 4-2. If Emily decides to retain the $25,000 of cash basis accounts receivable rather than transferring them to the newly formed corporation, she will recognize $25,000 of ordinary income upon their collection. Alternatively, if the receivables are transferred to the corporation as the facts suggest, the corporation will recognize the ordinary income. However, a subsequent corporate distribution to Emily of the cash collected could be subject to double taxation as a dividend (see Chapter 5 for further discussion). Given the alternatives available, Emily needs to evaluate which approach is better for the parties involved. ■

Another way to shift income to other taxpayers is by the use of corporate debt. Shareholder debt in a corporation can be given to family members in a lower tax bracket. This technique also causes income to be shifted without a loss of control of the corporation.

4.7 Debt in the Capital Structure

The advantages and disadvantages of debt as opposed to equity have previously been noted. To increase debt without incurring the thin capitalization problem, consider the following:

- Preserve the formalities of the debt. This includes providing for written instruments, realistic interest rates, and specified due dates.
- If possible, have the corporation repay the debt when it comes due. If this is not possible, have the parties renegotiate the arrangement. Try to proceed as a nonshareholder creditor would. It is not unusual, for example, for bondholders of publicly held corporations to extend due dates when default occurs. The alternative is to foreclose and perhaps seriously impair the amount the creditors will recover.
- Avoid provisions in the debt instrument that make the debt convertible to equity in the event of default. These provisions are standard practice when nonshareholder creditors are involved. They serve no purpose if the shareholders are also the creditors and hold debt in proportion to ownership shares.

EXAMPLE 36

Gail, Cliff, and Ruth are equal shareholders in Magenta Corporation. Each transfers cash of $100,000 to Magenta in return for its bonds. The bond agreement provides that the holders will receive additional voting rights in the event Magenta Corporation defaults on its bonds. The voting rights provision is worthless and merely raises the issue of thin capitalization. Gail, Cliff, and Ruth already control Magenta Corporation, so what purpose is served by increasing their voting rights? The parties probably used a "boilerplate" bond agreement that was designed for third-party lenders (e.g., banks and other financial institutions). ■

- Pro rata holding of debt is difficult to avoid. For example, if each of the shareholders owns one-third of the stock, then each will want one-third of the debt. Nevertheless, some variation is possible.

EXAMPLE 37

Assume the same facts as Example 36 except that only Gail and Cliff acquire the bonds. Ruth leases property to Magenta Corporation at an annual rent that approximates the yield on the bonds. Presuming the rent passes the arm's length test (i.e., what unrelated parties would charge), all parties reach the desired result. Gail and Cliff withdraw corporate profits in the form of interest income, and Ruth is provided for with rent income. Magenta Corporation can deduct both the interest and the rent payments. ■

- Try to keep the debt-equity ratio within reasonable proportions. A problem frequently arises when the parties form the corporation. Often the amount invested in capital stock is the minimum required by state law. For example, if the state of incorporation permits a minimum of $1,000, limiting the investment to this amount does not provide much safety for later debt financing by the shareholders.
- Stressing the fair market value of the assets rather than their tax basis to the corporation can be helpful in preparing to defend debt-equity ratios.

EXAMPLE 38

Emily, Josh, and Miles form Black Corporation with the following capital investments: cash of $200,000 from Emily; land worth $200,000 (basis of $20,000) from Josh; and a patent worth $200,000 (basis of $0) from Miles. To state that the equity of Black Corporation is $220,000 (the tax basis to the corporation) does not reflect reality. The equity account is more properly stated at $600,000 ($200,000 + $200,000 + $200,000). ■

- The nature of the business can have an effect on what is an acceptable debt-equity ratio. Capital-intensive industries (e.g., manufacturing, transportation) characteristically rely heavily on debt financing. Consequently, larger debt should be tolerated.

What if a corporation's efforts to avoid the thin capitalization problem fail and the IRS raises the issue on audit? What steps should the shareholders take? They should hedge their position by filing a protective claim for refund claiming dividend treatment on the previously reported interest income. In such an event, ordinary income would be converted to preferential dividend income treatment. Otherwise, the IRS could ultimately invoke the statute of limitations and achieve the best of all possible worlds—the shareholders would have been taxed on the interest income at the ordinary income rates while the corporation would receive no deduction for what is now reclassified as a dividend. By filing the claim for refund, the shareholders have kept the statute of limitations from running until the thin capitalization issue is resolved at the corporate level.

4.8 Investor Losses

Be aware of the danger of losing § 1244 attributes. Only the original holder of § 1244 stock is entitled to ordinary loss treatment. If, after a corporation is formed, the owner transfers shares of stock to family members to shift income within the family group, the benefits of § 1244 are lost.

EXAMPLE 39

Norm incorporates his business by transferring property with a basis of $100,000 for 100 shares of stock. The stock qualifies as § 1244 stock. Norm later gives 50 shares each to his children, Susan and Paul. Eventually, the business fails, and the shares of stock become worthless. If Norm had retained the stock, he would have had an ordinary loss deduction of $100,000 (assuming he filed a joint return). Susan and Paul, however, have a capital loss of $50,000 each because the § 1244 attributes are lost as a result of the gift (i.e., neither Susan nor Paul was an original holder of the stock). ■

REFOCUS ON THE BIG PICTURE

TAX ISSUES CAN BE NEUTRALIZED WHEN GROWING INTO THE CORPORATE FORM

Emily, the sole property transferor, must acquire at least 80 percent of the stock issued by the new corporation in order for the transaction to receive tax-deferred treatment under § 351. Otherwise, a tremendous amount of gain (up to $300,000) will be recognized. As a corollary, David must not receive more than 20 percent of the corporation's stock in exchange for his services (see Examples 9 and 10). However, even if § 351 is available, any corporate debt issued by the corporation will be treated as boot and will trigger gain recognition to Emily (see Example 4). Therefore, she must evaluate the cost of recognizing gain now versus the benefit of the corporation obtaining an interest deduction later.

What If?

Can the § 351 transaction be modified to further reduce personal and business tax costs, both at the time of formation and in future years? Several strategies may be worth considering.

- Instead of having the corporation issue debt on formation, Emily might withhold certain assets. If the building is not transferred, for example, it can be leased to the corporation. The resulting rent payment would mitigate the double tax problem by producing a tax deduction for the corporation.
- An additional benefit results if Emily does not transfer the cash basis receivables to the corporation. This approach avoids a tax at the corporate level and a further tax when the receipts are distributed to Emily in the form of a dividend. If the receivables are withheld, their collection is taxed only to Emily (see Example 35).
- No mention is made as to the existence (or nonexistence) of any accounts payable outstanding at the time of corporate formation. If they do exist, which is likely, it could be wise for Emily to transfer them to the corporation. The subsequent corporate payment of the liability produces a corporate deduction that will reduce any corporate tax.

Double taxation can be mitigated in certain situations with a modest amount of foresight!

KEY TERMS

Built-in loss property, 4–13
Capital contribution, 4–17
Control, 4–6
Investor loss, 4–20
Liabilities in excess of basis, 4–10
Nonbusiness bad debts, 4–21
Property, 4–4
Qualified small business corporation, 4–24
Qualified small business stock, 4–24
Section 1244 stock, 4–23
Securities, 4–5
Thin capitalization, 4–19

DISCUSSION QUESTIONS

1. **LO.1** In terms of justification and effect, § 351 (transfer to a controlled corporation) and § 1031 (like-kind exchange) are much alike. Explain.

2. **LO.1** Under what circumstances will gain and/or loss be recognized on a § 351 transfer?

3. **LO.1** Presley agrees to serve as the chief financial officer for newly formed Red Corporation. As compensation for the services he renders, Red will issue 60 shares of stock to Presley. What is the tax effect to Presley of this transaction?

4. **LO.1** Can the receipt of boot ever be taxable in a § 351 transfer in the absence of realized gain? Explain.

5. **LO.1** Does the receipt of a 10-year note in exchange for the transfer of appreciated property to a controlled corporation cause recognition of gain? Explain.

6. **LO.1** What is the control requirement of § 351? Describe the effect of the following in satisfying this requirement:
   a. A shareholder renders only services to the corporation for stock.
   b. A shareholder both renders services and transfers property to the corporation for stock.
   c. A shareholder has only momentary control after the transfer.
   d. A long period of time elapses between the transfers of property by different shareholders.

7. **LO.1** Kate transfers appreciated property to Crow Corporation in exchange for 50% of its stock, while Kevin transfers a secret process and services for the remainder of Crow's stock. Kevin's services relate to expertise he will provide in corporate operations *after* Crow's formation. What are the tax issues? **ISSUE ID**

8. **LO.1, 2, 7** Four friends plan to form a corporation for purposes of constructing a shopping center. Charlie will be contributing the land for the project and wants more security than shareholder status provides. He is contemplating two possibilities: receive corporate bonds for his land, or take out a mortgage on the land before transferring it to the corporation. Comment on the choices Charlie is considering. What alternatives can you suggest? **ISSUE ID** **DECISION MAKING**

9. **LO.1** Duane and Sally form Robin Corporation by transferring appreciated property in exchange for 60% and 40% of Robin stock, respectively. Are the exchanges taxable if Duane donates his shares to the United Way (a charity) immediately after the exchange?

10. **LO.1** Mary and Paul transfer property while Matt renders services in forming Falcon Corporation. Each receives one-third of its stock. Will the exchanges be taxable? Explain.

11. **LO.1** At a point when Robin Corporation has been in existence for six years, shareholder Ted transfers real estate (adjusted basis of $20,000 and fair market value of $100,000) to the corporation for additional stock. At the same time, Peggy, the other shareholder, acquires one share of stock for cash. After the two transfers, the percentages of stock ownership are as follows: 79% by Ted and 21% by Peggy. **ISSUE ID**
    a. What were the parties trying to accomplish?
    b. Will it work? Explain.

12. **LO.2** Does the transfer of property subject to a mortgage to a controlled corporation trigger gain? Explain.

13. **LO.2** Before incorporating her apartment rental business, Libbie takes out second mortgages on several of the units. She uses the mortgage proceeds to make capital improvements to the units. Along with all of the rental units, Libbie transfers the mortgages to the newly formed corporation in return for all of its stock. Discuss the tax consequences of these procedures.

14. **LO.2** Why does § 357(c) require recognition of gain when liabilities assumed by a corporation exceed the adjusted basis of the assets transferred?

15. **LO.3** Discuss how each of the following affects the calculation of the basis of stock received by a shareholder in a § 351 transfer:
    a. The transfer of a liability to the corporation along with property.
    b. Property transferred has built-in losses.
    c. The basis in the property transferred to the corporation.
    d. The receipt of "other property" (i.e., boot) in addition to stock.

16. **LO.3** Identify a situation when a corporation can deduct the value of the stock it issues for the rendition of services. Identify a situation when a deduction is not available.

17. **LO.3** Pursuant to a § 351 transfer, Pedro transfers property to Goose Corporation in exchange for Goose stock and $15,000 cash. What is Goose's holding period for the property it receives from Pedro? What is Pedro's holding period for the Goose stock?

18. **LO.4** A corporation acquires property as a contribution to capital from a shareholder and from a nonshareholder. Are the rules pertaining to the property's basis the same? Explain.

19. **LO.5** In structuring the capitalization of a corporation, what are the advantages and disadvantages of utilizing debt rather than equity?

20. **LO.5** In determining whether debt of a corporation should be reclassified as stock, comment on the relevance of the following:
    a. The loan is on open account.
    b. The loan is payable on demand.
    c. The corporation does not make timely repayments.
    d. Payments are contingent on earnings.
    e. The loans are in the same proportion as the shareholdings, and the corporation uses the funds to purchase a new building.
    f. The corporation's debt-equity ratio is 5:1.

21. **LO.6** Assuming § 1244 does not apply, what is the tax treatment of stock that has become worthless?

22. **LO.6** Under what circumstances, if any, may a shareholder deduct a business bad debt on a loan made to the corporation?

DECISION MAKING

23. **LO.6** Four years ago, Nelson purchased stock in Black Corporation for $37,000. The stock has a current value of $5,000. Nelson needs to decide which of the following alternatives to pursue. Determine the tax effect of each.
    a. Without selling the stock, Nelson deducts $32,000 for the partial worthlessness of the Black Corporation investment.
    b. Nelson sells the stock to his aunt for $5,000 and deducts a $32,000 long-term capital loss.
    c. Nelson sells the stock to a third party and deducts an ordinary loss.
    d. Nelson sells the stock to his mother for $5,000 and deducts a $32,000 long-term capital loss.
    e. Nelson sells the stock to a third party and deducts a $32,000 long-term capital loss.

ISSUE ID

24. **LO.1, 7** Keith's sole proprietorship holds assets that, if sold, would yield a gain of $100,000. It also owns assets that would yield a loss of $30,000. Keith incorporates his business using only the gain assets. Two days later, Keith sells the loss assets to the newly formed corporation. What is Keith trying to accomplish? Will he be successful?

25. **LO.7** Sarah incorporates her small business, but does not transfer the machinery and equipment the business uses to the corporation. Subsequently, the machinery and equipment are leased to the corporation for an annual rent. What tax reasons might Sarah have for not transferring the machinery and equipment to the corporation when the business was incorporated?

ISSUE ID

PROBLEMS

26. **LO.1, 3** Sam, John, Lucy, and Sylvia form Pine Corporation with the following consideration:

	Consideration Transferred		
	Basis to Transferor	Fair Market Value	Number of Shares Issued
From Sam—			
Inventory	$30,000	$97,000	30*
From John—			
Equipment ($30,000 of depreciation taken by John in previous years)	55,000	99,000	30**
From Lucy—			
Secret process	25,000	90,000	30
From Sylvia—			
Cash	30,000	30,000	10

*Sam receives $7,000 cash in addition to the 30 shares.
**John receives $9,000 cash in addition to the 30 shares.

Assume the value of each share of Pine Corporation stock is $3,000. As to these transactions, provide the following information:

a. Sam's recognized gain or loss. Identify the nature of any such gain or loss.
b. Sam's basis in the Pine stock.
c. Pine Corporation's basis in the inventory.
d. John's recognized gain or loss and its classification.
e. John's basis in the Pine stock.
f. Pine Corporation's basis in the equipment.
g. Lucy's recognized gain or loss.
h. Lucy's basis in the Pine stock.
i. Pine Corporation's basis in the secret process.
j. Sylvia's recognized gain or loss.
k. Sylvia's basis in the Pine stock.

27. **LO.1, 3** Mark and Gail form Maple Corporation with the following consideration:

	Consideration Transferred		
	Basis to Transferor	Fair Market Value	Number of Shares Issued
From Mark—			
Cash	$ 40,000	$ 40,000	
Installment obligation	140,000	360,000	40
From Gail—			
Cash	140,000	140,000	
Equipment	120,000	180,000	
Patent	4,000	280,000	60

The installment obligation has a face amount of $360,000 and was acquired last year from the sale of land held for investment purposes (adjusted basis of $140,000). As to these transactions, provide the following information:

a. Mark's recognized gain or loss.
b. Mark's basis in the Maple Corporation stock.
c. Maple Corporation's basis in the installment obligation.
d. Gail's recognized gain or loss.
e. Gail's basis in the Maple Corporation stock.
f. Maple Corporation's basis in the equipment and the patent.
g. How would your answers to the preceding questions change if Mark received common stock and Gail received preferred stock?
h. How would your answers change if Gail was a partnership?

DECISION MAKING

28. **LO.1, 7** Jane, Jon, and Clyde incorporate their respective businesses and form Starling Corporation. On March 1 of the current year, Jane exchanges her property (basis of $50,000 and value of $150,000) for 150 shares in Starling Corporation. On April 15, Jon exchanges his property (basis of $70,000 and value of $500,000) for 500 shares in Starling. On May 10, Clyde transfers his property (basis of $90,000 and value of $350,000) for 350 shares in Starling.
    a. If the three exchanges are part of a prearranged plan, what gain will each of the parties recognize on the exchanges?
    b. Assume Jane and Jon exchanged their property for stock four years ago while Clyde transfers his property for 350 shares in the current year. Clyde's transfer is not part of a prearranged plan with Jane and Jon to incorporate their businesses. What gain will Clyde recognize on the transfer?
    c. Returning to the original facts, if the property that Clyde contributes has a basis of $490,000 (instead of $90,000), how might the parties otherwise structure the transaction?

COMMUNICATIONS

29. **LO.1** Michael Robertson (1635 Maple Street, Syracuse, NY 13201) exchanges property (basis of $200,000 and fair market value of $850,000) for 75% of the stock of Red Corporation. The other 25% is owned by Sarah Mitchell, who acquired her stock several years ago. You represent Michael, who asks whether he must report gain on the transfer. Prepare a letter to Michael and a memorandum for the tax files documenting your response.

ISSUE ID

30. **LO.1** Barbara exchanges property (basis of $20,000 and fair market value of $500,000) for 65% of the stock of Pelican Corporation. Alice, Barbara's daughter, who acquired her stock last year, owns the other 35% of Pelican. What are the tax issues?

31. **LO.1** Three years ago, Irene and Julie formed Hummingbird Corporation. Each transferred property to Hummingbird in exchange for 50 shares of its stock. In the current year, Jaime transfers property worth $600,000 (basis of $90,000) for 50 shares (a one-third interest) in Hummingbird Corporation. What are the tax consequences to Jaime and to Hummingbird on the transfer in the current year?

32. **LO.1, 3** Ann and Bob form Robin Corporation. Ann transfers property worth $420,000 (basis of $150,000) for 70 shares in Robin Corporation. Bob receives 30 shares for property worth $165,000 (basis of $30,000) and for legal services (worth $15,000) in organizing the corporation.
    a. What gain or income, if any, will the parties recognize on the transfer?
    b. What basis do Ann and Bob have in the stock in Robin Corporation?
    c. What is Robin Corporation's basis in the property and services it received from Ann and Bob?

33. **LO.1, 3** Assume in Problem 32 that the property Bob transfers to Robin Corporation is worth $15,000 (basis of $3,000) and his services in organizing the corporation are worth $165,000. What are the tax consequences to Ann, Bob, and Robin Corporation?

34. **LO.3** Kim is an employee of Azure Corporation. In the current year, she receives a salary of $30,000 and is also given 10 shares of Azure stock for services she renders to the corporation. The shares in Azure Corporation are worth $1,000 each. How will the transfer of the 10 shares to Kim be handled for tax purposes by Kim? What is Azure Corporation's total compensation deduction for Kim's services?

DECISION MAKING

35. **LO.1, 7** Rhonda Johnson owns 50% of the stock of Peach Corporation. She and the other 50% shareholder, Rachel Powell, have decided that additional contributions of capital are needed if Peach is to remain successful in its competitive industry. The two shareholders have agreed that Rhonda will contribute assets having a value of $200,000 (adjusted basis of $15,000) in exchange for additional shares of stock. After the transaction, Rhonda will hold 75% of Peach Corporation and Rachel's interest will fall to 25%.
   a. What gain is realized on the transaction? How much of the gain will be recognized?
   b. Rhonda is not satisfied with the transaction as proposed. How would the consequences change if Rachel agrees to transfer $1,000 of cash in exchange for additional stock? In this case, Rhonda will own slightly less than 75% of Peach and Rachel's interest will be slightly more than 25%.
   c. If Rhonda still is not satisfied with the result, what should be done to avoid any gain recognition?

36. **LO.1, 2, 3** Natalie was engaged in a consulting business as a sole proprietor and reported her income on the cash basis. On March 1, 2011, she incorporates the business. In exchange for all of the assets and liabilities of her business, Natalie obtains all of the stock of newly formed Brown Corporation. Included in the transfer are the unrealized receivables and payables of the business. The balance sheet of Brown immediately following its formation is as follows:

Brown Corporation
Balance Sheet
March 1, 2011

Assets

	Basis to Brown	Fair Market Value
Cash	$100,000	$ 100,000
Unrealized accounts receivable	–0–	220,000
Equipment (cost $210,000; depreciation claimed $60,000)	150,000	320,000
Building (straight-line depreciation)	160,000	400,000
Land	40,000	160,000
Total	$450,000	$1,200,000

Liabilities and Equity

Liabilities:	
Accounts payable—trade	$ 120,000
Notes payable—bank	360,000
Stockholder's equity:	
Common stock	720,000
Total	$1,200,000

Discuss the tax consequences of the incorporation to Natalie and to Brown Corporation.

ISSUE ID

37. **LO.1, 2, 3** Four years ago, Gene exchanged commercial real estate worth $1.5 million (basis of $300,000) and subject to a mortgage of $200,000, for land worth $1.15 million, subject to a mortgage of $150,000, and cash of $300,000. In the current year, Gene transfers the land that he received in the exchange to newly formed Bronze Corporation for all of its stock. Bronze Corporation assumes the original mortgage on the land, current face amount of $100,000, and a second mortgage, face amount of $20,000. Gene had placed the second mortgage on the land to secure the purchase of some equipment that he used in this business. What are the tax issues?

38. **LO.1, 2, 3** David organizes White Corporation with a transfer of land (basis of $200,000, fair market value of $600,000) that is subject to a mortgage of $150,000. A month before the incorporation, David borrowed $100,000 for personal purposes and gave the bank a lien on the land. White Corporation issues stock worth $350,000 to David and assumes the mortgage of $150,000 and the personal loan of $100,000. What are the tax consequences of the incorporation to David and to White Corporation?

DECISION MAKING

39. **LO.1, 3** Michael transfers the following assets to Peach Corporation in exchange for all of its stock. (Assume neither Michael nor Peach plans to make any special tax elections at the time of incorporation.)

Assets	Michael's Adjusted Basis	Fair Market Value
Inventory	$ 60,000	$ 90,000
Delivery vehicles	150,000	100,000
Shelving	80,000	70,000

a. What is Michael's recognized gain or loss?
b. What is Michael's basis in the stock?
c. What is Peach's basis in the inventory, delivery vehicles, and shelving?
d. If Michael has no intentions of selling his Peach stock for at least 15 years, what action would you recommend that Michael and Peach Corporation consider? How does this change the previous answers?

40. **LO.1, 2, 3** Fay, a sole proprietor, is engaged in a cash basis, service business. In the current year, she incorporates the business to form Robin Corporation. She transfers assets with a basis of $400,000 (fair market value of $1.2 million), a bank loan of $360,000 (which Robin assumes), and $80,000 in trade payables in return for all of Robin's stock. What are the tax consequences of the incorporation of the business?

41. **LO.1, 3** Sara and Jane form Wren Corporation. Sara transfers property, basis of $25,000 and value of $200,000, for 50 shares in Wren Corporation. Jane transfers property, basis of $10,000 and value of $185,000, and agrees to serve as manager of Wren for one year; in return, Jane receives 50 shares in Wren. The value of Jane's services to Wren is $15,000.
a. What gain or income do Sara and Jane recognize on the exchange?
b. What is Wren Corporation's basis in the property transferred by Sara and Jane? How does Wren treat the value of the services Jane renders?

42. **LO.1, 3** Assume in Problem 41 that Jane receives the 50 shares of Wren Corporation stock in consideration for the appreciated property and for providing legal services in organizing the corporation. The value of Jane's services is $15,000.
a. What gain or income does Jane recognize?
b. What is Wren Corporation's basis in the property transferred by Jane? How does Wren treat the value of the services Jane renders?

43. **LO.1, 3** On January 7, 2011, Donna transferred machinery worth $100,000 (basis of $30,000) to a controlled corporation, Jay, in a transfer that qualified under § 351. Donna had deducted depreciation on the machinery in the amount of $80,000 when she held the machinery for use in her proprietorship. On November 16, 2011, Jay Corporation sells the machinery for $95,000. What are the tax consequences to Donna and to Jay Corporation on the sale of the machinery?

44. **LO.4** RetailMart Corporation desires to set up a distribution facility in a western state. After considerable negotiations with a small town in Oregon, RetailMart accepts the following offer: land and building (fair market value of $4 million) and cash of $1.5 million.
a. How much gain, if any, must RetailMart Corporation recognize?
b. What basis will RetailMart Corporation have in the land and building?
c. Within one year of the contribution, RetailMart renovates the building for $800,000 and purchases inventory for $300,000. What basis will RetailMart Corporation have in each of these assets?
d. What is the treatment of the $400,000 in cash that RetailMart received from the town but did not use?

COMMUNICATIONS

45. **LO.5, 6** Emily Patrick (36 Paradise Road, Northampton, MA 01060) formed Teal Corporation a number of years ago with an investment of $200,000 cash, for which she received $20,000 in stock and $180,000 in bonds bearing interest of 8% and maturing in nine years. Several years later, Emily lent the corporation an additional $50,000 on open account. In the current year, Teal Corporation becomes insolvent and is declared

bankrupt. During the corporation's existence, Emily was paid an annual salary of $60,000. Write a letter to Emily in which you explain how she would treat her losses for tax purposes.

46. **LO.5, 6** Stock in Jaybird Corporation (555 Industry Lane, Pueblo, CO 81001) is held equally by Vera, Wade, and Wes. Jaybird seeks additional capital in the amount of $900,000 to construct a building. Vera, Wade, and Wes each propose to lend Jaybird Corporation $300,000, taking from Jaybird a $300,000 four-year note with interest payable annually at two points below the prime rate. Jaybird Corporation has current taxable income of $2 million. You represent Jaybird Corporation. Jaybird's president, Steve Ferguson, asks you how the payments on the notes might be treated for tax purposes. Prepare a letter to Ferguson and a memo to your tax files where you document your conclusions.

COMMUNICATIONS

47. **LO.6** Sam, a single taxpayer, acquired stock in a corporation that qualified as a small business corporation under § 1244, at a cost of $100,000 three years ago. He sells the stock for $10,000 in the current tax year.
    a. How will the loss be treated for tax purposes?
    b. Assume instead that Sam sold the stock to his sister, Kara, a few months after it was acquired for $100,000 (its fair market value). If Kara sells the stock for $60,000 in the current year, how should she treat the loss for tax purposes?

48. **LO.6** Three years ago and at a cost of $40,000, Paul Sanders acquired stock in a corporation that qualified as a small business corporation (under § 1244). A few months after he acquired the stock, when it was still worth $40,000, he gave it to his brother, Mike Sanders. Mike, who is married and files a joint return, sells the stock for $25,000 in the current tax year. Mike asks you, his tax adviser, how the sale will be treated for tax purposes. Prepare a letter to your client and a memo to the file. Mike's address is 10 Hunt Wood Drive, Hadley, PA 16130.

COMMUNICATIONS

49. **LO.6** Susan transfers property (basis of $50,000 and fair market value of $25,000) to Thrush Corporation in exchange for shares of § 1244 stock. (Assume the transfer qualifies under § 351.)
    a. What is the basis of the stock to Susan? (Susan and Thrush do not make an election to reduce her stock basis.)
    b. What is the basis of the stock to Susan for purposes of § 1244?
    c. If Susan sells the stock for $20,000 two years later, how will the loss be treated for tax purposes?

50. **LO.5, 7** Frank, Cora, and Mitch are equal shareholders in Purple Corporation. The corporation's assets have a tax basis of $50,000 and a fair market value of $600,000. In the current year, Frank and Cora each loan Purple Corporation $150,000. The notes to Frank and Cora bear interest of 8% per annum. Mitch leases equipment to Purple Corporation for an annual rental of $12,000. Discuss whether the shareholder loans from Frank and Cora might be reclassified as equity. Consider in your discussion whether Purple Corporation has an acceptable debt-equity ratio.

DECISION MAKING

RESEARCH PROBLEMS

Note: Solutions to Research Problems can be prepared by using the **Checkpoint® Student Edition** online research product, which is available to accompany this text. It is also possible to prepare solutions to the Research Problems by using tax research materials found in a standard tax library.

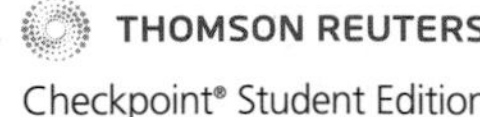

Research Problem 1. Lynn Jones, Shawn, Walt, and Donna are trying to decide whether they should organize a corporation and transfer their shares of stock in several corporations to this new corporation. All their shares are listed on the New York Stock Exchange and are readily marketable. Lynn would transfer shares in Brown Corporation; Shawn would transfer stock in Rust Corporation; Walt would transfer stock in White Corporation; and Donna would transfer stock in several corporations. The stock would be held by the newly formed corporation for investment purposes. Lynn asks you, her tax adviser, if she would have gain on the transfer of her substantially appreciated shares in Brown Corporation if she transfers the shares to a newly formed corporation. She also asks whether there will be

DECISION MAKING

COMMUNICATIONS

tax consequences if she, Shawn, Walt, and Donna form a partnership, rather than a corporation, to which they would transfer their readily marketable stock. Your input will be critical as they make their decision. Prepare a letter to the client, Lynn Jones, and a memo for the firm's files. Lynn's address is 1540 Maxwell Avenue, Highland, KY 41099.

Research Problem 2. Joel has operated his business as a sole proprietorship for many years but has decided to incorporate the business in order to limit his exposure to personal liability. The balance sheet of his business is as follows:

	Adjusted Basis	Fair Market Value
Assets:		
Cash	$ 50,000	$ 50,000
Accounts receivable	40,000	40,000
Inventory	30,000	60,000
Fixed assets	10,000	200,000
	$130,000	$350,000
Liabilities:		
Trade accounts payable	$ 25,000	$ 25,000
Notes payable	175,000	175,000
Owner's equity	(70,000)	150,000
	$130,000	$350,000

One problem with this plan is that the liabilities of his sole proprietorship exceed the basis of the assets to be transferred to the corporation by $70,000 ($200,000 − $130,000). Therefore, Joel would be required to recognize a gain of $70,000. He is not pleased with this result and asks you about the effect of drawing up a $70,000 note that he would transfer to the corporation. Would the note, which promises a future payment to the corporation of $70,000, enable Joel to avoid recognition of the gain?

Partial list of research aids:
§ 357(c).

Research Problem 3. Tim is a real estate broker who specializes in commercial real estate. Although he usually buys and sells on behalf of others, he also maintains a portfolio of property of his own. He holds this property, mainly unimproved land, either as an investment or for sale to others.

In early 2010, Irene and Al contact Tim regarding a tract of land located just outside the city limits. Tim bought the property, which is known as the Moore farm, several years ago for $600,000. At that time, no one knew that it was located on a geological fault line. Irene, a well-known architect, and Al, a building contractor, want Tim to join them in developing the property for residential use. They are aware of the fault line but believe they can circumvent the problem by using newly developed design and construction technology. Because of the geological flaw, however, they regard the Moore farm as being worth only $450,000. Their intent is to organize a corporation to build the housing project, and each party will receive stock commensurate to the property or services contributed.

After consulting his tax adviser, Tim agrees to join the venture if certain modifications to the proposed arrangement are made. The transfer of the land would be structured as a sale to the corporation. Instead of receiving stock, Tim would receive a note from the corporation. The note would be interest bearing and be due in five years. The maturity value of the note would be $450,000—the amount that even Tim concedes is the fair market value of the Moore farm.

What income tax consequences ensue from Tim's suggested approach? Compare this result with what would happen if Tim merely transferred the Moore farm in return for stock in the new corporation.

Research Problem 4. After considerable research, Brock and Louise decided to open a well-known franchise restaurant, Sammy's Sandwich Shop. Before opening the shop in a nearby strip shopping center, Brock and Louise paid $1,000 to an attorney to incorporate their business as B&L, Inc. They also paid a franchise fee of $20,000 to SSS Franchisor for the right to operate as Sammy's Sandwich Shop.

Soon, however, they learned that many Sammy's Sandwich Shop locations across the country were failing. In large measure, these failures were due to difficulties in dealing with the franchisor, SSS Franchisor. Brock and Louise also realized that to be successful, they would need to raise an additional $150,000 of capital. Ultimately, they closed the business and sought a refund of the franchise fee. As SSS Franchisor has repeatedly refused to refund their fee and any legal recourse appears fruitless, Brock and Louise have no hope of any recovery. How should the legal and franchise fees be treated for tax purposes?

Partial list of research aids:
Alami El Moujahid, 97 TCM 1165, T.C.Memo. 2009–42.

Use the tax resources of the Internet to address the following questions. Do not restrict your search to the Web, but include a review of newsgroups and general reference materials, practitioner sites and resources, primary sources of the tax law, chat rooms and discussion groups, and other opportunities.

Research Problem 5. Identify two publicly traded corporations that have issued more than one class of stock to their shareholders. Was the issuance of the additional classes of stock part of the original incorporation, or did it occur later? Determine the rationale for the corporations' actions.

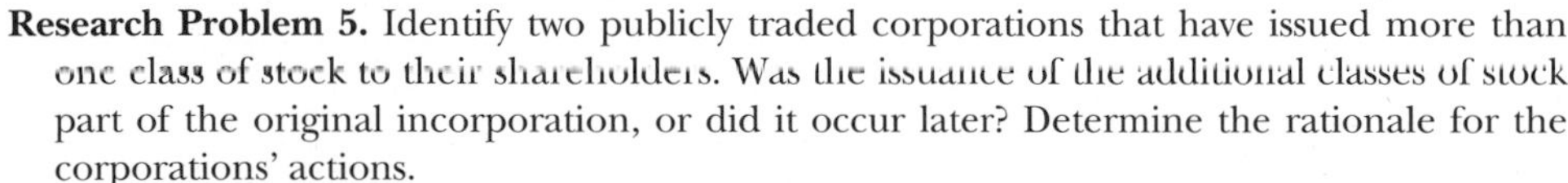

Research Problem 6. Have the provisions of § 1202, which relate to qualified small business stock, been widely used since their enactment? What leads you to this conclusion? What rationale did Congress provide as a justification for the provision's enactment? What justification was offered for increasing the exclusion percentage in 2009 and 2010?

Research Problem 7. Limited liability company (LLC) status has become a very popular form of operating a business in recent years. Investigate how the growing popularity of LLC status has affected the relative number of new businesses that have chosen to operate as a corporation.

[illegible]

Use the tax resources of the Internet to address the following questions. Do not restrict your search to the Web, but include a review of newsgroups and general reference materials, practitioner sites and resources, primary sources of the tax law, chat rooms and discussion groups, and other opportunities.

[illegible]

CHAPTER 5

Corporations: Earnings & Profits and Dividend Distributions

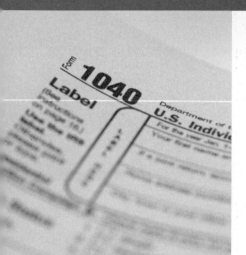

LEARNING OBJECTIVES

After completing Chapter 5, you should be able to:

LO.1

Explain the role that earnings and profits play in determining the tax treatment of distributions.

LO.2

Compute a corporation's earnings and profits.

LO.3

Apply the rules for allocating earnings and profits to distributions.

LO.4

Describe the tax treatment of dividends for individual shareholders.

LO.5

Evaluate the tax impact of property dividends on the recipient shareholder and the corporation making the distribution.

LO.6

Identify the nature and treatment of constructive dividends.

LO.7

Discuss the tax treatment of stock dividends and stock rights.

LO.8

Structure corporate distributions in a manner that minimizes the tax consequences to the parties involved.

OUTLINE

For the latest in changes to tax legislation, visit **www.cengage.com/taxation/swft.**

THE BIG PICTURE **Tax Solutions for the Real World**

TAXING CORPORATE DISTRIBUTIONS

Lime Corporation, an ice cream manufacturer, has had a very profitable year. To share its profits with its two shareholders, Orange Corporation and Gustavo, it distributes cash of $200,000 to Orange and real estate worth $300,000 (adjusted basis of $20,000) to Gustavo. The real estate is subject to a mortgage of $100,000, which Gustavo assumes. The distribution is made on December 31, Lime's year-end.

Lime Corporation has had both good and bad years in the past. More often than not, however, it has lost money. Despite this year's banner profits, the GAAP-based balance sheet for Lime indicates a year-end deficit in retained earnings. Consequently, the distribution of cash and land is treated as a liquidating distribution for financial reporting purposes, resulting in a reduction of Lime's paid-in capital account.

The tax consequences of the distributions to the corporation and its shareholders depend on a variety of factors that are not directly related to the financial reporting treatment. Identify these factors and explain the tax effects of the distributions to both Lime Corporation and its two shareholders. **Read the chapter and formulate your response.**

Chapter 4 examined the tax consequences of corporate formation. In Chapters 5 and 6, the focus shifts to the tax treatment of corporate distributions, a topic that plays a leading role in tax planning. The importance of corporate distributions derives from the variety of tax treatments that may apply. From the shareholder's perspective, distributions received from the corporation may be treated as ordinary income, preferentially taxed dividend income, capital gain, or a nontaxable recovery of capital. From the corporation's perspective, distributions made to shareholders are generally not deductible. However, a corporation may recognize losses in liquidating distributions (see Chapter 6), and gains may be recognized at the corporate level on distributions of appreciated property. In the most common scenario, a distribution triggers dividend income to the shareholder and provides no deduction to the paying corporation, resulting in a double tax (at both the corporate and the shareholder level). This double tax may be mitigated by a variety of factors including the corporate dividends received deduction and preferential tax rates on qualified dividends paid to individuals.

As will become apparent in the subsequent discussion, the tax treatment of corporate distributions can be affected by a number of considerations:

- The availability of earnings to be distributed.
- The basis of the shareholder's stock.
- The character of the property being distributed.
- Whether the shareholder gives up ownership in return for the distribution.
- Whether the distribution is liquidating or nonliquidating.
- Whether the distribution is a "qualified dividend."
- Whether the shareholder is an individual or another kind of taxpaying entity.

This chapter discusses the tax rules related to nonliquidating distributions of cash and property. Distributions of stock and stock rights are also addressed. Chapter 6 extends the discussion to the tax treatment of stock redemptions and corporate liquidations.

5.1 Corporate Distributions—Overview

LO.1

Explain the role that earnings and profits play in determining the tax treatment of distributions.

To the extent that a distribution is made from corporate earnings and profits (E & P), the shareholder is deemed to receive a dividend, taxed as ordinary income or as preferentially taxed dividend income.[1] Generally, corporate distributions are presumed to be paid out of E & P (defined later in this chapter) and are treated as dividends *unless* the parties to the transaction can show otherwise. Distributions not treated as dividends (because of insufficient E & P) are nontaxable to the extent of the shareholder's stock basis, which is reduced accordingly. The excess of the distribution over the shareholder's basis is treated as a gain from sale or exchange of the stock.[2]

EXAMPLE 1

At the beginning of the year, Amber Corporation (a calendar year taxpayer) has E & P of $15,000. The corporation generates no additional E & P during the year. On July 1, the corporation distributes $20,000 to its sole shareholder, Bonnie, whose stock basis is $4,000. In this situation, Bonnie recognizes dividend income of $15,000 (the amount of E & P distributed). In addition, she reduces her stock basis from $4,000 to zero, and she recognizes a taxable gain of $1,000 (the excess of the distribution over the stock basis). ■

5.2 Earnings and Profits (E & P)—§ 312

LO.2

Compute a corporation's earnings and profits.

The notion of **earnings and profits** is similar in many respects to the accounting concept of retained earnings. Both are measures of the firm's accumulated capital (E & P includes both the accumulated E & P of the corporation since February 28, 1913, and the current year's E & P). A difference exists, however, in the way these figures are calculated. The computation of retained earnings is based on financial accounting rules while E & P is determined using rules specified in the tax law.

E & P fixes the upper limit on the amount of dividend income that shareholders must recognize as a result of a distribution by the corporation. In this sense, E & P represents the corporation's economic ability to pay a dividend without impairing its capital. Thus, the effect of a specific transaction on E & P can often be determined by assessing whether the transaction increases or decreases the corporation's capacity to pay a dividend.

COMPUTATION OF E & P

The Code does not explicitly define the term *earnings and profits.* Instead, a series of adjustments to taxable income are identified to provide a measure of the corporation's economic income. Both cash basis and accrual basis corporations use the same approach when determining E & P.[3]

Additions to Taxable Income

To determine current E & P, it is necessary to add *all* previously excluded income items back to taxable income. Included among these positive adjustments are interest on municipal bonds, excluded life insurance proceeds (in excess of cash surrender value), and Federal income tax refunds from tax paid in prior years.

EXAMPLE 2

A corporation collects $100,000 on a key employee life insurance policy (the corporation is the owner and beneficiary of the policy). At the time the policy matured on the death of the insured employee, it possessed a cash surrender value of $30,000. None of

[1] §§ 301(c)(1), 316, and 1(h)(11).
[2] §§ 301(c)(2) and (3).
[3] Section 312 describes many of the adjustments to taxable income necessary to determine E & P. Regulation § 1.312–6 addresses the effect of accounting methods on E & P.

the $100,000 is included in the corporation's taxable income, but $70,000 is added to taxable income when computing current E & P. The distribution of the $30,000 cash surrender value does not increase E & P because it does not reflect an increase in the corporation's dividend-paying capacity. Instead, it represents a shift in the corporation's assets from life insurance to cash. ■

In addition to excluded income items, the dividends received deduction and the domestic production activities deduction are added back to taxable income to determine E & P. Neither of these deductions decreases the corporation's assets. Instead, they are partial exclusions for specific types of income (dividend income and income from domestic production activities). Since they do not impair the corporation's ability to pay dividends, they do not reduce E & P.

Subtractions from Taxable Income

When calculating E & P, it is also necessary to subtract certain nondeductible expenses from taxable income. These negative adjustments include the nondeductible portion of meal and entertainment expenses, related-party losses, expenses incurred to produce tax-exempt income, Federal income taxes paid, nondeductible key employee life insurance premiums (net of increases in cash surrender value), nondeductible fines, penalties, and lobbying expenses.

EXAMPLE 3

A corporation sells property with a basis of $10,000 to its sole shareholder for $8,000. Because of § 267 (disallowance of losses on sales between related parties), the $2,000 loss cannot be deducted when calculating the corporation's taxable income. However, since the overall economic effect of the transaction is a decrease in the corporation's assets by $2,000, the loss reduces the current E & P for the year of sale. ■

EXAMPLE 4

A corporation pays a $10,000 premium on a key employee life insurance policy covering the life of its president. As a result of the payment, the cash surrender value of the policy is increased by $7,000. Although none of the $10,000 premium is deductible for tax purposes, current E & P is reduced by $3,000. The $7,000 increase in cash surrender value is not subtracted because it does not represent a decrease in the corporation's ability to pay a dividend. Instead, it represents a shift in the corporation's assets, from cash to life insurance. ■

Timing Adjustments

Some E & P adjustments shift the effect of a transaction from the year of its inclusion in or deduction from taxable income to the year in which it has an economic effect on the corporation. Charitable contributions, net operating losses, and capital losses all necessitate this kind of adjustment.

EXAMPLE 5

During 2011, a corporation makes charitable contributions, $12,000 of which cannot be deducted when calculating the taxable income for the year because of the 10% taxable income limitation. Consequently, the $12,000 is carried forward to 2012 and fully deducted in that year. The excess charitable contribution reduces the corporation's current E & P for 2011 by $12,000 and increases its current E & P for 2012 (when the deduction is allowed) by the same amount. The increase in E & P in 2012 is necessary because the charitable contribution carryover reduces the taxable income for that year (the starting point for computing E & P) and already has been taken into account in determining the E & P for 2011. ■

Gains and losses from property transactions generally affect the determination of E & P only to the extent that they are recognized for tax purposes. Thus, gains and losses deferred under the like-kind exchange provision and deferred involuntary conversion gains do not affect E & P until recognized. Accordingly, no timing adjustment is required for these items.

CONCEPT SUMMARY 5.1

E & P Adjustments

Nature of the Transaction	Adjustment to Taxable Income to Determine Current E & P	
	Addition	Subtraction
Tax-exempt income	X	
Dividends received deduction	X	
Domestic production activities deduction	X	
Collection of proceeds from insurance policy on life of corporate officer (in excess of cash surrender value)	X	
Deferred gain on installment sale (all gain is added to E & P in year of sale)	X	
Future recognition of installment sale gross profit		X
Excess charitable contribution (over 10% limitation) and excess capital loss in year incurred		X
Deduction of charitable contribution, NOL, or capital loss carryovers in succeeding taxable year (increase E & P because deduction reduces taxable income while E & P was reduced in a prior year)	X	
Federal income taxes paid		X
Federal income tax refund	X	
Loss on sale between related parties		X
Nondeductible fines, penalties, and lobbying expenses		X
Nondeductible meal and entertainment expenses		X
Payment of premiums on insurance policy on life of corporate officer (in excess of increase in cash surrender value of policy)		X
Realized gain (not recognized) on an involuntary conversion	No effect	
Realized gain or loss (not recognized) on a like-kind exchange	No effect	
Excess percentage depletion (only cost depletion can reduce E & P)	X	
Accelerated depreciation (E & P is reduced only by straight-line, units-of-production, or machine hours depreciation)	X	X
Additional first-year depreciation	X	
Section 179 expense in year elected (80%)	X	
Section 179 expense in four years following election (20% each year)		X
Increase (decrease) in LIFO recapture amount	X	X
Intangible drilling costs deducted currently (reduce E & P in future years by amortizing costs over 60 months)	X	
Mine exploration and development costs (reduce E & P in future years by amortizing costs over 120 months)	X	

development costs be amortized over a period of 60 months and 120 months, respectively. For income tax purposes, however, these costs can be deducted in the current year.[13]

SUMMARY OF E & P ADJUSTMENTS

E & P serves as a measure of a corporation's earnings that are available for distribution as taxable dividends to the shareholders. Current E & P is determined by making a series of adjustments to the corporation's taxable income that are outlined in Concept Summary 5.1. Other items that affect E & P, such as property dividends, are covered later in the chapter. The effect of stock redemptions on E & P is covered in Chapter 6.

[13] § 312(n)(2).

CURRENT VERSUS ACCUMULATED E & P

Accumulated E & P is the total of all previous years' current E & P (since February 28, 1913) reduced by distributions made from E & P in previous years. It is important to distinguish between **current E & P** and **accumulated E & P** because the taxability of corporate distributions depends on how these two accounts are allocated to each distribution made during the year. A complex set of rules governs the allocation process.[14] These rules are described in the following section and summarized in Concept Summary 5.2.

LO.3

Apply the rules for allocating earnings and profits to distributions.

ALLOCATING E & P TO DISTRIBUTIONS

When a positive balance exists in both the current and the accumulated E & P accounts, corporate distributions are deemed to be made first from current E & P and then from accumulated E & P. When distributions exceed the amount of current E & P, it becomes necessary to allocate current and accumulated E & P to each distribution made during the year. Current E & P is applied first on a pro rata basis (using dollar amounts) to each distribution. Then, accumulated E & P is applied in chronological order, beginning with the earliest distribution. As seen in the following example, this allocation is important if any shareholder sells stock during the year.

EXAMPLE 8

On January 1 of the current year, Black Corporation has accumulated E & P of $10,000. Current E & P for the year amounts to $30,000. Megan and Matt are sole *equal* shareholders of Black from January 1 to July 31. On August 1, Megan sells all of her stock to Helen. Black makes two distributions to shareholders during the year: $40,000 to Megan and Matt ($20,000 to each) on July 1, and $40,000 to Matt and Helen ($20,000 to each) on December 1. Current and accumulated E & P are applied to the two distributions as follows:

	Source of Distribution		
	Current E & P	Accumulated E & P	Return of Capital
July 1 distribution ($40,000)	$15,000	$10,000	$15,000
December 1 distribution ($40,000)	15,000	—	25,000

Since 50% of the total distributions are made on July 1 and December 1, respectively, one-half of current E & P is applied to each of the two distributions. Accumulated E & P is applied in chronological order, so the entire amount attaches to the July 1 distribution. The tax consequences to the shareholders are presented below.

	Shareholder		
	Megan	Matt	Helen
July distribution ($40,000)			
Dividend income—			
From current E & P ($15,000)	$ 7,500	$ 7,500	$ -0-
From accumulated E & P ($10,000)	5,000	5,000	-0-
Return of capital ($15,000)	7,500	7,500	-0-
December distribution ($40,000)			
Dividend income—			
From current E & P ($15,000)	-0-	7,500	7,500
From accumulated E & P ($0)	-0-	-0-	-0-
Return of capital ($25,000)	-0-	12,500	12,500
Total dividend income	$12,500	$20,000	$ 7,500
Nontaxable return of capital (assuming sufficient basis in the stock investment)	$ 7,500	$20,000	$12,500

[14] Regulations relating to the source of a distribution are at Reg. § 1.316–2.

Because the balance in the accumulated E & P account is exhausted when it is applied to the July 1 distribution, Megan has more dividend income than Helen, even though both receive equal distributions during the year. In addition, each shareholder's basis is reduced by the nontaxable return of capital; any excess over basis results in taxable gain. ■

When the tax years of the corporation and its shareholders are not the same, it may be impossible to determine the amount of current E & P on a timely basis. For example, if shareholders use a calendar year and the corporation uses a fiscal year, then current E & P may not be ascertainable until after the shareholders' returns have been filed. To address this timing issue, the allocation rules presume that current E & P is sufficient to cover every distribution made during the year until the parties can show otherwise.

EXAMPLE 9

Green Corporation uses the fiscal year of July 1 through June 30 for tax purposes. Carol, Green's only shareholder, uses a calendar year. On July 1, 2011, Green Corporation has a zero balance in its accumulated E & P account. For fiscal year 2011–2012, the corporation suffers a $5,000 deficit in current E & P. On August 1, 2011, Green distributed $10,000 to Carol. The distribution is dividend income to Carol and is reported when she files her income tax return for the 2011 calendar year, on or before April 15, 2012. Because Carol cannot prove until June 30, 2012, that the corporation has a deficit for the 2011–2012 fiscal year, she must assume the $10,000 distribution is fully covered by current E & P. When Carol learns of the deficit, she can file an amended return for 2011 showing the $10,000 as a return of capital. ■

Additional difficulties arise when either the current or the accumulated E & P account has a deficit balance. In particular, when current E & P is positive and accumulated E & P has a deficit balance, accumulated E & P is *not* netted against current E & P. Instead, the distribution is deemed to be a taxable dividend to the extent of the positive current E & P balance.

EXAMPLE 10
THE BIG PICTURE

Return to the facts of *The Big Picture* on p. 5–2. Recall that Lime Corporation had a deficit in GAAP-based retained earnings at the start of the year and banner profits during the year. Assume that these financial results translate into an $800,000 deficit in accumulated E & P at the start of the year and current E & P of $600,000. In this case, current E & P would exceed the $500,000 of cash and property distributed to the shareholders. The distributions are treated as taxable dividends; they are deemed to be paid from current E & P even though Lime still has a deficit in accumulated E & P at the end of the year. ■

In contrast to the previous rule, when a deficit exists in current E & P and a positive balance exists in accumulated E & P, the accounts are netted at the date of distribution. If the resulting balance is zero or negative, the distribution is a return of capital. If a positive balance results, the distribution is a dividend to the extent of the balance. Any loss in current E & P is deemed to accrue ratably throughout the year unless the parties can show otherwise.

EXAMPLE 11

At the beginning of the current year, Gray Corporation (a calendar year taxpayer) has accumulated E & P of $10,000. During the year, the corporation incurs a $15,000 deficit in current E & P that accrues ratably. On July 1, Gray Corporation distributes $6,000 in cash to Hal, its sole shareholder. To determine how much of the $6,000 cash distribution represents dividend income to Hal, the balances of both accumulated and current E & P as of July 1 are determined and netted. This is necessary because of the deficit in current E & P.

CONCEPT SUMMARY 5.2

Allocating E & P to Distributions

1. Current E & P is applied first to distributions on a pro rata basis; then, accumulated E & P is applied (as necessary) in chronological order beginning with the earliest distribution. See Example 8.
2. Until the parties can show otherwise, it is presumed that current E & P covers all distributions. See Example 9.
3. When a deficit exists in accumulated E & P and a positive balance exists in current E & P, distributions are regarded as dividends to the extent of current E & P. See Example 10.
4. When a deficit exists in current E & P and a positive balance exists in accumulated E & P, the two accounts are netted at the date of distribution. If the resulting balance is zero or a deficit, the distribution is treated as a return of capital, first reducing the basis of the stock to zero, then generating taxable gain. If a positive balance results, the distribution is a dividend to the extent of the balance. Any loss in current E & P is deemed to accrue ratably throughout the year unless the corporation can show otherwise. See Example 11.

	Source of Distribution	
	Current E & P	Accumulated E & P
January 1		$10,000
July 1 (½ of $15,000 net loss)	($7,500)	2,500
July 1 distribution of $6,000:		
Dividend income: $2,500		
Return of capital: $3,500		

The balance in E & P just before the July 1 distribution is $2,500. Thus, of the $6,000 distribution, $2,500 is taxed as a dividend, and $3,500 represents a return of capital. ■

5.3 Dividends

LO.4

Describe the tax treatment of dividends for individual shareholders.

As noted earlier, distributions by a corporation from its E & P are treated as dividends. The tax treatment of dividends varies, depending on whether the shareholder receiving them is a corporation or another kind of taxpaying entity. All corporations treat dividends as ordinary income and are permitted a dividends received deduction (see Chapter 2). Through 2012, qualified dividend income earned by individuals is taxed at reduced tax rates. Beginning in 2013, dividends will be taxed as ordinary income for individuals if Congress does not act to extend the reduced tax rate.

Is the Double Tax on Dividends Fair?

As noted in this chapter, the double tax on dividends remains controversial. The tax rate on qualified dividends has, in the past, been as high as 70 percent, and it is possible that the current 15 percent tax rate will be increased when it expires at the end of 2012. Yet, in most countries throughout the world, there is no double tax on dividend income. Many arguments for and against the double tax have been made, usually reflecting the vested interests of the individuals or organizations involved. Arguments supporting repeal of the double tax focus on capital formation and economic stimulus, while those against repeal are based on equity. What do *you* believe? Is the double tax imposed on dividends fair? Why or why not?

RATIONALE FOR REDUCED TAX RATES ON DIVIDENDS

The double tax on corporate income has always been controversial. Arguably, taxing dividends twice creates several undesirable economic distortions, including:

- An incentive to invest in noncorporate rather than corporate entities.
- An incentive for corporations to finance operations with debt rather than with equity since interest payments are deductible. Notably, this behavior increases the vulnerability of corporations in economic downturns because of higher leverage.
- An incentive for corporations to retain earnings and structure distributions of profits to avoid the double tax.

Collectively, these distortions raise the cost of capital for corporate investments. Estimates are that eliminating the double tax would increase capital stock in the corporate sector by as much as $500 billion.[15] In addition, some argue that elimination of the double tax would make the United States more competitive globally. Bear in mind that a majority of our trading partners assess only one tax on corporate income.

While many support a reduced or no tax rate on dividends, others contend that the double tax should remain in place because of the concentration of economic power held by publicly traded corporations. Furthermore, many of the distortions noted above can be avoided through the use of deductible payments by C corporations and by utilizing other forms of doing business (e.g., partnerships, limited liability companies, and Subchapter S corporations). Those favoring retention of the double tax also note that the benefits of reduced tax rates on dividends flow disproportionately to the wealthy.[16]

The United States continues to struggle to find the appropriate course to follow on the taxation of dividends. The reduced tax rate on **qualified dividends** for individuals applicable through 2012 reflects a compromise between the complete elimination of tax on dividends and the treatment of dividends as ordinary income. At this time, the tax treatment of dividends is uncertain. Congress may act to extend the current reduced rates on qualified dividends for individuals. If new legislation is not enacted, however, beginning in 2013 qualified dividends will once again be taxed as ordinary income.

QUALIFIED DIVIDENDS

Qualified Dividends—Application and Effect

Under current law, dividends that meet certain requirements are subject to a 15 percent tax rate for most individual taxpayers from 2003 through 2012. Individuals in the 10 or 15 percent rate brackets were subject to a 5 percent rate on dividends paid from 2003 through 2007. Beginning in 2008, dividends are exempt from tax for these lower-income taxpayers.[17]

Qualified Dividends—Requirements

To be taxed at the lower rates, dividends must be paid by either domestic or certain qualified foreign corporations. Qualified foreign corporations include those traded on a U.S. stock exchange or any corporation located in a country that

[15]Integration of Individual and Corporate Tax Systems, Report of the Department of the Treasury (January 1992).

[16]The Urban Institute–Brookings Institution Tax Policy Center estimates that more than one-half—53%—of the benefits from the reduced tax rate on dividends go to the 0.2% of households with incomes over $1 million.

[17]See §§ 1(h)(1) and (11).

GLOBAL
Tax Issues

Corporate Integration

From an international perspective, the double taxation of dividends is unusual. Most countries have adopted a policy of corporate integration, which imposes a single tax on corporate profits. Corporate integration takes several forms. One popular approach is to impose a tax at the corporate level, but allow shareholders to claim a credit for corporate-level taxes paid when dividends are received. A second alternative is to allow a corporate-level deduction for dividends paid to shareholders. A third approach is to allow shareholders to exclude corporate dividends from income. A fourth alternative suggested in the past by the U.S. Treasury is the "comprehensive business income tax," which excludes both dividend and interest income while disallowing deductions for interest expense.

(1) has a comprehensive income tax treaty with the United States, (2) has an information-sharing agreement with the United States, and (3) is approved by the Treasury.[18]

Two other requirements must be met for dividends to qualify for the favorable rates. First, dividends paid to shareholders who hold both long and short positions in the stock do not qualify. Second, the stock on which the dividend is paid must be held for more than 60 days during the 121-day period beginning 60 days before the ex-dividend date.[19] To allow for settlement delays, the ex-dividend date is typically 2 days before the date of record on a dividend. This holding period rule parallels the rule applied to corporations that claim the dividends received deduction.[20]

EXAMPLE 12

In June of the current year, Green Corporation announces that a dividend of $1.50 will be paid on each share of its common stock to shareholders of record on July 15. Amy and Corey, two unrelated shareholders, own 1,000 shares of the stock on the record date (July 15). Consequently, each receives $1,500 (1,000 shares × $1.50). Assume Amy purchased her stock on January 15 of this year, while Corey purchased her stock on July 1. Both shareholders sell their stock on July 20. To qualify for the lower dividend rate, stock must be held for more than 60 days during the 121-day period beginning 60 days prior to July 13 (the ex-dividend date). The $1,500 Amy receives is subject to preferential 15%/0% treatment. The $1,500 Corey receives, however, is not. Corey did not meet the 60-day holding requirement, so her dividend will be taxed as ordinary income. ■

Qualified dividends are not considered investment income for purposes of determining the investment interest expense deduction. Taxpayers can, however, elect to treat qualified dividends as ordinary income (taxed at regular rates) and include them in investment interest income. Thus, taxpayers subject to an investment interest expense limitation must evaluate the relative benefits of taxing qualified dividends at low rates versus using the dividends as investment income to increase the amount of deductible investment interest expense.

[18] In Notice 2006–101, 2006–2 C.B. 930, the Treasury identified 55 qualifying countries (among those included in the list are the members of the European Union, the Russian Federation, Canada, and Mexico). Nonqualifying countries not on the list include most of the former Soviet republics (except Kazakhstan), Bermuda, and the Netherlands Antilles.

[19] § 1(h)(11)(B)(iii)(I).

[20] See § 246(c).

TAX *in* the NEWS

Higher Taxes on Dividends Don't Mean Lower Dividends

The potential expiration of the reduced tax rate on dividends in 2013 is not likely to have much impact on corporations' dividend policies. The sensitivity of some companies to how the market may react to dividend cuts will likely deter them from reducing their dividends. In addition, shareholders who are not subject to individual tax rates, such as pension funds and foreign investors, own a large portion of U.S. equities. Reuvan Avi-Yonah, a professor at the University of Michigan Law School, suggests that during the last decade companies pandered to foreign hedge fund shareholders by favoring stock redemptions over dividends as a means of paying assets to shareholders. As a result, he argues, the tax cut was not effective in encouraging companies to pay out dividends.

Other research by three accounting professors (Doug Shackelford, Jennifer Blouin, and Jana Raedy) found that the dividend tax cut did lead to larger dividend payouts by firms. However, the effect was greatest when corporate officers and directors held large interests in the company. This suggests that the increased dividend payouts in these companies was motivated by the self-interested behavior of those who set dividend policies. Even if the tax cuts spurred dividend payments by corporations, most academics agree that the effect was not as large as anticipated.

Source: Martin Vaughan, "Higher Taxes May Not Push Firms to Cut Dividends," *Wall Street Journal,* August 30, 2010.

PROPERTY DIVIDENDS

LO.5

Evaluate the tax impact of property dividends on the recipient shareholder and the corporation making the distribution.

Although most corporate distributions are cash, a corporation may distribute a **property dividend** for various reasons. The shareholders could want a particular property that is held by the corporation. Similarly, a corporation with low cash reserves may still wish to distribute a dividend to its shareholders.

Property distributions have the same impact as distributions of cash except for effects attributable to any difference between the basis and the fair market value of the distributed property. In most situations, distributed property is appreciated, so its sale would result in a gain to the corporation. Distributions of property with a basis that differs from fair market value raise several tax questions.

- For the shareholder:
  - *What is the amount of the distribution?*
  - *What is the basis of the property in the shareholder's hands?*
- For the corporation:
  - *Is a gain or loss recognized as a result of the distribution?*
  - *What is the effect of the distribution on E & P?*

Property Dividends—Effect on the Shareholder

When a corporation distributes property rather than cash to a shareholder, the amount distributed is measured by the fair market value of the property on the date of distribution.[21] As with a cash distribution, the portion of a property distribution covered by existing E & P is a dividend, and any excess is treated as a return of capital. If the fair market value of the property distributed exceeds the corporation's E & P and the shareholder's basis in the stock investment, a capital gain usually results.

The amount distributed is reduced by any liabilities to which the distributed property is subject immediately before and immediately after the distribution and by any liabilities of the corporation assumed by the shareholder. The basis of the distributed property for the shareholder is the fair market value of the property on the date of the distribution.

EXAMPLE 13
THE BIG PICTURE

Return to the facts of *The Big Picture* on p. 5–2. Lime Corporation distributed property with a $300,000 fair market value and $20,000 adjusted basis to one of its shareholders, Gustavo. The property was subject to a $100,000 mortgage, which Gustavo assumed. As a result, Gustavo has a taxable dividend of $200,000 [$300,000 (fair market value) – $100,000 (liability)]. The basis of the property to Gustavo is $300,000. ■

[21] Section 301 describes the tax treatment of corporate distributions to shareholders.

EXAMPLE 14

Red Corporation owns 10% of Tan Corporation. Tan has ample E & P to cover any distributions made during the year. One distribution made to Red Corporation consists of a vacant lot with an adjusted basis of $75,000 and a fair market value of $50,000. Red has a taxable dividend of $50,000, and its basis in the lot becomes $50,000. ■

Distributing property that has depreciated in value as a property dividend may reflect poor planning. Note what happens in Example 14. Basis of $25,000 disappears due to the loss (adjusted basis of $75,000, fair market value of $50,000). As an alternative, Tan Corporation could sell the lot and use the loss to reduce its taxes. Then, Tan could distribute the $50,000 of proceeds to shareholders.

Property Dividends—Effect on the Corporation

All distributions of appreciated property generate gain to the distributing corporation.[22] In effect, a corporation that distributes gain property is treated as if it had sold the property to the shareholder for its fair market value. However, the distributing corporation does *not* recognize loss on distributions of property.

EXAMPLE 15
THE BIG PICTURE

Return to the facts of *The Big Picture* on p. 5-2. Lime Corporation distributed property with a fair market value of $300,000 and an adjusted basis of $20,000 to Gustavo, one of its shareholders. As a result, Lime recognizes a $280,000 gain on the distribution. ■

EXAMPLE 16

A corporation distributes land with a basis of $30,000 and a fair market value of $10,000. The corporation does not recognize a loss on the distribution. ■

If the distributed property is subject to a liability in excess of basis or the shareholder assumes such a liability, a special rule applies. For purposes of determining gain on the distribution, the fair market value of the property is treated as not being less than the amount of the liability.[23]

EXAMPLE 17

Assume the land in Example 16 is subject to a liability of $35,000. The corporation recognizes gain of $5,000 on the distribution. ■

Corporate distributions reduce E & P by the amount of money distributed or by the greater of the fair market value or the adjusted basis of property distributed, less the amount of any liability on the property.[24] E & P is increased by gain recognized on appreciated property distributed as a property dividend.

EXAMPLE 18

Crimson Corporation distributes property (basis of $10,000 and fair market value of $20,000) to Brenda, its shareholder. Crimson Corporation recognizes a gain of $10,000. Crimson's E & P is increased by the $10,000 gain and decreased by the $20,000 fair market value of the distribution. Brenda has dividend income of $20,000 (presuming sufficient E & P). ■

EXAMPLE 19

Assume the same facts as in Example 18, except that the adjusted basis of the property in the hands of Crimson Corporation is $25,000. Because loss is not recognized and the adjusted basis is greater than fair market value, E & P is reduced by $25,000. Brenda reports dividend income of $20,000. ■

EXAMPLE 20

Assume the same facts as in Example 19, except that the property is subject to a liability of $6,000. E & P is now reduced by $19,000 [$25,000 (adjusted basis) – $6,000 (liability)]. Brenda has a dividend of $14,000 [$20,000 (amount of the distribution) – $6,000 (liability)], and her basis in the property is $20,000. ■

[22]Section 311 describes how corporations are taxed on distributions.
[23]§ 311(b)(2).
[24]§§ 312(a), (b), and (c).

TAX *in* the NEWS

The Case of the Disappearing Dividend Tax

During the last few years, U.S. banks and offshore hedge funds have developed a novel technique for avoiding the tax on dividends entirely. The strategy involves the use of financial derivatives. A simple version of the strategy is called a dividend swap. In the swap, a U.S. bank buys a block of stock from an offshore hedge fund. The bank and the hedge fund also enter into a derivatives contract. The contract requires the bank to make payments to the hedge fund equal to the total return on the stock (both increases in fair market value and dividends) for a designated time period. These payments equal the income and gain the stock would have provided to the hedge fund if it had continued to own the stock. In exchange for these payments, the hedge fund agrees to pay the bank an amount based on some benchmark interest rate. The hedge fund also agrees that it will pay the bank an amount equal to the loss if the fair market value of the stock declines.

After purchasing the stock from the hedge fund, the bank receives taxable dividend income. For tax purposes, however, the dividend income is completely offset by the expense of payments made to the hedge fund under the derivatives contract. In return, the bank receives compensation from the hedge fund equal to a benchmark interest rate. The overseas hedge fund no longer receives taxable dividend income, and the swap payments received are not subject to U.S. taxation. As a result, taxable dividend income is converted to tax-free income.

Some experts estimate that the strategy has allowed hedge funds to avoid paying more than $1 billion a year in taxes on U.S. dividends. Recent legislation (the Foreign Account Tax Compliance Act of 2009) attacks this approach to avoiding taxes on dividends by treating payments made to the hedge fund as taxable equivalents to dividends.

Source: Kevin E. Packman and Mauricio D. Rivero, "The Foreign Account Tax Compliance Act: Taxpayers Face More Disclosures and Potential Penalties," *Journal of Accountancy*, August 2010.

Under no circumstances can a distribution, whether cash or property, either generate a deficit in E & P or add to a deficit in E & P. Deficits can arise only through corporate losses.

EXAMPLE 21

Teal Corporation has accumulated E & P of $10,000 at the beginning of the current tax year. During the year, it has current E & P of $15,000. At the end of the year, it distributes cash of $30,000 to its sole shareholder, Walter. Teal's E & P at the end of the year is zero. The accumulated E & P of $10,000 is increased by current E & P of $15,000 and reduced $25,000 by the dividend distribution. The remaining $5,000 of the distribution to Walter does not reduce E & P because a distribution cannot generate a deficit in E & P. ■

CONSTRUCTIVE DIVIDENDS

LO.6

Identify the nature and treatment of constructive dividends.

Any measurable economic benefit conveyed by a corporation to its shareholders can be treated as a dividend for Federal income tax purposes even though it is not formally declared or designated as a dividend. Also, it need not be issued pro rata to all shareholders[25] or satisfy the legal requirements of a dividend. Such a benefit, often described as a **constructive dividend**, is distinguishable from actual corporate distributions of cash and property in form only.

For tax purposes, constructive distributions are treated the same as actual distributions.[26] Thus, corporate shareholders are entitled to the dividends received deduction (see Chapter 2), and other shareholders receive preferential tax rates (0 or 15 percent) through 2012 on qualified constructive dividends. The constructive distribution is taxable as a dividend only to the extent of the corporation's

[25]See *Lengsfield v. Comm.*, 57–1 USTC ¶9437, 50 AFTR 1683, 241 F.2d 508 (CA–5, 1957).

[26]*Simon v. Comm.*, 57–2 USTC ¶9989, 52 AFTR 698, 248 F.2d 869 (CA–8, 1957).

current and accumulated E & P. The burden of proving that the distribution constitutes a return of capital because of inadequate E & P rests with the taxpayer.[27]

Constructive dividend situations usually arise in closely held corporations. Here, the dealings between the parties are less structured, and frequently, formalities are not preserved. The constructive dividend serves as a substitute for actual distributions and is usually intended to accomplish some tax objective not available through the use of direct dividends. The shareholders may be attempting to distribute corporate profits in a form deductible to the corporation.[28] Alternatively, the shareholders may be seeking benefits for themselves while avoiding the recognition of income. Although some constructive dividends are disguised dividends, not all are deliberate attempts to avoid actual and formal dividends; many are inadvertent. Thus, an awareness of the various constructive dividend situations is essential to protect the parties from unanticipated, undesirable tax consequences. The most frequently encountered types of constructive dividends are summarized below.

Shareholder Use of Corporate-Owned Property

A constructive dividend can occur when a shareholder uses corporation property for personal purposes at no cost. Personal use of corporate-owned automobiles, airplanes, yachts, fishing camps, hunting lodges, and other entertainment facilities is commonplace in some closely held corporations. In these situations, the shareholder has dividend income equal to the fair rental value of the property for the period of its personal use.[29]

Bargain Sale of Corporate Property to a Shareholder

Shareholders often purchase property from a corporation at a cost below the fair market value. These bargain sales produce dividend income equal to the difference between the property's fair market value on the date of sale and the amount the shareholder paid for the property.[30] These situations might be avoided by appraising the property on or about the date of the sale. The appraised value should become the price paid by the shareholder.

Bargain Rental of Corporate Property

A bargain rental of corporate property by a shareholder also produces dividend income. Here the measure of the constructive dividend is the excess of the property's fair rental value over the rent actually paid. Again, appraisal data should be used to avoid any questionable situations.

Payments for the Benefit of a Shareholder

If a corporation pays an obligation of a shareholder, the payment is treated as a constructive dividend. The obligation in question need not be legally binding on the shareholder; it may, in fact, be a moral obligation.[31] Forgiveness of shareholder indebtedness by the corporation creates an identical problem.[32] Also, excessive rentals paid by a corporation for the use of shareholder property are treated as constructive dividends.

Unreasonable Compensation

A salary payment to a shareholder-employee that is deemed to be **unreasonable compensation** is frequently treated as a constructive dividend. As a consequence, it is not deductible by the corporation. In determining the reasonableness of salary payments, the following factors are considered:

[27] *DiZenzo v. Comm.*, 65–2 USTC ¶9518, 16 AFTR 2d 5107, 348 F.2d 122 (CA–2, 1965).

[28] Recall that dividend distributions do not provide the distributing corporation with an income tax deduction, although they do reduce E & P.

[29] See *Daniel L. Reeves*, 94 TCM 287, T.C.Memo. 2007–273.

[30] Reg. § 1.301–1(j).

[31] *Montgomery Engineering Co. v. U.S.*, 64–2 USTC ¶9618, 13 AFTR 2d 1747, 230 F.Supp. 838 (D.Ct. N.J., 1964), *aff'd* in 65–1 USTC ¶9368, 15 AFTR 2d 746, 344 F.2d 996 (CA–3, 1965).

[32] Reg. § 1.301–1(m).

- The employee's qualifications.
- A comparison of salaries with dividend distributions.
- The prevailing rates of compensation for comparable positions in comparable business concerns.
- The nature and scope of the employee's work.
- The size and complexity of the business.
- A comparison of salaries paid with both gross and net income.
- The taxpayer's salary policy toward all employees.
- For small corporations with a limited number of officers, the amount of compensation paid to the employee in question in previous years.
- Whether a reasonable shareholder would have agreed to the level of compensation paid.[33]

The last factor above, known as the "reasonable investor test," is a relatively new development in the law on reasonable compensation.[34] Its use by the courts has been inconsistent. In some cases, the Seventh Circuit Court of Appeals has relied solely on the reasonable investor test in determining reasonableness, whereas the Tenth Circuit Court of Appeals has largely ignored this factor. Other Federal circuits have used an approach that considers all of the factors in the list.[35]

Loans to Shareholders

Advances to shareholders that are not bona fide loans are constructive dividends. Whether an advance qualifies as a bona fide loan is a question of fact to be determined in light of the particular circumstances. Factors considered in determining whether the advance is a bona fide loan include the following:[36]

- Whether the advance is on open account or is evidenced by a written instrument.
- Whether the shareholder furnished collateral or other security for the advance.
- How long the advance has been outstanding.
- Whether any repayments have been made.
- The shareholder's ability to repay the advance.
- The shareholder's use of the funds (e.g., payment of routine bills versus nonrecurring, extraordinary expenses).
- The regularity of the advances.
- The dividend-paying history of the corporation.

Even when a corporation makes a bona fide loan to a shareholder, a constructive dividend may be triggered, equal to the amount of imputed (forgone) interest on the loan.[37] Imputed interest equals the amount by which the interest paid by the Federal government on new borrowings, compounded semiannually, exceeds the interest charged on the loan. When the imputed interest provision applies, the shareholder is deemed to have made an interest payment to the corporation equal to the amount of imputed interest, and the corporation is deemed to have repaid the imputed interest to the shareholder through a constructive dividend. As a result, the corporation receives interest income and makes a nondeductible dividend payment, and the shareholder has taxable dividend income that might be offset with an interest deduction.

EXAMPLE 22

Mallard Corporation lends its principal shareholder, Henry, $100,000 on January 2 of the current year. The loan is interest-free and payable on demand. On December 31,

[33]All but the final factor in this list are identified in *Mayson Manufacturing Co. v. Comm.*, 49–2 USTC ¶9467, 38 AFTR 1028, 178 F.2d 115 (CA–6, 1949).

[34]For example, see *Alpha Medical, Inc. v. Comm.*, 99–1 USTC ¶50,461, 83 AFTR 2d 99–697, 172 F.3d 942 (CA–6, 1999).

[35]See *Vitamin Village, Inc.*, 94 TCM 277, T.C.Memo. 2007–272, for an example of a case that uses both the reasonable investor test and other factors.

[36]*Fin Hay Realty Co. v. U.S.*, 68–2 USTC ¶9438, 22 AFTR 2d 5004, 398 F.2d 694 (CA–3, 1968). But see *Nariman Teymourian*, 90 TCM 352, T.C.Memo. 2005–302, for an example of how good planning can avoid constructive dividends in the shareholder loan context.

[37]See § 7872.

the imputed interest rules are applied. Assuming the Federal rate is 6%, compounded semiannually, the amount of imputed interest is $6,090. This amount is deemed paid by Henry to Mallard in the form of interest. Mallard is then deemed to return the amount to Henry as a constructive dividend. Thus, Henry has dividend income of $6,090, which might be offset with a deduction for the interest paid to Mallard. Mallard has interest income of $6,090 for the interest received, with no offsetting deduction for the dividend payment. ■

Loans to a Corporation by Shareholders

Shareholder loans to a corporation may be reclassified as equity because the debt has too many features of stock. Any interest and principal payments made by the corporation to the shareholder are then treated as constructive dividends. This topic was covered more thoroughly in the discussion of "thin capitalization" in Chapter 4.

LO.7

Discuss the tax treatment of stock dividends and stock rights.

STOCK DIVIDENDS AND STOCK RIGHTS

Stock Dividends—§ 305

Historically, **stock dividends** were excluded from income on the theory that the ownership interest of the shareholder was unchanged as a result of the distribution.[38] Recognizing that some distributions of stock could affect ownership interests, the 1954 Code included a provision (§ 305) taxing stock dividends where (1) the stockholder could elect to receive either stock or property or (2) the stock dividends were in discharge of preference dividends. However, because this provision applied to a narrow range of transactions, corporations were able to develop an assortment of alternative methods that circumvented taxation and still affected shareholders' proportionate interests in the corporation.[39] In response, the scope of § 305 was expanded.

In its current state, the provisions of § 305 are based on the proportionate interest concept. As a general rule, stock dividends are excluded from income if they are pro rata distributions of stock or stock rights, paid on common stock. Listed below are five exceptions to this general rule. Each represents a disproportionate distribution situation in which the stock distribution may be taxed.

1. Distributions payable in either stock or property at the election of the shareholder.
2. Distributions of property to some shareholders with a corresponding increase in the proportionate interest of other shareholders in either assets or E & P of the distributing corporation.
3. Distributions of preferred stock to some common shareholders and of common stock to other common shareholders.
4. Distributions of stock to preferred shareholders. However, changes in the conversion ratio of convertible preferred stock to account for a stock dividend or stock split are not taxable in some circumstances.
5. Distributions of convertible preferred stock unless it can be shown that the distribution will not result in a disproportionate distribution.

Holders of convertible securities are considered shareholders. Thus, under the second exception above, when interest is paid on convertible debentures and stock dividends are paid on common stock, the stock dividends are taxable. This result is avoided if the conversion ratio or conversion price is adjusted to reflect the price of the stock dividend.[40]

[38]See *Eisner v. Macomber*, 1 USTC ¶32, 3 AFTR 3020, 40 S.Ct. 189 (USSC, 1920).

[39]See "Stock Dividends," Senate Report 91–552, 1969–3 C.B. 519.

[40]See Reg. § 1.305–3(d) for illustrations of how to compute required adjustments of conversion ratios or prices.

Deemed Dividends from Controlled Foreign Corporations

As described in the "Global Tax Issues" feature earlier in this chapter, the tax law requires a U.S. parent corporation to recognize some of the unrepatriated earnings of a controlled foreign corporation (CFC) as income. The U.S. parent's basis in the CFC stock is increased by the amount of the taxed but unrepatriated earnings. Subsequently, when cash or property is actually paid to the U.S. parent (i.e., when taxed earnings are repatriated), no income results. Thus, the CFC rules preclude some deferral but do not lead to double taxation.

In an effort to boost the economy, in 2004 Congress introduced a temporary one-year tax break for CFCs. The provision allowed an 85 percent deduction for cash dividends paid from untaxed earnings by CFCs to U.S. corporate shareholders. For many corporations, this provision reduced the tax on repatriated foreign earnings from 35 percent to 5.25 percent. By all accounts, the tax break was a resounding success as an estimated $300 billion additional foreign money flowed into the United States during 2005.

If stock dividends are not taxable, the corporation's E & P is not reduced.[41] If the stock dividends are taxable, the distributing corporation treats the distribution in the same manner as any other taxable property dividend.

If a stock dividend is taxable, the shareholder's basis for the newly received shares is fair market value, and the holding period starts on the date of receipt. If a stock dividend is not taxable, the basis of the stock on which the dividend is distributed is reallocated.[42] If the dividend shares are identical to these formerly held shares, basis for the old stock is reallocated by dividing the taxpayer's cost in the old stock by the total number of shares. If the dividend stock is not identical to the underlying shares (e.g., a stock dividend of preferred on common), basis is determined by allocating the basis of the formerly held shares between the old and new stock according to the fair market value of each. The holding period includes the holding period of the formerly held stock.[43]

EXAMPLE 23

Gail bought 1,000 shares of common stock two years ago for $10,000. In the current tax year, Gail receives 10 shares of common stock as a nontaxable stock dividend. Gail's basis of $10,000 is divided by 1,010. Each share of stock has a basis of $9.90 instead of the pre-dividend $10 basis. ■

EXAMPLE 24

Assume Gail received, instead, a nontaxable preferred stock dividend of 100 shares. The preferred stock has a fair market value of $1,000, and the common stock, on which the preferred is distributed, has a fair market value of $19,000. After the receipt of the stock dividend, the basis of the common stock is $9,500, and the basis of the preferred is $500, computed as follows:

Fair market value of common	$19,000
Fair market value of preferred	1,000
	$20,000
Basis of common: $^{19}/_{20} \times$ $10,000	$ 9,500
Basis of preferred: $^{1}/_{20} \times$ $10,000	$ 500

■

[41]§ 312(d)(1).
[42]§ 307(a).
[43]§ 1223(5).

Stock Rights

The rules for determining taxability of **stock rights** are identical to those for determining taxability of stock dividends. If the rights are taxable, the recipient has income equal to the fair market value of the rights. The fair market value then becomes the shareholder-distributee's basis in the rights.[44] If the rights are exercised, the holding period for the new stock begins on the date the rights (whether taxable or nontaxable) are exercised. The basis of the new stock is the basis of the rights plus the amount of any other consideration given.

If stock rights are not taxable and the value of the rights is less than 15 percent of the value of the old stock, the basis of the rights is zero. However, the shareholder may elect to have some of the basis in the formerly held stock allocated to the rights.[45] The election is made by attaching a statement to the shareholder's return for the year in which the rights are received.[46] If the fair market value of the rights is 15 percent or more of the value of the old stock and the rights are exercised or sold, the shareholder *must* allocate some of the basis in the formerly held stock to the rights.

EXAMPLE 25

A corporation with common stock outstanding declares a nontaxable dividend payable in rights to subscribe to common stock. Each right entitles the holder to purchase one share of stock for $90. One right is issued for every two shares of stock owned. Fred owns 400 shares of stock purchased two years ago for $15,000. At the time of the distribution of the rights, the market value of the common stock is $100 per share, and the market value of the rights is $8 per right. Fred receives 200 rights. He exercises 100 rights and sells the remaining 100 rights three months later for $9 per right.

Fred need not allocate the cost of the original stock to the rights because the value of the rights is less than 15% of the value of the stock ($1,600 ÷ $40,000 = 4%). If Fred does not allocate his original stock basis to the rights, the tax consequences are as follows:

- Basis of the new stock is $9,000 [$90 (exercise price) × 100 (shares)]. The holding period of the new stock begins on the date the stock was purchased.
- Sale of the rights produces long-term capital gain of $900 [$9 (sales price) × 100 (rights)]. The holding period of the rights starts with the date the original 400 shares of stock were acquired.

If Fred elects to allocate basis to the rights, the tax consequences are as follows:

- Basis of the stock is $14,423 [$40,000 (value of stock) ÷ $41,600 (value of rights and stock) × $15,000 (cost of stock)].
- Basis of the rights is $577 [$1,600 (value of rights) ÷ $41,600 (value of rights and stock) × $15,000 (cost of stock)].
- When Fred exercises the rights, his basis for the new stock will be $9,288.50 [$9,000 (cost) + $288.50 (basis for 100 rights)].
- Sale of the rights would produce a long-term capital gain of $611.50 [$900 (sales price) − $288.50 (basis in the remaining 100 rights)]. ■

TAX PLANNING:
5.4 Corporate Distributions

LO.8

Structure corporate distributions in a manner that minimizes the tax consequences to the parties involved.

The following points are especially important when planning for corporate distributions.

- Because E & P is the pool of funds from which dividends may be distributed, its periodic determination is essential to corporate planning. Thus, an E & P account should be established and maintained, particularly if the possibility exists that a corporate distribution might be a return of capital.

[44] Reg. § 1.305–1(b).
[45] § 307(b)(1).
[46] Reg. § 1.307–2.

TAX *in* the NEWS

THE BAILOUT PAID BIG DIVIDENDS

In October 2008, nine American banks received $125 billion from the Federal government in exchange for shares of preferred stock to shore up their finances. At the time of the bailout, some pointed out that the agreement did not impose any restrictions on dividends paid by the banks receiving the bailout money. Estimates were that any such dividends would redirect more than 20 percent of the Federal money to shareholders of the banks in 2009 alone. Since the money would be distributed to shareholders, it would not be available to improve the banks' financial position—ostensibly, the purpose of the bailout. Interestingly, David Scharfstein (a finance professor at Harvard) estimated that the officers and directors of the nine banks involved would receive about $250 million of the bailout cash in dividend payments in the first year as a result of the shares they owned in the banks.

Management at these banks argued that dividend payments were necessary to support stock prices and make the raising of additional capital possible. While shareholders of healthy companies should be indifferent to dividend payments (from an economic perspective), at distressed companies (e.g., banks), dividends favor the interests of shareholders over lenders. Each dollar paid out as a dividend is not available to creditors in a bankruptcy proceeding. Thus, the dividend payments represent "an attempt by shareholders to beat creditors out the door."

During 2009, some banks responded to government and public pressure and reduced or eliminated their dividend payouts. Not all banks reduced their dividends, however. As of early 2009, a number of banks continued to pay out significant amounts. Wells Fargo, which took $25 billion in bailout funds, maintained its dividend payouts until March 2009. PNC Financial Services Group, U.S. Bancorp, Capital One Financial, Goldman Sachs Group, and Morgan Stanley also continued to pay significant dividends to shareholders.

Source: Adapted from David Scharfstein and Jeremy C. Stein, "This Bailout Doesn't Pay Dividends," *New York Times,* October 20, 2008.

- Accumulated E & P is the sum of all past years' current E & P. Because there is no statute of limitations on the computation of E & P, the IRS can redetermine a corporation's current E & P for a tax year long since passed. Such a change affects accumulated E & P and has a direct impact on the taxability of current distributions to shareholders.
- Distributions can be planned to avoid or minimize dividend exposure.

EXAMPLE 26

Flicker Corporation has accumulated E & P of $100,000 as of January 1 of the current year. During the year, it expects to have earnings from operations of $80,000 and to sell an asset for a loss of $100,000. Thus, it anticipates a current E & P deficit of $20,000. Flicker Corporation also expects to make a cash distribution of $60,000. The best approach is to recognize the loss as soon as possible and, immediately thereafter, make the cash distribution to the shareholders. Suppose these two steps take place on January 1. Because the current E & P has a deficit, the accumulated E & P account must be updated (refer to Example 11 in this chapter). Thus, at the time of the distribution, the combined E & P balance is zero [$100,000 (beginning balance in accumulated E & P) – $100,000 (existing deficit in current E & P)], and the $60,000 distribution to the shareholders constitutes a return of capital. Current deficits are deemed to accrue pro rata throughout the year unless the parties can prove otherwise; here, they can. ■

EXAMPLE 27

After several unprofitable years, Darter Corporation has a deficit in accumulated E & P of $100,000 as of January 1, 2011. Starting in 2011, Darter expects to generate annual E & P of $50,000 for the next four years and would like to distribute this amount to its shareholders. The corporation's cash position (for dividend purposes) will correspond to the current E & P generated. Consider the following two distribution schedules:

1. On December 31 of 2011, 2012, 2013, and 2014, Darter Corporation distributes cash of $50,000.
2. On December 31 of 2012 and 2014, Darter Corporation distributes cash of $100,000.

The two alternatives are illustrated below.

Year	Accumulated E & P (First of Year)	Current E & P	Distribution	Amount of Dividend
		Alternative 1		
2011	($ 100,000)	$50,000	$ 50,000	$50,000
2012	(100,000)	50,000	50,000	50,000
2013	(100,000)	50,000	50,000	50,000
2014	(100,000)	50,000	50,000	50,000
		Alternative 2		
2011	($ 100,000)	$50,000	$ –0–	$ –0–
2012	(50,000)	50,000	100,000	50,000
2013	(50,000)	50,000	–0–	–0–
2014	–0–	50,000	100,000	50,000

Alternative 1 produces $200,000 of dividend income because each $50,000 distribution is fully covered by current E & P. Alternative 2, however, produces only $100,000 of dividend income for the shareholders. The remaining $100,000 is a return of capital. Why? At the time Darter Corporation made its first distribution of $100,000 on December 31, 2012, it had a deficit of $50,000 in accumulated E & P (the original deficit of $100,000 is reduced by the $50,000 of current E & P from 2011). Consequently, the $100,000 distribution yields a $50,000 dividend (the current E & P for 2012), and $50,000 is treated as a return of capital. As of January 1, 2013, Darter's accumulated E & P now has a deficit balance of $50,000 since a distribution cannot increase a deficit in E & P. After adding the remaining $50,000 of current E & P from 2013, the balance on January 1, 2014, is zero. Thus, the second distribution of $100,000, made on December 31, 2014, also yields $50,000 of dividends (the current E & P for 2014) and a $50,000 return of capital. ■

5.5 Planning for Qualified Dividends

RETIREMENT PLANS

The reduced tax rates available to individual taxpayers on net capital gain and qualified dividend income reinforce the inadvisability of funding retirement accounts with stock. Since income in § 401(k) plans and IRAs is not taxed when earned, the benefits of the lower tax rates on these forms of income are lost. Instead, distributions from the plans are taxed at ordinary income tax rates.

INDIVIDUAL ALTERNATIVE MINIMUM TAX

The lower rates on dividends and long-term capital gains through 2012 apply under both the regular income tax and the alternative minimum tax. This increases the exposure of many individuals to the alternative minimum tax, particularly those with significant income from dividends or long-term capital gain. As a result, individual taxpayers who pay the alternative minimum tax should reconsider their investment strategies to manage the mix of ordinary income, dividend income, and capital gain.

CLOSELY HELD CORPORATIONS

Closely held corporations have considerable discretion regarding their dividend policies. In the past, the double tax result provided strong motivation to avoid the payment of dividends. Instead, the incentive was to bail out corporate profits in a manner that provided tax benefits to the corporation. Hence, liberal use was made of compensation, loan, and lease arrangements because salaries, interest, and rent are deductible. Under current law, however, shareholders prefer dividends because salaries, interest, and rent are fully taxed while dividends receive preferential treatment. Thus, the question becomes this: *Should the corporation or the shareholders benefit?* In general, the best strategy considers the tax consequences to both parties.

EXAMPLE 28

Consider a corporation paying tax at the 34% rate and an individual shareholder in the 35% tax bracket. A deductible $10,000 payment to the shareholder will *save* the corporation $3,400 in tax, resulting in an after-tax cost of $6,600. The shareholder will pay $3,500 in tax, resulting in after-tax income of $6,500. This creates a joint tax burden of $100 ($3,500 tax paid by the shareholder − $3,400 tax saved by the corporation). If, instead, the corporation paid a $10,000 qualified dividend (subject to a 15% tax rate) to the shareholder, no tax savings would be realized by the corporation, resulting in an after-tax cost of $10,000. The shareholder would owe $1,500 in taxes, leaving $8,500 of income. Considering both the corporation and the shareholder, a dividend creates $1,400 more tax liability than a deductible payment, so the deductible payment is more tax efficient. ■

In Example 28, when the deductible payment is made, the shareholder bears an increased tax burden of $2,000 ($3,500 tax due from the deductible payment − $1,500 tax due from the dividend) while the corporation saves $3,400 ($3,400 tax saved because of the deductible payment − $0 tax saved because of the dividend). Both parties could actually benefit if the corporation transfers part of its benefit to the shareholder through a larger deductible payment.

EXAMPLE 29

Assume the same facts as in Example 28, except that the corporation pays a $14,000 deductible payment. In this case, the corporation will save $4,760 ($14,000 × 34%) in tax, resulting in an after-tax cost of $9,240. From the corporation's perspective, this is preferable to a $10,000 dividend because it costs $760 less after tax ($10,000 dividend cost − $9,240 after-tax cost of a $14,000 deductible payment). The shareholder will pay taxes of $4,900 on the deductible payment, resulting in after-tax income of $9,100. The shareholder will also prefer this payment to a dividend because it generates $600 more after-tax income ($9,100 − $8,500 from a dividend). ■

Thus, if properly structured, deductible payments by the corporation to the shareholder still appear to be preferable to dividends in most situations (unless the corporation faces a low tax rate). The benefit of this strategy will be even greater if the shareholder is paying alternative minimum tax.

5.6 Constructive Dividends

Tax planning can be particularly effective in avoiding constructive dividend situations. Shareholders should try to structure their dealings with the corporation on an arm's length basis. For example, reasonable rent should be paid for the use of corporate property, and a fair price should be paid for its purchase. The parties should make every effort to support the amount involved with appraisal data or market information obtained from reliable sources at or near the time of the transaction. Dealings between shareholders and a closely held corporation should be as formal as possible. In the case of loans to shareholders, for example, the parties should provide for an adequate rate of interest and written evidence of the debt. Shareholders also should establish and follow a realistic repayment schedule.

If shareholders wish to bail out corporate profits in a form deductible to the corporation, a balanced mix of the possible alternatives lessens the risk of constructive dividend treatment. Rent for the use of shareholder property, interest on amounts borrowed from shareholders, or salaries for services rendered by shareholders are all feasible substitutes for dividend distributions. Overdoing any one approach, however, may attract the attention of the IRS. Too much interest, for example, may mean the corporation is thinly capitalized, and some of the debt may be reclassified as equity investment.

Much can be done to protect against the disallowance of unreasonable compensation. Example 30 is an illustration, all too common in a family corporation, of what *not* to do.

EXAMPLE 30

Bob Cole wholly owns Eagle Corporation. Corporate employees and annual salaries include Mrs. Cole ($120,000), Cole Jr. ($80,000), Bob Cole ($640,000), and Ed ($320,000). The operation of Eagle Corporation is shared about equally between Bob Cole and Ed, who is an unrelated party. Mrs. Cole performed significant services for Eagle during its formative years, but now merely attends the annual meeting of the board of directors. Cole Jr., Bob Cole's son, is a full-time student and occasionally signs papers for the corporation in his capacity as treasurer. Eagle Corporation has not distributed a dividend for 10 years although it has accumulated substantial E & P. Mrs. Cole, Cole Jr., and Bob Cole run the risk of a finding of unreasonable compensation, based on the following factors:

- Mrs. Cole's salary is vulnerable unless proof is available that some or all of her $120,000 annual salary is payment for services rendered to the corporation in prior years and that she was underpaid for those years.[47]
- Cole Jr.'s salary is also vulnerable; he does not appear to earn the $80,000 paid to him by the corporation. Neither Cole Jr. nor Mrs. Cole is a shareholder, but each one's relationship to Bob Cole is enough of a tie-in to raise the unreasonable compensation issue.
- Bob Cole's salary appears susceptible to challenge. Why is he receiving $320,000 more than Ed when it appears that they share equally in the operation of the corporation?
- The fact that Eagle Corporation has not distributed dividends over the past 10 years, even though it is capable of doing so, increases the likelihood of a constructive dividend. ■

What could have been done to improve the tax position of the parties in Example 30? Mrs. Cole and Cole Jr. are not entitled to a salary as neither seems to be performing any services for the corporation. Paying them a salary simply aggravates the problem. The IRS is more apt to consider *all* the family members' salaries excessive under the circumstances. Bob Cole should probably reduce his compensation to correspond with that paid to Ed. He can then attempt to distribute corporate earnings to himself in some other form.

Paying some dividends to Bob Cole would also help alleviate the problem raised in Example 30. The IRS has been successful in denying a deduction for salary paid to a shareholder-employee, even when the payment was reasonable, in a situation where the corporation had not distributed any dividends.[48] Most courts, however, have not denied deductions for compensation solely because a dividend was not paid. A better approach is to compare an employee's compensation with the level of compensation prevalent in the particular industry.

The corporation can provide *indirect* compensation to Bob Cole by paying expenses that benefit him personally, but are nevertheless deductible to the corporation. For example, premiums paid by the corporation for sickness, accident, and hospitalization insurance for Bob Cole are deductible to the corporation and nontaxable to him.[49] Any payments under the policy are not taxable to Bob Cole unless they exceed his medical expenses.[50] The corporation can also pay for travel and entertainment expenses incurred by Cole on behalf of the corporation. If these expenses are primarily for the benefit of the corporation, Bob Cole will not recognize any taxable income, and the corporation will receive a deduction.[51]

When testing for reasonableness, the IRS looks at the total compensation package, including indirect compensation payments to a shareholder-employee. Thus, indirect payments must not be overlooked.

[47] See, for example, *R.J. Nicoll Co.*, 59 T.C. 37 (1972).

[48] *McCandless Tile Service v. U.S.*, 70–1 USTC ¶9284, 25 AFTR 2d 70–870, 422 F.2d 1336 (Ct.Cls., 1970). The court in *McCandless* concluded that a return on equity of 15% of net profits was reasonable.

[49] Reg. § 1.162–10.

[50] The medical reimbursement plan must meet certain nondiscrimination requirements of § 105(h)(2).

[51] Reg. § 1.62–2(c)(4).

Forgetting About the Past

Michael is the CEO and sole shareholder of Cormorant Corporation. Michael recently approached you, a tax adviser in private practice, about taking on Cormorant as a client.

In your initial interview with Michael, you learn that Cormorant claimed a $1 million deduction for his salary last year. In an audit last month, the IRS disallowed $800,000 of the salary deduction as unreasonable compensation. In the future, Cormorant fully intends to take the same salary deduction of $1 million for Michael, given his active role in the organization. In short, Cormorant believes that the salary is appropriate.

Should you accept Cormorant Corporation as a new client? If so, can you claim the same salary deduction of $1 million?

EXAMPLE 31

Cora, the president and sole shareholder of Willet Corporation, is paid an annual salary of $100,000 by the corporation. Cora would like to draw funds from the corporation, but is concerned that additional salary payments might cause the IRS to contend her salary is unreasonable. Cora does not want Willet to pay any dividends. She also wishes to donate $50,000 to her alma mater to establish scholarships for needy students. In this situation, Willet Corporation can make the contribution on Cora's behalf. The payment clearly benefits Cora, but she will not be taxed on the amount of the contribution,[52] and Willet can take a charitable contribution deduction for the payment. ■

EXAMPLE 32

Assume in Example 31 that Cora has made an individual pledge to the university to provide $50,000 for scholarships for needy students. Willet Corporation satisfies Cora's pledge by paying the $50,000 to the university, but she will be taxed on the amount.[53] In this context, the $50,000 payment to the university may be treated as *indirect* compensation to Cora. In determining whether Cora's salary is unreasonable, both the *direct* payment of $100,000 and the *indirect* $50,000 payment will be considered—a total compensation package of $150,000. ■

REFOCUS ON THE BIG PICTURE

TAXING CORPORATE DISTRIBUTIONS

A number of factors affect the tax treatment of Lime Corporation's distributions. The amount of current and accumulated E & P (which differ from the financial reporting concept of retained earnings) partially determines the tax effect on the shareholders. Given that Lime Corporation has had a highly profitable year, it is likely that there is sufficient current E & P to cover the distributions. If so, they are dividends to the shareholders rather than a return of capital. Orange Corporation receives $200,000 of dividend income that is mostly offset by the dividends received deduction. The amount of the offsetting deduction depends on the ownership percentage that Orange has in Lime. Gustavo has $200,000 of dividend income (i.e., $300,000 value of the land less the $100,000 mortgage). Assuming that Lime is a domestic corporation and that Gustavo has held his stock for the entire year, the land is a qualified dividend. As a result, the dividend is either tax-free (if Gustavo has a marginal rate of 10 or 15 percent) or subject to a 15 percent tax rate. Gustavo's basis in the land is its fair market value at distribution, or $300,000.

CONTINUED

[52] *Henry J. Knott*, 67 T.C. 681 (1977).

[53] *Schalk Chemical Co. v. Comm.*, 62–1 USTC ¶9496, 9 AFTR 2d 1579, 304 F.2d 48 (CA–9, 1962).

From Lime Corporation's perspective, the distribution of appreciated property creates a deemed gain. Thus, a $280,000 gain results ($300,000 fair market value of the land less its adjusted basis of $20,000). While the gain increases Lime's E & P, the distributions to the shareholders reduce it by $200,000 for the cash and $200,000 for the land ($300,000 fair market value reduced by the $100,000 mortgage).

What If?

What if current E & P is less than the cash and land distributed to the shareholders? Current E & P is applied pro rata to the cash and the land. Since the amounts received by the two shareholders are equal ($200,000 each), the current E & P applied is taxed as a dividend and is treated as described above. To the extent that the distributions are not covered by current E & P, accumulated E & P is then applied in a pro rata fashion (since both distributions were made on December 31). However, Lime probably has a deficit in accumulated E & P. As a result, the remaining amounts distributed to the two shareholders are first a tax-free recovery of stock basis, and any excess is taxed as a sale of the stock (probably classified as capital gain).

KEY TERMS

Accumulated earnings and profits, 5–8

Constructive dividend, 5–15

Current earnings and profits, 5–8

Earnings and profits (E & P), 5–3

Property dividend, 5–13

Qualified dividends, 5–11

Stock dividends, 5–18

Stock rights, 5–20

Unreasonable compensation, 5–16

DISCUSSION QUESTIONS

1. **LO.2** What is meant by the term *earnings and profits*?

2. **LO.1** What factors affect the tax treatment of corporate distributions?

3. **LO.2** In determining Blue Corporation's current E & P for 2011, how should taxable income be adjusted as a result of the following transactions?
   a. A capital loss carryover from 2010, fully used in 2011.
   b. Nondeductible meal expenses in 2011.
   c. Interest on municipal bonds received in 2011.
   d. Nondeductible lobbying expenses in 2011.
   e. Loss on a sale between related parties in 2011.
   f. Federal income tax refund received in 2011.

4. **LO.5** Discuss the impact each of the following has on generating or adding to a deficit in E & P:
   a. An operating loss of the corporation.
   b. A dividend distribution by the corporation.

5. **LO.2** In what ways does the computation of E & P require more conservative accounting than the computation of taxable income?

6. **LO.3** Describe the effect of a distribution in a year when the distributing corporation has:
   a. A deficit in accumulated E & P and a positive amount in current E & P.
   b. A positive amount in accumulated E & P and a deficit in current E & P.
   c. A deficit in both current and accumulated E & P.
   d. A positive amount in both current and accumulated E & P.

7. **LO.3** A calendar year corporation has no accumulated E & P, but expects to earn current E & P for the year. A cash distribution to its shareholders on January 1 should result in a return of capital. Comment on the validity of this statement.

8. **LO.4** Discuss the rationale for the reduced tax rates on dividends paid to individuals.

9. **LO.1, 2, 3, 4, 5** Red Corporation distributes $500,000 in cash to each of its three shareholders: Jack, Susan, and Orange Corporation. What factors must be considered when determining how the distribution is treated for tax purposes by the shareholders? **ISSUE ID**

10. **LO.5** Assume the same facts as in Question 9 except that property is distributed. What factors must be considered when determining how the distribution is treated for tax purposes by Red Corporation? **ISSUE ID**

11. **LO.5** Why would a corporation distribute a property dividend?

12. **LO.5** Seagull Corporation owns three machines that it uses in its business. It no longer needs two of these machines and is considering distributing them to its two shareholders as a property dividend. All three machines have a fair market value of $40,000 each. The basis of each machine is as follows: machine A, $47,000; machine B, $40,000; and machine C, $32,000. The corporation has asked you for advice. What do you recommend? **DECISION MAKING**

13. **LO.5** What is the effect on the corporation when it makes a property distribution?

14. **LO.5** A corporation is contemplating a possible property distribution to its shareholders. If appreciated property is to be used, does it matter to the distributing corporation whether the property distributed is a long-term capital asset or depreciable property subject to recapture? **ISSUE ID**

15. **LO.6** To be treated as a dividend for tax purposes, must a corporation's distribution to its shareholders meet the legal requirements of a dividend, be formally declared, or be issued pro rata to all shareholders? Discuss.

16. **LO.6** Judy is the president and sole shareholder of Parakeet Corporation. She is paid an annual salary of $600,000, while her son, Mike, the company's chief financial officer, is paid a salary of $375,000. Mike works for Parakeet on a part-time basis and spends most of his time training for triathlons. Parakeet advances $80,000 to Judy as an interest-free loan. What are the tax issues? **ISSUE ID**

17. **LO.6** Whether compensation paid to a corporate employee is reasonable is a question of fact to be determined from the surrounding circumstances. How would the resolution of this problem be affected by each of the following factors?
    a. The employee owns no stock but is the mother-in-law of the sole shareholder.
    b. The shareholder-employee does not have a college degree.
    c. The shareholder-employee works 40 hours per week for another unrelated employer.
    d. The shareholder-employee was underpaid for services during the formative period of the corporation.
    e. The corporation has never paid a dividend.
    f. Year-end bonuses are paid to all employees, but officer-shareholders receive disproportionately larger bonuses.

18. **LO.4, 8** Orange Corporation would like to transfer excess cash to its sole shareholder, Danielle, who is also an employee. Danielle is in the 28% tax bracket, and Orange is in the 34% bracket. Because Danielle's contribution to the business is substantial, Orange believes that a $50,000 bonus in the current year is reasonable compensation and should be deductible by the corporation. However, Orange is considering paying Danielle a $50,000 dividend because the tax rate on dividends is lower than the tax rate on compensation. Is Orange correct in believing that a dividend is the better choice? Why or why not? **DECISION MAKING**

19. **LO.6, 8** Green Corporation has several employees. Their names and salaries are listed below.

Samantha	$600,000
Chris (Samantha's daughter)	100,000
Joey (Samantha's son)	100,000
Jack (an unrelated third party)	250,000

Chris and Joey are the only shareholders of Green Corporation. Samantha and Jack share equally in the management of the company's operations. Chris and Joey are both full-time college students at a university 200 miles away. Green has substantial E & P and has never distributed a dividend. Discuss problems related to Green's salary arrangement.

20. **LO.6, 8** Condor Corporation pays its president and sole shareholder, Katrina, an annual salary of $500,000. Katrina wishes to avoid dividends because of the double tax result. However, she is concerned that if she were to receive any more salary, the IRS might treat it as unreasonable compensation and a constructive dividend. Instead, Katrina is thinking of having Condor contribute $150,000 to her favorite charity. Would there be a problem if Katrina makes a pledge for this amount and Condor pays it on her behalf? Explain.

COMMUNICATIONS

21. **LO.7** Your client, Gull Corporation, declares a dividend permitting its common shareholders to elect to receive 12 shares of cumulative preferred stock or 4 additional shares of Gull common stock for every 20 shares of common stock held. Gull has only common stock outstanding (fair market value of $50 per share). One shareholder elects to receive preferred stock, and the remaining shareholders choose the common stock. Gull asks you whether the shareholders have any taxable income on the receipt of the stock. Prepare a letter to Gull and a memo to the file regarding this matter. Gull's address is 626 White Hill, Marathon, TX 79842.

22. **LO.7** Describe the rationale underlying the tax treatment of stock distributions.

23. **LO.7** How are nontaxable and taxable stock rights handled for tax purposes?

PROBLEMS

24. **LO.1, 4** At the start of the current year, Indigo Corporation (a calendar year taxpayer) has accumulated E & P of $240,000. Indigo's current E & P is $160,000, and at the end of the year, it distributes $440,000 ($220,000 each) to its equal shareholders, Sarah and Mason. Their basis in the stock is $8,000 for Sarah and $32,000 for Mason. How is the distribution treated for tax purposes?

25. **LO.2** Capon Corporation, a calendar year taxpayer, receives dividend income of $600,000 from a corporation in which it holds a 12% interest. Capon also receives interest income of $90,000 from municipal bonds. (The municipality used the proceeds from the bond issue to construct a library.) Capon borrowed funds to purchase the municipal bonds and pays $50,000 of interest on the loan. Excluding these items, Capon's taxable income is $1.2 million.
    a. What is Capon Corporation's taxable income after these items are taken into account?
    b. What is Capon Corporation's accumulated E & P at the start of next year if its beginning balance this year is $400,000?

26. **LO.1, 2, 3** On September 30, Jade Corporation, a calendar year taxpayer, sold a parcel of land (basis of $300,000) for a $900,000 note. The note is payable in five installments, with the first payment due next year. Because Jade did not elect out of the installment method, none of the $600,000 gain is taxed this year.

    Jade Corporation had a $400,000 deficit in accumulated E & P at the beginning of the year. Before considering the effect of the land sale, Jade had a deficit in current E & P of $100,000.

    Robert, the sole shareholder of Jade, has a basis of $150,000 in his stock. If Jade distributes $950,000 to Robert on December 31, how much income must he report for tax purposes?

27. **LO.2** Sparrow Corporation (a calendar year, accrual basis taxpayer) had the following transactions in 2011, its second year of operation.

Taxable income	$330,000
Federal income tax liability paid	112,000
Tax-exempt interest income	5,000
Meals and entertainment expenses (total)	3,000
Premiums paid on key employee life insurance	3,500
Increase in cash surrender value attributable to life insurance premiums	700

Proceeds from key employee life insurance policy	$130,000
Cash surrender value of life insurance policy at distribution	20,000
Excess of capital losses over capital gains	13,000
MACRS deduction	26,000
Straight-line depreciation using ADS lives	16,000
Section 179 expense elected during 2010	100,000
Organizational expenses incurred during 2010	14,000
Dividends received from domestic corporations (less than 20% owned)	25,000

Sparrow uses the LIFO inventory method, and its LIFO recapture amount increased by $10,000 during 2011. In addition, Sparrow sold property on installment during 2010. The property was sold for $40,000 and had an adjusted basis at sale of $32,000. During 2011, Sparrow received a $15,000 payment on the installment sale. Finally assume that Sparrow elected to amortize qualified organizational expenses during 2010 and that no additional first-year depreciation was claimed. Compute Sparrow's current E & P.

28. **LO.2** In each of the following *independent* situations, indicate the effect on taxable income and E & P, stating the amount of any increase (or decrease) as a result of the transaction. Assume E & P has already been increased by taxable income.

Transaction	Taxable Income Increase (Decrease)	E & P Increase (Decrease)
a. Realized gain of $90,000 on involuntary conversion of building ($20,000 of gain is recognized).	________	________
b. Mining exploration costs incurred on June 1 of the current year; $36,000 is deductible from current-year taxable income.	________	________
c. Sale of equipment to unrelated third party for $350,000; basis is $210,000 (no election out of installment method; no payments are received in the current year).	________	________
d. Dividends of $30,000 received from 5%-owned corporation, together with dividends received deduction (assume taxable income limit does not apply).	________	________
e. Domestic production activities deduction of $60,000 claimed in current year.	________	________
f. Section 179 expense deduction of $60,000 in current year.	________	________
g. Impact of current-year § 179 expense deduction for item (f) in succeeding year.	________	________
h. MACRS depreciation of $90,000. ADS depreciation would have been $100,000.	________	________
i. Federal income taxes paid in the current year of $50,000.	________	________

29. **LO.2** Osprey Corporation, a calendar year taxpayer, made estimated tax payments of $12,000 for 2011 ($3,000 per quarter). Osprey filed its Federal income tax return for 2011 reflecting a tax liability of $5,000. Due to its overpayments, in 2012 Osprey received a $7,000 refund. What is the impact on Osprey's E & P of the payment of estimated taxes and the receipt of the Federal income tax refund?

30. **LO.1, 3** Lark Corporation is a calendar year taxpayer. At the beginning of the current year, Lark has accumulated E & P of $330,000. The corporation incurs a deficit in current E & P of $460,000 that accrues ratably throughout the year. On June 30, Lark distributes $200,000 to its sole shareholder, Adrienne. If Adrienne's stock has a basis of $40,000, how is she taxed on the distribution?

31. **LO.1, 3** At the beginning of its taxable year, Turkey Corporation had E & P of $405,000. For the calendar year, Turkey incurred a deficit in current E & P of $550,000, which includes a $405,000 loss on the sale of an asset on June 30. If Turkey made a distribution of $75,000 to its sole shareholder on July 1, how is the shareholder taxed?

32. **LO.1, 3** Cardinal Corporation (a calendar year taxpayer) had a deficit in accumulated E & P of $500,000 at the beginning of the current year. Its net profit for the period January 1 through July 30 was $600,000, but its E & P for the entire taxable year was only $80,000. If Cardinal made a distribution of $120,000 to its sole shareholder on August 1, how will the shareholder be taxed?

33. **LO.1, 3** Bunting Corporation and Jennifer each own 50% of Sparrow Corporation's common stock. On January 1, Sparrow has a deficit in accumulated E & P of $150,000. Its current E & P is $65,000. During the year, Sparrow makes cash distributions of $30,000 each to Bunting and Jennifer.
    a. How are the two shareholders taxed on the distribution?
    b. What is Sparrow Corporation's accumulated E & P at the end of the year?

34. **LO.1, 3** Complete the following schedule for each case. Assume the shareholders have ample basis in the stock investment.

	Accumulated E & P Beginning of Year	Current E & P	Cash Distributions (All on Last Day of Year)	Dividend Income	Return of Capital
a.	($150,000)	$ 70,000	$130,000	$ ______	$ ______
b.	200,000	(60,000)	210,000	______	______
c.	130,000	50,000	150,000	______	______
d.	120,000	(40,000)	130,000	______	______
e.	Same as (d) except the distribution of $130,000 is made on June 30, and the corporation uses the calendar year for tax purposes.			______	______

35. **LO.1, 3** Mike, the sole shareholder of Daffodil Corporation, sold his Daffodil stock to Steve on July 30 for $200,000. Mike's basis in the stock was $150,000 at the beginning of the year. Daffodil had accumulated E & P of $110,000 on January 1 and current E & P of $170,000. During the year, Daffodil made the following distributions: $300,000 cash to Mike on July 1 and $100,000 cash to Steve on December 30. How will Mike and Steve be taxed on the distributions? How much gain will Mike recognize on the sale of his stock to Steve?

DECISION MAKING

36. **LO.4** Sarah, a shareholder of Cardinal Corporation, is in the 35% tax bracket. This year, she receives a $10,000 qualified dividend from Cardinal, incurs investment interest expense of $21,000, and has net investment income of $11,000 (not including the qualified dividend). Assume that Sarah does not expect to have any investment income in the foreseeable future. Should Sarah treat the distribution as a qualified dividend or classify it as net investment income?

37. **LO.4** In November of the current year, Emerald Corporation declared a dividend of $2 per share (the shareholder record date is December 15). Assume that Emerald has sufficient current E & P to cover the dividend payment. If Judy purchases 500 shares of Emerald stock on December 5 and sells the stock on December 25, how is she taxed on the $1,000 dividend?

38. **LO.1, 5** Heather, an individual, owns all of the outstanding stock in Silver Corporation. Heather purchased her stock in Silver nine years ago, and her basis is $56,000. At the beginning of this year, the corporation has $76,000 of accumulated E & P and no current E & P (before considering the effect of the distributions). What are the tax consequences to Heather (amount and type of income and basis in property received) and Silver Corporation (gain or loss and effect on E & P) in each of the following situations?

a. Silver distributes land to Heather. The land was held as an investment and has a fair market value of $54,000 and an adjusted basis of $42,000.
b. Assume that Silver Corporation has no current or accumulated E & P prior to the distribution. How would your answer to (a) change?
c. Assume that the land distributed in (a) is subject to a $46,000 mortgage (which Heather assumes). How would your answer change?
d. Assume that the land has a fair market value of $54,000 and an adjusted basis of $62,000 on the date of the distribution. How would your answer to (a) change?
e. Instead of distributing land in (a), assume that Silver decides to distribute equipment used in its business. The equipment has a $14,000 market value, a $1,200 adjusted basis for income tax purposes, and a $5,200 adjusted basis for E & P purposes. When the equipment was purchased four years ago, its original fair market value was $18,000.

39. **LO.1, 5** Peach Corporation distributes property ($250,000 basis and $300,000 fair market value) to its sole shareholder, Karla. The property is subject to a liability of $400,000, which Karla assumes. Peach has E & P of $650,000 prior to the distribution.
   a. What gain, if any, does Peach recognize on the distribution, and what is Peach's accumulated E & P at the start of the following year?
   b. What is the amount of Karla's dividend income on the distribution, and what is her basis in the property received?

40. **LO.1, 5** Green Corporation, with E & P of $600,000, distributes land (worth $300,000, adjusted basis of $340,000) to Michael, its sole shareholder. The land is subject to a liability of $130,000, which Michael assumes. What are the tax consequences to Green and to Michael?

41. **LO.1, 3** At the beginning of the current year, Cornflower Corporation (a calendar year taxpayer) has accumulated E & P of $54,000. During the year, Cornflower incurs a $28,000 loss from operations that accrues ratably. On October 1, Cornflower distributes $43,000 in cash to Roy, its sole shareholder. How will Roy be taxed on the distribution?

42. **LO.1, 5** Penguin Corporation distributes equipment (adjusted basis of $80,000; fair market value of $65,000) to its shareholder, Holly. What are the tax consequences to Penguin Corporation and to Holly?

43. **LO.1, 2, 3, 4, 5** Cerulean Corporation has two equal shareholders, Eloise and Olivia. Eloise acquired her Cerulean stock three years ago by transferring property worth $700,000, basis of $300,000, for 70 shares of the stock. Olivia acquired 70 shares in Cerulean Corporation two years ago by transferring property worth $660,000, basis of $110,000. Cerulean Corporation's accumulated E & P as of January 1 of the current year is $350,000. On March 1 of the current year, the corporation distributed to Eloise property worth $120,000, basis to Cerulean of $50,000. It distributed cash of $220,000 to Olivia. On July 1 of the current year, Olivia sold her stock to Magnus for $820,000. On December 1 of the current year, Cerulean distributed cash of $90,000 each to Magnus and Eloise. What are the tax issues? **ISSUE ID**

44. **LO.1, 2, 5** Purple Corporation has accumulated E & P of $65,000 at the beginning of the year. Its current-year taxable income is $320,000. On December 31, Purple distributed business property (worth $140,000, adjusted basis of $290,000) to Peter, its sole shareholder. Peter assumes an $80,000 liability on the property. Included in the determination of Purple's current taxable income is $16,000 of income recognized from an installment sale in a previous year. In addition, the corporation incurred a Federal income tax liability of $112,000, paid life insurance premiums of $3,500, and received term life insurance proceeds of $55,000 on the death of an officer. **DECISION MAKING**
   a. What is Peter's gross income from the distribution?
   b. What is the E & P of Purple Corporation after the property distribution?
   c. What is Peter's tax basis in the property received?
   d. How would your answers to (a) and (b) change if Purple had sold the property at its fair market value, used $80,000 of the proceeds to pay off the liability, and then distributed the remaining cash and any tax savings to Peter?

45. **LO.5** Iris Corporation owns 30% of Fresia Corporation's stock. On November 15, Fresia Corporation, with current E & P of $320,000, distributes land (fair market value of $100,000; basis of $160,000) to Iris. The land is subject to a liability of $80,000, which Iris assumes.
   a. How is Iris Corporation taxed on the distribution?
   b. What is Fresia Corporation's E & P after the distribution?

46. **LO.6** Wren Corporation makes a loan evidenced by a written note to its sole shareholder, James. The loan is collateralized by James's cabin in the Lake Superior area, but the loan is interest-free. Discuss whether the advance is a bona fide loan. Will you need additional information to complete your analysis? If so, describe what information you would need.

47. **LO.6** Parrot Corporation is a closely held company with accumulated E & P of $300,000 and current E & P of $350,000. Tom and Jerry are brothers; each owns a 50% share in Parrot, and they share management responsibilities equally. What are the tax consequences of each of the following independent transactions involving Parrot, Tom, and Jerry? How does each transaction affect Parrot's E & P?
   a. Parrot sells an office building (adjusted basis of $350,000; fair market value of $300,000) to Tom for $275,000.
   b. Parrot lends Jerry $250,000 on March 31 of this year. The loan is evidenced by a note and is payable on demand. No interest is charged on the loan (the current applicable Federal interest rate is 7%).
   c. Parrot owns an airplane that it leases to others for a specified rental rate. Tom and Jerry also use the airplane for personal use and pay no rent. During the year, Tom used the airplane for 120 hours, and Jerry used it for 160 hours. The rental value of the airplane is $350 per hour, and its maintenance costs average $80 per hour.
   d. Tom leases equipment to Parrot for $20,000 per year. The same equipment can be leased from another company for $9,000 per year.

48. **LO.7** Katie purchased 5,000 shares of Grebe Corporation common stock six years ago for $80,000. In the current year, Katie received a preferred stock dividend of 400 shares, while the other holders of common stock received a common stock dividend. The preferred stock Katie received has a fair market value of $40,000, and her common stock has a fair market value of $120,000. Assume that Grebe has ample E & P to cover any distributions made during the year. What is Katie's basis in the preferred and common stock after the dividend is received? When does her holding period commence for the preferred stock?

COMMUNICATIONS

49. **LO.7** Julie Swanson bought 5,000 shares of Great Egret Corporation stock two years ago for $12,000. Last year, Julie received a nontaxable stock dividend of 1,000 shares in Great Egret Corporation. In the current tax year, Julie sold all of the stock received as a dividend for $9,000. Prepare a letter to Julie and a memo to the file describing the tax consequences of the stock sale. Julie's address is 3737 Canyon Drive, Minneapolis, MN 55434.

50. **LO.7** Denim Corporation declares a nontaxable dividend payable in rights to subscribe to common stock. One right and $60 entitle the holder to subscribe to one share of stock. One right is issued for every two shares of stock owned. At the date of distribution of the rights, the market value of the stock is $110 per share, and the market value of the rights is $55 per right. Lauren owns 300 shares of stock that she purchased two years ago for $9,000. Lauren receives 150 rights, of which she exercises 105 to purchase 105 additional shares. She sells the remaining 45 rights for $2,475. What are the tax consequences of this transaction to Lauren?

DECISION MAKING

51. **LO.4, 8** Ivana, the president and a shareholder of Robin Corporation, has earned a salary bonus of $15,000 for the current year. Because of the lower tax rates on qualifying dividends, Robin is considering substituting a dividend for the bonus. Assume the tax rates are 28% for Ivana and 34% for Robin Corporation.
   a. How much better off would Ivana be if she were paid a dividend rather than salary?
   b. How much better off would Robin Corporation be if it paid Ivana salary rather than a dividend?
   c. If Robin Corporation pays Ivana a salary bonus of $20,000 instead of a $15,000 dividend, how would your answers to (a) and (b) change?
   d. What should Robin do?

COMMUNICATIONS

52. **LO.1, 3, 8** Your client, Heron Corporation, has a deficit in accumulated E & P of $300,000. Starting this year, it expects to generate annual E & P of $150,000 for the next four years and would like to distribute this amount to its shareholders. How should Heron Corporation distribute the $600,000 over the four-year period to provide the least amount of dividend income to its shareholders (all individuals)? In a letter to your client, make appropriate suggestions on how this should be done. Also, prepare a memo for your firm's file. Heron Corporation's address is 12 Nature Trail Way, Daytona Beach, FL 32114.

RESEARCH PROBLEMS

Note: Solutions to Research Problems can be prepared by using the **Checkpoint® Student Edition** online research product, which is available to accompany this text. It is also possible to prepare solutions to the Research Problems by using tax research materials found in a standard tax library.

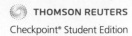

THOMSON REUTERS
Checkpoint® Student Edition

COMMUNICATIONS

Research Problem 1. Patrick Zimbrick and his son, Dan, own all of the outstanding stock of Osprey Corporation. Both Dan and Patrick are officers in the corporation and, together with their uncle, John, comprise the entire board of directors. Osprey uses the cash method of accounting and has a calendar year-end. In late 2007, the board of directors adopted the following legally enforceable resolution (agreed to in writing by each of the officers):

> Salary payments made to an officer of the corporation that shall be disallowed in whole or in part as a deductible expense for Federal income tax purposes shall be reimbursed by such officer to the corporation to the full extent of the disallowance. It shall be the duty of the board of directors to enforce payment of each such amount.

In 2008, Osprey paid Patrick $560,000 in compensation. Dan received $400,000. On an audit in late 2011, the IRS found the compensation of both officers to be excessive. It disallowed deductions for $200,000 of the payment to Patrick and $150,000 of the payment to Dan. The IRS recharacterized the disallowed payments as constructive dividends. Complying with the resolution by the board of directors, both Patrick and Dan repaid the disallowed compensation to Osprey Corporation in early 2012. Dan and Patrick have asked you to determine how their repayments should be treated for tax purposes. Dan is still working as a highly compensated executive for Osprey while Patrick is retired and living off his savings. Prepare a memo to your firm's client files describing the results of your research.

Partial list of research aids:
§ 1341.
Vincent E. Oswald, 49 T.C. 645 (1968).

COMMUNICATIONS

Research Problem 2. Oriole Corporation wholly owns Canary Corporation, which was formed six years ago with the transfer of several assets and a substantial amount of cash. Oriole's basis in the Canary stock is $11.5 million. Since it was formed, Canary has been a very successful manufacturing company and currently has accumulated E & P of $8 million. The company's principal assets are property, plant, and equipment (worth $11 million) and cash and marketable securities of $8.5 million, for a total fair market value of $19.5 million.

Oriole and Canary are members of an affiliated group and have made the election under § 243(b) to entitle Oriole to a 100% dividends received deduction. From a strategic perspective, Oriole is no longer interested in manufacturing and is considering a sale of Canary. In anticipation of a sale in the next year or two, the management of Oriole has contacted you for advice. If Canary is sold outright, Oriole will have a capital gain of $8 million ($19.5 million fair market value less a basis of $11.5 million). As an alternative, taxes on a future sale would be minimized if Canary first pays Oriole an $8 million dividend equal to its E & P. With the 100% dividends received deduction, the payment would be tax-free to Oriole. Subsequent to the dividend payment, Canary can be sold for its remaining value of $11.5 million ($11 million in property, plant, and equipment plus $500,000 in cash), resulting in no gain or loss to Oriole.

a. Prepare a letter to Louise Jones, the president of Oriole Corporation, describing the results of the proposed plan. Oriole's address is 974 State Street, La Crosse, WI 53786.
b. Prepare a memo for your firm's client files.

Partial list of research aids:
Waterman Steamship Corp. v. Comm., 70–2 USTC ¶9514, 26 AFTR 2d 70–5185, 430 F.2d 1185 (CA–5, 1970).

Research Problem 3. Your client, White Corporation, has done well since its formation 20 years ago. This year, it recognized a $50 million capital gain from the sale of a subsidiary. White's CEO has contacted you to discuss a proposed transaction to reduce the tax on the capital gain. Under the proposal, White will purchase all of the common stock in Purple Corporation for $200 million. Purple is a profitable corporation that has $63 million in

cash and marketable securities, $137 million in operating assets, and approximately $280 million in E & P. After its acquisition, Purple will distribute $50 million in cash and marketable securities to White. Due to the 100% dividends received deduction, no taxable income results to White from the dividend. White will then resell Purple for $150 million. The subsequent sale of Purple generates a $50 million capital loss [$200 million (stock basis) – $150 million (sales price)]. The loss from the stock sale can then be used to offset the preexisting $50 million capital gain. Will the proposed plan work?

Partial list of research aids:
§ 1059.

COMMUNICATIONS

Research Problem 4. Emerald Corporation is required to change its method of accounting for Federal income tax purposes. The change will require an adjustment to income to be made over three tax periods. Jonas, the sole shareholder of Emerald Corporation, wants to better understand the implications of this adjustment for E & P purposes, as he anticipates a distribution from Emerald in the current year. Prepare a memo for your firm's client files describing the results of your research.

Partial list of research aids:
§ 481(a).
Rev.Proc. 97–27, 1997–1 C.B. 680.

INTERNET *activity*

Use the tax resources of the Internet to address the following questions. Do not restrict your search to the Web, but include a review of newsgroups and general reference materials, practitioner sites and resources, primary sources of the tax law, chat rooms and discussion groups, and other opportunities.

Research Problem 5. Just how common are dividend distributions? Are dividends concentrated in the companies traded on the New York Stock Exchange, or do closely held corporations pay dividends with the same frequency and at the same rates? Did dividends increase following the reduction in tax rates in 2003? Did dividends decrease during the financial downturn of 2008 and 2009? Financial institutions and observers are acutely interested in these issues. Search for comments on such questions at various commercial websites as well as one or two academic journals or newsgroups.

Research Problem 6. The law allowing a reduced tax rate on dividends (part of the "Bush tax cuts") was scheduled to expire at the end of 2010. During the year leading up to the scheduled expiration, there was considerable debate surrounding the desirability of extending the reduced rate beyond 2010. Search the Internet for arguments for and against extending the reduced rates on dividends for individuals. Summarize the arguments made on both sides. Which side do you agree with? Why?

Research Problem 7. Over the last few years, there have been several proposals to reform the Federal income tax. Use the Internet to ascertain how these proposals have addressed the tax treatment of corporate distributions.

CHAPTER

6

Corporations: Redemptions and Liquidations

LEARNING OBJECTIVES

After completing Chapter 6, you should be able to:

LO.1

Identify the stock redemptions that qualify for sale or exchange treatment.

LO.2

Understand the tax impact of stock redemptions on the distributing corporation.

LO.3

Recognize the restrictions on sale or exchange treatment for certain redemption-like transactions.

LO.4

Understand the tax consequences of complete liquidations for both the corporation and its shareholders.

LO.5

Understand the tax consequences of subsidiary liquidations for both the parent and the subsidiary corporations.

LO.6

Identify planning opportunities available to minimize the tax impact in stock redemptions and complete liquidations.

OUTLINE

For the latest in changes to tax legislation, visit **www.cengage.com/taxation/swft.**

THE BIG PICTURE **Tax Solutions for the Real World**

FAMILY CORPORATIONS AND STOCK REDEMPTIONS

Christina Flores formed Orange Corporation 15 years ago, and she continues to own all 10,000 shares of Orange stock outstanding (basis of $400,000). Christina has been employed full-time with Orange since its inception, handling all of the corporation's management and strategy decisions during that time. Christina receives an annual salary of $250,000 from Orange for this work. Within the next five to seven years, Christina would like to retire and transfer ownership in Orange to her two children, ages 24 and 22. The children have worked full-time with Orange over the last two years and have demonstrated both the capacity and the willingness to take over the business after their mother's retirement. Currently, the Orange stock is worth $6 million, and it is expected to be worth $8 million by the time of Christina's retirement. The stock represents approximately 80 percent of Christina's net worth. Orange Corporation (E & P of $2 million) generates strong positive cash flow, but a significant investment in property, plant, and equipment will be required over the next several years. The children are not expected to have the financial wherewithal to purchase the Orange stock from their mother at the time of her retirement, although Christina would be receptive to taking notes in exchange for her Orange stock.

How could a stock redemption be used to assist Christina in achieving her goal of transferring control of Orange to the children upon her retirement? **Read the chapter and formulate your response.**

Sandra is the sole shareholder of Mockingbird Corporation, having acquired 1,000 shares in the corporation 10 years ago at a cost of $400,000. Mockingbird has been profitable for most of those years and has earnings and profits (E & P) of $800,000. Currently, the Mockingbird shares are worth $1 million.

Sandra needs $500,000 for another investment opportunity, and to obtain the necessary funds, she has considered several alternatives involving her ownership interest in Mockingbird:

- Mockingbird could declare a dividend, but Sandra wants to avoid having the entire distribution taxed as a dividend, if possible (see Chapter 5).
- Sandra could sell one-half of her stock to an unrelated third party, but she does not want to give up control of the corporation.
- Sandra could sell one-half of her stock directly to Mockingbird in a stock redemption.

Sandra prefers the stock redemption as she believes it would provide her with the following favorable tax consequences while allowing her to retain sole control of Mockingbird:

- Return of capital treatment to the extent of her basis in the stock sold ($200,000).
- Long-term capital gain treatment on the excess of the amount realized over the basis ($300,000).

These tax outcomes typically apply to sales or exchanges of stock held for the required long-term holding period. For example, Sandra would be taxed in this manner on a sale of the stock to an unrelated third party. In the sale to Mockingbird, however, a key characteristic inherent in typical stock sales—a reduction in ownership interest—is missing. Because Sandra would still own 100 percent of Mockingbird after the proposed stock redemption, the Code treats the transaction as a $500,000 dividend distribution (i.e., a return *from* her investment), not as a sale or exchange. However, *certain* kinds of stock redemptions do qualify under the Code for sale or exchange treatment (i.e., a return *of* the owner's investment). In these transactions, as a general rule, the shareholder's ownership interest must be diminished as a result of the redemption. Additionally, a disposition of stock in a complete liquidation of a corporation will generally produce sale or exchange treatment. This chapter examines the tax implications of corporate distributions that are stock redemptions and complete liquidations.

6.1 Stock Redemptions—In General

LO.1

Identify the stock redemptions that qualify for sale or exchange treatment.

Under § 317(b), a **stock redemption** occurs when a corporation acquires its stock from a shareholder in exchange for cash or other property. In a stock redemption, the shareholder is selling stock back to the issuing corporation, and it resembles a sale of stock to an unrelated third party. However, while a sale of stock to an outsider invariably results in sale or exchange treatment, only a *qualifying* stock redemption is treated as a sale for tax purposes.

Nonqualified stock redemptions are denied sale or exchange treatment because they are deemed to have the same effect as dividend distributions. For example, if a shareholder owns all the stock of a corporation and sells a portion of that stock to the corporation, the shareholder's ownership interest in the corporation does not change. After the redemption, the shareholder still owns all the outstanding stock of the corporation. In this situation, the stock redemption resembles a dividend distribution and is taxed as such.

Stock redemptions occur for a variety of reasons. Publicly traded corporations often reacquire their shares with the goal of increasing shareholder value. For corporations where the stock is closely held, redemptions frequently occur to achieve shareholder objectives. For instance, a redemption might be used to acquire the stock of a deceased shareholder of a closely held corporation. Using corporate funds to purchase the stock from the decedent's estate relieves the remaining shareholders of the need to use their own money to acquire the stock. Stock redemptions also frequently occur as a result of property settlements in divorce actions. When spouses jointly own 100 percent of a corporation's shares, a divorce decree may require that the stock interest of one spouse be bought out. A redemption of that spouse's shares relieves the other spouse from having to use his or her own funds for the transaction.

6.2 Stock Redemptions—Sale or Exchange Treatment

Noncorporate shareholders generally prefer to have a stock redemption treated as a sale or exchange rather than as a dividend distribution. For individual taxpayers, the maximum tax rate for long-term capital gains is currently 15 percent (0 percent for taxpayers in the 10 or 15 percent marginal tax bracket). The preference for qualifying stock redemption treatment is based on the fact that such transactions result in (1) the tax-free recovery of the redeemed stock's basis and (2) capital gains that can be offset by capital losses. In a nonqualified stock redemption, the *entire* distribution is taxed as dividend income (assuming adequate E & P), which, although generally taxed at the same rate as long-term capital gains, cannot be offset by capital losses.

EXAMPLE 1

Abby, an individual in the 35% tax bracket, acquired stock in Quail Corporation four years ago for $300,000. In the current year, Quail Corporation (E & P of $1 million) redeems her shares for $450,000. If the redemption qualifies for sale or exchange treatment, Abby will have a long-term capital gain of $150,000 [$450,000 (redemption amount) − $300,000 (basis)]. Her tax liability on the $150,000 gain will be $22,500 ($150,000 × 15%). If the stock redemption does not qualify as a sale or

TAX *in* the NEWS — Corporations Flush with Cash Increase Stock Buyback Programs

When the economy went bad, businesses slashed costs and reduced capital expenditures. As a result of these cuts, corporate profits and cash flows have improved dramatically, and many corporations are carrying record amounts of cash on their books. Hesitant to increase capital and other expenditures in the current economic environment, many corporations have decided, instead, to use surplus cash to repurchase shares of their stock. Reasons cited for stock buyback programs include a desire to offset the dilution to earnings per share associated with employee stock option plans, a desire to enhance shareholder value, and a perception that a corporation's stock is undervalued in the marketplace. The qualifying stock redemption provisions must be considered in determining the proper tax treatment for a shareholder participating in a stock buyback program. In the case of stock of a publicly traded corporation, however, a shareholder's ownership interest likely is so minuscule that sale or exchange treatment will be the result.

exchange, the entire distribution will be treated as a dividend, and her tax liability will be $67,500 ($450,000 × 15%). Thus, Abby will save $45,000 ($67,500 − $22,500) in income taxes if the transaction is a qualifying stock redemption. ■

EXAMPLE 2

Assume in Example 1 that Abby has a capital loss carryover of $100,000 in the current tax year. If the transaction is a qualifying stock redemption, Abby can offset the entire $100,000 capital loss carryover against her $150,000 long-term capital gain. As a result, only $50,000 of the gain will be taxed, and her tax liability will be only $7,500 ($50,000 × 15%). On the other hand, if the transaction does not qualify for sale or exchange treatment, the entire $450,000 will be taxed as a dividend at 15%. In addition, assuming she has no capital gains in the current year, Abby will be able to deduct only $3,000 of the $100,000 capital loss carryover to offset her ordinary income. ■

In contrast, however, *corporate* shareholders normally receive more favorable tax treatment from a dividend distribution than would result from a qualifying stock redemption. Corporate taxpayers typically report only a small portion of a dividend distribution as taxable income because of the dividends received deduction (see Chapter 2). Further, the preferential tax rate applicable to dividend and long-term capital gain income is not available to corporations. Consequently, tax planning for stock redemptions must consider the different preferences of corporate and noncorporate shareholders.

EXAMPLE 3

Assume in Example 1 that Abby is a corporation, that the stock represents a 40% ownership interest in Quail Corporation, and that Abby has corporate taxable income of $850,000 before the redemption transaction. If the transaction is a qualifying stock redemption, Abby will have a long-term capital gain of $150,000 that will be subject to tax at 34%, or $51,000. On the other hand, if the $450,000 distribution is treated as a dividend, Abby will have a dividends received deduction of $360,000 ($450,000 × 80%), so only $90,000 of the payment will be taxed. Consequently, Abby's tax liability on the transaction will be only $30,600 ($90,000 × 34%). ■

When a qualifying stock redemption results in a *loss* to the shareholder rather than a gain, § 267 disallows loss recognition if the shareholder owns (directly or indirectly) more than 50 percent of the corporation's stock. A shareholder's basis in property received in a stock redemption, qualifying or nonqualified, generally will be the property's fair market value, determined as of the date of the redemption. Further, the holding period of the property begins on that date.

The Code establishes the criteria for determining whether a transaction is a qualifying stock redemption for tax purposes. The terminology in an agreement between the parties is not controlling, nor is state law. Section 302(b) provides four types of

GLOBAL *Tax Issues*

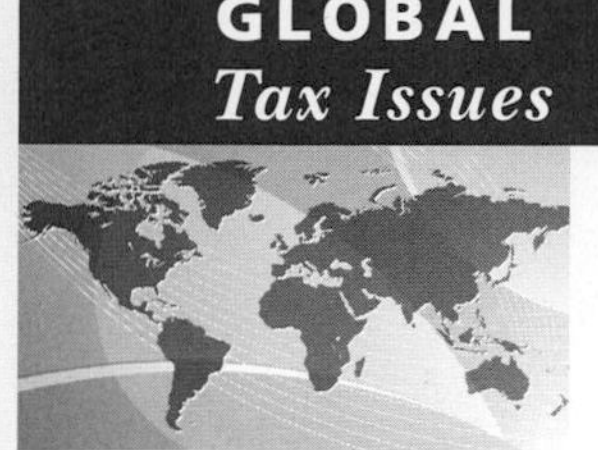

Foreign Shareholders Prefer Sale or Exchange Treatment in Stock Redemptions

As a general rule, foreign shareholders are subject to U.S. tax on dividend income from U.S. corporations but not on capital gains from the sale of U.S. stock. In some situations, a nonresident alien is taxed on a capital gain from the disposition of stock in a U.S. corporation, but only if the stock was effectively connected with the conduct of a U.S. trade or business of the individual. Foreign corporations are similarly taxed on gains from the sale of U.S. stock investments. Whether a stock redemption qualifies for sale or exchange treatment therefore takes on added significance for foreign shareholders. If one of the qualifying stock redemption rules can be satisfied, the foreign shareholder typically will avoid U.S. tax on the transaction. If, instead, dividend income is the result, a 30 percent withholding tax typically applies. For further details, see Chapter 9.

qualifying stock redemptions. Additionally, certain distributions of property to an estate in exchange for a deceased shareholder's stock are treated as qualifying stock redemptions under § 303.

HISTORICAL BACKGROUND AND OVERVIEW

Under prior law, the *dividend equivalency rule* was used to determine which stock redemptions qualified for sale or exchange treatment. Under that rule, if the facts and circumstances of a redemption indicated that it was essentially equivalent to a dividend, the redemption did not qualify for sale or exchange treatment. Instead, the entire amount received by the shareholder was taxed as dividend income to the extent of the corporation's E & P.

The uncertainty and subjectivity surrounding the dividend equivalency rule led Congress to enact several objective tests for determining the status of a redemption. Currently, the following five types of stock redemptions qualify for sale or exchange treatment:

- Distributions not essentially equivalent to a dividend ("not essentially equivalent redemptions").
- Distributions substantially disproportionate in terms of shareholder effect ("disproportionate redemptions").
- Distributions in complete termination of a shareholder's interest ("complete termination redemptions").
- Distributions to noncorporate shareholders in partial liquidation of a corporation ("partial liquidations").
- Distributions to pay a shareholder's death taxes ("redemptions to pay death taxes").

Concept Summary 6.1 later in this chapter summarizes the requirements for each of the qualifying stock redemptions.

STOCK ATTRIBUTION RULES

To qualify for sale or exchange treatment, a stock redemption generally must result in a substantial reduction in the shareholder's ownership interest in the corporation. In the absence of this reduction in ownership interest, the redemption proceeds are taxed as dividend income. In determining whether a stock redemption has sufficiently reduced a shareholder's interest, the stock owned by certain related parties is attributed to the redeeming shareholder.[1] Thus, the stock **attribution** rules must be

[1] § 318.

EXHIBIT 6.1 Stock Attribution Rules

	Deemed or Constructive Ownership
• Family	An individual is deemed to own the stock owned by his or her spouse, children, grandchildren, and parents (not siblings or grandparents).
• Partnership	A partner is deemed to own the stock owned by a partnership to the extent of the partner's proportionate interest in the partnership.
	Stock owned by a partner is deemed to be owned in full by a partnership.
• Estate or trust	A beneficiary or heir is deemed to own the stock owned by an estate or trust to the extent of the beneficiary or heir's proportionate interest in the estate or trust.
	Stock owned by a beneficiary or heir is deemed to be owned in full by an estate or trust.
• Corporation	Stock owned by a corporation is deemed to be owned proportionately by any shareholder owning 50% or more of the corporation's stock.
	Stock owned by a shareholder who owns 50% or more of a corporation is deemed to be owned in full by the corporation.

considered in applying the stock redemption provisions. Under these rules, related parties are defined to include the following family members: spouses, children, grandchildren, and parents. Attribution also takes place *from* and *to* partnerships, estates, trusts, and corporations (50 percent or more ownership required in the case of regular corporations). Exhibit 6.1 summarizes the stock attribution rules.

EXAMPLE 4
THE BIG PICTURE

Return to the facts of *The Big Picture* on p. 6-2. Assume instead that Christina owns only 80% of the stock in Orange Corporation, with the other 20% being held by her two children. For purposes of the stock attribution rules, Christina is treated as owning 100% of the stock in Orange Corporation. She owns 80% directly and, because of the family attribution rules, 20% indirectly through her children. ■

EXAMPLE 5

Chris owns 40% of the stock in Gray Corporation. The other 60% is owned by a partnership in which Chris has a 20% interest. Chris is deemed to own 52% of Gray Corporation: 40% directly and, because of the partnership interest, 12% indirectly (20% × 60%). ■

As discussed later, the *family* attribution rules (refer to Example 4) can be waived in the case of some complete termination redemptions. In addition, the stock attribution rules do not apply to partial liquidations or redemptions to pay death taxes.

NOT ESSENTIALLY EQUIVALENT REDEMPTIONS

Under § 302(b)(1), a redemption qualifies for sale or exchange treatment if it is "not essentially equivalent to a dividend." This provision represents a continuation of the dividend equivalency rule applicable under prior law. The earlier redemption language was retained principally for redemptions of preferred stock because shareholders often have no control over when corporations call in such stock.[2] Like its predecessor, the **not essentially equivalent redemption** lacks an objective test. Instead, each case must be resolved on a facts and circumstances basis.[3]

[2]See S.Rept. No. 1622, 83d Cong., 2d Sess. 44 (1954).

[3]Reg. § 1.302–2(b)(1).

Based upon the Supreme Court's decision in *U.S. v. Davis*,[4] a redemption will qualify as a not essentially equivalent redemption only when the shareholder's interest in the redeeming corporation has been meaningfully reduced. In determining whether the **meaningful reduction test** has been met, the stock attribution rules apply. A decrease in the redeeming shareholder's voting control appears to be the most significant indicator of a meaningful reduction,[5] but reductions in the rights of redeeming shareholders to share in corporate earnings or to receive corporate assets upon liquidation are also considered.[6] The meaningful reduction test is applied whether common stock or preferred stock is being redeemed.

EXAMPLE 6

Pat owns 58% of the common stock of Falcon Corporation. As a result of a redemption of some of his stock, Pat's ownership interest in Falcon is reduced to 51%. Since Pat continues to have dominant voting rights in Falcon after the redemption, the distribution is treated as essentially equivalent to a dividend. The entire amount of the distribution therefore is taxed as dividend income (assuming adequate E & P). ■

EXAMPLE 7

Maroon Corporation redeems 2% of its stock from Maria. Before the redemption, Maria owned 10% of Maroon Corporation. In this case, the redemption may qualify as a not essentially equivalent redemption. Maria experiences a reduction in her voting rights, her right to participate in current earnings and accumulated surplus, and her right to share in net assets upon liquidation. ■

When a redemption *fails* to satisfy any of the qualifying stock redemption rules, the basis of the redeemed shares does not disappear. Typically, the basis will attach to the basis of the redeeming shareholder's remaining shares in the corporation. If, however, the redeeming shareholder has terminated his or her direct stock ownership and the redemption is nonqualified due to the attribution rules, the basis of the redeemed shares will attach to the basis of the constructively owned stock.[7] In this manner, a nonqualified stock redemption can result in stock basis being shifted from one taxpayer (the redeeming shareholder) to another taxpayer (the shareholder related under the attribution rules).

EXAMPLE 8

Floyd and Fran, husband and wife, each own 50 shares in Grouse Corporation, representing 100% of the corporation's stock. All the stock was purchased for $50,000. Both Floyd and Fran serve as directors of the corporation. The corporation redeems Floyd's 50 shares, but he continues to serve as a director of the corporation. The redemption is treated as a dividend distribution (assuming adequate E & P) because Floyd constructively owns Fran's stock, or 100% of the Grouse stock outstanding. Floyd's $25,000 basis in the 50 shares redeemed attaches to Fran's stock; thus, Fran now has a basis of $50,000 in the 50 shares she owns in Grouse. ■

DISPROPORTIONATE REDEMPTIONS

A stock redemption qualifies for sale or exchange treatment under § 302(b)(2) as a **disproportionate redemption** if the following conditions are met:

- After the distribution, the shareholder owns *less than* 80 percent of the interest owned in the corporation before the redemption. For example, if a shareholder owns a 60 percent interest in a corporation that redeems part of the stock, the shareholder's ownership interest after the redemption must be less than 48 percent (80 percent of 60 percent).
- After the distribution, the shareholder owns *less than* 50 percent of the total combined voting power of all classes of stock entitled to vote.

[4]70–1 USTC ¶9289, 25 AFTR 2d 70–827, 90 S.Ct. 1041 (USSC, 1970).

[5]See, for example, *Jack Paparo*, 71 T.C. 692 (1979).

[6]See, for example, *Grabowski Trust*, 58 T.C. 650 (1972).

[7]Reg. § 1.302–2(c). But see Prop.Reg. § 1. 302–5.

In determining a shareholder's ownership interest before and after a redemption, the attribution rules apply.

EXAMPLE 9

Bob, Carl, and Dan, unrelated individuals, own 30 shares, 30 shares, and 40 shares, respectively, in Wren Corporation. Wren has 100 shares outstanding and E & P of $200,000. The corporation redeems 20 shares of Dan's stock for $30,000. Dan paid $200 a share for the stock two years ago. Dan's ownership in Wren Corporation before and after the redemption is as follows:

	Total Shares	Dan's Ownership	Ownership Percentage	80% of Original Ownership
Before redemption	100	40	40% (40 ÷ 100)	32% (80% × 40%)
After redemption	80	20	25% (20 ÷ 80)*	

*Note that the denominator of the fraction is reduced after the redemption (from 100 to 80).

Dan's 25% ownership after the redemption meets both tests of § 302(b)(2). It is less than 80% of his original ownership and less than 50% of the total voting power. The distribution therefore qualifies as a disproportionate redemption and receives sale or exchange treatment. As a result, Dan has a long-term capital gain of $26,000 [$30,000 – $4,000 (20 shares × $200)]. ■

EXAMPLE 10

Assume that Carl and Dan are father and son. The redemption described above would not qualify for sale or exchange treatment because of the effect of the attribution rules. Dan is deemed to own Carl's stock before and after the redemption. Dan's ownership in Wren Corporation before and after the redemption is as follows:

	Total Shares	Dan's Direct Ownership	Carl's Ownership	Dan's Direct and Indirect Ownership	Ownership Percentage	80% of Original Ownership
Before redemption	100	40	30	70	70% (70 ÷ 100)	56% (80% × 70%)
After redemption	80	20	30	50	62.5% (50 ÷ 80)	

Dan's direct and indirect ownership of 62.5% fails to meet either of the tests of § 302 (b) (2). After the redemption, Dan owns more than 80% of his original ownership and more than 50% of the voting stock. Thus, the redemption does not qualify for sale or exchange treatment and results in a dividend distribution of $30,000 to Dan. The basis in the 20 shares redeemed is added to Dan's basis in his remaining 20 shares. ■

A redemption that does not qualify as a disproportionate redemption may still qualify as a not essentially equivalent redemption if it meets the meaningful reduction test (see Example 7).

COMPLETE TERMINATION REDEMPTIONS

A redemption that terminates a shareholder's *entire* stock ownership in a corporation qualifies for sale or exchange treatment under § 302(b)(3). The attribution rules generally apply in determining whether the shareholder's stock ownership has been completely terminated. However, the *family* attribution rules do not apply to a **complete termination redemption** if the following conditions are met:

- The former shareholder has no interest, other than that of a creditor, in the corporation for at least 10 years after the redemption (including an interest as an officer, director, or employee).
- The former shareholder files an agreement to notify the IRS of any prohibited interest acquired within the 10-year postredemption period and to retain all necessary records pertaining to the redemption during this time period.

Acquisition of stock in the corporation by bequest or inheritance will not constitute a prohibited interest. The required agreement should be in the form of a separate statement signed by the former shareholder and attached to the return for the year in which the redemption occurs. The agreement should state that the former shareholder agrees to notify the IRS within 30 days of acquiring a prohibited interest in the corporation during the 10-year postredemption period.[8]

EXAMPLE 11

Kevin owns 50% of the stock in Green Corporation, while the remaining interest in Green is held as follows: 40% by Wilma (Kevin's wife) and 10% by Carmen (a key employee). Green redeems all of Kevin's stock for its fair market value. As a result, Wilma and Carmen are the only remaining shareholders, now owning 80% and 20%, respectively. If the requirements for the family attribution waiver are met, the transaction will qualify as a complete termination redemption and result in sale or exchange treatment. If the waiver requirements are not satisfied, Kevin will be deemed to own Wilma's (his wife's) stock, and the entire distribution will be taxed as a dividend (assuming adequate E & P). ■

EXAMPLE 12

Assume in Example 11 that Kevin qualifies for the family attribution waiver for the redemption. In the year of the redemption, Kevin treats the transaction as a sale or exchange. However, if he purchases Carmen's stock seven years after the redemption, he has acquired a prohibited interest, and the redemption distribution is reclassified as a dividend. Kevin will owe additional taxes due to this revised treatment. ■

Convertible Preferred Stock—Conversion or Redemption?

Four years ago, a corporation that does not sell its stock publicly sold some convertible preferred stock to a small investment group. At the option of the shareholders, the preferred stock can be converted into common stock at any time. The preferred stock also has a call feature, allowing the corporation to call (redeem) the stock at any time during the first five years after its issuance.

The corporation recently developed a successful invention that it has not yet publicly disclosed. The corporate board of directors expects that the corporation will experience significant earnings growth in the future as a result of the invention. The directors, all of whom own common stock in the corporation, would like to call the preferred stock so that those shares cannot be converted into common stock and otherwise participate in the corporation's future earnings growth. The call price set out in the preferred stock indenture provides a premium to the shareholders upon redemption. The directors vote to redeem all of the outstanding preferred stock and notify the preferred shareholders of the board's decision. Did the board of directors act ethically?

PARTIAL LIQUIDATIONS

Under § 302(b)(4), a *noncorporate* shareholder is allowed sale or exchange treatment for a distribution that qualifies as a **partial liquidation**. A partial liquidation is a distribution that (1) is *not essentially equivalent to a dividend* and (2) is both pursuant to a plan and made within the plan year or within the succeeding taxable year. A stock redemption pursuant to a partial liquidation may be pro rata with respect to the shareholders. In the case of a pro rata distribution, an actual surrender of stock is not required to qualify the transaction as a partial liquidation.[9]

[8]Reg. § 1.302–4(a).

[9]See *Fowler Hosiery Co. v. Comm.*, 62–1 USTC ¶9407, 9 AFTR 2d 1252, 301 F.2d 394 (CA–7, 1962); and Rev.Rul. 90–13, 1990–1 C.B. 65.

In determining whether a distribution is not essentially equivalent to a dividend, the effect of the distribution on the *corporation* is examined.[10] Consequently, to qualify as a partial liquidation, the distribution must result in a *genuine contraction* of the business of the corporation.

EXAMPLE 13

Dove Corporation owned a building with seven floors. Part of the building was rented, and part was used directly in Dove's business. A fire destroyed the two top floors, and Dove received insurance proceeds in reimbursement for the damage sustained. For business reasons, Dove did not rebuild the two floors and, instead, chose to operate on a smaller scale than before the fire. Pursuant to a plan adopted in the current year, Dove uses the insurance proceeds to redeem some stock from its shareholders. The distribution is not essentially equivalent to a dividend and qualifies as a partial liquidation.[11] ■

Applying the genuine contraction of a corporate business concept has proved difficult due to the lack of objective tests. The IRS has ruled that neither the sale of investments nor the sale of excess inventory will satisfy the genuine contraction test.[12] To minimize uncertainty, the genuine contraction test should be relied upon only after obtaining a favorable ruling from the IRS.

EXAMPLE 14
THE BIG PICTURE

Return to the facts of *The Big Picture* on p. 6-2. Assume that Orange Corporation loses a major customer and a severe drop in sales occurs. The corporation reduces its inventory investment and has $600,000 of excess cash on hand as a result. It distributes the excess cash to Christina in redemption of 10% of her stock. Since Christina's ownership interest in Orange remains unchanged (100%), the redemption does not qualify as a not essentially equivalent redemption, a disproportionate redemption, or a complete termination redemption. Further, the reduction in inventory does not qualify as a general contraction of Orange Corporation's business; thus, the distribution is not a partial liquidation. Therefore, the $600,000 is dividend income to Christina. The $40,000 basis in the stock redeemed (10% × $400,000) attaches to the basis of Christina's remaining shares of Orange. ■

A safe-harbor rule, the *termination of a business* test, will satisfy the not essentially equivalent to a dividend requirement. In contrast to the genuine contraction test, the termination of a business test does follow objective requirements. A distribution will qualify under the termination of a business test if the following conditions are met:

- The corporation has two or more qualified trades or businesses. A qualified trade or business is any trade or business that (1) has been actively conducted for the five-year period ending on the date of the distribution and (2) was not acquired in a taxable transaction during that five-year period.
- The distribution consists of the assets of a qualified trade or business or the proceeds from the sale of such assets.
- The corporation is actively engaged in the conduct of a qualified trade or business immediately after the distribution.

EXAMPLE 15

Loon Corporation, the owner and operator of a wholesale grocery business with a substantial amount of excess cash, purchased a freight-hauling concern. Six years later,

[10] § 302(e)(1)(A).

[11] See *Joseph W. Imler*, 11 T.C. 836 (1948), *acq.* 1949–1 C.B. 2; and Reg. § 1.346–1(a)(2).

[12] Rev.Rul. 60–322, 1960–2 C.B. 118.

CONCEPT SUMMARY 6.1

Summary of the Qualifying Stock Redemption Rules

Type of Redemption	Requirements to Qualify
Not essentially equivalent to a dividend [§ 302(b)(1)]	Meaningful reduction in shareholder's voting interest. Reduction in shareholder's right to share in earnings or in assets upon liquidation also considered. Stock attribution rules apply.
Substantially disproportionate [§ 302(b)(2)]	Shareholder's interest in the corporation, after the redemption, must be less than 80% of interest before the redemption and less than 50% of total combined voting power of all classes of stock entitled to vote. Stock attribution rules apply.
Complete termination [§ 302(b)(3)]	Entire stock ownership terminated. In general, stock attribution rules apply. However, *family* attribution rules are waived when former shareholder has no interest, other than as a creditor, in the corporation for at least 10 years and files an agreement to notify IRS of any prohibited interest acquired during 10-year period. Shareholder must retain all necessary records during 10-year period.
Partial liquidation [§ 302(b)(4)]	Not essentially equivalent to a dividend. • Genuine contraction of corporation's business. • Termination of a business. – *Corporation has two or more qualified trades or businesses.* – *Corporation terminates one qualified trade or business while continuing another qualified trade or business.* Distribution may be in form of cash or property. Redemption may be pro rata. Stock attribution rules do not apply.
Redemption to pay death taxes [§ 303]	Value of stock of one corporation in gross estate exceeds 35% of value of adjusted gross estate. Stock of two or more corporations treated as stock of a single corporation in applying the 35% test if decedent held a 20% or more interest in the stock of the corporations. Redemption limited to sum of death taxes and funeral and administration expenses. Generally tax-free because tax basis of stock is FMV on date of decedent's death and value is unchanged at redemption. Stock attribution rules do not apply.

Loon distributes the freight-hauling assets in kind on a pro rata basis to its shareholders. The distribution satisfies the termination of a business test. Loon had conducted both businesses for at least five years and continues to conduct the wholesale grocery business. Thus, for noncorporate shareholders, the distribution qualifies as a partial liquidation and is treated as a sale or exchange to the shareholders. For corporate shareholders of Loon, the distribution will be taxed as dividend income (assuming adequate E & P). ■

REDEMPTIONS TO PAY DEATH TAXES

Section 303 provides sale or exchange treatment to a redemption of stock included in, and representing a substantial part of, a decedent's gross estate. The purpose of this provision is to provide an estate with liquidity to pay death-related expenses when a significant portion of the estate consists of stock in a closely held corporation. Often such stock is not easily marketable, and a stock redemption represents the only viable option for its disposition. The redemption might not satisfy any of the other qualifying stock redemption provisions because of the attribution rules (e.g., attribution to estate from beneficiaries). A **redemption to pay death taxes** provides sale or exchange treatment without regard to the attribution rules, but the provision limits this treatment to the sum of the death taxes and funeral and administration expenses. A redemption in excess of these expenses may qualify for sale or exchange treatment under one of the § 302 provisions.

An estate's basis in property acquired from a decedent is generally the property's fair market value on the date of death.[13] Typically, there is little change in the fair market value of stock from the date of a decedent's death to the date of a redemption to pay death taxes. When the redemption price in a redemption to pay death taxes is the same as the estate's basis in the stock, the estate will recognize no gain (or loss) on the transaction.

Section 303 applies only to a distribution made with respect to stock of a corporation that is included in the gross estate of a decedent and whose value *exceeds* 35 percent of the value of the adjusted gross estate. (For definitions of "gross estate" and "adjusted gross estate," see the Glossary in Appendix C.)

EXAMPLE 16

Juan's adjusted gross estate is $7 million. The death taxes and funeral and administration expenses of the estate total $720,000. Included in the gross estate is stock of Yellow Corporation valued at $2.8 million. Juan had acquired the stock nine years ago at a cost of $300,000. Yellow redeems $720,000 of the stock from Juan's estate. Because the value of the Yellow stock in Juan's estate exceeds the 35% threshold ($2.8 million ÷ $7 million = 40%), the redemption qualifies under § 303 as a sale or exchange to Juan's estate. Assuming the value of the stock has remained unchanged since the date of Juan's death, there is no recognized gain (or loss) on the redemption [$720,000 (amount realized) – $720,000 (estate's stock basis)]. ■

In determining whether the value of stock of one corporation exceeds 35 percent of the value of the adjusted gross estate, the stock of two or more corporations in which the decedent held a 20 percent or more interest is treated as the stock of one corporation.[14] When this exception applies, the stock redeemed can be that of any of the 20 percent or more shareholder interests.

EXAMPLE 17

The adjusted gross estate of a decedent is $8 million. The gross estate includes stock of Owl and Robin Corporations valued at $1.6 million and $1.4 million, respectively. Unless the two corporations are treated as a single corporation for purposes of the 35% test, § 303 does not apply to a redemption of the stock of either corporation. If the decedent owned at least 20% of the stock of both Owl and Robin, § 303 can apply to a redemption of such stock. The 35% test is met when the stock of Owl and Robin is treated as that of a single corporation [($1.6 million + $1.4 million) ÷ $8 million = 37.5%]. The stock of Owl or Robin (or both) can be redeemed under § 303, to the extent of the sum of the death taxes and funeral and administration expenses. ■

6.3 Effect on the Corporation Redeeming Its Stock

LO.2

Understand the tax impact of stock redemptions on the distributing corporation.

Thus far, the discussion has focused on the tax consequences of stock redemptions to the *shareholder*. There are also several tax issues surrounding the redeeming *corporation* that must be addressed, including the recognition of gain or loss on property distributed pursuant to a redemption, the effect on a corporation's E & P from a

[13] If available and elected, an alternate valuation date would apply. § 1014(a).

[14] § 303(b)(2)(B).

distribution that is a qualifying stock redemption, and the deductibility of expenditures incurred in connection with a redemption. These issues are discussed in the following paragraphs.

RECOGNITION OF GAIN OR LOSS

Section 311 provides that corporations recognize *gain* on all nonliquidating distributions of appreciated property as if the property had been sold for its fair market value. Distributions in redemption of stock, qualifying or not, are nonliquidating distributions. When distributed property is subject to a corporate liability, the fair market value of that property is treated as not being less than the amount of the liability.

Losses are not recognized on nonliquidating distributions of property. Therefore, a corporation should avoid distributing loss property (fair market value less than basis) as consideration in the redemption of a shareholder's stock. However, the corporation could sell the property in a taxable transaction in which it can recognize a loss and then distribute the proceeds.

EXAMPLE 18

To carry out a stock redemption, Blackbird Corporation distributes land (basis of $80,000, fair market value of $300,000) to a shareholder. Blackbird has a recognized gain of $220,000 ($300,000 – $80,000). If the land is subject to a liability of $330,000, Blackbird has a recognized gain of $250,000 ($330,000 – $80,000). If the value of the property distributed was less than its adjusted basis, the realized loss would not be recognized. ■

EFFECT ON EARNINGS AND PROFITS

In a qualifying stock redemption, the E & P of the distributing corporation is reduced by an amount not in excess of the ratable share of the corporation's E & P attributable to the stock redeemed.[15]

EXAMPLE 19

Navy Corporation has 100 shares of stock outstanding. In a qualifying stock redemption, Navy distributes $200,000 in exchange for 30 of its shares. At the time of the redemption, Navy has paid-in capital of $120,000 and E & P of $450,000. The charge to E & P is limited to 30% of the corporation's E & P ($135,000), and the remainder of the redemption price ($65,000) is a reduction of the Navy paid-in capital account. If, instead, the 30 shares were redeemed for $80,000, the charge to E & P would be limited to $80,000, the amount paid by the corporation to carry out the stock redemption. ■

REDEMPTION EXPENDITURES

In redeeming its shares, a corporation may incur certain expenses such as accounting, brokerage, legal, and loan fees. Section 162(k) specifically denies a deduction for expenditures incurred in connection with a stock redemption. The disallowance does not apply to amounts otherwise deductible as interest under § 163.

6.4 Stock Redemptions— Additional Limitations

LO.3

Recognize the restrictions on sale or exchange treatment for certain redemption-like transactions.

Stock redemptions that do not fall under any of the qualifying stock redemption provisions are treated as dividend distributions to the extent of the corporation's E & P. Resourceful taxpayers, however, devised ways to circumvent the redemption provisions. Two types of these transactions involved structuring what was, in effect, a stock redemption or a dividend distribution as a sale of the stock. The widespread use of these

[15] § 312(n)(7).

TAX in the NEWS

The Demise of a Loophole?

Section 162(k) disallows a deduction for expenditures incurred in connection with a stock redemption. Section 404(k) allows a corporation a deduction for certain cash dividends made with respect to its stock held by an employee stock ownership plan (ESOP). If a corporation distributes cash in redemption of its stock from an ESOP and the redemption fails the qualifying redemption provisions, the distribution qualifies as a dividend for purposes of the § 404(k) deduction. The first judicial review of whether the § 162(k) disallowance trumps the § 404(k) deduction resulted in a taxpayer victory [*Boise Cascade Corp. v. U.S.*, 2003–1 USTC ¶50,472, 91 AFTR 2d 2003–2280, 329 F.3d 751 (CA–9, 2003)].

Emboldened by the *Boise Cascade* decision, other taxpayers asserted § 404(k) deductions related to stock redemption distributions. However, the IRS has prevailed in all subsequent disputes in the area, including a recent Eighth Circuit decision [*Nestlé Purina Petcare Co. v. Comm.*, 2010–1 USTC ¶50,213, 105 AFTR 2d 2010–912, 594 F.3d 968 (CA–8, 2010), *cert. den.* 131 S.Ct. 86 (2010)]. In addition to the Eighth Circuit, the Third Circuit [*Conopco, Inc. v. U.S.*, 2009–2 USTC ¶50,942, 104 AFTR 2d 2009–5315, 572 F.3d 162 (CA–3, 2009)] and the Tax Court, in that court's earlier decision in *Nestlé Purina Petcare* [*Ralston Purina Co.*, 131 T.C. 29 (2008)], have rejected the Ninth Circuit's analysis in *Boise Cascade*. Taxpayers seeking a favorable review of the issue in any of the remaining judicial venues are likely to be disappointed, as the *Boise Cascade* decision appears to be of no value outside the Ninth Circuit.

Note: For a thorough review of the issue, see M. Persellin and S. Novak, "Death of a Loophole: Do Recent Decisions Portend Doom for Ninth Circuit's Rationale in *Boise Cascade*?" *Corporate Taxation* (September/October 2010): 17–24.

approaches to obtain sale or exchange treatment led to the enactment of § 306, dealing with preferred stock bailouts, and § 304, dealing with sales of stock to related corporations. These two loophole-closing provisions are explained next. Some corporate divisions resemble stock redemptions, and those distributions are also briefly discussed.

PREFERRED STOCK BAILOUTS

When a corporation's stock is owned entirely (or predominantly) by a few family members and/or related entities, the attribution rules severely limit the opportunities for effecting a qualifying stock redemption. Nonetheless, clever taxpayers devised a scheme called the **preferred stock bailout** in an attempt to obtain the benefits of a qualifying stock redemption without the attendant limitations.[16] Under this scheme, a corporation issued a nontaxable (nonvoting) preferred stock dividend on common stock,[17] the shareholder assigned a portion of his or her basis in the common stock to the preferred stock,[18] and the preferred stock was sold to a third party. Since the disposition did not take the form of a stock redemption, the related limitations on sale or exchange treatment did not apply. As a result, the sale of the preferred stock was treated like any other capital asset disposition where the sales proceeds were offset by the stock's basis and the gain was taxed using the favorable capital gains rate. Unlike a sale of common shares, however, the sale of the preferred stock did not reduce the shareholder's ownership interest in the corporation.

The tax avoidance possibilities of the preferred stock bailout led to the enactment of § 306. In the case of a sale of *§ 306 stock* to a third party, the shareholder generally has ordinary income on the sale equal to the fair market value of the preferred stock on the date of the stock dividend.[19] The ordinary income is *treated* as a dividend for purposes of the 15 percent (or 0 percent) maximum tax rate on dividend income[20] but has no effect on the issuing corporation's E & P. No loss is recognized on the sale of the preferred stock;[21] instead, the unrecovered basis in the

[16]See, e.g., *Chamberlin v. Comm.*, 53–2 USTC ¶9576, 44 AFTR 494, 207 F.2d 462 (CA–6, 1953), *cert. den.* 74 S.Ct. 516 (USSC, 1954).

[17]See § 305(a).

[18]See § 307(a).

[19]The ordinary income taint is limited to the stock's ratable share of the corporation's E & P at the date of the distribution. § 306(a)(1).

[20]§ 306(a)(1)(D).

[21]§ 306(a)(1)(C).

preferred stock sold is added to the basis of the shareholder's common stock.[22] If, instead of a sale to a third party, the issuing corporation redeems the preferred stock from the shareholder, the redemption proceeds constitute dividend income to the extent of the corporation's E & P (see Chapter 5).[23]

EXAMPLE 20
THE BIG PICTURE

Return to the facts of *The Big Picture* on p. 6-2. Assume that on January 3 of the current year, Orange Corporation (E & P of $2 million) declares and issues a nontaxable preferred stock dividend of 1,000 shares to Christina. After the stock dividend, the fair market value of one share of common is $540, and the fair market value of one share of preferred is $600. Two days later, Christina sells the 1,000 shares of preferred stock to Emily, an unrelated party, for $600,000. Section 306 produces the following results:

- After the distribution and before the sale, the preferred stock has a basis to Christina of $40,000 [($600,000 value of preferred ÷ $6 million value of preferred and common) × $400,000 (original basis of common stock)]. At this time, the common stock has a new basis of $360,000.
- The sale of the preferred stock generates $600,000 of ordinary income to Christina. This is the amount of dividend income Christina would have recognized had cash been distributed instead of preferred stock (i.e., the § 306 taint). The 15% maximum tax rate on dividend income is applicable to the $600,000.
- The $40,000 basis allocated to the preferred stock is added back to the basis of the common stock; thus, the common stock basis is increased back to $400,000.
- Orange Corporation's E & P is unaffected by either the stock dividend or its subsequent sale. ■

Section 306 stock is stock other than common that (1) is received as a nontaxable stock dividend, (2) is received tax-free in a corporate reorganization or separation to the extent that either the effect of the transaction was substantially the same as the receipt of a stock dividend or the stock was received in exchange for § 306 stock, or (3) has a basis determined by reference to the basis of § 306 stock (e.g., a gift of § 306 stock). (Corporate reorganizations are discussed in Chapter 7.) If a corporation has no E & P on the date of distribution of a nontaxable preferred stock dividend, the stock will not be § 306 stock.[24]

REDEMPTIONS THROUGH THE USE OF RELATED CORPORATIONS

A shareholder possessing a controlling interest (i.e., direct or indirect ownership of at least 50 percent)[25] in two or more corporations could, in the absence of any statutory limitation, obtain sale or exchange treatment by having one corporation purchase some of the shareholder's stock in a second related corporation. This result could occur even if the shareholder's ownership interest in the corporation whose stock is sold has not been substantively reduced. Section 304 closes this loophole by treating the sale of stock of one corporation to a related corporation as a stock redemption subject to the rules discussed earlier in this chapter. This provision applies to a transfer involving brother-sister corporations as well as to parent-subsidiary situations (see Chapters 2 and 8).

In general, § 304 requires a redemption through the use of related corporations to result in a reduction of ownership interest that would satisfy one of the qualifying stock redemptions of § 302 (e.g., disproportionate redemption) or § 303.[26] If the redemption does not qualify under those rules, the transaction is characterized as a dividend distribution.[27] When brother-sister corporations are involved, the

[22]Reg. § 1.306–1(b)(2), Example (2).
[23]See § 306(a)(2).
[24]§ 306(c).
[25]§ 304(c).
[26]See § 304(a)(1).
[27]The distribution is given dividend income treatment to the extent of the sum of E & P of the two related corporations. § 304(b)(2).

shareholder increases the basis in the stock of the acquiring corporation by the basis of the stock surrendered in the transaction. Likewise, the acquiring corporation's basis in the stock acquired is equal to the basis the shareholder had in such shares.[28]

DISTRIBUTION OF STOCK AND SECURITIES OF A CONTROLLED CORPORATION

If one corporation controls another corporation, stock in the subsidiary corporation can be distributed to the shareholders of the parent corporation tax-free under § 355. When a subsidiary is newly formed to perfect a corporate division, this provision applies through the divisive corporate reorganization rules discussed in Chapter 7. When a subsidiary already exists, § 355 alone applies, and the transaction can resemble either a dividend, a stock redemption, or a complete liquidation. The rules surrounding these transactions are covered in detail in Chapter 7.

6.5 Liquidations—In General

LO.4

Understand the tax consequences of complete liquidations for both the corporation and its shareholders.

When a corporation makes a nonliquidating distribution (e.g., stock redemption), the entity typically will continue as a going concern. With a complete liquidation, however, corporate existence terminates, as does each shareholder's ownership interest. A complete liquidation, like a qualifying stock redemption, produces sale or exchange treatment to the *shareholder*. However, the tax effects of a liquidation to the *corporation* vary somewhat from those of a redemption. Sale or exchange treatment is the general rule for the liquidating corporation, although some losses are disallowed.

THE LIQUIDATION PROCESS

A **corporate liquidation** exists when a corporation ceases to be a going concern. The corporation continues solely to wind up affairs, pay debts, and distribute any remaining assets to its shareholders. Legal dissolution under state law is not required for a liquidation to be complete for tax purposes. A liquidation can exist even if the corporation retains a nominal amount of assets to pay remaining debts and preserve legal status.[29]

Shareholders may decide to liquidate a corporation for one or more reasons, including the following:

- The corporate business has been unsuccessful.
- The shareholders wish to acquire the corporation's assets.
- Another person or corporation wants to purchase the corporation's assets. The purchaser may buy the shareholders' stock and then liquidate the corporation to acquire the assets. Alternatively, the purchaser may buy the assets directly from the corporation. After the assets are sold, the corporation distributes the sales proceeds to its shareholders and liquidates.

As one might expect, the different means used to liquidate a corporation produce varying tax results.

LIQUIDATING AND NONLIQUIDATING DISTRIBUTIONS COMPARED

As noted previously, a *nonliquidating* property distribution produces gain (but not loss) to the distributing corporation. For the shareholder, the receipt of cash or property produces dividend income to the extent of the corporation's E & P or, in the case of a qualifying stock redemption, results in sale or exchange treatment.

[28] Reg. § 1.304–2(a) and § 362(a).

[29] Reg. § 1.332–2(c).

TAX *in the NEWS*

GENERAL MOTORS LIVES ON—OR DOES IT?

Most Americans are aware that the U.S. government bailed out General Motors Corporation (GM). The government provided a $50 billion infusion of capital in an effort to stave off the automaker's demise. "New GM" was formed, and it purchased most of the operating assets of Motors Liquidation Company (MLC), "former GM" in bankruptcy. U.S. taxpayers received a 61 percent ownership interest in new GM for their investment. But what about former GM's less desirable assets and its liabilities? MLC was left with many old factory buildings and other unwanted assets, in addition to the liabilities, of former GM. Outdated factories fraught with environmental problems have proved to be a hard sale for MLC, and many other assets (e.g., factory robots, an abandoned church, a golf course) also remain on MLC's balance sheet. (For a look at the properties available for purchase, check out MLC's website at **www.motorsliquidation.com**.) On August 31, 2010, MLC filed a plan of liquidation in bankruptcy court that would result in the transfer of substantially all of its cash and remaining unsold assets to four trusts, including a trust funded with more than $800 million for environmental cleanup work related to the old factories.

Similar to a qualifying stock redemption, a *liquidation* produces sale or exchange treatment for the shareholders. E & P has no impact on the gain or loss to be recognized by the shareholder in either type of distribution.[30] However, a liquidation produces different tax consequences to the distributing corporation. With certain exceptions, a liquidating corporation recognizes gain *and* loss upon the distribution of its assets.

EXAMPLE 21

Goose Corporation, with E & P of $40,000, makes a cash distribution of $50,000 to its sole shareholder. The shareholder's basis in the Goose stock is $20,000. If the distribution is not a qualifying stock redemption or in complete liquidation, the shareholder recognizes dividend income of $40,000 (the amount of Goose's E & P) and treats the remaining $10,000 of the distribution as a return of capital. If the distribution is a qualifying stock redemption or is pursuant to a complete liquidation, the shareholder has a capital gain of $30,000 ($50,000 distribution − $20,000 stock basis). In the case of these distributions, Goose's E & P is of no consequence to the shareholder's tax result. ■

In the event a corporate distribution results in a *loss* to the shareholder, another distinction exists between nonliquidating distributions and liquidations. Section 267 disallows recognition of losses between related parties in nonliquidating distributions but not in complete liquidations.

EXAMPLE 22

The stock of Tern Corporation is owned equally by three brothers, Rex, Sam, and Ted. When Ted's basis in his stock is $40,000, the corporation distributes $30,000 to him in cancellation of all his shares. If the distribution is a qualifying stock redemption, the $10,000 realized loss is not recognized because Ted and Tern Corporation are related parties. Under § 267, Ted is deemed to own more than 50% in value of the corporation's outstanding stock. Ted's direct ownership is limited to 33⅓%, but through his brothers he owns indirectly another 66⅔% for a total of 100%. On the other hand, if the distribution is pursuant to a complete liquidation, Ted's $10,000 realized loss is recognized. ■

The rules governing the basis of property received from a corporation are identical for both nonliquidating and liquidating distributions. Section 301(d) specifies that the basis of property received in a nonliquidating distribution is its fair market

[30] § 331.

value on the date of distribution, while § 334(a) provides the same treatment for property received in a liquidating distribution.

In the following pages, the tax consequences of a complete liquidation are examined, first from the view of the distributing corporation and then in terms of the shareholder. Because the tax rules differ when a subsidiary corporation is liquidated, the rules relating to the liquidation of a subsidiary corporation are discussed separately.

6.6 Liquidations—Effect on the Distributing Corporation

THE GENERAL RULE

Section 336(a) provides that a corporation recognizes *gain or loss* on the distribution of property in a complete liquidation. The property is treated as if it were sold at its fair market value. This treatment is consistent with the notion of double taxation that is inherent in operating a business as a C corporation—once at the corporate level and again at the shareholder level.

As in the case of a nonliquidating distribution, when property distributed in a complete liquidation is subject to a liability of the liquidating corporation, the fair market value used to calculate gain or loss may not be less than the amount of the liability.

EXAMPLE 23

Pursuant to a complete liquidation, Warbler Corporation distributes to its shareholders land held as an investment (basis of $200,000, fair market value of $300,000). If no liability is involved, Warbler has a gain of $100,000 on the distribution ($300,000 – $200,000). Likewise, if the land is subject to a liability of $250,000, Warbler Corporation has a gain of $100,000. If, instead, the liability were $350,000, Warbler's gain on the distribution would be $150,000 ($350,000 – $200,000). ■

There are four exceptions to the general rule of gain and loss recognition by a liquidating corporation:

- *Losses* are not recognized on certain liquidating distributions to related-party shareholders.
- *Losses* are not recognized on certain sales and liquidating distributions of property that was contributed to the corporation with a built-in loss shortly before the adoption of a plan of liquidation.
- A subsidiary corporation does not recognize *gains or losses* on liquidating distributions to its parent corporation.
- A subsidiary corporation does not recognize *losses* on liquidating distributions to its minority shareholders.

The first two exceptions, referred to as the "antistuffing rules," are discussed in detail in the next section and are summarized in Figure 6.1 at the end of the section. The last two exceptions, dealing with the liquidation of a subsidiary corporation, are discussed later in this chapter.

ANTISTUFFING RULES

When property is transferred to a corporation in a § 351 transaction or as a contribution to capital, carryover and substituted basis rules generally apply (see Chapter 4). Generally, the transferee corporation takes a basis in the property equal to that of the transferor-shareholder, and the shareholder takes an equal basis in the stock received in the exchange (or adds such amount to existing stock basis in the case of a capital contribution). Without special limitations, a transfer of loss property (fair market value less than basis) in a carryover basis transaction would present opportunities for the duplication of losses.

EXAMPLE 24
THE BIG PICTURE

Return to the facts of *The Big Picture* on p. 6-2. Assume that Christina transfers property (basis of $100,000, fair market value of $55,000) to Orange Corporation in exchange for additional stock. The exchange qualifies under § 351. Absent any exceptions to the contrary, the general rule of carryover basis would apply, and Orange would take a carryover basis of $100,000 in the property while Christina would take a $100,000 basis in the additional stock. A sale or liquidating distribution of the property by Orange Corporation would result in a $45,000 loss [$55,000 (fair market value of property) − $100,000 (property basis)]. Similarly, a sale by Christina of the stock acquired in the § 351 exchange would also result in a $45,000 loss [$55,000 (fair market value of stock) − $100,000 (stock basis)]. ■

Congress addressed this loss duplication issue in the Tax Reform Act of 1986 by enacting two loss limitation ("antistuffing") rules under § 336(d) that apply to corporations upon liquidation. The effect of these rules is to disallow some or all of a loss realized by a corporation in liquidating distributions (and, in some cases, sales) of certain property.

The antistuffing rules limited the duplication of losses realized upon a corporation's liquidation, but loss trafficking was still possible if the corporation sold high-basis property in the normal course of business instead of upon or pursuant to liquidation. As a result, Congress revisited the loss duplication issue and, in the American Jobs Creation Act of 2004, enacted limitations to the general basis rules in § 351 and contribution to capital transactions. Unlike the antistuffing rules that disallow losses, the § 362(e)(2) rules require a corporation to step down the basis of property acquired in a § 351 or contribution to capital transaction by the amount of any net built-in loss embodied in such property. The basis step-down is required when a shareholder transfers properties having an aggregate basis in excess of their aggregate fair market value ("net built-in loss"), and it is allocated proportionately among the properties having built-in losses. Alternatively, the transferor-shareholder can elect to reduce his or her stock basis by the amount of net built-in loss. (See Chapter 4 for further discussion of the basis adjustment rules.) The antistuffing rules of § 336(d) continue to apply in the case of liquidating distributions (and certain sales) of loss property, but their bite has been lessened somewhat by the § 362(e)(2) basis step-down rules.

Related-Party Loss Limitation

Losses are disallowed on distributions to *related parties* in either of the following cases:

- The distribution is *not* pro rata, or
- The property distributed is disqualified property.[31]

A corporation and a shareholder are considered related if the shareholder owns (directly or indirectly) more than 50 percent in value of the corporation's outstanding stock.[32]

A *pro rata distribution* is one where *each* shareholder receives his or her proportionate share of the corporate asset distributed. *Disqualified property* is property that is acquired by the liquidating corporation in a § 351 or contribution to capital transaction during the five-year period ending on the date of the distribution. The related-party loss limitation can apply even if the property was appreciated (fair market value greater than basis) when it was transferred to the corporation.

[31] § 336(d)(1).

[32] Section 267 provides the definition of a related party for purposes of this provision. The rules are similar to the stock attribution rules discussed earlier in this chapter; one exception, however, is that stock owned by a sibling is treated as owned by the taxpayer under § 267.

EXAMPLE 25

Bluebird Corporation stock is owned by Ana and Sanjay, who are unrelated. Ana owns 80% and Sanjay owns 20% of the stock in the corporation. Bluebird has the following assets (none of which were acquired in a § 351 or contribution to capital transaction) that are distributed in complete liquidation of the corporation:

	Adjusted Basis	Fair Market Value
Cash	$600,000	$600,000
Equipment	150,000	200,000
Building	400,000	200,000

Assume Bluebird Corporation distributes the equipment to Sanjay and the cash and the building to Ana. Bluebird recognizes a gain of $50,000 on the distribution of the equipment. The loss of $200,000 on the building is disallowed because the property is distributed to a related party and the distribution is not pro rata (i.e., the building is not distributed 80% to Ana and 20% to Sanjay). ■

EXAMPLE 26

Assume in Example 25 that Bluebird Corporation distributes the cash and equipment to Ana and the building to Sanjay. Again, Bluebird recognizes the $50,000 gain on the equipment. However, it now recognizes the $200,000 loss on the building because the property is not distributed to a related party (i.e., Sanjay does not own more than 50% of the stock in Bluebird Corporation). ■

EXAMPLE 27

Wren Corporation's stock is held equally by three brothers. Four years before Wren's liquidation, the shareholders transfer jointly owned property (basis of $150,000, fair market value of $200,000) to the corporation in return for stock in a § 351 transaction. When the property is worth $100,000, it is transferred pro rata to the brothers in a liquidating distribution. Because each brother owns directly and indirectly more than 50% (i.e., 100% in this situation) of the stock and disqualified property is involved, none of the $50,000 realized loss [$100,000 (fair market value) – $150,000 (basis)] is recognized by Wren Corporation. ■

EXAMPLE 28

Assume in Example 27 that the property's fair market value is $100,000 at the time of the § 351 transfer and $75,000 at the time of the liquidating distribution to the brothers. As a result of the § 362(e)(2) basis step-down rules, Wren Corporation's basis in the property is $100,000 [$150,000 (basis to brothers) – $50,000 (net built-in loss of property transferred)]. In a liquidating distribution of the property to the brothers, Wren would realize a loss of $25,000 [$75,000 (fair market value of property at distribution) – $100,000 (Wren's stepped-down basis in property)]. Because this is a distribution of disqualified property to related parties, none of the $25,000 loss is recognized by Wren. ■

Built-in Loss Limitation

A second loss limitation applies to sales, exchanges, or distributions of built-in loss property (fair market value less than basis) that is transferred to a corporation shortly before the corporation is liquidated. The built-in loss limitation applies when the following conditions are met:

- The property was acquired by the corporation in a § 351 or contribution to capital transaction.
- Such acquisition was part of a plan whose principal purpose was to recognize a loss on that property by the liquidating corporation. A tax avoidance purpose is presumed in the case of transfers occurring within two years of the adoption of a plan of liquidation.

This disallowance rule applies only to the extent that a property's built-in loss at transfer is not eliminated by a stepped-down basis. Some built-in losses on property transfers will avoid the basis step-down either because built-in gain properties were also transferred by the shareholder (see Chapter 4, Example 22) or because the shareholder elected to step down the basis of his or her stock instead. Any loss attributable to a decline in a property's value after its transfer to the corporation is not subject to the built-in loss limitation.[33]

EXAMPLE 29

On January 4, 2011, Brown Corporation acquires two properties from a shareholder in a transaction that qualifies under § 351.

	Shareholder's Basis	Fair Market Value	Built-in Gain/(Loss)
Land	$100,000	$50,000	($50,000)
Securities	10,000	35,000	25,000
			($25,000)

The net built-in loss of $25,000 results in a stepped-down basis of $75,000 in the land for Brown Corporation [$100,000 (shareholder's basis) – $25,000 (step-down equal to net built-in loss)]. Brown adopts a plan of liquidation on July 8, 2011, and distributes the land to an unrelated shareholder on November 11, 2011, when the land is worth $30,000. Of the $45,000 loss realized [$30,000 (value of land on date of distribution) – $75,000 (basis in land)] by Brown on the distribution, $25,000 is disallowed by the built-in loss limitation [$50,000 (value of land when acquired by Brown) – $75,000 (stepped-down basis in land)], and $20,000 is recognized (equal to the decline in value occurring after acquisition by Brown). ■

The built-in loss limitation applies to a broader range of transactions than the related-party exception, which disallows losses only on certain distributions to related parties (i.e., more-than-50 percent shareholders). The built-in loss limitation can apply to distributions of property to any shareholder, including an unrelated party, and to a *sale or exchange* of property by a liquidating corporation. However, the limitation is narrower than the related-party exception in that it applies only to property that had a built-in loss upon its acquisition by the corporation and only as to the amount of the built-in loss (as adjusted by the basis step-down rules).

EXAMPLE 30

Assume in Example 29 that the land was worth $120,000 on the date Brown Corporation acquired the property. As there is no net built-in loss on the transfer, Brown will have a basis of $100,000 in the land. If the distribution is to an unrelated shareholder, Brown Corporation will recognize the entire $70,000 loss [$30,000 (fair market value on date of distribution) – $100,000 (basis)]. However, if the distribution is to a related party, Brown cannot recognize any of the loss under the related-party loss limitation because the property is disqualified property. When the distribution is to a related party, the loss is disallowed even though the entire decline in value occurred during the period the corporation held the property. ■

The built-in loss limitation will apply only in rare cases if the corporation has held the property more than two years prior to liquidation. The presumption of a tax avoidance purpose for property transferred to a corporation in the two years preceding the liquidation can be rebutted if there is a clear and substantial relationship between the contributed property and the (current or future) business of the corporation. When there was a business reason for the transfer, the built-in loss limitation will not apply.

[33] § 336(d)(2).

FIGURE 6.1 Distributions of Loss Property by a Liquidating Corporation

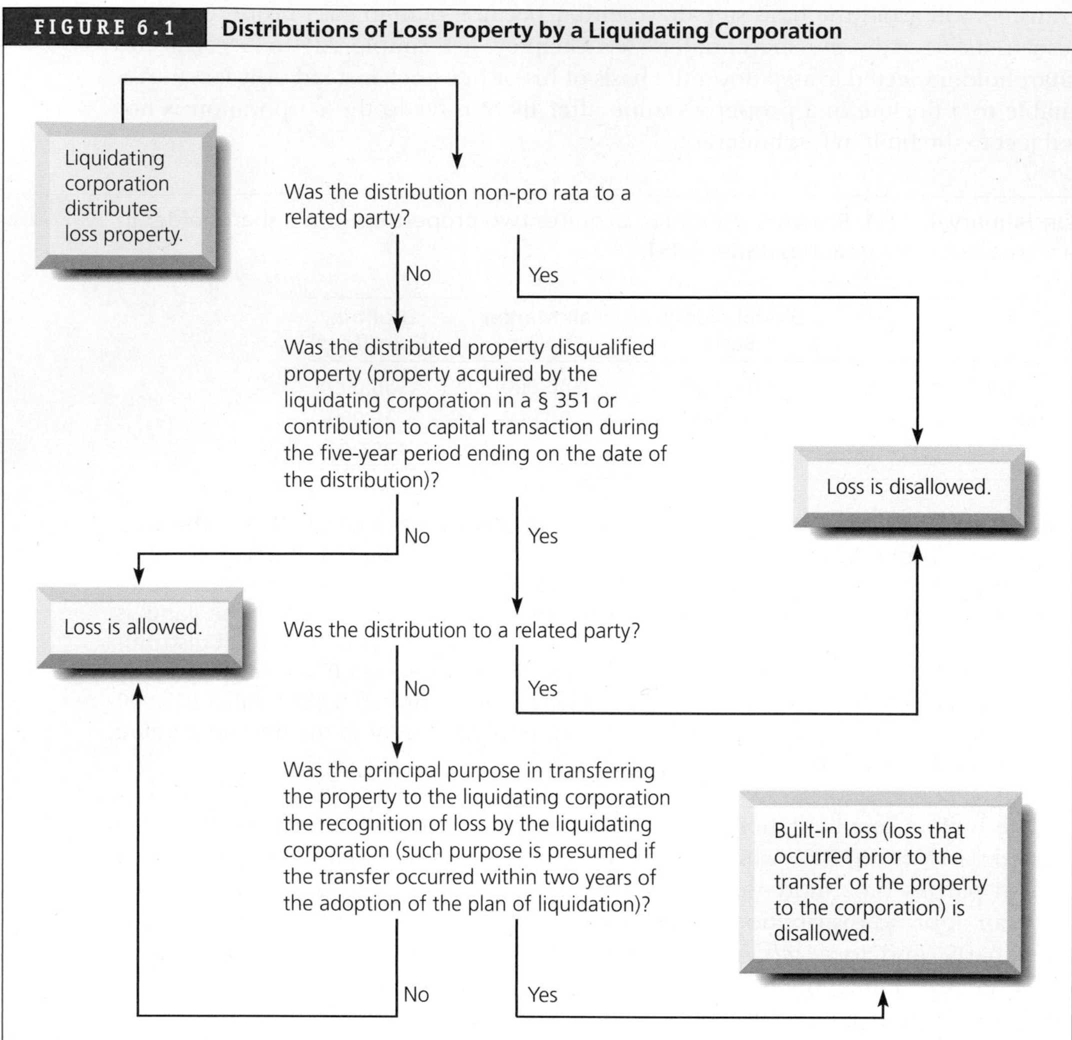

EXAMPLE 31

Cardinal Corporation's stock is held by two unrelated individuals: 60% by Manuel and 40% by Jack. One year before Cardinal's liquidation, Manuel transfers land (basis of $150,000, fair market value of $100,000) and equipment (basis of $10,000, fair market value of $70,000) to the corporation as a contribution to capital. As there is no net built-in loss on the transfer, Cardinal will have a basis of $150,000 in the land. There is no business reason for the transfer. In liquidation, Cardinal distributes the land (now worth $90,000) to Jack. Even though the distribution is to an unrelated party, the built-in loss of $50,000 is not recognized. However, Cardinal Corporation can recognize the loss of $10,000 ($90,000 – $100,000) that occurred while it held the land. If, instead, the land is distributed to Manuel, a related party, the entire $60,000 loss is disallowed under the related-party loss limitation. ■

EXAMPLE 32

Assume in Example 31 that the land and equipment are transferred to Cardinal Corporation because a bank required the additional capital investment as a condition to making a loan to the corporation. Because there is a business purpose for the transfer, all of the $60,000 loss is recognized if the land is distributed to Jack in liquidation. If, instead, the land is distributed to Manuel, a related party, the entire loss is still disallowed under the related-party loss limitation. ■

Tax Paid on Net Gain

To the extent that a corporation pays tax on the net amount of gain recognized as a result of its liquidation, the proceeds available to be distributed to the shareholders are likewise reduced. This reduction for the payment of taxes will reduce the amount realized by the shareholders, which will then reduce their gain (or increase the loss) recognized.

EXAMPLE 33

Purple Corporation's assets are valued at $2 million after payment of all corporate debts except for $300,000 of taxes payable on net gains it recognized on the liquidation. Therefore, the amount realized by the shareholders is $1.7 million ($2,000,000 – $300,000). As described below, in determining the gain or loss recognized by a shareholder, the amount realized is offset by the stock's adjusted basis. ■

REPORTING BUSINESS ACTIVITIES—LIQUIDATION CONSEQUENCES?

In 2004, Thomas Johnson incorporated his bagel shop and became the sole shareholder of Bagels by Thomas, Inc. For the tax years 2004–2008, Bagels by Thomas, Inc., properly filed and paid corporate income taxes (Form 1120). In early 2009, Thomas read an article on the "check-the-box" Regulations that allow a taxpayer to choose the entity form of doing business for tax purposes (see Chapter 2). Having tired of the additional complexities and requirements of the corporate form, Thomas took advantage of the "check-the-box" Regulations and reported all of the 2009 business activity for Bagels by Thomas, Inc., on his individual income tax return (Form 1040) as a sole proprietorship (Schedule C). Thomas repeated this treatment for 2010 as well. No corporate returns were filed for the business for 2009 or 2010, but the corporation was not formally liquidated. You are preparing Thomas's individual income tax return for 2011 and become aware of these facts. How should you proceed?

6.7 LIQUIDATIONS—EFFECT ON THE SHAREHOLDER

The tax consequences to the shareholders of a corporation in the process of liquidation are governed either by the general rule of § 331 or by the exception of § 332 relating to the liquidation of a subsidiary.

THE GENERAL RULE

In the case of a complete liquidation, § 331(a) provides for sale or exchange treatment for the shareholders. Thus, the difference between the fair market value of the assets received from the corporation and the adjusted basis of the stock surrendered is the gain or loss recognized by the shareholder. The fair market value of property received subject to a corporate liability is reduced by the amount of such liability. Typically, the stock is a capital asset in the hands of the shareholder, and capital gain or loss results. The burden of proof is on the taxpayer to furnish evidence as to the adjusted basis of the stock. In the absence of such evidence, the stock is deemed to have a zero basis, and the full amount of the liquidation proceeds equals the amount of the gain recognized.[34] The basis of property received in a liquidation is the property's fair market value on the date of distribution.[35]

SPECIAL RULE FOR CERTAIN INSTALLMENT OBLIGATIONS

Corporations often sell assets pursuant to a plan of liquidation, and sometimes these sales are made on the installment basis. If the installment notes are then distributed in liquidation, the corporation recognizes gain (or loss) equal to the

[34] *John Calderazzo*, 34 TCM 1, T.C.Memo. 1975–1.

[35] § 334(a).

difference between the fair market value of the notes and the corporation's basis in the notes.[36] However, shareholders can use the installment method to defer to the point of collection the portion of their gain that is attributable to the notes. This treatment requires the shareholders to allocate their stock basis between the installment notes and the other assets received from the corporation.[37]

EXAMPLE 34

After a plan of complete liquidation has been adopted, Beige Corporation sells its only asset, unimproved land held as an investment. The land has appreciated in value and is sold to Jane (an unrelated party) for \$100,000. Under the terms of the sale, Beige Corporation receives cash of \$25,000 and Jane's notes for the balance of \$75,000. The notes are payable over 10 years (\$7,500 per year) and carry an appropriate rate of interest. Immediately after the sale, Beige Corporation distributes the cash and notes to Earl, the sole shareholder. Earl has an adjusted basis of \$20,000 in the Beige stock, and the installment notes have a value equal to their face amount (\$75,000). These transactions have the following tax results:

- Beige Corporation recognizes gain on the distribution of the installment notes, measured by the difference between the \$75,000 fair market value and the basis Beige had in the notes.
- Earl may defer the gain on the receipt of the notes to the point of collection.
- Earl must allocate the adjusted basis in his stock (\$20,000) between the cash and the installment notes as follows:

$$\frac{\text{Cash}}{\text{Total receipts}} = \frac{\$25{,}000}{\$100{,}000} \times \$20{,}000 = \$5{,}000 \text{ basis allocated to the cash}$$

$$\frac{\text{Notes}}{\text{Total receipts}} = \frac{\$75{,}000}{\$100{,}000} \times \$20{,}000 = \$15{,}000 \text{ basis allocated to the notes}$$

- On the cash portion of the transaction, Earl must recognize \$20,000 of gain [\$25,000 (cash received) − \$5,000 (basis allocated to the cash)] in the year of liquidation.
- Over the next 10 years, Earl must recognize a total gain of \$60,000 on the collection of the notes, computed as follows:

$$\$75{,}000 \text{ (fair market value)} - \$15{,}000 \text{ (basis allocated to the notes)} = \$60{,}000 \text{ (gross profit)}$$

- The gross profit percentage on the notes is 80%, computed as follows:

$$\frac{\$60{,}000 \text{ (gross profit)}}{\$75{,}000 \text{ (contract price)}} = 80\%$$

  Thus, Earl must report a gain of \$6,000 [\$7,500 (amount of note) × 80% (gross profit percentage)] on the collection of each note over the next 10 years.
- The interest element is accounted for separately. ■

6.8 Liquidations—Parent-Subsidiary Situations

LO.5

Understand the tax consequences of subsidiary liquidations for both the parent and the subsidiary corporations.

Section 332, an exception to the general rule of § 331, provides that a parent corporation does *not* recognize gain or loss on a liquidation of a subsidiary. In addition, the subsidiary corporation recognizes *neither gain nor loss* on distributions of property to its parent.[38]

[36] § 453B(a). Gain is not recognized in the distribution of installment notes by a subsidiary liquidating pursuant to § 332. See the discussion below and §§ 337(a) and 453B(d).

[37] § 453(h). Installment notes attributable to the sale of inventory qualify only if the inventory was sold in a bulk sale to one person.

[38] § 337(a). This is an exception to the general rule of § 336.

The requirements for applying § 332 are as follows:

- The parent must own at least 80 percent of the voting stock of the subsidiary and at least 80 percent of the value of the subsidiary's stock.
- The subsidiary must distribute all its property in complete cancellation of all its stock within the taxable year or within three years from the close of the tax year in which the first distribution occurred.
- The subsidiary must be solvent.[39]

If these requirements are met, nonrecognition of gains and losses becomes mandatory. However, if the subsidiary is insolvent, the parent corporation will have an ordinary loss deduction under § 165(g).

When a series of distributions occurs in the liquidation of a subsidiary corporation, the parent corporation must own the required amount of stock (80 percent) on the date the plan of liquidation is adopted and at all times until all property has been distributed.[40] If the parent fails the control requirement at any time, the provisions for nonrecognition of gain or loss do not apply to any distribution.[41]

MINORITY SHAREHOLDER INTERESTS

In a § 332 parent-subsidiary liquidation, up to 20 percent of the subsidiary's stock can be owned by minority shareholders. In such liquidations, a distribution of property to a minority shareholder is treated in the same manner as a *nonliquidating* distribution. That is, the subsidiary corporation recognizes gain (but not loss) on the property distributed to the minority shareholder.[42]

EXAMPLE 35

The stock of Tan Corporation is held as follows: 80% by Mustard Corporation and 20% by Arethia. Tan Corporation is liquidated on December 9, 2011, pursuant to a plan adopted on January 7, 2011. At the time of its liquidation, Tan Corporation has assets with a basis of $100,000 and fair market value of $500,000. Tan Corporation distributes the property pro rata to Mustard Corporation and to Arethia. Tan must recognize gain of $80,000 [($500,000 fair market value − $100,000 basis) × 20% minority interest]. Since the corporate tax due in this liquidation relates entirely to the minority shareholder distribution, that amount will most likely be deducted from the $100,000 distribution ($500,000 × 20%) going to Arethia. The remaining gain of $320,000 is not recognized because it is attributable to property being distributed to Mustard, the parent corporation. ■

A minority shareholder is subject to the general rule requiring the recognition of gain or loss in a liquidation. Accordingly, the difference between the fair market value of the assets received and the basis of the minority shareholder's stock is the amount of gain or loss recognized. Further, the basis of property received by the minority shareholder is the property's fair market value on the date of distribution.[43]

INDEBTEDNESS OF THE SUBSIDIARY TO THE PARENT

If a subsidiary transfers appreciated property to its parent to satisfy a debt, it must recognize gain on the transaction unless the subsidiary is liquidating and the conditions of § 332 (discussed above) apply. When § 332 applies, the subsidiary does not recognize gain or loss upon the transfer of properties to the parent in satisfaction of indebtedness.[44]

[39] § 332(b) and Reg. §§ 1.332–2(a) and (b).

[40] Establishing the date of the adoption of a plan of complete liquidation could be crucial in determining whether § 332 applies. See, for example, *George L. Riggs, Inc.*, 64 T.C. 474 (1975).

[41] § 332(b)(3) and Reg. § 1.332–2(a).

[42] §§ 336(a) and (d)(3).

[43] § 334(a).

[44] § 337(b)(1).

GLOBAL *Tax Issues*

Basis Rules for Liquidations of Foreign Subsidiaries

The basis of property acquired by a parent corporation in the liquidation of a subsidiary corporation is generally equal to the basis the subsidiary had in such property. However, the American Jobs Creation Act of 2004 modified the basis rules regarding property acquired by a U.S. parent in some § 332 liquidations of foreign subsidiaries. In general, if the aggregate basis in a foreign subsidiary's assets exceeds their aggregate fair market value, the U.S. parent will take a fair market value basis in the property acquired. The purpose of this amendment is to deny the importation of built-in losses (excess of basis over fair market value). [See §§ 334(b)(1)(B) and 362(e)(1)(B).]

EXAMPLE 36

Eagle Corporation owes its parent, Finch Corporation, $20,000. It satisfies the obligation by transferring land (basis of $8,000, fair market value of $20,000) to Finch. Normally, Eagle would recognize a gain of $12,000 on the transaction. However, if the transfer is made pursuant to a liquidation under § 332, Eagle does not recognize a gain. ■

This nonrecognition provision does not apply to the parent corporation. The parent corporation recognizes gain or loss on the receipt of property in satisfaction of indebtedness, even if the property is received during liquidation of the subsidiary.

EXAMPLE 37

Pelican Corporation owns bonds (basis of $95,000) of its subsidiary, Crow Corporation, that were acquired at a discount. Upon liquidation of Crow pursuant to § 332, Pelican receives a distribution of $100,000, the face amount of the bonds. The transaction has no tax effect on Crow. However, Pelican Corporation recognizes gain of $5,000 [$100,000 (amount realized) – $95,000 (basis in bonds)]. ■

BASIS OF PROPERTY RECEIVED BY THE PARENT CORPORATION—THE GENERAL RULE

Property received in the complete liquidation of a subsidiary has the same basis it had in the hands of the subsidiary.[45] Unless the parent corporation makes a § 338 election (discussed below), this carryover basis in the assets generally will differ significantly from the parent's basis in the stock of the subsidiary. Since the liquidation is a nontaxable exchange, the parent's gain or loss on the difference in basis is not recognized. Further, the parent's basis in the stock of the subsidiary disappears.

EXAMPLE 38

Lark Corporation has a basis of $200,000 in the stock of Heron Corporation, a subsidiary in which it owns 85% of all classes of stock. Lark purchased the Heron stock 10 years ago. In the current year, Lark liquidates Heron Corporation and acquires assets that are worth $800,000 and have a tax basis to Heron of $500,000. Lark Corporation takes a basis of $500,000 in the assets, with a potential gain upon their sale of $300,000. Lark's $200,000 basis in Heron's stock disappears. ■

EXAMPLE 39

Indigo Corporation has a basis of $600,000 in the stock of Kackie Corporation, a wholly owned subsidiary acquired 10 years ago. It liquidates Kackie Corporation and receives assets that are worth $400,000 and have a tax basis to Kackie of $300,000. Indigo Corporation takes a basis of $300,000 in the assets it acquires from Kackie. If Indigo sells the assets, it has a gain of $100,000 even though its basis in the Kackie stock was $600,000. Indigo's loss on its stock investment in Kackie will never be recognized. ■

[45] § 334(b)(1) and Reg. § 1.334–1(b). But see § 334(b)(1)(B) (exception for property acquired in some liquidations of foreign subsidiaries).

In addition to the parent corporation taking the subsidiary's basis in its assets, the carryover rules of § 381 apply (see Chapter 7). Under that provision, the parent acquires other tax attributes of the subsidiary, including the subsidiary's net operating loss carryover, business credit carryover, capital loss carryover, and E & P.

BASIS OF PROPERTY RECEIVED BY THE PARENT CORPORATION—§ 338 ELECTION

Background

As discussed above, the liquidation of a subsidiary generally is a nontaxable transaction, resulting in the nonrecognition of gain or loss for both the parent and the subsidiary corporations and the carryover of the subsidiary's asset bases (and other tax attributes). This treatment reflects the fact that such a liquidation often is merely a change in corporate structure and not a change in substance. This is particularly the case when the parent has owned the stock of the subsidiary since the subsidiary's inception. In such cases, the carried-over bases are comparable to what the parent would have in the subsidiary's assets if the parent, and not the subsidiary, had originally acquired the assets.

The carryover basis rule for § 332 liquidations can result in some inequities when the subsidiary has been in existence for some time prior to the parent's acquisition of the subsidiary's stock. The parent's basis in the stock of the subsidiary will reflect the fair market value of the subsidiary's assets (and goodwill) at the time of the stock purchase. As a result, the parent's basis in the stock of the subsidiary will usually be greater than the subsidiary's basis in its assets. Under the carryover basis rule, a liquidation of the subsidiary would result in the parent taking a basis in the subsidiary's assets that is less than the parent's basis in the stock of the subsidiary. This is the case even if the parent acquired the subsidiary stock solely to obtain the subsidiary's assets.

If the parent could treat the purchase of the subsidiary stock as a purchase of its assets, the parent could take a basis in the assets equal to the acquisition cost of the stock. In most cases, this would mean a higher asset basis and, as a result, larger depreciation deductions and lower gains upon disposition for the parent. To obtain this stock-basis-for-asset-basis result, taxpayers successfully devised stock purchase/subsidiary liquidation transactions that fell outside the purview of § 332.[46] Congress codified this treatment by enacting § 338, which permits the purchase of a controlling interest of stock to be treated as a purchase of the subsidiary's assets.

Requirements for Application

A corporation (the "parent") may *elect* the provisions of § 338 if it acquires stock representing at least 80 percent of the voting power and at least 80 percent of the value of another corporation (the "subsidiary") within a 12-month period ("*qualified stock purchase*"). The stock must be acquired in a taxable transaction (i.e., § 351 and other nonrecognition provisions do not apply). An acquisition of stock by any member of an affiliated group that includes the parent corporation is considered to be an acquisition by the parent. The **§ 338 election** must be made by the fifteenth day of the ninth month beginning after the month in which a qualified stock purchase occurs. If made, the election is irrevocable.

Tax Consequences

Upon a § 338 election, the subsidiary is treated as having sold its assets on the qualified stock purchase date for a value that is determined with reference to the parent's

[46]See, e.g., *U.S. v. M.O.J. Corp.*, 60–1 USTC ¶9209, 5 AFTR 2d 535, 274 F.2d 713 (CA–5, 1960). See also *Kimbell-Diamond Milling Co.*, 14 T.C. 74 (1950), *aff'd* 51–1 USTC ¶9201, 40 AFTR 328, 187 F.2d 718 (CA–5, 1951), *cert. den.* 72 S.Ct. 50 (USSC, 1951) (IRS argued stock-for-asset basis).

basis in the subsidiary stock plus any liabilities of the subsidiary ("aggregate deemed sale price").[47] The subsidiary is then treated as a new corporation that purchased those assets for a similarly computed amount ("adjusted grossed-up basis") on the day following the qualified stock purchase date.[48] The deemed sale results in gain (or loss) recognition to the subsidiary, and the deemed purchase results in a stepped-up (or -down) basis for the subsidiary's assets.[49] The subsidiary may, but need not, be liquidated. If the subsidiary is liquidated, the parent will obtain a carryover of the stepped-up (or -down) basis of the subsidiary's assets.

A Comparison of the General Rule and the § 338 Election

Under the general rule of nonrecognition, the liquidation of a subsidiary is tax-free to both the subsidiary (except for any minority interest) and the parent corporation. Under § 338, the subsidiary recognizes gain (or loss) on the deemed disposition of its assets. A liquidation of the subsidiary remains tax-free to the parent. While a carryover basis rule applies in both cases, the subsidiary's assets generally will have a stepped-up basis as a result of the § 338 election, and a liquidation of the subsidiary will result in a carryover of the stepped-up basis to the parent. Further, a liquidation of the subsidiary results in a carryover of its other tax attributes (e.g., E & P) to the parent whether or not a § 338 election is made. However, when the election is made, the subsidiary is treated as a new corporation as of the day following the qualified stock purchase date; as a result, any tax attributes acquired by the parent are likely to be nominal (or zero) in amount.

The holding period of the subsidiary's assets is determined with reference to the substance of the transaction. When the subsidiary is liquidated and there is no § 338 election, the subsidiary's historical holding period in its assets carries over to the parent. This is the typical carryover rule found in other nonrecognition provisions. A § 338 election, however, assumes a sale and repurchase of the subsidiary's assets. As a result of these deemed transactions, the holding period starts anew. If there is a § 338 election and the subsidiary is liquidated, the holding period of the property received by the parent begins on the date of the qualified stock purchase. On the other hand, if there is a § 338 election and the subsidiary is not liquidated, the holding period of the assets begins on the day after the qualified stock acquisition date. The parent-subsidiary liquidation rules are set out in Concept Summary 6.2.

TAX PLANNING:

6.9 Stock Redemptions

LO.6

Identify planning opportunities available to minimize the tax impact in stock redemptions and complete liquidations.

Stock redemptions offer several possibilities for tax planning:

- The alternative to a qualifying stock redemption is dividend treatment. The 15 percent (0 percent for taxpayers in the 10 or 15 percent marginal tax bracket) preferential tax rate on dividend income reduces some of the adverse consequences of a nonqualified stock redemption.
- A nonqualified redemption may be preferable to one that produces sale or exchange treatment if the distributing corporation has little or no E & P or the distributee-shareholder is another corporation. In the latter situation, dividend treatment may be preferred due to the availability of the dividends received deduction.
- Stock redemptions are particularly well suited for purchasing the interest of a retiring or deceased shareholder. Rather than the remaining shareholders buying the stock of the retiring or deceased shareholder, corporate funds are used to redeem the stock from the retiring shareholder or from the decedent shareholder's estate. A corporate buy-sell agreement can be

[47] See §§ 338(a)(1) and (b) and Reg. § 1.338–4.

[48] See §§ 338(a)(2) and (b) and Reg. § 1.338–5.

[49] For the rules governing the allocation of the purchase price to the assets, see § 338(b)(5) and Reg. § 1.338–6.

CONCEPT SUMMARY 6.2

Summary of Liquidation Rules

Effect on the Shareholder	Basis of Property Received	Effect on the Corporation
§ 331—The general rule provides for gain or loss treatment on the difference between the FMV of property received and the basis of the stock in the corporation. Gain allocable to installment notes received can be deferred to point of collection.	§ 334(a)—Basis of assets received by the shareholder will be the FMV on the date of distribution (except for installment obligations on which gain is deferred to the point of collection).	§ 336—Gain or loss is recognized for distributions in kind and for sales by the liquidating corporation. Losses are not recognized for distributions to related parties if the distribution is not pro rata or if disqualified property is distributed. Losses may be disallowed on sales and distributions of built-in loss property even if made to unrelated parties.
§ 332—In liquidation of a subsidiary, no gain or loss is recognized to the parent. Subsidiary must distribute all of its property within the taxable year or within three years from the close of the taxable year in which the first distribution occurs. Minority shareholders taxed under general rule of § 331.	§ 334(b)(1)—Property has the same basis as it had in the hands of the subsidiary. Parent's basis in the stock disappears. Carryover rules of § 381 apply. Minority shareholders get FMV basis under § 334(a).	§ 337—No gain or loss is recognized to the subsidiary on distributions to the parent. Gain (but not loss) is recognized on distributions to minority shareholders.
	§ 338—Subsidiary need not be liquidated. If subsidiary is liquidated, parent's basis is new stepped-up (or -down) basis. Parent's basis in the stock disappears. Carryover rules of § 381 apply, but such amounts are likely to be nominal.	§ 338—Gain or loss is recognized to the subsidiary. Subsidiary is treated as a new corporation, and its basis in assets is stepped up (or down) to reflect parent's basis in subsidiary stock plus subsidiary's liabilities. New basis is allocated among various asset classes.

used to effect a redemption of a retiring or deceased shareholder's stock. The ability to use the corporation's funds to buy out a shareholder's interest is also advantageous in property settlements between divorcing taxpayers. The redeeming corporation need not finance the redemption entirely with cash as it can issue its own notes as consideration in the transaction without adverse tax consequences to the shareholder.

- A third party who wishes to purchase all the stock of a corporation can utilize a stock redemption to finance some of the stock acquisition cost. This technique is referred to as a "bootstrap acquisition." The third party first purchases a small amount of stock from the shareholders. The corporation then redeems all of its outstanding stock except that of the third party. The third party becomes the sole shareholder of the corporation, but corporate funds finance most of the acquisition.
- A not essentially equivalent redemption provides minimal utility and generally should be relied upon only as a last resort. Instead, a redemption should be structured to satisfy the objective tests required of one of the other qualifying redemptions.
- The timing and sequence of a redemption should be considered carefully as a series of redemptions may have the effect of a dividend distribution. The following example illustrates this point.

GLOBAL Tax Issues

Exception to § 332 for Liquidations of U.S. Subsidiaries of Foreign Corporations

When a U.S. subsidiary is liquidated into a U.S. parent, gains (or losses) are not recognized immediately, but rather are deferred as a result of the carryover basis rule. Gains inherent in the transferred assets will be recognized upon their disposition by the parent. Foreign corporations generally are not subject to U.S. taxation, so the liquidation of a U.S. subsidiary into a foreign parent could avoid gain recognition entirely if § 332 were to apply unabated. Section 367(b) overrides § 332 when a U.S. subsidiary is liquidated into a foreign parent, however. Under § 367(b), the subsidiary will recognize gain on the transfer of certain "tainted" assets. Tainted assets include inventory, installment obligations, accounts receivable, and depreciable property (to the extent of depreciation recapture). For further details, see Chapter 9.

EXAMPLE 40

Sparrow Corporation's stock is held by three unrelated shareholders: Alma (60 shares), Antonio (20 shares), and Ali (20 shares). The corporation redeems 24 of Alma's shares. Shortly thereafter, it redeems 5 of Antonio's shares. Does Alma's redemption qualify as a disproportionate redemption? Taken in isolation, it satisfies the 80% and 50% tests. Yet, if the IRS takes into account the later redemption of Antonio's shares, Alma has not satisfied the 50% test; she still owns $^{36}/_{71}$ of the corporation after the two redemptions. A greater time lag between the redemptions places Alma in a better position to argue against collapsing the two redemptions as parts of one integrated plan. ■

- For a family corporation in which all of the shareholders are related to each other, the only hope of achieving sale or exchange treatment may lie in the use of a redemption that completely terminates a shareholder's interest or one that follows a shareholder's death. In a complete termination redemption, it is important that the family stock attribution rules be avoided. Here, strict compliance with the requirements for the family attribution waiver (e.g., the withdrawing shareholder does not acquire a prohibited interest in the corporation within 10 years) is crucial.
- In a redemption to pay death taxes, the amount to be sheltered from dividend treatment is limited to the sum of death taxes and funeral and administration expenses. However, a redemption in excess of the limitation does not destroy the applicability of § 303. Further, if the transaction is structured properly, the excess amount can qualify for sale or exchange treatment under one of the other redemption rules.

6.10 Disposing of § 306 Stock

Distributing the preferred stock dividend at a time when the corporation has no E & P avoids the § 306 taint altogether. Otherwise, avoiding ordinary income on the disposition of § 306 stock is a difficult feat. Unless the corporation's E & P was nominal at the time of the stock dividend (in the case of a § 306 stock sale) or at the time of the redemption (in the case of a § 306 stock redemption), the disposition of § 306 stock typically produces only ordinary income. The 15 percent (or 0 percent) tax rate applicable to dividend income lessens the bite of such treatment. A gift of § 306 stock does not defeat the ordinary income taint as the taint remains with the stock. However, if the donee is in the 10 or 15 percent marginal tax bracket, the tainted income at disposition would be taxed at the 0 percent tax rate applicable to dividends for the lowest-bracket taxpayers. In a charitable contribution of § 306 stock, the deduction is reduced under § 170(e) by the amount of the ordinary income taint.

A sale of § 306 stock in a transaction that terminates the shareholder's entire direct and indirect stock interest (common and preferred) in the corporation will avoid ordinary income treatment, as will a disposition in liquidation of the corporation. Similarly, a redemption of § 306 stock in a complete termination redemption or a partial liquidation avoids the ordinary income result. However, these exceptions are of limited use in the typical disposition of § 306 stock.

6.11 Corporate Liquidations

With the exception of parent-subsidiary liquidations, distributions in liquidation are taxed at both the corporate level and the shareholder level. When a corporation liquidates, it can, as a general rule, claim losses on assets that have depreciated in value. These assets should not be distributed in the form of a property dividend or stock redemption because losses are not recognized on nonliquidating distributions.

Shareholders faced with large prospective gains in a liquidation may consider shifting part or all of that gain to other taxpayers. One approach is to donate stock to charity. A charitable contribution of the stock produces a deduction equal to the stock's fair market value (see Chapter 2). Alternatively, the stock may be given to family members. If the family member is in the 10 or 15 percent marginal tax bracket, some or all of the gain on liquidation could be taxed at the 0 percent preferential rate on long-term capital gains. Whether these procedures will be successful in shifting the liquidation-related gain from the taxpayer depends on the timing of the transfer. If the donee of the stock is not in a position to prevent the liquidation of the corporation, the donor may be deemed to have made an anticipatory assignment of income. In such a case, the gain is still taxed to the donor. In addition, possible gift tax issues on the stock transfer must be considered (see Chapter 18). Advance planning of stock transfers therefore is crucial in arriving at the desired tax result.

The installment sale provisions provide some relief from the general rule that a shareholder recognizes all gain upon receiving a liquidating distribution. If the assets of the liquidating corporation are not to be distributed in kind, a sale of the assets in exchange for installment notes should be considered. Shareholders receiving the notes in a liquidation can then report their gain on the installment method as the notes are collected. Gain deferred under the installment method is subject to the tax rates applicable in each year of collection. Under current tax law, the preferential tax rate for long-term capital gains is scheduled to increase to 20 percent (from 15 percent) after 2012. Thus, the deferral of gain on installment obligations received in a liquidation must be weighed against the anticipated 5 percentage point increase in the applicable tax rate for gains deferred beyond 2012.

6.12 Parent-Subsidiary Liquidations

The nonrecognition provision applicable to the liquidation of a subsidiary, § 332, is not elective. Nevertheless, some flexibility may be available:

- Whether § 332 applies depends on the 80 percent stock ownership test. A parent corporation may be able to avoid § 332 by reducing its stock ownership in the subsidiary below this percentage to allow for recognition of a loss. On the other hand, the opposite approach may be desirable to avoid gain recognition. A corporate shareholder possessing less than the required 80 percent ownership may want to acquire additional stock to qualify for § 332 treatment.
- Once § 332 becomes effective, less latitude is allowed in determining the parent's basis in the subsidiary's assets. Generally, the subsidiary's existing basis in its assets carries over to the parent. If a timely § 338 election is made, the subsidiary's basis in its assets is stepped up to reflect, in part, the parent's basis in the subsidiary stock. If the subsidiary also is liquidated, the parent obtains assets with the stepped-up basis.

- An election to have the § 338 rules apply should be carefully weighed as the election can be detrimental. The income tax liability on the subsidiary's recognized gain that results from the deemed sale of its assets is the cost under § 338 for obtaining the stepped-up basis. As a result, a § 338 election may be a viable option only when the subsidiary possesses loss and/or credit carryovers that can be used to offset the associated tax.

6.13 Asset Purchase versus Stock Purchase

The acquisition of a corporation's assets generally takes one of two forms. In one form, the acquiring corporation purchases the stock of the target corporation, and then the target (subsidiary) is liquidated. In the other form, the acquiring corporation purchases the assets of the target corporation, and then the target distributes the proceeds to its shareholders in liquidation. Nontax considerations may affect the form of acquisition, with each form having both favorable and unfavorable aspects.

An asset purchase requires that title be transferred and that creditors be notified. Further, an asset purchase may not be feasible if valuable nontransferable trademarks, contracts, or licenses are involved. Alternatively, an asset purchase may be preferable to a stock purchase if the target's shareholders refuse to sell their stock. Additionally, an asset purchase avoids the transfer of liabilities (including unknown liabilities) generally inherent in stock acquisitions. An asset purchase also has the advantage of allowing the purchaser to avoid the acquisition of unwanted assets, whereas a stock purchase would involve all of a target's assets.

REFOCUS ON THE BIG PICTURE

A FAMILY ATTRIBUTION WAIVER IS A VALUABLE TOOL IN SUCCESSION PLANNING

With proper planning, a complete termination redemption could be utilized to achieve Christina's objectives. In the years remaining before her retirement, Christina should ensure that her children are actively involved in the management and strategy decisions of Orange Corporation. Also, an ownership interest in Orange should be shifted to each of the children so that they are in minority shareholder positions by the time Christina retires. The children could purchase Orange shares from Christina or newly issued shares from Orange. Alternatively, Christina could make annual gifts of Orange stock to the children. In addition to eliminating the need for the children to raise capital for a stock purchase, this alternative would produce favorable estate tax consequences. Upon Christina's retirement, Orange would redeem her remaining ownership interest, and the two children would be the sole shareholders of Orange Corporation. Assuming that Christina satisfies the requirements of the family attribution waiver, the transaction would qualify as a complete termination redemption. Orange Corporation could issue notes to finance the stock redemption, and Christina could use the installment method to report her gain. (The notes should specify a reasonable rate of interest.)

What If?

What if Christina passes away before her retirement date? A redemption to pay death taxes could be utilized to redeem Orange stock from Christina's estate, as it appears that the requirements of § 303 would be satisfied. However, a redemption would qualify under § 303 only to the extent of the estate's death taxes and funeral and administration expenses. A redemption of an amount greater than the sum of these expenditures probably would not satisfy any of the § 302 qualifying stock redemption provisions, as the children would be the primary or sole beneficiaries of Christina's estate. After the redemption to pay death taxes, the estate's remaining shares of Orange would be distributed to the children, and they would control 100 percent of the outstanding shares of the corporation.

KEY TERMS

Attribution, 6–5
Complete termination redemption, 6–8
Corporate liquidation, 6–16
Disproportionate redemption, 6–7
Meaningful reduction test, 6–7
Not essentially equivalent redemption, 6–6
Partial liquidation, 6–9
Preferred stock bailout, 6–14
Redemption to pay death taxes, 6–12
Section 338 election, 6–27
Stock redemption, 6–3

DISCUSSION QUESTIONS

1. **LO.1** Contrast the tax treatment of distributions that are a return *from* an investment with the treatment of those that are a return *of* an investment.
2. **LO.1** A disposition of stock in a redemption is equivalent to a sale of stock to a third party, so the tax treatment should be the same for both types of transactions. Assess the validity of this statement.
3. **LO.1, 2, 6** Joseph and Erica, husband and wife, jointly own all of the stock in Velvet Corporation. The two are currently involved in divorce proceedings, and pursuant to those negotiations they have agreed that only one of them will remain a shareholder in Velvet after the divorce. Since Erica has been more involved in Velvet's management and operations over the years, the parties have agreed that Joseph's ownership should be acquired by either Erica or Velvet. What issues should be considered in determining whether Erica or Velvet should acquire Joseph's shares in the corporation? **ISSUE ID**
4. **LO.1** During the current year, Gnatcatcher, Inc., distributed $100,000 each to Brandi and Yuen in redemption of some of their Gnatcatcher stock. The two shareholders acquired their shares five years ago. Each shareholder is in the 28% tax bracket, and each had a $40,000 basis in her redeemed stock. Brandi incurred $9,000 of tax on her redemption, but Yuen incurred $15,000 on her redemption. Discuss the likely reason for the difference in tax liabilities arising from the stock redemptions.
5. **LO.1** Would a shareholder prefer a qualifying stock redemption or a nonqualified stock redemption? Why?
6. **LO.1** Is a loss realized in a qualifying stock redemption recognized by the shareholder?
7. **LO.1** A shareholder's basis in property received in a qualifying stock redemption is the property's fair market value on the date of the redemption, but a shareholder's basis in property received in a nonqualified stock redemption is the basis the distributing corporation had in such property. Comment on the validity of this statement.
8. **LO.1** Would qualifying stock redemption treatment be ensured if the distribution was treated as a sale or exchange of the stock under applicable state law?
9. **LO.1** How do the § 318 stock attribution rules apply to corporations and their shareholders?
10. **LO.1** The stock attribution rules apply to all stock redemptions. Assess the validity of this statement.
11. **LO.1** What happens to the basis of stock redeemed in a nonqualified stock redemption?
12. **LO.1** Explain the requirements for a disproportionate redemption.
13. **LO.1, 2** Tammy and Barry formed Pheasant Corporation several years ago in a transaction that qualified under § 351. Both shareholders serve as officers and on the board of directors of Pheasant. In the current year, Pheasant Corporation redeemed all of Barry's shares in the corporation with a property distribution. What are the tax issues for Barry and Pheasant? **ISSUE ID**
14. **LO.1** Discuss the requirements for the family attribution waiver in a complete termination redemption.

15. **LO.1** The termination of a business test is a safe-harbor rule that satisfies the not essentially equivalent to a dividend requirement for a partial liquidation. Briefly outline the requirements for the termination of a business test.

ISSUE ID

16. **LO.1, 2** Brown Corporation operates several trades and businesses. In the current year, Brown discontinues the operation of one of its trades and businesses. Brown is considering distributing to its shareholders either the assets of the discontinued business or the proceeds from the sale of such assets. Considering both of these alternatives, what are the tax issues for Brown Corporation and its shareholders?

17. **LO.1** Why is § 303 (redemption to pay death taxes) of particular importance for shareholders of closely held corporations?

18. **LO.1, 2** Explain the requirements for a redemption to pay death taxes. What are the tax consequences of a redemption to pay death taxes for the shareholder and the corporation?

ISSUE ID

19. **LO.1, 2** Angie and her daughter, Ann, who are the only shareholders of Bluebird Corporation, each paid $100,000 four years ago for their shares in Bluebird. Angie also owns 20% of the stock in Redbird Corporation. The Redbird stock is worth $500,000, and Angie's basis in the stock is $50,000. Angie dies in 2011 leaving all her property to her husband, Gary, but Ann wants to be the sole shareholder of Bluebird Corporation. Bluebird has assets worth $4 million (basis of $700,000) and E & P of $1 million. Angie's estate is worth approximately $6 million. Angie has made gifts during her lifetime to Ann. What are the tax issues for Angie's estate, Ann, and Bluebird?

DECISION MAKING

20. **LO.2, 6** Indigo Corporation desires to transfer cash of $100,000 or property worth $100,000 to one of its shareholders, Linda, in a redemption transaction that will be treated as a qualifying stock redemption. If Indigo distributes property, the corporation will choose between two assets that are each worth $100,000 and are no longer needed in its business: Property A (basis of $121,000) and Property B (basis of $53,000). Indigo is indifferent as to the form of the distribution, but Linda prefers a cash distribution. Considering the tax consequences to Indigo on the distribution to redeem Linda's shares, what should Indigo distribute?

ISSUE ID

21. **LO.2** Kackie Corporation (E & P of $1 million) is currently in negotiations to redeem stock from one or more of its shareholders. The form (i.e., cash and/or property) and amount of the distribution(s) to the shareholder(s) are key points of the negotiations. What are the tax issues for Kackie Corporation?

22. **LO.2** Discuss the deductibility of expenditures, such as legal, accounting, transfer agent, brokerage, and appraisal fees, a corporation might incur in connection with a redemption of its stock.

23. **LO.3** What is § 306 stock, and what is the relevance of such classification?

24. **LO.3** What issues arise when a shareholder sells shares owned in one corporation to another corporation in which he or she is a shareholder?

25. **LO.4** Discuss when a corporate liquidation occurs for tax purposes.

26. **LO.4** Briefly discuss whether a corporation recognizes gains or losses on the distribution of property in liquidation.

27. **LO.1, 2, 4** One difference between the tax treatment of a liquidation and a qualifying stock redemption is the applicability of § 267. Explain this statement from the perspective of both the shareholder and the corporation.

28. **LO.4** Can the related-party loss limitation in a complete liquidation apply to a realized loss attributable to a decline in a property's fair market value that occurred after the property was acquired by the liquidating corporation?

29. **LO.4** When properties transferred by a shareholder in a § 351 transaction have a net built-in loss (aggregate fair market value less than aggregate basis), the basis step-down rule must be applied. Discuss the relevance of the built-in loss limitation given the enactment of the basis step-down rule.

30. **LO.4** Explain the tax consequences to a shareholder of a corporation in the process of liquidation under the general rule of § 331. May a shareholder use the installment method to report gain on a complete liquidation?

31. **LO.5** Discuss the tax consequences to the parent corporation in a § 332 liquidation of a subsidiary.

32. **LO.5** Does § 332 apply to the liquidation of an insolvent subsidiary? If not, then how does the parent corporation treat such a liquidation?

33. **LO.5** A subsidiary corporation is liquidated under § 332. Pursuant to its liquidation, the subsidiary transferred property to a minority shareholder. With respect to this distribution, what are the tax consequences to the subsidiary corporation and to the minority shareholder?

34. **LO.5** Condor Corporation pays $950,000 for 100% of the stock in Dove Corporation. Dove has a basis of $800,000 in its assets and E & P of $220,000. If Condor liquidates Dove and makes no special election, what are the tax consequences to Condor and to Dove?

35. **LO.5** What happens to a subsidiary's tax attributes (e.g., net operating loss, E & P, capital loss carryover) upon a § 332 liquidation?

36. **LO.5** What are the requirements for the application of § 338?

37. **LO.5** In general, what are the tax consequences of a § 338 election?

PROBLEMS

38. **LO.1, 2, 6** Teal Corporation, with E & P of $1.9 million, distributes property with a basis of $180,000 and a fair market value of $250,000 to Grace, a 28% shareholder. **DECISION MAKING**
    a. What are the tax consequences to Teal Corporation and to Grace if the distribution is a property dividend?
    b. What are the tax consequences in (a) if Grace is a corporation?
    c. What are the tax consequences to Teal Corporation and to Grace if the distribution is a qualifying stock redemption? Assume that half of Grace's stock (basis of $70,000) is redeemed in the transaction.
    d. What are the tax consequences in (c) if Grace is a corporation?
    e. If the parties involved could choose from among the preceding options, which would they choose and why?

39. **LO.1** Julio is in the 35% tax bracket. He acquired 1,000 shares of stock in Gray Corporation seven years ago at a cost of $250 per share. In the current year, Julio received a payment of $500,000 from Gray Corporation in exchange for 600 of his shares in Gray. Gray has E & P of $1 million. What tax liability would Julio incur on the $500,000 payment in each of the following situations? Assume that Julio has no capital losses.
    a. The payment qualifies for stock redemption (i.e., sale or exchange) treatment.
    b. The payment does not qualify for stock redemption (i.e., sale or exchange treatment is not applicable) treatment.

40. **LO.1** How would your answer to Problem 39 differ if Julio were a corporate shareholder (in the 34% tax bracket) rather than an individual shareholder and the stock ownership in Gray Corporation represented a 15% interest?

41. **LO.1** Assume in Problem 39 that Julio has a capital loss carryover of $110,000 in the current tax year. Julio has no other capital gain transactions during the year. What amount of the capital loss may Julio deduct in the current year in the following situations? **DECISION MAKING**
    a. The $500,000 payment from Gray Corporation is a qualifying stock redemption for tax purposes (i.e., receives sale or exchange treatment).
    b. The $500,000 payment from Gray Corporation does not qualify as a stock redemption for tax purposes (i.e., does not receive sale or exchange treatment).
    c. If Julio had the flexibility to structure the transaction as described in either (a) or (b), which form would he choose?

42. **LO.1** How would your answer to parts (a) and (b) of Problem 41 differ if Julio were a corporate shareholder (in the 34% tax bracket) rather than an individual shareholder and the stock ownership in Gray Corporation represented a 15% interest?

43. **LO.1** Magpie Corporation has 3,000 shares of common stock outstanding. Josephina owns 800 shares, Josephina's daughter owns 500 shares, Josephina's brother owns 800 shares, Tern Corporation owns 600 shares, and Petrel Partnership owns 300 shares. Josephina owns 45% of the stock of Tern Corporation, and she owns a 60% interest in Petrel Partnership.
    a. Applying the § 318 stock attribution rules, how many shares does Josephina own in Magpie Corporation?
    b. Assume Josephina owns 75% of the stock of Tern Corporation. How many shares does Josephina own, directly and indirectly, in Magpie Corporation?

44. **LO.1** Pedro owns 700 of the 1,000 shares outstanding of Indigo Corporation (E & P of $950,000). Pedro paid $170 per share for the stock 12 years ago. The remaining stock in Indigo is owned by unrelated individuals. What are the tax consequences to Pedro in the following independent situations?
    a. Indigo redeems 350 shares of Pedro's stock for $175,000.
    b. Indigo redeems 450 shares of Pedro's stock for $225,000.

COMMUNICATIONS

45. **LO.1, 2** Stork Corporation (E & P of $850,000) has 1,000 shares of common stock outstanding. The shares are owned by the following individuals: Lana Johnson, 450 shares; Lori Johnson (Lana's sister), 450 shares; and Leo Johnson (Lana's son), 100 shares. Lana paid $200 per share for the Stork stock eight years ago. Lana is interested in reducing her stock ownership in Stork via a stock redemption for $1,000 per share, the fair market value of the stock. Stork Corporation would distribute cash for the entire redemption transaction. Lana has inquired as to the minimum number of shares that she would have to redeem in order to obtain favorable long-term capital gain treatment and the overall tax consequences of such a redemption to both her and Stork Corporation. Prepare a letter to Lana (1000 Main Street, Oldtown, MN 55166) and a memo for the file in which you explain your conclusions.

46. **LO.1** Thrush Corporation (E & P of $450,000) has 3,000 shares of common stock outstanding. The shares are owned as follows: John Thompson, 1,300 shares; Edward Thompson (John's father), 1,000 shares; and Georgia Simpson (John's sister), 700 shares. In the current year, Thrush redeems all of John's shares. Determine whether the redemption can qualify for sale or exchange treatment under the complete termination redemption rules in each of the following independent circumstances.
    a. John does not file an agreement with his tax return (for the year of redemption) to notify the IRS of any prohibited interest acquired in Thrush during the 10-year post-redemption period.
    b. Seven years after the redemption, Georgia dies, and John purchases the 700 shares in Thrush Corporation from her estate.
    c. John receives a five-year note receivable from Thrush Corporation in exchange for the redeemed stock.

47. **LO.1, 2** Robert and Lori (Robert's sister) own all the stock in Swan Corporation (E & P of $700,000). Each owns 500 shares and has a basis of $25,000 in the shares. Robert wants to sell his stock for $400,000, the fair market value, but he will continue to be employed as an officer of Swan Corporation after the sale. Lori would like to purchase Robert's shares and, thus, become the sole shareholder in Swan, but Lori is short of funds. What are the tax consequences to Robert, Lori, and Swan Corporation under the following circumstances?
    a. Swan Corporation distributes cash of $400,000 to Lori, and she uses the cash to purchase Robert's shares.
    b. Swan Corporation redeems all of Robert's shares for $400,000.

48. **LO.1, 2** Sean owns 1,000 shares or 40% of the outstanding stock of Crane Corporation (E & P of $900,000). Sean purchased the stock 15 years ago for $50,000. For the last eight years, Crane has owned and operated three different trades or businesses. Pursuant to a plan adopted in the current year, Crane Corporation sells one of those trades or businesses and distributes the proceeds from such sale to its shareholders pursuant to a stock redemption. Sean received a distribution of $200,000 in redemption of 500 shares

of Crane stock. Determine the tax consequences of the redemption to Sean and to Crane Corporation under the following independent circumstances.

a. Sean is an individual shareholder.
b. Sean is a corporate shareholder.

49. **LO.1, 2** The gross estate of Tanya, decedent, includes stock of Finch Corporation (E & P of $2 million) valued at $1.4 million. At the time of her death in 2011, Tanya owned 40% of the Finch stock outstanding, and she had a basis of $220,000 in the stock. The death taxes and funeral and administration expenses related to Tanya's estate amount to $1.4 million, and the adjusted gross estate is $7 million. The remainder of the Finch stock is owned by shareholders unrelated to Tanya (or her estate). Tanya named her son, Taylor, as the sole heir of her estate. In the current year, Finch Corporation distributes $1.4 million to the estate in redemption of all of its stock in the corporation. What are the tax consequences of the redemption to Tanya's estate and to Finch Corporation?

50. **LO.1** The gross estate of Bridgett, decedent, includes stock of Crane Corporation (E & P of $1.3 million) and Eagle Corporation (E & P of $1 million) valued at $750,000 and $2 million, respectively. At the time of her death in 2011, Bridgett owned 26% of the Crane stock outstanding and 32% of the Eagle stock outstanding. Bridgett had a basis of $240,000 in the Crane stock and $165,000 in the Eagle stock. Bridgett's adjusted gross estate is $7.5 million, and the death taxes and funeral and administration expenses total $750,000. What are the tax consequences to Bridgett's estate if Crane Corporation redeems all of the Crane Corporation stock for $750,000?

51. **LO.1, 2** Teal Corporation (E & P of $900,000) has 2,000 shares of common stock outstanding. The shares are owned by the following individuals: Ann, 800 shares; Bonnie, 600 shares; and Lucy, 600 shares. Each of the shareholders paid $20 per share for the Teal stock nine years ago. In the current year, Teal distributes $90,000 to Ann in redemption of 300 of her shares. Determine the tax consequences of the redemption to Ann and to Teal Corporation under the following independent circumstances.

a. The three shareholders are unrelated.
b. Ann and Bonnie are mother and daughter.

52. **LO.2** Crane Corporation has 2,000 shares of stock outstanding. It redeems 500 shares for $370,000 when it has paid-in capital of $300,000 and E & P of $1.2 million. The redemption qualifies for sale or exchange treatment for the shareholder. Crane incurred $13,000 of accounting and legal fees in connection with the redemption transaction. What is the effect of the distribution on Crane Corporation's E & P? Also, what is the proper tax treatment of the redemption expenditures? Prepare a letter to the president of Crane Corporation (506 Wall Street, Winona, MN 55987) and a memo for the file in which you explain your conclusions. **COMMUNICATIONS**

53. **LO.3** Ramon and Sophie are the sole shareholders of Gull Corporation. Ramon and Sophie each have a basis of $75,000 in their 500 shares of Gull common stock. When its E & P was $500,000, Gull Corporation issued a preferred stock dividend on the common shares of Ramon and Sophie, giving each 500 shares of preferred stock with a par value of $200 per share. Fair market value of one share of common was $300, and fair market value of one share of preferred was $200.

a. What are the tax consequences of the distribution to Ramon and Sophie?
b. What are the tax consequences to Ramon if he later sells his preferred stock to Anthony for $100,000? Anthony is not related to Ramon.
c. What are the tax consequences if, instead of Ramon selling the preferred stock to Anthony, Gull Corporation redeems the stock from Ramon for $100,000? Assume Gull's E & P at the time of the redemption is $550,000.

54. **LO.3** Martin owns 1,000 shares of stock in Black Corporation and 500 shares of stock in Blue Corporation, representing 100% ownership of Black and 50% ownership of Blue. Martin sells 200 Blue shares to Black Corporation for $300,000. Martin purchased the Blue stock four years ago at a cost of $600 per share. What are the tax consequences of the sale, assuming Black Corporation has E & P of $800,000 and Blue Corporation has E & P of $1 million?

55. **LO.1, 2, 4** Dove Corporation (E & P of $650,000) has 1,000 shares of stock outstanding. The shares are owned as follows: Julia, 600 shares; Maxine (Julia's daughter), 300 shares; and Janine (Julia's granddaughter), 100 shares. Dove Corporation owns land (basis of

$470,000, fair market value of $330,000) that it purchased as an investment seven years ago. Dove distributes the land to Julia in exchange for all her shares in the corporation. Julia had a basis of $350,000 in the shares. What are the tax consequences for both Dove Corporation and Julia if the distribution is:

a. A qualifying stock redemption?
b. A liquidating distribution?

56. **LO.4** Pursuant to a complete liquidation, Oriole Corporation distributes to its shareholders land held for three years as an investment (adjusted basis of $310,000, fair market value of $420,000). The land is subject to a liability of $200,000.
    a. What are the tax consequences to Oriole Corporation on the distribution of the land?
    b. If the land is, instead, subject to a liability of $500,000, what are the tax consequences to Oriole on the distribution?

57. **LO.4** Bronze Corporation's stock is held equally by three brothers, Mitchell, Alex, and Ron. Four years ago, the brothers transferred to Bronze Corporation land in which they had owned equal interests. The transfer of the land (basis of $260,000, fair market value of $300,000) qualified under § 351. Pursuant to a liquidation in the current year, Bronze distributed the land pro rata to the three brothers. The land had a fair market value of $215,000 on the date of the distribution. What amount of loss may Bronze Corporation recognize on the distribution of the land?

58. **LO.4** On April 21, 2010, Crow Corporation acquired land and equipment in a § 351 transaction. At that time, the land had a basis of $300,000 and a fair market value of $225,000, and the equipment had a basis of $20,000 and a fair market value of $100,000. The land and equipment were transferred to Crow Corporation for use as security for a loan the corporation was in the process of obtaining from a local bank. The bank required the additional capital investment as a condition for making the loan. Crow Corporation adopted a plan of liquidation on October 3, 2011. On December 2, 2011, Crow Corporation distributes the land to Ali, a 40% shareholder. On the date of the distribution, the land had a fair market value of only $150,000. What amount of loss may Crow Corporation recognize on the distribution of the land?

59. **LO.4** On January 5, 2010, Grackle Corporation acquired equipment as a contribution to capital. At that time, the equipment had an adjusted basis of $360,000 and a fair market value of $290,000. This was the only property transferred to Grackle at that time. On July 22, 2011, Grackle Corporation adopted a plan of liquidation. On November 10, 2011, Grackle sold the equipment to Chris, an unrelated party, for its current fair market value of $200,000. Grackle Corporation never used the equipment for any business purpose during the time it owned the equipment. What amount of loss may Grackle Corporation recognize on the sale of the equipment?

DECISION MAKING

60. **LO.4** Pink Corporation acquired land and securities in a § 351 tax-free exchange in 2010. On the date of the transfer, the land had a basis of $800,000 and a fair market value of $980,000, and the securities had a basis of $70,000 and a fair market value of $200,000. Pink Corporation has two shareholders, Maria and Paul, unrelated individuals. Maria owns 70% of the stock in Pink Corporation, and Paul owns 30%. The corporation adopts a plan of liquidation in 2011. On this date, the value of the land has decreased to $640,000. What is the effect of each of the following on Pink Corporation? Which option should be selected?
    a. Distribute all the land to Maria.
    b. Distribute all the land to Paul.
    c. Distribute 70% of the land to Maria and 30% to Paul.
    d. Distribute 50% of the land to Maria and 50% to Paul.
    e. Sell the land and distribute the proceeds of $640,000 proportionately to Maria and to Paul.

DECISION MAKING

61. **LO.4** Assume in Problem 60 that the land had a fair market value of $700,000 on the date of its transfer to Pink Corporation. On the date of the liquidation, the land's fair market value has decreased to $640,000. How would your answer to Problem 60 change if:
    a. All the land is distributed to Maria?
    b. All the land is distributed to Paul?
    c. The land is distributed 70% to Maria and 30% to Paul?
    d. The land is distributed 50% to Maria and 50% to Paul?
    e. The land is sold and the proceeds of $640,000 are distributed proportionately to Maria and to Paul?

62. **LO.4** Pursuant to a complete liquidation in the current year, Oriole Corporation distributes to Samantha land held for four years as an investment (basis of $225,000, fair market value of $480,000). The land is subject to a liability of $150,000. Samantha, who owned 20% of the Oriole shares outstanding, had a basis of $90,000 in the stock. What are the tax consequences of the liquidating distribution to Oriole Corporation and to Samantha?

63. **LO.4** After a plan of complete liquidation has been adopted, Purple Corporation sells its only asset, land, to Rex (an unrelated party) for $800,000. Under the terms of the sale, Purple receives cash of $200,000 and Rex's note in the amount of $600,000. The note is payable over five years ($120,000 per year) and carries an appropriate rate of interest. Immediately after the sale, Purple distributes the cash and note to Helen, the sole shareholder of Purple Corporation. Helen has a basis of $80,000 in the Purple stock. What are the tax results to Helen if she wishes to defer as much gain as possible on the transaction? Assume the installment note possesses a value equal to its face amount.

64. **LO.4, 5** The stock of Magenta Corporation is owned by Fuchsia Corporation (90%) and Marta (10%). Magenta is liquidated on September 2, 2011, pursuant to a plan of liquidation adopted earlier in the same year. In the liquidation, Magenta distributes various assets worth $1,620,000 (basis of $1,950,000) to Fuchsia (basis of $1.2 million in Magenta stock) and a parcel of land worth $180,000 (basis of $165,000) to Marta (basis of $35,000 in Magenta stock). Assuming the § 338 election is not made, what are the tax consequences of the liquidation to Magenta, Fuchsia, and Marta?

65. **LO.4, 5** The stock in Ivory Corporation is owned by Gold Corporation (80%) and Imelda (20%). Gold Corporation purchased its shares in Ivory nine years ago at a cost of $650,000, and Imelda purchased her shares in Ivory four years ago at a cost of $175,000. Ivory Corporation has the following assets that are distributed in complete liquidation:

	Adjusted Basis	Fair Market Value
Cash	$600,000	$600,000
Inventory	80,000	200,000
Equipment	350,000	200,000

a. Assume that Ivory Corporation distributes the cash and inventory to Gold Corporation and the equipment to Imelda. What are the tax consequences of the distributions to Ivory Corporation, to Gold Corporation, and to Imelda?
b. Assume that Ivory Corporation distributes the cash and equipment to Gold Corporation and the inventory to Imelda. What are the tax consequences of the distributions to Ivory Corporation, to Gold Corporation, and to Imelda?

66. **LO.5** Orange Corporation purchased bonds (basis of $185,000) of its wholly owned subsidiary, Green Corporation, at a discount. Upon liquidation of Green pursuant to § 332, Orange receives payment in the form of land worth $200,000, the face amount of the bonds. Green had a basis of $220,000 in the land. What are the tax consequences of this land transfer to Green Corporation and to Orange Corporation?

67. **LO.5** At the time of its liquidation under § 332, Cardinal Corporation (E & P of $560,000) had the following assets and liabilities: cash ($175,000); marketable securities (fair market value of $230,000, basis of $250,000); unimproved land (fair market value of $600,000, basis of $300,000); unsecured note payable ($50,000); and mortgage on the unimproved land ($270,000). Cardinal also had a net operating loss carryover of $45,000. Wren Corporation acquired all the stock of Cardinal seven years ago for $160,000.
a. How much gain (or loss) will Cardinal Corporation recognize upon the liquidating distribution of its assets and liabilities to Wren Corporation?
b. How much gain (or loss) will Wren Corporation recognize in the liquidation of Cardinal?
c. What basis will Wren have in the marketable securities and unimproved land it receives in the liquidation?
d. What happens to Cardinal's E & P and net operating loss carryover?

68. **LO.5** On August 9, 2011, Egret Corporation acquired 100% of the outstanding stock of Aqua Corporation for $1 million and made a qualified § 338 election. On that date, Aqua Corporation had assets with a basis of $700,000 and E & P of $400,000. Assume that the aggregate deemed sale price and the adjusted grossed-up basis each equal $1.2 million and that Aqua Corporation is immediately liquidated. In general, what are the tax consequences to Egret and to Aqua of the § 338 election and the liquidation of Aqua?

RESEARCH PROBLEMS

THOMSON REUTERS
Checkpoint® Student Edition

Note: Solutions to Research Problems can be prepared by using the **Checkpoint® Student Edition** online research product, which is available to accompany this text. It is also possible to prepare solutions to the Research Problems by using tax research materials found in a standard tax library.

COMMUNICATIONS

Research Problem 1. Tanya Anderson (4100 E. 6th Street, Tucson, AZ 85711) owns 50% of the common stock of Lavender Corporation. Joseph Hansen, an individual unrelated to Tanya, owns the remaining shares in Lavender. Both shareholders are active in the management of the corporation. Currently, the shareholders do not have an agreement limiting the disposition of either individual's stock interest in Lavender. The two are contemplating a buy-sell agreement that would require a retired or deceased shareholder to sell his or her shares to the other shareholder ("continuing shareholder") at a price fixed by the agreement. The goal is to provide sole ownership of Lavender to the continuing shareholder, but both shareholders have expressed concerns about being able to finance the stock purchase required under the agreement. Lavender Corporation (E & P of $1 million) generates significant profits and positive cash flow annually, and its financial position is excellent. Tanya has contacted you regarding the best way to structure the buy-sell agreement given the shareholders' goals and concerns. Prepare a letter to Tanya and a memo for the file documenting your recommendations.

COMMUNICATIONS

Research Problem 2. Six years ago, Coastal Drillers, Inc., redeemed all of the stock owned directly by Jeremiah Cranston (6870 Vinton Court, Los Angeles, CA 90034). At the time of the redemption, Jeremiah and his immediate family members owned 100% of the stock of Coastal Drillers. Jeremiah satisfied all of the requirements of the family attribution waiver [under § 302(c)(2)]; thus, the transaction qualified as a complete termination redemption and resulted in a significant long-term capital gain. Coastal Drillers' E & P at the time of the transaction exceeded the redemption proceeds. Treatment of the redemption proceeds as a dividend would have resulted in a $200,000 greater tax liability for Jeremiah. Now, six years later, Coastal Drillers has offered Jeremiah a consulting engagement. The consulting engagement would be for a one-year term, but options to renew could extend the contract to a total of five years. Assuming all options are exercised, Jeremiah would earn $150,000 under the contract. Based on the terms of the contract, Jeremiah would properly be classified as an independent contractor, not as an employee of Coastal Drillers. Jeremiah has contacted you regarding the effect, if any, of the proposed consulting engagement on the tax treatment of his earlier stock redemption. Prepare a letter to Jeremiah and a memo for the file documenting your conclusions.

Research Problem 3. Tammy Olsen has owned 100% of the common stock of Green Corporation (basis of $75,000) since the corporation's formation in 2002. In 2008, when Green had E & P of $320,000, the corporation distributed to Tammy a nontaxable dividend of 500 shares of preferred stock (value of $100,000 on date of distribution) on her common stock interest (value of $400,000 on date of distribution). In 2009, Tammy donated the 500 shares of preferred stock to her favorite charity, State University. Tammy deducted $100,000, the fair market value of the stock on the date of the gift, as a charitable contribution on her 2009 income tax return. Tammy's adjusted gross income for 2009 was $420,000. Six months after the contribution, Green Corporation redeemed the preferred stock from State University for $100,000. Upon audit of Tammy's 2009 return, the IRS disallowed the entire deduction for the gift to State University, asserting that the preferred stock was § 306 stock and that § 170(e)(1)(A) precluded a deduction for contributions of such stock. What is the proper tax treatment for Tammy's contribution of Green Corporation preferred stock?

Partial list of research aids:
Reg. § 1.170A–4(b)(1).
§ 306(b)(4).

Research Problem 4. Berta Jackson owns 100% of the common stock of Almond Corporation (E & P of $1.5 million), having purchased the stock 15 years ago. Berta is contemplating a gift of 45% of her shares in Almond (basis of $100,000, fair market value of $1 million) to a qualified charitable organization. Under Berta's plan, Almond would then redeem the charitable organization's shares in the corporation, and the charity would use the redemption proceeds to finance the construction of a soccer complex in a low-income neighborhood. Berta's objectives are to claim a charitable contribution deduction of $1 million for the gift of the Almond shares and retain sole ownership in Almond after the corporation's redemption of stock from the charitable organization. However, a CPA friend of Berta's has warned her to be careful to avoid the assignment of income doctrine. Uncertain as to the meaning of her friend's warning, Berta has asked you for advice as to how to proceed with her plan. What advice would you give Berta so that she can achieve her objectives?

Use the tax resources of the Internet to address the following questions. Do not restrict your search to the Web, but include a review of newsgroups and general reference materials, practitioner sites and resources, primary sources of the tax law, chat rooms and discussion groups, and other opportunities.

COMMUNICATIONS

Research Problem 5. Buy-sell agreements are frequently used to address the disposition of a retiring or deceased shareholder's stock in a closely held corporation. Using the Internet as your sole research source, prepare an outline on the planning opportunities and pitfalls of using a buy-sell agreement in conjunction with the qualifying stock redemption provisions.

COMMUNICATIONS

Research Problem 6. Economic downturns mean an increase in corporate bankruptcy filings. Although many corporations are able to use Chapter 11 of the Bankruptcy Code to restructure, the recent credit crunch has limited such restructurings, and more and more bankruptcies are ending up in a liquidation of the corporate entity. Liquidating trusts are often utilized for the disposition of assets of a corporation going through bankruptcy. Using the Internet as your sole research source, prepare an outline discussing the use of liquidating trusts and their advantages.

CHAPTER 7

Corporations: Reorganizations

LEARNING OBJECTIVES

After completing Chapter 7, you should be able to:

LO.1 Understand the general requirements of corporate reorganizations.

LO.2 Determine the tax consequences of a corporate reorganization.

LO.3 Explain the statutory requirements for the different types of reorganizations.

LO.4 Delineate the judicial and administrative conditions for a nontaxable corporate reorganization.

LO.5 Apply the rules pertaining to the carryover of tax attributes in a corporate reorganization.

LO.6 Structure corporate reorganizations to obtain the desired tax consequences.

OUTLINE

For the latest in changes to tax legislation, visit **www.cengage.com/taxation/swft.**

THE BIG PICTURE **Tax Solutions for the Real World**

STRUCTURING ACQUISITIONS

Rock & Water Corporation (R&W) specializes in industrial park landscaping featuring rock walls, holding ponds, water fountains, and indigenous vegetation. One of R&W's central missions is to cause as little negative impact on the environment as possible. Until recently, R&W applied this policy only to its own work, but the new CEO, Tony Turner, wants to extend its corporate responsibility to its suppliers. R&W uses several types of chemicals and fertilizers in its business and is aware that three of its suppliers do not use environmentally sound practices. Realizing that simply changing suppliers will not eliminate these polluting practices, R&W is considering acquiring these three suppliers. Using this strategy, R&W would control the production practices of these corporations.

R&W is unsure of how to structure these potential acquisitions of its suppliers and seeks your advice. R&W gives you the following information about these potential acquisitions. BrineCo is a profitable corporation that has been owned predominantly by the Adams family since its incorporation in 1950. AcidCo started up in 1967. AcidCo has been having legal troubles and has continually been fined since more stringent EPA standards came into existence. Besides chemicals used by R&W, AcidCo produces acids for the mining industry.

Lastly, ChemCo is a new fertilizer producer with the technology to produce environmentally safe products. Its management is inexperienced, however, and the result has been inefficiencies in production and unintended harm to its surroundings. ChemCo has yet to show a profit. How will you advise R&W to approach each of these acquisitions? **Read the chapter and formulate your response.**

One tenet of U.S. tax policy is to encourage business development. Accordingly, the tax laws allow entities to form without taxation, assuming certain requirements are met. As an extension of this policy, corporate restructurings are also favored with tax-free treatment. Corporations may engage in a variety of acquisitions, combinations, consolidations, and divisions tax-free, as long as the "reorganization" requirements in the Code are met.

Since the dollar value of most reorganizations is substantial, the tax implications are significant, and thus the tax law often dictates the form of the restructuring. The taxable gain for shareholders is likely to be treated as either a dividend or a capital gain. For individual shareholders, both dividends and capital gains are subject to lower tax rates than apply to ordinary income. Corporate shareholders are allowed the dividends received deduction, if the gains are categorized as a dividend. However, since corporations receive no tax rate reduction for capital gains, corporate shareholders and the corporations involved in the restructuring would be taxed at their highest marginal rate on any gains classified as capital.

Careful planning can reduce or totally eliminate the tax possibilities for both the corporations and their shareholders. Consequently, when feasible, parties contemplating a corporate reorganization should apply for and obtain from the IRS a letter ruling determining the income tax effect of the transactions. Assuming the parties proceed with the transactions as proposed in the ruling request, a favorable ruling provides, in effect, an insurance policy as to the tax treatment of the restructuring.[1]

Courts originally concluded that even minor changes in a corporation's structure would produce taxable gains for the shareholders involved.[2] Congress, however, determined that businesses should be allowed to make necessary capital adjustments

[1] To expedite the letter ruling process, the IRS attempts to issue rulings within 10 weeks from the date of request. Rev.Proc. 2005–68, 2005–2 C.B. 694.

[2] *U.S. v. Phellis*, 1 USTC ¶54, 3 AFTR 3123, 42 S.Ct. 63 (USSC, 1921).

TAX in the NEWS

Mergers and Acquisitions Come in Waves

Merger and acquisition (M&A) transactions do not occur at a steady rate year after year. Rather, M&A activity comes in waves. Economists have identified five clearly distinct waves since the late 1800s. Generally, after a wave crests, there is a low tide of M&A activity for several years. The first two waves are documented only for the United States, the third includes the United Kingdom, the fourth adds the rest of Europe, and the last is considered truly international. A summary of these eras of M&A activity follows.

- *First wave (Great Merger Wave).* The economic expansion created by dramatic technical innovations, the beginning of industrial stock trading, and the passage of the Sherman Antitrust Act started this wave. This M&A activity predominantly involved firms in similar industries consolidating to form monopolies and decrease competition. It ended when the equity market crashed in 1903.
- *Second wave.* This wave, beginning just before World War I, was fueled by the small to mid-size firms left after the first wave. These mergers produced firms large enough to compete with the giant firms; thus, oligopolies dominated by a few firms were created. The stock market crash of 1929 put the brakes on this wave.
- *Third wave.* The Great Depression and World War II held off the next wave until the 1950s. Once this wave began, however, it lasted for nearly two decades, making it the longest period of sustained M&A activity. These acquisitions focused on business diversification, leading to large conglomerates. Because these conglomerates never achieved the expected benefits from diversification, conglomerate stocks crashed in 1969–1970. Then, the 1973 oil crisis pushed the world economy into a recession and ended this wave.
- *Fourth wave.* This wave started with the deregulation of financial services and the creation of financial instruments such as junk bonds. It was characterized by corporate raiders, divestitures, and leveraged and management buyouts. As with other waves, its end was announced by a stock market crash—the crash of 1987.
- *Fifth wave.* The last wave was energized by increasing economic globalization, technological innovation, deregulation, and privatization. These M&As were mega-mergers with a substantial proportion of them being cross-border transactions. The fifth wave halted when the dot-coms and the financial industry collapsed, leading to numerous corporate scandals.

Source: Adapted from Marina Martynova and Luc Renneboog, "A Century of Corporate Takeovers: What Have We Learned and Where Do We Stand?" *Journal of Banking and Finance* (2008), and "Historical Merger and Acquisition Activity," *Mergerstat Review* (2006).

without being subject to taxation.[3] The theory for nonrecognition in certain corporate restructurings or "reorganizations" is similar to that underlying § 351 treatment and like-kind exchanges. As the Regulations state:

> the new property is substantially a continuation of the old investment . . . and, in the case of reorganizations, . . . the new enterprise, the new corporate structure, and the new property are substantially continuations of the old.[4]

7.1 Reorganizations—In General

LO.1
Understand the general requirements of corporate reorganizations.

Although the term **reorganization** is commonly associated with a corporation in financial difficulty, for tax purposes the term refers to any corporate restructuring that may be tax-free under § 368. To qualify as a tax-free reorganization, a corporate restructuring transaction must meet not only the specific requirements of § 368 but also several general requirements. These requirements include the following.

[3] Reg. § 1.368–1(b). See S.Rept. No. 275, 67th Cong., 1st Sess. (1921), at 1939–1 C.B. 181.

[4] Reg. § 1.1002–1(c).

1. There must be a *plan of reorganization.*
2. The reorganization must meet the *continuity of interest* and the *continuity of business enterprise* tests provided in the Regulations.
3. The restructuring must meet the judicial doctrine of having a *sound business purpose.*
4. The court-imposed *step transaction* doctrine should not apply to the reorganization.

All of these concepts are discussed in this chapter. The initial and most important consideration, however, is whether the reorganization qualifies for nonrecognition status under § 368.

SUMMARY OF THE DIFFERENT TYPES OF REORGANIZATIONS

Section 368(a) specifies seven corporate restructurings or *reorganizations* that will qualify as nontaxable exchanges. If the transaction fails to qualify as a reorganization, it will not receive the special tax-favored treatment. Therefore, a corporation considering a business reorganization must determine in advance if the proposed transaction specifically falls within one of these seven types.

The Code states, in § 368(a)(1), that the term *reorganization* applies to any of the following.

A. A statutory merger or consolidation.
B. The acquisition by a corporation of another using solely stock of each corporation (voting-stock-for-stock exchange).
C. The acquisition by a corporation of substantially all of the property of another corporation in exchange for voting stock (voting-stock-for-asset exchange).
D. The transfer of all or part of a corporation's assets to another corporation when the original corporation's shareholders are in control of the new corporation immediately after the transfer (divisive exchange, also known as a spin-off, split-off, or split-up).
E. A recapitalization.
F. A mere change in identity, form, or place of organization.
G. A transfer by a corporation of all or a part of its assets to another corporation in a bankruptcy or receivership proceeding.

These seven types of tax-free reorganizations typically are designated by their identifying letters: "Type A," "Type B," "Type C," and so on. Each will be described in more detail later in the chapter.

LO.2

Determine the tax consequences of a corporate reorganization.

SUMMARY OF TAX CONSEQUENCES IN A TAX-FREE REORGANIZATION

The tax treatment for the parties involved in a tax-free reorganization almost exactly parallels the treatment under the like-kind exchange provisions of § 1031. In the simplest like-kind exchange, neither gain nor loss is recognized on the exchange of "like-kind" property. When "boot" (defined as non-like-kind property) is received, gain may be recognized. The four-column template of Concept Summary 7.1 computes the amount of gain recognized and the adjusted basis in the new asset received in the like-kind exchange.

Unfortunately, the like-kind exchange provisions do not apply to the exchange of stock or securities.[5] Therefore, the general rule is that when an investor exchanges stock in one corporation for stock in another, the exchange is a taxable transaction. If the transaction qualifies as a reorganization under § 368, however, the exchange receives tax-deferred treatment. Thus, a § 368 reorganization, in substance, is similar to a nontaxable exchange of like-kind property, and the four-column template of Concept Summary 7.1 is useful for reorganizations as well.

[5] § 1031(a)(2)(B).

CONCEPT SUMMARY 7.1

Gain and Basis Rules for Nontaxable Exchanges

(1) Realized Gain/Loss	(2) Recognized Gain (Not Loss)	(3) Postponed Gain/Loss	(4) Basis of New Asset
Amount realized – Adjusted basis of asset(s) surrendered	Lesser of boot received or gain realized	Realized gain/loss (column 1) – Recognized gain (column 2)	FMV of asset (stock) received – Postponed gain (column 3) or + Postponed loss (column 3)
Realized gain/loss	Recognized gain	Postponed gain/loss	Adjusted basis in new asset (stock)

EXAMPLE 1

José holds 1,000 shares of Lotus stock that he purchased for $10,000 several years ago. In a merger of Lotus into Blossom, Inc., José exchanges his 1,000 Lotus shares for 1,000 Blossom shares. Both investments are valued at $18 per share. Thus, José's stock is valued at $18,000($18 per share × 1,000 shares). Assuming that this exchange qualifies for tax-free treatment under § 368, José's recognized gain and basis in his Blossom stock are computed as follows.

Realized Gain	Recognized Gain	Postponed Gain	Basis in Blossom Stock
$18,000	$-0-	$8,000	$18,000
– 10,000			– 8,000
$ 8,000			$10,000

The exchange of José's stock has no tax consequences for Lotus or Blossom. ■

Gain or Loss

Corporations meeting the § 368 requirements do not recognize gain or loss on a restructuring. There are exceptions to the nonrecognition rule, however. If the acquiring corporation transfers property to the target corporation along with its stock and securities, gain, but not loss, may be recognized. When the target receives other property (called *boot*) in the restructuring and fails to distribute it, or distributes its own appreciated property to its shareholders, gain, but not loss, is recognized. *Other property* for restructurings is any asset other than stock or securities and, thus, is treated as boot.[6]

EXAMPLE 2

In a qualifying reorganization, Acquiring Corporation exchanges $800,000 of stock and land with a $200,000 fair market value and a $150,000 basis for all of Target Corporation's assets, which have a $1 million fair market value and a $600,000 basis. Due to the *other property* (land) it used in the transfer, Acquiring recognizes a $50,000 gain ($200,000 – $150,000) on the reorganization. If Target distributes the land to its shareholders, it does not recognize gain. If Target retains the land, however, it recognizes gain to the extent of the *other property* received, $200,000. ■

Generally, the shareholders of corporations involved in a tax-free reorganization do not recognize gain or loss when exchanging their stock unless they receive cash or other property in addition to stock. The cash or other property is considered boot, and the gain recognized by the stockholder is the lesser of the boot received or the realized gain. This is analogous to the treatment of boot in a like-kind exchange.

[6]§§ 361(a) and (b).

GLOBAL Tax Issues

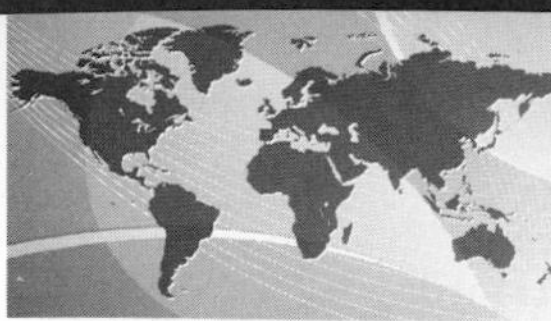

Mining M&As Are Good as Gold

When the economy is weak, gold is strong. And when gold is strong, merger and acquisition (M&A) activity spikes in the mining industry. Currently, the gold mining industry is undergoing a remarkable consolidation. Globally, M&A activity for this sector topped $60 billion in 2010, accounting for more than 38 percent of all M&A mining deals for the year.

China, Australia, South Africa, the United States, Russia, and Peru are the world's largest gold producers. Together, they account for almost 50 percent of the global total. At one time, South Africa produced more than 50 percent of the total, and Africa continues to be a magnet for mining companies. Barrick Gold Corporation (the world's largest gold producer), its spin-off, African Barrick Gold, and Kinross Gold, Newcrest Mining, KazakhGold, and Newmont Mining are all major players in the current gold M&A mania.

One of the fuels for this M&A activity is the diminishing likelihood of discovering new gold deposits that are economically feasible. With the amount of gold on the planet finite and the demand for gold increasing, mining corporations are using M&A activities to add to their reserves. Using this method, a company can concentrate its capital on extracting from proven mines rather than on risky prospecting for new gold fields, which is becoming increasingly more expensive.

Sources: Liezel Hill, "African Barrick Looking in West, North-East Africa for Potential M&A," *miningweekly.com*, October 29, 2010; and Scott Wright (Zeal Intelligence, LLC), "Gold Mining M&A," October 29, 2010.

The only instance when shareholders may recognize losses in reorganizations is when they receive solely boot and no stock.

EXAMPLE 3

Kalla, the sole shareholder of Target Corporation in Example 2, has a $700,000 basis in her stock. She exchanges her Target stock for the $800,000 of Acquiring stock plus the land ($200,000) transferred by Acquiring to Target. Kalla has a $200,000 recognized gain due to receiving the land (boot). The computations are as follows.

Realized Gain	Recognized Gain	Postponed Gain	Basis in Acquiring Stock
$1,000,000*	$200,000	$100,000	$800,000
− 700,000			−100,000
$ 300,000			$700,000

* $800,000 stock + $200,000 land. ■

Once the gain is recognized, its character must be determined. The following are the possibilities for gain characterization.

- Dividend to the extent of the shareholder's proportionate share of a positive balance in the corporation's earnings and profits (E & P). The remaining gain is generally capital gain.
  - *The distinction between dividends and long-term capital gain is important when the taxpayer has capital losses to offset, or when the capital gain would be classified as short term and therefore not subject to the special tax rates.*
- If the requirements of § 302(b) can be met, the transaction will qualify for stock redemption treatment (see Chapter 6).

A White Knight Turns Black

Retail Corporation is a small regional chain of upscale clothing stores. As business casual has become the accepted dress for professionals, Retail has become very profitable. Consequently, it has substantial liquid assets and few liabilities. Retail is so encouraged by its profitability that it is considering becoming a national chain.

Retail's success has not gone unnoticed in the marketplace. Mega Corporation, a privately owned conglomerate, makes an unsolicited tender offer for the Retail stock. In the past, Mega has made such offers for other small corporations with substantial liquid assets. Once it owns enough stock to take control of the board of directors, Mega forces the liquidation of the company to obtain its liquid assets. Therefore, Retail is very concerned about Mega's tender offer. To avoid being taken over by Mega, Retail negotiates with Cotton Corporation, one of its suppliers, for a merger of the two companies. Cotton is fully aware of the dangers faced by Retail as it was the target of an unsuccessful takeover by Mega in the past. It was rescued from the takeover by a similar "white knight" merger with one of its competitors.

Through an informer at Cotton, Mega discovers Retail's plan to foil its hostile takeover. To sabotage the Retail-Cotton merger, Mega offers Cotton an exclusive contract for producing its line of children's school clothes for Mega's national chain of discount department stores. The contract requires that Cotton not be affiliated with any other corporation in the retail clothing business. Cotton's directors believe this contract could boost profits by 20 percent. Therefore, the board votes to enter into the contract with Mega and abandon its merger negotiations with Retail. Retail ultimately is taken over by Mega and liquidated. All of its 1,000 employees lose their jobs. What ethical issues, if any, did Cotton's directors face in their dealings with Mega and Retail?

- *Gains from qualifying stock redemptions are treated as capital gains.*
- *In computing the shareholder's ownership reduction, shares actually received in the acquiring corporation are compared with the number of shares the shareholder would have received if solely the acquiring corporation's stock had been distributed in the reorganization.*[7]

EXAMPLE 4
THE BIG PICTURE

Return to the facts of *The Big Picture* on p. 7-2. R&W proceeds with its acquisition of BrineCo. Sam acquired a 30% interest in BrineCo 15 years ago for $80,000. He exchanges his BrineCo stock for $25,000 cash and stock in R&W worth $125,000. At the time of the reorganization, BrineCo's E & P is $50,000. Sam has a $70,000 realized gain ($150,000 cash and stock received − $80,000 BrineCo stock basis) and a $25,000 recognized gain (cash boot received). The first $15,000 ($50,000 BrineCo E & P × 30%) is taxable as a dividend, and the remaining $10,000 is treated as capital gain. Both are taxed at special tax rates.

Suppose instead that Sam receives 10% of the R&W stock with a $100,000 fair market value and $50,000 cash. If Sam had received solely stock, he would have received 15% of the R&W stock. Since Sam owns less than 80% of the stock he would have owned if solely stock had been distributed (10% ÷ 15% is 67%) and less than 50% of R&W, he qualifies for sale or exchange treatment under § 302(b)(2). Therefore, Sam's $50,000 recognized gain is a long-term capital gain. ■

Debt security holders receive treatment similar to shareholders. They recognize gain only when the principal (face) amount of the securities received is greater than the principal (face) amount of the securities surrendered. If securities are received and none are relinquished, gain will be recognized.

The term *security* is not defined in the Code or the Regulations. Generally, however, debt instruments with terms longer than 10 years (e.g., bonds) are treated as securities, and those with terms of 5 years or less (e.g., notes) are not. An exception to this general rule occurs when the debt instrument issued by the acquiring corporation is exchanged for target securities having the same term and/or maturity date.[8]

[7] *Comm. v. Clark*, 89–1 USTC ¶9230, 63 AFTR 2d 89–860, 109 S.Ct. 1455 (USSC, 1989), and Rev.Rul. 93–61, 1993–2 C.B. 118.

[8] Rev.Rul. 2004–78, 2004–2 C.B. 108.

CONCEPT SUMMARY 7.2

Basis Rules for a Tax-Free Reorganization

Basis to Acquiring Corporation of Property Received	
Target's basis in property transferred	$xx,xxx
Plus: Gain recognized by target on the transaction	x,xxx
Equals: Basis of property to acquiring corporation	$xx,xxx

Basis to Target Shareholders of Stock and Securities Received	
Basis of stock and securities transferred	$xx,xxx
Plus: Gain and dividend income recognized	x,xxx
Minus: Money and fair market value of other property received	(x,xxx)
Equals: Basis of stock and securities received	$xx,xxx

EXAMPLE 5

Alejandra holds a debt instrument from Hibiscus Corporation. The debt's principal value is $10,000, and its maturity date is December 31, 2014. In connection with the merger of Hibiscus and Tea Corporation, Alejandra exchanges her Hibiscus debt for a $10,000 Tea note that matures on December 31, 2014. Even though these notes do not have a term remaining of more than five years, they qualify for tax-free reorganization treatment because they have the same term. ■

EXAMPLE 6

Assume the same facts as in Example 5, except that in exchange for her $10,000 debt instrument, Alejandra receives a note from Tea with a $15,000 principal value. Alejandra recognizes a $5,000 capital gain on the exchange. ■

Basis

The assets transferred from the target corporation to the acquiring corporation retain their basis. The acquiring corporation's carryover basis is increased by any gain recognized by the target corporation on the reorganization. Concept Summary 7.2 shows this computation.

EXAMPLE 7

Target exchanges its assets with a $5 million fair market value and a $3 million basis for $4.5 million of Acquiring stock and $500,000 of land. Target does not distribute the land to its shareholders. Target recognizes a $500,000 gain on the reorganization (due to the other property not being distributed). Acquiring's basis in the assets received from Target is $3.5 million [$3,000,000 (Target's basis) + $500,000 (Target's gain recognized)]. ■

The tax basis of the stock and securities received by a shareholder pursuant to a tax-free reorganization generally is the same as the basis of those surrendered. This basis is decreased by the fair market value of boot received and increased by the gain and/or dividend income recognized on the transaction. Concept Summary 7.2 provides a summary of these calculations. Another way to compute the basis in the stock and securities received, using the Concept Summary 7.1 template, is to subtract the gain (or add the loss) postponed from the fair market value of the

CONCEPT SUMMARY 7.3

Tax Consequences of Tax-Free Reorganizations

Treatment is similar to like-kind exchanges.

- No gain or loss is recognized by the acquiring or target corporation unless other property (i.e., boot) is transferred or received by any parties to the reorganization.
- Basis in the assets received by the acquiring corporation is generally carried over from the target corporation.
- The stock received by the target corporation's shareholders takes a substituted basis, derived from their target stock basis.
- Gain, but not loss, may be recognized when boot is transferred by the acquiring corporation.
- Gain, but not loss, may be recognized when the target corporation receives boot and does not distribute the boot to its shareholders.
- Gain, but not loss, may be recognized when target shareholders receive anything other than stock (i.e., boot) in exchange for their target stock.

stock and securities received. This basis computation ensures that the postponed gain or loss will be recognized when the new stock or securities are disposed of in a taxable transaction.

EXAMPLE 8

Quinn exchanges all of his Target Corporation stock for Acquiring Corporation stock plus $3,000 cash. The exchange is pursuant to a tax-free reorganization. Quinn paid $10,000 for the Target stock two years ago. The Acquiring stock received by Quinn has a $12,000 fair market value. Quinn has a $5,000 realized gain, which is recognized to the extent of the boot received, $3,000. Quinn's basis in the Acquiring stock is $10,000. This can be computed as follows.

Realized Gain	Recognized Gain	Postponed Gain	Basis in Acquiring Stock
$15,000*	$3,000	$2,000	$12,000
−10,000			−2,000
$ 5,000			$10,000

* $12,000 stock + $3,000 cash. ■

EXAMPLE 9

Assume the same facts as in Example 8, except that Quinn's Target stock basis was $16,000. Quinn realizes a $1,000 loss on the exchange, none of which is recognized. His basis in the Acquiring stock is $13,000, computed as follows.

Realized Gain	Recognized Loss	Postponed Loss	Basis in Acquiring Stock
$15,000*	$−0−	($1,000)	$12,000
− 16,000			+ 1,000
($ 1,000)			$13,000

* $12,000 stock + $3,000 cash. ■

Concept Summary 7.3 reviews the tax consequences for tax-free reorganizations.

7.2 Types of Tax-Free Reorganizations

LO.3

Explain the statutory requirements for the different types of reorganizations.

TYPE A

"Type A" reorganizations can be classified as either mergers or consolidations. A **merger** is the union of two or more corporations, with one of the corporations retaining its corporate existence and absorbing the others. The other corporations cease to exist by operation of law. A **consolidation** occurs when a new corporation is created to take the place of two or more corporations. The "Type A" reorganizations are illustrated in Figure 7.1. To qualify as a "Type A" reorganization, mergers and consolidations must comply with the requirements of foreign, state, or Federal statutes.

EXAMPLE 10

Acquiring Corporation obtains all the assets of Target Corporation, a French corporation, in exchange for 5,000 shares of Acquiring stock. Target is liquidated by distributing the Acquiring stock to its shareholders in exchange for their shares in Target. All French law requirements are met. This transaction qualifies as a "Type A" statutory merger. ■

EXAMPLE 11
THE BIG PICTURE

Return to the facts of *The Big Picture* on p. 7-2. The Rock & Water Corporation (R&W) formation occurred as follows. Roca and Agua Corporations were united under state law into new R&W Corporation by transferring all of their assets to R&W in exchange for all of R&W's stock. By operation of state law, Roca and Agua liquidated by distributing R&W stock to their shareholders in exchange for the shareholders' stock in Roca and Agua. This "Type A" reorganization is a consolidation. ■

Advantages and Disadvantages

The "Type A" reorganization allows more flexibility than the other types of reorganizations.

- Unlike both "Type B" and "Type C" reorganizations, the acquiring stock transferred to the target need not be voting stock.
- The acquiring corporation can transfer money or other property to the target corporation without destroying tax-free treatment for the stock also exchanged.
  - *Money or other property, however, constitutes boot and may cause gain recognition by the acquiring corporation, the target, and/or the target's shareholders.*
- When consideration other than stock is given by the acquiring corporation, care must be taken not to run afoul of the **continuity of interest test**.
  - *This test, promulgated by the courts and the Treasury, requires that the consideration given by the acquiring corporation be a substantial proprietary interest, i.e., at least 40 percent stock.*[9]
- There is no requirement that "substantially all" of the target's assets be transferred to the acquiring corporation as in a "Type C" reorganization.
  - *Thus, the target can sell or otherwise dispose of assets not desired by the acquiring corporation without affecting the tax-free nature of the restructuring.*

A "Type A" is not without its disadvantages.

- Each corporation involved in the restructuring must obtain the approval of the majority of its shareholders.
- In almost every state, dissenting shareholders can require that their shares be appraised and purchased.
  - *Meeting the demands of objecting shareholders can become so cumbersome and expensive that the parties may be forced to abandon the "Type A" reorganization.*
- The acquiring corporation must assume *all* liabilities (including unknown and contingent liabilities) of the target corporation as a matter of state law.

[9]Prop.Reg. 146247–06, 2007–1 C.B. 977 (TD 9316); Ltr. Rul. 200610007; Notice 2010–25, 2010–14 I.R.B. 527.

FIGURE 7.1 "Type A" Reorganization

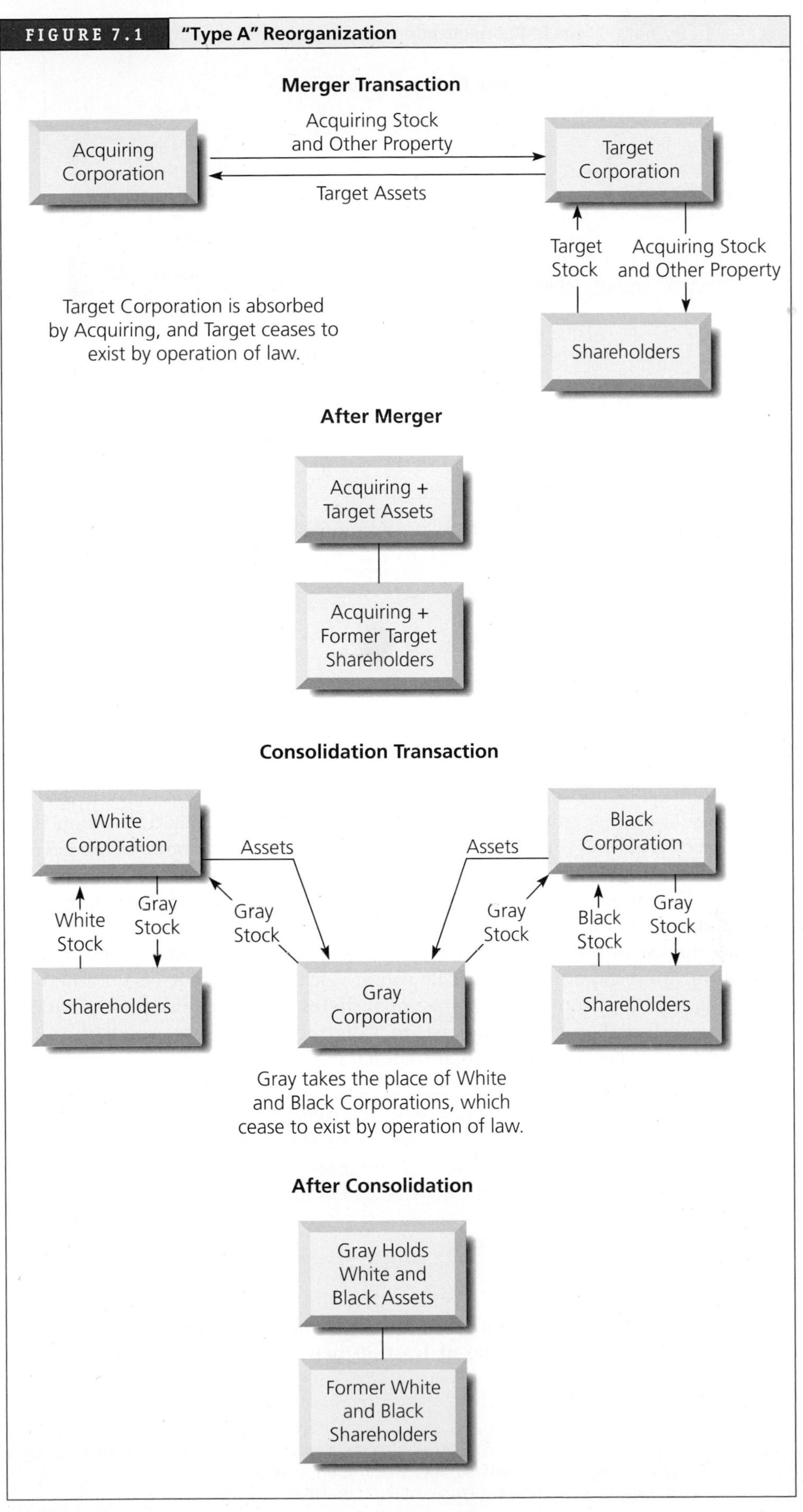
Merger Transaction
Acquiring Corporation
Acquiring Stock and Other Property
Target Assets
Target Corporation
Target Stock
Acquiring Stock and Other Property
Shareholders
Target Corporation is absorbed by Acquiring, and Target ceases to exist by operation of law.
After Merger
Acquiring + Target Assets
Acquiring + Former Target Shareholders
Consolidation Transaction
White Corporation
Assets
Assets
Black Corporation
White Stock
Gray Stock
Gray Stock
Gray Stock
Black Stock
Gray Stock
Shareholders
Gray Corporation
Shareholders
Gray takes the place of White and Black Corporations, which cease to exist by operation of law.
After Consolidation
Gray Holds White and Black Assets
Former White and Black Shareholders

FIGURE 7.2 "Type B" Reorganization

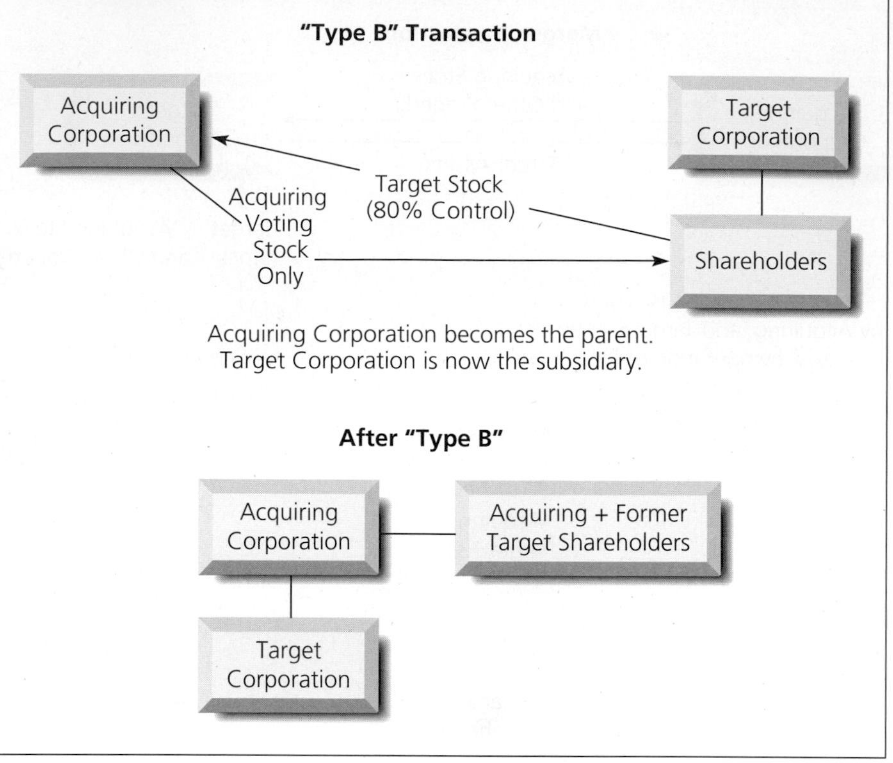

TYPE B

In a "Type B" reorganization, the acquiring corporation obtains "control" of the target corporation in an exchange involving solely stock. Both corporations survive and a parent-subsidiary relationship is created. In simple terms, this transaction is an exchange of acquiring voting stock for target stock. Voting stock must be the *sole* consideration given by the acquiring corporation,[10] a requirement that is strictly construed.[11] The target's stock relinquished in the transaction may be common or preferred, voting or nonvoting.

Since the use of boot is precluded, gain is never recognized in a "Type B" reorganization. An exception to the solely voting stock requirement occurs when the target shareholders would receive fractional shares of the acquiring corporation's stock. Cash rather than fractional shares of acquiring stock may be paid to the target shareholders.[12] The "Type B" reorganization is illustrated in Figure 7.2.

EXAMPLE 12
THE BIG PICTURE

Return to the facts of *The Big Picture* on p. 7-2. R&W Corporation proceeds with the acquisition of AcidCo. In the transaction between R&W and AcidCo shareholders, 20% of R&W voting stock is exchanged for 90% of all classes of stock in AcidCo. The exchange qualifies as a "Type B" reorganization. R&W becomes the parent of AcidCo. ■

Control Requirements

The "Type B" reorganization requires that the acquiring corporation be in "control" of the target corporation immediately after the reorganization. **Control** for this purpose requires owning at least 80 percent of all classes of the target

[10] The exchange of the acquiring corporation's bonds for the target's bonds may be considered a separate and distinct transaction from a "Type B" reorganization according to Rev.Rul. 98–10, 1998–1 C.B. 643. Consequently, this exchange will not affect an otherwise qualifying "Type B" reorganization.

[11] *A. S. Heverly v. Comm.*, 80–1 USTC ¶9322, 45 AFTR 2d 80–1122, 621 F.2d 1227 (CA–3, 1980), and *E. S. Chapman v. Comm.*, 80–1 USTC ¶9330, 45 AFTR 2d 80–1290, 618 F.2d 856 (CA–1, 1980).

[12] Rev.Rul. 66–365, 1966–2 C.B. 116.

FINANCIAL DISCLOSURE *Insights*

Creating the King of Sweets

In 2008, two of the largest candy companies united to become the Sugar King. Publicly held William Wrigley Jr. Company became a subsidiary of privately held Mars, Inc., when Mars paid approximately $23 billion for 100 percent of the Wrigley stock. After the acquisition, Wrigley was no longer a listed company. The acquisition was backed by Goldman Sachs, and Warren Buffett's Berkshire Hathaway Corporation became a minority shareholder in Mars as part of the financing. Although all of the shareholders recognized gains on the sale of their Wrigley stock, neither Mars nor Wrigley had any gain or loss recognition. Since Wrigley continues to exist, there was no change in the tax basis of its assets. Thus, Wrigley is essentially the same; it just has different shareholders.

The transaction was designed as a sale so that Mars could remain a privately held company. If Mars instead had used its voting stock to acquire the Wrigley stock, the deal would have qualified as a "Type B" voting stock-for-stock reorganization. The resulting organizational structure would have been the same as in the taxable transaction—a parent-subsidiary relationship. With a "Type B," the only difference is that the Wrigley shareholders would not have recognized any gain. Wrigley and Mars would have the same treatment, and Wrigley's assets would take the same carryover basis as in the taxable transaction.

What is the financial accounting treatment for this transaction? Even though Wrigley is a subsidiary of Mars, the acquisition method of accounting treats this transaction as if Mars had purchased Wrigley's assets. Thus, every asset was stepped up or down to its fair value at the time of the transaction. If Mars paid more for the assets than their individual fair values, the excess created a goodwill asset. On the other hand, if Mars paid less than the fair value of the assets, Mars had a bargain purchase. The excess of the fair value of the assets over the amount paid would have been recognized as income! This result is very different from the tax outcome where Wrigley and Mars recognized no gain or loss and the basis in Wrigley's assets remains the same as before the restructuring.

corporation's stock. The 80 percent-control-after-reorganization requirement does not mean that all 80 percent must be "acquired" in the restructuring transaction. Stock previously purchased in separate transactions can be counted in determining the 80 percent ownership.[13] Further, the stock may be acquired from the shareholders directly or from the target corporation.

EXAMPLE 13

Acquiring Corporation purchased 30% of Target's stock for cash six years ago. It acquires another 55% in the current year by exchanging its voting stock with Target's shareholders. Thus, even though some of the Target shares were acquired with cash, the "Type B" requirements are satisfied through the current 55% exchange.

What if Acquiring Corporation purchased 30% of Target's stock for cash three months ago? Now the acquisition of the additional 55% of Target's stock for voting stock seems to be part of a two-step transaction. The acquisition of the remaining stock for voting stock is probably not tax-free due to the step transaction doctrine. ■

Disadvantages and Advantages

The solely voting stock consideration requirement is a substantial disadvantage of the "Type B" reorganization. Another disadvantage is that if the acquiring corporation does not obtain 100 percent control of the target corporation, problems may arise with the minority interest remaining in the target.

Nevertheless, the voting-stock-for-stock acquisition has the advantage of simplicity. Generally, the target corporation's shareholders act individually in transferring their stock to the acquiring corporation. Thus, the target corporation itself and the acquiring corporation's shareholders are not directly involved as long as the acquiring corporation has sufficient treasury or unissued shares to effect the transaction.

[13] Reg. § 1.368–2(c).

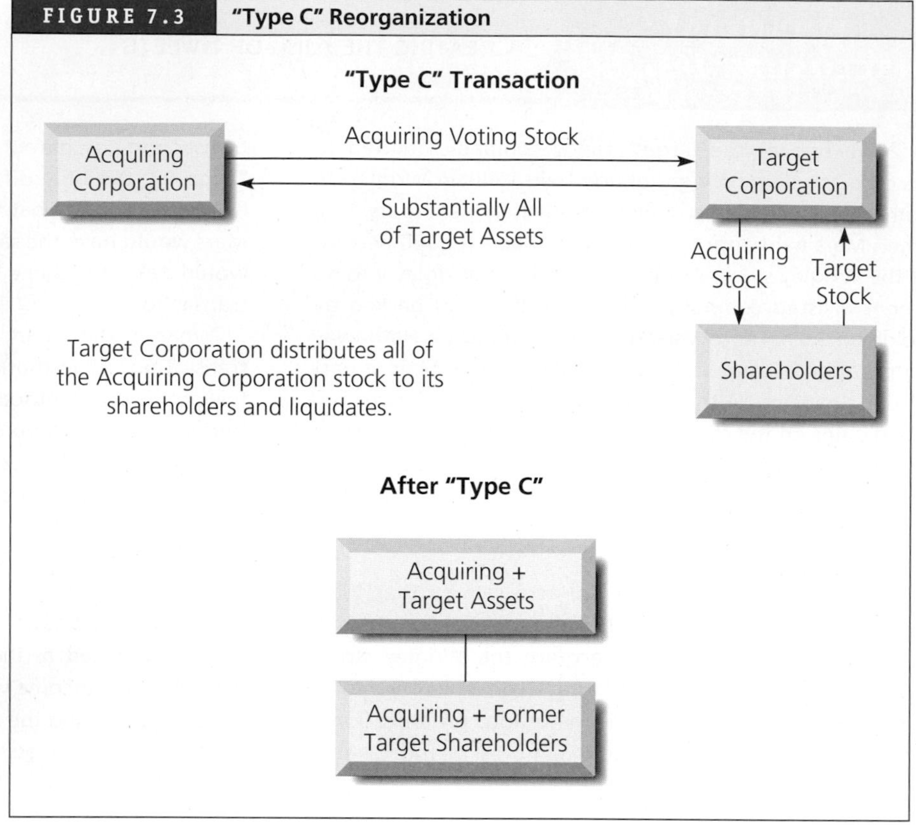

TYPE C

In the "Type C" reorganization, the acquiring corporation obtains substantially all of the target corporation's assets in exchange for acquiring voting stock and a limited amount of other property. The target corporation must distribute all assets received in the reorganization, as well as any of its own property retained. The target corporation then liquidates.[14] Thus, a "Type C" reorganization is essentially a voting-stock-for-assets exchange followed by liquidation of the target corporation. The exchange is a taxable transaction for the shareholders to the extent that they receive assets other than acquiring corporation stock. The "Type C" reorganization is illustrated in Figure 7.3.

EXAMPLE 14
THE BIG PICTURE

Return to the facts of *The Big Picture* on p. 7-2. R&W Corporation proceeds with the acquisition of ChemCo. R&W transfers voting stock representing a 30% ownership interest to ChemCo for substantially all of ChemCo's assets. After the exchange, ChemCo's only assets are cash and R&W voting stock. ChemCo distributes the R&W stock and cash to its shareholders in exchange for their ChemCo stock. The exchange qualifies as a "Type C" reorganization if ChemCo liquidates after the distribution. The exchange is taxable to the shareholders to the extent of the cash they received. ■

"Type A" and "Type C" Reorganizations Compared

A "Type C" reorganization's outcome is similar to that of a "Type A" merger, as can be seen by comparing the diagrams for these reorganizations (Figure 7.3 versus Figure 7.1). However, their requirements differ. A "Type C" has more restrictions regarding the consideration that may be used by the acquiring corporation. Nevertheless, the "Type C" can be preferable to the "Type A," because in the "Type C" the acquiring corporation assumes only the target liabilities for which it negotiates. Normally, the acquiring corporation is not liable for unknown or contingent

[14] Distributions may be to creditors as well as to shareholders. § 368(a)(2)(G).

liabilities of the target. Thus, when the target liquidates, the unknown liabilities become the responsibility of the former target shareholders, causing them additional risks.[15] Lastly, in many states, the restructuring only needs to be approved by a majority of the target shareholders. Thus, unlike in a "Type A" merger, the acquiring shareholders' vote of approval is not necessary for the restructuring.

Consideration in the "Type C" Reorganization

The acquiring corporation's consideration in a "Type C" reorganization normally consists of voting stock. However, there are exceptions to this rule. Cash and other property do not destroy a "Type C" reorganization if at least 80 percent of the fair market value of the target's property is obtained with voting stock.

Although the acquiring corporation has more freedom in the consideration given in a "Type C" than in a "Type B," this freedom is not without a cost. When the acquiring corporation gives solely voting stock for the target corporation's assets, the target corporation's liabilities assumed by the acquiring corporation are not considered *other property* (i.e., boot) in the exchange.[16] The transaction is a voting-stock-for-assets exchange, and the 80 percent-of-property requirement is met. However, liabilities assumed by the acquiring corporation *are* treated as *other property* if the target corporation receives any property other than voting stock in the reorganization.[17] Target liabilities assumed by the acquiring corporation are likely to exceed 20 percent of the fair market value of the target assets acquired and, consequently, destroy the "Type C" reorganization.

EXAMPLE 15

Target Corporation exchanges $850,000 assets and a $250,000 liability for Acquiring stock worth $600,000. Target distributes the stock to its shareholders and liquidates. The transaction qualifies as a "Type C" reorganization. The liability is not treated as *other property* received. Acquiring obtained 100% of Target's assets for voting stock. The liability assumed by Acquiring is disregarded as boot in this situation.

Suppose that Target Corporation exchanged its $850,000 assets and $250,000 liability for Acquiring stock worth $590,000 and $10,000 in cash. The liability now is considered *other property* because Target also received cash. *Other property* amounts to $260,000, which exceeds 20% of the fair market value of Target's assets ($850,000 × 20% = $170,000). This transaction would not qualify as a "Type C" reorganization.

If Acquiring had given voting stock worth $800,000 and $50,000 in cash for all of Target's assets, the transaction would qualify as a "Type C" reorganization. No liabilities are assumed, and the *other property* transferred is less than 20% of the fair market value of the assets ($50,000 < $170,000). ■

The acquiring corporation's prior ownership of the target's stock will not prevent the transaction from meeting the "solely-for-voting-stock" requirement in a "Type C" reorganization. If the acquiring corporation purchased stock in the target corporation in an earlier unrelated transaction, the previously acquired stock will not be considered in determining whether 80 percent of the target's assets were obtained with the acquiring corporation's stock.[18]

EXAMPLE 16

Acquiring Corporation purchased 30% of Target Corporation's stock five years ago. In the current year, the fair market value of Target's assets is $1 million. Acquiring transfers $700,000 of its voting stock to Target in exchange for the 70% of Target's assets that Acquiring currently does not own. This qualifies as a "Type C" reorganization. The previous purchase of Target stock is not considered to be part of the reorganization transaction. Therefore, Acquiring is exchanging solely voting stock for 100% control over Target's assets. ■

[15] Byron F. Egan, "Acquisition Agreement Issues," 7th Annual Institute on Corporate, Securities, and Related Aspects of Mergers and Acquisitions, October 8, 2010.

[16] § 368(a)(1)(C).

[17] § 368(a)(2)(B).

[18] Reg. § 1.368–2(d).

Asset Transfers

The "Type C" reorganization requires that substantially all of the target corporation's assets be transferred to the acquiring corporation. However, there is no statutory definition of "substantially all." To receive a favorable IRS ruling, the target must transfer to the acquiring corporation at least 90 percent of its net asset value and 70 percent of its gross asset value.[19] Smaller percentages may qualify depending on the facts and circumstances of the reorganization.[20]

GIVING VOICE TO ETHICAL VALUES

Through a "Type C" reorganization, Blue I Corporation (a distributor of contact lenses) merged with I Glass Corporation (a distributor of eyeglasses). Blue I acquired all the assets ($1 million) and liabilities ($400,000) of I Glass for $600,000 of Blue I's common voting stock. The transaction was completed on June 1 of the current year. As a staff accountant with the firm preparing the first consolidated tax return for the combined entity, you find a document dated December of last year indicating that, in anticipation of the "Type C" reorganization, Blue I acquired 5 percent of I Glass's stock for cash. The stock was acquired from a shareholder who would have been against the merger. Considering this acquisition as part of the "Type C" reorganization would cause the liabilities to be considered boot, and the 80-percent-of-assets-for-voting-stock requirement would not be met.

You bring your findings to your manager, Joe Fitswaller. Joe has always been a good manager to work for, and you like him. That is why you are surprised when Joe tells you that what you have found is none of your concern. Besides, the IRS will never figure out what happened because the stock was acquired in a different tax year. As you discuss this issue with Joe, you realize that he already knew about the transaction before you brought it to his attention. On returning to your work, you find correspondence between Joe and Blue I regarding the December stock acquisition. You also discover that the shareholder from whom the stock was purchased is also named Fitswaller. You suspect that Joe is covering up this issue because he has given advice to Blue I to benefit his relative and has subjected the firm to possible liability for the taxes of Blue I's failed tax-free acquisition of I Glass. Joe will likely lose his job if the partners find out about this.

You know that you must tell the partner on the engagement about what you have found. The risk to the firm is just too great not to divulge this information. What would you write in a memo to the partner explaining what you have learned and the possible risks to the firm?

TYPE D

The first three types of tax-free corporate reorganizations are designed for corporate combinations. The "Type D" reorganization is different; it is generally used to effect a corporate division, called a "divisive" reorganization. However, the "Type D" can also be used to combine corporations—an "acquisitive" reorganization. In contrast with other restructurings, in the "Type D" acquisitive reorganization, the entity transferring assets is considered the acquiring corporation, and the corporation receiving the property is the target.

Acquisitive Type D Reorganization

If a combination meets the following requirements, it will be treated as a "Type D" reorganization.

- Substantially all of the acquiring corporation's property must be transferred to the target corporation.
- The acquiring corporation must be in control (at least 50 percent) of the target.[21]

[19] Rev.Proc. 77–37, 1977–2 C.B. 568, amplified by Rev.Proc. 86–42, 1986–2 C.B. 722

[20] Where 70% of the assets were transferred and 30% were retained to discharge the target's liabilities prior to liquidation, the IRS found that substantially all of the assets were transferred. Rev.Rul. 57–518, 1957–2 C.B. 253.

[21] No attribution of ownership is used in determining whether there is 50% control. §§ 368(a)(2)(H) and 304(c).

FIGURE 7.4 Acquisitive "Type D" Reorganization

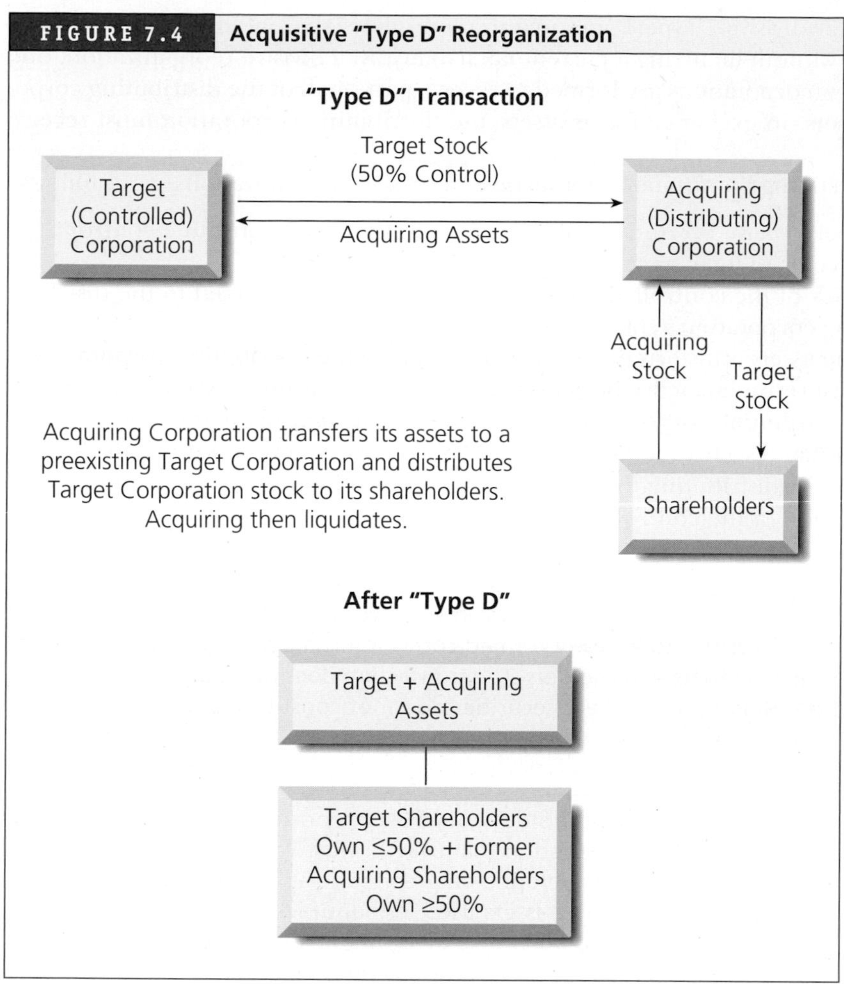

- Target stock received by the acquiring corporation, as well as any remaining assets of the acquiring corporation, must be distributed to its shareholders.
- The acquiring corporation must liquidate.

This type of transaction may also meet the "Type C" requirements (from the target's viewpoint). If the transaction can be classified as both a "Type C" and a "Type D" reorganization, it is treated as a "Type D" reorganization.[22] The "Type D" acquisitive reorganization is diagrammed in Figure 7.4. A comparison of Figure 7.4 with Figure 7.3 will illustrate how a "Type D" may also qualify as a "Type C" reorganization.

EXAMPLE 17

Acquiring Corporation wishes to control Target Corporation ($300,000 value), but Target holds a nontransferable license. Thus, Target must be the surviving corporation. Acquiring transfers all its assets valued at $700,000 to Target for 70% of Target's stock. Acquiring then distributes all the Target stock to its shareholders in exchange for their Acquiring stock and liquidates. The transaction qualifies as a "Type D" reorganization. ■

Divisive Type D Reorganization

Rather than combining, shareholders may wish to divide the corporation by distributing its assets among two or more corporations. This might occur for many reasons including antitrust problems, differences of opinion among the shareholders, product liability concerns, increasing shareholder value, or family tax planning. The

[22]Reg. § 1.368–2(d)(3).

more typical divisive "Type D" reorganization allows shareholders to accomplish their goals without incurring a current tax liability. In a divisive reorganization, one or more new corporations are formed to receive part or all of the distributing corporation's assets. In exchange for its assets, the distributing corporation must receive stock.

The remaining requirements for divisive "Type D" reorganizations are as follows.

- The stock received by the distributing corporation must constitute control (80 percent) of the new corporation(s).
- The stock of the controlled corporation(s) must be transferred to the distributing corporation's shareholders.
- Both the assets transferred and those retained by the distributing corporation must represent active businesses that have been owned and conducted by the distributing corporation for at least five years before the transfer.
- The stock and securities transfers to the shareholders cannot be principally a device for distributing the earnings and profits of either the distributing corporation or the controlled corporation(s).[23]

EXAMPLE 18

Bell is a manufacturing corporation. It also owns investment securities. Bell transfers the investment securities to a newly formed corporation and distributes the stock of the new corporation to its shareholders. The transaction does not qualify as a "Type D" reorganization. Holding investment securities does not constitute a trade or business. The Bell shareholders are taxed on the stock they receive. ■

EXAMPLE 19

Jane and Ivan are the sole shareholders of WB Corporation. WB was organized 10 years ago and is actively engaged in manufacturing two products, widgets and bolts. Considerable friction has developed between Jane and Ivan, who now wish to divide the business. Jane wants the assets used in manufacturing widgets, and Ivan wants to continue manufacturing bolts. The division of the business assets between the shareholders can be accomplished tax-free using one of the divisive "Type D" reorganizations. ■

EXAMPLE 20

Cube, Inc., has manufactured a single product at two plants for the past 10 years. It transfers one plant and related activities to a new corporation, Square, Inc. Cube then distributes the Square stock to its shareholders. Each plant's activities constitute a trade or business. The transaction qualifies as a "Type D" reorganization. ■

Spin-Offs, Split-Offs, and Split-Ups

There are three different types of divisive "Type D" reorganizations: spin-offs, split-offs, and split-ups.

- In a **spin-off**, a new corporation is formed to receive some of the distributing corporation's assets in exchange for the new corporation's stock.[24] The distributing corporation's shareholders receive the new corporation's stock without surrendering any of their distributing corporation stock. The shareholders' basis in their distributing corporation stock is allocated between the distributing corporation stock and the new stock, based on the relative fair market value of each.
- A **split-off** resembles a spin-off except that in a split-off the shareholders surrender distributing corporation stock in exchange for stock in the new corporation. Stock basis is computed in the same manner as for a spin-off.
- In a **split-up**, two or more new corporations are formed to receive substantially all of the distributing corporation's assets. The stock of each new corporation is exchanged for the distributing corporation stock. The

[23] § 355(a)(1)(B) and Reg. § 1.355–2(b)(4).

[24] An existing corporation can be the target instead of a new corporation.

distributing corporation is then liquidated. The shareholders' basis in the relinquished distributing corporation stock carries over as the basis of stock in the new corporations.

The spin-off and split-off are illustrated in Figure 7.5, and the split-up is illustrated in Figure 7.6.

EXAMPLE 21

Shawnee purchased 10% (500 shares) of DistributingCo eight years ago for $60,000. Before the spin-off reorganization, DistributingCo's stock value was $900,000, and Shawnee's shares were valued at $90,000, or $180 per share ($90,000 ÷ 500 shares). DistributingCo spins off 30% of its business assets into NewCo (fair value $270,000) and distributes 10,000 shares of NewCo stock to its shareholders. Shawnee's 1,000 NewCo shares are worth $27,000. After the spin-off, the value of DistributingCo is reduced to $630,000, and therefore the value of Shawnee's stock in DistributingCo is $63,000. Shawnee's $60,000 beginning basis in DistributingCo is allocated to the two companies' stock as follows: $18,000 to NewCo stock [$60,000 × ($27,000/$90,000)] and $42,000 to DistributingCo stock [$60,000 × ($63,000/$90,000)]. ■

EXAMPLE 22

Assume the same facts as in Example 21, except that DistributingCo creates NewCo through a split-off. Shawnee is required to surrender 30% of her DistributingCo stock (150 shares) to receive the 1,000 NewCo shares. Shawnee's 350 DistributingCo shares (500 − 150) now have a value of $63,000 ($180 × 350), and her NewCo stock is worth $27,000 ($90,000 − $63,000). Shawnee's $60,000 beginning basis in DistributingCo is allocated to the two companies' stock as follows: $42,000 to the DistributingCo stock [$60,000 × ($63,000/$90,000)] and $18,000 to the 1,000 NewCo shares [$60,000 × ($27,000/$90,000)]. ■

EXAMPLE 23
THE BIG PICTURE

Return to the facts of *The Big Picture* on p. 7-2. R&W Corporation proceeds with its acquisition of AcidCo. Gail and Gary are equal shareholders of AcidCo, which was organized six years ago. To prepare for the restructuring transaction with R&W, AcidCo creates two new corporations to receive its business lines. AbraseCo will receive all of the assets related to the landscaping chemical business. These are the assets desired by R&W. The remaining mining acid assets are transferred to MineCo.

The AbraseCo and MineCo stock received in exchange for AcidCo's assets is transferred equally to Gary and Gail in exchange for all of their shares in AcidCo. Gail and Gary now are 100% owners of both AbraseCo and MineCo. Having no assets, AcidCo liquidates.

This transaction qualifies as a "Type D" split-up. Neither Gary nor Gail recognizes any gain or loss on the exchange. Gary and Gail take a basis in the AcidCo stock equal to their basis in the stock of AbraseCo and MineCo. The allocation between AbraseCo and MineCo is performed in the manner utilized in Examples 21 and 22. ■

TYPE E

The "Type E" reorganization is a **recapitalization**—a major change in the character and amount of outstanding capital stock, securities, or paid-in capital of a corporation. The transaction is significant only for the stock- or bondholders who exchange their equity or securities. Since no property, stocks, or bonds are exchanged with another corporation, the "Type E" reorganization has no tax implications for the corporation involved. Further, transactions in a corporation's own stock or bonds are not taxable events.[25]

The following types of exchanges qualify for nonrecognition treatment as "Type E" reorganizations: bonds for stock, stock for stock, and bonds for bonds. A corporation can exchange its common stock for preferred stock or its preferred stock for common stock tax-free. The exchange of bonds for other bonds is tax-free when the principal (face) amount of the debt received is not more than the surrendered debt's principal (face) amount.

[25]Reg. §§ 1.1032–1(a) and (c).

FIGURE 7.5 "Type D" Reorganizations: Spin-Off and Split-Off

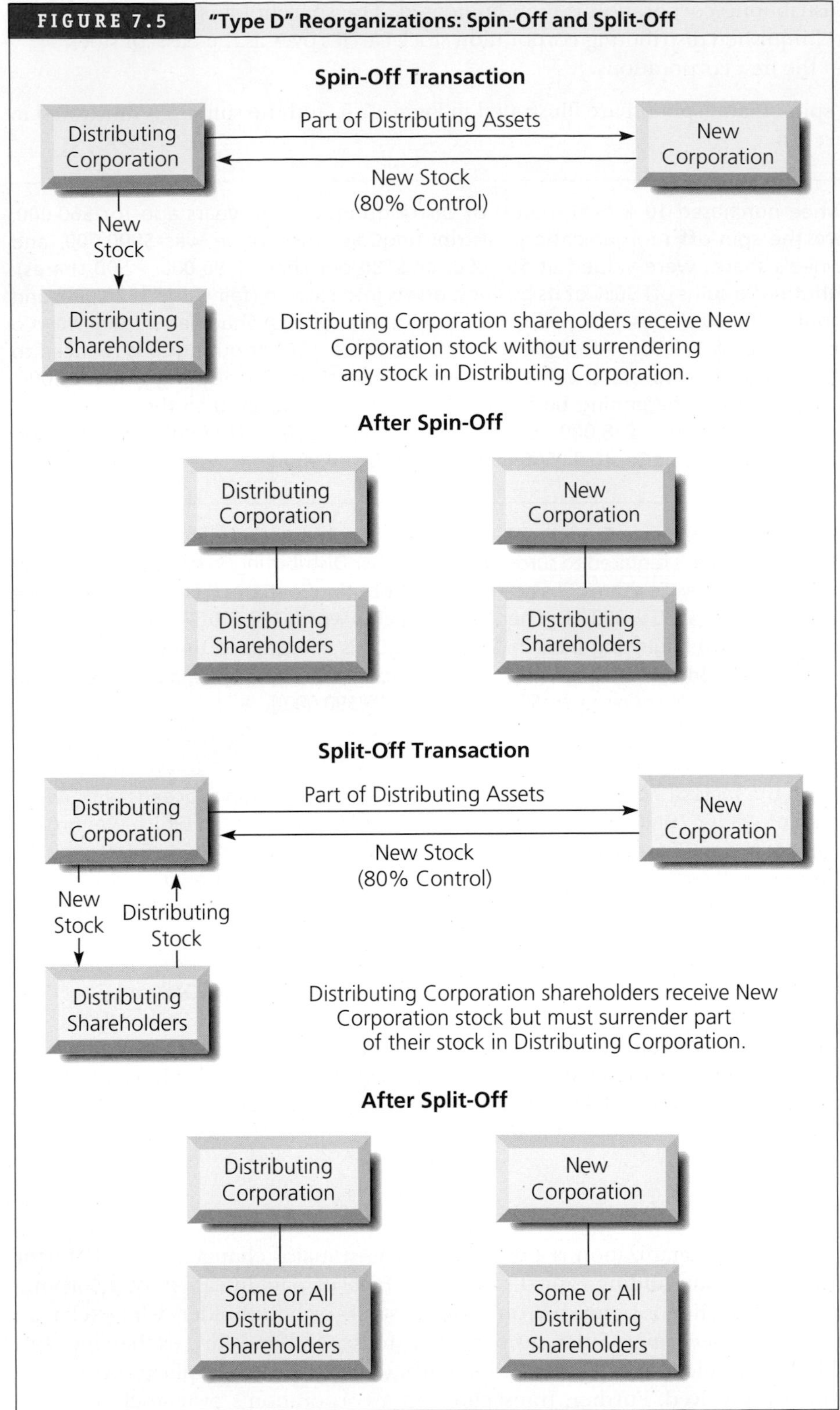

EXAMPLE 24

All of Mesquite Corporation's bondholders exchange their $1,000, 3% interest-bearing bonds for $1,000, 4% interest-bearing bonds. This qualifies as a "Type E" reorganization because the surrendered bonds' face amount is equal to the face amount of the bonds received. ■

FIGURE 7.6 "Type D" Reorganization: Split-Up

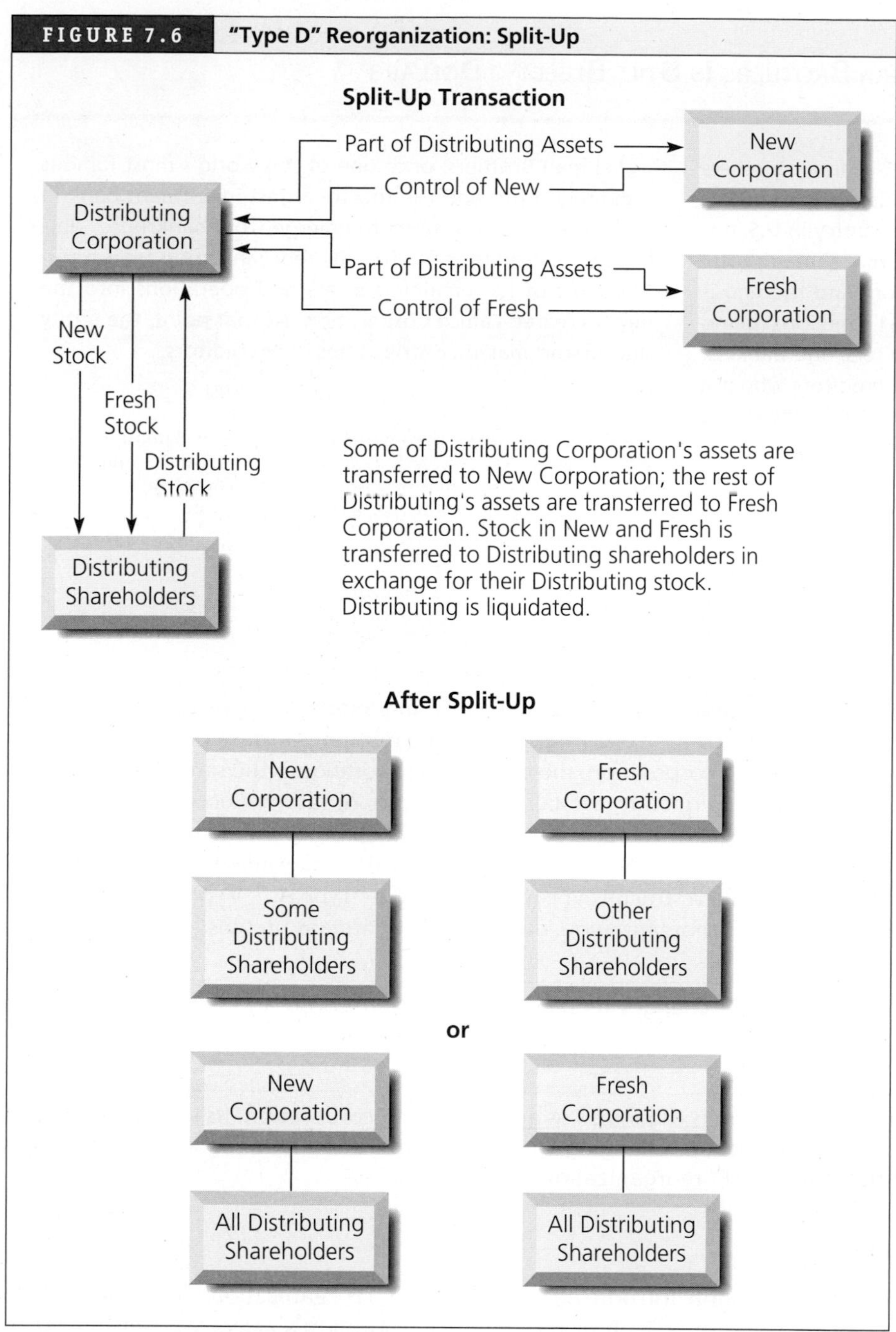

EXAMPLE 25
THE BIG PICTURE

Return to the facts of *The Big Picture* on p. 7-2. BrineCo's stock is owned 80% by Gomez Adams and 20% by his children. Gomez wants to relinquish his corporate control to his children. He exchanges his common voting stock for nonvoting preferred stock. The exchange qualifies as a "Type E" reorganization. However, any difference in value between stock received and stock surrendered could be treated as compensation to Gomez or as a gift to Gomez's children. ■

EXAMPLE 26

Cedar Corporation exchanges each of its $1,000 bonds for 10 shares of common stock worth $100 per share. This qualifies as a "Type E" reorganization, and no gain is recognized because the bond value given up is equal to the stock value received ($1,000 = 10 × $100). ■

TAX *in* the NEWS

Lehman Brothers Is Still Bleeding Dollars

More than two years after the collapse of Lehman Brothers Holdings, Inc., the bankruptcy proceedings still continue. It has now become the most expensive bankruptcy in U.S. history, even bigger than Enron or WorldCom. Lehman's total bankruptcy costs have exceeded $1 billion, and the end is not in sight. Every day of the year, about $1.3 million is being paid to Lehman's legions of lawyers, advisers, and bankers. All of these fees come at the expense of creditors who are hoping that eventually they will be repaid. Every dollar that is being paid to the advisers is a dollar not available to pay the creditors. At the present, it appears that the creditors may eventually recover less than 16 cents on the dollar.

Lehman Brothers, once one of the world's most famous brokerage firms and the fourth-largest investment bank in the United States, expects to emerge from bankruptcy during the first quarter of 2011. Its reorganization plan transfers most of its remaining assets and operations into the newly created Lamco Corporation. At that point, the entity should start making distributions to its creditors.

Sources: Adapted from Caroline Humer, "Lehman Bankruptcy a $1 Billion Payday for Advisers," *Reuters*, October 15, 2010; and Linda Sandler, "Lehman Bankruptcy Advisers' Fees Top $1 Billion in 24½ Months," *Bloomberg*, October 19, 2010.

TYPE F

The "Type F" reorganization is "a mere change in identity, form, or place of organization . . . however effected."[26] Since "Type F" reorganizations involve only slight changes to a single operating corporation, the successor corporation is the same corporation as its predecessor. Consequently, the tax characteristics of the predecessor carry over to the successor. A "Type F" reorganization does not jeopardize the status of § 1244 stock, nor will it terminate a valid S corporation election unless termination is desired. The IRS has ruled that if a restructuring could qualify as a "Type A," "Type C," or "Type D" as well as a "Type F" reorganization, the "Type F" treatment prevails.[27]

EXAMPLE 27

Conifer Corporation changes its name to Evergreen Corporation. This is a "Type F" reorganization. ■

EXAMPLE 28

Orchard Corporation is organized as a Subchapter S corporation. Its shareholders wish to revoke its S election. Changing from an S corporation to a regular C corporation qualifies as a "Type F" reorganization. ■

TYPE G

Bankruptcy legislation introduced the "Type G" reorganization. In an acquisitive restructuring, substantially all of the debtor corporation's assets are transferred to an acquiring corporation in exchange for its stock and securities. This stock and securities are distributed to the senior creditors in exchange for their claims against the debtor corporation. To qualify for "Type G" reorganization treatment, the debtor corporation must be insolvent before the reorganization and may be in Chapter 11 bankruptcy or a similar Federal or state court proceeding.

Like other reorganizations, the "Type G" must meet the sound business purpose, continuity of business, and continuity of interest requirements. However, the continuity of interest test is more lenient for "Type G" reorganizations. When a corporation is insolvent, the creditors become the true owners of the corporate assets.[28] Thus,

[26] § 368(a)(1)(F).
[27] Rev.Rul. 57–276, 1957–1 C.B. 126.
[28] *Helvering v. Alabama Asphaltic Limestone Co.*, 42–1 USTC ¶9245, 28 AFTR 567, 62 S.Ct. 540 (USSC, 1942).

TAX *in the NEWS* ANATOMY OF A CORPORATE BANKRUPTCY

You have often heard of publicly held corporations filing for bankruptcy protection under Chapter 11. Have you ever wondered what that actually means?

The Federal bankruptcy laws control how companies attempt to recover from debilitating debt. Chapter 11 allows a troubled corporation to restructure using a "Type G" reorganization to try to become profitable again. By filing under Chapter 11, the corporation can remain in business, and corporate management can continue to run its day-to-day operations. Although Chapter 11 gives some control over the bankruptcy process to the corporation, a bankruptcy court must approve all significant business decisions. The corporation's stock and bonds will still trade in the securities markets, so the corporation must continue to file SEC reports. A corporation declaring bankruptcy must file a Form 8–K, within 15 days.

As part of the Justice Department, the U.S. Trustee appoints committees to represent the creditors and stockholders. These committees work with the corporation to develop a plan of reorganization. The plan must be accepted by two-thirds of the stockholders before the bankruptcy court will confirm it. Dissenting shareholders cannot be bought out, as often occurs in other types of reorganizations; they must accept the majority's decisions. The plan includes a negotiated settlement of the corporation's debt that delineates the amounts of debt being relieved.

The SEC reviews the disclosure statement for completeness and to ensure shareholder representation. Before the plan is confirmed and implemented, the bankruptcy court must determine that the settlement complies with the Bankruptcy Code. This relief of debt through bankruptcy filing will give the corporation a chance to recover and survive.

rather than the shareholders, the creditors should be the ones with the continuing interest in the property of the insolvent corporation. The former shareholders need not receive stock in the acquiring corporation for the restructuring to qualify as a "Type G" reorganization.[29]

The acquiring corporation in a "Type G" reorganization must reduce the tax attributes carried over from the bankrupt corporation to the extent of the cancellation-of-debt-income relief. The tax attributes reduced include the following.

- Net operating losses (NOLs).
- General business credits (GBCs).
- Minimum tax credits (MTCs).
- Capital loss carryovers.
- Basis in property.

These attributes are reduced in the order listed above; however, the acquiring corporation may elect to reduce the basis of depreciable property first.

EXAMPLE 29

Worthless Corporation files for Chapter 11 protection when its liabilities exceed its assets by $100,000 (cancellation-of-debt-income relief). Worthless has a $60,000 NOL carryover and a $30,000 capital loss carryover at the time of its restructuring. Through a "Type G" reorganization, NewStart, Inc., becomes the successor corporation to Worthless. NewStart must reduce the carryover attributes by $100,000. Consequently, NewStart has no NOL or capital loss carryovers from Worthless, and it must reduce the basis in the assets by $10,000 ($100,000 total carryovers reduction − $60,000 NOL − $30,000 capital losses = $10,000 basis reduction). ■

A summary of the advantages and disadvantages of the various corporate reorganizations described in this chapter is found in Concept Summary 7.4.

[29]Private Letter Ruling 8909007; Reg. § 1.368–1(e)(8), Example 10.

CONCEPT SUMMARY 7.4

Summary of Corporate Reorganization Advantages and Disadvantages

Reorganization	Type	Advantages	Disadvantages
A	Merger or consolidation	• No requirement that consideration be voting stock. As much as 60% of consideration can be cash and property without tax consequences for the stock received (cash and other property received *are* taxed).	• All liabilities of target corporation are assumed by acquiring corporation as a matter of law. • Acquiring approval of majority shareholders, dealing with dissenters' rights, and holding shareholder meetings, as required by foreign, state, or Federal law, may present problems.
B	Voting-stock-for-stock exchange	• Stock may be acquired from shareholders. • Procedures to effect reorganization are not complex.	• *Only* voting stock of acquiring corporation may be used. • Must have 80% control of a target corporation. • May have minority interest remaining in target corporation.
C	Stock-for-assets exchange	• Less complex than "Type A"; no foreign, state, or Federal law to follow. • Cash or property consideration for 20% or less of fair market value of property transferred is acceptable. • Acquiring corporation assumes only the target's liabilities that it chooses.	• *Substantially all* assets of target corporation must be transferred. • Liabilities count as *other property* for 20% rule if any consideration other than stock and liabilities is used. • The target corporation must distribute the stock, securities, and other properties it receives in the reorganization to its shareholders.
D	Corporate division: spin-off, split-off, split-up	• Permits corporate division without tax consequences if no *boot* is involved.	• Control requirements of 50% for an acquisitive reorganization and 80% for a divisive reorganization must be met.
	Acquisitive	• Allows smaller target corporation to retain its existence.	
E	Recapitalization	• Allows for major changes in corporate equity structure.	
F	Change in identity, form, or place of organization	• Survivor is treated as same entity as predecessor; thus, tax attributes of predecessor are retained.	
G	Court-approved reorganization of bankrupt corporation	• Creditors can exchange debts for stock tax-free. • State merger laws need not be followed.	• Planning for use is limited.

7.3 Judicial Doctrines

LO.4

Delineate the judicial and administrative conditions for a nontaxable corporate reorganization.

Besides the statutory requirements for reorganizations, several judicially created doctrines have become basic requirements for tax-free treatment. These doctrines include the sound business purpose, continuity of interest, and continuity of business enterprise doctrines. The courts have also formulated the step transaction doctrine to determine the tax status of a reorganization that occurs through a series of related transactions. In addition, a reorganization plan that is consistent with one of the Code reorganizations is required.

SOUND BUSINESS PURPOSE

Even if the statutory reorganization requirements are literally followed, a transaction will not be tax-free unless it exhibits a **business purpose**.[30] The business purpose requirement is meant to limit nonrecognition treatment to transactions that are motivated, at least in part, by valid corporate needs. The transaction must have economic consequences germane to the businesses that go beyond mere tax avoidance. Although tax avoidance is not, by itself, considered a business purpose, the absence of a tax avoidance motive does not establish that there was the requisite business purpose.[31]

Given that a business purpose is required for a tax-free treatment, whose business purpose must it be—the corporation's or the shareholders'? The Regulations indicate that the corporation's business purpose should be paramount. However, the courts have considered both corporate and shareholder purposes because it is sometimes impossible to distinguish between them.[32]

The Damage from Structural Problems

Your firm is involved in structuring a reorganization for your client, Eagle Corporation. Your manager has mentioned several times that this reorganization is very important to Eagle as it provides a solution to Eagle's financial problems.

Quail Corporation, the other party to the reorganization, requests information about the structural stability of an apartment building, which is a significant part of the transaction. Jeanne Smith, Eagle's tax director, tells you that no structural problems with the building have been documented. After you have given this information to Quail, you find out from a friend that the consensus in the construction community is that the building has substantial hidden structural damage. The steel used in the building was produced by a company whose products have caused structural instability in other buildings.

In your research, you have determined that this reorganization is a huge transaction for Quail and that if problems occur, Quail could face bankruptcy, not to mention that innocent renters could be harmed. Quail's managers have said that they are impressed with your firm's integrity. After the merger, Quail will be looking for a new auditing firm, and, based on their interactions with you, Quail would consider your firm. Your manager thinks this will be a good business opportunity once the transaction is completed and no conflict of interest remains.

What will you do with your information about the structural instability of the apartment building? Address how your actions will affect Eagle, Quail, your firm, and you.

[30]Reg. §§ 1.368–1(c) and 1.355–2. See also *Gregory v. Helvering*, 35–1 USTC ¶9043, 14 AFTR 1191, 55 S.Ct. 266 (USSC, 1935). The doctrine as developed in the *Gregory* case became a precedent for all transactions that might be shams devised merely for tax avoidance purposes. It brought about the principle of substance over form. All business transactions must have a sound business purpose.

[31]Reg. § 1.355–2(b) and *Comm. v. Marne S. Wilson*, 66–1 USTC ¶9103, 16 AFTR 2d 6030, 353 F.2d 184 (CA–9, 1966).

[32]*Lewis Trustee v. Comm.*, 49–2 USTC ¶9377, 38 AFTR 377, 176 F.2d 646 (CA–1, 1949); *Estate of Parshelsky v. Comm.*, 62–1 USTC ¶9460, 9 AFTR 2d 1382, 303 F.2d 14 (CA–2, 1962).

CONTINUITY OF INTEREST

The *continuity of interest* requirement prevents transactions that appear to be sales from qualifying as nontaxable reorganizations. Therefore, the continuity of interest test provides that if the shareholders have substantially the same investment after the restructuring as before, the transaction may qualify as a nontaxable event. To qualify for tax-favored status, the target corporation shareholders must receive an equity interest in the acquiring corporation.[33]

The Regulations deem that the continuity of interest test is met when the target corporation shareholders receive acquiring corporation stock equal to at least 40 percent of their prior stock ownership in a merger with the target.[34] Not all target shareholders need to receive stock in the surviving corporation. The requirement is applied to the aggregate consideration given by the acquiring corporation.

EXAMPLE 30

Target Corporation merges into Acquiring Corporation pursuant to state statutes. Under the merger plan, Target's shareholders can elect to receive either cash or stock in Acquiring. The shareholders who hold 45% of Target's outstanding stock elect to receive cash; the remaining 55% of the shareholders elect to receive Acquiring stock. This plan satisfies the continuity of interest test. The shareholders receiving cash are taxed on the transaction. Those receiving stock are not taxed. ■

EXAMPLE 31

Juanita owns 100% of Target Corporation. Target merges into Acquiring Corporation. Juanita receives 1% of Acquiring's outstanding stock in exchange for all of her Target stock. The continuity of interest test is met; Juanita received only stock for her interest. ■

If the continuity of interest requirement is met at the time of the reorganization, a sale of stock to an unrelated party immediately before or after the restructuring will not destroy the continuity of interest. Unrelated parties here include individuals, noncorporate entities, and corporations that are not part of either the acquirer's or the target's affiliated group.[35]

EXAMPLE 32

Pursuant to a preexisting contract, Juanita, in Example 31, sells all her Acquiring Corporation stock to Ying for its value. This sale occurs one week after the reorganization. Since Ying is not considered a party related to Juanita, the sale to Ying does not affect the continuity of interest test. ■

CONTINUITY OF BUSINESS ENTERPRISE

The **continuity of business enterprise** test ensures that tax-free reorganization treatment is limited to situations where there is a continuing interest in the target's business. Specifically, this test requires the acquiring corporation to either (1) continue the target corporation's historic business (business test) or (2) use a significant portion of the target corporation's assets in its business (asset use test). Continuing one of the target corporation's significant business lines satisfies the business test. Determining whether the acquiring corporation's use of the target's assets is "significant" is based on the relative importance of the assets to the target's former business or their net fair market value.[36] Thus, meeting the asset use test depends on facts and circumstances.

[33] *Pinellas Ice & Cold Storage v. Comm.*, 3 USTC ¶1023, 11 AFTR 1112, 53 S.Ct. 257 (USSC, 1933), and *LeTulle v. Scofield*, 40–1 USTC ¶9150, 23 AFTR 789, 60 S.Ct. 313 (USSC, 1940). In *LeTulle*, a corporation transferred all its assets to another corporation for cash and bonds. The Court held that the transaction was not a tax-free reorganization if the transferor's only retained interest was that of a creditor. This concept is now in Reg. §§ 1.368–1(b) and (c).

[34] See footnote 9.

[35] Reg. § 1.368–1(e)(3).

[36] Reg. § 1.368–1(d).

Brewers Are Consolidating Globally

In 2000, one-third of global beer sales were divided among the top 10 brewers. Now, due to mergers and acquisitions (M&A), almost 50 percent of global beer sales by volume and 75 percent of the profits belong to four mega-beverage companies—Anheuser-Busch InBev, SABMiller, Heineken, and Carlsberg. The highlights of the big M&A activity in the brewing industry include:

- **2002:** South African Breweries (SAB) buys U.S. Miller Brewing from Philip Morris. Through this combination, SABMiller becomes the world's second-largest brewer after Anheuser-Busch.
- **2004:** Belgium's Interbrew (ranked third) merges with Brazil-based AmBev (ranked fifth) to create the world's largest brewer. Originally, the company was called InterbrewAmBev, but wisely it was renamed InBev.
- **2005:** The U.S. company Adolph Coors and the Canadian Molson merge to create Molson Coors Brewing and become the world's fifth-largest brewer.
- **2008 (June):** SABMiller combines its U.S. breweries with the U.S. operations of Molson Coors to create MillerCoors.
- **2008 (July):** InBev makes an unsolicited offer for Anheuser-Busch, at the time the world's second-largest brewer. The maker of Budweiser, the world's top-selling beer, Anheuser-Busch controls almost 50 percent of the U.S. market. After much legal maneuvering, the two companies negotiate a friendly $52 billion takeover that creates the world's largest brewer.
- **2010 (April):** Heineken (currently ranked second by revenue and third by volume) acquires Femsa, Latin America's largest brewer with labels such as Sol and Dos Equis. The $5.5 billion deal boosts Heineken sales in Mexico, the world's fourth-largest beer market by profits. Heineken also becomes a top brewer in Brazil, the second-largest beer market behind the United States.

Sources: Adapted from Theresa Howard, "Beer's Been Going Global for Years; Consolidation Has Long Been the Name of the Game," *USA Today*, July 14, 2008; "For Heineken, Femsa Deal Is a Beer Balancing Act," *New York Times*, January 12, 2010.

The continuity of interest and business doctrines apply to reorganizations that involve two or more corporations. In these situations, there can be a discontinuance because the transaction may really be a sale rather than a corporate restructuring. When the reorganization involves only one corporation, the continuation of the interest or business is not a concern. Accordingly, these two doctrines do not apply to "Type E" and "Type F" reorganizations.

STEP TRANSACTION

The **step transaction** doctrine prevents taxpayers from engaging in a series of transactions for the purpose of obtaining tax benefits that would not be allowed if the transaction was accomplished in a single step. When the steps are so interdependent that the accomplishment of one step would be fruitless without the completion of the series of steps, the transactions may be collapsed into a single step.[37]

The step transaction doctrine presents problems for reorganizations when the acquiring corporation does not want all of the target's assets. For a "Type C" and

[37] *American Bantam Car Co.*, 11 T.C. 397 (1948), *aff'd* in 49–2 USTC ¶9471, 38 AFTR 820, 177 F.2d 513 (CA–3, 1949), *cert. den.* 70 S.Ct. 622 (USSC, 1950). If the steps have independent economic significance, the doctrine does not apply. See *Esmark, Inc.*, 90 T.C. 171 (1988) and Rev.Rul. 79–250, 1979–2 C.B. 156.

FINANCIAL DISCLOSURE *Insights*

CORPORATE RESTRUCTURINGS AND THE EFFECTIVE TAX RATE

Book-tax differences often are created by corporate reorganizations falling under § 368. The tax-free nature of the § 368 reorganizations leads to temporary differences due to the timing of income/loss recognition—current for books and postponed for tax. The expenses incurred in corporate restructurings are capitalized for tax purposes but are allowed as expenses for financial accounting, thus resulting in permanent book-tax differences.

While acquisition and divestiture strategies are utilized to achieve corporate goals, the results of these restructurings influence the financial statements and ultimately the effective income tax rates. For example, the effective tax rate of Ryder Systems recently increased by 1.7 percentage points due to its restructuring transactions. Cisco's realignments boosted its effective rate by over 2 percentage points in one year. This increase occurred because the foreign restructuring costs Cisco incurred did not create tax deductions in the United States.

Ford took a bigger hit due to its restructuring. Over a three-year period, its effective tax rate increased by about 6 percentage points due to its capital transactions.

acquisitive "Type D," the target (acquirer for "Type D") must transfer substantially all of its assets to the acquiring (target for "Type D") corporation. If the target corporation attempts to dispose of its unwanted assets before a reorganization, the step transaction doctrine could ruin the reorganization's tax-favored status. The acquiring corporation would have failed to obtain substantially all of the target corporation's assets. Without direct evidence to the contrary, the IRS generally views any transactions occurring within one year of a reorganization as part of the restructuring.[38]

7.4 Tax Attribute Carryovers

LO.5

Apply the rules pertaining to the carryover of tax attributes in a corporate reorganization.

Some target corporation tax features (loss carryovers, tax credits, and E & P deficits) are welcomed by the successor corporation. Others may prove less desirable (positive E & P and assumption of liabilities). The mandatory carryover rules should be carefully considered in every corporate acquisition; they may, in fact, determine the form of the transaction.

ASSUMPTION OF LIABILITIES

Since a corporate reorganization must result in some continuation of the previous corporation's business activities, existing liabilities are rarely liquidated (a "Type G" reorganization is the exception). The acquiring corporation either assumes the target corporation's liabilities or takes the target's assets subject to their liabilities. These liabilities are generally not considered boot when determining gain recognition for the corporations involved in the restructuring. Liabilities are problematic only in the "Type C" reorganization, when the acquiring corporation transfers other property to the target as well as stock. In this situation, the liabilities are considered boot and, therefore, can cause a violation of the 80 percent-of-assets-for-voting-stock requirement.

ALLOWANCE OF CARRYOVERS

When a corporation acquires a target corporation's property, it also acquires the target's tax attributes. This occurs in the "Type A," "Type C," acquisitive "Type D," and "Type G" reorganizations. Section 381 determines which of the target corporation's tax benefits can be carried over to the successor. The "Type B," "Type E," and

[38]Reg. § 1.368–2(c), but in Rev.Rul. 69–48, 1969–1 C.B. 106, the IRS applied the step transaction doctrine to transactions that were 22 months apart.

Culture Shock Results in Merger and Acquisition Failures

Cross-border mergers and acquisitions (M&A) are becoming increasingly popular as the dollar has declined against other global currencies and companies seek to take advantage of expanding opportunities in emerging markets such as Eastern Europe and the BRIC economies (Brazil, Russia, India, and China). Nevertheless, the success rates of cross-border M&A remain dismally low because cultural issues frequently derail seemingly perfect M&A marriages.

Companies bent on acquisitions in developing economies are aware of the well-known risks such as questionable business practices, environmental exposures, and lack of intellectual property protection. But they're less prepared to evaluate the risks associated with cultural differences. A mistake that companies often make is to go into an M&A deal assuming that the practices that made them successful in their home territory will work in another country. This simply is not the case. Research indicates that ignoring the "soft" cultural issues often leads to failed deals.

When M&A facilitators were asked to identify the most significant issues they faced in their most recent transaction, one of the top responses was cultural differences. Organizations should overhaul their due diligence processes to include cultural integration issues and pay close attention to those challenges at every step of the transaction.

Source: Adapted from John Cummings, "Cross-Border M&A: Insulating against Culture Shock," *Business Strategy*, April 24, 2008.

"Type F" reorganizations do not fall under the § 381 carryover rules because the original target corporation remains intact and retains its own tax attributes. In a "Type B" reorganization, the target corporation merely becomes a subsidiary of the acquiring corporation. The "Type E" and "Type F" reorganizations involve only the original corporation; thus, no assets or tax attributes are being acquired. A divisive "Type D" reorganization also is not subject to § 381. In a spin-off or split-off, the old distributing corporation retains its tax attributes, and the new corporation starts fresh with regard to its tax attributes (with the exception of E & P). In a split-up, on the other hand, the tax attributes of the distributing corporation disappear when it liquidates.

NET OPERATING LOSS CARRYOVERS

A target corporation's NOL is one of the beneficial tax attributes (and sometimes its most valuable asset) that may be carried forward to the acquiring corporation. Although the NOL cannot be carried back to a prior acquiring corporation tax year, it can be used prospectively. Thus, an NOL is a valuable target corporation asset to the acquirer, because it can offset future income of the combined successor corporation.

EXAMPLE 33
THE BIG PICTURE

Return to the facts of *The Big Picture* on p. 7-2. R&W Corporation proceeds with its acquisition of ChemCo. Prior to the merger, ChemCo accumulated a $3 million NOL. After the reorganization, R&W generates $5 million of taxable income. ChemCo's $3 million NOL carries over to offset the $5 million taxable income, reducing it to $2 million. R&W saves $1,020,000 in Federal income taxes by being able to utilize ChemCo's NOL carryover ($3 million NOL carryover × 34%). Thus, the $3 million NOL is a valuable asset that may be worth more than $1 million to R&W. ■

TAX *in* the NEWS

GM Emerges from Bankruptcy with Billions of Dollars in Tax Benefits

General Motors has paid off its government loans and is relisted on the stock exchange after an initial public offering (IPO) of stock in the "New GM" Corporation. As permitted with a "Type G" reorganization, the "New GM" will carry over "Old GM" tax benefits (NOLs, general business credits, foreign tax credits, etc.) worth more than $45 billion. The use of these tax benefits, however, is limited by § 382 if there is a more than a 50-percentage-point ownership change for the shareholders owning 5 percent or more of the stock.

Given that the Treasury acquired about 61 percent of GM through the Troubled Asset Relief Program (TARP), it would seem that the limitations should apply. Not so! Notice 2010-2 indicates that the § 382 limits will not apply to the Treasury's acquisition and disposal of the GM stock. The ability to use these benefits to offset future income for years should make GM more attractive to investors, thus supporting a higher price for the stock. As the Treasury is selling an undisclosed portion of its stock, a higher stock price will provide the government coffers with a larger return. The strategy appears to be beneficial to both GM and the Treasury.

Although the Treasury is losing billions of future tax dollars due to the carryover tax benefits, consider that if GM had not emerged from bankruptcy, it would never have produced future taxable income, and all of its employees would be in the unemployment lines. Thus, the tax benefits are shielding income that would otherwise never have been earned!

Sources: Adapted from Notice 2010–2; Randall Smith, "GM to Get Tax Break Worth Billions," *Wall Street Journal,* November 2, 2010; and Robert Willens, "Treasury Fixed Snag Prior to GM IPO," *CFO.com,* September 27, 2010.

Ownership Changes

To curtail the tax benefits received from NOL carryovers, § 382 limits the yearly amount of NOL that may be utilized by the successor corporation. The **§ 382 limitation** applies when there is a more than 50-percentage-point ownership change (by value) for the common shareholders of the target (loss) corporation. An **ownership change** takes place on the day (*change date*) that either an *owner shift* or an *equity structure shift* occurs.

- An **owner shift** is any change in the common stock ownership of shareholders owning at least 5 percent. Owner shifts can be caused by purchases, stock issuances, redemptions, recapitalizations, transfers to controlled corporations, and equity structure shifts.
- An **equity structure shift** occurs in tax-free reorganizations other than "Type F," divisive "Type D," or divisive "Type G" restructurings. The change date for determining the equity structure shift is the date when the reorganization is considered to have occurred.
- Although equity structure shifts and owner shifts are defined as separate ownership changes, the end result of an equity structure shift most likely is to create an owner shift. The treatment for both types of shifts is the same.

Whether an ownership change has occurred is determined by examining the common stock ownership during the testing period, generally the prior three years.[39] Shareholders owning less than a 5 percent interest during the testing period are aggregated and treated as one shareholder for determining an owner shift. Thus, transfers between shareholders who own less than 5 percent do not influence the percentage-point ownership change computation.

EXAMPLE 34

Target Corporation is merged into Acquiring Corporation in a "Type A" reorganization. At the time of the merger, Target had an NOL of $100,000. Pursuant to the merger, Target's shareholders, none of whom own a 5% interest, receive 40% of Acquiring's stock. An equity structure shift has taken place. Since all of Target's shareholders owned less

[39] The testing period is the period following the most recent ownership change if that change occurred within the past three years. Further, the testing period cannot begin before the year in which the carryforward being tested occurs. See § 382(i).

than 5%, they are aggregated in determining the owner shift. As a group, these shareholders owned 100% of the loss corporation prior to the restructuring and only 40% of the successor corporation after the reorganization. A more than 50-percentage-point ownership change has occurred because of the equity structure shift.

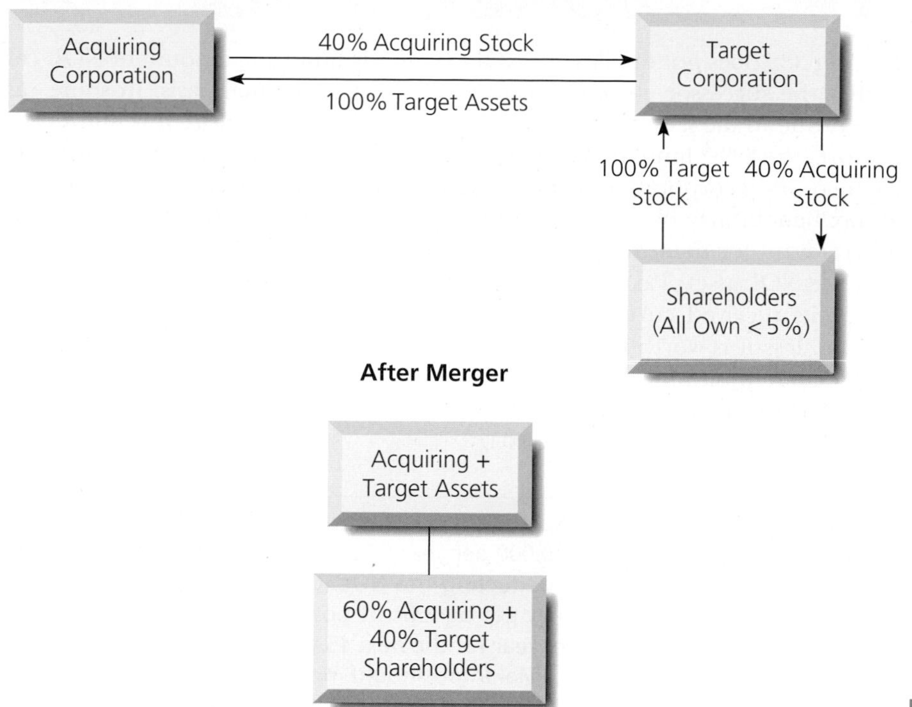

■

When an ownership change occurs, the yearly NOL amount usable by the successor corporation is restricted. The limit is based on the fair market value of the loss corporation's stock (both common and preferred) multiplied by the **long-term tax-exempt rate** (the highest adjusted Federal long-term rate for the prior three-month period).[40] The stock received in a reorganization or the price paid for the loss corporation's stock generally indicates its fair market value.

Since the § 382 limitation is based on the loss corporation's value, there is an incentive to inflate its value prior to the ownership change. This could be accomplished through capital contributions. The so-called anti-stuffing rules prohibit this behavior by disregarding assets contributed in the two years prior to the change date.

EXAMPLE 35

Winner Corporation acquires Loser Corporation when Loser has a $250,000 NOL carryforward. Winner exchanges 30% of its stock valued at $600,000 for all of Loser's stock. The applicable long-term tax-exempt rate at the change date is 5%. Several months before the acquisition by Winner, Loser's shareholders contributed investment assets with a fair market value of $100,000, thus increasing Loser's value from $500,000 to $600,000. The § 382 limitation computation will not include the recent increase in Loser's fair market value. Consequently, the yearly § 382 limitation is $25,000($500,000 × 5%). ■

The objective of the § 382 *limitation* is to restrict NOL use to a hypothetical future income stream from the loss corporation. This future income stream is defined as the yield that would be received if the stock was sold and the proceeds were invested in long-term tax-exempt securities. Thus, the formula for computing the § 382 limitation is as follows.

[40] The determination of value occurs immediately *after* the ownership change in the case of redemptions or other contractions that are associated with the ownership change.

Loss corporation's FMV on change date
× Federal long-term tax-exempt rate
= Yearly § 382 limitation

Section 382 does not disallow an NOL. It merely limits the amount of NOL carryover that the successor corporation can utilize on an annual basis. In some cases, however, due to the § 382 limitation, the NOL may expire before it is utilized fully. Therefore, the § 382 limitation should be considered when determining the tax benefit an acquiring corporation receives from the target corporation's NOL. Since the NOL tax benefit may be the target's most valuable asset, a present value analysis is highly relevant for determining the amount the acquiring corporation is willing to pay for the NOL asset. Tax benefits received in future years are not worth as much as tax benefits received currently. The farther in the future the NOL deduction is taken, the less it is worth today. At some point, depending on the discount factor used, the NOL postponed to distant future years may be almost worthless in present value dollar terms. Present value table excerpts are found in Tables 7.1 and 7.2 (located at the end of the chapter text).

EXAMPLE 36

MakingIt Corporation acquires WashedUp Corporation in a transaction that subjects WashedUp's $600,000 NOL to a $40,000 per year § 382 limitation. After the acquisition, there are 15 years remaining for deducting the NOL. Given that MakingIt uses a discount factor of 10% for evaluating the benefit of possible transactions, the present value of a $40,000 deduction every year for the next 15 years, assuming a corporate tax rate of 35%, is $106,484. Thus, MakingIt should not pay WashedUp more than $106,484 for the $210,000 NOL tax benefits ($600,000 NOL × 35% tax rate). This means that because of the time value of money, the NOL is worth about half of its face value! The present value of the NOL is computed as follows.

$40,000 × 35% tax rate = $14,000 tax saving per year × 7.606 (discount factor for present value of annuity for 15 years at a 10% discount rate) = $106,484

Suppose that the § 382 yearly limitation is $120,000 rather than $40,000. Now the NOL can be fully deducted in 5 years rather than 15 years. Using the same discount factor (10%), the value of the NOL benefit to MakingIt increases to $159,222, computed as follows.

$120,000 × 35% tax rate = $42,000 tax saving per year × 3.791 (discount factor for present value of annuity for 5 years at a 10% discount rate) = $159,222 ■

If the successor corporation's current-year taxable income is insufficient to offset the authorized NOL deduction, the amount not utilized may be carried forward and added to the next year's § 382 limitation.

EXAMPLE 37

Profit Corporation acquires Loss Corporation and its $300,000 NOL in a transaction causing an equity structure shift. Loss's value on the change date is $500,000, and the applicable long-term tax-exempt rate is 5%. Therefore, the yearly § 382 limitation is $25,000 ($500,000 × 5%). During the current year, Profit/Loss successor corporation has $20,000 net income before the NOL deduction. The successor corporation may offset its taxable income by $20,000 of the NOL. Since the § 382 limit is $25,000, the NOL limit for next year will be $30,000 ($25,000 current + $5,000 prior-year carryover) rather than $25,000. ■

A further limitation on the ability to utilize the NOL carryforward arises in the year that the ownership change occurs (change year). The NOL amount available to the successor corporation in the change year is limited to the percentage of days remaining in the tax year after the change day. The § 382 yearly NOL limitation is multiplied by this percentage.

CONCEPT SUMMARY 7.5

Summary of Carryover Rules

Tax attributes that carry over from a loss corporation to the successor corporation:

1. Loss carryovers—subject to the § 382 limitation.
   A. Annual limitations on carryover use are evoked when there is an ownership change—a more than 50-percentage-point owner shift or an equity structure shift.
      - Owner shift is a change in the ownership of shareholders owning 5% or more of the corporate stock.
      - Equity shift occurs in tax-free reorganizations, other than a divisive "Type D" and "Type G" or a "Type F."

   B. Annual carryover usage cannot exceed the value of the old loss corporation on the change date (date of transfer) multiplied by the highest long-term tax-exempt Federal rate for the three calendar months prior to the structure change.
   C. Year of transfer. The loss claimed in the year of transfer is limited to the annual limitation multiplied by a percentage representing the remaining days in the year of transfer.
   D. Loss corporation carryovers are applied to the § 382 limitation in this order: built-in capital losses, capital loss carryovers, built-in ordinary losses, NOL carryovers, foreign tax credits, business credit carryovers, and lastly minimum tax credit carryovers.
2. Earnings and profits.
   A. Positive E & P of an acquired corporation carries over.
   B. If either corporation has a deficit in E & P, the successor corporation will have two E & P accounts. One account contains the total positive accumulated E & P as of the date of the transfer. The other contains the total deficit as of the date of the transfer. Future positive E & P may offset the deficit E & P account.
3. Other tax attributes.
   A. Depreciation and cost recovery methods carry over.
   B. The installment method of reporting carries over.

The formula for this computation is as follows.

Yearly § 382 limitation
× Number of days remaining in year/365 (366 in leap year)
= Initial year § 382 limitation

Lastly, the NOL carryover is disallowed for future taxable years if the successor corporation fails to satisfy the continuity of business enterprise requirement for at least two years following any ownership change.[41] The continuity of business enterprise test is the same as for tax-free reorganizations. That is, a significant historical line of the loss corporation's business must be continued, or the successor corporation must use a significant amount of the loss corporation's assets in its business.

EXAMPLE 38

On December 1, Minus transfers all of its assets to Plus (a calendar year corporation) in exchange for 40% of Plus's stock. At the time of the merger, Minus is valued at $900,000 and has an NOL carryover of $200,000. The long-term tax-exempt rate is 5%. Since a more than 50-percentage-point ownership change has occurred for Minus's shareholders, the amount of NOL available for use in the merger year is $3,699 [$900,000 × 5% = $45,000 × (30/365)]. The NOL available to reduce the successor corporation's taxable income in the next year is $45,000. If Plus fails to continue Minus's historical business or use substantially all of its assets for a two-year period, Plus is not allowed to use any of Minus's NOL. ■

[41] § 382(c)(1).

EARNINGS AND PROFITS

The E & P of an acquired corporation carries over to a successor corporation.[42] Thus, the positive E & P of the acquiring and target corporations are added together and become the accumulated E & P for the successor corporation. However, a successor corporation is not permitted to apply the acquired corporation's E & P deficit against its own E & P.[43] Thus, the E & P of a deficit corporation is deemed to be received by the successor corporation as of the takeover date. A deficit may be used only to offset E & P accumulated by the successor corporation after the change date.[44]

Consequently, the successor corporation must maintain two separate E & P accounts after the change date: one account contains the prior accumulated E & P as of the change date, and the other contains the deficit transferred and E & P accumulated since the change date. The deficit in the post-transfer account may not be used to reduce accumulated E & P in the pre-transfer account.

EXAMPLE 39

Target Corporation is merged into Acquiring Corporation on December 31, 2011. On that date, the E & P balance for Target is a negative $75,000, and for Acquiring it is a positive $400,000. In 2012, current E & P for Acquiring is $50,000. Acquiring now has two E & P balances: pre-2012 $400,000 and post-2011 negative $25,000 ($50,000 – $75,000).

	12/31/2011	E & P 2012	12/31/2012
Post-2011 E & P	($ 75,000)	$50,000	($ 25,000)
Pre-2012 E & P	400,000		400,000

■

In corporate "Type D" divisions, the E & P of the distributing corporation must be allocated among the newly created corporations and the distributing corporation based on the fair market value in each entity.[45]

EXAMPLE 40

Gaming Corporation distributes its computer gaming line of business to the newly created Compgame in a transaction qualifying as a "Type D" spin-off reorganization. Before the distribution, Gaming is worth $1 million and holds E & P of $300,000. After the spin-off, Gaming's value is $600,000 and Compgame's value is $400,000. Compgame starts with an E & P balance of $120,000 ($300,000 × $400,000/$1,000,000), and Gaming retains an E & P balance of $180,000 ($300,000 – $120,000). ■

OTHER CARRYOVERS

The capital losses and excess tax credits carried over to the successor corporation are also limited by § 382, if there is an ownership change for the loss corporation's shareholders.[46] The year-of-transfer limitations also apply to the use of capital losses and excess credits. When a corporation has several types of loss corporation carryovers, they are applied to the § 382 limitation in the following order.

1. Built-in capital losses.
2. Capital losses.
3. Built-in ordinary losses.
4. NOLs.
5. Foreign tax credits.
6. Business credits.
7. Minimum tax credits.[47]

[42] *Comm. v. Sansome*, 3 USTC ¶978, 11 AFTR 854, 60 F.2d 931 (CA–2, 1931), *cert. den.* 53 S.Ct. 291 (USSC, 1932).

[43] *Comm. v. Phipps*, 49–1 USTC ¶9204, 37 AFTR 827, 69 S.Ct. 616 (USSC, 1949).

[44] § 381(c)(2) and Reg. § 1.381(c)(2)–1(a)(5).

[45] Reg. § 1.312–10.

[46] § 383.

[47] Reg. § 1.383–1(d).

Computing the amount of excess credits allowable in the current year is more complicated than determining the capital loss or NOL carryover, as the steps below indicate.

1. Calculate regular tax liability after allowable losses.
2. Compute regular tax liability as if the full § 382 limitation is deductible.
3. Subtract the tax liability in step 2 from the tax liability in step 1. The remainder is the § 382 limitation applicable to excess credits.

EXAMPLE 41
THE BIG PICTURE

Return to the facts of *The Big Picture* on p. 7-2. R&W Corporation proceeds with the acquisition of ChemCo, and it acquires $100,000 of general business credits from ChemCo. Assume that the § 382 limitation for the year is $200,000 and that R&W's taxable income is $800,000 before applying this limitation. If the full deduction allowable by § 382 were utilized, R&W's taxable income would be $600,000 ($800,000 – $200,000). The amount of general business credit that R&W may take in the current year is $68,000, computed as follows.

Step 1. Regular tax liability ($800,000 × 34% tax rate)	$272,000
Step 2. Tax liability with full § 382 limitation ($600,000 × 34% tax rate)	204,000
Step 3. Subtract step 2 from step 1	$ 68,000

■

EXAMPLE 42

Two years ago, Gain Corporation acquired Loss Corporation in a transaction causing an ownership change. The § 382 limitation is $150,000 for the current year. Gain Corporation's taxable income before considering carryovers is $400,000 ordinary income and $100,000 capital gain. The Loss Corporation carryovers to the current year include a $20,000 capital loss, a $60,000 NOL, and $30,000 of excess business credits. The capital loss is utilized first to offset the capital gain, and then the NOL is used against the ordinary income. Taxable income becomes $420,000 [($100,000 – $20,000) + ($400,000 – $60,000)]. If the full § 382 limitation were utilized, taxable income would be $350,000 [($400,000 + $100,000) – $150,000]. The amount of excess business credit allowable in the current year would be $23,800, computed as follows.

Step 1. Regular tax liability ($420,000 × 34%)	$142,800
Step 2. Tax liability with full § 382 limitation ($350,000 × 34%)	119,000
Step 3. Subtract step 2 from step 1	$ 23,800

■

The benefit from all loss corporation carryovers taken in the current year cannot, in total, exceed the calculated yearly § 382 limitation. Nor can the loss carryovers exceed the year-of-transfer limitation.

DISALLOWANCE OF CARRYOVERS

Irrespective of the carryover rules, the IRS can utilize § 269 to disallow the carryover of tax benefits if a tax avoidance scheme is apparent. Such items are disallowed when a corporation acquires property of another corporation primarily to evade or avoid Federal income tax by securing the benefits that the acquiring corporation would not otherwise enjoy. Whether the principal purpose is tax evasion or avoidance is a question of fact. If the loss corporation's business is promptly discontinued after a corporate reorganization, the IRS may use § 269 to disallow the loss carryovers.

FINANCIAL DISCLOSURE *Insights*

TAKEOVERS GONE WRONG

Not all corporate takeovers live up to their financial expectations or possibilities. Notorious examples such as the acquisition of Time Warner by AOL, and of Snapple by Quaker Oats, are still talked about, long after the combined group failed and the target company was sold.

Corporate deals that fail to succeed have financial accounting results as well. AOL had high hopes when it acquired the social networking site Bebo, but visitors to Facebook and Twitter far exceeded those to Bebo, so AOL sold its subsidiary within about two years. A private equity group was the buyer, so the precise sales price is not available, but industry estimates put it at less than $10 million, much less than AOL's initial acquisition price of $850 million.

A loss on subsidiary stock like the Bebo sale is claimed under GAAP rules, and the stock market rewarded AOL with a share price increase of more than 2 percent after the sale. But such a loss is not immediately deductible in full for Federal income taxes. This timing difference created a deferred tax asset for AOL of about $300 million.

Another GAAP result of the Bebo sale was a hit to AOL's intangible assets. AOL determined that it would test whether its goodwill had been impaired due to the unwise investment in Bebo. Often, corporate failures such as this mean that former employees receive severance packages. These benefits usually are treated using GAAP reserves, which would create another temporary book-tax difference for AOL.

TAX PLANNING:
7.5 ASSESSING THE POSSIBLE BENEFITS OF RESTRUCTURING OPTIONS

LO.6

Structure corporate reorganizations to obtain the desired tax consequences.

Reorganizations are valuable tools in corporate tax-free restructurings. However, it may not be possible to achieve the desired corporate structure by utilizing a single reorganization type. For this reason, reorganizations should not be seen as mutually exclusive transactions; they can be combined with other tax-favored transactions into a comprehensive plan. The tax law allows a series of tax-favored transactions to be recognized as legitimate separate steps when the statutory requirements for each are met. Thus, the step transaction doctrine can be beneficially applied to facilitate the tax treatment desired by the taxpayer.

EXAMPLE 43

Black Corporation operates two businesses, both of which have been in existence for five years. One business is a manufacturing operation; the other is a wholesale distributorship. White Corporation wishes to acquire only the manufacturing business and refuses to purchase all of Black's assets. ■

What course of action might be advisable to transfer the manufacturing operation from Black to White with the least, if any, tax costs? Compare the following three possibilities.

1. Black Corporation transfers the manufacturing operation to White Corporation in return for some of the latter's stock.
2. Black Corporation forms Orange Corporation and transfers the manufacturing business to it in return for all of Orange's stock. The Orange stock is then distributed to Black's shareholders. This portion of the arrangement is a nontaxable spin-off. Orange now transfers the manufacturing operation to White Corporation in exchange for some of the latter's stock.
3. Rather than transferring the manufacturing business as described in possibility 2, Black transfers the wholesale distributorship. White exchanges some of its voting stock for the Black stock. Black is now a subsidiary of White.

CONCEPT SUMMARY 7.6

Summary of Corporate Reorganization Requirements

Reorganization Type	Type of Consideration	Amount of Stock Ownership	Carryover of Tax Attributes	Treatment of E & P	Resulting Corporation(s)
"Type A" merger	Stock, cash, and property	At least 40% continuing interest by target shareholders	Yes	Combine if positive	Acquiring corporation continues, and target corporation ceases to exist.
"Type A" consolidation	Stock, cash, and property	At least 40% continuing interest by contributing corporations' shareholders	Yes	Combine if positive	New corporation continues, and contributing corporations cease to exist.
"Type B"	Solely voting stock	At least 80% control of target corporation	No, remain with target	Remains with target	Parent-subsidiary relationship
"Type C"	Voting stock and limited other cash and property	At least 80% of target corporation assets acquired with voting stock	Yes	Combine if positive	Acquiring corporation continues, and target corporation ceases to exist.
"Type D" acquisitive	Substantially all assets of distributing corporation	At least 50% control of target corporation	Yes	Combine if positive	Target corporation continues, and distributing corporation ceases to exist.
"Type D" divisive	Assets of distributing corporation	At least 80% control of target corporations	No	Allocate among entities	Distributing corporation and target corporations continue except for split-up; only target corporations continue.
"Type E"	Stock for stock Bonds for bonds Bonds for stock	N/A	Yes, same corporation	N/A	Original corporation continues.
"Type F"	N/A	N/A	Yes	Carries over	Old corporation continues as new corporation.
"Type G"	Stock	At least 40% continuing interest by creditors	Yes	N/A	Acquiring corporation continues, and debtor corporation ceases to exist.

Possibility 1 probably will not fit within the definition of a "Type C" reorganization, because Black does not transfer substantially all of the assets in return for White stock. The manufacturing operation is transferred, but the wholesale distributorship is not. As a result, Black continues to exist. A "Type C" usually requires that the target corporation liquidate after the reorganization.

Possibility 2 is a spin-off of the assets *desired* by White, followed by a "Type C" reorganization between Orange and White. This approach is acceptable to the IRS even though White does not acquire "substantially all" of Black's assets. The transaction is treated as successfully creating a separate corporation (Orange) through a

"Type D" reorganization. The "Type C" is considered to be only between White and Orange. Black is not a party to the latter reorganization.[48]

Possibility 3 follows a different approach. It starts with the spin-off of the *unwanted* assets and concludes with White obtaining the *wanted* assets by exchanging its stock for the Black stock. Taken by itself, this last step satisfies the voting-stock-for-stock requirement of a "Type B" reorganization. If, however, the step transaction doctrine is applied and the spin-off is disregarded, the Orange stock distributed to Black's shareholders might be considered as property *other than voting stock* in White. The IRS has not chosen to take this position and probably will recognize the nontaxability of a spin-off of *unwanted* assets followed by a "Type B" reorganization.[49]

EXAMPLE 44

Major and Minor are unrelated corporations in separate lines of business. For valid business purposes, Major would like to acquire Minor through a nontaxable transaction. Major will continue Minor's line of business after the reorganization and, in light of product liability issues, would like to keep the companies separate. However, there are substantial investment assets in Minor that Major would like to possess. How can Major acquire Minor's investments and still keep Minor as a separate entity? ■

Combining a corporate reorganization with a distribution allows Major to receive the investments and have Minor continue as a corporation. Major exchanges its voting stock for all of Minor's stock. This is accomplished either by a direct exchange with the Minor shareholders, or by Minor recalling its stock and distributing the Major voting stock to its shareholders. Since Major exchanges only voting stock for Minor's stock, the transaction qualifies as a tax-deferred "Type B" reorganization. Minor is now a wholly owned subsidiary of Major. Minor then distributes the investment assets as a dividend to its parent, Major. This distribution qualifies for the 100 percent dividends received deduction. The IRS will not recast this as an acquisition of Minor's assets and stock for voting stock of Major.[50]

CARRYOVER CONSIDERATIONS

Careful consideration of the restructuring alternative can help to preserve desirable tax carryover attributes.

EXAMPLE 45

Acquiring Corporation wants to obtain the assets of Target Corporation. These assets have a $600,000 basis to Target and a $500,000 fair market value. Target has incurred losses in its operations during the past several years and possesses $250,000 in NOLs, with 15 years of carryovers remaining. Acquiring plans to continue the business conducted by Target, hoping to do so on a profitable basis. ■

To accomplish the planned acquisition of Target's assets, Acquiring could consider the following alternatives.

1. Using cash and/or other property, Acquiring purchases the assets directly from Target. Following the purchase, Target liquidates and distributes the cash and/or property to its shareholders.
2. Acquiring purchases for cash and/or other property all of the stock in Target from its shareholders. Shortly thereafter, Acquiring liquidates Target.
3. Utilizing a "Type A" reorganization, Target merges into Acquiring. In exchange for their stock, Target's shareholders receive stock in Acquiring.
4. Under a "Type C" reorganization, Target transfers all of its assets to Acquiring in return for the latter's voting stock. Target distributes the Acquiring stock to its shareholders and liquidates.

[48] Rev.Rul. 2003–79, I.R.B. 2003–29.
[49] Rev.Rul. 70–434, 1970–2 C.B. 83.
[50] Rev.Rul. 74–35, 1974–1 C.B. 85.

A satisfactory solution must center around the preservation of Target Corporation's favorable tax attributes—the high basis in the assets and the NOL carryovers. Alternative 1 is highly unsatisfactory. It will not retain Target's favorable tax attributes. The purchase price (probably $500,000) becomes the basis of the assets in the hands of Acquiring Corporation. Further, any unused NOLs disappear upon Target's liquidation. Target has a realized loss of $100,000 [$600,000 (basis in the assets) − $500,000 (sale proceeds)] from the sale of its assets. Yet the realized loss may generate little, if any, tax savings to Target. In view of Target's unabsorbed NOL carryovers, it appears doubtful that the company will generate much taxable income in the year of sale.

Alternative 2 appears to be a better solution but has a major risk. When a subsidiary is liquidated under § 332, the subsidiary's basis in its assets carries over to the acquiring corporation.[51] Therefore, Target's $600,000 basis in its assets becomes Acquiring's basis in the assets. What Acquiring paid for the Target stock becomes irrelevant. Target's NOLs also carry over to Acquiring. However, § 269 (disallowing any deduction or credit when the acquisition was made to evade or avoid income tax) could present a problem. Section 269(b) specifically applies to a liquidation within two years after the acquisition date.

Alternatives 3 and 4 should accomplish the same tax result, but with less tax risk. Presuming Acquiring can establish a business purpose for the "Type A" or "Type C" reorganization, § 269 can be avoided. The preservation of favorable tax attributes, such as the NOL carryover, should be considered when acquiring a small corporation.

How much should Acquiring offer for Target Corporation in Alternatives 3 and 4? By preserving the NOL tax attribute, Acquiring is obtaining a value greater than the fair market value of the assets of $500,000. Assume the following facts.

- The Federal long-term interest rate is 4 percent.
- Acquiring uses a 6 percent discount factor for business decisions.
- Acquiring's marginal income tax rate is 35 percent for all years involved.

The § 382 limitation would allow Acquiring to utilize $20,000 of the NOL each year ($500,000 × 4%). Thus, it would take Acquiring 12.5 years to utilize the NOL ($250,000 ÷ $20,000). The net present value of the NOL to Acquiring is $63,378 computed as follows.

$20,000 × 35% = $7,000 tax benefit × 8.384 factor (12-year annuity at 6%) = $58,688
$250,000 − ($20,000 × 12 years) = $10,000 available for use in year 13
$10,000 × .469 factor (year 13 value of $1 at 6%) = $4,690
$58,688 + $4,690 = $63,378

The alternatives are illustrated in Figure 7.7.

EXAMPLE 46

Cardinal Corporation, worth $200,000, has a $150,000 NOL. The stock in Cardinal is owned by Kevin, 55%, and Fran, 45%. Kevin wants to sell his interest in Cardinal and retire. But what happens to the NOL if Kevin sells his entire interest? There would be a more than 50-percentage-point change in the ownership of Cardinal Corporation. Therefore, the § 382 limitation would be $200,000 times the long-term tax-exempt rate. Assume the rate is 10%. The loss of $150,000 is now limited to $20,000 annually. Can a sale be structured so that the NOL is not so limited?

An owner shift is calculated for the three-year testing period. Kevin could sell 35% of Cardinal stock in Year 1, 5% in Year 2, 5% in Year 3, and 10% in Year 4. None of the three-year testing periods has a more than 50-percentage-point change in the ownership of the corporation. Thus, there is no § 382 limitation. Cardinal can deduct the entire $150,000 NOL sooner rather than later. ■

[51] § 334(b)(1).

FIGURE 7.7 Four Alternatives for Acquiring Corporate Assets

Alternative 1: Purchase of Target Assets

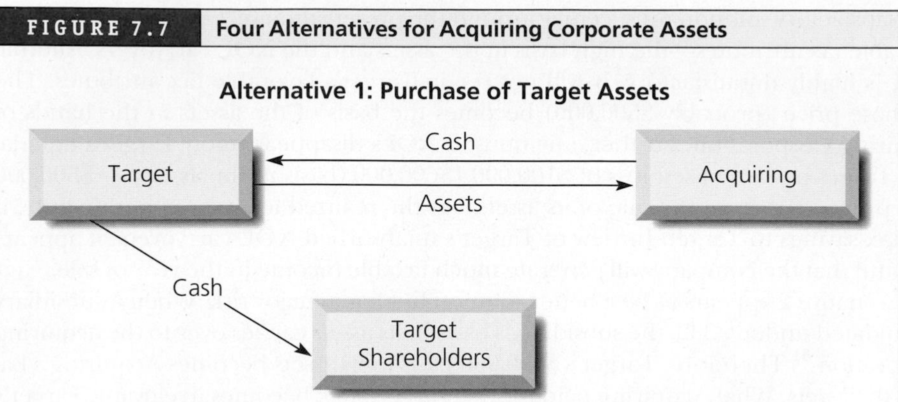

In a purchase of Target's assets for their fair market value of $500,000, Acquiring Corporation has a $500,000 basis in the assets. Target's higher basis of $600,000 is lost. In addition, its NOL of $250,000 disappears. Although Target recognizes a loss on the liquidation, the loss is not beneficial, as Target does not have taxable income that the loss can offset.

Alternative 2: Purchase of Target Stock— Liquidation of Target by Acquiring

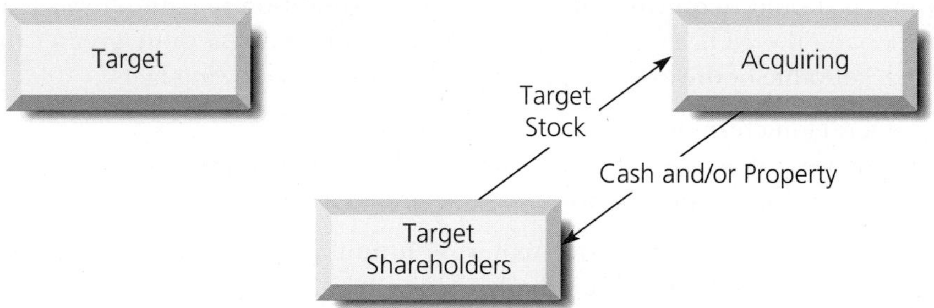

If Acquiring obtains all of Target's stock from the shareholders and liquidates Target, thereby obtaining all of Target's assets, there is a carryover of Target's basis in its assets. Thus, Acquiring has a basis of $600,000 in the assets. Target's NOL of $250,000 carries over to Acquiring, subject to the § 382 limitation. However, § 269 may be applied to disallow the basis carryover and NOL carryover.

Alternatives 3 and 4: "Type A" or "Type C" Reorganization

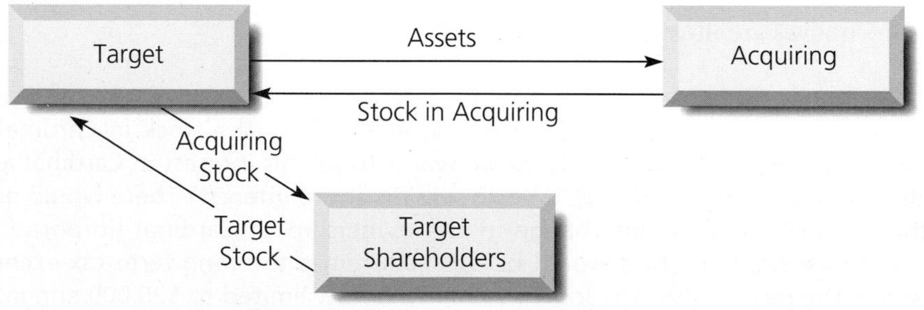

In a "Type A" or a "Type C" reorganization, the $600,000 basis in Target's assets will carry over to Acquiring. In addition, the $250,000 NOL carries over to Acquiring, subject to the § 382 limitation. Section 269 is less of a problem than in a subsidiary liquidation under § 332.

TABLE 7.1 Present Value of $1 per Period at *i*% for *n* Periods, PVIF(*i*,*n*)

Period	1%	2%	3%	4%	5%	6%	7%	8%	9%	10%	11%	12%	13%	14%	15%
1	0.990	0.980	0.971	0.962	0.952	0.943	0.935	0.926	0.917	0.909	0.901	0.893	0.885	0.877	0.870
2	0.980	0.961	0.943	0.925	0.907	0.890	0.873	0.857	0.842	0.826	0.812	0.797	0.783	0.769	0.756
3	0.971	0.942	0.915	0.889	0.864	0.840	0.816	0.794	0.772	0.751	0.731	0.712	0.693	0.675	0.658
4	0.961	0.924	0.888	0.855	0.823	0.792	0.763	0.735	0.708	0.683	0.659	0.636	0.613	0.592	0.572
5	0.951	0.906	0.863	0.822	0.784	0.747	0.713	0.681	0.650	0.621	0.593	0.567	0.543	0.519	0.497
6	0.942	0.888	0.837	0.790	0.746	0.705	0.666	0.630	0.596	0.564	0.535	0.507	0.480	0.456	0.432
7	0.933	0.871	0.813	0.760	0.711	0.665	0.623	0.583	0.547	0.513	0.482	0.452	0.425	0.400	0.376
8	0.923	0.853	0.789	0.731	0.677	0.627	0.582	0.540	0.502	0.467	0.434	0.404	0.376	0.351	0.327
9	0.914	0.837	0.766	0.703	0.645	0.592	0.544	0.500	0.460	0.424	0.391	0.361	0.333	0.308	0.284
10	0.905	0.820	0.744	0.676	0.614	0.558	0.508	0.463	0.422	0.386	0.352	0.322	0.295	0.270	0.247
11	0.896	0.804	0.722	0.650	0.585	0.527	0.475	0.429	0.388	0.350	0.317	0.287	0.261	0.237	0.215
12	0.887	0.788	0.701	0.625	0.557	0.497	0.444	0.397	0.356	0.319	0.286	0.257	0.231	0.208	0.187
13	0.879	0.773	0.681	0.601	0.530	0.469	0.415	0.368	0.326	0.290	0.258	0.229	0.204	0.182	0.163
14	0.870	0.758	0.661	0.577	0.505	0.442	0.388	0.340	0.299	0.263	0.232	0.205	0.181	0.160	0.141
15	0.861	0.743	0.642	0.555	0.481	0.417	0.362	0.315	0.275	0.239	0.209	0.183	0.160	0.140	0.123
16	0.853	0.728	0.623	0.534	0.458	0.394	0.339	0.292	0.252	0.218	0.188	0.163	0.141	0.123	0.107
17	0.844	0.714	0.605	0.513	0.436	0.371	0.317	0.270	0.231	0.198	0.170	0.146	0.125	0.108	0.093
18	0.836	0.700	0.587	0.494	0.416	0.350	0.296	0.250	0.212	0.180	0.153	0.130	0.111	0.095	0.081
19	0.828	0.686	0.570	0.475	0.396	0.331	0.277	0.232	0.194	0.164	0.138	0.116	0.098	0.083	0.070
20	0.820	0.673	0.554	0.456	0.377	0.312	0.258	0.215	0.178	0.149	0.124	0.104	0.087	0.073	0.061
25	0.780	0.610	0.478	0.375	0.295	0.233	0.184	0.146	0.116	0.092	0.074	0.059	0.047	0.038	0.030
30	0.742	0.552	0.412	0.308	0.231	0.174	0.131	0.099	0.075	0.057	0.044	0.033	0.026	0.020	0.015
35	0.706	0.500	0.355	0.253	0.181	0.130	0.094	0.068	0.049	0.036	0.026	0.019	0.014	0.010	0.008
40	0.672	0.453	0.307	0.208	0.142	0.097	0.067	0.046	0.032	0.022	0.015	0.011	0.008	0.005	0.004
50	0.608	0.372	0.228	0.141	0.087	0.054	0.034	0.021	0.013	0.009	0.005	0.003	0.002	0.001	0.001

TABLE 7.2 Present Value of an (Ordinary) Annuity of $1 per Period at *i*% for *n* Periods, PVIFA(*i*,*n*)

Period	1%	2%	3%	4%	5%	6%	7%	8%	9%	10%	11%	12%	13%	14%	15%
1	0.990	0.980	0.971	0.962	0.952	0.943	0.935	0.926	0.917	0.909	0.901	0.893	0.885	0.877	0.870
2	1.970	1.942	1.913	1.886	1.859	1.833	1.808	1.783	1.759	1.736	1.713	1.690	1.668	1.647	1.626
3	2.941	2.884	2.829	2.775	2.723	2.673	2.624	2.577	2.531	2.487	2.444	2.402	2.361	2.322	2.283
4	3.902	3.808	3.717	3.630	3.546	3.465	3.387	3.312	3.240	3.170	3.102	3.037	2.974	2.914	2.855
5	4.853	4.713	4.580	4.452	4.329	4.212	4.100	3.993	3.890	3.791	3.696	3.605	3.517	3.433	3.352
6	5.795	5.601	5.417	5.242	5.076	4.917	4.767	4.623	4.486	4.355	4.231	4.111	3.998	3.889	3.784
7	6.728	6.472	6.230	6.002	5.786	5.582	5.389	5.206	5.033	4.868	4.712	4.564	4.423	4.288	4.160
8	7.652	7.325	7.020	6.733	6.463	6.210	5.971	5.747	5.535	5.335	5.146	4.968	4.799	4.639	4.487
9	8.566	8.162	7.786	7.435	7.108	6.802	6.515	6.247	5.995	5.759	5.537	5.328	5.132	4.946	4.772
10	9.471	8.983	8.530	8.111	7.722	7.360	7.024	6.710	6.418	6.145	5.889	5.650	5.426	5.216	5.019
11	10.368	9.787	9.253	8.760	8.306	7.887	7.499	7.139	6.805	6.495	6.207	5.938	5.687	5.453	5.234
12	11.255	10.575	9.954	9.385	8.863	8.384	7.943	7.536	7.161	6.814	6.492	6.194	5.918	5.660	5.421
13	12.134	11.348	10.635	9.986	9.394	8.853	8.358	7.904	7.487	7.103	6.750	6.424	6.122	5.842	5.583
14	13.004	12.106	11.296	10.563	9.899	9.295	8.745	8.244	7.786	7.367	6.982	6.628	6.302	6.002	5.724
15	13.865	12.849	11.938	11.118	10.380	9.712	9.108	8.559	8.061	7.606	7.191	6.811	6.462	6.142	5.847
16	14.718	13.578	12.561	11.652	10.838	10.106	9.447	8.851	8.313	7.824	7.379	6.974	6.604	6.265	5.954
17	15.562	14.292	13.166	12.166	11.274	10.477	9.763	9.122	8.544	8.022	7.549	7.120	6.729	6.373	6.047
18	16.398	14.992	13.754	12.659	11.690	10.828	10.059	9.372	8.756	8.201	7.702	7.250	6.840	6.467	6.128
19	17.226	15.678	14.324	13.134	12.085	11.158	10.336	9.604	8.950	8.365	7.839	7.366	6.938	6.550	6.198
20	18.046	16.351	14.877	13.590	12.462	11.470	10.594	9.818	9.129	8.514	7.963	7.469	7.025	6.623	6.259
25	22.023	19.523	17.413	15.622	14.094	12.783	11.654	10.675	9.823	9.077	8.422	7.843	7.330	6.873	6.464
30	25.808	22.396	19.600	17.292	15.372	13.765	12.409	11.258	10.274	9.427	8.694	8.055	7.496	7.003	6.566
35	29.409	24.999	21.487	18.665	16.374	14.498	12.948	11.655	10.567	9.644	8.855	8.176	7.586	7.070	6.617
40	32.835	27.355	23.115	19.793	17.159	15.046	13.332	11.925	10.757	9.779	8.951	8.244	7.634	7.105	6.642
50	39.196	31.424	25.730	21.482	18.256	15.762	13.801	12.233	10.962	9.915	9.042	8.304	7.675	7.133	6.661

REFOCUS ON THE BIG PICTURE

STRUCTURING ACQUISITIONS

Rock & Water Corporation (R&W) is unsure how to structure the potential acquisitions of its three suppliers. The first target is BrineCo, a profitable corporation that has been owned predominantly by the Adams family since its incorporation in 1950. In negotiations with BrineCo, R&W determines that it has virtually no debt because most of its assets date from its incorporation. Senior Adams family members are ready to retire, and the younger generation has no interest in the business. Consequently, all members would like some cash in the transaction. The "Type A" reorganization would be a good choice for this acquisition. R&W can exchange cash, preferred stock, and voting stock for only those assets it wants to acquire. Since BrineCo has few liabilities, acquiring all of them will not be an issue nor will obtaining the approval of the BrineCo shareholders. The assets not transferred to R&W will be distributed to the Adams family, along with the stock and cash received from R&W in complete liquidation of BrineCo.

The next target, AcidCo, has been struggling financially and is having legal liability issues related to its failure to meet environmental standards. Since its landscaping chemical and mining acid lines of business are active and have been in existence for more than five years, AcidCo can, through a divisive "Type D" reorganization, spin off or split off its mining acid business and retain the landscaping chemical line. Once this is accomplished, R&W can acquire AcidCo stock from its shareholders by exchanging R&W voting stock in a "Type B" reorganization. This restructuring would protect R&W's assets from AcidCo's legal liability issues until R&W can clean up the environmental problems.

Lastly, ChemCo has the technology to produce environmentally safe products, but its inexperienced management has resulted in it being unprofitable. R&W can use a "Type C" reorganization to acquire substantially all of ChemCo's assets and can select which liabilities it assumes. To avoid having the liability assumption treated as boot, R&W should use solely voting stock for the exchange. ChemCo must terminate after the reorganization. Given that ChemCo has NOL, capital loss, and business credit carryovers, R&W must be sure to meet the continuity of business enterprise requirement for at least two years. Most likely the § 382 limitation will apply as ChemCo shareholders will experience an equity structure shift of greater than 50 percentage points; thus, the amount of carryover tax attributes that R&W may use in any one year will be limited. A net present value analysis should be performed to determine what R&W is willing to pay for ChemCo's tax attributes. Finally R&W will need to keep two E & P accounts: one for its pre-reorganization E & P and another with ChemCo's negative E & P that will be offset by future profits of the combined company.

KEY TERMS

Business purpose, 7–25
Consolidation, 7–10
Continuity of business enterprise, 7–26
Continuity of interest test, 7–10
Control, 7–12
Equity structure shift, 7–30
Long-term tax-exempt rate, 7–31
Merger, 7–10
Owner shift, 7–30
Ownership change, 7–30
Recapitalization, 7–19
Reorganization, 7–3
Section 382 limitation, 7–30
Spin-off, 7–18
Split-off, 7–18
Split-up, 7–18
Step transaction, 7–27

DISCUSSION QUESTIONS

1. **LO.1** Explain why it is wise to obtain a private letter ruling from the IRS when structuring a corporate reorganization.

2. **LO.1, 2** What type of treatment do corporate shareholders and individual shareholders desire when there is a taxable gain from a corporate restructuring? How is the character of the shareholders' gain determined?

3. **LO.1** Identify the nontaxable types of corporate reorganizations.

4. **LO.2** Summarize the tax consequences of a § 368 reorganization.

5. **LO.2** How is the four-column template in Concept Summary 7.1 used to determine a shareholder's basis in the new stock received in a corporate restructuring?

ISSUE ID

6. **LO.1, 2, 3** Five years ago, Mervin purchased 1,000 shares of Fern Corporation, which represents 20% of Fern's outstanding stock. As part of a restructuring agreement between Fern and Ivy Corporation, Mervin receives 10% of Ivy's stock (valued at $100,000) and a $30,000 bond in exchange for all of his Fern stock. Fern is liquidated after the restructuring. What are the tax issues regarding this transaction?

7. **LO.3** How does a "Type A" reorganization differ from a "Type B" with regard to the consideration that is permissible in the restructuring?

8. **LO.3** Compare the relationship between the acquiring and target corporations immediately after a "Type B" and a "Type C" reorganization.

9. **LO.3** What is the difference in the treatment of liabilities between a "Type A" and a "Type C" reorganization?

10. **LO.3** A "Type C" reorganization requires that substantially all of the target's assets be transferred to the acquiring corporation. Explain what is meant by "substantially all" of the assets.

11. **LO.3** What are the different types of "Type D" reorganizations? Describe each type.

12. **LO.3** What types of transactions receive tax-free treatment in "Type E" reorganizations?

13. **LO.3** What types of restructurings qualify as "Type F" reorganizations?

14. **LO.3** Discuss the continuity of interest requirement for the "Type G" reorganization.

ISSUE ID

15. **LO.3, 4, 5** Air Corporation is interested in acquiring Water Corporation. Water produces equipment for scuba diving, and Air manufactures parachutes for skydiving. Water has had some setbacks on its investments and has a substantial capital loss carryforward. Conversely, Air's investments have increased in value and have considerable built-in gains.

    If a restructuring occurs, Air will exchange 20% of its stock and some liquid assets for most of Water's assets. Air would also like to have Water switch to producing air tanks to be used by the military in extremely high ejections from fighter planes.

    As the tax manager for Air, what concerns do you have regarding this proposed transaction between Air and Water?

16. **LO.3, 4, 6** Six years ago, Circle Corporation developed a chemical process that Square Corporation would like to own. Square wants to acquire all of the assets used in producing chemicals from this process. Circle is not willing to sell the process or assets due to the large gain it would recognize. Circle suggests a merger, but Square is not interested in Circle's other lines of business.

    Circle is considering splitting off its other business assets into a new corporation for the benefit of those shareholders who are against the proposed merger with Square. This split-off would occur just prior to Circle entering into a "Type C" reorganization with Square. For the assets retained in Circle after the split-off, the remaining shareholders will receive Square stock.

    Explain whether this transaction will run afoul of either the "Type C" statutory reorganization requirements or the continuity of interest doctrine, due to the application of the step transaction doctrine.

17. **LO.5** What types of reorganizations are subject to the § 381 limitation?

18. **LO.5** For § 382, what is the testing period for determining ownership shifts? How are shareholders owning less than 5% treated in determining ownership shifts?

19. **LO.5** The § 382 limitation is intended to restrict the use of tax attributes to a hypothetical future income stream from the loss corporation. How is the future income stream defined?

20. **LO.4** Emily Arson is the president and sole shareholder of Emar Corporation, a small shoe production company. Though Emar's manufacturing equipment is old and not of much value, Emar's plant has a very favorable location. Mega Tires, Inc., is interested in acquiring Emar solely to obtain the land. Mega Tires would likely junk Emar's manufacturing equipment and demolish the plant so that it could build a new tire retail outlet at the location. The plant and land are 90% of Emar's asset value. Mega Tires has proposed exchanging $1 million of its stock for Emar's assets.

COMMUNICATIONS

Emily has heard of the continuity of business enterprise requirement that must be met for a corporate reorganization to receive tax-free treatment. She is concerned that the proposed transaction will not meet this requirement. Write Emily Arson a letter explaining what she must include in her contract with Mega Tires to ensure that the proposed reorganization will satisfy the continuity of business enterprise doctrine. Emily's address is 510 S. Market Street, Alton, MO 65606.

21. **LO.4** Briefly describe the judicial doctrines of sound business purpose, continuity of business enterprise, and the step transaction doctrine.

22. **LO.5** Why does the calculation of the § 382 limitation for business credits require calculations beyond what is necessary for NOLs?

23. **LO.5** How is a target corporation's negative E & P balance treated when it is carried over to the successor corporation?

24. **LO.5, 6** Garden Corporation is considering acquiring Flower Corporation. Flower has a good product line and a fairly new production plant; however, it has made some unprofitable investments. Currently, Flower holds a five-year capital loss carryforward of $50,000. Garden holds its own $20,000 capital loss carryover that will expire in two years. In its acquisition of Flower, what should Garden consider when determining Flower's fair market value?

25. **LO.5, 6** Under what circumstances will the acquiring corporation have two or more E & P accounts after a reorganization?

PROBLEMS

26. **LO.3** Determine whether the following transactions are taxable. If a transaction is not taxable, indicate what type of reorganization is effected, if any.

DECISION MAKING

   a. Chow Corporation has two divisions that have been in existence for seven years. The nail division has assets valued at $455,000 and liabilities of $75,000, whereas the hammer division has assets valued at $670,000 and liabilities of $50,000. Chow would like the two divisions to be separate corporations. It creates Spitz Corporation and transfers all of the hammer division assets and liabilities in exchange for 100% of Spitz's stock. Chow then distributes the Spitz stock to its shareholders.
   b. Kees Corporation has not been able to pay its creditors in the last year. To avoid foreclosure, Kees transfers its assets valued at $720,000 and liabilities of $700,000 to a new corporation, Corgi, Inc., in accordance with a state court proceeding. The creditors receive shares of Corgi voting stock valued at $500,000 and cancel the outstanding debt. The former Kees shareholders receive the remaining shares in Corgi.
   c. Plott Corporation owns assets valued at $400,000 and liabilities of $100,000. Saluki Corporation transfers $160,000 of its voting stock and $40,000 in cash for 75% of Plott's assets and all of its liabilities. Plott distributes its remaining assets and the Saluki stock to its shareholders. Plott then liquidates.
   d. Akita Corporation holds assets valued at $750,000 with liabilities of $300,000, and Griffon Corporation holds assets valued at $1.5 million with liabilities of $225,000. Akita transfers 75% of its voting stock to Griffon in exchange for $1,350,000 of its assets. Griffon distributes the Akita stock, its remaining assets, and all of its liabilities to its shareholders. Griffon then liquidates.

e. York Corporation owns assets valued at $300,000 with liabilities of $100,000, and Anatol Corporation holds assets valued at $800,000 with liabilities of $200,000. York exchanges 75% of its voting stock for 100% of Anatol's assets and liabilities. Anatol distributes the York stock to its shareholders. Anatol then liquidates.

f. Canaan Corporation obtained 200,000 shares of Bouvier Corporation's stock 10 years ago. In the current year, Canaan exchanges 40% of its stock for 500,000 of the remaining 800,000 shares of Bouvier stock. After the transaction, Canaan owns 700,000 of the 800,000 Bouvier shares outstanding.

27. **LO.2** Cole acquired 55% of Dane Corporation for $400,000 eight years ago. In the current year, Dane merges with Great Corporation, and Cole receives 7.5% of Great's stock plus $300,000 in land. The Great stock received by Cole is valued at $900,000. At the time of the transaction, Dane's E & P is $450,000, and Great's E & P is $1.8 million. As an individual shareholder, how should Cole treat this transaction for tax purposes?

28. **LO.2** Tri Corporation and Angle Corporation are combining to form Triangle Corporation in a restructuring that qualifies as a "Type A" consolidation reorganization. Tyron, the sole shareholder of Tri, has a basis of $250,000 in his stock, which he purchased 10 years ago. Anna is the sole shareholder of Angle and also has a basis of $250,000 in her stock. She purchased the stock four months ago. Tri transfers all of its assets valued at $650,000 (adjusted basis of $280,000) and $250,000 in liabilities to Triangle for $50,000 in cash and $350,000 in Triangle stock.

    Angle transfers all of its assets valued at $250,000 (adjusted basis of $200,000) and $50,000 in liabilities to Triangle for $30,000 in cash and $170,000 in Triangle stock. Upon completion of the consolidation, the Triangle stock and cash are transferred to Tyron and Anna, and both Tri and Angle cease to exist by operation of law.

    Determine the gain or loss that Tri, Angle, Tyron, Anna, and Triangle recognize from the reorganization. What are Triangle's bases in the assets it receives and Tyron's and Anna's new bases in their Triangle stock?

29. **LO.2** Sahara Corporation acquires Oasis Corporation in a "Type A" reorganization by exchanging 35% of its stock for all of the Oasis assets (fair market value of $950,000), liabilities ($300,000), and accumulated E & P ($140,000). Rama, a 60% shareholder of Oasis, exchanges her interest in Oasis (basis of $225,000) for Sahara stock and $100,000 cash. What is the tax treatment of Rama's exchange of Oasis stock for Sahara stock and cash?

DECISION MAKING

30. **LO.2, 3** Spinone Corporation directs its sole shareholder to exchange all of his common stock valued at $200,000 (basis of $50,000) for $100,000 of common stock, $80,000 of preferred stock, and $20,000 in cash. In addition, Spinone directs its sole bondholder to exchange her $150,000 of bonds paying 6.0% for $170,000 of bonds paying 5.3%. How are these transactions treated for tax purposes by the shareholder, the bondholder, and Spinone?

31. **LO.2** Quail Corporation was created in 2000 through contributions from Kasha ($800,000) and Frank ($200,000). In a transaction qualifying as a reorganization, Quail exchanges all of its assets currently valued at $2 million (basis of $1.5 million) for Covey Corporation stock valued at $1.9 million plus $100,000 in Covey bonds. Quail distributes the Covey stock and bonds proportionately to Frank and Kasha in exchange for their stock in Quail. Quail's current and accumulated E & P before the reorganization amounts to $70,000.
    a. How do Kasha and Frank treat this transaction for tax purposes?
    b. How do Quail and Covey treat this transaction for tax purposes? What is Covey's basis in the assets it receives from Quail?

32. **LO.2** Rosa owns 30% of Pine Corporation's stock (basis of $50,000), and the other 70% was recently purchased by Arvid (basis of $620,000). Pine enters into a reorganization with Lodgepole Corporation, in which Rosa will receive a 5% interest (value of $300,000) in Lodgepole and Arvid will receive a 10% interest (value of $600,000) plus assets worth $100,000. Lodgepole's basis in these assets is $60,000. At the time of the reorganization, Pine's value is $1 million, and Lodgepole's value is $6 million.
    a. What are Rosa's and Arvid's bases in their new Lodgepole stock?
    b. What is the amount of gain (loss) recognized by Rosa, Arvid, Pine, and Lodgepole on the reorganization?

33. **LO.2** Lemon Corporation enters into a merger with Lime Corporation. Lemon has assets valued at $900,000 (basis of $980,000) and liabilities of $600,000. Lime transfers its stock for 90% of Lemon's assets and liabilities. Lemon distributes the Lime stock and its remaining asset (value of $90,000, adjusted basis of $80,000) subject to a liability ($60,000) to its shareholder, Lea, in exchange for her Lemon stock. Lea's basis in her Lemon stock is $350,000. Lemon liquidates after collecting all of its stock from Lea.
   a. What is the value of stock transferred from Lime to Lemon?
   b. What is the amount of gain (loss) realized and recognized by Lea from the merger? What is Lea's basis in her Lime stock?
   c. What is the amount of gain (loss) realized and recognized by Lemon and Lime from the merger? What is Lime's basis in Lemon's assets?

34. **LO.3** Determine whether the following transactions are taxable. If a transaction is not taxable, indicate what type of reorganization is effected, if any. **DECISION MAKING**
   a. Bichon Frise Corporation moves its headquarters and state of legal incorporation from Omaha, Nebraska, to Phoenix, Arizona. It also changes its name to Chihuahua, Inc.
   b. Tzu, Inc., owns assets valued at $600,000 and liabilities of $150,000. Whippet Corporation exchanges $270,000 of its voting stock and investments worth $180,000 for all of Tzu's assets and liabilities. Tzu distributes the Whippet stock to its shareholders for 60% of their stock and retains the investments.
   c. Borzoi Company holds assets valued at $850,000 and liabilities of $50,000. Mastiff, Inc., transfers $790,000 of its voting stock and $10,000 of nonvoting stock for all of Borzoi's voting and nonvoting stock. Borzoi becomes a subsidiary of Mastiff.
   d. Rottweiler Corporation owns two lines of business that it has conducted for the last eight years. For liability protection, Rottweiler's shareholders decide that it would be best to separate into two corporations. The assets and liabilities of the garbage collection division are transferred to Rott Corporation in exchange for all of its stock. The manufacturing division's assets and liabilities are exchanged for all of the stock of Weiler Corporation. The Rott and Weiler stocks are distributed to the Rottweiler shareholders in return for all of their Rottweiler stock. Then Rottweiler liquidates.
   e. Sharpei Company holds assets valued at $3 million and liabilities of $100,000. LowChen Company transfers $2.85 million of its voting stock for 95% of Sharpei's assets. Sharpei distributes the LowChen stock, the remaining assets, and the liabilities to its shareholders and then liquidates.
   f. Spaniel, Inc., owns assets valued at $1 million and liabilities of $450,000. Cocker Corporation transfers $590,000 of its voting stock and $5,000 in cash for all of Spaniel's assets and assumes 90% of its liabilities. Spaniel distributes the Cocker stock, cash, and remaining liabilities to its shareholders and then liquidates.

35. **LO.3, 6** Several years ago, Apso, Inc., was organized with equal contributions from April, ShibCo, and Otter Corporation. Last year, April purchased additional Apso stock from Otter, such that her Apso ownership percentage now is 57%. Otter currently owns 10% of Apso and ShibCo owns 33%. In the current year, ShibCo decides that it wants a controlling interest in Apso. April is willing to exchange her Apso stock for ShibCo stock. Otter does not want to be a shareholder of ShibCo. It prefers to remain a shareholder of Apso, but if there is no other solution, it will liquidate its interest. Apso currently holds assets worth $12 million (basis of $6.5 million) and $2 million of liabilities. Explain whether ShibCo can accomplish the restructuring using a "Type B" or "Type C" reorganization. **DECISION MAKING**

36. **LO.3, 6** Birdie Corporation has obtained a patent on a revolutionary putter that is sure to be an instant success with serious golfers. Unfortunately, Birdie does not have the capital to market the new putter adequately. Therefore, it is considering joining forces with Bogie Corporation, a company with substantial liquid assets and experience in marketing golfing products. Although Bogie has had some unfavorable press lately that has tarnished its reputation, Birdie believes a union between the two would be beneficial to both corporations. **COMMUNICATIONS**

    Birdie's president, Xanna Jackson, requests your guidance as to what type of reorganization Birdie and Bogie should consider. She provides you with the following information.

Corporation	FMV of Assets	Adjusted Basis	Liabilities
Birdie	$200,000	$160,000	$150,000
Bogie	800,000	600,000	100,000

Write a letter to Ms. Jackson, explaining the appropriateness of using a "Type A" consolidation, a "Type C" reorganization, or an acquisitive "Type D" reorganization. Birdie's address is 460 Lakeview Drive, Lake Oswego, OR 97034.

ISSUE ID

37. **LO.3, 6** PeekCo enters into a transaction to acquire Poodle, Inc., by exchanging $1.5 million of its voting stock for all remaining common ($900,000) and preferred stock ($600,000) outstanding. PeekCo currently owns 30% of Poodle that it bought three years ago for $250,000 from one of the original owners (basis of $50,000). The owner sold when she found out that PeekCo might have intentions of acquiring Poodle. Identify the tax issues in the proposed transaction.

COMMUNICATIONS

38. **LO.3, 6** Frame Corporation, a publicly held entity, has approached Lisa Springs, the CEO of WireCo, regarding the acquisition of its manufacturing plant and equipment contained therein plus any liabilities associated with these assets. Not wanting to recognize a $300,000 gain on the disposition of these assets ($850,000 value − $550,000 basis), Lisa suggests that Frame acquire WireCo using a "Type C" reorganization. However, Frame is not interested in acquiring the building housing WireCo's headquarters that is located adjacent to the plant. The building is valued at $150,000, and its basis is $130,000. WireCo has $200,000 of liabilities associated with the plant and equipment and a $100,000 mortgage on the headquarters building.

    Lisa Springs requests your advice on whether the transaction can be structured as a "Type C" reorganization if Frame does not acquire the headquarters. WireCo's address is 3443 E. Riverbank Road, Walla Walla, WA 99362. Write a letter to Ms. Springs indicating how to arrange this transaction and meet the requirements of a "Type C" reorganization.

DECISION MAKING

39. **LO.3, 6** In 2000, Shelty Corporation was organized to manufacture dog food with equal contributions from Jane, Claire, and Brian. In 2002, Shelty opened retail pet stores in North Dakota. In 2004, Shelty developed a line of healthy snacks for dogs. Each line of business has a net value of $1 million. In the current year, there have been substantial disagreements among the three shareholders as to Shelty's future direction, and consequently, the shareholders have decided to go their separate ways. Shelty must cease to exist, as none of the shareholders wants the others to obtain the Shelty name. Develop, diagram, and explain a plan to divide the corporation among the shareholders while incurring the least amount of current Federal income tax.

ISSUE ID

COMMUNICATIONS

40. **LO.3** Stapelia Corporation has been operating eight landfills in three different states for the past 30 years. Lately, the states have changed their laws governing landfills, making it cumbersome for Stapelia to ensure that all the landfills meet the various environmental requirements. Stapelia's president, Robin Fernandez, would like to divide Stapelia into three corporations by incorporating the landfills in the states in which they are located. Write Robin Fernandez a letter explaining Stapelia's choices in accomplishing its goal of becoming three separate corporations. Robin's address is 2500 Cactus Road, Dodge City, KS 67801.

DECISION MAKING

41. **LO.2, 3** The Komondor Corporation was incorporated in 2001 by Tyee and Danette. Tyee received 5,000 shares of common stock for his $100,000 contribution, and Danette received 5,000 shares of common stock and 500 shares of preferred for her $200,000 contribution. In 2005, both Tyee and Danette acquired $50,000 of Komondor bonds paying 3% interest.

    In the current year, Komondor's common stock is valued at $500,000, and its preferred stock is worth $100,000. SheenCo would like to acquire a 50% interest in Komondor through the purchase of common stock for $500,000. Tyee and Danette see this as a good time to restructure Komondor's capital. They would like to own bonds paying 5% interest, and Tyee would like to receive $50,000 of preferred stock for some of his common stock. What advice would you give to Komondor?

42. **LO.3** The Titan Arum Corporation was incorporated by Sia two years ago in Boston, Massachusetts. Titan Arum has not been very successful even though its products are in great demand. Sia named the company Titan Arum after the plant that has the largest flower in the world. However, unbeknownst to Sia, the flower smells like rotting meat. Upon learning this vital information, Sia decides that his corporation needs a new name and a new start in a state with no state corporate income tax. He creates a new corporation, Rose, in Washington State. Explain how to transfer all of Titan Arum's assets and liabilities to Rose using a tax-favored reorganization. **ISSUE ID**

43. **LO.3** TinCo has product liability problems and has filed for bankruptcy protection in the state court. Currently, its liabilities are $1 million, and its depreciable assets are valued at $550,000 (basis of $400,000). Through the "Type G" reorganization, a new entity, ZinCo, has been created to succeed TinCo. At the time of the restructuring, TinCo has an NOL carryforward of $200,000, general business credits of $50,000, and a capital loss carryforward of $100,000. Explain the tax consequences for TinCo and ZinCo if ZinCo elects to reduce the basis of the depreciable property first in the "Type G" reorganization.

44. **LO.3, 4** Joe, Greg, Lynn, and Shanna each own a 25% interest in Norwich Corporation, which manufactures shoe polish. Joe is irascible and often argues with the other three shareholders. They tend to give in to Joe because he is so persistent. Now Joe has caused Norwich to acquire a wine store by exchanging 30% of the Norwich stock for all of the assets ($300,000) of the wine store. The Norwich stock was distributed to the wine store's owner, and then the wine store entity liquidated. After Joe has run the wine business for a few months, the other shareholders vote to drop the wine business into a separate corporation, with Joe receiving all of the stock for his 25% interest in Norwich. Joe no longer will be a shareholder of Norwich. Identify the tax issues regarding these transactions. **ISSUE ID**

45. **LO.2, 3, 4, 5, 6** Float Corporation is in the luxury yacht business and has been hit hard by the downturn in the economy. It has been barely breaking even, and its investments of its previous profits have substantial built-in capital losses. It has not sold these investment assets because it cannot utilize the resulting tax losses. Float's attorney suggests that it try to merge with a profitable company, specifically one with built-in capital gains. A profitable company would be willing to acquire Float just for its built-in capital losses. **ISSUE ID**

    Float advertises for a merger partner, and Fierce, Inc., contacts Float. Fierce manufactures and installs home security systems. In the discussion, Float determines that Fierce could use a small fraction of Float's business assets and might consider developing security systems for yachts, but is not at all interested in manufacturing yachts. Most important, Fierce is very interested in acquiring Float's built-in capital losses.

    Fierce offers 10% of its stock and $500,000 in exchange for all of Float's assets. Float can use the cash to buy the stock of the shareholders who oppose the merger. What tax issues should Fierce and Float consider before agreeing to this merger as structured?

46. **LO.5** Through a "Type B" reorganization, Golden Corporation acquired 90% of RetrieverCo stock by October 2 of the current tax year ending December 31. At the time the 90% was acquired, RetrieverCo was worth $800,000, and the Federal long-term tax-exempt rate was 3%. RetrieverCo holds capital loss carryovers of $50,000. If Golden reports taxable income of $300,000 which includes $30,000 of capital gains, how much of the RetrieverCo capital loss carryover may Golden use in the current year to offset its income?

47. **LO.5** Through an acquisitive "Type D" reorganization, Border, Inc., is merged into Collie Corporation on September 2 of the current calendar tax year. The Federal long-term tax-exempt rate for September 2 is 5%. Border shareholders receive 70% of the Collie stock in exchange for all of their Border shares. Border liquidates immediately after the exchange. At the time of the merger, Border was worth $1 million and held a $500,000 NOL.

    If Collie reports taxable income of $400,000 for the current year, how much of the Border NOL can be utilized in the current year? How much of the Border NOL may Collie utilize next year if its taxable income remains the same?

48. **LO.3, 5** Through a "Type C" reorganization, Springer Corporation was merged into Spaniel Corporation last year. Springer shareholders received 40% of the Spaniel stock in exchange for all of their Springer shares. Springer liquidated immediately after the exchange. At the time of the merger, Springer was worth $2 million and held a $500,000 NOL. If Spaniel reports taxable income of $800,000 for the current year, how much of the

Springer NOL can be utilized by Spaniel? Assume that the applicable Federal long-term tax-exempt rate is 4%.

DECISION MAKING

49. **LO.5** Five years ago, Jack purchased an Inu Corporation 15-year bond having a face value of $150,000 and paying 6% annual interest. In a "Type E" reorganization, Inu is going to exchange Jack's bond with 10 years remaining for a 5-year bond having a face value of $180,000 and paying 4% annual interest. Jack uses a 6% discount factor and is in the 25% tax bracket for all years. The capital gain rate is 15% for all years. Determine if this is an equitable exchange for Jack.

50. **LO.5** Global Corporation is negotiating a merger ("Type A" reorganization) with State Corporation, to be effective on December 31 of the current year. Global is a profitable corporation with $10 million in assets and taxable income of approximately $5 million, whereas State is struggling with built-up NOLs of $560,000 and net assets valued at $800,000. If Global's discount rate for investment decisions is 7%, what is the maximum value to Global of State's NOL? Assume that the Federal long-term tax-exempt rate is 5% for this merger.

DECISION MAKING

51. **LO.5** Taipa Corporation is interested in acquiring Kers Corporation through a "Type C" reorganization on January 2 of the current year. Taipa's stock is valued at $10 million and generates $1 million of taxable income yearly. Kers holds plant and equipment valued at $780,000 and liabilities of $230,000. It also reports a $346,500 NOL with 10 years remaining of the carryover period. If Taipa uses a 12% discount rate for its business investment decisions and the Federal long-term tax-exempt rate is 9%, what percentage of its stock should be exchanged for Kers's assets?

52. **LO.5** On January 2 of the current year, Tulip, Inc., merged with Tree, Inc., receiving $2 million in Tree stock for all of its assets and liabilities. The Tulip shareholders now own 25% of Tree. At the time of the merger, Tulip held a capital loss carryforward of $80,000 and excess business credits of $35,000. At the end of the current year, Tree computes its taxable income before any carryovers as $600,000: $60,000 capital gains and $540,000 operating income. If the Federal long-term rate is 6%, how much of the Tulip carryovers may Tree utilize in the current year?

53. **LO.5** Through a "Type A" reorganization, VizslaCo acquires 100% of Puli Corporation by exchanging 30% of its stock for all of Puli's assets and liabilities. The VizslaCo stock was exchanged for all of the stock of the Puli shareholders. Then Puli liquidated. The net value of Puli's assets at the time of the restructuring was $500,000, and the Federal long-term tax-exempt rate was 5%. Puli held business tax credit carryovers of $61,250. If VizslaCo is always in the 35% tax bracket, what is the value of these credits to VizslaCo, assuming that it uses a discount rate of 8%?

54. **LO.5** Shepherd Corporation is considering acquiring RentCo by exchanging its stock (value of $10 per share) for RentCo's only asset, a tract of land (adjusted basis of $150,000 and no liability). The yearly net rent that RentCo receives on the land is $50,000. Shepherd anticipates that it will receive the same net rent for the land over the next 20 years. At the end of that time, it would sell the land for $400,000.

    What is the maximum number of shares that RentCo shareholders can expect Shepherd to offer for 100% of their RentCo stock? Assume that Shepard uses a 10% discount rate and is in the 34% tax bracket for all years. What type of reorganization is this contemplated transaction?

ISSUE ID

55. **LO.3, 4, 5, 6** Henri and Simone started Manx Corporation in 2002 with each investing $500,000. Manx develops and manufactures pet toys and supplies. The business has been very profitable (now valued at $5 million) due to Henri's marketing abilities and Simone's knack for inventing toys that pets love. Since Henri and Simone feel that Manx cannot expand further in the pet product industry, they are in the market to acquire another company.

    Henri hears about LaPerm Corporation from one of their customers. LaPerm is a beauty supply manufacturer. It has a great line of products but has suffered substantial losses due to a lack of strategic marketing and ineffective management. It is a small company with net assets valued at $200,000, but it has a $300,000 NOL and a $100,000 business credit carryover. All the shares of LaPerm are held by Marcel, who started LaPerm 40 years ago. Marcel is 66 and is no longer interested in running the business.

    Before Henri and Simone enter into negotiations with Marcel regarding the acquisition of LaPerm using a tax-deferred reorganization, what issues should be considered?

RESEARCH PROBLEMS

Note: Solutions to Research Problems can be prepared by using the **Checkpoint® Student Edition** online research product, which is available to accompany this text. It is also possible to prepare solutions to the Research Problems by using tax research materials found in a standard tax library.

THOMSON REUTERS
Checkpoint® Student Edition

Research Problem 1. New Gate Corporation desires to acquire Old Post in a nontaxable transaction. Prior to entering into the transaction with New Gate, Old Post issues $800,000 worth of 15-year bonds paying 6% annually. The bonds are purchased by most of Old Post's shareholders and also by many individuals who have no affiliation with Old Post. New Gate makes an offer to the shareholders to exchange two shares of its common voting class A stock for each common share of Old Post and 20 shares of common voting class B stock for each preferred share of Old Post.

Most of the shareholders are reluctant to make the exchange because of the favorable terms of the Old Post bonds they are holding. Consequently, New Gate offers to acquire all of the Old Post outstanding bonds in exchange for New Gate bonds paying 6% interest annually, with an equal principal amount and a 15-year term. All of the Old Post bondholders exchange their debentures, and 90% of the Old Post shareholders exchange their stock. Can these transactions qualify as nontaxable corporate reorganizations? How should these transactions be treated by New Gate, Old Post, and Old Post's shareholders?

Research Problem 2. Pan, an S corporation, is in the home construction business and has sustained $500,000 in losses in excess of the shareholders' bases in their stock. Thus, these losses have been suspended and are not likely to be available to the shareholders in the near future. To finance its construction in the last couple of years, Pan has issued notes for $1 million, and it is currently in default on these notes. Pan sells its investment assets and accounts receivables. It uses the proceeds to partially pay the note holders.

Once Pan realizes that it is no longer a viable going concern, it files a petition for bankruptcy under Chapter 11 with the bankruptcy court. To rehabilitate its business, Pan is considering the following. It will create a new C corporation, called Clipper, into which Pan will merge. Thus, Clipper will be the surviving corporation. The note holders will receive 80% of the Clipper stock in exchange for relinquishing their rights to the outstanding principals on their notes. The other 20% of the stock will be exchanged with the former shareholders of Pan. Clipper will acquire 60% of the fair market value of Pan's gross assets and 100% of the fair market value of the operating assets held at the bankruptcy filing date. The operating assets are all of Pan's assets except those previously sold to pay the note holders. Following the merger, Clipper will continue in the home construction industry.

Will the merger, as described, meet the requirements of the "Type G" reorganization? Specifically, does the proposed reorganization meet the requirement that substantially all of the assets of the old corporation be transferred to the new corporation?

Research Problem 3. Marula Corporation was formed in 2000, with Adede contributing $34,000 of machinery, Buru contributing $33,000 cash, and Chipo $33,000 of land. Marula has been a very successful firm and now is valued at $1 million. Based on the success of Marula, Adede, Buru, and Chipo join with Dube to create the Kudu Corporation this year. Adele, Buru, and Chipo each contribute $132,000 for 99% of the stock (33% each). Dube contributes $4,000 for 1% of the shares.

Through Dube's contacts, Kudu is able to obtain a very lucrative government contract. Unfortunately, Kudu does not have the facilities to service this contract. Marula easily could fulfill the government orders, but Dube had the contract written in such a manner that it is not transferable. Consequently, Marula transfers all of its assets to Kudu in exchange for $200,000 of cash and immediately liquidates. Will this restructuring qualify as a "Type D" reorganization, even though no stock was transferred from Kudu to Marula's shareholders? What gain or loss do the Marula shareholders recognize on this transaction?

COMMUNICATIONS

Research Problem 4. Pyramid Corporation wishes to acquire one of Pharaoh, Inc.'s active lines of business that Pharaoh has run since its incorporation in 1952. In contemplation of the acquisition, Pharaoh creates TutCo by transferring the desired line of business to TutCo in exchange for all of its stock. This stock is distributed to part of the Pharaoh shareholders in exchange for their shares.

Meanwhile, Pyramid arranges financing to repurchase enough of its own stock to complete the acquisition of 85% of TutCo with voting stock. After the exchange of Pyramid stock for TutCo stock in December of the current year, TutCo is a subsidiary of Pyramid.

To orchestrate this acquisition, Pyramid, Pharaoh, and TutCo have incurred substantial legal fees, asset and stock valuation costs, state fees, and financing fees. Determine how the costs paid to facilitate the acquisition of TutCo are treated for Federal income tax purposes. Provide citations to primary tax sources in a research memo to the tax file.

INTERNET *activity*

Use the tax resources of the Internet to address the following questions. Do not restrict your search to the Web, but include a review of newsgroups and general reference materials, practitioner sites and resources, primary sources of the tax law, chat rooms and discussion groups, and other opportunities.

COMMUNICATIONS

Research Problem 5. State income tax law may include provisions for corporate reorganizations that differ from those of the Federal income tax rules. Find your state's statutes that indicate the treatment of reorganizations that are tax-deferred for Federal purposes. Provide a written summary of the provision(s) with citations in a memo to the tax research file.

COMMUNICATIONS

Research Problem 6. Find a recent merger or acquisition that has received financing support from Berkshire Hathaway. Prepare a written summary of the transaction, including the companies involved and the manner in which Berkshire Hathaway provided support for the transaction, and send your document to your classmates.

COMMUNICATIONS

Research Problem 7. Find a news article discussing a recent spin-off, split-off, or split-up. Prepare a one-page summary of the reorganization, including the names of the companies, the value of the transaction, and the reason (if given) for the divestiture. Send your report to your classmates.

COMMUNICATIONS

Research Problem 8. When corporations are contemplating reorganization transactions, it is suggested that they obtain a private letter ruling (PLR) from the IRS to ensure the treatment they desire. How does a taxpayer request a PLR? E-mail a one-page memo to your professor explaining the current procedures by which to request a PLR.

CHAPTER 8

Consolidated Tax Returns

LEARNING OBJECTIVES

After completing Chapter 8, you should be able to:

LO.1 Apply the fundamental concepts of consolidated tax returns.

LO.2 Identify the sources of the rules for consolidated taxable income.

LO.3 Recognize the major advantages and disadvantages of filing consolidated tax returns.

LO.4 Describe the corporations that are eligible to file on a consolidated basis.

LO.5 Explain the compliance aspects of consolidated returns.

LO.6 Compute a parent's investment basis in a subsidiary.

LO.7 Account for intercompany transactions of a consolidated group.

LO.8 Identify limitations that restrict the use of losses and credits of group members derived in separate return years.

LO.9 Derive deductions and credits on a consolidated basis.

LO.10 Demonstrate tax planning opportunities available to consolidated groups.

OUTLINE

For the latest in changes to tax legislation, visit **www.cengage.com/taxation/swft.**

THE BIG PICTURE **Tax Solutions for the Real World**

A CORPORATION CONTEMPLATES A MERGER

Alexander Corporation has had a long-term association with one of its suppliers, Hamilton Corporation. In the past, Hamilton was a highly profitable operation and was even able to make loans to Alexander to cover short-term working capital needs. Recently, however, Hamilton has been consistently late in meeting current obligations. Alexander has had to grant extensions of up to nine months on Hamilton's payables. Several vendors have even ceased doing business with Hamilton. Nevertheless, Alexander feels confident that Hamilton's fortunes will improve. If this financial turnaround occurs, Alexander will continue dealing with Hamilton in the same manner as in the past.

But Alexander's tax advisers have suggested another alternative. They say that Alexander should consider acquiring Hamilton in a merger or other takeover that qualifies as a tax-favored reorganization (see Chapter 7), so as to avoid any immediate Federal income tax liability. Hamilton's downturn has left it with sizable net operating losses that would be attractive to Alexander for use on future joint tax returns. Since Hamilton's name, reputation, and location still have value in the marketplace, it could continue as a separate division or subsidiary of Alexander. Furthermore, the takeover would give other businesses greater assurance of Hamilton's financial viability. Lastly, there could be tax advantages to Alexander, the new parent of a two-corporation group.

Evaluate this and other viable alternatives for Alexander taking into account various possible outcomes (e.g., the success or failure of Hamilton's business). **Read the chapter and formulate your response.**

8.1 Context of the Consolidated Return Rules

To this point, the discussion has centered on the computation of the tax liability of individual corporations under the regular tax calculation, along with specific penalty taxes and the alternative minimum tax. This is an appropriate approach to the study of corporate taxation, as more than 90 percent of the roughly 7 million U.S. corporations are closely held (i.e., either by a small group of operators/investors or by members of the same family).

Although some of these family businesses operate in a multiple-corporation environment, the vast majority of the assets held by businesses nationwide are owned by no more than 50,000 large corporate conglomerates. These corporations conduct the bulk of the country's "big business" and generate most of the taxable income earned by corporate taxpayers. In addition, these corporate groups face some special tax rules, which are the subject of this chapter.

MOTIVATIONS TO CONSOLIDATE

Corporate conglomerates are present in every aspect of life. The local dairy or bakery is likely to be owned by General Mills or General Foods. Oil and insurance companies own movie-making corporations. Professional sports teams are corporate cousins of the newspapers and television/radio stations that carry their games. The same corporate group that produces night lights for a child's nursery may manufacture control equipment for bombers and other elements of the Defense Department's arsenal.

What brings together these sometimes strange corporate bedfellows? For the most part, nontax motivations provide the strongest incentives for multiple-corporation acquisitions and holdings. Among the many commonly encountered motivations are the following.

- A desire to isolate assets of other group members from the liabilities of specific operating divisions (e.g., to gain limited liability for a tobacco or asbestos company within an operating conglomerate).
- A need to carry out specific estate planning objectives (e.g., by transferring growth or high-risk assets to younger-generation shareholders).
- A wish to isolate the group's exposure to losses and liabilities incurred in joint ventures with "outside" entities (especially when such venturers are not based in the United States).
- A perception that separate divisions/group members will be worth more on the market if they maintain unique identities or otherwise avoid a commingling of assets and liabilities with other group members (e.g., where a trade name or patent is especially valuable or carries excessive goodwill in the marketplace).
- Conversely, an attempt to shield the identities of a subsidiary's true owners from the public where negative goodwill exists (e.g., with respect to the consequences of a nuclear or industrial accident, or the use of a long-held name of an oil or a tobacco company).

LO.1

Apply the fundamental concepts of consolidated tax returns.

Although nontax concerns may be the primary reason for the creation of many conglomerates, tax incentives may also play a role. To a large extent, these incentives can be found in the rules that control the filing of **consolidated returns**. In general terms, the IRS allows certain corporate groups to be treated as a single entity for Federal income tax purposes. This enables the group to use available tax exemptions and brackets optimally among its members and to shelter the income of profitable members with the losses of other members. Thus, through the consolidated return rules, corporate taxpayers have an opportunity to manage the combined tax liability of the members of the group.

The consolidated return rules may be available to a taxpayer as a result of various business decisions.

- A consolidated return may result from a merger, acquisition, or other corporate combination (discussed in Chapter 7).

EXAMPLE 1

When Dover Corporation acquires all of the stock of Edwards Corporation, a new corporate group, Dover and Edwards Corporation, is formed. The two group members can elect to file their tax return on a consolidated basis. ■

- A group of business taxpayers may be restructured to comply with changes in regulatory requirements, meet the demands of a competitive environment, or gain economies of scale and operate more efficiently in a larger arrangement. Consequently, an election to file a consolidated return becomes available.

EXAMPLE 2

External Corporation, a retailer, acquires Internal Corporation, a wholesaler, in an effort to control its flow of inventory in unstable economic times. The two group members can elect to file their tax returns on a consolidated basis. ■

- The taxpayers may be seeking to gain tax, financial reporting, and other financial advantages that are more readily available to corporate combinations.

EXAMPLE 3

Over the next three years, Mary Corporation will be selling a number of its business assets at a loss. If Norbert Corporation acquires all of Mary's stock and the group elects to file its tax returns on a consolidated basis, Norbert will be able to combine its gains from the sale of business property with Mary's losses in computing the group's consolidated § 1231 gain/loss for the year. ■

TAX *in* the NEWS — Do Conglomerates Create Conflicts of Interest?

The Internet may have brought dark days for the journalism profession, but the media still can perform a "watchdog" function that keeps governments and businesses under the microscope. Conglomerates that have communications subsidiaries often argue that it takes a lot of capital to staff news bureaus in Europe or to produce movies with expensive special effects. Thus, some of the most recognizable television networks and news organizations have been acquired by large corporations with multiple subsidiaries.

But can the disparate members of a conglomerate resist the temptation to act in concert for the good of the entire group? Charges of "soft reporting" among corporate cousins often arise when critical reporting seems lacking. Given that General Electric owns an interest in NBC Universal, will we ever see a *Dateline* segment about how GE may bend the rules to obtain Defense Department contracts? Can ABC online critics comment negatively on the 3-D version of *A Christmas Carol*, a movie from Disney, its corporate parent?

SOURCE AND PHILOSOPHY OF CONSOLIDATED RETURN RULES

Some form of consolidated corporate tax return has been allowed for Federal purposes since World War I. At that time, the Treasury became suspicious that conglomerates were shifting taxable income to a number of smaller entities to avoid the high marginal rates of the excess profits tax that had been imposed to finance the war effort. Thus, the consolidated return rules can be seen as perhaps the earliest effort of the IRS to limit the tax benefits available to multiple corporations.

EXAMPLE 4

Assume that the marginal Federal income tax rate is 10% on the first $100,000 of taxable income and 15% on any taxable income in excess of $100,000. The additional 5 percentage points constitute a war profits tax, and the revenue raised is used for the war effort.

Further assume that the tax law includes no restrictions on the tax computations of related corporations. A corporation with annual taxable income of $1 million can eliminate its entire exposure to the war profits tax by splitting its business evenly among 10 separate corporations. ■

LO.2

Identify the sources of the rules for consolidated taxable income.

At various times, Congress has modified the pertinent Regulations and imposed a higher tax rate or surcharge on consolidated groups to increase the cost of making the consolidation election. During World War II, when it feared "too much" income of profiteers was being sheltered within consolidated groups, Congress suspended the application of the rules for most taxpayers. On other occasions, including the present, complex limitations were placed on the use and timing of positive tax benefits, such as net operating loss (NOL) carryovers, that were acquired in a corporate consolidation. Congress imposed these limits to discourage profitable corporations from "trafficking" in businesses that had generated net losses.

Currently, Congress has delegated most of its legislative authority involving consolidated returns to the Treasury. As a result, the majority of the rules that affect consolidated groups are found in the Regulations. The Code provisions dealing with consolidated returns are strictly definitional in nature and broad in scope,[1] while the related Regulations dictate the computational and compliance requirements of the group.[2]

As discussed in Chapter 1, "legislative" Regulations of this sort carry the full force and effect of law. Challenges to the content of these Regulations seldom are supported by the courts. Consequently, taxpayers generally participate actively in the hearings process in an effort to have their interpretations included in the final Regulations.

[1] §§ 1501–1505.

[2] Reg. §§ 1.1501–1, 1.1502–0 through 1.1502–100, 1.1503–1 through 1.1503–2T, and 1.1504–1.

FINANCIAL DISCLOSURE *Insights*

GAAP AND TAX TREATMENT OF CONSOLIDATIONS

Both U.S. financial accounting and tax rules use the term *consolidation*, but there is only a slight resemblance in the content of those rules. Here are some of the key similarities and differences between the book and tax treatment of conglomerates.

- GAAP consolidations for the most part are *mandatory* when specified ownership levels are met. Federal income tax consolidation is an *election* by the affiliates to join the parent's tax return.
- GAAP consolidations can include entities such as partnerships and non-U.S. entities. Federal income tax rules generally limit the consolidated return only to U.S. C corporations.
- Ownership levels required for a target to consolidate with a parent generally are 50 percent for GAAP and 80 percent for Federal income tax.
- Tax rules treat a merger or acquisition of a target corporation by a parent as a like-kind exchange, assuming that the requirements of a § 368 reorganization are met (see Chapter 7). Under GAAP, the transaction usually is reported as a purchase of the target's identifiable assets and liabilities.
- After a takeover occurs, book cost amounts are assigned at fair market value, and any excess purchase price is deemed to be goodwill. For Federal income tax purposes, if reorganization treatment is available, the target's basis in its assets carries over to the parent's accounts.
- Goodwill is treated differently under book and tax rules. Financial accounting goodwill cannot be amortized, but impairments to its value are reported as operating losses. Book income results if that impairment of the goodwill is reversed, fox example, because the value of the goodwill has increased. For Federal income tax purposes, purchased goodwill is amortized over 15 years.

The length and detail of these Regulations make the consolidated return rules among the most complex in the entire Federal income tax law. For the most part, the underlying objective of the rules remains one of organizational neutrality; that is, a group of closely related corporations should have neither a tax advantage nor a disadvantage relative to taxpayers who file separate corporate returns.

DELEGATING AUTHORITY TO THE NONELECTED

In no other area of the tax law has Congress given the Treasury such leeway in crafting both major principles and details as in the area of consolidated returns. Since Treasury staff members are not elected officials, this delegation of authority might appear to be a shirking of congressional duty and a dangerous assignment of legislative power to an isolated group of individuals.

To what extent should Congress delegate its powers over the country's largest businesses (not only the largest players in the global economy but also the largest contributors to campaign and reelection funds)? Can the delegation of congressional powers to Washington-based civil servants, who are virtually immune to the checks and balances of the election process, be healthy for all taxpayers?

You are a member of the House Ways and Means Committee, and your chances of reelection are jeopardized when you must take a position on a consolidated tax return issue: Taxes on old-line manufacturers would increase, while those on more environmentally friendly, high-tech industries would fall. Should you avoid the debate altogether by deferring the issue to the Regulations process?

The derivation of a set of consolidated financial statements for a conglomerate and the computation of its consolidated taxable income correspond only slightly. The equity method that is followed for financial accounting purposes has a role in the consolidated return rules, but exceptions to accounting conventions are both critical and numerous. Thus, a knowledge of financial accounting consolidation procedures is not necessarily of great assistance in computing consolidated taxable income, nor is a lack of familiarity with accounting conventions a hindrance.

EXAMPLE 5

Dividends paid by SubCo to its 100% owner, Parent Corporation, are eliminated from the separate taxable income computations of both group members in deriving consolidated taxable income. This treatment parallels the eliminating entry that is made in developing the group's consolidated financial statements.

Later, SubCo sells an asset to its 100% owner, Parent Corporation, at a tax and accounting gain of $100,000. The asset appreciates by another $20,000 before Parent sells it to an unrelated party, Outsider Corporation.

No tax or accounting gain is reported by the group members until the ultimate sale by Parent to Outsider. In constructing the consolidated financial statements, Parent realizes a $120,000 gain. For tax purposes, however, SubCo is assigned $100,000 of the gain, and Parent recognizes only "its" $20,000. ■

8.2 Assessing Consolidated Return Status

LO.3

Recognize the major advantages and disadvantages of filing consolidated tax returns.

As Concept Summary 8.1 illustrates, all of the members of a corporate group must meet three broad requirements to be eligible to elect, and maintain the right, to file a consolidated income tax return.

- The corporations must meet the statutory ownership requirements to be classified as an affiliated group.[3]
- The corporations must be eligible to make a consolidation election.[4]
- The group must meet various tax accounting and compliance requirements.[5]

Before making an election to file consolidated tax returns, related taxpayers must weigh the resulting tax advantages and disadvantages.

The potential advantages of filing consolidated returns are many.

- The operating and capital loss carryovers of one group member may be used to shelter the corresponding income of other group members.
- The taxation of all intercompany dividends may be eliminated.
- Recognition of income from certain intercompany transactions can be deferred.
- Certain deductions and credits may be optimized by using consolidated amounts in computing pertinent limitations (e.g., the deductions for charitable contributions and dividends received, and foreign tax credits).
- The tax basis of investments in the stock of subsidiaries is increased as the members contribute to consolidated taxable income.
- The domestic production activities deduction of a group might be greater than the sum of the deductions for all of the affiliates, as the formula for determining the deduction permits various components to be aggregated.
- The alternative minimum tax (AMT) attributes of all group members can be used in deriving consolidated alternative minimum taxable income (AMTI). This can reduce the adjusted current earnings (ACE) adjustment and optimize other AMT preferences and adjustments.
- The share holdings of all group members can be used in meeting other statutory requirements.[6]

Consolidated returns also have a number of potential disadvantages.

- The election is binding on all subsequent tax years of the group members, unless either the makeup of the affiliated group changes or the IRS consents to a revocation of the election.
- Capital and operating losses of one group member are applied against the corresponding income of the other group members even when assigning

[3]§§ 1504(a)(1) and (2).

[4]This is a negative definition, rooted in §§ 1504(b) through (f).

[5]See especially Reg. §§ 1.1502–75, –76, and –77.

[6]E.g., for purposes of the § 165(g)(3) ordinary deduction for losses from worthlessness of securities. For the 80% corporate control requirement of § 351, see the discussion in Chapter 4.

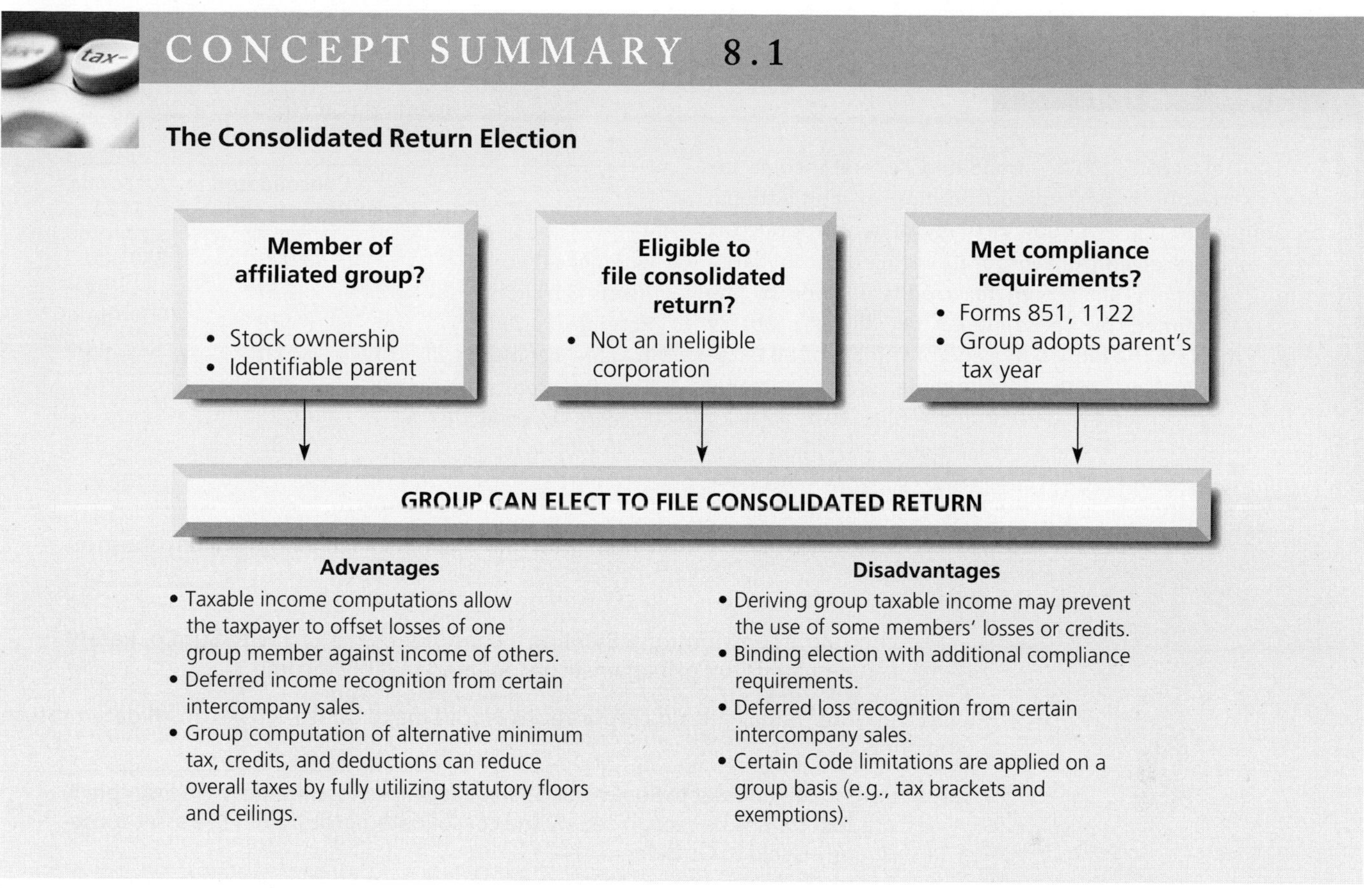

the losses to separate return years would produce a greater tax benefit. The benefit might be due, for instance, to rate discounts or changes in tax rates.

CONCEPT SUMMARY 8.1
The Consolidated Return Election
Member of affiliated group?
• Stock ownership
• Identifiable parent
Eligible to file consolidated return?
• Not an ineligible corporation
Met compliance requirements?
• Forms 851, 1122
• Group adopts parent's tax year
GROUP CAN ELECT TO FILE CONSOLIDATED RETURN
Advantages
• Taxable income computations allow the taxpayer to offset losses of one group member against income of others.
• Deferred income recognition from certain intercompany sales.
• Group computation of alternative minimum tax, credits, and deductions can reduce overall taxes by fully utilizing statutory floors and ceilings.
Disadvantages
• Deriving group taxable income may prevent the use of some members' losses or credits.
• Binding election with additional compliance requirements.
• Deferred loss recognition from certain intercompany sales.
• Certain Code limitations are applied on a group basis (e.g., tax brackets and exemptions).

- Recognition of losses from certain intercompany transactions is deferred.
- Using consolidated amounts in computing the limitations may decrease the amounts of certain deductions and credits.
- Return elections made by the parent (e.g., to claim a credit for foreign tax payments rather than a deduction) are binding on all members of the filing group for the year.
- The tax basis of investments in the stock of subsidiaries is decreased when the members generate operating losses and by distributions from members' E & P.
- The requirement that all group members use the parent's tax year creates short tax years for the subsidiaries. As a result, a subsidiary's income may be bunched together needlessly, and one of the years of its charitable contribution and loss carryforward periods may be lost.
- Additional administrative costs may be incurred in complying with the consolidated return Regulations.

EXAMPLE 6

The following taxpayers should consider filing consolidated returns.

- Major Insurance Corporation generates billions of dollars of taxable income every year. Independent Movie Productions, Ltd., is concerned with artistic integrity, and its annual taxable loss totals $40 to $45 million per year. The accumulated losses are of no use to Independent, but Major can use them to effect an immediate tax reduction at its 35% marginal tax rate.
- Every year, Parent contributes $1.2 million of its $10 million taxable income to charity. Thus, because of the 10% of taxable income limitation, Parent cannot deduct the full amount of the gift in computing taxable income. SubCo generates $3 million of taxable income every year, and it makes no

TAX in the NEWS

Consolidated Return Statistics

Tax data related to 2007 consolidated Federal income tax returns show the important contribution of multinational corporations to U.S. revenues. Virtually all net corporate tax revenues are received from corporations filing consolidated returns. Essentially all foreign tax credits allowed by the Code are claimed by consolidated tax filers, probably because they are the most active and profitable of all C corporations operating in the international sector. Yet only about 43,000 consolidated returns are filed every year—a minuscule portion considering that about 1.85 million C corporations file Form 1120.

	Consolidated Returns Only	All Forms 1120
Number of returns	43,000	1,850,000
Assets ($ trillions)	57	54
Receipts ($ trillions)	18	20
Taxable income ($ trillions)	1.1	1.1
Tax after credits ($ billions)	293	294
Foreign tax credits ($ billions)	85	83

charitable contributions. By filing a consolidated return with SubCo, Parent can deduct its full gift against consolidated taxable income.

On the other hand, certain corporations would make unattractive consolidated return partners.

- Parent sells an asset to SubCo at a $500,000 realized loss. As shown in Example 5, this loss cannot be recognized by the consolidated group until the asset subsequently is sold to Outsider.
- ParentCo holds a large NOL carryforward, and SubCo generates a steady level of taxable income every year. Both corporations are involved in international commerce and make significant tax payments to other countries. SubCo would use these payments to compute a foreign tax credit. But if the corporations file a consolidated return, ParentCo effectively makes the tax accounting elections for the group. It is likely that the ParentCo group will claim the foreign tax payments as deductions against consolidated taxable income, so as to use the NOL carryforward more quickly. ■

8.3 Electing Consolidated Return Status

A corporation can join in a consolidated tax return if it meets three requirements, as shown in Concept Summary 8.1.

- It must be a member of an **affiliated group**.
- It cannot be ineligible to file on a consolidated basis.
- It must meet the initial and ongoing compliance requirements specified in the Code and Regulations.

AFFILIATED GROUP

An affiliated group exists when one corporation owns at least 80 percent of the voting power and stock value of another corporation.[7] This stock ownership test must be met on every day of the tax year. Multiple tiers and chains of corporations are allowed as long as the group has an identifiable parent corporation (i.e., at least 80 percent of one corporation must be owned by another).

[7] §§ 1504(a)(1) and (2).

EXAMPLE 7

Two corporate group structures are illustrated below. Both meet the 80% stock ownership test, but the structure on the right is not an affiliated group because there is no identifiable parent entity.

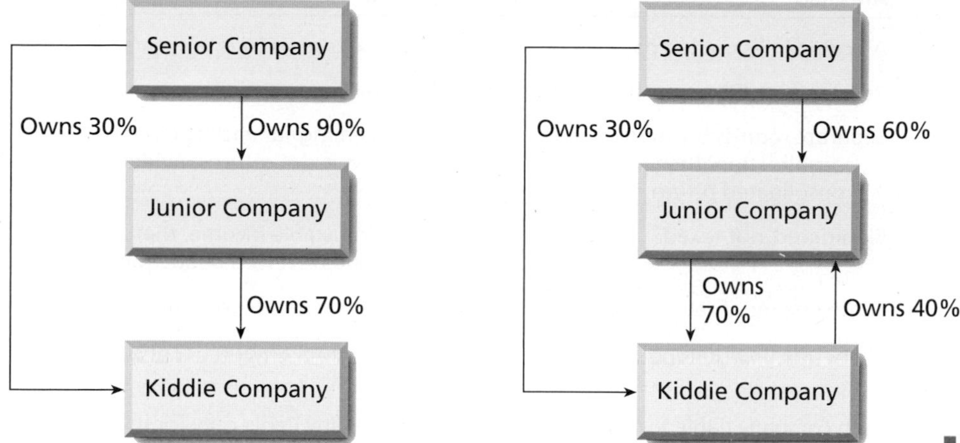

■

Members of an affiliated group can file tax returns in either of two ways.

- File a separate tax return for each member of the group and claim a 100 percent dividends received deduction for payments passing among them.
- Elect to file income tax returns on a consolidated basis. No 100 percent dividends received deduction is allowed for payments among group members.

Table 8.1 provides additional details as to the tax effects of making a consolidated return election.

A Federal election to form a consolidated group may not be binding for state income tax purposes. Some states allow only separate return filing, and others may define the members of an electing group or tax their income differently than the Federal rules do. See Chapter 16 for additional discussion of the multistate taxation of related corporations.

AFFILIATED VERSUS CONTROLLED GROUP

An affiliated group is similar but not identical to a *parent-subsidiary controlled group*, as discussed in Chapter 2. Members of a controlled group are required to share a number of tax benefits, including the following.

- Discounted marginal tax rates on the first $75,000 of taxable income.[8]
- The $150,000 or $250,000 accumulated earnings credit.[9]
- The $40,000 exemption in computing the alternative minimum tax liability.[10]

In addition, members of a controlled group must defer the recognition of any realized loss on intercompany sales until a sale is made at a gain to a nongroup member.[11] Similarly, any gain on the sale of depreciable property between members of a controlled group is recognized as ordinary income.[12]

A parent-subsidiary controlled group exists when one corporation owns at least 80 percent of the voting power or stock value of another corporation on the last day of the tax year.[13] Multiple tiers of subsidiaries and chains of ownership are allowed, as long as the group has an identifiable parent corporation.

[8]§§ 11(b)(1) and 1561(a)(1).
[9]§§ 535(c)(2) and 1561(a)(2).
[10]§§ 55(d)(2) and 1561(a)(3).
[11]§§ 267(a)(1), (b)(3), and (f).
[12]§§ 1239(a) and (c).
[13]§ 1563(a)(1). For this purpose, stock attribution rules apply. In addition, all stock options are considered to be exercised by their holders. §§ 1563(d)(1) and (e)(1) through (3).

TABLE 8.1 Comparison of Tax Effects Available to Affiliated Group

Attribute	Treatment If Consolidated Returns Are Filed	Treatment If Separate Returns Are Filed
Tax year	All companies use the parent's tax year.	Companies use various tax years.
Change to common tax year	Required, no IRS permission needed.	Requires IRS permission.
Returns of acquired companies	Separate returns through date of consolidation, then join in consolidated return.	Continue filing for each company's tax year. No extra returns needed.
Intercompany dividend	Eliminated, not taxed.	Include in taxable income, then claim dividends received deduction.
Lower tax brackets	Share one set of rates among the group.	Share one set of rates among the group.
Accumulated earnings credit, $150,000/$250,000 floor	Share one floor among the group.	Share one floor among the group.
Liability for tax	Each company liable for the entire consolidated tax liability.	Each company liable only for its own tax.
Statute of limitations	Extension for one company applies to all in the group.	Each company retains its own statute of limitations.
Accounting methods	Need not conform to parent.	Need not conform to parent.
NOLs, capital gains/losses, § 1231 gains/losses, charitable contribution deductions, § 199 domestic production activities deduction, dividends received deductions, foreign tax credit payments and baskets, etc.	Computed on a consolidated basis.	Computed separately for each company.
Gain/loss on intercompany transactions	Deferred.	Not deferred.
Basis of parent's investment	Changes due to subsidiary operating gain/loss, taxes, and distributions.	No adjustments.

EXAMPLE 8

Aqua Corporation owns 80% of White Corporation. Aqua and White Corporations are members of a parent-subsidiary controlled group. Aqua is the parent corporation, and White is the subsidiary. ■

The parent-subsidiary relationship described in Example 8 is easy to recognize because Aqua Corporation is the direct owner of White Corporation. Real-world business organizations often are much more complex, sometimes including numerous corporations with chains of ownership connecting them. In these complex corporate structures, determining whether the controlled group classification is appropriate becomes more difficult. The ownership requirements can be met through direct ownership (as in Example 8) or through indirect ownership.

EXAMPLE 9

Red Corporation owns 80% of the voting stock of White Corporation, and White Corporation owns 80% of the voting stock of Blue Corporation. Red, White, and Blue Corporations constitute a controlled group in which Red is the common parent and

TAX *in* the NEWS

Some States Don't Allow Consolidation

Some states have been hesitant to allow a corporate conglomerate doing business within their boundaries to make a consolidation election when computing state taxable income. Perhaps these states question their constitutional ability to tax the income generated by an affiliate that is incorporated elsewhere. Another consideration may be that consolidation would permit losses generated in other states to be applied against taxable income originating within the state.

There is no real consensus among the states as to how to tax a group consolidated for Federal tax purposes. Some states require the group to make a separate election to file on a consolidated basis. Others reserve the right to force the consolidation treatment on a Federal group for state purposes. The diversity that exists is evident in the following table showing a sample of 2009 state rules applicable to consolidated returns.

State	Consolidation Allowed?
Alabama	A Federal electing group can make a separate election to file on a consolidated basis for state purposes. With no such election, all must file separate returns.
Alaska	If the unitary group files consolidated returns for Federal purposes, it must do so for state purposes.
Arizona	A Federal electing group can elect to file on a consolidated basis in the state. The state can require a consolidated return to protect its revenues.
Arkansas	A Federal electing group can elect to file a consolidated return in the state so long as it shows some Arkansas taxable income.
Connecticut	A Federal electing group can elect to file a consolidated return in the state, but it is called a "combined return."
District of Columbia	Consolidation is allowed for a Federal electing group only with prior approval of the revenue department. All affiliates must have nexus with D.C. Special rules apply to high-tech entities.
Georgia	A Federal consolidating group can file a state consolidated return only with the revenue department's prior permission.
Kansas	A Federal electing group must file a Kansas consolidated return if all of the taxable income of all of the affiliates is derived in-state. If out-of-state taxable income is present, permission must be received from the state before the group can file on a consolidated basis.
Louisiana	The state can require a consolidated return, but the taxpayer cannot elect to file one.
Minnesota	No consolidation allowed.
North Carolina	The taxpayer cannot elect to file a consolidated return, but the state can require one if the "true net earnings" of the group are not disclosed.

White and Blue are subsidiaries. The same result would occur if Red Corporation, rather than White Corporation, owned the Blue Corporation stock.

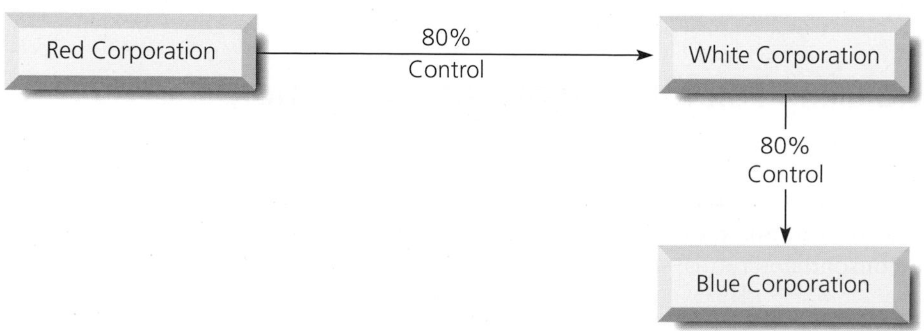

Red is the common parent of a parent-subsidiary controlled group consisting of Red, White, and Blue Corporations. ■

EXAMPLE 10

Brown Corporation owns 80% of the stock of Green Corporation, which owns 30% of Blue Corporation. Brown also owns 80% of White Corporation, which owns 50% of Blue Corporation. Brown, Green, Blue, and White Corporations constitute a parent-subsidiary controlled group in which Brown is the common parent and Green, Blue, and White are subsidiaries.

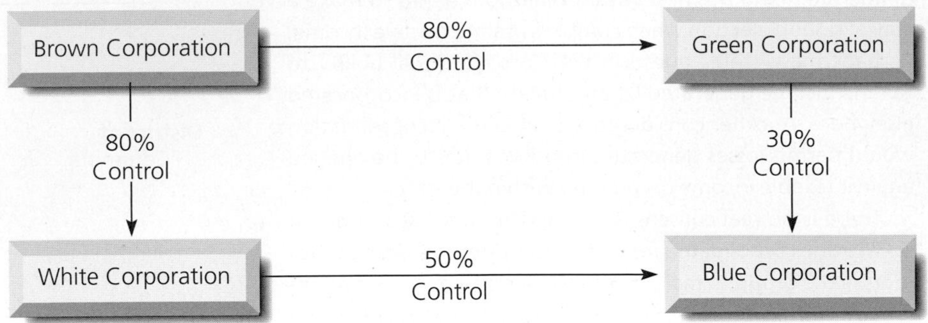

Brown is the common parent of a parent-subsidiary controlled group consisting of Brown, Green, Blue, and White Corporations. ■

The tax effects brought about by electing to file on a consolidated basis include all of the benefit-sharing effects of controlled group membership. In addition, membership in a consolidated group leads to a much more complex set of controlling tax rules, as discussed in the remainder of this chapter.

EXAMPLE 11

ParentCo owns all of the stock of SubCo, and TopCo owns all of the stock of BottomCo. Both pairs of corporations constitute affiliated groups, as well as controlled groups. ParentCo and SubCo elect to file Federal income tax returns on a consolidated basis. TopCo and BottomCo do not so elect. Consequently, they file separate Federal income tax returns.

Both groups share the lower tax rates on the first $75,000 of combined taxable income—ParentCo and SubCo because they file a combined tax return, and TopCo and BottomCo because of the controlled group rules. Neither group can deduct a loss realized on an intercompany sale. But accounting for the taxable income of the consolidated group is much more complex, as indicated by the rules summarized in Table 8.1. ■

The most important differences between an affiliated group and a parent-subsidiary controlled group include the following. In each case, the affiliated group definition is more difficult to meet.

- The stock attribution rules applied in meeting the controlled group stock ownership test are not required for the affiliated group definition. In an affiliated group, the identifiable parent corporation itself must meet the stock ownership test.
- Affiliated group members must meet the stock ownership tests on *every day* of the tax year. The corresponding controlled group tests are applied only on the last day of the year.[14]

LO.4

Describe the corporations that are eligible to file on a consolidated basis.

ELIGIBILITY FOR THE CONSOLIDATION ELECTION

The Code lists a number of corporations that may *not* use a consolidated return to report their taxable income.[15] Thus, these corporations cannot be used to meet the stock ownership tests, and their taxable incomes cannot be included in a consolidated return. Some of the most frequently encountered entities that are ineligible for consolidated return status include:

[14] §§ 1501 and 1563(b)(1).

[15] § 1504(b).

- Corporations established outside the United States or in a U.S. possession.
- Tax-exempt corporations.[16]
- Insurance companies.
- Partnerships, trusts, estates, limited liability entities, and any other noncorporate entities.[17]

EXAMPLE 12

In the first ownership structure in the accompanying figure, Phillips, Rhesus, Todd, and Valiant form an affiliated group, with Phillips as the parent, under the stock ownership rules. Valiant, a life insurance company, cannot be included in a consolidated return, however, so the consolidation election is available only to Phillips, Rhesus, and Todd. In the second structure, Phillips, Rhesus, and Todd form an affiliated group, and all of them can be included in a properly executed consolidated return. Phillips is the identifiable parent of the group. Rhesus and Todd essentially form a brother-sister group below Phillips.

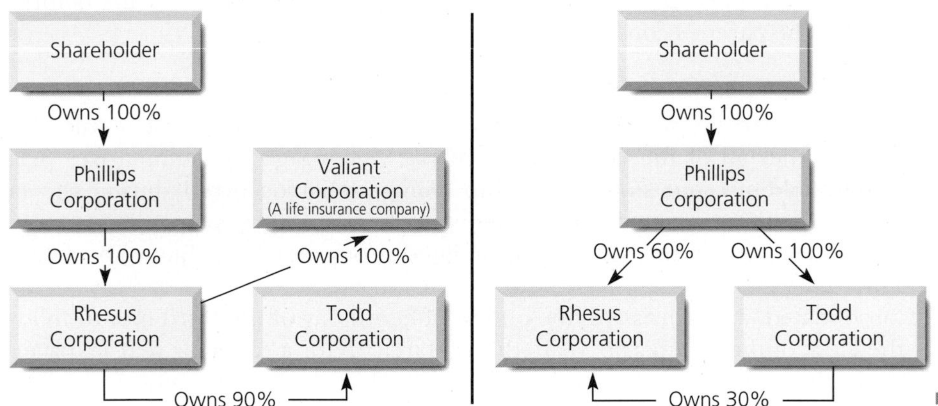

■

COMPLIANCE REQUIREMENTS

LO.5

Explain the compliance aspects of consolidated returns.

An eligible entity that meets the stock ownership test can be included in a consolidated group if several compliance requirements are met.

The Initial Consolidated Return

The first consolidated tax return of an affiliated group must meet certain requirements.

- The Form 1120 for the tax year of the consolidated group should include the taxable results of the operations of all of the members of the consolidated group.[18] This return is filed in lieu of the separate returns of the group members.[19] The identified group then continues to file on a consolidated basis until an eligible group no longer exists or an election to "deconsolidate" is made.[20]
- A Form 1122 should be attached to the first consolidated tax return for each of the subsidiaries included in the group.[21] This form represents a consent by the affiliate to be included in the consolidated group.

The election must be made no later than the extended due date of the parent's return for the year. Only in the case of an inadvertent error can the election to consolidate be rescinded once this extended due date passes.

[16]This includes any entity that is exempt from tax under § 501. See Chapter 15 for a discussion of the qualification of organizations for exempt status.

[17]Some less frequently encountered entities also are prohibited from filing on a consolidated basis. These include regulated investment companies (mutual funds) and real estate investment trusts. §§ 1504(b)(4) through (7).

[18]A consolidation election is inferred, even when specific aspects of pertinent forms are completed incorrectly, as long as the members' combined operations are reported on the Form 1120. *American Pacific Whaling Co. v. Comm.*, 35–1 USTC ¶9065, 14 AFTR 887, 74 F.2d 613 (CA–9, 1935).

[19]Reg. § 1.1502–75(a)(1).

[20]Reg. § 1.1502–75(c). The IRS permits such an election only rarely, on the parent's assertion of (1) a good-cause reason to disengage from consolidated status or (2) a substantial change in the tax law that adversely affects the consolidated tax liability.

[21]Reg. § 1.1502–75(b).

EXAMPLE 13
THE BIG PICTURE

Return to the facts of *The Big Picture* on p. 8-2. Assume that both Alexander and Hamilton use calendar tax years, and that they wish to file their Federal income tax returns on a consolidated basis starting with the 2011 tax year. Alexander does not elect an extended due date for its 2011 return.

If the consolidation election is to be effective, Alexander must file a Form 1120 that includes the taxable income/(loss) for both corporations by March 15, 2012. Hamilton must execute a Form 1122 and attach it to the consolidated Form 1120.

If Alexander and Hamilton convert their separate tax returns to the consolidated format in this manner, the election to consolidate is in force for all future tax years, or until the IRS approves Alexander's application to revoke it. ■

An application to terminate the consolidation election must be filed at least 90 days prior to the extended due date of the consolidated return.[22] Generally, when a subsidiary leaves an ongoing consolidated group, it must wait five years before it can reenter the parent's consolidated group.[23]

Subsequent Consolidated Returns

Each consolidated tax return must include Form 851, Affiliations Schedule. This report identifies all of the corporations in the electing group, summarizes pertinent shareholdings and stock ownership changes that occurred during the tax year, and lists the estimated tax payments made by the group members for the year. Affiliates joining an existing consolidated group need not file a Form 1122, though.

Consolidated tax returns are due on the fifteenth day of the third month following the close of the group's tax year (this is March 15 for a calendar year taxpayer). A six-month extension to file the return can be obtained by executing Form 7004, but an estimated payment of the remaining tax liability for the group must accompany the extension application.

Liability for Taxes

Group members are jointly and severally liable for the entire consolidated income tax liability.[24] This rule applies to interest and penalties imposed as a result of audits as well as to tax liabilities. Furthermore, the IRS is not bound to follow internal agreements among group members in apportioning the liability.[25]

EXAMPLE 14

Parent Corporation, a calendar year taxpayer, acquired 100% of the stock of calendar year SubCo on December 20, 2011. The group filed on a consolidated basis from that date until December 31, 2013, when all of the SubCo stock was sold to Foreign Corporation.

An IRS audit determined that Parent owed an additional $10 million in Federal income taxes, relating to a sale it made on December 30, 2011. By mid-2014, however, Parent's cash-flow difficulties had brought it close to bankruptcy and forced it to cease activities.

Due to the consolidation election, the IRS can assess the delinquent taxes from SubCo (and Foreign Corporation). SubCo is liable for the full amount of any consolidated tax liability, even when it is not the source of the income that led to the tax. ■

Starting with the third consolidated return year, estimated tax payments must be made on a consolidated basis.[26] Prior to that year, estimates can be computed and paid on either a separate or a consolidated basis.

[22]Reg. § 1.1502–75(c)(1)(i).
[23]§ 1504(a)(3); Rev.Proc. 2002–32, 2002–1 C.B. 959.
[24]Reg. § 1.1502–6(a).
[25]Reg. § 1.1502–6(c).
[26]Reg. § 1.1502–5(a)(1).

Regular tax liability is computed applying the graduated tax rates to consolidated taxable income, following the requirements of controlled group status. In this regard, contributions to the actual payment of the tax liability often are arranged to correspond to contributions to consolidated taxable income.

EXAMPLE 15

Parent Corporation owns 100% of the stock of SubCo, and the two corporations file a consolidated tax return beginning in Year 2. Over the course of a five-year period, the corporations generate the following taxable income/(loss). The low marginal rates that apply to the group's first $75,000 of taxable income might be assigned in various ways.

Year	Parent's Taxable Income	SubCo's Taxable Income	Low Brackets Assigned to Parent	Low Brackets Assigned to SubCo
1	$100,000	($ 10,000)	$37,500	$37,500
2	100,000	(10,000)	75,000	–0–
3	50,000	10,000	65,000	10,000
4	(15,000)	10,000	65,000	10,000
5	100,000	100,000	37,500	37,500

In Year 1, the consolidated group has not yet been formed. Separate returns are filed, and the low tax brackets are apportioned equally between the two entities. Once consolidated returns begin to be filed in Year 2, the indicated elections are made. For Year 2, all of the low brackets are assigned to Parent, rather than wasting any on SubCo, which has a negative taxable income.

For Years 3 and 4, the majority of the low brackets are assigned to Parent, because the group believes that Parent's taxable income is more likely to be adjusted upward on an audit. The apportionment is made to create a cushion for Parent in the event that additional tax liability occurs after the initial return is filed. When group members' taxable incomes are close in value and/or exceed $75,000 in total, as in Year 5, a simple equal apportionment of the low brackets is suggested. ■

Benefits accruing from the graduated corporate tax rates are apportioned equally among the group members unless all members consent to some other method through an annual election. The most commonly used tax-sharing agreements are the *relative taxable income* and *relative tax liability* methods. Under the relative taxable income method,[27] the consolidated tax liability is allocated among the members based on their relative amounts of separate taxable income. When the relative tax liability method is used,[28] the consolidated tax liability is allocated based on the relative hypothetical separate tax liabilities of the members. IRS permission is required for the group to change from one allocation method to another.

EXAMPLE 16

The Parent consolidated group reports the following results for the tax year. Assume a 35% marginal tax rate.

	Parent	SubOne	SubTwo	SubThree	Consolidated
Ordinary income	$400	$100	$–0–	($ 20)	$480
Capital gain/loss	–0–	–0–	100	(25)	75
§ 1231 gain/loss	50	–0–	(50)	–0–	–0–
Separate taxable incomes	$450	$100	$ 50	($ 20) with a $25 capital loss carryover	

[27]§ 1552(a)(1); Reg. § 1.1552–1(a)(1).

[28]§ 1552(a)(2); Reg. § 1.1552–1(a)(2).

	Parent	SubOne	SubTwo	SubThree	Consolidated
Consolidated taxable income					$555
Consolidated tax liability					$194
Foreign tax credit, from SubOne					(19)
Net tax due					$175

If the group has consented to the relative taxable income method, the consolidated tax liability is allocated as follows.

	Separate Taxable Income	Allocation Ratio	Allocated Tax Due
Parent	$450	450/600	$131
SubOne	100	100/600	29
SubTwo	50	50/600	15
SubThree	–0–	–0–	–0–
Totals	$600		$175

The results are different if the relative tax liability method is in effect. Specifically, SubOne gets an immediate tax benefit for the tax credit that it brings to the group. Under neither method, though, does SubThree get any tax benefit from the losses that it brings to the consolidated group.

	Separate Taxable Income	Separate Tax Liability	Allocation Ratio	Allocated Tax Due
Parent	$450	$157.5	157.5/191	$144
SubOne	100	16.0*	16/191	15
SubTwo	50	17.5	17.5/191	16
SubThree	–0–	–0–	–0–	–0–
Totals	$600	$191.0		$175

*After applying foreign tax credit

Alternative minimum tax (AMT) liability for group members is computed on the basis of consolidated AMTI. The group is allowed only one $40,000 AMT exemption, which is phased out at a rate of 25 percent of the amount by which consolidated AMTI exceeds $150,000. Similarly, the AMT adjustment for adjusted current earnings (ACE), which is 75 percent of the excess of ACE over pre-ACE AMTI, is computed using consolidated amounts.

Tax Accounting Periods and Methods

All the members of a consolidating group must use the parent's tax year.[29] As a result, the group may be required to file a short-year return for the first year a subsidiary is included in the consolidated return, so that the parent's year-end can be adopted.

When a mid-year acquisition occurs, both short years are used in tracking the carryforward period of unused losses and credits. Short-year income and deductions are apportioned between the pre- and post-acquisition periods. The apportionment

[29]Reg. § 1.1502–76(a)(1).

may be done either on a daily basis or as the items are recorded for financial accounting purposes, at the election of the corporation being acquired.[30]

EXAMPLE 17

All of the stock of calendar year SubCo is acquired by Parent Corporation on July 15, 2011. The corporations elect to file a consolidated return immediately upon the acquisition.

SubCo had generated a long-term capital loss in its 2008 tax year. As of January 1, 2012, only one year remains in the five-year carryforward period for the capital loss.

According to SubCo's financial accounting records, \$400,000 of its \$1 million accounting and taxable income for the year was generated in 2011 after the acquisition. At SubCo's election, either \$400,000 (the "books" apportionment method) or \$465,753 [(170 postacquisition days/365 days) × \$1 million income] (the "daily" method) can be included in the first consolidated return. ■

Members of a consolidated group can continue to use the tax accounting methods that were in place prior to the consolidation election.[31] Thus, the members of a consolidated group may use different accounting methods. On the other hand, because the \$5 million gross-receipts test with respect to use of the cash method of accounting is applied on a consolidated basis,[32] some of the group members may need to switch from the cash to the accrual method of tax accounting.

8.4 Stock Basis of Subsidiary

LO.6

Compute a parent's investment basis in a subsidiary.

Upon acquiring a subsidiary, the parent corporation records a stock basis on its tax balance sheet equal to the acquisition price. At the end of every consolidated return year, the parent records one or more adjustments to this stock basis, as in the financial accounting "equity" method. This treatment prevents double taxation of gain (or deduction of loss) upon the ultimate disposal of the subsidiary's shares.[33] The adjustments are recorded on the last day of the consolidated return year or on the (earlier) date of the disposal of the shares.[34]

In this regard, positive adjustments to stock basis include:

- An allocable share of consolidated taxable income for the year.
- An allocable share of the consolidated operating or capital loss of a subsidiary that could not utilize the loss through a carryback to a prior year.

Negative adjustments to stock basis include:

- An allocable share of a consolidated taxable loss for the year.
- An allocable share of any carryover operating or capital losses that are deducted on the consolidated return and have not previously reduced stock basis.
- Dividends paid by the subsidiary to the parent out of the subsidiary's E & P.

EXAMPLE 18
THE BIG PICTURE

Return to the facts of *The Big Picture* on p. 8-2. Assume that Alexander acquired all of the outstanding Hamilton stock on January 1, 2010, for \$1 million. The parties immediately elected to file consolidated Federal income tax returns. Hamilton reported a 2010 taxable loss of \$100,000, but it generated \$40,000 taxable income in 2011 and \$65,000 in 2012. Hamilton paid a \$10,000 dividend to Alexander in mid-2012.

Alexander holds the following stock bases in Hamilton on the last day of each of the indicated tax years.

2010	\$900,000	2011	\$940,000	2012	\$995,000 ■

[30] Reg. § 1.1502–76(b)(4).

[31] Reg. § 1.1502–17(a).

[32] §§ 448(a)(1) and (c)(2).

[33] This procedure parallels the accounting for tax basis in a partnership or S corporation. See Chapters 10 and 12.

[34] Reg. § 1.1502–32(a). Basis adjustments also are allowed when necessary to determine a tax liability (e.g., when member stock is bought or sold).

When accumulated postacquisition negative adjustments to the stock basis of the subsidiary exceed the acquisition price plus prior positive adjustments, an **excess loss account** is created.[35] This account (1) allows the consolidated return to recognize the losses of the subsidiary in the current year and (2) enables the group to avoid the need to reflect a negative stock basis on its tax-basis balance sheet. If the subsidiary stock is redeemed or sold to a nongroup member while an excess loss account exists, the seller recognizes the balance of the account as capital gain income.[36]

EXAMPLE 19

Parent Corporation acquired all of the stock of SubCo early in Year 1, for $100,000. As a result of SubCo's operations, the group records the amounts listed.

Year	Operating Gain/(Loss)	Stock Basis	Excess Loss Account
1	($ 40,000)	$60,000	$ -0-
2	(80,000)	-0-	20,000
3	30,000	10,000	-0-

If Parent sells the SubCo stock for $50,000 at the end of Year 2, Parent recognizes a $70,000 capital gain ($50,000 amount realized − $0 adjusted basis in stock + $20,000 recovery of excess loss account). If the sale takes place at the end of Year 3, the capital gain is $40,000.[37] ■

In a chain of more than one tier of subsidiaries, the computation of the stock basis amounts starts with the lowest-level subsidiary, then proceeds up the ownership structure to the parent's holdings.[38]

There is no such concept as consolidated E & P in the Federal income tax law. Rather, each entity accounts for its own share of consolidated taxable income on an annual basis, immediately recognizing within E & P any gain or loss on intercompany transactions and reducing E & P by an allocable share of the consolidated tax liability.[39]

8.5 Computing Consolidated Taxable Income

When an affiliated group computes its taxable income for the year, it does not simply add together the separate taxable income amounts of its members. Two groups of transactions are removed from the members' tax returns and receive special treatment. Then the special items are recombined with the remaining items of members' taxable incomes to obtain the group's consolidated taxable income for the year. Figure 8.1 illustrates how consolidated taxable income is constructed using this sequential approach.

1. Taxable income is computed for each member on a separate basis.
2. "Group items" and "intercompany items" are isolated and receive special treatment.
3. The remaining separate incomes are combined with the group and intercompany items, resulting in consolidated taxable income.

The Code requires this computational procedure to accomplish several goals.

- Certain transactions are accounted for on a consolidated basis (e.g., charitable contributions and capital gains and losses). This requires that the transactions be isolated from the separate tax returns and computed on a groupwide basis.

[35] Reg. § 1.1502–19.

[36] Reg. §§ 1.1502–19(a)(1) and (2).

[37] The Year 3 subsidiary income is used first to eliminate the excess loss account (i.e., before it creates new stock basis). Reg. § 1.1502 32(e)(3).

[38] Reg. § 1.1502–19(b)(3).

[39] Reg. § 1.1502–33(d). In the absence of an election to use some other allocation method, the consolidated tax liability is allocated to each group member according to the relative taxable income method.

FIGURE 8.1 Computing Consolidated Taxable Income

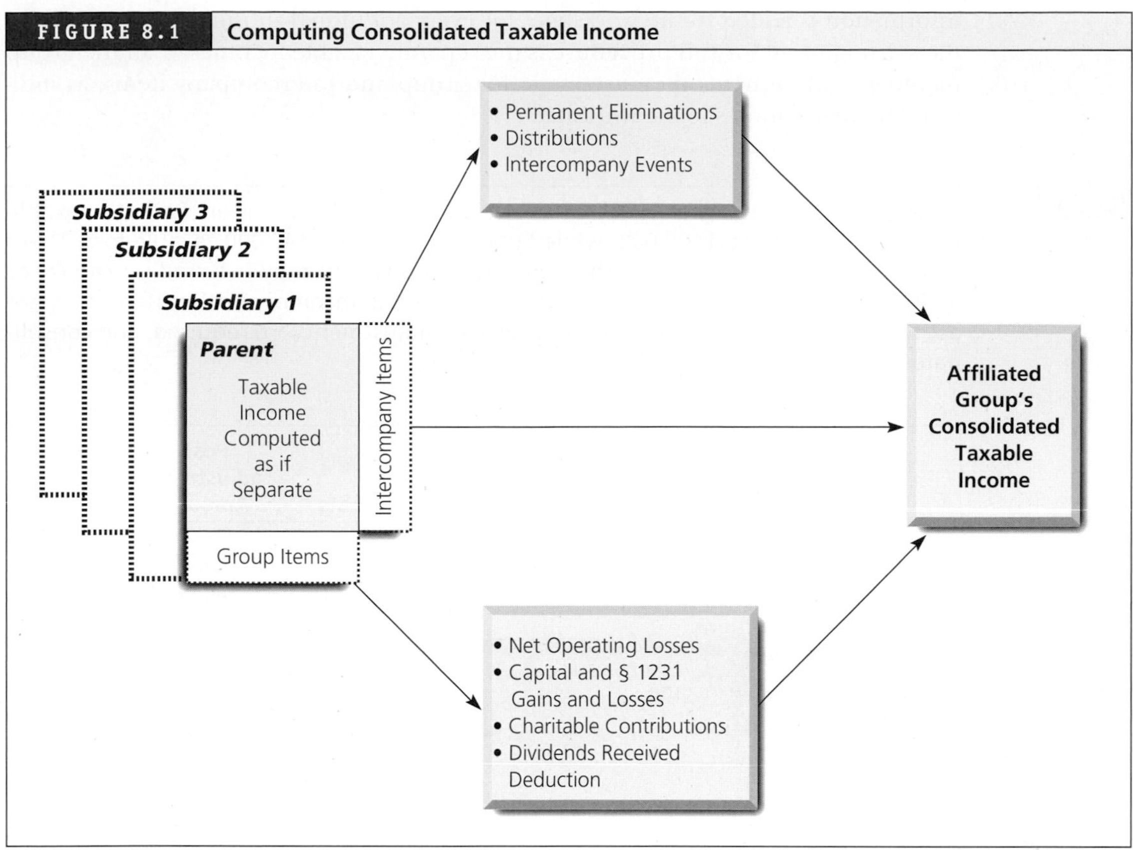

FIGURE 8.2 Consolidated Taxable Income Worksheet

	Separate Taxable Income	Adjustments	Post-adjustment Amounts
Parent information	______	______	______
Subsidiary information	______	______	______
Group-basis transactions	______	______	______
Intercompany events	______	______	______
Consolidated taxable income	______	______	______

*Permanent eliminations. **Group-basis transaction. †Matching rule.

- Gains and losses from certain intercompany transactions are deferred until a later tax year. Consequently, they are removed from the tax returns of the members that generated them.
- A few intercompany transactions (e.g., dividend payments) are removed from the taxable income calculation altogether, never to appear in a consolidated return.

COMPUTATIONAL PROCEDURE

The remainder of this chapter will follow the computational procedure suggested in Figure 8.1. Figure 8.2 presents a skeleton worksheet for this computational procedure to be used in examples throughout the remainder of this chapter. Additional information is added to the worksheet for every additional subsidiary. In each case, the starting point for this procedure is the separate taxable incomes of all the group members. Adjustments then are made for group and intercompany items, as indicated in the footnotes to the worksheet.

EXAMPLE 20

Parent Corporation owns 100% of the stock of SubCo. This year, Parent's taxable income amounted to $100,000, while SubCo generated a $40,000 taxable loss. There were no transactions between the two corporations, and they incurred no capital or § 1231 gains/losses, charitable contributions, dividend income, or other items that are accounted for on a group basis. Accordingly, no adjustments are required, and consolidated taxable income is $60,000.

	Separate Taxable Income	Adjustments	Post-adjustment Amounts
Parent information	$100,000		$100,000
SubCo information	(40,000)		(40,000)
Group-basis transactions			
Intercompany events			
Consolidated taxable income			$ 60,000
*Permanent eliminations.	**Group-basis transaction.	†Matching rule.	

■

LO.7

Account for intercompany transactions of a consolidated group.

TYPICAL INTERCOMPANY TRANSACTIONS

General Rules

When one member of a consolidated group engages in a transaction with another member of the group, an intercompany transaction occurs. In contrast to the financial accounting treatment of most such transactions, the most commonly encountered items *remain in* the members' separate taxable incomes and therefore cancel each other out on a consolidated basis. For instance, when one group member performs services for another member during the year, the purchaser of the services incurs a deductible expenditure, while the service provider generates includible income. The net result is a zero addition to consolidated taxable income.[40]

This two-step procedure prevents the group from avoiding any related-party loss disallowances. Furthermore, when the members involved in the transaction are using different tax accounting methods, the payor's deduction for the expenditure is deferred until the year in which the recipient recognizes the related gross income.[41]

EXAMPLE 21

In the current year, Parent Corporation provided consulting services to its 100%-owned subsidiary, SubCo, under a contract that requires no payments to Parent until next year. Both parties use the accrual method of tax accounting. The services that Parent rendered are valued at $100,000. In addition, Parent purchased $15,000 of supplies from SubCo.

Including these transactions, Parent's taxable income for the year amounted to $500,000. SubCo reported $150,000 of separate taxable income. The group is not required to make any eliminating adjustments. The members' deductions incurred offset the income included by the other party to the intercompany transaction. The

[40] Reg. §§ 1.1502–13(a)(1)(i) and (b)(1).

[41] §§ 267(a)(2) and (b)(3); Reg. § 1.1502–13(b)(2).

consolidated taxable income includes both Parent's $15,000 deduction for supplies and SubCo's $15,000 gross receipts from the sale, so the consolidated taxable income computation *de facto* results in an elimination similar to the kind made in financial accounting. No further adjustment is needed.

	Separate Taxable Income	Adjustments	Post-adjustment Amounts
Parent information	$500,000		$500,000
SubCo information	150,000		150,000
Group-basis transactions			
Intercompany events			
Consolidated taxable income			$650,000
*Permanent eliminations.	**Group-basis transaction.		†Matching rule.

Assume instead that Parent is a cash basis taxpayer. Since Parent will not recognize the $100,000 of service income earned in the current year until the next tax period, SubCo's related deduction also is deferred until the following year. Thus, the intercompany item—SubCo's deduction—must be eliminated from consolidated taxable income. Additional record keeping is required to keep track of this intercompany transaction (and all others like it), so that the deduction is claimed in the appropriate year.

	Separate Taxable Income	Adjustments	Post-adjustment Amounts
Parent information	$400,000		$400,000
SubCo information	150,000	+ $100,000 due to use of different tax accounting methods	250,000 /
Group-basis transactions			
Intercompany events			
Consolidated taxable income			$650,000
*Permanent eliminations.	**Group-basis transaction.		†Matching rule.

■

Several other rules also apply to intercompany transactions. Dividends received from other group members are eliminated from the recipients' separate taxable incomes, and no dividends received deduction is allowed.[42] When the distribution consists of noncash assets, the subsidiary payor realizes (but defers recognition of) any gain on the distributed property until the asset leaves the group, and the (eliminated) dividend amount equals the fair market value of the asset.[43]

EXAMPLE 22

Parent Corporation received a $50,000 cash dividend from 100%-owned SubCo in the current year. Including this item, Parent's separate taxable income amounted to $200,000, and SubCo reported $240,000 separate taxable income.

Parent cannot claim a dividends received deduction for this payment, but the dividend is eliminated in computing consolidated taxable income. No elimination is required for SubCo, as dividend payments are nondeductible.

[42]Reg. § 1.1502–13(f)(2). If the distribution exceeds the payor's E & P, the stock basis of the payor is reduced. When the basis reaches zero, an excess loss account is created. Reg. § 1.1502–19(a). Dividends received from non-group members may result in a dividends received deduction; they constitute a group-basis item (discussed later in the chapter).

[43]§§ 301(b)(1) and (d); § 311(b)(1); Reg. §§ 1.1502–13(c)(7) and (f)(7).

	Separate Taxable Income	Adjustments	Post-adjustment Amounts
Parent information	$200,000	–$50,000 dividend received from SubCo*	$150,000
SubCo information	240,000		240,000
Group-basis transactions			
Intercompany events			
Consolidated taxable income			$390,000

*Permanent eliminations. **Group-basis transaction. †Matching rule.

■

LO.8

Identify limitations that restrict the use of losses and credits of group members derived in separate return years.

Members' Net Operating Losses

Often, the election to file consolidated returns is at least partly motivated by the parent corporation's desire to use the positive tax attributes of the subsidiary corporation, especially its NOLs. A number of provisions, however, discourage corporate acquisitions that are solely tax motivated.[44]

The usual corporate NOL computations are available for the losses of the consolidated group.[45] Excess losses are carried back 2 years and then forward 20 years, although the parent may elect to forgo the carryback deductions for all members of the group. The NOL is derived after removing any consolidated charitable contribution deduction and capital gain or loss from consolidated taxable income. These items are removed because they have their own carryover periods and rules.[46] The consolidated dividends received deduction remains a part of the consolidated NOL.[47]

EXAMPLE 23

Parent Corporation and SubCo have filed consolidated returns since both entities were incorporated in 2009. Neither group member incurred any capital gain or loss transactions during 2009–2011, nor did they make any charitable contributions. Taxable income computations for the members include the following.

Year	Parent's Taxable Income	SubCo's Taxable Income	Consolidated Taxable Income
2009	$100,000	$ 40,000	$140,000
2010	100,000	(40,000)	60,000
2011	100,000	(140,000)	?
2012	100,000	210,000	?

The 2011 consolidated loss of $40,000 can be carried back to offset 2009 consolidated taxable income. Alternatively, Parent can elect to carry the loss forward to 2012, forgoing any carryback computation. This might be appropriate given an increase in statutory tax rates effective for 2012 or an application of the AMT in 2009 and 2010.

Examine SubCo's 2011 NOL of $140,000. The amount resulted from the following combination of transactions for the year. Unused contributions and capital gain/loss items are subject to their own carryover periods, and they constitute group-basis items, as identified in Figure 8.1.

Operating loss	($ 140,000)
Net capital gain	15,000
Charitable contributions	20,000
Separate taxable income	(125,000)

■

[44]See Chapter 7 and §§ 269, 381, 382, and 482.

[45]As part of the economic stimulus package, a 2008 or 2009 loss may be carried back at the parent's election for 3, 4, or 5 years. "TARP" recipients cannot make this election. Special limitations apply in the case of the fifth year—see Chapter 2. § 172(b)(1)(H).

[46]Reg. § 1.1502–24(c). No election is available that would enable the parent to forgo the net capital loss carryback.

[47]Reg. § 1.1502–21(f).

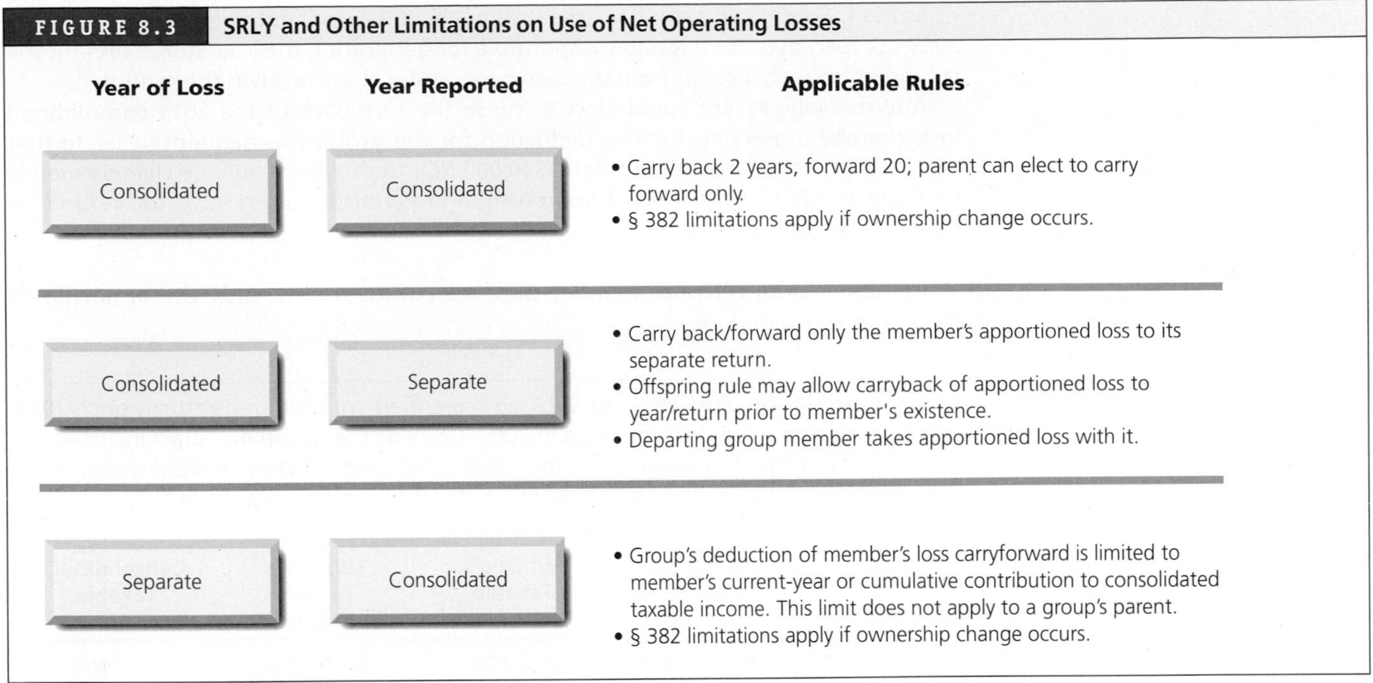

FIGURE 8.3 SRLY and Other Limitations on Use of Net Operating Losses
Year of Loss
Year Reported
Applicable Rules
Consolidated
Consolidated
• Carry back 2 years, forward 20; parent can elect to carry forward only.
• § 382 limitations apply if ownership change occurs.
Consolidated
Separate
• Carry back/forward only the member's apportioned loss to its separate return.
• Offspring rule may allow carryback of apportioned loss to year/return prior to member's existence.
• Departing group member takes apportioned loss with it.
Separate
Consolidated
• Group's deduction of member's loss carryforward is limited to member's current-year or cumulative contribution to consolidated taxable income. This limit does not apply to a group's parent.
• § 382 limitations apply if ownership change occurs.

Complications arise, however, when the corporations enter or depart from a consolidated group, so that members' operating losses are either incurred in a "separate return year" and deducted in a "consolidated return year," or vice versa. A variety of restrictions limit the availability of such deductions to discourage profitable corporations from acquiring unprofitable entities simply to file immediate refund claims based on loss and credit carryforwards. Figure 8.3 summarizes the applicable SRLY (separate return limitation year) limitations.

In any case where the members of a consolidated group change over time, the taxpayer must apportion the consolidated NOL among the group members. When more than one group member generates a loss for the consolidated year, the following formula is used to apportion the loss among the electing group's members.

EXAMPLE 24

Parent Corporation and SubCo have filed consolidated returns since 2010. Both entities were incorporated in 2009. Neither group member incurred any capital gain or loss transactions during 2009–2012, nor did they make any charitable contributions. Taxable income computations for the members are listed below.

Year	Parent's Taxable Income	SubCo's Taxable Income	Consolidated Taxable Income
2009*	$100,000	$ 40,000	N/A
2010**	100,000	(40,000)	$60,000
2011**	100,000	(140,000)	?
2012**	100,000	210,000	?

*Separate return year. **Consolidated return year.

In 2011, SubCo can carry back the entire $40,000 consolidated NOL to its separate 2009 tax year, because it is solely responsible for generating the loss. SubCo files for the refund of taxes that result from the carryback, and it alone receives the refund.[48]

Alternatively, Parent could elect to forgo the carryback of the 2011 consolidated loss, thereby preserving the loss deduction for the group's subsequent years. In that case, the 2012 tax reduction from the $40,000 NOL deduction would be claimed merely by filing the 2012 consolidated tax return, and Parent would receive the refund on behalf of the group. ■

In years when a group member files a separate return, only the apportioned NOL may be carried over.

EXAMPLE 25

Parent Corporation, SubOne, and SubTwo have filed consolidated returns since 2010. All of the entities were incorporated in 2009. None of the group members incurred any capital gain or loss transactions during 2009–2012, nor did they make any charitable contributions. Taxable income computations for the members are listed below.

Year	Parent's Taxable Income	SubOne's Taxable Income	SubTwo's Taxable Income	Consolidated Taxable Income
2009*	$100,000	$100,000	$ 40,000	N/A
2010**	100,000	100,000	(40,000)	$160,000
2011**	100,000	(60,000)	(120,000)	?
2012**	100,000	100,000	210,000	?

*Separate return year. **Consolidated return year.

If Parent does not elect to forgo the carryback of the 2011 consolidated NOL of $80,000, both subsidiaries can carry losses back to their 2009 separate return years and receive separate refunds. SubOne can carry back a $26,667 loss [(SubOne's NOL $60,000/aggregate NOLs $180,000) × consolidated NOL $80,000], and SubTwo can carry back a $53,333 loss. ■

Under the so-called offspring rule, the consolidated group can use a carryback loss that is apportioned to a member of the electing group, even though that member did not exist in the carryback year.[49] If the member joined the group immediately upon its incorporation, but cannot use an apportioned loss in the carryback period because it was not in existence, that loss is still available to the group.[50]

EXAMPLE 26

Parent Corporation, SubOne, and SubTwo have filed consolidated returns since 2010. The first two entities were incorporated and consolidated in 2009, and SubTwo came into existence in 2010 through an asset spin-off from Parent. None of the group members incurred any capital gain or loss transactions during 2009–2012, nor did they make any charitable contributions. Taxable income computations for the members are listed below.

Year	Parent's Taxable Income	SubOne's Taxable Income	SubTwo's Taxable Income	Consolidated Taxable Income
2009*	$100,000	$ 40,000	—	$140,000
2010*	100,000	100,000	($ 40,000)	160,000
2011*	100,000	(60,000)	(120,000)	?
2012*	100,000	100,000	210,000	?

*Consolidated return year.

[48]Reg. §§ 1.1502–78(b)(1) and (c), Example 4.

[49]Reg. § 1.1502–79(a)(2).

[50]Reg. § 1.1502–21(b)(2)(ii)(B) restricts the use of this loss to the parent, if the carryback year is a separate return year for the parties.

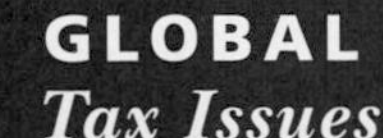

CONSOLIDATED RETURNS AND NOLs

Very few countries outside the United States allow the use of consolidated returns. In the view of most countries, tax deductions for operating losses should be used only by those who generated them, not by some sister or other related corporation. This is as much a social principle (the sanctity of the corporate entity) as a revenue-raising provision (NOL deductions mean lower tax collections).

The way European business is conducted makes this result more understandable, as the tax laws of the various countries must ensure that operating losses generated in Tedesco, for instance, are not shifted to Cadenza and converted to deductions there.

This restrictive approach to the trading of operating loss deductions is found in U.S. multistate tax law as well, where tax-oriented border incentives can be especially important. Some states (like Pennsylvania) have, over a specified time period, disallowed the use of loss carryovers of any sort, whereas others (like Ohio) require the taxpayer to deduct only losses assigned to the taxpayer's in-state operations. Multistate tax issues are addressed in Chapter 16.

If Parent does not elect to forgo the carryback of the 2011 consolidated NOL of $80,000, SubOne can carry its $26,667 loss back to 2009. SubTwo's $53,333 share of the loss can also be carried back to 2009 and used by members of the consolidated group. Under the offspring rule, SubTwo is treated as being a member of the group for the entire *group* carryback period because its existence is rooted in Parent's assets. ■

When a corporation leaves a consolidated group, it takes with it any apportioned share of any unused loss carryforwards, to be used on its subsequent separate returns.

EXAMPLE 27

Parent Corporation, SubOne, and SubTwo have filed consolidated returns since 2009, the year in which all of the entities were incorporated. None of the group members incurred any capital gain or loss transactions during 2009–2012, nor did they make any charitable contributions. Taxable income computations for the members are listed below.

Parent elects to forgo any loss carryback for the group's 2011 operations. On the first day of the 2012 tax year, a non-U.S. investor purchases all of the stock of SubTwo. On its 2012 separate return, SubTwo can deduct its $53,333 share of the 2011 NOL carryforward.[51]

Year	Parent's Taxable Income	SubOne's Taxable Income	SubTwo's Taxable Income	Consolidated Taxable Income
2009*	$100,000	$100,000	$ 40,000	$240,000
2010*	100,000	100,000	(40,000)	160,000
2011*	100,000	(60,000)	(120,000)	?
2012**	100,000	100,000	210,000	N/A

*Consolidated return year. **Separate return year. ■

[51]SubTwo cannot take the entire $120,000 NOL that is attributable to it. Reg. §§ 1.1502–79(a)(1)(ii) and (b)(2)(ii). Losses and carryovers first must be absorbed within the current consolidated return year before any loss apportionment occurs.

When an NOL is carried forward from a separate return year onto a consolidated return, another set of limitations, known as the **separate return limitation year (SRLY)** rules, applies.[52] The consolidated return can include an NOL carryforward from the member's SRLY period only to the extent of the lesser of its (1) current-year or (2) cumulative positive contribution to consolidated taxable income.[53]

The SRLY limitations never apply to the electing group's identifiable parent.[54]

EXAMPLE 28

Parent Corporation and SubCo have filed consolidated returns since 2010. Both entities were incorporated in 2009. Neither group member incurred any capital gain or loss transactions during 2009–2012, nor did they make any charitable contributions. Taxable income computations for the members are listed below.

Year	Parent's Taxable Income	SubCo's Taxable Income	Consolidated Taxable Income
2009*	$100,000	($40,000)	N/A
2010**	100,000	(10,000)	$90,000
2011**	100,000	15,000	?
2012**	100,000	70,000	?

*Separate return year. **Consolidated return year.

The thrust of the SRLY rules is to limit Parent's deduction of SubCo's losses from a separate return year against consolidated income. Accordingly, none of SubCo's separate return loss from 2009 can be deducted in computing 2010 consolidated taxable income; the deduction is limited to the lesser of SubCo's current-year (zero) or cumulative (zero) contribution to consolidated taxable income.

In computing 2011 consolidated taxable income, the SubCo SRLY loss deduction is limited to $5,000, the lesser of SubCo's current-year ($15,000) or cumulative ($5,000) contribution to consolidated taxable income. The remaining SRLY deduction reduces consolidated taxable income beginning in 2012. ■

EXAMPLE 29

Parent Corporation and SubCo have filed consolidated returns since 2010. Both entities were incorporated in 2009. Neither group member incurred any capital gain or loss transactions during 2009–2012, nor did they make any charitable contributions. Taxable income computations for the members are listed below.

Year	Parent's Taxable Income	SubCo's Taxable Income	Consolidated Taxable Income
2009*	($ 40,000)	$100,000	N/A
2010**	(100,000)	(10,000)	($110,000)
2011**	20,000	165,000	?
2012**	100,000	70,000	?

*Separate return year. **Consolidated return year.

The 2011 consolidated return can include a deduction for Parent's entire 2009 NOL of $40,000. The deduction is not limited to the lesser of Parent's current-year ($20,000) or cumulative (zero) contribution to consolidated taxable income. SRLY rules do not apply to the group's parent. ■

[52] Reg. § 1.1502–21(c). The SRLY rules apply to capital loss and credit carryforwards as well.

[53] Reg. § 1.1502–21(c).

[54] Reg. § 1.1502–1(f)(2)(i), known as the "lonely parent" rule.

When both the SRLY rules and a § 382 limitation apply because an ownership change has occurred (see Chapter 7), the § 382 provisions override the SRLY limits.[55]

EXAMPLE 30

The Parent consolidated group includes SubTwo, which was acquired as part of a § 382 ownership change. SubTwo brought with it to the group a $180,000 NOL carryforward, $125,000 of which is available this year under the SRLY rules due to SubTwo's positive contribution to the group's taxable income. The § 382 limitation with respect to SubTwo is $100,000. Accordingly, only $100,000 of the SubTwo NOL can be used to reduce consolidated taxable income this year.

If the § 382 limitation had been $200,000 instead, the full $180,000 NOL deduction would have been allowed. The § 382 rules prevail even with respect to SRLY losses that overlap with the same tax year. ■

COMPUTATION OF GROUP ITEMS

LO.9

Derive deductions and credits on a consolidated basis.

Several income and deduction items are derived on a consolidated-group basis. Therefore, statutory limitations and allowances are applied to the group as though it were a single corporation. This computational convention allows group members to match various types of gains and losses and to increase specific limitations, required by the Code, in a manner that optimizes the overall tax benefit.

Specifically, the following items are computed on a group basis with the usual C corporation tax effects applied to the combined group amounts (see Chapter 2).

- Net capital gain/loss.
- Section 1231 gain/loss.
- Domestic production activities deduction.
- Casualty/theft gain/loss.
- Charitable contributions.
- Dividends received deduction.
- Net operating loss.
- AMT adjustments and preferences.

Following the computational procedure of Figures 8.1 and 8.2, all of the group-basis items are removed from each member's separate taxable income. Then, using the consolidated taxable income figure to that point, statutory limitations are applied to determine group-basis gains, losses, income, and deductions.

EXAMPLE 31

Parent Corporation's current-year taxable income included $300,000 net income from operations and a $50,000 net long-term capital gain. Parent also made a $40,000 contribution to State University. Accordingly, its separate taxable income amounted to $315,000.

Income from operations	$300,000
Capital gain income	+50,000
Charitable contribution (maximum)	−35,000
Separate taxable income	$315,000

SubCo generated $170,000 income from operations and incurred a $45,000 short-term capital loss. Thus, its separate taxable income was $170,000, and aggregate separate taxable income for the group amounted to $485,000.

Upon consolidation, a larger amount of Parent's charitable contribution is deductible, and its capital gain is almost fully sheltered from current-year tax.

[55] Reg. §§ 1.1502–21(g) and –22(g).

	Separate Taxable Income	Adjustments	Post-adjustment Amounts
Parent information	$315,000	−$50,000 capital gain income** +$35,000 charitable contribution deduction**	$300,000
SubCo information	170,000	$45,000 short-term capital loss**	170,000
Group-basis transactions		+$5,000 net long-term capital gain −$40,000 charitable contribution deduction (maximum for group is $47,500)	−35,000
Intercompany events			
Consolidated taxable income			$435,000
*Permanent eliminations.		**Group-basis transaction.	†Matching rule.

■

Computing these items on a group basis does not always result in a reduction of aggregate group taxable income. Nevertheless, the possibility of using the group-basis computations may affect transactions by group members late in the tax year when it becomes apparent that planning opportunities may be available. It also may encourage the taxpayer to seek out fellow group members that bring complementary tax attributes to the consolidated return.

EXAMPLE 32

Parent Corporation owns 15% of the stock of Outsider Corporation throughout the year. Outsider paid a $150,000 dividend to Parent during the year. Parent also generated $400,000 of taxable operating income and sold a § 1231 asset at a $10,000 gain. Parent's separate taxable income is computed below.

Operating income	$ 400,000
Dividend income	+150,000
§ 1231 gain	+10,000
Dividends received deduction (70%)	−105,000
Separate taxable income	$ 455,000

A 10% owner of Outsider, SubCo also received a $100,000 dividend. SubCo's operations produced a $20,000 net taxable loss for the year, and it sold a § 1231 asset at a $4,000 loss. Thus, SubCo's separate taxable income is computed as follows.

Operating income	($ 20,000)
Dividend income	+100,000
§ 1231 loss	−4,000
Dividends received deduction[56]	−53,200
Separate taxable income	$ 22,800

A consolidated return increases the group's dividends received deduction,[57] but it wastes the opportunity to claim SubCo's § 1231 loss as an ordinary deduction.

[56]Limited to 70% of taxable income before the deduction. § 246(b)(1).

[57]The group cannot apply an 80% rate for the dividends received deduction, even though aggregate group ownership in Outsider now exceeds 20%. Reg. § 1.1502–26(a)(1)(i).

	Separate Taxable Income	Adjustments	Post-adjustment Amounts
Parent information	$455,000	−$150,000 dividend received from Outsider**	$400,000
		−$10,000 § 1231 gain**	
		+$105,000 dividends received deduction**	
SubCo information	22,800	−$100,000 dividend received from Outsider**	(20,000)
		+$4,000 § 1231 loss	
		+$53,200 dividends received deduction	
Group-basis transactions		+$250,000 dividend received from Outsider	+81,000
		−$175,000 dividends received deduction (70% × $250,000)	
		+$6,000 § 1231 gain	
Intercompany events			
Consolidated taxable income			$461,000

*Permanent eliminations. **Group-basis transaction. †Matching rule.

The domestic production activities deduction, or DPAD (see Chapter 3), is allowed for an **expanded affiliated group (EAG).**[58] If such a group files a Form 1120 as a consolidated group, the DPAD is another group item. The DPAD is computed on the basis of consolidated taxable income, not the separate taxable income amounts of the members, and the taxable income limitation is applied to this amount. The DPAD then is allocated to the group members on the basis of the qualified production activities income (QPAI) of each, regardless of whether the member has a separate taxable gain or loss for the year.[59] If the member's QPAI is negative, it is treated as zero for this purpose.

EXAMPLE 33

Except for the DPAD, the members of an electing consolidated group report the following data.

Affiliate	Taxable Income ($ Million)	Qualified Production Activities Income (QPAI) ($ Million)	W–2 Wages ($ Million)
Brown, parent	50	80	60
Coral	(20)	40	20
Drake	10	30	-0-
Totals	40	150	80

The DPAD is computed at the group level, and then it is allocated to the affiliates based on the relative amount of each member's QPAI. Members' separate taxable incomes are recomputed for these amounts, and consolidated taxable income then is determined.

- Brown is allocated 80/150 of the group's DPAD.
- Coral is allocated 40/150 of the group's DPAD.
- Drake is allocated 30/150 of the group's DPAD.

[58]An expanded affiliated group includes any group of parent-subsidiary corporations in which more than 50% of each member is owned directly or indirectly by a parent corporation. An EAG can include corporations that are ineligible to elect to file a consolidated return, such as an insurance company. § 199(d)(4)(B).

[59]Intercompany sales among group members are included in qualified production activities income, but receipts from intercompany leases, rentals, and licensing are not. Reg. § 1.199–7(c).

Although Coral reported an NOL for the year, it is not separately subject to the taxable income limitation. Further, note that Drake separately would not be entitled to any DPAD because of the W–2 wage limitation. These member-level limitations are not relevant in the EAG determination of the DPAD. The DPAD is a group item on the consolidated return. ■

Other items computed on a consolidated basis include all elements of the general business and research credits, any recapture of those credits, the foreign tax credit, the percentage depletion deduction, and all elements of AMTI.

THE MATCHING RULE

A special class of intercompany transactions receives deferral treatment under the Regulations.[60] The gain or loss realized on these transactions is removed from consolidated taxable income until the sold asset leaves the affiliated group. The purpose of this **matching rule** is to prevent group members from accelerating loss deductions that relate to sales of assets within the group. In effect, for purposes of these intercompany transactions the group is treated as a single corporation with multiple operating divisions.

The matching rule applies to sales of assets or the performance of services among group members. The entire deferred gain or loss enters the consolidated taxable income computation when, say, the asset is transferred outside the group through a subsequent sale. Full gain or loss recognition also can be triggered under the "acceleration rule" when the transferor of the property leaves the group or the consolidation election is terminated.[61] The acceleration rule applies when it no longer is possible to produce a proper result under the matching rule.

Generally, the gain or loss on the sale outside the group is recognized in the same manner as it would have been on the initial transfer.[62]

EXAMPLE 34

Parent Corporation sold a plot of land to SubCo in the current year for $100,000. Parent had acquired the land 10 years ago for $40,000. The consolidated return also reflects the operating results of the parties: Parent generated $10,000 income, and SubCo produced a $100,000 gain.

This intercompany transaction triggers the matching rule: Parent's $60,000 realized gain is deferred through an elimination in the computation of consolidated taxable income. The $60,000 gain is recognized by the group when SubCo later sells the land to Outsider Corporation.

	Separate Taxable Income	Adjustments	Post-adjustment Amounts
Parent information	$ 70,000	______	$ 70,000
SubCo information	100,000	______	100,000
Group-basis transactions			
Intercompany events		–$60,000 gain on intercompany sale to SubCo†	–60,000
Consolidated taxable income			$110,000
*Permanent eliminations.	**Group-basis transaction.		†Matching rule.

SubCo sold the land to Outsider for $110,000 in a year in which its operating income totaled $60,000 (exclusive of the sale of the land), and Parent's operating income amounted to $170,000.

60 Reg. § 1.1502–13.

61 Reg. § 1.1502–13(d)(1)(i).

62 Sections 267 and 1239 may convert other types of gain into ordinary income. See especially Reg. §§ 1.267(f)–1 and 1.1239–1(a) and (b)(3).

	Separate Taxable Income	Adjustments	Post-adjustment Amounts
Parent information	$170,000		$170,000
SubCo information	70,000		70,000
Group-basis transactions			
Intercompany events		+$60,000 restored gain on Parent's sale to SubCo†	+60,000
Consolidated taxable income			$300,000
*Permanent eliminations.	**Group-basis transaction.		†Matching rule.

Generally, the matching rule is attractive to the group when intercompany sales take place at a gain. When such sales generate losses, however, the mandatory nature of the rule may become burdensome.

TAX PLANNING:

8.6 Choosing Consolidated Return Partners

Taxpayers should optimize their overall tax benefits when choosing consolidated return partners. Within the limitations of the rules discussed earlier in the chapter, attributes of potential target corporations might include some of the following.

LO.10

Demonstrate tax planning opportunities available to consolidated groups.

- Loss and credit carryovers.
- Passive activity income, loss, or credits.
- Gains that can be deferred through intercompany sales.
- Contributions to consolidated ACE adjustments.
- Excess limitation amounts (e.g., with respect to charitable contributions).
- Section 1231 gains, losses, and lookback profiles.

8.7 Consolidation versus 100 Percent Dividends Received Deduction

When adequate ownership is held, a 100 percent dividends received deduction is available for payments received from subsidiaries with whom a consolidated return is *not* filed. Thus, this tax benefit is still available when the taxpayer wishes to affiliate with an insurance company, foreign entity, or other ineligible corporation. A taxpayer that cannot find potential group partners with the desired level of complementary tax attributes may also take advantage of this benefit.

8.8 Protecting the Group Members' Liability for Tax Payments

Because all group members are responsible for consolidated tax liabilities, interest, and penalties, target subsidiaries and their (present and potential) shareholders should take measures to protect their separate interests.

EXAMPLE 35

Return to the facts of Example 14. Exposure by SubCo and its successive shareholders to tax (and all other) liabilities of Parent Corporation should be minimized by including appropriate clauses in purchase contracts and related documents. For instance, (1) Foreign Corporation could alter its negotiating position so that it pays less to acquire the

CONCEPT SUMMARY 8.2

The Consolidated Tax Return

1. Groups of corporations form for a variety of tax and nontax reasons. The election to file Federal income tax returns on a consolidated basis allows certain group members to use their positive tax attributes (e.g., loss or credit carryovers) to offset negative tax attributes (e.g., positive taxable income) of other members.
2. Consolidated tax returns are limited to eligible corporations that satisfy stock ownership tests and meet various compliance requirements. For instance, all group members must conform their tax years to that of the parent of the group. Group members may use different tax accounting methods, however.
3. Group members are jointly and severally liable for the overall income tax liability of the group. For the most part, computations of estimated tax liabilities must be made on a consolidated basis.
4. The stock basis of a subsidiary is derived from the acquisition price of the stock, increased by the taxable income (or decreased by the losses) of the subsidiary, and decreased by dividend distributions. An excess loss account is created when aggregate losses of the subsidiary exceed both the purchase price and ensuing income amounts. The excess loss account is recaptured as capital gain when the subsidiary stock is disposed of.
5. Under the § 382 or SRLY rules, NOL carryforwards may be deferred when they relate to subsidiaries acquired by the group. When both restrictions apply, the § 382 rules prevail.
6. In computing consolidated taxable income, certain items, such as charitable contributions and § 1231 gains and losses, are computed on a consolidated basis, while other gains and losses are deferred until later tax periods. The group is subject to severe restrictions in using any operating losses of a subsidiary that has been acquired or disposed of.

SubCo stock, or (2) SubCo might attempt to recover any Parent taxes that it pays through courts other than the Tax Court. ■

A short tax year may be created when a member with a nonmatching tax year joins or leaves the group. When this occurs, the group should consider measures to limit the ensuing negative tax consequences. For instance, additional income can be accelerated into the short year of acquisition. This will reduce any loss carryforwards when the carryover period is effectively shortened due to the takeover. The group also should make suitable income-allocation elections in assigning income to the short year. Finally, group estimated tax payments should be computed using both consolidated and separate liability amounts to determine the more beneficial method. In this way, only the minimum quarterly tax payments are made, and the benefits of the time value of money are maximized.

In the context of a corporate takeover, the controlling intercompany documents should address the tax-sharing agreement. Members should allow for reimbursement between affiliates when a member cannot pay its allocated portion of the group's income tax liability. Another provision in the agreement should address the allocation of taxes caused by the takeover itself. For example, should some of the resulting tax liability be paid by affiliates, or should it be paid entirely by the target corporation?

8.9 Documentation Requirements

Adjustments to the basis of subsidiary stock must be fully documented, with detailed workpapers retained by the taxpayer.[63] If a tax understatement results from poor documentation of the subsidiary's stock basis, a penalty is added to the amount of tax due.[64] Because of the importance of the stock basis computations for this and other reasons, contemporaneous documentation by the parent corporation must be maintained.

[63]Reg. § 1.1502–32(q). An earlier proposed rule, not adopted, would have required the details of the basis computations to be attached to the consolidated return.

[64]The preamble to the Regulation specifies that the penalty applies to misstatements of basis due to negligence and substantial or gross misconduct by the taxpayer. TD 8560, 1994–2 C.B. 200.

REFOCUS ON THE BIG PICTURE

SHOULD THE AFFILIATED GROUP FILE A CONSOLIDATED RETURN?

If Alexander and Hamilton are restructured as an affiliated group in a qualifying reorganization, and both corporations continue to exist as separate entities, the parties should consider an election to file their Federal income tax returns on a consolidated basis. Assuming that Hamilton begins to generate positive taxable income in the near future as expected, the NOLs and other attractive tax attributes that Hamilton brings to the group will be of great benefit to both corporations.

The group also may benefit from other aspects of Hamilton's tax situation, including its accumulated capital and passive losses and credits that have been carried forward due to a lack of tax liability. In all likelihood, Alexander and Hamilton are a "good match" as potential consolidated return partners.

What If?

But what if Alexander's expectations for a turnaround in Hamilton's business fortunes prove to be incorrect and the subsidiary continues to generate NOLs? The SRLY rules will prevent the deductions and credits acquired from Hamilton from being of immediate use to the affiliated group. A consolidation election will be beneficial only if the Hamilton subsidiary generates positive postacquisition taxable income.

KEY TERMS

Affiliated group, 8–8
Consolidated returns, 8–3
Excess loss account, 8–18
Expanded affiliated group (EAG), 8–29
Matching rule, 8–30
Separate return limitation year (SRLY), 8–26

DISCUSSION QUESTIONS

1. **LO.1** You are making a presentation to the board of directors of HugeCo about the merits of acquiring Bitty, Ltd., an important supplier. One board member knowing that you are a tax specialist, asks you to list some of the nontax reasons to make the acquisition. List at least four such motivations in a PowerPoint slide. **COMMUNICATIONS**

2. **LO.1** Describe how a corporate entity might be restructured to enable the resulting group to qualify for a consolidation election. (Hint: Recall the corporate changes discussed in Chapter 7, such as the "Type A" reorganization.) **DECISION MAKING**

3. **LO.2** Only a few sections in the Internal Revenue Code are devoted to the rules that control how consolidated income tax returns are filed. In contrast, the Regulations that explain and clarify those Code sections are voluminous. Given the complexity of the entities and transactions that consolidated returns involve, comment on whether this is a proper balancing of the tax-writing responsibilities in this area.

4. **LO.2** Financial accounting rules do not always match the tax treatment of transactions involving groups of U.S. corporations. List at least two areas where tax and accounting rules differ when groups of affiliated corporations are involved.

5. **LO.3** The local CPA Society is presenting its annual tax conference. Most of the attendees will be career tax professionals who work with smaller clients. You have been asked to submit an outline for your talk, "When to Use a Consolidated Tax Return: Federal Tax Law Issues." Organize an outline that lists the advantages and disadvantages of a consolidation election. Include at least five points in each category. Keep your points at the introductory level, as the members of your audience know the tax law well, but do not work regularly in this area. **COMMUNICATIONS**

6. **LO.3, 4** List the steps that are required under Federal income tax law before a parent and its affiliates are allowed to file on a consolidated basis. Consider only the requirements for the group to file its *first* consolidated return.

ISSUE ID

7. **LO.3, 10** Black, Brown, and Red Corporations are considering a corporate restructuring that would allow them to file Federal income tax returns on a consolidated basis. Black holds significant NOL carryforwards from several years ago. Brown has always been profitable and is projected to remain so. Red has been successful, but its product cycles are mature and operating losses are likely to begin three years from now and last for a decade. What tax issues should the corporations consider before electing to file on a consolidated basis?

ISSUE ID

8. **LO.3, 10** Continue with the facts presented in Question 7. In addition, assume that Brown Corporation has a history of making large, continuous charitable contributions in its community. In the next three years, Brown's largest investment assets will be priced such that they will be attractive candidates for sale. Modify your list of tax issues to include these considerations.

9. **LO.3, 9** Indicate whether each of the following would make good consolidated return partners in computing the affiliated group's Federal income tax.
   a. SubCo has a number of appreciated assets that it wants to sell to its parent, Huge Corporation.
   b. SubCo has a number of assets that it wants to sell to its parent, Huge. The assets have declined in market value since SubCo purchased them.
   c. ParentCo claims a tax credit with respect to its payment of foreign income taxes. SubCo wishes to continue to claim a deduction for these tax payments.
   d. ParentCo uses a calendar tax year, while SubTwo has been using a September 30 tax year-end.

10. **LO.3, 5** Indicate whether each of the following would make good partners for electing to file a consolidated return for Federal income tax purposes. Explain why or why not.
   a. SubCo cannot claim its full domestic production activities deduction, because of the taxable income limitation. ParentCo is highly profitable every tax year.
   b. ParentCo would like to file on a consolidated basis with SubOne, because the subsidiary will be generating sizable operating losses in the next two tax years. Starting with the third tax year, though, SubOne will enter a highly profitable period.
   c. ParentCo has $2 million in suspended foreign tax credits that will expire in two more tax years. Its wholly owned subsidiary, ShortCo, generates $5 million in foreign-source income every year.
   d. This year, ParentCo generated $4 million in taxable income, and its wholly owned subsidiary, Small Corporation, reported a $3 million operating loss. Next year, though, Small is projected to start a four-year period with $20 million total taxable profits.

11. **LO.4** Provide the information required to complete the following chart.

Group of Entities	Eligible to Join a Consolidated Group?	Why or Why Not Eligible?
a. Mercy Hospital	________	________
b. Columbus United Health Insurance, Ltd.	________	________
c. Bethke Services, Inc.	________	________
d. Tequila Teléfono, organized in El Salvador	________	________
e. Vermont, South Carolina, and Utah Barber Shops, Inc.	________	________
f. Boston Yankees Partnership	________	________
g. Henry Pontiac Trust	________	________

12. **LO.5** The Flamingo Group cannot decide whether to start to file on a consolidated basis for Federal income tax purposes, effective for its tax year beginning January 1, 2012. Its computational study of the effects of consolidation is taking longer than expected. What is the latest date by which the group must make this critical decision?

13. **LO.5** The Penguin Group cannot decide whether to cease to file on a consolidated basis for Federal income tax purposes, effective for its tax year beginning January 1, 2012. Its computational study of the effects of such a "de-consolidation" is taking longer than expected. What is the latest date by which the group must make this critical decision?

14. **LO.5** Lavender and Azure began to file a calendar year consolidated return for tax year 2009. The group never extends the due date of its tax returns. Lavender acquires all of the stock of Rose on January 1, 2010, and immediately joins the consolidated group. All of the Rose stock is sold to another investor at the end of 2012. Explain the significance of the following dates. Which of your answers can change if the taxpayers so elect? **DECISION MAKING**
    a. March 15, 2010.
    b. January 1, 2011.
    c. March 15, 2011.
    d. January 1, 2018.

15. **LO.5** The consolidated tax liability for most affiliated groups is assigned among the parent and its subsidiaries—each entity is responsible for "its share" of the tax. The Regulations allow several methods to be used to compute these allocations. Identify and describe the two most commonly used tax allocation methods.

16. **LO.5** Parent Corporation and its wholly owned subsidiary, Child Corporation, file Federal tax returns on a separate basis. Parent manufactures postage meters, and Child provides mail-order services to a cross section of clients in the state. **ISSUE ID**

    Parent uses a calendar tax year, while Child files using an April 30 year-end. Parent's gross receipts for the year total $10 million, and Child's are $2.5 million. Identify some Federal income tax issues as to accounting periods and methods that the group would face if the corporations elect to consolidate.

17. **LO.6** Your firm has assigned you to work with Jeri Byers, the tax director of a small group of corporations. The group qualifies to file on a consolidated basis and plans to make its first election to file in that manner. In a memo to Jeri's tax file, describe some of the more important adjustments that she will need to make, to keep track of the parent corporation's basis in the stock of each of the subsidiaries. **COMMUNICATIONS**

18. **LO.6** An *excess loss account* is used by a parent in computing its basis in the stock it holds in a subsidiary, so that the stock basis never can be less than zero. Explain.

19. **LO.6** Your client, MegaCorp, has asked for your assistance in filing the current-year consolidated Federal income tax return. MegaCorp provides you with the following items for the parent and each of the affiliates. Comment.
    - Gross income items.
    - Deductions and credit amounts.
    - Beginning and ending balance in E & P.
    - Cash distributions from the subsidiaries to the parent, MegaCorp.

20. **LO.6** Outline the process by which a consolidated group computes its Federal taxable income. Your description should match the approach taken in Figure 8.1.

21. **LO.7** Parent Corporation and its wholly owned subsidiary, Child Corporation, have filed Federal income tax returns on a consolidated basis since Child was incorporated many years ago. Both entities use calendar tax years. Parent uses accrual tax accounting, but Child uses the cash method. **ISSUE ID**

    In December 2011, Parent renders services worth $750,000 to Child. Parent's operations for 2011 result in a $2 million loss. Parent sends Child an invoice for the services in December 2011, and Child pays it in January 2012. What tax consequences are the parties trying to accomplish? Will this plan work?

22. **LO.7** In December 2011, Child Corporation prepays Parent Corporation $750,000 for use of a common database system in 2012. Child is a wholly owned subsidiary of Parent, with whom Child has filed a consolidated Federal income tax return since Child was spun off from Parent many years ago. While both entities have calendar tax years, Parent uses the accrual method, and Child employs the cash method of tax accounting. **ISSUE ID**

    Both entities are profitable for the 2011 tax year. What tax consequences are the parties trying to accomplish? Will this plan work?

23. **LO.8** Tiny Corporation brought a $4 million NOL carryforward into the Mucho Group of corporations that elected to file on a consolidated basis as of the beginning of this year. Combined results for the year generated $15 million taxable income, $1.5 million of which was attributable to Tiny's activities for the year. Has Tiny been a good consolidation partner?

DECISION MAKING

24. **LO.8** Parent and Child Corporations have filed on a consolidated basis since the mid-1970s. Junior Corporation was formed at the beginning of this year through an asset split-off from Parent. Operations this year resulted in a $2 million operating loss, one-fourth of which can be traced to Junior.

    Should Junior join the consolidated group this year? Will the group be able to carry back and claim a refund for the $500,000 NOL that is attributable to Junior?

25. **LO.8** Beige owned all of the stock of White when the two corporations were formed a decade ago. The group immediately elected to file on a consolidated basis. Now White's management team has purchased the company from the parent and intends to carry on and expand the business into new markets.

    When White left the Beige consolidated group, the group held a $3 million NOL carryforward, $800,000 of which was attributable to White's operations under formulas used by all of the parties. White will generate $300,000 on each of its first five years' worth of separate returns.

    Advise White as to who "owns" the carryforwards after the corporate division.

26. **LO.8** The consolidated return Regulations employ the "SRLY" rules to limit the losses that a parent can claim with respect to a newly acquired subsidiary. Explain the tax policy behind the SRLY rules, and describe how they affect the timing of loss deductions after an acquisition.

COMMUNICATIONS

27. **LO.9** The computational method of Figure 8.1 indicates that consolidated taxable income includes a number of group items, where limitations are applied on an aggregate basis. In no more than two PowerPoint slides, list as many group items as you can.

DECISION MAKING

28. **LO.9, 10** Intercompany transactions of a consolidated group can be subject to a "matching rule" and an "acceleration rule."
    a. Define both of these terms.
    b. As a tax planner structuring an intercompany transaction, when would it be beneficial to use either rule?

COMMUNICATIONS

29. **LO.9** Use a timeline to diagram the gain/loss recognition by this affiliated group.
    - Year 1: SubCo purchases an asset for $100.
    - Year 3: SubCo sells the asset to Parent for $175.
    - Year 4: Parent sells the asset to Stranger (not an affiliate) for $160.

COMMUNICATIONS

30. **LO.9** Use a timeline to diagram the gain/loss recognition by this affiliated group.
    - Year 1: SubCo purchases an asset for $100.
    - Year 3: SubCo sells the asset to Parent for $75.
    - Year 4: Parent sells the asset to Stranger (not an affiliate) for $40.

COMMUNICATIONS

31. **LO.9, 10** Junior was a member of the Rice consolidated group for many years. It left the group effective for the 2011 tax year. In 2009, Junior sold a plot of land to Parent at a $600,000 realized loss. Recognition of that loss by the group was deferred under the matching rule. As a departing group member, does Junior have any right to take the loss with it to be used on its subsequent separate returns? Prepare two memos for the tax research file, outlining the arguments both in Junior's favor and in the remaining group's favor.

32. **LO.10** At a meeting of local tax executives last week, you heard several of the tax professionals complaining about the sizable costs that they incur in meeting and maintaining an election to file Federal consolidated income tax returns. Examine these comments in more detail. Under what circumstances might a group of affiliates decide *not* to make a consolidation election? List three or more reasons that might make a corporate group question whether it should make such an election.

COMMUNICATIONS

33. **LO.10** Findlay Corporation was formed by three engineers. Sally brings entrepreneurial skills to the ownership group, while Patricia is the "idea person." Lois makes prototypes and works with potential manufacturers of Findlay products. Unfortunately, Findlay cannot exploit its operations due to lack of capital.

    Huge Corporation has the needed capital and recognizes Findlay's potential. It has sent takeover overtures to the Findlay board of directors. As the chief of Findlay's tax matters, you have been asked to prepare a list of items that will be necessary should the acquisition by Huge occur. Present your list of at least three items in a PowerPoint slide.

PROBLEMS

34. **LO.2** Your client, Big Corporation, and its wholly owned subsidiary, LittleCo, file a consolidated return for Federal income tax purposes. Indicate both the financial accounting and the tax treatment of the following transactions.
    a. LittleCo pays a $1 million dividend to Big.
    b. LittleCo sells investment land to Big. LittleCo's basis in the land is $200,000. The sale price is $500,000.
    c. Six months after purchasing the land from LittleCo, Big sells the investment land to Phillips, an unrelated party, for $650,000.

35. **LO.3** Giant Corporation owns all of the stock of PebbleCo, so they constitute a Federal affiliated group and a parent-subsidiary controlled group. By completing the following chart, delineate for Giant's tax department some of the effects of an election to file Federal consolidated income tax returns.

Situation	If the Group Files a Consolidated Return	If Separate Income Tax Returns Continue to Be Filed
a. PebbleCo pays a $1 million cash dividend to Giant.	________	________
b. Taxable income for both group members this year is $50,000.	________	________
c. Giant's tax liability is $95,000, and Pebble's liability totals $75,000.	________	________
d. Giant uses the LIFO method for its inventories, but Pebble wants to use FIFO for its own inventories.	________	________

36. **LO.3** Giant Corporation owns all of the stock of PebbleCo, so they constitute a Federal affiliated group and a parent-subsidiary controlled group. By completing the following chart, delineate for Giant's tax department some of the effects of an election to file Federal consolidated income tax returns.

Situation	If the Group Files a Consolidated Return	If Separate Income Tax Returns Continue to Be Filed
a. Giant and PebbleCo both produce taxable profits from manufacturing activities.	________	________
b. PebbleCo pays Giant an annual royalty for use of the Giant trademarks.	________	________
c. Giant uses a calendar tax year, while PebbleCo's tax year-end is March 31.	________	________
d. Giant claims a credit for its foreign tax payments, while Pebble claims a deduction for them.	________	________

37. **LO.3, 4** Apply the controlled and affiliated group rules to determine whether a parent-subsidiary controlled group or an affiliated group exists in each of the following independent situations. Circle Y for yes and N for no.

	Situation	Parent-Subsidiary Controlled Group?	Affiliated Group?
a.	Throughout the year, Parent owns 65% of the stock of SubCo.	Y N	Y N
b.	Parent owns 70% of SubCo. The other 30% of SubCo stock is owned by Senior, a wholly owned subsidiary of Parent.	Y N	Y N
c.	For 11 months, Parent owns 75% of the stock of SubCo. For the last month of the tax year, Parent owns 100% of the SubCo stock.	Y N	Y N

38. **LO.5** Senior Corporation owns all of the stock of Junior, Ltd., a corporation that has been declared bankrupt and has no net assets. Junior still owes $1 million to Wholesale, Inc., one of its suppliers, and $2.5 million to the IRS for unpaid Federal income taxes. Senior and Junior have always filed Federal income tax returns on a consolidated basis. What is Senior's exposure concerning Junior's outstanding income tax liabilities?

39. **LO.5** Parent and Sub Corporations file their Federal income tax returns on a consolidated basis. Parent, a calendar year taxpayer, owns all of the outstanding stock of Sub. The consolidation election was effective in January 2010. Both companies are profitable, and tax projections for the future appear below. How much must be remitted to the IRS for estimated payments in each year?

Tax Year	Parent's Federal Tax Estimate	Sub's Federal Tax Estimate
2010	$500,000	$150,000
2011	500,000	170,000
2012	600,000	200,000
2013	750,000	300,000

40. **LO.5** The Parent consolidated group reports the following results for the tax year. Dollar amounts are listed in millions.

	Parent	SubOne	SubTwo	SubThree	Consolidated
Ordinary income	$700	$200	$ 140	($90)	$ 950
Capital gain/loss	–0–	–0–	60	(25)	35
§ 1231 gain/loss	150	–0–	(50)	–0–	100
Separate taxable incomes	$850	$200	$ 150	($90) with a $25 capital loss carryover	
Consolidated taxable income					$1,085
Consolidated tax liability					$ 380
Energy tax credit, from SubOne					(20)
Net tax due					$ 360

Determine each member's share of the consolidated tax liability, assuming that the members all have consented to use the relative taxable income method. Assume a 35% marginal tax rate.

41. **LO.5** Assume the same facts as in Problem 40, except that the group members have adopted the relative tax liability tax-sharing method.

42. **LO.5** ParentCo owns all of the stock of DaughterCo, and the group files its Federal income tax returns on a consolidated basis. Both taxpayers are subject to the AMT this year due to active operations in oil and gas development. No intercompany transactions were incurred this year. If the affiliates filed separate returns, they would report the following amounts.

Company	Adjusted Current Earnings (ACE)	AMT Income before the ACE Adjustment
ParentCo	$1,500,000	$1,000,000
DaughterCo	250,000	400,000
Totals	$1,750,000	$1,400,000

How does the consolidation election affect the overall AMT liability of the group?

43. **LO.6** Senior, Ltd., acquires all of the stock of JuniorCo for $30 million at the beginning of 2010. The group immediately elects to file income tax returns on a consolidated basis. Senior's operations generate a $50 million profit every year. In 2011, JuniorCo pays its parent a $9 million dividend. Operating results for JuniorCo are as follows.

2010	$ 4 million
2011	12 million
2012	15 million

a. Compute Senior's basis in the JuniorCo stock as of the end of 2010, 2011, and 2012.
b. Same as (a), except that JuniorCo's 2011 tax year produced a $6 million NOL.
c. Same as (a), except that JuniorCo's 2011 tax year produced a $40 million NOL.

44. **LO.6** WhaleCo acquired all of the common stock of MinnowCo early in Year 1, for $500,000, and MinnowCo immediately elected to join WhaleCo's consolidated Federal income tax return. As part of the takeover, WhaleCo also acquired $800,000 of MinnowCo bonds. The results of MinnowCo for the first few years of the group operations were reported as follows.

Tax Year	Operating Gain/(Loss)	Stock Basis
1	$ 100,000	______
2	(400,000)	______
3	(300,000)	______

Determine WhaleCo's basis in its MinnowCo stock as of the end of each tax year.

45. **LO.6** Continue with the facts of Problem 44. WhaleCo has determined that it will sell all of its MinnowCo stock at the end of Year 3 for $250,000. Taking into account the rules regarding excess loss accounts, determine WhaleCo's gain/loss from its sale of the MinnowCo stock.

46. **LO.7** Compute consolidated taxable income for the calendar year Teal Group, which elected consolidated status immediately upon creation of the two member corporations in January 2010. All recognized income relates to the consulting services of the firms. No intercompany transactions were completed during the indicated years.

Year	Teal Corporation	Orange Corporation
2010	$250,000	($ 50,000)
2011	250,000	(60,000)
2012	250,000	(240,000)
2013	250,000	90,000

47. **LO.7, 8** Compute consolidated taxable income for the calendar year Moose Group, which elected consolidated status immediately upon the creation of the two member corporations on January 1, 2010. All recognized income is ordinary in nature, and no intercompany transactions were completed during the indicated years.

Year	Moose Corporation	Elk Corporation
2010	$250,000	$ 50,000
2011	250,000	(110,000)
2012	250,000	(400,000)
2013	250,000	75,000

48. **LO.8** Cougar, Jaguar, and Ocelot Corporations have filed on a consolidated, calendar year basis for many years. At the beginning of the 2011 tax year, the group elects to de-consolidate. The group's $4 million NOL carryforward can be traced in the following manner: one-half to Cougar's operations and one-quarter each to Jaguar's and Ocelot's. How will Ocelot treat the NOL on its 2011 separate tax return?

49. **LO.8** The Parent consolidated group includes SubTwo, which was acquired as part of a § 382 ownership change. SubTwo brought with it to the group a large NOL carryforward, $2.5 million of which is available this year under the SRLY rules due to SubTwo's positive contribution to the group's taxable income. The § 382 limitation with respect to SubTwo is $400,000. How much of SubTwo's NOL can be used this year to reduce consolidated taxable income?

50. **LO.8** Child Corporation joined the Thrust consolidated group in 2010. At the time it joined the group, Child held a $900,000 NOL carryforward. On a consolidated basis, the members of Thrust generated significant profits for many years.

    Child's operating results during the first few consolidated return years were as follows.

2010	($100,000)
2011	600,000
2012	500,000

The § 382 rules do not apply to the group.

How will Child's NOLs affect consolidated taxable income for these years? Is any refund available with respect to the NOL that Child brought into the group?

51. **LO.9** Parent Corporation sold a plot of undeveloped land to SubCo this year for $100,000. Parent had acquired the land several years ago for $20,000. The consolidated return also reflects the operating results of the parties: Parent generated $130,000 income from operations, and SubCo produced a $20,000 operating loss.
    a. Use the computational worksheet of Figure 8.2 to derive the group members' separate taxable incomes and the group's consolidated taxable income.
    b. Same as (a), except that SubCo sold the land to Outsider Corporation for $110,000 in a subsequent year, when its operating income totaled $30,000 (exclusive of the sale of the land), and Parent's operating income amounted to $90,000.

RESEARCH PROBLEMS

THOMSON REUTERS
Checkpoint® Student Edition

Note: Solutions to Research Problems can be prepared by using the **Checkpoint® Student Edition** online research product, which is available to accompany this text. It is also possible to prepare solutions to the Research Problems by using tax research materials found in a standard tax library.

COMMUNICATIONS

Research Problem 1. LargeCo owns stock in Small Corporation. The voting shares and value of the Small stock owned by LargeCo are as follows.

- Common stock, 100%.
- Preferred stock, 60%.

Under Small's corporate bylaws, the board of directors manages all of the entity's operations and investments. A majority vote of the board is required before any new policy or practice is adopted.

Board members are elected in the following manner: the common shareholders elect five of the eight board members, and the preferred shareholders separately elect the other three directors.

LargeCo would like to file a consolidated tax return with Small. Is the § 1504 stock ownership test met (i.e., does LargeCo own 80% of the voting power and value of the Small stock)? Prepare a memo to your firm's tax research file that addresses this affiliated group issue.

Research Problem 2. The calendar year Thor Group files its Federal income tax returns on a consolidated basis. The group's members elected to file on a consolidated basis because some of them were generating income, while others were generating losses. To utilize the deductions for the losses, the group began filing a consolidated return.

Now market conditions have changed. Currently, group members are all producing positive Federal taxable incomes. Various groups of shareholders desire to purchase the affiliates of the now-profitable group. If this occurs, the group no longer will meet the ownership requirements for consolidation starting in tax year 2012.

Is it possible to effect a de-consolidation of the group for tax year 2011? Why not just file separate returns for each member of the group for that year? The parent would claim the 100% dividends received deduction on its own return, and this should void the election.

The breakup of the group will take place by the end of June 2012, so no consolidated group will exist for that calendar tax year. But, by using the suggested strategy, the de-consolidation can be effective all the way back to January 2011. Do you agree?

Research Problem 3. The Cardinal Group had filed on a consolidated basis for several years. Parent Cardinal, Ltd., had a wholly owned subsidiary, Swallow, Inc. The group used a calendar tax year.

COMMUNICATIONS

On January 25, 2011, Heron acquired all of the stock of Cardinal, including its ownership in Swallow, an important supplier for Heron's manufacturing process. All parties in the new group intended to file on a consolidated basis immediately and, indeed, used consolidated amounts in filing the 2011 Heron Group return on September 10, 2012.

During the audit of Heron Group's 2011 tax return, the IRS disallowed the use of the consolidated method because no Forms 1122 had ever been filed for the affiliates in the new group. In a memo to the tax research file, summarize the possibilities for the Heron Group to be granted an extension to elect consolidated return status.

Research Problem 4. Last year, Cutlinger, Inc., acquired Donte Corporation in a state-law merger. Donte immediately joined the Cutlinger consolidated return group for state and Federal income tax purposes. Both parties use the calendar tax year.

COMMUNICATIONS

At the time of the acquisition, Donte held some undeveloped land, known as Whispering Aspens, about 35 miles out of town, that it had purchased for speculation three years earlier. Donte's basis in the land was $40 million, and a recent appraisal put its value on the date of the acquisition at $4 million.

The decline in the value of Whispering Aspens reflected the generally poor operating results that Donte had been experiencing. Exclusive of the sale of the land, Donte had generated a $2 million operating loss for the two years prior to being acquired by Cutlinger, and it projected the same results for the next two years as well, now as a Cutlinger subsidiary.

The Donte board of directors had wanted to sell off Whispering Aspens for $4 million before Cutlinger made the acquisition, but Cutlinger sweetened the per-share acquisition price and convinced them to wait. Cutlinger had learned from an inside source that the tollway authority that operated a road abutting Whispering Aspens had decided to build a new interchange nearby and that Whispering Aspens now would be much more valuable in an outright sale to developers.

After the takeover, Cutlinger quickly sold off Whispering Aspens to a strip mall developer for $24 million in cash. On its consolidated tax return, the Cutlinger group reported a $16 million loss. On audit, the IRS disallowed the entire loss deduction. Mary Ellen Rogers, tax director of Cutlinger, wants your analysis of the tax results of the land sale. Write a letter to her addressing the IRS's position. Cutlinger's corporate offices are at 1101 Office Strip Lane, Suite 3, Hudson OH, 44237.

Research Problem 5. Super Corporation acquired all of the stock of Lesser Corporation in 2008, and the entities have filed a state and Federal consolidated income tax return ever since. In 2011, an audit notice from the state unemployment tax administration makes it clear that Lesser underpaid its 2009 payroll taxes by $750,000. Lesser's cash flow at this time is poor, and it has insufficient funds to pay the $750,000. Can the state revenue agency collect the outstanding payroll tax from Super, under the "joint and several liability" rule for tax obligations of consolidated return affiliates?

Use the tax resources of the Internet to address the following questions. Do not restrict your search to the Web, but include a review of newsgroups and general reference materials, practitioner sites and resources, primary sources of the tax law, chat rooms and discussion groups, and other opportunities.

COMMUNICATIONS

Research Problem 6. Find a thread in a tax blog involving consolidated returns. Post an entry to the site concerning acceptable tax allocation formulas. Which tax-sharing methods have been most popular with the blogger's clients? Why? Have specific tax-sharing methods become more or less popular over time? What difficulties are encountered in gaining the affiliates' consent to a tax-sharing method? Has the blogger created any variations on the most common tax-sharing methods? How and why did these new formulas come about? Write an e-mail to your professor summarizing the following.

a. The text of your posted message.
b. The responses that you received in the first week after posting.
c. The titles of other posters to the group and the type of questions that they are discussing.

Research Problem 7. Determine whether the income tax laws of your state, and those of two of its neighbors, allow Federal affiliated groups to use capital loss, passive loss, and NOL deductions. What are the NOL carryback and carryforward periods? What other limitations apply?

COMMUNICATIONS

Research Problem 8. Find several journal articles and Web postings addressing the consolidation election. Construct a list titled "Consolidated Returns: Compliance Tips and Traps," and submit this document to your instructor. Provide citations for your research.

COMMUNICATIONS

Research Problem 9. Identify the key details of the evolution and development of the Federal consolidated tax return rules. When were consolidated returns elective? Required? What political forces were at work when the major 1966 and 1995 changes to the pertinent Federal income tax Regulations were adopted? When were NOL deduction limitations tightened or relaxed? Why? Arrange your findings using a timeline and no more than three PowerPoint slides.

COMMUNICATIONS

Research Problem 10. Complete a review of the evolution of your state's tax laws concerning consolidated returns. Use a format similar to the one described in Research Problem 9.

CHAPTER

9

Taxation of International Transactions

LEARNING OBJECTIVES

After completing Chapter 9, you should be able to:

LO.1

Explain the framework underlying the U.S. taxation of cross-border transactions.

LO.2

Understand the interaction between Internal Revenue Code provisions and tax treaties.

LO.3

Apply the rules for sourcing income and deductions into U.S. and foreign categories.

LO.4

Explain how foreign currency exchange affects the tax consequences of international transactions.

LO.5

Work with the U.S. tax provisions affecting U.S. persons earning foreign-source income, including the rules relating to cross-border asset transfers, antideferral provisions, and the foreign tax credit.

LO.6

Apply the U.S. tax provisions concerning nonresident alien individuals and foreign corporations.

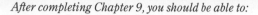

OUTLINE

For the latest in changes to tax legislation, visit **www.cengage.com/taxation/swft.**

THE BIG PICTURE Tax Solutions for the Real World

GOING INTERNATIONAL

VoiceCo, a domestic corporation, designs, manufactures, and sells specialty microphones for use in theaters. All of its activities take place in Florida, although it ships products to customers all over the United States. When it receives some inquiries about its products from foreign customers, VoiceCo decides to test the foreign market and places ads in foreign trade journals. Soon it is taking orders from foreign customers.

VoiceCo is concerned about its potential foreign income tax exposure. Although it has no assets or employees in the foreign jurisdictions, it now is involved in international commerce. Is VoiceCo subject to income taxes in foreign countries? Must it pay U.S. income taxes on the profits from its foreign sales? What if VoiceCo pays taxes to other countries? Does it receive any benefit from these payments on its U.S. tax return?

Suppose that VoiceCo establishes a manufacturing plant in Ireland to meet the European demand for its products. VoiceCo incorporates the Irish operation as VoiceCo-Ireland, a foreign corporation. Ireland imposes only a 12.5 percent tax on VoiceCo-Ireland's profits. So long as VoiceCo-Ireland does not distribute profits to VoiceCo, will the profits escape U.S. taxation? What are the consequences to VoiceCo of being the owner of a so-called controlled foreign corporation? Does it have any reporting requirements with the IRS? **Read the chapter and formulate your response.**

9.1 Overview of International Taxation

LO.1

Explain the framework underlying the U.S. taxation of cross-border transactions.

In today's global business environment, most large businesses are truly international in scope. Consider the most recent financial results of three "all-American" companies: Coca-Cola, Ford Motor Company, and Microsoft. Coca-Cola reported that 70 percent of its total net income is from offshore operations, Ford earned $1.2 billion in pretax profits from non-U.S. operations, and Microsoft earned $15.4 billion in profits (62 percent of its book net income before tax) from operations outside the United States. Honda, a Japanese company, reported that 44 percent of its sales were in North America; Toyota, another Japanese company, earned 29 percent of its net revenues from automobile sales in North America.

Global trade is an integral part of the U.S. economy. In 2009, U.S. exports and imports of goods and services totaled $1.6 trillion and $1.9 trillion, respectively. This international trade creates significant U.S. tax consequences for both U.S. and foreign entities. In the most recent year for which data are available, U.S. corporations reported $402 billion in foreign-source income, paid $112 billion in taxes to foreign governments, and claimed foreign tax credits in excess of $84 billion. Foreign individual recipients reported $69 billion in U.S.-source income subject to withholding and paid $8.4 billion in U.S. taxes. U.S. corporations controlled by foreign owners reported $46 billion in U.S. taxable income.

Cross-border transactions create the need for special tax considerations for both the United States and its trading partners. From a U.S. perspective, international tax laws should promote the global competitiveness of U.S. enterprises and at the same time protect the tax revenue base of the United States. These two objectives sometimes conflict, however. The need to deal with both contributes to the complexity of the rules governing the U.S. taxation of cross-border transactions.

EXAMPLE 1

U.S. persons engage in activities outside the United States for many different reasons. Consider two U.S. corporations that have established sales subsidiaries in foreign countries. Dedalus, Inc., operates in Germany, a high-tax country, because customers demand local attention from sales agents. Mulligan, Inc., operates in the Cayman Islands, a low-tax country, simply to shift income outside the United States. U.S. tax law must fairly address both situations with the same law. ■

FIGURE 9.1 U.S. Taxation of Cross-Border Transactions

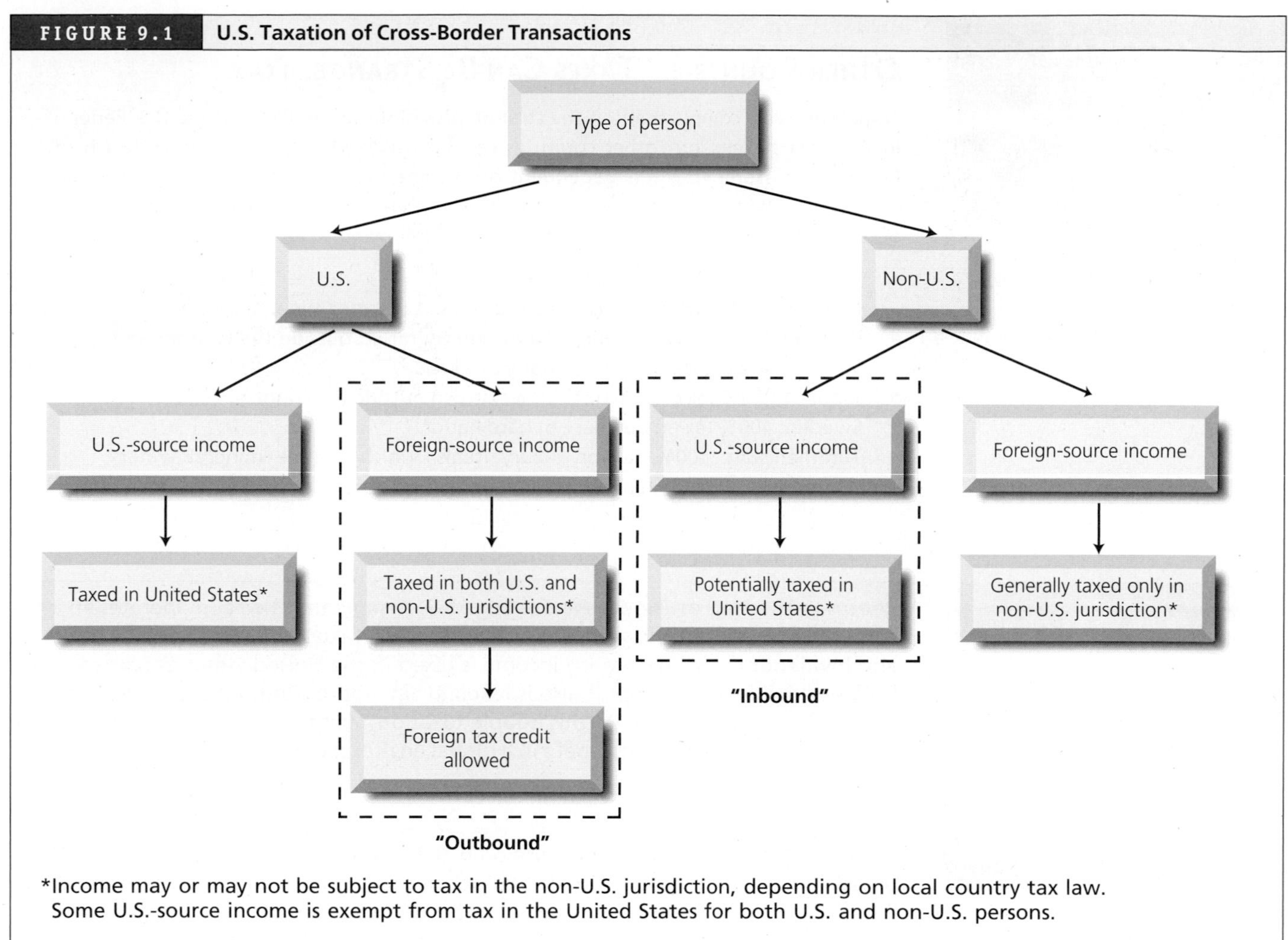

*Income may or may not be subject to tax in the non-U.S. jurisdiction, depending on local country tax law. Some U.S.-source income is exempt from tax in the United States for both U.S. and non-U.S. persons.

U.S. international tax provisions are concerned primarily with two types of potential taxpayers: U.S. persons earning foreign-source income and foreign persons earning U.S.-source income.[1] U.S. persons earning U.S.-source income are taxed under the purely domestic provisions of the Internal Revenue Code. Foreign persons earning foreign-source income are not within the taxing jurisdiction of the United States (unless this income is somehow connected to a U.S. trade or business). Figure 9.1 illustrates this categorization.

The United States taxes the worldwide income of U.S. taxpayers. Because foreign governments may also tax some of this income, these taxpayers may be subjected to double taxation. Special provisions such as the foreign tax credit can mitigate this problem. For foreign taxpayers, the United States generally taxes only income earned within its borders. The U.S. taxation of cross-border transactions can be organized in terms of "outbound" and "inbound" taxation. **Outbound taxation** refers to the U.S. taxation of foreign-source income earned by U.S. taxpayers. **Inbound taxation** refers to the U.S. taxation of U.S.-source income earned by foreign taxpayers.

[1]The term "person" includes an individual, corporation, partnership, trust, estate, or association. § 7701(a)(1). The terms "domestic" and "foreign" are defined in §§ 7701(a)(4) and (5).

GLOBAL Tax Issues

Other Countries' Taxes Can Be Strange, Too

Some observers complain about the strange provisions or workings of the U.S. Federal income tax system, but other countries can be criticized in the same way. Much of Europe, for example, is less dependent on income taxes than the United States and more dependent on transaction and wealth taxes, and these can take unusual forms. A quick survey of taxes around the globe finds the following.

- Australia: 68% tax on cigarette purchases.
- China: 80–100% tax on purchase of autos built outside China.
- Costa Rica: 170% tax on purchase of poultry raised outside the country and 96% tax on purchase of foreign dairy products.
- Japan: 1,000% tax on purchase of rice grown outside the country.
- Sweden: 400% tax on purchase of hard liquor.
- Turkmenistan: 100% tax on luxury items, which include mineral water, cotton mittens, saws, blankets, pillows, and mattresses.

EXAMPLE 2
THE BIG PICTURE

Return to the facts of *The Big Picture* on p. 9-2. Assume that VoiceCo operates an unincorporated manufacturing branch in Singapore to take advantage of local materials and low labor costs. This branch income is taxed in the United States as part of VoiceCo's worldwide income, but it also is taxed in Singapore. Without the availability of a foreign tax credit to mitigate this double taxation, VoiceCo would suffer an excessive tax burden and could not compete in a global environment. ■

EXAMPLE 3
THE BIG PICTURE

Return to the facts of *The Big Picture* on p. 9-2. VoiceCo's major competitor is a Swiss-based foreign corporation with operations in the United States. Although not a U.S. person, the Swiss competitor is taxed in the United States on its U.S.-source business income. If the Swiss competitor could operate free of U.S. tax, VoiceCo would face a serious competitive disadvantage. ■

9.2 Tax Treaties

LO.2

Understand the interaction between Internal Revenue Code provisions and tax treaties.

The U.S. tax rules governing cross-border transactions are based on both the Internal Revenue Code and **tax treaties**. Tax treaties are bilateral agreements between countries that provide tax relief for those persons covered by the treaties. Tax treaty provisions generally override the treatment otherwise called for under the Internal Revenue Code or foreign tax statutes. Taxpayers should attempt to resolve any conflicts between a treaty and local law. A common way of doing so is to apply the "later-in-time" rule, under which preference is given to whichever is newer, the treaty or the law.

More than 50 income tax treaties between the United States and other countries are in effect (see Exhibit 9.1). These treaties generally provide *taxing rights* with regard to the taxable income of residents of one treaty country who have income sourced in the other treaty country. For the most part, neither country is prohibited from taxing the income of its residents. The treaties generally give one country primary taxing rights and require the other country to allow a credit for the taxes paid on the twice-taxed income.

EXAMPLE 4

ForCo, Ltd., a resident of a foreign country with which the United States has an income tax treaty, earns income attributable to a permanent establishment (e.g., place of business) in the United States. Under the treaty, the United States has primary taxing rights with regard to this income. The other country can also require that the income be included in gross income and can subject the income to its income tax, but it must allow a credit for the taxes paid to the United States on the income. ■

FINANCIAL DISCLOSURE *Insights* — EFFECTIVE TAX STRATEGIES USING OVERSEAS OPERATIONS

In a global economy, publicly traded business entities can operate in many taxing jurisdictions. For instance, General Electric reports that it files current-year tax returns with more than 250 countries, amounting to over 7,000 income tax returns at the Federal and local levels worldwide. Note that this tax activity does not take into account the sales, value added, property, and other tax returns that are required by the U.S. states and localities!

The financial reports of profitable U.S. companies indicate that overseas operations can produce tax benefits of their own, not taking into account the effects of increased market share and financial stability. For instance, the trucking firm Ryder Systems recently reported current tax refunds of about $235,000 and deferred tax savings of about $500,000 on non-U.S. profits of about $11.5 million. In a recent period, Eli Lilly reduced its effective tax rate by about one-third due to overseas operations. And General Electric reduced its 2009 effective tax rate to a negative amount because of various income deferrals related to overseas earnings. We will address these deferral techniques later in the chapter.

Which country receives primary taxing rights usually depends on the residence of the taxpayer or the presence of a permanent establishment in a treaty country to which the income is attributable. Generally, a permanent establishment is a branch, office, factory, workshop, warehouse, or other fixed place of business.

Most U.S. income tax treaties reduce the withholding tax rate on certain items of investment income, such as interest and dividends. For example, treaties with France and Sweden reduce the withholding on portfolio dividends to 15 percent and on certain interest income to zero. Many newer treaties (e.g., with the United Kingdom, Australia, and Japan) provide for no withholding on dividend payments to parent

EXHIBIT 9.1 U.S. Income Tax Treaties in Force as of April 2010

Australia	Iceland	Pakistan
Austria	India	Philippines
Barbados	Indonesia	Poland
Belgium	Ireland	Portugal
Canada	Israel	Romania
China	Italy	Russia
Commonwealth of Independent States*	Jamaica	Slovak Republic
Cyprus	Japan	Slovenia
Czech Republic	Kazakhstan	South Africa
Denmark	Korea, Republic of	Spain
Egypt	Latvia	Sweden
Estonia	Lithuania	Switzerland
Finland	Luxembourg	Thailand
France	Mexico	Trinidad and Tobago
Germany	Morocco	Tunisia
Greece	Netherlands	Turkey
Hungary	New Zealand	United Kingdom
	Norway	Venezuela

*The income tax treaty between the United States and the former Soviet Union now applies to the countries of Armenia, Azerbaijan, Belarus, Georgia, Kyrgyzstan, Moldova, Tajikistan, Turkmenistan, Ukraine, and Uzbekistan. The Commonwealth of Independent States is an association of many of the former constituent republics of the Soviet Union.

corporations. The United States has developed a Model Income Tax Convention as the starting point for negotiating income tax treaties with other countries.[2]

9.3 Sourcing of Income and Deductions

LO.3

Apply the rules for sourcing income and deductions into U.S. and foreign categories.

The sourcing of income and deductions inside or outside the United States has a direct bearing on a number of tax provisions affecting both U.S. and foreign taxpayers. For example, foreign taxpayers generally are taxed only on income sourced inside the United States, and U.S. taxpayers receive relief from double taxation under the foreign tax credit rules based on their foreign-source income. Accordingly, an examination of sourcing rules is often the starting point in addressing international tax issues.

INCOME SOURCED INSIDE THE UNITED STATES

The determination of the source of income depends on the type of income realized (e.g., income from the sale of property versus income for the use of property). This makes the classification of income an important consideration. Section 861 contains source rules for most types of income.[3]

Interest

Interest income received from the U.S. government, from the District of Columbia, and from noncorporate U.S. residents or domestic corporations is sourced inside the United States. There are a few exceptions to this rule. Certain interest received from a U.S. corporation that earned 80 percent or more of its active business income from foreign sources over the prior three-year period is treated as foreign-source income. Interest received on amounts deposited with a foreign branch of a U.S. corporation is also treated as foreign-source income if the branch is engaged in the commercial banking business.

EXAMPLE 5

John holds a bond issued by Delta, a domestic corporation. For the immediately preceding three tax years, 82% of Delta's gross income has been active foreign business income. The interest income that John receives for the current tax year from Delta is foreign-source income. ■

Dividends

Dividends received from domestic corporations (other than certain U.S. possessions corporations) are sourced inside the United States. Generally, dividends paid by a foreign corporation are foreign-source income. However, if a foreign corporation earned 25 percent or more of its gross income from income effectively connected with a U.S. trade or business for the three tax years immediately preceding the year of the dividend payment, that percentage of the dividend is treated as U.S.-source income.

EXAMPLE 6

Ann receives dividend income from the following corporations for the current tax year.

Amount	Corporation	Effectively Connected U.S. Income for Past Three Years	U.S.-Source Income
$500	Green, domestic	85%	$500
600	Brown, domestic	13%	600
300	Orange, foreign	92%	276

[2] Treasury Department Model Income Tax Convention (November 15, 2006).

[3] Other rules pertaining to the sourcing of income are found in §§ 862–865.

WHY THE TREATY PROCESS STALLS

GLOBAL *Tax Issues*

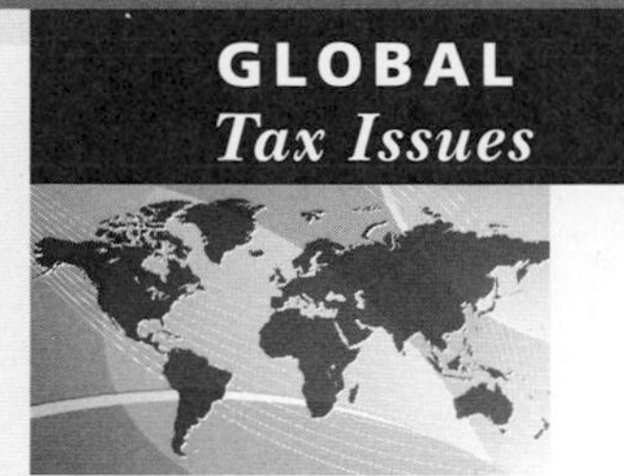

The United States has negotiated several income tax treaties that have never been signed or ratified (e.g., with Argentina, Bangladesh, and Brazil). The treaty process sometimes stalls for several reasons.

One is the desire on the part of some less developed countries for a tax-sparing provision in the treaty. In other words, these countries want the United States to allow a foreign tax credit against U.S. taxes even though U.S. companies operating there actually pay no foreign taxes due to local tax reduction agreements (i.e., tax holidays).

Another reason is the exchange of information provision. Some countries, for example, have anonymous bank rules that would preclude the exchange of information. Not long ago, the Parliament of Kazakhstan voted on a provision to eliminate secret bank accounts so that the United States–Kazakhstan income tax treaty could be ratified.

Because Green Corporation and Brown Corporation are domestic corporations, the dividends they pay are U.S.-source income. Orange Corporation is a foreign corporation that earned 92% of its business income over the prior three years from income effectively connected with a U.S. trade or business. Because Orange meets the 25% threshold, 92% of its dividend is U.S. source. ■

Personal Services Income

The source of income from personal services is determined by the location in which the services are performed (inside or outside the United States). A limited *commercial traveler* exception is available. Under this exception, personal services income must meet all the following requirements to avoid being classified as U.S.-source income.

- The services must be performed by a nonresident alien who is in the United States for 90 days or less during the taxable year.
- The compensation may not exceed $3,000 in total for the services performed in the United States.
- The services must be performed on behalf of:
  - *a nonresident alien, foreign partnership, or foreign corporation that is not engaged in a U.S. trade or business or*
  - *an office or place of business maintained in a foreign country or possession of the United States by an individual who is a citizen or resident of the United States, a domestic partnership, or a domestic corporation.*

EXAMPLE 7

Mark, a nonresident alien, is an engineer employed by a foreign oil company. He spent four weeks in the United States arranging the purchase of field equipment for his company. His salary for the four weeks was $3,500. Even though the oil company is not engaged in a U.S. trade or business, and Mark was in the United States for less than 90 days during the taxable year, the income is U.S.-source income because it exceeds $3,000. ■

The issue of whether income is derived from the performance of personal services is important in determining the income's source. The courts have held that a corporation can perform personal services.[4] In addition, in the absence of capital as an income-producing factor, personal services income can arise even though there is no recipient of the services.[5] If payment is received for services performed partly inside and partly outside the United States, the income must be allocated for source

[4]See *British Timken Limited,* 12 T.C. 880 (1949), and Rev.Rul. 60–55, 1960–1 C.B. 270.

[5]See *Robida v. Comm.,* 72–1 USTC ¶9450, 29 AFTR 2d 72–1223, 460 F.2d 1172 (CA–9, 1972). The taxpayer was employed in military PXs around the world. He had large slot machine winnings and claimed the foreign earned income exclusion. The IRS challenged the exclusion on the grounds that the winnings were not earned income because there was no recipient of Robida's services. The court, however, found that, in the absence of capital, the winnings were earned income.

purposes on some reasonable basis that clearly reflects income under the facts and circumstances. The number of days worked in each country is generally acceptable.[6]

Rents and Royalties

The source of income received for the use of tangible property is the country in which the property is located. The source of income received for the use of intangible property (e.g., patents, copyrights, secret processes and formulas) is the country in which the property is used.

Sale or Exchange of Property

Generally, the location of real property determines the source of any income derived from the property. Income from the disposition of U.S. real property interests is U.S.-source income.

The source of income from the sale of personal property (assets other than real property) depends on several factors, including the following.

- Whether the property was produced by the seller.
- The type of property sold (e.g., inventory or a capital asset).
- The residence of the seller.

Generally, income, gain, or profit from the sale of personal property is sourced according to the residence of the seller. Income from the sale of purchased inventory, however, is sourced in the country in which the sale takes place.[7]

When the seller has produced the inventory property, the income must be apportioned between the country of production and the country of sale. Gross income is sourced under a 50/50 allocation method unless the taxpayer elects to use the independent factory price (IFP) method or the separate books and records method. The 50/50 method assigns one-half of the inventory profits from export sales to the location of the production assets and one-half to the place of title passage. The IFP method may be elected only where an IFP exists.[8] If the manufacturer or producer regularly sells to wholly independent distributors, this can establish an *independent* factory or production price.

Under § 865, income from the sale of personal property other than inventory is sourced at the residence of the seller unless one of the following exceptions applies.

- Gain on the sale of depreciable personal property is sourced according to prior depreciation deductions to the extent of the deductions. Any excess gain is sourced the same as the sale of inventory.
- Gain on the sale of intangibles is sourced according to prior amortization deductions to the extent of the deductions. Contingent payments, however, are sourced as royalty income.
- Gain attributable to an office or fixed place of business maintained outside the United States by a U.S. resident is foreign-source income.
- Income or gain attributable to an office or fixed place of business maintained in the United States by a nonresident is U.S.-source income.

The sourcing of losses is complicated and depends on the nature of the property. Different rules exist for the disposition of stock versus other personal property.[9]

Transportation and Communication Income

Income from transportation beginning *and* ending in the United States is U.S.-source income. Fifty percent of the income from transportation beginning *or* ending in the United States is U.S.-source income, unless the U.S. point is only an intermediate stop. This rule does not apply to personal services income unless the

[6]Reg. § 1.861–4(b). See *Stemkowski*, 76 T.C. 252 (1981).

[7]§§ 861(a)(6) and 865. The sale is deemed to take place where title passes. See Reg. § 1.861–7(c) regarding title passage. There has been considerable conflict in this area of tax law. See, for example, *Liggett Group, Inc.*, 58 TCM 1167, T.C.Memo. 1990–18.

[8]§ 863(b)(2), Reg. § 1.863–3, and Notice 89–10, 1989–1 C.B. 631.

[9]See Reg. § 1.861–8(e)(7) and Temp.Reg. § 1.865–1T(a)(1). See Reg. §§ 1.865–(2)(a)(1) and (2) regarding the source of losses on the disposition of stock.

TAX *in the NEWS*

Sourcing Income in Cyberspace

The use of the Internet for more and more consumer and business transactions is posing problems for the taxing authorities. Consumers purchase books, music, clothing, and food from online retailers. Businesses negotiate with suppliers via online auctions of products and services. Consultants provide services to their clients over the Internet. Very few transactions do not have a counterpart that takes place in cyberspace. The existing income-sourcing rules were developed long before the existence of the Internet, and taxing authorities are finding it challenging to apply these rules to Internet transactions. Where does a sale take place when the web server is in the Cayman Islands, the seller is in Singapore, and the customer is in Texas? Where is a service performed when all activities take place online? These questions and more must be answered by the United States and its trading partners as e-commerce grows in size and importance.

transportation is between the United States and a possession. Income from space and ocean activities conducted outside the jurisdiction of any country is sourced according to the residence of the person conducting the activity.

International communication income derived by a U.S. person is sourced 50 percent in the United States when transmission is between the United States and a foreign country. International communication income derived by foreign persons is foreign-source income unless it is attributable to an office or other fixed place of business in the United States. In that case, it is U.S.-source income.

Software Income

Income from the sale or license of software is sourced depending on how the income is classified. A transfer of software is classified as either the transfer of a copyright (e.g., the right to the computer program itself) or the transfer of a copyrighted article (the right to use a copy of the computer program).[10] If the transfer is considered a transfer of a copyright, the income is sourced using the royalty income rules. If the transfer is considered a transfer of a copyrighted article, the income is treated as resulting from a sale of the article and is sourced based on the personal property sales rules.

INCOME SOURCED OUTSIDE THE UNITED STATES

The provisions for sourcing income outside the United States are not as detailed and specific as those for determining U.S.-source income. Basically, § 862 provides that if interest, dividends, compensation for personal services, income from the use or sale of property, or other income is not U.S.-source income, then it is foreign-source income.

ALLOCATION AND APPORTIONMENT OF DEDUCTIONS

The United States levies a tax on *taxable income.* Deductions and losses, therefore, must be allocated and apportioned between U.S.- and foreign-source gross income to determine U.S.- and foreign-source taxable income. Deductions directly related to an activity or property are allocated to classes of income. This is followed by apportionment between the statutory and residual groupings (e.g., foreign versus domestic) on some reasonable basis.[11] A deduction not definitely related to any class of gross income is ratably allocated to all classes of gross income and apportioned between U.S.- and foreign-source income.

[10]Reg. § 1.861–18.

[11]Reg. § 1.861–8.

EXAMPLE 8

Ace, Inc., a domestic corporation, has $2 million gross income and a $50,000 expense, all related to real estate activities. The expense is allocated and apportioned using gross income as a basis as follows.

	Gross Income			Apportionment	
	Foreign	U.S.	Allocation	Foreign	U.S.
Sales	$1,000,000	$500,000	$37,500*	$25,000	$12,500**
Rentals	400,000	100,000	12,500	10,000	2,500***
			$50,000	$35,000	$15,000

*$50,000 × ($1,500,000/$2,000,000).
**$37,500 × ($500,000/$1,500,000).
***$12,500 × ($100,000/$500,000).

If Ace could show that $45,000 of the expense was directly related to sales income, the $45,000 would be allocated to that class of gross income, with the remainder allocated and apportioned ratably based on gross income. ■

Interest expense is allocated and apportioned based on the theory that money is fungible. With limited exceptions, interest expense is attributable to all the activities and property of the taxpayer, regardless of the specific purpose for incurring the debt on which interest is paid. Taxpayers must allocate and apportion interest expense on the basis of assets, using either the fair market value or the tax book value of the assets.[12] Once the fair market value is used, the taxpayer must continue to use this method. Special rules apply in allocating and apportioning interest expense in an affiliated group of corporations.

EXAMPLE 9
THE BIG PICTURE

Return to the facts of *The Big Picture* on p. 9-2. Assume that VoiceCo generates U.S.-source and foreign-source gross income for the current year. VoiceCo's assets (tax book value) are as follows.

Assets generating U.S.-source income	$18,000,000
Assets generating foreign-source income	5,000,000
	$23,000,000

VoiceCo incurs interest expense of $800,000 for the current year. Using the tax book value method, interest expense is apportioned to foreign-source income as follows.

$$\frac{\$5{,}000{,}000 \text{ (foreign assets)}}{\$23{,}000{,}000 \text{ (total assets)}} \times \$800{,}000 = \$173{,}913$$

■

Specific rules also apply to research and development (R&D) expenditures, certain stewardship expenses, legal and accounting fees and expenses, income taxes, and losses. Although U.S. companies incur about 90 percent of their R&D expenditures at U.S. facilities, several billion dollars are spent on foreign R&D each year. The Regulations provide that a portion of a U.S. company's R&D expenditures must be treated as foreign-source expense if the R&D relates to foreign product sales.

TRANSFER PRICING

Taxpayers may be tempted to minimize taxation by manipulating the source of income and the allocation of deductions arbitrarily through **transfer pricing.** This manipulation is more easily accomplished between or among related persons. The IRS uses § 482 to counter such actions. The provision gives the IRS the power to

[12]Reg. § 1.861–9T. Reg. § 1.861–10T(b) describes circumstances in which interest expense can be directly allocated to specific debt. This exception to the fungibility concept is limited to cases in which specific property is purchased or improved with nonrecourse debt.

reallocate gross income, deductions, credits, or allowances between or among organizations, trades, or businesses owned or controlled directly or indirectly by the same interests. This can be done whenever the IRS determines that reallocation is necessary to prevent the evasion of taxes or to reflect income more clearly. Section 482 is a "one-edged sword" available only to the IRS. The taxpayer generally cannot invoke it to reallocate income and expenses.[13]

WHEN CAN 1 + 1 = 3?

Pharma, Inc., a U.S. pharmaceutical company, operates in the United States and in Ireland through a wholly owned Irish subsidiary corporation. Pharma manufactures certain aspects of a drug in the United States at a cost of $50 million and sells this product to its Irish subsidiary for $70 million, producing a $20 million profit in the United States. The Irish subsidiary completes the manufacturing of the drug at a cost of $10 million and sells the final product to unrelated customers in Europe for $85 million, producing a $5 million profit in Ireland [$85 million sales price − $70 million cost of goods sold (purchased inventory) − $10 million additional processing costs]. In the aggregate, Pharma and its Irish subsidiary have produced a product at a cost of $60 million and sold it for $85 million, resulting in $25 million in total profits.

What if the IRS decides that the transfer price of $70 million was too low and should have been $74 million? This would indicate that $24 million of the profit should have been in the United States and $1 million in Ireland. Should the tax authorities in Ireland automatically make the transfer pricing adjustment on their side (i.e., reduce the Irish subsidiary's income to $1 million from $5 million)? What if the IRS and the Irish tax authorities disagree and Pharma and its subsidiary end up paying tax on $29 million in profits ($24 million in the United States and $5 million in Ireland) even though only $25 million of economic profits actually exist? Is this fair to the taxpayer? What recourse should Pharma have when it is caught between two governments that disagree?

EXAMPLE 10

Consider the transaction depicted in Figure 9.2. A U.S. corporation manufactures and sells inventory to an unrelated foreign customer. The sales price for the inventory is $1,000 and the related cost of goods sold (COGS) is $600. The resulting profit of $400 is all taxed to the U.S. corporation, resulting in a $140 U.S. income tax liability ($400 × 35%). If the U.S. corporation has no business presence in the foreign jurisdiction and is merely selling to a customer located there, the foreign government is unlikely to impose any local income tax on the U.S. corporation. Consequently, the total tax burden imposed on the inventory sale is $140.

Suppose instead that the U.S. corporation attempts to reduce its total tax expense by channeling the inventory sale through a foreign subsidiary in the same country as the foreign customer. In this case, because the U.S. corporation controls the foreign subsidiary, it chooses an intercompany sales price (the transfer price) that moves a portion of the profits from the United States to the foreign country.

By selling the inventory it manufactured to its 100%-owned foreign subsidiary for $700, the U.S. corporation reports only $100 of profits and an associated U.S. tax liability of $35. The foreign subsidiary then sells the inventory to the ultimate customer for $1,000 and, with a $700 COGS, earns a $300 profit. In this example, the foreign country imposes only a 10% tax on corporate profits, resulting in a foreign income tax of $30 ($300 × 10%). By using a related foreign entity in a lower-tax jurisdiction, the U.S. corporation has lowered its overall tax liability on the sale from $140 (all U.S.) to $65 ($35 U.S. and $30 foreign).

The critical question is whether the IRS will view the $700 intercompany sales price as the appropriate transfer price. Under § 482, the IRS may question why the foreign corporation deserved to earn $300 of the total $400 profit related to the manufacture and sale of the inventory. In general, the U.S. corporation must document the

[13]Reg. § 1.482–1(a)(3).

FIGURE 9.2 Transfer Pricing Example

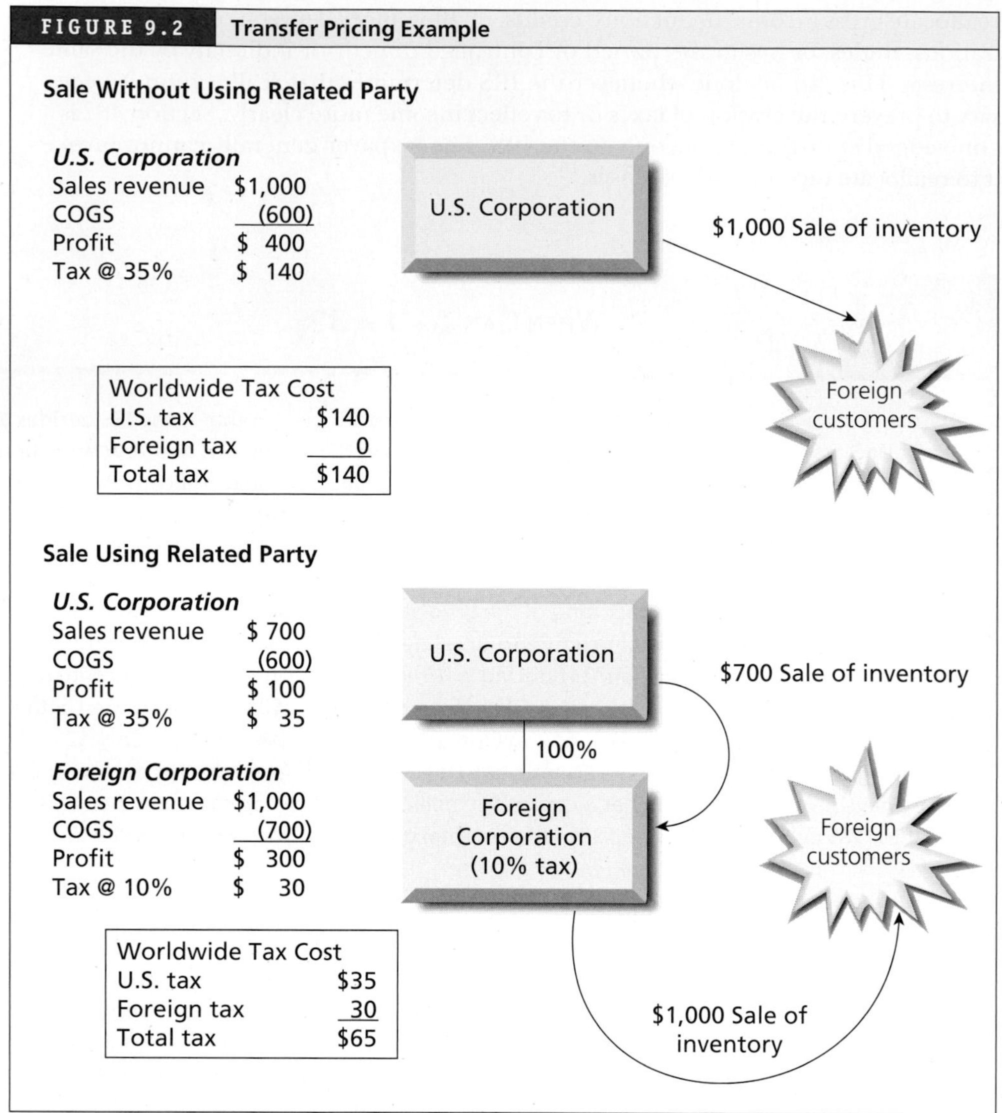

functions performed by the foreign corporation, the assets it owns that assist in producing the income, or the risks it takes (e.g., credit risk).

Without documentation of significant functions, assets, or risks of the foreign subsidiary, the IRS will not consider the $300 profit earned by the foreign corporation to be appropriate, and it will adjust the transfer price upward. If the IRS determines that the transfer price should have been, say, $990, then the U.S. corporation reports a $390 profit (with $136.50 U.S. income tax), and the foreign corporation earns a $10 profit (with $1 in foreign income tax). With this change in transfer price, the U.S. corporation does not succeed in transferring a meaningful portion of its profits to the lower-tax jurisdiction and reduces its tax liability by only $2.50. ■

The reach of § 482 is quite broad. The IRS takes the position that a corporation and its sole shareholder who works full-time for the corporation can be treated as two separate trades or businesses for purposes of § 482.[14] Two unrelated shareholders who each owned 50 percent of a corporation were held to be acting in concert for their common good and, thus, together controlled the corporation.[15]

[14]Rev.Rul. 88–38, 1988–1 C.B. 246. But see *Foglesong v. Comm.*, 82–2 USTC ¶9650, 50 AFTR 2d 82–6016, 691 F.2d 848 (CA–7, 1982), *rev'g* 77 T.C. 1102 (1981).

[15]See *B. Forman Co., Inc. v. Comm.*, 72–1 USTC ¶9182, 29, AFTR 2d 72–403, 453 F.2d 1144 (CA–2, 1972).

TAX *in* *the NEWS*

APAs Reduce Uncertainty in Transfer Pricing Disputes

The first Advance Pricing Agreement (APA) was approved in January 1991. The IRS reports that 904 APAs have been executed and 352 others are in negotiation. The taxpayers participating in the APA program come from many different industries. The five most represented industries are financial institutions, computer items and software, chemicals, transportation equipment, and electrical equipment.

Only 10 percent of the largest taxpayers involved in international intercompany transactions have participated in the APA process. However, the volume of intercompany transactions represented by these taxpayers constitutes over 40 percent of the total dollar value of international intercompany transactions. About 10 percent of all active APA cases involve small businesses with annual gross income under $200 million.

The APA process is not simple or quick. The IRS reports that the APAs approved in 2009 took an average of 38 months to complete.

Source: Announcement and Report Concerning Advance Pricing Agreements, March 29, 2010 (Announcement 2010–21).

In applying § 482, an arm's length price must be determined to assign the correct profits to related entities. Several alternative methods can be used in determining an arm's length price on the sale of tangible or intangible property. The major problem with most pricing methods is that uncontrolled comparable transactions are needed as a benchmark.

An accuracy-related penalty of 20 percent is provided by § 6662 for net § 482 transfer price adjustments (changes in profit allocations by the IRS) for a taxable year that exceed the lesser of $5 million or 10 percent of the taxpayer's gross receipts. In addition, there is a 40 percent penalty for "gross misstatements."

As an aid to reducing pricing disputes, the IRS initiated the Advance Pricing Agreement (APA) program whereby the taxpayer can propose a transfer pricing method for certain international transactions. The taxpayer provides relevant data, which are then evaluated by the IRS. If accepted, the APA provides a safe-harbor transfer pricing method for the taxpayer. Apple Computer, Inc., accomplished the first successful APA submission in 1991.

9.4 Foreign Currency Transactions

LO.4

Explain how foreign currency exchange affects the tax consequences of international transactions.

The relative value of a foreign currency and the U.S. dollar is described by the foreign exchange rate. Changes in this rate affect the dollar value of foreign property held by the taxpayer, the dollar value of foreign debts, and the dollar amount of gain or loss on a transaction denominated in a foreign currency. Almost every international tax issue requires consideration of currency exchange implications.

EXAMPLE 11

Dress, Inc., a domestic corporation, purchases merchandise for resale from Fiesta, Inc., a foreign corporation, for 50,000K (a foreign currency). On the date of purchase, 1K is equal to $1 U.S. (1K:$1). At this time, the account payable is $50,000. On the date of payment by Dress (the foreign exchange date), the exchange rate is 1.25K:$1. In other words, the foreign currency has been devalued in relation to the U.S. dollar, and Dress will pay Fiesta 50,000K, which will cost Dress only $40,000. Dress must record the purchase of the merchandise at $50,000 and recognize a foreign currency gain of $10,000 ($50,000 − $40,000). ■

In recent years, U.S. currency abroad has amounted to more than 50 percent of the U.S. currency in circulation. Taxpayers may find it necessary to translate amounts denominated in foreign currency into U.S. dollars for any of the following purposes.

- Purchase of goods, services, and property.
- Sale of goods, services, and property.

CONCEPT SUMMARY 9.1

Recognition of Foreign Exchange Gain or Loss

Transaction	Date of Recognition
Purchase or sale of inventory or business asset	Date of disposition of foreign currency
Branch profits	Remittance of branch profits
Subpart F income	Receipt of previously taxed income (accumulated E & P)
Dividend from untaxed current or accumulated E & P	No exchange gain or loss to recipient

- Collection of foreign receivables.
- Payment of foreign payables.
- Foreign tax credit calculations.
- Recognition of income or loss from foreign branch activities.

The foreign currency exchange rates, however, have no effect on the transactions of a U.S. person who arranges all international transactions in U.S. dollars.

EXAMPLE 12

Sellers, Inc., a domestic corporation, purchases goods from Rose, Ltd., a foreign corporation, and pays for these goods in U.S. dollars. Rose then exchanges the U.S. dollars for the currency of the country in which it operates. Sellers has no foreign exchange considerations with which to contend. If instead Rose required Sellers to pay for the goods in a foreign currency, Sellers would have to exchange U.S. dollars to obtain the foreign currency to make payment. If the exchange rate changed from the date of purchase to the date of payment, Sellers would have a foreign currency gain or loss on the currency exchange. ■

The following concepts are important when dealing with the tax aspects of foreign exchange.

- Foreign currency is treated as property other than money.
- Gain or loss on the exchange of foreign currency is considered separately from the underlying transaction (e.g., the purchase or sale of goods).
- No gain or loss is recognized until a transaction is closed.

TAX ISSUES

The following major tax issues must be considered when dealing with foreign currency exchange.

- The date of recognition of any gain or loss (see Concept Summary 9.1).
- The source (U.S. or foreign) of the foreign currency gain or loss.
- The character of the gain or loss (ordinary or capital).

FUNCTIONAL CURRENCY

The Code generally adopted the Financial Accounting Standards Board standard on foreign currency translation. ASC 830 (SFAS 52) introduced the **functional currency** approach. For accounting and tax purposes, the currency of the economic environment in which the foreign entity operates generally is used as the monetary unit to measure gains and losses.

Under § 985, all income tax determinations are to be made in the taxpayer's functional currency. A taxpayer's default functional currency is the U.S. dollar. In most cases, a **qualified business unit (QBU)** operating in a foreign country uses that country's

FINANCIAL DISCLOSURE *Insights*

Tax Rates in Non-U.S. Jurisdictions

When Congress changes the U.S. tax law, it seldom applies tax rate changes retroactively or prospectively—the rate changes almost always are applicable on the date that the tax bill is effective. Other countries do not always enact tax law changes in this way. Sometimes a country will adopt a schedule of tax rate increases or decreases to go into effect over a period of years.

Tax legislation of this sort can have an important effect on the U.S. taxpayer's effective tax rate as computed in the footnotes to the financial statements. When another country adopts prospective tax rate changes, an increase or decrease in the effective tax rate is reported with respect to the deferred tax accounts for GAAP purposes. Specifically, the effective tax rate decreases when a tax rate cut is scheduled in a country that does business with the U.S. party, and the rate increases when a tax rate increase is adopted for future tax years. In the last three decades, most developed countries have been cutting business income tax rates.

A recent effective tax rate computation for Berkshire Hathaway showed a decrease of about one percentage point due to scheduled tax rate cuts in Germany and the United Kingdom. Allied Healthcare Products showed a similar adjustment of about two percentage points. In contrast, the effective tax rate increased by about one percentage point for American Travellers Life Insurance Company.

currency as its functional currency. A QBU is a separate and clearly identified unit of a taxpayer's trade or business (e.g., a foreign branch). An individual is not a QBU; however, a trade or business conducted by an individual may be a QBU.[16]

BRANCH OPERATIONS

When a foreign branch (QBU) uses a foreign currency as its functional currency, profit or loss is computed in the foreign currency each year and translated into U.S. dollars for tax purposes. The entire amount of profit or loss, not taking remittances into account, is translated using the average exchange rate for the taxable year. Exchange gain or loss is recognized on remittances from the QBU. The U.S. dollar amount of the remittance at the exchange rate in effect on the date of remittance is compared with the U.S. dollar value (basis pool) of the equity pool of the branch. The rules outline a "foreign exchange exposure pool method" to compute any exchange gain or loss.[17] This exchange gain or loss is ordinary, and it is sourced according to the income to which the remittance is attributable.

DISTRIBUTIONS FROM FOREIGN CORPORATIONS

An actual distribution of E & P from a foreign corporation is included in income by the U.S. recipient at the exchange rate in effect on the date of distribution.[18] Thus, no exchange gain or loss is recognized. Deemed dividend distributions under Subpart F (discussed later in the chapter) are translated at the average exchange rate for the corporation's tax year to which the deemed distribution is attributable. Exchange gain or loss can result when an actual distribution of this previously taxed income is made.

FOREIGN TAXES

For purposes of the foreign tax credit, foreign taxes accrued generally are translated at the average exchange rate for the tax year to which the taxes relate. Under exceptions to this rule, foreign taxes must be translated at the exchange rate in effect when the foreign taxes were paid.[19] If foreign taxes are paid within two years of accrual, and if they differ from the accrued amount merely because of currency

[16]Reg. § 1.989(a)–1(b).

[17]Prop.Reg. §§ 1.987–1 and –2.

[18]§ 986(b).

[19]§§ 986(a)(1)(B) and (C).

exchange fluctuation, no redetermination is required, even though the actual dollar value paid may differ from the accrued amount. In other cases, when the taxes paid differ from the amount accrued, a redetermination is required.

EXAMPLE 13
THE BIG PICTURE

Return to the facts of *The Big Picture* on p. 9-2. Assume that VoiceCo operates a foreign branch. Foreign taxes attributable to branch income amount to 5,000K (a foreign currency). The taxes are paid within two years of being accrued. The average foreign exchange rate for the tax year to which the foreign taxes relate is .5K:$1. On the date the taxes are paid, the rate is .6K:$1. No redetermination is required, and VoiceCo reports foreign taxes of $10,000 for purposes of the foreign tax credit. ■

9.5 U.S. Persons with Foreign Income

LO.5

Work with the U.S. tax provisions affecting U.S. persons earning foreign-source income, including the rules relating to cross-border asset transfers, antideferral provisions, and the foreign tax credit.

U.S. taxpayers often "internationalize" gradually over time. A U.S. business may operate on a strictly domestic basis for several years, then explore foreign markets by exporting its products abroad, and later license its products to a foreign manufacturer or enter into a joint venture with a foreign partner. If its forays into foreign markets are successful, the U.S. business may create a foreign subsidiary and move a portion of its operations abroad by establishing a sales or manufacturing facility.

A domestically controlled foreign corporation can have significant U.S. tax consequences for the U.S. owners, and any U.S. taxpayer paying foreign taxes must consider the foreign tax credit provisions. Foreign businesses likewise enter the U.S. market in stages. In either case, each step generates increasingly significant international tax consequences. Figure 9.3 shows a typical timeline for "going global."

EXPORT PROPERTY

The easiest way for a U.S. enterprise to engage in global commerce is simply to sell U.S.-produced goods and services abroad. These sales can be conducted with little or no foreign presence and allow the business to explore foreign markets without making costly financial commitments to foreign operations.

The U.S. tax consequences of simple export sales are straightforward. All such income is taxed in the United States to the U.S. taxpayer. Whether foreign taxes must be paid on this export income depends on the particular law of the foreign jurisdiction and whether the U.S. taxpayer is deemed to have a foreign business presence there (often called a "permanent establishment"). In many cases, such export income is not taxed by a foreign jurisdiction.

FIGURE 9.3 Global Activities Timeline

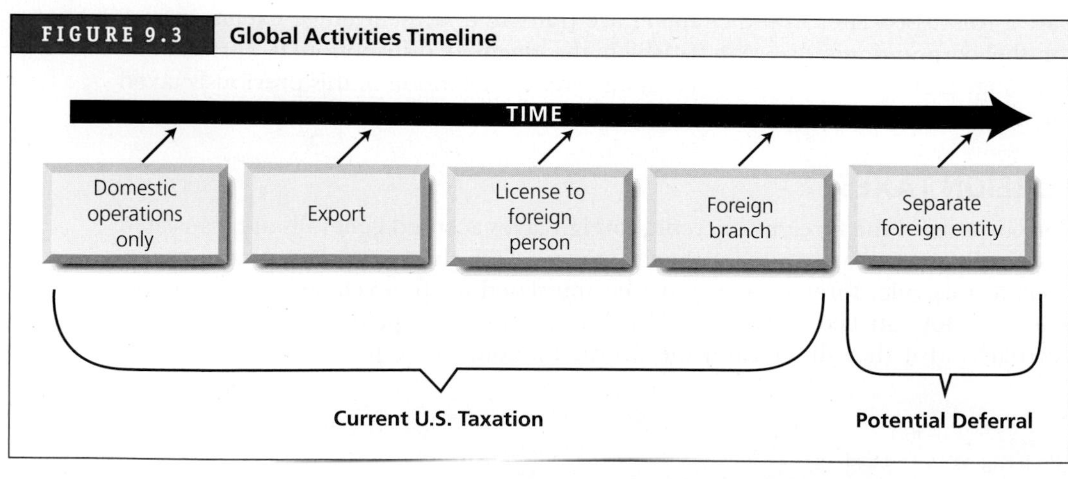

FIGURE 9.4 Taxation of Cross-Border Asset Transfers

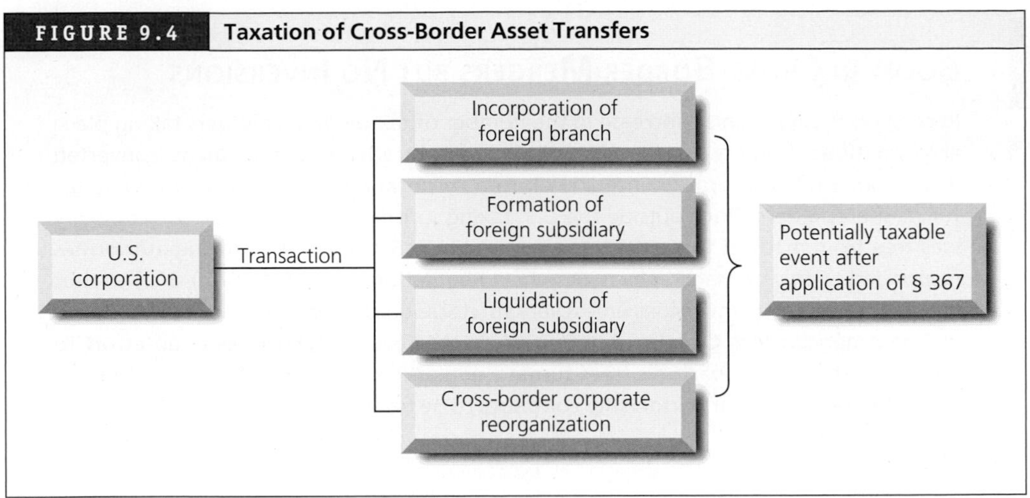

CROSS-BORDER ASSET TRANSFERS

As part of "going international," a U.S. taxpayer may decide to transfer assets outside the United States so that any foreign business will be conducted outside the U.S. tax jurisdiction. To originate investment through, or transfer investment to, a foreign entity, the U.S. taxpayer must make some sort of transfer to the foreign entity. This may take the form of a cash investment or a transfer of assets of a U.S. entity.

In situations where potential taxable income is transferred to a corporation outside the U.S. taxing jurisdiction, the exchange may trigger a tax. The tax result of transferring property to a foreign corporation depends on the nature of the exchange, the assets involved, the income potential of the property, and the character of the property in the hands of the transferor or transferee. Figure 9.4 summarizes the taxation of cross-border asset transfers.

Outbound Transfers

As discussed in Chapters 6 and 7, when assets are exchanged for corporate stock in a domestic transaction, realized gain or loss may be deferred rather than recognized. Similarly, deferral treatment may be available when the following "outbound" capital changes occur, i.e., moving corporate business across country borders and outside the United States.

- A U.S. corporation starts up a new corporation outside the United States (§ 351).
- A U.S. corporation liquidates a U.S. subsidiary into an existing foreign subsidiary (§ 332).
- A U.S. corporation incorporates a non-U.S. branch of a U.S. corporation, forming a new foreign corporation (§ 351).
- A foreign corporation uses a stock swap to acquire a U.S. corporation (Type "B" reorganization).
- A foreign corporation acquires substantially all of a U.S. corporation's net assets (Type "C" reorganization).

These otherwise tax-deferred transactions may trigger current taxation when foreign corporations are involved. Under § 367, the general rule is that gain deferral is not allowed when assets are leaving the U.S. taxing jurisdiction. However, a major exception allows continued tax deferral for assets transferred to a foreign corporation to be used in a trade or business carried on outside the United States.

The trade or business exception does not apply to certain "tainted" assets, and the transfer of these assets outside the United States triggers immediate gain (but not loss) recognition. The following are "tainted" assets under § 367.

GLOBAL
Tax Issues

Boom in Cross-Border Mergers but No Inversions

Recent years have seen an increase in the number of tax-deferred mergers taking place across national borders. Helen of Troy, the publicly traded cosmetics giant, converted itself from a U.S. corporation into a tax haven corporation without triggering any tax for its shareholders. Once outside the U.S. taxing jurisdiction, the "inverted" company was free from many of the restrictions imposed by U.S. tax law. U.S. taxing authorities responded to this transaction by issuing new Regulations [Reg. § 1.367(a)–3(c)] to shut down these so-called inversions unless very strict standards were met.

The American Jobs Creation Act of 2004 created even stricter rules in an effort to deter shareholders or partners from turning domestic entities into foreign entities. A domestic corporation or partnership continues to be treated as domestic if:

- A foreign corporation acquires substantially all of its properties after March 4, 2003.
- The former shareholders (or partners) of the U.S. corporation (or partnership) hold 80 percent or more of the foreign corporation's stock after the transaction.
- The foreign corporation does not have substantial business activities in its country of incorporation.

If the former shareholders or partners own at least 60 percent but less than 80 percent of the new corporation, the foreign entity remains foreign, but other restrictions may apply.

- Inventory (raw goods, work-in-progress, and finished goods).
- Installment obligations and unrealized accounts receivable.
- Foreign currency.
- Property leased by the transferor unless the transferee is the lessee.

These tainted assets are likely to turn over quickly once the asset transfer is completed, and any appreciation is likely to be recognized outside the U.S. taxing jurisdiction. Consequently, § 367 requires recognition of this gain upon transfer of the asset outside the United States.

EXAMPLE 14

Amelia, Inc., a domestic corporation, incorporates its profitable Irish manufacturing branch and creates a new wholly owned foreign corporation, St. George, Ltd., to engage in manufacturing activities in Ireland. The transfer qualifies as tax deferred under § 351. The branch assets have always been used in Ireland. Amelia transfers the following branch assets to St. George upon its creation.

Asset	Tax Basis	Market Value	Built-in Gain/Loss
Raw materials inventory	$100	$ 400	$ 300
Accounts receivable	200	250	50
Manufacturing equipment	450	925	475
Furniture and fixtures	150	50	(100)
Total	$900	$1,625	$ 725

Although the $725 in realized gain is deferred under § 351, the gain is potentially taxable under § 367 because the assets are leaving the U.S. taxing jurisdiction. The general rule of § 367 is that all the realized gain is recognized by Amelia. However, because St. George will use the transferred assets in the active conduct of a foreign trade or business, the realized gain remains potentially deferred. As the inventory and accounts receivable are "tainted assets," Amelia must recognize $350 of gain upon the transfer ($300 gain attributable to inventory and $50 gain from the accounts receivable). Gain is recognized on an asset-by-asset basis with no offset for losses on other assets. ■

In addition to gain on the tainted assets listed above, any U.S. depreciation and other types of recapture potential in the assets transferred must be recognized to the extent of gain realized. This provision applies only to appreciated assets for which the depreciation or other deduction has resulted in a tax benefit. The U.S. depreciation is the portion of the depreciation attributable to use of the property in the United States. Prior branch losses are also recaptured to the extent that they are not recaptured under the § 904(f) provisions.

The transfer of intangibles is treated separately as a transfer pursuant to a sale for contingent payments.[20] These amounts are treated as received by the transferor over the life of the intangible and are ordinary income. They are recognized by the transferor and must be commensurate with the income attributable to the intangible. A subsequent disposition by the transferee triggers income recognition to the initial transferor.

Inbound and Offshore Transfers

One objective of § 367 is to prevent E & P that has accumulated in U.S.-owned foreign corporations from escaping U.S. taxation. Section 367(b) covers the tax treatment of inbound and offshore transfers with regard to stock of a controlled foreign corporation (CFC). (CFCs are discussed in more detail in a later section.) Examples of inbound transactions include the following.

- The liquidation of a foreign corporation into a domestic parent under § 332.
- The acquisition of the assets of a foreign corporation by a domestic corporation in a Type "C" or Type "D" reorganization.

Offshore transfers include the following.

- A foreign corporation acquisition of a first- or lower-tier foreign corporation in exchange for stock of a non-CFC.
- A foreign corporate Type "B," Type "C," or Type "D" acquisition of a foreign corporation in exchange for CFC stock.
- A foreign § 351 transfer of stock or other property in a foreign corporation having a U.S. shareholder.

U.S. persons that are directly or indirectly parties to an inbound or offshore transfer involving stock of a CFC generally recognize dividend income to the extent of their pro rata share of the previously untaxed E & P of the foreign corporation. In some circumstances, income can be deferred by entering into a gain recognition agreement with the IRS. Special rules apply to the outbound transfer of domestic or foreign shares.

TAX HAVENS

Many outbound transfers of assets to foreign corporations are to countries with tax rates higher than or equal to the U.S. rate. Thus, tax avoidance is not the motive for such transfers. Some U.S. corporations, however, make their foreign investment in (or through) a tax haven. A **tax haven** is a country where either locally sourced income or residents are subject to no or low internal taxation.

One method of potentially avoiding taxation is to invest through a foreign corporation incorporated in a tax haven. Because the foreign corporation is a resident of the tax haven, the income it earns is subject to no or low internal taxes. Tax haven

[20] § 367(d).

FIGURE 9.5 Use of a Tax Haven Corporation

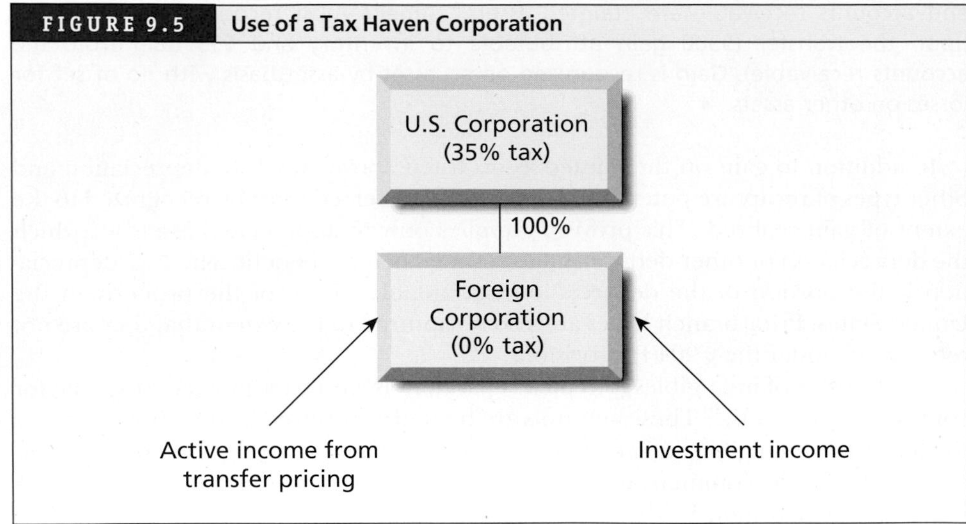

countries may also have provisions limiting the exchange of financial and commercial information.

Figure 9.5 illustrates this use of a tax haven by a U.S. corporation. The U.S. corporation uses a foreign subsidiary corporation in a low- or no-tax country to earn either investment income or a portion of income from business activities (as illustrated previously in the transfer pricing discussion). Because the foreign subsidiary is not consolidated with the domestic parent under U.S. tax law (i.e., the foreign corporation is not a member of the U.S. corporation's affiliated group) and is not itself engaged in any U.S. trade or business, the foreign corporation is not subject to U.S. taxation. Without the application of the transfer pricing rules or the Subpart F rules (discussed later), the foreign corporation's income will escape U.S. taxation until the time that any foreign profits are repatriated back to the U.S. parent as a dividend or similar payment.

A tax haven also can, in effect, be created by an income tax treaty. For example, under an income tax treaty between Country A and Country B, residents of Country A are subject to a withholding tax of only 5 percent on dividend and interest income sourced in Country B. The United States and Country A have a similar treaty. The United States does not have a treaty with Country B, and the withholding tax is 30 percent. A U.S. corporation can create a foreign subsidiary in Country A and use that subsidiary to make investments in Country B. This practice is referred to as **treaty shopping**. If the Country B investment income had been earned directly by the U.S. corporation, it would be subject to a 30 percent withholding tax. As a result of investing through the foreign subsidiary created in Country A, the U.S. parent corporation pays only 10 percent in foreign taxes on the income earned, that is, 5 percent to Country B and 5 percent to Country A.

In recent years, many countries have enacted "treaty shopping" provisions. Under the provisions, treaty benefits for withholding taxes are not available to a resident corporation unless a certain percentage of its beneficial interests are owned, directly or indirectly, by one or more individual residents of the country in which the corporation is resident. The most controversial article in the U.S. Model Treaty is Article 22, Limitation on Benefits, which is meant to prevent treaty shopping. Article 22 disallows treaty benefits to an entity unless more than 50 percent of the beneficial interest in the entity is owned, directly or indirectly, by one or more individual residents of the treaty country in which the entity is resident.[21]

[21]Additional limitations on the use of treaty benefits are contained in § 894(c).

TAX *in* the NEWS

Taxpayers Came Clean on Foreign Bank Accounts

Some U.S. persons have attempted to evade U.S. income taxes on foreign income through the use of undisclosed foreign bank accounts. In 2009, the IRS offered an opportunity for these noncompliant taxpayers to come forward and voluntarily disclose their foreign bank accounts and settle their tax bills.

The IRS provided an example of the advantages of coming forward voluntarily. If a U.S. person voluntarily disclosed $1 million in a foreign bank account and $50,000 per year in unreported interest for six years, that taxpayer would pay $386,000 in taxes and penalties (plus interest). Without voluntary disclosure, however, once discovered, the taxpayer would pay $2,306,000 in taxes and penalties (plus interest) and face the possibility of other penalties and criminal prosecution.

Another voluntary disclosure period was offered by the IRS early in 2011.

FOREIGN CORPORATIONS CONTROLLED BY U.S. PERSONS

To minimize current tax liability, taxpayers often attempt to defer the recognition of taxable income. One way to do this is to shift the income-generating activity to a foreign entity that is not within the U.S. tax jurisdiction. A foreign corporation is the most suitable entity for such an endeavor because, unlike a partnership, it is not a conduit through which income is taxed directly to the owner. Because of the potential for abuse, Congress has enacted various provisions to limit the availability of deferral.

Exporting U.S. Jobs or Improving U.S. Competitiveness?

U.S.-owned foreign corporations with exclusively overseas operations are not subject to U.S. corporate income tax on their profits. Such profits are taxed to the U.S. shareholders only upon repatriation back to the United States as dividends. In some cases, the U.S. shareholders are taxed on profits deemed to be repatriated before any actual distribution (so-called Subpart F income). When there is no Subpart F income, however, U.S. owners of foreign corporations are able to defer indefinitely any U.S. tax on all of their foreign profits. When politicians complain that companies that export jobs are receiving tax breaks, they often are referring to this deferral privilege associated with tax-savvy foreign operations.

U.S. owners of foreign corporations point out that they must compete in a global environment. Many other countries, such as the Netherlands, do not tax the offshore profits of foreign subsidiaries even if the profits are brought home. If a U.S.-owned foreign corporation cannot at least defer its U.S. taxes, it suffers a competitive disadvantage relative to a Dutch-owned subsidiary, for example. Others argue that the deferral privilege simply creates an unwarranted advantage for companies operating offshore compared with their U.S.-based counterparts.

Which argument do you find more compelling? How do you explain the incentive of tax deferral to U.S. workers whose jobs have moved offshore? How would you explain loss of tax deferral to the U.S. shareholders of a company that pays triple the corporate tax rate of its global competitors?

Controlled Foreign Corporations

Subpart F, §§ 951–964 of the Code, provides that certain types of income generated by controlled foreign corporations (CFCs) are currently included in gross income by the U.S. shareholders without regard to actual distributions. For Subpart F to apply, the foreign corporation must have been a CFC for an uninterrupted period of 30 days or more during the taxable year. When this is the case, U.S. shareholders must include in gross income their pro rata share of Subpart F income and increase in earnings that the CFC has invested in U.S. property for the tax year. This rule applies to U.S. shareholders who own stock in the corporation on the last day of the tax year or on the last day the foreign corporation is a CFC. The gross income inclusion must be made for their taxable year in which the taxable year of the CFC ends.

EXAMPLE 15

Gray, Inc., a calendar year corporation, is a CFC for the entire tax year. Chance Company, a U.S. corporation, owns 60% of Gray's one class of stock for the entire year. Subpart F income is $100,000, and no distributions have been made during the year. Chance, a calendar year taxpayer, includes $60,000 in gross income as a constructive dividend for the tax year. ■

EXAMPLE 16

Gray, Inc., is a CFC until July 1 of the tax year (a calendar year) and earns $100,000 in Subpart F income. Terry, a U.S. citizen, owns 30% of its one class of stock for the entire year. She includes $14,877 [$100,000 × 30% × (181 days/365 days)] in gross income as a constructive dividend for the tax year. ■

A **CFC** is any foreign corporation in which more than 50 percent of the total combined voting power of all classes of stock entitled to vote or the total value of the stock of the corporation is owned by U.S. shareholders on any day during the taxable year of the foreign corporation. The foreign subsidiaries of most multinational U.S. parent corporations are CFCs. For purposes of determining if a foreign corporation is a CFC, a **U.S. shareholder** is defined as a U.S. person who owns, or is considered to own, 10 percent or more of the total combined voting power of all classes of voting stock of the foreign corporation. Stock owned directly, indirectly, and constructively is counted.

Indirect ownership involves stock held through a foreign entity, such as a foreign corporation, foreign partnership, or foreign trust. This stock is considered to be actually owned proportionately by the shareholders, partners, or beneficiaries. Constructive ownership rules, with certain modifications, apply in determining if a U.S. person is a U.S. shareholder, in determining whether a foreign corporation is a CFC, and for certain related-party provisions of Subpart F.[22]

EXAMPLE 17

A non-U.S. corporation has the following shareholders.

Shareholders	Voting Power	Classification
Alan	30%	U.S. person
Bill	9%	U.S. person
Carla	40%	Non-U.S. person
Dora	20%	U.S. person
Ed	1%	U.S. person

Bill is Alan's son. Alan, Bill, and Dora are U.S. shareholders. Alan owns 39%, 30% directly and 9% constructively through Bill. Bill also owns 39%, 9% directly and 30% constructively through Alan. Thus, Bill is a U.S. shareholder. Dora owns 20% directly. The corporation is a CFC because U.S. shareholders own 59% of the voting power. Ed, a U.S. person, owns 1% and is not related to any of the other shareholders. Thus, Ed is not a U.S. shareholder and would not have to include any of the Subpart F income in gross income. If Bill were not related to Alan or to any other U.S. persons who were shareholders, Bill would not be a U.S. shareholder, and the corporation would not be a CFC. ■

U.S. shareholders must include their pro rata share of the applicable income in their gross income only to the extent of their actual ownership. Stock held indirectly (but not constructively) is considered actually owned for this purpose.

[22] §§ 958 and 318(a).

EXAMPLE 18

Bill, in Example 17, would recognize only 9% of the Subpart F income as a constructive dividend. Alan would recognize 30%, and Dora would recognize 20%. If instead Bill were a foreign corporation wholly owned by Alan, Alan would recognize 39% as a constructive dividend. ■

Subpart F Income A U.S. shareholder of a CFC does not necessarily lose the ability to defer U.S. taxation of income earned by the CFC. Only certain income earned by the CFC triggers immediate U.S. taxation as a constructive dividend. This tainted income, referred to as Subpart F income, can be characterized as income with little or no economic connection with the CFC's country of incorporation. **Subpart F** income consists of the following.

- Insurance income (§ 953).
- Foreign base company income (§ 954).
- International boycott factor income (§ 999).
- Illegal bribes.
- Income derived from a § 901(j) foreign country.

Insurance Income Income attributable to insuring risk of loss outside the country in which the CFC is organized is Subpart F income. This rule precludes U.S. corporations from setting up offshore insurance companies in tax havens to convert expenditures for self-insurance into a deductible insurance premium.

Foreign Base Company Income Foreign base company income (FBCI) provisions target transactions whereby a CFC earns income that lacks any economic connection to its country of organization. FBCI includes:

- Foreign personal holding company income.
- Foreign base company sales income.
- Foreign base company services income.
- Foreign base company oil-related income.

Foreign personal holding company (FPHC) income consists of the following.

- Dividends, interest, royalties, rents, and annuities.
- Excess gains over losses from the sale or exchange of property (including an interest in a trust or partnership) that gives rise to FPHC income or that does not give rise to any income.
- Excess of foreign currency gains over foreign currency losses (other than any transaction directly related to the business needs of the CFC).
- Income from notional principal contracts.
- Certain payments in lieu of dividends.
- Certain personal service contract income.

Certain FPHC income does not trigger a Subpart F inclusion under exceptions for same-country payments, payments out of non-Subpart F E & P of related CFCs, and active rent and royalty income.

Foreign base company (FBC) sales income is income derived by a CFC where the CFC has very little connection with the process that generates the income and a related party is involved. If the CFC earns income from the sale of property to customers outside the CFC's country of incorporation, and either the supplier or the customer is related to the CFC, such income is FBC sales income.

EXAMPLE 19

Ulysses, Ltd., is a CFC organized in the United Kingdom and owned 100% by Joyce, Inc., a U.S. corporation. Ulysses purchases finished inventory from Joyce and sells the inventory to customers in Hong Kong. This sales income constitutes FBC sales income. ■

An exception applies to property that is manufactured, produced, grown, or extracted in the country in which the CFC was organized or created and also to property sold for use, consumption, or disposition within that country. In both these situations, the CFC has participated in the economic process that generates the income.

EXAMPLE 20

If Ulysses, from Example 19, purchases raw materials from Joyce and performs substantial manufacturing activity in the United Kingdom before selling the inventory to customers in Hong Kong, the income is not FBC sales income.

Even without the manufacturing activity, sales to customers within the United Kingdom would not produce FBC sales income. ■

Certain income derived by a branch of the CFC in another country can be deemed FBC sales income. This is the case when the effect of using the branch is the same as if the branch were a wholly owned subsidiary.[23]

FBC services income is income derived from the performance of services for or on behalf of a related person and performed outside the country in which the CFC was created or organized. Income from services performed in connection with the sale of property by a CFC that has manufactured, produced, grown, or extracted such property is not FBC services income.

FBC oil-related income is income, other than extraction income, derived in a foreign country by large oil producers in connection with the sale of oil and gas products and sold by the CFC or a related person for use or consumption outside the country in which the oil or gas was extracted.

Subpart F Income Exceptions A *de minimis* rule provides that if the total amount of a foreign corporation's FBCI and gross insurance income for the taxable year is less than the lesser of 5 percent of gross income or $1 million, none of its gross income is treated as FBCI for the tax year. At the other extreme, if a foreign corporation's FBCI and gross insurance income exceed 70 percent of total gross income, all the corporation's gross income for the tax year is treated as Subpart F income.

FBCI and insurance income subject to high foreign taxes are not included under Subpart F if the taxpayer establishes that the income was subject to an effective rate, imposed by a foreign country, of more than 90 percent of the maximum corporate rate under § 11. For example, the rate must be greater than 31.5 percent (90% × 35%), where 35 percent represents the highest U.S. corporate rate.

Investment in U.S. Property In addition to Subpart F income, U.S. shareholders must include in gross income their pro rata share of the CFC's increase in investment in U.S. property for the taxable year.[24] U.S. property generally includes U.S. real property, debt obligations of U.S. persons, and stock in certain related domestic corporations. The CFC must have sufficient E & P to support a deemed dividend.

EXAMPLE 21

Fleming, Ltd., a CFC, earned no Subpart F income for the taxable year. If Fleming lends $100,000 to Lynn, its sole U.S. shareholder, this debt is considered an investment in U.S. property by Fleming because it now owns a U.S. note receivable. Holding the note triggers a constructive dividend of $100,000 to Lynn, assuming Fleming has sufficient E & P. ■

Distributions of Previously Taxed Income Distributions from a CFC are treated as being first from E & P attributable to increases in investment in U.S. property previously taxed as a constructive dividend, second from E & P attributable to previously taxed Subpart F income, and last from other E & P. Thus, distributions of previously taxed income are not taxed again as a dividend but reduce E & P. Any increase in investment in U.S. property is considered attributable first to Subpart F income and thus is not taxed twice.

[23] § 954(d)(2).

[24] § 956.

TAX in the NEWS

Bring It Home

A tax law change in 2004 provided a one-time opportunity to bring offshore profits home to the United States. U.S. shareholders of foreign corporations were allowed to repatriate certain profits of their foreign subsidiaries and receive an 85 percent dividends received deduction. At a 35 percent tax rate, these recipients paid a U.S. tax of only 5.25 percent (35% × 15%).

Many U.S. corporations thought this was a great idea. U.S. corporations brought home $362 billion in cash dividends eligible for this special deduction. Foreign subsidiaries in the Netherlands provided the largest percentage of repatriated profits (26 percent). Second and third on the list of sources of repatriated profits were Switzerland (9.9 percent) and Bermuda (9.6 percent).

EXAMPLE 22

In the current year, Jet, Inc., a U.S. shareholder, owns 100% of a CFC, from which Jet receives a $100,000 distribution. The CFC's E & P is composed of the following amounts.

- $50,000 attributable to previously taxed investment in U.S. property.
- $30,000 attributable to previously taxed Subpart F income.
- $40,000 attributable to other E & P.

Jet has a taxable dividend of only $20,000, all attributable to other E & P. The remaining $80,000 is previously taxed income. The CFC's E & P is reduced by $100,000. The remaining $20,000 E & P is all attributable to other E & P. ■

A U.S. shareholder's basis in CFC stock is increased by constructive dividends and decreased by subsequent distributions of previously taxed income. U.S. corporate shareholders who own at least 10 percent of the voting stock of a foreign corporation are allowed an indirect foreign tax credit for foreign taxes deemed paid on constructive dividends included in gross income under Subpart F. The indirect credit also is available for Subpart F income attributable to certain lower-tier foreign corporations. See the foreign tax credit discussion later in this chapter. The various constructive dividend possibilities for CFC income appear in Concept Summary 9.2.

Dispositions of Stock of a CFC Under the Subpart F provisions, Subpart F income of a CFC is currently taxed to U.S. shareholders to the extent of their pro rata share. This rule, however, does not reach the earnings of the CFC that are not included in the taxable income of the shareholders under Subpart F (e.g., active trade or business income not involving related persons). Section 1248 prevents the gain from the disposition of CFC stock from escaping taxation as ordinary income. This provision requires that gain on the sale or other disposition of stock of a CFC by a U.S. shareholder be treated as dividend income to the extent of the transferor's share of undistributed nonpreviously taxed E & P of the corporation.

Other Antideferral Provision

Congress has enacted another provision to limit the deferral benefits associated with earning investment income through a foreign corporation. The passive foreign investment company (PFIC) rules can trigger constructive dividends to U.S. persons.

A PFIC is similar in theory to a CFC, but the rules are more restrictive. Any level of ownership can subject a U.S. person to taxation under the PFIC provisions if the foreign corporation earns substantial levels of investment income or holds significant investment assets.[25] Foreign mutual funds are often PFICs to their U.S. owners.

[25] § 1297.

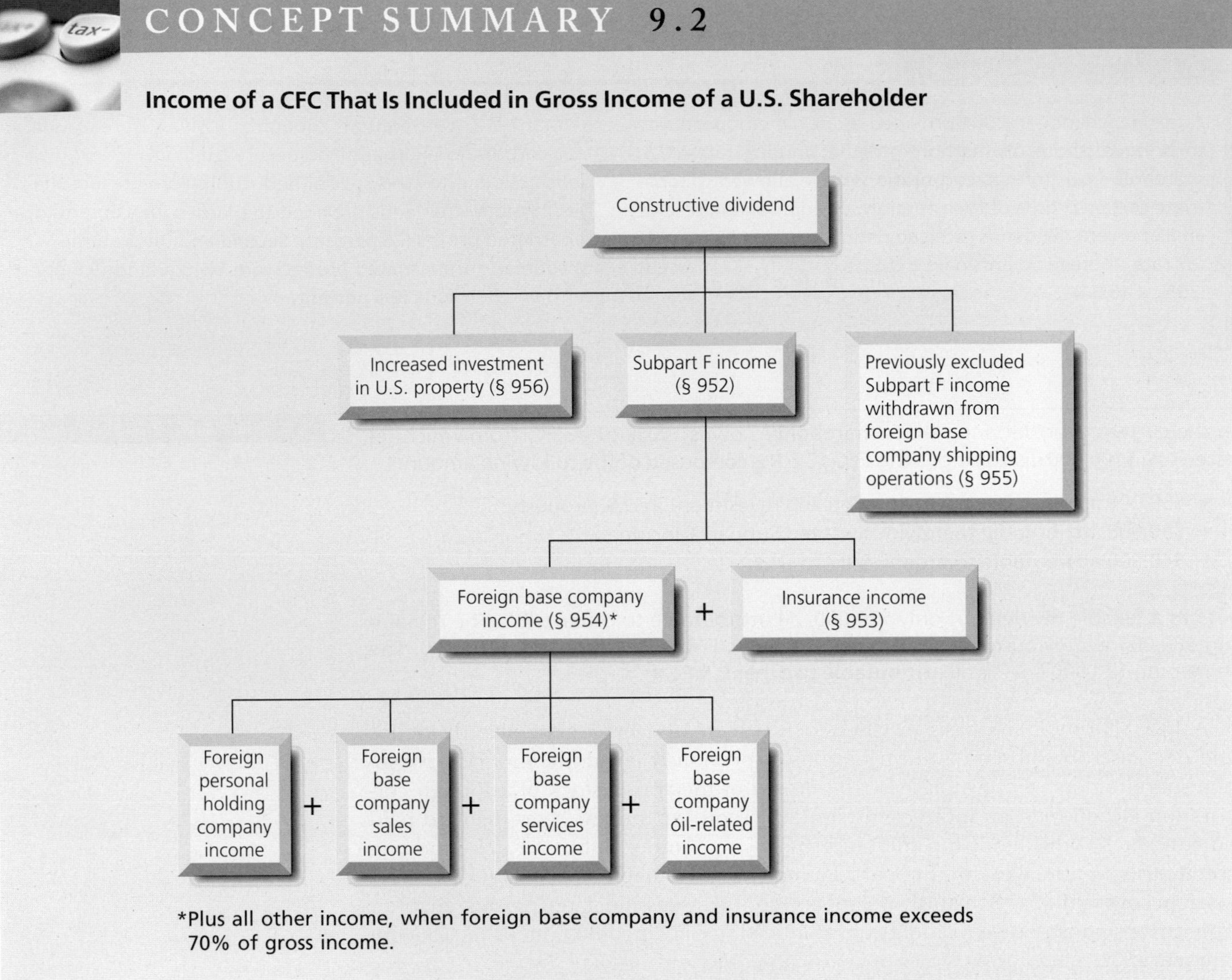

Income falling under both Subpart F and the PFIC provisions is taxed only under Subpart F to U.S. shareholders of a CFC.

THE FOREIGN TAX CREDIT

The United States retains the right to tax its citizens and residents on their total taxable income. This approach can result in double taxation, presenting a potential problem to U.S. persons who work or invest abroad.

To reduce the possibility of double taxation, Congress enacted the **foreign tax credit (FTC)** provisions. Under these provisions, a qualified taxpayer is allowed a tax credit for foreign income taxes paid. The credit is a dollar-for-dollar reduction of U.S. income tax liability.

EXAMPLE 23

Ace Tools, Inc., a U.S. corporation, has a branch operation in Mexico, from which it earns taxable income of $750,000 for the current year. Ace pays income tax of $150,000 on these earnings to the Mexican tax authorities. Ace must also include the $750,000 in gross income for U.S. tax purposes. Assume that, before considering the FTC, Ace owes $255,000 in U.S. income taxes on this foreign-source income. Thus, total taxes on the $750,000 could equal $405,000 ($150,000 + $255,000), a 54% effective rate. But Ace takes an FTC of $150,000 against its U.S. tax liability on the foreign-source income. Ace's total taxes on the $750,000 now are $255,000 ($150,000 + $105,000), a 34% effective rate. ■

The FTC is elective for any particular tax year.[26] If the taxpayer does not "choose" to take the FTC, § 164 allows a deduction for foreign taxes paid or incurred. A taxpayer cannot take a credit and a deduction for the same foreign income taxes.[27] However, a taxpayer can take a deduction in the same year as an FTC for foreign taxes that are not creditable (e.g., non-income taxes).

The Direct Credit

Section 901 provides a direct FTC to U.S. taxpayers that pay or incur a foreign income tax. For purposes of the direct credit, only the taxpayer that bears the legal incidence of the foreign tax is eligible for the credit.

EXAMPLE 24

Snowball, Inc., a U.S. corporation, operates an unincorporated branch manufacturing operation in Australia. On its U.S. tax return, Snowball, Inc., reports $450,000 of taxable income from the Australian branch and $650,000 of taxable income from its U.S. operations. Snowball paid $135,000 in Australian income taxes related to the $450,000 in branch income. This $135,000 is a direct FTC because Snowball directly paid the foreign tax. Snowball's U.S. tax liability after the FTC is determined as follows.

Australian branch income	$ 450,000
U.S. operations income	650,000
Total taxable income	$1,100,000
U.S. tax rate	× 34%
U.S. income tax before FTC	$ 374,000
FTC	(135,000)
Net U.S. tax liability	$ 239,000

Because the effective foreign tax rate (30%) is less than the U.S. rate (34%), the $135,000 FTC is fully creditable without limitation (see the discussion under FTC Limitations below). ■

Section 903 provides U.S. taxpayers with a direct FTC for foreign taxes imposed in lieu of an income tax by the foreign government. A credit for withholding tax is the most common example of a § 903 credit. Many governments impose a withholding tax on the gross amount of certain payments of passive income to nonresidents of their countries. This withholding tax also triggers a direct credit. Even though the tax is withheld by the payor of the income, the tax is imposed directly on the recipient.

EXAMPLE 25

MettCo, Inc., a domestic corporation, receives a $5,000 dividend from DeanCo, Ltd., a foreign corporation. The foreign country imposes a 20% withholding tax on dividend payments to nonresidents. Accordingly, DeanCo withholds $1,000 ($5,000 × 20%) from the dividend and remits this tax to the local country tax authorities. DeanCo pays the remaining $4,000 to MettCo.

Although MettCo did not directly pay the $1,000 in foreign tax, the entire amount is allowed as a direct tax to MettCo for FTC purposes. MettCo reports $5,000 in dividend income on its U.S. tax return (the gross amount of the dividend) but receives an FTC against any U.S. tax for the $1,000 in foreign withholding tax. ■

[26] § 901(a).

[27] § 275.

The Indirect Credit

If a U.S. corporation operates in a foreign country through a branch, the direct credit is available for foreign taxes paid. If, however, a U.S. corporation operates in a foreign country through a foreign subsidiary, the direct credit is not available for foreign taxes paid by the foreign corporation. An indirect credit is available to U.S. corporate taxpayers that receive actual or constructive dividends from foreign corporations that have paid foreign income taxes.[28] These foreign taxes are deemed paid by the corporate shareholders in the same proportion as the dividends actually or constructively received bear to the foreign corporation's post-1986 undistributed E & P.

$$\text{Indirect FTC} = \frac{\text{Actual or constructive dividend}}{\text{Post-1986 undistributed E \& P}} \times \text{Post-1986 foreign taxes}$$

Section 78 requires a domestic corporation that chooses the FTC for deemed-paid foreign taxes to *gross up* (add to income) dividend income by the amount of deemed-paid taxes.

EXAMPLE 26

Wren, Inc., a domestic corporation, owns 50% of Finch, Inc., a foreign corporation. Wren receives a dividend of $120,000 from Finch. Finch paid foreign taxes of $500,000 on post-1986 E & P. Finch's post-1986 E & P totals $1.2 million. Wren's deemed-paid foreign taxes for FTC purposes are $50,000.

Cash dividend from Finch	$120,000
Deemed-paid foreign taxes	
$\left(\frac{\$120{,}000}{\$1{,}200{,}000} \times \$500{,}000\right)$	50,000
Gross income to Wren	$170,000

In addition to the $120,000 cash dividend, Wren must include the $50,000 in gross income for the § 78 gross-up adjustment if the FTC is elected. ■

Certain ownership requirements must be met before the indirect credit is available to a domestic corporation. The domestic corporation must own 10 percent or more of the voting stock of the foreign corporation. The credit is also available for deemed-paid foreign taxes of second- and third-tier foreign corporations if the 10 percent ownership requirement is met at the second- and third-tier level. A 5 percent indirect ownership requirement must also be met. The indirect credit is also available for foreign taxes paid by fourth- through sixth-tier foreign corporations if additional requirements are met, including the requirement that these corporations be CFCs. The § 902 ownership requirements are summarized in Figure 9.6.

FTC Limitations

To prevent taxpayers from crediting foreign taxes against U.S. taxes levied on U.S.-source taxable income, the FTC is subject to a limitation. The FTC for any taxable year cannot exceed the lesser of two amounts: (1) the actual foreign taxes paid or accrued or (2) the U.S. taxes (before the FTC) on foreign-source taxable income. The FTC limitation is derived in the following manner.

$$\text{FTC limitation} = \frac{\text{Foreign-source taxable income}}{\text{Total taxable income}^{29}} \times \text{U.S. tax before FTC}$$

[28] § 902.

[29] For FTC purposes, the taxable income of an individual, estate, or trust is computed without any deduction for personal exemptions. § 904(b)(1).

FIGURE 9.6 Section 902 Ownership Requirements

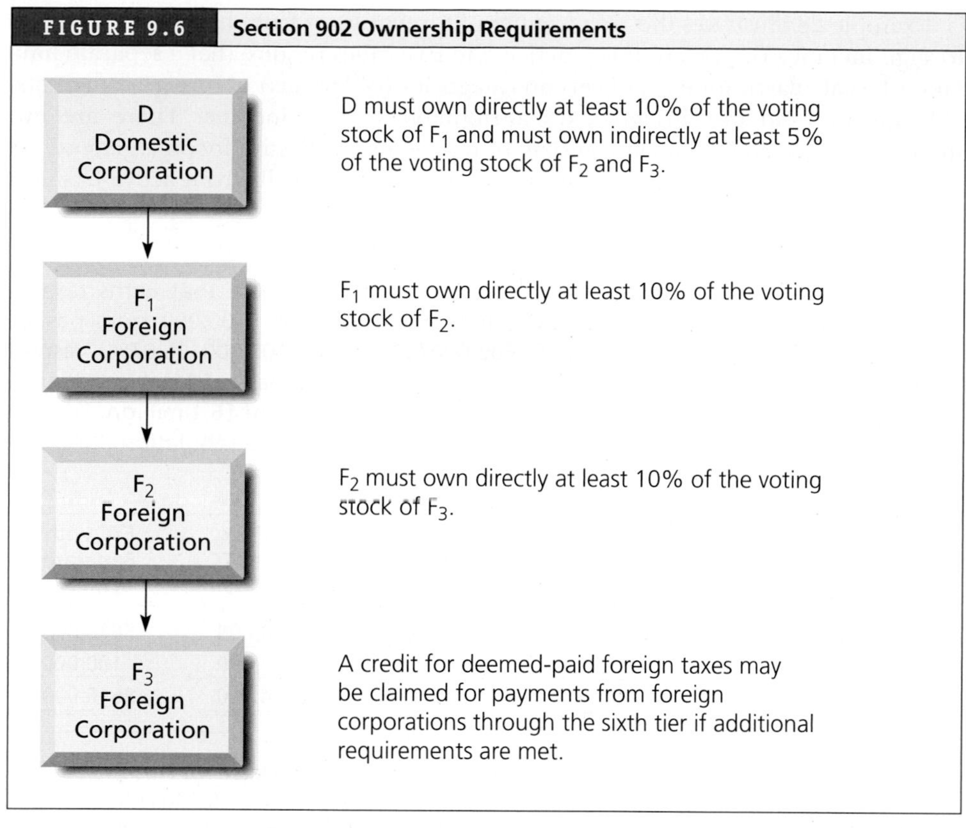
D
Domestic
Corporation
D must own directly at least 10% of the voting stock of F_1 and must own indirectly at least 5% of the voting stock of F_2 and F_3.
F_1
Foreign
Corporation
F_1 must own directly at least 10% of the voting stock of F_2.
F_2
Foreign
Corporation
F_2 must own directly at least 10% of the voting stock of F_3.
F_3
Foreign
Corporation
A credit for deemed-paid foreign taxes may be claimed for payments from foreign corporations through the sixth tier if additional requirements are met.

EXAMPLE 27

Charlotte, Inc., a domestic corporation that invests in foreign securities, has total taxable income for the tax year of $120,000, consisting of $100,000 in U.S.-source business profits and $20,000 of income from foreign sources. Foreign taxes of $9,500 were withheld by foreign tax authorities. Assume that Charlotte's U.S. tax before the FTC is $42,000. The company's FTC is limited to $7,000 [$42,000 × ($20,000/$120,000)]. Charlotte's net U.S. tax liability is $35,000. ■

As Example 27 illustrates, the limitation can prevent the total amount of foreign taxes paid in high-tax jurisdictions from being credited. Taxpayers could overcome this problem by generating additional foreign-source income that is subject to no, or low, foreign taxation.

EXAMPLE 28

Compare Domestic Corporation's FTC situations. In one, the corporation has only $500,000 of highly taxed foreign-source income. In the other, Domestic also has $100,000 of low-taxed foreign-source interest income.

	Only Highly Taxed Income	With Low-Taxed Interest Income
Foreign-source income	$500,000	$600,000
Foreign taxes	275,000	280,000
U.S.-source income	700,000	700,000
U.S. taxes (34%)	408,000	442,000
FTC limitation	170,000*	204,000**

*$408,000 × ($500,000/$1,200,000).
**$442,000 × ($600,000/$1,300,000).

Domestic's foreign taxes increase by only $5,000 ($280,000 − $275,000), but its FTC limitation increases by $34,000 ($204,000 − $170,000). ■

Example 28 illustrates the *cross-crediting* of foreign taxes from high- and low-taxed foreign income. To prevent this practice, the FTC rules require that a separate limitation be calculated for each of certain categories (or baskets) of foreign-source taxable income and the foreign taxes attributable to that income. There are two income baskets: passive income and all other (general). Passive income generally is investment-type income; general limitation income is typically from active business sources.

EXAMPLE 29

BenCo, Inc., a U.S. corporation, has a foreign branch in France that earns taxable income of $1.5 million from manufacturing operations and $600,000 from passive activities. BenCo pays foreign taxes of $600,000 (40%) and $100,000 (16.67%), respectively, on this foreign-source income. The corporation also earns $4 million of U.S.-source taxable income, resulting in worldwide taxable income of $6.1 million. BenCo's U.S. taxes before the FTC are $2,074,000 (at 34%). The following tabulation illustrates the effect of the separate limitation baskets on cross-crediting.

Foreign Income Category	Net Taxable Amount	Foreign Taxes	U.S. Tax before FTC at 34%	FTC with Separate Limits
General	$1,500,000	$600,000	$510,000	$510,000
Passive	600,000	100,000	204,000	100,000
Total	$2,100,000	$700,000	$714,000	$610,000

Without the separate limitation provisions, the FTC would be the lesser of (1) $700,000 foreign taxes or (2) $714,000 share of U.S. tax [$2,074,000 × ($2,100,000/$6,100,000)]. The separate limitation provisions reduce the FTC by $90,000 ($700,000 − $610,000). The effect of the separate limitation rules is that the foreign-source income taxed at the foreign tax rate of 40% cannot be aggregated with foreign-source income taxed at only 16.67%. ■

A partner's distributive share of partnership income generally also is categorized in separate limitation baskets based on the character of the partnership's income.

FTC Carryovers

The various FTC limitations can result in unused (noncredited) foreign taxes for the tax year. The carryback period is 1 year, and the carryforward period is 10 years.[30] The taxes can be credited in years when the formula limitation for that year exceeds the foreign taxes attributable to the same tax year.

The carryback and carryforward provisions are available only within a specific basket. In other words, excess foreign taxes in one basket cannot be carried over unless there is an excess limitation in the same basket for the carryover year.

Foreign Losses

Citizens and residents of the United States who hold foreign investments or operations directly (e.g., through a branch operation) or through a conduit entity (e.g., a partnership) have the opportunity to offset foreign losses against U.S.-source income, thereby reducing the U.S. income tax due on U.S.-source income. If the foreign country in which the loss is generated (sourced) taxes subsequent income from these foreign operations, the FTC could reduce or eliminate any U.S. tax on the income.

To prevent this loss of tax revenue to the United States, the tax law provides that the overall foreign losses should be recaptured as U.S.-source income for FTC purposes.[31] This is accomplished by reducing the numerator of the FTC limitation formula. Foreign-source taxable income is reduced by the lesser of (1) the remaining unrecaptured overall foreign loss or (2) 50 percent of foreign-source taxable income

[30] § 904(c).

[31] § 904(f)(1).

for the taxable year (unless the taxpayer elects to recapture a greater percentage). Unrecaptured foreign losses are carried over indefinitely until recaptured.

EXAMPLE 30

Shannon, Inc., a domestic corporation, operates a branch in Japan. The earnings record of the branch is as follows.

Year	Taxable Income (Loss)	Foreign Taxes Paid
2008	($ 15,000)	–0–
2009	(20,000)	–0–
2010	(20,000)	–0–
2011	40,000	$20,000

For 2008–2011, Shannon has U.S.-source taxable income of $300,000 each year. Shannon's 2011 U.S. tax liability before the FTC is $115,600. Its overall foreign loss is $55,000 for 2008–2011. The FTC limitation for 2011 is $6,800 {$115,600 × [$40,000 – (50% × $40,000)]/$340,000}. ■

A situation may arise in which overall foreign losses have been incurred and the U.S. taxpayer disposes of trade or business property used predominantly outside the United States before any or all of the loss is recaptured. The provisions described above will not necessarily reach such a situation. The statutory solution to this problem is that upon disposal the U.S. taxpayer generates U.S.-source income. The amount of income generated is the lesser of (1) the fair market value of the property less its adjusted basis or (2) the remaining amount of unrecaptured overall foreign losses.[32]

When a taxpayer has a loss for the tax year in one or more foreign-source categories (baskets), the loss must be apportioned pro rata to foreign-source categories with income for the tax year. If there is an overall foreign loss (i.e., foreign losses exceed foreign income in all categories), the overall foreign loss then reduces U.S.-source income. A U.S. loss for the tax year is apportioned pro rata to foreign-source income in each category, but only after the apportionment of any foreign losses to those income categories.

EXAMPLE 31

During 2011, Bloom, Inc., a U.S. corporation, incurred a $10,000 loss in its manufacturing activities and had $25,000 in passive income. The loss in the general basket is apportioned to the passive basket as follows.

Foreign Income Category	Income or Loss	Foreign-Source Taxable Income
General	($10,000)	$ –0–
Passive	25,000	15,000
Total	$15,000	$15,000

In 2012, Bloom earns $25,000 in manufacturing income and $24,000 in passive income. So the previously apportioned loss must be reallocated back to the affected basket as follows.

Foreign Income Category	Income or Loss	Previously Apportioned Loss	Foreign-Source Taxable Income
General	$25,000	($10,000)	$15,000
Passive	24,000	10,000	34,000
Total	$49,000		$49,000

■

[32] § 904(f)(3).

FINANCIAL DISCLOSURE *Insights*

Overseas Operations and Book-Tax Differences

Non-U.S. operations account for a large portion of the permanent book-tax differences of U.S. business entities. These differences may relate to different tax bases, different tax rate structures, or special provisions concerning tax-based financing with the other country. For instance, lower tax rates applied by non-U.S. countries recently reduced Berkshire Hathaway's current-year tax liabilities by about one-half percentage point.

Tax planning strategies using non-U.S. operations also are found in the deferred tax asset and liability accounts. Tax deferrals allowed under current U.S. tax rules and carryforwards of the foreign tax credit can be substantial for some businesses. For example, IBM recently reported a deferred tax asset relating to delays in using its FTCs amounting to about $500 million. For the operating arm of General Electric, that amount was about $2 billion.

A symmetric treatment is used for overall domestic losses (i.e., when U.S.-source losses exceed all foreign-source income). In this case, future U.S.-source income is recharacterized as foreign source.

The Alternative Minimum Tax FTC

For purposes of the alternative minimum tax (AMT), the FTC limitation is calculated by using foreign-source alternative minimum taxable income (AMTI) in the numerator and total AMTI in the denominator of the formula and the tentative minimum tax rather than the regular tax.

$$\text{AMT FTC limitation} = \frac{\text{Foreign-source AMTI}}{\text{Total AMTI}} \times \text{Tentative minimum tax}$$

The taxpayer may elect to use regular foreign-source taxable income in the numerator if it does not exceed total AMTI. The AMT FTC limit must also be determined on a basket-by-basket basis.

Other Considerations

For a foreign levy to qualify for the FTC, it must be a tax, and its predominant character must be that of an income tax in the U.S. sense.[33] A levy is a tax if it is a compulsory payment, rather than a payment for a specific economic benefit such as the right to extract oil. A tax's predominant character is that of an income tax in the U.S. sense if it reaches realized net gain and is not a *soak-up* tax, that is, does not depend on being credited against the income tax of another country. A tax that is levied in lieu of an income tax is also creditable.[34]

EXAMPLE 32

JonesCo, a domestic corporation, generates $2 million of taxable income from operations in Larissa, a foreign country. Larissan law levies a tax on income generated in Larissa by foreign residents only in cases in which the country of residence (such as the United States) allows a tax credit for foreign taxes paid. JonesCo will not be allowed an FTC for taxes paid to Larissa, because the foreign tax is a soak-up tax. ■

For purposes of the FTC, foreign taxes are attributable to the year in which they are paid or accrued. Under § 905, taxpayers using the cash method of accounting for tax purposes may elect to take the FTC in the year in which the foreign taxes accrue. The election is binding on the taxpayer for the year in which it is made and for all subsequent years. Foreign taxes generally must be translated to U.S. dollars at the average exchange rate for the tax year to which the taxes relate.[35]

[33] Reg. § 1.901–2.

[34] § 903 and Reg. § 1.903–1.

[35] § 986(a).

9.6 U.S. Taxation of Nonresident Aliens and Foreign Corporations

LO.6

Apply the U.S. tax provisions concerning nonresident alien individuals and foreign corporations.

Generally, only the U.S.-source income of nonresident alien individuals and foreign corporations is subject to U.S. taxation. This reflects the reach of the U.S. tax jurisdiction. The constraint, however, does not prevent the United States from also taxing the foreign-source income of nonresident alien individuals and foreign corporations when that income is effectively connected with the conduct of a U.S. trade or business.[36] Concept Summary 9.3 at the end of this section summarizes these tax rules.

NONRESIDENT ALIEN INDIVIDUALS

A **nonresident alien (NRA)** individual is an individual who is not a citizen or resident of the United States. For example, Prince William is an NRA, because he is not a citizen or resident of the United States. Citizenship is determined under the immigration and naturalization laws of the United States.[37] Basically, the citizenship statutes are broken down into two categories: nationality at birth or through naturalization.

Residency

A person is a resident of the United States for income tax purposes if he or she meets either the green card test or the substantial presence test.[38] If either of these tests is met for the calendar year, the individual is deemed a U.S. resident for the year.

A foreign person issued a green card is considered a U.S. resident on the first day he or she is physically present in the United States after issuance. The green card is Immigration Form I–551. Newly issued cards are no longer green, but the form still is referred to as the "green card." Status as a U.S. resident remains in effect until the green card has been revoked or the individual has abandoned lawful permanent resident status.

The substantial presence test is applied to an alien without a green card. It is a mathematical test involving physical presence in the United States. An individual who is physically present in the United States for at least 183 days during the calendar year is a U.S. resident for income tax purposes. This 183-day requirement can also be met over a three-year period that includes the two immediately preceding years and the current year, as long as the individual is present in the United States at least 31 days during the current year.[39] For this purpose, each day of the current calendar year is counted as a full day, each day of the first preceding year as one-third day, and each day of the second preceding year as one-sixth day.

EXAMPLE 33

Li, a foreign citizen, was present in the United States for 90 days in 2009, 180 days in 2010, and 110 days in 2011. For Federal income tax purposes, Li is a U.S. resident for 2011, because she was physically present for 185 days [(90 days × $^1/_6$) + (180 days × $^1/_3$) + (110 days × 1)] during the three-year period. ■

Under the substantial presence test, residence begins the first day the individual is physically present in the United States and ends the last day of physical presence for the calendar year (assuming the substantial presence test is not satisfied for the next calendar year). Nominal presence of 10 days or less can be ignored in determining whether the substantial presence test is met.

The substantial presence test allows for several exceptions. Commuters from Mexico and Canada who are employed in the United States but return home each day are excepted. Also excepted are individuals who are prevented from leaving the United States by medical conditions that arose while the individuals were in the United States. Some individuals are exempt from the substantial presence test,

[36] §§ 871, 881, and 882.

[37] Title 8, Aliens and Nationality, *United States Code.*

[38] § 7701(b).

[39] § 7701(b)(3)(A).

including foreign government-related individuals (e.g., diplomats), qualified teachers, trainees and students, and certain professional athletes.

Should There Be Some "Heart" in Tax Law?

In determining whether an alien is a U.S. resident for U.S. income tax purposes under the substantial presence test, days on which a medical condition prevents the person from leaving the United States are not counted as days present in the United States. The medical condition (e.g., illness or injury) must have arisen after the NRA arrived in the United States. In other words, it generally must be an unexpected illness or accident. No such exception is available, however, for a family member or other NRA who is significant to the person who becomes ill or injured. Thus, under this rule, the relative or other significant person may have to either risk being classified as a U.S. resident for the tax year or leave the ill person (or accident victim) alone in the United States. Does this limited exception ignore the human element in illness and recovery?

Nonresident Aliens Not Engaged in a U.S. Trade or Business

Certain U.S.-source income that is *not* effectively connected with the conduct of a U.S. trade or business is subject to a flat 30 percent tax. This income includes dividends, interest, rents, royalties, certain compensation, premiums, annuities, and other fixed, determinable, annual or periodic (FDAP) income. This tax generally is levied by a withholding mechanism that requires the payors of the income to withhold 30 percent of gross amounts.[40] This method eliminates the problems of assuring payment by nonresidents, determining allowable deductions, and, in most instances, the filing of tax returns by nonresidents. Interest received from certain portfolio debt investments, even though U.S.-sourced, is exempt from taxation. Interest earned on deposits with banking institutions is also exempt as long as it is not effectively connected with the conduct of a U.S. trade or business.

Capital gains *not* effectively connected with the conduct of a U.S. trade or business are exempt from tax, as long as the NRA individual was not present in the United States for 183 days or more during the taxable year. If an NRA has not established a taxable year, the calendar year is used. NRAs are not permitted to carry forward capital losses.[41]

Nonresident Aliens Engaged in a U.S. Trade or Business

Two important definitions determine the U.S. tax consequences to NRAs with U.S.-source income: "the conduct of a **U.S. trade or business**" and "**effectively connected income.**" Specifically, in order for an NRA's noninvestment income to be subject to U.S. taxation, the NRA must be considered engaged in a U.S. trade or business and must earn income effectively connected with that business.

General criteria for determining if a U.S. trade or business exists include the location of production activities, management, distribution activities, and other business functions. Trading in commodities and securities ordinarily does not constitute a trade or business. Dealers, however, need to avoid maintaining a U.S. trading office and trading for their own accounts. Corporations (other than certain personal holding companies) that are not dealers can trade for their own accounts. There are no restrictions on individuals who are not dealers.

The Code does not explicitly define a U.S. trade or business, but case law has defined the concept as activities carried on in the United States that are regular, substantial, and continuous.[42] Once an NRA is considered engaged in a U.S. trade or

[40] §§ 871 and 1441.

[41] § 871(a)(2).

[42] See, for example, *Higgins v. Comm.*, 41–1 USTC ¶9233, 25 AFTR 1160, 61 S.Ct. 475 (1941), and *Continental Trading, Inc. v. Comm.*, 59–1 USTC ¶9316, 3 AFTR 2d 923, 265 F.2d 40 (CA–9, 1959).

business, all U.S.-source income other than FDAP and capital gain income is considered effectively connected to that trade or business and is therefore subject to U.S. taxation.

EXAMPLE 34

Vito, an NRA, produces wine for export. During the current year, Vito earns $500,000 from exporting wine to unrelated wholesalers in the United States. The title to the wine passes to the U.S. wholesalers in New York. Vito has no offices or employees in the United States. The income from wine sales is U.S.-source income, but because Vito is not engaged in a U.S. trade or business, the income is not subject to taxation in the United States.

Assume that Vito begins operating a hot dog cart in New York City. This activity constitutes a U.S. trade or business. Consequently, all U.S.-source income other than FDAP or capital gain income will be taxed in the United States as income effectively connected with a U.S. trade or business. Thus, both the hot dog cart profits and the $500,000 in wine income will be taxed in the United States. ■

FDAP and capital gain income may be considered effectively connected income if the assets that generate this income are used in, or held for use in, the trade or business (the asset-use test) or if the activities of the trade or business are a material factor in the production of the income (the business-activities test).[43] As long as FDAP and capital gain income are not effectively connected with a U.S. trade or business, the tax treatment of these income items is the same whether NRAs are engaged in a U.S. trade or business or not.

EXAMPLE 35

Ingrid, an NRA, operates a U.S. business. During the year, cash funds accumulate. Ingrid invests these funds on a short-term basis so that they remain available to meet her business needs. Under the asset-use test, any income earned from these investments is effectively connected income. ■

Effectively connected income is taxed at the same rates that apply to U.S. citizens and residents, and deductions for expenses attributable to that income are allowed. NRAs with effectively connected income are also allowed a deduction for casualty and theft losses related to property located within the United States, a deduction for qualified charitable contributions, and one personal exemption. NRAs with income effectively connected with the conduct of a U.S. trade or business may also be subject to the alternative minimum tax.

Withholding Provisions

The 30 percent U.S. tax on FDAP income is generally administered by requiring the payor of the income to withhold the tax and remit it to the U.S. tax authorities. This assures the government of timely collection and relieves it of jurisdictional problems that could arise if it had to rely on recipients residing outside the United States to pay the tax. As explained earlier, income tax treaties with other countries provide for reduced withholding on certain types of FDAP income (see Exhibit 9.2 for some examples of withholding rates).

FOREIGN CORPORATIONS

Definition

The classification of an entity as a foreign corporation for U.S. tax purposes is an important consideration. A corporation created or organized in the United States is a domestic corporation. A foreign corporation is one that is not domestic. Thus,

[43] § 864(c).

EXHIBIT 9.2 Selected Tax Treaty Withholding Rates

	Interest	Dividends in General	Dividends Paid by U.S. Subsidiary to a Foreign Parent Corporation
Australia	10%	15%	0%
Canada	10	15	5
Ireland	0	15	5
Japan	10	15	0
Mexico	15	15	0
Philippines	15	25	20

though McDonald's is, in reality, a global corporation, it is considered a domestic corporation for U.S. tax purposes, solely because it was organized in the United States.

Income Not Effectively Connected with a U.S. Trade or Business

U.S.-source FDAP income of foreign corporations is taxed by the United States in the same manner as that of NRA individuals—at a flat 30 percent rate. Generally, foreign corporations qualify for the same exemptions from U.S. taxation for investment income as do NRA individuals. The U.S.-source capital gains of foreign corporations are exempt from the Federal income tax if they are not effectively connected with the conduct of a U.S. trade or business.

Effectively Connected Income

Foreign corporations conducting a trade or business in the United States are subject to Federal income taxation on any U.S.-source income effectively connected with the trade or business. As with NRAs, any FDAP or capital gain income is not considered effectively connected unless the income meets the asset-use or business-activities test.[44] Foreign corporations are subject to the same tax rates on their effectively connected income as domestic corporations.

Branch Profits Tax

The objective of the **branch profits tax** is to afford equal tax treatment to income generated by a domestic corporation controlled by a foreign corporation and to income generated by other U.S. operations controlled by foreign corporations. If the foreign corporation operates through a U.S. subsidiary (a domestic corporation), the income of the subsidiary is taxable by the United States when earned and is also subject to a withholding tax when repatriated (returned as dividends to the foreign parent). Before the branch profits tax was enacted, a foreign corporation with a branch in the United States paid only the initial tax on its U.S. earnings; remittances were not taxed.

In addition to the income tax imposed under § 882 on effectively connected income of a foreign corporation, a tax equal to 30 percent of the **dividend equivalent amount (DEA)** for the taxable year is imposed on any foreign corporation with effectively connected income.[45] The DEA is the foreign corporation's effectively connected earnings for the taxable year, adjusted for increases and decreases in the corporation's U.S. net equity (investment in the U.S. operations).

The DEA is limited to current E & P and post-1986 accumulated E & P that is effectively connected, or treated as effectively connected, with the conduct of a U.S. trade or business. U.S. net equity is the sum of money and the aggregate adjusted

[44] § 864(c).

[45] § 884.

basis of assets and liabilities directly connected to U.S. operations that generate effectively connected income.

EXAMPLE 36

Robin, Inc., a foreign corporation, has a U.S. branch operation with the following tax results and other information for the year.

Pretax earnings effectively connected with a U.S. trade or business	$2,000,000
U.S. corporate tax (at 34%)	680,000
Remittance to home office	1,000,000
Increase in U.S. net equity	320,000

Robin's DEA and branch profits tax are computed as follows.

E & P effectively connected with a U.S. trade or business ($2,000,000 – $680,000)	$1,320,000
Less: Increase in U.S. net equity	(320,000)
Dividend equivalent amount	$1,000,000
Branch profits tax rate	× 30%
Branch profits tax	$ 300,000

■

The 30 percent rate of the branch profits tax may be reduced or eliminated by a treaty provision. If a foreign corporation is subject to the branch profits tax, no other U.S. tax is levied on the dividend actually paid by the corporation during the taxable year.

THE FOREIGN INVESTMENT IN REAL PROPERTY TAX ACT

Prior to 1980, NRAs and foreign corporations could avoid U.S. taxation on gains from the sale of U.S. real estate if the gains were treated as capital gains and were not effectively connected with the conduct of a U.S. trade or business. In the mid-1970s, midwestern farmers pressured Congress to eliminate what they saw as a tax advantage that would allow nonresidents to bid up the price of farmland. This and other concerns about foreign ownership of U.S. real estate led to the enactment of the Foreign Investment in Real Property Tax Act (FIRPTA) of 1980.

Under **FIRPTA**, gains and losses realized by NRAs and foreign corporations from the sale or other disposition of U.S. real property interests are treated as effectively connected with the conduct of a U.S. trade or business even when those individuals or corporations are not actually so engaged. NRA individuals must pay a tax equal to the lesser of two amounts: (1) 26 (or 28) percent of their alternative minimum taxable income or (2) regular U.S. rates on the net U.S. real property gain for the taxable year.[46] For purposes of this provision, losses are taken into account only to the extent they are deductible as business losses, losses on transactions entered into for profit, or losses from casualties and thefts.

U.S. Real Property Interest (USRPI)

Any direct interest in real property situated in the United States and any interest in a domestic corporation (other than solely as a creditor) are U.S. real property interests (USRPIs). This definition applies unless the taxpayer can establish that a domestic corporation was not a U.S. real property holding corporation (USRPHC) during the shorter of two periods: (1) the period during which the taxpayer held an interest in the corporation or (2) the five-year period ending on the date on which the interest was disposed of (the base period). A domestic corporation is not a USRPHC if it holds no USRPIs on the date of disposition of its stock and if any USRPIs held by the corporation during the base period were disposed of in a transaction in which gain, if any, was fully recognized.

[46] § 897.

EXAMPLE 37

From January 1, 2006, through January 1, 2011, Francis (a foreign investor) held shares in Door, Inc., a U.S. corporation. During this period, Door held two parcels of U.S. real estate and stock of Sash, Inc., another U.S. corporation. Sash also owned U.S. real estate. The two parcels of real estate held directly by Door were disposed of on December 15, 2007, in a nontaxable transaction. Sash disposed of its U.S. real estate in a taxable transaction on January 1, 2011.

An interest in Door is treated as a USRPI because Door did not recognize gain on the December 15, 2007 disposition of the USRPIs. If Door's ownership of U.S. real estate had been limited to its indirect ownership through Sash, an interest in Door would not have constituted a USRPI as of January 2, 2011. This result would occur because Sash disposed of its USRPIs in a taxable transaction in which gain was fully recognized. ■

A USRPHC is any corporation (whether foreign or domestic) where the fair market value of the corporation's USRPIs equals or exceeds 50 percent of the aggregate of fair market value of certain specified assets. These assets are the corporation's USRPIs, its interests in real property located outside the United States, and any other of its assets that are used or held for use in a trade or business. Stock regularly traded on an established securities market is not treated as a USRPI if a person holds no more than 5 percent of the stock.

Gain on a disposition of stock of a foreign real property holding corporation is not subject to tax under FIRPTA. However, gain on a disposition of a USRPI by such a foreign corporation is subject to FIRPTA.

Withholding Provisions

The FIRPTA withholding provisions require any purchaser or agent acquiring a USRPI from a foreign person to withhold 10 percent of the amount realized on the disposition.[47] A domestic partnership, trust, or estate with a foreign partner, foreign grantor treated as owner, or foreign beneficiary generally must withhold 35 percent of the gain allocable to that person on a disposition of a USRPI.

Foreign corporations also are subject to withholding provisions on certain distributions. Without this withholding, NRAs could sell USRPIs, receiving the sales proceeds outside the United States, and jurisdictional issues could make it difficult for the U.S. tax authorities to collect any U.S. tax that might be due on gains. Certain exceptions to FIRPTA withholding are allowed.

Failure to withhold can subject the purchaser or the purchaser's agent to interest on any unpaid amount.[48] A civil penalty of 100 percent of the amount required to be withheld and a criminal penalty of up to $10,000 or five years in prison can be imposed for willful failure to withhold.[49]

EXPATRIATION TO AVOID U.S. TAXATION

Section 877 provides for U.S. taxation of U.S.-source income earned by individuals who relinquished their U.S. citizenship within 10 years of deriving that income if they gave up their citizenship to avoid U.S. taxation. Furthermore, NRAs who lost U.S. citizenship within a 10-year period immediately preceding the close of the tax year must pay taxes on their U.S.-source income as though they were still U.S. citizens. This provision applies only if the expatriation had as one of its principal purposes the avoidance of U.S. taxes. Individuals are presumed to have a tax avoidance purpose if they meet either of the following criteria.[50]

- Average annual net income tax for the five taxable years ending before the date of loss of U.S. citizenship is more than $147,000 (in 2011).
- Net worth as of that date is at least $2 million.

[47] § 1445.

[48] §§ 6601, 6621, and 6651.

[49] §§ 6672 and 7202.

[50] § 877(a)(2). The dollar amounts are adjusted for inflation.

FINANCIAL DISCLOSURE *Insights*

DEFERRED TAX ASSETS OVERSEAS

U.S. corporations are not the only entities that can have balance sheets with excessive deferred tax accounts. Restrictive regulatory rules as to how non-U.S. banks compute their capital amounts tend to create large deferred tax assets for them. These accounts attract more attention from regulators in a "down" economy, when the financial stability of the banking system is even more critical than usual.

Deferred tax assets do not affect the entity's actual cash balances, but they can affect the stock price in the short term. Even professional equity analysts can have difficulty understanding announcements of tax adjustments to the balance sheet. Regulations limit the level of deferred tax assets that banks can have in a given country, and political pressure to increase those limits is appearing, as the proportion of shareholder equity that is made up of deferred tax assets has grown significantly in the last five years.

The following are estimates from JPMorgan Chase of the magnitude of deferred tax asset balances for selected banks overseas and banks in the United States.

	Percentage of Shareholder Equity Constituted by Deferred Tax Assets
Dexia	44%
Deutsche Bank	24
Monte dei Paschi	23
UBS	21
Credit Suisse	20
U.S. banks, average	11

These provisions also apply to "long-term lawful permanent residents" who cease to be taxed as U.S. residents. A long-term permanent resident is an individual (other than a citizen of the United States) who is a lawful permanent resident of the United States in at least 8 taxable years during the 15-year period ending with the taxable year in which the individual either ceases to be a lawful permanent resident of the United States or begins to be treated as a resident of another country under an income tax treaty between the United States and the other country (and does not waive the benefits of the treaty to residents of that country). An exception applies to certain individuals with dual citizenship.

The United States continues to treat individuals as U.S. citizens or residents until the taxpayers provide required information and an expatriation notice. Expatriates who are subject to the 10-year rule outlined above must file an information disclosure statement annually. If an expatriate is physically present in the United States for more than 30 days during a calendar year during the 10-year period, the individual is taxed as a U.S. citizen or resident.[51] These expatriation rules, taken as a whole, make it difficult to give up U.S. citizenship or residency simply to avoid U.S. taxation.

9.7 REPORTING REQUIREMENTS

The U.S. tax provisions in the international area include numerous reporting requirements. Furthermore, civil and criminal penalties for noncompliance can apply.[52]

A domestic corporation that is 25 percent or more foreign owned must file an information return and maintain certain records where they will be accessible to the IRS.[53] Additionally, any foreign corporation carrying on a trade or business in the United States must file an information return and maintain records in a similar manner.[54]

U.S. shareholders of a CFC must file a Form 5471. The U.S. partners of a controlled foreign partnership must file an information return.[55] A foreign partnership

[51] § 877(g)(1).
[52] See Chapter 17.
[53] § 6038A.
[54] § 6038C.
[55] § 6038.

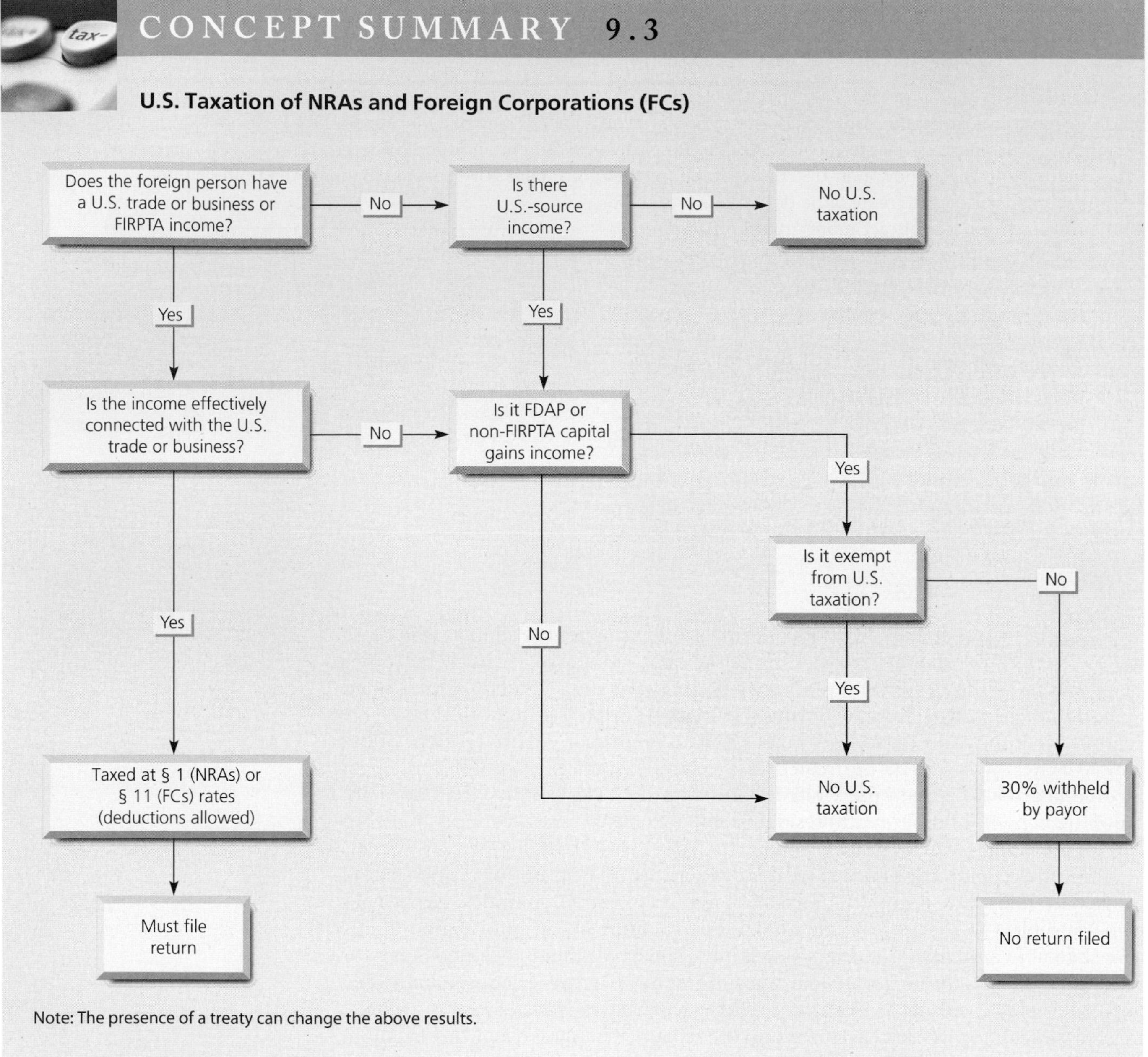

that has gross income that is either U.S.-source or effectively connected with a U.S. trade or business must file a partnership return.[56] Changes in ownership of interests in foreign partnerships (acquisitions or dispositions) must also be reported if a 10 percent or greater interest is involved.[57]

Asset transfers to foreign corporations or partnerships under certain tax-deferred transactions require information returns at the time of the transfer.[58] U.S. taxpayers that control foreign corporations or partnerships must also file annual information returns related to these entities.[59] Creation of, or a transfer to, a foreign trust by a U.S. person necessitates the filing of a Form 3520.[60]

[56] § 6031(e).
[57] § 6046A.
[58] § 6038B.
[59] § 6038.
[60] § 6048.

GLOBAL *Tax Issues*

Filing Deadlines When You're Overseas

What if you are situated outside the United States when you file a tax return? Working with a non-U.S. postal service can be challenging even on a good day. The established rule still seems to be that the date of the non-U.S. postmark determines whether the return is filed in a timely manner or whether a failure to file penalty will be assessed (Rev.Rul. 80–218).

The IRS seems to be having some trouble digesting this rule, though. In *Pekar*, 113 TC 158, where the non-U.S. postmark indicated that the return had been mailed before its due date, the IRS seemed to be taking a date-received position with the Tax Court. But the Service admitted its mistake in ITA 2000121085, where the reliance-on-postmark test is applied as expected.

No ruling to date has specifically addressed the application of this rule to a private express delivery service like UPS, but neither the Code nor rulings restrict the when-delivered to the carrier rule to domestic shipments, either. Thus, if a U.S. taxpayer living overseas uses a private delivery service, some form of date stamping is a good idea.

TAX PLANNING:

Over time, legislation has tended to reduce the ability to plan transactions and operations in a manner that minimizes tax liability. However, taxpayers who are not limited by the constraints of a particular transaction or operation can use the following suggestions to plan for maximum tax benefits.

9.8 The Foreign Tax Credit Limitation and Sourcing Provisions

The FTC limitation is partially based on the amount of foreign-source taxable income in the numerator of the limitation ratio. Consequently, the sourcing of income is extremely important. Income that is taxed by a foreign tax jurisdiction benefits from the FTC only to the extent that it is classified as foreign-source income under U.S. tax law. Thus, elements that affect the sourcing of income, such as the place of title passage, should be considered carefully before a transaction is undertaken.

It may be possible for a U.S. corporation to alleviate the problem of excess foreign taxes by using the following techniques.

- Generate "same basket" foreign-source income that is subject to a tax rate lower than the U.S. tax rate.
- Reduce highly taxed foreign-source income in favor of foreign-source income that is taxed at a lower rate by shifting operations or intangibles.
- Time the repatriation of foreign-source earnings to coincide with excess limitation years.
- Deduct foreign taxes for years when the deduction benefit would exceed the FTC benefit.
- Convert deductions related to foreign-source income so that they are related to U.S.-source income instead.

EXAMPLE 38

Della, Inc., a U.S. corporation, reports U.S.-source taxable income of $200,000, total taxable income of $300,000, and a U.S. tax liability (before the FTC) of $105,000. Della receives foreign-source taxable income, pays foreign income taxes, and computes an FTC as shown.

GLOBAL *Tax Issues*

A Deferral for an End to Deferral?

The Obama administration is interested in reforming the U.S. taxation of foreign income. It has indicated a particular concern with scaling back the benefits resulting from the deferral of income earned by the foreign subsidiaries of U.S. corporations, believing that about $3 trillion cash in unrepatriated profits remain overseas as a result of this tax rule.

In May 2009 the Treasury Department released *General Explanations of the Administration's Fiscal Year 2010 Revenue Proposals*. This publication—widely known as the "Green Book"—outlined several far-reaching proposed changes to the U.S. international tax rules. Key ideas included reducing the availability of the "check-the-box" election, disallowing certain U.S. tax deductions until associated foreign income is repatriated, and reducing the ability for certain opportunities involving the foreign tax credit. The net effect of these changes would be an increase in the U.S. tax on the foreign profits of U.S. corporations.

The President's 2010 revenue proposals also contained suggestions for international tax reform. Despite the administration's desire for change in this area, significant international tax reform remained stalled at the end of 2010.

Basket	Amount	Foreign Taxes	FTC Limitation	Allowed FTC
Passive	$ 80,000	$ 8,000	$28,000	$ 8,000
General	20,000	8,000	7,000	7,000
	$100,000	$16,000		$15,000

If Della can shift $10,000 of passive income into the general basket, the FTC is increased by $1,000. The FTC limitation for the general basket increases to $10,500 [($30,000/$300,000) × $105,000]. This allows all $8,000 of foreign taxes related to the general basket to be credited in the current year. The allowed FTC for the passive basket remains unchanged at $8,000. ■

EXAMPLE 39

Donohoe, Inc., a U.S. corporation, reports U.S. total taxable income of $100,000, classified as follows.

	Total	U.S.-Source Income	Foreign-Source Income—General
Gross income	$150,000	$100,000	$ 50,000
Deductions	(50,000)	(40,000)	(10,000)
Taxable income	$100,000	$ 60,000	$ 40,000

U.S. income tax before the FTC is $34,000, and Donohoe's FTC limitation is $13,600 ($40,000/$100,000 × $34,000). If, through planning and analysis, Donohoe is able to convert $5,000 of the deductions related to foreign-source income to U.S. source, the total taxable income would remain the same, but the FTC limitation would increase to $15,300 ($45,000/$100,000 × $34,000). ■

TAX *in* the NEWS

So Long, It's Been Nice Knowing You

Did you ever wonder who gives up U.S. citizenship? It is easy to find out. Section 877 requires that U.S. citizens and long-term permanent residents inform the IRS of their expatriation on Form 8854, Initial and Annual Expatriation Information Statement, in the year of expatriation and certain years thereafter.

Expatriating individuals must also give notice of an expatriating act or termination of residency to the Department of State or the Department of Homeland Security.

The government publishes the names of these individuals in the *Federal Register* each quarter. Several hundred people abandoned U.S. citizenship in the second quarter of 2010 alone.

9.9 The Foreign Corporation as a Tax Shelter

An NRA who is able to hold U.S. investments through a foreign corporation can accomplish much in the way of avoiding U.S. taxation. Capital gains (other than dispositions of U.S. real property interests) are not subject to U.S. taxation. This assumes that they are not effectively connected with a U.S. trade or business. The NRA can dispose of the stock of a foreign corporation that holds U.S. real property and not be subject to taxation under § 897 (FIRPTA). Furthermore, the stock of a foreign corporation is not included in the U.S. gross estate of a deceased NRA, even if all the assets of the foreign corporation are located in the United States.

Caution is advised when the foreign corporation may generate income effectively connected with the conduct of a U.S. trade or business. The income may be taxed at a higher rate than if the NRA individually generated the income. The tradeoff between a higher U.S. tax on this income and protection from the U.S. estate tax and § 897 must be weighed.

9.10 Planning under Subpart F

The *de minimis* rule allows a CFC to avoid the classification of income as FBC income or insurance income and prevents the U.S. shareholder from having to include it in gross income as a constructive dividend. Thus, a CFC with total FBC income and insurance income in an amount close to the 5 percent or $1 million level should monitor income realization to assure that the *de minimis* rule applies for the tax year. At least as important is avoiding the classification of all the gross income of the CFC as FBC income or insurance income. This happens when the sum of the FBC income and gross insurance income for the taxable year exceeds 70 percent of total gross income.

Careful timing of investment in U.S. property can reduce the potential for constructive dividend income to U.S. shareholders. The gross income of U.S. shareholders attributable to investment in U.S. property is limited to the E & P of the CFC.[61] E & P that is attributable to amounts that have been included in gross income as Subpart F income in either the current year or a prior tax year is not taxed again when invested in U.S. property.

[61]§§ 959(a)(1) and (2).

9.11 Using the Check-the-Box Regulations

The check-the-box Regulations under § 7701 provide a great deal of flexibility for U.S.-based multinational corporations. Corporations are allowed to organize their branches and subsidiaries around the world in ways that optimize both local country and U.S. taxation. For example, a U.S. corporation may choose to treat its subsidiary in the United Kingdom as a partnership or unincorporated branch for U.S. tax purposes (thus taking advantage of loss flow-throughs) and a corporation under United Kingdom law (where certain tax and liability benefits may exist). The flurry of multinational restructurings since the issuance of the check-the-box Regulations has led to some cries of foul by U.S. taxing authorities who claim that these provisions are being used in inappropriate ways. The Treasury Department and the IRS are currently exploring ways to curb some of these perceived abuses.

9.12 Transferring Intangible Assets Offshore

In many industries, a company's intangible assets, such as licenses and patents, produce a relatively large share of total income. For example, the license to use a software program is much more valuable than the actual disc the customer purchases; thus, a large part of the profit from the sale of software accrues to the license holder.

Unlike manufacturing plants, intangible assets can be easily transferred to related entities outside the United States. Congress recognized this potential, and § 367 requires gain to be recognized if intangibles are transferred outside the United States. To avoid this § 367 "toll charge," companies should consider creating their intangibles offshore so that no subsequent transfer is required. Companies may choose to perform their R&D activities within subsidiaries located in tax haven countries in order to create and keep their valuable intangibles in low-tax jurisdictions.

9.13 Transfer Pricing

U.S. multinational companies earn income across many different jurisdictions and operate through several different types of entities (e.g., subsidiary corporations, joint ventures, partnerships). With proper planning and documentation, a U.S. corporation can organize its intercompany payments for goods and services, interest on debt, and royalties for use of intangible property in such a way as to minimize its worldwide tax burden. For example, a U.S. multinational may choose to borrow in high-tax jurisdictions (where the interest deduction will be more valuable) and earn royalty income in low-tax jurisdictions (where the income escapes heavy taxation).

Such decisions can be made within the legal framework of the tax laws of the United States and other countries. In the United States, § 482 provides the guidelines that must be met to justify and document appropriate transfer pricing. In general, these guidelines require an entity to demonstrate that it deserved to earn its profits based on the functions it performs, the assets it owns, or the risks it takes.

REFOCUS ON THE BIG PICTURE

GOING INTERNATIONAL

Now you can address the questions about VoiceCo's activities that were posed at the beginning of the chapter. Simply selling into a foreign jurisdiction may not trigger any overseas income tax consequences, but such income is taxed currently to VoiceCo in the United States. When VoiceCo sets up an Irish corporation, it benefits from deferral because as a manufacturer it can avoid deemed dividends under Subpart F. However, there may be passive-basket income earned by the Irish subsidiary.

VoiceCo must file Form 5471 to report on the activities of its foreign subsidiary. If VoiceCo receives dividends from its foreign subsidiary, it can claim § 902 foreign tax credits (so-called indirect credits). What are the foreign tax implications if VoiceCo "checks the box" on its foreign subsidiary? The U.S. tax implications?

What If?

Suppose that although VoiceCo's European sales become a substantial part of its total revenues, it decides not to create a foreign subsidiary. Instead, because shipping costs are high and customers demand quick turnaround on product orders, VoiceCo decides to license its design and manufacturing process to a local European musical instruments company for sales in Europe. The European company pays VoiceCo a royalty equal to 25 percent of the sales price on all its sales of microphones based on VoiceCo's design. The royalty income is foreign-source income (as the underlying intangible property is exploited outside the United States).

The European country imposes a 5 percent withholding tax on all royalty payments to VoiceCo. The royalties are part of its worldwide income and so are currently taxed to VoiceCo in the United States. Will VoiceCo receive a foreign tax credit for the withholding tax?

KEY TERMS

Branch profits tax, 9–36
CFC (controlled foreign corporation), 9–22
Dividend equivalent amount (DEA), 9–36
Effectively connected income, 9–34
FIRPTA, 9–37
Foreign tax credit (FTC), 9–26
Functional currency, 9–14
Inbound taxation, 9–3
Nonresident alien (NRA), 9–33
Outbound taxation, 9–3
Qualified business unit (QBU), 9–14
Subpart F, 9–23
Tax haven, 9–19
Tax treaties, 9–4
Transfer pricing, 9–10
Treaty shopping, 9–20
U.S. shareholder, 9–22
U.S. trade or business, 9–34

DISCUSSION QUESTIONS

1. **LO.1** What is the meaning of the statement "U.S. persons are taxed on their worldwide income"?

2. **LO.1** Liang, a U.S. citizen, owns 100% of ForCo, a foreign corporation not engaged in a U.S. trade or business. In the absence of any dividends or Subpart F inclusions, is Liang subject to any U.S. income tax on the profits of ForCo?

3. **LO.2** Kelly, a U.S. citizen, earns interest income that is sourced in Germany. How could a U.S. tax treaty with Germany reduce Kelly's taxes on the interest?

4. **LO.3** When is dividend income paid by a non-U.S. entity to a U.S. investor *not* foreign-source income? Be specific.

ISSUE ID

COMMUNICATIONS

5. **LO.3** Write a memo outlining the issues that arise when attempting to source income that is earned from Internet-based activities.

6. **LO.3** Generally, U.S. taxpayers with foreign operations desire to increase foreign-source income and reduce deductions against that foreign-source income in order to increase their FTC limitations. How does § 482 enable the IRS to prevent taxpayers from manipulating the source of income and allocation of deductions? Explain.

7. **LO.4** Weinke is a business organized in Austria, where the local currency is the euro. Nevertheless, Weinke's U.S. branch uses the U.S. dollar as its functional currency. How can this be?

8. **LO.4** When dealing with the rules concerning gain and loss from foreign currency transactions, the taxpayer must identify its qualified business units (QBUs). What is a QBU? How many QBUs can a business operate?

9. **LO.4** Douglass is a business organized in the United States, and its functional currency is the U.S. dollar. On a January sale to a customer in Finland, the closing price for the goods is expressed in euros, payable to Douglass on March 1. Does Douglass record a foreign currency gain or loss on this transaction?

ISSUE ID

10. **LO.5** What are the important concepts to be considered when U.S. assets are transferred outside the country to be used in starting a new business?

COMMUNICATIONS

11. **LO.5** Write a memo to a U.S. client explaining why some of the profit that it generates from a non-U.S. subsidiary still is included in its U.S. taxable income.

12. **LO.5** Summarize the ownership rules that apply in determining whether a non-U.S. entity is a controlled foreign corporation (CFC) under the U.S. Federal income tax rules.

ISSUE ID

13. **LO.5** Joanna owns 5% of Axel, a foreign corporation. Joanna's son, Fred, is considering acquiring 15% of Axel from an NRA. The remainder of Axel is owned 27% by unrelated U.S. persons and 53% by unrelated NRAs. Currently, Fred operates (as a sole proprietorship) a manufacturing business that sells goods to Axel for resale outside the United States and outside Axel's country of residence. Joanna is not concerned about the concentration of investment because she expects to sell her stock in Axel in three years at a significant capital gain. Are there tax issues that Joanna and Fred, both U.S. citizens, need to address?

14. **LO.5** Is a foreign corporation owned equally by 100 unrelated U.S. citizens considered to be a CFC?

15. **LO.5** QuinnCo could not claim all of the income taxes that it paid to Japan as a foreign tax credit (FTC) this year. What computational limit probably kept QuinnCo from taking its full FTC?

16. **LO.5** SwitchCo, a U.S. business, paid income taxes to France relative to profitable sales that it made in that country. Can it claim a deduction for these taxes in computing U.S. taxable income? A tax credit? Both? Explain.

17. **LO.5** USCo, a domestic corporation, receives a $10,000 dividend from ForCo, a wholly owned foreign corporation. The § 902 deemed-paid FTC associated with this dividend is $4,000. What is the total gross income included in USCo's tax return as a result of this dividend?

ISSUE ID

18. **LO.5** Molly, Inc., a domestic corporation, owns 15% of PJ, Inc., and 12% of Emma, Inc., both foreign corporations. Molly is paid gross dividends of $35,000 and $18,000 from PJ and Emma, respectively. PJ withheld and paid more than $10,500 in foreign taxes on the $35,000 dividend. PJ's country of residence levies a 20% tax on dividends paid to nonresident corporations. However, the tax rate is increased to 30% if the recipient is a resident of a country that provides an FTC. Taxes of $3,600 are withheld on the dividend from Emma. What tax issues must be considered in determining the availability and amount of the FTC allowed to Molly, Inc.?

19. **LO.5** Working with the FTC may involve "baskets" of foreign-source income and deductions. Explain this term.

20. **LO.6** In general terms, how is a non-U.S. person taxed on its U.S. business income? Investment income? Do not take any tax treaties into account in your answer.

21. **LO.3, 6** Creek, Inc., a foreign corporation, sells vacuum tubes in several countries, including the United States. In fact, currently 25% of Creek's sales income is sourced in the United States (through branches in New York and Chicago). Creek is considering opening additional branches in San Francisco and Phoenix to increase U.S. sales. What tax issues must Creek consider before making this move?

ISSUE ID

22. **LO.3, 6** Write a short memo on the difference between "inbound" and "outbound" activities in the context of U.S. taxation of international income.

COMMUNICATIONS

23. **LO.1, 3, 5** If a U.S. taxpayer is subject to U.S. income tax on profits earned outside the United States and such profits also are subject to income tax in the foreign jurisdiction, how does the U.S. taxpayer escape double taxation? Draft a short speech that you will give to your university's Business Club.

COMMUNICATIONS

PROBLEMS

24. **LO.4, 5** RedCo, a domestic corporation, incorporates GreenCo, a new wholly owned entity in Germany. Under both German and U.S. legal principles, this entity is a corporation. RedCo faces a 35% U.S. tax rate.

    GreenCo earns $800,000 in net profits from its German activities and makes no dividend distributions to RedCo. How much U.S. tax will RedCo pay for the current year as a result of GreenCo's earnings, assuming no deemed dividend under Subpart F? Ignore any FTC implications.

25. **LO.3** Madison, a U.S. resident, received the following income items for the current tax year. Identify the source of each income item as either U.S. or foreign.
    a. $3,000 dividend from U.S. Flower Company, a U.S. corporation that operates solely in the eastern United States.
    b. $6,000 dividend from Stern Corporation, a U.S. corporation that had total gross income of $4 million from the active conduct of a foreign trade or business for the immediately preceding three tax years. Stern's total gross income for the same period was $5 million.
    c. $2,000 dividend from International Consolidated, Inc., a foreign corporation that had gross income of $3 million effectively connected with the conduct of a U.S. trade or business for the immediately preceding three tax years. International's total gross income for the same period was $6 million.
    d. $600 interest from a savings account at a Florida bank.
    e. $5,000 interest on Warren Corporation bonds. Warren is a U.S. corporation that derived $6 million of its gross income for the immediately preceding three tax years from operation of an active foreign business. Warren's total gross income for this same period was $7.2 million.

26. **LO.3** Gloria Wang, an NRA, is a professional golfer. She played in seven tournaments in the United States in the current year and earned $200,000 in prizes from these tournaments. She deposited the winnings in a bank account she opened in Mexico City after her first tournament win.

    Gloria played a total of 30 tournaments for the year and earned $300,000 in total prize money. She spent 40 days in the United States, 60 days in England, 20 days in Scotland, and the rest of the time in South America. Write a letter to Gloria explaining how much U.S.-source income she will generate, if any, from her participation in these tournaments and whether any of her winnings are subject to U.S. taxation. Gloria's address is AV Rio Branco, 149-4#, Rio de Janeiro, RJ 22421, Brazil.

COMMUNICATIONS

27. **LO.3** Determine whether the source of income for the following sales is U.S. or foreign.
    a. Suarez, an NRA, sells stock in Home Depot, a U.S. corporation, through a broker in San Antonio.
    b. Chris sells stock in IBM, a U.S. corporation, to her brother, Rich. Both Chris and Rich are NRAs, and the sale takes place outside the United States.

c. Crows, Inc., sells inventory produced in the United States to customers in Europe. Title passes in the international waters of the Atlantic Ocean.
d. Doubles, Inc., a U.S. corporation, manufactures equipment in Malaysia and sells the equipment to customers in the United States.

28. **LO.3, 6** Determine whether the source of income in each of the following situations is U.S. or foreign.
   a. Development, Inc., a U.S. corporation, earns $400,000 in royalty income from Far East, Ltd., a foreign corporation, for the use of several patented processes in Far East's manufacturing business, located in Singapore.
   b. Marion, an NRA, is an employee of a foreign corporation. During the tax year, she spends 75 days in the United States purchasing cloth for her employer, a clothing manufacturer. Her yearly salary is $150,000 (translated to U.S. dollars). Marion spends a total of 250 days working during the year. Her employer has no other business contacts with the United States.
   c. Jacques, an NRA, sells an apartment building to Julie, a U.S. resident. The building is located in Denver. The closing takes place in Jacques's country of residence.
   d. A domestic corporation sells depreciable personal property that it has been using in its foreign branch operations. The property sells for $180,000, has a tax basis of $75,000, and has been depreciated for tax purposes to the extent of $77,000. The property is located in a foreign country but is sold to another domestic corporation. The sales transaction takes place in the United States.

29. **LO.3** USCo, a domestic corporation, purchases inventory for resale from distributors within the United States and resells this inventory to customers outside the United States, with title passing outside the United States. What is the sourcing of USCo's inventory sales income?

30. **LO.3** USCo, a domestic corporation, owns the rights to a patent related to a medical device. USCo licenses the rights to use the patent to IrishCo, a foreign corporation. IrishCo uses the patent in a manufacturing facility located in Ireland. What is the sourcing of the royalty income received by USCo from IrishCo for the use of the patent?

31. **LO.3** USCo incurred $100,000 in interest expense for the current year. The tax book value of USCo's assets generating foreign-source income is $20 million. The tax book value of USCo's assets generating U.S.-source income is $80 million. How much of the interest expense is allocated and apportioned to foreign-source income?

DECISION MAKING

32. **LO.3** Create, Inc., produces inventory in its foreign manufacturing plants for sale in the United States. Its foreign manufacturing assets have a tax book value of $5 million and a fair market value of $15 million. Its assets related to the sales activity have a tax book value of $200,000 and a fair market value of $50,000. Create's interest expense totaled $300,000 for the current year.
   a. What amount of interest expense is allocated and apportioned to foreign-source income using the tax book value method? What amount of Create's interest expense is allocated and apportioned to foreign-source income using the fair market method?
   b. If Create wishes to maximize its FTC, which method should it use?

33. **LO.4** Peck, Inc., a U.S. corporation, purchases weight-lifting equipment for resale from HiDisu, a Japanese corporation, for 75 million yen. On the date of purchase, 150 yen is equal to $1 U.S. (¥150:$1). The purchase is made on December 15, 2011, with payment due in 90 days. Peck is a calendar year taxpayer. On December 31, 2011, the foreign exchange rate is ¥250:$1. What amount of foreign currency gain or loss, if any, must Peck recognize for 2011 as a result of this transaction?

COMMUNICATIONS

34. **LO.4** Table, Inc., a U.S. corporation, operates a manufacturing branch in Mexico and a sales branch in Canada. The Mexican branch uses the peso for all its activities, and the Canadian branch uses the Canadian dollar for all its activities. Write a letter to Karen Burns, Table's tax director, explaining the number of foreign qualified business units the company will have from these activities. Table's address is 840 Logan Avenue, Madison, WI 53705.

35. **LO.4** Chair, Inc., a U.S. corporation, operates a sales branch in Ireland. Although the operations are located in Ireland, where the euro is the local currency, all the branch's sales are to customers in the United Kingdom. The revenue is collected in British

pounds, and the sales branch's employees are paid in British pounds. What functional currency should Chair use for its Irish sales branch?

36. **LO.4** Harold is a citizen and resident of the United States. He pays all of his living expenses in U.S. dollars. He operates an unincorporated trade or business buying and selling rare books over the Internet to Canadian customers. All income and expenses of the rare book business are in Canadian dollars. Explain to Harold the number of qualified business units he has and the related functional currency of the QBUs.

37. **LO.4, 6** Carroll Manufacturing, Inc., a calendar year domestic corporation, operates a branch in Ireland. In the current year, the branch generated 750,000 euros in net profit. On December 31 of the current year, one euro equaled 85 cents. The average exchange rate for the current year between the euro and the dollar was 90 cents. Write a memo to Margaret Zhang, the controller of Carroll, explaining (1) how and when the Irish profits will be taxed to Carroll in the United States and (2) under what conditions a foreign currency gain or loss will be recognized.

ISSUE ID

COMMUNICATIONS

38. **LO.4, 5** Teal, Inc., a foreign corporation, pays a dividend to its shareholders on November 30. Red, Inc., a U.S. corporation and 7% shareholder in Teal, receives a dividend of 10,000K (a foreign currency). Pertinent exchange rates are as follows.

November 30	.9K:$1
Average for year	.7K:$1
December 31	2K:$1

What is the dollar amount of the dividend received by Red, Inc.? Does Red have a foreign exchange gain or loss on receipt of the dividend?

39. **LO.5** Hometown, a U.S. C corporation, makes a sale to a customer in Sustainia, a country that applies a 25% income tax to business profits. The customer found out about Hometown through an Internet search. Hometown has no facilities or employees outside the United States. Hometown's profit on the sale totals $1,000. Where is the tax levied on this $1,000 profit?

40. **LO.5** USCo incorporated its foreign branch operations in Italy by transferring the branch's assets to a foreign corporation in return solely for stock in the new corporation. All of the branch's assets are located outside the United States and are used in the active conduct of a foreign trade or business. Is this transaction automatically eligible for tax deferral under § 351?

41. **LO.5** Buckeye Corporation transferred inventory (basis of $10, fair market value of $40) and machinery used in a U.S. factory (basis of $50, fair market value of $85) to MapleLeaf, a newly formed corporation in Canada, in exchange for all of MapleLeaf's stock. Buckeye previously deducted $30 of depreciation related to the machinery on its U.S. tax return. How much gain, if any, must Buckeye recognize on the transfers of the property to MapleLeaf?

42. **LO.5** WorldCo, a domestic corporation, is planning to incorporate a branch that it has been operating in a foreign country. WorldCo's branch has a large amount of inventory. In no more than three PowerPoint slides, outline the tax results of transferring this inventory to a newly formed foreign corporation.

COMMUNICATIONS

43. **LO.5** Beach, Inc., a domestic corporation, operates a branch in Mexico. Over the last 10 years, this branch has generated $50 million in losses. For the last 3 years, however, the branch has been profitable and has earned enough income to entirely offset the prior losses. Most of the assets are fully depreciated, and a net gain would be recognized if the assets were sold.

    Beach's CFO believes that Beach should incorporate the branch now so that this potential gain can be transferred to a foreign corporation, thereby avoiding U.S. tax and, as an added benefit, avoiding U.S. taxes on future income. Draft a memo to Claire Quinty, the CFO, addressing the tax issues involved in the proposed transaction.

ISSUE ID

COMMUNICATIONS

44. **LO.5** USCo owns 55% of the voting stock of LandCo, a Country X corporation. Irishco, an unrelated Country Y corporation, owns the other 45% of LandCo. LandCo owns 100% of the voting stock of OceanCo, a Country Z corporation. Assuming USCo is a U.S. shareholder, do LandCo and OceanCo meet the definition of a CFC?

45. **LO.5** Hart Enterprises, a U.S. corporation, owns 100% of OK, Ltd., an Irish corporation. OK's gross income for the year is $10 million. Determine OK's Subpart F income (before any expenses) from the transactions that it reported this year.
    a. OK received $600,000 from sales of products purchased from Hart and sold to customers outside Ireland.
    b. OK received $1 million from sales of products purchased from Hart and sold to customers in Ireland.
    c. OK received $400,000 from sales of products purchased from unrelated suppliers and sold to customers in Germany.
    d. OK purchased raw materials from Hart, used these materials to manufacture finished goods, and sold these goods to customers in Italy. OK earned $300,000 from these sales.
    e. OK received $100,000 for the performance of warranty services on behalf of Hart. These services were performed in Japan for customers located in Japan.
    f. OK received $50,000 in dividend income from investments in Canada and Mexico.

46. **LO.5** Round, Inc., a U.S. corporation, owns 80% of the only class of stock of Square, Inc., a CFC. Square is a CFC until May 1 of the current tax year (not a leap year). Round has held the stock since Square was organized and continues to hold it for the entire year. Round and Square are both calendar year taxpayers. Square's Subpart F income for the tax year is $1 million, current E & P is $2.5 million, and no distributions have been made for the tax year. What amount, if any, must Round include in gross income under Subpart F for the tax year?

ISSUE ID

COMMUNICATIONS

47. **LO.5** Mary Beth Alessio, a U.S. citizen, has placed all her investments in a Cayman Island corporation owned 1% by Mary Beth and 99% by a foreign individual. She pays no income tax in the Cayman Islands on this income. The foreign corporation earns only interest and dividends. Prepare a letter informing Mary Beth of the U.S. tax consequences of her foreign investments. Her address is 941 Windom Lane, Hagerstown, MD 21740.

48. **LO.5** Weather, Inc., a domestic corporation, operates in both Mexico and the United States. This year, the business generated taxable income of $600,000 from foreign sources and $900,000 from U.S. sources. All of Weather's foreign-source income is in the general limitation basket. Weather's total taxable income is $1.5 million. Weather pays Mexican taxes of $228,000. What is Weather's FTC for the tax year? Assume a 34% U.S. income tax rate.

49. **LO.5** Blunt, Inc., a U.S. corporation, earned $600,000 in total taxable income including $80,000 in foreign-source taxable income from its German branch's manufacturing operations and $30,000 in foreign-source taxable income from its Swiss branch's engineering services operations. Blunt paid $32,000 in German income taxes and $1,800 in Swiss income taxes. Compute Blunt's U.S. tax liability after any available FTCs. Assume the U.S. tax rate is 34%.

50. **LO.5** Dunne, Inc., a U.S. corporation, earned $400,000 in total taxable income, including $50,000 in foreign-source taxable income from its branch manufacturing operations in Brazil and $20,000 in foreign-source income from interest earned on bonds issued by Dutch corporations. Dunne paid $25,000 in Brazilian income taxes and $3,000 in Dutch income taxes. Compute Dunne's U.S. tax liability after any available FTCs. Assume the U.S. tax rate is 34%.

51. **LO.5** ABC, Inc., a domestic corporation, has $50 million of taxable income, including $15 million of general limitation foreign-source taxable income, on which ABC paid $5 million in foreign income taxes. The U.S. tax rate is 35%. What is ABC's foreign tax credit?

52. **LO.5** Mary, a U.S. citizen, is the sole shareholder of CanCo, a Canadian corporation. During its first year of operations, CanCo earns $14 million of foreign-source taxable income, pays $6 million of Canadian income taxes, and distributes a $2 million dividend to Mary. Can Mary claim a deemed-paid (indirect) FTC on her Form 1040 with respect to receipt of the dividend distribution from CanCo?

53. **LO.5** ABC, Inc., a domestic corporation, owns 100% of HighTax, a foreign corporation. HighTax has $50 million of post-1986 undistributed earnings, all of which is attributable

to general limitation income, and $50 million of post-1986 foreign income taxes. HighTax distributes a $5 million dividend to ABC. The dividend, which is subject to a 5% foreign withholding tax, is ABC's only item of income during the year. The U.S. tax rate is 35%. What amount of excess FTCs is produced by the dividend?

54. **LO.5** USCo, a domestic corporation, has worldwide taxable income of $1.5 million, including a $300,000 dividend from ForCo, a wholly owned foreign corporation. ForCo has $16 million in post-1986 undistributed E & P, and it has paid $10 million of foreign income taxes attributable to these earnings. All foreign income is in the general limitation basket. What is USCo's deemed-paid FTC related to the dividend received (before consideration of any limitation)?

55. **LO.5** USCo, a domestic corporation, has worldwide taxable income of $500,000, including a $100,000 dividend from ForCo, a wholly owned foreign corporation. ForCo has $1 million in post-1986 undistributed E & P, and it has paid $200,000 of foreign income taxes attributable to these earnings. All foreign income is in the general limitation basket. What is USCo's deemed-paid FTC related to the dividend received (before consideration of any limitation)?

56. **LO.5** Plane, Inc., a U.S. corporation, earned $600,000 in total taxable income for the current year. This total includes $750,000 in U.S.-source income, $50,000 in foreign-source income in the passive basket, and a $200,000 loss in the general limitation basket. Plane paid $5,000 in foreign income taxes related to the passive basket and incurred no taxes related to the general limitation basket. What is Plane's allowed FTC for the current year?

57. **LO.5** Elmwood, Inc., a domestic corporation, owns 15% of Correy, Ltd., a Hong Kong corporation. The remaining 85% of Correy is owned by Fortune Enterprises, a Canadian corporation. At the end of the current year, Correy has $400,000 in post-1986 undistributed E & P and $200,000 in foreign taxes related to this E & P. On the last day of the year, Correy pays a $30,000 dividend to Elmwood. Elmwood's taxable income before the dividend is $200,000. What is Elmwood's tax liability after consideration of the dividend and any allowed FTC, assuming a 34% U.S. tax rate?

58. **LO.5** Your client Chips, Inc., is engaged in the cookie production business, with production plants in Florida and Singapore. The U.S. plant has always produced profits, but the Singapore operation has generated $80,000 in losses since inception. This year, the Singapore operation began producing net profits. Draft a brief memo to Sally, the CFO of Chips, explaining why a portion of the current-year foreign-source income must be recharacterized as U.S.-source for FTC limitation purposes.

COMMUNICATIONS

59. **LO.5** Skills, Inc., a U.S. corporation, earns current foreign-source income classified in two different FTC income baskets. It earns $50,000 in passive foreign-source income and suffers a net loss of $30,000 in the general limitation basket. What is the numerator of the FTC limitation formula for the passive basket in the current year? Explain.

60. **LO.5** Canteen, Inc., a U.S. corporation, owns 100% of NewGrass, Ltd., a foreign corporation. NewGrass earns only general limitation income. During the current year, NewGrass paid Canteen a $10,000 dividend. The § 902 credit associated with this dividend is $3,000. The foreign jurisdiction requires a withholding tax of 20%, so Canteen received only $8,000 in cash as a result of the dividend. What is Canteen's total U.S. gross income reported as a result of the $8,000 cash dividend?

61. **LO.5** For which of the following foreign income inclusions is a U.S. corporation potentially allowed an indirect FTC under § 902?
    a. Interest income from a 5%-owned foreign corporation.
    b. Interest income from a 60%-owned foreign corporation.
    c. Dividend income from a 5%-owned foreign corporation.
    d. Dividend income from a 60%-owned foreign corporation.

62. **LO.5** Night, Inc., a domestic corporation, earned $300,000 from foreign manufacturing activities on which it paid $90,000 of foreign income taxes. Night's foreign sales income is taxed at a 50% foreign tax rate. What amount of foreign sales income can Night earn without generating any excess FTCs for the current year? Assume a 34% U.S. tax rate.

DECISION MAKING

63. **LO.4, 5** Partin, Inc., a foreign subsidiary of Jones, Inc., a U.S. corporation, has pretax income of 200,000 euros for 2011. Partin accrues 50,000 euros in foreign taxes on this

income. The average exchange rate for the tax year to which the taxes relate is .95 €$1. None of the income is Subpart F income. If the net earnings of 150,000 euros are distributed when the exchange rate is 1.05 €$1, what are the deemed-paid taxes available to Jones? Assume that 2011 is Partin's first year of operation.

64. **LO.5** Collins, Inc., a domestic corporation, operates a manufacturing branch in Singapore. During the current year, the manufacturing branch produces a loss of $300,000. Collins also earns interest income from investments in Europe, where it earns $800,000 in passive income. Collins paid no foreign income taxes related to the Singapore branch, but it paid $64,000 in foreign income taxes related to the passive income. Collins pays U.S. income taxes at the 34% tax rate. What is Collins's allowable FTC for the current year?

COMMUNICATIONS

65. **LO.3, 4, 5** You are the head tax accountant for the Venture Company, a U.S. corporation. The board of directors is considering expansion overseas and asks you to present a summary of the U.S. tax consequences of investing overseas through a foreign subsidiary. Prepare a detailed outline of the presentation you will make to the board.

DECISION MAKING

COMMUNICATIONS

66. **LO.5** Money, Inc., a U.S. corporation, has $500,000 to invest overseas for 2011. For U.S. tax purposes, any additional income earned by Money will be taxed at 34%. Two possibilities for investment are:
    a. Invest the $500,000 in common stock of Exco (a foreign corporation). Exco common stock pays a dividend of $3 per share each year. The $500,000 would purchase 10,000 shares (or 10%) of Exco's only class of stock (voting common). Exco expects to earn $10 million before taxes for 2011 and to be taxed at a flat rate of 40%. Its 2011 E & P before taxes is estimated to be $9.4 million. Exco's government does not withhold on dividends paid to foreign investors.
    b. Invest the $500,000 in Exco bonds that pay interest at 7% per year. Assume that the bonds will be acquired at par, or face, value. Exco's government withholds 25% on interest paid to foreign investors.

    Analyze these two investment opportunities and determine which would give Money the better return after taxes. Be sure to consider the effect of the FTC. Write a memorandum to Money, Inc., advising the corporation of your findings.

67. **LO.2, 6** IrishCo, a manufacturing corporation resident in Ireland, distributes products through a U.S. office. Current-year taxable income from such sales in the United States is $12 million. IrishCo's U.S. office deposits working capital funds in short-term certificates of deposit with U.S. banks. Current-year interest income from these deposits is $150,000.

    IrishCo also invests in U.S. securities traded on the New York Stock Exchange. This investing is done by the home office. For the current year, IrishCo has realized capital gains of $300,000 and dividend income of $50,000 from these stock investments. Compute IrishCo's U.S. tax liability, assuming that the U.S.-Ireland income tax treaty reduces withholding on dividends to 15% and on interest to 5%. Assume a 34% U.S. tax rate.

68. **LO.6** Vanguard, S.A., a Peruvian corporation, manufactures inventory in Peru. The inventory is sold to independent distributors in the United States, with title passing to the purchaser in the United States. Vanguard has no employees or operations within the United States. All sales activities are conducted through telephone, fax, and Internet communication between Vanguard's home office and its U.S. customers. Explain whether Vanguard has any income effectively connected with a U.S. trade or business.

69. **LO.6** Clario, S.A., a Peruvian corporation, manufactures furniture in Peru. It sells the furniture to independent distributors in the United States. Because title to the furniture passes to the purchasers in the United States, Clario has $1 million in U.S.-source income. Clario has no employees or operations in the United States related to its furniture business.

    As a separate line of business, Clario buys and sells antique toys. Clario has a single employee operating a booth on weekends at a flea market in Waldo, Florida. The antique toy business generated $9,000 in net profits from U.S. sources during the current year.

    What is Clario's effectively connected income for the current year?

70. **LO.6** Palm, Ltd., a foreign corporation, operates a sales branch in the United States that constitutes a U.S. trade or business. Rather than return the profits from the sales branch

to the foreign home office, Palm invests the profits in certificates of deposit at U.S. banks. Explain whether the interest earned on these CDs is considered effectively connected with Palm's U.S. trade or business.

71. **LO.6** Trace, Ltd., a foreign corporation, operates a trade or business in the United States. Trace's U.S.-source income effectively connected with this trade or business is $800,000 for the current year. Trace's current-year E & P is $650,000. Trace's net U.S. equity was $8.2 million at the beginning of the year and $8.6 million at year-end. Trace is a resident in a country that has no income tax treaty with the United States. Prepare a brief memo to Trace's Tax VP, reporting Trace's branch profits tax liability for the current year, along with a planning idea for reducing the branch profits tax. **COMMUNICATIONS**

72. **LO.6** Brenda, an NRA individual, owns 30% of the stock of Jeff, Inc., a U.S. corporation. Jeff's balance sheet on the last day of the taxable year is as follows.

		Adjusted Basis	Fair Market Value
Cash (used as working capital)		$ 200,000	$ 200,000
Investment in foreign land		300,000	800,000
Investment in U.S. real estate:			
Land		150,000	400,000
Buildings	$2,300,000		
Less: Depreciation	300,000	2,000,000	5,000,000
		$2,650,000	$6,400,000
Accounts payable		$ 300,000	$ 300,000
Notes payable		500,000	500,000
Capital stock		400,000	4,150,000
Retained earnings		1,450,000	1,450,000
		$2,650,000	$6,400,000

Brenda was in the United States only 40 days in the tax year. She sold all of her stock in Jeff on the last day of the tax year for $6.4 million. Brenda's adjusted basis in the stock sold was $500,000. She sold the stock for cash. What are the U.S. tax consequences, if any, to Brenda?

73. **LO.6** In Problem 72, what are the U.S. tax consequences, if any, to Brenda if Jeff, Inc., is a foreign corporation instead of a domestic corporation?

74. **LO.6** John McPherson is single, an attorney, and a U.S. citizen. He recently attended a seminar where he learned he could give up his U.S. citizenship, move to Bermuda (where he would pay no income tax), and operate his law practice long distance via the Internet with no U.S. tax consequences. Write a letter informing John of the tax consequences of his proposed actions. His address is 1005 NE 10th Street, Gainesville, GA 32812. **ISSUE ID** **COMMUNICATIONS**

75. **LO.6** ForCo, a foreign corporation not engaged in a U.S. trade or business, received a $500,000 dividend from USCo, a domestic corporation. ForCo incurred $20,000 in expenses related to earning the dividend. USCo's income is all from U.S. sources. ForCo is not eligible for any treaty benefits. What is the withholding tax on the dividend paid to ForCo?

76. **LO.6** ForCo, a foreign corporation not engaged in a U.S. trade or business, received a $200,000 dividend from USCo, a domestic corporation. ForCo incurred $5,000 in expenses related to earning the dividend. USCo's income is all from U.S. sources. ForCo is not eligible for any treaty benefits. What is the withholding tax on the dividend paid to ForCo?

77. **LO.6** ForCo, a foreign corporation not engaged in a U.S. trade or business, received an $800,000 dividend from USCo, a domestic corporation. ForCo incurred $40,000 in expenses related to earning the dividend. USCo's income is all from U.S. sources. ForCo is eligible for an income tax treaty that limits withholding on dividends to 10%. What is the withholding tax on the dividend paid to ForCo?

TAX RETURN PROBLEMS

1. Fleming Products, Inc., a U.S. corporation, has a branch in Canada. The branch earns taxable income of $1 million from manufacturing operations and $500,000 from passive investment. Fleming Products pays Canadian income tax of $400,000 (40%) and $100,000 (20%), respectively, on this foreign-source income. The corporation also earns U.S.-source taxable income from manufacturing operations of $4 million, resulting in worldwide taxable income of $5.5 million. The U.S. taxes before the FTC are $1.87 million (at 34%). Fleming Products (employer ID number 11–1111111) accrues taxes for purposes of the FTC. This information is summarized below.

Income Category	Gross Income	Direct Expenses	Indirect Expenses	Taxable Income	Foreign Taxes
U.S. manufacturing	$ 9,000,000	$4,460,000	$540,000	$4,000,000	NA
Foreign manufacturing	5,000,000	3,700,000	300,000	1,000,000	$400,000
Passive investment	1,000,000	440,000	60,000	500,000	100,000
Total	$15,000,000	$8,600,000	$900,000*	$5,500,000	$500,000

*This $900,000 represents expenses not definitely allocable to any of the corporation's activities. It is allocated and apportioned based on relative gross income.

Complete a Form 1118 to compute Fleming's FTC in the general limitation income and passive categories. Use the fill-in forms at **www.irs.gov**.

2. Cotton Export, Inc., a domestic corporation, has the following taxable income amounts for the current tax year and incurs foreign income taxes as shown.

Type of Income	Source	Amount	Foreign Taxes
Sales	Canada	$ 830,000	$339,000
	U.S.	300,000	–0–
Dividends*	Canada	20,000	5,100**
	U.S.†	25,000	–0–
		$1,175,000	$344,100

U.S. taxes before FTC = $399,500.

*From a portfolio of foreign stocks, all owned less than 1% by vote or value.
**Included in dividend amount (i.e., the $20,000 is before the $5,100 in withholding taxes).
†Net of dividends received deduction.

Gross foreign-source sales income is $1.2 million. Deductions allocable to foreign sales income total $320,000, and the apportioned share of deductions not definitely allocable to foreign sales income is $50,000.

Gross foreign-source dividend income is $21,000. There are no deductions definitely allocable to dividend income. The apportioned share of deductions not definitely allocable to foreign-source dividend income is $1,000.

Determine Cotton's FTC by completing the appropriate Form 1118s. Use the fill-in forms at **www.irs.gov**.

RESEARCH PROBLEMS

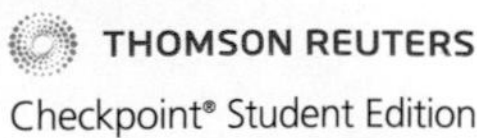

Checkpoint® Student Edition

Note: Solutions to Research Problems can be prepared by using the **Checkpoint® Student Edition** online research product, which is available to accompany this text. It is also possible to prepare solutions to the Research Problems by using tax research materials found in a standard tax library.

COMMUNICATIONS

Research Problem 1. Jerry Jeff Keen, the CFO of Boots Unlimited, a Texas corporation, has come to you regarding a potential restructuring of business operations. Boots has long manufactured its western boots in plants in Texas and Oklahoma. Recently, Boots has explored the possibility of setting up a manufacturing subsidiary in Ireland, where manufacturing profits are taxed at 10%. Jerry Jeff sees this as a great idea, given that the alternative is to continue all manufacturing in the United States, where profits are taxed at 34%. Boots plans to continue all the cutting, sizing, and hand tooling of leather in its U.S. plants. This material will be shipped to Ireland for final assembly, with the finished product shipped to retail outlets all over Europe and Asia. Your initial concern is whether the income generated by the Irish subsidiary will be considered foreign base company income. Address this issue in a research memo, along with any planning suggestions.

Partial list of research aids:
§ 954(d).
Reg. § 1.954–3(a).
Bausch & Lomb, 71 TCM 2031, T.C.Memo. 1996–57.

Research Problem 2. NewCar.com, Inc., an innovative, Internet-based automobile retailer based in Ghana, is beginning to seek customers in the United States. Currently, it has no sales personnel or assets located in the United States, but it makes a few sales to U.S. customers based on orders over its website. NewCar.com is considering sending a few sales agents to the United States to set up sales offices in large cities. The offices will have no inventory and will merely provide a place for the sales agents to meet with interested customers. Ghana has no income tax treaty with the United States. How would you advise NewCar.com, Inc., on the tax consequences of its proposed U.S. venture?

DECISION MAKING

Partial list of research aids:
§ 882(a)(1).
Higgins v. Comm., 41–1 USTC ¶9233, 25 AFTR 1160, 61 S.Ct. 475 (1941).
Continental Trading, Inc. v. Comm., 59–1 USTC ¶9316, 3 AFTR 2d 923, 265 F.2d 40 (CA–9, 1959).
Piedras Negras Broadcasting Co., 43 BTA 297 (1941), *aff'd* 127 F.2d 260 (CA–5, 1942).

Use the tax resources of the Internet to address the following questions. Do not restrict your search to the Web, but include a review of newsgroups and general reference materials, practitioner sites and resources, primary sources of the tax law, chat rooms and discussion groups, and other opportunities.

Research Problem 3. Locate data on the size of the international economy, including data on international trade, foreign direct investment by U.S. firms, and investment in the United States by foreign firms. Useful web locations include **www.census.gov** and **www.bea.gov**. Prepare an analysis of the data for a three-year period using spreadsheet and graphing software, and e-mail the results to your instructor.

COMMUNICATIONS

Research Problem 4. The IRS's web page at **www.irs.gov** contains many useful links to publications, tax forms and instructions, and tax revenue statistics. Locate web pages for at least three other countries' taxing authorities. In no more than three PowerPoint slides, show your classmates the web address for each of these pages and describe how these web pages compare with the IRS's page in terms of content and ease of use.

COMMUNICATIONS

Research Problem 5. For your analysis, choose 10 countries, one of which is the United States. Create a table showing whether each country applies a worldwide or territorial approach to international income taxation. Then list the country's top income tax rate on business profits. Send a copy of your table to your instructor.

COMMUNICATIONS

Research Problem 6. Find the text of various tax treaties currently in force in the United States. In an e-mail to your instructor, address the following items.

COMMUNICATIONS

a. How does the U.S. income tax treaty with Germany define "business profits" for multinational businesses?
b. How does the U.S. income tax treaty with Japan treat the branch profits tax?
c. List five countries with which the United States has entered into an estate tax treaty.
d. What is the effective date of the latest income tax treaty with the United Kingdom?

Part 3

Flow-Through Entities

Unlike C corporations, some business entities are taxed under the conduit principle. Generally, this means the tax attributes of various transactions are retained as they flow through the entity to the owners. With limited exceptions, no tax is imposed at the entity level. Part 3 discusses two types of flow-through entities—partnerships and corporations that make the Subchapter S election. Part 3 also integrates the material on corporations (Part 2) with flow-through entities in regard to the decision-making process. By comparing the tax attributes of C corporations, S corporations, and partnerships, the owners are provided with the tools needed to choose the appropriate form for conducting a business.

CHAPTER

10

Partnerships: Formation, Operation, and Basis

LEARNING OBJECTIVES

After completing Chapter 10, you should be able to:

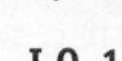

LO.1 Distinguish among the various types of entities treated as partnerships for tax purposes.

LO.2 Describe how partnership income is reported and taxed.

LO.3 Discuss governing principles and theories of partnership taxation.

LO.4 Describe the tax effects of forming a partnership with cash and property contributions.

LO.5 Identify elections available to a partnership, and specify the tax treatment of expenditures of a newly formed partnership.

LO.6 Specify the accounting methods available to a partnership and the methods of determining a partnership's tax year.

LO.7 Calculate partnership taxable income and describe how partnership items affect a partner's income tax return.

LO.8 Determine a partner's basis in the partnership interest.

LO.9 Explain how liabilities affect a partner's basis.

LO.10 Describe the limitations on deducting partnership losses.

LO.11 Describe the treatment of transactions between a partner and the partnership.

LO.12 Provide insights regarding advantageous use of a partnership.

OUTLINE

For the latest in changes to tax legislation, visit **www.cengage.com/taxation/swft.**

THE BIG PICTURE **Tax Solutions for the Real World**

WHY USE A PARTNERSHIP, ANYWAY?

For 15 years, Maria has owned and operated a seaside bakery and café called The Beachsider. Each morning, customers line up on the boardwalk in front of the building and enjoy fresh coffee and croissants while waiting for a table. "The building is too small," Maria commented to her landlord, Kyle. "Is there any way we can expand?" The Beachsider is one of several older buildings on 3 acres of a 10-acre parcel that Kyle's family has owned for years. The remaining 7 acres are undeveloped.

Kyle and Maria talked to Josh, a real estate developer, and he proposed an expansion to The Beachsider and upgrades to the other buildings. The improvements would preserve the character of the original shopping center, and the remaining acreage would be available for future expansion. Kyle and Maria were impressed with Josh's vision and excited about the plans to upgrade the property and expand Maria's business.

The parties agreed to form a partnership to own and operate The Beachsider and to improve and lease the other buildings. Josh summarized the plan as follows: "Kyle and Maria will each contribute one-half of the capital we need. Kyle's real estate is valued at about $2 million. Maria's bakery equipment and the café furnishings are valued at about $500,000. The improvements will cost about $1.5 million, which Maria has agreed to contribute to the partnership."

Josh continued, "You have agreed that I do not need to contribute any capital to the partnership. Instead, I will manage the construction and the operation of the partnership in exchange for 5 percent of the capital and 20 percent of the ongoing profits. My capital interest will be valued at $200,000."

What are the tax consequences if the trio forms Beachside Properties as a partnership to own and operate the shopping center? What issues might arise later in the life of the entity? **Read the chapter and formulate your response.**

10.1 Overview of Partnership Taxation

COMPARISON OF PARTNERSHIPS AND SUBCHAPTER C CORPORATIONS

This chapter and the next two chapters analyze two types of entities that may offer advantages over regular corporations. These entities are partnerships and S corporations, which are called *flow-through* or *pass-through* entities because the owners of the trade or business choose to avoid treating the enterprise as a separate taxable entity. Instead, the owners are taxed on a proportionate share of the entity's taxable income at the end of each of its taxable years.

Often a partnership may provide tax advantages over a C, or regular, corporation. A partnership is subject to only a single level of taxation, while C corporation income is subject to *double taxation.* Corporate income is taxed at the entity level at rates up to 35 percent. Any after-tax income that is distributed to corporate owners as a dividend is taxed again at the owner level. Though partnership income may be subject to high tax rates at the partner level, the resulting tax will generally be lower than a combined corporate-level tax and a second tax on a dividend distribution.

A partnership offers certain planning opportunities not available to other entities. Both C and S corporations are subject to rigorous allocation and distribution requirements. Generally, each income or loss allocation or distribution is proportionate to the ownership interest of each shareholder. A partnership, though, may adjust its allocations of income and cash flow among the partners each year according to their needs, as long as certain standards, discussed later in this chapter, are met. Also, any previously unrealized income of an S or C corporation, such as appreciation of corporate assets, is recognized at the entity level when the corporation liquidates. However, a partnership generally may liquidate tax-free.

TAX *in* *the NEWS*

THE EXTENT OF PARTNERSHIP USAGE

Partnerships come in all flavors and sizes! In less than a decade, the number of U.S. partnerships increased by 50 percent—from about 2 million entities in 2000 to over 3 million entities in 2008. In 2008 (the last year for which data are available), partnership entities owned assets with a combined gross book value of almost $20 trillion. Over 60 percent (almost 1.9 million) of these entities are limited liability companies; the vast majority of the rest are either general partnerships or limited partnerships. The balance includes limited liability partnerships, limited liability limited partnerships, and specialty entities (such as real estate investment trusts, or REITs). (See the discussion of the various types of partnerships on pp. 10-3 and 10-4.)

The "partner mix" is shifting. Corporations are increasingly using the partnership entity form to expand operations or to create joint ventures with other entities. In 2006, for the first time, more than half of partnership income and losses was allocated to corporations.

Partnerships are used in almost every type of industry—from agriculture to health care to waste management. Almost half of all partnerships are engaged in some sort of real estate business. Certain elements of the tax law make partnerships especially appealing for activities such as research and development, and oil and gas exploration and extraction. All kinds of service activities are operated through some sort of partnership (especially limited liability partnerships): partnerships are common in the accounting, law, education, and transportation services industries.

Source: IRS, *Statistics of Income Bulletin*, Fall 2002 and Fall 2010 reports based on 2000 and 2008 filing years.

In addition, administrative and filing requirements are usually relatively simple for a partnership. Many states impose reporting and licensing requirements on corporate entities, including S corporations. These include franchise or capital stock tax returns that may require annual assessments and costly professional preparation assistance.[1] Partnerships, on the other hand, often have no reporting requirements beyond Federal and state informational tax returns.

For smaller business operations, a partnership enables several owners to combine their resources at low cost. It also offers simple filing requirements, the taxation of income only once, and the ability to discontinue operations relatively inexpensively.

For larger business operations, a partnership offers a unique ability to raise capital with low filing and reporting costs compared to, for example, corporate bond issuances. Special allocations of income and cash-flow items may be used by partnerships to meet the objectives of the owners. As described in the accompanying "Tax in the News" feature, partnerships are used in almost every imaginable industry, and use of these entities is on the rise.

This chapter addresses partnership formation and operations. Chapter 11 focuses on dispositions of partnership interests, partnership distributions, and optional basis adjustments. Chapter 12 discusses the taxation of S corporations.

WHAT IS A PARTNERSHIP?

LO.1

Distinguish among the various types of entities treated as partnerships for tax purposes.

A partnership is an association formed by two or more persons to carry on a trade or business, with each contributing money, property, labor, or skill, and with all expecting to share in profits and losses. A "person" can be an individual, trust, estate, corporation, association, or another partnership.[2] For Federal income tax purposes, a partnership includes a syndicate, group, pool, joint venture, or other unincorporated organization through which any business, financial operation, or venture is carried on. The entity must not be otherwise classified as a corporation, trust, or estate.

The types of entities that may be taxed as partnerships include general partnerships, limited partnerships, limited liability partnerships, limited liability limited partnerships, and limited liability companies. These entities are typically

[1]Certain states treat limited liability companies (LLCs) as corporations for purposes of state franchise taxes.

[2]§§ 7701(a)(1) and (2).

distinguished based on the types of business permitted to be conducted by the entity and the extent to which the partners are personally liable for the entity's debts.

- A **general partnership** (GP) consists of two or more partners who are **general partners;** there are no **limited partners.** Creditors of a general partnership can collect from both the partnership's assets and the personal assets of the owner-partners. A general partner can be subject to a malpractice judgment brought against the partnership, even though the partner was not personally involved in the malpractice. General partnerships are used for both operating activities (e.g., product manufacturing or sales) and for service businesses (e.g., accounting, law, or medicine).
- A **limited partnership** (LP) is a partnership with at least one general partner and one or more limited partners. These partnerships often have numerous limited partners and are used to raise capital for real estate development, oil and gas exploration, research and development, and various financial product investment vehicles. Typically, only the general partners are personally liable to creditors; each limited partner's risk of loss is restricted to that partner's equity investment in the entity.
- A **limited liability company** (LLC) combines the corporate benefit of limited liability for the owners with the benefits of partnership taxation, including the single level of tax and special allocations of income, losses, and cash flows. Owners are technically considered to be "members" rather than partners, but a properly structured LLC is generally treated as a partnership for all Federal tax purposes. Almost all states permit capital-intensive companies as well as nonprofessional service-oriented businesses and some professional service-providing companies to operate as LLCs.
- A **limited liability partnership** (LLP) is treated similarly to a general partnership in most states. The primary difference between an LLP and a general partnership is that an LLP partner is not personally liable for any malpractice committed by other partners. The LLP is currently the organizational form of choice for the large accounting firms. LLPs are discussed in more detail in Chapter 11.
- A **limited liability limited partnership** (LLLP) is an extension of the limited partnership form in which all partners, whether general or limited, are accorded limited liability. At this writing, about half of U.S. states permit formation of LLLPs or recognize LLLPs formed in another state. Existing limited partnerships can acquire LLLP status by filing a proper request with the appropriate state jurisdiction.

A partnership is governed by a **partnership agreement**, which should explain the rights and obligations of the partners; the allocation of income, deductions, and cash flows; initial and future capital contribution requirements; conditions for terminating the partnership; and other matters. The governing agreement of an LLC has a similar structure and is known as an **operating agreement**.

EXAMPLE 1
THE BIG PICTURE

Return to the facts of *The Big Picture* on p. 10-2. When Beachside Properties is formed, Kyle, Maria, and Josh must decide which type of partnership to utilize.

With a general partnership, Kyle, Maria, and Josh would each be jointly and severally liable for all entity debts. With a limited partnership, one of the partners would be designated as a general partner and would be liable for all entity debts. Because all three partners want to have limited liability, they decide not to use a general or limited partnership.

They do not consider a limited liability partnership because that entity form is typically reserved for service-providing entities.

With a limited liability company (or, if their state permits, a limited liability limited partnership), each partner's losses will be limited to the partner's contributed capital. Therefore, Kyle, Maria, and Josh decide to form Beachside Properties as an LLC. ■

ELECTIONS RELATED TO PARTNERSHIP STATUS

The IRS's "check-the-box" Regulations allow most unincorporated business entities—such as general partnerships, limited partnerships, LLPs, LLLPs, and LLCs—to select their Federal tax status.[3] If an unincorporated entity has two or more owners, it generally can choose to be taxed as either a partnership or a C corporation. By default, a newly formed noncorporate entity with two or more owners is generally treated as a partnership. Alternatively, the entity may file Form 8832 and "check the box" to elect to be treated as a corporation. This provides the entity with flexibility regarding its Federal tax classification. The Regulations, however, do not permit all unincorporated business or investment entities to choose their tax status. Newly formed publicly traded partnerships, for example, must be taxed as corporations.

A partnership generally may elect out of the partnership taxation rules if it is involved in one of the following activities:

- Investment (rather than the active conduct of a trade or business).
- Joint production, extraction, or use of property.
- Underwriting, selling, or distributing a specific security issue.[4]

If a proper election is made, the partnership is disregarded for Federal tax purposes, and its operations are reported directly on the owners' tax returns. Such elections "out" of partnership status are not common.

TAXATION OF PARTNERSHIP INCOME

LO.2

Describe how partnership income is reported and taxed.

A partnership is not a taxable entity.[5] Rather, the taxable income or loss of the partnership flows through to the partners at the end of the entity's tax year.[6] Partners report their allocable share of the partnership's income or loss for the year on their tax returns. As a result, the partnership itself pays no Federal income tax on its income; instead, the partners' individual tax liabilities are affected by the activities of the entity.

EXAMPLE 2

Adam is a 40% partner in the ABC Partnership. Both Adam's and the partnership's tax years end on December 31. In 2011, the partnership generates $200,000 of ordinary taxable income. However, because the partnership needs capital for expansion and debt reduction, Adam makes no cash withdrawals during 2011. He meets his living expenses by reducing his investment portfolio. Adam is taxed on his $80,000 allocable share of the partnership's 2011 income, even though he received no distributions from the entity during 2011. This allocated income is included in Adam's gross income. ■

EXAMPLE 3

Assume the same facts as in Example 2, except that the partnership recognizes a 2011 taxable loss of $100,000. Adam's $40,000 proportionate share of the loss flows through to him from the partnership, and he can deduct the loss. (Note: Loss limitation rules discussed later in the chapter may result in some or all of this loss being deducted by Adam in a later year.) ■

Many items of partnership income or expense, gain, or loss retain their identity as they flow through to the partners. This separate flow-through of certain items is required because such **separately stated items** *might* affect any two partners' tax liabilities in different ways. When preparing a personal tax return, a partner takes each of these items into account separately.[7] For example, charitable contributions are separately stated because partners need to compute their own personal limitation on charitable contributions. Some partners are able to deduct the entire amount they are allocated. Others are limited in what they can deduct by the amount of their adjusted gross income (AGI).

[3] Reg. §§ 301.7701–1 to –3.
[4] § 761(a).
[5] § 701.
[6] § 702.
[7] § 703(a)(1).

EXAMPLE 4

Brittany is a 25% partner in the BR Partnership. The cash basis entity collected sales income of $60,000 during 2010 and incurred $15,000 in business expenses. In addition, it sold a corporate bond, in June, for a $9,000 long-term capital gain. Finally, the partnership made a $1,000 contribution to the local Performing Arts Fund. The fund is a qualifying charity. BR and all of its partners use a calendar tax year.

For 2010, Brittany is allocated ordinary taxable income of $11,250 [($60,000 − $15,000) × 25%] from the partnership. She also reports her allocated share of the partnership's long-term capital gain ($2,250) and charitable contributions ($250). The ordinary income increases Brittany's gross income. The long-term capital gain and charitable contribution are separately stated because they could be treated differently on her tax return from the way they are treated on the tax returns of the other partners. For example, Brittany may have capital losses to offset the capital gain or may be subject to a percentage limitation on charitable contribution deductions for 2010. Other partners may have no capital losses or percentage limitations on charitable contribution deductions. ■

Typically, a partnership combines income and expenses related to the partnership's trade or business activities into a single income or loss amount that is passed through to the partners. Most other partnership items are separately stated. For example, net income (loss) from rental real estate activities and net short-term capital gains (losses) are each determined at the partnership level and reported separately to the partners.

Other items that are allocated separately to the partners include recognized gains and losses from property transactions; qualified and ordinary dividend income; tax preferences and adjustments for the alternative minimum tax; expenditures that qualify for the foreign tax credit; information the partner needs to calculate the domestic production activities deduction of § 199; and expenditures that the partners would treat as itemized deductions.

PARTNERSHIP REPORTING

Even though it is not a taxpaying entity, a partnership must file an information tax return, Form 1065. This return is due by the fifteenth day of the fourth month following the end of the tax year. For a calendar year partnership, this deadline is April 15. An automatic five-month extension is available (to September 15 for a calendar year partnership). As part of this return, the partnership prepares a **Schedule K–1** for each partner that shows that partner's share of partnership items. Each partner receives a copy of Schedule K–1 for use in preparing the respective tax return.

Look at Form 1065 for 2010 in Appendix B, and refer to it during the following discussion. The ordinary income and expense items generated by the partnership's trade or business activities are netted to produce a single income or loss amount. The partnership reports this ordinary income or loss from its trade or business activities on Form 1065, page 1. Schedule K (page 4 of Form 1065) accumulates all items that must be separately reported to the partners, including net trade or business income or loss (from page 1). The amounts on Schedule K are allocated among the partners on the partners' Schedules K–1.

EXAMPLE 5

The BR Partnership in Example 4 reports its $60,000 sales income on Form 1065, page 1, line 1. The $15,000 of business expenses are reported in the appropriate amounts on page 1, line 2 or lines 9–20. Partnership ordinary income of $45,000 is shown on page 1, line 22, and on Schedule K, line 1. The $9,000 net long-term capital gain and the $1,000 charitable contribution are reported only on Schedule K, on lines 9a and 13a, respectively.

Brittany receives a Schedule K–1 from the partnership that shows her shares of partnership ordinary income of $11,250, long-term capital gain of $2,250, and charitable contributions of $250 on lines 1, 9a, and 13 (Code A), respectively.

She combines these amounts with similar items from sources other than BR in her personal tax return. For example, if she has a $5,000 long-term capital loss from a stock transaction during the year, her overall net capital loss calculated on Schedule D of her 1040 is

$2,750. She evaluates this net amount to determine the amount she may deduct on her Form 1040. She reports the $250 of charitable contributions on her Schedule A. ■

As this example shows, one must look at both page 1 and Schedule K to get complete information regarding a partnership's operations for the year.

The partnership reconciles book income with income reported on the return by preparing Schedule M–1 or Schedule M–3. This reconciliation is similar to the reconciliation between financial (book) and taxable income prepared by a corporation. On the corporate return, taxable income is shown on Form 1120, page 1, and it is reconciled to book income on either Schedule M–1 or Schedule M–3 (see Chapter 2).

For a partnership, book income must be reconciled to the partnership's *equivalent* of taxable income. The partnership prepares the Analysis of Net Income (Loss) (page 5 of Form 1065) to determine the partnership's taxable income equivalent. Certain amounts shown on Schedule K are netted and entered on the Net Income (Loss) line (line 1) of this Analysis. This is the amount to which book income must be reconciled on Schedule M–1 or Schedule M–3.

Schedule M–1 is found on page 5 of Form 1065. Schedule M–3 is a separate three-page form. Schedule M–3 is required in lieu of Schedule M–1 if the partnership has $10 million or more in assets at the end of the year, if it has $35 million of receipts during the year, or if certain other situations exist. In addition, Schedule M–3 is required if a partner owns a 50 percent or more interest in partnership profits, loss, or capital and is required to file its own Schedule M–3. If a partnership is required to file Schedule M–3, it must also answer various questions on Schedule C.

The net taxable income calculated on the Analysis of Net Income (Loss) schedule should agree with the reconciled taxable income on Schedule M–1 (line 9) or the reconciled amount from Schedule M–3, Part II. Schedule L generally shows an accounting-basis balance sheet.

Schedule M–2 reconciles partners' beginning and ending capital accounts. The analysis of capital accounts on Schedule M–2 reflects contributions to and distributions from the partnership as well as the partnership's income, gains, losses, and deductions. Schedule M–2 can be prepared using any of several methods, including the tax basis, generally accepted accounting principles (GAAP), or the "§ 704(b) book" method. The method used on Schedule M–2 should also be used in preparing the partners' Schedules K–1. If this method differs from the method used for the balance sheet (Schedule L), a reconciling schedule should be provided.

CONCEPTUAL BASIS FOR PARTNERSHIP TAXATION

LO.3

Discuss governing principles and theories of partnership taxation.

The unique tax treatment of partners and partnerships can be traced to two legal concepts that evolved long ago: the **aggregate concept** (or conduit) and the **entity concept**. These concepts influence practically every partnership tax rule.

Aggregate (or Conduit) Concept

The aggregate (or conduit) concept treats the partnership as a channel through which income, credits, deductions, and other items flow to the partners. Under this concept, the partnership is regarded as a collection of taxpayers joined in an agency relationship with one another. The imposition of the income tax on individual partners reflects the influence of this doctrine.

Entity Concept

The entity concept treats partners and partnerships as separate units and gives the partnership its own tax "personality" by (1) requiring a partnership to file an information tax return and (2) treating partners as separate and distinct from the partnership in certain transactions between a partner and the entity. A partner's recognition of capital gain or loss on the sale of the partnership interest illustrates this doctrine.

Combined Concepts

Some rules governing the formation, operation, and liquidation of a partnership contain a blend of the entity and aggregate concepts.

PARTNER'S OWNERSHIP INTEREST IN A PARTNERSHIP

In keeping with the aggregate theory, each partner typically owns both a **capital interest** and a **profits (loss) interest** in the partnership. A capital interest is measured by a partner's **capital sharing ratio**, which is the partner's percentage ownership of the capital of the partnership. A partner's capital interest can be determined in several ways. The most widely accepted method measures the capital interest as the percentage of net asset value (asset value remaining after payment of all partnership liabilities) a partner would receive on immediate liquidation of the partnership.

A profits (loss) interest is simply the partner's percentage allocation of current partnership operating results. **Profit and loss sharing ratios** are usually specified in the partnership agreement and are used to determine each partner's allocation of partnership ordinary taxable income and separately stated items.[8] The partnership can change its profit and loss allocations at any time simply by amending the partnership agreement.

Each partner's profit, loss, and capital sharing ratios must appear on the partner's Schedule K–1. In many cases, the three ratios are the same. A partner's capital sharing ratio generally equals the partner's profit and loss sharing ratios if all profit and loss allocations, for each year of the partnership's existence, are in the same proportion as the partner's initial contributions to the partnership. These ratios can differ for a number of reasons, however. For example, a partner may receive an interest in future profits (and no interest in partnership capital) in exchange for services rendered to the partnership. On its website, the IRS has issued answers to "frequently asked questions" (FAQs) about the determination of partners' capital, profit, and loss sharing ratios. As the IRS's responses make clear, many methods are acceptable, provided the method is consistently applied.

The partnership agreement may, in some cases, provide for a **special allocation** of certain items to specified partners, or it may allocate items in a different proportion from general profit and loss sharing ratios. These items are separately reported to the partner receiving the allocation. As indicated in the answers to the FAQs mentioned above, these special allocations should generally be considered in determining the partners' capital, profit, and loss sharing ratios.

For a special allocation to be recognized for tax purposes, it must produce nontax economic consequences to the partners receiving the allocation.[9]

EXAMPLE 6

When the George-Amy Partnership was formed, George contributed cash and Amy contributed some City of Iuka bonds that she had held for investment purposes. The partnership agreement allocates all of the tax-exempt interest income from the bonds to Amy as an inducement for her to remain a partner. This is an acceptable special allocation for income tax purposes; it reflects the differing economic circumstances that underlie the partners' contributions to the capital of the entity. Since Amy would have received the exempt income if she had not joined the partnership, she can retain the tax-favored treatment by means of the special allocation. ■

EXAMPLE 7

Assume the same facts as in Example 6. Three years after it was formed, the George-Amy Partnership purchased some City of Butte bonds. The municipal bond interest income of $15,000 flows through to the partners as a separately stated item, so it retains its tax-exempt status. The partnership agreement allocates all of this income to George because he is subject to a higher marginal income tax bracket than is Amy. The partnership also allocates $15,000 more of the partnership taxable income to Amy than to George. These allocations are not effective for income tax purposes because they have no purpose other than reduction of the partners' combined income tax liability. ■

[8] § 704(a).

[9] § 704(b).

INSIDE AND OUTSIDE BASES

Throughout these chapters, reference is made to the partnership's inside basis and the partners' outside basis. **Inside basis** refers to the adjusted basis of each partnership asset, as determined from the partnership's tax accounts. **Outside basis** represents each partner's basis in the partnership interest. In keeping with the aggregate theory, each partner "owns" a share of the partnership's inside basis for all its assets. In many cases—especially on formation of the partnership—the total of the partnership's inside bases for all of its assets equals the total of all the partners' outside bases in their partnership interests.

Consider a partner's outside basis. When income flows through to a partner from the partnership, the partner's basis in the partnership interest increases. When a loss flows through to a partner, basis is reduced.

EXAMPLE 8

Paul contributes $20,000 cash to acquire a 30% capital and profits interest in the Blue Jay Partnership. In its first year of operations, the partnership earns ordinary income of $40,000 and makes no distributions to Paul. Paul's initial basis is the $20,000 he paid for the interest. He reports ordinary income of $12,000 (30% × $40,000 partnership income) on his individual return and increases his basis by the same amount, to $32,000. ■

The Code provides for the increase and decrease in a partner's basis so that the income or loss from partnership operations is taxed only once. In Example 8, if Paul sold his interest at the end of the first year for $32,000, he would have no gain or loss. If the Code did not provide for an adjustment of a partner's basis, Paul's basis would be $20,000, and he would be taxed on the gain of $12,000 in addition to being taxed on his $12,000 share of income. In other words, without the basis adjustment, partnership income would be subject to double taxation.

Specific rules for calculating the partner's outside basis are discussed later in the chapter. As these discussions indicate, a partner's basis is important for determining the treatment of distributions from the partnership to the partner, establishing the deductibility of partnership losses, and calculating gain or loss on the partner's disposition of the partnership interest.

A partner's basis is not reflected anywhere on the Schedule K–1. Instead, each partner should maintain a personal record of adjustments to basis. As mentioned previously, Schedule K–1 reconciles a partner's capital account, but the ending capital account balance is rarely the same amount as the partner's basis. Just as the tax and accounting bases of a specific asset may differ, a partner's capital account and basis in partnership interest may not be equal for a variety of reasons. For example, a partner's basis includes the partner's share of partnership liabilities; these liabilities are not reported as part of the partner's capital account. The partner's share of partnership liabilities is shown separately in Part II of the Schedule K–1.

ANTI-ABUSE PROVISIONS

As Chapters 10 and 11 reflect, partnership taxation is often flexible. For example, partnership operating income or losses can sometimes be shifted among partners, and partnership capital gains and losses can sometimes be shifted from one partner to another. The Code contains many provisions designed to thwart unwarranted allocations, but the IRS believes opportunities still abound for tax avoidance. As Chapter 11 notes, the IRS has adopted Regulations that allow it to recharacterize transactions that it considers to be "abusive."[10]

Concept Summary 10.1 reviews the general concepts of partnership taxation.

[10]Reg. § 1.701–2.

CONCEPT SUMMARY 10.1

Overview of Partnerships

1. Compared with a Subchapter C corporation, a partnership may offer some advantages, including a single level of taxation, the availability of certain planning opportunities, and simplified administration and reporting.
2. Entities treated as a partnership for tax purposes include general partnerships, limited partnerships, limited liability companies, limited liability partnerships, and limited liability limited partnerships.
3. The various types of partnerships are distinguished based on the types of businesses that can be conducted and the extent to which the partners are liable for entity debts. Both considerations are determined based on state law.
4. Partnership income and losses flow through to the partners and are reported on the partners' tax returns. The partnership reports ordinary income or loss as well as *separately stated items* to the partners. Under certain conditions, items may be *specially allocated* to specified partners.
5. The partnership files Form 1065 as an information return and prepares a Schedule K–1 to report each partner's share of income and deductions.
6. The *entity concept* treats partners and partnerships as separate units. The nature and amount of partnership gains and losses and most partnership tax elections are determined at the partnership level.
7. The *aggregate concept* allows partnership income, gains, losses, credits, deductions, etc., to flow through to the partners for separate tax reporting.
8. Sometimes both the aggregate concept and the entity concept apply to the same transaction, but usually one dominates.
9. A partner has an *outside basis* in the partnership interest. The partnership has an *inside basis* in partnership assets.
10. Each partner has a *profit* and *loss sharing ratio*, which is the partner's share of income and losses. The partner also has a *capital sharing ratio*, which, in general terms, equals the percentage of the partner's rights to partnership property upon liquidation of the partnership.

10.2 FORMATION OF A PARTNERSHIP: TAX EFFECTS

LO.4

Describe the tax effects of forming a partnership with cash and property contributions.

GAIN OR LOSS ON CONTRIBUTIONS TO THE PARTNERSHIP

When a taxpayer transfers property to an entity in exchange for valuable consideration, a taxable exchange normally results. Typically, both the taxpayer and the entity realize and recognize gain or loss on the exchange.[11] The gain or loss recognized by the transferor is the difference between the fair market value of the consideration received and the adjusted basis of the property transferred.[12]

In most situations, however, neither the partner nor the partnership recognizes the gain or loss that is realized when a partner contributes property to a partnership in exchange for a partnership interest. Instead, the realized gain or loss is deferred.[13]

There are two reasons for this nonrecognition treatment. First, forming a partnership allows investors to combine their assets toward greater economic goals than could be achieved separately. Only the form of ownership, rather than the amount owned by each investor, has changed. Requiring that gain be recognized on such transfers would make the formation of some partnerships economically unfeasible. Second, because the partnership interest received is typically not a liquid asset, the partner may not have sufficient cash with which to pay the tax. Thus, deferral of the gain recognizes the economic realities of the business world and follows the wherewithal to pay principle of taxation.

[11] § 1001(c).
[12] § 1001(a).
[13] § 721.

EXAMPLE 9

Alicia transfers two assets to the Wren Partnership on the day the entity is created, in exchange for a 60% profit and loss interest worth $60,000. She contributes cash of $40,000 and retail display equipment (basis to her as a sole proprietor, $8,000; fair market value, $20,000). Since an exchange has occurred between two parties, Alicia *realizes* a $12,000 gain on this transaction. The gain realized is the fair market value of the partnership interest of $60,000 less the basis of the assets that Alicia surrendered to the partnership [$40,000 (cash) + $8,000 (equipment)].

Under § 721, Alicia *does not recognize* the $12,000 realized gain in the year of contribution. This makes sense because, in the exchange, she received only an illiquid partnership interest; she received no cash with which to pay any resulting tax liability. ■

EXAMPLE 10

Assume the same facts as in Example 9, except that the equipment Alicia contributes to the partnership has an adjusted basis of $25,000. She has a $5,000 *realized* loss [$60,000 – ($40,000 + $25,000)], but she cannot deduct the loss. Realized losses, as well as realized gains, are deferred by § 721.

Alternatively, Alicia could have sold the equipment to a third party. This would have allowed her to deduct a $5,000 loss in the year of the sale. Alicia then could have contributed $60,000 cash (including the proceeds from the sale) for her interest in the partnership, and the partnership would have funds to purchase similar equipment. ■

EXAMPLE 11

Five years after the Wren Partnership (Examples 9 and 10) was created, Alicia contributes another piece of equipment to the entity. This property has a basis of $35,000 and a fair market value of $50,000. Alicia will defer the recognition of the $15,000 realized gain. Section 721 is effective whenever a partner makes a contribution to the capital of the partnership. ■

If a partner contributes only capital and § 1231 assets, the partner's holding period in the partnership interest is the same as that partner's holding period for these assets. If cash or assets that are not capital or § 1231 assets are contributed, the holding period in the partnership interest begins on the date the partnership interest is acquired. If multiple assets are contributed, the partnership interest is apportioned, and a separate holding period applies to each portion.

EXCEPTIONS TO § 721

The nonrecognition provisions of § 721 do not apply when

- appreciated stocks are contributed to an investment partnership;
- the transaction is essentially a taxable exchange of properties;
- the transaction is a disguised sale of properties; or
- the partnership interest is received in exchange for services rendered to the partnership by the partner.

Investment Partnership

If the transfer consists of appreciated stocks and securities and the partnership is an investment partnership, it is possible that the realized gain on the stocks and securities will be recognized by the contributing partner at the time of contribution.[14] This provision prevents multiple investors from using the partnership form to diversify their investment portfolios on a tax-free basis. A similar provision, § 351(e), applies to corporations (see Chapter 4).

Exchange

If a transaction is essentially a taxable exchange of properties, tax on the gain is not deferred under the nonrecognition provisions of § 721.[15]

[14] § 721(b).

[15] Reg. § 1.731–1(c)(3).

EXAMPLE 12

Sara owns land, and Brandon owns stock. Sara would like to have Brandon's stock, and Brandon wants Sara's land. If Sara and Brandon both contribute their property to newly formed SB Partnership in exchange for interests in the partnership, the tax on the transaction appears to be deferred under § 721. The tax on a subsequent distribution by the partnership of the land to Brandon and the stock to Sara also appears to be deferred under § 731 (discussed in Chapter 11). Not so! The IRS will disregard the passage of the properties through the partnership and will hold, instead, that Sara and Brandon exchanged the land and stock directly. Thus, the transactions will be treated as any other taxable exchange. ■

Disguised Sale

A similar result occurs in a **disguised sale** of property or of a partnership interest. A disguised sale may occur when a partner contributes appreciated property to a partnership and soon thereafter receives a distribution from the partnership. This distribution may be viewed as a payment by the partnership for purchase of the property.[16]

EXAMPLE 13

Kim transfers property to the KLM Partnership. The property has an adjusted basis of $10,000 and a fair market value of $30,000. Two weeks later, the partnership makes a distribution of $30,000 cash to Kim. Under the distribution rules of § 731, the distribution would not be taxable to Kim if the basis for her partnership interest prior to the distribution was greater than the $30,000 cash distributed. However, the transaction appears to be a disguised purchase-sale transaction, rather than a contribution and distribution. Therefore, Kim must recognize gain of $20,000 on transfer of the property, and the partnership is deemed to have purchased the property for $30,000. ■

A disguised sale of a partnership interest could occur where Partner A contributes property to the partnership and the partnership makes a distribution of the property to Partner B in liquidation of Partner B's interest in the partnership. This transaction may be viewed as a sale of Partner B's partnership interest to Partner A.

Extensive Regulations under § 707 outline situations in which the IRS will presume a disguised sale has occurred. For example, a disguised sale is presumed to exist if both the following occur:

- A contractual agreement requires a contribution by one partner to be followed within two years by a specified distribution from the partnership.
- The distribution is to be made without regard to partnership profits. In other words, the forthcoming distribution is not subject to significant "entrepreneurial risk."

The Regulations also outline situations in which a distribution generally will *not* be deemed to be part of a disguised sale. They include a distribution that occurs more than two years after the property is contributed and a distribution that is deemed "reasonable" in relation to the capital invested by the partner and in relation to distributions made to other partners.

Services

A final exception to the nonrecognition provision of § 721 occurs when a partner receives a capital interest (i.e., liquidation rights) in the partnership as compensation for services rendered to the partnership. This is not a tax-deferred transaction because services are not treated as "property" that can be transferred to a partnership on a tax-free basis. Instead, the partner performing the services recognizes ordinary compensation income equal to the fair market value of the partnership interest received.[17]

[16] § 707(a)(2)(B)

[17] § 83(a).

The partnership may deduct the amount included in the service partner's income if the services are of a deductible nature. If the services are not deductible to the partnership, they must be capitalized to an asset account. For example, architectural plans created by a partner are capitalized as part of the structure built with those plans. Alternatively, day-to-day management services performed by a partner for the partnership are usually deductible by the partnership.

EXAMPLE 14

Bill, Carlos, and Dave form the BCD Partnership, with each receiving a one-third interest in the entity. Dave receives his one-third interest as compensation for tax planning services he will render after the formation of the partnership. The value of a one-third capital interest in the partnership (for each of the parties) is $20,000. Dave recognizes $20,000 of compensation income, and he has a $20,000 basis in his partnership interest. The same result would occur if the partnership had paid Dave $20,000 for his services and he immediately contributed that amount to the entity for a one-third ownership interest. In either case, the partnership will probably be able to deduct $20,000 in calculating its ordinary business income. ■

EXAMPLE 15
THE BIG PICTURE

Return to the facts of *The Big Picture* on p. 10-2. Assume that Kyle has a basis of $600,000 in the $2 million of real estate he contributed and that Maria has a $0 basis in the bakery equipment and the café furnishings.

When Beachside Properties, LLC, is formed, no tax results for the LLC or for Kyle or Maria. Kyle does not recognize his $1.4 million realized gain nor does Maria recognize her $500,000 realized gain.

Kyle takes a substituted basis of $600,000 for his interest, and Maria takes a substituted basis of $1.5 million ($1.5 million for contributed cash + $0 for contributed property). Beachside Properties assumes a carryover basis of $600,000 for the real estate contributed by Kyle and $0 for the property contributed by Maria. To the extent that the buildings and other land improvements are depreciable, the LLC "steps into Kyle's shoes" in calculating depreciation deductions.

Because Josh receives his 5% capital interest in the LLC in exchange for services, the $200,000 is taxable to him. Beachside Properties either capitalizes or expenses the cost of the services, depending on their nature. Josh's 20% profits interest will be taxed to him as profits are allocated to him. ■

TAX ISSUES RELATIVE TO CONTRIBUTED PROPERTY

When a partner makes a tax-deferred contribution of an asset to the capital of a partnership, the tax law assigns a carryover basis to the property.[18] The partnership's basis in the asset (inside basis) is equal to the partner's basis in the property prior to its transfer to the partnership. The partner's outside basis in the new partnership interest is the same as the partner's basis in the contributed asset. The tax term for this basis concept is *substituted basis.* Thus, two assets are created out of one when a partnership is formed, namely, the property in the hands of the new entity and the new asset (the partnership interest) in the hands of the partner. Both assets are assigned a basis that is derived from the partner's basis in the contributed property.

To understand the logic of these rules, consider what Congress was attempting to accomplish with the deferral approach. Recall that gain or loss is deferred when property is contributed to a partnership in exchange for a partnership interest. The basis amounts are the amounts necessary to allow for recognition of the deferred gain or loss if the property or the partnership interest is subsequently disposed of in a taxable transaction. This treatment is similar to the treatment of assets transferred to a controlled corporation[19] and the treatment of like-kind exchanges.[20]

[18] § 723.
[19] § 351.
[20] § 1031.

EXAMPLE 16

On June 1, 2011, Luis transfers property to the JKL Partnership in exchange for a one-third interest in the partnership. The property has an adjusted basis to Luis of $10,000 and a fair market value of $30,000 on June 1. Luis has a $20,000 realized gain on the exchange ($30,000 – $10,000), but under § 721, he does not recognize any of the gain. Luis's basis for his partnership interest is the amount necessary to recognize the $20,000 deferred gain if his partnership interest is subsequently sold for its $30,000 fair market value. This amount, $10,000, is referred to as substituted basis. The basis of the property contributed to the partnership is the amount necessary to allow for the recognition of the $20,000 deferred gain if the property is subsequently sold for its $30,000 fair market value. This amount, also $10,000, is referred to as carryover basis. ■

The holding period for the contributed asset carries over to the partnership. Thus, the partnership's holding period for the asset includes the period during which the partner owned the asset.

Depreciation Method and Period

If depreciable property is contributed to the partnership, the partnership is usually required to use the same cost recovery method and life used by the partner. The partnership merely "steps into the shoes" of the partner and continues the same cost recovery calculations. The partnership may not elect under § 179 to immediately expense any part of the basis of depreciable property it receives from the transferor partner.

Intangible Assets

If a partner contributes an existing "§ 197" intangible asset to the partnership, the partnership generally will "step into the shoes" of the partner in determining future amortization deductions. Section 197 intangible assets include goodwill, going-concern value, information systems, customer- or supplier-related intangible assets, patents, licenses obtained from a governmental unit, franchises, trademarks, covenants not to compete, and other items.

EXAMPLE 17

On September 1, 2009, at a cost of $120,000, James obtained a license to operate a television station from the Federal Communications Commission. The license is effective for 20 years. On January 1, 2011, he contributes the license to the JS Partnership in exchange for a 60% interest. The value of the license is still $120,000 at that time.

The license is a § 197 asset because it is a license with a term greater than 15 years. The cost is amortized over 15 years. James claims amortization for 4 months in 2009 and 12 months in 2010. Thereafter, the partnership steps into James's shoes in claiming amortization deductions. ■

Intangible assets that do not fall under the § 197 rules are amortized over their useful life, if any.[21]

Receivables, Inventory, and Losses

To prevent ordinary income from being converted into capital gain, gain or loss is treated as ordinary when the partnership disposes of either of the following:[22]

- Contributed receivables that were unrealized in the contributing partner's hands at the contribution date. Such receivables include the right to receive payment for goods or services delivered or to be delivered.
- Contributed property that was inventory in the contributor's hands on the contribution date, if the partnership disposes of the property within *five years of the contribution.* For this purpose, inventory includes all tangible property except capital assets and real or depreciable business assets.

[21]Reg. § 1.167(a)–3.

[22]§ 724. For this purpose, § 724(d)(2) waives the holding period requirement in defining § 1231 property.

EXAMPLE 18

Deon operates a cash basis retail electronics store as a sole proprietor. Raul is an enterprising individual who likes to invest in small businesses. On January 2 of the current year, Deon and Raul form the DR Partnership. Their partnership contributions are as follows:

	Adjusted Basis	Fair Market Value
From Deon:		
Receivables	$ -0-	$ 20,000
Land used as parking lot*	12,000	50,000
Inventory	25,000	50,000
From Raul:		
Cash	120,000	120,000

*The parking lot had been held for nine months at the contribution date.

Within 30 days of formation, DR collects the receivables and sells the inventory for $50,000 cash. It uses the land for the next 10 months as a parking lot, then sells it for $35,000 cash. DR realized the following income in the current year from these transactions:

- Ordinary income of $20,000 from collecting receivables.
- Ordinary income of $25,000 from sale of inventory.
- § 1231 gain of $23,000 from sale of land.

Since the land takes a carryover holding period, it is treated as having been held 19 months at the sale date. ■

A similar rule is designed to prevent a capital loss from being converted into an ordinary loss. Under the rule, if contributed property is disposed of at a loss and the property had a "built-in" capital loss on the contribution date, the loss is treated as a capital loss if the partnership disposes of the property *within five years of the contribution*. The capital loss is limited to the amount of the "built-in" loss on the date of contribution.

EXAMPLE 19

Assume the same facts as Example 18, except for the following:

- Deon held the land for investment purposes. It had a fair market value of $8,000 at the contribution date.
- DR used the land as a parking lot for 10 months and sold it for $6,500.

DR realizes the following income and loss from the land contribution and sale transactions:

- Capital loss of $4,000 from sale of the land ($12,000 – $8,000).
- § 1231 loss of $1,500 from sale of the land ($8,000 – $6,500).

Since the land was sold within five years of the contribution date, the $4,000 built-in loss is a capital loss. The postcontribution loss of $1,500 is a § 1231 loss because DR used the property in its business. ■

Concept Summary 10.2 reviews the rules that apply to partnership asset contribution and basis adjustments.

TAX ACCOUNTING ELECTIONS

LO.5

Identify elections available to a partnership, and specify the tax treatment of expenditures of a newly formed partnership.

A newly formed partnership must make numerous tax accounting elections. These elections are formal decisions on how a particular transaction or tax attribute should be handled. Most of these elections must be made by the partnership rather than by the partners individually.[23] The *partnership* makes the elections involving the following items:

[23] § 703(b).

CONCEPT SUMMARY 10.2

Partnership Formation and Initial Basis Computation

1. Generally, partners or partnerships do not recognize gain or loss when property is contributed for capital interests.
2. Partners contributing property for partnership interests take the contributed property's adjusted basis for their *outside basis* in their partnership interest. The partners are said to take a substituted basis in their partnership interest.
3. The partnership will continue to use the contributing partner's basis for the *inside basis* in property it receives. The contributed property is said to take a carryover basis.
4. The holding period of a partner's interest includes that of contributed property when the property was a § 1231 asset or capital asset in the partner's hands. Otherwise, the holding period starts on the day the interest is acquired. The holding period of an interest acquired by a cash contribution starts at acquisition.
5. The partnership's holding period for contributed property includes the contributing partner's holding period.

- Taxable year and accounting method (cash, accrual, or hybrid).
- Inventory method.
- Cost or percentage depletion method, excluding oil and gas wells.
- Cost recovery methods and assumptions.
- Treatment of research and experimentation costs [§§ 174(a) or (b) or § 41 credit, if available].
- Amortization of organizational costs and amortization period.
- Amortization of startup expenditures and amortization period.
- Method of cost allocation under § 199[24] and, for certain partnerships, determination of "qualified production activities income" (QPAI) and production-related wages.
- Optional basis adjustments for property (§ 754, discussed in Chapter 11).
- Section 179 deductions for certain tangible personal property.
- Nonrecognition treatment for involuntary conversion gains.
- Election out of partnership rules.

Each partner is bound by the decisions made by the partnership relative to the elections. If the partnership fails to make an election, a partner cannot compensate for the error by making the election individually.

Though most elections are made by the partnership, each *partner* individually is required to make a specific election on the following relatively narrow tax issues:

- Whether to reduce the basis of depreciable property first when excluding income from discharge of indebtedness.
- Whether to claim cost or percentage depletion for oil and gas wells.
- Whether to take a deduction or a credit for taxes paid to foreign countries and U.S. possessions.

INITIAL COSTS OF A PARTNERSHIP

In its initial stages, a partnership incurs expenses relating to some or all of the following: forming the partnership (organizational costs), admitting partners to the partnership, marketing and selling partnership units to prospective partners (syndication costs), acquiring assets, starting business operations (startup costs), negotiating contracts, and other items. Many of these expenditures are not currently deductible.

[24]Reg. §§ 1.199–4 and 5.

However, the Code permits a deduction or ratable amortization (i.e., straight-line) of "organizational" and "startup" costs; acquisition costs for depreciable assets are included in the initial basis of the acquired assets; and costs related to some intangible assets may be amortized. "Syndication costs" may be neither amortized nor deducted.

Organizational Costs

Organizational costs include expenditures that are (1) incident to the creation of the partnership; (2) chargeable to a capital account; and (3) of a character that, if incident to the creation of a partnership with an ascertainable life, would be amortized over that life. Organizational costs include accounting fees and legal fees connected with the partnership's formation. The expenditures must be incurred within a period that starts a reasonable time before the partnership begins business. The period ends with the due date (without extensions) of the tax return for the initial tax year.

For organizational costs incurred after October 22, 2004, the partnership may elect to deduct up to $5,000 of the costs in the year in which it begins business. This amount must be reduced, however, by the organizational costs that exceed $50,000. Any organizational costs that cannot be deducted under this provision are amortizable over 180 months beginning with the month in which the partnership begins business.[25]

In general, the partnership is deemed to have elected the $5,000 deduction and 180-month amortization treatment simply by deducting the proper amounts on the tax return.[26]

Startup Costs

Startup costs include operating costs that are incurred after the entity is formed but before it begins business. Such costs include marketing surveys prior to conducting business, pre-operating advertising expenses, costs of establishing an accounting system, costs incurred to train employees before business begins, and salaries paid to executives and employees before the start of business.

The partnership may elect to deduct up to $5,000 ($10,000 for tax years beginning in 2010 only) of startup costs in the year in which it begins business. This amount must be reduced, however, by the startup costs that exceed $50,000 ($60,000 for tax years beginning in 2010 only).[27] Costs that are not deductible under this provision are amortizable over 180 months beginning with the month in which the partnership begins business.

As with organizational costs, the partnership, in general, is treated as making a deemed election to deduct and/or amortize these costs simply by treating the amounts as specified in the tax return.[28]

EXAMPLE 20

The calendar year Bluejay Partnership was formed on July 1, 2011, and immediately started business. Bluejay incurred $4,000 in legal fees for drafting the partnership agreement and $2,200 in accounting fees for tax advice of an organizational nature. In addition, the partnership incurred $20,000 of pre-opening advertising expenses and $34,000 of salaries and training costs for new employees before opening for business. The partnership selected the accrual method of accounting and will deduct and amortize organizational and startup costs as permitted under §§ 709 and 195.

Bluejay incurred $6,200 ($4,000 + $2,200) of organizational costs in 2011. The partnership may deduct $5,040 of these costs on its 2011 tax return. This deduction is the sum of the $5,000 permitted deduction and the $40 ($1,200 × 6/180) amortization deduction for the $1,200 of organizational costs that exceed the $5,000 base amount.

Bluejay incurred $54,000 ($20,000 + $34,000) of startup costs in 2011. The partnership may deduct $2,767 of these costs on its tax return for 2011. This deduction is the sum of

[25] § 709.

[26] Reg. § 1.709–1T. This Regulation is scheduled to expire in July 2011. If it is not finalized or extended, a formal election to amortize organizational costs will be required after that date.

[27] §§ 195(b)(1) and (b)(3).

[28] Reg. § 1.195–1T. This Regulation is scheduled to expire in July 2011. If it is not finalized or extended, a formal election to amortize startup costs will be required after that date.

- $5,000 reduced by the $4,000 ($54,000 – $50,000) amount by which the startup costs exceed $50,000.
- $1,767 ($53,000 × 6/180) amortization of the remaining $53,000 ($54,000 – $1,000) of startup costs for 6 months. ■

Acquisition Costs of Depreciable Assets

Expenditures may be incurred in changing the legal title in which certain assets are held from that of the contributing partner to the partnership name. These costs include legal fees incurred to transfer assets and transfer taxes imposed by some states. Such costs are added to the partnership's basis for the depreciable assets and increase the amount the partnership may depreciate. As mentioned earlier, the partnership typically determines its depreciation deductions by "stepping into the shoes" of the contributing partner. If additional costs are incurred, though, the additional basis is treated as a new MACRS asset, placed in service on the date the cost is incurred (e.g., the date the asset is transferred to the partnership).

Syndication Costs

Syndication costs are capitalized, but no amortization election is available. Syndication costs include the following expenditures incurred for promoting and marketing partnership interests:

- Brokerage fees.
- Registration fees.
- Legal fees paid for security advice or advice on the adequacy of tax disclosures in the prospectus or placement memo for securities law purposes.
- Accounting fees related to offering materials.
- Printing costs of prospectus, placement memos, and other selling materials.

LO.6

Specify the accounting methods available to a partnership and the methods of determining a partnership's tax year.

METHOD OF ACCOUNTING

Like a sole proprietorship, a newly formed partnership may adopt either the cash or the accrual method of accounting, or a hybrid of these two methods.

However, a few special limitations on cash basis accounting apply to partnerships.[29] The cash method of accounting may not be adopted by a partnership that

- has one or more C corporation partners or
- is a tax shelter.

A C corporation partner does *not* preclude cash basis treatment if

- the partnership meets the $5 million gross receipts test described below,
- the C corporation partner(s) is a qualified personal service corporation, such as an incorporated attorney, or
- the partnership is engaged in the business of farming.

A partnership meets the $5 million gross receipts test if it has not received average annual gross receipts of more than $5 million for all tax years beginning after December 31, 1985. "Average annual gross receipts" is the average of gross receipts for the three tax years ending with the tax period prior to the tax year in question. For new partnerships, the period of existence is used. Gross receipts are annualized for short taxable periods. A partnership must change to the accrual method the first year after the year in which its average annual gross receipts exceed $5 million and must use the accrual method thereafter.

A tax shelter is a partnership whose interests have been sold in a registered offering or a partnership in which 35 percent of the losses are allocated to limited partners.

[29] § 448

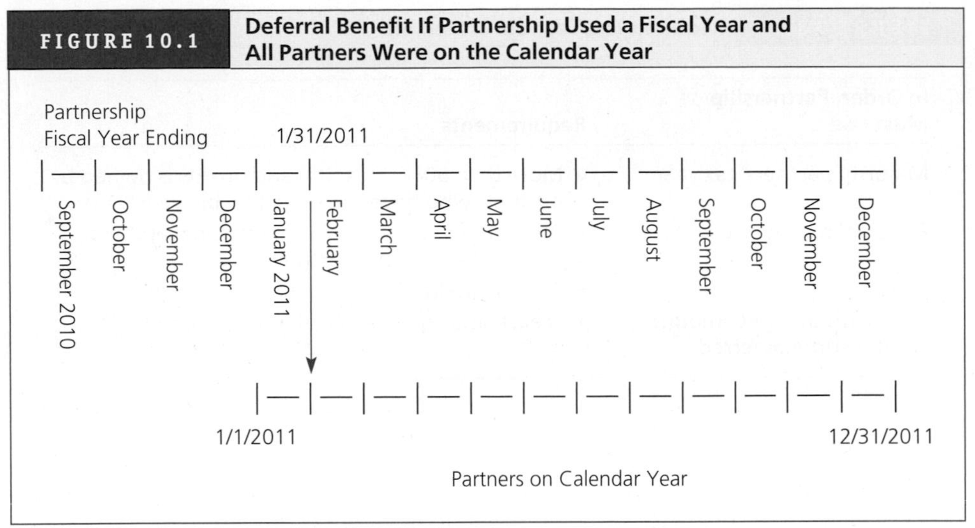

FIGURE 10.1 Deferral Benefit If Partnership Used a Fiscal Year and All Partners Were on the Calendar Year

EXAMPLE 21

Jason and Julia are both attorneys. In 2008, each of them formed a professional personal service corporation to operate their separate law practices. In 2011, the two attorneys decide to form the JJ Partnership, which consists of the two professional corporations. In 2011, JJ's gross receipts are $6 million. JJ may adopt the cash method of accounting, as it is a partnership consisting of qualified personal service corporations. Because JJ has no C corporate partners that are not personal service corporations, the cash method is available even though JJ's average annual gross receipts are greater than $5 million. JJ may also adopt the accrual method of accounting or a hybrid of the cash and accrual methods. ■

TAXABLE YEAR OF THE PARTNERSHIP

Partnership taxable income (and any separately stated items) flows through to each partner at the end of the *partnership's* taxable year. A *partner's* taxable income, then, includes the distributive share of partnership income for any *partnership* taxable year that ends within the partner's tax year.

When all partners use the calendar year, it would be beneficial in present value terms for a profitable partnership to adopt a fiscal year ending with January 31. Why? As Figure 10.1 illustrates, when the adopted year ends on January 31, the reporting of income from the partnership and payment of related taxes can be deferred for up to 11 months. For instance, income earned by the partnership in September 2010 is not taxable to the partners until January 31, 2011. It is reported in the partner's tax return for the year ended December 31, 2011, which is not due until April 15, 2012. Even though each partner may be required to make quarterly estimated tax payments, some deferral is still possible.

Required Taxable Years

To prevent excessive deferral of taxation of partnership income, Congress and the IRS have adopted a series of rules that prescribe the *required* taxable year an entity must adopt if no alternative tax years (discussed on the next page) are selected.

Three rules are presented in Figure 10.2.[30] The partnership must consider each rule in order. The partnership's required taxable year is the taxable year determined under the first rule that applies. The partnership uses the tax year of the "majority partners" if partners owning more than 50 percent of partnership capital and profits have the same tax year. The partnership uses the tax year of the "principal partners" if all partners who own 5 percent or more of capital or profits have the same tax year.

[30]§ 706(b).

FIGURE 10.2 Required Tax Year of Partnership

In Order, Partnership Must Use	Requirements
Majority partners' tax year	• More than 50% of capital *and* profits is owned by partners who have the same taxable year.
Principal partners' tax year	• All partners who own 5% or more of capital *or* profits are principal partners. • All principal partners must have the same tax year.
Year with smallest amount of income deferred	• "Least aggregate deferral rule" (Example 22).

If no year-end is determined under either of these tests, the partnership determines a year under the **least aggregate deferral rule**. Under this rule, the partnership tests the year-ends that are used by the various partners to determine the weighted-average deferral of partnership income. The year-end that offers the least amount of deferral is the *required tax year* under this rule.

EXAMPLE 22

Anne and BonnieCo are equal partners in the AB Partnership. Anne uses the calendar year, and BonnieCo uses a fiscal year ending August 31. Neither Anne nor BonnieCo is a majority partner as neither owns more than 50%. Although Anne and BonnieCo are both principal partners, they do not have the same tax year. Therefore, the general rules indicate that the partnership's required tax year must be determined by the "least aggregate deferral rule." The following computations support August 31 as AB's tax year, because the 2.0 product using that year-end is less than the 4.0 product when December 31 is used.

Test for 12/31 Year-End

Partner	Year Ends	Profit Interest		Months of Deferral		Product
Anne	12/31	50%	×	–0–	=	0.0
BonnieCo	8/31	50%	×	8	=	4.0
Aggregate number of deferral months						4.0

Test for 8/31 Year-End

Partner	Year Ends	Profit Interest		Months of Deferral		Product
Anne	12/31	50%	×	4	=	2.0
BonnieCo	8/31	50%	×	–0–	=	0.0
Aggregate number of deferral months						2.0

■

Alternative Tax Years

If the required tax year is undesirable to the entity, three other alternative tax years may be available:

- Establish to the IRS's satisfaction that a *business purpose* exists for a different tax year. This will typically be a "natural business year" (as defined)[31] that ends following a peak season or shortly thereafter.
- Elect a tax year so that taxes on partnership income are deferred for not more than *three months* from the *required* tax year.[32] Then, have the

[31] Rev.Proc. 2006–46, 2006–2 C.B. 859, § 5.07.

[32] § 444.

partnership maintain with the IRS a prepaid, non-interest-bearing deposit of estimated deferred taxes.[33] This alternative may not be desirable as the deposit is based on the highest individual tax rate plus one percentage point.
- Elect a 52- to 53-week taxable year that ends with reference to the required taxable year or to the taxable year elected under the three-month deferral rule.

10.3 Operations of the Partnership

LO.7

Calculate partnership taxable income and describe how partnership items affect a partner's income tax return.

An individual, corporation, trust, estate, or another partnership can become a partner in a partnership. Since a partnership is a tax-reporting, rather than a taxpaying, entity for purposes of its Federal (and state) income tax computations, the partnership's income, deductions, credits, and alternative minimum tax (AMT) preferences and adjustments can ultimately be reported and taxed on any of a number of income tax returns (e.g., Forms 1040 [individuals], 1041 [fiduciaries, see Chapter 20], 1120 [C corporations], and 1120S [S corporations]).

A partnership is subject to all other taxes in the same manner as any other business. Thus, the partnership files returns and pays the outstanding amount of pertinent sales taxes and property taxes. For employees (not partners), the partnership files returns and pays Social Security, unemployment, and other payroll taxes.

MEASURING AND REPORTING INCOME

The partnership's Form 1065 organizes and reports the transactions of the entity for the tax year. Each of the partnership's tax items is reported on Schedule K of that return. Each partner receives a Schedule K–1 that reports the partner's allocable share of partnership income, credits, and preferences for the year. The IRS also receives a copy of each K–1.

Income Measurement

The measurement and reporting of partnership income require a two-step approach. Certain items must be netted at the partnership level, and other items must be segregated and reported separately on the partnership return and each partner's Schedule K–1.

Among the many income and deduction items passed through separately are the following:

- Net short-term and net long-term capital gains or losses.
- Section 1231 gains and losses.
- Charitable contributions.
- Portfolio income items (qualified and ordinary dividends, interest, and royalties).
- Expenses related to portfolio income.
- Immediately expensed tangible personal property (§ 179).
- Items allocated among the partners in a different ratio from the general profit and loss ratio.
- Recovery of items previously deducted (tax benefit items).
- Guaranteed payments, discussed later in the chapter.
- Passive activity items, such as rental real estate income or loss.
- Intangible drilling and development costs.
- Taxes paid to foreign countries and U.S. possessions.[34]

The reason for separately reporting the preceding items is rooted in the aggregate or conduit concept. These items affect various exclusions, deductions, and credits at the partner level and must pass through without loss of identity so that the proper tax for each partner may be determined.[35]

[33] § 7519.

[34] § 702(a).

[35] § 702(b).

In addition, the partnership must report any information the partner needs in order to prepare a complete and accurate income tax return. This information includes the partner's share of the following:

- Information necessary to calculate the domestic production activities deduction (§ 199), such as qualified production activities income (QPAI) and W–2 wages (discussed later in the chapter).
- AMT preferences and adjustments, for use in calculating the partner's alternative minimum tax.
- Self-employment income, for use in calculating the partner's self-employment tax.
- Foreign-source income, for use in calculating the partner's foreign tax credits.

A partnership is not allowed the following deductions:

- Net operating losses (NOLs).
- Depletion of oil and gas interests.
- Dividends received deduction.

In addition, items that are only allowed by legislative grace to individuals, such as standard deductions or personal exemptions, are not allowed to the partnership. Also, if a partnership makes a payment on behalf of a partner, such as for alimony, medical expenses, or other items that constitute itemized deductions to individuals, the partnership treats the payment as a distribution or guaranteed payment (discussed later) to the partner, and the partner determines whether to claim the deduction.

EXAMPLE 23
THE BIG PICTURE

Return to the facts of *The Big Picture* on p. 10-2. In its second year of operations, Beachside Properties, LLC, reports income and expenses from operating the café as well as rent income and expenses from leasing the other buildings. Beachside's activities are summarized as follows:

Sales revenue	$600,000
Cost of sales	200,000
Salaries to employees	100,000
Cost recovery deductions	60,000
Utilities, supplies, and repairs	40,000
Taxes and licenses (including payroll taxes)	20,000
Contribution to art museum	6,000
Short-term capital gain	12,000
Net income from rental real estate	300,000
Qualified dividends received	4,000
Exempt income (bond interest)	2,100
AMT adjustment (cost recovery)	5,000
Payment of medical expenses on behalf of partner Kyle	4,000

The LLC experienced a $20,000 net loss from operations last year, its first year of business.

Refer to Form 1065 in Appendix B. Beachside's ordinary income is determined and reported on the partnership return as follows:

Nonseparately Stated Items (Ordinary Income)—Form 1065, Pages 1 and 4	
Sales revenue	$600,000
Cost of sales	(200,000)
Salaries to employees	(100,000)
Cost recovery deductions	(60,000)
Utilities, supplies, and repairs	(40,000)
Taxes and licenses (including payroll taxes)	(20,000)
Ordinary income (Form 1065, page 1, line 22, and Form 1065, page 4 [Schedule K], line 1)	$180,000

Beachside's separately stated income and deduction items are:

Separately Stated Income and Deductions (Schedule K)	
Net income from rental real estate (Line 2)	$300,000
Qualified dividends received (Line 6)	4,000
Short-term capital gain (Line 9a)	12,000
Contribution to art museum (Line 13a)	6,000

Beachside is not a allowed a deduction for last year's $20,000 NOL—this item was passed through to the LLC members in the previous year. Moreover, the LLC is not allowed a deduction for payment of Kyle's medical expenses. This payment is probably handled as a distribution to Kyle, who may report it as a medical expense on his Schedule A in determining his itemized deductions. The AMT adjustment is not a separate component of the LLC's income, and it must be reported by Beachside's members so that they can properly calculate any AMT liability.

The LLC reports the following additional information that the partners must report or utilize in preparing their tax returns:

Additional Information (Schedule K)	
AMT adjustment—cost recovery (Line 17a)	$5,000
Tax-exempt income—bond interest (Line 18a)	2,100

■

EXAMPLE 24
THE BIG PICTURE

Continue with the facts in Example 23, but now consider the book-tax reconciliation. Beachside Properties, LLC, must prepare the Analysis of Income (Loss) and Schedule M–1 on Form 1065, page 5. In preparing these schedules, the LLC combines the ordinary income of $180,000 and the four separately stated income and deduction amounts in Example 23 to arrive at "net income" of $490,000. This amount is shown on line 1 of the Analysis of Income (Loss) and is the amount to which book income is reconciled on Schedule M–1, line 9. ■

EXAMPLE 25
THE BIG PICTURE

Assume the same facts as in Example 23, but now consider the effect of the LLC's operations on one of its members. Maria, a 40% owner, will receive a Schedule K–1 from Beachside Properties, on which she is allocated a 40% share of ordinary income and separately stated items. Thus, on her Form 1040, Maria includes $72,000 of ordinary income, a $2,400 charitable contribution, a $4,800 short-term capital gain, $120,000 of passive rent income, and $1,600 of qualified dividend income.

Maria will disclose her $840 share of tax-exempt interest on the first page of Form 1040. In determining her AMT liability (if any), Maria will take into account a $2,000 positive adjustment. ■

Domestic Production Activities Deduction (§ 199)

As noted in Chapter 3, the conduct of certain businesses, usually manufacturing activities, can yield a domestic production activities deduction (DPAD). To determine the base for the deduction, domestic production gross receipts (DPGR) is first computed and then is reduced by related cost of goods sold and direct and indirect expenses to arrive at qualified production activities income (QPAI). The deduction (or DPAD) is 9 percent (6 percent in 2007 to 2009) of the lesser of QPAI or taxable income.[36] (Starting in 2010, lower rates apply for oil-related production activities.)

[36] § 199(a).

GLOBAL
Tax Issues

Various Withholding Procedures Applicable to Foreign Partners

A U.S. partnership may have foreign partners, and these partners will be taxed on their U.S. income. Because it might be difficult for the IRS to collect the tax owed by such foreign partners, several Code sections provide for various withholding procedures. The procedures differ depending on whether the income is "effectively connected with a U.S. trade or business," derived from investment property, or related to real estate transactions.

If the partnership purchases real property from a foreign seller, for example, the partnership is required to withhold 10 percent of the purchase price. If a partnership sells a U.S. real property interest, it must typically withhold 35 percent of the gain allocated to a foreign partner. Further, if the partnership receives "fixed and determinable annual or periodic payments" (FDAP), such as dividends, interest, or rents, it is required to withhold 30 percent of the amounts paid to any foreign person. (The 30 percent withholding rate is often reduced to a lower rate by a tax treaty between the United States and the foreign country.)

Finally, under Regulations issued in 2005 and 2008, if the partnership has U.S. business income, it must withhold and pay an amount equal to the highest U.S. tax rate applicable to the foreign taxpayer's allocable share of partnership income less certain certified losses and deductions. For a foreign individual or corporate partner, the partnership would generally withhold 35 percent of any amounts related to a U.S. business.

When the taxpayer is not a corporation, modified AGI is substituted for taxable income. In no event, however, may the DPAD exceed 50 percent of the W–2 wages paid that are attributable to domestic production activities.[37]

When pass-through entities are involved (i.e., partnerships, S corporations, estates, and trusts), special rules apply.[38] Specifically, in the case of partnerships, the following rules govern the DPAD computation and allowance:

- Whether an activity qualifies for the DPAD is determined at the entity level. The actual deduction is determined at the partner level.
- For many types of partnerships, QPAI and W–2 wages related to production can be calculated at the entity level.[39] Unless otherwise indicated, assume throughout this chapter that the entity-level calculation applies.
- The partnership calculates QPAI by taking into account all separately stated and nonseparately stated items. Income and deduction inclusion and limitations are, for this purpose, determined at the partnership level.
- The Regulations outline specific methods for allocating costs between production-related and non-production-related activities. An "eligible § 861 partnership" must use the § 861 method, as defined. An "eligible widely held pass-through entity" must use the "simplified deduction method." An "eligible small pass-through entity" must use the "small business simplified overall method."
- On Schedule K–1, each partner is allocated his or her share of QPAI and W–2 wages related to domestic production activities (or additional information if the § 861 method is used). The entity allocates QPAI among the partners using the allocation method used for gross income. The entity allocates W–2 production-related wages among the partners using the allocation method used for allocating wage expense.

[37] § 199(b).

[38] The rules applicable to pass-through entities are contained in § 199(d)(1) and Reg. § 1.199–5.

[39] Rev.Proc. 2007–34, 2007–1 C.B. 1345.

- An individual partner will list this pass-through information on Form 8903 (Domestic Production Activities Deduction).
- A partner combines the partnership pass-through items with those from other sources (e.g., a partner has his or her own factory).
- Guaranteed payments made by a partnership to a partner are not considered to be W–2 wages for DPAD purposes.

EXAMPLE 26

For tax year 2011, the BR Partnership had QPAI of $200,000 and W–2 wages related to QPAI of $37,500. Brian is a 40% partner in BR and, as such, is allocated QPAI of $80,000 and W–2 wages of $15,000. If Brian's modified AGI (before the DPAD) is $160,000, his DPAD is determined as follows: 9% × the lesser of $80,000 (QPAI) or $160,000 (MAGI), or $7,200. This amount cannot exceed 50% of Brian's allocable share of W–2 wages, or $7,500 (50% × $15,000). Brian's DPAD, reported as an above-the-line deduction on his Form 1040, is $7,200; the amount is not reduced by the W–2 wages paid limitation. ■

EXAMPLE 27

Assume the same facts as in Example 26, except that Brian also earns income from a qualified production activity he conducts individually (i.e., apart from the partnership). This activity generates QPAI of $60,000, but there are no W–2 wages—Brian uses contract labor (independent contractors). Now the DPAD calculation is 9% of the lesser of $140,000 ($60,000 + $80,000), or $160,000 (MAGI), or $12,600. But because the wage limitation remains the same (see computation in Example 26), Brian's DPAD is limited to $7,500. ■

Withdrawals

Capital withdrawals by partners during the year do not affect the partnership's income measuring and reporting process. These items usually are treated as distributions made on the last day of the partnership's tax year. Distributions are discussed in Chapter 11.

Penalties

A partner's share of each partnership item should be reported on the partner's tax return in the same manner as presented on the Form 1065. If a partner treats an item differently, the IRS must be notified of the inconsistent treatment.[40] If a partner fails to notify the IRS, a negligence penalty may be added to the tax due.

To encourage the filing of a partnership return, a penalty of $195, per partner, per month (or fraction thereof, but not to exceed 12 months) is imposed on the partnership for failure to file a complete and timely information return without reasonable cause.[41]

A "small partnership" with 10 or fewer partners who are individuals (other than nonresident aliens), corporations, or an estate of a partner is exempt from these penalties.[42]

PARTNERSHIP ALLOCATIONS

Economic Effect

As shown by the example of Beachside Properties in *The Big Picture,* a partnership agreement or an LLC's operating agreement can provide that any partner may share capital, profits, and losses in different ratios. For example, a partner could have a 25 percent capital sharing ratio, yet be allocated 30 percent of the profits and 20 percent of the losses of the partnership. Such special allocations have, at times, been used in an attempt to manipulate the allocation of tax benefits among partners. The Regulations[43] are designed to prevent unfair use of such manipulation. Although these rules are too complex to discuss in detail, the general outline of one of these rules—the **economic effect test**—can be easily understood.

[40] § 6222.
[41] § 6698.
[42] § 6231(a)(1)(B).
[43] Reg. § 1.704–1(b).

In general, the economic effect test requires the following:

- An allocation of income or gain to a partner must increase the partner's capital account, and an allocation of deduction or loss must decrease the partner's capital account.
- When the partner's interest is liquidated, the partner must receive net assets that have a fair market value equal to the positive balance in the capital account.
- A partner with a negative capital account must restore that account upon liquidation of the interest. Restoration of a negative capital account can best be envisioned as a contribution of cash to the partnership equal to the negative balance.

These requirements are designed to ensure that a partner bears the economic burden of a loss or deduction allocation and receives the economic benefit of an income or gain allocation.

EXAMPLE 28

Eli and Sanjay each contribute $20,000 cash to the newly formed ES Partnership. The partnership uses the cash to acquire a depreciable asset for $40,000. The partnership agreement provides that the depreciation is allocated 90% to Eli and 10% to Sanjay. Other items of partnership income, gain, loss, or deduction are allocated equally between the partners. Upon liquidation of the partnership, property will be distributed to the partners in accordance with their positive capital account balances. Any partner with a negative capital account must restore the capital account upon liquidation. Assume the first-year depreciation on the equipment is $4,000. Also, assume nothing else happens in the first year that affects the partners' capital accounts.

Eli's capital account is $16,400 ($20,000 – $3,600), and Sanjay's capital account has a balance of $19,600 ($20,000 – $400) after the first year of partnership operations. The Regulations require that a hypothetical sale of the asset for its $36,000 adjusted basis on the last day of the year and an immediate liquidation of the partnership should result in Eli and Sanjay receiving distributions equal to their capital accounts. According to the partnership agreement, Eli would receive $16,400, and Sanjay would receive $19,600 of the cash in a liquidating distribution. Eli, therefore, bears the economic burden of $3,600 depreciation since he contributed $20,000 to the partnership and would receive only $16,400 upon liquidation. Likewise, Sanjay's economic burden is $400 since he would receive only $19,600 of his original $20,000 investment. The agreement, therefore, has economic effect. ■

EXAMPLE 29

Assume the same facts as in Example 28, except that the partnership agreement provides that Eli and Sanjay will receive equal amounts of cash upon liquidation of the partnership. The hypothetical sale of the asset for its $36,000 adjusted basis and the immediate liquidation of the partnership would result in each partner receiving $18,000 cash. Since each partner contributed $20,000 to the partnership and each partner would receive $18,000 upon liquidation, each partner bears the economic burden of $2,000 of depreciation. The original 90%/10% allocation of depreciation to the two partners is defective, and the IRS will require that the depreciation be reallocated equally ($2,000 each) to the two partners to reflect the economic burden borne by each partner. ■

Precontribution Gain or Loss

Certain income, gain, loss, and deductions relative to contributed property may not be allocated under the rules described above. Instead, **precontribution gain or loss** must be allocated among the partners to take into account the variation between the basis of the property and its fair market value on the date of contribution.[44] The partnership keeps track of these differences in its "§ 704(b) book" accounting records. For nondepreciable property, *built-in* gain or loss on the date of contribution must be allocated to the contributing partner when the property is eventually disposed of by the partnership in a taxable transaction. If the property is depreciable, Regulations describe allowable methods of allocating depreciation deductions.[45]

[44] § 704(c)(1)(A).

[45] Reg. § 1.704–3.

EXAMPLE 30
THE BIG PICTURE

Return to the facts of *The Big Picture* on p. 10-2. When Beachside Properties, LLC, was formed, Kyle contributed property valued at $2 million with a basis of $600,000. Maria contributed equipment and furnishings with a $0 basis and a $500,000 value. For § 704 (b) book accounting purposes, Beachside records the land and other properties at their fair market values. For tax purposes, the LLC takes carryover bases in the properties. The LLC must keep track of the differences between the basis in each property and the value at the contribution date. If any of this property is sold, the gain must be allocated to the contributing partner to the extent of any previously unrecognized built-in gain.

For example, if Beachside sells the land contributed by Kyle for $2.3 million, the gain would be calculated and allocated as follows:

	§ 704 (b) Book	Tax
Amount realized	$2,300,000	$2,300,000
Less: Adjusted basis	2,000,000	600,000
Gain realized	$ 300,000	$1,700,000
Built-in gain to Kyle	–0–	1,400,000
Remaining gain (allocated proportionately)	$ 300,000	$ 300,000

For tax purposes, Kyle would recognize $1,520,000 of the gain [($300,000 × 40%) + $1,400,000]; Maria would recognize $120,000 ($300,000 × 40%); and Josh would recognize $60,000 ($300,000 × 20%). ■

If contributed property has built-in losses at the contribution date, allocations related to the built-in loss can be made only to the contributing partner. For purposes of allocations to other partners, the partnership's basis in the loss property is treated as being the fair market value of the property at the contribution date.[46]

Concept Summary 10.3 reviews the tax reporting rules for partnership activities.

BUILT-IN APPRECIATION ON CONTRIBUTED PROPERTY

In the "old days," one partner could contribute cash and another partner could contribute an equal value of appreciated property with no subsequent record-keeping requirements. Future depreciation deductions and gains on sale of the property could be allocated to both partners equally, thereby shifting income from one taxpayer to another. A partner in a lower tax bracket (or with expiring net operating losses and the like) could report the share of the gain on sale of the asset with a relatively low corresponding tax burden.

Section 704(c)(1)(A) was added to the Code to ensure that the partner contributing the property pays tax on any built-in gain. This prevents income shifting among taxpayers and loss of revenue to the IRS.

There is no corresponding provision for S corporations—gains and losses and depreciation expense are allocated among the shareholders without regard to any built-in appreciation on contributed property.

What theory of partnership taxation supports this difference in treatment?

BASIS AND CAPITAL ACCOUNT FOR A PARTNERSHIP INTEREST

LO.8

Determine a partner's basis in the partnership interest.

Previously, this chapter discussed how to compute a partner's adjusted basis when the partnership is formed. It was noted that the partner's adjusted basis in the newly formed partnership usually equals (1) the adjusted basis in any property contributed to the partnership plus (2) the fair market value of any services the partner performed for the partnership (i.e., the amount of ordinary income reported by the partner for services rendered to the partnership).

[46] § 704(c)(1)(C).

CONCEPT SUMMARY 10.3

Tax Reporting of Partnership Activities

Event	Partnership Level	Partner Level
1. Compute partnership ordinary income or loss.	Form 1065, line 22, page 1. Schedule K, Form 1065, line 1, page 4.	Schedule K–1 (Form 1065), line 1. Each partner's share is passed through for separate reporting. Some amounts may be specially allocated to specific partners. For income: Each partner's basis is increased. For losses: Each partner's basis is decreased • The amount of a partner's loss deduction may be limited. • Losses that may not be deducted are carried forward for use in future years.
2. Separately reported income and deduction items like portfolio income, capital gain and loss, and § 179 deductions.	Schedule K, Form 1065, various lines, page 4.	Schedule K–1 (Form 1065), various lines. Each partner's share of each item is passed through for separate reporting.
3. Net earnings from self-employment (see p. 10-40).	Schedule K, Form 1065, line 14, page 4.	Schedule K–1 (Form 1065), line 14.
4. Additional calculations that partner is required to make (e.g., AMT, foreign tax credits).	Schedule K, Form 1065, various lines, page 4.	Schedule K–1 (Form 1065), various lines. Each partner's share of each item is passed through and considered in various calculations.

A partnership interest also can be acquired after the partnership has been formed. The method of acquisition controls how the partner's initial basis is computed. If the partnership interest is purchased from another partner, the purchasing partner's basis is the amount paid (cost basis) for the partnership interest. The basis of a partnership interest acquired by gift is the donor's basis for the interest plus, in certain cases, some or all of the transfer (gift) tax paid by the donor. The basis of a partnership interest acquired through inheritance generally is the fair market value of the interest on the date the partner dies.

After the partner is admitted to the partnership, the partner's basis is adjusted for numerous items. The following operating results *increase* a partner's adjusted basis:

- The partner's proportionate share of partnership income (including capital gains and tax-exempt income).
- The partner's proportionate share of any increase in partnership liabilities. (This provision is discussed in the next section.)

The following operating results *decrease* the partner's adjusted basis in the partnership:

- The partner's proportionate share of partnership deductions and losses (including capital losses).
- The partner's proportionate share of nondeductible expenses.
- The partner's proportionate share of any reduction in partnership liabilities.[47]

[47] §§ 705 and 752.

Under no circumstances can the partner's adjusted basis for the partnership interest be reduced below zero.

Increasing the adjusted basis for the partner's share of partnership taxable income is logical since the partner has already been taxed on the income. By increasing the partner's basis, this ensures that the partner is not taxed again on the income when he or she sells the interest or receives a distribution from the partnership.

It is also logical that the tax-exempt income should increase the partner's basis. If the income is exempt in the current period, it should not contribute to the recognition of gain when the partner either sells the interest or receives a distribution from the partnership.

EXAMPLE 31

Tyler is a one-third partner in the TUV Partnership. His proportionate share of the partnership income during the current year consists of $20,000 of ordinary taxable income and $10,000 of tax-exempt income. None of the income is distributed to Tyler. The adjusted basis of Tyler's partnership interest before adjusting for his share of income is $35,000, and the fair market value of the interest before considering the income items is $50,000.

The unrealized gain inherent in Tyler's investment in the partnership is $15,000 ($50,000 − $35,000) before adjusting for his share of income. Tyler's proportionate share of the income items should increase the fair market value of the interest to $80,000 ($50,000 + $20,000 + $10,000). By increasing the adjusted basis of Tyler's partnership interest to $65,000 ($35,000 + $20,000 + $10,000), this ensures that the unrealized gain inherent in Tyler's partnership investment remains at $15,000. This makes sense because the $20,000 of ordinary taxable income is taxed to Tyler this year and should not be taxed again when Tyler either sells his interest or receives a distribution. Similarly, the exempt income is exempt this year and should not increase Tyler's gain when he either sells his interest or receives a distribution from the partnership. ■

Decreasing the adjusted basis for the partner's share of deductible losses, deductions, and noncapitalizable, nondeductible expenditures is logical for the same reasons. An item that is deductible currently should not contribute to creating a loss when the partnership interest is sold or when a distribution is received from the partnership. Similarly, a noncapitalizable, nondeductible expenditure should never be deductible nor contribute to a loss when a subsequent sale or distribution transaction occurs.

Liability Sharing

LO.9

Explain how liabilities affect a partner's basis.

A partner's adjusted basis is affected by the partner's share of partnership debt.[48] Partnership debt includes any partnership obligation that creates an asset, results in an expense to the partnership, or results in a nondeductible, noncapitalizable item at the partnership level. This definition includes certain contingent liabilities.[49] The definition also includes most debt that is considered a liability under financial accounting rules except for accounts payable of a cash basis partnership.

Under § 752, an increase in a partner's share of partnership debt is treated as a cash contribution by the partner to the partnership. A partner's share of partnership debt increases as a result of increases in the total amount of partnership debt. A decrease in a partner's share of partnership debt is treated as a cash distribution from the partnership to the partner. A partner's share of partnership debt decreases as a result of (1) decreases in the total amount of partnership debt and (2) assumption of the partner's debt by the partnership.

[48] § 752.

[49] Reg. § 1.752–1(a)(4)(ii).

EXAMPLE 32

Jim and Becky contribute property to form the JB Partnership. Jim contributes cash of $30,000. Becky contributes land with an adjusted basis and fair market value of $45,000, subject to a liability of $15,000. The partnership borrows $50,000 to finance construction of a building on the contributed land. At the end of the first year, the accrual basis partnership owes $3,500 in trade accounts payable to various vendors. Assume no other operating activities occurred. If Jim and Becky share equally in liabilities, the partners' bases in their partnership interests are determined as follows:

Jim's Basis		Becky's Basis	
Contributed cash	$30,000	Basis in contributed land	$ 45,000
Share of debt on land (assumed by partnership)	7,500	Less: Debt assumed by partnership	(15,000)
		Share of debt on land (assumed by partnership)	7,500
Initial basis	$37,500	Initial basis	$ 37,500
Share of construction loan	25,000	Share of construction loan	25,000
Share of trade accounts payable	1,750	Share of trade accounts payable	1,750
Basis, end of first year	$64,250	Basis, end of first year	$ 64,250

In this case, it is reasonable that the parties have an equal basis, because each is a 50% owner and they contributed property with identical *net* bases and identical *net* fair market values. ■

EXAMPLE 33

Assume the same facts as in Example 32. In the second year, the partnership generates $70,000 of taxable income from operations and repays both the $50,000 construction loan and the $3,500 trade accounts payable. The taxable income is allocated equally to each partner and increases each partner's basis by $35,000. The $26,750 ($25,000 + $1,750) reduction of each partner's share of liabilities is treated as a cash distribution to each partner and reduces each partner's adjusted basis by that amount. The $72,500 adjusted basis for each partner at the end of the second year is computed as follows:

Jim's Basis		Becky's Basis	
Basis, beginning of second year	$ 64,250	Basis, beginning of second year	$ 64,250
Share of taxable income	35,000	Share of taxable income	35,000
Share of construction loan paid	(25,000)	Share of construction loan paid	(25,000)
Share of trade accounts payable paid	(1,750)	Share of trade accounts payable paid	(1,750)
Basis, end of second year	$ 72,500	Basis, end of second year	$ 72,500

■

Partnership debt is classified as either recourse or nonrecourse. **Recourse debt** is partnership debt for which the partnership or at least one of the partners is personally liable. This personal liability can exist, for example, through the operation of state law or through personal guarantees that a partner makes to the creditor. Personal liability of a party related to a partner (under attribution rules) is treated as the personal liability of the partner. **Nonrecourse debt** is debt for which no partner (or party related to a partner) is personally liable. Lenders of nonrecourse debt generally require that collateral be pledged against the loan. Upon default, the lender can claim only the collateral, not the partners' personal assets. Note that for an LLC most debt will be treated as nonrecourse debt because the LLC members typically are not personally liable for the debt.

Recourse Debt Rules Recourse debt is allocated in a manner designed to recognize the extent to which a partner bears the "economic risk of loss." Under the Regulations, recourse debt created after January 29, 1989, is shared in accordance with a **constructive liquidation scenario.**[50]

Under this scenario, the following events are *deemed* to occur at the end of each taxable year of the partnership:

1. Most partnership assets (including cash) become worthless.
2. The worthless assets are sold at fair market value ($0), and losses on the deemed sales are determined.
3. These losses are allocated to the partners according to their loss sharing ratios. These losses reduce the partners' capital accounts.
4. Any partner with a (deemed) negative capital account balance is treated as contributing cash to the partnership to restore that negative balance to zero.
5. The cash deemed contributed by the partners with negative capital balances is used to pay the liabilities of the partnership.
6. The partnership is deemed to be liquidated immediately, and any remaining cash is distributed to partners with positive capital account balances.

A partner's share of partnership recourse liabilities equals the amount of that partner's cash contribution that would be used (in step 5 above) to pay partnership recourse liabilities.

EXAMPLE 34

On January 1 of the current year, Hannah and Ian each contribute $20,000 cash to the newly created HI Partnership. Each partner has a 50% interest in partnership capital and profits. Losses are allocated 60% to Hannah and 40% to Ian. The first year of partnership operations resulted in the following balance sheet as of December 31:

	Basis	FMV		Basis	FMV
Cash	$12,000	$12,000	Recourse payables	$30,000	$30,000
Receivables	7,000	7,000	Hannah, capital	19,500	19,500
Land and buildings	50,000	50,000	Ian, capital	19,500	19,500
	$69,000	$69,000		$69,000	$69,000

The recourse debt is shared in accordance with the constructive liquidation scenario. All of the partnership assets (including cash) are deemed to be worthless and sold for $0. This creates a loss of $69,000 ($12,000 + $7,000 + $50,000).

The constructive liquidation scenario results in the $69,000 loss being allocated $41,400 to Hannah and $27,600 to Ian. As a consequence, Hannah's capital account has a negative balance of $21,900, and Ian's account has a negative balance of $8,100. Each partner is deemed to contribute cash equal to these negative capital accounts, and the cash would be used to pay the recourse liabilities under the liquidation scenario. Accordingly, Hannah and Ian share $21,900 and $8,100, respectively, in the recourse debt. The debt allocation percentages (73% to Hannah and 27% to Ian) are different from the partners' 60%/40% loss sharing ratios.

Note that if the partners shared losses equally, the intuitive result would arise. The $69,000 constructive liquidation loss would be allocated equally ($34,500 each) to Hannah and Ian. As a result, each partner would have a $15,000 negative capital account that would correspond to that partner's share of the partnership's recourse debt. ■

[50]See Reg. § 1.752–2. Other rules (beyond the scope of this text) apply to debt created before January 30, 1989, and between January 29, 1989, and December 28, 1991.

Nonrecourse Debt Rules As previously noted, most debt of an LLC will fall into the nonrecourse category. Nonrecourse debt is allocated in three stages. First, an amount of debt equal to the amount of *minimum gain* is allocated to partners who share in minimum gain. The calculation of minimum gain is complex, and details of the calculation are beyond the scope of this text. In general, minimum gain approximates the amount of nonrecourse (mortgage) liability on a property in excess of the "book" basis of the property. Generally, the "book" basis for a property item is the same as the "tax" basis, although sometimes the amounts are different. For example, the "book" basis for contributed property on the date of contribution is its fair market value at that date.

If a lender forecloses on partnership property, the result is treated as a deemed sale of the property for the mortgage balance. Gain is recognized for at least the amount of the liability in excess of the property's "book" basis—hence, minimum gain. Allocation of minimum gain among the partners should be addressed in the partnership agreement.

Second, the amount of nonrecourse debt equal to the remaining *precontribution gain* under § 704(c) is allocated to the partner who contributed the property and debt to the partnership. For this purpose, the remaining precontribution gain is the excess of the current nonrecourse debt balance on the contributed property over the current tax basis of the contributed property.[51] Note that this calculation is only relevant when the "book" and "tax" bases of the contributed property are different.

Third, any remaining nonrecourse debt generally is allocated to the partners in accordance with their profit sharing ratios.

EXAMPLE 35

Ted contributes a nondepreciable asset to the TK Partnership in exchange for a one-third interest in the capital, profits, and losses of the partnership. The asset has an adjusted tax basis to Ted and the partnership of $24,000 and a fair market value and "book" basis on the contribution date of $50,000. The asset is encumbered by a nonrecourse note (created January 1, 2010) of $35,000. Because the "book" basis exceeds the nonrecourse debt, there is no minimum gain. Under § 704(c) principles, the Regulations provide that the first $11,000 of the nonrecourse debt ($35,000 debt − $24,000 basis) is allocated to Ted. The remaining $24,000 nonrecourse debt is allocated according to the profit sharing ratio, and Ted's share is $8,000. Therefore, Ted shares in $19,000 ($11,000 + $8,000) of the nonrecourse debt.

Ted's basis in his partnership interest is determined as follows:

Substituted basis of contributed property	$ 24,000
Less: Liability assumed by partnership	(35,000)
Plus: Allocation of § 704(c) debt	11,000
Basis before remaining allocation	$ -0-
Plus: Allocation of remaining nonrecourse debt	8,000
Basis in partnership interest	$ 8,000

The § 704(c) allocation of nonrecourse debt prevents Ted from receiving a deemed distribution ($35,000) in excess of his basis in property he contributed ($24,000). Without this required allocation of nonrecourse debt, in some cases, a contributing partner would be required to recognize gain on a contribution of property encumbered by nonrecourse debt. ■

Other Factors Affecting Basis Calculations

The partner's basis is also affected by (1) postacquisition contributions of cash or property to the partnership; (2) postacquisition distributions of cash or property from the partnership; and (3) special calculations that are designed to allow the full deduction of

[51] Reg. § 1.704–3.

percentage depletion for oil and gas wells. Postacquisition contributions of cash or property affect basis in the same manner as contributions made upon the creation of the partnership. Postacquisition distributions of cash or property reduce basis.

Figure 10.3 on the next page summarizes the rules for computing a partner's basis in a partnership interest.

EXAMPLE 36
THE BIG PICTURE

Return to the facts of *The Big Picture* on p. 10-2. Example 25 described how the income and deduction items of Beachside Properties, LLC, are allocated to Maria on her Schedule K–1. But how is Maria's basis affected by those items?

Assume that at the beginning of that tax year (Beachside's second year of operations), Maria's basis in her LLC interest was $1.6 million, including a $200,000 share of the LLC's $500,000 of nonrecourse debt. At the end of the year, Beachside had $600,000 of debt, which was again treated as nonrecourse to all the LLC members.

During the year, Maria contributes to the LLC cash of $100,000 and additional property (basis of $0 and fair market value of $50,000). On December 31, the LLC distributes $20,000 cash to her. Maria's share of Beachside's income, gain, and deductions is as described in Example 25.

Maria's basis can be calculated using the ordering rules shown in Figure 10.3. At the end of the year, Maria's basis is as follows:

Beginning basis	$1,600,000
Contributions, including increase in share of liabilities:	
Share of net increase in LLC liabilities [40% × ($600,000 – $500,000)]	40,000
Cash contribution to LLC capital	100,000
Maria's basis in noncash capital contribution	-0-
Share of LLC income items:	
Ordinary LLC income	72,000
LLC's net passive income from rental real estate	120,000
Tax-exempt income	840
Short-term capital gain	4,800
Qualified dividend income	1,600
Distributions and withdrawals:	
Capital withdrawal	(20,000)
Share of LLC deduction items:	
Charitable contribution	(2,400)
Ending basis	$1,916,840

As will be explained in Chapter 11, Maria could withdraw cash from the LLC up to the amount of her basis without paying tax on the distribution.

Maria's basis does not appear on the LLC's tax return or on her Schedule K–1. All partners are responsible for maintaining their own basis calculations. ■

A partner is required to compute the adjusted basis only when necessary and thus can avoid the inconvenience of making day-to-day calculations of basis. When a partnership interest is sold, exchanged, or retired, however, the partner must compute the adjusted basis as of the date the transaction occurs. Computation of gain or loss requires an accurate calculation of the partner's adjusted basis on the transaction date.

Partner's Capital Account Analysis

As mentioned earlier in the chapter, the partner's basis is not the same as the partner's capital account. Think of the capital account as an accounting calculation of the partner's ownership in the entity.

The capital account analysis (sometimes called a "rollforward" or "reconciliation") is shown on the partner's Schedule K–1. (See Appendix B) This calculation shows the

FIGURE 10.3 Partner's Basis in Partnership Interest

Basis is generally adjusted in the following order:

Initial basis. Amount paid for partnership interest, or gift or inherited basis (including share of partnership debt). Amount paid can be amount contributed to the partnership or amount paid to another partner or former partner.

+ Partner's subsequent contributions
+ Since interest acquired, partner's share of the partnership's
  - Debt increase
  - Taxable income items
  - Exempt income items
  - Excess of depletion deductions over adjusted basis of property subject to depletion

− Partner's distributions and withdrawals

− Since interest acquired, partner's share of the partnership's
  - Debt decrease
  - Separately stated deductions
  - Nondeductible items not chargeable to a capital account
  - Special depletion deduction for oil and gas wells
  - Loss items

The basis of a partner's interest can never be negative.

change in the partner's capital account from the beginning to the end of the tax year. The capital account does not include the taxpayer's share of partnership debts, and it might differ from the basis calculation for other reasons as well.

On Schedule K–1, the partner's capital account analysis can be prepared using any of several methods, including the tax basis, GAAP, or the § 704(b) book method. The method selected, which is indicated on the Schedule K–1, should be the same method that was used in preparing Schedule M–2. In some cases, the partner's ending basis in the partnership interest will equal the sum of the partner's Schedule K–1 amounts for the partner's share of liabilities and the partner's ending capital account. This could happen, for example, when the partner has been in the partnership since its inception, there have been no transfers of the partner's interest, and the capital account analysis is prepared on a tax basis.

EXAMPLE 37
THE BIG PICTURE

The last example illustrated the calculation of Maria's basis in her interest in Beachside Properties, LLC. Maria's Schedule K–1 will show her capital account rollforward from the prior year to the current year. Assume that her capital account is calculated on a tax basis and that the beginning capital account balance was $1.4 million. The reconciliation shown on Schedule K–1 will be as follows:

Beginning capital account	$1,400,000
Capital contributed during the year	100,000
Current-year increase (decrease)	196,840
Withdrawals and distributions	(20,000)
Ending capital account	$1,676,840

Although this will not always be the case, Maria's ending capital account balance differs from her ending basis by the amount of her $240,000 share of the LLC's nonrecourse debt. ■

LOSS LIMITATIONS

LO.10

Describe the limitations on deducting partnership losses.

Partnership losses flow through to the partners for use on their tax returns. However, the amount and nature of the losses allowed in a partner's tax computations may be limited. When limitations apply, all or a portion of the losses are held in suspension until a triggering event occurs. Only then can the losses be used to determine the partner's tax liability. No time limit is imposed on such carryforwards of losses.

Three different limitations may apply to partnership losses that are passed through to a partner:

- The first is the overall limitation contained in § 704(d). This limitation allows the deduction of losses only to the extent the partner has adjusted basis for the partnership interest. Recall that the partner's basis is not the same as the capital account shown on the partner's Schedule K–1.
- Losses that are deductible under the overall limitation may then be subject to the at-risk limitation of § 465. Losses are deductible under this provision only to the extent the partner is at risk for the partnership interest.
- Any losses that survive this second limitation may be subject to a third limitation, the passive loss rules of § 469.

Only losses that make it through all these applicable limitations are eligible to be deducted on the partner's tax return.

EXAMPLE 38

Megan is a partner in a partnership that does not invest in real estate. On January 1, 2011, Megan's adjusted basis for her partnership interest is $50,000, and her at-risk amount is $35,000. Her share of losses from the partnership for 2011 is $60,000, all of which is passive. She has one other passive income-producing investment that produced $25,000 of passive income during 2011.

Megan will be able to deduct $25,000 of partnership losses on her Form 1040 for 2011. Her deductible loss is calculated as follows:

Applicable Provision	Deductible Loss	Suspended Loss
§ 704(d) overall limitation	$50,000	$10,000
§ 465 at-risk limitation	35,000	15,000
§ 469 passive loss limitation	25,000	10,000

Megan can deduct only $50,000 under the overall limitation. Of this $50,000, only $35,000 is deductible under the at-risk limitation. Under the passive loss limitation, passive losses can be deducted only against passive income. Thus, Megan can deduct only $25,000 on her return in 2011. ■

Overall Limitation

A partner may deduct losses flowing through from the partnership only to the extent of the partner's adjusted basis in the partnership. A partner's adjusted basis in the partnership is determined at the end of the partnership's taxable year. It is adjusted for distributions and any partnership gains during the year, but it is determined *before considering any losses for the year.*

Losses that cannot be deducted because of this rule are suspended and carried forward (never back) for use against future increases in the partner's adjusted basis. Such increases might result from additional capital contributions, from sharing in additional partnership debts, or from future partnership income.

EXAMPLE 39

Courtney and Daniel do business as the CD Partnership, sharing profits and losses equally. All parties use the calendar year. At the start of the current year, the basis of Courtney's partnership interest is $25,000. The partnership sustains an operating loss of $80,000 in the current year. For the current year, only $25,000 of Courtney's $40,000 allocable share of the partnership loss can be deducted under the overall limitation. As a result, the basis of Courtney's partnership interest is zero as of January 1 of the following year, and Courtney must carry forward the remaining $15,000 of partnership losses. ■

EXAMPLE 40

Assume the same facts as in Example 39, and that the partnership earns a profit of $70,000 for the next calendar year. Courtney reports net partnership income of $20,000 ($35,000 distributive share of income – the $15,000 carryforward loss). The basis of Courtney's partnership interest becomes $20,000. ■

At-Risk Limitation

Under the at-risk rules, the partnership losses from business and income-producing activities that individual partners and closely held C corporation partners can deduct are limited to amounts that are economically invested in the partnership. Invested amounts include the adjusted basis of cash and property contributed by the partner and the partner's share of partnership earnings that has not been withdrawn.[52] A closely held C corporation exists when five or fewer individuals own more than 50 percent of the entity's stock under appropriate attribution and ownership rules.

When some or all of the partners are personally liable for partnership recourse debt, that debt is included in the adjusted basis of those partners. Usually, those partners also include the debt in their amount at risk.

No partner, however, carries any financial risk on nonrecourse debt. Therefore, as a general rule, partners cannot include nonrecourse debt in their amount at risk even though that debt is included in the adjusted basis of their partnership interest. This rule has an exception, however, that applies in many cases. Real estate nonrecourse financing provided by a bank, retirement plan, or similar party or by a Federal, state, or local government generally is deemed to be at risk.[53] Such debt is termed **qualified nonrecourse debt**. In summary, although the general rule provides that nonrecourse debt is not at risk, the overriding exception may provide that it is deemed to be at risk.

When determining a partner's loss deduction, the overall limitation rule is invoked first. That is, the deduction is limited to the partner's outside basis at the end of the partnership year. Then, the at-risk provisions are applied to see if the remaining loss is still deductible. Suspended losses are carried forward until a partner has a sufficient amount at risk in the activity to absorb them.[54]

EXAMPLE 41

Kelly invests $5,000 in the Kelly Green Limited Partnership as a 5% general partner. Shortly thereafter, the partnership acquires the master recording of a well-known vocalist for $250,000 ($50,000 from the partnership and $200,000 secured from a local bank by means of a *recourse* mortgage). Assume Kelly's share of the recourse debt is $10,000, and her basis in her partnership interest is $15,000 ($5,000 cash investment + $10,000 debt share). Since the debt is recourse, Kelly's at-risk amount is also $15,000. Kelly's share of partnership losses in the first year of operations is $11,000. Kelly is entitled to deduct the full $11,000 of partnership losses under both the overall and the at-risk limitations because this amount is less than both her outside basis and at-risk amount.

If, instead, the bank loan had been nonrecourse, Kelly would be able to deduct only $5,000 of the flow-through loss. The amount she has at risk in the partnership does not include the nonrecourse debt. (The debt does not relate to real estate so it is not qualified nonrecourse debt.) ■

Passive Activity Rules

A partnership loss share may be disallowed under the passive activity rules. These rules apply to partners who are individuals, estates, trusts, closely held

[52] § 465(a).
[53] § 465(b)(6).
[54] § 465(a)(2).

C corporations, or personal service corporations. The rules require the partners to separate their interests in partnership activities into three groups:

- *Active.* Earned income, such as salary and wages; income or loss from a trade or business in which the partner materially participates; and guaranteed payments received by the partner for services.
- *Portfolio.* Annuity income, interest, dividends, guaranteed payments from a partnership for interest on capital, royalties not derived in the ordinary course of a trade or business, and gains and losses from disposal of investment assets.
- *Passive.* Income from a trade or business activity in which the partner does not materially participate on a regular, continuous, and substantial basis,[55] or income from many rental activities.

Material participation in an activity is determined annually. The burden is on the partner to prove material participation. The IRS has provided a number of objective tests for determining material participation. In general, these tests require the partner to have substantial involvement in daily operations of the activity. Thus, a Maine vacation resort operator investing in a California grape farm or an electrical engineer employed in Virginia investing in an Iowa corn and hog farm may have difficulty proving material participation in the activities. By default, a partner treated as a limited partner is typically considered *not* to materially participate in partnership activities.[56]

Rent income from real or personal property generally is passive income, regardless of the partner's level of participation. Exceptions are made for rent income from activities where substantial services are provided (e.g., certain developers, resorts); from hotels, motels, and other transient lodging; from short-term equipment rentals; and from certain developed real estate. In addition, rental real estate is not treated as a passive activity for a person who qualifies as a real estate professional.

Usually, passive activity losses can be offset only against passive activity income.[57] In determining the net passive activity loss for a year, losses and income from all passive activities are aggregated. The amount of suspended losses carried forward from a particular activity is determined by the ratio of the net loss from that activity to the aggregate net loss from all passive activities for the year. A special rule for rental real estate (discussed in the following section) allows a limited $25,000 offset against nonpassive income.[58]

A partner making a taxable disposition of an entire interest in a passive activity takes a full deduction for suspended passive activity losses from that activity in the year of disposal.[59] Suspended losses are deductible against income in the following order: income or gain from the passive activity, net income or gain from all passive activities, and other income. When a passive activity is transferred in a primarily nontaxable exchange (e.g., a like-kind exchange or contribution to a partnership), suspended losses are deductible only to the extent of gains recognized on the transfer. Remaining losses are deducted on disposal of the activity received in the exchange.

EXAMPLE 42

Jamie has several investments in passive activities that generate aggregate losses of $10,000 in the current year. One of her long-time friends, Sarah, an entrepreneur in the women's apparel business, is interested in opening a new apparel store in a nearby community. Jamie is willing to finance a substantial part of the expansion but does not want to get involved with day-to-day operations. Jamie also wants to limit any possible loss to her initial investment.

Jamie and Sarah decide to form a limited liability limited partnership, which will own the new store. Sarah will be the general partner, and Jamie will be a limited partner. Jamie invests $100,000, and Sarah invests $50,000 and provides managerial skills and know-how. Each has a 50% interest in profits and losses. In the first year of

[55] §§ 469(c)(1) and (2).
[56] § 469(h)(2).
[57] § 469(a)(1).
[58] § 469(i).
[59] § 469(g).

TAX in the NEWS

LLC Members Not Automatically Treated as Passive

Under § 469(h)(2), "no interest in a limited partnership as a limited partner shall be treated as an interest with respect to which a taxpayer materially participates." The IRS has taken the position that because a member of an LLC has limited liability with respect to the entity's debts, that member has an "interest in a limited partnership" and cannot, by definition, be a material participant in an LLC's activities.

To illustrate, in Example 43 in the text, if the entity had been an LLC rather than an LLLP, the IRS's position might have been that *neither* Jamie nor Sarah met the material participation requirements, even though Sarah contributed substantial time and energy to the venture.

In *Paul D. Garnett*, 132 T.C. 368 (2009), the Tax Court ruled that the taxpayer's mere status as a member of an LLC did not lead to a presumption that he should be treated as *not* being a material participant in the LLC's activities. The court stated that the determinative test was whether the LLC member participated in LLC activities and not whether the LLC member was protected from entity liabilities.

The effect of this ruling is that it will be much easier for an LLC member to claim a loss from the LLC. The member will not automatically be treated as a passive, non-material participant, resulting in a disallowed loss.

operations, the store generates a profit of $30,000. Because Jamie's share of the profit ($15,000) is passive activity income, it can be fully utilized against her passive activity losses on other investments. Thus, Jamie's share of the apparel store profits enables her to obtain a full deduction of her $10,000 of passive activity losses. ■

EXAMPLE 43

Assume the same facts as in Example 42, except that the entity generates a loss of $30,000. Jamie's $15,000 share of the loss is treated as a passive loss and is suspended until such time as she has offsetting passive income. Sarah's loss is an active loss that is deductible if it otherwise meets the §§ 704(d) and 465 loss limitations. ■

Rental Real Estate Losses

In any one year, individuals can offset up to $25,000 of passive losses from rental real estate against active and portfolio income. The $25,000 maximum is reduced by 50 percent of the difference between the taxpayer's modified AGI and $100,000. Thus, when the taxpayer's modified AGI reaches $150,000, the offset is eliminated.

The offset is available to those who actively (rather than materially) participate in rental real estate activities. Active participation is an easier test to meet. Unlike material participation, it does not require regular, continuous, and substantial involvement with the activity. However, the taxpayer must own at least 10 percent of the fair market value of all interests in the rental property and either contribute to the activity's management decisions in a significant and bona fide way or actively participate in arranging for others to make such decisions.

EXAMPLE 44

José invests $10,000 cash in the Sparrow Limited Partnership in the current year for a 10% limited interest in capital and profits. Shortly thereafter, the partnership purchases rental real estate subject to a qualified nonrecourse mortgage of $120,000 obtained from a commercial bank. José has no other passive loss activities during the current year.

José does not participate in any of Sparrow's activities. His share of losses from Sparrow's first year of operations is $27,000. His modified AGI before considering the loss is $60,000. Before considering the loss, José's basis in the partnership interest is $22,000 [$10,000 cash + (10% × $120,000 debt)], and his loss deduction is limited to this amount under the overall limitation. The debt is included in José's amount at risk because it is qualified nonrecourse financing. It may seem that José should be allowed to deduct the $22,000 loss share from portfolio or active income under the rental real estate exception to the passive losses. However, the loss may not be offset against this income because José is not an active participant in the partnership. ■

10.4 Transactions between Partner and Partnership

LO.11

Describe the treatment of transactions between a partner and the partnership.

Many types of transactions occur between a partnership and one of its partners. The partner may contribute property to the partnership, perform services for the partnership, or receive distributions from the partnership. The partner may borrow money from or lend money to the partnership. Property may be bought and sold between the partner and the partnership. Several of these transactions were discussed earlier in the chapter. The remaining types of partner-partnership transactions are the focus of this section.

GUARANTEED PAYMENTS

If a partnership makes a payment to a partner, the payment may be a draw against the partner's share of partnership income; a return of some or all of the partner's original capital contribution; or a guaranteed payment, among other treatments. A **guaranteed payment** is a payment for services performed by the partner or for the use of the partner's capital. The payment may not be determined by reference to partnership income. Guaranteed payments are usually expressed as a fixed-dollar amount or as a percentage of capital that the partner has invested in the partnership. Whether the partnership deducts or capitalizes the guaranteed payment depends on the nature of the payment.

EXAMPLE 45

David, Derek, and Danielle formed the accrual basis DDD Partnership in 2011. The partnership and each of the partners are calendar year taxpayers. According to the partnership agreement, David is to manage the partnership and receive a $21,000 distribution from the entity every year, payable in 12 monthly installments. Derek is to receive an amount that is equal to 18% of his capital account, as it is computed by the firm's accountant at the beginning of the year, payable in 12 monthly installments. Danielle is the partnership's advertising specialist. She withdraws approximately 4% of the partnership's net income for her personal use. David and Derek receive guaranteed payments from the partnership, but Danielle does not. ■

Guaranteed payments resemble the salary or interest payments of other businesses.[60] Deductible guaranteed payments, like any other deductible expenses of a partnership, can create an ordinary loss for the entity. If the partnership distributes appreciated property to pay the guaranteed payment, the partnership must recognize a gain on the transfer.[61]

A partner who receives guaranteed payments during a partnership year must include the payments in income as if they were received on the last day of the partnership year. Guaranteed payments are always taxable as ordinary income to the recipient partner. The partner's guaranteed payment is reported on Schedule K–1. The partner uses this information (in lieu of a Form W–2 or 1099) to report the income on the partner's tax return.

EXAMPLE 46

Continue with the situation introduced in Example 45. For calendar year 2011, David receives the $21,000 as provided by the partnership agreement, Derek's guaranteed payment for 2011 is $17,000, and Danielle withdraws $20,000. Before considering these amounts, the partnership's ordinary income for 2011 is $650,000.

The partnership can deduct its payments to David and Derek, so the final amount of its 2011 ordinary income is $612,000 ($650,000 – $21,000 – $17,000). Thus, each of the equal partners is allocated $204,000 of ordinary partnership income for their 2011

[60] § 707(c).

[61] Rev.Rul. 2007–40, 2007–1 C.B. 1426.

individual income tax returns ($612,000 ÷ 3). In addition, David reports the $21,000 guaranteed payment as income on his 2011 tax return, and Derek similarly includes the $17,000 guaranteed payment in his 2011 income. Danielle's partnership draw is deemed to have come from her allocated $204,000 (or from the accumulated partnership income that was taxed in prior years) and is not taxed separately to her. Danielle's basis, though, is reduced by the $20,000 distribution. ■

EXAMPLE 47

Assume the same facts as in Example 46, except that the partnership has a "natural business year" that ends on March 31, 2012. The total amount of the guaranteed payments is taxable to the partners on that date. Thus, even though David received 9 of his 12 payments for fiscal 2012 in calendar 2011, all of his guaranteed payments are taxable to him in 2012. Similarly, all of Derek's guaranteed payments are taxable to him in 2012 and not when they are received. The deduction for, and the gross income from, guaranteed payments is allowed on the same date that all of the other income and expense items relative to the partnership are allocated to the partners (on the last day of the entity's tax year). ■

SELF-EMPLOYMENT TAX OF PARTNERS

A partner usually does not qualify as an employee for tax purposes. Thus, a partner receiving guaranteed payments is not regarded as an employee of the partnership for purposes of withholding taxes. Moreover, because a partner is not an employee, the partnership cannot deduct its payments for any of a partner's fringe benefits.

Certain partnership income reported by a partner who is an individual taxpayer may be considered "net earnings from self-employment" and is subject to self-employment (SE) tax. Section 1402 provides that SE income includes the partner's distributive share of income from a partnership's trade or business, whether or not that income is distributed. This provision applies to income allocated to a "general partner" and income earned by a "limited partner" that is in the nature of compensation for services performed for or on behalf of the partnership.[62]

For a general partner, both the partner's allocable share of income and any guaranteed payments for services are subject to the SE tax. For a limited partner, any guaranteed payment for services rendered to the partnership is subject to the SE tax. Recall that an LLC member often is treated similarly to a limited partner.

Proposed Regulations provide guidance regarding how to determine whether a partner or LLC member should be treated as a general partner or a limited partner. These regulations provide, in general, that a partner or LLC member will be treated as a general partner if

- the partner has personal liability for partnership debts by virtue of status as a partner,
- the partner can enter into contractual relationships on behalf of the partnership, or
- the partner works more than 500 hours in the partnership's trade or business during the tax year.

If the partner is treated as a general partner solely because of the "hours worked" limitation, the interest can still be treated as a limited interest (for purposes of classifying the partner's distributive share of income) if there is at least one other limited partner with identical rights.

Because of the proposed status of these Regulations, taxpayers are not required to comply with them or disclose any noncompliance. These Regulations are highly controversial and have existed since 1997 without being finalized. At this point, however, they are the only guidance available.

[62] §§ 1402(a) and (a)(13). See also Prop.Reg. § 1.1402(a)–2(h).

EXAMPLE 48
THE BIG PICTURE

Return to the facts of *The Big Picture* on p. 10-2. Assume that Josh was elected the managing member of Beachside Properties, LLC; he has the sole authority to contract for the LLC and works 1,000 hours per year in the business. Maria works 1,000 hours per year in the café. After surrendering his land to Beachside, Kyle has generally not been involved in the LLC's operations.

Kyle and Josh each receive a guaranteed payment of $5,000 per month from the LLC. Josh's payment is for services, and Kyle's is for use of his $2 million of land. Maria receives a guaranteed payment of $10,000 per month, of which $5,000 is for services and $5,000 is for the use of her $2 million of capital.

If Beachside follows the Proposed Regulations, the members' distributive shares and guaranteed payments will be treated as follows:

	Distributive Share (Proposed Regulations)	Guaranteed Payments [§ 1402(a)(13)]
Kyle	Not SE income	Not SE income (payment is for capital; not services)
Maria	Not SE income*	$5,000 SE income (services) and $5,000 not SE income (capital)
Josh	SE income	SE income (payment is for services to the LLC)

* Under the Proposed Regulations, Maria's distributive share is not SE income for two reasons: (1) she is a general partner by virtue of working more than 500 hours per year; and (2) Kyle, a "limited partner," has an interest with identical rights to Maria ■

OTHER TRANSACTIONS BETWEEN A PARTNER AND A PARTNERSHIP

Certain transactions between a partner and the partnership are treated as if the partner were an outsider, dealing with the partnership at arm's length.[63] Loan transactions, rental payments, and sales of property between the partner and the partnership are generally treated in this manner. In addition, payments for services are treated this way when the services are short-term technical services that the partner also provides for parties other than the partnership.

EXAMPLE 49

Chad, a one-third partner in the ABC Partnership, owns a tract of land that the partnership wishes to purchase. The land has a fair market value of $30,000 and an adjusted basis to Chad of $17,000. If Chad sells the land to the partnership, he recognizes a $13,000 gain on the sale, and the partnership takes a $30,000 cost basis in the land. If the land has a fair market value of $10,000 on the sale date, Chad recognizes a $7,000 loss. ■

The time for deducting a payment by an accrual basis partnership to a cash basis service partner depends upon whether the amount is a guaranteed payment or a payment to a partner who is treated as an outsider. A guaranteed payment is includible in the partner's income on the last day of the partnership year when it is properly accrued by the partnership, even though the payment may not be made to the partner until the next taxable year. Conversely, the *partner's* method of accounting controls the timing of the deduction if the payment is treated as made to an outsider. This is because a deduction cannot be claimed for such amounts until the recipient partner is required to include the amount in income under the partner's method of accounting.[64] Thus, a partnership cannot claim a deduction until it actually makes

[63] § 707(a).

[64] § 267(a)(2).

CONCEPT SUMMARY 10.4

Partner-Partnership Transactions

1. Partners can transact business with their partnerships in a nonpartner capacity. These transactions include the sale and exchange of property, rentals, loans of funds, etc.
2. A payment to a partner may be classified as a guaranteed payment if it is for services or use of the partner's capital and is not based on partnership income. A guaranteed payment may be deductible by the partnership and is included in the partner's income on the last day of the partnership's taxable year.
3. Partners may be subject to self-employment tax on their distributive shares of partnership income if they are treated as general partners.
4. A partner may be subject to self-employment tax on guaranteed payments if the payments are for services, regardless of whether the partner is a general or a limited partner.
5. A payment to a partner may be treated as being to an outside (though related) party. Such a payment is deductible or capitalizable by the partnership at the time it must be included in income under the partner's method of accounting.
6. Guaranteed payments and payments to a partner that are treated as being to an outside party are only deductible if the underlying reason for the payment constitutes an ordinary and necessary (rather than capitalizable) business expense.
7. Losses are disallowed between a partner or related party and a partnership when the partner or related party owns more than a 50% interest in the partnership's capital or profits.
8. When there is income from a related-party sale, it is treated as ordinary income if the property is not a capital asset to both the transferor and the transferee.

the payment to the cash basis partner, but it could accrue and deduct a payment due to an accrual basis partner even if payment was not yet made.

EXAMPLE 50

Rachel, a cash basis taxpayer, is a partner in the accrual basis RTC Partnership. On December 31, 2011, the partnership accrues but does not pay $10,000 for deductible services that Rachel performed for the partnership during the year. Both Rachel and the partnership are calendar year taxpayers.

If the $10,000 accrual is a guaranteed payment, the partnership deducts the $10,000 in its calendar year ended December 31, 2011, and Rachel includes the $10,000 in her income for the 2011 calendar year. That Rachel is a cash basis taxpayer and does not actually receive the cash in 2011 is irrelevant.

If the payment is classified as a payment to an outsider, the partnership cannot deduct the payment until Rachel actually receives the cash. If, for example, Rachel performs janitorial services (i.e., not in her capacity as a partner) and receives the cash on March 25, 2012, the partnership deducts the payment and Rachel recognizes the income on that date. ■

Sales of Property

Certain sales of property fall under special rules. No loss is recognized on a sale of property between a person and a partnership when the person owns, directly or indirectly, more than 50 percent of partnership capital or profits.[65] The disallowed loss may not vanish entirely, however. If the transferee eventually sells the property at a gain, the disallowed loss reduces the gain that the transferee would otherwise recognize.

EXAMPLE 51

Blake sells land (adjusted basis to him, $30,000; fair market value, $45,000) to a partnership in which he controls a 60% capital interest. The partnership pays him only $20,000 for the land. Blake cannot deduct his $10,000 realized loss. The sale apparently was not at arm's length, but the taxpayer's intentions are irrelevant. Blake and the partnership are related parties, and the loss is disallowed.

When the partnership sells the land to an outsider at a later date, it receives a sales price of $44,000. The partnership can offset the recognition of its $24,000 realized gain

[65] § 707(b).

on the subsequent sale ($44,000 sales proceeds − $20,000 adjusted basis) by the amount of the $10,000 prior disallowed loss ($30,000 − $20,000). Thus, the partnership recognizes a $14,000 gain on its sale of the land. ■

Using a similar rationale, any gain that is realized on a sale or exchange between a partner and a partnership in which the partner controls a capital or profits interest of more than 50 percent must be recognized as ordinary income, unless the asset is a capital asset to both the seller and the purchaser.[66]

EXAMPLE 52

Kristin purchases some land (adjusted basis, $30,000; fair market value, $45,000) for $45,000 from a partnership in which she controls a 90% profits interest. The land was a capital asset to the partnership. If Kristin holds the land as a capital asset, the partnership recognizes a $15,000 capital gain. However, if Kristin is a land developer and the property is not a capital asset to her, the partnership must recognize $15,000 ordinary income from the sale, even though the property was a capital asset to the partnership. ■

Concept Summary 10.4 on the previous page reviews partner-partnership transactions.

TAX PLANNING:

10.5 Choosing Partnership Taxation

LO.12

Provide insights regarding advantageous use of a partnership.

Concept Summary 10.5 enumerates various factors that the owners of a business should consider in deciding whether to use a C corporation, S corporation, or partnership as a means of doing business. The reader should refer back to this list after reading Chapters 11 (advanced partnership topics) and 12 (S corporations). Chapter 13 includes a more elaborate discussion of the tax effects of various forms of conducting business.

10.6 Formation and Operation of a Partnership

Potential partners should be cautious in transferring assets to a partnership to ensure that they are not required to recognize any gain upon the creation of the entity. The nonrecognition provisions of § 721 are relatively straightforward and resemble the provisions under § 351, which permit certain tax-free property transfers to corporations. However, any partner can make a tax-deferred contribution of assets to the entity either at the inception of the partnership or later. This possibility is not available to less-than-controlling shareholders in a corporation.

The partners should anticipate the tax benefits and pitfalls that are presented in Subchapter K and should take appropriate actions to resolve any potential problems before they arise. Typically, all that is needed is an appropriate provision in the partnership agreement (e.g., with respect to differing allocation percentages for gains and losses). Recall, however, that a special allocation of income, expense, or credit items in the partnership agreement must satisfy certain requirements before it is acceptable to the IRS.

10.7 Basis Considerations and Loss Deduction Limitations

If a partnership incurs a loss for the taxable year, careful planning will help ensure that the partners can claim the deduction.

A partner can contribute capital to the partnership before the end of the tax year. Alternatively, the partnership could incur additional debt. The partner's cash contribution or share of debt increases the partner's basis in the partnership interest. If the loss also meets the "at-risk" and "passive" hurdles, the loss can be deducted.

[66] § 707(b)(2).

CONCEPT SUMMARY 10.5

Advantages and Disadvantages of the Partnership Form

The partnership form may be attractive when one or more of the following factors is present:

- The entity is generating net taxable losses and/or valuable tax credits, which will be of use to the owners.
- The owners want to avoid complex corporate administrative and filing requirements.
- Other means of reducing the effects of the double taxation of corporate business income (e.g., compensation to owners, interest, and rental payments) have been exhausted.
- The entity does not generate material amounts of tax preference and adjustment items, which increase the alternative minimum tax liabilities of its owners.
- The entity is generating net passive income, which its owners can use to claim immediate deductions for net passive losses that they have generated from other sources.
- The owners wish to make special allocations of certain income or deduction items that are not possible under the C or S corporation forms.
- The owners anticipate liquidation of the entity within a short period of time. Liquidation of a C or S corporation would generate entity-level recognized gains on appreciated property distributed.
- The owners have adequate bases in their ownership interests to facilitate the deduction of flow-through losses and the assignment of an adequate basis to assets distributed in kind to the owners.

The partnership form may be less attractive when one or more of the following factors is present:

- The tax paid by the individual owners on the entity's income is greater than the tax the entity would pay if it were a C corporation, and the income is not expected to be distributed soon. (If distributed by a C corporation, double taxation would likely occur.)
- The entity is generating net taxable income without distributing any cash to the owners. The owners may not have sufficient cash with which to pay the tax on the entity's earnings.
- The type of income that the entity is generating (e.g., business and portfolio income) is not as attractive to its owners as net passive income would be because the owners could use net passive income to offset the net passive losses that they have generated on their own.
- The entity is in a high-exposure business, and the owners desire protection from personal liability. An LLC, LLP, or LLLP structure may be available, however, to limit personal liability.
- The owners want to avoid Federal self-employment tax.
- The entity has already been formed as a corporation, and conversion to partnership status could result in significant taxes in the course of liquidation.
- Partnership operations are complex (indicating that Form 1065 might not be filed until near the due date for the return), but partners with the same tax year need to file their returns as early as possible for personal reasons (e.g., to meet debt requirements or to receive a tax refund).

In the following year, if the partnership is expected to report taxable income, the partner could withdraw cash or pay off debt equal to the income. The partner's cash contribution would have to be invested in the partnership for only a short time. Similarly, the partnership's additional debt would not have to be maintained for a long period of time.

10.8 Partnership Reporting Requirements

For most small (under 100 partners) partnerships, the tax return is due by the fifteenth day of the fourth month following the tax year (April 15 for a calendar year partnership). If all partners and the partnership have the same tax year, the partnership tax return will be due on the same date as the return for any partners who are individual taxpayers. The partnership return will be due one month *after* the due date for the return of a partner that is a Subchapter C or Subchapter S corporation. For example, suppose that a partnership has an individual and a Subchapter S corporation as partners, and all taxpayers use the calendar year. The individual partner's tax return

Partnerships Around the World—and Beyond

Technology continues to act as a catalyst—and incentive—for the creation of joint ventures. From web kiosks at gas stations to global satellite networks, high-tech companies are forging alliances to bring technology to consumers.

Both Microsoft and Time Warner have teamed up with various gas stations, pizza parlors, and numerous other retail outlets to offer programming. These ventures appear to be spurred by a desire to capture larger shares of the ever-expanding advertising market.

Meanwhile, the largest U.S. telecommunications companies are continuing to align themselves with partners in foreign markets: each wants to have the widest possible service coverage area so that it can offer efficient communications and computer networking to business clients with a global presence.

Recent partnerships (Verizon or AT&T and Apple, for example) have unleashed cell phones that provide tower-based navigation and browser systems. A more recent venture aims to provide these services to cell phones from satellites. In a few years, we will be able to "connect" anywhere, anytime—courtesy of an "out of this world" partnership.

will be due on April 15 (the same date as the partnership's return), but the S corporation's tax return will be due on March 15 (a month earlier).

The partners cannot file an accurate return until they receive the Schedule K–1 from the partnership. A good accountant will pay attention to the partners' status and will attempt to schedule completion of partnership tax returns to accommodate the partners' filing requirements. Still, in some situations the partners may have to obtain extensions for filing their tax returns because they have not received their Schedule K–1 in time.

In extreme cases, a partner may need to file a return by the original due date (e.g., to meet debt financing requirements or to request a refund of overpaid taxes). In that case, the partner can estimate income from the partnership in the original return and then file an amended return when the Schedule K–1 from the partnership is received.

10.9 Transactions between Partners and Partnerships

Partners should be careful when engaging in transactions with the partnership to ensure that no negative tax results occur. A partner who owns a majority of the partnership generally should not sell property at a loss to the partnership because the loss is disallowed. Similarly, a majority partner should not sell a capital asset to the partnership at a gain, if the asset is to be used by the partnership as other than a capital asset. The gain on this transaction is taxed as ordinary income to the selling partner rather than as capital gain.

As an alternative to selling property to a partnership, the partner should consider a lease arrangement. The partner recognizes rent income, and the partnership has a rent expense. A partner who needs more cash immediately can sell the property to an outside third party; then the third party can lease the property to the partnership for a fair rental.

The timing of the deduction for a payment by an accrual basis partnership to a cash basis partner varies depending on whether the payment is a guaranteed payment or is treated as a payment to an outsider. If the payment is a guaranteed payment, the deduction occurs when the partnership makes the accrual. If the payment is treated as a payment to an outsider, the actual date the payment is made controls the timing of the deduction.

10.10 Drafting the Partnership Agreement

Although a written partnership agreement (or LLC operating agreement) is not always required, many rules governing the tax consequences to partners and their partnerships refer to such an agreement. Remember that a partner's distributive share of income, gain, loss, deduction, or credit is determined in accordance with the partnership agreement. Consequently, if taxpayers operating a business in partnership form want a measure of certainty as to the tax consequences of their activities, a carefully drafted partnership agreement is crucial. An agreement that sets forth the obligations, rights, and powers of the partners should prove invaluable in settling controversies among them and provide some degree of certainty as to the tax consequences of the partners' actions.

REFOCUS ON THE BIG PICTURE

WHY USE A PARTNERSHIP, ANYWAY?

After considering the various types of partnerships, Kyle, Maria, and Josh decide to form Beachside Properties as an LLC (see Example 1). On formation of the entity, there was no tax to the LLC or to any of its members (see Example 15). Beachside Properties computes its income as shown in Example 23 and allocates the income as illustrated in Examples 24 and 25. The LLC's income affects the members' bases and capital accounts as shown in Examples 30 and 36. An important consideration for the LLC members is whether their distributive shares and guaranteed payments will be treated as self-employment income (see Example 48).

What If?

What happens in the future when the LLC members decide to expand or renovate Beachside's facilities? At that time, the existing members can contribute additional funds, the LLC can obtain new members, or the entity can solicit third-party financing. An LLC is not subject to the 80 percent control requirement applicable to the formation of and subsequent transfers to a corporation. Therefore, new investors can contribute cash or other property in exchange for interests in the LLC—and the transaction will qualify for tax-deferred treatment under § 721.

KEY TERMS

Aggregate concept, 10–7
Capital interest, 10–8
Capital sharing ratio, 10–8
Constructive liquidation scenario, 10–31
Disguised sale, 10–12
Economic effect test, 10–25
Entity concept, 10–7
General partners, 10–4
General partnership, 10–4
Guaranteed payment, 10–39
Inside basis, 10–9
Least aggregate deferral rule, 10-20
Limited liability company, 10–4
Limited liability limited partnership, 10–4
Limited liability partnership, 10–4
Limited partners, 10–4
Limited partnership, 10–4
Nonrecourse debt, 10–30
Operating agreement, 10–4
Outside basis, 10–9
Partnership agreement, 10–4
Precontribution gain or loss, 10–26
Profit and loss sharing ratios, 10–8
Profits (loss) interest, 10–8
Qualified nonrecourse debt, 10–36
Recourse debt, 10–30
Schedule K-1, 10–6
Separately stated items, 10–5
Special allocation, 10–8
Syndication costs, 10–18

DISCUSSION QUESTIONS

1. **LO.1** What is a partnership?

2. **LO.1** Name the five types of partnerships discussed in this chapter. What factors are considered in determining the type of partnership entity to utilize?

3. **LO.1** What are the differences and similarities between a general partnership (GP) and a limited liability partnership (LLP)?

4. **LO.2** What is a separately stated item, and where is it reported on the partnership return?

5. **LO.2** Describe how a partnership reports its taxable income.

6. **LO.2** Describe how book income is reconciled with a partnership's "taxable income."

7. **LO.3** Describe the differences and similarities between the entity concept and the aggregate or conduit concept of partnership taxation.

8. **LO.3, 7, 11** Orange, LLC, was formed when Green, Inc., contributed $400,000 of cash and Rose contributed nondepreciable assets valued at $200,000 with a basis of $10,000. In addition, Rose will perform significant management services for the LLC. For most items, the members intend to allocate profits, losses, and liquidating distributions equally. How can (or must) special allocations be used to compensate the members for the differences between the bases and values of contributed property and time devoted to LLC activities? **ISSUE ID**

9. **LO.3** What is a partner's capital account? Describe how a partner's ending capital account balance is determined. In addition to the material in the chapter, refer to Schedule K–1 in Appendix B.

10. **LO.4** When can the formation of a partnership result in a taxable gain to one or more of the new partners?

11. **LO.4** Compare the provision for the nonrecognition of gain or loss on contributions to a partnership (i.e., § 721) with the similar provision related to corporate formation (i.e., § 351). What are the major differences and similarities?

12. **LO.4** Kelsey and Christopher are forming the KC Partnership, in which Kelsey will own a 40% interest and Christopher will own a 60% interest. Kelsey will contribute appreciated land, and Christopher will contribute cash. What is the tax effect of the formation to Kelsey, Christopher, and the partnership? **ISSUE ID**

13. **LO.4** Jonathan owns property (basis of $200,000, value of $300,000). He plans to contribute the property to the JJG Partnership in exchange for a 25% interest. **ISSUE ID**
    a. What issues arise if the partnership distributes $150,000 of cash to Jonathan three months after the property contribution? **DECISION MAKING**
    b. How can the risk of adverse tax consequences be minimized?

14. **LO.5** Tina and Rex plan to form the TR Partnership to acquire, own, and manage a certain rental real estate property. The financial information has been accumulated into an Offering Memorandum that is currently being brokered to investors (for a 6% commission). What types of costs is the partnership likely to incur, and how will those costs be treated? **ISSUE ID**

15. **LO.6** How is the taxable year of a newly formed partnership determined?

16. **LO.7** What is the purpose of the three rules that implement the economic effect test?

17. **LO.8, 9** Discuss the adjustments that must be made to a partner's basis in the partnership interest. When are such adjustments made?

18. **LO.9** Describe, in general terms, how a partnership's liabilities affect a partner's basis in the partnership interest.

19. **LO.10** Describe the three limitations that apply to the deductibility of a loss from a partnership. In what order are these limitations applied?

20. **LO.11** What is a guaranteed payment? When is it deducted by the partnership? When is it reported in the recipient partners' income?

21. **LO.11** When is partnership income subject to self-employment tax for an individual partner?

22. **LO.9, 10, 12** Discuss situations in which the partnership entity form might be more advantageous (or disadvantageous) than operating as a Subchapter C or S corporation.

23. **LO.4, 6, 7, 9, 10, 11** Comment on the validity of the following statements:
    a. Because a partnership is not a taxable entity, it is not required to file any type of tax return.
    b. Generally, a transfer of appreciated property to a partnership results in recognized gain to the contributing partner at the time of the transfer.
    c. When a partner renders services to the entity in exchange for an unrestricted interest in future profits of the partnership, that partner recognizes gross income.
    d. Property that was held as inventory by a contributing partner, but is a capital asset in the hands of the partnership, results in a capital gain if the partnership immediately sells the property.
    e. The partnership generally chooses the methods of accounting and those for computing depreciation in determining the income from the partnership.
    f. A partnership may choose a year that results in the least aggregate deferral of tax to the partners, unless the IRS requires the use of an alternative tax year under the "business purpose" test.
    g. Built-in gains related to nondepreciable property contributed to a partnership must be allocated to the contributing partner to the extent the gain is eventually recognized by the partnership.
    h. A partner's capital account for a partnership interest includes that partner's share of partnership recourse and nonrecourse liabilities.
    i. A partner can carry forward, for an unlimited period of time, the share of any partnership operating losses that exceed the partner's basis in the entity, provided the partner retains an ownership interest in the partnership.
    j. Losses on sales between a partner and the partnership are never deductible.

PROBLEMS

24. **LO.4** Justin and Tiffany form the equal TJ Partnership. Justin contributes cash of $300,000. Tiffany contributes property with an adjusted basis of $200,000 and a fair market value of $300,000.
    a. How much gain, if any, must Justin recognize on the transfer? Must Tiffany recognize any gain?
    b. What is Justin's basis in his partnership interest?
    c. What is Tiffany's basis in her partnership interest?
    d. What basis does the partnership take in the property transferred by Tiffany?

DECISION MAKING

25. **LO.4, 12** Scott and Amber form the equal Toucan, LLC, with a cash contribution of $100,000 from Scott and a property contribution (adjusted basis of $110,000, fair market value of $100,000) from Amber.
    a. How much gain or loss, if any, does Amber realize on the transfer? Does Amber recognize any gain or loss?
    b. What is Scott's basis in his LLC interest?
    c. What is Amber's basis in her LLC interest?
    d. What basis does the LLC take in the property transferred by Amber?
    e. Are there more effective ways to structure the formation?

26. **LO.4** Drew and Emma formed the equal D&E Partnership on January 1 of the current year. Drew contributed $50,000 of cash and land with a fair market value of $100,000 and an adjusted basis of $80,000. Emma contributed equipment with a fair market value of $150,000 and an adjusted basis of $60,000. Emma had previously used the equipment in her sole proprietorship.
    a. How much gain or loss will Drew, Emma, and the partnership realize?
    b. How much gain or loss will Drew, Emma, and the partnership recognize?
    c. What bases will Drew and Emma take in their partnership interests?
    d. What bases will D&E take in the assets it receives?
    e. Are there any differences between inside and outside basis?
    f. How will the partnership depreciate any assets it receives from the partners?

27. **LO.4** Jared and Chelsea form the equal JC Partnership. Jared contributes cash of $20,000 and land (fair market value of $80,000, adjusted basis of $65,000), and Chelsea contributes the assets of her sole proprietorship (value of $100,000, adjusted basis of $125,000). What are the tax consequences of the partnership formation to Jared, Chelsea, and JC Partnership? **ISSUE ID**

28. **LO.4** Assume the same facts as in Problem 27, except that Chelsea sells her assets to a third party for $100,000 and then contributes that cash to the partnership. The partnership locates equivalent assets that it purchases for $110,000. How do these changes affect the tax result for Chelsea and the partnership? How does the economic result differ? **ISSUE ID** **DECISION MAKING**

29. **LO.4, 8, 12** Ben and Beth are equal partners in BB, LLC, formed on June 1 of the current year. Ben contributed land that he inherited from his father three years ago. Ben's father purchased the land in 1950 for $6,000. The land was worth $50,000 when Ben's father died. The fair market value of the land was $75,000 at the date it was contributed to the partnership.

    Beth has significant experience developing real estate. After the LLC is formed, she will prepare a plan for developing the property and secure zoning approvals for the LLC. She would normally bill a third party $25,000 for these efforts. Beth will also contribute $50,000 cash in exchange for her 50% interest in the LLC. The value of her 50% interest is $75,000.

    a. How much gain or income will Ben recognize on his contribution of the land to the LLC? What is the character of any gain or income recognized?
    b. What basis will Ben take in his LLC interest?
    c. How much gain or income will Beth recognize on the formation of the LLC? What is the character of any gain or income recognized?
    d. What basis will Beth take in her LLC interest?

30. **LO.4, 12** Continue with the facts presented in Problem 29. **DECISION MAKING**
    a. Construct an opening balance sheet for BB, LLC, reflecting the LLC's basis in assets and the fair market value of these assets.
    b. Outline any planning opportunities that may minimize current taxation to any of the parties.

31. **LO.4, 12** Continue with the facts presented in Problem 29. At the end of the first year, the LLC distributes $50,000 cash to Ben. No distribution is made to Beth. **DECISION MAKING**
    a. Under general tax rules, how would the payment to Ben be treated?
    b. How much income or gain would Ben recognize as a result of the payment?
    c. Under general tax rules, what basis would the LLC take in the land Ben contributed?
    d. What alternative treatment might the IRS try to impose?
    e. Under the alternative treatment, how much income or gain would Ben recognize?
    f. Under the alternative treatment, what basis would the LLC take in the land contributed by Ben?
    g. How can the transaction be restructured to minimize risk of IRS recharacterization?

32. **LO.4** The JM Partnership was formed to acquire land and subdivide it as residential housing lots. On March 1, 2011, Jessica contributed land valued at $600,000 to the partnership in exchange for a 50% interest. She had purchased the land in 2003 for $420,000 and held it for investment purposes (capital asset). The partnership holds the land as inventory.

    On the same date, Matt contributed land valued at $600,000 that he had purchased in 2001 for $720,000. He became a 50% owner. Matt is a real estate developer, but he held this land personally for investment purposes. The partnership holds this land as inventory.

    In 2012, the partnership sells the land contributed by Jessica for $620,000. In 2013, the partnership sells the real estate contributed by Matt for $580,000.

    a. What is each partner's initial basis in his or her partnership interest?
    b. What is the amount of gain or loss recognized on the sale of the land contributed by Jessica? What is the character of this gain or loss?
    c. What is the amount of gain or loss recognized on the sale of the land contributed by Matt? What is the character of this gain or loss?
    d. How would your answer in (c) change if the property was sold in 2018?

ISSUE ID

33. **LO.5** In 2011, Tim and Molly form TM Partnership, Ltd. (an LLLP), to own and operate certain real estate. Tim contributed land, and Molly contributed cash to be used for setting up the entity and creating a plan for developing the property. Once a development plan was in place, the partnership sold interests in the partnership to investors to raise funds for constructing a shopping center. The partnership incurred expenses of $12,000 for forming the entity and $52,000 for starting the business (e.g., setting up the accounting systems, locating tenants, and negotiating leases). It also paid $18,000 in transfer taxes for changing the ownership of the property to the partnership's name. The brokerage firm that sold the interests to the limited partners charged a 6% commission, which totaled $600,000. The calendar year partnership started business in September 2011. Describe how all these initial expenses are treated by the partnership.

ISSUE ID

34. **LO.4, 5, 6, 7** Finch, Inc., a calendar year general contractor, and Cardinal, Inc., a development corporation with a July 31 year-end, formed the equal FC, LLC, on January 1 of the current year. Both LLC members are C corporations. The LLC was formed to construct and lease shopping centers in Seattle, Washington. Finch contributed cash of $1 million, equipment (basis of $200,000, fair market value of $500,000), building permits, and architectural designs created by Finch's employees (basis of $0, fair market value of $200,000). Cardinal contributed land (basis of $500,000, fair market value of $700,000) and cash of $1 million. The cash was used as follows:

Legal fees for drafting LLC agreement	$ 20,000
Materials and labor costs for construction in progress on shopping center	1,900,000
Office expense (utilities, rent, overhead, etc.)	80,000

What issues must the LLC address in preparing its initial tax return?

ISSUE ID

35. **LO.6** Browne and Red, both C corporations, formed the BR Partnership on January 1, 2009. Neither Browne nor Red is a personal service corporation, and BR is not a tax shelter. BR's gross receipts were $4.6 million, $5 million, $6 million, and $7 million, respectively, for the four tax years ending in 2009, 2010, 2011, and 2012. Describe the methods of accounting available to BR in each tax year.

36. **LO.5** On July 1 of the current year, the R & R Partnership (an LLLP) was formed to operate a bed and breakfast inn. The partnership paid $3,000 in legal fees for drafting the partnership agreement and $5,000 for accounting fees related to organizing the entity. It also paid $10,000 in syndication costs to locate and secure investments from limited partners. In addition, before opening the inn for business, the entity paid $15,500 for advertising and $36,000 in costs related to an open house just before the grand opening of the property. The partnership opened the inn for business on October 1.
    a. How are these expenses classified?
    b. How much may the partnership deduct in its initial year of operations?
    c. How are costs treated that are not deducted currently?

ISSUE ID

37. **LO.4, 5, 6** The Heron Partnership was formed on July 1 of the current year and admitted Carl and Megan as equal partners on that date. The partners each contributed $200,000 of cash to establish a children's clothing store in a local shopping mall. The partners spent July and August buying inventory, equipment, supplies, and advertising for their "Grand Opening" on October 1. Following are some of the costs the partnership incurred during its first year of operations:

Legal fees to form partnership	$ 2,000
Advertising for "Grand Opening"	15,000
Advertising after opening	10,000
Consulting fees for establishing accounting system	5,000
Rent, six months at $2,000/month	12,000
Utilities at $600 per month	3,600
Salaries to sales clerks	30,000
Payments to Carl and Megan for services ($5,000/month each for three months, beginning in October)	30,000
Tax return preparation expense	5,000

In addition, the partnership purchased all of the assets of Granny Newcombs, Inc. Of the total purchase price for these assets, $60,000 was allocated to the trade name and logo.

Determine how each of the above costs is treated by the partnership, and identify the period over which the costs can be deducted, if any.

38. **LO.6** AzureCo, AuburnCo, and AquamarineCo form the AAA Partnership on January 1 of the current year. AzureCo is a 50% partner, and AuburnCo and AquamarineCo are each 25% partners. All of the partners and AAA use the cash method of accounting. For reporting purposes, AzureCo uses a fiscal year with a June 30 year-end, AuburnCo uses a fiscal year with an October 31 year-end, and AquamarineCo uses a calendar year. What is AAA's required tax year under the least aggregate deferral method?

39. **LO.4, 7** Phoebe and Parker are equal members of Phoenix Investors, LLC. They are real estate investors who formed the LLC several years ago with equal cash contributions. Phoenix then purchased a piece of land.

    On January 1 of the current year, to acquire a one-third interest in the entity, Reece contributed to the LLC some land she had held for investment. Reece purchased the land five years ago for $75,000; its fair market value at the contribution date was $90,000. No special allocation agreements were in effect before or after Reece was admitted to the LLC. Phoenix holds all land for investment.

    Immediately before Reece's property contribution, the balance sheet of Phoenix Investors, LLC, was as follows:

	Basis	FMV		Basis	FMV
Land	$30,000	$180,000	Phoebe, capital	$15,000	$ 90,000
			Parker, capital	15,000	90,000
	$30,000	$180,000		$30,000	$180,000

    a. At the contribution date, what is Reece's basis in her interest in the LLC?
    b. When does the LLC's holding period begin for the contributed land?
    c. On June 30 of the current year, the LLC sold the land contributed by Reece for $90,000. How much is the recognized gain or loss, and how is it allocated among the LLC members?
    d. Prepare a balance sheet reflecting basis and fair market value for the LLC immediately after the land sale described in (c). Assume no other transactions occurred during the tax year.

40. **LO.7** Assume the same facts as in Problem 39, with the following exceptions.

    - Reece purchased the land five years ago for $120,000. Its fair market value was $90,000 when it was contributed to the LLC.
    - Phoenix sold the land contributed by Reece for $84,000.

    a. How much is the recognized gain or loss, and how is it allocated among the LLC members?
    b. Prepare a balance sheet reflecting basis and fair market value for the LLC immediately after the land sale. Also prepare schedules that support the amount in each LLC member's capital account.

41. **LO.7, 8, 9** Andrea and Michael are equal partners in the accrual basis AM Partnership. At the beginning of the current tax year, Andrea's capital account has a balance of $200,000, and the partnership has recourse debts of $100,000 payable to unrelated parties. Assume all partnership recourse debt is shared equally between the partners. The following information about AM's operations for the current year is obtained from the partnership's records:

Taxable income	$320,000
Tax-exempt interest income	6,000
§ 1231 gain	9,000
Short-term capital loss	2,000
Political contribution	1,000
Charitable contribution to Big Brothers Big Sisters	2,000
Cash distribution to Andrea	50,000

Assume that year-end partnership debt payable to unrelated parties is $140,000. If all transactions are reflected in her beginning capital and basis in the same manner, what is Andrea's basis in the partnership interest:

a. At the beginning of the year?
b. At the end of the year?

42. **LO.7, 8, 11** The KL Partnership is owned equally by Kayla and Lisa. Kayla's basis is $20,000 at the beginning of the tax year. Lisa's basis is $16,000 at the beginning of the year. KL reported the following income and expenses for the current tax year:

Sales revenue	$150,000
Cost of sales	80,000
Distribution to Lisa	15,000
Depreciation expense	20,000
Utilities	14,000
Rent expense	18,000
Long-term capital gain	6,000
Payment to Mercy Hospital for Kayla's medical expenses	12,000

a. Determine the ordinary partnership income and separately stated items for the partnership.
b. Calculate Kayla's basis in her partnership interest at the end of the tax year. What items should Kayla report on her Federal income tax return?
c. Calculate Lisa's basis in her partnership interest at the end of the tax year. What items should Lisa report on her Federal income tax return?

43. **LO.7, 8, 10, 11** How would the answers in Problem 42 change if partnership revenues were $100,000 instead of $150,000?

44. **LO.4, 7, 8, 9** Celeste contributed business-related assets valued at $250,000 (basis of $100,000) in exchange for her 50% interest in the Celestine Partnership. Christine contributed land and a building valued at $400,000 (basis of $200,000) in exchange for the remaining 50% interest. Christine's property was encumbered by a qualified nonrecourse debt of $150,000, which was assumed by the partnership. The partnership reports the following income and expenses for the current tax year:

Sales	$350,000
Utilities, salaries, and other operating expenses	190,000
Short-term capital gain	6,000
Tax-exempt interest income	2,000
Charitable contributions	1,000
Distribution to Celeste	20,000
Distribution to Christine	10,000

At the end of the current tax year, Celestine had recourse debt of $100,000 for partnership accounts payable and qualified nonrecourse debt of $140,000.

a. What is Celeste's basis after formation of the partnership? Christine's basis?
b. What income and separately stated items does the partnership report on Celeste's Schedule K–1? What items does Celeste report on her tax return?
c. Assume all partnership debts are shared equally. At the end of the tax year, what are Celeste's basis and amount at risk in her partnership interest?

ISSUE ID

45. **LO.4, 7, 8, 9** Continue with the facts presented in Problem 44, except that Celestine was formed as an LLC instead of a general partnership.

a. How would Celestine's ending liabilities be treated?
b. How would Celeste's basis and amount at risk be different?

DECISION MAKING

46. **LO.7, 8, 9, 10** As of January 1 of last year, Dylan's outside basis and at-risk limitation for his 40% interest in the DEF Partnership were $60,000. Dylan and the partnership use the calendar year for tax purposes. The partnership incurred an operating loss of $200,000 for last year and a profit of $120,000 for the current year. Dylan is a material participant in the partnership.

a. How much loss, if any, may Dylan recognize for last year?
b. How much net reportable income must Dylan recognize for the current year?

c. What is Dylan's basis in the partnership as of December 31 of last year?
d. What is Dylan's basis in the partnership as of December 31 of the current year?
e. What year-end tax planning would you suggest to ensure that Dylan can deduct his share of partnership losses?

47. **LO.4, 7, 8, 10** Bryan and Cody each contribute $120,000 to the newly formed BC Partnership in exchange for a 50% interest. The partnership uses the available funds to acquire equipment costing $200,000 and to fund current operating expenses. The partnership agreement provides that depreciation will be allocated 80% to Bryan and 20% to Cody. All other items of income and loss will be allocated equally between the partners. Upon liquidation of the partnership, property will be distributed to the partners in accordance with their capital account balances. Any partner with a negative capital account must contribute cash in the amount of the negative balance to restore the capital account to $0. **DECISION MAKING**

In its first year, the partnership reported an ordinary loss (before depreciation) of $80,000 and depreciation expense of $36,000. In its second year, the partnership reported $40,000 of income from operations (before depreciation), and it reported depreciation expense of $57,600.

a. Calculate the partners' bases in their partnership interests at the end of the first and second tax years. Are any losses suspended?
b. Does the allocation provided in the partnership agreement have economic effect?

48. **LO.7, 8, 10** Continue with the facts presented in Problem 47. On the first day of the third tax year, the partnership sold the equipment for $150,000 and distributed the cash in accordance with the partnership agreement. The partnership was liquidated at this time. **ISSUE ID**

a. Calculate the partners' bases in their partnership interests after reflecting any gain or loss on disposal of the equipment.
b. How will partnership cash balances be distributed to the partners on liquidation?
c. What observations can you make regarding the value of a deduction to each partner?

49. **LO.7, 8** Chris and Lauren each contributed $90,000 cash to the cash basis CL Partnership. The partnership uses all $180,000 of the cash to purchase a depreciable asset. The partnership agreement provides that depreciation is allocated 60% to Chris and 40% to Lauren. All other items of partnership income, gain, loss, or deduction are allocated equally between the two partners. During the first year of operations, the partnership produces $30,000 of income before depreciation and deducts $30,000 of depreciation. At the end of the first year, the partnership sells the depreciable asset for its $150,000 book value. Following these transactions, the partnership has $180,000 of cash ($150,000 from sale of the asset and $30,000 from operations). Assume nothing else happens in the first year that affects the partners' capital accounts. The partnership then distributes all cash to the partners and liquidates at the end of the first year.

a. How much cash is distributed to each partner in the liquidating distribution under the economic effect test?
b. If the partnership distributes $30,000 cash to Lauren on June 30 of the current year, how much cash is distributed to each partner in the liquidating distribution under the economic effect test?

50. **LO.7, 8, 9, 10** Your client, the Williams Institute of Technology (WIT), is a 60% partner in the Research Industries Partnership (RIP). WIT is a widely held Subchapter C corporation and is not subject to the passive loss limitation. WIT is located at 76 Bradford Lane, St. Paul, MN 55164. The controller, Jeanine West, has sent you the following note and a copy of WIT's 2010 Schedule K–1 from the partnership. **DECISION MAKING** **COMMUNICATIONS**

Excerpt from client's note:
"RIP expects its 2011 operations to include the following:

Net loss from operations	$200,000
Capital gain from sale of land	100,000

The land was contributed by DASH, the other partner, when its value was $260,000. The partnership sold the land for $300,000. The partnership used this cash to repay all the partnership debt and pay for operating expenditures, which a tax partner in your firm has said RIP can deduct this year. The net loss of $200,000 reflects that deduction.

We want to be sure we can deduct our full share of this loss, but we do not believe we will have enough basis."

Items Reported on the 2010 Schedule K–1	
WIT's share of partnership recourse liabilities	$90,000
WIT's ending capital account balance	30,000

Draft a letter to the controller that describes the following:

- WIT's allocation of partnership items.
- WIT's basis in the partnership interest following the allocation.
- Any limitations on loss deductions.
- Any recommendations you have that would allow WIT to claim the full amount of losses in 2011.

Assume WIT's 2010 K–1 accurately reflects the information needed to compute its basis in the partnership interest. Also assume the operating expenditures are fully deductible this year, as the partner said.

Your client has experience researching issues in the Internal Revenue Code, so you may use some citations. However, be sure the letter is written in layperson's terms and cites are minimized.

51. **LO.9** The MGP General Partnership was created on January 1 of the current year by having Melinda, Gabe, and Pat each contribute $10,000 cash to the partnership in exchange for a one-third interest in partnership income, gains, losses, deductions, and credits. On December 31 of the current year, the partnership balance sheet reads as follows:

	Basis	FMV		Basis	FMV
Assets	$60,000	$75,000	Recourse debt	$30,000	$30,000
			Melinda, capital	14,000	19,000
			Gabe, capital	14,000	19,000
			Pat, capital	2,000	7,000
				$60,000	$75,000

Pat's capital account is less than Melinda's and Gabe's capital accounts because Pat has withdrawn more cash than the other partners.

How do the partners share the recourse debt as of December 31 of the current year?

COMMUNICATIONS

52. **LO.4, 8, 9** Paul and Anna plan to form the PA General Partnership by the end of the current year. The partners will each contribute $80,000 cash, and in addition, the partnership will borrow $240,000 from First State Bank. The $400,000 will be used to buy an investment property. The property will serve as collateral, and both partners will be required to personally guarantee the debt.

The tentative agreement provides that 60% of operating income, gains, losses, deductions, and credits will be allocated to Paul for the first five years the partnership is in existence. The remaining 40% is allocated to Anna. Thereafter, all partnership items will be allocated equally. The agreement also provides that capital accounts will be properly maintained and that each partner must restore any deficit in the capital account upon the partnership's liquidation.

The partners would like to know, before the end of the tax year, how the $240,000 liability will be allocated for basis purposes. Using the format (1) facts, (2) issues, (3) conclusion, and (4) law and analysis, draft a memo to the tax planning file for the PA Partnership that describes how the debt will be shared between the partners for purposes of computing the adjusted basis of each partnership interest.

ISSUE ID

DECISION MAKING

53. **LO.8, 9, 10, 12** The BCD Partnership plans to distribute cash of $20,000 to partner Brad at the end of the tax year. The partnership reported a loss for the year, and Brad's share of the loss is $10,000. At the beginning of the tax year, Brad's basis in his partnership interest, including his share of partnership liabilities, was $15,000. The partnership expects to report substantial income in future years.
    a. What rules are used to calculate Brad's ending basis in his partnership interest?
    b. How much gain or loss will Brad report for the tax year?

c. Will the deduction for the $10,000 loss be suspended?
d. Could any planning opportunities be used to minimize any negative tax ramifications of the distribution?

54. **LO.9, 10** Jasmine Gregory is a 20% member in Sparrow Properties, LLC, which is a lessor of residential rental property. Her share of the LLC's losses for the current year is $100,000. Immediately before considering the deductibility of this loss, Jasmine's capital account (which, in this case, corresponds to her basis excluding liabilities) reflected a balance of $50,000. Jasmine has personally guaranteed a $10,000 debt of the LLC that is allocated to her as a recourse debt. Her share of the LLC's nonrecourse debt is $30,000. This debt cannot be treated as qualified nonrecourse debt. Jasmine spends several hundred hours a year working for Sparrow Properties. **COMMUNICATIONS**

    Jasmine is also a managing member of Skylark Rentals, LLC, which is engaged in long-term (more than 30 days) equipment rental activities. (This is considered a passive activity.) Jasmine's share of Skylark's income is $36,000.

    Jasmine's modified adjusted gross income before considering the LLCs' activities is $300,000. Determine how much of Sparrow's $100,000 loss Jasmine can deduct on her current calendar year return. Using the format (1) facts, (2) issues, (3) conclusion, and (4) law and analysis, draft a memo to the client's tax file describing the loss limitations. Identify the Code sections under which losses are suspended.

55. **LO.11** FredCo and Fran are equal partners in the calendar year F & F Partnership. FredCo uses a fiscal year ending June 30, and Fran uses a calendar year. FredCo receives an annual guaranteed payment of $50,000 for use of capital contributed by FredCo. F & F's taxable income (after deducting FredCo's guaranteed payment) is $40,000 for 2011 and $50,000 for 2012.
    a. What is the amount of income from the partnership that FredCo must report for its tax year ending June 30, 2012?
    b. What is the amount of income from the partnership that Fran must report for her tax year ending December 31, 2012?

56. **LO.11** Continue with the facts presented in Problem 55. Assume FredCo's annual guaranteed payment is increased to $60,000 starting on January 1, 2012, and the partnership's taxable income for 2011 and 2012 (after deducting FredCo's guaranteed payment) is the same (i.e., $40,000 and $50,000, respectively). What is the amount of income from the partnership that FredCo must report for its tax year ending June 30, 2012?

57. **LO.7, 11** Nicole, a calendar year individual, owns 30% of Creole Cravings, Inc., a C corporation that was formed on February 1, 2011. She receives a $5,000 monthly salary from the corporation, and Creole Cravings generates $200,000 of taxable income (after accounting for payments to Nicole) for its tax year ending January 31, 2012.
    a. How do these activities affect Nicole's 2011 adjusted gross income?
    b. Assume, instead that Creole Cravings is a partnership (January 31 year-end) and that it classifies Nicole's salary as a guaranteed payment. How do these activities affect Nicole's 2011 and 2012 adjusted gross income?

58. **LO.11** Four GRRLs Partnership is owned by four sisters. Leah holds a 70% interest; each of the others owns 10%. Leah sells investment property to the partnership for its fair market value of $100,000 (Leah's basis is $150,000).
    a. How much loss, if any, may Leah recognize?
    b. If the partnership later sells the property for $160,000, how much gain must it recognize?
    c. If Leah's basis in the investment property was $20,000 instead of $150,000, how much, if any, gain would she recognize on the sale, and how would the gain be characterized?

TAX RETURN PROBLEMS

1. Ryan Marshall (111–11–1111), Samantha Evans (222–22–2222), and Tyler Armstrong (333–33–3333) are equal members in Tile Doctors, LLC (TDL), a limited liability company engaged in residential tile installation in San Diego, California. TDL's Federal employer identification number (EIN) is 11–1111111. The LLC uses the accrual method of accounting and the calendar year for reporting purposes. It began business operations on October 15, 2008. Its current address is 5917 East Cienega Boulevard, San Diego, CA, 92101. TDL's 2010 income statement reflected net income of $149,400. The following information was taken from the LLC's financial records for the current year: **H&R BLOCK** At Home

Receipts:	
Sales revenues	$740,375
Tax-exempt interest income	2,700
Long-term capital gain	1,825
Long-term capital loss	(300)
Total revenues	$744,600
Cash payments related to cost of goods sold:	
Materials purchases	$162,250
Salaries and wages (production-related W–2 wages)	278,300
Direct job costs	26,450
Additional § 263A costs	2,950
Total cash payments for jobs (all completed)	$469,950
Other cash disbursements (net of additional § 263A costs):	
Rent (including $1,000 payment for rent accrued in December 2009)	$ 14,200
Utilities (including $500 payment for utilities accrued in December 2009)	7,100
Office employee salaries (nonproduction W–2 wages)	25,400
Contribution to Red Cross	1,500
Meals and entertainment (subject to 50% disallowance)	1,200
Guaranteed payment, Tyler Armstrong, managing member	30,000
Office expense	2,820
Legal and professional fees	3,575
Payroll taxes	2,625
Business interest on operating line of credit	9,500
Repairs	1,410
Tile cutting equipment (eligible for §179 deduction)	9,000
Total other cash disbursements	$108,330
Noncash expenses:	
Accrual of ending accounts payable ($1,200 rent; $600 utilities)	$ 1,800
Depreciation on equipment purchased in previous years (reported on Schedule A)	16,620

The beginning and ending balance sheets for the LLC were as follows for 2010:

	Beginning	Ending
Cash	$ 11,360	$ 22,680
Long-term investments	46,000	42,000
Equipment	95,000	104,000
Accumulated depreciation	(26,660)	(52,280)
Total assets	$125,700	$116,400
Accounts payable	$ 1,500	$ 1,800
Recourse operating line of credit (note payable in less than one year)	75,000	60,000
Capital, Marshall	16,400	18,200
Capital, Evans	16,400	18,200
Capital, Armstrong	16,400	18,200
Total liabilities and capital	$125,700	$116,400

TDL closes its offices during the last two weeks of December each year. The LLC receives payment upon completion of each project and has no jobs in progress, inventory, or accounts receivable at the end of most tax years. Accounts payable relate to rent and utilities, which may be deducted in the current tax year under the recurring item exception of § 461(h)(3).

The LLC uses the lower of cost or market method for valuing inventory. TDL is subject to § 263A; for simplicity, assume § 263A costs are reflected in the same manner for book and tax purposes. TDL did not change its inventory accounting method during the year. There were no writedowns of inventory items, and TDL does not use the LIFO method.

The LLC claimed $16,620 of depreciation expense for both tax and financial accounting purposes; all $16,620 should be reported on Schedule A. The depreciation creates a "post-1986 depreciation adjustment" of $2,400 for AMT purposes. The LLC will claim a § 179 deduction for the tile cutting equipment purchased during the year.

All capital gains and losses resulted from sales of investment assets and will be taxed at regular capital gains rates. All line-of-credit borrowings were used exclusively for business operations; consequently, none of the interest expense is considered investment interest expense.

All guaranteed payments were paid to Tyler Armstrong. In addition, each member (including Armstrong) withdrew $4,000 per month as a distribution (draw) of operating profits.

TDL's business activities are eligible for the domestic production activities deduction (DPAD) of § 199. The LLC uses the "small business simplified overall method" and reports qualified production activities income (QPAI) and production-related W–2 wages to the LLC members on Schedule K–1. Assume that QPAI is $147,275.

The operating line of credit was guaranteed by all the LLC members; the accounts payable were not guaranteed. Assume the members share equally in all LLC liabilities, because all initial contributions and all ongoing allocations and distributions are pro rata.

All members are classified as "active individuals" and "LLC member-managers" on Schedule K–1. The capital account analysis on Schedule K–1 is prepared on a tax basis. On the Analysis of Income (Loss), the IRS's instructions indicate that the amounts for any LLC members should be reported on the line for limited partners.

None of the members sold any portion of their interests in TDL during 2010. There were no distributions of noncash property or interests in the LLC. None of the members contributed cash or other property to the LLC during the year. The LLC has never participated in a like-kind exchange. The LLC has not previously made an election under § 754. The LLC has not made a basis adjustment under §§ 734(b) or 743(b) and is not required to make such an adjustment.

TDL's operations are entirely restricted to Southern California. All members are U.S. citizens who are unrelated to one another. The LLC does not own more than 20% (directly or indirectly) of any other entity. No debt of the LLC's was canceled, forgiven, or modified during the tax year. The LLC had no foreign operations, no foreign bank accounts, and no interest in any foreign trusts or other partnerships. The LLC is not publicly traded. No Forms 8805 or 8865 are required to be attached to the return, and the LLC has not filed (and is not required to file) Forms 8893, 8858, or 8918 for the tax year.

The IRS's business code for "tile contractors" is 236110. Tyler Armstrong has agreed to serve as the tax matters partner. The LLC files its tax return in Ogden, Utah. Member Tyler Armstrong lives at 14231 N. Los Alamos Boulevard, San Diego, CA 92101.

a. Prepare pages 1–5 of Form 1065 for TDL. Do not prepare Form 4562 or Schedule D. Leave any items blank where insufficient information has been provided. Prepare supporting schedules as necessary if adequate information is provided. *Hint:* Prepare Schedule A first to determine cost of goods sold.
b. Prepare Schedule K–1 for member Tyler Armstrong.

2. On January 1, 2005, the Branson Company (EIN 22–2222222) and Porto Engineering, Inc. (EIN 33–3333333), formed Branto, LLC (an equally owned joint venture). During its first four years, the LLC worked with the U.S. Department of Homeland Security and the National Transportation Safety Board to design and develop a specific device for airport passenger screening. Porto provides engineering expertise, and Branson provides high-tech manufacturing, selling, and distribution expertise. Early in 2009, the two governmental agencies recommended the product. In 2010, Branto's screening device is being succesfully marketed, sold, delivered, and installed in airports around the United States.

The LLC uses the accrual method of accounting and the calendar year for reporting purposes. Its current address is 3750 Airport Boulevard, Seattle, WA, 98124. The following information was taken from the trial balance supporting the LLC's GAAP-basis (audited) financial statements for the 2010 calendar year:

Revenues:	
Sales revenues	$40,000,000
Interest income	50,000
Total revenues	$40,050,000
Amounts related to cost of goods sold:	
Beginning inventory	$ 2,000,000
Materials purchases	8,000,000
Labor	9,000,000
Additional § 263A costs	–0–
Other costs: Various items	2,700,000
Book depreciation	1,275,000
Less: Ending inventory	(3,000,000)
Total amounts re: work-in-progress	$19,975,000
Other costs *not* related to production:	
Salaries and wages	$ 1,000,000
Taxes and licenses	300,000
Charitable contributions	100,000
Interest expense	200,000
Meals and entertainment (subject to 50% disallowance)	1,200,000
Travel expenses	800,000
Employee benefit programs	300,000
Insurance (including key employee life insurance of $100,000)	300,000
Legal and professional fees	600,000
Office expenses	2,000,000
Sales and promotion expenses	2,500,000
Utilities	800,000
Warranty expense (increase to reserves; not fixed and determinable)	300,000
Total other costs disbursements	$10,400,000
Net income per books and GAAP-basis audited financial statements	$ 9,675,000

The beginning and ending GAAP-basis balance sheets for the LLC were as follows at December 31, 2010:

	Beginning	Ending
Cash	$ 975,000	$ 1,825,000
Accounts receivable	620,000	2,600,000
Inventories	2,000,000	3,000,000
U.S. government obligations	1,000,000	1,000,000
Land	600,000	600,000
Buildings and equipment	12,000,000	15,000,000
Accumulated depreciation	(6,375,000)	(7,650,000)
Total assets	$10,820,000	$16,375,000
Accounts payable	$ 420,000	$ 800,000
Other current liabilities:		
Operating line of credit (guaranteed by LLC members)	1,000,000	2,000,000
Warranty reserves (not guaranteed by members)	200,000	500,000
Mortgage notes on building	5,000,000	6,000,000
Capital, Branson Company	2,100,000	3,537,500
Capital, Porto Engineering, Inc.	2,100,000	3,537,500
Total liabilities and capital	$10,820,000	$16,375,000

The LLC uses the lower of cost or market method for valuing inventory. Branto is subject to § 263A; for simplicity, assume § 263A costs are reflected in the same manner for book and tax purposes. Branto did not change its inventory accounting method during the year. There were no writedowns of inventory items, and Branto does not use the LIFO method.

The LLC claimed $2,499,270 of depreciation expense for tax purposes (book depreciation is $1,275,000). All tax depreciation expense should be reported on Schedule A. The LLC placed $3 million of assets in service during the current year; this exceeds the threshold for eligibility for a § 179 deduction. Tax depreciation amounts reflect bonus depreciation deductions (and these assets are not subject to AMT adjustments). Depreciation for assets placed in service in prior years creates an adjustment of ($276,900) for AMT purposes. (This is a negative amount—book depreciation for these assets is greater than tax depreciation.)

All borrowings were used exclusively for business operations; consequently, none of the interest expense is considered investment interest expense. The LLC members were required to guarantee the debt related to the operating line of credit. The accounts payable, accrued warranty claim liabilities, and the mortgage were not guaranteed by the members. The mortgage relates to the real property and is considered qualified nonrecourse financing. The partners share equally in all LLC liabilities, because all initial contributions and all ongoing allocations and distributions are pro rata.

The LLC's activities are eligible for the domestic production activities deduction (DPAD). For simplicity, assume the LLC's qualified production activities income (QPAI) is $9.5 million. The LLC's production-related W–2 wages are $10 million.

No guaranteed payments were paid to either of the LLC members. Instead, the members each withdrew $3.4 million of cash during the year. The LLC has never made a distribution to the partners of noncash property. Cash distributions were not subject to the disclosure requirements of Reg. § 1.707–8. The LLC has not made a § 754 election and had no transactions during the current year that would warrant such an election. None of the members sold any portion of their interests in the LLC during the year.

During the current tax year, the LLC did not sell or acquire intangible assets, restructure debt, or distribute any property received in a like-kind exchange. It did not change any accounting method for tax or financial reporting purposes. Both LLC members are U.S. Subchapter C corporations. The LLC's operations are entirely restricted to the United States, and all sales were to U.S. businesses. The LLC had no foreign operations, no foreign bank accounts, and no interest in any foreign trusts or other LLCs.

None of the members contributed cash or other property to the LLC during the year. The LLC has not made a basis adjustment under §§ 734(b) or 743(b) and is not required to make such an adjustment. The LLC does not own more than 20% (directly or indirectly) of any other entity. The LLC is not publicly traded. No Forms 8805 or 8865 are required to be attached to the return, and the LLC has not filed (and is not required to file) Forms 8893, 8858, or 8918 for the tax year.

Both members are classified as "corporations" and "LLC member-managers" on Schedule K–1. The capital account analysis on Schedule K–1 is prepared on a tax basis. On the Analysis of Income (Loss), the IRS's instructions indicate that the amounts for any LLC members should be reported on the line for limited partners.

The IRS's business code for "Other specialty trade contractors" is 238900. The LLC files its tax return in Ogden, Utah. Branson Company is located at 3750 Airport Boulevard, Seattle, WA 98124 (the same as the LLC's address). Porto Engineering, Inc., is located at 42100 Highway 980 West, Tacoma, WA 98401. The LLC member corporations are each owned by several unrelated individual taxpayers. Branson Company is the tax matters partner.

The capital account reconciliation on the partners' Schedules K–1 is prepared on a GAAP basis. The LLC is required to file Schedule M–3, Form 8916–A (Supplemental Attachment to Schedule M–3), and Schedule C with its Form 1065. Schedule L must be prepared on a financial reporting basis.

a. Prepare pages 1–5 of Form 1065 for Branto, LLC. Do not prepare Form 4562. Leave any items blank where insufficient information has been provided. Prepare supporting schedules as necessary if adequate information is provided.
b. Prepare Schedule M–3, Form 8916–A (page 1), and Schedule C. Hint: You will find four book-tax differences (two temporary differences and two permanent differences).
c. Prepare Schedule K–1 for 50% LLC member Branson Company.

RESEARCH PROBLEMS

THOMSON REUTERS
Checkpoint® Student Edition

Note: Solutions to Research Problems can be prepared by using the **Checkpoint® Student Edition** online research product, which is available to accompany this text. It is also possible to prepare solutions to the Research Problems by using tax research materials found in a standard tax library.

COMMUNICATIONS

Research Problem 1. Your clients, Grayson Investments, Inc. (Ana Marks, President), and Blake Caldwell, each contributed $200,000 of cash to form the Realty Management Partnership, a limited partnership. Grayson is the general partner, and Blake is the limited partner. The partnership used the $400,000 cash to make a down payment on a building. The rest of the building's $4 million purchase price was financed with an interest-only nonrecourse loan of $3.6 million, which was obtained from an independent third-party bank.

The partnership allocates all partnership items equally between the partners except for the MACRS deductions and building maintenance, which are allocated 70% to Blake and 30% to Grayson. The partnership definitely wishes to satisfy the "economic effect" requirements of Reg. §§ 1.704–1 and 1.704–2 and will reallocate MACRS, if necessary, to satisfy the requirements of the Regulations.

Under the partnership agreement, liquidation distributions will be paid in proportion to the partners' positive capital account balances. Capital accounts are maintained as required in the Regulations. Grayson Investments has an unlimited obligation to restore its capital account while Blake is subject to a qualified income offset provision.

Assume all partnership items, except for MACRS, will net to zero throughout the first three years of the partnership operations. Also, assume that each year's MACRS deduction will be $200,000 (to simplify the calculations).

Draft a letter to the partnership evaluating the allocation of MACRS in each of the three years under Reg. §§ 1.704–1 and –2. The partnership's address is 53 East Marsh Ave., Smyrna, GA 30082. Do not address the "substantial" test.

Research Problem 2. Franklin Industries, Inc., and George Weldon have formed the FG Partnership to operate a retail establishment selling antique household furnishings. Franklin Industries is the general partner, and George is the limited partner. Both partners contribute $15,000 to form the partnership. The partnership uses the $30,000 contributed by the partners and a recourse loan of $100,000 obtained from an unrelated third-party lender to acquire $130,000 of initial inventory.

The partners believe they will have extensive losses in the first year due to advertising and initial cash-flow requirements. Franklin and George have agreed to share losses equally. To make sure the losses can be allocated to both partners, they have included a provision in the partnership agreement requiring each partner to restore any deficit balance in that partner's partnership capital account upon liquidation of the partnership.

Franklin was also willing to include a provision that requires Franklin to make up any deficit balance within 90 days of liquidation of the partnership. As a limited partner, George argued that he should not be subject to such a time requirement. The partners compromised and included a provision that requires George to restore a deficit balance in his capital account within two years of liquidation of the partnership. No interest will be owed on the deferred restoration payment.

How is the debt allocated to the partners' respective bases? Describe the rules that apply and cite your references. Hint: You will find that FG cannot allocate the $100,000 recourse debt equally to the two partners. Where appropriate, assume that a 10% interest rate, compounded semiannually, applies.

Research Problem 3. Harrison has considerable experience as a leasing agent for residential rental properties. Alameda Properties (not a publicly traded partnership) has offered Harrison a position handling leasing activities for a new limited liability limited partnership that is being formed to construct and manage three apartment complexes. Alameda is willing to hire Harrison for a minimum of two years to lease and manage the properties, but the partnership is unable to pay the $100,000 annual salary Harrison requires without impairing its ability to pay necessary cash distributions to the limited partners.

Alameda is willing to pay Harrison a $60,000 salary for two years, increasing to a market salary thereafter. Alameda is also willing to allow Harrison to purchase a 10%

interest in the partnership, but Harrison cannot afford the required $25,000 capital contribution.

The partnership expects to have income and cash flows from operations of approximately $200,000 per year. The annual cash flows will be distributed to the partners each year during the estimated seven-year holding period of the properties.

Harrison and Alameda Properties have approached you for assistance in structuring a mutually satisfactory arrangement. You are aware that a partner can be awarded an interest in the future profits of a partnership and have learned from a colleague that in 2005, the IRS issued a Notice and Proposed Regulations that outline procedures for structuring an arrangement to avoid current taxation of the expected future profits. You have suggested that, in lieu of requiring Harrison to pay the $25,000 purchase price, Alameda could grant Harrison a 10% interest in Alameda's future profits.

a. Under Notice 2005–43, what actions must the partnership take to ensure the profits interest is nontaxable? What is the tax result for receipt of a nonforfeitable future profits interest?
b. Alameda has an interest in making sure that Harrison remains with the company and wants to attach a three-year forfeiture clause to the profits interest. In other words, if Harrison leaves the company within three years, his profits interest is terminated. What additional considerations arise under Notice 2005–43 if the profits interest is not fully vested?
c. What are the advantages and disadvantages of the proposed structure to each party?
d. At this writing, one of the IRS's targeted items in its "priority guidance plan" is to issue guidelines related to a partner's receipt of a profits interest or an interest in the capital of the partnership (also called a "carried interest"). Review the current tax rules and regulations to determine whether the IRS has acted on this. If so, how would those rules affect Harrison if he had received a 10% interest in partnership capital rather than future partnership profits?

Use the tax resources of the Internet to address the following questions. Do not restrict your search to the Web, but include a review of newsgroups and general reference materials, practitioner sites and resources, primary sources of the tax law, chat rooms and discussion groups, and other opportunities.

Research Problem 4. Print an article posted by a law firm that comments on pitfalls to avoid in drafting partnership agreements. Ideally, use the home page of a firm that has offices in your state.

Research Problem 5. Use the search feature on your favorite news site on the Web (e.g., CNN, ABC News, Fox News, etc.) and search for news on partnerships, LLCs, or limited partnerships. What entities did you find that are taking advantage of the partnership entity form? (Be sure these entities are truly legal partnerships. Some entities called "partnerships" by the news media actually involve transfers of stock or formation of a corporation to manage the joint venture.)

Research Problem 6. Find the home page of a partnership that seems to be soliciting financing from new partners. Comment on the portrayal of the pertinent tax law that is included in the materials, especially with respect to the at-risk rules and the passive activity limitations.

Partnerships: Distributions, Transfer of Interests, and Terminations

CHAPTER 11

LEARNING OBJECTIVES

After completing Chapter 11, you should be able to:

LO.1 Determine the tax treatment of proportionate nonliquidating distributions from a partnership to a partner.

LO.2 Determine the tax treatment of proportionate distributions that liquidate a partnership.

LO.3 Describe the tax treatment that applies to distributions treated as disguised sales and distributions of marketable securities and precontribution gain property.

LO.4 Discuss the general concepts governing tax treatment of disproportionate distributions.

LO.5 Determine the tax treatment under § 736 of payments from a partnership to a retiring or deceased partner.

LO.6 Calculate the selling partner's amount and character of gain or loss on the sale or exchange of a partnership interest.

LO.7 Describe tax issues related to other dispositions of partnership interests.

LO.8 Calculate the optional adjustments to basis under § 754.

LO.9 Outline the methods of terminating a partnership.

LO.10 Identify the special considerations of a family partnership.

LO.11 Describe the application of partnership provisions to limited liability companies (LLCs) and limited liability partnerships (LLPs).

LO.12 Evaluate tax planning considerations related to partnership distributions and sales of partnership interests.

OUTLINE

For the latest in changes to tax legislation, visit **www.cengage.com/taxation/swft.**

THE BIG PICTURE **Tax Solutions for the Real World**

THE LIFE CYCLE OF A PARTNERSHIP

In the previous chapter, Josh, Kyle, and Maria created Beachside Properties, LLC, to own and operate the Beachsider Café and to own, manage, and lease the remaining properties in the Shorefront Center. The 10-acre center includes 3 developed acres (including the Beachsider Café) and 7 acres being held for expansion. Josh, Kyle, and Maria own, respectively, 20 percent, 40 percent, and 40 percent shares in the LLC's profits and losses and 5 percent, 47.5 percent, and 47.5 percent interests in its capital. The entity was formed as an LLC to achieve some measure of limited liability as to potential losses (see Chapter 10).

Several years have passed since the LLC was formed. The LLC interests and the net underlying assets are currently valued at approximately $10 million (including $1 million of goodwill for the Beachsider Café). During this period, the LLC has made significant distributions of cash and property to its members.

The population in the area has grown substantially, and it appears to be a good time to develop the remaining seven acres of the property. The cost of development is estimated at $10 million. Josh wants to manage the expansion, but Kyle and Maria are nearing retirement age and would prefer to dispose of their interests (valued at $9.5 million, or 95 percent of the net LLC value). Josh has been approached by a group of developers who are willing to invest the $19.5 million necessary to make the improvements and to purchase Kyle's and Maria's interests.

The transfer of Kyle's and Maria's interests and the admission of the new LLC members can be accomplished in two ways. First, the LLC could admit the new members for $19.5 million of cash and use $9.5 million to redeem the interests of Kyle and Maria. Second, Kyle and Maria could sell their LLC interests directly to the new members for $9.5 million; the new members would also contribute $10 million of cash to the LLC for the expansion. Although the two alternatives have identical economic effects, the tax results could differ substantially.

How are the distributions of cash and property to the LLC members treated over the years? What are the tax consequences of admitting the new members to the LLC and redeeming the interests of Kyle and Maria? What are the results if the new members acquire the interests directly from Kyle and Maria and contribute the cash for expansion to the LLC? **Read the chapter and formulate your response.**

The previous chapter examined the tax effects of partnership formation and operations. Most operating transactions of a partnership present few tax problems; under the aggregate theory of partnership taxation, revenues earned and expenses paid by the partnership flow through to the tax returns of the partners. If the partners are individuals, the transactions are then handled like other individual tax matters.

However, a number of special tax provisions, many of them complex, govern the effects of the following transactions, which are discussed in this chapter:

- Nonliquidating distributions, or routine distributions from the partnership to the partners. In most cases, these distributions create no recognized gain or loss to the partner receiving the distribution. This treatment contrasts with that of corporate distributions, which may result in dividend income to the shareholder.
- Liquidating distributions, after which the recipient of the distribution is no longer a partner. The general rule here is that gain or loss is not recognized by either the liquidated partner or the partnership. There are exceptions, however, and these may result in gains or losses that are usually capital in nature.
- Sale of a partnership interest to a new or existing partner. This results in the selling partner receiving a return of capital and capital gain or loss. The result follows both the aggregate and the entity theories discussed in the last chapter. The general tax treatment is similar to that of a stock sale made by a

shareholder in a C or S corporation; the taxpayer recognizes a gain or loss. The gain or loss is allocated between capital and ordinary amounts based on the partnership's underlying assets—an example of the aggregate theory at work.

This chapter also discusses an optional election a partnership may make concerning adjustments to basis when a partnership interest is sold. Partnership terminations and special problems associated with family partnerships are also explained. The chapter closes with discussions of two specialized business forms, limited liability companies and limited liability partnerships.

11.1 Distributions from a Partnership

The tax treatment of distributions from a partnership to a partner was introduced in Chapter 10 in the context of routine cash withdrawals (or "draws") and cash distributions from a continuing partnership to a continuing partner. These draws and distributions reduce the partner's outside basis by the amount of the cash received. The partnership's inside basis in assets is similarly reduced.

EXAMPLE 1
THE BIG PICTURE

Return to the facts of *The Big Picture* on p. 11-2. Assume that Josh's basis in his interest in Beachside Properties, LLC, is $300,000. The LLC distributes $50,000 cash to Josh at the end of the year. Josh does not recognize any gain on the distribution and reduces his basis by $50,000 (the amount of the distribution) to $250,000. Josh's basis in the cash he received is $50,000, and the LLC's inside basis for his assets is reduced by the $50,000 cash distributed. ■

The result in Example 1 arises whether or not a similar distribution is made to Kyle or Maria, the other members of Beachside Properties, LLC. In a partnership or LLC, it is not critical that all partners or members receive a distribution at the same time as long as capital account balances are maintained appropriately, and final distributions are in accordance with ending capital account balances (see Chapter 10). Capital account maintenance requirements ensure that each partner eventually receives the proper amount, even though current distributions are not in accordance with ownership percentages.

A payment from a partnership to a partner is not necessarily treated as a distribution. For example, as discussed in Chapter 10, a partnership may pay interest or rent to a partner for use of the partner's capital or property, make a guaranteed payment to a partner, or purchase property from a partner.

If a payment *is* treated as a distribution from the partnership to the partner, however, it will fall into one of two categories:

- Liquidating distributions.
- Nonliquidating distributions.

These distributions may consist of cash or partnership property. Whether a distribution is a **liquidating** or **nonliquidating distribution** depends solely on whether the partner remains a partner in the partnership after the distribution is made. A *liquidating* distribution occurs either (1) when a partnership itself liquidates and distributes all of its property to its partners or (2) when an ongoing partnership redeems the interest of one of its partners. This second type of liquidating distribution occurs, for example, when a partner retires from a partnership, or when a deceased partner's interest is liquidated. The two types of liquidating distributions receive differing tax treatment, as later sections of the chapter will explain.

A *nonliquidating* distribution is any other distribution from a continuing partnership to a continuing partner—that is, any distribution that is not a liquidating distribution. Nonliquidating distributions are of two types: draws or partial liquidations. A *draw* is a distribution of a partner's share of current or accumulated partnership profits that have been taxed to the partner in current or prior taxable years of the partnership. A *partial liquidation* is a distribution that reduces the partner's interest in partnership capital but does not liquidate the partner's entire interest in the partnership. The distinction between the two types of nonliquidating distributions is largely semantic, as the basic tax treatment typically does not differ.

EXAMPLE 2

Kate joins the calendar year KLM Partnership on January 1, 2011, by contributing $40,000 cash to the partnership in exchange for a one-third interest in partnership capital, profits, and losses. Her distributive share of partnership income for the year is $25,000. If the partnership distributes $65,000 ($25,000 share of partnership profits + $40,000 initial capital contribution) to Kate on December 31, 2011, the distribution is a nonliquidating distribution as long as Kate continues to be a partner in the partnership. This is true even though Kate receives her share of profits plus her entire investment in the partnership. In this case, $25,000 is considered a draw, and the remaining $40,000 is a partial liquidation of Kate's interest. If, instead, the partnership is liquidated or Kate ceases to be a partner in the ongoing partnership, the $65,000 distribution is a liquidating distribution. ■

A distribution is generally tax deferred. However, in certain circumstances, the partner may recognize capital gain (or loss) and ordinary income (or loss) when a distribution is received from the partnership.

A distribution may be either proportionate or disproportionate. In a **proportionate distribution**, a partner receives the appropriate share of certain ordinary income-producing assets of the partnership. A **disproportionate distribution** occurs when the distribution increases or decreases the distributee partner's interest in certain ordinary income-producing assets. The tax treatment of disproportionate distributions is very complex.

The initial discussion and examples in this chapter describe the treatment of proportionate current and liquidating distributions. Special rules related to property distributions are discussed next. The discussion of distributions concludes with a brief overview of the rules pertaining to disproportionate distributions.

LO.1

Determine the tax treatment of proportionate nonliquidating distributions from a partnership to a partner.

PROPORTIONATE NONLIQUIDATING DISTRIBUTIONS

In general, neither the partner nor the partnership recognizes gain or loss when a proportionate nonliquidating distribution occurs.[1] The partner usually takes a carryover basis for the assets distributed.[2] The distributee partner's outside basis is reduced (but not below zero) by the amount of cash and the adjusted basis of property distributed to the partner by the partnership.[3] As the following example illustrates, a distribution does not change a partner's overall economic position.

EXAMPLE 3

Steven is a one-fourth partner in the SP Partnership. On December 31 of the current tax year, his basis in his partnership interest is $40,000. The fair market value of the interest is $70,000. The partnership distributes $25,000 cash to him on that date. The distribution is not taxable to Steven or the partnership. The distribution reduces Steven's adjusted basis in the partnership to $15,000 ($40,000 − $25,000), and the fair market value of his partnership interest is, arguably, reduced to $45,000 ($70,000 − $25,000). ■

EXAMPLE 4

Assume the same facts as in Example 3, except that, in addition to the $25,000 cash, the partnership distributes land with an adjusted basis to the partnership of $13,000 and a fair market value of $30,000 on the date of distribution. The distribution is not taxable to Steven or the partnership. Steven reduces his basis in the partnership to $2,000 [$40,000 − ($25,000 + $13,000)] and takes a carryover basis of $13,000 in the land. The fair market value of Steven's remaining interest in the partnership is, arguably, reduced to $15,000 [$70,000 − ($25,000 + $30,000)].

If Steven had sold his partnership interest for $70,000 rather than receiving the distributions, he would have realized and recognized gain of $30,000 ($70,000 selling price − $40,000 outside basis). Because he has not recognized any gain or loss on the

[1]§§ 731(a) and (b).

[2]§ 732(a)(1).

[3]§ 733.

distribution of cash and land, he should still have the $30,000 of deferred gain to recognize at some point in the future. This is exactly what will happen. If Steven sells the cash, land, and remaining partnership interest on January 1 of the next year (the day after the distribution), he realizes and recognizes gains of $17,000 ($30,000 – $13,000) on the land and $13,000 ($15,000 – $2,000) on the partnership interest. These gains total $30,000, which is the amount of the original deferred gain. ■

Note the difference between the tax theory governing distributions from C corporations and partnerships. In a C corporation, a distribution from current or accumulated income (earnings and profits) is taxable as a dividend to the shareholder, and the corporation does not receive a deduction for the amount distributed. This is an example of corporate income being subject to double taxation. In a partnership, a distribution from current or accumulated profits is not taxable because Congress has decided that partnership income should be subject to only a single level of taxation. Because a partner pays taxes when the share of income is earned by the partnership, this income is not taxed again when distributed.

These results make sense under the entity and aggregate concepts. The entity concept is applicable to corporate dividends, so any amount paid as a dividend is treated as a transfer by the corporate entity to the shareholder and is taxed accordingly. Under the aggregate theory, though, a partner receiving a distribution of partnership income is treated as merely receiving something already owned. Whether the partner chooses to leave the income in the partnership or receive it in a distribution makes no difference.

Cash Distributions

Gain Recognition A proportionate nonliquidating distribution of cash is taxable to the partner if the distributed cash exceeds the outside basis of the partner's interest in the partnership.[4]

EXAMPLE 5

Samantha is a one-third partner in the SMP Partnership. Her basis in this ownership interest is $50,000 on December 31, 2011, after accounting for the calendar year partnership's 2011 operations and for Samantha's 2011 capital contributions. On December 31, 2011, the partnership distributes $60,000 cash to Samantha. She recognizes a $10,000 gain from this distribution ($60,000 cash received – $50,000 basis in her partnership interest). Most likely, this gain is taxed as a capital gain.[5] ■

As you can see, distributions *from* current and accumulated earnings are taxed differently to shareholders and partners, but cash distributions *in excess* of accumulated profits are taxed similarly for corporate shareholders and partners in partnerships. Both shareholders and partners are allowed to recover the cumulative capital invested in the entity tax-free.

Liability Reduction Treated as Cash Distribution Recall from Chapter 10 that the reduction of a partner's share of partnership debt is treated as a distribution of cash from the partnership to the partner. A reduction of a partner's share of partnership debt, then, first reduces the partner's basis in the partnership. Any reduction of a share of debt in excess of a partner's basis in the partnership is taxable to the partner as a gain.

EXAMPLE 6

Returning to the facts of Example 5, assume that Samantha's $50,000 basis in her partnership interest included a $60,000 share of partnership liabilities. If the partnership repays all of its liabilities, Samantha is treated as receiving a $60,000 distribution from the partnership. The first $50,000 of this distribution reduces her basis to $0. The last $10,000 distributed creates a taxable gain to her of $10,000. ■

[4] § 731(a)(1).

[5] § 731(a). If the partnership holds any "hot assets," however, Samantha will probably recognize some ordinary income. See § 751(b) and the related discussion of ordinary income ("hot") assets and disproportionate distributions later in this chapter.

Marketable Security Distributions Treated as Cash A distribution of marketable securities can also be treated as a distribution of cash. Determining the treatment of such distributions is complicated because several exceptions may apply and the basis in the distributed stock must be calculated. Such distributions are discussed later under Property Distributions with Special Tax Treatment: Marketable Securities.

Loss Recognition The distributee partner cannot recognize a loss on a proportionate nonliquidating distribution. This loss is deferred because tax law typically does not permit losses to be recognized until the loss is certain to occur and the amount is known. After the nonliquidating distribution, the partner still owns the partnership interest, which has an indeterminate future value. Only when a final liquidating distribution is received is the loss certain and known in amount—and potentially deductible.

EXAMPLE 7

Henry has a $50,000 basis in his partnership interest. Assume that on December 31 he receives a distribution of $10,000 cash. As a result of the distribution, his basis in the partnership interest is reduced to $40,000.

Henry knows the partnership has fallen on hard times and that future distributions will probably not amount to more than a few hundred dollars. He may not recognize a loss, even though a loss probably exists. The amount of the loss is not fixed and determinable because he still owns the partnership interest. ■

Property Distributions

In general, a distributee partner does not recognize gain from a property distribution. If the basis of property distributed by a partnership exceeds the partner's basis in the partnership interest, the distributed asset takes a substituted basis. This ensures that the partner does not receive asset basis that is not "paid for."

EXAMPLE 8

Amanda has a $50,000 basis in her partnership interest. The partnership distributes land it owns with a basis and a fair market value of $60,000. Amanda does not recognize any gain on this distribution because it is a distribution of property. However, Amanda should not be allowed to take a carryover basis of $60,000 in the land, when her basis in her partnership interest is only $50,000. Therefore, Amanda takes a substituted basis of $50,000 in the land. Her basis in her partnership interest is reduced by the basis she takes in the asset received, or $50,000. Therefore, Amanda has a $50,000 basis in the land and a $0 basis in her partnership interest, and she recognizes no gain on this distribution. ■

The rule that no gain or loss is recognized on a property distribution from a partnership has several exceptions. These situations may arise for either a current or a liquidating distribution, so discussion of these exceptions is deferred until all the general rules are discussed (see Property Distributions with Special Tax Treatment later in the chapter).

Ordering Rules

When the inside basis of the distributed assets exceeds the distributee partner's outside basis, the assets are deemed distributed in the following order:

- Cash is distributed first.
- Unrealized receivables and inventory are distributed second.
- All other assets are distributed last.

Unrealized receivables are receivables that have a value to the partnership, but for which the related income has not yet been realized or recognized under the partnership's method of accounting. The term *unrealized receivables* applies only to amounts that will ultimately be realized and recognized as ordinary income. If the partnership uses the cash method of accounting, trade receivables from services or sales are unrealized receivables. If the partnership uses the accrual method, income has already been recognized, so trade receivables are not unrealized receivables. Unrealized receivables include receivables from sales of ordinary income property and rights to payments for services. For some purposes, unrealized receivables also include depreciation recapture income that would arise if the partnership sold its depreciable assets. Installment gains are unrealized receivables if the gain will be taxed as ordinary income when realized.

Inventory, for purposes of these ordering rules, includes any partnership assets except cash, capital, or § 1231 assets. For example, all accounts receivable are considered to be inventory, although only cash basis receivables are "unrealized receivables."

Because the partner typically does not recognize a gain from a *property* distribution, the Code provides that the partner's basis for property received cannot exceed the partner's basis in the partnership interest immediately before the distribution. For each level of asset distribution, the relevant adjustments are made to the partner's basis in the interest. In other words, after a cash distribution, the partner's basis in the interest is recomputed before determining the effect of a distribution of unrealized receivables or inventory. The basis is again recomputed before determining the effect of a distribution of other assets. If the remaining outside basis at the end of any step is insufficient to cover the entire inside basis of the assets in the next step, that remaining outside basis is allocated among the assets within that class.[6]

EXAMPLE 9

Lindsey has a $48,000 basis in her partnership interest. On October 10, 2011, the partnership distributes to her cash of $12,000, cash basis receivables with an inside basis of $0 and a fair market value of $10,000, and a parcel of land with a basis to the partnership of $60,000 and a fair market value of $100,000. Lindsey has a realized gain on the distribution of $74,000 ($12,000 + $10,000 + $100,000 – $48,000). None of that gain is recognized, however, because the $12,000 cash distribution does not exceed her $48,000 adjusted basis for her partnership interest. In determining the basis effects of the distribution, the cash is treated as being distributed first, reducing Lindsey's adjusted basis to $36,000 ($48,000 – $12,000). The receivables are distributed next, taking a $0 carryover basis to Lindsey. Her adjusted basis remains at $36,000. The land is distributed last, taking a substituted basis of $36,000 and reducing her adjusted basis for her partnership interest to $0. ■

When more than one asset in a particular class is distributed, special rules apply. Usually, if the partner's remaining adjusted basis for the partnership interest is less than the partnership's adjusted basis for the distributed assets in the particular class, the partner's adjusted basis for each distributed asset is computed by following three steps:

Step 1 Each distributed asset within the class initially takes a carryover basis.

Step 2 If necessary, this carryover basis for each of these assets is reduced in proportion to their respective amounts of unrealized depreciation (amount that carryover basis is greater than fair market value). Under no circumstances, however, can the basis of any asset be reduced below its fair market value in step 2.

Step 3 Any remaining decrease in basis is allocated among all the distributed assets in the class in proportion to their respective adjusted bases (as determined in step 2).

EXAMPLE 10

Assume the same facts as in Example 9, except that Lindsey receives two parcels of land, rather than a single parcel. The partnership's basis for the parcels is $15,000 for Parcel 1 and $45,000 for Parcel 2. Each parcel has a fair market value of $30,000. Lindsey has a realized gain on the distribution of $34,000 ($12,000 + $10,000 + $60,000 – $48,000). None of that gain is recognized, however, because the $12,000 cash distribution does not exceed her $48,000 adjusted basis.

As in Example 9, Lindsey takes a $12,000 basis for the cash and a $0 carryover basis for the receivables and has a $36,000 adjusted basis for her partnership interest after

[6]§ 732.

these two items are distributed. Because two parcels of land are distributed, and because Lindsey's remaining $36,000 adjusted basis for her partnership interest is less than the partnership's $60,000 total basis for the two parcels of land, Lindsey's adjusted basis for each parcel of land is computed by following these steps:

Step 1 She initially takes a carryover basis of $15,000 for Parcel 1 and $45,000 for Parcel 2.

Step 2 She reduces the basis of Parcel 2 to its lower fair market value of $30,000. The basis for Parcel 1 is not adjusted in this step because Parcel 1 has a fair market value greater than its basis.

Step 3 The remaining $9,000 difference between her $36,000 basis for the partnership interest and the $45,000 ($15,000 + $30,000) basis for the land parcels after step 2 is allocated to the two parcels in proportion to their respective bases (as computed in step 2). Therefore, the amount of the step 3 basis reduction allocated to Parcel 1 is:

$$\$9,000 \times \frac{\$15,000}{\$45,000} = \$3,000$$

Lindsey's basis for Parcel 1 is $12,000 ($15,000 – $3,000). The amount of the step 3 basis reduction allocated to Parcel 2 is:

$$\$9,000 \times \frac{\$30,000}{\$45,000} = \$6,000$$

Lindsey's basis for Parcel 2 is $24,000 ($30,000 – $6,000). ■

EXAMPLE 11

Assume the same facts as in Example 10, and that Lindsey sells both parcels of land early in 2012 for their fair market values, receiving proceeds of $60,000 ($30,000 + $30,000). She also collects $10,000 from the cash basis receivables. Now she recognizes all of the $34,000 gain that she deferred upon receiving the property from the partnership [$60,000 amount realized – $36,000 basis for the two parcels ($12,000 + $24,000) + $10,000 collected – $0 basis for the receivables]. ■

Review the tax results of Examples 9 and 10. Although Lindsey does not recognize any of the gain she realizes from the distribution, she has a zero outside basis for her partnership interest. If Lindsey expects the partnership to generate net losses in the near future, she will *not* find this zero basis attractive. She may be unable to deduct her share of these future losses when they flow through to her on the last day of the partnership's subsequent tax year.

The low basis that Lindsey has assigned to the parcels of land is of no significant detriment to her if she does not intend to sell the land in the near future. Because land does not generate cost recovery deductions, the substituted basis is used only to determine Lindsey's gain or loss upon her disposition of the land in a taxable sale or exchange.

Concept Summary 11.1 reviews the general rules that apply to proportionate nonliquidating partnership distributions.

Arranging Tax-Advantaged Distributions

The Sparrow Partnership plans to distribute $200,000 cash to its partners at the end of the year. Marjorie is a 40 percent partner and would receive $80,000. Her basis in the partnership is only $10,000, however, so she would be required to recognize a $70,000 gain if she receives a cash distribution. She has asked the partnership instead to purchase a parcel of land she has found on which she will build her retirement residence. The partnership will then distribute that land to her. Under the partnership distribution rules, Marjorie would take a $10,000 basis in land worth $80,000. Her basis in the partnership would be reduced to $0, and the $70,000 gain is deferred. Do you think this is an appropriate transaction?

CONCEPT SUMMARY 11.1

Proportionate Nonliquidating Distributions (General Rules)

1. Neither the distributee partner nor the partnership recognizes any gain or loss on a proportionate nonliquidating distribution. However, if cash distributed exceeds the distributee partner's outside basis, gain is recognized. Property distributions generally do not result in gain recognition.
2. The distributee partner usually takes the same basis in the distributed property that the property had to the partnership (carryover basis). However, where the inside basis of distributed property exceeds the partner's outside basis, the basis assigned to the distributed property cannot exceed that outside basis (substituted basis).
3. Gain recognized by the distributee partner on a proportionate nonliquidating distribution is capital in nature.
4. Loss is never recognized on a proportionate nonliquidating distribution.

Calculations

1.	Partner's outside basis.	______
2.	Less: Cash distributed to partner.	______
3.	Gain recognized by partner (excess of Line 2 over Line 1).	______
4.	Partner's remaining outside basis (Line 1 – Line 2). If less than $0, enter $0.	______
5.	Partner's basis in unrealized receivables and inventory distributed (enter lesser of Line 4 or the partnership's inside basis in the unrealized receivables and inventory).	______
6.	Basis available to allocate to other property distributed (Line 4 – Line 5).	______
7.	Partnership's inside basis of other property distributed.	______
8.	Basis to partner of other property distributed (enter lesser of Line 6 or Line 7).	______
9.	Partner's remaining outside basis (Line 6 – Line 8).	______

PROPORTIONATE LIQUIDATING DISTRIBUTIONS

LO.2

Determine the tax treatment of proportionate distributions that liquidate a partnership.

Proportionate liquidating distributions consist of a single distribution or a series of distributions that result in the termination of the partner's entire interest in the partnership. If the partnership continues in existence after the partner's interest is liquidated, the rules of § 736 govern the classification of the liquidating payments. These rules are discussed later in the chapter. Other rules apply, however, if the partner's interest is liquidated because the partnership is also liquidating. This section examines the latter type of liquidating distribution.

The partnership itself does not recognize either gain or loss on a proportionate liquidating distribution. The following discussion outlines rules for allocation of basis and possible gain or loss recognition by partners. These rules are summarized in Concept Summary 11.2 at the end of this section.

Gain Recognition and Ordering Rules

When a partnership liquidates, the liquidating distributions to a partner usually consist of an interest in several or all of the partnership assets. The gain recognition and ordering rules parallel those for nonliquidating distributions, except that the partner's *entire* basis in the partnership interest is allocated to the assets received in the liquidating distribution, unless the partner is required to recognize a loss. A loss may be recognized when *only* cash, unrealized receivables, or inventory is received in the distribution. As a result of the ordering rules, the basis of some assets may be adjusted upward or downward to absorb the partner's remaining outside basis. Unrealized receivables or inventory are never "stepped up," although they may be "stepped down."

The general ordering and gain recognition rules for a proportionate liquidating distribution are summarized as follows:

- Cash is distributed first and results in a capital gain if the amount distributed exceeds the partner's basis in the partnership interest. The cash distributed reduces the liquidated partner's outside basis dollar for dollar. The partner's basis cannot be reduced below zero.
- The partner's remaining outside basis is then allocated to unrealized receivables and inventory up to an amount equal to the partnership's adjusted bases in those properties. If the partnership's bases in the unrealized receivables and inventory exceed the partner's remaining outside basis, the remaining outside basis is allocated to the unrealized receivables and inventory.
- Finally, if the liquidating partner has any remaining outside basis, that basis is allocated to the other assets received.[7]

EXAMPLE 12

When Tara's basis in her partnership interest is $70,000, she receives cash of $15,000, a proportionate share of inventory, and land in a distribution that liquidates both the partnership and her entire partnership interest. The inventory has a basis to the partnership of $20,000 and a fair market value of $30,000. The land's basis is $8,000, and the fair market value is $12,000. Under these circumstances, Tara recognizes no gain or loss. After reducing Tara's $70,000 basis by the $15,000 cash received, the remaining $55,000 is allocated first to the inventory and then to the land. The basis of the inventory in Tara's hands is $20,000, and the basis of the land is $35,000. ■

When more than one asset in a particular class is distributed in a proportionate liquidating distribution, special rules may apply. If the partner's remaining basis for the partnership interest is less than the partnership's basis for the distributed assets in the particular class, the partner's basis for each distributed asset is computed as illustrated in Example 10. If, however, the partner's remaining basis for the partnership interest is greater than the partnership's basis for the distributed assets in the "other assets" class, the partner's basis for each remaining distributed asset is computed by following three steps:

Step 1 Each distributed asset within the "other assets" class initially takes a carryover basis.

Step 2 Then, this carryover basis for each of these assets is increased in proportion to their respective amounts of unrealized appreciation (amount that fair market value is greater than carryover basis). Under no circumstances, however, can the basis of any asset be increased above its fair market value in step 2.

Step 3 Any remaining increase in basis is allocated among all the distributed assets in the "other assets" class in proportion to their respective fair market values.

EXAMPLE 13

Assume the same facts as in Example 12, except that Tara receives two parcels of land instead of one. The partnership's basis for the parcels is $2,000 for Parcel 1 and $6,000 for Parcel 2. Each parcel has a fair market value of $6,000.

Tara takes a $15,000 basis for the cash and a $20,000 carryover basis for the inventory. She has a $35,000 basis for her partnership interest after these two items are distributed. Because two parcels of land are distributed, and because Tara's remaining $35,000 basis for her partnership interest exceeds the partnership's $8,000 basis for the two parcels of land, Tara's basis for each parcel of land is computed by following these steps:

[7] §§ 731 and 732.

Step 1 She initially takes a carryover basis of $2,000 for Parcel 1 and $6,000 for Parcel 2.

Step 2 She increases the basis of Parcel 1 by $4,000 to its fair market value of $6,000. The basis for Parcel 2 is not affected in this step because Parcel 2 has a fair market value equal to its basis.

Step 3 Tara's $23,000 ($35,000 − $6,000 − $6,000) remaining basis for her partnership interest is allocated to each land parcel in proportion to each parcel's respective $6,000 fair market value. Therefore, $11,500 [($6,000/$12,000) × $23,000] is allocated to each parcel. Tara's basis in Parcel 1 is $17,500 ($2,000 + $4,000 + $11,500). Her basis in Parcel 2 is also $17,500 ($6,000 + $11,500). ■

Loss Recognition

The distributee partner recognizes a *loss* on a liquidating distribution if both of the following are true:

1. The partner receives *only* cash, unrealized receivables, or inventory.
2. The partner's outside basis in the partnership interest exceeds the partnership's inside basis for the assets distributed. This excess amount is the loss recognized by the distributee partner.[8]

The word "only" is important. A distribution of any other property precludes recognition of the loss.

EXAMPLE 14

When Ramon's outside basis is $40,000, he receives a liquidating distribution of $7,000 cash and a proportionate share of inventory having a partnership basis of $3,000 and a fair market value of $10,000. Ramon is not allowed to "step up" the basis in the inventory, so it is allocated a $3,000 carryover basis. Ramon's unutilized outside basis is $30,000 ($40,000 − $7,000 − $3,000). Because he received a liquidating distribution of *only* cash and inventory, he recognizes a capital loss of $30,000 on the liquidation. ■

EXAMPLE 15

Assume the same facts as in Example 14, except that in addition to the cash and inventory, Ramon receives the desk he used in the partnership. (Assume the distribution is proportionate to the partners.) The desk has an adjusted basis of $100 to the partnership. Applying the rules outlined above to this revised fact situation produces the following results:

Step 1 Cash of $7,000 is distributed to Ramon and reduces his outside basis to $33,000.

Step 2 Inventory is distributed to Ramon. He takes a $3,000 carryover basis in the inventory and reduces his outside basis in the partnership to $30,000.

Step 3 The desk is distributed to Ramon. Because the desk is not cash, an unrealized receivable, or inventory, he cannot recognize a loss. Therefore, Ramon's remaining basis in his partnership interest is allocated to the desk. He takes a $30,000 basis for the desk. ■

What can Ramon do with a $30,000 desk? If he continues to use it in a trade or business, he can depreciate it. Once he has established his business use of the desk, he could sell it and recognize a large § 1231 loss. If the loss is isolated in the year of the sale, it is an ordinary loss. Thus, with proper planning, no liquidated partner should be forced to recognize a capital loss instead of an ordinary loss.

Gain recognized by the withdrawing partner on the subsequent disposition of inventory is ordinary income unless the disposition occurs more than five years after the distribution.[9] The withdrawing partner's holding period for all other property received in a liquidating distribution includes the partnership's related holding period.

[8] § 731(a)(2).

[9] § 735(a)(2).

CONCEPT SUMMARY 11.2

Proportionate Liquidating Distributions When the Partnership Also Liquidates (General Rules)

1. Generally, neither the distributee partner nor the partnership recognizes gain or loss when a partnership liquidates. However, a partner recognizes gain if the cash received exceeds the partner's outside basis. A partner recognizes loss when (a) the partner receives only cash, unrealized receivables, or inventory and (b) the partner's outside basis is greater than the partnership's inside basis of the assets distributed.
2. A partner's basis in distributed assets must be determined in a certain order. Cash is distributed first, inventory and unrealized receivables second, and all other assets last. Assets in the last category take a substituted basis equal to the distributee partner's remaining outside basis.
3. Gain or loss recognized by a distributee partner in a distribution that liquidates a partnership is usually capital in nature.

Calculations

1.	Partner's outside basis.	______
2.	Less: Cash distributed to partner.	______
3.	Gain recognized by partner (excess of Line 2 over Line 1).	______
4.	Partner's remaining outside basis (Line 1 – Line 2). If less than $0, enter $0.	______
5.	Partner's basis in unrealized receivables and inventory distributed (enter lesser of Line 4 or the inside basis in the unrealized receivables and inventory).	______
6.	Basis to partner of other property distributed (Line 4 – Line 5).	______
7.	Loss recognized by partner (if no other property was distributed, enter amount from Line 6).	______
8.	Partner's remaining outside basis.	$0

Concept Summary 11.2 outlines the general rules that apply to proportionate liquidating partnership distributions.

LO.3

Describe the tax treatment that applies to distributions treated as disguised sales and distributions of marketable securities and precontribution gain property.

PROPERTY DISTRIBUTIONS WITH SPECIAL TAX TREATMENT

Recall that a distribution from a partnership to a partner usually does not result in taxable gain. This section discusses three exceptions in which a proportionate distribution, either liquidating or nonliquidating, may result in gain to the partner.

Disguised Sales

As discussed in Chapter 10, a disguised sale is a transaction in which a partner contributes appreciated property to a partnership and soon thereafter receives a distribution of cash or property from the partnership. If the IRS determines the payment is part of a "purchase" of the property, rather than a distribution from the partnership, the usual sale or exchange rules apply. The partner is treated as having sold the property and must report a gain on the sale. The partnership takes a cost basis in the property purchased. See Chapter 10 for additional discussion.

Marketable Securities

The fair market value of a marketable security distributed to a partner is generally treated as a cash distribution.[10] Some or all of the value of the security over the partner's outside basis prior to the distribution is a taxable gain. The partner must assign a basis to the security received in the distribution, so the distribution ordering rules must be taken into account.

[10] § 731(c).

The term *marketable securities* is broadly defined and includes almost any debt or equity interest that is actively traded, including options, futures contracts, and derivatives. Marketable securities are *not* treated as cash if (1) they were originally contributed by the partner to whom they are now distributed (certain exceptions apply to this provision), (2) the property was not a marketable security when acquired by the partnership, or (3) the partner is an eligible partner of an investment partnership, as defined in Chapter 10.

The primary purpose of this rule is to stop the tax avoidance that otherwise would occur if a partnership purchased marketable securities with the intent of immediately distributing them to the partner. As the "Ethics & Equity" feature earlier in this chapter indicated, a partnership can purchase property desired by a partner, distribute that property to the partner, and allow the partner to defer tax on any appreciation inherent in the partnership interest. This rule prevents a partnership from arranging such a transaction with marketable securities.

If, on the distribution date, the marketable security is appreciated, it probably was not acquired by the partnership in an effort to assist the distributee partner in reducing the tax on the distribution. The portion of the security value treated as cash is reduced by a proportionate share of the appreciation inherent in the distributed security. The amount of the reduction is the excess of (1) the partner's share of appreciation in this particular security before the distribution over (2) the partner's share of appreciation in the portion of the security retained by the partnership. If the partner's interest in the partnership is liquidated, the gain on the partner's share of the distributed security is deferred. The "reduction" is intended to take into account the partnership's intent, or lack thereof, to reduce the partner's gains.

EXAMPLE 16

Assume the A to Z Partnership has the following balance sheet:

	Basis	FMV		Basis	FMV
ZYX Corporation security	$4,000	$10,000	Andrew, capital	$ 500	$ 2,000
Land	1,000	10,000	Other partners, capital	4,500	18,000
Total	$5,000	$20,000	Total	$ 5,000	$20,000

The partnership distributes $2,000 (value) of the ZYX stock to 10% partner Andrew in liquidation of his partnership interest. The amount of the distribution treated as cash is the $2,000 fair market value of the stock reduced by Andrew's decrease in his share of the inside appreciation in the stock. Before the distribution, Andrew's share of appreciation in this stock was $600 [10% × ($10,000 − $4,000)]. *His share* of appreciation in the stock retained by the partnership is $0, because he no longer owns an interest in the partnership. The $2,000 value of the stock is reduced by $600 ($600 appreciation before − $0 after distribution). Andrew is treated as if he received a cash distribution of $1,400.

Andrew's outside basis was $500 before the distribution. The $1,400 deemed cash distribution triggers gain recognition of $900. ■

The distributee partner's basis in the security is the sum of (1) the basis in the stock as determined under the regular distribution rules (see the discussion under Ordering Rules above) and (2) the gain recognized on the distribution.

EXAMPLE 17

In Example 16, the stock would take a substituted basis of $500 to Andrew under the distribution ordering rules. This basis is the lesser of the partnership's inside basis in the stock of $800 (20% × $4,000) or Andrew's outside basis of $500 (see Concept Summary 11.2). The recognized gain of $900 increases Andrew's basis in the stock to $1,400 ($500 + $900).

This basis determination preserves the inherent built-in gain in Andrew's partnership interest. Before the distribution, Andrew has $1,500 of appreciation in his interest ($2,000 − $500). After considering the $900 gain on the stock distribution, he should have $600 of untaxed appreciation. The stock value is $2,000, and Andrew's basis is $1,400, so the untaxed appreciation is the expected $600 amount. ■

Unless otherwise indicated, the remaining examples in this chapter assume the partnership is not distributing marketable securities.

Precontribution Gain

Taxable gains may arise on a distribution of property to a partner where precontribution (built-in) gains exist. Specifically, if a partner contributes appreciated property to a partnership, the contributing partner recognizes gain in two situations:

1. If the contributed appreciated property is distributed to another partner within seven years of the contribution date, the contributing partner recognizes the remaining net precontribution gain on the property.[11] The contributing partner's basis in the partnership interest is increased by the amount of gain recognized. Also, the basis of the distributed property is increased by this same amount to prevent double taxation of this precontribution gain when the distributee partner later sells the asset.

EXAMPLE 18

In 2011, Rick contributes nondepreciable property with an adjusted basis of $10,000 and a fair market value of $40,000 to the RTCO Partnership in exchange for a one-fourth interest in profits and capital. In 2012, when the property's fair market value is $50,000, the partnership distributes the property to Tom, another one-fourth partner. Because the property was contributed to the partnership within seven years of the date the property was distributed, and precontribution gain of $30,000 ($40,000 – $10,000) was attributable to the property, the built-in gain on the property is taxable to Rick. Therefore, Rick must pay tax on the $30,000 built-in gain in 2012, the year the property was distributed to Tom. Rick increases his basis in his partnership interest by the $30,000 gain recognized. Tom also increases his basis in the property received by $30,000.

Note that if the partnership were to sell the property to an unrelated third party for $40,000 in 2012, the result would be the same for Rick. Under § 704(c)(1)(A), recognized built-in gains must be allocated to the partner who contributed the property, and the partner's outside basis is increased accordingly. ■

2. The second situation occurs where the partnership distributes *any* property other than cash to a partner within seven years after *that* partner contributes appreciated property to the partnership. In this case, the partner recognizes the lesser of (a) the remaining net precontribution (built-in) gain or (b) the excess of the fair market value of the distributed property over the partner's basis in interest before the distribution.[12] The distributee partner's basis in his or her partnership interest is increased by the amount of gain recognized. To maintain a parity between inside and outside basis, the partnership is allowed to increase its basis in the precontribution gain property remaining in the partnership.

   An exception applies if the partner originally contributed the distributed property. The partnership is merely returning property to the original contributor, and the partner is not required to recognize built-in gain. The general rules that govern property distributions apply.

EXAMPLE 19

In 2009, Bill contributed land to the BMC Partnership. His basis in the land was $16,000. The fair market value at the contribution date was $40,000. In 2011, the partnership distributes other property with an adjusted basis of $16,000 and fair market value of $65,000 to Bill. Bill's basis in his partnership interest was $12,000 immediately before the distribution. Because Bill contributed precontribution gain property within seven years of receiving the distribution of other property, he recognizes gain on the

[11] § 704(c)(1)(B).

[12] § 737.

TAX *in* the *NEWS*

SIMPLIFYING PARTNERSHIP TAXATION—A LOSING BATTLE?

Partnership taxation has become increasingly complex over the past decade. The tax treatment of a distribution differs depending on the type of property being distributed, the appreciation inherent in the property, to whom the property is distributed, and how the partnership originally acquired the property. Liability sharing rules vary depending on the type of liability, the type of partner (general or limited), and when the liability was created. And the "substantial economic effect" rules include numerous pages of guidelines on when and how to allocate income and loss among the partners.

The U.S. Treasury Department and other parties have called for simplification of the rules. For example, the IRS has presented plans for simplifying some areas (e.g., the disproportionate distribution rules discussed below). Yet none of the recently enacted tax legislation or IRS Regulations have simplified partnership taxation. Furthermore, the IRS is currently considering additional changes to the Regulations that will add considerable complexity to this already difficult area.

Source: 2009–2010 Priority Guidance Plan, Department of the Treasury (First Periodic Update, March 16, 2010).

distribution. The maximum he must recognize is the net precontribution gain, or $24,000 ($40,000 fair market value − $16,000 adjusted basis of property contributed). He compares this amount to the excess of the fair market value of the distributed property over his basis in his partnership interest, or $53,000 ($65,000 fair market value of property − $12,000 adjusted basis in interest prior to distribution).

Because the $24,000 precontribution gain is less than the $53,000 inherent gain, Bill recognizes gain of $24,000. His basis in his partnership interest increases by the $24,000 gain recognized to $36,000, and the partnership's basis in the "precontribution gain" property Bill originally contributed also increases by $24,000 to $40,000. ■

EXAMPLE 20

Assume the same facts as in Example 19, except that Bill's basis in his partnership interest was $60,000 before the distribution. In this case, the excess value of the distributed property is only $5,000 ($65,000 − $60,000), so Bill only recognizes gain of $5,000, with corresponding adjustments to the basis of his partnership interest and the partnership's basis in the precontribution gain property.

The remaining precontribution gain of $19,000 ($24,000 − $5,000) is charged to Bill at some point in the future if the partnership sells the precontribution gain property or distributes it to another partner within seven years of its contribution. Some or all of the remaining precontribution gain may also be recognized if other appreciated property is distributed to Bill within seven years of the original contribution. ■

If the distribution occurs more than seven years after the original contribution, Bill recognizes no gain, and the distribution is handled under the general distribution rules described earlier in this section.

DISPROPORTIONATE DISTRIBUTIONS

LO.4

Discuss the general concepts governing tax treatment of disproportionate distributions.

An additional exception to the general gain and loss nonrecognition rule arises when a partnership makes a "disproportionate distribution" of assets. A disproportionate distribution occurs when a partnership makes a distribution of cash or property to a partner and that distribution increases or decreases the distributee partner's proportionate interest in certain of the partnership's ordinary income-producing assets.

These ordinary income-producing assets, called **hot assets**, include substantially **appreciated inventory** and unrealized receivables. Unrealized receivables are rights to receive future amounts that will result in ordinary income when the income is recognized. Inventory, as the term is used here, has a much broader meaning than usual. It includes all assets that are not cash, capital, or § 1231 assets. Substantially appreciated inventory is inventory that has a fair market value in excess of 120 percent of the partnership's adjusted basis for the inventory.

The taxation of disproportionate distributions is based on the aggregate theory of taxation. Under this theory, each partner is deemed to own a proportionate share of the underlying assets of the partnership. In line with this concept, each partner is responsible for recognizing and reporting the proportionate share of ordinary income potential of these assets, such as would arise on the sale of substantially appreciated inventory or on the collection of cash basis receivables.

Section 751(b) maintains each partner's proportionate share of ordinary income by recasting any transaction in which a disproportionate distribution of hot assets is made. If the distributee partner receives less than a proportionate share of hot assets, the transaction is treated as if two separate events occurred: (1) the partnership made a distribution of some of the hot assets to the distributee partner, and (2) that partner immediately sold these hot assets back to the partnership. The partner recognizes ordinary income on the sale of the hot assets, and the partnership takes a cost basis for the hot assets purchased.

EXAMPLE 21

The balance sheet of the AB Partnership is as follows on December 31 of the current tax year:

	Basis	FMV		Basis	FMV
Cash	$26,000	$26,000	Abby, capital	$13,000	$26,000
Unrealized receivables	–0–	26,000	Bob, capital	13,000	26,000
Total	$26,000	$52,000	Total	$26,000	$52,000

Abby and Bob are equal partners in the partnership. The partnership makes a liquidating distribution of the unrealized receivables to Abby and the cash to Bob. Because the unrealized receivables are a hot asset, Abby has received more than her proportionate share of the hot asset, and Bob has received less than his proportionate share. Section 751 recasts the transaction into two separate events. First, Bob is deemed to receive a current distribution of his 50% share of hot assets (basis = $0; fair market value = $13,000), which he then immediately sells back to the partnership for $13,000 of the cash. Bob recognizes $13,000 ordinary income on the sale, and the partnership takes a $13,000 basis in the receivables purchased. The remaining $13,000 cash received by Bob reduces his adjusted basis for his partnership interest to $0 ($13,000 cash distributed – $13,000 adjusted basis).

Abby receives both the $13,000 receivables that the partnership purchased from Bob and her share of the remaining $13,000 unrealized receivables. She takes a substituted basis of $13,000 in the receivables and reduces her adjusted basis for her partnership interest to $0. When she collects all $26,000 of the receivables, she will recognize $13,000 of ordinary income ($26,000 cash collected – $13,000 basis for receivables).

Although the mechanical rules of § 751(b) are complicated, the application of the rules in this example has ensured that each partner eventually recognizes his or her $13,000 share of ordinary income. Bob recognizes his share at the time the partnership is liquidated. Abby's share is recognized when she collects the unrealized receivables. ■

Although most of the problems and examples in this text involve proportionate distributions, be aware that disproportionate distributions occur frequently in practice. The calculation of ordinary income in disproportionate distributions can become extremely complex. These more difficult calculations are not discussed in this text.

PARTNERSHIPS AS TAX SHELTERS

"Tax shelter" investments offer benefits both through the economic performance potential of the investment asset or activity and through the tax savings afforded by utilizing various tax provisions. Some types of tax shelters are operated through partnerships. For example, in some industries (e.g., research and development, oil and gas, and real estate), the partnership form provides a means of efficiently raising capital, and various provisions in Subchapter K (and elsewhere in the Code) offer additional tax advantages.

In the case of certain real estate investments, the liabilities included in the partner's basis can be used to shield the partnership's losses resulting from depreciation deductions and operations of the entity. If the partnership agreement is carefully drafted, active partners may be able to claim ordinary losses greatly in excess of their capital contributions. As long as the liability provides adequate basis, the partner can continue to claim losses.

When the liabilities are repaid or forgiven, the situation changes. The partner is treated as receiving a current distribution of cash and recognizes a capital gain on the payment or forgiveness of the debt. This has been called a "phantom gain" because the partner must recognize a gain with no corresponding cash with which to pay the tax. Partnerships have been known to refinance debt over extensive periods of time simply to avoid this result.

As a tax planning strategy, these real estate ventures offer the partners an ordinary loss deduction during the earlier operating years (at up to about a 36 percent Federal savings rate), with capital gains being recognized (generally as unrecaptured § 1250 gains taxed at up to 25 percent) when the debt is repaid!

What are your thoughts on this potential for tax rate arbitrage? What do you think of the practice of using certain types of partnerships to take advantage of various provisions of the tax law?

11.2 LIQUIDATING DISTRIBUTIONS TO RETIRING OR DECEASED PARTNERS

LO.5

Determine the tax treatment under § 736 of payments from a partnership to a retiring or deceased partner.

Payments made by an ongoing partnership in complete liquidation of a retiring partner's interest are classified under § 736 as either *income* or *property* payments. Payments made to a successor to the interest of a deceased partner are similarly classified by § 736.[13] It is critical to observe that § 736 only classifies the payments. Other Code Sections provide the rules for computing the tax effects of these payments. Although these payments can be made in cash, property, or both cash and property, this discussion assumes that all payments are made in cash.

From a practical standpoint, the partnership and the retiring partner negotiate a total buyout package. The retiring partner expects compensation for the partner's proportionate share of the fair market value of each partnership asset. The partner also expects to be compensated for a share of the partnership's going-concern value. *Property* payments [called § 736(b) payments] represent the former type of buyout provision, and *income* payments [§ 736(a) payments] typically represent the latter. Once the total buyout price is determined, § 736 provides rules for determining the allocation between income and property payments, but leaves some room for negotiation between the partner and the partnership over which component of the buyout represents each type of payment.

The following provides an overview of property and income payments:

- *Property payments—in general.* In general, property payments [§ 736(b) payments] are cash distributions paid by the partnership to the partner in exchange for the partner's interest in partnership assets. The partnership may not deduct these amounts. If the partnership owns no hot assets, the property payment is treated under the normal proportionate distribution rules. If the partnership owns certain hot assets (e.g., depreciation recapture or substantially appreciated inventory), and the retiring partner receives only cash, the distribution is not proportionate. In this case, the

[13]A successor is typically the estate of the deceased or the party who inherits the decedent's interest.

property payments to the partner are allocated between cash payments for the partner's share of (1) hot assets and (2) other assets. The hot asset portion is treated as if there is a distribution of the partner's proportionate share of all hot assets and a sale of these hot assets back to the partnership, as illustrated in Example 21. The income recognized in the hot asset sale is ordinary income, and the gain or loss recognized on the rest of the property payments is capital gain or loss.

- *Income payments—in general.* Income payments [§ 736(a) payments] are treated as a partner's distributive share of partnership income or, alternatively, as a guaranteed payment to the retiring partner. Recall from Chapter 10 that the partner receiving a guaranteed payment recognizes ordinary income. Depending on whether the amount is a distributive share or a guaranteed payment, either (1) the remaining partners report a lesser share of partnership income (distributive share), or (2) the partnership deducts the guaranteed payment.

EXAMPLE 22

Pamela receives cash of $15,000 in liquidation of her partnership interest, in which she has a basis of $10,000. The partnership owns no hot assets. After following all the classification requirements of § 736, $12,000 of this amount is classified as a property payment, and $3,000 is classified as a guaranteed payment. The $12,000 property payment is treated as a distribution from the partnership in exchange for her partnership interest, so Pamela recognizes a $2,000 capital gain on this part of her liquidation proceeds ($12,000 property payment − $10,000 basis in interest). She recognizes $3,000 ordinary income for the guaranteed payment, and the partnership deducts the same amount. ■

PROPERTY PAYMENTS

Cash payments made for the partner's pro rata share of the fair market value of each partnership asset are classified as § 736(b) payments. The following items are not treated as § 736(b) payments, however, if (1) the partnership is primarily a service provider (i.e., "capital is *not* a material income-producing factor for the partnership") and (2) the retiring or deceased partner was a general partner in the partnership:

- Payments made for the partner's pro rata share of unrealized receivables. For purposes of this rule, unrealized receivables do *not* include potential depreciation recapture.
- Payments made for the partner's pro rata share of the partnership goodwill, unless the partnership agreement states that the payments are for goodwill. This exception applies only to payments for goodwill that exceed the partner's pro rata share of the partnership's inside basis for goodwill.
- Certain annuities and lump-sum payments made to retiring partners or a deceased partner's successors.

If such payments are made by a service-oriented partnership to a general partner, they are classified as § 736(a) payments. Conversely, if these payments are made by a capital-intensive partnership or to a limited partner, they are classified as § 736(b) payments.

EXAMPLE 23

The ABC Partnership has the following balance sheet at the end of the current tax year:

	Basis	FMV		Basis	FMV
Cash	$36,000	$36,000	Anne, capital	$15,000	$27,000
Unrealized receivables	–0–	18,000	Bonnie, capital	15,000	27,000
Land	9,000	27,000	Cindy, capital	15,000	27,000
Total	$45,000	$81,000	Total	$45,000	$81,000

Partner Anne is a general partner retiring from the service-oriented partnership. She receives $36,000 cash, none of which is stated to be for goodwill. Because the fair market value of Anne's share of the three recorded assets is only $27,000 (1/3 × $81,000), the $9,000 excess payment is for unstated goodwill.

The payment Anne receives for her interest in the cash and land is a § 736(b) property payment. This payment is $21,000, consisting of $12,000 paid for the cash (1/3 × $36,000) and $9,000 paid for Anne's share of the fair market value of the land (1/3 × $27,000). The remaining cash of $15,000 is for her $6,000 interest in the unrealized receivables and for $9,000 unstated goodwill and is a § 736(a) payment. ■

Section 736(b) payments for "nonhot" assets are treated first as a return of the partner's outside basis in the partnership.[14] Once the entire basis is returned, any additional amounts are taxed to the partner as capital gain. If the cash distributions are not sufficient to return the partner's entire outside basis, the shortfall is taxed to the partner as a capital loss.[15]

EXAMPLE 24

In Example 23, the property payment of $21,000 cash includes amounts for Anne's share of land and cash only, neither of which is a hot asset. If Anne's outside basis is $15,000, she recognizes capital gain of $6,000 [($12,000 + $9,000) – $15,000] on the distribution. However, if Anne's outside basis is $25,000, she recognizes a $4,000 capital loss on the distribution [($12,000 + $9,000) – $25,000]. The partnership cannot deduct any part of the $21,000 property payment. ■

If part of the property payment is for the partner's share of hot assets, the § 736(b) payment is allocated between the portion related to hot assets and the portion related to other assets. The portion of the payment *not* related to hot assets is treated as described in Example 24. The portion of the payment related to hot assets is treated as discussed earlier under Disproportionate Distributions. Distributions that are disproportionate to the partner's share of hot assets of the partnership are treated as two separate transactions:

- First, the partner's proportionate share of hot assets is deemed to be distributed. A partner cannot step up the basis in hot assets, so on the distribution, the hot assets take the lesser of the partnership's inside basis for the hot assets or the partner's outside basis in the interest.
- Second, these hot assets are deemed to be sold back to the partnership at fair market value. A portion of the § 736(b) payment is allocated to the partnership's deemed purchase of the hot assets.

EXAMPLE 25

If, in Example 23, Anne was a limited partner or the partnership was capital-intensive, the entire payment of $36,000 is a § 736(b) property payment. The $36,000 payment is allocated between hot assets and other assets. The payment for cash and land is a payment for Anne's other assets, as is the payment for partnership goodwill. The payment for the unrealized receivables, however, is a payment for Anne's share of the partnership's hot assets.

The partnership is treated first as distributing Anne's $6,000 proportionate share of unrealized receivables. Anne's carryover basis in the receivables is $0.

Anne then resells the unrealized receivables to the partnership for their $6,000 fair market value. She reports $6,000 of ordinary income on this sale. The partnership now has a basis of $6,000 in its $18,000 of accounts receivable.

The partnership paid Anne $36,000. Of this amount, $6,000 is to "repurchase" her share of receivables; the remaining $30,000 is in exchange for the partnership's other assets ($12,000 for cash + $9,000 for land + $9,000 for goodwill). Anne calculates and reports a $15,000 capital gain ($30,000 payment – $15,000 basis) in addition to the $6,000 ordinary income. ■

[14] §§ 736(b) and 731(a)(1).

[15] § 731(a)(2).

INCOME PAYMENTS

All payments that are not classified as § 736(b) property payments are categorized as § 736(a) income payments. These income payments are further classified into two categories. Payments that are *not* determined by reference to partnership income are treated as guaranteed payments. They are fully taxable as ordinary income to the distributee partner and are fully deductible by the continuing partnership.

Section 736(a) income payments that are determined by reference to partnership income are treated as distributive shares of that income (i.e., an allocation of partnership income for the year). They are taxed to the distributee partner according to their character to the partnership. Thus, for example, they may be taxed as capital gain as well as ordinary income.[16] Because this capital gain and ordinary income are allocated to the liquidated partner, the payments reduce the amount of partnership capital gain and ordinary income allocated to the remaining partners.[17]

EXAMPLE 26

Continue with the same facts as in Example 23 where the partnership is service oriented. The $6,000 cash payment ($18,000 × 1/3) for Anne's pro rata share of the unrealized receivables is classified as a § 736(a) income payment, as is the $9,000 payment for unstated goodwill.

Because the $15,000 § 736(a) income payment ($6,000 + $9,000) is not determined by reference to partnership income, the payment is classified as a guaranteed payment. It is included as ordinary income on Anne's tax return and is deductible by the partnership. ■

The following table summarizes the taxation results of Examples 23 through 26, for a partnership where capital is not a material income-producing factor and where it is. In both cases, Anne's basis in her partnership interest was $15,000 before the distribution.

	Tax Character to Anne		Deduction to ABC
Service-oriented partnership:			
§ 736(b)(Example 24)	$ 6,000	capital gain	None
§ 736(a)(Example 26)	15,000	ordinary income	$15,000
Total gain	$21,000		
Capital-intensive partnership:			
§ 736(b)(Example 25)	$15,000	capital gain	None
§ 736(b)(Example 25)	6,000	ordinary income	None
§ 736(a)(Example 25)	–0–	ordinary income	None
Total gain	$21,000		

As this table illustrates, the characterization under § 736 does not change the overall gain; in both cases Anne recognizes total gain of $21,000. This is appropriate because she receives $36,000 cash against a basis of $15,000.

The character of Anne's income differs solely as a result of the characterization of goodwill. For the service-oriented partnership with unstated goodwill, the payment for goodwill results in ordinary income to the partner. For the capital-intensive partnership, or if the partner is a limited partner, goodwill results in capital gain.

From the partnership's point of view, it is entitled to a deduction for goodwill payments only if it is a service partnership and the retiring partner is a general partner, and then only if the goodwill payment is not stated in the partnership agreement.

The partnership's position also differs as a result of the treatment of unrealized receivables. As a service partnership, it can claim a current deduction for the

[16] § 702(b).

[17] Reg. § 1.736–1 (a)(4).

amount of the distribution related to the receivables. As a capital-intensive partnership, ABC has a cost basis in the receivables when it is deemed to repurchase them from Anne. When the receivables are collected, the partnership's ordinary income is reduced.

EXAMPLE 27
THE BIG PICTURE

Return to the facts of *The Big Picture* on p. 11-2. Recall that the members of Beachside Properties, LLC, are considering two alternatives for its future expansion. Assume that they decide to admit new partners for $19.5 million and use $9.5 million of the cash to redeem the interests of Kyle and Maria.

Because the LLC itself is not liquidating, the distribution to Kyle and Maria is classified under § 736. The current balance sheet for Beachside Properties, LLC, is as follows:

	Basis	Fair Market Value
Cash	$1,000,000	$ 1,000,000
Accounts receivable and inventory	500,000	1,000,000
Land	500,000	6,000,000
Buildings and other § 1231 property	2,000,000	3,000,000
Goodwill	-0-	1,000,000
Total assets	$4,000,000	$12,000,000
Debt	$2,000,000	$2,000,000
Capital, Josh	300,000*	500,000
Capital, Kyle	400,000*	4,750,000
Capital, Maria	1,300,000*	4,750,000
Net assets	$4,000,000	$12,000,000

*The LLC members' capital accounts correspond to their bases, excluding their shares of the LLC's liabilities. The members' bases are not proportionate because the bases of the contributed properties were not proportionate. Also, over time, some LLC income was retained to provide operating cash flows, and some of the members have withdrawn more cash than others.

Capital is a "material income-producing factor" for Beachside Properties, LLC. Therefore, in this redemption scenario, the entire $9.5 million distribution from the LLC to Kyle and Maria is a § 736(b) payment for their interests in the partnership's property. Kyle and Maria will recognize a gain to the extent that this cash distribution (including forgiveness of their shares of the LLC's debt) exceeds their bases in the LLC interests.

Because Kyle and Maria receive cash in lieu of their shares of the LLC's unrealized receivables (including potential depreciation recapture) and inventory, this is a disproportionate distribution. They will recognize ordinary income to the extent that their gain relates to these receivables and inventory. The remaining gain will be a capital gain.

As there are no § 736(a) payments, the LLC cannot claim any deductions. Absent a § 754 election (discussed later), the basis of the LLC's property will not be affected. ■

SERIES OF PAYMENTS

Frequently, the partnership and retiring partner agree that the buyout payment may be made over several years in specified installments. This minimizes the negative cash-flow impact on the partnership and allows the retiring partner to maximize the dollar amount of the buyout arrangement. In certain cases, such as where a retiring partner has been instrumental in developing a business relationship with specific clients, the parties can agree that the buyout payments will be determined by reference to the future income generated by those clients or by reference to overall partnership income, rather than being fixed in amount. If the partners deal at arm's length and specifically agree to the §§ 736(a) and (b) allocation and timing of each class of payment, the agreement normally controls.[18] In the absence of an agreement classifying the payments under

[18]Reg. § 1.736–1 (b)(5).

CONCEPT SUMMARY 11.3

Liquidating Distributions of Cash When the Partnership Continues

1. Payments made by an ongoing partnership to a liquidating partner are classified as § 736(a) income payments or as § 736(b) property payments.
2. Section 736(b) property payments are payments made for the liquidated partner's share of partnership assets.
3. If the partnership is a service provider and the partner is a general partner, payments made for the liquidated partner's share of certain unrealized receivables, certain goodwill that is not provided for in the partnership agreement, and certain annuity payments are classified as § 736(a) income payments.
4. Section 736(a) income payments are the payments mentioned in Item 3 above and any other payments that are not classified as § 736(b) property payments.
5. To the extent the § 736(b) property payment is for the partner's share of partnership hot assets, the partner is deemed to have received and sold his or her share of such assets to the partnership. The partner reports ordinary income on this transaction, and the partnership will have a cost basis in the hot asset.
6. To the extent the § 736(b) property payments are classified as a payment for the partner's share of the partnership's "nonhot" assets, the payment is taxed as a return of the partner's outside basis. Any excess cash received over the partner's outside basis is taxed as capital gain.
7. Section 736(a) income payments are further classified as either guaranteed payments or distributive shares. Guaranteed payments are taxable as ordinary income to the partner and are deductible by the partnership. Distributive shares retain the same tax character to the partner as they had to the partnership. Distributive shares paid to the liquidated partner are excludible from the continuing partners' tax returns.

§ 736, Regulations specify classification rules for each payment. In either situation, certain tax planning opportunities arise that are beyond the scope of this text.

Concept Summary 11.3 reviews the rules for liquidating distributions under § 736.

11.3 Sale of a Partnership Interest

LO.6

Calculate the selling partner's amount and character of gain or loss on the sale or exchange of a partnership interest.

A partner can sell or exchange a partnership interest, in whole or in part. The transaction can be between the partner and a third party; in this case, it is similar in concept to a sale of corporate stock. Or, as described in the last section, the transaction can be between the partner and the partnership, in which case it is similar in concept to a redemption of corporate stock by the entity. The transfer of a partnership interest produces different results from the transfer of corporate stock because both the entity and aggregate concepts apply to the partnership situation, whereas only the entity concept applies to a sale of stock. The effect of the different rules is that gain or loss resulting from a sale of a partnership interest may be divided into capital gain or loss and ordinary income or loss.

GENERAL RULES

Generally, the sale or exchange of a partnership interest results in gain or loss, measured by the difference between the amount realized and the selling partner's adjusted basis in the partnership interest.[19]

Liabilities

In computing the amount realized and the adjusted basis of the interest sold, the selling partner's share of partnership liabilities must be determined, as discussed in Chapter 10. The purchasing partner includes any assumed indebtedness as a part of the consideration paid for the partnership interest.[20]

[19] § 741.

[20] § 742.

EXAMPLE 28

Cole originally contributed $50,000 in cash for a one-third interest in the CDE Partnership. During the time Cole was a partner, his share of partnership income was $90,000, and he withdrew $60,000 cash. Cole's capital account balance is now $80,000, and partnership liabilities are $45,000, of which Cole's share is $15,000. Cole's outside basis is $95,000 ($80,000 capital account + $15,000 share of partnership debts).

Cole sells his partnership interest to Stephanie for $110,000 cash, with Stephanie assuming Cole's share of partnership liabilities. The total amount realized by Cole is $125,000 ($110,000 cash received + $15,000 of partnership debts transferred to Stephanie). Cole's gain on the sale is $30,000 ($125,000 realized – adjusted basis of $95,000).

Stephanie's adjusted basis for her partnership interest is the purchase price of $125,000 ($110,000 cash paid + $15,000 assumed partnership debt). ■

Income Allocation

When a partner sells an entire interest in the partnership:

- Income for the partnership interest for the tax year is allocated between the buying partner and the selling partner, and
- The partnership's tax year "closes" with respect to the selling partner.

The closing of the tax year causes the selling partner to report the share of income on the sale date rather than at the end of the partnership's tax year.

The selling partner's basis is adjusted for the allocated income or loss before the partner calculates the gain or loss on the sale of the interest.

EXAMPLE 29

On September 30, 2011, Erica sells her 20% interest in the Evergreen Partnership to Jason for $25,000. Erica is a calendar year taxpayer. Evergreen owns no hot assets, and its tax year ends on June 30.

On July 1, 2011, Erica's basis in the partnership interest was $8,000. Her share of current partnership income is $10,000 for the period she owned the partnership interest (July 1 to September 30). Because the partnership's tax year closes with respect to Erica, she must report $10,000 of income on her 2011 tax return. Her basis in the partnership interest is increased to $18,000, and she recognizes a $7,000 capital gain on the sale.

Note that Erica will also report income from Evergreen's tax year ending on June 30, 2011, on her 2011 tax return. ■

There are several acceptable methods of determining the partner's share of income.[21] Under one method, the partnership merely prorates annual income and allocates an amount to the buying and selling partners based on the number of days (or months) in the partnership's tax year in which they were partners. Another method is called the *interim closing of the books* method. As the name implies, the partnership determines its actual income through the date the selling partner sold the interest and allocates a proportionate share of that income to the partner. If partnership earnings are seasonal, the two methods can produce vastly different results.

EXAMPLE 30

Trevor sold his 40% interest in the Owl Partnership to Megan on July 1 of the current tax year. Both Trevor and the partnership report on a calendar year basis. The partnership's income was $60,000 through June 30, and its income for the last half of the year was $2,000. Under the annual proration method, the partnership's income for the year is $62,000, of which 40%, or $24,800, is allocated to the 40% interest. Based on the number of months each was a partner, both Trevor and Megan report income of $12,400 for the current year.

Under the interim closing method, Trevor is allocated 40% of $60,000, or $24,000, and Megan is allocated 40% of $2,000, or $800 of partnership income. ■

[21] § 706(d)(1) and Regulations and 2009 Proposed Regulations thereunder.

If the partnership uses the cash method for certain items such as interest, taxes, rent, or other amounts that accrue over time, it must allocate these items to each day in the tax year over which they economically accrue and use the interim closing method for these items in determining the amount allocated to a selling partner.[22]

The partnership is not required to issue a Schedule K–1 to the selling partner until the normal filing of its tax return. The partner, though, is required to include the share of partnership income as of the sale date. Consequently, the partner may have to obtain an extension for filing his or her personal return until the partnership provides a Schedule K–1. If the partnership uses an IRS-approved fiscal year and the partner uses a calendar year, income bunching may occur, as described in Example 29.

Tax Reporting

Partners who sell or exchange a partnership interest must promptly notify the partnership of the transfers. After notification is received, the partnership may be required to file an information statement with the IRS for the calendar year in which the transfers took place. The statement lists the names and addresses of the transferors and transferees. The partnership provides all parties with a copy of the statement.

EFFECT OF HOT ASSETS

A major exception to capital gain or loss treatment on the sale or exchange of a partnership interest arises when a partnership has hot assets. As noted previously, *hot assets* are *unrealized receivables* and *inventory*, assets that, when collected or disposed of by the partnership, would cause it to recognize ordinary income or loss. When a partner sells the interest in a partnership, it is as if the partnership had sold its hot assets and allocated to the selling partner the partner's proportionate share of the ordinary income or loss created by the sale. The primary purpose of this rule is to prevent a partner from converting ordinary income into capital gain through the sale of a partnership interest.[23]

Unrealized Receivables

The term "unrealized receivables" generally has the same meaning as in the earlier discussion of disproportionate distributions. As previously noted, unrealized receivables include the accounts receivable of a cash basis partnership and, for sale or exchange purposes, depreciation recapture potential.[24]

EXAMPLE 31

The cash basis Thrush Partnership owns only a $10,000 receivable for rendering health care advice. Its basis in the receivable is zero because no income has been recognized. This item is a hot asset because ordinary income is not generated until Thrush collects on the account.

Jacob, a 50% partner, sells his interest to Mark for $5,000. If Jacob's basis in his partnership interest is $0, his total gain is $5,000. The entire gain is attributable to Jacob's share of the unrealized receivable, so his gain is taxed as ordinary income. ■

Depreciation recapture represents ordinary income the partnership would recognize if it sold depreciable property. Under the aggregate theory, the selling partner's share of depreciation recapture potential is treated as an unrealized receivable and is taxed to the selling partner as ordinary income, rather than capital gain. (Recall that depreciation recapture is *not* treated as an unrealized receivable for § 736 purposes, discussed previously.)

[22] § 706(d)(2).
[23] § 751(a).
[24] § 751(a)(1).

EXAMPLE 32

Andrew sells his 40% interest in the accrual basis Wren Partnership. The partnership has a depreciable business asset that it originally purchased for $25,000. The asset now has an adjusted basis of $15,000 and a market value of $30,000. Depreciation recapture potential is $10,000 ($25,000 − $15,000). In this case, Wren holds a $10,000 unrealized receivable with a zero basis and a $20,000 ($30,000 − $10,000) nonhot asset with an adjusted basis of $15,000. If Wren sold the asset for $30,000, it would recognize $10,000 of ordinary income and $5,000 of § 1231 gain. Therefore, Andrew recognizes $4,000 ($10,000 × 40%) of ordinary income when he sells his partnership interest. ■

The effect of the hot asset rule is that a partner selling an interest in a partnership with hot assets must usually recognize both ordinary income (loss) and capital gain (loss).

EXAMPLE 33

Ahmad sells his interest in the equal ABC Partnership to Dave for $17,000 cash. On the sale date, the partnership's cash basis balance sheet reflects the following:

	Basis	FMV		Basis	FMV
Cash	$10,000	$10,000	Liabilities	$ 9,000	$ 9,000
Accounts receivable (for services)	–0–	30,000	Capital accounts		
Nonhot assets	14,000	20,000	Ahmad	5,000	17,000
			Beth	5,000	17,000
			Chris	5,000	17,000
Total	$24,000	$60,000	Total	$24,000	$60,000

The total amount realized by Ahmad is $20,000 ($17,000 cash price + $3,000 of debt assumed by Dave). Because Ahmad's basis for his partnership interest is $8,000 ($5,000 capital account + $3,000 debt share), the total gain recognized on the sale is $12,000 ($20,000 − $8,000).

Because the partnership has an unrealized receivable, the hot asset rule applies. If ABC sold the accounts receivable for $30,000, Ahmad's proportionate share of the ordinary income recognized on this sale would be $10,000 ($30,000 × 1/3). Consequently, $10,000 of the $12,000 recognized gain on the sale relates to Ahmad's interest in the unrealized receivables and is taxed to him as ordinary income. The remaining gain of $2,000 is taxed to him as a capital gain.

Note that under the hot asset rule, Ahmad still reports $12,000 of income or gain; the hot asset rule merely reclassifies part of the gain as ordinary income. The effect of the rule is that the partnership's inherent ordinary income is allocated to the partner who earned it. ■

EXAMPLE 34

Assume the same facts as in Example 33, except that Ahmad's basis in his partnership interest is $10,000. Under these circumstances, Ahmad's capital gain or loss is zero. Ahmad still has $10,000 of ordinary income because of the unrealized receivables.

If Ahmad's basis in the partnership interest is $11,000 (instead of $10,000), an unusual result occurs. Ahmad has a $9,000 overall gain ($20,000 amount realized − $11,000 basis). The receivables generate $10,000 of ordinary income, and Ahmad recognizes a capital *loss* of $1,000 on the rest of the sale. ■

Inventory

For a sale or exchange of a partnership interest, the term *inventory* includes all partnership property except money, capital assets, and § 1231 assets. Receivables of an accrual basis partnership are included in the definition of inventory, as they are neither capital assets nor § 1231 assets.[25] This definition also is broad enough to include all items considered to be unrealized receivables.

[25] § 751(d).

CONCEPT SUMMARY 11.4

Sale of a Partnership Interest

1. A partnership interest is a capital asset and generally results in capital gain or loss on disposal.
2. The outside bases of the selling and buying partners, as well as the pertinent selling price and purchase price, include an appropriate share of partnership debt.
3. Partnership income or loss for the interest is allocated between the selling and buying partners. The selling partner's basis is adjusted before the gain or loss on the sale is calculated.
4. The partnership's tax year closes with respect to the selling partner on the sale date; the seller reports partnership income at that time, and income "bunching" may occur.
5. When hot assets are present, the selling partner's overall gain or loss is reclassified into a capital gain or loss portion and an ordinary income or loss amount related to the partnership's underlying hot assets.
6. Hot assets consist of unrealized receivables and inventory.
7. Unrealized receivables include amounts earned by a cash basis taxpayer from services rendered. They also include depreciation recapture potential that would result if an asset were sold at a gain.
8. Inventory includes all partnership property except cash, capital assets, and § 1231 assets. Inventory also includes unrealized receivables.

EXAMPLE 35

Jan sells her one-third interest in the JKL Partnership to Matt for $20,000 cash. On the sale date, the partnership balance sheet reflects the following:

	Basis	FMV		Basis	FMV
Cash	$10,000	$10,000	Jan, capital	$15,000	$20,000
Inventory	21,000	30,000	Kelly, capital	15,000	20,000
Capital assets	14,000	20,000	Luis, capital	15,000	20,000
Total	$45,000	$60,000	Total	$45,000	$60,000

The overall gain on the sale is $5,000 ($20,000 – $15,000). Jan's share of the appreciation in the inventory is $3,000 [($30,000 – $21,000) × $^1/_3$]. Therefore, she recognizes $3,000 of ordinary income because of the inventory and $2,000 of capital gain from the rest of the sale. ■

EXAMPLE 36
THE BIG PICTURE

Return to the facts of *The Big Picture* on p. 11-2. Recall that the second restructuring option for Beachside Properties, LLC, is for Kyle and Maria to sell their interests directly to the new members of the LLC. The new members will pay $4.75 million each to Kyle and Maria in exchange for their interests in the LLC. They will then contribute $10 million of cash to Beachside Properties for the expansion.

Refer back to the balance sheet in Example 27. Kyle and Maria will receive cash of $9.5 million (total) plus relief of their shares of the LLC's debt. Their bases in the LLC interests equal their capital account balances plus their shares of the LLC's liabilities. The difference must be recognized as a gain.

The gain is ordinary income to the extent that it relates to Kyle's and Maria's shares of the LLC's accounts receivable, inventory, and depreciation recapture. The remaining gain is a capital gain. Absent a § 754 election (discussed later), the basis of the LLC's property will not be affected. ■

Concept Summary 11.4 enumerates the rules that apply to sales of partnership interests.

11.4 Other Dispositions of Partnership Interests

LO.7

Describe tax issues related to other dispositions of partnership interests.

Partnership interests may be reduced or terminated, and partnerships liquidated, in a variety of other ways, including the following:

- Transfer of the interest to a corporation when the partners control the corporation after the transfer.
- Transfer of the interest to a corporation when the partners *do not* control the corporation after the transfer.
- Like-kind exchanges.
- Death of a partner.
- Gifts.

TRANSFERS TO A CORPORATION

Transfers of a partnership interest to a corporation may take place when one or all partners are ready to retire from the business; they may exchange the partnership interest for stock in an existing corporation and cease to be involved in the day-to-day operations of the business. Alternatively, many partnerships incorporate simply to obtain the protection from liability or other advantages of the corporate form and make no real changes in business operations. Incorporation may occur at a time when the business is expanding and wants to obtain equity capital from issuing shares to outsiders. The corporate form may also provide tax advantages for a successful business that prefers to retain some earnings for internal expansion without having them taxed at the high individual tax rates of the owners.

Recall from Chapter 4 the controlled corporation rules of § 351. These rules provide that gain or loss is not recognized on the transfer of property to a corporation solely in exchange for stock in that corporation if, immediately after the exchange, the stockholders are in control of the corporation.

In many cases, including most of those in which an existing partnership is incorporated and continues to operate, § 351 conditions are met, and the transfer of the partnership interest to the corporation is a nontaxable exchange. If the partners transferring the property do not satisfy the 80 percent control requirements of § 351, they recognize gain or loss on the transfer according to standard rules for sales or exchanges.

If the partnership interest transferred represents 50 percent or more of the total interest in capital or profits, the partnership is terminated. Partnership termination is discussed later in the chapter.

Incorporation Methods

Consider the situation where the partners decide to incorporate an existing partnership by creating a new corporation owned entirely by the partners. At least three alternative methods are available for structuring the incorporation transaction:

- Each partner's interest is transferred to the corporation in exchange for stock under the usual § 351 rules. As a result, the partnership terminates, and the corporation owns all partnership assets and liabilities. The corporation takes a substituted basis for the assets, and the old partners have a substituted basis for the stock.
- The partnership transfers all of its assets to the corporation in exchange for stock and the assumption of partnership liabilities. The stock then is distributed to the partners (generally in a liquidating distribution) in proportion to their partnership interests. The corporation takes a carryover basis for the assets, and the old partners have a substituted basis for the stock.

- The partnership makes a pro rata distribution of all of its assets and liabilities to its partners in complete liquidation. The partners then transfer their undivided interests in the assets and liabilities to the corporation in exchange for stock under § 351. The corporation's basis for the assets is the substituted basis of those assets to the partners. The partners have a substituted basis for the stock.

Assuming that existing partnership debt does not exceed the basis of transferred assets, none of the three incorporation methods generates a recognized gain or loss. They may, however, result in different inside and outside basis amounts. Thus, selecting the appropriate incorporation method is crucial.

LIKE-KIND EXCHANGES

The nontaxable like-kind exchange rules do not apply to the exchange of interests in different partnerships.[26] These exchanges are fully taxable under the sale or exchange rules discussed previously. However, an exchange of interests in the same partnership is generally a nontaxable event.[27]

DEATH OF A PARTNER

If a partner dies, the taxable year of the partnership closes with respect to that partner on the date of death.[28] The deceased partner's share of partnership income or loss is computed to that date and is reported on the partner's final Form 1040.

In professional partnerships, local law may prohibit an estate or other successor from continuing as a partner (beyond a certain time period). In most cases, the remaining partners want to buy out or liquidate the deceased partner's interest in the partnership. The previously discussed rules pertaining to sales and liquidations of partnership interests apply to these transactions.

GIFTS

Generally, the donor of a partnership interest recognizes neither gain nor loss. If the donor's entire interest is transferred, all items of partnership income, loss, deduction, or credit attributable to the interest are prorated between the donor and donee.

The taxable year of the partnership does not close with respect to the donor, however, so the donor reports his or her share of partnership income or loss at the end of the partnership's tax year.

As the following "Ethics & Equity" feature indicates, the gift of an interest in a partnership owning unrealized receivables can be problematic.

Assignment of Income

Jim is a partner in a cash basis partnership that specializes in personal injury matters. Cases are accepted on a contingent fee basis. If the client wins, the firm gets 30 percent of the recovery. If the client loses, no fee results. Just before a large judgment is awarded, Jim gives half of his partnership interest to his son, an attorney. The son recognizes as income the portion of the award attributable to the partnership interest he received as a gift. What is Jim trying to accomplish? Will it work?

[26] § 1031 (a)(2)(D).

[27] Rev.Rul. 84–52, 1984–1 C.B. 157

[28] § 706(c)(2)(A).

11.5 Optional Adjustments to Property Basis

LO.8

Calculate the optional adjustments to basis under § 754.

When a partner purchases a partnership interest, the purchase price reflects what the acquiring partner believes the interest in the partnership is worth. This price reflects, to a large extent, the value the partner places on the partnership's assets. Because the value of the assets probably differs from their inside bases, a discrepancy exists between the purchasing partner's outside basis and that partner's share of the inside basis of partnership assets.

If the partnership makes an **optional adjustment election** or **§ 754 election**, the inside basis of the partnership property can be adjusted to reflect the purchase price paid by the partner. If the election is not made, the statute produces some inequitable results.

EXAMPLE 37

A partnership owns a building with an adjusted basis of $450,000 and a fair market value of $900,000. George buys a one-third interest in the partnership for $300,000 (an amount equal to one-third of the value of the building). The partnership does not make an election under § 754. Although the price George paid for the interest was based on fair market value, the building's depreciation continues to be determined on the partnership's adjusted basis of $450,000, of which George's share is only $150,000. ■

EXAMPLE 38

In contrast, assume that the building in Example 37 had an adjusted basis of $300,000 and a fair market value of $150,000. Assume also that George purchased the one-third interest for $50,000 (an amount equal to one-third of the value of the building). Although the purchase price was based on fair market value, George obtains the benefit of *double* depreciation deductions because these deductions are calculated on the adjusted basis of the depreciable property ($300,000), which is twice the property's market value. ■

A result similar to that in Example 37 can take place when a partnership purchases a retiring partner's interest with a cash payment that is greater than that partner's outside basis for the partnership interest. Without a § 754 election, the partnership cannot increase the adjusted basis of its assets for the excess cash paid to the retiring partner.[29]

An optional adjustment-to-basis election can be made for any year in which a transfer or distribution occurs by attaching a statement to a timely filed partnership return (including extensions).[30] An election is binding for the year for which it is made and for all subsequent years, unless the IRS consents to its revocation. Permission to revoke is granted for business reasons, such as a substantial change in the nature of the business or a significant increase in the frequency of interest transfers. Permission is not granted if it appears the primary purpose is to avoid downward adjustments to basis otherwise required under the election.

In one type of situation, a basis adjustment must generally be made even if the partnership has not made a § 754 election. A basis adjustment is generally *required* if a sale or distribution occurs on or after October 23, 2004, and the partnership has a substantial built-in loss. A substantial built-in loss exists when the partnership's adjusted basis for all partnership property exceeds the fair market value of the property by more than $250,000. If in Example 38, the fair market value of partnership property had been less than $50,000 and George had purchased the partnership interest on or after October 23, 2004, a basis adjustment would have been required.

[29] §§ 743(a) and 734(a), respectively.

[30] § 754.

ADJUSTMENT: SALE OR EXCHANGE OF AN INTEREST

If the § 754 optional adjustment-to-basis election is in effect and a partner's interest is sold to or exchanged with a third party, or a partner dies, the partnership adjusts the basis of its assets as illustrated in the following calculation:[31]

Transferee's outside basis in the partnership	$ xxx
Less: Transferee's share of the inside basis of all partnership property	(xxx)
Adjustment	$ xxx

If the amount calculated is positive, the partnership increases the adjusted basis of its assets. If the amount is negative, the basis of the assets is decreased. In either case, the adjustment affects the basis of partnership property with respect to the transferee partner only. When a portion of the optional adjustment results in a step-up of depreciable property, the step-up amount is depreciated as if it were a newly acquired asset. The transferee partner, therefore, shares in the depreciation taken by the partnership on the original asset and, in addition, reports all of the depreciation taken on the step-up basis created by the optional adjustment.

The partner's basis in each property item for which an optional adjustment has been made equals the partner's share of the inside basis for the property item plus or minus the partner's optional basis adjustment that is allocated to that property.

EXAMPLE 39

Keith is a member of the KLM Partnership, and all partners have equal interests in capital and profits. The partnership has made an optional adjustment-to-basis election. Keith's interest is sold to Sean for $76,000. The balance sheet of the partnership immediately before the sale shows the following:

	Basis	FMV		Basis	FMV
Cash	$ 15,000	$ 15,000	Capital accounts		
Depreciable assets	150,000	213,000	Keith	$ 55,000	$ 76,000
			Leah	55,000	76,000
			Morgan	55,000	76,000
Total	$165,000	$228,000	Total	$165,000	$228,000

The adjustment is the difference between the basis of Sean's interest in the partnership and his share of the adjusted basis of partnership property. The basis of Sean's interest is his purchase price, or $76,000. His one-third share of the adjusted basis of partnership property is $55,000 ($165,000 × 1/3). The optional adjustment that is added to the basis of partnership property is $21,000.

Transferee's outside basis in partnership	$ 76,000
Less: Transferee's share of inside basis of all partnership property	(55,000)
Adjustment	$ 21,000

The $21,000 basis increase is treated as a new depreciable asset. Depreciation on this asset is allocated to Sean. If the partnership later sells all the underlying assets, Sean's share of the gain takes into account the remaining (undepreciated) balance of the $21,000 step-up. ■

ADJUSTMENT: PARTNERSHIP DISTRIBUTIONS

Optional adjustments to basis are also available to the partnership when property is distributed to a partner. If a § 754 optional adjustment-to-basis election is in effect, the basis of partnership property is *increased* by the following:[32]

[31] § 743(b).

[32] § 734(b).

- Any gain recognized by a distributee partner.
- The excess of the partnership's adjusted basis for any distributed property over the adjusted basis of that property in the hands of the distributee partner.

Conversely, the basis of partnership property is *decreased* by the following:

- Any loss recognized by a distributee partner.
- In the case of a liquidating distribution, the excess of the distributee partner's adjusted basis of any distributed property over the basis of that property to the partnership.

EXAMPLE 40

Ryan has a basis of $50,000 in his partnership interest and receives a building with an adjusted basis to the partnership of $120,000 in termination of his interest. (The partnership has no hot assets.) The building's basis in Ryan's hands is $50,000 under the proportionate liquidating distribution rules. If an optional adjustment-to-basis election is in effect, the partnership increases the basis of its remaining property by $70,000.

Partnership's adjusted basis in distributed property	$120,000
Less: Distributee's basis in distributed property	(50,000)
Increase	$ 70,000

■

EXAMPLE 41

Assume the same facts as in Example 40, except the partnership's basis in the building was $40,000. Ryan's basis in the building is still $50,000, and the partnership reduces the basis of its remaining property by $10,000.

Distributee's basis in distributed property	$ 50,000
Less: Partnership's adjusted basis in distributed property	(40,000)
Decrease	$ 10,000

■

Although these rules may seem confusing at first reading, understanding the theory on which they are based helps to clarify the situation. Section 734(b) assumes that the inside basis for all partnership assets equals the outside basis for all of the partners' interests immediately before the distribution. When this equality exists both before and after a distribution, no adjustment to the basis of partnership property is necessary. However, when the equality does not exist after the distribution, an adjustment can bring the inside and outside bases back into equality. This is the adjustment that is made by the two increases and the two decreases described in the bulleted lists above.

EXAMPLE 42

Assume the Cardinal Partnership has an inside basis of $12,000 for its assets, which have a fair market value of $15,000. Aaron, Bill, and Chelsea each have outside bases of $4,000 for their partnership interests. If the partnership liquidates partner Aaron's interest with a $5,000 cash distribution, the resulting balance sheet is unbalanced as follows:

	Inside (Assets)		Outside (Capital)
Before	$12,000	=	$12,000
Distribution	(5,000)	≠	(4,000)
After	$ 7,000	≠	$ 8,000

This unbalanced situation can be eliminated by adding $1,000 to the inside basis of the formula. Note that this is the same amount as the gain that Aaron recognizes on the distribution ($5,000 cash − $4,000 outside basis = $1,000 gain). Therefore, by adding the amount of Aaron's gain to the inside basis of the partnership assets, the inside basis = outside basis formula is back in balance.

Inside (Assets)		Outside (Capital)
$7,000	≠	$8,000
+1,000		
$8,000	=	$8,000

Note that if the partnership liquidates Aaron's interest with a distribution of land having a $5,000 inside basis, the same unbalanced situation occurs. Although this transaction does not create any recognized gain for Aaron, the $1,000 optional adjustment is the excess of the $5,000 inside basis of the distributed property over the $4,000 substituted basis of that property to Aaron. ■

The two optional adjustment decreases are also explained by this type of analysis.

The basis adjustments created by distributions affect the bases of all remaining partnership properties. Therefore, any depreciation deductions taken on such basis adjustments are allocated to all partners remaining in the partnership after the distribution. The *partnership* also takes these basis adjustments into account in determining any gains or losses on subsequent sales of partnership properties.

EXAMPLE 43
THE BIG PICTURE

Return to the facts of *The Big Picture* on p. 11-2. Recall that the members of Beachside Properties, LLC, are considering two restructuring options. For either option, Beachside Properties could make a § 754 election and reflect an adjustment to the basis of the LLC's property.

- *Step-up related to sale of interests.* On a sale of the interests to the new LLC members, the step-up would equal the difference between the $9.5 million paid and Kyle's and Maria's share of the inside basis of the LLC's property. This step-up of approximately $7.6 million [$9.5 million − (95% × $2 million net assets)] would be allocated to the various partnership properties under the rules of § 755 (not discussed in this chapter). Deductions related to the step-up, such as depreciation, would be allocated to the new developer group.
- *Step-up related to distribution in liquidation of the partners' interests.* If the LLC redeems the interests of Kyle and Maria, the LLC can step up the bases of its remaining assets by the amount of gain recognized by Kyle and Maria. This step-up is approximately $7.8 million [$9.5 million distribution − $1.7 million total basis in partnership interests (Kyle's basis of $400,000 + Maria's basis of $1.3 million)], and benefits all the remaining partners in the partnership.

Note that the step-up differs depending on whether there is a sale or redemption, because Kyle's and Maria's share of the basis of the assets differs from their basis in the LLC interests. ■

11.6 Termination of a Partnership

LO.9

Outline the methods of terminating a partnership.

When does a partnership's final tax year end? Technically, it ends when the partnership terminates, which occurs on either of the following events:

- No part of the business continues to be carried on by any of the partners in a partnership.
- Within a 12-month period, there is a sale or exchange of 50 percent or more of the partnership's capital and profits.[33]

The partnership terminates and its tax year closes when the partnership incorporates or when one partner in a two-party partnership buys out the other partner, thereby creating a sole proprietorship. A termination also occurs when the partnership ceases operations and liquidates.

[33] § 708(b)(1).

The partnership taxable year usually does not close upon the death of a partner or upon the liquidation of a partner's interest, unless the liquidation of the interest of one partner in a two-partner partnership effectively terminates the partnership on the liquidation date. However, the partnership year will close in respect to the deceased or liquidated partner.[34] The deceased or liquidated partner's share of partnership income or loss is computed to the date of death or liquidation and reported on the partner's tax return for the year in which the death or liquidation occurs.

The partnership year does not close upon the entry of a new partner to the partnership. It also does not close upon the sale or exchange of an existing partnership interest unless the transaction results in 50 percent or more of the interests in the partnership capital and profits being sold within a 12-month period.

EXAMPLE 44

Partner Olaf, who held a one-third interest in the Oriole Partnership, died on November 20, 2011. The partnership uses an approved fiscal year ending September 30. Olaf used a calendar year. The partnership agreement does not contain a buy-sell provision that is triggered upon the death of a partner. The partnership's tax year does not close with Olaf's death. The partnership tax year does close, however, with respect to Olaf. His share of partnership income or loss for the period from October 1, 2011, to November 20, 2011, is reported on his final Form 1040. The partnership income or loss from November 21, 2011, to September 30, 2012, is taxed to Olaf's estate or other successor. Income from the partnership's fiscal year ending September 30, 2011, is reported on Olaf's final income tax return, which covers the period from January 1 to November 20, 2011. The executor of Olaf's estate elected that the taxable year for Olaf's estate will end on October 31.

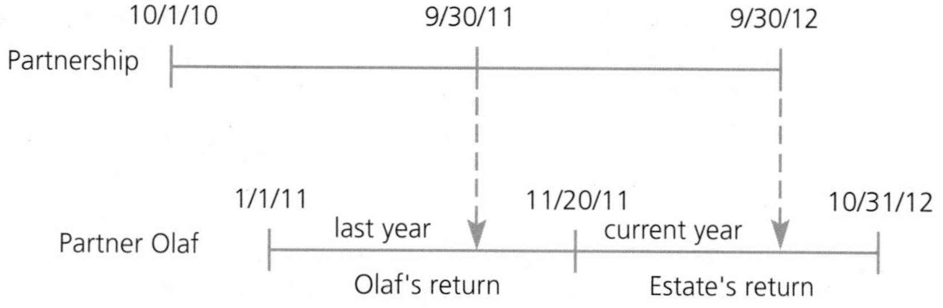

A **technical termination of a partnership** occurs when the partnership business operations continue but the partnership terminates because there has been a sale or exchange of the requisite 50 percent capital and profits interests within 12 months. If the same interest (less than 50 percent) is sold more than once, only one sale is considered in determining whether more than 50 percent has been sold within 12 months. The terminated partnership is deemed to liquidate by transferring its assets and liabilities to a newly formed partnership, which continues its business operations.[35] A technical termination may have numerous consequences, such as creating a different taxable year for the new partnership or modifying the cost recovery methods to be used by the new partnership.

EXAMPLE 45
THE BIG PICTURE

Return to the facts of *The Big Picture* on p. 11-2. Before the sale or redemption, Kyle's and Maria's combined interests equal 95% of the LLC's capital and 80% of the LLC's profits interests. If they both sell their interests within a 12-month period, they will cause a technical termination of the existing LLC, and a new LLC will be deemed to be formed. Though not a devastating result, it must be dealt with by redetermining the LLC's basis in its assets and reestablishing the (new) LLC as an entity. (Note: The partners could structure the sale so that the termination did not occur, for example, by having Kyle and Maria sell less than a 50% interest in the LLC in one year and the remaining interest more than 12 months later.)

If the LLC redeems the interests, there is no sale or exchange transaction, and no technical termination of the LLC. ■

[34] § 706(c)(2)(A).

[35] Reg. § 1.708–1(b).

11.7 OTHER ISSUES

LO.10

Identify the special considerations of a family partnership.

Partnership rules also generally apply to family partnerships, limited liability companies, and limited liability partnerships. This section examines the special considerations applicable to these entities.

FAMILY PARTNERSHIPS

Family partnerships are owned and controlled primarily by members of the same family. Such partnerships may be established for a variety of reasons. A daughter may have a particular expertise that, coupled with her parents' abilities, allows them to establish a successful business. Often, however, one primary reason for establishing a family partnership is the desire to save taxes. If the parents are in higher marginal tax brackets than the children, family tax dollars are saved by funneling some of the partnership income to the children.

Valid family partnerships are difficult to establish for tax purposes. A basic tenet of tax law is that income must be taxed to the person who performs the services or owns the capital that generates the income. A parent, therefore, cannot transfer only a profits interest to a child and expect the transfer to be recognized for tax purposes.

Capital versus Services

Because of the concern that family partnerships are established primarily for tax avoidance purposes, a family member is recognized as a partner only in the following cases:

- Capital is a material income-producing factor in the partnership, and the family member's capital interest is acquired in a bona fide transaction (even if by gift or purchase from another family member) in which ownership and control are received.
- Capital is not a material income-producing factor, but the family member contributes substantial or vital services.[36]

If a partnership derives a substantial portion of its gross income from the use of capital, such as inventories or investments in plant, machinery, or equipment, the capital is considered to be a material income-producing factor. Ordinarily, capital is not a material income-producing factor if the partnership's income consists principally of fees, commissions, or other compensation for personal services performed by partners or employees.

Children as Partners

When capital is a material income-producing factor and a partnership interest is transferred by gift or sale to a child who is under age 19 (or a student under age 24), the kiddie tax may apply. Under the kiddie tax, some of the dependent child's distributive share of partnership income may be taxed at the parent's tax rate, unless the income share constitutes earned income. Regardless of age, if the child provides bona fide services to a partnership and the income share constitutes earned income, the parent-partner's tax rate is avoided.

EXAMPLE 46

Karen operates a first-floor-window-washing business in a summer lakeside resort city. Relatively small amounts of capital are required to operate the sole proprietorship (buckets, sponges, squeegees, etc.). During the summer, Karen normally hires middle and high school students to wash windows. Her 17-year-old daughter and 15-year-old son want to work in the business during the summer to earn money for spending and for college. Each obtains the necessary summer work permit. Karen creates the KDS Partnership and gives each child a 5% interest.

[36] § 704(e).

Karen figures that if her children were paid an hourly rate, about 5% of KDS's profits would be distributed to them as wages. Karen believes that an ownership interest will help the children learn what running a profitable business entails and prepare them for an active business life after their education is completed.

Because capital is not a material income-producing factor in the business, and the children's profit percentages approximate what they would earn if they were paid an hourly rate, all of the income is classified as earned income. Thus, the kiddie tax is avoided. ■

Gift of Capital Interest

If a family member acquires a capital interest by gift in a family partnership in which capital is a material income-producing factor, only part of the income may be allocated to this interest. First, the donor of the interest is allocated an amount of partnership income that represents reasonable compensation for services to the partnership. Then, the remaining income is divided among the partners in accordance with their capital interests in the partnership. An interest purchased by one family member from another is considered to be created by gift for this purpose.[37]

EXAMPLE 47

A partnership in which a parent transferred a 50% interest by gift to a child generated a profit of $90,000. Capital is a material income-producing factor. The parent performed services valued at $20,000. The child performed no services. Under these circumstances, $20,000 is allocated to the parent as compensation. Of the remaining $70,000 of income attributable to capital, at least 50%, or $35,000, is allocated to the parent. ■

LIMITED LIABILITY COMPANIES

LO.11

Describe the application of partnership provisions to limited liability companies (LLCs) and limited liability partnerships (LLPs).

Owners of small businesses often wish to combine the limited liability of a corporation with the pass-through provisions of a partnership. S corporations, described in Chapter 12, provide some of these advantages. The limited liability company is a form of entity that goes further in combining partnership taxation with limited personal liability for all owners of the entity. All of the states and the District of Columbia have passed legislation permitting the establishment of LLCs.

Taxation of LLCs

A properly structured LLC with two or more owners is generally taxed as a partnership. Because none of the LLC members are personally liable for any debts of the entity, the LLC is effectively treated as a limited partnership with no general partners. As described in Chapter 10, this results in unusual application of partnership taxation rules in such areas as allocation of liabilities to the LLC members, inclusion or exclusion of debt for at-risk purposes, passive or active status of a member for passive loss purposes, and determination of a member's liability for self-employment tax.

Converting to an LLC

A partnership can convert to an LLC with few, if any, tax ramifications: the old elections of the partnership continue, and the partners retain their bases and ownership interests in the new entity. However, a C or an S corporation that reorganizes as an LLC is treated as having liquidated prior to forming the new entity. The transaction is taxable to both the corporation and the shareholders. See the "Tax in the News" feature on the next page for considerations related to converting a C or S corporation to partnership or LLC status.

[37] § 704(e)(3).

TAX in the NEWS

Converting a C or S Corporation to a Partnership Entity

Shareholders may decide to convert their existing C or S corporation to a partnership for various reasons (e.g., to avoid double taxation or to pass through losses). Unfortunately, this process is not as tax neutral as the incorporation of a partnership. In general, the conversion is treated as a liquidation of the corporate entity and the formation of a partnership.

Recall from earlier chapters that the liquidation of a corporation (C or S) is a taxable event (§§ 331 and 336). The assets are distributed from the corporation, and this triggers gain at the entity level (and a corporate-level tax if the entity is a C corporation). The gain is the difference between the basis and the fair market value of the distributed assets.

The tax resulting from a conversion, however, is less burdensome when the economy is depressed and asset values are low (corporate-level gain is minimized or possibly eliminated). Also beneficial are the current relatively low tax rates—capital gains are generally taxed to individuals at only a 15 percent maximum tax rate. Thus, taxpayers may be able to take advantage of difficult economic times and lower tax rates by converting a double-taxed corporate entity to a more tax-efficient LLC or LLP.

Advantages of an LLC

An LLC offers certain advantages over a limited partnership, including the following:

- Generally, none of the owners of an LLC are personally liable for the entity's debts. General partners in a limited partnership have personal liability for partnership recourse debts.
- Limited partners cannot participate in the management of the partnership. All owners of an LLC have the legal right to participate in the entity's management.

The advantages of an LLC over an S corporation are discussed in Chapter 13.

Disadvantages of an LLC

The disadvantages of an LLC stem primarily from the entity's relative newness. There is only a limited body of case law interpreting the various state statutes, so the application of some provisions is uncertain. An additional uncertainty for LLCs that operate in more than one jurisdiction is which state's law will prevail and how it will be applied.

Among other factors, statutes differ from state to state as to the type of business an LLC can conduct—particularly as to the extent to which certain service-providing firms can operate as LLCs. A service entity may find it can operate as an LLC in one state but not in another.

LIMITED LIABILITY PARTNERSHIPS

Although the name is similar, a limited liability partnership (LLP) is quite different from a limited partnership. In 1991, Texas became the first state to allow professionals to organize their practices as registered LLPs. All states now permit LLPs to be formed. Also, as described in Chapter 10, about 20 states have adopted legislation authorizing a variation known as a limited liability limited partnership (LLLP). The difference between a general partnership and an LLP is small, but very significant. Recall that general partners are jointly and severally liable for all partnership debts. In some states, partners in a registered LLP are jointly and severally liable for contractual liability (i.e., they are treated as general partners for commercial debt). They are also always personally liable for their own malpractice or other torts. They are not, however, personally liable for the malpractice and torts of their partners. As a result, the exposure of their personal assets to lawsuits filed against other partners and the partnership is considerably reduced.

An LLP must have formal documents of organization and register with the state. Because the LLP is a general partnership in other respects, it does not have to pay any state franchise taxes on its operations—an important difference between LLPs and LLCs in states that impose franchise taxes on LLCs. LLPs are taxed as partnerships under Federal tax statutes.

The conversion of a general partnership into a registered LLP is a continuation of the old partnership for tax purposes if all the general partners become LLP partners and hold the same proportionate interests in the LLP that they held in the general partnership. This means that all the old partnership's elections continue in the LLP, including accounting methods, the taxable year-end, and the § 754 election.

ANTI-ABUSE REGULATIONS

The IRS has issued Regulations that allow it to disregard the form of a partnership transaction when it believes that the transaction (or series of transactions) is abusive.[38] Under the Regulation, a transaction is abusive if it satisfies two tests. First, it must have a principal purpose of substantially reducing the present value of the partners' aggregate Federal tax liability. In addition, the potential tax reduction must be inconsistent with the intent of Subchapter K. If the IRS disregards the form of a transaction, it will recast the transaction in a manner that reflects the transaction's underlying economic arrangement.

It is often difficult to determine whether a proposed transaction will substantially reduce the present value of the partners' aggregate tax liability. Partners may not know their personal tax situations until the transaction occurs and the partner's tax return is completed. Practitioners are concerned that the IRS could try to use "perfect hindsight" to determine if a transaction should be recast. This could make it difficult to anticipate the ultimate tax treatment of many partnership transactions.

The IRS says it will not recast transactions that are bona fide business arrangements and offers several examples in the Regulation. The IRS has also announced that a field examiner cannot invoke the Regulation without approval. Review by a partnership specialty group within the IRS is required before the IRS will challenge a taxpayer's treatment of a transaction under this Regulation.

TAX PLANNING:

11.8 Sales and Exchanges of Partnership Interests

LO.12

Evaluate tax planning considerations related to partnership distributions and sales of partnership interests.

DELAYING ORDINARY INCOME

A partner planning to dispose of a partnership interest in a taxable transaction might consider either an installment sale or a pro rata distribution of hot assets, followed by a sale of the remaining interest in the partnership. Although the partner will have ordinary income when these hot assets are collected or sold, the partner can spread the income over more than one tax year by controlling the collection or disposal dates.

BASIS ADJUSTMENT FOR TRANSFEREE

If a partnership interest is acquired by purchase, the purchaser may want to condition the acquisition on the partnership's promise to make an election to adjust the basis of partnership assets. Making the election under § 754 results in the basis in the partner's ratable share of partnership assets being adjusted to reflect the purchase price. Failure to do so could result in the loss of future depreciation deductions or could convert ordinary losses into capital losses.

[38] Reg. § 1.701–2.

TAX *in* the NEWS

Tax Treatment of "Carried Interests"

Limited partnerships are often used as vehicles for raising capital. For example, investors might purchase interests in a limited partnership created to purchase a specific rental real estate property (or properties).

This partnership might be formed by a real estate property management firm using funds loaned by a mortgage banking firm, and with the partnership interests marketed by a brokerage house. The developer, lender, and promoter are often noncorporate firms that accept a "carried interest"—typically, a capital interest in the partnership—in lieu of receiving current compensation for their services. The investment is structured so that there is no value in the carried interest at the time it is awarded—therefore, receipt of the carried interest in exchange for services does not result in current taxation. When the limited partnership is eventually sold or liquidated, these parties receive a gain allocation or a liquidating distribution from the partnership.

For example, say Real Property Developers Group, LLC, accepts a 5 percent interest (at no current cost) in the capital of Rental Property, Ltd. The LLC performs all services entailed in acquiring, managing, and syndicating the limited partnership offering. (Assume the LLC does not receive any allocations of the limited partnership's operating income or expenses.)

When Rental Property, Ltd., is liquidated, the LLC receives a $10 million liquidating distribution. This results in a capital gain because the LLC had no basis in the partnership interest. The arrangement is very attractive as it yields a $10 million capital gain at the end instead of ordinary income when the entity is formed and during the life of the partnership.

For several years, this type of arrangement has been under fire in the financial press. Congress has made several attempts to pass legislation that would result in ordinary income treatment for "carried interests." In recent years, several bills have been proposed that would have adopted this treatment. It may be just a matter of time before one of these bills is passed by both houses of Congress and signed by the President.

The current treatment does have supporters, though. Venture capital firms accept a tremendous amount of risk and incur substantial expenses in forming such ventures, many of which are unsuccessful. The question to be resolved is one of characterization. Should the risk-bearing developer, syndicator, and lender be forced to recognize ordinary income for the performance of services? Or should they be awarded capital gains treatment when the partnership is terminated, reflecting the risk inherent in the venture?

Source: Present Law and Analysis Relating to Tax of Partnership Carried Interests, Joint Committee on Taxation, JCX-41-07, July 10, 2007.

11.9 Planning Partnership Distributions

GENERAL GUIDELINES

In planning for any partnership distributions, be alert to the following possibilities:

- When gain recognition is undesirable, ascertain that cash distributions from a partnership, including any debt assumptions or repayments, do not exceed the basis of the receiving partner's interest.
- Distributions of marketable securities may also result in gain, but the current gain can be minimized if the securities *are* appreciated.
- When a partner is to receive a liquidating distribution and the full basis of the interest will not be recovered, the partner's capital loss can be ensured by providing that the only assets received by the partner are cash, unrealized receivables, and inventory. If a capital loss is undesirable, however, the partnership should also distribute a capital or § 1231 asset that will take the partner's remaining basis in the interest. This may result in a more desirable ordinary deduction or loss in the future.
- Current and liquidating distributions may result in ordinary income recognition for either the receiving partner or the partnership if hot assets are present. When such income is undesirable, consider making a distribution of hot assets pro rata to the receiving partner.
- If precontribution gain property is contributed to a partnership, gain to the contributing partner can be further deferred if the partnership waits

seven years before (1) distributing the precontribution gain property to another partner or (2) distributing other partnership property to the precontribution gain partner if the value of the other property exceeds the partner's basis in the partnership.

- When the partnership agreement initially is drafted, consider including provisions that govern liquidating distributions of partnership income and property. The specifics of the agreement generally will be followed by the IRS if these and other relevant points are addressed early in the life of the entity.

VALUATION PROBLEMS

Both the IRS and the courts usually consider the value of a partner's interest or any partnership assets agreed upon by all partners to be correct. Thus, when planning the sale or liquidation of a partnership interest, the results of the bargaining process should be documented. To avoid valuation problems on liquidation, include a formula or agreed-upon valuation procedure in the partnership agreement or in a related buy-sell agreement.

11.10 Comparing Sales to Liquidations

When a partner disposes of an entire interest in a partnership for a certain sum, the *before-tax* result of a sale of that interest to another partner or partners is the same as the liquidation of the interest under § 736. In other words, if both transactions result in the partner receiving the same amount of pre-tax dollars, the partner should be ambivalent about which form the transaction takes unless one form offers tax savings that the other does not.

The *after-tax* result of a sale of a partnership interest and a liquidation of a partner's interest by an ongoing partnership may differ considerably. One difference occurs when the payment for that interest is extended over several years. When a partner sells the partnership interest to another partner, the selling partner can postpone the recognition of income under the installment sale rules. These rules are very restrictive and require that gain and income be recognized at least as quickly as the proportionate share of the receivable is collected. However, in a liquidation, more flexibility may be available. Under § 736, the § 736(b) payments for partnership property can be made before the income payments under § 736(a). Furthermore, the § 736(b) payments can be treated as a return of basis first with gain recognized only after the distributee partner has received amounts equal to the basis. This treatment results in a deferral of gain and income recognition under § 736 that is not available under the installment sale provisions.

PAYMENTS FOR GOODWILL

The partner who purchases a partnership interest often pays an amount that can be attributed, in part, to partnership goodwill. Purchased goodwill is included in a purchasing partner's outside basis for the partnership interest. The partner cannot amortize the goodwill unless (1) the asset qualifies as a § 197 intangible, amortizable over 15 years, and (2) the partnership makes an election under § 754 to adjust the basis of partnership assets to reflect the purchase price paid. In many cases, the purchasing partner will not obtain a tax benefit from the goodwill until the partnership interest is disposed of.

Under § 736, amounts paid by a service partnership for a general partner's share of partnership goodwill can be treated as a § 736(a) payment. If this payment is a guaranteed payment, it is deductible by the partnership. If it is a distributive share, it is excludible from the income stream of the remaining partners. In effect, this is also like a deduction. If (1) capital is a material income-producing factor of the partnership or (2) the distributee partner was a limited partner, payments for goodwill constitute § 736(b) property payments. These payments are not deductible by the partnership and result in increased capital gain (or decreased capital loss) to the retiring partner.

TERMINATION OF PARTNERSHIP

A partnership terminates if 50 percent or more of the total interest in partnership capital and profits is sold within a 12-month period. A liquidation under § 736, however, is not considered a sale or exchange under this rule. Therefore, a partnership can liquidate a partner's interest without terminating a three-partner partnership, even if the liquidated partner had a 98 percent interest in partnership capital and profits immediately before the liquidating distribution.

A sale and a liquidation of a partnership interest also differ in other respects that are beyond the scope of this text. The point to remember is that differences exist that may result in considerable after-tax savings for the partners. Careful planning can result in a properly structured transaction.

11.11 Other Partnership Issues

CHOICE OF ENTITY

The partnership liquidation rules demonstrate the tax advantages of the partnership form over the C corporation in the final stage of the business's life:

- A service partnership can effectively claim deductions for its payment to a retiring general partner for goodwill.
- The partnership liquidation itself is not a taxable event. Under corporate rules, however, liquidating distributions and sales in preparation for a distribution are fully taxable.
- Tax liability relative to the liquidation is generated at the partner level, but only upon a recognition event (such as receipt of cash in excess of basis, or sale of an asset received in a distribution). The timing of this event is usually under the control of the (ex-)partner. In this manner, the tax obligations can be placed into the most beneficial tax year and rate bracket.

FAMILY PARTNERSHIPS

If possible, make certain that very young and elderly members of a family partnership contribute services to the entity, so as to justify their income allocations. These services can comprise the most routine facets of the business, including monitoring and operating copy and fax machines and providing ongoing maintenance of the indoor and outdoor landscaping environments. Although no more than a market level of compensation can be assigned for this purpose, the services themselves constitute evidence of the active role that the partner plays in the operations of the entity.

As there is no equivalent of the kiddie tax for elderly taxpayers, retention of the founding members of the partnership past the nominal retirement age often facilitates the income-shifting goals of the family.

REFOCUS ON THE BIG PICTURE

THE LIFE CYCLE OF A PARTNERSHIP

Two things are happening when the new developers become members of Beachside Properties, LLC. The developers are buying out the interests of two existing LLC members, and they are providing cash with which to expand the LLC's operations.

The expansion itself raises no specific tax problems. An LLC can admit new members with no immediate tax consequences. In addition to the issues addressed earlier in the chapter, the LLC's operating agreement should be modified to ensure that there is no shift in ownership rights between Josh and the new LLC members.

What If?

Changing the facts, assume the developers have only $5 million in cash, with good prospects for receiving an additional $5 million over the next two years, and $9.5 million more in the third year. The LLC has found a bridge loan and temporary financing of $10 million to cover costs during this interim period. This loan, though, is not large enough to also completely buy out Kyle's and Maria's interests. Thus, Kyle and Maria have agreed to accept installment payments for the sale or redemption of their interests.

Now the buyout of Kyle and Maria can be treated either as an installment sale or as a redemption under § 736 requiring a series of payments. While the specific results of these arrangements are beyond the scope of this chapter, different tax consequences might arise as to the timing and character of Kyle's and Maria's gain recognition.

KEY TERMS

Appreciated inventory, 11–15
Disproportionate distribution, 11–4
Hot assets, 11–15
Liquidating distribution, 11–3
Nonliquidating distribution, 11–3
Optional adjustment election, 11–29
Proportionate distribution, 11–4
§ 754 Election, 11–29
Technical termination of a partnership, 11–33
Unrealized receivables, 11–6

DISCUSSION QUESTIONS

1. **LO.1** Describe the tax treatment to the partner of a proportionate nonliquidating distribution of cash, land, and inventory. When might the partner recognize a gain or loss?

2. **LO.1** How is the basis determined for land and inventory received in a proportionate nonliquidating distribution? How is the partner's basis in the partnership interest affected?

3. **LO.1** What is the effect on a partnership of a proportionate nonliquidating distribution of cash, land and inventory?

4. **LO.2** Describe the tax treatment to the partner of a proportionate liquidating distribution (where the partnership also liquidates) of cash, land, and inventory. When might the partner recognize a gain or loss?

5. **LO.2** How is the basis determined for land and inventory received in a proportionate liquidating distribution (where the partnership also liquidates)? How is the partner's basis in the partnership interest affected?

6. **LO.2** What is the effect on a partnership of a proportionate liquidating distribution of cash, and appreciated land and inventory where the partnership also liquidates? How does this compare with liquidating distributions from a corporation?

ISSUE ID

7. **LO.1, 2** The LizMack Partnership distributes the following assets to partner Liz:
   - $20,000 cash.
   - Inventory with a $20,000 value and a $10,000 basis to the partnership.
   - A parcel of land with a $30,000 value and a $35,000 basis to the partnership.

   What issues must be considered in determining the tax treatment of the distribution?

8. **LO.1, 4, 6** Describe, in general terms, two types of assets regarded as "hot assets." When is characterization as a "hot asset" relevant?

ISSUE ID

9. **LO.1, 2** What theories of taxation underlie the rules related to proportionate liquidating and nonliquidating distributions? (In other words, what are these distribution rules trying to accomplish?)

ISSUE ID

10. **LO.3** What issues arise if a partner contributes appreciated property to a partnership and that property is later distributed to another partner?

ISSUE ID

11. **LO.3** What issues arise if a partner contributes appreciated property to a partnership and other appreciated property is later distributed to the contributing partner?

12. **LO.4** What is a disproportionate distribution? What is the theory underlying the disproportionate distribution rules, and what are they trying to accomplish?

13. **LO.5** Distinguish between the treatment of § 736 income and property payments. What are the tax consequences of such payments to the retiring partner, the remaining partners, and the partnership?

ISSUE ID

14. **LO.6, 8** Jody sells her partnership interest to Bill for $10,000. What issues must be addressed by Jody, Bill, and the partnership?

15. **LO.6** Identify amounts that are included in the sales proceeds when a partner sells an interest in the partnership to an unrelated third party. How is the character of the selling partner's gain or loss determined?

16. **LO.7** What are the consequences to the donor and the donee partner when a partnership interest is gifted during the year? How is income allocated between the two partners?

17. **LO.8** Who makes the optional adjustment-to-basis election? How is the election made, and what is its effect on future years?

18. **LO.9** Describe the various types of events that can cause a partnership termination. Which of these can cause a "technical" termination?

19. **LO.1, 2, 3, 4, 5, 6, 8, 10, 11** Comment on the validity of each of the following statements.
    a. A partner may recognize ordinary income if a proportionate current distribution of cash exceeds the partner's basis in the partnership interest.
    b. A partner may recognize a capital loss in a proportionate current distribution if the only assets received are cash, unrealized receivables, and/or inventory.
    c. In a proportionate liquidating distribution, if a partner receives cash equal to the basis in the partnership interest, any other property received will take a $0 basis.
    d. If a partner contributes property with a precontribution gain and that property is later distributed to that same partner, the partner must recognize a capital gain in the amount of the precontribution gain.
    e. In a disproportionate distribution, either the partnership or the distributee partner might be required to recognize ordinary income.
    f. In a redemption of a partnership interest under § 736, a payment to a general partner in a service partnership for goodwill that is provided for in the partnership agreement is treated as a § 736(b) property payment.
    g. Under § 736 all payments to a retiring partner are either property payments [§ 736(b)] or income payments [§ 736(a)].
    h. In a sale of a partnership interest, the partner will recognize capital gain to the extent that the selling price exceeds the partner's basis in the partnership interest.

i. A partner may make a § 754 election if gain is recognized on a distribution of cash from the partnership.
j. A § 754 election might be appropriate if a partner purchases a partnership interest from another partner for substantially more than the partner's share of the underlying basis in partnership assets.
k. A family member can be recognized as a partner in a partnership in which capital is *not* a material income-producing factor only if that partner provides substantial services to the partnership.
l. Both the tax and the economic consequences are the same, whether a partnership redeems the partner's interest in the partnership or that interest is sold to a new partner for an equivalent amount of cash.

20. **LO.11** To what extent are the personal assets of a general partner, limited partner, or member of an LLC subject to (a) contractual liability claims, such as trade accounts payable, and (b) malpractice claims against the entity? Answer the question for partners or members in a general partnership, LLP, nonprofessional LLC, and limited partnership.

PROBLEMS

21. **LO.1** Greg's outside basis in his interest in the GO Partnership is $360,000. In a proportionate nonliquidating distribution, the partnership distributes to him cash of $60,000, inventory (fair market value of $200,000, basis to the partnership of $160,000), and land (fair market value of $50,000, basis to the partnership of $80,000). The partnership continues in existence.
    a. Does the partnership recognize any gain or loss as a result of this distribution?
    b. Does Greg recognize any gain or loss as a result of this distribution?
    c. Calculate Greg's basis in the land, in the inventory, and in his partnership interest immediately following the distribution.

22. **LO.1** When Tiffany's outside basis in the TMF Partnership is $120,000, the partnership distributes to her $30,000 cash, an account receivable (fair market value of $75,000, inside basis to the partnership of $0), and a parcel of land (fair market value of $150,000, inside basis to the partnership of $125,000). Tiffany remains a partner in the partnership, and the distribution is proportionate to the partners.
    a. Determine the recognized gain or loss to the partnership as a result of this distribution.
    b. Determine the recognized gain or loss to Tiffany as a result of the distribution.
    c. Determine Tiffany's basis in the land, account receivable, and TMF Partnership after the distribution.

23. **LO.1** In each of the following independent cases in which the partnership owns no hot assets, indicate:

    - Whether the partner recognizes gain or loss.
    - Whether the partnership recognizes gain or loss.
    - The partner's adjusted basis for the property distributed.
    - The partner's outside basis in the partnership after the distribution.

    a. Brooke receives $10,000 cash in partial liquidation of her interest in the partnership. Brooke's outside basis for her partnership interest immediately before the distribution is $6,000.
    b. Brianna receives $30,000 cash and land with an inside basis to the partnership of $50,000 (value of $100,000) in partial liquidation of her interest. Brianna's outside basis for her partnership interest immediately before the distribution is $90,000.
    c. Assume the same facts as in (b), except that Brianna's outside basis for her partnership interest immediately before the distribution is $40,000.
    d. Bonnie receives $100,000 cash and inventory with a basis of $50,000 and a fair market value of $60,000 in partial liquidation of her partnership interest. Her basis was $80,000 before the distribution. All partners received proportionate distributions.

24. **LO.8** Assume the facts of Problem 23. In each independent case, are additional planning opportunities available to the partnership to maximize its inside basis in its assets? If so, by how much can the basis be increased? What is the effect of any basis increase to the distributee partner or the other partners? **DECISION MAKING**

25. **LO.1** Mark's basis in his partnership interest is $39,000. In a proportionate nonliquidating distribution, Mark receives $30,000 cash and two inventory items with bases of $10,000 each to the partnership. The values of the inventory items are $15,000 and $5,000.
   a. How much gain or loss, if any, must Mark recognize on the distribution?
   b. What basis will Mark take in each inventory item?

COMMUNICATIONS

26. **LO.1** Heloise Hawkins is a 50% partner in the calendar year Hawkins-Henry Partnership. On January 1, 2011, her basis in her partnership interest is $150,000. The partnership has no taxable income or loss for the current year. In a nonliquidating distribution, the partnership distributes $140,000 cash to Heloise on December 15. It also distributes inventory proportionately to all partners. Heloise receives inventory with a basis of $25,000 and a fair market value of $20,000. In January 2012, Heloise, your client, asks your advice regarding treatment of 2011 operations and distributions. Using the format (1) facts, (2) issues, and (3) conclusion and analysis, draft a letter to Heloise at the Hawkins-Henry Partnership (1622 E. Henry Street, St. Paul, MN 55163). Your letter should address the following points and provide enough information for the client to understand the applicable tax provisions but without including specific citations.
   a. How much gain or loss does the partnership recognize as a result of 2011 activities?
   b. How much gain or loss must Heloise recognize in 2011?
   c. What is Heloise's basis in inventory received?
   d. What is Heloise's basis in her partnership interest at the end of 2011?

27. **LO.1, 2** At the beginning of the tax year, Monica's basis in the MIP LLC was $100,000, including Monica's $50,000 share of the LLC's liabilities. At the end of the year, MIP distributed to Monica cash of $20,000 and inventory (basis of $10,000, fair market value of $16,000). In addition, MIP repaid all of its liabilities by the end of the year.
   a. If this is a proportionate nonliquidating distribution, what is the tax effect of the distribution to Monica and MIP? After the distribution, what is Monica's basis in the inventory and in her MIP interest?
   b. Would your answers to (a) change if this had been a proportionate liquidating distribution?

ISSUE ID

28. **LO.1, 2, 3, 4, 5, 6, 8, 10, 12** Vincent is a 50% partner in the TAV Partnership. He became a partner three years ago when he contributed land with a value of $60,000 and a basis of $30,000 (current value is $100,000). Tyler and Anita each contributed $30,000 cash for a 25% interest. Vincent's basis in his partnership interest is currently $150,000; the other partners' bases are each $75,000. The partnership has the following assets:

	Basis	FMV
Cash	$200,000	$200,000
Accounts receivable	–0–	200,000
Marketable securities	70,000	100,000
Land	30,000	100,000
Total	$300,000	$600,000

In general terms, describe the tax result if TAV distributes a $50,000 interest in the land each to Tyler and Anita and $100,000 of accounts receivable to Vincent at the end of the current year. Calculations are not required.

ISSUE ID

29. **LO.1, 3, 4** Assume the same facts as in Problem 28, except that TAV distributes $100,000 of cash to Vincent, $50,000 of marketable securities to Tyler, and $50,000 of accounts receivable to Anita. In general terms, describe the tax result of the distribution.

ISSUE ID

30. **LO.1, 3, 4** Assume the same facts as Problem 28, except that TAV distributes a $50,000 interest in the land and $50,000 of accounts receivable to Vincent and $25,000 of cash and $25,000 of accounts receivable each to Anita and Tyler. In general terms, describe the tax result of the distribution.

ISSUE ID

31. **LO.2, 3, 4, 12** Use the assets and partners' bases from Problem 28. Assume the partnership distributes all its assets in a liquidating distribution. In deciding the allocation of assets, what issues should the partnership consider to minimize each partner's taxable gains?

32. **LO.2** In each of the following independent liquidating distributions in which the partnership also liquidates, determine the amount and character of any gain or loss to be

recognized by each partner and the basis of each asset (other than cash) received. In each case, assume distributions of hot assets are proportionate to the partners.

a. Brandon has a partnership basis of $60,000 and receives a distribution of $75,000 in cash.
b. Barry has a partnership basis of $80,000 and receives $30,000 cash and a capital asset with a basis to the partnership of $40,000 and a fair market value of $50,000.
c. Bryan has a partnership basis of $100,000 and receives $30,000 cash, inventory with a basis to the partnership of $20,000, and a capital asset with a partnership basis of $30,000. The inventory and capital asset have fair market values of $25,000 and $40,000, respectively.
d. Blake has a partnership basis of $60,000 and receives a distribution of $20,000 cash and an account receivable with a basis of $0 to the partnership (value is $30,000).

33. **LO.2, 12** The basis of Jesse's partnership interest is $90,000. Jesse receives a pro rata liquidating distribution consisting of $30,000 cash, land with a basis of $50,000 and a fair market value of $60,000, and his proportionate share of inventory with a basis of $20,000 to the partnership and a fair market value of $22,000. Assume the partnership also liquidates. **DECISION MAKING**
    a. How much gain or loss, if any, must Jesse recognize as a result of the distribution?
    b. What basis will Jesse take in the inventory and land?
    c. If the land is sold two years later for $60,000, what are the tax consequences to Jesse?
    d. What are the tax consequences to the partnership as a result of the liquidating distribution?
    e. Is any planning technique available to the partnership to avoid any "lost basis" results?
    f. Would your answer to (b) change if this had been a nonliquidating distribution?

34. **LO.2** Assume the same facts as in Problem 33, except that Jesse's basis in the partnership is $120,000 instead of $90,000.
    a. How much gain or loss, if any, must Jesse recognize on the distribution?
    b. What basis will Jesse take in the inventory and land?
    c. What are the tax consequences to the partnership?
    d. Would your answer to (a) or (b) change if this had been a nonliquidating distribution?

35. **LO.2, 12** Jamie's basis in her partnership interest is $30,000. In liquidation of her interest, the partnership distributes to Jamie cash of $10,000 and inventory (basis of $6,000 and value of $12,000). **DECISION MAKING**
    a. How much gain or loss, if any, must Jamie recognize as a result of the distribution?
    b. What basis will Jamie take in the inventory?
    c. What are the tax consequences to the partnership?
    d. Can you recommend an alternative distribution?
    e. Would your answer to (a) or (b) change if this had been a nonliquidating distribution?

36. **LO.2** Julie's basis in her partnership interest is $108,000. In a proportionate distribution in liquidation of the partnership, Julie receives $50,000 cash and two parcels of land with bases of $20,000 each to the partnership. The partnership holds both parcels of land for investment, and the parcels have fair market values of $10,000 and $30,000.
    a. How much gain or loss, if any, must Julie recognize on the distribution?
    b. What basis will Julie take in each parcel?
    c. If the land had been held as inventory by the partnership, what effect, if any, would it have on your responses to (a) and (b)?

37. **LO.2, 12** Assume the same facts as in Problem 36, except that Julie receives $50,000 cash and a desk having a basis of $1,200 to the partnership and a fair market value of $2,000. **DECISION MAKING**
    a. How much loss, if any, may Julie recognize on the distribution?
    b. What basis will Julie take in the desk?
    c. Suppose Julie's 15-year-old son uses the desk for his personal use for one year before Julie sells it for $1,000. How much loss may Julie recognize on the sale of the desk? What tax planning procedures could have prevented this result?

38. **LO.3** In 2008, Adrianna contributed land with a basis of $16,000 and a fair market value of $25,000 to the A&I Partnership in exchange for a 25% interest in capital and profits. In 2011, the partnership distributes this property to Isabel, also a 25% partner, in a nonliquidating distribution. The fair market value has increased to $30,000 at the time the property is distributed. Isabel's and Adrianna's bases in their partnership interests are each $40,000 at the time of the distribution.
    a. How much gain or loss, if any, does Adrianna recognize on the distribution to Isabel? What is Adrianna's basis in her partnership interest following the distribution?
    b. What is Isabel's basis in the land she received in the distribution?
    c. How much gain or loss, if any, does Isabel recognize on the distribution? What is Isabel's basis in her partnership interest following the distribution?
    d. How much gain or loss would Isabel recognize if she later sells the land for its $30,000 fair market value? Is this result equitable?
    e. Would your answers to (a) and (b) change if Adrianna originally contributed the property to the partnership in 2000?

39. **LO.3** Derek contributed a tract of undeveloped land to the Nightingale Partnership in 2008. He originally paid $20,000 for the property in 1999, but its value was $70,000 at the date of the contribution. In 2011, the partnership distributes another parcel of land to Derek; the land has a basis to the partnership of $30,000. The fair market value of the distributed property is $100,000 in 2011. Derek's basis in his partnership interest is $60,000 immediately before the distribution.
    a. How much gain or loss, if any, does Derek recognize on the distribution?
    b. What is Derek's basis in his partnership interest following the distribution?
    c. What is Derek's basis in the property he receives in the distribution?
    d. After the distribution, what is the partnership's basis in the property originally contributed by Derek?
    e. Would your answers to (b), (c), and (d) change if Derek originally contributed the property to the partnership in 2000?

40. **LO.3, 5** The FABB Partnership distributes a marketable security to 25% partner Fred in complete liquidation of his interest in the partnership. Use the following facts to answer the questions that follow:

    - The partnership's basis in the security is $10,000, and its value is $20,000. The partnership did not own any of this particular security following the distribution.
    - Fred's basis in the partnership interest is $5,000 immediately prior to the distribution.
    - Fred is a general partner, and capital is a material income-producing factor to the partnership.
    - The partnership owns no hot assets.

    a. How is the security classified under § 736?
    b. What is the amount of the security distribution that is treated as a cash distribution?
    c. How much gain does Fred report on the distribution?
    d. What is Fred's basis in the security he receives in the distribution?

DECISION MAKING

41. **LO.5, 12** Maurice is a 10% general partner in the Chartreuse Partnership, which provides consulting services. The partnership distributes $100,000 cash to Maurice in complete liquidation of his partnership interest. Maurice's share of partnership unrealized receivables immediately before the distribution is $40,000. The partnership has no other hot assets. Assume none of the cash payment is for goodwill. Maurice's basis for his partnership interest immediately before the distribution is $50,000.
    a. How is the cash payment treated under § 736?
    b. How much gain or loss must Maurice recognize on the distribution, and what is the character of these amounts?
    c. How does the partnership treat the distribution to Maurice?
    d. What planning opportunities might the partnership wish to consider?

42. **LO.6** RBP Partnership is a service-oriented partnership that has three equal general partners. One of them, Barry, sells his interest to another partner, Dale, for $90,000 cash and the assumption of Barry's share of partnership liabilities. On the sale date, the partnership's cash basis balance sheet is as shown below. Assume that the capital accounts *before* the sale reflect the partners' bases in their partnership interests, excluding liabilities. The payment exceeds the stated fair market value of the assets because of goodwill that is not recorded on the books.

	Basis	FMV		Basis	FMV
Cash	$120,000	$120,000	Note payable	$ 30,000	$ 30,000
Accounts receivable	–0–	90,000	Capital accounts		
Capital assets	30,000	75,000	Barry	40,000	85,000
			David	40,000	85,000
			Dale	40,000	85,000
Total	$150,000	$285,000	Total	$150,000	$285,000

a. What is the total amount realized by Barry on the sale?
b. How much, if any, ordinary income must Barry recognize on the sale?
c. How much capital gain must Barry report?
d. What is Dale's basis in the partnership interest acquired?

43. **LO.5** Assume in Problem 42 that Barry's partnership interest is not sold to another partner. Instead, the partnership makes a liquidating distribution of $90,000 cash to Barry, and the remaining partners assume his share of the liabilities. How much gain or loss must Barry recognize, and how is it characterized? Assume Barry is a general partner, there is no provision for the payment for goodwill in the partnership agreement, and capital is not a material income-producing factor to the partnership.

44. **LO.6, 8** Diana, a partner in the cash basis HDA Partnership, has a one-third interest in partnership profits and losses. The partnership's balance sheet at the end of the current year is as follows:

	Basis	FMV		Basis	FMV
Cash	$120,000	$120,000	Hannah, capital	$ 90,000	$250,000
Receivables	–0–	240,000	Diana, capital	90,000	250,000
Land	150,000	390,000	Alexis, capital	90,000	250,000
Total	$270,000	$750,000	Total	$270,000	$750,000

Diana sells her interest in the HDA Partnership to Kenneth at the end of the current year for cash of $250,000.

a. How much income must Diana report on her tax return for the current year from the sale, and what is its nature?
b. If the partnership does not make an optional adjustment-to-basis election, what are the type and amount of income that Kenneth must report in the next year when the receivables are collected?
c. If the partnership did make an optional adjustment-to-basis election, what are the type and amount of income that Kenneth must report in the next year when the receivables are collected? When the land (which is used in the HDA Partnership's business) is sold for $420,000? Assume no other transactions occurred that year.

45. **LO.6, 7, 9** At the end of last year, Ben, a 40% partner in the four-person BBJR Partnership, has an outside basis of $50,000 in the partnership, including a $40,000 share of partnership debt. Ben's share of the partnership's § 1245 recapture potential is $25,000. All parties use the calendar year. Describe the income tax consequences to Ben in each of the following independent situations that take place in the current year:
a. On the first day of the tax year, Ben sells his partnership interest to Marilyn for $80,000 cash and the assumption by Marilyn of the appropriate share of partnership liabilities.
b. Ben dies after a lengthy illness on April 1 of the current year. Ben's brother immediately takes Ben's place in the partnership.

46. **LO.6, 7, 9** Briefly discuss how your responses in Problem 45 would change if the BBJR Partnership had $200,000 of unrealized receivables at the end of the current year, including the § 1245 recapture potential.

47. **LO.9** For each of the following independent fact patterns, indicate whether a termination of the partnership has occurred for tax purposes. Assume no other partnership interests are sold either one year before or one year after the transactions described.

a. Paige sells her interest in capital and profits of the PQR Partnership. She owns a 48% interest in capital and a 60% interest in the partnership's profits.
b. Ryan and Rob are equal partners in the R & R Partnership. Ryan dies on January 15, 2011. Rob purchases Ryan's interest from his estate on March 15, 2011. Answer for January 15, 2011.
c. Answer (b), for March 15, 2011.
d. Joel, a 52% partner in the profitable J & D Partnership, gives his entire interest to his son on July 1, 2011.
e. Jessica sells her 50% interest in the FJK Partnership to new partner Ashley.
f. Carol, Cora, and Chris are equal partners in the Canary Partnership. On January 22, 2011, Cora sells her entire interest to Ted. On December 29, 2011, Carol sells a 15% interest to Earl. On January 25, 2012, Chris sells his interest to Frank.

48. **LO.10** Fred and Samuel, father and son, operate a local restaurant as an LLC. The FS, LLC earned a profit of $120,000 in the current year. Samuel's equal partnership interest was acquired by gift from Fred. Assume that capital is a material income-producing factor and that Fred manages the day-to-day operations of the restaurant without any help from Samuel. Reasonable compensation for Fred's services is $60,000.
a. How much of the LLC's income is allocated to Fred?
b. What is the maximum amount of the LLC's income that can be allocated to Samuel?
c. Assuming that Samuel is 15 years old, has no other income, and is claimed as a dependent by Fred, how is Samuel's income from the LLC taxed?

RESEARCH PROBLEMS

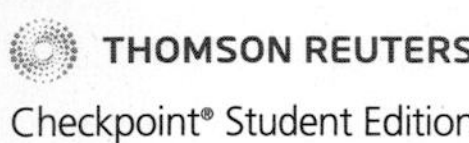

Checkpoint® Student Edition

Note: Solutions to Research Problems can be prepared by using the **Checkpoint® Student Edition** online research product, which is available to accompany this text. It is also possible to prepare solutions to the Research Problems by using tax research materials found in a standard tax library.

DECISION MAKING

Research Problem 1. Your client, Paul, owns a one-third interest as a managing (general) partner in the service-oriented PRE, LLP. He would like to retire from the limited liability partnership at the end of the current year and asks your help in structuring the buyout transaction.

Based on interim financial data and revenue projections for the remainder of the year, the LLP's balance sheet is expected to approximate the following at year-end:

	Basis	FMV		Basis	FMV
Cash	$ 60,000	$ 60,000	Paul, capital	$ 60,000	$150,000
Accounts receivable	-0-	180,000	Rachel, capital	60,000	150,000
Land (capital asset)	120,000	210,000	Erik, capital	60,000	150,000
Total assets	$180,000	$450,000	Total capital	$180,000	$450,000

Although the LLP has some cash, the amount is not adequate to purchase Paul's entire interest in the current year. The LLP has proposed to pay Paul, in liquidation of his interest, according to the following schedule:

December 31, 2011	$50,000
December 31, 2012	$50,000
December 31, 2013	$50,000

Paul has agreed to this payment schedule, but the parties are not sure of the tax consequences of the buyout and have temporarily halted negotiations to consult with their tax advisers. Paul has retained you to ascertain the income tax ramifications of the buyout and to make sure he secures the most advantageous result available. Using the IRS Regulations governing partnerships, answer the following questions.

a. If the buyout agreement between Paul and PRE is silent as to the treatment of each payment, how will each payment be treated by Paul and the partnership?
b. As Paul's adviser, what payment schedule should Paul negotiate to minimize his current tax liability?

c. Regarding the LLP, what payment schedule would ensure that the remaining partners receive the earliest possible deductions?
d. What additional planning opportunity might be available to the partnership?

Research Problem 2. The accrual basis Four Winds Partnership owned and operated three storage facilities in Milwaukee, Wisconsin. The partnership did not have a § 754 election in effect when partner Taylor sold her 25% interest to Patrick for $250,000. The partnership has no debt. There are no § 197 assets, and assume there is no depreciation recapture potential on the storage facility buildings.

At the time of the transfer, the partnership's asset bases and fair market values were as follows:

	Basis	Fair Market Value
Cash	$ 50,000	$ 50,000
Accounts receivable	150,000	150,000
Storage facility #1	500,000	200,000
Storage facility #2	400,000	500,000
Storage facility #3	300,000	100,000
Total assets	$1,400,000	$1,000,000

The value of two of the properties is less than the partnership's basis because of downturns in the real estate market in the area.

Patrick's share of the inside basis of partnership assets is $350,000, and his share of the fair market value of partnership assets is $250,000.

a. What adjustment is required regarding Patrick's purchase of the partnership interest? Must a § 754 election be made?
b. Using the basis allocation rules of § 755 and the Regulations thereunder, calculate the amount of the total adjustment to be allocated to each of the partnership's assets.
c. Would an adjustment be required if the partnership was a venture capital firm and, instead of storage facilities, its three primary assets were equity interests owned in target firms? What requirements would have to be satisfied in order to avoid making a basis adjustment?

Research Problem 3. ABC Partnership is engaged exclusively in providing consulting services, and capital is not a material income-producing factor. The ABC General Partnership agreement, which was drafted in 2008, did not explain how a retiring partner would be paid for his or her share of partnership goodwill. In 2010, the partnership executed an "Amendment of General Partnership Agreement," which provided that Partner Adam was to receive $100,000 cash from the partnership on July 1, 2011. The payment was to be made to retire Adam's interest in the partnership. Of that amount, $30,000 was in return for Adam's one-third interest in the fair market value of the net assets of the partnership. The other $70,000 was referred to as "a guaranteed payment, or a payment for goodwill."

Saying that the "Amendment of General Partnership Agreement" is not clear, the IRS wants to treat the payment for goodwill as ordinary income to Adam and deductible by the partnership (this approach maximizes the tax revenue for the government). Presuming the taxpayers would prefer a return of basis and capital gain, what authority is available to support this position?

Use the tax resources of the Internet to address the following questions. Do not restrict your search to the Web, but include a review of newsgroups and general reference materials, practitioner sites and resources, primary sources of the tax law, chat rooms and discussion groups, and other opportunities.

COMMUNICATIONS

Research Problem 4. Print an article written by a tax adviser discussing the merits of the family limited partnership. Write a memo discussing one of the following issues.

a. The effects of Revenue Ruling 93–12 on the use of the entity.
b. The effects of § 704(e) on income computations for the entity.
c. The accuracy of the computations made by the author in the article.

Your memo should include a summary of the findings presented in the article and a summary and discussion of your thoughts. For example, you may wish to address situations in which family limited partnerships may be beneficial or pitfalls in structuring such an entity.

Research Problem 5. On what form or attachment does a partnership report that it has made a § 754 election? Prepare such a form using the facts of Example 39 in the text.

Research Problem 6. Download a copy of the legislation with which your state began to allow the formation of limited liability companies. What types of business activities can an LLC conduct in your state?

S Corporations

CHAPTER 12

LEARNING OBJECTIVES

After completing Chapter 12, you should be able to:

LO.1 Explain the tax effects that S corporation status has on shareholders.

LO.2 Identify corporations that qualify for the S election.

LO.3 Explain how to make an S election.

LO.4 Explain how an S election can be terminated.

LO.5 Compute nonseparately stated income and identify separately stated items.

LO.6 Allocate income, deductions, and credits to shareholders.

LO.7 Determine how distributions to S corporation shareholders are taxed.

LO.8 Calculate a shareholder's basis in S corporation stock.

LO.9 Explain the tax effects that losses have on shareholders.

LO.10 Compute the built-in gains and passive investment income penalty taxes.

LO.11 Engage in tax planning for S corporations.

OUTLINE

For the latest in changes to tax legislation, visit **www.cengage.com/taxation/swft.**

THE BIG PICTURE **Tax Solutions for the Real World**

DEDUCTIBILITY OF LOSSES AND THE CHOICE OF BUSINESS ENTITY

Cane, Inc., has been a C corporation for a number of years, earning taxable income of less than $100,000 per year. Thus, the business has been subject to the lower C corporation tax rates, but due to cheap imports from China, Cane's two owners, Smith and Jones, expect operating losses for the next two or three years. They hope to outsource some of the manufacturing to Vietnam and turn the company around. How can they deduct these anticipated future losses?

The corporation receives some tax-exempt income, generates a small domestic production activities deduction (DPAD), and holds some C corporation earnings and profits. Each owner draws a salary of $92,000. Cane has two classes of stock, voting and non-voting common stock. Should Smith and Jones elect to be taxed as an S corporation? Do they need to liquidate or go through some type of reorganization to do so? **Read the chapter and formulate your response.**

12.1 Choice of Business Entity

LO.1

Explain the tax effects that S corporation status has on shareholders.

An individual establishing a business has a number of choices as to the form of business entity under which to operate. Chapters 2 through 7 outline many of the rules, advantages, and disadvantages of operating as a regular corporation. Chapters 10 and 11 discuss the partnership entity, and Chapter 11 covers the limited liability company (LLC) and limited liability partnership (LLP) forms.

Another alternative, the **S corporation**, provides many of the benefits of partnership taxation and at the same time gives the owners limited liability protection from creditors. The S corporation rules, which are contained in **Subchapter S** of the Internal Revenue Code (§§ 1361–1379), were enacted to allow flexibility in the entity choice that businesspeople face. Thus, S status combines the legal environment of C corporations with taxation similar to that applying to partnerships. S corporation status is obtained through an election by a *qualifying* corporation with the consent of its shareholders.

S corporations are treated as corporations under state law. They are recognized as separate legal entities and generally provide shareholders with the same liability protection afforded by C corporations. For Federal income tax purposes, however, taxation of S corporations resembles that of partnerships. As with partnerships, the income, deductions, and tax credits of an S corporation flow through to shareholders annually, regardless of whether distributions are made. Thus, income is taxed at the shareholder level and not at the corporate level. Payments to S shareholders by the corporation are distributed tax-free to the extent that the distributed earnings were previously taxed. Further, C corporation penalty taxes like the accumulated earnings tax, personal holding company tax, and alternative minimum tax do not apply to an S corporation.

Although the Federal tax treatment of S corporations and partnerships is similar, it is not identical. For instance, liabilities affect an owner's basis differently, and S corporations may incur a tax liability at the corporate level. Furthermore, an S corporation may not allocate income like a partnership, and distributions of appreciated property are taxable in an S corporation situation (see Concept Summary 12.2 later in this chapter). In addition, a variety of C corporation provisions apply to S corporations. For example, the liquidation of C and S corporations is taxed in the same way. As a rule, where the S corporation provisions are silent, C corporation rules apply.

TAX in the NEWS

S Corporations by the Numbers

In 2007, a total of 3.99 million S corporation returns were filed—a modest 3 percent increase from 2006. The wholesale/retail (645,114) and construction (569,361) industries accounted for the largest number of returns. There were more than 6.83 million S corporation shareholders. Total receipts were more than $6 trillion, with $400 billion of net income and $82.8 billion of deficits. In 2009, 0.4 percent of all S corporation returns were audited by the IRS.

Today, the choice of a flow-through entity for a closely held business often is between an S corporation (a Federal tax entity) and an LLC (a state tax entity). Although an S corporation resembles an LLC, there are differences. A two-or-more-member LLC operates under partnership tax principles, whereas, as just explained, partnership taxation rules do not always apply to an S corporation.

AN OVERVIEW OF S CORPORATIONS

As the following examples illustrate, S corporations can be advantageous even when the individual tax rate exceeds the corporate tax rate.

EXAMPLE 1

An S corporation earns $300,000 in 2011. The marginal individual tax rate applicable to shareholders is 35% on ordinary income and 15% on dividends. The applicable marginal corporate tax rate is 34%. All after-tax income is distributed currently.

	C Corporation	S Corporation
Earnings	$ 300,000	$ 300,000
Less: Corporate tax	(102,000)	–0–
Available for distribution	$ 198,000	$ 300,000
Less: Tax at owner level	(29,700)	(105,000)
Available after-tax earnings	$ 168,300	$ 195,000

The S corporation generates an extra $26,700 of after-tax earnings ($195,000 – $168,300), when compared with a similar C corporation. The C corporation might be able to reduce this disadvantage, however, by paying out its earnings as compensation, rents, or interest expense. Tax at the owner level can also be deferred or avoided by not distributing after-tax earnings. ■

EXAMPLE 2

A new corporation elects S status and incurs a net operating loss (NOL) of $300,000. The shareholders may use their proportionate shares of the NOL to offset other taxable income in the current year, providing an immediate tax savings. In contrast, a newly formed C corporation is required to carry the NOL forward for up to 20 years and does not receive any tax benefit in the current year. Hence, an S corporation can accelerate NOL deductions and thereby provide a greater present value for tax savings generated by the loss. ■

WHEN TO ELECT S CORPORATION STATUS

The planner begins by determining the appropriateness of an S election. The following factors should be considered.

- If shareholders have *high marginal rates* relative to C corporation rates, it may be desirable to avoid S corporation status. Although C corporation earnings can be subject to double taxation, good tax planning mitigates this result, e.g., when the owners take profits out as salary. Likewise, profits of the corporation may be taken out by the shareholders as capital gain income through stock redemptions, liquidations, or sales of stock to others. Alternatively, C corporation profits may be paid out as dividends, subject to a 15 percent maximum tax rate. Any distribution of profits or sale of stock can be deferred to a later year, thereby reducing the present value of shareholder taxes. Finally, potential shareholder-level tax on corporate profits can be eliminated by a step-up in the basis of the stock upon the shareholder's death.

- S corporation status allows shareholders to *realize tax benefits from corporate losses immediately*—an important consideration in new business enterprises where losses are common. Thus, if corporate NOLs are anticipated and there is unlikely to be corporate income over the near term to offset with the NOLs, S corporation status is advisable. However, the deductibility of the losses to shareholders must also be considered. The *at-risk* and *passive loss limitations apply to losses* generated by an S corporation. In addition, as discussed later in this chapter, shareholders may not deduct losses in excess of the basis in their stock. Together these limits may significantly reduce the benefits of an S election in a loss setting.
- If the entity electing S status is currently a C corporation, *NOL carryovers* from prior years *cannot be used* in an S corporation year. Even worse, S corporation years reduce the 20-year carryover period. And the corporation may be subject to some corporate-level taxes if it elects S status (see the discussion of the built-in gains tax later in this chapter).
- Because S corporations are flow-through entities, separately stated deduction and income items *retain any special tax characteristics* when they are reported on shareholders' returns. Whether this consideration favors S status depends upon the character of income and deductions of the S corporation. For instance, it may be an advantage to receive the flow-through of passive income, or the qualified domestic production activities deduction, on the shareholder's tax return, making the S election more attractive. *Charitable contributions are not subject to the 10 percent limitation* at the corporate level, but an S corporation cannot take advantage of special provisions for contributions of inventory and scientific equipment.
- *State and local tax laws also should be considered* when making the S election. Although an S corporation usually escapes Federal income tax, it may not be immune from state and local taxes. State taxation of S corporations varies. Some states, including Michigan, treat them the same as C corporations, resulting in a corporate tax liability from an income or franchise tax.
- The choice of S corporation status is *affected by a variety of other factors*. For example, the corporate alternative minimum tax (see Chapter 3) may be avoided in an S corporation. An in-depth discussion of entity choice is provided in Chapter 13.

12.2 Qualifying for S Corporation Status

LO.2

Identify corporations that qualify for the S election.

DEFINITION OF A SMALL BUSINESS CORPORATION

To achieve S corporation status, a corporation *first* must qualify as a **small business corporation**. If each of the following requirements is met, then the entity can elect S corporation status.

- Is a domestic corporation (incorporated and organized in the United States).
- Is an eligible corporation (see below for ineligible types).
- Issues only one class of stock.

TAX *in the NEWS*

GAO Attacks S Corporations

According to the U.S. Government Accountability Office (GAO), S corporations are not only one of the fastest growing business types, but they are also likely to make errors on their tax returns. In a report to the Senate Finance Committee, the GAO said that 68 percent of S corporation returns filed for tax years 2003 and 2004 misreported at least one item. About 80 percent of the time, such misreporting favored the taxpayer.

A majority of S corporations used paid preparers. Nevertheless, 71 percent of those returns were noncompliant. Mistakes in calculating shareholder basis were one of the major problems. Some S corporations also failed to pay adequate wages to shareholders, underreporting roughly $23.6 billion. This underreporting resulted in billions of dollars in lost employment taxes to the government.

Source: Government Accountability Office, *Tax Gap: Actions Needed to Address Noncompliance with S Corporation Tax Rules,* December 15, 2009.

- Is limited to a theoretical maximum of 100 shareholders.
- Has only individuals, estates, and certain trusts and exempt organizations as shareholders.
- Has no nonresident alien shareholders.

Unlike other provisions in the tax law (e.g., § 1244), no maximum or minimum dollar sales or capitalization restrictions apply to small business corporations.

Ineligible Corporations

Small business corporation status is not permitted for non-U.S. corporations, nor for certain banks and insurance companies.

Any domestic corporation that is not an ineligible corporation can be a qualified Subchapter S corporation subsidiary (QSSS), if the S corporation holds 100 percent of its stock and elects to treat the subsidiary as a QSSS.[1] The QSSS is viewed as a division of the parent, so the parent S corporation can own a QSSS through another QSSS. QSSSs have a separate existence for legal purposes, but they exist only within the parent S corporation for tax purposes.

One Class of Stock

A small business corporation may have only one class of stock issued and outstanding.[2] This restriction permits differences in voting rights, but not differences in distribution or liquidation rights.[3] Thus, two classes of common stock that are identical except that one class is voting and the other is nonvoting would be treated as a single class of stock for small business corporation purposes. In contrast, voting common stock and voting preferred stock (with a preference on dividends) would be treated as two classes of stock. Authorized and unissued stock or treasury stock of another class does not disqualify the corporation. Likewise, unexercised stock options, phantom stock, stock appreciation rights, warrants, and convertible debentures usually do not constitute a second class of stock.

The determination of whether stock provides identical rights as to distribution and liquidation proceeds is made based on the provisions governing the operation of the corporation. These *governing provisions* include the corporate charter, articles of incorporation, bylaws, applicable state law, and binding agreements relating to distribution and liquidation proceeds. Employment contracts, loan agreements, and other commercial contracts are *not* considered governing provisions.[4]

[1] § 1361(b)(3)(B).
[2] § 1361(b)(1)(D).
[3] § 1361(c)(4).
[4] Reg. § 1.1361–1(l)(2).

EXAMPLE 3
THE BIG PICTURE

Return to the facts of *The Big Picture* on p. 12–2. Cane, Inc., could elect to be an S corporation as long as the two classes of common stock are identical except that one class is voting and the other class is nonvoting.

You learn that both shareholders have binding employment contracts with Cane, Inc. The amount of compensation paid by the corporation to Jones under her employment contract is reasonable, but the amount paid to Smith under his employment contract is excessive, resulting in a constructive dividend. Smith's employment contract was not prepared to circumvent the one-class-of-stock requirement.

Because employment contracts are not considered governing provisions, Cane still is treated as though it has only one class of stock if an S election is made. ■

Although the one-class-of-stock requirement seems straightforward, it is possible for debt to be reclassified as stock, resulting in an unexpected loss of S corporation status.[5] To mitigate concern over possible reclassification of debt as a second class of stock, the law provides a set of *safe-harbor provisions.*

First, straight debt *issued in an S corporation year* will not be treated as a second class of stock and will not disqualify the S election.[6] The characteristics of straight debt include the following.

- The debtor is subject to a written, unconditional promise to pay on demand or on a specified date a sum certain in money.
- The interest rate and payment date are not contingent on corporate profits, management discretion, or similar factors.
- The debt is not convertible into stock.
- The debt is held by a creditor who is an individual (other than a nonresident alien), an estate, or a qualified trust.
- Straight debt can be held by creditors actively and regularly engaged in the business of lending money.

In addition to straight debt under the safe-harbor rules, short-term unwritten advances from a shareholder that do not exceed $10,000 in the aggregate at any time during the corporation's taxable year generally are not treated as a second class of stock. Likewise, debt that is held by stockholders in the same proportion as their stock is not treated as a second class of stock, even if it would be reclassified as equity otherwise.[7]

Number of Shareholders

A small business corporation theoretically is limited to 100 shareholders. If shares of stock are owned jointly by two individuals, they will generally be treated as separate shareholders.

Family members may be treated as one shareholder for purposes of determining the number of shareholders. The term "members of the family" is defined as the common ancestor, the lineal descendants of the common ancestor, and the spouses (or former spouses) of the lineal descendants or common ancestor.[8] An estate of a family member also may be treated as a family member for purposes of determining the number of shareholders.

EXAMPLE 4

Fred and Wilma (husband and wife) jointly own 10 shares in Marlins, Inc., an S corporation, with the remaining 290 shares outstanding owned by 99 other unrelated shareholders. Fred and Wilma get divorced; pursuant to the property settlement approved

[5]Refer to the discussion of debt-versus-equity classification in Chapter 4.

[6]§ 1361(c)(5)(A).

[7]Reg. § 1.1361–1(l)(4).

[8]§§ 1361(c)(1)(A)(ii) and (B)(i). The need for an affirmative election to treat family members as a single shareholder was eliminated in 2005. Notice 2005–91, 2005 51 I.R.B. 1164 provides insight into the determination of who is a family member.

by the court, the 10 shares held by Fred and Wilma are divided between them—5 to each. Before the divorce settlement, Marlins had 100 shareholders under the small business corporation rules. After the settlement, it still has 100 shareholders and continues to qualify as a small business corporation. A former spouse is treated as being in the same family as the individual to whom he or she was married. ■

Type of Shareholder Limitation

Small business corporation shareholders may be resident individuals, estates, certain trusts, and certain tax-exempt organizations.[9] Charitable organizations, employee benefit trusts exempt from taxation, and a one-person LLC classified as a disregarded entity also all can qualify as shareholders of an S corporation. This limitation prevents partnerships, corporations, limited liability partnerships, most LLCs, and most IRAs and Roth IRAs from owning S corporation stock. Partnerships and corporate shareholders could easily circumvent the 100-shareholder limitation as illustrated in the following example.

EXAMPLE 5

Saul and 105 of his close friends wish to form an S corporation. Saul reasons that if he and his friends form a partnership, the partnership can then form an S corporation and act as a single shareholder, thereby avoiding the 100-shareholder rule. Saul's plan will not work because partnerships cannot own stock in a small business corporation. ■

Although partnerships and corporations cannot own small business corporation stock, small business corporations can be partners in a partnership or shareholders in a corporation. This ability allows the 100-shareholder requirement to be bypassed in a limited sense. For example, if two small business corporations, each with 100 shareholders, form a partnership, then the shareholders of both corporations can enjoy the limited liability conferred by S corporation status and a single level of tax on partnership profits.

Nonresident Aliens

Nonresident aliens cannot own stock in a small business corporation.[10] That is, individuals who are not U.S. citizens *must live in the United States* to own S corporation stock. Therefore, shareholders with nonresident alien spouses in community property states[11] cannot own S corporation stock because the nonresident alien spouse would be treated as owning half of the community property.[12] Similarly, if a resident alien shareholder moves outside the United States, the S election will be terminated.

MAKING THE ELECTION

LO.3

Explain how to make an S election.

To become an S corporation, a *small business corporation* (defined above) must file a valid election with the IRS. The election is made on Form 2553. For the election to be valid, it should be filed on a timely basis, and all shareholders must consent.

For S corporation status to apply in the current tax year, the election must be filed either in the previous year or on or before the fifteenth day of the third month of the current year.

[9] § 1361(b)(1)(B). Foreign trusts, charitable remainder trusts, and charitable lead trusts cannot be shareholders.

[10] § 1362(b)(1)(C).

[11] Assets acquired by a married couple are generally considered community property in these states: Arizona, California, Idaho, Louisiana, Nevada, New Mexico, Texas, Washington, Wisconsin, and (if elected by the spouses) Alaska.

[12] See *Ward v. U.S.*, 81–2 USTC ¶9674, 48 AFTR 2d 81–5942, 661 F.2d 226 (Ct.Cls., 1981), where the court found that the stock was owned as community property. Since the taxpayer-shareholder (a U.S. citizen) was married to a citizen and resident of Mexico, the nonresident alien prohibition was violated. If the taxpayer-shareholder had held the stock as separate property, the S election would have been valid.

EXAMPLE 6
THE BIG PICTURE

Return to the facts of *The Big Picture* on p. 12–2. Suppose that in 2011 shareholders Smith and Jones decide to become an S corporation beginning January 1, 2012. Since the C corporation uses a calendar tax year, the S election can be made at any time in 2011 or by March 15, 2012. An election after March 15, 2012, will not be effective until the 2013 calendar tax year. ■

There is a simplified method of requesting relief for late S elections that were intended to be effective as of the date of the election. The entity must file a properly completed Form 2553 with a Form 1120S no later than six months after the due date of the tax return (excluding extensions) of the entity for the first tax year in which the S election was intended. The Form 2553 must explain the reason for the failure to timely file the election. Sufficient reasonable cause might occur, for example, where both the corporation's accountant and its attorney failed to file the election because each believed the other had done so, or because there was miscommunication as to who was responsible for filing.

Even if the 2½-month deadline is met, an S election is not valid unless the corporation qualifies as a small business corporation for the *entire* tax year. Otherwise, the election will be effective for the following tax year.

A corporation that does not yet exist cannot make an S corporation election.[13] Thus, for new corporations, a premature election may not be effective. A new corporation's 2½-month election period begins at the earliest occurrence of any of the following events.

- When the corporation has shareholders.
- When it acquires assets.
- When it begins doing business.[14]

EXAMPLE 7

Several individuals acquire assets on behalf of Rock Corporation on June 29, 2011, and begin doing business on July 3, 2011. They subscribe to shares of stock, file articles of incorporation for Rock, and become shareholders on July 7, 2011. The S election must be filed no later than 2½ months after June 29, 2011 (i.e., on or before September 12) to be effective for 2011. ■

The IRS can correct errors in electing S status, where a taxpayer can show that the mistake was inadvertent, the entity otherwise was qualified to be an S corporation, and it acted as if it were an S corporation. Under certain conditions, automatic relief is granted without the need for a letter ruling request and the normal user fee.

An LLC that makes a timely and valid election to be classified as an S corporation need not "check the box" on a Form 8832. The LLC must meet all of the other S corporation requirements.

SHAREHOLDER CONSENT

A qualifying election requires the consent of all of the corporation's shareholders.[15] Consent must be in writing, and it must generally be filed by the election deadline. A consent extension is available only if Form 2553 is filed on a timely basis, reasonable cause is given, and the interests of the government are not jeopardized.[16]

[13] See, for example, *T.H. Campbell & Bros., Inc.*, 34 TCM 695, T.C.Memo. 1975–149; Ltr.Rul. 8807070.

[14] Reg. § 1.1372–2(b)(1). Also see, for example, *Nick A. Artukovich*, 61 T.C. 100 (1973).

[15] § 1362(a)(2).

[16] Rev.Rul. 60–183, 1960–1 C.B. 625; *William Pestcoe*, 40 T.C. 195 (1963); Reg. § 1.1362–6(b)(3)(iii).

EXAMPLE 8

Vern and Yvonne decide to convert their C corporation into a calendar year S corporation for 2011. At the end of February 2011 (before the election is filed), Yvonne travels to Ukraine and forgets to sign a consent to the election. Yvonne will not return to the United States until June and cannot be reached by fax or e-mail.

Vern files the S election on Form 2553 and also requests an extension of time to file Yvonne's consent to the election. Vern indicates that there is a reasonable cause for the extension: a shareholder is out of the country. Since the government's interest is not jeopardized, the IRS probably will grant Yvonne an extension of time to file the consent. Vern must file the election on Form 2553 on or before March 15, 2011, for the election to be effective for the 2011 calendar year. ■

Both husband and wife must consent if they own their stock jointly (as joint tenants, tenants in common, tenants by the entirety, or community property). This requirement has led to considerable taxpayer grief—particularly in community property states where the spouses may not realize that their stock is jointly owned as a community asset.

EXAMPLE 9

Three shareholders, Amy, Monty, and Dianne, incorporate in January and file Form 2553. Amy is married and lives in California. Monty is single and Dianne is married; both live in South Carolina. Because Amy is married and lives in a community property state, her husband also must consent to the S election. South Carolina is not a community property state, so Dianne's husband need not consent. ■

Finally, for current-year S elections, persons who were shareholders during any part of the taxable year before the election date, but were not shareholders when the election was made, must also consent to the election.[17]

EXAMPLE 10

On January 15, 2011, the stock of Columbus Corporation (a calendar year C corporation) was held equally by three individual shareholders: Jim, Sally, and LuEllen. On that date, LuEllen sells her interest to Jim and Sally. On March 14, 2011, Columbus Corporation files Form 2553. Jim and Sally indicate their consent by signing the form. Columbus cannot become an S corporation until 2012 because LuEllen did not indicate consent. Had all three shareholders consented by signing Form 2553, S status would have taken effect as of January 1, 2011. ■

LOSS OF THE ELECTION

LO.4

Explain how an S election can be terminated.

An S election remains in force until it is revoked or lost. Election or consent forms are not required for future years. However, an S election can terminate if any of the following occurs.

- Shareholders owning a majority of shares (voting and nonvoting) voluntarily revoke the election.
- A new shareholder owning more than one-half of the stock affirmatively refuses to consent to the election.
- The corporation no longer qualifies as a small business corporation.
- The corporation does not meet the passive investment income limitation.

Voluntary Revocation

A **voluntary revocation** of the S election requires the consent of shareholders owning a majority of shares on the day that the revocation is to be made.[18] A revocation filed

[17] § 1362(b)(2)(B)(ii).

[18] § 1362(d)(1).

up to and including the fifteenth day of the third month of the tax year is effective for the entire tax year, unless a later date is specified. Similarly, unless an effective date is specified, revocation made after the first 2½ months of the current tax year is effective for the following tax year.

EXAMPLE 11

The shareholders of Petunia Corporation, a calendar year S corporation, voluntarily revoke the S election on January 5, 2011. They do not specify a future effective date in the revocation. Assuming the revocation is properly executed and timely filed, Petunia will be a C corporation for the entire 2011 calendar year. If the election is not made until June 2011, Petunia will remain an S corporation in 2011 and will become a C corporation at the beginning of 2012. ■

A corporation can revoke its S status *prospectively* by specifying a future date when the revocation is to be effective. A revocation that designates a future effective date splits the corporation's tax year into a short S corporation year and a short C corporation year. The day on which the revocation occurs is treated as the first day of the C corporation year. The corporation allocates income or loss for the entire year on a pro rata basis, based on the number of days in each short year.

EXAMPLE 12

Assume the same facts as in the preceding example, except that Petunia designates July 1, 2011, as the revocation date. Accordingly, June 30, 2011, is the last day of the S corporation's tax year. The C corporation's tax year runs from July 1, 2011, to December 31, 2011. Income or loss for the 12-month period is allocated between the two short years, i.e., 184/365 to the C corporation year. ■

Rather than allocating on a pro rata basis, the corporation can elect to compute actual income or loss attributable to the two short years. This election requires the consent of everyone who was a shareholder at any time during the S corporation's short year and everyone who owns stock on the first day of the C corporation's year.[19]

EXAMPLE 13

Assume the same facts as in the preceding example, except that all of Petunia's shareholders consent to allocate the income or loss to the two short tax years based on its actual realization. Assume further that Petunia experiences a total loss of $102,000, of which $72,000 is incurred in the first half of the year. Since $72,000 of the loss occurs before July 1, this amount is allocated to the S corporation short year, and only $30,000 is allocated to the C corporation year. ■

Loss of Small Business Corporation Status

If an S corporation fails to qualify as a small business corporation at any time after the election has become effective, its status as an S corporation ends. The termination occurs on the day that the corporation ceases to be a small business corporation.[20] Thus, if the corporation ever has more than 100 shareholders, a second class of stock, or a nonqualifying shareholder, or otherwise fails to meet the definition of a small business corporation, the S election is immediately terminated.

EXAMPLE 14

Peony Corporation has been a calendar year S corporation for three years. On August 13, 2011, one of its 100 shareholders sells *some* of her stock to an outsider. Peony now

[19] § 1362(e)(3).

[20] § 1362(d)(2)(B).

has 101 shareholders, and it ceases to be a small business corporation. For 2011, Peony is an S corporation through August 12, 2011, and a C corporation from August 13 to December 31, 2011. ■

Passive Investment Income Limitation

The Code provides a **passive investment income (PII)** limitation for S corporations that were previously C corporations or for S corporations that have merged with C corporations. If an S corporation has C corporation E & P and passive income in excess of 25 percent of its gross receipts for three consecutive taxable years, the S election is terminated as of the beginning of the fourth year.[21]

EXAMPLE 15

For 2008, 2009, and 2010, Diapason Corporation, a calendar year S corporation, received passive income in excess of 25% of its gross receipts. If Diapason holds accumulated E & P from years in which it was a C corporation, its S election is terminated as of January 1, 2011. ■

PII includes dividends, interest, rents, gains and losses from sales of capital assets, and royalties net of investment deductions. Rents are not considered PII if the corporation renders significant personal services to the occupant.

EXAMPLE 16

Violet Corporation owns and operates an apartment building. The corporation provides utilities for the building, maintains the lobby, and furnishes trash collection for tenants. These activities are not considered significant personal services, so any rent income earned by the corporation will be considered PII.

Alternatively, if Violet also furnishes maid services to its tenants (personal services beyond what normally would be expected from a landlord in an apartment building), the rent income would no longer be PII. ■

Reelection after Termination

After an S election has been terminated, the corporation must wait five years before reelecting S corporation status. The five-year waiting period is waived if:

- there is a more-than-50-percent change in ownership of the corporation after the first year for which the termination is applicable, or
- the event causing the termination was not reasonably within the control of the S corporation or its majority shareholders.

12.3 Operational Rules

S corporations are treated much like partnerships for tax purposes. With a few exceptions,[22] S corporations generally make tax accounting and other elections at the corporate level. Each year, the S corporation determines nonseparately stated income or loss and separately stated income, deductions, and credits. These items are taxed only once, at the shareholder level. All items are allocated to each shareholder based on average ownership of stock throughout the year. The *flow-through* of each item of income, deduction, and credit from the corporation to the shareholder is illustrated in Figure 12.1.

[21] § 1362(d)(3)(A)(ii).

[22] A few elections can be made at the shareholder level (e.g., the choice between a foreign tax deduction or credit).

FIGURE 12.1 Flow-Through of Separate Items of Income and Loss to S Corporation Shareholders

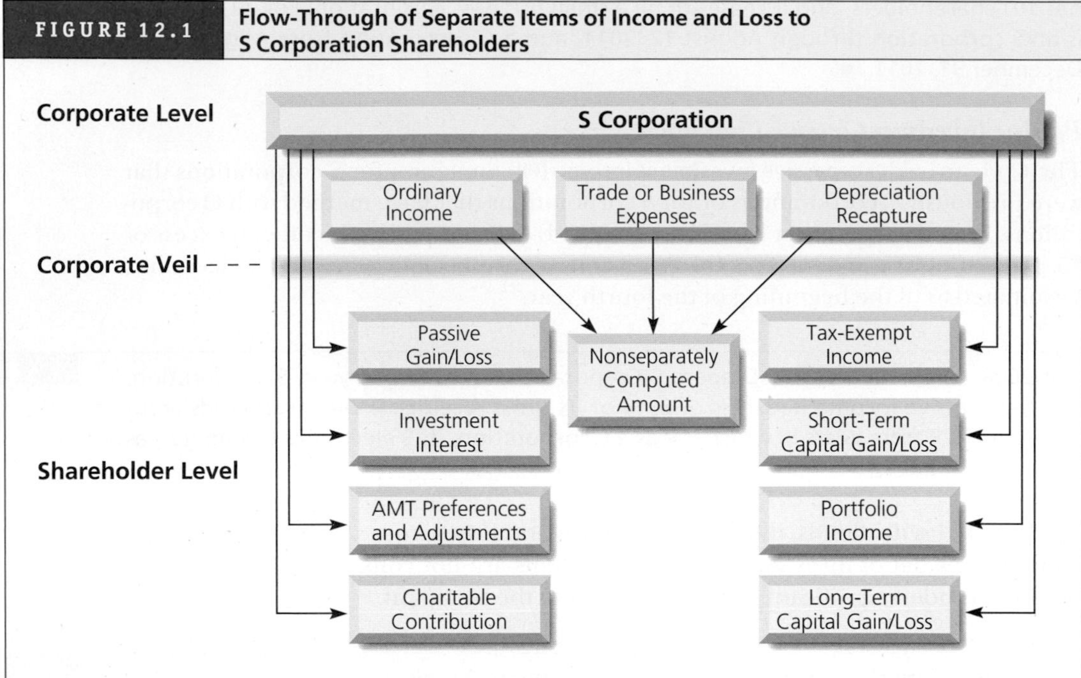

LO.5

Compute nonseparately stated income and identify separately stated items.

COMPUTATION OF TAXABLE INCOME

Subchapter S taxable income or loss is determined in a manner similar to the tax rules that apply to partnerships, except that S corporations amortize organizational expenditures under the C corporation rules[23] and must recognize gains, *but not losses*, on distributions of appreciated property to shareholders.[24] Other special provisions affecting only the computation of C corporation income, such as the dividends received deduction, do not extend to S corporations.[25] Finally, as with partnerships, certain deductions of individuals are not permitted, including alimony payments, personal moving expenses, certain dependent care expenses, the personal exemption, and the standard deduction.

In general, S corporation items are divided into (1) nonseparately stated income or loss and (2) separately stated income, losses, deductions, and credits that could affect the tax liability of any shareholder in a different manner, depending on other factors in the shareholder's tax situation. In essence, nonseparate items are aggregated into an undifferentiated amount that constitutes Subchapter S ordinary income or loss. An S corporation's separately stated items are identical to those separately stated by partnerships. These items retain their tax attributes on the shareholder's return. Separately stated items are listed on Schedule K of the 1120S. They include the following.

- Tax-exempt income.
- Long-term and short-term capital gains and losses.
- Section 1231 gains and losses.
- Charitable contributions (no grace period).
- Passive gains, losses, and credits.
- Certain portfolio income.
- Section 179 expense deduction.
- Domestic production gross receipts and deductions.
- Tax preferences and adjustments for the alternative minimum tax.
- Depletion.
- Foreign income or loss.

[23]§§ 248 and 1363(b).
[24]§ 1363(b).
[25]§ 703(a)(2).

- Recoveries of tax benefit items.
- Intangible drilling costs.
- Investment interest, income, and expenses.

EXAMPLE 17

The following is the income statement for Jersey, Inc., an S corporation.

Sales		$ 40,000
Less cost of sales		(23,000)
Gross profit on sales		$ 17,000
Less: Interest expense	$ 1,200	
Charitable contributions	400	
Advertising expenses	1,500	
Other operating expenses	2,000	(5,100)
Book income from operations		$ 11,900
Add: Tax-exempt interest	$ 300	
Dividend income	200	
Long-term capital gain	500	1,000
Less: Short-term capital loss		(150)
Net income per books		$ 12,750

Subchapter S ordinary income for Jersey is calculated as follows, using net income for book purposes as the starting point.

Net income per books		$ 12,750
Separately stated items		
Deduct: Tax-exempt interest	$ 300	
Dividend income	200	
Long-term capital gain	500	(1,000)
Add: Charitable contributions	$ 400	
Short-term capital loss	150	550
Subchapter S ordinary income		$ 12,300

The $12,300 of Subchapter S ordinary income, as well as each of the five separately stated items, are divided among the shareholders based upon their stock ownership. ■

ALLOCATION OF INCOME AND LOSS

LO.6

Allocate income, deductions, and credits to shareholders.

Each shareholder is allocated a pro rata portion of nonseparately stated income or loss and all separately stated items. The pro rata allocation method assigns an equal amount of each of the S items to each day of the year. If a shareholder's stock holding changes during the year, this allocation assigns the shareholder a pro rata share of each item for *each* day the stock is owned. On the date of transfer, the transferor (and not the transferee) is considered to own the stock.[26]

The per-day allocation must be used, unless the shareholder disposes of his or her entire interest in the entity.[27] In case of a complete termination, a short year may result. If a shareholder dies during the year, his or her share of the pro rata items up to and including the date of death is reported on the final individual income tax return.

[26]Reg. § 1.1377–1(a)(2)(ii).

[27]§§ 1366(a)(1) and 1377(a)(1).

EXAMPLE 18

Assume in the previous example that Pat, a shareholder, owned 10% of Jersey's stock for 100 days and 12% for the remaining 265 days. Using the required per-day allocation method, Pat's share of the S corporation items is as follows.

	Schedule K Totals	Pat's Share		Pat's Schedule K–1 Totals
		10%	12%	
Ordinary income	$12,300	$337	$1,072	$1,409
Tax-exempt interest	300	8	26	34
Dividend income	200	5	17	22
Long-term capital gain	500	14	44	58
Charitable contributions	400	11	35	46
Short-term capital loss	150	4	13	17

Pat's share of the Subchapter S ordinary income is the total of $12,300 × [0.10 × (100/365)] plus $12,300 × [0.12 × (265/365)], or $1,409. Each of the Schedule K–1 totals from the right-hand column flows through to the appropriate lines on Pat's individual income tax return (Form 1040). ■

EXAMPLE 19

If Pat in the previous example dies after owning the stock 100 days, his share of the S corporation items is reported on his final individual income tax return (Form 1040). Thus, only the items in the column labeled 10% in Example 18 are reported on Pat's final tax return. S corporation items that occur after Pat's death most likely would flow through to the income tax return of Pat's estate (Form 1041). ■

The Short-Year Election

If a shareholder's interest is completely terminated by disposition or death during the tax year, all shareholders holding stock during the year and the corporation may elect to treat the S taxable year as two taxable years. The first year ends on the date of the termination. Under this election, an interim closing of the books is undertaken, and the shareholders report their shares of the S corporation items as they occurred during the short tax year.[28]

The short-year election provides an opportunity to shift income, losses, and credits between shareholders. The election is desirable in circumstances where more loss can be allocated to taxpayers with higher marginal rates.

EXAMPLE 20

Alicia, the owner of all of the shares of an S corporation, transfers her stock to Cindy halfway through the tax year. There is a $100,000 NOL for the entire tax year, but $30,000 of the loss occurs during the first half of the year. Without a short-year election, $50,000 of the loss is allocated to Alicia, and $50,000 is allocated to Cindy. If the corporation makes the short-year election, Cindy is allocated $70,000 of the loss. Of course, the sales price of the stock would probably be increased to recognize the tax benefits being transferred from Alicia to Cindy. ■

In the case of the death of a shareholder, a short-year election prevents the income and loss allocation to a deceased shareholder from being affected by postdeath events.

EXAMPLE 21

Joey and Karl equally own Rose, Inc., a calendar year S corporation. Joey dies on June 29 of a year that is not a leap year. Rose has income of $250,000 for January 1 through June 29 and $750,000 for the remainder of the year. Without a short-year election, the income is allocated by assigning an equal portion of the annual income of $1 million to each day (or $2,739.73 per day) and allocating the daily portion between the shareholders.

[28] § 1377(a)(2).

Joey is allocated 50% of the daily income for the 180 days from January 1 to June 29, or $246,575.70 [($2,739.73/2) × 180]. Joey's *estate* is allocated 50% of the income for the 185 days from June 30 to December 31, or $253,425.02 [($2,739.73/2) × 185].

If the short-year election is made, the income of $250,000 from January 1 to June 29 is divided equally between Joey and Karl, so that each is taxed on $125,000. The income of $750,000 from June 30 to December 31 is divided equally between Joey's estate and Karl, or $375,000 to each.

Under either alternative, Karl reports income of $500,000. However, with the short-year election, $375,000 is allocated to Joey's estate versus only $253,425.02 without the election. Since the estate income tax rates are more progressive than the income tax rates on individuals, Joey's heirs would prefer that the election not be made. ■

TAX TREATMENT OF DISTRIBUTIONS TO SHAREHOLDERS

The amount of any distribution to an S corporation shareholder is equal to the cash plus the fair market value of any other property distributed. How the distribution is taxed depends upon whether the S corporation has C corporation **accumulated earnings and profits** (AEP, described in Chapter 5).

No C Corporation AEP

If the S corporation has never been a C corporation or if it has no C corporation AEP, the distribution is a tax-free recovery of capital to the extent that it does not exceed the shareholder's adjusted basis in the stock of the S corporation. When the amount of the distribution exceeds the adjusted basis of the stock, the excess is treated as a gain from the sale or exchange of property (capital gain in most cases). The vast majority of S corporations fall into this favorable category.

EXAMPLE 22

Twirl, Inc., a calendar year S corporation, has no AEP. During the year, Juan, an individual shareholder of the corporation, receives a cash distribution of $12,200 from Twirl. Juan's basis in his stock is $9,700. Juan recognizes a capital gain of $2,500, the excess of the distribution over the stock basis ($12,200 − $9,700). The remaining $9,700 is tax-free, but it reduces Juan's basis in his stock to zero. ■

C Corporation AEP

S corporations with C corporation AEP blend the entity and conduit approaches to taxation. This blending treats distributions of pre-election (C corporation) and post-election (S corporation) earnings differently. Distributions of C corporation AEP are taxed as dividends (0/15% rate), while distributions of previously taxed S corporation earnings are tax-free to the extent of the shareholder's adjusted basis in the stock.

Concept Summary 12.1 outlines the taxation of distributions. These rules are intended to prevent two problems that result when a C corporation has been converted to an S corporation.

- Tax manipulation could result in AEP from the C corporation years being withdrawn without taxation, since S corporation shareholders are taxed on income, not on distributions.
- On the other hand, double taxation could occur. Earnings from the S corporation years might both flow to the shareholders' tax returns as income and be taxed as dividends as if the corporation were a C corporation.

A special account is required to track undistributed earnings of an S corporation that have been taxed to shareholders previously. Distributions from this account, known as the **accumulated adjustments account (AAA)**, are tax-free. The AAA begins with a zero balance on the first day of an S corporation's first tax year. Essentially, the AAA is the cumulative total of undistributed nonseparately and separately stated items for S corporation taxable years beginning after 1982. Thus, the account parallels the calculation of C corporation AEP. Calculation of the AAA applies to all S corporations, but the AAA is most important to those that have been C corporations.

CONCEPT SUMMARY 12.1

Classification Procedures for Distributions from an S Corporation

Where No Earnings and Profits Exist	Where Earnings and Profits Exist
	1. Distributions are tax-free to the extent of the AAA.
	2. Distributions from AEP constitute dividend income.†
	3. Distributions are tax-free to the extent of the other adjustments account (OAA).
1. Distributions are nontaxable to the extent of shareholder's basis of stock.*	4. Any residual distribution amount is nontaxable to the extent of shareholder's basis of stock.*
2. Excess is treated as gain from a sale or exchange of stock (capital gain in most cases).	5. Excess is treated as gain from a sale or exchange of stock (capital gain in most cases).

*The distribution reduces the stock basis. Once stock basis reaches zero, any distribution from the AAA is treated as a gain from the sale or exchange of stock. Thus, the shareholder's stock basis is an upper limit on what a shareholder may receive tax-free.

†The AAA bypass election is available to pay out AEP before reducing the AAA [§ 1368(e)(3)].

The AAA provides a mechanism to ensure that the earnings of an S corporation are taxed to shareholders only once.

The AAA is computed by making adjustments in the order specified in Exhibit 12.1. Its balance is determined at the end of each year rather than at the time distributions are made. When more than one distribution occurs in the same year, a pro rata portion of each distribution is treated as having been made out of the AAA.

In calculating the amount in the AAA for purposes of determining the tax treatment of current-year distributions, the net negative adjustments (e.g., the excess of losses and deductions over income) for that tax year are ignored. Tax-exempt income and related expenses (e.g., insurance proceeds and premiums paid for life insurance) do not affect AAA.

A shareholder has a proportionate interest in the AAA, regardless of the size of his or her stock basis.[29] However, since the AAA is a corporate account, no connection exists between the prior accumulated S corporation income and any specific shareholder.[30] Thus, the benefits of the AAA can be shifted from one shareholder to another shareholder. For example, when one S shareholder transfers stock to another shareholder, any AAA on the purchase date may be distributed tax-free to the purchaser. Similarly, issuing additional stock to a new shareholder in an S corporation having AAA dilutes the account relative to the existing shareholders.

The AAA (unlike the stock basis) can have a negative balance. All losses decrease the AAA balance, even those in excess of the shareholder's stock basis. However, *distributions* may not make the AAA negative or increase a negative balance.

Distribution Ordering Rules

A cash distribution from an S corporation with AEP comes first from the AAA (limited to stock basis).[31] Distributions from the AAA are tax-free. The remaining distribution is taxed as a dividend to the extent of AEP. After AEP is fully distributed, any residual amount is applied against the other adjustments account (OAA, discussed below) and then the shareholder's remaining stock basis. The reduction in the shareholder's stock basis is a tax-free recovery of capital.[32] Any distributions once the stock basis reaches zero are taxed as capital gains.

[29] § 1368(c).

[30] § 1368(e)(1)(A).

[31] §§ 1368(c)(1) and (e)(1). Before 1983, an account similar to the AAA was in place, namely, **previously taxed income** (PTI). An S corporation in existence before 1983 might still hold some PTI.

[32] § 1368(c).

EXHIBIT 12.1 Adjustments to the Corporate AAA

Increase by:

1. Schedule K income items other than tax-exempt income.
2. Nonseparately computed income.
3. Depletion in excess of basis in the property.

Decrease by:

4. Negative Schedule K adjustments other than distributions (e.g., losses, deductions).
5. Any portion of a distribution that is considered to be tax-free from AAA (but not below zero).

Note: When the combination of items 1 through 4 results in a negative number, the AAA is adjusted first for the distribution and then for the adjustments in items 1 through 4.

EXAMPLE 23

Short, a calendar year S corporation, distributes $1,300 cash to its only shareholder, Otis, on December 31, 2011. Otis's basis in his stock is $1,400, Short's AAA balance is $500, and Short holds $750 AEP before the distribution.

According to the distribution ordering rules, the first $500 is a tax-free recovery of basis from the AAA. The next $750 is a taxable dividend distribution from AEP. The remaining $50 of cash is a tax-free recovery of basis. Immediately after the distribution, Short holds a zero balance in its AAA and AEP. Otis's stock basis now is $850.

	Corporate AAA	Corporate AEP	Otis's Stock Basis*
Balance, before the distribution	$ 500	$ 750	$1,400
Distribution ($1,300)			
From AAA	(500)		(500)
From AEP		(750)	
From stock basis			(50)
Balance, after the distribution	$ -0-	$ -0-	$ 850

*Details of basis adjustments are discussed later in the chapter. ■

EXAMPLE 24

Assume the same facts as in the preceding example. During the following year, Short reports zero ordinary income and distributes $1,000 to Otis. Of the distribution, $850 is a tax-free recovery of basis, and $150 is taxed to Otis as a capital gain. ■

With the consent of all of its shareholders, an S corporation can elect to have a distribution treated as if it were made from AEP rather than from the AAA. This mechanism is known as an AAA **bypass election**. This election may be desirable as a simple means by which to eliminate a small AEP balance.

EXAMPLE 25

Collett, a calendar year S corporation, has AEP of $12,000 and a balance of $20,000 in the AAA. Collett Corporation may elect to distribute the AEP first, creating a $12,000 dividend for its shareholders, before using the AAA. ■

Schedule M-2

S corporations report changes in the AAA on Schedule M-2 of Form 1120S. Schedule M-2 contains a column labeled **other adjustments account (OAA)**. This account includes items that affect basis but not the AAA, such as tax-exempt income and any related nondeductible expenses. For example, life insurance proceeds received and insurance premiums paid are traced through the OAA. Distributions are made from the OAA after AEP and the AAA are depleted to zero. Distributions from the OAA generally are tax-free.

EXAMPLE 26

During 2011, Sparrow, an S corporation, records the following items.

AAA, beginning of the year	$ 8,500
Ordinary income	25,000
Tax-exempt interest	4,000
Key employee life insurance proceeds received	5,000
Payroll penalty expense	2,000
Charitable contributions	3,000
Unreasonable compensation	5,000
Premiums on key employee life insurance	2,100
Distributions to shareholders	16,000

Sparrow's Schedule M-2 for the current year appears as follows.

Schedule M-2 **Analysis of Accumulated Adjustments Account, Other Adjustments Account, and Shareholders' Undistributed Taxable Income Previously Taxed**

	(a) Accumulated adjustments account	(b) Other adjustments account	(c) Shareholders' undistributed taxable income previously taxed
1 Balance at beginning of tax year	8,500		6,250
2 Ordinary income from page 1, line 21	25,000		
3 Other additions		9,000**	
4 Loss from page 1, line 21	( )		
5 Other reductions	(10,000*)	(2,100)	
6 Combine lines 1 through 5	23,500	6,900	
7 Distributions other than dividend distributions	16,000		
8 Balance at end of tax year. Subtract line 7 from line 6	7,500	6,900	6,250

**$2,000 (payroll penalty) + $3,000 (charitable contributions) + $5,000 (unreasonable compensation).*
***$4,000 (tax-exempt interest) + $5,000 (life insurance proceeds).*

■

Schedule M-3: Net Income or Loss Reconciliation

S corporations that have total assets on Schedule L at the end of the tax year that equal or exceed $10 million must file Schedule M-3 in lieu of Schedule M-1. For purposes of measuring total assets at the end of the year, assets are not netted or offset against liabilities. Total assets are determined using the accrual method of accounting unless both (1) the tax return of the corporation is prepared using an overall cash method of accounting, and (2) no entity includible in the U.S. tax return prepares or is included in financial statements prepared on an accrual basis.

The Schedule M-3 for S corporations is not identical to that for C corporations. Part I asks certain questions about the corporation's financial statements, and it reconciles book net income or loss to the income or loss for the tax year of the entity's U.S. tax return. Parts II and III reconcile specific book income or loss items with corresponding amounts on the U.S. tax return.

The IRS estimates that it takes about 87 hours to complete the Schedule M-3 of an S corporation, but many practitioners believe that more time may be required. A more complete discussion of Schedule M-3 is found in Chapter 2.

Avoiding Schedule M-3

Your S corporation client has read that a Schedule M-3 is now required for all S corporations with at least $10 million of assets. He says that the new schedule will reveal between 75 to 90 percent of the company's book-tax differences. Although this new schedule will help IRS agents find abusive transactions, your client is concerned that it will impose additional compliance burdens. The client's S corporation is approaching $10 million of assets, and he is thinking of either distributing some of the entity's business assets to himself or engaging in a spin-off. Are these techniques ethical?

Effect of Terminating the S Election

Normally, distributions to shareholders from a C corporation are taxed as dividends to the extent of E & P. However, any distribution of *cash* by a corporation to shareholders during a one-year period[33] following S election termination receives special treatment. Such a distribution is treated as a tax-free recovery of stock basis to the extent that it does not exceed the AAA.[34] Since *only* cash distributions reduce the AAA during this *postelection termination period*, a corporation should not make property distributions during this time. Instead, the entity should sell property and distribute the proceeds to shareholders. However, post-termination distributions that are charged against the OAA do not get tax-free treatment. To take advantage of post-termination benefits, an S corporation must know the amount of both the AAA and the OAA as of the date that the election terminates.

EXAMPLE 27

Quinn, the sole shareholder of Roman, Inc., a calendar year S corporation, elects during 2011 to terminate the S election, effective January 1, 2012. As of the end of 2011, Roman has an AAA of $1,300. Quinn can receive a nontaxable distribution of cash during a post-termination period of approximately one year to the extent of Roman's AAA. Although a cash distribution of $1,300 during 2012 would be nontaxable to Quinn, it would reduce the adjusted basis of his stock. ■

TAX TREATMENT OF NONCASH PROPERTY DISTRIBUTIONS BY THE CORPORATION

LO.7

Determine how distributions to S corporation shareholders are taxed.

An S corporation recognizes a gain on any liquidating or nonliquidating distribution of appreciated property in the same manner as if the asset had been sold to the shareholder at its fair market value.[35] The corporate gain is passed through to the shareholders. The character of the gain—capital gain or ordinary income—depends upon the type of asset being distributed. There is an important reason for this gain recognition rule. Without it, property might be distributed tax-free (other than for certain recapture items) and later sold without income recognition to the shareholder because the shareholder's basis equals the asset's fair market value.

The S corporation does not recognize a loss when distributing assets that are worth less than their basis. As with gain property, the shareholder's basis is equal to the asset's fair market value. Thus, the potential loss is postponed until the shareholder sells the stock of the S corporation. Since loss property receives a step-down in basis without any loss recognition by the S corporation, distributions of loss property should be avoided.

EXAMPLE 28

Turnip, Inc., an S corporation for 10 years, distributes a tract of land held as an investment to Chang, its majority shareholder. The land was purchased for $22,000 many years ago and is currently worth $82,000. Turnip recognizes a capital gain of $60,000, which increases the AAA by $60,000. The gain appears on Turnip's Schedule K, and a proportionate share of it passes through to the shareholders' tax returns. Then the property dividend reduces the AAA by $82,000 (the fair market value). The tax consequences are the same for appreciated property, whether it is distributed to the shareholders and they dispose of it, or the corporation sells the property and distributes the proceeds to the shareholders.

[33]The period is approximately one year in length. The post-termination transition period is discussed later in the chapter.

[34]§§ 1371(e) and 1377(b).

[35]§ 311(b).

CONCEPT SUMMARY 12.2

Consequences of Noncash Distributions

	Appreciated Property	Depreciated Property
S corporation	Realized gain is recognized by the corporation, which passes it through to the shareholders. Such gain increases a shareholder's stock basis, generating a basis in the property equal to FMV. On the distribution, the shareholder's stock basis is reduced by the FMV of the property (but not below zero).	Realized loss is not recognized. The shareholder takes an FMV basis in the property.
C corporation	Realized gain is recognized under § 311(b) and increases E & P (net of tax). The shareholder reports a taxable dividend to the extent of corporate E & P equal to the property's FMV. The shareholder takes an asset basis equal its FMV.	Realized loss is not recognized. The shareholder takes an FMV basis in the property.
Partnership	No gain to the partnership or partner. The partner takes a carryover basis in the asset, but the asset basis is limited to the partner's basis in the partnership.	Realized loss is not recognized. The partner takes a carryover basis in the asset, but the asset basis is limited to the partner's basis in the partnership.

If the land had been purchased for $82,000 and was currently worth $22,000, Chang takes a $22,000 basis in the land. The $60,000 realized loss is not recognized at the corporate level. The loss does not reduce Turnip's AAA. Only when the S corporation sells the asset does it recognize the loss and reduce AAA. ■

EXAMPLE 29

Assume the same facts as in the previous example, except that Turnip is a C corporation ($1 million E & P balance) or a partnership. The partner's basis in the partnership interest is $100,000.

	Appreciated Property		
	S Corporation	C Corporation	Partnership
Entity gain/loss	$60,000	$60,000	$ –0–
Owner's gain/loss/dividend	60,000	82,000	–0–
Owner's basis in land	82,000	82,000	22,000

	Property That Has Declined in Value		
	S Corporation	C Corporation	Partnership
Entity gain/loss	$ –0–	$ –0–	$ –0–
Owner's gain/loss/dividend	–0–	22,000	–0–
Owner's basis in land	22,000	22,000	82,000

■

LO.8

Calculate a shareholder's basis in S corporation stock.

SHAREHOLDER'S BASIS

The calculation of the initial tax basis of stock in an S corporation is similar to that for the basis of stock in a C corporation and depends upon the manner in which the shares are acquired (e.g., gift, inheritance, purchase, exchange under § 351, etc.). Once the initial tax basis is determined, various transactions during the life of the corporation affect the shareholder's basis in the stock. Although each shareholder is required to compute his or her own basis in the S shares, neither Form 1120S nor Schedule K–1 provides a place for deriving this amount.

A shareholder's basis is increased by stock purchases and capital contributions. Operations during the year cause the following upward adjustments to basis.[36]

- Nonseparately computed income.
- Separately stated income items (e.g., nontaxable income).
- Depletion in excess of basis in the property.

Basis then is reduced by distributions not reported as income by the shareholder (e.g., an AAA distribution). Next, the following items reduce basis (*but not below zero*).

- Nondeductible expenses of the corporation (e.g., fines, penalties, illegal kickbacks).
- Nonseparately computed loss.
- Separately stated loss and deduction items.

As under the partnership rule, basis first is increased by income items; then it is decreased by distributions and finally by losses.[37] In most cases, this *losses last* rule is advantageous to the S shareholder.

EXAMPLE 30

In its first year of operations, Iris, Inc., a calendar year S corporation in Clemson, South Carolina, earns income of $2,000. On February 2 in its second year of operations, Iris distributes $2,000 to Marty, its sole shareholder. During the remainder of the second year, the corporation incurs a $2,000 loss.

Under the S corporation ordering rules, the $2,000 distribution is tax-free AAA to Marty, and the $2,000 loss is *not* passed through because the stock basis cannot be reduced below zero. ■

A shareholder's basis in the stock can never be reduced below zero. Once stock basis is zero, any additional basis reductions from losses or deductions, but *not* distributions, decrease (but not below zero) the shareholder's basis in loans made to the S corporation. Any excess of losses or deductions over both bases is *suspended* until there are subsequent bases. Once the basis of any debt is reduced, it is later increased (only up to the original amount) by the subsequent *net* increase resulting from *all* positive and negative basis adjustments. The debt basis is adjusted back to the original amount by any "net increase" before any increase is made in the stock basis.[38] "Net increase" for a year is computed after taking distributions (other than those from AEP) into consideration. A distribution in excess of stock basis does not reduce any debt basis. If a loss and a distribution occur in the same year, the loss reduces the stock basis last, *after* the distribution.

EXAMPLE 31

Stacey, a sole shareholder, has a $7,000 stock basis and a $2,000 basis in a loan that she made to a calendar year S corporation with no AEP. At the beginning of 2011, the corporation's AAA and OAA balances are $0. Subchapter S ordinary income for 2011 is $8,200. During 2011, the corporation received $2,000 of tax-exempt interest income.

Cash of $17,300 is distributed to Stacey on November 15, 2011. Stacey recognizes only a $100 capital gain.

[36] § 1367(a).

[37] Reg. § 1.1367–1(f).

[38] § 1367(b)(2); Reg. § 1.1367–2(e).

	Corporate AAA	Corporate OAA	Stacey's Stock Basis	Stacey's Loan Basis
Beginning balance	$ -0-	$ -0-	$ 7,000	$2,000
Ordinary income	8,200		8,200	
Exempt income		2,000	2,000	
Subtotal	$ 8,200	$ 2,000	$ 17,200	$2,000
Distribution ($17,300)				
From AAA	(8,200)		(8,200)	
From OAA		(2,000)	(2,000)	
From stock basis			(7,000)	
Ending balance	$ -0-	$ -0-	$ -0-	$2,000
Distribution in excess of basis = Capital gain			$ 100	

Pass-through losses can reduce loan basis, but distributions do not. Stock basis cannot be reduced below zero, but the $100 excess distribution does not reduce Stacey's loan basis. ■

The basis rules for an S corporation are similar to the rules for determining a partner's interest basis in a partnership. However, a partner's basis in the partnership interest includes the partner's direct investment plus a *ratable share* of any partnership liabilities.[39] If a partnership borrows from a partner, the partner receives a basis increase as if the partnership had borrowed from an unrelated third party.[40] In contrast, except for loans from the shareholder to the corporation, corporate borrowing has no effect on S corporation shareholder basis. Loans from a shareholder to the S corporation have a tax basis only for the shareholder making the loan.

The fact that a shareholder has guaranteed a loan made to the corporation by a third party has no effect upon the shareholder's loan basis, unless payments actually have been made as a result of that guarantee.[41] If the corporation defaults on indebtedness and the shareholder makes good on the guarantee, the shareholder's indebtedness basis is increased to that extent.

A flow-through deduction is available for a shareholder loan only where there is clear evidence that the S corporation is liable to the shareholder. A shareholder looking for this result should borrow the money from the bank and then loan the money to the S corporation.

If a loan's basis has been reduced and is not restored, income is recognized when the S corporation repays the shareholder. If the corporation issued a note as evidence of the debt, repayment constitutes an amount received in exchange for a capital asset, and the amount that exceeds the shareholder's basis is entitled to capital gain treatment.[42] However, if the loan is made on open account, the repayment constitutes ordinary income to the extent that it exceeds the shareholder's basis in the loan.[43] Each repayment is prorated between the gain portion and the repayment of the debt.[44] Thus, a note should be given to ensure capital gain treatment for the income that results from a loan's repayment.

EXAMPLE 32

Sammy is a 57% owner of Falcon, an S corporation in Brooklyn, New York. At the beginning of the year, his stock basis is zero. Sammy's basis in a $12,000 loan made to Falcon and evidenced by Falcon's note has been reduced to $0 by prior losses. At the end

[39] § 752(a).

[40] Reg. § 1.752–1(e).

[41] See, for example, *Estate of Leavitt*, 90 T.C. 206 (1988), *aff'd* 89–1 USTC ¶9332, 63 AFTR 2d 89–1437, 875 F.2d 420 (CA–4, 1989); *Selfe v. U.S.*, 86–1 USTC ¶9115, 57 AFTR 2d 86–464, 778 F.2d 769 (CA–11, 1985); *James K. Calcutt*, 91 T.C. 14 (1988).

[42] *Joe M. Smith*, 48 T.C. 872 (1967), *aff'd* and *rev'd* in 70–1 USTC ¶9327, 25 AFTR 2d 70–936, 424 F.2d 219 (CA–9, 1970); Rev.Rul. 64–162, 1964–1 C.B. 304.

[43] Reg. § 1.1367–2. Open account debt is treated as if it were evidenced by a note if the shareholder's principal balance exceeds $25,000 at the end of the tax year.

[44] Rev.Rul. 68–537, 1968–2 C.B. 372.

of the year, he receives a $13,000 distribution. During the year, his net share of corporate taxable income is $11,000. Because there is no "net increase" (i.e., his share of income is less than the amount of the distribution), Sammy's debt basis is not restored. Instead, his share of income increases his stock basis to $11,000. Therefore, on receipt of the $13,000 distribution, $11,000 is a tax-free recovery of his stock basis, and $2,000 is a capital gain.[45] ■

EXAMPLE 33

Assume in the previous example that the distribution that Sammy receives is only $8,000. Since the "net increase" is $3,000 ($11,000 income share in excess of $8,000 distribution), the debt basis is restored by $3,000. Accordingly, the remaining income share not used to increase debt basis ($8,000) is used to increase Sammy's stock basis to $8,000. Therefore, on receipt of the $8,000 distribution, all $8,000 is tax-free, reducing the stock basis back to zero. ■

TREATMENT OF LOSSES

LO.9

Explain the tax effects that losses have on shareholders.

Net Operating Loss

One major advantage of an S election is the ability to pass through any net operating loss of the corporation directly to the shareholders. A shareholder can deduct an NOL for the year in which the S corporation's tax year ends. The corporation is not entitled to any deduction for the NOL. A shareholder's basis in the stock is reduced to the extent of any pass-through of the NOL, and the shareholder's AAA is reduced by the same deductible amount.[46]

EXAMPLE 34
THE BIG PICTURE

Return to the facts of *The Big Picture* on p. 12-2. If Smith and Jones make the S election for Cane, Inc., they will be able to pass through any NOLs to the extent of the shareholder's adjusted stock basis. If the new S corporation incurs an NOL of $84,000 during 2011, both shareholders are entitled to deduct $42,000 against other income for the tax year in which Cane's tax year ends. Any NOL incurred before the S election is in effect does not flow through to the two shareholders, as long as the S election is maintained. ■

Deductions for an S corporation's loss pass-throughs (e.g., NOL, capital loss, charitable contributions) cannot exceed a shareholder's adjusted basis in the stock *plus* the basis of any loans made by the shareholder to the corporation. If a taxpayer is unable to prove the tax basis, the loss pass-through can be denied.[47] As noted previously, once a shareholder's adjusted stock basis has been eliminated by a loss pass-through, any excess loss reduces the shareholder's basis for any loans made to the corporation (*but never below zero*). The basis for loans is established by the actual advances made to the corporation, and not by indirect loans.[48] If the shareholder's basis is insufficient to allow a full flow-through and there is more than one type of loss (e.g., in the same year the S corporation incurs both a passive loss and a net capital loss), the flow-through amounts are determined on a pro rata basis.

EXAMPLE 35

Ralph is a 50% owner of an S corporation for the entire year. His stock basis is $10,000, and his shares of the various corporate losses are as follows.

Ordinary loss from operations	$8,000
Capital loss	5,000
§ 1231 loss	3,000
Passive loss	2,000

[45] § 1367(b)(2)(B); Reg. § 1.1367–2(e).
[46] §§ 1368(a)(1)(A) and (e)(1)(A).
[47] See *Donald J. Sauvigne*, 30 TCM 123, T.C.Memo. 1971–30.
[48] *Ruth M. Prashker*, 59 T.C. 172 (1972); *Frederick G. Brown v. U.S.*, 83–1 USTC ¶9364, 52 AFTR 2d 82–5080, 706 F.2d 755 (CA–6, 1983).

Based upon a pro rata approach, the total $10,000 allocable flow-through would be split among the various losses as follows.

$$\text{Ordinary loss} = \frac{\$8{,}000}{\$18{,}000} \times \$10{,}000 = \$\ 4{,}444.44$$

$$\text{Capital loss} = \frac{\$5{,}000}{\$18{,}000} \times \$10{,}000 = \$\ 2{,}777.78$$

$$\S\ 1231\ \text{loss} = \frac{\$3{,}000}{\$18{,}000} \times \$10{,}000 = \$\ 1{,}666.67$$

$$\text{Passive loss} = \frac{\$2{,}000}{\$18{,}000} \times \$10{,}000 = \$\ 1{,}111.11$$

Total allocated loss $10,000.00 ■

Distributions made by an S corporation are taken into account *before* applying the loss limitations for the year. Thus, distributions reduce the shareholder's stock basis used in determining the allowable loss for the year, but a flow-through loss does *not* reduce stock basis when accounting for distributions made during the year.

EXAMPLE 36

Pylon, Inc., a calendar year S corporation, is partly owned by Doris, who has a beginning stock basis of $10,000. During the year, Doris's share of a long-term capital gain (LTCG) is $2,000, and her share of an ordinary loss is $9,000. If Doris receives a $6,000 distribution, her deductible loss is calculated as follows.

Beginning stock basis	$10,000
Add: LTCG	2,000
Subtotal	$12,000
Less: Distribution	(6,000)
Basis for loss limitation purposes	$ 6,000
Deductible loss	($ 6,000)
Unused loss	($ 3,000)

Doris's stock now has a basis of zero. ■

A shareholder's share of an NOL may be greater than both stock basis and loan basis. A shareholder is entitled to carry forward a loss to the extent that the loss for the year exceeds basis. Any loss carried forward may be deducted *only* by the *same* shareholder if and when the basis in the stock of or loans to the corporation is restored.[49]

EXAMPLE 37

Dana has a stock basis of $4,000 in an S corporation. He has loaned $2,000 to the corporation and has guaranteed another $4,000 loan made to the corporation by a local bank. Although his share of the S corporation's NOL for the current year is $9,500, Dana may deduct only $6,000 of the NOL on his individual tax return. Dana may carry forward $3,500 of the NOL, to be deducted when the basis in his stock or loan to the corporation is restored. Dana has a zero basis in both the stock and the loan after the flow-through of the $6,000 NOL. ■

Any loss carryover due to insufficient basis remaining at the end of an approximately one-year post-termination transition period is *lost forever*. The post-termination period includes the 120-day period beginning on the date of any determination pursuant to an audit of a taxpayer that follows the termination of the S corporation's election and that adjusts a Subchapter S item.[50] Thus, if a shareholder has a loss

[49] § 1366(d).

[50] § 1377(b)(1).

carryover, he or she should increase the stock or loan basis and flow through the loss before disposing of the stock.

Net operating losses from C corporation years cannot be utilized at the corporate level (except with respect to built-in gains, discussed later in this chapter), nor can they be passed through to the shareholders. Further, the carryforward period continues to run during S status.[51] Consequently, the S election may not be appropriate for a C corporation with NOL carryforwards. When a corporation is expecting losses in the future, an S election should be made *before* the loss years.

At-Risk Rules

S corporation shareholders, like partners, are limited in the amount of loss that they may deduct by their "at-risk" amounts. The rules for determining at-risk amounts are similar, but not identical, to the partner at-risk rules. These rules apply to the shareholders, but not to the corporation. An amount at risk is determined separately for each shareholder. The amount of the corporate losses that are passed through and deductible by the shareholders is not affected by the amount the corporation has at risk.

EXAMPLE 38

Shareholder Ricketts has a basis of $35,000 in his S corporation stock. He takes a $15,000 nonrecourse loan from a local bank and lends the proceeds to the S corporation. Ricketts now has a stock basis of $35,000 and a debt basis of $15,000. However, due to the at-risk limitation, he can deduct only $35,000 of losses from the S corporation. ■

Passive Losses and Credits

Section 469 provides that net passive losses and credits are not deductible when incurred and must be carried over to a year when there is passive income. Thus, one must be aware of three major classes of income, losses, and credits—active, portfolio, and passive. S corporations are not directly subject to the limits of § 469, but corporate rental activities are inherently passive, and other activities of an S corporation may be passive unless the shareholder(s) materially participate(s) in operating the business. An S corporation may engage in more than one such activity. If the corporate activity involves rentals or the shareholders do not materially participate, any loss or credit that flows through is passive. The shareholders are able to apply such losses or credits only against income from other passive activities.

A shareholder's stock basis is reduced by passive losses that flow through to the shareholder, even though the shareholder may not be entitled to a current deduction due to the passive loss limitations. The existence of material participation is determined at the shareholder level. There are seven tests for material participation, including a need to participate in the activity for more than 500 hours during the taxable year.[52]

EXAMPLE 39

Heather is a 50% owner of an S corporation engaged in a passive activity. A nonparticipating shareholder, she receives a salary of $6,000 for services as a result of the passive activity. Heather has $6,000 of earned income as a result of the salary. The $6,000 salary creates a $6,000 deduction/passive loss, which flows through to the shareholders. Heather's $3,000 share of the loss may not be deducted against the $6,000 of earned income. Under § 469(e)(3), earned income is not taken into account in computing the income or loss from a passive activity. ■

TAX ON PRE-ELECTION BUILT-IN GAIN

LO.10

Compute the built-in gains and passive investment income penalty taxes.

Normally, an S corporation does *not* pay an income tax, since all items flow through to the shareholders. But an S corporation that was previously a C corporation may be required to pay a built-in gains tax, LIFO recapture tax, general business credit recapture, or passive investment income tax.

[51] § 1371(b).

[52] Reg. § 1.469–5T(a).

TAX in the NEWS — S Corporations Pay Taxes, Too

S corporations, like partnerships and limited liability entities, are pass-through entities, and are supposed to pay zero entity-level Federal income tax. But certain penalty taxes apply to S corporations and their shareholders, as discussed later in the chapter. And when there is a tax liability, there are audit adjustments.

Here are some approximate amounts of tax payments by and for S corporations in recent tax years. Not even one-half of 1 percent of all Forms 1120S are liable for one or more of these taxes!

	2006	2007
Built-in gains tax	$585,000,000	$845,000,000
Excess net passive income tax	45,000,000	70,000,000
Audit adjustments	9,500,000	11,500,000
Other	775,000	–0–
Total tax liability	$640,275,000	$926,500,000

Source: IRS Tax Stats.

Without the **built-in gains tax** (§ 1374), it would be possible to avoid the corporate double tax on a disposition of appreciated property, by electing S corporation status.

The § 1374 tax generally applies to C corporations converting to S status after 1986. It is a *corporate-level* tax on any built-in gain recognized when the S corporation disposes of an asset in a taxable disposition within 10 calendar years after the date on which the S election took effect. The 10-year holding period is reduced to 7 years for tax years beginning in 2009 and 2010, and to 5 years for 2011.[53] The holding period begins on the date of the S election.

General Rules

The base for the § 1374 tax includes any unrealized gain on appreciated assets (e.g., real estate, cash basis receivables, and goodwill) held by a corporation on the day it elects S status. The highest corporate tax rate (currently 35 percent) is applied to the unrealized gain when any of the assets are sold. Furthermore, the gain on the sale (net of the § 1374 tax)[54] passes through as a taxable gain to shareholders.

EXAMPLE 40

Zinnia, Inc., a C corporation, owns a single asset with a basis of $100,000 and a fair market value of $500,000. Zinnia elects S corporation status. Section 1374 imposes a corporate-level tax that must be paid by Zinnia if it sells the asset after electing S status. Upon sale of the asset, the corporation owes a tax of $140,000 ($400,000 × 35%). The shareholders have a $260,000 taxable gain ($400,000 − $140,000). Hence, the built-in gains tax effectively imposes a double tax on Zinnia and its shareholders. ■

The maximum amount of gain that is recognized over the required (5-, 7-, or 10-year) holding period is limited to the *aggregate net* built-in gain of the corporation at the time it converted to S status. Thus, at the time of the S election, unrealized gains of the corporation are offset against unrealized losses. The net amount of gains and losses sets an upper limit on the tax base for the built-in gains tax. Any appreciation after the conversion to S status is subject to the regular S corporation pass-through rules.

Contributions of assets with realized losses on the date of conversion reduce the maximum built-in gain and any potential tax under § 1374.[55] In addition, built-in losses and built-in gains are netted each year to determine the annual § 1374 tax base. Thus, an incentive exists to contribute loss assets to a corporation before

[53] § 1374(d)(7)(B).

[54] § 1366(f)(2).

[55] §§ 1374(c)(2) and (d)(1).

CONCEPT SUMMARY 12.3

Calculation of the Built-in Gains Tax Liability

Step 1. Select the smaller of built-in gain or taxable income (C corporation rules).*

Step 2. Deduct unexpired NOLs and capital losses from C corporation tax years.

Step 3. Multiply the tax base obtained in step 2 by the top corporate income tax rate.

Step 4. Deduct any business credit carryforwards and AMT credit carryovers arising in a C corporation tax year from the amount obtained in step 3.

Step 5. The corporation pays any tax resulting from step 4.

*Any net recognized built-in gain in excess of taxable income is carried forward to the next year, as long as the next year is within the 5-, 7-, or 10-year recognition period.

electing S status. However, the IRS position is that contributions of loss property within two years before the earlier of the date of conversion or the date of filing an S election are presumed to have a tax avoidance motive and will not reduce the corporation's net unrealized built-in gain.

Normally, tax attributes of a C corporation do *not* carry over to a converted S corporation. For purposes of the tax on built-in gains, however, certain carryovers are allowed. In particular, an S corporation can offset built-in gains with unexpired NOLs or capital losses from C corporation years.

EXAMPLE 41
THE BIG PICTURE

Return to the facts of *The Big Picture* on p. 12-2. If Cane, Inc., becomes an S corporation, a built-in gain may be recognized. Assuming that Cane reports a $50,000 built-in gain on conversion, and that it holds a $20,000 NOL carryforward for C corporation years before the S election, the NOL carryforward is applied against the built-in gain. Cane's built-in gains tax applies only to $30,000. ■

Concept Summary 12.3 summarizes the calculation of the built-in gains tax.

LIFO Recapture Tax

To preclude deferral of gain recognition by a C corporation that is electing S status, any LIFO recapture amount at the time of the S election is subject to a corporate-level tax.

The taxable LIFO recapture amount equals the excess of the inventory's value under FIFO over the LIFO value. No negative adjustment is allowed if the LIFO value is higher than the FIFO value.

The resulting tax is payable in four equal installments, with the first payment due on or before the due date for the corporate return for the last C corporation year (without regard to any extensions). The remaining three installments are paid on or before the due dates of the succeeding corporate returns. No interest is due if payments are made by the due dates, and no estimated taxes are due on the four tax installments. The basis of the LIFO inventory is adjusted to account for this LIFO recapture amount, but the AAA is not decreased by payment of the tax.

PASSIVE INVESTMENT INCOME PENALTY TAX

A tax is imposed on the excess passive income of S corporations that possess AEP from C corporation years. The tax rate is the highest corporate rate for the year

TAX in the NEWS — THE SELF-EMPLOYMENT INCOME ADVANTAGE

A significant advantage of an S corporation involves the current definition of self-employment income. Although compensation for services rendered to an S corporation is subject to FICA taxes, a shareholder's share of income from an S corporation is not self-employment income. The rationale for this S corporation loophole is that the S shareholder does not personally carry on the entity's trade or business. In contrast, the earned income of a partnership or proprietorship is treated as self-employment income to the partner or proprietor.

The choice between a salary and pass-through income is not clear-cut, however.

- Although a salary is subject to payroll tax and pass-through income is not [*P.B. Ding v. Comm.,* 200 F.3d 587 (CA–9, 1999)], this nonearned income does not accrue Social Security benefits for its recipient.
- S corporation income distributions do not count as compensation for computing an employee's contribution formula for a retirement plan.
- The IRS and the courts require a shareholder to take a reasonable salary (see footnote 68).
- If a partner or proprietor reports salary income from other sources, and the aggregate salaries exceed the annual FICA ceiling, a partnership or proprietorship entity may provide tax savings over an S corporation.

(35 percent in 2011). The rate is applied to excess net passive income (ENPI), which is determined using the following formula:

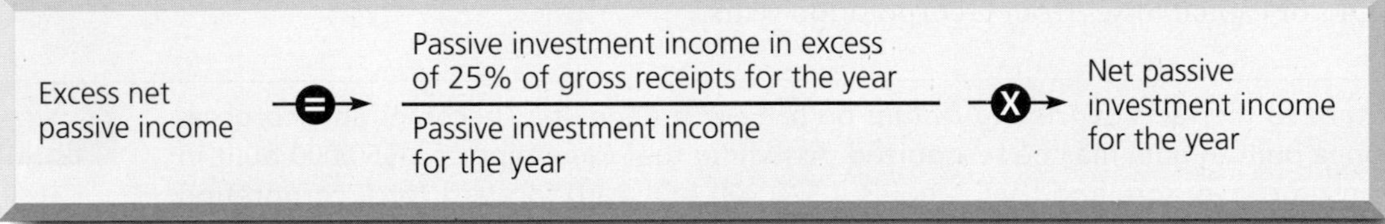

$$\text{Excess net passive income} = \frac{\text{Passive investment income in excess of 25\% of gross receipts for the year}}{\text{Passive investment income for the year}} \times \text{Net passive investment income for the year}$$

Passive investment income (PII) includes gross receipts derived from royalties, passive rents, dividends, interest, and annuities. Only the net gain from the disposition of capital assets is taken into account in computing PII gross receipts.[56] Passive investment income does not include built-in gains (or losses) recognized during the 5-, 7-, or 10-year waiting period. Net passive income is passive income reduced by any deductions directly connected with the production of that income. Any passive income tax reduces the amount the shareholders must take into income.

The excess net passive income cannot exceed the C corporate taxable income for the year before considering any NOL deduction or the special deductions allowed by §§ 241–250 (except the organizational expense deduction).[57]

EXAMPLE 42

Barnhardt Corporation, an S corporation, has gross receipts for the year totaling $264,000 (of which $110,000 is PII). Expenditures directly connected to the production of the PII total $30,000. Therefore, Barnhardt has net PII of $80,000 ($110,000 − $30,000), and its PII for the tax year exceeds 25% of its gross receipts by $44,000 [$110,000 PII − (25% × $264,000)]. Excess net passive income (ENPI) is $32,000, calculated as follows.

$$\text{ENPI} = \frac{\$44{,}000}{\$110{,}000} \times \$80{,}000 = \$32{,}000$$

Barnhardt's PII tax is $11,200 ($32,000 × 35%). ■

[56] § 1362(d)(3)(B) and (C).

[57] §§ 248, 1374(d)(4), and 1375(a) and (b).

OTHER OPERATIONAL RULES

Several other points may be made about the possible effects of various Code provisions on S corporations.

- An S corporation is required to make estimated tax payments with respect to tax exposure because of any recognized built-in gain and excess passive investment income.
- An S corporation may own stock in another corporation, but an S corporation may not have a C corporation shareholder. An S corporation is *not* eligible for a dividends received deduction.
- An S corporation is *not* subject to the 10 percent of taxable income limitation applicable to charitable contributions made by a C corporation.
- Any family member who renders services or furnishes capital to an S corporation must be paid reasonable compensation. Otherwise, the IRS can make adjustments to reflect the value of the services or capital.[58] This rule may make it more difficult for related parties to shift Subchapter S taxable income to children or other family members.
- Although § 1366(a)(1) provides for a flow-through of S items to a shareholder, it does not create self-employment income.[59] This treatment of earned income of S corporations is attractive compared to the treatment of a proprietorship or a partnership whose income is taxed as self-employment income to the owners. Compensation for services rendered to an S corporation is, however, subject to FICA taxes. Congress is considering a change to this rule.

EXAMPLE 43

Cody and Dana each own one-third of a fast-food restaurant, and their 14-year-old son owns the other shares. Both parents work full-time in the restaurant operations, but the son works infrequently. Neither parent receives a salary this year, when the taxable income of the S corporation is $160,000. The IRS can require that reasonable compensation be paid to the parents to prevent the full one-third of the $160,000 from being taxed to the son. Otherwise, this would be an effective technique to shift earned income to a family member to reduce the total family tax burden. Furthermore, low or zero salaries can reduce FICA taxes due to the Federal government. ■

EXAMPLE 44

Dave is a professor at a southeastern university earning a salary of $150,000. He also has consulting income of $80,000. If the consulting business is organized as an S corporation, Dave should withdraw a reasonable salary from the S corporation for his services. The S corporation pays payroll and withholding tax on the salary. Dave receives a tax credit for any overpayment of the employee share of the FICA tax, but the S corporation does not receive a similar credit.

If the business is operated as a proprietorship, Dave is exempt from the Social Security portion of the self-employment tax because his university salary exceeds the annual FICA ceiling. Here, operating as a proprietorship offers a tax advantage over an S corporation. ■

- An S corporation is placed on the cash method of accounting for purposes of deducting business expenses and interest owed to a cash basis related party.[60] Thus, the timing of the shareholder's income and the corporate deduction must match.
- An S corporation may not deduct a payment to one of its shareholders, e.g., a year-end performance bonus, until the payee reports the income.

[58] § 1366(e). In addition, beware of an IRS search for the "real owner" of the stock under Reg. § 1.1373–1(a)(2).

[59] Rev.Rul. 59–221, 1959–1 C.B. 225.

[60] § 267(b).

- The S election is not recognized by the District of Columbia and several states, including Connecticut, Michigan, New Hampshire, and Tennessee. Thus, some or all of the entity's income may be subject to a state-level income tax (e.g., a "sting tax" on large S corporations in Massachusetts).
- If § 1244 stock is issued to an S corporation, the S corporation and its shareholders may not treat losses on such stock as ordinary losses. However, an S corporation may issue § 1244 stock to its shareholders to obtain ordinary loss treatment.
- The § 1202 exclusion of gain on disposition of small business stock is *not* available for S stock.
- Losses may be disallowed due to a lack of a profit motive. If the activities at the corporate level are not profit motivated, the losses may be disallowed under the hobby loss rule of § 183.[61]
- A penalty is imposed for failure to file (including extensions) timely S corporation returns. The penalty is $195 per month times the number of S corporation shareholders. The penalty is assessed against the corporation for a maximum of 12 months.[62]
- Code § 1372(a) applies partnership treatment for certain fringe benefits to more-than-2 percent shareholder-employees of S corporations. Thus, these shareholders are not entitled to exclude certain fringe benefits from gross income. A more-than-2 percent shareholder-employee is allowed an above-the-line (*for* AGI) deduction on Form 1040 for accident and health insurance premiums.[63]
- If an S corporation excludes cancellation of debt (COD) income from gross income, the excluded amount is applied to reduce S corporation tax attributes.[64]

TAX PLANNING:

12.4 When the Election Is Advisable

LO.11

Engage in tax planning for S corporations.

Effective tax planning with S corporations begins with the determination of whether the election is appropriate. In this context, one should consider the following factors.

- Are losses from the business anticipated? If so, the S election may be highly attractive because these losses pass through to the shareholders.
- What are the tax brackets of the shareholders? If the shareholders are in high individual income tax brackets, it may be desirable to avoid S corporation status and have profits taxed to the corporation at lower C rates (e.g., 15 percent or 25 percent). However, the income still is not in the owners' hands.
- When the shareholders are in low individual income tax brackets, the pass-through of corporate profits is attractive, and reducing the combined income tax becomes the paramount consideration. Under these circumstances, the S election could be an effective tax planning tool. Note, however, that although an S corporation usually escapes Federal taxes, it may not be immune from state and local taxes imposed on corporations, or from several Federal penalty taxes.
- Does a C corporation have an NOL carryover from a prior year? Such a loss cannot be used in an S year (except for purposes of the built-in gains tax). Even worse, S years count in the 20-year carryover limitation. Thus, even if the S election is made, one might consider terminating the election before

[61] *Michael J. Houston*, 69 TCM 2360, T.C.Memo. 1995–159; *Mario G. De Mendoza, III*, 68 TCM 42, T.C.Memo. 1994–314.

[62] § 6699.

[63] Notice 2008–1, 2008–2 I.R.B. 251.

[64] §§ 108(a), 108(b)(2).

the carryover limitation expires. Such a termination would permit the loss to be utilized by what is now a C corporation.

- Both individuals and C corporations are subject to the alternative minimum tax. Many of the tax preference and adjustment items are the same, but some apply only to corporate taxpayers while others are limited to individuals. The alternative minimum tax adjustment relating to adjusted current earnings could create havoc with some C corporations (refer to Chapter 3). S corporations themselves are not subject to this tax.
- S corporations and partnerships have limited flexibility in the choice of a tax accounting period.[65]

12.5 Making a Proper Election

Once the parties have decided the election is appropriate, it becomes essential to ensure that the election is made properly.

- Make sure all shareholders consent. If any doubt exists concerning the shareholder status of an individual, it would be wise to have that party issue a consent anyway.[66] Too few consents are fatal to the election; the same cannot be said for too many consents.
- Be sure that the election is timely and properly filed. Either hand carry the election to an IRS office or send it by certified or registered mail. The date used to determine timeliness is the postmark date, not the date the IRS receives the election. A copy of the election should become part of the corporation's permanent files.
- Be careful to ascertain when the timely election period begins to run for a newly formed corporation. An election made too soon (before the corporation is in existence) is worse than one made too late. If serious doubts exist as to when this period begins, filing more than one election might be considered a practical means of guaranteeing the desired result.
- It still is beneficial for an S corporation to issue § 1244 stock (refer to Chapter 4). This type of stock allows the original shareholder to obtain an ordinary deduction for a loss on the sale or worthlessness of the stock, rather than long-term capital loss treatment. Shareholders have nothing to lose by complying with § 1244.

12.6 Preserving the Election

Recall that an election can be lost intentionally or unintentionally in several ways, and that a five-year waiting period generally is imposed before another S election is available. To preserve an S election, the following points should be kept in mind.

- As a starting point, all parties concerned should be made aware of the various transactions that lead to the loss of an election.
- Watch for possible disqualification of a small business corporation. For example, the death of a shareholder could result in a nonqualifying trust becoming a shareholder. The latter circumstance might be avoided by utilizing a buy-sell agreement or binding the deceased shareholder's estate to turn in the stock to the corporation for redemption or, as an alternative, to sell it to the surviving shareholders.[67]

---

[65] Entity tax-year constraints are discussed in Chapter 10.

[66] See *William B. Wilson*, 34 TCM 463, T.C.Memo. 1975–92.

[67] See Chapter 19 for a discussion of buy-sell agreements. Most such agreements do not create a second class of S stock. Rev.Rul. 85–161, 1985–2 C.B. 191; *Portage Plastics Co. v. U.S.*, 72–2 USTC ¶9567, 30 AFTR 2d 72–5229, 470 F.2d 308 (CA–7, 1973).

12.7 Planning for the Operation of the Corporation

Operating an S corporation to achieve optimum tax savings for all parties involved requires a great deal of care and, most important, an understanding of the applicable tax rules.

ACCUMULATED ADJUSTMENTS ACCOUNT

Although the corporate-level accumulated adjustments account (AAA) is used primarily by an S corporation with accumulated earnings and profits (AEP) from a Subchapter C year, all S corporations should maintain an accurate record of the AAA. Because there is a grace period for distributing the AAA after termination of the S election, the parties must be in a position to determine the balance of the account.

EXAMPLE 45

Nobles, Inc., an S corporation, has no C corporation AEP. Over the years, Nobles made no attempt to maintain an accurate accounting for the AAA. Now, the S election has been terminated, and Nobles has a grace period for distributing the AAA tax-free to its shareholders. A great deal of time and expense may be necessary to reconstruct the AAA balance. ■

When AEP is present, a negative AAA may cause double taxation of S corporation income. With a negative AAA, the recognition of current income restores the negative AAA balance to zero, but a subsequent distribution then is considered to be in excess of AAA and is taxable as a dividend to the extent of AEP. Distributions during the year reduce the stock basis for determining the allowable loss for the year, but the loss does *not* reduce the stock basis for determining the tax status of distributions made during the year. In determining the tax treatment of distributions by an S corporation having AEP, any net adjustments (e.g., excess of losses and deductions over income) for the tax year are ignored.

The AAA bypass election may be used to reduce exposure to the accumulated earnings tax or personal holding company tax in post-S years. This bypass election allows AEP to be distributed instead.

EXAMPLE 46

Zebra, Inc., an S corporation during 2010, has a significant amount in its AEP account. The shareholders expect to terminate the election in 2011, when Zebra will be subject to the lower corporate income tax rates. Since Zebra as a C corporation may be subject to the accumulated earnings penalty tax in 2011, the shareholders may wish to use the AAA bypass election to distribute some or all of the AEP. Of course, any distributions of the AEP account in 2010 would be taxable to the shareholders. ■

A net loss allocated to a shareholder reduces the AAA. This required adjustment should encourage an S corporation to make annual distributions of net income to avoid the reduction of an AAA by a future net loss.

SALARY STRUCTURE

The amount of salary paid to a shareholder-employee of an S corporation can have varying tax consequences and should be considered carefully. Larger amounts might be advantageous if the maximum contribution allowed for the shareholder-employee under the corporation's retirement plan has not been reached. Smaller amounts may be beneficial if the parties are trying to shift taxable income to lower-bracket shareholders, reduce payroll taxes, curtail a reduction of Social Security benefits, or restrict losses that do not pass through because of the basis limitation.

A strategy of decreasing compensation and correspondingly increasing distributions to shareholder-employees often results in substantial savings in employment taxes. However, a shareholder of an S corporation cannot always perform substantial services and arrange to receive distributions rather than compensation so that the corporation may avoid paying employment taxes. The IRS may deem the shareholder to be an employee, with any distributions recharacterized as wages subject to FICA and FUTA taxes.[68] In effect, the IRS requires that reasonable compensation be paid to shareholder-employees. For planning purposes, some level of compensation should be paid to all shareholder-employees to avoid any recharacterization of nonpassive distributions as deductible salaries—especially in personal service corporations.

The IRS can require that reasonable compensation be paid to family members who render services or provide capital to the S corporation. The IRS also can adjust the items taken into account by family-member shareholders to reflect the value of services or capital they provided. Refer to Example 43.

Unreasonable compensation traditionally has not been a problem for S corporations, but deductible compensation under § 162 reduces an S corporation's taxable income, which is relevant to the built-in gains tax. Compensation may be one of the larger items that an S corporation can use to reduce taxable income to minimize any built-in gains penalty tax. Thus, IRS agents may attempt to classify compensation as unreasonable to increase the § 1374 tax.

Deductions for various tax-free fringe benefits are denied to a more-than-2 percent shareholder-employee of an S corporation. Such benefits include group term life insurance, medical insurance, and meals and lodging furnished for the convenience of the employer. These items are treated as wages and are subject to most payroll taxes. The employee can deduct medical insurance premiums on his or her tax return.

LOSS CONSIDERATIONS

A net loss in excess of tax basis may be carried forward and deducted only by the same shareholder in succeeding years. Thus, before disposing of the stock, a shareholder should increase the basis of such stock/loan to flow through the loss. The next shareholder does not obtain the loss carryover.

Any unused loss carryover in existence upon the termination of the S election may be deducted only in the next tax year and is limited to the individual's *stock* basis (not loan basis) in the post-termination year.[69] The shareholder may wish to purchase more stock to increase the tax basis in order to absorb the loss.

The NOL provisions create a need for sound tax planning during the last election year and the post-termination transition period. If it appears that the S corporation is going to sustain an NOL or use up any loss carryover, each shareholder's basis should be analyzed to determine if it can absorb the share of the loss. If basis is insufficient to absorb the loss, further investments should be considered before the end of the post-termination transition year. Such investments can be accomplished through additional stock purchases from the corporation, or from other shareholders, to increase basis. This action ensures the full benefit from the NOL carryover.

EXAMPLE 47

A calendar year C corporation has an NOL of $20,000 in 2010. The corporation makes a valid S election in 2011 and has another $20,000 NOL in that year. At all times during 2011, the stock of the corporation was owned by the same 10 shareholders, each of whom owned 10% of the stock. Tim, one of the 10 shareholders, has a stock basis of $1,800 at the beginning of 2011. None of the 2010 NOL may be carried forward into the S year. Although Tim's share of the 2011 NOL is $2,000, the deduction for the loss is limited to $1,800 in 2011 with a $200 carryover. ■

AVOIDING THE PASSIVE INVESTMENT INCOME TAX

Too much passive investment income (PII) may cause an S corporation to incur a § 1375 penalty tax and/or terminate the S election. Several planning techniques can

[68] Rev.Rul. 74–44, 1974–1 C.B. 287; *Spicer Accounting, Inc. v. U.S.*, 91–1 USTC ¶50,103, 66 AFTR 2d 90–5806, 918 F.2d 90 (CA–9, 1990); *Radtke v. U.S.*, 90–1 USTC ¶50,113, 65 AFTR 2d 90–1155, 895 F.2d 1196 (CA–7, 1990); *Joseph M. Grey Public Accountant, P.C.*, 119 T.C. 121 (2002); *Watson, P.C. v. U.S.*, 2010–1 USTC ¶50,444, 105 AFTR 2d 2010–2624 (D.C. S.IA), 714 F.Supp.2d 954.

[69] § 1366(d)(3).

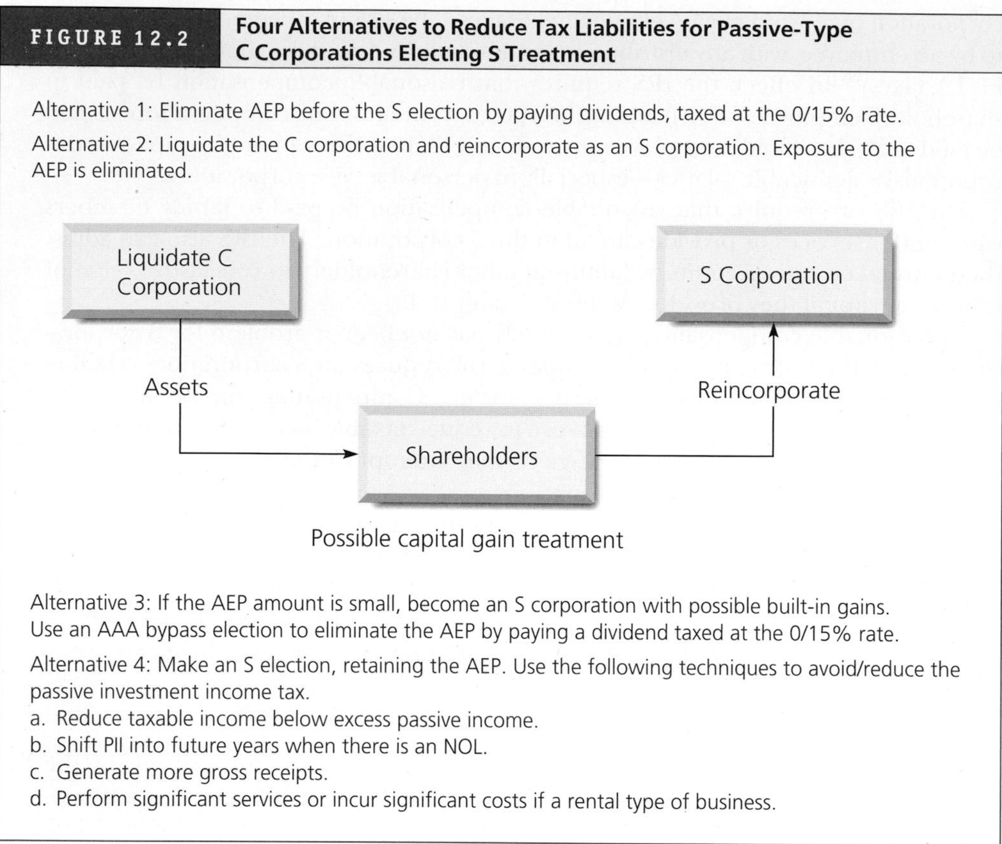

Alternative 1: Eliminate AEP before the S election by paying dividends, taxed at the 0/15% rate.
Alternative 2: Liquidate the C corporation and reincorporate as an S corporation. Exposure to the AEP is eliminated.
Liquidate C Corporation
S Corporation
Assets
Reincorporate
Shareholders
Possible capital gain treatment
Alternative 3: If the AEP amount is small, become an S corporation with possible built-in gains.
Use an AAA bypass election to eliminate the AEP by paying a dividend taxed at the 0/15% rate.
Alternative 4: Make an S election, retaining the AEP. Use the following techniques to avoid/reduce the passive investment income tax.
a. Reduce taxable income below excess passive income.
b. Shift PII into future years when there is an NOL.
c. Generate more gross receipts.
d. Perform significant services or incur significant costs if a rental type of business.

FIGURE 12.2 **Four Alternatives to Reduce Tax Liabilities for Passive-Type C Corporations Electing S Treatment**

be used to avoid both of these unfavorable events. Where a small amount of AEP exists, an AAA bypass election may be appropriate to purge the AEP, thereby avoiding the passive income tax altogether. Alternatively, the corporation might reduce taxable income below the excess net passive income; similarly, PII might be accelerated into years in which there is an offsetting NOL. In addition, the tax can be avoided if the corporation manufactures needed gross receipts. By increasing gross receipts without increasing PII, the amount of PII in excess of 25 percent of gross receipts is reduced. Finally, performing significant services or incurring significant costs with respect to rental real estate activities can elevate the rent income to nonpassive.

EXAMPLE 48

An S corporation has paid a passive investment income penalty tax for two consecutive years. In the next year, the corporation has a large amount of AAA. If the AEP account is small, a bypass election may be appropriate to purge the corporation of the AEP. Without any AEP, no passive investment income tax applies, and the S election is not terminated. Any distribution of AEP to the shareholders constitutes taxable dividends, however.

Another alternative is to manufacture a large amount of gross receipts without increasing PII through an action such as a merger with a grocery store. If the gross receipts from the grocery store are substantial, the amount of the PII in excess of 25% of gross receipts is reduced. ■

Figure 12.2 shows four alternatives that a C corporation that intends to elect S treatment may use to reduce its tax liability.

MANAGING THE BUILT-IN GAINS TAX

The taxable income limitation encourages an S corporation to create deductions or accelerate deductions in the years that built-in gains are recognized. Although the postponed built-in gain is carried forward to future years, the time value of money makes the postponement beneficial. For example, payment of compensation, rather than a distribution, creates a deduction that reduces taxable income and postpones the built-in gains tax.

EXAMPLE 49

Mundy, Inc., an S corporation converted from a C corporation, has built-in gain of $110,000 and taxable income of $120,000 before payment of salaries to its two shareholders. If Mundy pays at least $120,000 in salaries to the shareholders (rather than a distribution), its taxable income drops to zero, and the built-in gains tax is postponed. Thus, Mundy needs to keep the salaries as high as possible to postpone the built-in gains tax in future years and reap a benefit from the time value of money. Of course, paying the salaries may increase the payroll tax burden if the salaries are below FICA and FUTA limits. ■

Giving built-in gain property to a charitable organization does not trigger the built-in gains tax. To reduce or eliminate the built-in gains tax, built-in *loss* property may be sold in the same year that built-in gain property is sold. Generally, the taxpayer should sell built-in loss property in a year when an equivalent amount of built-in gain property is sold. Otherwise, the built-in loss could be wasted.

EXAMPLE 50

Green Corporation elects S status effective for calendar year 2010. As of January 1, 2010, Green's only asset has a basis of $40,000 and a fair market value of $100,000. If this asset is sold for $120,000 in 2011, Green recognizes an $80,000 gain, of which $60,000 is subject to the corporate built-in gains tax. The other $20,000 of gain is subject to the S corporation pass-through rules and is not subject to the corporate income tax.

Unless the taxpayer can show otherwise, any appreciation existing at the date of the sale or exchange is presumed to be preconversion built-in gain. Therefore, Green incurs a built-in gain of $80,000 unless it can prove that the $20,000 gain developed after the effective date of the election. ■

CONTROLLING ADJUSTMENTS AND PREFERENCE ITEMS

The individual alternative minimum tax (AMT) affects more taxpayers than ever before because the tax base has expanded and the difference between regular tax rates and the individual AMT rate has been narrowed. In an S corporation setting, tax preferences flow through proportionately to the shareholders, who, in computing the individual AMT, treat the preferences as if they were directly realized. Thus, the S corporation may not take advantage of the AMT exemption available to a small corporation, but there is no ACE adjustment. Further, if an S corporation has a built-in gain under § 1374, the entity does not pay an AMT on the transaction.

DOMESTIC PRODUCTION ACTIVITIES DEDUCTION

Domestic production gross receipts (DPGR), attributable cost of goods sold (CGS), and allocable deductions earned by the S corporation are passed through to the shareholders. These corporate-level DPGR, CGS, and allocable deductions are combined with any DPGR, CGS, and allocable deductions that the shareholder has from other sources.

An allocable portion of the S corporation's W–2 wages is passed through to the shareholder, but only those wages that are properly allocable to DPGR. See Chapter 3 for the calculation of the qualified domestic production activities deduction (DPAD).

EXAMPLE 51

An S corporation has $100,000 DPGR and $75,000 of wages, and its qualified production activities income (QPAI) is $25,000. Shareholder Kirby has a 50% interest in the S corporation. All expenses that reduce DPGR are from wages, and all wages paid relate to DPGR.

Kirby is allocated $12,500 of QPAI and $37,500 of wages. ■

The DPAD has no effect on a shareholder's stock basis. Further, an S corporation may qualify for the small business simplified overall method to apportion cost of goods sold and deductions between DPGR and non-DPGR at the entity level. The IRS may permit an S corporation to calculate a shareholder's share of QPAI at the entity level, to be combined with the shareholder's QPAI. A specific shareholder is not allowed to use another cost allocation method to reallocate the costs of the

S corporation, regardless of the method used by the specific shareholder to allocate or apportion costs.

TERMINATION ASPECTS

It is always advisable to avoid accumulated earnings and profits (AEP) in an S corporation. There is the ever-present danger of terminating the election because of excess passive investment income in three consecutive years. Further, the § 1375 penalty tax is imposed on excess passive net income. Thus, one should try to eliminate such AEP through a dividend distribution or liquidation of the S corporation with a subsequent reincorporation. If the AEP account is small, to eliminate the problem all of the shareholders may consent under § 1368(e)(3) to have distributions treated as made first from AEP rather than from the AAA (the AAA bypass election).

LIQUIDATION OF AN S CORPORATION

S corporations are subject to many of the same liquidation rules applicable to C corporations (refer to Chapter 6). In general, the distribution of appreciated property to S shareholders in complete liquidation is treated as if the property were sold to the shareholders in a taxable transaction. Unlike a C corporation, however, the S corporation itself incurs no incremental tax on the liquidation gains, because such gains flow through to the shareholders subject only to the built-in gains tax of § 1374. Any corporate gain increases the shareholder's stock basis by a like amount and reduces any gain realized by the shareholder when he or she receives the liquidation proceeds. Thus, an S corporation usually avoids the double tax that is imposed on C corporations. However, when an S corporation liquidates, all of its special tax attributes disappear (e.g., AAA, AEP, C corporation NOLs, suspended losses).

REFOCUS ON THE BIG PICTURE

USING A FLOW-THROUGH ENTITY TO ACHIEVE DEDUCTIBILITY OF LOSSES

As long as Smith and Jones, the owners of Cane, Inc., maintain C corporation status, they cannot deduct any NOLs that the business incurs on their individual tax returns. For the owners to deduct any future NOLs on their Forms 1040, Cane needs to be operated as a flow-through entity. The most logical alternatives are to make an S election or to become a limited liability company.

An S election may be appropriate for Cane. Cane should make a timely election on Form 2553 (see Appendix B), and both shareholders must consent to the election. The owners should make the election on or before the fifteenth day of the third month of the current year.

Normally, an S corporation does not pay any income tax because all items (including NOLs) flow through to the shareholders. A C corporation making an S election may be required to pay a built-in gains tax or a LIFO recapture tax. The base for the built-in gains tax includes any unrealized gain on appreciated assets held by Cane on the day the owners elect S status. The highest corporate rate is applied to the unrealized gain when any of the built-in gain assets are sold. If the corporation uses the LIFO inventory method, any LIFO recapture amount at the time of the S election is subject to a corporate-level tax.

Cane does not need to liquidate or engage in a tax-deferred reorganization when converting to an S corporation. An S corporation can have voting and nonvoting common stock, provided that all shares have the same economic rights to corporate income or loss. Data used to compute a DPAD flows through to the shareholders.

Cane might get rid of the tax-exempt income, which will not be reflected in AAA. Although it is reflected in stock basis, tax-exempt income (as part of OAA) is distributed to the shareholders only after the S corporation has distributed all of its C corporation earnings and profits.

KEY TERMS

Accumulated adjustments account (AAA), 12–15

Accumulated earnings and profits, 12–15

Built-in gains tax, 12–26

Bypass election, 12–17

Other adjustments account (OAA), 12–17

Passive investment income (PII), 12–11

Previously taxed income, 12-16

S corporation, 12–2

Small business corporation, 12–4

Subchapter S, 12–2

Voluntary revocation, 12–9

DISCUSSION QUESTIONS

1. **LO.1** Which of these apply to an S corporation?
   a. Alternative minimum tax.
   b. Accumulated earnings tax.
   c. Personal holding company tax.
   d. Flow-through of NOLs.
   e. Unlimited liability.

2. **LO.1** Distributions by an S corporation to its shareholders are always tax-free. Discuss this statement.

3. **LO.1** Why is an S corporation treated more favorably than a C corporation, relative to the Federal corporate income tax?

4. **LO.1** If shareholders have higher marginal income tax rates relative to the C corporation brackets, it always is desirable to be an S corporation. Discuss the validity of this statement.

5. **LO.1** What effects do C corporation NOLs have on an S corporation?

6. **LO.1** How are charitable contributions treated by an S corporation?

7. **LO.2** What requirements must an entity meet to elect S corporation status?

8. **LO.2** Would any of these items be considered a second class of stock for an S corporation?
   a. Voting preferred stock (with a preference on dividends).
   b. Treasury stock of another class.
   c. Phantom stock.
   d. Unexercised stock options.
   e. Warrants.
   f. Stock appreciation rights.
   g. Convertible debentures.

9. **LO.2** Outline the characteristics of an S corporation's *straight debt.*

10. **LO.2** Would any of these items be considered a second class of stock for an S corporation?
    a. Short-term unwritten advances from a shareholder that do not exceed $10,000 in the aggregate at any time during the corporation's taxable year.
    b. Debt that is held by shareholders in the same proportion as their stock holdings.
    c. Section 1244 stock.

11. **LO.2** Which of the following can be a shareholder of an S corporation?
    a. Limited liability partnership.
    b. Corporation.
    c. Nonresident alien.
    d. Estate.
    e. Charitable organization exempted from taxation.
    f. Roth IRA.
    g. Minor child.

ISSUE ID

COMMUNICATIONS

12. **LO.2, 11** Bob Roman, the major owner of an S corporation, approaches you for some tax planning help. He would like to exchange some real estate in a like-kind transaction under § 1031 for some real estate that may have some environmental liabilities. Prepare a letter to Bob outlining your suggestion. Bob's address is 8411 Huron Boulevard, West Chester, PA 19382.

ISSUE ID

13. **LO.2, 3** On March 2, the two 50% shareholders of a calendar year corporation decide to elect S status. One of the shareholders, Terry, purchased her stock from a previous shareholder (a nonresident alien) on January 18. Identify any potential problems for Terry or the corporation.

COMMUNICATIONS

14. **LO.4** Caleb Samford calls you and says that his two-person S corporation was involuntarily terminated in February 2010. He asks you if they can make a new S election now, in November 2011. Draft a memo for the file, outlining what you told Caleb.

15. **LO.5** Indicate whether each of the following items is available to an S corporation.
    a. Amortization of organizational expenditures.
    b. Dividends received deduction.
    c. Standard deduction.
    d. Personal exemption.
    e. Section 179 expense deduction.

16. **LO.6** Using the categories in the following legend, classify each transaction as a plus (+) or minus (−) on Schedule M-2 of Form 1120S. An answer might look like one of these: "+AAA" or "−OAA."

Legend		
AAA	=	Accumulated adjustments account
OAA	=	Other adjustments account
NA	=	No direct effect on Schedule M-2

    a. Receipt of tax-exempt interest income.
    b. Unreasonable compensation determined.
    c. Depreciation recapture income.
    d. Nontaxable life insurance proceeds.
    e. Expenses related to tax-exempt securities.
    f. Charitable contributions.
    g. Business gifts in excess of $25.
    h. Nondeductible fines and penalties.
    i. Selling expenses.

ISSUE ID

17. **LO.6, 11** Collett's S corporation has a small amount of accumulated earnings and profits (AEP), requiring the use of the more complex distribution rules. His accountant tells him that this AEP forces the maintenance of the AAA figure each year. Identify relevant tax issues facing Collett.

COMMUNICATIONS

18. **LO.6, 8** Scott Roberts owns 10% of an S corporation. He is confused with respect to the amounts of the corporate AAA and his stock basis. Write a brief memo to Scott identifying the key differences between AAA and an S shareholder's stock basis.

19. **LO.8** For each of the following independent statements, indicate whether the transaction will increase (+), decrease (−), or have no effect (*NE*) on the adjusted basis of a shareholder's stock in an S corporation.
    a. Expenses related to tax-exempt income.
    b. Long-term capital gain.
    c. Nonseparately computed loss.
    d. Section 1231 gain.
    e. Depletion *not* in excess of basis.
    f. Separately computed income.
    g. Nontaxable return-of-capital distribution by the corporation.
    h. Selling expenses.
    i. Business gifts in excess of $25.

j. Depreciation recapture income.
k. Dividends received by the S corporation.
l. LIFO recapture tax computed at the date of the S election.
m. Recovery of a bad debt previously deducted.
n. Short-term capital loss.
o. Corporate distribution out of AAA.

20. **LO.9** Sheila Jackson is a 50% shareholder in Washington, Inc., an S corporation. This year, Jackson's share of the Washington loss is $100,000. Jackson has income from several other sources. Identify at least four tax issues related to the effects of the S corporation loss on Jackson's tax return. **ISSUE ID**

21. **LO.1, 11** One of your clients is considering electing S status. Texas, Inc., is a six-year-old company with two equal shareholders, both of whom paid $30,000 for their stock. Going into 2011, Texas has a $110,000 NOL carryforward from prior years. Estimated income is $40,000 for 2011 and $25,000 for each of the next three years. Should Texas make an S election for 2011? **DECISION MAKING**

22. **LO.10** There is no advantage for an S corporation to have § 1244 stock. Discuss the validity of this statement.

23. **LO.6, 11** What is the purpose of the AAA bypass election?

PROBLEMS

24. **LO.5, 6** Sentilles, Inc., a calendar year S corporation, incurred the following items this year.

§ 1231 gain	$ 11,000
Tax-exempt interest income	7,000
Net sales	140,020
Depreciation recapture income	14,000
Long-term capital gain	20,000
Cost of goods sold	(42,000)
Administrative expenses	(15,000)
Depreciation expenses	(13,000)
Charitable contribution	(10,000)
Distributions to shareholders	(34,000)

a. Calculate Sentilles's nonseparately computed income.
b. How much ordinary income or loss is reported by Brittany Nelson, a 25% shareholder?

25. **LO.5, 6** Neely, Inc., a calendar year S corporation, incurred the following items this year.

Operating income	$100,400
Cost of goods sold	(40,000)
Depreciation expense	(10,000)
Administrative expenses	(5,000)
§ 1231 gain	21,000
Tax-exempt interest income	12,000
Dividends received	8,600
Depreciation recapture income	20,000
Short-term capital loss from stock sale	(6,000)
Long-term capital loss from stock sale	(4,000)
Long-term capital gain from stock sale	15,000
Charitable contributions	(4,500)

Jake Neely is a 40% shareholder of the S corporation throughout the year.
a. Calculate Jake's share of nonseparately computed income.
b. Calculate Jake's share of any net long-term capital gain.

26. **LO.5, 6** Whip, Inc., is a calendar-year S corporation. Whip's book income this year totals $90,000. Whip is owned equally by three shareholders. From supplemental data, you obtain the following information about items that are included in book income.

Selling expenses	($21,200)
Tax-exempt interest	2,200
Dividends received	9,000
§ 1231 gain	6,000
Depreciation recapture income	12,000
Recovery of bad debts	4,000
Long-term capital loss	(6,000)
Salary to owners (each)	(10,000)
Cost of goods sold	(95,000)
Distributions to shareholders	(6,300)

a. Compute Whip's Subchapter S income or loss for 2011.
b. How much ordinary income or loss is reported by Nicole, one of Whip's shareholders?
c. How much dividend income is reported on Nicole's Schedule K-1?

27. **LO.6, 8, 9** Betty is a shareholder in a calendar year S corporation. At the beginning of the year, her stock basis is $10,000, her share of AAA is $2,000, and her share of corporate AEP is $6,000. She receives a $6,000 distribution, and her share of S corporation items includes a $2,000 long-term capital gain and a $9,000 ordinary loss. Determine the effects of these events on AAA, stock basis, and AEP.

28. **LO.6** Noon, Inc., a calendar year S corporation, is equally owned by Ralph and Thomas. Thomas dies on April 1 (not a leap year), and his estate selects a March 31 fiscal year. Noon has $400,000 of income for January 1 through March 31 and $600,000 for the remainder of the year.
a. Determine how income is allocated to Ralph and Thomas under the pro rata approach.
b. Determine how income is allocated to Ralph and Thomas under the per-books method.

DECISION MAKING

29. **LO.5, 6** Goblins, Inc., is a calendar year S corporation. Its AAA balance is zero.
a. Goblins holds $90,000 of AEP. Tobias, the sole shareholder, has an adjusted basis of $80,000 in his stock. Determine the tax aspects if a $90,000 salary is paid to Tobias.
b. Same as part (a), except that Goblins pays Tobias a $90,000 dividend from AEP.

30. **LO.6, 7, 8** Tiger, Inc., a calendar year S corporation, is owned equally by four shareholders: Ann, Becky, Chris, and David. Tiger owns a piece of investment land that was purchased for $160,000 four years ago. On September 14, 2011, when the land is worth $240,000, it is distributed to David. Assuming that David's basis in his S corporation stock is $270,000 on the distribution date, discuss any tax ramifications.

31. **LO.6, 11** During the year, Wheel, a calendar year S corporation in Stillwater, Oklahoma, generates the following AMT items: a positive adjustment of $66,000 for mining exploration costs, an excess depletion tax preference of $96,000, and a positive certified pollution control facility adjustment of $36,000. The firm's positive ACE adjustment is $102,000. If Pam Epstein is a one-third Wheel shareholder, what effect do these items have on her individual tax return?

COMMUNICATIONS

32. **LO.6, 8, 9, 11** In 2011, Spence, Inc., a calendar year S corporation, generates an ordinary loss of $110,000 and makes a distribution of $140,000 to its sole shareholder, Storm Nelson. Nelson's stock basis at the beginning of the year is $200,000. Write a memo to your senior manager, Aaron McMullin, discussing the tax treatment of Spence's activities.

33. **LO.6** Lonergan, Inc., a calendar year S corporation in Athens, Georgia, had a balance in AAA of $200,000 and AEP of $110,000 on December 31, 2011. During 2012, Lonergan, Inc., distributes $140,000 to its shareholders, while sustaining an ordinary loss of $120,000. Calculate the balance in Lonergan's AAA and AEP accounts at the end of 2012.

34. **LO.6** If the beginning balance in Talker, Inc.'s OAA is $3,900, and the following transactions occur, what is Talker's ending OAA balance?

Depreciation recapture income	$21,000
Payroll tax penalty	(4,200)
Tax-exempt interest	5,300
Nontaxable life insurance proceeds	50,000
Life insurance premiums paid (nondeductible)	(2,800)

35. **LO.6** Stockstill, Inc., a calendar year S corporation, holds an AAA balance of $715,000 at the beginning of 2011. During the year the following items occur.

Sales income	$206,000
Loss from real estate operations	(5,000)
Officers' life insurance proceeds	100,000
Dividend income	17,000
Interest income	3,000
Charitable contributions	(22,000)
§ 179 depreciation expense	(2,500)
Administrative expenses	(41,000)
Premiums paid for officers' life insurance	(3,600)
Cash distribution to shareholders	(69,220)

Calculate Stockstill's ending AAA balance.

36. **LO.6, 7, 8** Money, Inc., a calendar year S corporation in Denton, Texas, has two unrelated shareholders, each owning 50% of the stock. Both shareholders have a $400,000 stock basis as of January 1, 2011. At the beginning of 2011, Money has AAA of $300,000 and AEP of $600,000. During 2011, Money has operating income of $100,000. At the end of the year, Money distributes securities worth $1 million, with an adjusted basis of $800,000. Determine the tax effects of these transactions.

37. **LO.6, 7, 8** Assume the same facts as in Problem 36, except that the two shareholders consent to an AAA bypass election.

38. **LO.8, 9** At the beginning of 2010, Christine Wheat has a basis of $5,000 in her stock of a calendar year S corporation, Zhou, Inc. She holds no debt of the S corporation. During 2010, Wheat's total share of Zhou's losses and deductions is $16,000, consisting of $10,000 of ordinary loss and $6,000 of nondeductible, noncapital expenses. For 2011, Wheat's share of Zhou's ordinary income is $12,000. Assuming no Reg. § 1.1367–1(g) election, how are these facts treated by Christine Wheat?

39. **LO.8, 9** Assume the same facts as in Problem 38, except that a Reg. § 1.1367–1(g) election is made. How does your answer change?

40. **LO.8** Jeff, a 52% owner of an S corporation, has a stock basis of zero at the beginning of the year. Jeff's basis in a $10,000 loan made to the corporation and evidenced by a corporate note has been reduced to zero by pass-through losses. During the year, his net share of the corporate taxable income is $11,000. At the end of the year, Jeff receives a $15,000 distribution. Discuss the tax effects of the distribution.

41. **LO.8** Assume the same facts as in Problem 40, except that there is no $15,000 distribution, but the corporation repays the loan principal to Jeff. Discuss the tax effects.

42. **LO.8** Assume the same facts as in Problem 40, except that Jeff's share of corporate taxable income is only $8,000, and there is no distribution. However, the corporation repays the $10,000 loan principal to Jeff. Discuss the tax effects. Assume there was no corporate note (i.e., only an account payable). Does this change your answer?

43. **LO.5, 6, 11** Red Lion, Inc., is an S corporation with a sizable amount of AEP from a C corporation year. The S corporation has $400,000 investment income and $400,000 investment expense in 2011. The company makes cash distributions to enable its sole shareholder to pay her taxes. What are the tax aspects to consider? **ISSUE ID**

44. **LO.6, 9** At the beginning of the year, Ann and Becky own equally all of the stock of Whitman, Inc., an S corporation. Whitman generates a $120,000 loss for the year (not a leap year). On the 189th day of the year, Ann sells her half of the Whitman stock to her son, Scott. How much of the $120,000 loss, if any, belongs to Scott?

45. **LO.6, 9** In Problem 44, how much of the Whitman loss belongs to Ann and Becky, assuming Becky's stock basis is $41,300?

COMMUNICATIONS

46. **LO.5, 6, 8, 9** A calendar year S corporation has an ordinary loss of $80,000 and a capital loss of $20,000. Ms. Freiberg owns 30% of the corporate stock and has a $24,000 basis in her stock. Determine the amounts of the ordinary loss and capital loss, if any, that flow through to Ms. Freiberg. Prepare a tax memo for the files.

47. **LO.5, 6, 8** Savoy, Inc., of Auburn, Alabama, is an accrual basis S corporation with three equal shareholders. The three cash basis shareholders have the following stock basis at the beginning of the year: Andre, $12,000; Crum, $22,000; and Barbara, $28,000. Savoy reports the following income and expense items.

Operating loss	($30,000)
Short-term capital gain	37,500
Long-term capital loss	(6,000)
Nondeductible fees and penalties	3,000

The electing corporation distributes $5,000 cash to each of the shareholders during the tax year. Calculate the shareholders' stock bases at the end of the year.

48. **LO.10** Rodeo, Inc., a cash basis S corporation in College Station, Texas, formerly was a C corporation. Rodeo has the following assets and liabilities on January 1, 2011, the date the S election is made.

	Adjusted Basis	Fair Market Value
Cash	$ 200,000	$ 200,000
Accounts receivable	–0–	105,000
Equipment	110,000	100,000
Land	1,800,000	2,500,000
Accounts payable	–0–	110,000

During 2011, Rodeo collects the accounts receivable and pays the accounts payable. The land is sold for $3 million, and taxable income for the year is $590,000. What is Rodeo's built-in gains tax?

49. **LO.10** In 2011, the excess net passive income of Cut-N-Shooters, Inc., an S corporation in Cut-N-Shoot, Texas, is $32,000. Cut-N-Shooters holds $50,000 of accumulated earnings and profits from a C corporation year, and it reports AMT adjustments of $17,000 this year. Calculate any passive investment income penalty tax.

ISSUE ID

50. **LO.5, 6, 11** Bonnie and Clyde each own one-third of a fast-food restaurant, and their 13-year-old daughter owns the other shares. Both parents work full-time in the restaurant, but the daughter works infrequently. Neither Bonnie nor Clyde receives a salary during the year, when the ordinary income of the S corporation is $180,000. An IRS agent estimates that reasonable salaries for Bonnie, Clyde, and the daughter are $30,000, $35,000, and $10,000, respectively. What adjustments would you expect the IRS to impose upon these taxpayers?

COMMUNICATIONS

51. **LO.11** Friedman, Inc., an S corporation, holds some highly appreciated land and inventory, and some marketable securities that have declined in value. It anticipates a sale of these assets and a complete liquidation of the company over the next two years. Arnold Schwartz, the CFO, calls you, asking how to treat these transactions. Prepare a tax memo indicating what you told Arnold in the phone conversation.

52. **LO.6, 10** Renae Crochet sold 1,000 shares of her stock in Blue, Inc., an S corporation. She sold the stock for $12,750, after she had owned it for four years. Renae had paid $97,000 for the stock, which was issued under § 1244. Renae is single and is the original owner of the 1,000 shares. Determine the appropriate tax treatment of any gain or loss on the stock sale.

DECISION MAKING

53. **LO.11** Opal is the owner of all of the shares of an S corporation. Opal is considering receiving a salary of $80,000 from the business. She will pay 7.65% FICA taxes on the salary, and the S corporation will pay the same amount of FICA tax. If Opal reduces her salary to $60,000 and takes an additional $20,000 as a distribution, how much total tax could be saved?

54. **LO.10** Blue Corporation elects S status effective for calendar year 2010. As of January 1, 2010, Blue holds two assets.

	Adjusted Basis	Fair Market Value
Land	$50,000	$110,000
IBM Stock	55,000	40,000

Blue sells the land in 2011 for $120,000. Calculate Blue's recognized built-in gain, if any, in 2011.

55. **LO.1, 6, 8, 9, 11** Orange, Inc., a calendar year corporation in Clemson, South Carolina, elects S corporation status for 2011. The company generated a $74,000 NOL in 2010 and another NOL of $43,000 in 2011. Orange recorded no other transactions for the year.

At all times in 2010 and 2011, the stock of the corporation is owned by the same four shareholders, each owning 25% of the stock. Pete, one of the shareholders, holds a $6,020 basis in the Orange stock at the beginning of 2011. Identify the Federal income tax issues that face Pete.

TAX RETURN PROBLEMS

1. Jacob Mitchell (123–45–6781) and Ryan Marshall (123–45–6782) are 70% and 30% owners of Special Treats, Inc. (11–1111111), a candy company located at 145 Avenue A, Dime Box, TX 77823. The company's S corporation election was made on January 15, 2005. The following information was taken from the income statement for 2010.

H&R BLOCK At Home

Interest income	$ 100,000
Gross sales receipts	1,100,000
Beginning inventory	9,600
Direct labor	103,100
Direct materials purchased	178,200
Other direct costs	49,400
Ending inventory	3,500
Salaries and wages	42,100
Officers' salaries	50,000
Repairs	16,100
Depreciation	15,300
Interest expense	5,200
Rent expense	40,000
Taxes	15,100
Charitable contributions (cash)	20,000
Advertising expenses	30,000
Other deductions	50,000
Book income	$ 579,400

A comparative book-basis balance sheet appears below.

	January 1, 2010	December 31, 2010
Cash	$ 47,800	$?
Accounts receivable	93,100	123,100
Inventories	9,600	3,500
Prepaid expenses	8,300	17,600
Building and equipment	138,200	185,300
Accumulated depreciation	(84,200)	?
Land	2,000	2,000
Total assets	$214,800	$719,200

	January 1, 2010	December 31, 2010
Accounts payable	$ 42,500	$ 72,300
Notes payable (less than 1 year)	4,500	2,100
Notes payable (more than 1 year)	26,700	24,300
Capital stock	30,000	30,000
Retained earnings	111,100	?
Total liabilities and capital	$214,800	$719,200

Jacob's accounting firm provides the following additional information.

Distributions to shareholders	$100,000

Using the above information, prepare a complete Form 1120S and a Schedule K–1 for Jacob Mitchell, 145 Avenue A, Dime Box, TX 77823. If any information is missing, make realistic assumptions and list them.

2. John Jacobs (111–11–1111), Sam Franklin (123–45–6789), and Sandra Moore (987–65–4321) are, respectively, 55%, 35%, and 10% owners of Textiles, Inc. (12–3456789), a textile manufacturing company located at 4044 Main Street, Kannapolis, NC 28083. The company's first S election was made on January 1, 1992. The following information was taken from the financial income statement for 2010.

Business income	$ 38,000
Interest income	230,000
Tax-exempt interest income	37,000
Distributive partnership income	9,000,000
Gross sales	111,831,710
Beginning inventory	500,000
Direct labor	41,200,000
Direct materials purchased	24,800,000
Ending inventory	1,100,000
Taxes (payroll)	3,923,500
Contributions to United Fund (public charity)	44,500
Meals and entertainment (before 50% limitation)	79,000
Fines on illegal activities	34,000
Life insurance premiums (Textiles is the beneficiary)	98,000
Compensation to shareholder-officers (proportionate to ownership)	2,820,910
Salaries and wages	7,500,000
Interest expense	1,722,200
Bad debt expense	820,000
Repairs	1,500,000
Depreciation (same amount for book and Federal income taxes)	1,615,400
Advertising	425,000
Pension plan contributions	600,000
Employee benefit programs	287,500
Amortization expenses	820,000
Other deductions	63,700
Book income	$39,383,000

A comparative book-basis balance sheet appears below.

	January 1, 2010	December 31, 2010
Cash	$ 4,784,000	$?
Accounts receivable	9,310,000	15,313,600
Inventories	500,000	1,100,000
Prepaid expenses	1,033,300	758,200
Loans to shareholders	31,300	72,700
Building and trucks	13,820,300	24,434,800
Accumulated depreciation	(8,423,500)	?
Land	180,900	1,651,300
Life insurance	1,156,600	1,834,400
Total assets	$22,392,900	$41,451,800
Accounts payable	$ 4,979,700	$ 8,296,500
Notes payable (less than one year)	512,200	898,900
Loans from shareholders	15,575,100	19,196,700
Notes payable (more than one year)	2,182,100	3,383,500
Loan on life insurance	531,200	1,620,600
Capital stock	100,300	100,300
Paid-in capital	955,900	955,900
Retained earnings	(831,400)	?
Treasury stock	(1,612,200)	(1,612,200)
Total liabilities and capital	$22,392,900	$41,451,800

You must determine whether a Schedule M-3 is to be prepared by the entity. If a Schedule M-3 is required, you can omit Form 8916-A.

Textiles's accounting firm and the corporate books and records provide the following additional information.

Distributions to shareholders	$18,900,000
Income from U.S. partnership	
Distributive share	9,000,000
Ordinary income	4,800,000
Charitable contributions	3,000,000
Accumulated adjustments account (AAA), beginning balance	(831,400)
Other adjustments account (OAA), beginning balance	–0–

- A Canadian subsidiary shows net income of $6 million, assets of $44 million, and liabilities of $12 million on Textiles' financial statement. The subsidiary is not an includible corporation.
- Salaries and wages include $1.2 million of deferred compensation.
- Of the amortization amount, only $90,000 is deductible currently.
- Of the bad debt expense, $230,000 is not deductible this year.
- Of other expenses, $3,700 is permanently not deductible.

Using the above information, prepare a complete Form 1120S and a Schedule K–1 for John Jacobs (1245 Brantley Road, Kannapolis, NC 28083). If any information is missing, make realistic assumptions and list them.

RESEARCH PROBLEMS

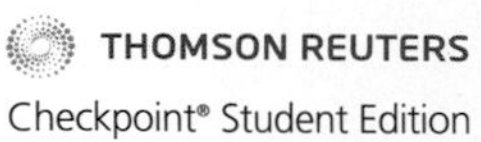

Checkpoint® Student Edition

Note: Solutions to Research Problems can be prepared by using the **Checkpoint® Student Edition** online research product, which is available to accompany this text. It is also possible to prepare solutions to the Research Problems by using tax research materials found in a standard tax library.

Research Problem 1. The tax treatment of fringe benefits for more-than-2% shareholder-employees of S corporations is less favorable than that for nonowners or employees of some other entities. What fringe benefits are subject to this limitation? What fringe benefits escape this limitation?

COMMUNICATIONS

Research Problem 2. Locate and summarize in an e-mail to your instructor the holdings of these items involving S corporations.

a. Ltr.Rul. 200834007.
b. TAM 200747018.
c. *Edward W. Arnold,* T.C.Memo 2005–256.
d. § 1374(b)(3)(B).

Research Problem 3. Bushong, Inc., a calendar year S corporation, has a "tax cash-flow" provision in its shareholder agreement. Bushong must make annual distributions by the December 31 following a tax year in which there is an income pass-through. Each distribution must be in an amount sufficient to enable shareholders to pay their state and Federal income taxes on the pass-through.

The agreement also provides that if an audit adjustment is made to items reported on the Schedule K–1, Bushong can make a discretionary distribution to handle the increased taxes resulting from the adjustment.

The shareholders want to change the agreement. Under the proposal, if an audit adjustment is made and Bushong makes a discretionary payment, the payment would be in accordance with the shareholders' ownership shares during the tax year the adjustment, rather than as of the distribution date.

Would the proposal create a second class of stock and terminate Bushong's S election?

COMMUNICATIONS

Research Problem 4. Sam is selling his S corporation, Superbody Fitness, Inc. He will receive 80% cash and 20% of another S corporation fitness center. As part of this transaction, should Sam liquidate Superbody Fitness? Outline your analysis in an e-mail to your instructor.

INTERNET *activity*

Use the tax resources of the Internet to address the following questions. Do not restrict your search to the Web, but include a review of newsgroups and general reference materials, practitioner sites and resources, primary sources of the tax law, chat rooms and discussion groups, and other opportunities.

Research Problem 5. Develop a list of the pros and cons for a proposal by Congress to restructure the Federal income tax law for flow-through entities and integrate Subchapters K and S.

COMMUNICATIONS

Research Problem 6. Go to the Internet site of a newspaper or business magazine and find a case study of how to start a small business and choose the best tax entity (e.g., C corporation, S corporation, etc.). Summarize your findings in an e-mail to your instructor.

COMMUNICATIONS

Research Problem 7. Determine how the recent health care legislation treats S corporations with respect to the self-employment tax. Present your findings in an e-mail of no more than 250 words to your instructor.

COMMUNICATIONS

Research Problem 8. Summarize in no more than five PowerPoint slides the purpose and provisions of the S Corporation Modernization Act of 2009.

CHAPTER 13

Comparative Forms of Doing Business

LEARNING OBJECTIVES

After completing Chapter 13, you should be able to:

LO.1

Identify the principal legal and tax forms for conducting a business.

LO.2

Appreciate the relative importance of nontax factors in making business decisions.

LO.3

Distinguish between the forms for conducting a business according to whether they are subject to single taxation or double taxation.

LO.4

Identify techniques for avoiding double taxation and for controlling the entity tax.

LO.5

Understand the applicability and the effect of the conduit and entity concepts on contributions to the entity, operations of the entity, entity distributions, passive activity loss and at-risk rules, and special allocations.

LO.6

Analyze the effect of the disposition of a business on the owners and the entity for each of the forms for conducting a business.

LO.7

Compare the tax consequences of the various forms of doing business.

OUTLINE

For the latest in changes to tax legislation, visit **www.cengage.com/taxation/swft.**

THE BIG PICTURE

SELECTION OF A TAX ENTITY FORM

Milly and Doug are going to start a dot.com business in which they both will participate on an active basis. They have an adequate amount in savings to finance the business. Limited liability is a significant factor for the business, but equally important is the minimization of income taxes. They have narrowed the choice of business forms to a C corporation or a general partnership. Annual earnings of the business before taxes are expected to be $200,000, and any after-tax profit will be distributed to Milly and Doug. Assume that both Milly and Doug are single and that their marginal tax rate is 28 percent. Advise Milly and Doug on the choice of business form. **Read the chapter and formulate your response**.

A variety of factors, both tax and nontax, affect the choice of the form of business entity. The form that is appropriate at one point in the life of an entity and its owners may not be appropriate at a different time.

EXAMPLE 1

Eva is a tax practitioner in Kentwood, the Dairy Center of the South. Many of her clients are dairy farmers. She recently had tax planning discussions with two of her clients, Jesse, a Line Creek dairy farmer, and Larry, a Spring Creek dairy farmer.

Jesse recently purchased his dairy farm. He is 52 years old and just retired after 30 years of service as a chemical engineer at an oil refinery in Baton Rouge. Eva recommended that he incorporate his dairy farm and elect S corporation status for Federal income tax purposes.

Larry has owned his dairy farm since 2005. He inherited it from his father. At that time, Larry retired after 20 years of service in the U.S. Air Force. He has a master's degree in Agricultural Economics from LSU. His farm is incorporated, and shortly after the date of incorporation, Eva had advised him to elect S corporation status. She now advises him to revoke the S election. ■

Example 1 raises a number of interesting questions. Does Eva advise all of her dairy farmer clients to initially elect S corporation status? Why has she advised Larry to revoke his S election? Will she advise Jesse to revoke his S election at some time in the future? Will she advise Larry to make another S election at some time in the future? Why did she not advise Larry to terminate his corporate status? Could Larry and Jesse have achieved the same tax consequences for their dairy farms if they had operated the farms as partnerships instead of incorporating? Does the way the farm is acquired (e.g., purchase versus inheritance) affect the choice of business entity for tax purposes?

This chapter provides the basis for comparatively analyzing the tax consequences of business decisions for five types of tax entities (sole proprietorship, partnership, corporation, S corporation, and limited liability company). Understanding the comparative tax consequences for the different types of entities and being able to apply them effectively to specific fact patterns can lead to effective tax planning, which is exactly what Eva was doing with her two clients. As the following discussion illustrates, a variety of potential answers may exist for each of the questions raised by Eva's advice.

13.1 Forms of Doing Business

LO.1

Identify the principal legal and tax forms for conducting a business.

The principal *legal* forms for conducting a business entity are a sole proprietorship, partnership, limited liability company, and corporation.[1] From a *Federal income tax* perspective, these same forms are available with the corporate form being divided into two types (S corporation and C or regular corporation). In most instances, the legal form and the tax form are the same. In some cases, however, the IRS may attempt to tax a business entity as a form different from its legal form. This reclassification normally takes one of two possible approaches:

- The IRS ignores the corporate form and taxes the owners directly (the corporate entity lacks substance).
- The IRS ignores the partnership form and taxes the partnership as if it were a corporation.

The IRS may try to reclassify a corporation for several reasons. One reason is to prevent taxpayers from taking advantage of the potential disparity between the corporate and individual tax rates. Although the highest corporate statutory rate and the highest individual statutory rate are now the same (35 percent), the specific corporate and individual rates applicable to a particular taxpayer may differ. For example, an individual may be in the 35 percent bracket, and the corporation may be in the 15 percent, 25 percent, or 34 percent bracket. Another reason for taxing the owners directly is to make them ineligible for favorable taxation of certain fringe benefits (see the subsequent discussion in Favorable Treatment of Certain Fringe Benefits).

In the case of a partnership, reclassification of a partnership as if it were a corporation can subject the business entity to double taxation. In addition, the resultant loss of conduit status prevents partnership losses from being passed through to the tax returns of the partners.

The taxpayer generally is bound for tax purposes by the legal form that is selected. A major statutory exception to this is the ability of an S corporation to receive tax treatment similar to that of a partnership.[2] In addition, taxpayers sometimes can control which set of tax rules will apply to their business operations. The "check-the-box" Regulations provide an elective procedure that enables certain entities to be classified as partnerships for Federal income tax purposes even though they have corporate characteristics.[3] These Regulations have greatly simplified the determination of entity classification.

A **limited liability company (LLC)** is a hybrid business form that combines the corporate characteristic of limited liability for the owners with the tax characteristics of a partnership.[4] All of the states now permit this legal form for conducting a business.

The most frequently cited benefit of an LLC is the limited liability of the owners. Compared to the other forms of ownership, LLCs offer additional benefits but also certain disadvantages. Refer to the coverage of the advantages and disadvantages of an LLC in Chapter 11 on p. 11-36.

An individual conducting a sole proprietorship files Schedule C of Form 1040. If more than one trade or business is conducted, a separate Schedule C is filed for each trade or business. A partnership files Form 1065. A corporation files Form 1120, and an S corporation files Form 1120S. An LLC that has elected to be taxed as a partnership files Form 1065.

[1] A business entity can also be conducted in the form of a trust or estate. These two forms are not discussed in this chapter. See the discussion of the income taxation of trusts and estates in Chapter 20.

[2] §§ 1361 and 1362.

[3] Reg. §§ 301.7701–1 through –4, and –6. Note that if the business has only one owner, the elective procedure enables the entity to be classified as a sole proprietorship.

[4] Depending on state law, an LLC may be organized as a limited liability corporation or a limited liability partnership.

TAX in the NEWS — PROFESSIONAL SERVICE FIRMS AND ORGANIZATIONAL FORM

Many professional service firms (e.g., accountants, architects, lawyers) have chosen to become limited liability partnerships (LLPs). In the accounting profession, this includes all of the Big 4 (i.e., Deloitte, Ernst & Young, KPMG, and PricewaterhouseCoopers) and most regional and local accounting firms.

An LLP helps to provide protection for the purely personal assets of the partners. Under the LLP organizational structure, the only partners whose personal assets are at risk to pay a judgment are those actually involved in the negligence or wrongdoing at issue. Note, however, that the entity is still responsible for the full judgment. Thus, the capital of the entity is still at risk.

13.2 NONTAX FACTORS

LO.2

Appreciate the relative importance of nontax factors in making business decisions.

Taxes are only one of many factors to consider in making any business decision. Above all, any business decision should make economic sense.

EXAMPLE 2

Albert is considering investing $10,000 in a limited partnership. He projects that he will be able to deduct the $10,000 within the next two years (his share of partnership losses). Since Albert's marginal tax rate is 35%, the deductions will produce a positive cash-flow effect of $3,500 ($10,000 × 35%). However, there is a substantial risk that he will not recover any of his original investment. If this occurs, his negative cash flow from the investment in the limited partnership is $6,500 ($10,000 – $3,500). Albert must decide if the investment makes economic sense. ■

CAPITAL FORMATION

The ability of an entity to raise capital is a factor that must be considered. A sole proprietorship is subject to obvious limitations. Compared to the sole proprietorship, the partnership has a greater opportunity to raise funds through the pooling of owner resources.

EXAMPLE 3

Adam and Beth decide to form a partnership, AB. Adam contributes cash of $200,000, and Beth contributes land with an adjusted basis of $60,000 and a fair market value of $200,000. The partnership is going to construct an apartment building at a cost of $800,000. AB pledges the land and the building to secure a loan of $700,000. ■

The limited partnership offers even greater potential than the general partnership form because a limited partnership can secure funds from investors (limited partners).

EXAMPLE 4

Carol and Dave form a limited partnership, CD. Carol contributes cash of $200,000, and Dave contributes land with an adjusted basis of $60,000 and a fair market value of $200,000. The partnership is going to construct a shopping center at a cost of $5 million. Included in this cost is the purchase price of $800,000 for land adjacent to that contributed by Dave. Thirty limited partnership interests are sold for $100,000 each to raise $3 million. CD also pledges the shopping center (including the land) and obtains nonrecourse creditor financing of $2 million. ■

Both the § 465 at-risk provision and the § 469 passive activity loss provision have reduced the tax attractiveness of investments in real estate, particularly in the limited partnership form. In effect, the tax consequences have a critical effect on the economic consequences.[5]

Of the different forms of business entities, the corporate form offers the greatest ease and potential for obtaining owner financing because it can issue additional shares of stock. The ultimate examples of this form are the large public companies that are listed on the stock exchanges.

LIMITED LIABILITY

A corporation offers its owners limited liability under state law. This absence of personal liability on the part of the owners is the most frequently cited advantage of the corporate form.

EXAMPLE 5

Ed, Fran, and Gabriella each invest $25,000 for all the shares of stock of Brown Corporation. Brown obtains creditor financing of $100,000. Brown is the defendant in a personal injury suit resulting from an accident involving one of its delivery trucks. The court awards a judgment of $2.5 million to the plaintiff. The award exceeds Brown's insurance coverage by $1.5 million. Even though the judgment will probably result in Brown's bankruptcy, the shareholders will have no personal liability for the unpaid corporate debts. ■

Limited liability is not available to all corporations. For many years, state laws did not permit professional individuals (e.g., accountants, attorneys, architects, and physicians) to incorporate. Even though professionals are now allowed to incorporate, the statutes do not provide limited liability for the performance of professional services.

Even if state law provides for limited liability, the shareholders of small corporations may have to forgo this benefit. Quite often, such a corporation may be unable to obtain external financing (e.g., a bank loan) unless the shareholders guarantee the loan.

The limited partnership form provides limited liability to the limited partners. Their liability is limited to the amount invested plus any additional amount that they agreed to invest. However, the general partner (or partners) has unlimited liability.

EXAMPLE 6

Hazel, the general partner, invests $250,000 in HIJ, a limited partnership. Iris and Jane, the limited partners, each invest $50,000. While the potential loss for Iris and Jane is limited to $50,000 each, Hazel's liability is unlimited. ■

Indirectly, it may be possible to provide the general partner with limited liability by having a corporation as the general partner (see Figure 13.1). When the entity is structured this way, the general partner (the corporation) has limited its liability under the corporate statutes. Therefore, individual A is protected from personal liability by being merely the shareholder of Corporation A. Prior to the issuance of the check-the-box Regulations, it was necessary to structure the entity very carefully in order to avoid the limited partnership being classified as an association and taxed as a corporation. With the check-the-box Regulations, the limited partnership depicted in Figure 13.1 can be taxed as a partnership.[6]

OTHER FACTORS

Other nontax factors may be significant in selecting an organization form including the following:

- Estimated life of the business.
- Number of owners and their roles in the management of the business.
- Freedom of choice in transferring ownership interests.
- Organizational formality including the related cost and extent of government regulation.

[5]See the related discussions in Chapters 10 and 11. For a comprehensive discussion of these provisions, see Chapter 11 in *South-Western Federal Taxation: Individual Income Taxes.*

[6]See the discussions of limited partnerships in Chapter 11. Also see Rev.Proc. 89–12, 1989–1 C.B. 798 and Rev.Rul. 88–76, 1988–2 C.B. 360.

FIGURE 13.1 Limited Partnership with a Corporate General Partner

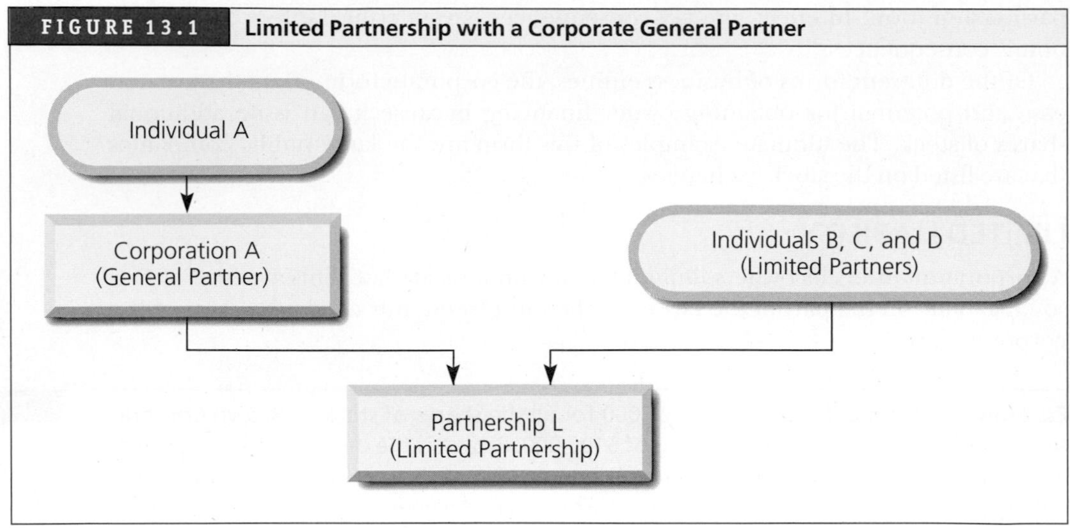

13.3 Single versus Double Taxation

LO.3

Distinguish between the forms for conducting a business according to whether they are subject to single taxation or double taxation.

OVERALL IMPACT ON ENTITY AND OWNERS

The sole proprietorship, partnership, and LLC are subject to *single* taxation. This result occurs because the owner(s) and the entity generally are not considered separate for tax purposes. Thus, the tax liability is levied at the owner level rather than at the entity level.

On the other hand, the corporate form is subject to *double* taxation. This is frequently cited as the major tax disadvantage of the corporate form. Under double taxation, the entity is taxed on the earnings of the corporation, and the owners are taxed on distributions to the extent they are made from corporate earnings. If the corporation is a personal service corporation (see Chapter 2), the corporation is subject to a flat tax rate of 35 percent.

The S corporation provides a way to attempt to avoid double taxation and to subject the earnings to a lower tax rate (the actual individual tax rate may be lower than the actual corporate tax rate). However, the ownership structure of an S corporation is restricted in both the number and type of shareholders. In addition, statutory exceptions subject the entity to taxation in certain circumstances. To the extent these exceptions apply, double taxation may result. Finally, the distribution policy of the S corporation may encounter difficulties with the *wherewithal to pay* concept.

EXAMPLE 7

Hawk Corporation has been operating as an S corporation since it began its business two years ago. For both of the prior years, Hawk incurred a tax loss. Hawk has taxable income of $75,000 for 2011 and expects that its earnings will increase each year in the foreseeable future. Part of this earnings increase will result from Hawk's expansion into other communities in the state. Since most of this expansion will be financed internally, no dividend distributions will be made to the shareholders.

Assuming all of Hawk's shareholders are in the 33% tax bracket, their tax liability for 2011 will be $24,750 ($75,000 × 33%). Although the S corporation election will avoid double taxation, the shareholders will have a wherewithal to pay problem. In addition, the actual tax liability for 2011 would have been less if Hawk had not been an S corporation [(15% × $50,000) + (25% × $25,000) = $13,750]. ■

The data in Example 7 can be used to illustrate two additional tax concepts. First, the current wherewithal to pay problem could be resolved by terminating the S corporation election. The tax liability would then be imposed at the corporate level. Since the

GLOBAL
Tax Issues

Tax Rates and Economic Activity

Tax rates affect economic activity. The maximum corporate income tax rates for selected countries are as follows:

Country	Tax Rate
France	33.33%
Germany	33%*
Hong Kong	16.5%
Japan	30%
Republic of Ireland	12.5%
Russia	20%
Singapore	18%
United States	35%**
Vietnam	25%
Industrial nations' average	27%

*Standard rate of 15% is increased to 33% by the trade tax and the solidarity tax.
**Plus state average of 4.3%.

Most of these countries except the United States have recently reduced their corporate tax rates. The primary motivation for doing so was to increase the country's attractiveness as a location for foreign investment.

corporation does not intend to make any dividend distributions, double taxation at the present time would be avoided. Terminating the election will also reduce the overall shareholder-corporation tax liability by $11,000 ($24,750 − $13,750).[7] Second, tax decisions on the form of business organization should consider more than the current taxable year. If the S election is terminated, another election will not be available for five years. If the earnings exceed the expansion needs, Hawk could encounter an accumulated earnings tax problem (at a 15 percent tax rate) if it is a C corporation. Thus, the decision to revoke the election should have at least a five-year time frame. Perhaps a better solution would be to retain the election and distribute enough dividends to the S corporation shareholders to enable them to pay the shareholder tax liability.

Two other variables that relate to the adverse effect of double taxation are the timing and form of corporate distributions. If no distributions are made in the short run, then only single taxation occurs in the short run.[8] To the extent that double taxation does occur in the future, the cash-flow effect should be discounted to the present. Second, when the distribution is made, is it in the form of a dividend or a return of capital (a stock redemption or a complete liquidation)?[9]

EXAMPLE 8

Gray Corporation has taxable income of $100,000 for 2011. Gray's tax liability is $22,250. All of Gray's shareholders are in the 33% bracket. If dividends of $77,750 are distributed in 2011, the shareholders will have a tax liability of $11,663 ($77,750 × 15%), assuming the dividends are qualified dividends. The combined corporation-shareholder tax liability is $33,913 ($22,250 + $11,663) for a combined effective tax rate of 33.9%. ■

[7]The absence of distributions to shareholders could create an accumulated earnings tax problem under § 531. However, as long as earnings are used to finance expansion, the "reasonable needs" provision will be satisfied, and the corporation will avoid any accumulated earnings tax.

[8]This assumes there is no accumulated earnings tax problem. See the subsequent discussion of distributions in Minimizing Double Taxation.

[9]See the coverage of dividends in Chapter 5 and the coverage of stock redemptions and complete liquidations in Chapter 6.

FIGURE 13.2 Bar Graph Illustration of Dividend versus Stock Redemption

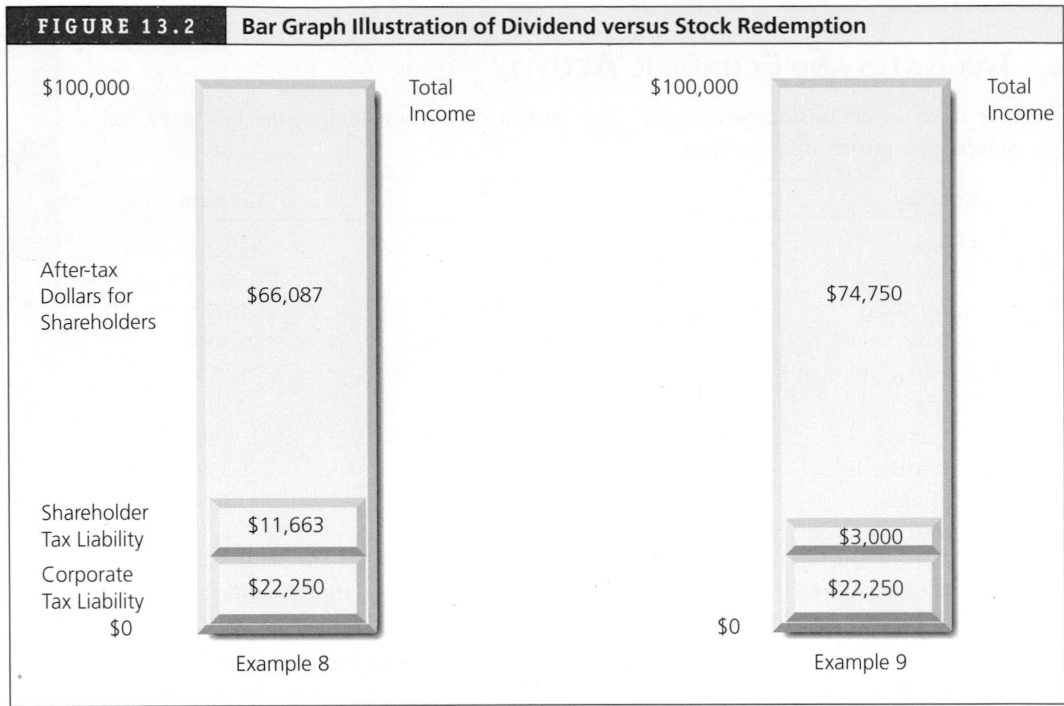

EXAMPLE 9

Assume the same facts as in Example 8, except that the form of the distribution is a stock redemption and the basis for the redeemed shares is $57,750. The shareholders have a recognized gain of $20,000 and a tax liability of $3,000 ($20,000 × 15% beneficial capital gain rate). The combined corporation-shareholder tax liability is $25,250 ($22,250 + $3,000) for a total effective tax rate of 25.25%. ■

The differences in the tax consequences in Examples 8 and 9 are even more obvious when illustrated in bar graph form (see Figure 13.2).

ALTERNATIVE MINIMUM TAX

All of the forms of business are directly or indirectly subject to the alternative minimum tax (AMT).[10] For the sole proprietorship and the C corporation, the effect is direct (the AMT liability calculation is attached to the tax form that reports the entity's taxable income—Form 1040 or Form 1120). For the partnership, LLC, and S corporation, the effect is indirect (the tax preferences and adjustments are passed through from the entity to the owners, and the AMT liability calculation is not attached to the tax form that reports the entity's taxable income—Form 1065 or Form 1120S).

When compared with the other forms of business, the C corporation appears to have a slight advantage. The corporate AMT rate of 20 percent is less than the individual AMT rates of 26 and 28 percent. An even better perspective is provided by comparing the maximum AMT rate with the maximum regular rate for both the individual and the corporation. For the individual, the AMT rate is 80 percent (28%/35%) of the maximum regular rate. The AMT rate for the corporation is 57 percent (20%/35%) of the maximum regular rate. Therefore, on the basis of comparative rates, the C corporation does have an advantage. In addition, as discussed below, under certain circumstances, a C corporation is exempt from the AMT.

The apparent corporate AMT rate advantage may be more than offset by the AMT adjustment that applies only to the C corporation. This is the adjustment for adjusted current earnings (ACE). The amount of the adjustment is 75 percent of the

[10] § 55.

excess of ACE over unadjusted alternative minimum taxable income (AMTI). If unadjusted AMTI exceeds ACE for the tax year, the adjustment is negative.[11]

If the ACE adjustment continually causes the C corporation to be subject to the AMT, the owners should consider electing S corporation status if the eligibility requirements can be satisfied. Since the S corporation does not have this item as an adjustment, it may be possible to reduce the tax liability.

The AMT does not apply to small corporations for tax years beginning after December 31, 1997. For this purpose, a C corporation is classified as a small corporation if it had average annual gross receipts of not more than $5 million for the three-year period beginning after December 1993. A corporation will continue to be classified as a small corporation if its average annual gross receipts for the three-year period preceding the current tax year and any intervening three-year periods do not exceed $7.5 million. Tax legislation enacted in 1998 provided an additional opportunity for a C corporation to be classified as a small corporation. A C corporation automatically is classified as a small corporation in its first year of existence.

If the AMT is going to apply for the taxable year, the entity should consider accelerating income into the current taxable year and delaying deductions so that the resultant increased taxable income will be taxed at the lower AMT rate. For the C corporation, the potential rate differential is 15 percentage points (20 percent AMT rate versus 35 percent regular rate). For the individual taxpayer (i.e., as a sole proprietor, as a partner, or as an S corporation shareholder), the potential tax rate differential is 7 percentage points (28 percent highest AMT rate versus 35 percent regular rate). A present value analysis should be used to assure that the acceleration of income and delaying of deductions do not increase actual tax liabilities.

STATE TAXATION

In selecting a form for doing business, the determination of the tax consequences should not be limited to Federal income taxes. Consideration should also be given to state income taxes and, if applicable, local income taxes.[12]

The S corporation provides a good illustration of this point. Suppose that the forms of business being considered are a limited partnership or a corporation. An operating loss is projected for the next several years. The owners decide to operate the business in the corporate form. The principal nontax criterion for the decision is the limited liability attribute of the corporation. The owners consent to an S corporation election, so the corporate losses can be passed through to the shareholders to deduct on their individual tax returns. However, assume that state law does not permit the S corporation election on the state income tax return. Thus, the owners will not receive the tax benefits of the loss deductions that would have been available on their state income tax returns if they had chosen the limited partnership form. As a result of providing limited liability to the owner who would have been the general partner for the limited partnership, the loss deduction at the state level is forgone.

13.4 Controlling the Entity Tax

LO.4

Identify techniques for avoiding double taxation and for controlling the entity tax.

Of the five forms of business entities, it appears at first glance that only the corporation needs to be concerned with controlling the entity tax. If control is defined in the narrow sense of double taxation, then this issue is restricted to the corporate form. However, from the broader perspective of controlling the tax liability related to the business entity's profits, whether that tax is imposed at the entity or the owner level, all five business forms are encompassed.

[11]§§ 56(c)(1) and (f). See the discussion of the corporate AMT in Chapter 3.

[12]See the discussion of multistate corporate taxation in Chapter 16.

Techniques that can be used to minimize the current-period tax liability include the following:

1. Distribution policy.
2. Recognizing the interaction between the regular tax liability and the AMT liability.
3. Utilization of special allocations.
4. Favorable treatment of certain fringe benefits.
5. Minimizing double taxation.

Some of the techniques apply to all five forms of business entities. Others apply to only one of the five forms. Even those that apply to all do not minimize taxes equally for all forms. Since the first three techniques are discussed elsewhere in this chapter, only the last two are discussed here.

FAVORABLE TREATMENT OF CERTAIN FRINGE BENEFITS

Ideally, a fringe benefit produces the following tax consequences:

- Deductible by the entity (employer) that provides the fringe benefit.
- Excludible from the gross income of the taxpayer (employee) who receives the fringe benefit.

From the perspective of the owner or owners of an entity, when the entity provides such favorably taxed fringe benefits to an owner, the benefits are paid for with *before-tax* dollars.

EXAMPLE 10

Rocky, the owner of Rocky's Ranch, a C corporation in the 34% tax bracket, is provided with meals and lodging that qualify for exclusion treatment under § 119. The annual cost of the meals and lodging to Rocky's Ranch is $10,000. Since the cost is deductible in calculating the taxable income of Rocky's Ranch on Form 1120, the after-tax cost to the corporation is only $6,600 [$10,000 − (34% × $10,000)]. Since the $10,000 is excluded in calculating Rocky's gross income, there is no additional tax cost at the owner level. If Rocky had paid for the meals and lodging himself, no deduction would have been permitted because these expenditures are nondeductible personal expenditures. Thus, from Rocky's perspective, the receipt of excludible meals and lodging of $10,000 is equivalent to receiving a distribution from the corporation of $15,385 [$10,000/(100% − 35%)], assuming he is in the 35% tax bracket. ■

Not all favorably taxed fringe benefits receive exclusion treatment. Although not as attractive to the recipient, another approach provided in the Code is deferral treatment (e.g., pension plans and profit sharing plans).

Example 10 illustrates how certain fringe benefits can be used to benefit the owner of an entity and at the same time have a beneficial impact on the combined tax liability of the entity and the owner. In recognition of this, Congress has enacted various nondiscrimination provisions that generally negate favorable tax treatment if the fringe benefit program is discriminatory. In addition, the Code includes several statutory provisions that make the favorably taxed fringe benefit treatment available only to *employees* (e.g., group term life insurance, meal and lodging exclusion).[13]

The IRS defines the term *employee* restrictively. For the owner of a business entity to be treated as an employee, the entity must be a corporation.[14] For this purpose, an S corporation is treated as a partnership, and a greater-than-2 percent shareholder is treated as a partner.[15]

[13] §§ 79 and 119.

[14] Reg. § 1.79–0(b). The IRS has not been completely successful with respect to this position.

[15] § 1372(a).

Classification of an owner as a nonemployee produces two negative results. First, the deduction for the cost of the fringe benefit to the entity is disallowed at the entity level. Second, the owner whose fringe benefit has been paid for by the entity must include the cost of the fringe benefit in gross income.

MINIMIZING DOUBLE TAXATION

Only the corporate form is potentially subject to double taxation. Several techniques are available for eliminating or at least reducing the second layer of taxation:

- Making distributions to the shareholders that are deductible to the corporation.
- Not making distributions to the shareholders.
- Making distributions that qualify for return of capital treatment at the shareholder level.
- Making the S corporation election.

Note that for distributions made in 2003 and thereafter the availability of the beneficial rate (15%/0% in 2008–2012 and 15%/5% before 2008) for qualified dividends reduces the potential negative impact of double taxation (see Chapter 5).

Making Deductible Distributions

Use of the first technique requires careful advance planning. Typical distribution forms that will result in a deduction to the corporation are (1) salary payments to shareholder-employees, (2) lease rental payments to shareholder-lessors, and (3) interest payments to shareholder-creditors.

A Technique for Getting a Bonus

Luis is the chief operating officer of an S corporation that has about $40 million in annual sales. During the five years he has been in his position, profits have increased between 15 and 20 percent each year. Luis owns 10 percent of the stock of the corporation, and Jay owns 90 percent. Although Luis's salary has increased each year, he has not received any bonuses.

Luis suggests that Jay establish a performance-based system that would enable him to receive a bonus based on the growth in the corporation's profitability. Jay believes that Luis is adequately compensated and that a bonus plan is unnecessary.

To demonstrate his displeasure with Jay's response, Luis is considering selling half of his stock to Marco, a cousin who is a citizen of Spain and a longtime resident of Madrid. Marco has expressed an interest in investing in the corporation. Luis believes that this proposed sale of stock to Marco may motivate Jay to change his mind regarding the bonus plan.

Comment on whether Luis's plan will work and on the ethics of such a plan.

Recognizing the tax benefit of this technique, the IRS scrutinizes these types of transactions carefully. All three types are evaluated in terms of *reasonableness.*[16] In addition, the interest payments may result in the IRS raising the **thin capitalization** issue and reclassifying some or all of the debt as equity.[17] IRS success with either approach raises the specter of double taxation.

[16] § 162(a)(1). *Mayson Manufacturing Co. v. Comm.*, 49–2 USTC ¶9467, 38 AFTR 1028, 178 F.2d 115 (CA–6, 1949); *Harolds Club v. Comm.*, 65–1 USTC ¶9198, 15 AFTR 2d 241, 340 F.2d 861 (CA–9, 1965).

[17] § 385; Rev.Rul. 83–98, 1983–2 C.B. 40; *Bauer v. Comm.*, 84–2 USTC ¶9996, 55 AFTR 2d 85–433, 748 F.2d 1365 (CA–9, 1984).

EXAMPLE 11

Donna owns all the stock of Green and is also the chief executive officer. Green's taxable income before salary payments to Donna is as follows:

2009	$ 80,000
2010	50,000
2011	250,000

During the year, Donna receives a monthly salary of $3,000. In December of each year, she reviews the operations for the year and determines the year-end bonus to be paid to the key officers (only Donna for bonus purposes). Donna's yearly bonuses are as follows:

2009	$ 44,000
2010	14,000
2011	214,000

The obvious purpose of Green's bonus program is to reduce the corporate taxable income to zero and thereby avoid double taxation. The examination of Green's tax return by the IRS would likely result in a deduction disallowance for unreasonable compensation. ■

EXAMPLE 12

Tom and Vicki each contribute $20,000 to TV Corporation for all the stock of TV. In addition, they each lend $80,000 to TV. The loan is documented by formal notes, the interest rate is 7%, and the maturity date is 10 years from the date of the loan.

The notes provide the opportunity for the corporation to make payments of $5,600 each year to both Tom and Vicki and for the payments not to be subject to double taxation. That is, the interest payments are includible in the gross income of Tom and Vicki, but are deductible by TV in calculating its taxable income. At the time of repayment in 10 years, neither Tom nor Vicki will have any gross income from the repayment since the $80,000 amount realized is equal to the basis for the note of $80,000 (return of capital concept).

If the IRS succeeded in reclassifying the notes as equity, Tom and Vicki's includible gross income of $5,600 each would remain the same (interest income would be reclassified as dividend income that may be taxed at the 15% rate). However, because the dividend payments are not deductible by TV, the corporation's taxable income would increase by $11,200 ($5,600 × 2). To make matters worse, the repayment of the notes in 10 years would not qualify for return of capital treatment and would likely result in dividend income treatment for Tom and Vicki. ■

Not Making Distributions

Double taxation will not occur unless the corporation makes (actual or deemed) distributions to the shareholders. A closely held corporation that does not make distributions will eventually encounter an accumulated earnings tax problem unless the reasonable needs requirement is satisfied. When making distribution policy decisions each year, the board of directors should be apprised of any potential accumulated earnings tax problem and take the appropriate steps to eliminate it. The accumulated earnings tax rate of 15 percent in 2011 is the same as the 15 percent rate for qualified dividends for individual taxpayers.[18]

EXAMPLE 13

According to an internal calculation made by Dolphin Corporation, its accumulated taxable income is $400,000. The board of directors would prefer not to declare any dividends, but is considering a dividend declaration of $400,000 to avoid the accumulated earnings tax. All of the shareholders are in the 35% bracket.

If a dividend of $400,000 is declared, the tax cost to the shareholders is $60,000 ($400,000 × 15%), assuming the dividends are qualified dividends. If a dividend is not

[18]§ 531. See the discussion of the accumulated earnings tax in Chapter 3.

declared and the IRS assesses the accumulated earnings tax, the tax cost to the corporation for the accumulated earnings tax also would be $60,000 ($400,000 × 15%).

To make matters worse, Dolphin will have incurred the accumulated earnings tax cost without getting any funds out of the corporation to the shareholders. If the unwise decision were now made to distribute the remaining $340,000 ($400,000 − $60,000) to the shareholders, the additional tax cost at the shareholder level would be $51,000 ($340,000 × 15%). Therefore, the combined shareholder-corporation tax cost would be $111,000 ($60,000 + $51,000). This is 185% ($111,000/$60,000) of the tax cost that would have resulted from an initial dividend distribution of $400,000. ■

The legislation that created the special tax rate of 15 percent for qualified dividends also lowered the accumulated earnings tax rate from 35 percent to 15 percent. This tax rate reduction has substantially lowered the impact of the accumulated earnings tax. In Example 13, the penalty tax at the corporate level prior to the legislative change would have been $140,000 ($400,000 × 35%). Assuming the remaining $260,000 was distributed to the shareholders, the additional tax cost at the shareholder level would have been $91,000 ($260,000 × 35%). Therefore, the combined shareholder-corporation tax cost would have been $231,000 ($140,000 + $91,000) rather than the current $111,000. Thus, by reducing both the tax rate for the accumulated earnings tax and the tax rate on qualified dividends, this legislative change has substantially lowered the tax burden of the accumulated earnings tax.

Assuming that the accumulated earnings tax can be avoided (e.g., a growth company whose reasonable needs justify its no dividend policy), a policy of no distributions to shareholders can avoid the second layer of taxation forever. This will occur if the shares of stock are bequeathed to the taxpayer's beneficiaries. As a result of the step-up in basis rules for inherited property, the basis of the stock for the beneficiaries will be the fair market value at the date of the decedent's death rather than the decedent's basis.

Return of Capital Distributions

The magnitude of the effect of double taxation can be reduced if the corporate distributions to the shareholders can qualify for return of capital rather than dividend treatment. For an ongoing corporation, the stock redemption provisions offer an opportunity to reduce the includible gross income at the shareholder level. The corporate liquidation provisions can be used if the business entity will cease to operate in corporate form. Under redemption and liquidation rules, the distribution may be treated as a sale of some or all of the shareholder's stock resulting in a tax-free recovery of basis and capital gain.

EXAMPLE 14

Copper Corporation makes a distribution of $60,000 to its shareholders. Mark and Kate, two of the shareholders, receive $25,000 and $10,000, respectively. The form of the distribution permits the shareholders to surrender a certain number of shares of stock. The potential exists that the distribution can qualify for stock redemption treatment at the shareholder level. Mark satisfies the requirements for a substantially disproportionate distribution under § 302. Kate does not because she is in control of the corporation after the distribution (she owns 60% of the stock). Assuming Mark's basis for the shares redeemed is $20,000, he has a capital gain of $5,000 ($25,000 − $20,000). Kate has dividend income of $10,000. She must allocate her stock basis among her remaining shares. ■

Electing S Corporation Status

Electing S corporation status generally eliminates double taxation by making the corporation a tax reporter rather than a taxpayer. Therefore, the only tax levy is at the shareholder level. Factors to consider in making this election include the following:

TAX in the NEWS

C Corporations versus S Corporations

Are there more C corporations than S corporations? If you answered yes, you are right, but not by much. According to IRS data, 47 percent of all corporations are S corporations. Most S corporations (81 percent) have only one or two shareholders.

When it comes to share of corporate net income, C corporations win hands down. C corporations report 82 percent of net income.

- Are all the shareholders willing to consent to the election?
- Can the qualification requirements under § 1361 be satisfied at the time of the election?
- Since the qualification requirements become maintenance requirements, can these requirements continue to be satisfied?
- For what period will the conditions that make the election beneficial continue to prevail?
- Will the corporate distribution policy create wherewithal to pay problems at the shareholder level?

EXAMPLE 15

Emerald Corporation commenced business in January 2011. The two shareholders, Diego and Jaime, are both in the 28% tax bracket. The following operating results are projected for the first five years of operations:

2011	($ 50,000)
2012	400,000
2013	600,000
2014	800,000
2015	1,000,000

The corporation plans to expand rapidly. Therefore, no distributions will be made to shareholders. In addition, beginning in 2012, preferred stock will be offered to a substantial number of investors to help finance the expansion.

If the S corporation election is made for 2011, the $50,000 loss can be passed through to Diego's and Jaime's tax returns. Therefore, the cash-flow effect would be $14,000 ($50,000 × 28%). Assume that the election is either revoked or is involuntarily terminated at the beginning of 2012 as a result of the issuance of the preferred stock. The corporate tax liability for 2012 would be $136,000 ($400,000 × 34%).

If the S corporation election is not made for 2011, the $50,000 loss will be a net operating loss. The amount can be carried forward to reduce the 2012 corporate taxable income to $350,000 ($400,000 − $50,000). The resultant tax liability is $119,000 ($350,000 × 34%).

Should the S corporation election be made for just the one-year period? The answer is unclear. With an assumed after-tax rate of return to Diego and Jaime of 10%, the value of the $14,000 one year hence is $15,400 ($14,000 × 110%). Even considering the time value of money, the combined corporation-shareholder negative cash-flow effect of $120,600 ($136,000 − $15,400) in the case of an S election is not significantly different from the $119,000 corporate tax liability that would result for a regular corporation. The differential is even less when related accounting and/or legal fees are considered. ■

Another benefit of electing S corporation status is that the corporation is not subject to the accumulated earnings or personal holding company taxes.

DIVORCE AND THE S ELECTION

Palm, Inc., is a calendar year S corporation. Counting married couples as one shareholder, Palm has 100 shareholders (none of whom are related). Palm's taxable income is about $2 million, and it normally distributes 80 percent of its earnings to shareholders. Valeria and Gus Sanders each own 10 percent of the stock of Palm.

After considerable marital discord and lengthy legal proceedings, Valeria and Gus's divorce was finalized on November 22, 2011. On Thanksgiving, however, they began a reconciliation that led to their remarriage on December 31, 2011. Even though the divorce meant that there were 101 shareholders for a little over one month in 2011, Palm files as an S corporation for 2011. According to Palm's accountant, the continued S status is justified because the remarriage "fixed the tax problem." She concludes that obtaining the IRS's approval not to terminate the S election is unnecessary because in substance Gus and Valeria were always husband and wife.

Evaluate the accountant's conclusion.

13.5 Conduit versus Entity Treatment

LO.5

Understand the applicability and the effect of the conduit and entity concepts on contributions to the entity, operations of the entity, entity distributions, passive activity loss and at-risk rules, and special allocations.

Under the **conduit concept**, the entity is viewed as merely an extension of the owners. Under the **entity concept**, the entity is regarded as being separate and distinct from its owners. The effects that these different approaches have in the following areas are examined for the partnership (and LLC), C corporation, and S corporation:

- Recognition at time of contribution to the entity.
- Basis of ownership interest.
- Results of operations.
- Recognition at time of distribution.
- Passive activity losses.
- At-risk rules.
- Special allocations.

The sole proprietorship is not analyzed separately because the owner and the business are in essence the same. In one circumstance, however, a tax difference does occur. Recognition does not occur when an owner contributes an asset to a sole proprietorship. Thus, the basis generally is a carryover basis. However, if the asset is a personal use asset, the sole proprietorship's basis is the *lower of* the adjusted basis or the fair market value at the date of contribution. Also note that if a personal use asset is contributed to a partnership or corporation, this *lower of* rule applies.

EFFECT ON RECOGNITION AT TIME OF CONTRIBUTION TO THE ENTITY

Since the conduit approach applies for the partnership and LLC, § 721 provides for no recognition on the contribution of property to the partnership or LLC in exchange for an ownership interest. Section 721 protects both a contribution associated with the formation of the partnership or LLC and later contributions. The partnership or LLC has a carryover basis for the contributed property, and the owners have a carryover basis for their ownership interests.[19]

Since the entity approach applies for the corporation, the transfer of property to a corporation in exchange for its stock is a taxable event. However, if the § 351 control requirement (80 percent) is satisfied, no gain or loss is recognized. In this case, both the corporate property and the shareholders' stock will have a carryover basis.[20] This control requirement makes it more likely that shareholders who contribute appreciated property to the corporation *after* the formation of the corporation will recognize gain.

[19]See the pertinent discussion in Chapter 10.

[20]See the pertinent discussion in Chapter 4.

TAX *in* the NEWS

A Tax Reversal: State Governments Pay for Jobs

State governments continue to offer direct and indirect subsidies (i.e., cash payments, infrastructure development, and tax holidays) in an effort to woo companies that will generate jobs for the area. Jon Corzine while governor of New Jersey promised to send a $3,000 check to every small business that hired a new employee. Minnesota Governor Tim Pawlenty called for an expansive package of tax cuts that would include tax-free zones for companies that create "green jobs."

Providing such incentives, particularly in the current recession, makes economic sense. For example, Texas recently put up $10 million to persuade Caterpillar to locate a new assembly plant, projected to employ 1,400 workers, in the small town of Seguin. Days after breaking ground, Caterpillar announced 20,000 job cuts worldwide, but stated that it remains committed to the new plant as a long-term growth strategy.

But what happens if companies do not keep their promises and the new jobs do not materialize? More and more states, including Texas, are inserting "clawback" provisions in their agreements. Clawback provisions require companies to return some or all of the funds provided by the state government if the promised jobs are not created.

Source: Adapted from Stephanie Simon, "More States Considering Tax Breaks to Woo Jobs," *Wall Street Journal*, February 2, 2009, p. A1.

To the extent that the fair market value of property contributed to the entity at the time of formation is not equal to the property's adjusted basis, it may be desirable to make a special allocation associated with the subsequent sale of the contributed property by the entity. With a special allocation, the owner contributing the property receives the tax benefit or detriment for any recognized gain or loss that subsequently results because of the initial difference between the adjusted basis and the fair market value. For the partnership or LLC, this special allocation treatment is mandatory. No such allocation is available for the C corporation form, since the gain or loss is recognized at the corporation level rather than at the shareholder level. For the S corporation, no such allocation is available. The recognized gain or loss will be reported on the shareholders' tax returns based on their stock ownership.

EXAMPLE 16

Khalid contributes land with an adjusted basis of $10,000 and a fair market value of $50,000 for a 50% ownership interest. At the same time, Tracy contributes cash of $50,000 for the remaining 50% ownership interest. Because the entity is unable to obtain the desired zoning, it subsequently sells the land for $50,000.

If the entity is a C corporation, Khalid has a realized gain of $40,000 ($50,000 – $10,000) and a recognized gain of $0 resulting from the contribution. His basis for his stock is $10,000, and the corporation has a basis for the land of $10,000. The corporation has a realized and recognized gain of $40,000 ($50,000 – $10,000) when it sells the land. Thus, what should have been Khalid's recognized gain becomes the corporation's taxable gain. There is no way that the corporation can directly allocate the recognized gain to Khalid. The corporation could distribute the land to Khalid and let him sell the land, but the distribution may be taxable to Khalid as a dividend, and gain may be recognized at the corporate level on the distribution.

If the entity is a partnership or LLC, the tax consequences are the same as in the C corporation illustration except for the $40,000 recognized gain on the sale of the land. The partnership or LLC has a realized and recognized gain of $40,000 ($50,000 – $10,000). However, even though Khalid's share of profits and losses is only 50%, all of the $40,000 recognized gain is allocated to him. If the entity is an S corporation, the tax consequences are the same as in the C corporation illustration except that Khalid reports $20,000 of the recognized gain on his tax return and Tracy reports $20,000 also. ■

Note that not all contributions of assets to corporations are made by shareholders. States and local governments continue to lure businesses to locate in a particular state or locality with promises of tax breaks and grants. See the additional discussion of this topic in the "Tax in the News" feature on the previous page.

EFFECT ON BASIS OF OWNERSHIP INTEREST

In the case of a partnership or an LLC, the contribution of property to the entity in exchange for an ownership interest is not a taxable event under § 721. Therefore, the owner's basis for the ownership interest is a carryover basis. For C and S corporations, the nontaxable and the related carryover basis results are appropriate only if the 80 percent control requirement of § 351 is satisfied. If the control requirement is not satisfied, any realized gain or loss on the transaction is recognized, and the stock basis is equal to the fair market value of the contributed property.

In a partnership or an LLC, since the owner is the taxpayer, profits and losses of the entity affect the owner's basis in the entity interest. Likewise, the owner's basis is increased by the share of entity liability increases and is decreased by the share of entity liability decreases. This liability effect enables the owner to potentially benefit from the leverage concept. Accordingly, the owner's basis changes frequently.[21]

For the C corporation, the corporation is the taxpayer. Therefore, the shareholder's basis for the stock is not affected by corporate profits and losses or corporate liability increases or decreases.

The treatment of an S corporation shareholder falls in between that of the owner of a partnership or LLC interest and the C corporation shareholder. The S corporation shareholder's stock basis is increased by the share of profits and decreased by the share of losses, but it is not affected by corporate liability increases or decreases. Thus, unlike the owner of a partnership or LLC interest, the S corporation shareholder does not potentially benefit from the leverage concept.

EXAMPLE 17
THE BIG PICTURE

Return to the facts of *The Big Picture* on p. 13-2. In the third year of operations, the entity chosen by Milly and Doug (either a partnership or a corporation) needs additional working capital. Consequently, they agree to admit Peggy as an owner. Peggy contributes cash of $100,000 to the entity for a 30% ownership interest. The entity borrows $50,000 and repays $20,000 of this amount by the end of the taxable year. The profits for the year are $90,000.

If the entity is a partnership, Peggy's basis at the end of the period is $136,000 ($100,000 investment + $9,000 share of net liability increase + $27,000 share of profits). (Note that Peggy's basis would be the same if the entity is an LLC—an entity form that Milly and Doug should have considered.) If Peggy is a C corporation shareholder instead, her stock basis is $100,000 ($100,000 original investment). If the corporation is an S corporation (another entity form that Milly and Doug should have considered), Peggy's stock basis is $127,000 ($100,000 + $27,000). ■

EFFECT ON RESULTS OF OPERATIONS

The entity concept is responsible for producing potential double taxation for the C corporation form (the corporation is taxed on its earnings, and the shareholders are taxed on the distribution of earnings). Thus, from the perspective of taxing the results of operations, the entity concept appears to be a disadvantage for the corporation. However, whether the entity concept actually produces disadvantageous results depends on the following:

- Whether the corporation generates positive taxable income.
- The tax rates that apply for the corporation and for the shareholders.
- The distribution policy of the corporation.

As discussed previously, techniques exist for getting cash out of the corporation to the shareholders without incurring double taxation (e.g., compensation payments to

[21] §§ 705 and 752.

shareholder-employees, lease rental payments to shareholder-lessors, and interest payments to shareholder-creditors). Since these payments are deductible to the corporation, they reduce corporate taxable income. If the payments can be used to reduce corporate taxable income to zero, the corporation will have no tax liability.

The maximum individual tax bracket is the same as the maximum corporate tax bracket (35 percent). However, in a specific situation, the corporate tax rates that apply may be greater than or less than the applicable individual rates. This opportunity for the corporation to be subject to a lower tax rate is less likely to be available for personal service corporations. There, the only rate available is 35 percent.[22]

Double taxation can occur only if distributions (actual or constructive) are made to the shareholders. Thus, if no distributions (actual or constructive) are made and if the entity can avoid the accumulated earnings tax (e.g., based on the statutory credit or the reasonable needs adjustment) and the personal holding company tax (e.g., the corporation primarily generates active income), only one current level of taxation will occur. If distributions do occur in the future with respect to current earnings, the resultant tax liability should be discounted for the interim period. If the distribution can qualify for return of capital treatment (stock redemption or liquidation) rather than dividend treatment, the shareholder tax liability is decreased. Ideally, taxation of the earnings at the shareholder level can be avoided permanently if the stock passes through the decedent shareholder's estate.

Application of the entity concept does result in the earnings components losing their identity when they are passed through to shareholders in the form of dividends. This may produce a negative result for capital gains. Since capital gains lose their identity when passed through in the form of dividends, they cannot be used to offset capital losses at the shareholder level. An even more negative result is produced when dividends are paid out of tax-exempt income. Tax-exempt income is excludible in calculating corporate taxable income, but is included in calculating current earnings and profits. Thus, what should not be subject to taxation (an exclusion) is taxed because of the entity concept.

The partnership, the LLC, and the S corporation use the conduit concept in reporting the results of operations. Any item that is subject to special treatment on the taxpayer-owners' tax return is reported separately to the owners. Other items are netted and reported as taxable income. Thus, taxable income merely represents those income and deduction items that are not subject to special treatment.[23]

Many of the problems that the entity concept may produce for the C corporation form are not present for the partnership, LLC, or S corporation. Included in this category are double taxation, problems with the reasonableness requirement, and loss of identity of the income or expense item at the owner level.

Only the partnership and LLC completely apply the conduit concept in reporting the results of operations. In several circumstances, the S corporation is subject to taxation at the corporate level, including the tax on built-in gains and the tax on certain passive investment income.[24] This limited application of the entity concept necessitates additional planning to attempt to avoid taxation at the corporate level.

EFFECT ON RECOGNITION AT TIME OF DISTRIBUTION

The application of the conduit concept results in distributions not being taxed to the owners. The application of the entity concept produces the opposite result. Therefore, distributions can be made to partners, to LLC owners, or to S corporation shareholders tax-free, whereas the same distribution would produce dividend income treatment for C corporation shareholders.

In this regard, a distinction must be made between distributions of earnings and other distributions for the S corporation. The S corporation generally is treated as a conduit with respect to its operations. However, as previously discussed, in several

[22] § 11(b)(2).
[23] §§ 701, 702, 1363, and 1366.
[24] §§ 1374 and 1375.

TAX *in* *the NEWS*

CERTAIN PARTNERSHIP DISTRIBUTIONS OF APPRECIATED PROPERTY

Section 311(b) of the Internal Revenue Code, which is applicable to C corporations and S corporations, provides that realized gain on the distribution of appreciated property to a shareholder results in recognized gain to the corporation. There is no similar statutory provision for the distribution of appreciated property made by a partnership to a partner.

However, the IRS has held that in one limited circumstance a distribution of appreciated property made by a partnership to a partner results in recognized gain to the partnership. If the appreciated property is distributed to the partner in satisfaction of a guaranteed payment under § 707(c), the distribution is treated as a sale or exchange under § 1001 rather than a distribution under § 731.

cases the entity concept is applied, and the S corporation becomes a taxpayer rather than merely a tax reporter. In effect, the conduit concept applies to S corporation operations unless otherwise specified in Subchapter S of the Code. Since distributions of earnings are included in the operations category, they are subject to conduit treatment through the application of the accumulated adjustments account (AAA).[25] Distributions in excess of earnings qualify for return of capital treatment.

A combination entity/conduit concept applies to property distributions to S corporation shareholders. As discussed above, the conduit concept applies with respect to the shareholder. However, if the property distributed is appreciated property, § 311(b) provides that the realized gain is recognized at the corporate level (same treatment as a C corporation). This corporate-level gain recognition is an application of the entity concept. Then, however, the conduit concept is applied to the pass-through of the gain to the shareholders.

EXAMPLE 18

Tan, an S corporation, is equally owned by Leif and Matt. Tan distributes two parcels of land to Leif and Matt. Tan has a basis of $10,000 for each parcel. Each parcel has a fair market value of $15,000. The distribution results in a $10,000 ($30,000 – $20,000) recognized gain for Tan. Leif and Matt each report $5,000 of the gain on their individual income tax returns. ■

Stock redemptions and complete liquidations are not covered by the provisions of Subchapter S. Therefore, the tax consequences of an S corporation stock redemption are determined under the C corporation provisions in § 302, while those for a complete liquidation are determined under the C corporation provisions in §§ 331 and 336.

EFFECT ON PASSIVE ACTIVITY LOSSES

The passive loss rules apply to the partnership, LLC, and S corporation, but apply to the C corporation only for personal service corporations and closely held corporations. A *closely held corporation* is defined as one that meets the stock ownership requirement under the personal holding company provisions. That is, more than 50 percent of the value of the outstanding stock at any time during the last half of the taxable year is owned by or for not more than five individuals. The definition of a personal service corporation is modified slightly from the standard definition under § 269A. A corporation is classified as a § 469 *personal service corporation* only if the following requirements are satisfied:

- The principal activity of the corporation is the performance of personal services.
- The services are substantially performed by owner-employees.

[25] § 1368.

TAX in the NEWS

When Rent Is Active Rather Than Passive

A major shareholder of a closely held S corporation leased an airplane to the corporation at a fair rental. As part of the lease agreement, the owner provided a pilot and crew. The lease also required that a replacement airplane be made available when repairs were needed for the leased aircraft. If the deductions associated with the airplane exceed the rent income, is any such loss active or passive? According to a recent Revenue Ruling, significant services are being provided. Thus, the lease activity is classified as active rather than passive, and the loss is not subject to the § 469 passive activity limits.

- Owner-employees own more than 10 percent in value of the stock of the corporation.

The general passive loss rules apply to the personal service corporation. Therefore, passive losses cannot be offset against either active income or portfolio income. For the closely held corporation, the application of the passive loss rules is less harsh. Although passive losses cannot be offset against portfolio income, they can be offset against active income.

The statutory language of § 469(a)(2), which describes the taxpayers subject to the passive loss rules, does not mention the partnership, LLC, or S corporation. Instead, it mentions the individual taxpayer. Since the conduit concept applies, the passive activity results are separately stated at the partnership, LLC, or S corporation level and are passed through to the owners with the identity maintained.

EFFECT OF AT-RISK RULES

The at-risk rules of § 465 apply to the partnership, LLC, and S corporation. Although the statutory language of § 465(a) mentions none of these, the conduit concept that applies to these entities results in the application of § 465. Section 465 also applies to closely held C corporations (defined the same as under the passive loss rules). However, exceptions are available for closely held corporations that are actively engaged in equipment leasing or are defined as qualified C corporations.

The application of the at-risk rules produces a harsher result for the partnership and the LLC than for the S corporation. This occurs because the partnership and the LLC, in the absence of § 465, would have a greater opportunity to use the leveraging concept.

EXAMPLE 19

Walt is the general partner, and Ira and Vera are the limited partners in the WIV limited partnership. Walt contributes land with an adjusted basis of $40,000 and a fair market value of $50,000 for his partnership interest, and Ira and Vera each contribute cash of $100,000 for their partnership interests. They agree to share profits and losses equally. To finance construction of an apartment building, the partnership obtains $600,000 of nonrecourse financing [not qualified nonrecourse financing under § 465(b)(6)] using the land and the building as the pledged assets. Each partner's basis for the partnership interest is as follows:

	Walt	Ira	Vera
Contribution	$ 40,000	$100,000	$100,000
Share of nonrecourse debt	200,000	200,000	200,000
Basis	$240,000	$300,000	$300,000

Without the at-risk rules, Ira and Vera could pass through losses up to $300,000 each even though they invested only $100,000 and have no personal liability for the nonrecourse debt. However, the at-risk rules limit the loss pass-through to the at-risk basis, which is $100,000 for Ira and $100,000 for Vera. Note that the at-risk rules can also affect the general partner. Since Walt is not at risk for the nonrecourse debt, his at-risk basis is $40,000. If the mortgage were recourse debt, his at-risk basis would be $640,000 ($40,000 + $600,000). Thus, as a result of the at-risk rules, leveraging is available only for recourse debt for partners who have potential personal liability. ■

EXAMPLE 20

Assume the same facts as in Example 19, except that the entity is an S corporation and Walt receives 20% of the stock and Ira and Vera each receive 40%. The basis for their stock is as follows:

Walt	$ 40,000
Ira	100,000
Vera	100,000

The nonrecourse debt does not affect the calculation of stock basis. The stock basis for each shareholder would remain the same even if the debt were recourse debt. Only direct loans by the shareholders increase the ceiling on loss pass-through (basis for stock plus basis for loans by shareholders). ■

EFFECT OF SPECIAL ALLOCATIONS

An advantage of the conduit concept over the entity concept is the ability to make special allocations. Special allocations are not permitted for the C corporation form. Indirectly, however, the corporate form may be able to achieve results similar to those produced by special allocations through payments to owners (e.g., salary payments, lease rental payments, and interest payments) and through different classes of stock (e.g., preferred, common). However, even in these cases, the breadth of the treatment and the related flexibility are less than that achievable under the conduit concept.

Although the S corporation is a conduit, it is treated more like a C corporation than a partnership or an LLC with respect to special allocations. This treatment results from the application of the per-share and per-day rule in § 1377(a). Although the S corporation is limited to one class of stock, it can still use the payments to owners procedure. However, the IRS has the authority to reallocate income among members of a family if fair returns are not provided for services rendered or capital invested.[26]

EXAMPLE 21

The stock of an S corporation is owned by Debra (50%), Helen (25%), and Joyce (25%). Helen and Joyce are Debra's adult children. Debra is in the 35% bracket, and Helen and Joyce are in the 15% bracket. Only Debra is an employee of the corporation. She is paid an annual salary of $20,000, whereas employees with similar responsibilities in other corporations earn $100,000. The corporation generates earnings of approximately $200,000 each year.

It appears that the reason Debra is paid a low salary is to enable more of the earnings of the S corporation to be taxed to Helen and Joyce, who are in lower tax brackets. Thus, the IRS could use its statutory authority to allocate a larger salary to Debra. ■

The partnership and LLC have many opportunities to use special allocations, including the following:

- The ability to share profits and losses differently from the share in capital.
- The ability to share profits and losses differently.
- The special allocation required under § 704(c) for the difference between the adjusted basis and the fair market value of contributed property.
- The special allocation of any item permitted under § 704(a) if the substantial economic effect rule of § 704(b) is satisfied.

[26] § 1366(e).

- The optional adjustment to basis permitted under § 754 and calculated under § 734 that results from distributions.
- The optional adjustment to basis permitted under § 754 and calculated under § 743 that results from an acquisition by purchase, taxable exchange, or inheritance.

13.6 FICA AND SELF-EMPLOYMENT TAXES

Payroll (employment) taxes can be a significant cost for a business and its owners, with a combined tax rate of 15.3 percent. Such costs can be classified into two categories.

- FICA taxes (Social Security and Medicare).
- Self-employment tax.

FICA

FICA (Federal Insurance Contribution Act) taxes are imposed on the wages of employees using the following rates.[27]

Social Security	6.2%
Medicare	1.45%

Such amounts are withheld by the employer from the employees' wages.

FICA withholding ceases for the Social Security portion once the employee has earned wages subject to the Social Security taxes of $106,800 in 2011 (indexed for inflation). All of the wages of an employee are subject to Medicare taxes. In addition, the employer must pay to the IRS an amount equal to the FICA tax withheld from employee wages (i.e., a matching 6.2% + 1.45%).[28]

SELF-EMPLOYMENT TAX

The purpose of the self-employment tax is to provide Social Security and Medicare benefits for self-employed individuals. For 2011, the self-employment tax is 13.3 percent (15.3 percent for years other than 2011) of self-employment income up to $106,800 (indexed for inflation) and 2.9 percent of self-employment income in excess of $106,800 (indexed for inflation).[29] In other words, for 2011 the self-employment tax is 10.4 percent of self-employment earnings up to $106,800 (for the Social Security portion) plus 2.9 percent of the total amount of self-employment earnings (for the Medicare portion).

IMPACT ON THE ENTITY AND ITS OWNERS

Depending on the type of tax entity, FICA taxes and self-employment taxes have different impacts on the entity and its owners as follows.

- *Sole proprietorship.* The wages of employees of the sole proprietorship are subject to FICA taxes, which must be matched by the sole proprietorship. The Schedule C income of the sole proprietorship is subject to the self-employment tax.
- *Partnership.* The wages of employees of the partnership are subject to FICA taxes, which must be matched by the partnership. A partner is not considered to be an employee. However, guaranteed payments (i.e., compensation for services rendered) made by the partnership to a partner are treated as self-employment income subject to the self-employment tax.[30]

[27] § 3101. The Tax Relief Act of 2010 reduced the employee's Social Security rate for 2011 from 6.2 percent to 4.2 percent.

[28] § 3111. The employer's Social Security rate for 2011 remains at 6.2%.

[29] §§ 1401 and 1402.

[30] § 707(c).

The partner's distributive share of the net earnings of the partnership is subject to self-employment tax.

- *Limited partnership.* The wages of employees of the limited partnership are subject to FICA taxes, which must be matched by the limited partnership. A limited partner is not considered to be an employee. However, guaranteed payments (i.e., compensation for services rendered) made by the limited partnership to a partner are treated as self-employment income subject to the self-employment tax.[31] A limited partner's distributive share of the net earnings of the limited partnership is not subject to self-employment tax.
- *C corporation.* The wages of employees of the corporation are subject to FICA taxes, which must be matched by the corporation. A shareholder who works for the corporation is an employee of the corporation and is subject to FICA taxes as an employee. The net earnings of the corporation have no effect on such a shareholder's self-employment income.
- *S corporation.* The wages of employees of the corporation are subject to FICA taxes, which must be matched by the corporation. A shareholder who works for the corporation is an employee of the corporation and is subject to FICA taxes as an employee. A shareholder's share of the net earnings of the corporation is not self-employment income, though the shareholder is subject to income tax on such earnings. In this respect, the shareholder of an S corporation receives more beneficial treatment than a sole proprietor or a partner whose share of the entity's net earnings is subject to self-employment tax.
- *LLC.* The wages of employees of an LLC are subject to FICA taxes, which must be matched by the LLC. If an LLC owner is treated as a limited partner, the LLC owner's distributive share of the net earnings of the LLC is not subject to the self-employment tax. Conversely, if an LLC owner is not treated as a limited partner, the LLC owner's distributive share of the net earnings of the LLC is subject to the self-employment tax.

13.7 Disposition of a Business or an Ownership Interest

LO.6

Analyze the effect of the disposition of a business on the owners and the entity for each of the forms for conducting a business.

A key factor in evaluating the tax consequences of disposing of a business is whether the disposition is viewed as the sale of an ownership interest or as a sale of assets. Generally, the tax consequences are more favorable if the transaction is treated as a sale of the ownership interest.

SOLE PROPRIETORSHIP

Regardless of the form of the transaction, the sale of a sole proprietorship is treated as the sale of individual assets. Thus, gains and losses must be calculated separately. Classification as capital gain or ordinary income depends on the nature and holding period of the individual assets. Ordinary income property such as inventory will result in ordinary gains and losses. Section 1231 property such as land, buildings, and machinery used in the business will produce § 1231 gains and losses (subject to depreciation recapture under §§ 1245 and 1250). Capital assets such as investment land and stocks qualify for capital gain or loss treatment.

If the amount realized exceeds the fair market value of the identifiable assets, the excess is attributed to goodwill, which produces capital gain for the seller. If instead the excess payment is attributed to a covenant not to compete, the related gain is classified as ordinary income rather than capital gain. Thus, the seller prefers the excess to be attributed to goodwill.

[31] § 707(c).

Unless the legal protection provided by a covenant not to compete is needed, the buyer is neutral as to whether the excess is attributed to goodwill or a covenant. Both goodwill and a covenant are § 197 intangibles and are amortized over a 15-year statutory period.

EXAMPLE 22

Seth, who is in the 35% tax bracket, sells his sole proprietorship to Wilma for $600,000. The identifiable assets are as follows:

	Adjusted Basis	Fair Market Value
Inventory	$ 20,000	$ 25,000
Accounts receivable	40,000	40,000
Machinery and equipment*	125,000	150,000
Buildings**	175,000	250,000
Land	40,000	100,000
	$400,000	$565,000

*Potential § 1245 recapture of $50,000.
**Potential § 1250 recapture of $20,000.

The sale produces the following results for Seth:

	Gain (Loss)	Ordinary Income	§ 1231 Gain	Capital Gain
Inventory	$ 5,000	$ 5,000		
Accounts receivable	-0-			
Machinery and equipment	25,000	25,000		
Buildings	75,000	20,000	$ 55,000	
Land	60,000		60,000	
Goodwill	35,000			$35,000
	$200,000	$50,000	$115,000	$35,000

If the sale is structured this way, Wilma can deduct the $35,000 paid for goodwill over a 15-year period. If instead Wilma paid the $35,000 to Seth for a covenant not to compete for a period of seven years, she still would amortize the $35,000 over a 15-year period. However, this would result in Seth's $35,000 capital gain being reclassified as ordinary income. If the covenant has no legal relevance to Wilma, in exchange for treating the payment as a goodwill payment, she should negotiate for a price reduction that reflects the benefit of the tax on capital gains to Seth. ■

PARTNERSHIP AND LIMITED LIABILITY COMPANY

The sale of a partnership or LLC can be structured as the sale of assets or as the sale of an ownership interest. If the transaction takes the form of an asset sale, it is treated the same as for a sole proprietorship (described above). The sale of an ownership interest is treated as the sale of a capital asset under § 741 (subject to ordinary income potential under § 751 for unrealized receivables and substantially appreciated inventory). Thus, if capital gain treatment can produce beneficial results for the taxpayer (e.g., has capital losses to offset or has beneficially treated net capital gain), the sale of an ownership interest is preferable.

From the buyers' perspective, the form does not produce different tax consequences. If the transaction is an asset purchase, the basis for the assets is the amount paid for them. Assuming the buyers intend to continue to operate in the partnership or LLC form, the assets can be contributed to the entity under § 721. Therefore, the owners' basis for their entity interest is equal to the purchase price for the assets. Likewise, if ownership interests are purchased, the owners' basis is the purchase price, and the entity's basis for the assets is the purchase price since the original entity will have terminated.[32]

[32] § 708(b)(1)(B).

A problem may arise if an individual purchases an entity interest from another partner or limited liability entity owner and the amount paid exceeds the new owner's pro rata share of the entity's basis for the assets. If the new owner does not acquire at least a 50 percent capital and profits interest, the old entity may not terminate.[33]

EXAMPLE 23

Paul purchases Sandra's partnership interest for $100,000. He acquires both a 20% capital interest and a 20% interest in profits and losses. At the purchase date, the assets of the partnership are as follows:

	Adjusted Basis	Fair Market Value
Cash	$ 10,000	$ 10,000
Inventory	30,000	35,000
Accounts receivable	15,000	15,000
Machinery and equipment	70,000	90,000
Buildings	100,000	150,000
Land	175,000	200,000
	$400,000	$500,000

In effect, Paul paid $100,000 for his 20% share of partnership assets ($500,000 × 20%). His basis for his partnership interest reflects the purchase price of $100,000. However, Paul's proportionate share of the partnership assets is based on the partnership's adjusted basis for the assets of $400,000 (i.e., $400,000 × 20% = $80,000). Since Paul's acquisition of his ownership interest from Sandra did not result in a termination of the partnership, the partnership's adjusted basis for the assets does not change. Therefore, if the partnership were to liquidate all of its assets immediately for $500,000, Paul's share of the recognized gain of $100,000 ($500,000 – $400,000) would be $20,000 ($100,000 × 20%). This result occurs even though Paul paid fair market value for his partnership interest.

The Code does provide an opportunity to rectify this inequity to Paul. If the partnership elects the optional adjustment to basis under § 754, the operational provisions of § 743 will result in Paul having a special additional basis for each of the appreciated partnership assets.

The amount is the excess of the amount Paul effectively paid for each of the assets over his pro rata share of the partnership's basis for the assets.

	Amount Paid (20% Share)	Pro Rata Share of Adjusted Basis	Special Basis Adjustment
Cash	$ 2,000	$ 2,000	$ –0–
Inventory	7,000	6,000	1,000
Accounts receivable	3,000	3,000	–0–
Machinery and equipment	18,000	14,000	4,000
Buildings	30,000	20,000	10,000
Land	40,000	35,000	5,000
	$100,000	$80,000	$20,000

Therefore, if the partnership sells the inventory, Paul's share of the ordinary income is $1,000 ($5,000 × 20%). He then reduces this amount by his special additional basis of $1,000. Thus, the net effect, as it equitably should be, is $0 ($1,000 – $1,000). ■

As Example 23 illustrates, the optional adjustment-to-basis election under § 754 provides a way to avoid the aforementioned problem. However, four additional factors need to be considered. First, the election must be made by the partnership (or

[33]§§ 708(b)(1)(A) and (B).

TAX *in the NEWS*

A One-Way Street for Partners

Janel paid $800,000 for Waldo's partnership interest in the DWT Partnership. Waldo's outside basis was $600,000, which equaled his share of the partnership's inside basis for the partnership assets. Unless the partnership makes a § 754 election, Janel will eventually pay income taxes on the $200,000 difference between her outside basis of $800,000 and her share of the inside basis of $600,000. However, a § 754 election will activate § 743 and provide her with a special basis adjustment of $200,000. But does she recognize the need for making the § 754 election, and will the other partners cooperate?

Suppose the amounts are reversed (i.e., Janel paid $600,000 for an inside basis of $800,000). In this situation, Janel would prefer to avoid making the § 754 election. Congress has limited the ability to make this choice. The statutory language of § 743 was modified to require an automatic downward basis adjustment if the partnership has a "substantial built-in loss" at the time of the transfer.

Note that this § 743 treatment applies only to losses. For built-in gains, an affirmative § 754 election still is necessary in order to receive a § 743 upward basis adjustment.

LLC), not just by the acquiring partner. Therefore, the acquiring partner should obtain a written agreement from the other partners indicating they will consent to the § 754 election. Second, the election is a continuing election. Thus, while the election benefits an acquiring partner if the partnership assets are appreciated at the date of acquisition, it produces detrimental consequences (i.e., a negative special basis adjustment) if the adjusted basis exceeds the fair market value of the assets at the acquisition date. Third, the election not only activates the operational provisions of § 743, it also activates the operational provisions of § 734 with respect to partnership distributions. Fourth, if the members of the partnership change frequently, record keeping can become complex.

C CORPORATION

The sale of the business held by a C corporation can be structured as either an asset sale or a stock sale. The stock sale has the dual advantage to the seller of being less complex both as a legal transaction and as a tax transaction. It also has the advantage of providing a way to avoid double taxation. Finally, the gain or loss on the sale of the stock is a capital gain or loss to the shareholder.

EXAMPLE 24

Jane and Zina each own 50% of the stock of Purple Corporation. They have owned the business for 10 years. Jane's basis for her stock is $40,000, and Zina's basis for her stock is $60,000. They agree to sell the stock to Rex for $300,000. Jane has a long-term capital gain of $110,000 ($150,000 − $40,000), and Zina has a long-term capital gain of $90,000 ($150,000 − $60,000). Rex has a basis for his stock of $300,000. Purple's basis for its assets does not change as a result of the stock sale. ■

Structuring the sale of the business as a stock sale may produce detrimental tax results for the purchaser. As Example 24 illustrates, the basis of the corporation's assets is not affected by the stock sale. If the fair market value of the stock exceeds the corporation's adjusted basis for its assets, the purchaser is denied the opportunity to step up the basis of the assets to reflect the amount in effect paid for them through the stock acquisition. Note that this is similar to the problem at the partnership (or LLC) level if the § 754 election is not made.

For an asset sale, the seller of the business can be either the corporation or the shareholders. If the seller is the corporation, the corporation sells the business (the assets), pays any debts not transferred, and makes a liquidating distribution to the shareholders. If the sellers are the shareholders, the corporation pays any debts that will not be transferred and makes a liquidating distribution to the shareholders; then the shareholders sell the business.

Regardless of the approach used for an asset sale, double taxation will occur. The corporation is taxed on the actual sale of the assets and is taxed as if it had sold the assets when it makes the liquidating distribution of the assets to the shareholders who then sell the assets. The shareholders are taxed when they receive cash or assets distributed in kind by the corporation.

The asset sale resolves the purchaser's problem of not being able to step up the basis of the assets to their fair market value. The basis for each asset is the amount paid for it. In order to operate in corporate form (assuming the purchaser is not a corporation), the purchaser needs to transfer the property to a corporation in a § 351 transaction.

From the perspective of the seller, the ideal form of the transaction is a stock sale. Conversely, from the purchaser's perspective, the ideal form is an asset purchase. Thus, a conflict exists between the buyer's and the seller's objectives regarding the form of the transaction. Therefore, the bargaining ability of the seller and the purchaser to structure the sale as a stock sale or an asset sale, respectively, has become more critical.

Rather than selling the entire business, an owner may sell his or her ownership interest. Since the form of the transaction is a stock sale, the results for the selling shareholder will be the same as if all the shareholders had sold their stock (i.e., capital gain or capital loss to the shareholder).

Selling Stock versus Selling Corporate Assets: Relevance of Double Taxation

Molly owns all of the stock of Peach, Inc., a C corporation that she wants to sell. Since she started the business, the fair market value of the corporate assets and the value of her stock investment have appreciated by about $7 million. The C corporation's marginal tax rate is 34 percent. Unfortunately, the buyer of the corporation is only interested in purchasing its assets and does not want to buy the stock.

Molly's objective is to avoid double taxation, and she is considering the following alternatives:

1. Sell the C corporation stock for its fair market value to her wholly owned S corporation. The S corporation will then liquidate the C corporation. As the value of the assets received will equal the purchase price of the stock, no gain will result, and only the C corporation will be subject to tax.
2. Have the C corporation elect S corporation status and then liquidate.
3. Liquidate the C corporation (i.e., sell the assets). Because the sale of the assets produces the same results as a sale of the stock, she will account for the liquidation as a stock sale.
4. Offer the buyer a $500,000 reduction in the purchase price if he will agree to purchase the stock rather than the corporate assets.

Evaluate these four alternatives in terms of achieving Molly's objective and from an ethical perspective.

S CORPORATION

Since the S corporation is a corporation, it is subject to the provisions for a C corporation discussed previously. Either an asset sale at the corporate level or a liquidating distribution of assets produces recognition at the corporate level. However, under the conduit concept applicable to the S corporation, the recognized amount is taxed at the shareholder level. Therefore, double taxation is avoided directly (only the shareholder is involved) for a stock sale and indirectly (the conduit concept ignores the involvement of the corporation) for an asset sale.

See Concept Summary 13.1 for a summary of the tax consequences of the disposition of a business.

CONCEPT SUMMARY 13.1

Tax Treatment of Disposition of a Business

Form of Entity	Form of Transaction	Tax Consequences	
		Seller	**Buyer**
Sole proprietorship	Sale of individual assets.	Gain or loss is calculated separately for the individual assets. Classification as capital or ordinary depends on the nature and holding period of the individual assets. If amount realized exceeds the fair market value of the identifiable assets, the excess is allocated to goodwill (except to the extent identified with a covenant not to compete), which is a capital asset.	Basis for individual assets is the allocated cost. Prefers that any excess of purchase price over the fair market value of identifiable assets be identified with a covenant not to compete if the covenant has legal utility. Otherwise, the buyer is neutral since both goodwill and covenants are amortized over a 15-year statutory period.
	Sale of the business.	Treated as if a sale of the individual assets (as above).	Treated as if a purchase of the individual assets (as above).
Partnership and limited liability company	Sale of individual assets.	Treatment is the same as for the sole proprietorship.	Treatment is the same as for the sole proprietorship. If the intent is to operate in partnership or LLC form, the assets can be contributed to a partnership or LLC under § 721.
	Sale of ownership interest.	Entity interest is treated as the sale of a capital asset under § 741 (subject to ordinary income potential under § 751 for unrealized receivables and substantially appreciated inventory).	Basis for new owner's ownership interest is the cost. The new entity's basis for the assets is also the pertinent cost (i.e., contributed to the entity under § 721), since the original entity will have terminated.
C corporation	Sale of corporate assets by corporation (i.e., corporation sells assets, pays debts, and makes liquidating distribution to the shareholders).	Double taxation occurs. Corporation is taxed on the sale of the assets with the gain or loss determination and the classification as capital or ordinary treated the same as for the sole proprietorship. Shareholders calculate gain or loss as the difference between the stock basis and the amount received from the corporation in the liquidating distribution. Capital gain or loss usually results, since stock typically is a capital asset.	Basis for individual assets is the allocated cost. If the intent is to operate in corporate form, the assets can be contributed to a corporation under § 351.
	Sale of corporate assets by the shareholders (i.e., corporation pays debts and makes liquidating distribution to the shareholders).	Double taxation occurs. At the time of the liquidating distribution to the shareholders, the corporation is taxed as if it had sold the assets. Shareholders calculate gain or loss as the difference between the stock basis and the fair market value of the assets received from the corporation in the liquidating distribution. Capital gain or loss usually results, since stock typically is a capital asset.	Same as above.

Tax Treatment of Disposition of a Business—Continued

Form of Entity	Form of Transaction	Tax Consequences	
		Seller	Buyer
	Sale of corporate stock.	Enables double taxation to be avoided. Since the corporation is not a party to the transaction, there are no tax consequences at the corporate level. Shareholders calculate gain or loss as the difference between the stock basis and the amount received for the stock. Capital gain or loss usually results, since stock typically is a capital asset.	Basis for the stock is its cost. The basis for the corporate assets is not affected by the stock purchase.
S corporation	Sale of corporate assets by corporation.	Recognition occurs at the corporate level on the sale of the assets with the gain or loss determination and the classification as capital or ordinary treated the same as for the sole proprietorship. Conduit concept applicable to the S corporation results in the recognized amount being taxed at the shareholder level. Double taxation associated with the asset sale is avoided, because the shareholder's stock basis is increased by the amount of gain recognition and decreased by the amount of loss recognition. Shareholders calculate gain or loss as the difference between the stock basis and the amount received from the corporation in the liquidating distribution. Capital gain or loss usually results, since stock typically is a capital asset.	Basis for individual assets is the allocated cost. If the intent is to operate in corporate form (i.e., as an S corporation), the assets can be contributed to a corporation under § 351.
	Sale of corporate assets by the shareholders.	At the time of the liquidating distribution to the shareholders, recognition occurs at the corporation level as if the corporation had sold the assets. The resultant tax consequences for the shareholders and the corporation are the same as for the sale of corporate assets by the S corporation.	Same as above.
	Sale of corporate stock.	Same as the treatment for the sale of stock of a C corporation.	Same as the treatment for the purchase of stock of a C corporation.

13.8 Converting to Other Entity Types

Rather than disposing of a business, the owners may decide to convert the tax entity form to a different tax entity form. This raises three primary issues.

- Does the conversion result in the recognition of gain or loss?
- What is the basis for the ownership interest in the new entity form?
- What is the basis of the assets of the new entity form?

SOLE PROPRIETORSHIP

The conversion of a sole proprietorship into another entity form can be achieved without any recognition of gain or loss at the entity level or at the owner level. This applies regardless of the new entity form. If the proprietorship is converted into a partnership or an LLC, nonrecognition can be achieved under the provisions of the Code.[34] If it is converted into a corporation (either an S corporation or a C corporation), nonrecognition can also be achieved.[35]

In transfers to a partnership, the basis of an ownership interest (partner or LLC owner) will be a carryover basis.[36] In transfers to a corporation, a shareholder's basis for stock will be a carryover basis.[37]

As to the entity, the partnership's or LLC's basis for its assets also is a carryover basis,[38] and the corporation's basis for its assets is likewise a carryover basis.[39]

C CORPORATION

A C corporation can convert to any of the following entity forms, which permit having multiple owners.

- Partnership or LLC.
- S corporation.

Converting to the S corporation tax entity form merely requires the election of S status.[40] As discussed in Chapter 12, the S election can be made only if all shareholders consent to the election and if the qualification requirements are satisfied.[41] Note that the qualification requirements become maintenance requirements that must be met in order to retain the S election.

Therefore, the election of S status produces the following tax consequences.

- No recognition of gain or loss.
- Carryover basis for the shareholders' stock.
- Carryover basis for the assets of the corporation.

A corporation can also convert to a partnership or LLC form. Unfortunately, in order to make this conversion, the corporation must be liquidated. This produces the following tax consequences.

- Recognition of gain or loss at the corporate level.[42]
- Recognition of gain or loss at the shareholder level.[43]
- Fair market value basis for the assets distributed in liquidation.[44]

After liquidation, it is necessary to contribute the assets to the new entity (i.e., the partnership or the LLC). The tax consequences to the owners and to the entity would be the same as those for a sole proprietorship that converts to a partnership or an LLC.

PARTNERSHIP

A partnership can convert to either of the following entity forms, which permit having multiple owners.

- C corporation.
- S corporation.

The partners can transfer their partnership interests to a corporation (either a C corporation or an S corporation) in exchange for the stock of the corporation.

[34] § 721(a).
[35] § 351(a).
[36] § 722.
[37] § 358(a).
[38] § 723.
[39] § 362(a).
[40] § 1362(a).
[41] §§ 1361(a), 1361(b), and 1362(a)(2).
[42] § 336(a).
[43] § 331(a).
[44] § 334(a).

Since this will satisfy the § 351 requirements, any realized gain or loss is not recognized.[45] If, however, the 80 percent control requirement is not satisfied, the realized gain or loss is recognized to the partners.[46]

Assuming the § 351 requirements for nonrecognition are satisfied, the following occur.

- The basis of the stock to the shareholders is a carryover basis.[47]
- The basis of the assets to the corporation is a carryover basis.[48]

13.9 Overall Comparison of Forms of Doing Business

See Concept Summary 13.2 for a detailed comparison of the tax consequences of the following forms of doing business: sole proprietorship, partnership, limited liability company, S corporation, and C corporation.

LO.7

Compare the tax consequences of the various forms of doing business.

CONCEPT SUMMARY 13.2

Tax Attributes of Different Forms of Business (Assume Partners and Shareholders Are All Individuals)

	Sole Proprietorship	Partnership/Limited Liability Company*	S Corporation**	Regular (C) Corporation***
Restrictions on type or number of owners	One owner. The owner must be an individual.	Must have at least 2 owners.	Only individuals, estates, certain trusts, and certain tax-exempt entities can be owners. Maximum number of shareholders limited to 100.****	None, except some states require a minimum of 2 shareholders.
Incidence of tax	Sole proprietorship's income and deductions are reported on Schedule C of the individual's Form 1040. A separate Schedule C is prepared for each business.	Entity not subject to tax. Owners in their separate capacity subject to tax on their distributive share of income. Entity files Form 1065.	Except for certain built-in gains and passive investment income when earnings and profits are present from C corporation tax years, entity not subject to Federal income tax. S corporation files Form 1120S. Shareholders are subject to tax on income attributable to their stock ownership.	Income subject to double taxation. Entity subject to tax, and shareholder subject to tax on any corporate dividends received. Corporation files Form 1120.
Highest tax rate	35% at individual level.	35% at owner level.	35% at shareholder level.	35% at corporate level plus 15%/0% on any corporate dividends at shareholder level (if qualified dividends; otherwise 35%).

[45] § 351(a).

[46] § 368(c).

[47] § 358(a).

[48] § 362(a).

Tax Attributes of Different Forms of Business—Continued

	Sole Proprietorship	Partnership/Limited Liability Company*	S Corporation**	Regular (C) Corporation***
Choice of tax year	Same tax year as owner.	Selection generally restricted to coincide with tax year of majority owners or principal owners, or to tax year determined under the least aggregate deferral method.	Restricted to a calendar year unless IRS approves a different year for business purposes or other exceptions apply.	Unrestricted selection allowed at time of filing first tax return.
Timing of taxation	Based on owner's tax year.	Owners report their share of income in their tax year with or within which the entity's tax year ends. Owners in their separate capacities are subject to payment of estimated taxes.	Shareholders report their shares of income in their tax year with or within which the corporation's tax year ends. Generally, the corporation uses a calendar year, but see "Choice of tax year" above. Shareholders may be subject to payment of estimated taxes. Corporation may be subject to payment of estimated taxes for the taxes imposed at the corporate level.	Corporation subject to tax at close of its tax year. May be subject to payment of estimated taxes. Dividends will be subject to tax at the shareholder level in the tax year received.
Basis for allocating income to owners	Not applicable (only one owner).	Profit and loss sharing agreement. Cash basis items of cash basis entities are allocated on a daily basis. Other entity items are allocated after considering varying interests of owners.	Pro rata share based on stock ownership. Shareholder's pro rata share is determined on a daily basis, according to the number of shares of stock held on each day of the corporation's tax year.	Not applicable.
Contribution of property to the entity	Not a taxable transaction.	Generally not a taxable transaction.	Is a taxable transaction unless the § 351 requirements are satisfied.	Is a taxable transaction unless the § 351 requirements are satisfied.
Character of income taxed to owners	Retains source characteristics.	Conduit—retains source characteristics.	Conduit—retains source characteristics.	All source characteristics are lost when income is distributed to owners.
Basis for allocating a net operating loss to owners	Not applicable (only one owner).	Profit and loss sharing agreement. Cash basis items of cash basis entities are allocated on a daily basis. Other entity items are allocated after considering varying interests of owners.	Prorated among shareholders on a daily basis.	Not applicable.
Limitation on losses deductible by owners	Investment plus liabilities.	Owner's investment plus share of liabilities.	Shareholder's investment plus loans made by shareholder to corporation.	Not applicable.

Tax Attributes of Different Forms of Business—Continued

	Sole Proprietorship	Partnership/Limited Liability Company*	S Corporation**	Regular (C) Corporation***
Subject to at-risk rules	Yes, at the owner level. Indefinite carryover of excess loss.	Yes, at the owner level. Indefinite carryover of excess loss.	Yes, at the shareholder level. Indefinite carryover of excess loss.	Yes, for closely held corporations. Indefinite carryover of excess loss.
Subject to passive activity loss rules	Yes, at the owner level. Indefinite carryover of excess loss.	Yes, at the owner level. Indefinite carryover of excess loss.	Yes, at the shareholder level. Indefinite carryover of excess loss.	Yes, for closely held corporations and personal service corporations. Indefinite carryover of excess loss.
Tax consequences of earnings retained by entity	Taxed to owner when earned and increases his or her investment in the sole proprietorship.	Taxed to owners when earned and increases their respective interests in the entity.	Taxed to shareholders when earned and increases their respective bases in stock.	Taxed to corporation as earned and may be subject to penalty tax if accumulated unreasonably.
Nonliquidating distributions to owners	Not taxable.	Not taxable unless money received exceeds recipient owner's basis in entity interest. Existence of § 751 assets may cause recognition of ordinary income.	Generally not taxable unless the distribution exceeds the shareholder's AAA or stock basis. Existence of accumulated earnings and profits could cause some distributions to be dividends.	Taxable in year of receipt to extent of earnings and profits or if exceeds basis in stock.
Capital gains	Taxed at owner level with opportunity to use alternative tax rate.	Conduit—owners must account for their respective shares.	Conduit, with certain exceptions (a possible penalty tax)—shareholders must account for their respective shares.	Taxed at corporate level with a maximum 35% rate. No other benefits.
Capital losses	Only $3,000 of capital losses can be offset each tax year against ordinary income. Indefinite carryover.	Conduit—owners must account for their respective shares.	Conduit—shareholders must account for their respective shares.	Carried back three years and carried forward five years. Deductible only to the extent of capital gains.
§ 1231 gains and losses	Taxable or deductible at owner level. Five-year lookback rule for § 1231 losses.	Conduit—owners must account for their respective shares.	Conduit—shareholders must account for their respective shares.	Taxable or deductible at corporate level only. Five-year lookback rule for § 1231 losses.
Foreign tax credits	Available at owner level.	Conduit—passed through to owners.	Generally conduit—passed through to shareholders.	Available at corporate level only.
§ 1244 treatment of loss on sale of interest	Not applicable.	Not applicable.	Available.	Available.
Basis treatment of entity liabilities	Includible in interest basis.	Includible in interest basis.	Not includible in stock basis.	Not includible in stock basis.
Built-in gains	Not applicable.	Not applicable.	Possible corporate tax.	Not applicable.
Special allocations to owners	Not applicable (only one owner).	Available if supported by substantial economic effect.	Not available.	Not applicable.

Tax Attributes of Different Forms of Business—Continued

	Sole Proprietorship	Partnership/Limited Liability Company*	S Corporation**	Regular (C) Corporation***
Availability of fringe benefits to owners	None.	None.	None unless a 2%-or-less shareholder.	Available within antidiscrimination rules.
Effect of liquidation/ redemption/ reorganization on basis of entity assets	Not applicable.	Usually carried over from entity to owner unless a § 754 election is made, excessive cash is distributed, or more than 50% of the capital interests are transferred within 12 months.	Taxable step-up to fair market value.	Taxable step-up to fair market value.
Sale of ownership interest	Treated as the sale of individual assets. Classification of recognized gain or loss depends on the nature of the individual assets.	Treated as the sale of an entity interest. Recognized gain or loss is classified as capital under § 741, subject to ordinary income treatment under § 751.	Treated as the sale of corporate stock. Recognized gain is classified as capital gain. Recognized loss is classified as capital loss, subject to ordinary loss treatment under § 1244.	Treated as the sale of corporate stock. Recognized gain is classified as capital gain. Recognized loss is classified as capital loss, subject to ordinary loss treatment under § 1244.
Distribution of appreciated property	Not taxable.	No recognition at the entity level.	Recognition at the corporate level to the extent of the appreciation. Conduit—amount of recognized gain is passed through to shareholders.	Taxable at the corporate level to the extent of the appreciation.
Splitting of income among family members	Not applicable (only one owner).	Difficult—IRS will not recognize a family member as an owner unless certain requirements are met.	Rather easy—gift of stock will transfer tax on a pro rata share of income to the donee. However, IRS can make adjustments to reflect adequate compensation for services.	Same as an S corporation, except that donees will be subject to tax only on earnings actually or constructively distributed to them. Other than unreasonable compensation, IRS generally cannot make adjustments to reflect adequate compensation for services and capital.
Organizational costs	Startup expenditures are eligible for $5,000 limited expensing (subject to phaseout) and amortizing balance over 180 months.	Organizational costs are eligible for $5,000 limited expensing (subject to phaseout) and amortizing balance over 180 months.	Same as partnership.	Same as partnership.
Charitable contributions	Limitations apply at owner level.	Conduit—owners are subject to deduction limitations in their own capacities.	Conduit—shareholders are subject to deduction limitations in their own capacities.	Limited to 10% of taxable income before certain deductions.

Tax Attributes of Different Forms of Business—Continued

	Sole Proprietorship	Partnership/Limited Liability Company*	S Corporation**	Regular (C) Corporation***
Alternative minimum tax	Applies at owner level. AMT rates are 26% and 28%.	Applies at the owner level rather than at the entity level. AMT preferences and adjustments are passed through from the entity to the owners.	Applies at the shareholder level rather than at the corporate level. AMT preferences and adjustments are passed through from the S corporation to the shareholders.	Applies at the corporate level. AMT rate is 20%. Exception for small corporations.
ACE adjustment	Does not apply.	Does not apply.	Does not apply.	The adjustment is made in calculating AMTI. The adjustment is 75% of the excess of adjusted current earnings over unadjusted AMTI. If the unadjusted AMTI exceeds adjusted current earnings, the adjustment is negative.
Tax preference items	Apply at owner level in determining AMT.	Conduit—passed through to owners who must account for such items in their separate capacities.	Conduit—passed through to shareholders who must account for such items in their separate capacities.	Subject to AMT at corporate level.

*Refer to Chapters 10 and 11 for additional details on partnerships and limited liability companies.
**Refer to Chapter 12 for additional details on S corporations.
***Refer to Chapters 2 through 9 for additional details on regular (C) corporations.
****Spouses and family members are treated as one shareholder.

TAX PLANNING:

Example 1 illustrated the relationship between tax planning and the choice of business form; it also raised a variety of questions about the advice given by the tax practitioner. By this time, the student should be able to develop various scenarios supporting the tax advice given. The actual fact situations that produced the tax adviser's recommendations were as follows:

- Jesse's experience in the dairy industry consists of raising a few heifers during the last five years he was employed. Eva anticipates that Jesse will have tax losses for the indeterminate future. In choosing between the partnership and the S corporation forms, Jesse indicated that he and his wife must have limited liability associated with the dairy farm.
- Larry was born and raised on his father's dairy farm. Both his education and his Air Force managerial experience provide him with useful tools for managing his business. However, Larry inherited his farm when milk prices were at a low for the modern era. Since none of her dairy farm clients were generating tax profits at that time, Eva anticipated Larry would operate his dairy farm at a loss. Larry, like Jesse, felt that limited liability was imperative. Thus, he incorporated the dairy farm and made the S corporation election.

For the first two years, Larry's dairy farm produced tax losses. Since then, the dairy farm has produced tax profits large enough to absorb the losses. Larry anticipates that his profits will remain relatively stable in the $50,000 to $75,000 range. Since he is in the 28 percent marginal tax bracket and anticipates no dividend distributions to him from the corporation, his tax liability associated with the dairy farm will be less if he terminates the S corporation election.

As Jesse and Larry's example illustrates, selection of the proper business form can result in both nontax and tax advantages. Both of these factors should be considered in making the selection decision. Furthermore, this choice should be reviewed periodically, since a proper business form at one point in time may not be the proper form at a different time. Note that another business form Eva could have considered for Jesse is the LLC.

In selecting the right entity for conducting any business, tax consequences are important. In looking at the attributes, consideration should be given to the tax consequences of the following:

- Contribution of assets to the entity by the owners at the time the entity is created and at later dates.
- Taxation of the results of operations.
- Distributions to owners.
- Disposition of an ownership interest.
- Termination of the entity.

REFOCUS ON THE BIG PICTURE

SELECTION OF A TAX ENTITY FORM

Although Milly and Doug have narrowed their choice of tax entity to either a C corporation or a general partnership, the tax adviser should not be so limited in suggesting which of the various entities achieve the clients' objectives. As the tax expert, the adviser has a much clearer perspective and may point out factors that the clients have overlooked.

Since Milly and Doug desire limited liability so that their other assets will not be at risk, this eliminates the use of a general partnership. Likewise, the limited partnership option (which does provide limited liability for the limited partner) is not feasible since both Milly and Doug intend to be active in operating the business.

Thus, the remaining choices to be reviewed are the following:

- C corporation.
- S corporation.
- LLC.

C Corporation

The C corporation satisfies the clients' limited liability objective. However, the C corporation is subject to the Federal income tax at the entity level. In addition, the shareholders are taxed (likely at a 15 percent rate) on the distributions of the after-tax earnings. Presuming taxable income of $200,000, the following takes place:

Tax at corporate level	$ 61,250
Tax at shareholder level	
Milly ($69,375 × 15%)	10,406
Doug ($69,375 × 15%)	10,406
Combined entity/owner tax liability	$ 82,062
After-tax cash flow ($200,000 – $82,062)	$117,938

CONTINUED

S Corporation

The S corporation also satisfies the limited liability objective. Since the S corporation is not subject to Federal income taxation at the entity level, only the shareholders are taxed on the earnings of the corporation. The following occurs:

Tax at corporate level	$ –0–
Tax at shareholder level	
Milly ($100,000 × 28%)	28,000
Doug ($100,000 × 28%)	28,000
Combined entity/owner tax liability	$ 56,000
After-tax cash flow ($200,000 – $56,000)	$144,000

LLC

The LLC also generally satisfies the limited liability objective. Under the check-the-box Regulations, the owners can elect to have the LLC taxed as a partnership. Since the LLC is not subject to Federal income taxation at the entity level, only the owners are taxed on the earnings of the LLC. The following occurs:

Tax at the LLC level	$ –0–
Tax at the owner level	
Milly ($100,000 x 28%)	28,000
Doug ($100,000 x 28%)	28,000
Combined entity/owner tax liability	$ 56,000
After-tax cash flow ($200,000 – $56,000)	$144,000

It appears that either the S corporation or the LLC meets Milly and Doug's objectives of having limited liability and minimizing their tax liability. The LLC offers an additional advantage in that an LLC does not have to satisfy the numerous statutory qualification requirements that must be met to elect and maintain S status. Based on the facts in this situation, however, it is unlikely that satisfying these requirements would create any difficulty for Milly and Doug.

KEY TERMS

Conduit concept, 13–15

Entity concept, 13–15

Limited liability company (LLC), 13–3

Thin capitalization, 13–11

DISCUSSION QUESTIONS

1. **LO.1** What are the principal legal forms for conducting a business entity? What are the principal Federal income tax forms for doing so?
2. **LO.1, 3** Compare C and S corporations as to the taxation of the entity and its owners.
3. **LO.1** Discuss the business and tax advantages of a limited liability company.
4. **LO.3** The maximum corporate tax rate of 35% is the same as the maximum rate applicable to individuals. Consequently, for any additional taxable income, the corporate tax liability will be the same as the individual tax liability. Do you agree? Why or why not?
5. **LO.2, 3** All of the Big 4 accounting firms changed their ownership form from a general partnership to a limited liability partnership. Discuss the legal and tax ramifications of this modification of ownership form.

6. **LO.2** Several taxpayers would like to conduct a business in partnership form with all of the owners having limited liability. Can a partnership, other than a limited liability partnership, be structured so that this objective is accomplished? If so, are there any tax pitfalls?

7. **LO.2** Samuel is considering opening a lawn-servicing business.
   a. What nontax factors should Samuel consider in choosing a business entity?
   b. Are nontax factors more important than tax factors to Samuel?

DECISION MAKING

8. **LO.1, 2, 3** Abe is an entrepreneur who likes to be actively involved in his business ventures. He is going to invest $500,000 in a business that he projects will produce a tax loss of approximately $100,000 per year in the short run. However, once consumers become aware of the new product being sold by the business and the quality of the service it provides, he is confident the business will generate a profit of at least $125,000 per year. Abe has substantial other income (from both business ventures and investment activities) each year. Advise Abe on the business form he should select for the short run. He will be the sole owner.

DECISION MAKING

9. **LO.3, 4, 7** Sam is trying to decide whether he should operate his business as a C corporation or as an S corporation. Due to potential environmental hazard problems, it is imperative that the business have limited liability. Sam is leaning toward the S corporation form because it avoids double taxation. However, he is concerned that he may encounter difficulty several years in the future when he may want to issue some preferred stock to his son as a way of motivating him to remain active in the business. Sue, a friend of his, says that he can maintain maximum flexibility by operating as a C corporation. According to her, Sam can avoid double taxation by paying himself a salary equal to the before-tax earnings. As Sam's tax adviser, what is your advice to him?

10. **LO.3** Answer the following questions.
    a. How does classification of a distribution as a dividend or as a return of capital affect the extent to which a C corporation and its shareholders are subject to double taxation?
    b. Does the same result apply to distributions of an S corporation (the entity has never been a C corporation)?

11. **LO.3** What AMT adjustment applies only to corporate taxpayers? Does it apply to both C corporations and S corporations?

12. **LO.3** Violet Corporation, a C corporation in the 34% tax bracket, will be subject to the AMT this year. Armen, Violet's president, has heard that it can be advantageous to accelerate income and defer deductions into a tax year in which the taxpayer is subject to the AMT. He wonders about the logic of doing this since it would increase Violet's total Federal income tax liability. Violet does not expect to be subject to the AMT next year, but will remain in the 34% bracket. Clarify this planning approach for Armen.

DECISION MAKING

13. **LO.3** Mary and Richert plan to establish a retail business that will have outlets in six cities in a southeastern state. Since the business probably will generate losses in at least the first three years, they want to use an entity that will pass the losses through to them for both Federal and state income tax purposes. They have narrowed their choices to an S corporation and a limited liability company. Advise Mary and Richert on selecting an entity form.

14. **LO.4** Why is achieving "employee status" important to the tax treatment of certain fringe benefits?

ISSUE ID

15. **LO.4** Tan, Inc., a C corporation, has been in existence for five years and has accumulated E & P of $990,000. It projects future earnings to continue at about $200,000 per year. David, Tan's sole shareholder and CEO, receives an annual salary of $400,000.
    a. What issues do David and Tan need to consider if their objective is to avoid double taxation?
    b. Should avoiding double taxation be a goal of David and Tan?

16. **LO.4** What techniques can the shareholders of a C corporation use to reduce its taxable income and thereby minimize or avoid double taxation? How can the IRS challenge these techniques?

DECISION MAKING

17. **LO.4** Teresa is considering contributing $800,000 to the capital of Mauve, Inc., a C corporation. A business acquaintance suggests that instead she should invest only $500,000 in capital and lend the $300,000 balance to the corporation. The interest rate

on the loan would be the Federal rate of 6%. Are there any tax benefits to this advice? Any tax pitfalls?

18. **LO.4** Is it possible to permanently avoid double taxation of a C corporation by never making distributions to shareholders (because the stock will appreciate in value and the heirs will receive a step-up in basis on the death of the shareholder)?

19. **LO.4** Orange and Rust have both been in business for approximately nine years. Each corporation has 14 shareholders and taxable income of about $350,000 per year. Neither corporation has made any dividend distributions nor plans to do so in the near future. Explain why Orange may have an accumulated earnings tax problem, while Rust does not.

20. **LO.4, 5** Arnold is going to conduct his business in corporate form. What factors should he consider in deciding whether to operate as a C corporation or as an S corporation? **DECISION MAKING**

21. **LO.4** Tammy and Arnold own 40% of the stock of Roadrunner, an S corporation. The other 60% is owned by 99 other shareholders (all are single and unrelated). Tammy and Arnold have agreed to a divorce and are in the process of negotiating a property settlement. **ISSUE ID**
    a. Identify the relevant tax issues for Tammy and Arnold.
    b. The divorce resulted in the Roadrunner stock being distributed equally to Tammy and Arnold. What could either party do to change the tax status of Roadrunner?

22. **LO.5** Sabrina is going to contribute an SUV to her wholly owned business. She purchased the SUV three years ago for $58,000 and used it exclusively for personal purposes during this period. The fair market value of the SUV is $40,000. Are the tax consequences different if Sabrina contributes the SUV to an S corporation in which she is a 100% shareholder rather than a C corporation in which she is a 100% shareholder? If the business is a sole proprietorship?

23. **LO.5** Answer the following questions.
    a. How are the nonrecognition rules for contributions of property to a partnership by a partner similar to those for contributions of property to a corporation by a shareholder?
    b. How, if at all, do the nonrecognition rules differ?

24. **LO.5** Why are special allocations either permitted or required for the partners in a partnership, yet are not permitted for the shareholders in a C corporation or an S corporation?

25. **LO.5** Entity liabilities have an effect on a partner's basis in the partnership interest. Yet entity liabilities do not have any effect on a corporate shareholder's stock basis (for either a C corporation or an S corporation). What is the reason for this difference?

26. **LO.5** Identify the effect of each of the following on a partner's basis for a partnership interest and a shareholder's (both C corporation and S corporation) basis for stock:

    - Profits.
    - Losses.
    - Liability increase.
    - Liability decrease.
    - Contribution of assets.
    - Distribution of assets.

27. **LO.5** The conduit concept applies to an S corporation. Are there any circumstances in which an S corporation is a taxpayer rather than merely a tax reporter?

28. **LO.5** Dexter, a partner in the Warbler Partnership, uses the cash method of accounting.
    a. Are the distributions of earnings by the partnership to Dexter taxed to him? Explain.
    b. Would the answer in (a) change if Dexter is a shareholder and Warbler, Inc., is a C corporation?

29. **LO.5** A partner's ability to pass through and deduct his or her share of the partnership loss is limited by the partnership interest basis.
    a. Does the Code further limit the loss pass-through and deduction with the § 465 at-risk rules?

b. In this regard, what effect do the § 469 passive activity loss rules have?
c. Which potentially are more restrictive: the § 465 at-risk rules or the § 469 passive activity loss rules?

30. **LO.6** Bruce wants to sell his sole proprietorship, a hair salon, to Eleanor for $375,000.
a. Does it matter to Bruce whether the form of the transaction is a sale of the business or a sale of the individual assets?
b. Is the answer in (a) affected by whether the assets have appreciated in value or declined in value?

ISSUE ID

31. **LO.6** Vladimir owns all the stock of Ruby, Inc., a C corporation. The fair market value of the stock (and Ruby's assets) is about four times Vladimir's adjusted basis for the stock. He is negotiating with an investor group for the sale of the corporation. Identify the relevant tax issues for Vladimir.

32. **LO.2, 3, 4, 5, 6, 7** Using the legend provided, indicate which form of business entity each of the following characteristics describes. Some of the characteristics may apply to more than one form of business entity.

Legend		
SP	=	Applies to sole proprietorship
P	=	Applies to partnership
S	=	Applies to S corporation
C	=	Applies to C corporation
N	=	Applies to none

a. Has limited liability.
b. Greatest ability to raise capital.
c. Subject to double taxation.
d. Not subject to double taxation.
e. Could be subject to accumulated earnings tax.
f. Limit on types and number of shareholders.
g. Has unlimited liability.
h. Sale of the business can be subject to double taxation.
i. Profits and losses affect the basis for an ownership interest.
j. Entity liabilities affect the basis for an ownership interest.
k. Distributions of earnings are taxed as dividend income to the owners.
l. Total invested capital cannot exceed $1 million.
m. AAA is an account that relates to this entity.

33. **LO.5** Using the legend provided, indicate which form of business entity each of the following characteristics describes. Some of the characteristics may apply to more than one form of business entity.

Legend		
P	=	Applies to partnership
S	=	Applies to S corporation
C	=	Applies to C corporation

The basis for an ownership interest is:
a. Increased by an investment by the owner.
b. Decreased by a distribution to the owner.
c. Increased by entity profits.
d. Decreased by entity losses.
e. Increased as the entity's liabilities increase.
f. Decreased as the entity's liabilities decrease.

34. **LO.5, 6** Green Partnership, a general partnership, has many opportunities to use special allocations. One of the special allocations available to Green is the optional adjustment-to-basis election under §§ 754 and 743 when a new partner acquires a partnership interest from an existing partner. Discuss the relevant factors that should be considered before making this election.

PROBLEMS

35. **LO.2** Sea Green Enterprises has the following assets and liabilities on its balance sheet:

	Net Book Value	Fair Market Value
Assets	$775,000	$975,000
Liabilities	250,000	250,000

Sea Green has just lost a product liability suit with damages of $7 million being awarded to the plaintiff. Although Sea Green will appeal the judgment, legal counsel indicates the judgment is highly unlikely to be overturned by the appellate court. The product liability insurance carried by Sea Green has a policy ceiling of $3 million. What is the amount of liability of Sea Green Enterprises and its owners if the form of the business entity is:

a. A sole proprietorship?
b. A partnership?
c. A C corporation?
d. An S corporation?

36. **LO.3** Red, White, Blue, and Magenta have taxable income as follows:

Corporation	Taxable Income
Red	$ 82,000
White	305,000
Blue	700,000
Magenta	40,000,000

a. Calculate the marginal tax rate and the effective tax rate for each of the C corporations.
b. Explain why the marginal tax rate for a C corporation can exceed 35%, but the effective tax rate cannot do so.

37. **LO.1, 2, 3** Amy and Jeff Barnes are going to operate their florist shop as a partnership or as an S corporation. After paying salaries of $45,000 to each of the owners, the shop's earnings are projected to be about $60,000. The earnings are to be invested in the growth of the business. Write a letter to Amy and Jeff Barnes (5700 Redmont Highway, Washington, D.C. 20024) advising them as to which of the two entity forms they should select. **DECISION MAKING** **COMMUNICATIONS**

38. **LO.2, 3** Jack, a married taxpayer, is going to establish a manufacturing business. He anticipates that the business will be profitable immediately due to a patent that he holds. He anticipates that profits for the first year will be about $250,000 and will increase at a rate of about 25% per year for the foreseeable future. He will be the sole owner of the business. Advise Jack on the form of business entity he should select. Assume Jack and his spouse will be in the 35% tax bracket. **DECISION MAKING**

39. **LO.3** Clay Corporation will begin operations on January 1. Earnings for the next five years are projected to be relatively stable at about $90,000 per year. The shareholders of Clay are in the 33% tax bracket. **DECISION MAKING**

a. Assume that Clay will reinvest its after-tax earnings in the growth of the company. Should Clay operate as a C corporation or as an S corporation?
b. Assume that Clay will distribute its after-tax earnings each year to its shareholders. Should Clay operate as a C corporation or as an S corporation?

40. **LO.3** Mabel and Alan, who are in the 35% tax bracket, recently acquired a fast-food franchise. Each of them will work in the business and receive a salary of $175,000. They anticipate that the annual profits of the business, after deducting salaries, will be approximately $450,000. The entity will distribute enough cash each year to Mabel and Alan to cover their Federal income taxes associated with the franchise.

a. What amount will the entity distribute if the franchise operates as a C corporation?
b. What amount will the entity distribute if the franchise operates as an S corporation?
c. What will be the amount of the combined entity/owner tax liability in (a) and (b)?

41. **LO.3** Owl is a closely held corporation owned by 8 shareholders (each has 12.5% of the stock). Selected financial information provided by Owl follows:

Taxable income	$6,250,000
Positive AMT adjustments (excluding ACE adjustment)	600,000
Negative AMT adjustments	(30,000)
Tax preferences	5,000,000
Retained earnings	900,000
Accumulated E & P	2,000,000
ACE adjustment	750,000

a. Calculate Owl's tax liability if Owl is a C corporation.
b. Calculate Owl's tax liability if Owl is an S corporation.
c. How would your answers in (a) and (b) change if Owl is not closely held (e.g., 5,000 shareholders with no shareholder owning more than 2% of the stock)?

DECISION MAKING

42. **LO.3** Falcon Corporation, a calendar year taxpayer, is a deepwater offshore drilling company that is planning to sell drilling equipment that it no longer needs. The drilling equipment has an adjusted basis of $400,000 ($700,000 – $300,000 depreciation) and a fair market value of $500,000. The AMT adjusted basis is $425,000. The buyer of the drilling equipment would like to close the transaction prior to the end of the calendar year. Falcon is uncertain whether the tax consequences would be better if the sale took place this year or next year and is considering the following options:

- $500,000 in cash payable on December 31, 2011.
- The sale is closed on December 31, 2011, with the consideration being a $500,000 note issued by the buyer. The maturity date of the note is January 2, 2012, with the equipment being pledged as security.

Falcon projects that its taxable income for 2011 and 2012 will be $400,000 (gross receipts of about $9.5 million) without the sale. Falcon has other AMT adjustments and tax preferences of $425,000 in 2011, which will not recur in 2012. Determine the tax consequences to Falcon under both options and recommend the option that is preferable.

43. **LO.4** Two sisters and their brother, all unmarried, own and operate a dairy farm. They live on the farm and take their meals on the farm for the "convenience of the employer." The fair market value of their lodging is $50,000, and the fair market value of their meals is $28,000. The meals are prepared for them by the farm cook who prepares their meals along with those of the eight other farm employees. Determine the tax consequences of the meals and lodging to the sisters and their brother if the farm is:
a. Incorporated.
b. Not incorporated.

44. **LO.4** A business entity's taxable income before the cost of certain fringe benefits paid to owners and other employees is $400,000. The amounts paid for these fringe benefits are as follows:

	Owners	Other Employees
Group term life insurance	$20,000	$40,000
Meals and lodging incurred for the convenience of the employer	50,000	75,000
Pension plan	30,000*	90,000

*H.R. 10 (Keogh) plan for partnership and S corporation.

The business entity is equally owned by four owners.
a. Calculate the taxable income of the business entity if the entity is a partnership, a C corporation, or an S corporation.
b. Determine the effect on the owners for each of the three business forms.

45. **LO.4** Turtle, a C corporation, has taxable income of $600,000 before paying salaries to the three equal shareholder-employees, Britney, Shania, and Alan. Turtle follows a policy of distributing all after-tax earnings to the shareholders.

a. Determine the tax consequences for Turtle, Britney, Shania, and Alan if the corporation pays salaries to Britney, Shania, and Alan as follows:

Option 1		Option 2	
Britney	$270,000	Britney	$135,000
Shania	180,000	Shania	90,000
Alan	150,000	Alan	75,000

b. Is Turtle likely to encounter any tax problems associated with either option?

46. **LO.4** Parrott, Inc., a C corporation, is owned by Abner (60%) and Freda (40%). Abner is the president, and Freda is the vice president for sales. All three are cash basis taxpayers. Late in 2010, Parrott encounters working capital difficulties. Therefore, Abner loans the corporation $540,000, and Freda loans the corporation $360,000. Each loan is on a 6% note that is due in five years with interest payable annually. Determine the tax consequences to Parrott, Abner, and Freda for 2011 if:
    a. The notes are classified as debt.
    b. The notes are classified as equity.

47. **LO.4** Marci and Jennifer each own 50% of the stock of Lavender, a C corporation. After paying each of them a "reasonable" salary of $125,000, the taxable income of Lavender is normally around $600,000. The corporation is about to purchase a $2 million shopping mall ($1.5 million allocated to the building and $500,000 allocated to the land). The mall will be rented to tenants at a net rent income (i.e., includes rental commissions, depreciation, etc.) of $500,000 annually. Marci and Jennifer will contribute $1 million each to the corporation to provide the cash required for the acquisition. Their CPA has suggested that Marci and Jennifer purchase the shopping mall as individuals and lease it to Lavender for a fair rental of $300,000. Both Marci and Jennifer are in the 35% tax bracket. The acquisition will occur on January 2, 2011. Determine whether the shopping mall should be acquired by Lavender or by Marci and Jennifer in accordance with their CPA's recommendation. Assume the depreciation on the shopping mall in 2011 is $37,000. **DECISION MAKING**

48. **LO.3, 4** Flower, Inc., a C corporation, has taxable income of $800,000 for 2011. It has used up the accumulated earnings credit and has no additional "reasonable needs of the business" for the current tax year. Determine the total potential tax liability for Flower:
    a. If it declares no dividends.
    b. If it declares and pays dividends equal to the after-tax earnings.
    c. In (a) and (b) if Flower is an S corporation.

49. **LO.4** Since Garnet Corporation was formed five years ago, its stock has been held as follows: 525 shares by Frank and 175 shares by Grace. Their basis in the stock is $350,000 for Frank and $150,000 for Grace. As part of a stock redemption, Garnet redeems 125 of Frank's shares for $175,000 and 125 of Grace's shares for $175,000. **DECISION MAKING**
    a. What are the tax consequences of the stock redemption to Frank and Grace?
    b. How would the tax consequences to Frank and Grace be different if, instead of the redemption, they each sell 125 shares to Chuck (an unrelated party)?
    c. What factors should influence their decision on whether to redeem or sell the 250 shares of stock?

50. **LO.4** Eagle Corporation has been an electing S corporation since its incorporation 10 years ago. During the first three years of operations, it incurred total losses of $250,000. Since then Eagle has generated earnings of approximately $150,000 each year. None of the earnings have been distributed to the three equal shareholders, Claire, Lynn, and Todd, because the corporation has been in an expansion mode. At the beginning of 2011, Claire sells her stock to Nell for $400,000. Nell has reservations about the utility of the S election. Therefore, Lynn, Todd, and Nell are discussing whether the election should be continued. They expect the earnings to remain at approximately $150,000 each year. However, since they perceive that the expansion period is over and Eagle has adequate working capital, they may start distributing the earnings to the shareholders. All of the shareholders are in the 33% tax bracket. Advise the three shareholders on whether the S election should be maintained. **DECISION MAKING**

DECISION MAKING

51. **LO.5** Andrew and Evans form a business entity with each contributing the following property:

	Andrew	Evans
Cash	$400,000	
Land		$400,000*

*Fair market value. Adjusted basis is $125,000.

Three months later, the land is sold for $465,000 because of unexpected zoning problems. The proceeds are to be applied toward the purchase of another parcel of land to be used for real estate development. Determine the tax consequences to the entity and to the owners upon formation and the later sale of the land if the entity is:

a. A partnership.
b. An S corporation.
c. A C corporation.
d. Is it possible to structure the disposition of the land so as to defer any recognition tax consequences?

52. **LO.5** Agnes, Becky, and Carol form a business entity with each contributing the following:

	Adjusted Basis	Fair Market Value	Ownership Percentage
Agnes: Cash	$100,000	$100,000	40%
Becky: Land	60,000	120,000	40%
Carol: Services		50,000	20%

Becky's land has a $20,000 mortgage that is assumed by the entity. Carol, an attorney, receives her ownership interest in exchange for legal services. Determine the recognized gain to the owners, the basis for their ownership interests, and the entity's basis for its assets if the entity is:

a. A partnership.
b. A C corporation.
c. An S corporation.

53. **LO.5** Melinda has a 30% ownership interest in an entity for which she initially contributed $180,000. She is one of the original owners of the business. None of the owners are related. During the life of the business, the following have occurred:

- Cumulative losses of $250,000 during the first three years.
- Profits of $200,000 in the next year.
- Distributions to owners of $90,000 at the end of year 3.
- Distribution to Melinda of $50,000 that redeems 25% of her ownership interest at the end of year 4. No other owners redeem any of their ownership interest.

Determine the tax consequences to Melinda if the entity is:

a. A partnership.
b. An S corporation.
c. A C corporation.

54. **LO.5** An entity engages in the following transactions during the taxable year:

- Sells stock held for three years as an investment for $30,000 (adjusted basis of $20,000).
- Sells land used in the business for $65,000. The land has been used as a parking lot and originally cost $40,000.
- Receives tax-exempt interest on municipal bonds of $5,000.
- Receives dividends on IBM stock of $80,000.

Describe the effect of these transactions on the entity and its owners if the entity is:

a. A partnership.
b. A C corporation.
c. An S corporation.

55. **LO.5** Swift Corporation distributes land (basis of $55,000 and fair market value of $120,000) to Sam and cash ($240,000) to Allison in exchange for part of their stock. Other shareholders do not redeem any of their stock. Sam surrenders shares of stock that have a basis of $25,000. Prior to the stock redemption, Sam owned 20% of the Swift stock, and after the redemption, he owns 15%. At the same time, Swift distributes cash to Allison, and she surrenders shares of stock with a basis of $40,000. Prior to the stock redemption, Allison owned 70% of the Swift stock, and after the redemption, she owns 60%. Determine the tax consequences to Swift, Sam, and Allison if Swift is:
    a. A C corporation.
    b. An S corporation.

56. **LO.5** Indigo, Inc., a personal service corporation, has the following types of income and losses for 2011:

Active income	$325,000
Portfolio income	49,000
Passive loss	333,000

    a. Calculate Indigo's taxable income for 2011.
    b. Assume that instead of being a personal service corporation, Indigo is a closely held corporation. Calculate Indigo's taxable income for 2011.
    c. Would the answer in (b) change if the passive loss is only $320,000 rather than $333,000?

57. **LO.5** Abby and Velma are equal owners of the AV Partnership with Abby investing $300,000 and Velma contributing land and a building (adjusted basis of $75,000; fair market value of $300,000). In addition, the entity borrows $300,000 using recourse financing and $100,000 using nonrecourse financing.
    a. What are Abby's and Velma's bases for their partnership interests (i.e., outside bases)?
    b. What are Abby's and Velma's at-risk bases?

58. **LO.5** Megan owns 60% and Vern owns 40% of a business entity. The owners would like to share profits with 60% for Megan and 40% for Vern and to share losses with 90% for Vern and 10% for Megan. Determine the tax consequences for 2011 if the entity has a tax loss of $100,000 and is:
    a. A partnership.
    b. A C corporation.
    c. An S corporation.

59. **LO.6** Emily and Freda are negotiating with George to purchase the business that he operates in corporate form (Pelican, Inc.). The assets of Pelican, Inc., a C corporation, are as follows:

Asset	Basis	FMV
Cash	$ 20,000	$ 20,000
Accounts receivable	50,000	50,000
Inventory	100,000	110,000
Furniture and fixtures*	150,000	170,000
Building**	200,000	250,000
Land	40,000	150,000

*Potential depreciation recapture under § 1245 is $45,000.
**The straight-line method was used to depreciate the building. The balance in the accumulated depreciation account is $340,000.

George's basis for the stock of Pelican, Inc., is $560,000. George is in the 35% tax bracket, and Pelican, Inc., is in the 34% tax bracket.
    a. Assume that Emily and Freda purchase the stock of Pelican from George and that the purchase price is $908,000. Determine the tax consequences to Emily and Freda, Pelican, and George.
    b. Assume that Emily and Freda purchase the assets from Pelican and that the purchase price is $908,000. Determine the tax consequences to Emily and Freda, Pelican, and George.

c. Assume that the purchase price is $550,000 because the fair market value of the building is $150,000, and the fair market value of the land is $50,000. Also, assume that no amount is assigned to goodwill. Emily and Freda purchase the stock of Pelican from George. Determine the tax consequences to Emily and Freda, Pelican, and George.

DECISION MAKING

60. **LO.6** Tom and Walt are purchasing the Copper Partnership from Jan and Gail for $650,000 with Tom and Walt being equal partners. Based on the negotiations, Jan and Gail have succeeded in having the transaction structured as the purchase of the partnership rather than the purchase of the individual assets. The adjusted basis of the individual assets of the Copper Partnership is $400,000.
    a. What are Tom's and Walt's bases for their partnership interests (i.e., outside bases)?
    b. What is Copper's adjusted basis for its assets after the transaction? Would a § 754 optional adjustment-to-basis election be helpful?

DECISION MAKING

61. **LO.6** Gail and Harry own the GH Partnership, which has conducted business for 10 years. The bases for their partnership interests are $100,000 for Gail and $150,000 for Harry. GH Partnership has the following assets:

Asset	Basis	FMV
Cash	$ 10,000	$ 10,000
Accounts receivable	30,000	28,000
Inventory	25,000	26,000
Building*	100,000	150,000
Land	250,000	400,000

*The straight-line method has been used to depreciate the building. Accumulated depreciation is $70,000.

Gail and Harry sell their partnership interests to Keith and Liz for $307,000 each.
    a. Determine the tax consequences of the sale to Gail, Harry, and GH Partnership.
    b. From a tax perspective, would it matter to Keith and Liz whether they purchase Gail's and Harry's partnership interests or the partnership assets from GH Partnership?

DECISION MAKING

COMMUNICATIONS

62. **LO.6** Damon Allred is going to purchase either the stock or the assets of Brass Corporation. All of the Brass stock is owned by Charley. Damon and Charley agree that Brass is worth $825,000. The tax basis for Brass's assets is $430,000. Write a letter to Damon advising him on whether he should negotiate to purchase the stock or the assets. Also, prepare a memo for the files. Damon's address is 100 Village Green, Chattanooga, TN 37403.

RESEARCH PROBLEMS

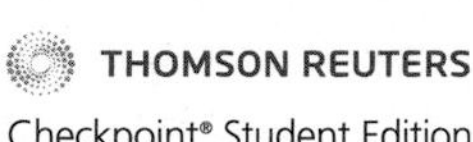

Checkpoint® Student Edition

Note: Solutions to Research Problems can be prepared by using the **RIA Checkpoint® Student Edition** online research product, which is available to accompany this text. It is also possible to prepare solutions to the Research Problems by using tax research materials found in a standard tax library.

Research Problem 1. The stock of Ebony, Inc., is owned as follows:

	Percent Ownership	Basis	FMV
Alma	30	$2,700	$270,000
Ben	30	2,700	270,000
Debbie	20	1,800	180,000
Clyde	20	1,800	180,000

Alma and Ben are the parents of Debbie and Clyde. Managerial positions in Ebony are as follows: Alma is the chief executive officer (CEO), Ben is the chief operating officer (COO), Debbie is the chief financial officer (CFO), and Clyde is the vice president for human resources. Alma and Ben have owned their stock for 30 years, and Debbie and Clyde have owned their stock for 10 years. Alma and Ben are considering disposing of their stock and would like to use the funds to acquire a more lucrative investment. Their initial plan was to have Ebony redeem their stock. However, their accountant has indicated that since they intend to retain their positions as officers, the redemption will not qualify under § 302(b)(3). The accountant suggests that they sell their stock to several outsiders who wish to acquire an interest in Ebony. As Debbie and Clyde expect to move into the CEO and COO positions in a few years, they oppose a sale to outsiders. They are concerned about the loss of family control that would result.

How can this family dilemma be resolved?

Research Problem 2. Dr. Sanders is a veterinarian who is the sole shareholder of Vet, Inc., an S corporation. The corporation offers consulting and surgical services to other veterinarians that Dr. Sanders provides. Dr. Sanders does not receive regular payments from the corporation but withdraws funds as the need arises. During the current year, he withdraws $118,000, and the net income of the corporation is $225,000. The corporation does not deduct the $118,000 nor does Dr. Sanders include it in his gross income. Dr. Sanders does, however, report the $225,000 in his gross income. Since Dr. Sanders has recognized all of the corporation's income, he sees no need to pay himself a salary. He justifies the treatment by arguing that he is not an employee (i.e., he is the owner) of the corporation, and the Federal income tax consequences are the same. Evaluate the approach taken by Dr. Sanders and Vet, Inc.

Research Problem 3. Amanda and Paul are equal owners in Talon, Inc., an S corporation, and each has an adjusted basis in the stock of $80,000. In the current year, Talon has a loss of $200,000, and its Schedule K–1s allocate $100,000 to each shareholder.

Amanda and Paul are also equal partners in a partnership. Two years ago, in order to provide additional working capital to Talon, the partnership loaned it $100,000. The loan bore all of the usual attributes of a bona fide loan (i.e., a formal note, market interest rate, payment schedule). The loan was recorded as a note receivable by the partnership and as a note payable on the S corporation accounting records. Formal minutes authorizing the loan stated that the partnership was acting as an agent for Amanda and Paul.

Amanda and Paul each deducted their share (i.e., $100,000) of the S corporation loss. They contend that their combined stock basis and debt basis for § 1366(d) purposes is $130,000 ($80,000 + $50,000). The IRS maintains that the basis of each shareholder is only $80,000 (the basis in the stock). The loan cannot count as part of the shareholder's debt basis as it was not made directly to the S corporation. Evaluate the positions of the taxpayers and the IRS.

Research Problem 4. Crane is a partner in the Cardinal Partnership. A dispute arose with the partnership regarding his share of current earnings. The partnership contends that the amount is $75,000, while Crane believes his share is $100,000.

Crane ceased being a partner on November 1, 2011. As a result of the dispute, the partnership distributed only $75,000 and placed the disputed $25,000 in escrow. However, Crane's Schedule K–1 from the partnership included the full $100,000. Crane feels that the K–1 should include only the $75,000 that is not in dispute. Is Crane correct?

Use the tax resources of the Internet to address the following questions. Do not restrict your search to the World Wide Web, but include a review of newsgroups and general reference materials, practitioner sites and resources, primary sources of the tax law, chat rooms and discussion groups, and other opportunities.

Research Problem 5. Find a newspaper article about a state that contributed assets to an auto company as a location inducement and later recovered some or all of the assets under a "clawback" provision. What are the tax consequences to the auto company when it returns these assets to the state?

Research Problem 6. Find an article describing how a specific business put together its employee fringe benefit package in light of the limitations presented by the tax law and its form of operation.

COMMUNICATIONS

Research Problem 7. Find a newspaper article that discusses the increasing regulation of "corporate America." Outline the pros and cons of such regulation from your viewpoint and that of the author. In this regard, does it matter whether S or C corporations are involved?

Research Problem 8. Determine how your state income tax deals with § 199 (domestic production activities deduction).

Part 4

Advanced Tax Practice Considerations

The tax professional interacts with a number of different groups and must abide by the rules of various agencies and governmental authorities when servicing clients. For publicly traded entities, additional reporting to shareholders is required as to tax consequences, requiring a reconciliation of tax and book income amounts. When the taxpayer is exempt from Federal income taxation, disclosure and operating requirements often differ from those applicable to the corporate tax model. Many businesses operate in more than one U.S. state and must account for the taxable activities in each. Lastly, the conduct of a tax professional's practice is bound by ethical and operational constraints, exposing both the taxpayer and the tax advisor to penalties, interest, and other sanctions. In this Part of the text, we examine in more detail these aspects of tax practice.

CHAPTER 14

Taxes on the Financial Statements

LEARNING OBJECTIVES

After completing Chapter 14, you should be able to:

LO.1 Recognize the differences between book and tax methods of computing income tax expense.

LO.2 Compute a corporation's book income tax expense.

LO.3 Describe the purpose of the valuation allowance.

LO.4 Recognize the effect of ASC 740-30 (APB 23) on effective tax rates.

LO.5 Interpret the disclosure information contained in an income tax footnote.

LO.6 Use financial statement income tax information to benchmark a company's tax position.

OUTLINE

For the latest in changes to tax legislation, visit **www.cengage.com/taxation/swft.**

THE BIG PICTURE **Tax Solutions for the Real World**

TAXES ON THE FINANCIAL STATEMENTS

Raymond Jones, the CEO of Arctic Corporation, would like some help in reconciling the amount of income tax expense on Arctic's financial statements with the amount of income tax reported on the company's corporate income tax return for its first year of operations. Mr. Jones does not understand why he can't simply multiply the financial statement income by the company's 35 percent marginal tax rate to get the financial tax expense. While the financial statements show book income before tax of $25 million, the reported Federal tax expense is only $7.7 million. In addition, the corporate tax return reports taxable income of $19 million and Federal income taxes payable of only $6.65 million.

Without knowing the specifics of the company's financial statements, does Arctic's situation look reasonable? Why is Arctic's financial tax expense not equal to $8.75 million ($25 million × 35%)? What causes the $1.05 million difference between the taxes shown on the financial statements and the taxes due on the tax return? **Read the chapter and formulate your response.**

GlobalCo is a U.S. corporation with operations in 40 different states and 27 different countries. It pays income taxes in virtually all these jurisdictions. GlobalCo's investors and competitors are interested in understanding GlobalCo's effective tax rate. An examination of its financial statements indicates that GlobalCo has a 28 percent effective tax rate. How much of GlobalCo's tax expense is related to U.S. Federal tax, state and local tax, or taxes in foreign countries? What portion of its tax cost is currently paid versus deferred to some future period? Has GlobalCo recorded any deferred tax assets, representing future tax savings, or deferred tax liabilities, representing future tax costs? How does GlobalCo's effective tax rate for the current year compare to prior years, or to other companies in the same industry? Why is GlobalCo's effective tax rate not simply 35 percent, the statutory corporate rate for large U.S. corporations?

The bottom line result of the many tax planning ideas, advice, and compliance efforts provided by tax professionals to their clients is captured in a simple summary number—income tax expense. A U.S. corporation's tax expense is reported in its annual Federal tax return, its financial statements, and other regulatory filings and is often the starting point for state and local tax returns. As it turns out, however, deriving a corporation's income tax expense is not so simple.

A corporation may report millions of dollars in tax expense in its financial statements and yet pay virtually nothing to the U.S., state, or foreign governments. Alternatively, a corporation may pay substantial amounts to the U.S., state, and foreign governments and report very little income tax expense in its financial statements. Why do such differences exist? Which income tax expense is the "correct" number? How can data regarding a corporation's income tax expense provide valuable information for the corporation, its competitors, and tax professionals assisting in the planning function? This chapter addresses these questions.

14.1 Book-Tax Differences

LO.1

Recognize the differences between book and tax methods of computing income tax expense.

A significant difference may exist between a corporation's Federal income tax liability as reported on its Form 1120 (tax) and the corporation's income tax expense as reported on its financial statements (book) prepared using **generally accepted accounting principles (GAAP)**. This book-tax difference is caused by any or all of the following.

TAX in the NEWS

Here, There, and Everywhere—Global Business Structures

The collapse of Enron Corporation gave the public a peek behind the scenes of a multinational corporation's financial and tax strategies. It turned out that Enron used many sophisticated techniques—some legal and some not—to increase its reported net income and decrease its taxes.

Enron used so-called special purpose entities, structured so that the income or loss of the entities was not included in Enron's financial statements. Enron had over 900 subsidiaries located in a number of tax haven countries around the world. For example, Enron had 692 subsidiaries incorporated in the Cayman Islands, 119 subsidiaries in the Turks and Caicos Islands, and 43 subsidiaries in Mauritius.

The $50 billion investment Ponzi scheme carried out by Bernard Madoff over the last decade reportedly involved dozens of offshore entities. Global operations are important to meet the legitimate needs of U.S. businesses. However, offshore entities add complexity that can be used to obscure actual results.

- Differences in reporting entities included in the calculation.
- Different definition of taxes included in the income tax expense amount.
- Different accounting methods.

A corporation's activities are captured in its accounting records, producing general ledger results. At the end of the year, these records are summarized to produce a trial balance. Adjustments to these accounting data may be necessary to produce both the corporation's financial statements and its corporate income tax return. These adjustments rarely are the same. As discussed below, different entities may be included for different purposes, and the book and tax rules can be quite different. On a tax return, Schedule M–1 or M–3 reconciles the difference between a corporation's book income and its taxable income. See Figure 14.1.

DIFFERENT REPORTING ENTITIES

A corporate group must consolidate all U.S. and foreign subsidiaries within a single financial statement for book purposes when the parent corporation controls more than 50 percent of the voting power of those subsidiaries.[1] In cases where the parent corporation owns between 20 and 50 percent of another corporation, the parent uses the **equity method** to account for the earnings of the subsidiary. Under the equity method, the parent currently records its share of the subsidiary's income or loss for the year.[2] Corporations that own less than 20 percent of other corporations typically use the *cost method* to account for income from these investments and include income only when actual dividends are received.

EXAMPLE 1
THE BIG PICTURE

Return to the facts of *The Big Picture* on p. 14-2. Arctic Corporation owns 100% of Gator, Inc., a domestic corporation; 100% of Hurricane, Ltd., a foreign corporation; and 40% of Beach, Inc., a domestic corporation. Arctic's combined financial statement includes its own net income and the net income of both Gator and Hurricane. In addition, Arctic's financial statement includes its 40% share of Beach's net income. Arctic's financial statement includes the income of these subsidiaries regardless of whether Arctic receives any actual profit distributions from its subsidiaries. ■

For Federal tax purposes, a U.S. corporation may elect to include any *domestic* subsidiaries that are 80 percent or more owned in its consolidated U.S. tax return.[3] The

[1] *Consolidation*, ASC Topic 810 (formerly *Consolidation of All Majority Owned Subsidiaries*, Statement of Financial Accounting Standards No. 94). Certain adjustments are made to reduce book income for the after-tax income related to minority shareholders.

[2] *Investments—Equity Method and Joint Ventures*, ASC Topic 323 (formerly *The Equity Method of Accounting for Investments in Common Stock*, Accounting Principles Board Opinion No. 18).

[3] §§ 1501–1504. The election to consolidate an 80% or more owned subsidiary generally can be changed only with the permission of the IRS.

TAX in the NEWS — A New Code?

Tax practitioners long have referred to the Internal Revenue Code simply as the "Code." Now there's a new code (or codification) to deal with—the long-awaited codification (or reorganization) of all the existing accounting standards. In June 2009, the Financial Accounting Standards Board (FASB) issued *The FASB Accounting Standards Codification and the Hierarchy of Generally Accepted Accounting Principles—a replacement of FASB Statement No. 162,* Statement of Financial Accounting Standards No. 168. The FASB Accounting Standards Codification (ASC) is now the major source of authoritative U.S. accounting and reporting standards (for other than certain nongovernmental entities). Guidance will continue to be issued by the Securities and Exchange Commission. This change is effective for financial statements for interim or annual periods ending on or after September 15, 2009.

The Accounting Standards Codification has made a major change in the way that the authoritative accounting literature is organized and referenced. Accounting for income tax guidance formerly referenced as SFAS 109, or APB 23, or FIN 48, is now combined in ASC Topic 740. Novices and experts alike will have much to learn as they use and cite the new code.

income of foreign subsidiaries and less than 80 percent owned domestic subsidiaries is not included in the consolidated tax return.

EXAMPLE 2
THE BIG PICTURE

Return to the facts of *The Big Picture* on p. 14-2. Also assume the facts presented in Example 1. If Arctic elects to include Gator as part of its consolidated Federal income tax return, Arctic's return includes its own taxable income and the taxable income generated by Gator. Hurricane's taxable income is not included in the consolidated return because it is a non-U.S. corporation. Beach, although a domestic corporation, cannot be consolidated with Arctic because Arctic owns only 40% of the stock. Income from Hurricane and Beach will be included in Arctic's U.S. taxable income only when Arctic receives actual or constructive dividends. ■

FIGURE 14.1 Flow of Accounting Data

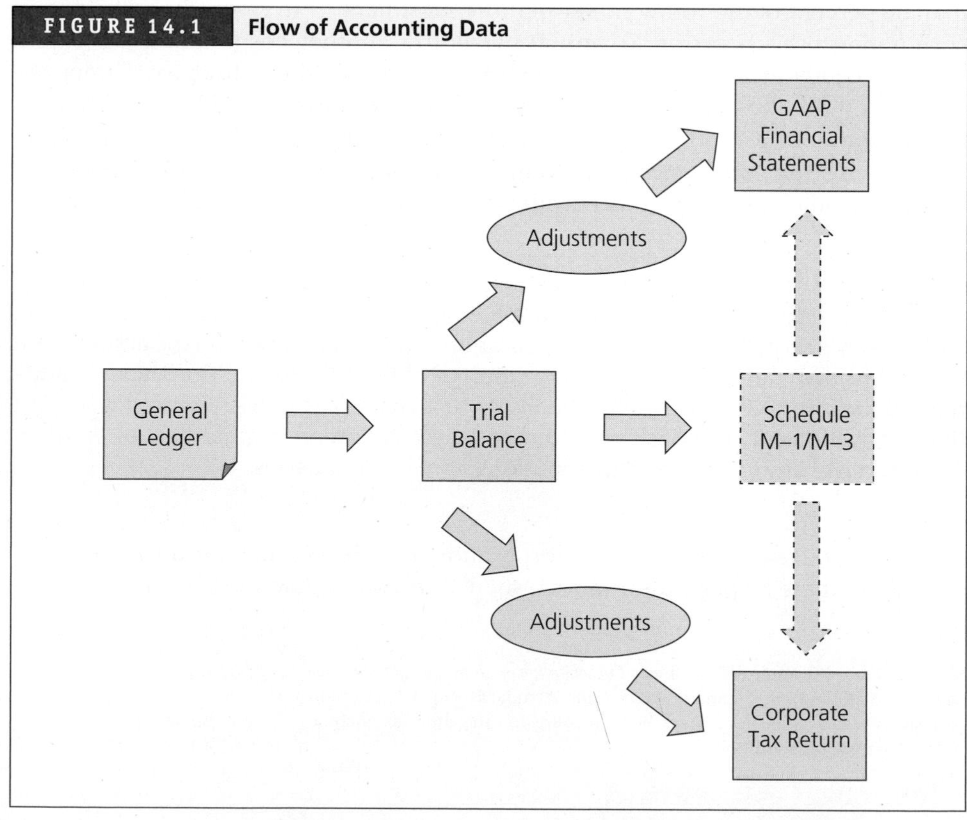

TAX *in* the NEWS

To Deduct or Not to Deduct—The Question Is Answered

In March 2004, the Financial Accounting Standards Board proposed that companies be required to report the value of options they provide to their employees as an expense on their financial statements beginning in 2005. The International Accounting Standards Board adopted a similar rule effective in 2004. Some companies feared the effect this rule might have on their share prices, with the lower net income that stock option expensing would produce. High-tech companies were particularly concerned about this proposal because they are heavy users of stock options to attract employees.

The opponents of stock option expensing lobbied Congress to intervene with the FASB and prevent the adoption of this rule. This is not the first time the option-expensing controversy has erupted. The FASB almost adopted a similar rule in 1994 but backed down after intervention by the U.S. Senate and the Securities and Exchange Commission. However, the recent history of corporate failure and fraud, combined with the push for more transparency in financial statements, made Congress hesitant to get involved this time around.

Ultimately, the FASB issued *Compensation—Stock Compensation*, ASC Topic 718-10 (formerly *Share-Based Payment*, Statement of Financial Accounting Standards No. 123R). The standard requires that the compensation cost relating to share-based payments be recognized as an expense in the income statement. The standard applies to many types of stock-based compensation, including stock options, restricted share plans, performance-based awards, share appreciation rights, and employee share purchase plans.

DIFFERENT TAXES

The income tax expense reported on a corporation's financial statement is the combination of the entity's Federal, state, local, and foreign income taxes. This tax expense number includes both current and deferred tax expense amounts. The distinction between current and deferred income taxes is discussed later in this chapter.

EXAMPLE 3
THE BIG PICTURE

Return to the facts of *The Big Picture* on p. 14-2. Also assume the facts presented in Example 1. For book purposes, Arctic, Gator, and Hurricane combine their income and expenses into a single financial statement. The book tax expense for the year includes all Federal, state, local, and foreign income taxes paid or accrued by these three corporations. In addition, the tax expense amount includes any future Federal, state, local, or foreign income tax expenses (or tax savings) on income reported in the current income statement. ■

The income tax expense computed on the Federal income tax return is the U.S. *Federal* income tax expense. This amount is based on the U.S. corporation's taxable income. State income taxes are reported on the Federal tax return, but as deductions in arriving at taxable income.

EXAMPLE 4
THE BIG PICTURE

Return to the facts of *The Big Picture* on p. 14-2. Also assume the facts presented in Example 1. Arctic and Gator file a consolidated Federal tax return. The tax expense reported on the Form 1120 is only the U.S. Federal income tax expense for the consolidated taxable income of Arctic and Gator. This tax expense does not include the income taxes that Arctic and its subsidiaries paid to state, local, or foreign governments. ■

DIFFERENT METHODS

Many differences exist between book and tax accounting methods. Some are simply **temporary differences**, with income and expenses appearing in both the financial statement and the tax return, but in different periods (i.e., a timing difference). Others are **permanent differences**, with items appearing in the financial statement or the tax return, but not both.

Examples of temporary differences include the following.

- *Depreciation on fixed assets.* Taxpayers may use an accelerated depreciation method under the modified accelerated cost recovery system (MACRS) rules but a straight-line method for book purposes. Even if identical methods are used, the period over which the asset is depreciated may differ between book and tax.

- *Compensation-related expenses.* Several differences exist in this category. For example, under GAAP, corporations must accrue the future expenses related to providing postretirement benefits other than pensions (e.g., health insurance coverage). However, these expenses are deductible for tax purposes only when paid.
- *Accrued income and expenses.* Although most income and expense items are recognized for tax and book purposes in the same period, a number of items potentially appear in different periods. For example, warranty expenses are accrued for book purposes but are not deductible for tax purposes until incurred. Inventory write-offs are accrued for book but are not deductible for tax until incurred. On the income side, different methods regarding the timing of income recognition may create temporary differences. For instance, GAAP recognizes income and loss when the *fair value* of most investment assets changes during the year, while tax rules recognize such realized gain or loss only upon a sale or other taxable disposition of the asset.
- *Net operating losses.* Operating losses from one tax year may be used to offset taxable income in another tax year. Thus, the losses incurred in one year for book purposes may be used as a deduction for tax purposes in a different year.
- *Intangible assets.* Goodwill and some other intangibles are not amortizable for book purposes. However, GAAP requires an annual determination of whether the intangible has suffered a reduction in value (i.e., impairment).[4] If an intangible has suffered an impairment, a current expense is required to reduce the intangible's book value to the lower level. For tax purposes, certain post-1993 intangibles are amortized over 15 years.[5]

Examples of permanent differences include the following.[6]

- *Nontaxable income.* A common example is municipal bond interest, which is income for book purposes but is not taxable.
- *Nondeductible expenses.* For example, the disallowed portion of meals and entertainment expense and certain penalties are not deductible for tax purposes but are expensed in arriving at book income.
- *Tax credits.* Credits such as the research activities credit reduce Federal income tax liability but have no corresponding book treatment.

EXAMPLE 5

Wise, Inc., reported the following results for the current year.

Book income (before tax)	$ 685,000
Tax depreciation in excess of book	(125,000)
Nondeductible warranty expense	65,000
Municipal bond interest income	(35,000)
Taxable income (Form 1120)	$ 590,000

Wise reports net income before tax of $685,000 on its financial statement but must adjust this amount for differences between book and tax income. Tax depreciation in excess of book is a tax deduction not deducted for book purposes, and warranty expense is deductible for book purposes but not yet deductible for tax. Both these items are temporary differences because they will eventually reverse (with book depreciation eventually exceeding tax depreciation and the warranty expense ultimately deducted for tax when incurred). The municipal bond interest is a permanent difference because this income will never be subject to tax. ■

[4] *Intangibles—Goodwill and Other,* ASC Topic 350 (formerly *Goodwill and Other Intangible Assets,* Statement of Financial Accounting Standards No. 142).

[5] § 197. Prior to 1994, goodwill and similar intangibles were not amortizable for tax purposes but were amortizable for book purposes over a maximum period of 40 years. Thus, goodwill acquired during this period triggered a permanent difference (amortizable for book but not for tax).

[6] Before the FASB changed the rules in 2004 for reporting stock options as an expense in financial statements, nonqualified stock option expenses also created a permanent difference because the corporation received a tax deduction on the date the employee exercised the option but was not required to deduct an expense for book purposes under prior GAAP.

TAX *in* the NEWS

Audit Roadmap Expands

The IRS audit roadmap now includes country lanes and alleyways in addition to major highways. Some U.S. corporations must disclose to the IRS much more detailed information about the differences between their book and taxable income. The book-tax reconciliation Schedule M–3 is used for consolidated tax groups with total year-end assets of $10 million or more. Schedule M–3 provides extensive detail on the differences between a corporation's book and taxable income, including information on entities included, income, and deductions (see Chapter 2).

The business community expressed concern over the compliance costs associated with providing this level of detail. These concerns did little to derail the expanded reporting requirements in an era of Sarbanes-Oxley, corporate fraud, and questions over whether corporations are paying their fair share of the tax burden.

Figure 14.2 contains the **Schedule M–1** from Form 1120, the corporate income tax return. The purpose of Schedule M–1 is to reconcile book income to the taxable income reported on the tax return. Line 1 is the net income or loss per books, and line 2 adds back the book tax expense in order to get back to book income before tax.[7] The remainder of Schedule M–1 contains positive and negative adjustments for both temporary and permanent differences until arriving at taxable income on line 10. For tax years after 2004, **Schedule M–3** is required for a consolidated tax group with total year-end assets of $10 million or more. Other corporations may file a Schedule M–3 voluntarily. Appendix B of this text includes a copy of the Schedule M–3.

The income tax note of the financial statements also contains a tax reconciliation, but as discussed later, the purpose and content of this reconciliation are quite different. The book-tax differences reported on Schedule M–1 or M–3 relate to *current-year* differences in book income and taxable income. These items are related to the temporary and permanent differences that occur in determining a corporation's book tax expense. However, for book purposes, the temporary differences are the result of the *cumulative* changes in deferred tax assets and liabilities (as discussed later).

The Schedule M–3 provides the IRS with more detailed information than is provided in the Schedule M–1. A more specific "book income" starting point is used, with the taxpayer identifying the source of the book net income amount by answering a series of questions in Part I. Detail then is provided on differences due to the income or loss from foreign entities, along with data about eliminated intercompany transactions.

FIGURE 14.2 Schedule M–1

Schedule M-1 **Reconciliation of Income (Loss) per Books With Income per Return**

Note: Schedule M-3 required instead of Schedule M-1 if total assets are $10 million or more—see instructions

1	Net income (loss) per books		7	Income recorded on books this year not included on this return (itemize):	
2	Federal income tax per books			Tax-exempt interest $ ______	
3	Excess of capital losses over capital gains .			______	
4	Income subject to tax not recorded on books this year (itemize): ______			______	
	______		8	Deductions on this return not charged against book income this year (itemize):	
5	Expenses recorded on books this year not deducted on this return (itemize):		a	Depreciation . . $ ______	
a	Depreciation . . . . $ ______		b	Charitable contributions $ ______	
b	Charitable contributions . $ ______			______	
c	Travel and entertainment . $ ______			______	
	______		9	Add lines 7 and 8	
6	Add lines 1 through 5		10	Income (page 1, line 28)—line 6 less line 9	

[7]Line 1, "Net income (loss) per books," is not defined in the instructions to the form, and corporations seem to use various starting points in the Schedule M–1 (e.g., only the book income from U.S. members of the group). The Schedule M–3 is more specific in defining book income.

CONCEPT SUMMARY 14.1

Income Amounts—Book versus Tax

Financial Statement	U.S. Federal Income Tax Return
Reporting entities	**Reporting entities**
• 50% or more owned domestic and foreign subsidiaries *must* be consolidated.	• 80% or more owned domestic subsidiaries *may* be consolidated.
• Share of income from 20 to 50% owned domestic and foreign corporations included in current income.	• Share of income from other corporations reported only when actual or constructive dividends are received.
Income tax expense	**Income tax expense**
• Federal income taxes.	• Federal income taxes.
• State income taxes.	• Current only.
• Local income taxes.	
• Foreign income taxes.	
• Current and deferred.	
Methods	**Methods**
• Temporary differences.	• Temporary differences.
• Permanent differences.	• Permanent differences.
• Income tax note reconciliation.	• Schedule M–1 or M–3 reconciliation.

The list of potential book-tax differences is significantly more comprehensive than that in the Schedule M–1, with income items reported in Part II and deduction items reported in Part III. And unlike the Schedule M–1, Schedule M–3 requires identification of whether a book-tax difference is temporary or permanent.

Schedule M–1 or M–3 typically is used as the starting point for IRS audits of corporations. Identifying large differences between book and taxable income may offer the IRS auditor insights into tax saving strategies (some perhaps questionable) employed by the taxpayer. Concept Summary 14.1 summarizes the book-tax differences in arriving at income tax expense.

14.2 Income Taxes in the Financial Statements

LO.2

Compute a corporation's book income tax expense.

GAAP PRINCIPLES

As pointed out earlier, a corporation's financial statements are prepared in accordance with GAAP. The purpose and objectives of these statements are quite different from the objective of the corporation's income tax return.

The **ASC 740 (SFAS 109)** approach produces a total income tax expense (also called the **income tax provision**) for the income currently reported on a corporation's combined financial statement.[8] This approach follows the matching principle, where all the expenses related to earning income are reported in the same period as the income without regard to when the expenses are actually paid.

EXAMPLE 6

PanCo, Inc., earns $100,000 in book income before tax. PanCo has a single temporary difference. Tax depreciation exceeds book depreciation by $20,000. Accordingly, PanCo's taxable income is $80,000 ($100,000 – $20,000 additional tax deduction). On its income

[8] *Income Taxes*, ASC Topic 740 (formerly *Accounting for Income Taxes*, Statement of Financial Accounting Standards No. 109).

TAX *in the NEWS*

THE BOOK-TAX INCOME GAP

The corporate financial scandals of Enron, WorldCom, and others heightened interest in whether corporations are making appropriate disclosures (i.e., transparency) and in whether they are shouldering their fair share of the tax burden. Adding fuel to the fire is the fact that the gap between book income and taxable income seems to be growing.

According to one study, over the last five years, 115 companies in the Standard and Poor's stock index incurred a Federal and state income tax rate of less than 20 percent. In fact, the rate for 39 of those companies was less than 10 percent.

Congress and the U.S. Treasury are concerned about the increased efforts by corporations to reduce U.S. income tax obligations and have issued regulations that require disclosure of certain "tax shelter" transactions. Corporations counter that the large differences in book and tax income are a function of the different rules and objectives of GAAP for financial statements and the Internal Revenue Code for tax returns. Actually, low effective tax rates often are traceable to one or more of the following.

- Use of NOL carryovers.
- Large investments in depreciable assets.
- Use of tax incentives, e.g., to encourage new companies and targeted industries like high-tech.
- The application of tax planning techniques.

tax return, PanCo reports total Federal tax expense of $28,000 ($80,000 × 35%). On its financial statement, PanCo reports a total tax expense of $35,000 ($100,000 × 35%). This $7,000 book-tax difference is the difference between the book and tax basis of the depreciable asset times the current corporate tax rate ($7,000 = $20,000 × 35%).

Although PanCo did not actually pay the $7,000 this year, in future years when the book-tax depreciation difference reverses, the $7,000 eventually is paid. Hence, the *future* income tax expense related to the current book income is reported in the current year. ■

The total book tax expense under ASC 740 (SFAS 109) is made up of both current and deferred components.[9] The **current tax expense** theoretically represents the taxes actually payable to (or refund receivable from) the governmental authorities for the current period. Although an oversimplification, think of this amount as the actual check the taxpayer writes to the government (or refund received) for the current year. Keep in mind, though, that the current portion of the book income tax expense rarely matches the taxpayer's actual tax liability.[10] Numerous items may lead to differences between actual current tax payments and the reported current tax expense. Figure 14.3 summarizes the computation of a corporation's current tax expense.

The deferred component of the book tax expense is called the **deferred tax expense** or **deferred tax benefit**. This component represents the future tax cost (or savings) connected with income reported in the current-period financial statement.

FIGURE 14.3 Current Tax Expense*

	Pretax book income
±	Schedule M–1/M–3 adjustment
	Taxable income before NOLs
−	NOL carryforwards
	Taxable income
×	Applicable tax rate
	Current tax expense (provision) before tax credits
−	Tax credits
	Current tax expense (tax provision)

*Simplified calculation.

[9]Corporations also may include a "cushion" in their provision for income tax expense, to account currently for potential tax costs in the future (e.g., deficiencies related to losing a potential IRS audit). See ASC 740-10 (formerly *FASB Interpretation 48 [FIN 48], Accounting for Uncertainty in Income Taxes—An Interpretation of FASB Statement No. 109,* Financial Accounting Standards Board).

[10]See G. A. McGill and E. Outslay, "Did Enron Pay Taxes? Using Accounting Information to Decipher Tax Status," *Tax Notes,* August 19, 2002, for a discussion of issues surrounding the interpretation of the current tax payable account.

GLOBAL Tax Issues

Accounting for Income Taxes in International Standards

The FASB and the International Accounting Standards Board (IASB) have worked to move the GAAP and IFRS treatment of income taxes closer together in light of the future convergence of GAAP and IFRS. Both ASC 740 (SFAS 109) and IAS 12 (the IFRS guidance for income taxes) are based on a balance sheet approach.

Nevertheless, several significant differences exist between the two standards. These include the thresholds for recognition and approach to valuation allowances, the treatment of foreign subsidiaries and undistributed earnings, and the measurement of uncertain tax positions.

One can keep up with the FASB and the IASB's work on the "Income Tax Project" by visiting the FASB website at **www.fasb.org** and searching for the "Technical Plan and Project Updates" section under "Projects."

Deferred tax expense or benefit is created as a result of temporary differences. More technically, ASC 740 (SFAS 109) adopts a **balance sheet approach** to measuring deferred taxes. Under this approach, the deferred tax expense or benefit is the change from one year to the next in the net **deferred tax liability** or **deferred tax asset.**

A deferred tax liability is the expected future tax liability related to current income (measured using enacted tax rates and rules).[11] A deferred tax liability is created in the following situations.

- An expense is deductible for tax in the current period but is not deductible for book until some future period.
- Income is includible currently for book purposes but is not includible in taxable income until a future period.

In essence, a deferred tax liability is created when the book basis of an asset exceeds its tax basis (the opposite results in a deferred tax asset).

EXAMPLE 7

PJ Enterprises earns net income before depreciation of $500,000 in 2010 and $600,000 in 2011. PJ has a single depreciable asset acquired in 2010 for $80,000. For tax purposes PJ may deduct $60,000 in depreciation expense for the first year and $20,000 in depreciation expense for the second year (i.e., it uses an accelerated method). For book purposes, assume that PJ depreciates the asset on a straight-line basis over two years ($40,000 depreciation expense per year).

2010

	Book	Tax
Income before depreciation	$500,000	$500,000
Depreciation	(40,000)	(60,000)
Income after depreciation	$460,000	$440,000
Corporate tax rate	× 35%	× 35%
Income tax expense	$161,000	$154,000
Current tax expense	$154,000	
Deferred tax expense	$ 7,000	
Starting adjusted basis in depreciable asset	$ 80,000	$ 80,000
Ending adjusted basis in depreciable asset	(40,000)	(20,000)
Change in adjusted basis	$ 40,000	$ 60,000

Book-tax balance sheet difference	$20,000
Corporate tax rate	× 35%
Deferred tax liability	$ 7,000

[11] If the tax rate will be different in future years, the *enacted* future tax rate should be used in the computation.

In this example, it is easy to "back into" the deferred tax expense amount of $7,000 by simply taking the difference between the tax expense per the tax return ($154,000) and the book tax expense ($161,000). This is referred to as the "APB 11" approach based on the method used before ASC 740 (SFAS 109). This may provide a quick check on the calculation in simple cases, but will not always be correct. The correct computation of the deferred tax expense is based on the difference between the book and tax asset basis numbers ($20,000) at the enacted corporate tax rate (35%).

2011

	Book	Tax
Income before depreciation	$600,000	$600,000
Depreciation	(40,000)	(20,000)
Income after depreciation	$560,000	$580,000
Corporate tax rate	× 35%	× 35%
Income tax expense	$196,000	$203,000
Current tax expense	$203,000	
Deferred tax expense	($ 7,000)	
Starting adjusted basis in depreciable asset	$ 40,000	$ 20,000
Ending adjusted basis in depreciable asset	(–0–)	(–0–)
Change in adjusted basis	$ 40,000	$ 20,000
Book-tax balance sheet difference	($20,000)	
Corporate tax rate	× 35%	
Deferred tax liability	($ 7,000)	

In 2011, the book-tax difference in asset basis reverses, with a resulting reverse in the deferred tax liability account. ■

EXAMPLE 8

Continue with the facts in Example 7. The following journal entries record the book tax expense (provision) for each year. Notice that the book total tax expense combines the current amount (income tax payable) and the future amount (deferred tax liability).

2010 journal entry		
Income tax expense (provision)	$161,000	
Income tax payable		$154,000
Deferred tax liability		7,000
2011 journal entry		
Income tax expense (provision)	$196,000	
Deferred tax liability	7,000	
Income tax payable		$203,000

At the end of 2010, the balance sheet reflects a net deferred tax liability of $7,000. At the end of 2011, the balance sheet contains no deferred tax liability because the temporary difference that created the deferred tax liability has reversed itself. ■

A deferred tax asset is the expected future tax benefit related to current book income (measured using enacted tax rates and rules). A deferred tax asset is created in the following situations.

- An expense is deductible for book in the current period but is not deductible for tax until some future period.
- Income is includible in taxable income currently but is not includible in book income until a future period.

EXAMPLE 9

MollCo, Inc., earns net income before warranty expense of $400,000 in 2010 and $450,000 in 2011. In 2010, MollCo deducts $30,000 in warranty expense for book purposes related to expected warranty repairs. This warranty expense is not deductible for tax purposes until actually incurred. Assume that the $30,000 warranty expense is paid in 2011 and that this is MollCo's only temporary difference.

2010

	Book	Tax
Income before warranty expense	$400,000	$400,000
Warranty expense	(30,000)	—
Income after warranty expense	$370,000	$400,000
Corporate tax rate	× 35%	× 35%
Income tax expense	$129,500	$140,000
Current tax expense	$140,000	
Deferred tax expense	($ 10,500)	
Basis in warranty expense payable	$ 30,000	$ –0–

Book-tax balance sheet difference	($30,000)
Corporate tax rate	× 35%
Deferred tax asset	($10,500)

In this example, it is easy to "back into" the deferred tax expense amount of $10,500 simply by taking the difference between the tax expense per the tax return ($140,000) and the book tax expense ($129,500). However, the correct computation of the deferred tax expense is based on the difference between the book and tax basis in the warranty expense payable ($30,000) at the corporate tax rate (35%).

2011

	Book	Tax
Income before warranty expense	$450,000	$450,000
Warranty expense	—	(30,000)
Income after depreciation	$450,000	$420,000
Corporate tax rate	× 35%	× 35%
Income tax expense	$157,500	$147,000
Current tax expense	$147,000	
Deferred tax expense	$ 10,500	
Basis in warranty expense payable	$ –0–	$ 30,000

Book-tax balance sheet difference	$ 30,000
Corporate tax rate	× 35%
Deferred tax asset	$ 10,500

In 2011, the book-tax difference in warranty expense payable reverses, with a resulting elimination of the deferred tax asset account. ■

EXAMPLE 10

Continue with the facts in Example 9. The following journal entries record the book tax expense (provision) for each year. Notice that the book total tax expense combines the current amount (income tax payable) and the future amount (deferred tax asset).

2010 journal entry		
Income tax expense (provision)	$129,500	
Deferred tax asset	10,500	
Income tax payable		$140,000
2011 journal entry		
Income tax expense (provision)	$157,500	
Deferred tax asset		$ 10,500
Income tax payable		147,000

FINANCIAL DISCLOSURE *Insights*: TAX LOSSES AND THE DEFERRED TAX ASSET

Although a current-year net operating loss (NOL) represents a failure of an entity's business model to some, others see it as an immediate tax refund. But when an NOL hits the balance sheet as a deferred tax asset, the story is not over. The NOL creates or increases a deferred tax asset that may or may not be used in future financial accounting reporting periods: the key question for a financial analyst is whether the entity will generate enough net revenue in future years to create a positive tax liability that can be offset by the NOL carryover amount.

For every reporting period, the managers of a business entity holding a loss carryforward must assess whether the loss is likely to be used to create cash flow in the future, as it offsets operating or other profits from future years. When it is more likely than not that a loss carryforward *will not be realized*, GAAP requires that a valuation allowance be created to reduce the deferred tax asset to a lower amount that is expected to be realized in the future. The valuation allowance is a contra-asset account (like accumulated depreciation on a fixed asset) against the deferred tax asset.

A valuation allowance against an NOL carryforward might be created when there is doubt as to the level of the entity's future net profits. The valuation allowance is reduced or eliminated, though, when it appears that the NOL will be fully realized due to any of the following.

- Future years' net income from operations or other activities.
- New product orders or contracts for business.
- The reversal of other temporary book-tax differences.
- An effective use of tax planning strategies.

Evidence that a loss carryforward might not be realized in the future includes the following.

- A series of operating losses in previous years for the reporting entity.
- A history of the entity's tax losses expiring unused.
- Open transactions, such as lawsuits and regulatory challenges, that might reduce future profits of the business.

The current version of IFRS does not allow for a valuation allowance. Under IAS 12, a deferred tax asset is recorded only when it is "probable" (a higher standard than GAAP's "more likely than not") that the deferred tax amount will be realized, and then only to the extent of that probable amount. Thus, no offsetting valuation allowance is needed.

At the end of 2010, the balance sheet reflects a net deferred tax asset of $10,500. At the end of 2011, the balance sheet contains no deferred tax asset because the temporary difference that created the deferred tax asset has reversed. ■

Deferred tax assets and liabilities are reported on the balance sheet just as any other asset or liability would be. However, the interpretation of these assets and liabilities is quite different. Typically, an asset is "good" because it represents a claim on something of value, and a liability is "bad" because it represents a future claim against the corporation's assets. In the case of deferred tax assets and liabilities, the interpretation is reversed. Deferred tax liabilities are "good" because they represent an amount that may be paid to the government in the future. In essence, deferred tax liabilities are like an interest-free loan from the government with a due date perhaps many years in the future. Deferred tax assets, on the other hand, are future tax benefits and thus are similar to a receivable from the government that may not be received until many years in the future.

VALUATION ALLOWANCE

LO.3 Describe the purpose of the valuation allowance.

Much of GAAP is based on the **conservatism principle**. That is, accounting rules are designed to provide assurance that assets are not overstated and liabilities are not understated. Current recognition of deferred tax liabilities does not require significant professional judgment because future tax liabilities always are expected to be settled. However, under ASC 740 (SFAS 109), deferred tax assets are recognized only when it is probable that the future tax benefits will be realized.

EXAMPLE 11

Warren, Inc., reported book income before tax of $2 million in 2010. Warren's taxable income is also $2 million (no temporary or permanent differences). Warren has a current U.S. income tax liability for 2010 of $700,000 before tax credits ($2 million × 35%). During 2010, Warren paid $100,000 in foreign income taxes that it is not able to use as a credit on its 2010 tax return because of the foreign tax credit (FTC) limitation (see Chapter 9). Warren's auditors believe it is more likely than not that Warren will be able to use the $100,000 in FTCs within the next 10 years before they expire. Consequently, the future tax benefit of the FTCs is accounted for in the current-year book tax expense as a $100,000 future tax benefit.

The current and deferred tax expense are calculated as follows.

	Book	Tax
Income tax expense	$600,000	$700,000
Current tax expense	$700,000	
Deferred tax expense (benefit)	($100,000)	

Warren makes the following journal entry to record the book income tax expense and deferred tax asset related to the expected use of the FTCs.

Income tax expense (provision)	$600,000	
Deferred tax asset	100,000	
Income tax payable		$700,000

Because Warren is able to record the benefit of the future FTCs, its effective tax rate is 30% ($600,000 tax expense/$2 million book income before tax). ■

When a deferred tax asset does not meet the *more likely than not* threshold for recognition, ASC 740 (SFAS 109) requires that a **valuation allowance** be created. The valuation allowance is a contra-asset account that offsets all or a portion of the deferred tax asset.

EXAMPLE 12

Assume that the auditors in Example 11 believe that Warren will be able to use only $40,000 of the FTCs, with the remaining $60,000 expiring. In this case, the future tax benefit recognized currently should be only $40,000 rather than the full $100,000. To implement this reduction in the deferred tax asset, Warren must record a valuation allowance of $60,000, resulting in a book tax expense of $660,000.

	Book	Tax
Income tax expense	$660,000	$700,000
Current tax expense	$700,000	
Deferred tax expense (benefit)	($ 40,000)	

Warren makes the following journal entry to record the book income tax expense and deferred tax asset related to the expected use of the FTCs.

Income tax expense (provision)	$660,000	
Deferred tax asset	100,000	
Valuation allowance		$ 60,000
Income tax payable		700,000

Warren must reduce the deferred tax asset by $60,000, which increases its effective tax rate to 33% ($660,000 tax expense/$2 million book income before tax), compared with the 30% effective tax rate in Example 11. ■

To determine whether a valuation allowance is required, both positive and negative evidence must be evaluated. Examples of negative evidence (i.e., evidence suggesting that the deferred tax asset will not be realized) include the following.

- History of losses.
- Expected future losses.

FINANCIAL DISCLOSURE *Insights*

Financial Accounting Effects of Tax Uncertainties

Companies take positions in their tax returns that may not ultimately survive the scrutiny of the IRS or other tax authorities. If a taxpayer loses the benefit of a favorable tax position after a future audit, the loss of this tax benefit may unfavorably affect the company's financial statement tax expense in that future year. The additional tax cost will become part of the current tax expense, yet the income this tax is related to would have been reported in the initial year. This result wreaks havoc with a company's effective tax rate.

To avoid this increase in effective tax rate, companies may book a reserve or "cushion" for the uncertain tax position in the initial year. That is, rather than book the entire tax benefit (and thus reduce tax expense in the current year), the company may book only a portion (or none) of the tax benefit. If the company later loses the actual tax benefit upon audit, to the extent the additional tax imposed is charged against the reserve (or "cushion"), the additional tax does not affect the future-year tax expense. If the company's tax position is not challenged in the future (or the company successfully defends any challenge), the reserve can be released. This release reduces the current tax expense in the future (release) year and lowers the company's effective tax rate in that year.

Prior to 2006, *FAS 5, Accounting for Contingencies,* addressed the accounting for uncertain events in the financial statements. Some of the FAS 5 rules addressed the use of a required reserve related to taxes. Even with FAS 5, the FASB was concerned that companies too freely used the tax reserve as a "cookie jar" to shift earnings from one period to another. To add more structure to the accounting for tax reserves, in July 2006 the FASB released Financial Interpretation No. 48 (FIN 48), *Accounting for Uncertainty in Income Taxes*. The approach required under ASC 740-10 (FIN 48) results in significantly more disclosure about uncertain tax positions by companies.

Application of ASC 740-10 (FIN 48) essentially is a two-step process. First, a tax benefit from an uncertain tax position may be recognized in the financial statements only if it is more likely than not that the position would be sustained on its technical merits. That is, audit or detection risk cannot be considered. This first step determines whether *any* of the tax benefit is recognized. If the uncertain tax position meets the more likely than not threshold, the second step is to determine the amount of the tax benefit to report (i.e., the measurement step).

Measurement is based on the probabilities associated with the position not being challenged, or being challenged with a negotiated settlement or litigation. All the relevant facts and circumstances as of the financial statement reporting date should be used in determining the probability of the ultimate outcome.

The recognition and measurement of uncertain tax positions must be reassessed at each reporting date. ASC 740-10 (FIN 48) requires a reconciliation of the beginning and ending balances of the unrecognized tax benefits and a discussion of potential changes in these unrecognized tax benefits that might occur over the next 12 months.

- Short carryback/carryforward periods.
- History of tax credits expiring unused.

Positive evidence (i.e., support for realizing the current benefit of future tax savings) includes the following.

- Strong earnings history.
- Existing contracts.
- Unrealized appreciation in assets.
- Sales backlog of profitable orders.

The valuation allowance is examined for appropriateness each year. The allowance may be increased or decreased if facts and circumstances change in the future.

EARNINGS OF FOREIGN SUBSIDIARIES

LO.4

Recognize the effect of ASC 740-30 (APB 23) on effective tax rates.

As discussed earlier, a corporate group's financial statements include both domestic and foreign controlled subsidiaries. However, foreign corporations, even those controlled by U.S. shareholders, are not part of a U.S. consolidated tax return. Consequently, U.S. taxpayers can achieve deferral of current U.S. taxes on foreign income if they operate their foreign activities through foreign subsidiary corporations in jurisdictions with lower tax rates than the United States (see Chapter 9). Although the *actual* U.S. taxes on foreign corporations' profits are deferred, the reported effective tax rate for financial statement purposes may not reflect this deferral because ASC 740 (SFAS 109) requires that a corporate group report both current and deferred income tax expense.

EXAMPLE 13

USCo, a domestic corporation, operates a manufacturing facility in Singapore through a Singapore corporation. Assume that the U.S. tax rate is 35% and the Singapore tax rate is 6%. For the current year, USCo earns $600,000 in taxable income. The Singapore corporation earns $400,000 in taxable income from its operations, pays $24,000 in taxes to Singapore, and makes no distributions to its U.S. parent. The Singapore corporation is not taxed in the United States because it is not a U.S. person and has no activities in the United States. USCo is not taxed on the Singapore profits because it has not received any distributions of these profits. Accordingly, USCo has achieved deferral and reduced its worldwide cash tax costs.

However, for financial statement purposes, the USCo group must include the $400,000 in Singapore profits in its net income and report both the Singapore tax and any *potential* U.S. tax (after allowable FTCs) as its total tax expense.

U.S. Tax Return		Potential U.S. Tax on Non-U.S. Income	
Income	$600,000	Income	$400,000
Tax rate	× 35%	Tax rate	× 35%
U.S. tax	$210,000	Total tax	$140,000
		Foreign tax credit	(24,000)
		Net U.S. tax	$116,000

Consequently, the total tax expense for financial statement purposes is $350,000. Keep in mind that the actual deferred tax liability is determined by multiplying the difference in the book and tax basis of the foreign subsidiary by the U.S. tax rate. There is a book-tax difference because the tax basis in the subsidiary is the original cost and the book basis has increased under the equity method of accounting by the equity in the subsidiary's earnings.

Current U.S. tax	$210,000
Current foreign tax	24,000
Deferred U.S. tax	116,000
Total tax expense	$350,000

The financial statement effective tax rate on global income is 35% ($350,000 total tax expense/$1,000,000 net income). Thus, although USCo paid only $234,000 in taxes, its effective tax rate (and thus its after-tax book income) does not reflect the savings generated from operating in Singapore, a low-tax country. ■

ASC 740-30 (APB 23) provides an exception to ASC 740 (SFAS 109) for income from foreign subsidiaries.[12] If a corporation documents that it is **permanently reinvesting** the earnings of its foreign subsidiaries outside the United States, the corporation does not record as an expense any future U.S. income tax that the corporation may pay on such earnings.

EXAMPLE 14

Assume that USCo, in Example 13, uses ASC 740-30 (APB 23) to avoid reporting the $116,000 in deferred taxes. Because USCo plans to reinvest its Singapore earnings indefinitely outside the United States, it is not required to include the deferred U.S. taxes as part of its total tax expense. Thus, USCo's total financial statement income remains $1 million, but its total tax expense is only $234,000 (the taxes currently paid to the United States and Singapore). The resulting financial statement effective tax rate is 23.4%

[12]Formerly *Opinion No. 23—Accounting for Income Taxes—Special Areas*, Accounting Principles Board.

TAX *in the NEWS*

Revealing the Tax Plan

The IRS requires that large corporations list the tax return positions that they have taken that may not be fully supported by the law. Schedule UTP ("uncertain tax positions") is added to the Form 1120 for all corporations with assets of at least $10 million, when the final transition period for the form is complete.

The Schedule UTP is the tax compliance analogue to the FIN 48 adjustments that corporations make to their financial statements. Tax returns have not included information of this sort before, and tax professionals worry that they will be alerting the IRS to specific items that will be most vulnerable to audit adjustments. Because tax returns are confidential documents, though, the public does not have access to a corporation's Schedule UTP.

Disclosures on the Schedule UTP include an enumeration of tax return positions for the current and prior tax years where:

- The taxpayer or a related party recorded a reserve against the Federal income tax expense on its audited financial statements.
- The taxpayer did not record a tax reserve based on its analysis of expected litigation. This means that, in the taxpayer's view, the probability of settling the item with the IRS is less than 50 percent, and the taxpayer determines that it is more likely than not (> 50% likelihood) to prevail on the merits of the issue in litigation.

Disclosures are not required for items that are immaterial under GAAP rules, or for which the filing position is sufficiently certain that no reserve is required. The Schedule UTP is required beginning with a corporation's 2010 tax year.

The IRS maintains that it will limit releases of the Schedule UTP to other taxing jurisdictions, and that it will not use Schedule UTP data to usurp the attorney-client and tax practitioner privileges of confidentiality, or the work-product doctrine. Taxpayers are not required to disclose the amounts of any reserves or the precise nature of the tax planning technique that led to the reserve for the filing position.

The Schedule UTP represents a new level of information exchange between the IRS and the taxpayer, focusing on filing-year disclosures rather than audit-year items. The IRS admits that it is directing its audit efforts toward large business entities and says that its compliance activities will be both more efficient and more effective as a result.

($234,000/$1,000,000), and the USCo group's after-tax book income reflects the Singapore tax savings. ■

Using ASC 740-30 (APB 23) is not an "all or nothing" decision. It can be adopted in some years and not others. Even within a year it may be used for only a portion of foreign subsidiary earnings.

EXAMPLE 15
THE BIG PICTURE

Return to the facts of *The Big Picture* on p. 14-2. Recall from Example 1 that Arctic Corporation has a wholly owned foreign subsidiary, Hurricane, Ltd. Assume that Arctic also owns 100% of another foreign corporation, Typhoon, Ltd. Arctic can choose to apply ASC 740-30 (APB 23) to both of its foreign subsidiaries in 2010 and to only Hurricane in 2011. In 2012, Arctic can choose to use ASC 740-30 (APB 23) for 40% of Hurricane's earnings and 80% of Typhoon's earnings. ■

ASC 740-30 (APB 23) is a major issue only when the foreign subsidiary is taxed at rates below the applicable U.S. tax rate. Otherwise, there is no deferral potential. However, using ASC 740-30 (APB 23) may limit the availability of creating deferred tax assets when foreign subsidiaries pay taxes at greater than the U.S. rate. Then the multinational group potentially could use these excess foreign taxes as credits on the U.S. tax return (see Chapter 9).

EXAMPLE 16

AmeriCo, a domestic corporation, operates a manufacturing facility in the Netherlands through Vander, a Dutch corporation. Assume that the U.S. tax rate is 35% and the Netherlands tax rate also is 35%. For the current year, AmeriCo earns $400,000 in taxable income. Vander earns $300,000 in taxable income from its operations, pays $105,000 in taxes to the Netherlands, and makes no distributions to its U.S. parent.

Vander is not taxed in the United States because it is not a U.S. person and has no activities in the United States. AmeriCo is not taxed on the Netherlands profits because it has not received any distributions of these profits.

For financial statement purposes, the AmeriCo group must include the $300,000 of Vander's profits in its net income and report both the Dutch tax and any *potential* U.S. tax (after allowable FTCs) as its total tax expense.

U.S. Tax Return		**Potential U.S. Tax on Foreign Income**	
Income	$400,000	Income	$ 300,000
Tax rate	× 35%	Tax rate	× 35%
U.S. tax	$140,000	Total tax	$ 105,000
		FTC	(105,000)
		Net U.S. tax	$ –0–

Consequently, the total tax expense for financial statement purposes is $245,000.

Current U.S. tax	$140,000
Current foreign tax	105,000
Total tax expense	$245,000

The financial statement effective tax rate on global income is 35% ($245,000 total tax expense/$700,000 book net income). Even without ASC 740-30 (APB 23), there is no deferred U.S. tax on the Dutch income, because AmeriCo would pay no additional U.S. tax upon the repatriation of Vander's earnings after its use of the available FTC.

Note that application of a valuation allowance against the deferred tax asset created by the FTC would affect the book effective tax rate. ■

Disclosing Aggressive Tax Positions

In 2010, Dickinson, Inc., reports an effective tax rate of 36 percent, and Badger, Inc., reports an effective tax rate of 21 percent. Both companies are domestic and operate in the same industry. Your initial examination of the financial statements of the two companies indicates that Badger apparently is doing a better job with its tax planning, explaining the difference in effective tax rates. Consequently, all else being equal, you decide to invest in Badger.

In a subsequent year, it comes to light that Badger had used some very aggressive tax planning techniques to reduce its reported tax expense. After examination by the IRS, Badger loses the tax benefits and reports a very large tax expense in that year. Over this multiple-year period, it turns out that Dickinson had the lower effective tax rate after all.

Do you believe Badger was ethical in not fully disclosing the aggressiveness of its tax positions in its 2010 financial statement? How does ASC 740 (FIN 48) affect Badger's disclosure requirement? Does ASC 740 (FIN 48) still leave room for ethical decision making by management in determining how to report uncertain tax positions?

LO.5

Interpret the disclosure information contained in an income tax footnote.

TAX DISCLOSURES IN THE FINANCIAL STATEMENTS

As illustrated earlier, any temporary differences create deferred tax liabilities or deferred tax assets, and these amounts appear in the corporation's balance sheet.

The Balance Sheet

As with any asset or liability, these accounts are classified as either current or noncurrent, based on the assets or liabilities that created the temporary difference. If the deferred tax liability or asset is not related to any asset, then the classification is based on the expected reversal period.

EXAMPLE 17

JenCo, Inc., has a deferred tax liability generated because tax depreciation exceeds book depreciation on manufacturing equipment. Because the equipment is classified as a noncurrent asset, the deferred tax liability is classified as noncurrent. JenCo also has a deferred tax asset related to bad debt expenses deductible for book purposes but not yet deductible for tax purposes. Because the bad debt expense is related to accounts receivable, a current asset, the associated deferred tax asset is classified as current.

If JenCo incurs an NOL, a deferred tax asset is created, because of the future tax benefit provided by the NOL deduction. The NOL is not related to any specific asset or liability. Accordingly, the deferred tax asset is classified based on when the corporation expects to use the NOL. If the expected use is more than one year in the future, the deferred tax asset is classified as noncurrent. ■

A corporation may have both deferred tax assets and liabilities, current and noncurrent. The corporation reports the *net* current deferred tax assets or liabilities, and the *net* noncurrent deferred tax assets or liabilities.

EXAMPLE 18
THE BIG PICTURE

Return to the facts of *The Big Picture* on p. 14-2. Arctic Corporation holds the following deferred tax asset and liability accounts for the current year.

Current deferred tax assets	$50,000
Current deferred tax liabilities	72,000
Noncurrent deferred tax assets	93,000
Noncurrent deferred tax liabilities	28,000

On its balance sheet, Arctic reports a $22,000 current net deferred tax liability ($72,000 – $50,000) and a $65,000 noncurrent net deferred tax asset ($93,000 – $28,000). ■

The Income Statement

In its income statement, a corporation reports a total income tax expense that consists of both the current tax expense (or benefit) and the deferred tax expense (or benefit). The tax expense must be allocated to income from continuing operations, discontinued operations, extraordinary items, prior-period adjustments, and the cumulative effect of accounting changes. Additional disclosures are required for tax expense allocated to income from continuing operations (e.g., current versus deferred, benefits of NOL deductions, changes in valuation allowances, etc.).

Financial Statement Footnotes

The income tax note contains a wealth of information, including the following.

- Breakdown of income between domestic and foreign.
- Detailed analysis of the provision for income tax expense.
- Detailed analysis of deferred tax assets and liabilities.
- Effective tax **rate reconciliation** (dollar amount or percentage).
- Information on use of ASC 740-30 (APB 23) for the earnings of foreign subsidiaries.
- Discussion of significant tax matters.

Rate Reconciliation

The purpose of the rate reconciliation is to demonstrate how a corporation's actual book effective tax rate relates to its "hypothetical tax rate" as if the book income were taxed at the U.S. corporate rate of 35 percent. Although similar to Schedule M–1 or M–3, the tax note rate reconciliation generally reports only differences triggered by permanent differences. As discussed in the benchmarking section later in this chapter, an analysis of the rate reconciliation can provide substantial clues as to the tax planning strategies adopted (or not adopted) by a company.

The steps in determining a corporation's income tax expense for book purposes are summarized in Concept Summary 14.2.

CONCEPT SUMMARY 14.2

Steps in Determining Book Tax Expense

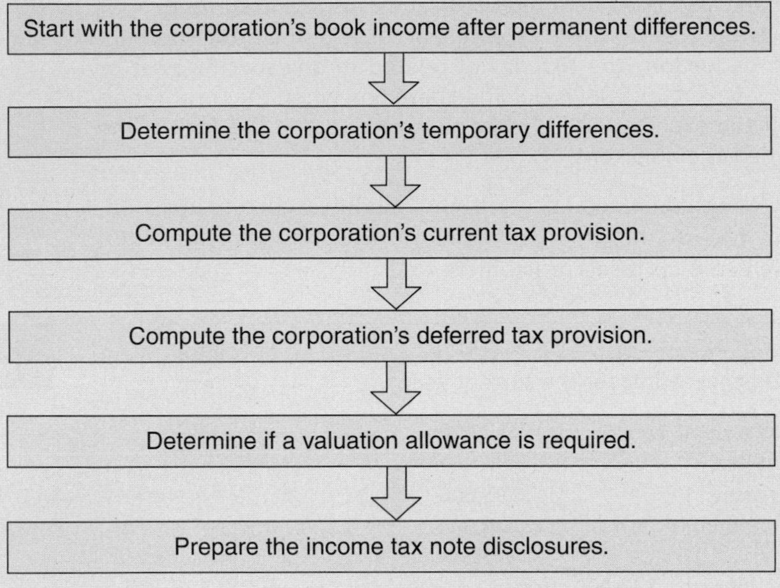

Start with the corporation's book income after permanent differences.
Determine the corporation's temporary differences.
Compute the corporation's current tax provision.
Compute the corporation's deferred tax provision.
Determine if a valuation allowance is required.
Prepare the income tax note disclosures.

EXAMPLE 19

BoxCo, Inc., a domestic corporation, owns 100% of PaperCo, Ltd., an Irish corporation. Assume that the U.S. corporate tax rate is 35% and the Irish rate is 10%. BoxCo is permanently reinvesting PaperCo's earnings outside the United States under ASC 740-30 (APB 23). The corporations' book income, permanent and temporary differences, and current tax expense are as follows.

	BoxCo	PaperCo
Book income before tax	$300,000	$200,000
Permanent differences		
Meals and entertainment expense	20,000	—
Municipal bond interest income	(50,000)	—
Book income after permanent differences	$270,000	$200,000
Temporary differences		
Tax > book depreciation	(50,000)	—
Book > tax bad debt expense	10,000	—
Taxable income	$230,000	$200,000
Tax rate	× 35%	× 10%
Current tax expense	$ 80,500	$ 20,000

Assume that the beginning-of-the-year difference between book and tax basis in the depreciable assets is $150,000 and the beginning-of-the-year difference between book and tax basis in the bad debt expense is $50,000. Thus, the beginning-of-the-year deferred tax liability is $35,000 [($150,000 − $50,000) × 35%]. To determine the deferred tax expense (benefit) for the current year, the change in these temporary differences from the beginning to the end of the year must be determined and then multiplied by the appropriate tax rate.

Temporary Differences	Beginning of Year	Change	End of Year
Depreciation	$150,000	$ 50,000	$200,000
Bad debts	(50,000)	(10,000)	(60,000)
Total temporary differences	$100,000	$ 40,000	$140,000
Tax rate	× 35%	× 35%	× 35%
	$ 35,000	$ 14,000	$ 49,000

The deferred tax liability increased by $14,000 for the year. Consequently, BoxCo's total tax expense for book purposes is $114,500.

Current tax expense	
Domestic	$ 80,500
Foreign	20,000
Deferred tax expense	
Domestic	14,000
Foreign	—
Total tax expense	$114,500

The journal entry to record the book income tax expense is constructed as follows.

Income tax expense (provision)	$114,500	
Income tax payable		$100,500
Deferred tax liability		14,000

BoxCo's book income is $500,000 (the combined book income of both BoxCo and PaperCo). The effective tax rate reconciliation is based on this book income, with the dollar amounts in the table representing the tax expense (benefit) related to the item, and the percentage representing the tax expense (benefit) as a percentage of book income. For example, the municipal bond interest of $50,000 reduces tax liability by $17,500 ($50,000 × 35%). This $17,500 as a percentage of the $500,000 book income is 3.5%.

	Effective Tax Rate Reconciliation	
	$	%
Hypothetical tax at U.S. rate	$175,000	35.0
Disallowed meals and entertainment expense	7,000	1.4
Municipal bond interest	(17,500)	(3.5)
Foreign income taxed at less than U.S. rate	(50,000)	(10.0)
Income tax expense (provision)	$114,500	22.9

Only permanent differences appear in the rate reconciliation. Temporary differences do not affect the *total* book income tax expense; they simply affect the amount of the tax expense that is current versus deferred. ■

EXAMPLE 20

Assume the same facts as Example 19, except that a new Federal income tax law is enacted before the end of the current year that will increase the corporate tax rate to 40% beginning next year. In this case, multiply the year-end total temporary differences of $140,000 by 40% rather than 35%. This results in an increase in the deferred tax liability of $21,000.

Temporary Differences	Beginning of Year	End of Year	Effect
Depreciation	$150,000	$200,000	
Bad debts	(50,000)	(60,000)	
Total temporary differences	$100,000	$140,000	
Tax rate	× 35%	× 40%	
Deferred tax liability	$ 35,000	$ 56,000	$21,000

The current-year deferred tax liability amount is a function of both the change in temporary differences at the enacted rate ($40,000 × 40%) and the additional 5% tax on the beginning temporary differences [$100,000 × (40% – 35%)]. This example illustrates the need for the "balance sheet" approach of ASC 740 (SFAS 109). Use of the APB 11 shortcut method would have produced the wrong answer with these facts. ■

EXAMPLE 21

LibbyCo, Inc., is a U.S. corporation that operates retail outlets selling eyeglasses. During the current year, LibbyCo reported pretax book income of $1,800. LibbyCo's U.S. corporate tax rate is 34%, it has no NOLs, credits, or foreign or state income taxes, and it is not subject to the alternative minimum tax.

LibbyCo's tax and book balance sheet is summarized below, along with book-tax basis differences for all assets and liabilities.

	Tax Debit/(Credit)	Book Debit/(Credit)	Difference
Assets			
Cash	$ 2,000	$ 2,000	$ –0–
Accounts receivable	5,400	5,400	–0–
Buildings	400,000	400,000	–0–
Accumulated depreciation	(315,000)	(330,000)	15,000
Furniture & fixtures	100,000	100,000	–0–
Accumulated depreciation	(70,000)	(45,000)	(25,000)
Total assets	$ 122,400	$ 132,400	($10,000)
Liabilities			
Accrued vacation pay	$ –0–	($ 25,000)	$25,000
Note payable	(16,400)	(16,400)	–0–
Total liabilities	($ 16,400)	($ 41,400)	$25,000
Stockholders' Equity			
Paid-in capital	($ 6,000)	($ 6,000)	
Retained earnings	(100,000)	(85,000)	
Total liabilities and stockholders' equity	($ 122,400)	($ 132,400)	

The difference between the book and tax basis of these assets and liabilities is the cumulative difference from all prior years. These differences are *not* the Schedule M–1 or M–3 differences. To determine the temporary differences for the current year and any associated deferred tax liability or deferred tax asset, these differences are compared to the basis differences at the beginning of the year.

Assume the following beginning-of-the-year book-tax differences. The end-of-the-year differences are calculated above. The differences are classified based on whether they produce a future tax benefit (deductible temporary differences) or a future tax cost (taxable temporary differences).

	Beginning of Year	Current-Year Difference	End of Year
Deductible Temporary Differences			
Buildings—accumulated depreciation	$ 10,000	$ 5,000	$ 15,000
Accrued vacation pay	17,000	8,000	25,000
Subtotal	$ 27,000	$13,000	$ 40,000
Applicable tax rate	× 34%		× 34%
Gross deferred tax asset	$ 9,180		$ 13,600
Change in deferred tax asset		$ 4,420	
Taxable Temporary Differences			
Furniture & fixtures—accumulated depreciation	($ 22,000)	$ 3,000	($ 25,000)
Subtotal	($ 22,000)	($ 3,000)	($ 25,000)
Applicable tax rate	× 34%		× 34%
Gross deferred tax liability	($ 7,480)		($ 8,500)
Change in deferred tax liability		($ 1,020)	
Net deferred tax asset / (deferred tax liability)	$ 1,700	$ 3,400	$ 5,100

The journal entry to record the deferred tax asset is constructed as follows.

Deferred tax asset	$3,400	
Income tax expense		$3,400

In addition to the temporary differences identified above, LibbyCo also reported two permanent differences between book and taxable income. It earned $1,400 in tax-exempt municipal bond interest, and it incurred $2,000 in nondeductible meals and entertainment expense. With this information, the current tax expense is determined as follows.

Pretax book income	$ 1,800
Book-tax adjustments	
Permanent items	
Tax-exempt Income	(1,400)
Nondeductible meals and entertainment	2,000
Temporary differences	
Building depreciation	5,000
Accrued vacation pay	8,000
Furniture & fixtures depreciation	(3,000)
Taxable income	$12,400
Current tax expense (34%)	$ 4,216

The building depreciation for book purposes exceeds tax depreciation, the furniture and fixtures depreciation for tax purposes exceeds book depreciation, and the accrued vacation pay is deductible for book purposes but not yet deductible for tax. These current-year temporary differences, combined with the two permanent items, also constitute the Schedule M–3 differences.

The journal entry to record the current tax expense is constructed as follows.

Income tax expense	$4,216	
Current income tax payable		$4,216

Assuming that no valuation allowance is required, the effect of these entries on the income statement is as follows. The current-year change in the deferred tax asset allows the book tax expense to be reduced by $3,400, producing a total book tax expense of $816 ($4,216 – $3,400).

Net income before tax	$1,800
Provision for income tax expense	(816)
Net income after tax	$ 984

The income tax footnote rate reconciliation is presented as follows.

Tax on book income at statutory rate	$612	34.00%
Tax-exempt income	(476)	(26.44)%
Nondeductible meals and entertainment	680	37.77%
Provision for income tax expense	$816	45.33%

With these facts, the "back-of-the-envelope" APB 11 method below produces the same results as the ASC 740 (SFAS 109) method. Note that this would not be true had there been changes to LibbyCo's applicable tax rate from the prior year, or if a valuation allowance had been required.

Pretax book income	$ 1,800
Permanent items	
Tax-exempt income	(1,400)
Nondeductible meals and entertainment	2,000
Book equivalent to taxable income	$ 2,400
Statutory tax rate	× 34%
Total book tax expense	$ 816

■

14.3 Benchmarking

LO.6

Use financial statement income tax information to benchmark a company's tax position.

As the *outcome* of the taxpayer's activities combined with the tax professional's advice, the income tax expense amount may appear to be of little interest to anyone beyond the taxpayer that makes the payment and the government agencies that collect it. The tax year is over, the transactions completed, and the final costs tallied. Still, this historical tax information may prove very valuable. A company's income tax expense is one of the single largest expense items on its income statement, and understanding the components of this expense is a critical activity for the tax professional.

Consider a typical baseball game. Two teams meet, interact following a specific set of rules, and ultimately complete the game generating a final score. Of course, the final score is of immediate interest to the teams and the fans, but once the game is over, the score and associated statistics (runs, hits, errors) are relegated to the history books. Yet these statistics are still quite useful. A team coach may use the game statistics to evaluate the strengths and weaknesses of the players to assist in improving performance. Other teams in the league may use the statistics to develop strategies for upcoming games. Players can use the statistics to benchmark themselves against their own performance in prior games or against players in other teams. In short, there is a wealth of information in these historical data.

A taxpayer's reported income tax expense is likewise a valuable source of information for the company, its tax advisers, and its competitors. The reported information provides clues about a company's operational and tax planning strategies.

Companies may benchmark their tax situation to other years' results or to other companies within the same industry. The starting point for a **benchmarking** exercise is the data from the income tax note rate reconciliation.

FIGURE 14.4 Tax Rate Reconciliation for Sears and Wal-Mart

	Sears		Wal-Mart	
	2009	2008	2009	2008
Hypothetical tax (benefit) at U.S. Federal rate	35.0%	35.0%	35.0%	35.0%
State and local income taxes, net of Federal benefit	6.0	7.2	1.9	1.7
Tax credits	(3.0)	(6.3)		
Resolution of income tax matters	(6.2)	(6.8)		
Basis difference in domestic subsidiary	—	(30.2)		
Non-U.S. income taxed at different rates	(0.9)	(2.3)	(1.7)	(1.6)
Nondeductible goodwill	—	50.0		
Other	(1.6)	(0.4)	(1.0)	(1.0)
	29.3%	46.2%	34.2%	34.1%
Book income before tax (in millions)	$420.0	$184.0	$20,898.0	$20,158.0

DYNAMIC BENCHMARKING

Figure 14.4 contains the tax rate reconciliation information from the income tax notes of Sears Holding Corporation (Sears) and Wal-Mart Stores, Inc. (Wal-Mart). Both companies are listed on the New York Stock Exchange, are in the same industry, and operate both inside and outside the United States. Although the income and tax expense amounts of both companies are quite different in magnitude, the tax amounts are converted to percentage of income numbers for comparability purposes. In 2008, Sears had an effective tax rate that was 12 percentage points higher than Wal-Mart's rate. In 2009, Sears's effective tax rate was 4.9 points below Wal-Mart's rate. What factors created these differences? Rate reconciliation information can provide clues.

Sears reported a higher effective tax rate in 2008 because its state and local income tax burden is higher, and because it suffered a goodwill impairment (the goodwill write-off is not tax deductible). These increase items were offset by reductions caused by certain basis differences in a domestic subsidiary, larger benefits from tax credits, and a larger benefit from a favorable resolution of tax matters.

When comparing effective tax rates, it is important to consider which components of the effective tax rate produce one-time effects. For example, for 2009, the effective tax rates of both companies were much more similar (Sears was about 5 percentage points lower than Wal-Mart). In particular, without the large effects of nondeductible goodwill and the domestic subsidiary basis difference, Sears approached the effective tax rate of Wal-Mart. Consequently, it appears that there are no long-term structural differences in the tax burdens faced by the two companies. This is not surprising given that both companies are incorporated in the United States, are in the same industry, and operate in many of the same jurisdictions.

However, items such as the nondeductible goodwill difference do indicate that there may be potential fundamental differences in how Sears's management deals with growth via expansion rather than acquisitions. It is acquired goodwill rather than the home-grown sort that faces potential impairment. The Sears example shows that the results of past and current strategic decisions eventually may show up in the income tax footnote.

REFINING THE ANALYSIS

In addition to comparing effective tax rates, companies can compare levels of deferred tax assets and liabilities.

EXAMPLE 22

Akiko Enterprises reports a net deferred tax liability of $280,000. Asare, Inc., a company in the same industry, reports a net deferred tax liability of $860,000. Seeing deferred tax liabilities on the balance sheet indicates that these companies are both benefiting from deferring actual tax payments (essentially, an interest-free loan from the government). At first glance it may appear that Asare is doing better in this regard. However, what if Akiko holds total assets of $2.6 million and Asare's assets total $19.2 million? This information indicates that Akiko has 10.8% ($280,000/$2.6 million) of its total assets "financed" with an interest-free loan from the government, while Asare has only 4.5% ($860,000/$19.2 million) of its assets "financed" with its deferred tax liabilities. ■

A company may do a more refined benchmarking analysis by examining each component of its deferred tax assets and liabilities as a percentage of total assets. For example, a company can examine how the deferred tax assets or liabilities related to property, plant, and equipment compare with its competitors. The nature of the components of deferred tax liabilities and deferred tax assets becomes quite important in a benchmarking analysis.

EXAMPLE 23

LinCo reports total book income before taxes of $10 million and a total tax expense of $3.2 million, producing a 32% effective tax rate. TuckCo also reports book income before taxes of $10 million. TuckCo's total tax expense is $3.1 million, producing an effective tax rate of 31%. At first glance it appears that both companies are similar with regard to effective tax rates. The total tax expense divided between current and deferred is as follows (in millions).

	LinCo	TuckCo
Current tax expense	$ 4.1	$ 4.2
Deferred tax benefit	(0.9)	(1.1)
Total tax expense	$ 3.2	$ 3.1

Again, it appears that both companies have created deferred tax assets in the current year that are expected to produce tax savings in the future. Knowing the nature of the underlying deferred tax assets will add greatly to the interpretation of the effective tax rates. The deferred tax asset generating LinCo's $900,000 expected future tax savings is the use of an NOL carryover. The deferred tax asset generating TuckCo's expected future tax savings is generated by different book and tax methods in accounting for warranty expense. This additional information reveals that LinCo has previously incurred losses and it is critical that it earn future income so as to use the NOL.

This is quite different from TuckCo's situation, which reveals only that common differences in accounting methods exist. Although the tax positions of LinCo and TuckCo seem very similar on the surface, a closer look reveals a striking difference. ■

EXAMPLE 24

WageCo and SalaryCo are both in the same industry and both report a 38% effective tax rate. Their book income and current, deferred, and total tax expense were reported as:

	WageCo	SalaryCo
Book income before tax	$1,500,000	$2,300,000
Current tax expense	$ 980,000	$ 24,000
Deferred tax expense (benefit)	(410,000)	850,000
Total tax expense	$ 570,000	$ 874,000
Effective tax rate	38%	38%

WageCo's total tax expense is highly dependent on the current recognition of future tax savings of $410,000. SalaryCo appears to be deferring a substantial portion of its tax expense to future years. Although both companies report a 38% effective tax rate, the details indicate that the two companies face very different tax situations. ■

SUSTAINING THE TAX RATE

It is important in benchmarking exercises to remove the effect of one-time items in comparing sustainable effective tax rates across time or companies. Examples of one-time items include restructuring costs, legal settlements, and IRS settlements. A one-time item may seem beneficial or detrimental to a company's effective tax rate. But the very nature of such an item implies that it has little to do with the company's long-term sustainable tax costs.

EXAMPLE 25

MetalCo and IronCo are both in the same industry and report the following tax rate reconciliations in their tax footnotes.

	MetalCo	IronCo
Hypothetical tax at U.S. rate	35.0%	35.0%
State and local taxes	2.2	2.1
Foreign income taxed at less than U.S. rate	(6.2)	(6.1)
Tax Court settlement on disputed tax issue	(18.6)	—
Effective tax rate	12.4%	31.0%

Although it appears that MetalCo has a significantly lower effective tax rate (12.4%) than IronCo's 31%, removing MetalCo's one-time item related to the court settlement indicates that both companies have a 31% effective tax rate (12.4% + 18.6% = 31%). ■

USES OF BENCHMARKING ANALYSIS

Benchmarking is part science and part art. A useful analysis requires both knowledge of how the underlying financial statements are constructed, including arriving at tax expense, and a detective's sense of where to look and what questions to ask.

In addition to benchmarking, financial analysts perform an important function for the capital markets in their detailed analyses of companies. The analyst combs through both the financial reports and other information about a company to produce an informed opinion on how a company is performing. Analysts' earnings forecasts often are an important metric to examine when making decisions about investing in companies.

An experienced financial analyst typically will have a good handle on interpreting financial statement information. However, even experienced analysts will often "punt" when it comes to interpreting the tax information contained in a financial statement, preferring to look at net income before taxes (or even EBITDA, earnings before interest, taxes, depreciation, and amortization). Lots of useful information about a company is contained in its tax footnote, and analysts might have an edge if they work at understanding the mysteries of taxes in the income statement.

TAX PLANNING:
14.4 Releasing Valuation Allowances

When a corporation records a valuation allowance, it loses the ability to recognize the benefit of future tax savings in the current period. However, all is not lost if the taxpayer can demonstrate that facts and circumstances have changed. For example, if a taxpayer generates an NOL, it records a deferred tax asset for the future tax savings related to using the NOL. However, if the evidence suggests that it is more likely than not that the NOL will expire unused, a valuation allowance must be recorded.

To reduce this valuation allowance, the taxpayer must demonstrate that there will be future taxable income sufficient to absorb the NOL within the carryforward period. Sources of future taxable income include reversals of temporary differences that will produce future taxable income and other sources of future profits. Taxpayers also may demonstrate that the adoption of new tax planning strategies will allow the use of deferred tax assets.

EXAMPLE 26
THE BIG PICTURE

Return to the facts of *The Big Picture* on p. 14-2. Arctic Corporation's $3 million deferred tax asset for an NOL carryforward has been offset by a $1 million valuation allowance, due to doubts over the levels of future sales and profitability. But this year, Arctic completed improvements to its inventory management system that are likely to increase the contribution margin of every product that Arctic sells. In addition, two of Arctic's largest customers have secured financing that will relieve the financial difficulties that have restricted them. In fact, Arctic just received purchase orders from those customers that will increase unit sales by 20% over the next 18 months. As a result, Arctic's auditors now support a release of $200,000 of the valuation allowance in the current quarter. ■

EXAMPLE 27

Assume that Warren, Inc., from Example 12, adopts new planning strategies in 2011 that will allow it ultimately to use all $100,000 of its FTC carryforward. Warren earns $2.3 million in book income before tax and reports $2.3 million in taxable income in 2011 (i.e., no permanent or temporary differences). The current tax expense is $805,000 ($2.3 million × 35%). Based on new evidence (implementation of tax planning strategies), the auditors determine that the entire $100,000 in FTCs will be used in the future before expiration. Accordingly, the $60,000 valuation allowance from 2010 is "released," and the tax benefit of this release affects the 2011 financial results as follows.

	Book	Tax
Income tax expense	$745,000	$805,000
Current tax expense	$805,000	
Deferred tax expense	($ 60,000)	

Warren makes the following journal entry to record the book income tax expense and valuation allowance release related to the expected use of the FTCs.

Income tax expense (provision)	$745,000	
Valuation allowance	60,000	
Income tax payable		$805,000

Warren's effective tax rate for 2011 is 32.4% ($745,000/$2.3 million). Without the valuation allowance release, Warren's effective tax rate would have been 35% ($805,000/$2.3 million). This tax rate benefit is realized even though the $100,000 in FTC carryforwards have yet to be actually used in Warren's tax return. ■

14.5 Reducing Effective Tax Rates with ASC 740-30 (APB 23)

Because ASC 740-30 (APB 23) allows for higher reported book earnings (no deferred U.S. tax expense is recorded), its use may be reflected in higher stock prices and increased shareholder wealth. Although academic studies find mixed

FINANCIAL DISCLOSURE *Insights*

Valuation Allowances for NOLs

Financial analysts use the valuation allowance system to help them determine an entity's expected future cash flows. Some critics of the GAAP rules for valuation allowances maintain that the process allows management to manipulate profits and earnings per share in an arbitrary fashion.

Only a few of the largest business entities, supported by going-concern assumptions and access to worldwide debt and equity capital, need to record a sizable valuation allowance. But valuation allowances also often are found in the financial reports of smaller entities and those in volatile industries, whose future profitability is likely to present questions.

In a recent reporting year, for instance, the following telecommunications businesses reported a valuation allowance related to expectations that their NOLs (for Federal and/or state taxing jurisdictions) would expire unused.

	Deferred Tax Assets ($000)	Valuation Allowance ($000)
Verizon	10,750	2,700
Bell South	2,100	1,100
AT&T	11,400	1,050
SBC Communications	3,900	150

Establishing a valuation allowance does not affect the entity's internal cash balances, but it might have an effect on the stock price. Valuation allowances can be "released" by management when evidence develops that the carryforwards are more likely to be used in the future, for example, if profitability improves and appears to be sustainable. For instance, the homebuilder Toll Brothers created a large valuation allowance when the real estate market collapsed, but it will release the allowance when housing prices stabilize and increase. Several corporations estimated that the 2010 health care reform legislation would force them to create a sizable valuation allowance, because the mandated expenditures would reduce future profitability. The following are examples of these estimates

	Reduction in Deferred Tax Assets due to Health Care Reform ($ million)
AT&T	1,000
John Deere	150
Caterpillar	100
3M	90

evidence on this effect, many U.S. multinationals with foreign subsidiaries do in fact use ASC 740-30 (APB 23) to avoid reporting U.S. deferred taxes on foreign earnings.

The "permanent reinvestment" exception should not be employed unless the corporation truly expects to keep its foreign earnings outside the United States. Using ASC 740-30 (APB 23) and then repatriating foreign profits after all can cause extreme spikes in a corporation's effective tax rate.

EXAMPLE 28

USCo, a domestic corporation, owns 100% of Shamrock, Ltd., an Irish corporation. Assume that the U.S. tax rate is 35% and the Irish tax rate is 10%. In 2010, USCo earns $100,000 in taxable income and pays $35,000 to the United States. Shamrock earns $400,000 in taxable income and pays $40,000 in taxes to Ireland. Shamrock makes no distributions to its U.S. parent and is not taxed in the United States because it is not a U.S. person and has no activities in the United States.

USCo is not taxed on the Irish profits because it has not received any distributions of these profits. Furthermore, USCo uses ASC 740-30 (APB 23) to avoid recording any deferred U.S. income tax expense on its financial statements. Accordingly, USCo has achieved deferral and reduced its worldwide cash tax costs and book income tax expense.

USCo's total tax expense for financial statement purposes is $75,000.

Current U.S. tax	$35,000
Current foreign tax	40,000
Total tax expense	$75,000

The financial statement effective tax rate on USCo's global income is 15% ($75,000 total tax expense/$500,000 net income). Thus, the USCo group has achieved higher after-tax book income and earnings per share.

In 2011, USCo earns $200,000 in taxable income and pays $70,000 to the United States. Shamrock breaks even for the year and pays no taxes to Ireland. In 2011, USCo decides to have Shamrock pay it a dividend of $360,000.

U.S. Tax Return	
U.S. income	$200,000
Foreign dividend*	400,000
Taxable income	$600,000
Tax rate	× 35%
	$210,000
FTC	(40,000)
Net U.S. tax	$170,000

* The total gross income is the $360,000 cash dividend grossed up by the $40,000 potential FTC (see Chapter 9).

For book purposes, USCo reports only $200,000 in net income (the $400,000 in Irish income was included in book income in 2010 and is not included again). The 2011 total tax expense for financial statement purposes is $170,000.

Current U.S. tax	$170,000
Current foreign tax	–0–
Total tax expense	$170,000

The financial statement effective tax rate on USCo's global income is 85% ($170,000 total tax expense/$200,000 net income). This extremely high effective rate is caused by the mismatching of the Irish income (reported in 2010) and the U.S. taxes on the Irish income (reported in 2011). ■

14.6 Comparing Tax Savings

Many different types of tax planning strategies can produce tax savings. Yet, even when planning ideas produce identical current cash-flow effects, some ideas may have an edge. CEOs and CFOs of public companies are very focused on the bottom line—the company's net income after tax and related earnings per share. A CFO is likely just as interested in an idea's effect on the company's bottom line income as on the cash tax savings.

For example, consider two tax planning ideas that each produce $700,000 of current tax savings. The first idea generates its $700,000 in tax savings by increasing tax depreciation relative to book depreciation by $2 million ($700,000 = $2 million × 35%). The second idea produces research activities tax credits of $700,000, thus reducing current-year tax by $700,000.

Idea 1 produces its current tax savings via a temporary difference. Accordingly, the book tax expense will not reflect the $700,000 in tax savings. Instead, this $700,000 simply moves from the current tax category into the deferred tax category. Even if the book-tax difference is not expected to reverse in the next 30 years (effectively generating "permanent" savings), the book tax expense does not reflect this savings.

In contrast, idea 2 produces its current tax savings via a permanent difference. Thus, the book tax expense also declines by $700,000. This item is a reconciling item in the income tax note rate reconciliation.

REFOCUS ON THE BIG PICTURE

TAXES ON THE FINANCIAL STATEMENTS

Raymond Jones should understand that the tax expense reported on the company's financial statements and the tax payable on the company's income tax returns are often different as a result of differences in the reporting entities used in the calculation and the different accounting methods used for book purposes and tax purposes. The use of different accounting methods may result in both temporary and permanent differences in financial statement income and taxable income. Examples of permanent differences include nontaxable income like municipal bond interest and tax credits. Temporary differences include depreciation differences and other amounts that are affected by the timing of a deduction or inclusion but ultimately will result in the same amount being reflected in the financial statements and income tax returns.

Permanent differences such as municipal bond interest cause Arctic's book income to be greater than its taxable income. In calculating the tax expense shown on the financial statements, Arctic's book income must be adjusted for these permanent differences. This results in an effective tax rate for financial statement purposes (30.8 percent) that is below the top U.S. statutory corporate income tax rate of 35 percent.

In this case, Arctic's income tax expense of $7.7 million is higher than the current Federal income tax payable. This results from timing differences and creates a $1.05 million deferred tax liability that is reported on the company's balance sheet. Unlike other liabilities, deferred tax liabilities are "good" in the sense that they represent an amount that may be paid to the government in the future rather than today.

What If?

Mr. Jones is concerned about a newspaper article that said that companies reporting less tax on their tax returns than on their financial statements were cheating the IRS. Is this an accurate assessment?

While differences in income taxes payable to the IRS and financial tax expense can result from aggressive and illegal tax shelters, differences also result from different methods of accounting that are required for financial statement reporting using GAAP and tax laws as enacted by Congress.

KEY TERMS

ASC 740 (SFAS 109), 14–8
ASC 740-30 (APB 23), 14–16
Balance sheet approach, 14–10
Benchmarking, 14–24
Conservatism principle, 14–13
Current tax expense, 14–9
Deferred tax asset, 14–10
Deferred tax benefit, 14–9
Deferred tax expense, 14–9
Deferred tax liability, 14–10
Equity method, 14-3
Generally accepted accounting principles (GAAP), 14–2
Income tax provision, 14–8
Permanent differences, 14–5
Permanently reinvesting, 14–16
Rate reconciliation, 14–19
Schedule M–1, 14–7
Schedule M–3, 14–7
Temporary differences, 14–5
Valuation allowance, 14–14

DISCUSSION QUESTIONS

1. **LO.1** Evaluate the following statement: For most business entities, book income differs from taxable income because "income" has different meanings for the users of the data in the income computation.

2. **LO.1** USCo, a domestic corporation, owns 100% of ForCo, a foreign corporation, and SubCo, a domestic corporation. USCo also owns 35% of InvestCo, a domestic corporation.

USCo receives no distributions from any of these corporations. Which of these entities' net income is included in USCo's income statement for current-year financial reporting purposes?

3. **LO.1** USCo, a domestic corporation, owns 100% of ForCo, a foreign corporation, and SubCo, a domestic corporation. USCo also owns 35% of InvestCo, a domestic corporation. USCo receives no distributions from any of these corporations. Which of these entities' taxable income is included in USCo's current-year Form 1120, U.S. income tax return? Assume USCo consolidates all eligible subsidiaries.

COMMUNICATIONS

4. **LO.1** Marcellus Jackson, the CFO of Mac, Inc., notices that the tax liability reported on Mac's tax return is less than the tax expense reported on Mac's financial statements. Provide a letter to Jackson outlining why these two tax expense numbers differ. Mac's address is 482 Linden Road, Paris, KY 40362.

ISSUE ID

5. **LO.1** Define the terms *temporary difference* and *permanent difference,* as they pertain to the financial reporting of income tax expenses. Describe how these two book-tax differences affect the gap between book and taxable income.

6. **LO.1** Identify two temporary book-tax differences and two permanent differences.

7. **LO.1** Indicate whether the following items create temporary or permanent differences.
   a. Book depreciation in excess of tax depreciation.
   b. Tax depreciation in excess of book depreciation.
   c. Municipal bond interest income.
   d. Disallowed meals and entertainment expense for tax purposes.
   e. Increase in the allowance for doubtful accounts.
   f. Increase in the reserve for warranty settlements.

8. **LO.2** Indicate whether the following temporary differences produce deferred tax assets or deferred tax liabilities (considered independently).
   a. Book depreciation in excess of tax depreciation.
   b. Tax depreciation in excess of book depreciation.
   c. Increase in the allowance for doubtful accounts.
   d. Increase in the reserve for warranty settlements.
   e. Foreign tax credits that are not allowed in the current year because of the FTC limitation.
   f. A current-year NOL.

9. **LO.5** Indicate whether the following temporary differences produce current or noncurrent deferred tax assets or deferred tax liabilities (considered independently).
   a. Book depreciation in excess of tax depreciation.
   b. Tax depreciation in excess of book depreciation.
   c. Increase in the allowance for doubtful accounts.
   d. Increase in the reserve for warranty settlements.
   e. Write-down for impairment of book goodwill.
   f. A current-year NOL.

10. **LO.1** Evaluate the following statement: The primary purpose of the Schedule M–1 and Schedule M–3 is to help the IRS craft its audits of the taxpayer. (Hint: Focus on the primary reason the IRS wants to see this information.)

11. **LO.2** Cramer, a stock analyst, wants to understand how the income tax expense reported in financial statements will affect stock prices. Briefly describe the objective of ASC 740 (SFAS 109) with regard to reporting income tax expense.

12. **LO.2** Skipper, Inc., earns pretax book net income of $500,000 in 2011. Skipper acquires a depreciable asset in 2011, and first-year tax depreciation exceeds book depreciation by $80,000. Skipper has no other temporary or permanent differences. Assuming the U.S. tax rate is 35%, compute Skipper's total income tax expense, current income tax expense, and deferred income tax expense.

13. **LO.2** Using the facts of Problem 12, determine the 2011 end-of-year balance in Skipper's deferred tax asset and deferred tax liability balance sheet accounts.

14. **LO.2** Skipper, in Problem 12, reports $600,000 of pretax book net income in 2012. Skipper's book depreciation exceeds tax depreciation in this year by $50,000. Skipper has no other

temporary or permanent differences. Assuming the U.S. tax rate is 35%, compute Skipper's total income tax expense, current income tax expense, and deferred income tax expense.

15. **LO.2** Using the facts of Problem 14, determine the 2012 end-of-year balance in Skipper's deferred tax asset and deferred tax liability balance sheet accounts.

16. **LO.2** Poco, Inc., earns pretax book net income of $250,000 in 2011. Poco deducted $30,000 in bad debt expense for book purposes. This expense is not yet deductible for tax purposes. Poco has no other temporary or permanent differences. Assuming the U.S. tax rate is 35%, compute Poco's total income tax expense, current income tax expense, and deferred income tax expense.

17. **LO.2** Using the facts of Problem 16, determine the 2011 end-of-year balance in Poco's deferred tax asset and deferred tax liability balance sheet accounts.

18. **LO.2** Poco, in Problem 16, reports $400,000 of pretax book net income in 2012. Poco did not deduct any bad debt expense for book purposes but did deduct $20,000 in bad debt expense for tax purposes. Poco has no other temporary or permanent differences. Assuming the U.S. tax rate is 35%, compute Poco's total income tax expense, current income tax expense, and deferred income tax expense.

19. **LO.2** Using the facts of Problem 18, determine the 2012 end-of-year balance in Poco's deferred tax asset and deferred tax liability balance sheet accounts.

20. **LO.3** What is a valuation allowance, and why is such a book account created? Be specific.

21. **LO.3** Timber, Inc., hopes to report a total book tax expense of $50,000 in the current year. This $50,000 expense consists of $80,000 in current tax expense and a $30,000 tax benefit related to the expected future use of an NOL by Timber. If the auditors determine that a valuation allowance of $10,000 must be placed against Timber's deferred tax assets, what is Timber's total book tax expense?

22. **LO.3** How does the release of a valuation allowance in a future year affect the book effective tax rate for that year?

23. **LO.4** RadioCo, a domestic corporation, owns 100% of TVCo, a manufacturing facility in Ireland. TVCo has no operations or activities in the United States. The U.S. tax rate is 35%, and the Irish tax rate is 15%. For the current year, RadioCo earns $400,000 in taxable income. TVCo earns $800,000 in taxable income from its operations, pays $120,000 in taxes to Ireland, and makes no distributions to RadioCo. **DECISION MAKING**
    a. Determine RadioCo's effective tax rate for book purposes with and without the permanent reinvestment assumption of ASC 740-30 (APB 23).
    b. Under what conditions should RadioCo adopt ASC 740-30 (APB 23) for TVCo's earnings?

24. **LO.4** Zhang, the CFO of TechCo, Inc., has used ASC 740-30 (APB 23) to avoid reporting any U.S. deferred tax expense on $30 million of the earnings of TechCo's foreign subsidiaries. All of these subsidiaries operate in countries with lower tax rates than the United States. Zhang wants to bring home $20 million in profits from these foreign subsidiaries in the form of dividends. How will this profit repatriation affect TechCo's book effective tax rate? **ISSUE ID**

25. **LO.4** Brian, the CFO of AutoCo, Inc., has used ASC 740-30 (APB 23) to avoid reporting any U.S. deferred tax expense on $60 million of the earnings of AutoCo's foreign subsidiaries. All of these subsidiaries operate in countries with higher tax rates than the ones that apply under U.S. law. Brian wants to bring home $20 million in profits from these foreign subsidiaries in the form of dividends. How will this profit repatriation affect AutoCo's book effective tax rate? **ISSUE ID**

26. **LO.1** Rufus Enterprises acquires another corporation. This acquisition created $10 million of goodwill for both book and tax purposes. The $10 million in goodwill is amortized over 15 years for tax purposes but is not deductible for book purposes unless impaired. Will this book-tax difference create a permanent or temporary difference?

27. **LO.6** Lydia is the CFO of FarmTime, Inc. FarmTime's tax advisers have recommended two tax planning ideas that will each provide $8 million of current-year cash tax savings. One idea is based on a timing difference and is expected to reverse 20 years in the future. The other idea creates a permanent difference that will never reverse. Determine **DECISION MAKING**

whether these ideas will allow FarmTime to reduce its reported book income tax expense for the current year. Illustrate your preference for one planning strategy over the other in a spreadsheet. Which idea will you recommend to Lydia?

COMMUNICATIONS

28. **LO.1, 5** Sam Taggart, the CEO of Skate, Inc., has reviewed Skate's tax return and its financial statement. He notices that both the Schedule M–3 and the rate reconciliation in the income tax note provide a reconciliation of tax information. However, he sees very little correspondence between the two schedules. Outline the differences between these two schedules in a letter to Sam. Skate's address is 499 Lucerne Avenue, Ocala, FL 34482.

29. **LO.6** RoofCo reports total book income before taxes of $20 million and a total tax expense of $8 million. FloorCo reports book income before taxes of $30 million and a total tax expense of $12 million. The companies' breakdown between current and deferred tax expense (benefit) is as follows.

	RoofCo	FloorCo
Current tax expense	$ 8.2	$12.4
Deferred tax benefit	(0.2)	(0.4)
Total tax expense	$ 8.0	$12.0

RoofCo's deferred tax benefit is from a deferred tax asset created because of differences in depreciation methods for equipment. FloorCo's deferred tax benefit is created by the expected future use of an NOL. Compare and contrast these two companies' effective tax rates. How are they similar, and how are they different?

COMMUNICATIONS

30. **LO.6** LawnCo and TreeCo operate in the same industry, and both report a 32% effective tax rate. Their book income and current, deferred, and total tax expense are reported below.

	LawnCo	TreeCo
Book income before tax	$ 500,000	$650,000
Current tax expense	$ 310,000	$ 17,000
Deferred tax expense (benefit)	(150,000)	191,000
Total tax expense	$ 160,000	$208,000
Effective tax rate	32%	32%

ShrubCo is a competitor of both these companies. Prepare a memo to Laura Collins, VP-Taxation, outlining your analysis of the two companies' effective tax rates, using only the information above.

31. **LO.6** RedCo and BlueCo operate in the same industry and report the following tax rate reconciliations in their tax footnotes.

	RedCo	BlueCo
Hypothetical tax at U.S. rate	35.0%	35.0%
State and local taxes	3.2	3.9
Foreign income taxed at less than U.S. rate	(12.3)	(7.8)
Tax Court settlement on disputed tax issue	5.3	—
Effective tax rate	31.2%	31.1%

Compare and contrast the effective tax rates of these two companies.

32. **LO.6** Comment on this statement: Benchmarking book-tax differences among entities is part science and part art.

PROBLEMS

33. **LO.2** Phillips, Inc., a cash basis C corporation, completes $100,000 in sales for Year 1, but only $70,000 of this amount is collected during Year 1. The remaining $30,000 from these sales is collected promptly during the first quarter of Year 2. The applicable income tax rate for Year 1 and thereafter is 25%. Compute Phillips's Year 1 current and deferred income tax expense.

34. **LO.2** Continue with the results of Problem 33. Prepare the GAAP journal entries for Phillips's Year 1 income tax expense.

35. **LO.2** Sing-Li, Inc., an accrual basis C corporation, sells widgets on credit. Its book and taxable income for Year 1 totals $42,000, before accounting for bad debts. Sing-Li's book allowance for uncollectible accounts increased for Year 1 by $12,000, but none of the entity's bad debts received a specific write-off for tax purposes. The applicable income tax rate for Year 1 and thereafter is 30%. Compute Sing-Li's Year 1 current and deferred income tax expense.

36. **LO.2** Continue with the results of Problem 35. Prepare the GAAP journal entries for Sing-Li's Year 1 income tax expense.

37. **LO.2** Rubio, Inc., an accrual basis C corporation, reports the following amounts for the tax year. The applicable income tax rate is 30%. Compute Rubio's taxable income.

Book and taxable income prior to the items below	$50,000
Increase in book allowance for anticipated warranty costs	8,000
Interest income from City of Westerville bonds	10,000
Bribes paid to Federal inspectors	17,000

38. **LO.2** Continue with the results of Problem 37. Determine Rubio's income tax expense and GAAP income for the year.

39. **LO.2** Willingham, Inc., an accrual basis C corporation, reports Year 1 book and taxable income of $2 million, before accounting for its investment activities. The applicable tax rate is 35% for Year 1 and thereafter. Compute Willingham's Year 1 current and deferred income tax expense.

    The entity owns one investment asset, which it purchased many years ago for $1 million. At the end of Year 1, the asset's fair value is $1.8 million. Willingham reports no other Year 1 book-tax differences.

40. **LO.2** Continue with the results of Problem 39. Prepare the GAAP journal entries for Willingham's Year 1 income tax expense.

41. **LO.2** Relix, Inc., is a domestic corporation with the following balance sheet for book and tax purposes at the end of the year. Based on this information, determine Relix's net deferred tax asset or net deferred tax liability at year end. Assume a 34% corporate tax rate and no valuation allowance.

	Tax Debit/(Credit)	Book Debit/(Credit)
Assets		
Cash	$ 500	$ 500
Accounts receivable	8,000	8,000
Buildings	750,000	750,000
Accumulated depreciation	(450,000)	(380,000)
Furniture & fixtures	70,000	70,000
Accumulated depreciation	(46,000)	(38,000)
Total assets	$ 332,500	$ 410,500

	Tax Debit/(Credit)	Book Debit/(Credit)
Liabilities		
Accrued litigation expense	$ -0-	($ 50,000)
Note payable	(78,000)	(78,000)
Total liabilities	($ 78,000)	($ 128,000)
Stockholders' Equity		
Paid-in capital	($ 10,000)	($ 10,000)
Retained earnings	(244,500)	(272,500)
Total liabilities and stockholders' equity	($332,500)	($ 410,500)

42. **LO.2** Based on the facts and results of Problem 41 and the beginning-of-the-year book-tax basis differences listed below, determine the change in Relix's deferred tax assets for the current year.

	Beginning of Year
Accrued litigation expense	$34,000
Subtotal	$34,000
Applicable tax rate	× 34%
Gross deferred tax asset	$11,560

43. **LO.2** Based on the facts and results of Problem 41 and the beginning-of-the-year book-tax basis differences listed below, determine the change in Relix's deferred tax liabilities for the current year.

	Beginning of Year
Building—accumulated depreciation	($57,000)
Furniture & fixtures—accumulated depreciation	(4,200)
Subtotal	($61,200)
Applicable tax rate	× 34%
Gross deferred tax liability	($20,808)

44. **LO.2** Based on the facts and results of Problems 41–43, determine Relix's change in net deferred tax asset or net deferred tax liability for the current year and provide the journal entry to record this amount.

45. **LO.2** In addition to the temporary differences identified in Problems 41–44, Relix, Inc., reported two permanent differences between book and taxable income. It earned $2,375 in tax-exempt municipal bond interest, and it incurred $780 in nondeductible meals and entertainment expense. Relix's book income before tax is $4,800. With this additional information, calculate Relix's current tax expense.

46. **LO.2** Provide the journal entry to record Relix's current tax expense as determined in Problem 45.

47. **LO.2** Based on the facts and results of Problems 41–46, calculate Relix's total provision for income tax expense reported in its financial statements and its book net income after tax.

48. **LO.2** Based on the facts and results of Problems 41–47, provide the income tax footnote rate reconciliation for Relix.

49. **LO.2** Kantner, Inc., is a domestic corporation with the following balance sheet for book and tax purposes at the end of the year. Based on this information, determine

Kantner's net deferred tax asset or net deferred tax liability at year-end. Assume a 34% corporate tax rate and no valuation allowance.

	Tax Debit/(Credit)	Book Debit/(Credit)
Assets		
Cash	$ 1,000	$ 1,000
Accounts receivable	9,000	9,000
Buildings	850,000	850,000
Accumulated depreciation	(700,000)	(620,000)
Furniture & fixtures	40,000	40,000
Accumulated depreciation	(10,000)	(8,000)
Total assets	$ 190,000	$ 272,000
Liabilities		
Accrued warranty expense	$ 0	($ 40,000)
Note payable	(16,000)	(16,000)
Total liabilities	($ 16,000)	($ 56,000)
Stockholders' Equity		
Paid-in capital	($ 50,000)	($ 50,000)
Retained earnings	(124,000)	(166,000)
Total liabilities and stockholders' equity	($ 190,000)	($ 272,000)

50. **LO.2** Based on the facts and results of Problem 49 and the beginning-of-the-year book-tax basis differences listed below, determine the change in Kantner's deferred tax assets for the current year.

	Beginning of Year
Accrued warranty expense	$30,000
Subtotal	$30,000
Applicable tax rate	× 34%
Gross deferred tax asset	$10,200

51. **LO.2** Based on the facts and results of Problem 49 and the beginning-of-the-year book-tax basis differences listed below, determine the change in Kantner's deferred tax liabilities for the current year.

	Beginning of Year
Building—accumulated depreciation	($62,000)
Furniture & fixtures—accumulated depreciation	(400)
Subtotal	($62,400)
Applicable tax rate	× 34%
Gross deferred tax liability	($21,216)

52. **LO.2** Based on the facts and results of Problems 49–51, determine Kantner's change in net deferred tax asset or net deferred tax liability for the current year. Provide the journal entry to record this amount.

53. **LO.2** In addition to the temporary differences identified in Problems 49–52, Kantner had two permanent differences between book and taxable income. It earned $7,800 in tax-exempt municipal bond interest, and it reported $850 in nondeductible meals and entertainment expense. Kantner's book income before tax is $50,000. With this additional information, calculate Kantner's current tax expense.

54. **LO.2** Provide the journal entry to record Kantner's current tax expense as determined in Problem 53.

55. **LO.2** Based on the facts and results of Problems 49–54, calculate Kantner's total provision for income tax expense reported on its financial statement and its book net income after tax.

56. **LO.2** Based on the facts and results of Problems 49–55, provide the income tax footnote rate reconciliation for Kantner.

RESEARCH PROBLEMS

Use the tax resources of the Internet to address the following questions. Do not restrict your search to the Web, but include a review of newsgroups and general reference materials, practitioner sites and resources, primary sources of the tax law, chat rooms and discussion groups, and other opportunities.

COMMUNICATIONS

Research Problem 1. Locate the web page of Citizens for Tax Justice and find the report "Corporate Income Taxes in the 1990s." Using this report, identify the effective tax rates of three companies, as estimated in the report. Also locate the financial statements of these three companies (using the companies' websites or the SEC's website **www.sec.gov**). From the financial statement income tax note, identify the reported effective tax rate from the rate reconciliation for each company. Compare and contrast the financial statement effective tax rates with those estimated by the Citizens for Tax Justice report. Summarize this information in an e-mail to your instructor.

COMMUNICATIONS

Research Problem 2. Locate the most recent financial statements of two companies in the same industry using the companies' websites or the SEC's website (**www.sec.gov**). Perform a benchmarking analysis of the two companies' effective tax rates, components of the effective tax rate reconciliation, levels of deferred tax assets and liabilities, and other relevant data. Summarize this information in an e-mail to your instructor.

COMMUNICATIONS

Research Problem 3. Search the news archives available on the Web and locate two articles addressing the controversy over whether fair value should be used to compute investment income on a company's income statement. Summarize these articles and send your report as an e-mail to your instructor.

COMMUNICATIONS

Research Problem 4. Both Schedule M–1 and Schedule M–3 of Form 1120 provide a reconciliation of book income to taxable income. Locate the instructions for both these schedules at the IRS website (**www.irs.gov**) and review the definition of book income for purposes of the two schedules. Identify three specific items included in the Schedule M–3 determination of book income and discuss why these items are useful in determining a corporation's appropriate book income to use in the reconciliation. Send your comments as an e-mail to your instructor.

COMMUNICATIONS

Research Problem 5. Use any available resources (databases, the Web, etc.) to locate articles or other discussions regarding the key differences between ASC 740 (SFAS 109) and International Accounting Standard No. 12 (related to income taxes). Summarize these key differences in an e-mail to your instructor, citing your sources.

COMMUNICATIONS

Research Problem 6. Locate the financial statements of three different companies that report information in the income tax footnote regarding uncertain tax positions under ASC 740 (FIN 48). Create a schedule that compares and contrasts the changes in uncertain tax positions reported by the three companies. E-mail the schedule to your instructor.

COMMUNICATIONS

Research Problem 7. Locate the financial statements of three different companies. Review the income tax footnote information on deferred tax assets (DTAs) and deferred tax liabilities (DTLs). Create a schedule that compares the end-of-the year amounts of DTAs and DTLs, including any valuation allowances. E-mail the schedule to your instructor.

Research Problem 8. Using publicly available web resources, locate summary financial information for two companies in the same industry. Compare and contrast the following items across the two companies: debt-to-equity ratio, return on assets, return on equity, inventory turnover ratio, and effective tax rate.

COMMUNICATIONS

Research Problem 9. Locate the financial statements of two different companies in two different industries that appear to have very different state and local tax burdens based on the rate reconciliation contained in the income tax footnote. Describe the difference in state and local effective rates and provide your thoughts on why the industry may be a factor in the differing state and local average tax rates. E-mail this discussion to your instructor.

Research Problem 10. Using publicly available web information, locate news or other items reporting financial analysts' forecasts or other information regarding two different companies. Determine whether the analyst appears to use tax information in the report. For example, does the analyst use pretax or after-tax earnings in the analysis? Draft an e-mail to your instructor describing your findings.

COMMUNICATIONS

Exempt Entities

CHAPTER 15

LEARNING OBJECTIVES

After completing Chapter 15, you should be able to:

LO.1

Identify the different types of exempt organizations.

LO.2

Enumerate the requirements for exempt status.

LO.3

Know the tax consequences of exempt status, including the different consequences for public charities and private foundations.

LO.4

Determine which exempt organizations are classified as private foundations.

LO.5

Recognize the taxes imposed on private foundations and calculate the related initial tax and additional tax amounts.

LO.6

Determine when an exempt organization is subject to the unrelated business income tax and calculate the amount of the tax.

LO.7

List the reports exempt organizations must file with the IRS and the related due dates.

LO.8

Identify tax planning opportunities for exempt organizations.

OUTLINE

For the latest in changes to tax legislation, visit **www.cengage.com/taxation/swft.**

THE BIG PICTURE Tax Solutions for the Real World

EFFECT OF A FOR-PROFIT BUSINESS ON A TAX-EXEMPT ENTITY

For an entity to be tax-exempt, it must serve the common good. This common good can include a mission as broad as that of a public charity such as the Red Cross or as narrow as that of a private foundation that operates a historic museum that depicts life in the eighteenth century. Most exempt organizations are exempt under § 501(c)(3).

Hopeful, Inc., is a § 501(c)(3) organization that provides temporary lodging and psychological services for abused women. Its annual operating budget is $12 million. More than two decades ago, Betty Jones was a recipient of the services provided by Hopeful. Now, Hopeful's administrator has been notified by the attorney for Betty's estate that her will transfers to Hopeful the legal ownership (100 percent of the outstanding stock) of Taste Good Ice Cream, a chain of 40 gourmet ice cream shops located in Virginia, North Carolina, and South Carolina. The business has been in existence for eight years and has produced substantially higher profits each year.

Hopeful's board is considering the following options regarding the inheritance from Betty and has hired you to provide an analysis of the tax consequences of each option.

- Sell the stock of Taste Good Ice Cream and contribute the net proceeds to Hopeful's endowment.
- Continue to conduct the Taste Good Ice Cream business as a division of Hopeful.
- Continue to conduct the business as a wholly owned subsidiary of Hopeful.

With the second and the third options, the existing management team will remain in place. After-tax profits not needed to expand the ice cream shop chain will be used by Hopeful in carrying out its exempt mission. **Read the chapter and formulate your response.**

Ideally, any entity that generates profit would prefer not to be subject to the Federal income tax. All of the types of entities discussed in Chapter 13 are subject to the Federal income tax at one level (e.g., sole proprietorships, partnerships, S corporations, and LLCs generally are subject only to single taxation) or more (e.g., C corporations are subject to double taxation). In contrast, entities classified as **exempt organizations** may be able to escape Federal income taxation altogether.

The tax-exempt sector is an important component of the U.S. economy. More than 2 million tax-exempt entities file tax returns with the IRS. These entities employ almost 12 million workers, representing about 10 percent of the total U.S. workforce. They control about $3.5 trillion in assets. The IRS audits about 8,000 of these entities every tax year.

Churches are among the types of organizations that are exempt from Federal income tax. Nevertheless, one must be careful not to conclude that anything labeled a church will qualify for exempt status.

During the 1970s and 1980s, a popular technique for attempting to avoid Federal income tax was the establishment of so-called mail-order churches. For example, in one scheme, a nurse obtained a certificate of ordination and a church charter from an organization that sold such documents.[1] The articles of incorporation stated that the church was organized exclusively for religious and charitable purposes, including a religious mission of healing the spirit, mind, emotions, and body. The nurse was the church's minister, director, and principal officer. Taking a vow of poverty, she transferred all of her assets, including a house and car, to the church. The church assumed all of the nurse's liabilities, including the mortgage on her house and her credit card bills. The nurse continued to work at a hospital and deposited her salary in the church's bank account. The church provided her with a living

[1] Rev.Rul. 81–94, 1981–1 C.B. 330.

TAX *in the NEWS*

Who Are the Donors?

Gifts are a major source of funds for many charities. Charitable giving by Americans in 2009 totaled $304 billion, about 2.1 percent of GDP. The bulk of charitable gifts are made by individuals and their estates.

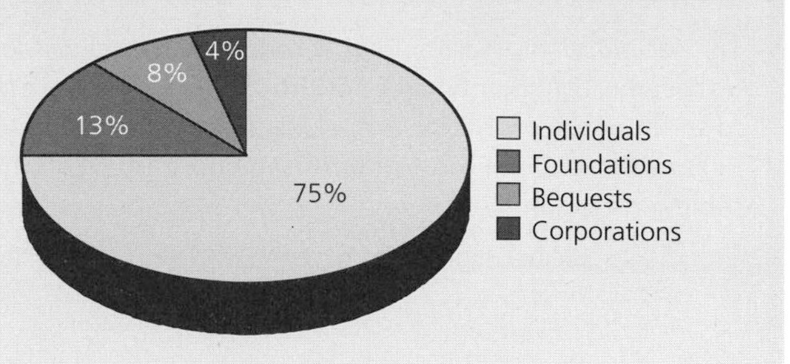

Source: Giving USA, 2011.

allowance sufficient to maintain or improve her previous standard of living. She was also permitted to use the house and car for personal purposes.

The IRS declared that such organizations were shams and not bona fide churches. For a church to be tax-exempt under § 501(c)(3), none of its net earnings may be used to the benefit of any private shareholder or individual. In essence, the organization should serve a public rather than a private interest. Though the courts have consistently upheld the IRS position, numerous avoidance schemes such as this have been attempted.

Another technique being marketed as a way to avoid Federal income taxes is to set up shop as a credit counselor. Credit counselors have an opportunity to qualify for tax-exempt status under § 501(c)(3). Supposedly, such tax-exempt organizations exist to help debt-laden consumers learn to practice sound financial management and become debt-free. Unfortunately, in reality some credit counseling organizations push consumers into debt repayment schedules with high, poorly disclosed fees that leave the debtor in worse financial shape than before the "counseling." Apparently, the primary motive of such techniques is to earn profits. These unsavory practices have caused Congress to call for greater IRS scrutiny. The IRS has revoked or is in the process of revoking the tax-exempt status of the 41 credit counselors it has audited. Such credit counselors have earned more than 40 percent of the industry's $1 billion in annual revenues.

As discussed in Chapter 1, the major objective of the Federal tax law is to raise revenue. If revenue raising were the only objective, however, the Code would not contain provisions that permit certain organizations to be either partially or completely exempt from Federal income tax. Social considerations also may affect the tax law. This objective bears directly on the decision by Congress to provide for exempt organization tax status. The House Report on the Revenue Act of 1938 explains:

> The exemption from taxation of money or property devoted to charitable and other purposes is based upon the theory that the Government is compensated for the loss of revenue by its relief from the financial burden which would otherwise have to be met by appropriations from public funds, and by the benefits resulting from the promotion of the general welfare.[2]

Recognizing this social consideration objective, Subchapter F (Exempt Organizations) of the Code (§§ 501–530) provides the authority under which certain organizations are exempt from Federal income tax. Exempt status is not open-ended in that two general limitations exist. First, the nature or scope of the organization may result in it being only partially exempt from tax.[3] Second, the organization may engage in activities that are subject to special taxation.[4]

[2]See 1939–1 (Part 2) C.B. 742 for a reprint of H.R. No. 1860, 75th Congress, 3rd Session.

[3]See the subsequent discussion of Unrelated Business Income Tax.

[4]See the subsequent discussions of Prohibited Transactions and Taxes Imposed on Private Foundations.

TAX *in the NEWS*

Who Are the Donees?

The recipients of charitable gifts can be classified as shown in the chart. Religious and educational organizations and foundations account for almost 60 percent of the donees. Religious organizations alone receive one-third of all charitable gifts.

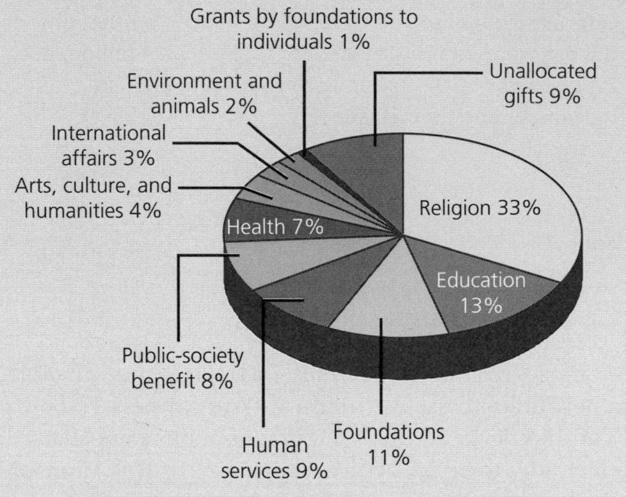

Source: Giving USA, 2011.

LO.1

Identify the different types of exempt organizations.

15.1 Types of Exempt Organizations

An organization qualifies for exempt status *only* if it fits into one of the categories provided in the Code. Examples of qualifying exempt organizations and the specific statutory authority for their exempt status are listed in Exhibit 15.1.[5]

LO.2

Enumerate the requirements for exempt status.

15.2 Requirements for Exempt Status

Exempt status frequently requires more than mere classification in one of the categories of exempt organizations. Many of the organizations that qualify for exempt status share the following characteristics.

TAX *in the NEWS*

A New Type of Nonprofit?

According to Senator Benjamin L. Cardin of Maryland, newspapers are vital to democracy. Thomas Jefferson reached the same conclusion centuries ago.

As more people turn to other media outlets, such as the Internet, for news, however, many newspapers are experiencing a decline in readership. Among those facing significant financial difficulty are the *Seattle Post-Intelligencer,* the *Rocky Mountain News,* the *Baltimore Examiner,* and the *San Francisco Chronicle.*

Convinced that newspapers play an important role in our society, Senator Cardin has introduced the Newspaper Revitalization Act. This measure would enable newspapers to operate as nonprofits under § 501(c)(3), if they choose to do so. Thus, their status would be similar to that now available to public broadcasting.

Under the bill, newspapers that choose this status still would be able to report freely on all issues including political campaigns, but they would not be allowed to make political endorsements. The bill is targeted to local newspapers and not to large newspaper conglomerates.

Source: Press release of Senator Benjamin Cardin.

[5]Section 501(a) provides for exempt status for organizations described in §§ 401 and 501. The orientation of this chapter is toward organizations that conduct business activities. Therefore, the exempt organizations described in § 401 (qualified pension, profit sharing, and stock bonus trusts) are outside the scope of the chapter and are not discussed.

EXHIBIT 15.1 **Types of Exempt Organizations**

Statutory Authority	Brief Description	Examples or Comments
§ 501(c)(1)	Federal and related agencies.	Commodity Credit Corporation, Federal Deposit Insurance Corporation, Federal Land Bank.
§ 501(c)(2)	Corporations holding title to property for and paying income to exempt organizations.	Corporation holding title to college fraternity house.
§ 501(c)(3)	Religious, charitable, educational, scientific, literary, etc., organizations.	Boy Scouts of America, Red Cross, Salvation Army, Episcopal Church, PTA, United Fund, University of Richmond.
§ 501(c)(4)	Civic leagues and employee unions.	Garden club, tenants' association promoting tenants' legal rights in entire community, League of Women Voters.
§ 501(c)(5)	Labor, agricultural, and horticultural organizations.	Teachers' association, organization formed to promote effective agricultural pest control, organization formed to test soil and to educate community members in soil treatment, garden club.
§ 501(c)(6)	Business leagues, chambers of commerce, real estate boards, etc.	Chambers of Commerce, American Plywood Association, National Football League (NFL), Professional Golfers Association (PGA) Tour, medical association peer review board, organization promoting acceptance of women in business and professions.
§ 501(c)(7)	Social clubs.	Country club, rodeo and riding club, press club, bowling club, college fraternities.
§ 501(c)(8)	Fraternal beneficiary societies.	Lodges. Must provide for the payment of life, sickness, accident, or other benefits to members or their dependents.
§ 501(c)(9)	Voluntary employees' beneficiary associations.	Provide for the payment of life, sickness, accident, or other benefits to members, their dependents, or their designated beneficiaries.
§ 501(c)(10)	Domestic fraternal societies.	Lodges. Must not provide for the payment of life, sickness, accident, or other benefits; and must devote the net earnings exclusively to religious, charitable, scientific, literary, educational, and fraternal purposes.
§ 501(c)(11)	Local teachers' retirement fund associations.	Only permitted sources of income are amounts received from (1) public taxation, (2) assessments on teaching salaries of members, and (3) income from investments.
§ 501(c)(12)	Local benevolent life insurance associations, mutual or cooperative telephone companies, etc.	Local cooperative telephone company, local mutual water company, local mutual electric company.
§ 501(c)(13)	Cemetery companies.	Must be operated exclusively for the benefit of lot owners who hold the lots for burial purposes.
§ 501(c)(14)	Credit unions.	Other than credit unions exempt under § 501(c)(1).
§ 501(c)(15)	Mutual insurance companies.	Mutual fire insurance company, mutual automobile insurance company.
§ 501(c)(16)	Corporations organized by farmers' cooperatives for financing crop operations.	Related farmers' cooperative must be exempt from tax under § 521.
§ 501(c)(19)	Armed forces members' posts or organizations.	Veterans of Foreign Wars (VFW), Reserve Officers Association.
§ 501(c)(20)	Group legal service plans.	Provided by a corporation for its employees.
§ 501(d)	Religious and apostolic organizations.	Communal organization. Members must include pro rata share of the net income of the organization in their gross income as dividends.
§ 501(e)	Cooperative hospital service organizations.	Centralized purchasing organization for exempt hospitals.
§ 501(f)	Cooperative service organization of educational institutions.	Organization formed to manage universities' endowment funds.
§ 529	Qualified tuition programs.	Prepaid tuition and educational savings programs.
§ 530	Coverdell Education Savings Accounts.	Qualified education savings accounts.

FINANCIAL DISCLOSURE *Insights*

Effects of Sarbanes-Oxley on Nonprofit Entities

The rules of the Sarbanes-Oxley Act do not apply to nonprofit entities. Nevertheless, some nonprofits voluntarily comply with its provisions. For example, New York's Julliard School and the International Swimming Hall of Fame in Fort Lauderdale have adopted the governance practices, code of ethics, and increased transparency required by Sarbanes-Oxley. Factors contributing to such adoption by nonprofits include the following.

- Accounting firms that audit nonprofits want to see the same financial controls now in place at for-profits.
- Nonprofit trustees are demanding more transparency.
- Nonprofit trustees are concerned that their professional reputations could be hurt if money is misused or the nonprofit falters.

- The organization serves some type of *common good.*[6]
- The organization is *not* a *for-profit* entity.[7]
- *Net earnings* do not benefit the members of the organization.[8]
- The organization does not exert *political influence.*[9]

SERVING THE COMMON GOOD

The underlying rationale for all exempt organizations is that they serve some type of *common good.* However, depending on the type of the exempt organization, the term *common good* may be interpreted broadly or narrowly. If the test is interpreted broadly, the group being served is the general public or some large subgroup thereof. If it is interpreted narrowly, the group is the specific group referred to in the statutory language. One of the factors in classifying an exempt organization as a private foundation is the size of the group it serves.

NOT-FOR-PROFIT ENTITY

The organization may not be organized or operated for the purpose of making a profit. For some types of exempt organizations, the *for-profit prohibition* appears in the statutory language. For other types, the prohibition is implied.

NET EARNINGS AND MEMBERS OF THE ORGANIZATION

What uses are appropriate for the net earnings of a tax-exempt organization? The logical answer would seem to be that the earnings should be used for the exempt purpose of the organization. However, where the organization exists for the good of a specific group of members, such an open-ended interpretation could permit net earnings to benefit specific group members. Therefore, the Code specifically prohibits certain types of exempt organizations from using their earnings in this way.

> ... no part of the net earnings ... inures to the benefit of any private shareholder or individual.[10]

In other instances, a statutory prohibition is unnecessary because the definition of the exempt organization in the Code effectively prevents such use.

> ... the net earnings of which are devoted exclusively to religious, charitable, scientific, literary, educational, and fraternal purposes.[11]

POLITICAL INFLUENCE

Religious, charitable, educational, etc., organizations are generally prohibited from attempting to influence legislation or participate in political campaigns.

[6]See, for example, §§ 501(c)(3) and (4).
[7]See, for example, §§ 501(c)(3), (4), (6), (13), and (14).
[8]See, for example, §§ 501(c)(3), (6), (7), (9), (10), (11), and (19).
[9]See, for example, § 501(c)(3).
[10]§ 501(c)(6).
[11]§ 501(c)(10).

Participation in political campaigns includes participation both *on behalf of* a candidate and *in opposition to* a candidate.

Only in limited circumstances are such exempt organizations permitted to attempt to influence legislation. See the subsequent discussion under Prohibited Transactions.

FOR THE GOOD OF THE PEOPLE

Matthew Ayres is the founder, and the man behind the throne, of the Church for Today television ministry. Ministry broadcasts originate from church services in California and New York and are transmitted via cable throughout the United States. Though the membership of the Church for Today is small (approximately 5,000 members), the typical member is quite wealthy. In addition to receiving contributions from its members, the church solicits and receives donations from viewers of the TV broadcasts. The church is tax-exempt under § 501(c)(3).

The stated mission of the church is religious in nature. However, Matthew firmly believes, as do the members of the board of deacons of the church, that certain societal goals must be accomplished for the prophecies of the church to come true (i.e., their divine being expects them to be active missionaries). Among its basic beliefs, the church advocates government control and possession of all guns, the legalization of drugs, abortion on demand once approved by the appropriate government agency, the withdrawal of all U.S. troops from foreign soil and the termination of all military alliances, the abolition of capital punishment, and the availability of tuition-free university education to all U.S. citizens.

The ministers of the Church for Today are expected to include these basic beliefs, at the subliminal level, in their sermons. Some do so more effectively and more frequently than others, but all are required to do so. Matthew and the board of deacons are dismayed that American society has not adopted many of their beliefs.

Accordingly, Matthew proposes to the board of deacons that the church take a more proactive role. The employment contract of the ministers now will require them to include the basic beliefs in their sermons in an active manner. No longer can the church's positions just be incorporated subliminally. All the beliefs must be covered quarterly, and every sermon must present at least one of the basic doctrines. The ministers will encourage the church members and TV viewers actively to support these positions at both the state and Federal levels.

As a new member of the board of deacons, you wholeheartedly support Matthew's position. However, you are concerned about the effects of this open advocacy of positions on the tax-exempt status of the church. Matthew responds that the "church has friends in high places" and assures you that the tax-exempt status will not be endangered. What should you do?

15.3 Tax Consequences of Exempt Status: General

LO.3

Know the tax consequences of exempt status, including the different consequences for public charities and private foundations.

An organization that is appropriately classified as one of the types of exempt organizations is generally exempt from Federal income tax. Four exceptions to this general statement exist, however. An exempt organization that engages in a *prohibited transaction* or is a so-called *feeder organization* is subject to tax. If the organization is classified as a *private foundation*, it may be partially subject to tax. Finally, an exempt organization is subject to tax on its *unrelated business taxable income.*

In addition to being exempt from Federal income tax, an exempt organization may be eligible for other benefits, including the following.

- The organization may be exempt from state income tax, state franchise tax, sales tax, or property tax.
- The organization may receive discounts on postage rates.
- Donors of property to the exempt organization may qualify for charitable contribution deductions on their Federal and state income tax returns. However, *not* all exempt organizations are qualified charitable contribution recipients (e.g., gifts to the National Football League, PGA Tour, and Underwriters Laboratories are not deductible).

TAX in the NEWS

The Effect of the Recession on Charitable Contributions

Tax-exempt entities have two key causes for concern associated with the contributions they receive. One is immediate and the other is in the future.

The first concern is the economy and its effect on contributions. In 2008, the amount of charitable contributions declined by 2 percent—the first time since 1987 (the year of the "Black Monday" stock market collapse) that contributions had declined. In 2009, contributions fell again, marking the first time in half a century that they had declined two years in a row. The obvious explanation was the recession. Logically, if people are earning less income, they may be inclined to give less.

According to the Chronicle of Philanthropy, donations dropped by 11 percent in 2009. However, according to a report by the Giving USA Foundation, the decline was only 3.6 percent. The reason for this difference may be that the Giving USA Foundation report includes donations to private foundations and smaller charities, while the Chronicle's report includes only gifts to the nation's 400 largest charities.

Sources: Adapted from "Charitable Gifts Declined Last Year," *Wall Street Journal*, June 10, 2009, p. D6; and Associated Press, "Donations Fell in 2009; Worst Decline in 20 Years," *Wall Street Journal*, October 18, 2010, p. A6.

PROHIBITED TRANSACTIONS

Engaging in a § 503 prohibited transaction can produce three negative results. First, part or all of the organization's income may be subject to Federal income tax. Second and even worse, the organization may forfeit its exempt status. Finally, intermediate sanctions may be imposed on certain exempt organization insiders.

Failure to Continue to Qualify

Organizations initially qualify for exempt status only if they are organized as indicated in Exhibit 15.1. The initial qualification requirements then effectively become maintenance requirements. Failure to continue to meet the qualification requirements results in the loss of the entity's exempt status.

New Faith, Inc., is an excellent example of an exempt organization that failed to continue to qualify for tax exemption.[12] The stated purposes of the organization were to feed and shelter the poor. In its application for exempt status, New Faith indicated that it would derive its financial support from donations, bingo games, and raffles. The IRS approved the exempt status.

New Faith's only source of income was the operation of several lunch trucks, which provided food to the general public in exchange for scheduled "donations." Evidence provided by the organization to the Tax Court did not show that the food from the lunch trucks was provided free of charge or at reduced prices. In addition, no evidence was presented to show that the people who received food for free or at below-cost prices were impoverished or needy. The court concluded that the primary purpose of the activity was the conduct of a trade or business. It upheld the IRS's revocation of New Faith's exempt status.

Election Not to Forfeit Exempt Status for Lobbying

Organizations exempt under § 501(c)(3) (religious, charitable, educational, etc., organizations) are subject to limits on their attempts to influence legislation (lobbying activities) and participate in political campaigns.[13] Substantial lobbying or political activity can result in the forfeiture of exempt status.

[12] *New Faith, Inc.*, 64 TCM 1050, T.C.Memo. 1992–601.

[13] § 501(c)(3). Even a single Internet link to a partisan political site can taint the exempt entity.

TAX *in* the NEWS — CONTRIBUTORS TO CHARITY?

Being a tax-exempt entity has several advantages. First and foremost, such entities generally are not subject to Federal income taxes. Second, donors are able to deduct on their Federal income tax returns contributions to the charity that qualify as charitable contributions. Such beneficial treatment is available to both public charities and private foundations. But is the deduction available if the donor benefits from making the contribution?

Kirk Herbstreit, the ESPN college football analyst, donated a house to a local fire department. Per the agreement, the firefighters torched the house as part of a training program. The expectation was that the Herbstreits would rebuild on the now-vacant site.

The Herbstreits claimed a charitable contribution deduction of $330,000 for the house, but the IRS disallowed the deduction. Now the couple has filed suit against the IRS over the deduction disallowance and the related interest charges.

Source: Adapted from "Herbstreit Sues IRS over Rejected Deduction," *USA Today*, July 24, 2009, p. 7C.

Certain exempt organizations are permitted to engage in lobbying (but not political) activities that are greater than an insubstantial part of their activities, by making a § 501(h) election.[14] Eligible for the election are most § 501(c)(3) organizations (educational institutions, hospitals, and medical research organizations; organizations supporting government schools; organizations publicly supported by charitable contributions; certain organizations that are publicly supported by various sources including admissions, sales, gifts, grants, contributions, or membership fees; and certain organizations that support certain types of public charities).

An eligible § 501(c)(3) organization must make an affirmative election to participate in lobbying activities on a limited basis. The lobbying expenditures of electing organizations are subject to a ceiling. Exceeding the ceiling can lead to the forfeiture of exempt status. Even when the ceiling is not exceeded, a tax may be imposed on some of the lobbying expenditures (as discussed subsequently).

Two terms are key to the calculation of the ceiling amount: **lobbying expenditures** and **grass roots expenditures**. Lobbying expenditures are made for the purpose of influencing legislation through either of the following.

- Attempting to affect the opinions of the general public or any segment thereof.
- Communicating with any legislator or staff member or with any government official or staff member who may participate in the formulation of legislation.

Grass roots expenditures are made for the purpose of influencing legislation by attempting to affect the opinions of the general public or any segment thereof.

The statutory ceiling is imposed on both lobbying expenditures and grass roots expenditures and is computed as follows.

- 150% × Lobbying nontaxable amount = Lobbying expenditures ceiling.
- 150% × Grass roots nontaxable amount = Grass roots expenditures ceiling.

The *lobbying nontaxable amount* is the lesser of (1) $1 million or (2) the amount determined in Figure 15.1.[15] The *grass roots nontaxable amount* is 25 percent of the lobbying nontaxable amount.[16]

An electing exempt organization is assessed a tax on **excess lobbying expenditures** as follows.[17]

- 25% × Excess lobbying expenditures = Tax liability.

[14] Religious organizations and private foundations cannot make this election.

[15] § 4911(c)(2).

[16] § 4911(c)(4).

[17] § 4911(a)(1).

FIGURE 15.1 Calculation of Lobbying Nontaxable Amount

Exempt Purpose Expenditures	Lobbying Nontaxable Amount Is
Not over $500,000	20% of exempt purpose expenditures*
Over $500,000 but not over $1 million	$100,000 + 15% of the excess of exempt purpose expenditures over $500,000
Over $1 million but not over $1.5 million	$175,000 + 10% of the excess of exempt purpose expenditures over $1 million
Over $1.5 million	$225,000 + 5% of the excess of exempt purpose expenditures over $1.5 million

*Exempt purpose expenditures generally are the amounts paid or incurred for the taxable year to accomplish the following purposes: religious, charitable, scientific, literary, educational, fostering national or international amateur sports competition, or the prevention of cruelty to children or animals.

Excess lobbying expenditures are the greater of the following.[18]

- Excess of the lobbying expenditures for the taxable year over the lobbying nontaxable amount.
- Excess of the grass roots expenditures for the taxable year over the grass roots nontaxable amount.

EXAMPLE 1

Tan, Inc., a qualifying § 501(c)(3) organization, incurs lobbying expenditures of $500,000 for the taxable year and grass roots expenditures of $0. Exempt purpose expenditures for the taxable year are $5 million. Tan elects to be eligible to make lobbying expenditures on a limited basis.

Applying the data in Figure 15.1, the lobbying nontaxable amount is $400,000 [$225,000 + 5%($5,000,000 − $1,500,000)]. The ceiling on lobbying expenditures is $600,000 (150% × $400,000). Therefore, the $500,000 of lobbying expenditures are under the permitted $600,000. However, the election results in the imposition of tax on the excess lobbying expenditures of $100,000 ($500,000 lobbying expenditures − $400,000 lobbying nontaxable amount). The resulting tax liability is $25,000 ($100,000 × 25%). ■

A § 501(c)(3) organization that makes disqualifying lobbying expenditures is subject to a 5 percent tax on the lobbying expenditures for the taxable year. A 5 percent tax may also be levied on the organization's management. The tax is imposed on management only if the managers knew that making the expenditures was likely to result in the organization no longer qualifying under § 501(c)(3), and if the managers' actions were willful and not due to reasonable cause. The tax does not apply to private foundations (see the subsequent discussion).[19] Concept Summary 15.1 capsulizes the rules on influencing legislation.

Intermediate Sanctions

Prior to 1996, the IRS had only two options available for dealing with exempt organizations (other than private foundations) engaging in prohibited transactions. First, it could attempt to subject part or all of the organization's income to Federal income tax. Second, it could revoke the exempt status of the organization. For private foundations, an additional option was available. The IRS could impose certain taxes on private foundations for engaging in so-called prohibited transactions (see Concept Summary 15.3 later in the chapter).

Tax legislation enacted in 1996 added another option to the IRS toolbox—**intermediate sanctions**—for so-called public charities.[20] The intermediate sanctions take the form of excise taxes imposed on disqualified persons (any individuals who are

[18] § 4911(b).
[19] § 4912.
[20] § 4958.

CONCEPT SUMMARY 15.1

Exempt Organizations and Influencing Legislation

Factor	Tax Result
Entity subject to rule	§ 501(c)(3) organization.
Effect of influencing legislation	Subject to tax on lobbying expenditures under § 4912.
	Forfeit exempt status under § 501(c)(3).
	Not eligible for exempt status under § 501(c)(4).
Effect of electing to make lobbying expenditures	Permitted to make limited lobbying expenditures.
	Subject to tax under § 4911.

in a position to exercise substantial influence over the affairs of the organization) who engage in *excess benefit transactions* and on exempt organization managers who participate in such a transaction knowing that it is improper. Such excess benefit transactions include transactions in which a disqualified person engages in a non-fair-market-value transaction with the exempt organization or receives unreasonable compensation.

The excise tax on the disqualified person is imposed at a rate of 25 percent of the excess benefit. For the exempt organization management, the excise tax is imposed at a rate of 10 percent of the excess benefit (unless such participation is not willful and is due to reasonable cause) with a statutory ceiling of $20,000 for any excess benefit transaction. These excise taxes are referred to as first-level taxes.

A second-level tax is imposed on the disqualified person if the excess benefit transaction is not corrected within the taxable period. This excise tax is imposed at a rate of 200 percent of the excess benefit.

FEEDER ORGANIZATIONS

A **feeder organization** carries on a trade or business for the benefit of an exempt organization and remits its profits to the exempt organization. Such organizations are not exempt from Federal income tax. This provision is intended to prevent an entity whose primary purpose is to conduct a trade or business for profit from escaping taxation merely because all of its profits are payable to one or more exempt organizations.[21]

Some income and activities are *not* subject to the feeder organization rules.[22]

- Rent income that would be excluded from the definition of the term *rent* for purposes of the unrelated business income tax (discussed subsequently).
- A trade or business where substantially all the work is performed by volunteers.
- The trade or business of selling merchandise where substantially all the merchandise has been received as contributions or gifts.

EXAMPLE 2
THE BIG PICTURE

Return to the facts of *The Big Picture* on p. 15–2. Recall that Hopeful, Inc., an exempt organization under § 501(c)(3) that provides temporary lodging and psychological services to abused women, is trying to decide what it should do with Taste Good Ice Cream, a chain of gourmet ice cream shops that it has received as a bequest. Assume that Hopeful has decided to operate Taste Good as a subsidiary, with the profits going to Hopeful to support its tax-exempt mission. The subsidiary will be a taxable entity (a feeder organization) subject to the Federal income tax using the corporate tax rates. ■

Concept Summary 15.2 highlights the consequences of exempt status.

[21] § 502(a).

[22] § 502(b).

CONCEPT SUMMARY 15.2

Consequences of Exempt Status

General	Exempt from Federal income tax. Exempt from most state and local income, franchise, sales, and property taxes. Qualify for reductions in postage rates. Gifts to the organization often can be deducted by donor.
Exceptions	May be subject to Federal income tax associated with the following. • Engaging in a prohibited transaction. • Being a feeder organization. • Being a private foundation. • Generating unrelated business taxable income.

15.4 Private Foundations

LO.4

Determine which exempt organizations are classified as private foundations.

TAX CONSEQUENCES OF PRIVATE FOUNDATION STATUS

Certain exempt organizations are classified as **private foundations**. This classification produces two negative consequences. First, the classification may have an adverse impact on the contributions received by the donee exempt organization. Contributions may decline because the tax consequences for donors may not be as favorable as if the entity were not a private foundation.[23] Second, the classification may result in taxation at the exempt organization level. The reason for this less beneficial tax treatment is that private foundations define common good more narrowly and therefore are seen as not being supported by, and operated for the good of, the public.

Definition of a Private Foundation

All § 501(c)(3) organizations are private foundations by default, unless one of the statutory exceptions applies. The following § 501(c)(3) organizations are *not* private foundations.[24]

1. Churches; educational institutions; hospitals and medical research organizations; charitable organizations receiving a major portion of their support from the general public or the United States, a state, or a political subdivision thereof that is operated for the benefit of a college or university; and governmental units (favored activities category).
2. Organizations that are broadly supported by the general public (excluding disqualified persons), by governmental units, or by organizations described in (1) above.
3. Entities organized and operated exclusively for the benefit of organizations described in (1) or (2) [a supporting organization].
4. Entities organized and operated exclusively for testing for public safety.

To meet the broadly supported requirement in (2) above, both the following tests must be satisfied.

- External support test.
- Internal support test.

Under the *external support test*, more than one-third of the organization's support each taxable year *normally* must come from the three groups listed in (2) above, in the following forms.

- Gifts, grants, contributions, and membership fees.

[23] § 170(e)(1)(B)(ii).

[24] § 509(a).

TAX *in* the NEWS

When Does a Charitable Mission Become Political Advocacy?

What is the role of a private foundation? The usual answer is to carry out some charitable mission. When the Council of Foundations held its 2010 annual conference in Denver, however, a number of the participants argued that foundations should be playing a more active role in society.

Although collaborative efforts between private philanthopy and the White House are certainly not new, the election of President Obama, a onetime community organizer, has given impetus to the movement. Not only has the President indicated that he is eager to work with charitable organizations, but many of the organizations have expressed a willingness to support his agenda. At the Council of Foundations conference, for example, many participants advocated actively supporting health care reform, migrant rights, initiatives to reduce income disparity, and efforts to combat global warming. At the same time, however, a few foundation leaders suggested that such active political involvement might have consequences that its advocates had not considered.

Source: Adapted from Anthony Paletta, "The Fawning of the Foundations," *Wall Street Journal,* April 30, 2010, p. W9.

- Gross receipts from admissions, sales of merchandise, performance of services, or the furnishing of facilities in an activity that is not an unrelated trade or business for purposes of the unrelated business income tax (discussed subsequently). However, such gross receipts from any person or governmental agency in excess of the greater of $5,000 or 1 percent of the organization's support for the taxable year are not counted in the numerator of the support fraction.
- Amounts received from disqualified persons are not included in the numerator of the support fraction. Disqualified persons include:
  - *Substantial contributors whose cumulative gifts and bequests to the exempt entity exceed both 2 percent of aggregate contributions received by the entity and $5,000.*
  - *Members of the governing body of the exempt entity including officers, directors, trustees, and their families.*
  - *Generally, corporations, partnerships, trusts, and estates that are affiliated with a disqualified person, using a 35 percent ownership/beneficiary control test.*

The *internal support test* limits the amount of support *normally* received from the following sources to one-third of the organization's support for the taxable year.[25]

- Gross investment income (gross income from interest, dividends, rents, and royalties).
- Unrelated business taxable income (discussed subsequently) minus the related tax.

EXAMPLE 3

Lion, Inc., a § 501(c)(3) organization, received the following support during the taxable year.

Governmental unit A for services rendered	$ 30,000
Governmental unit B for services rendered	20,000
General public for services rendered	20,000
Gross investment income	15,000
Contributions from individual substantial contributors (disqualified persons)	15,000
Total support	$100,000

For purposes of the *external support test,* the support from A is counted only to the extent of $5,000 (greater of $5,000 or 1% of $100,000 support). Likewise, for B, only

[25]The external and internal support tests generally must be met in each of the four preceding tax years. When these tests are met, public charity status is granted for the current year and for the subsequent year. Reg. §§ 1.509(a)–3(c) and 1.170A–9(e)(4)(i).

TAX in the NEWS

Donor-Advised Funds: A Hot Topic

Suppose that a wealthy taxpayer would like to make a substantial charitable contribution and qualify for the charitable contribution deduction this year. However, he has not yet identified the recipient of the contribution. Or the taxpayer has identified the recipient, but wants the charity to disburse the funds over a number of years. Or the taxpayer wants to make the contribution this year, but be permitted to advise the charitable organization in future years as to the possible use of the donated funds. Can the taxpayer achieve any of these goals and still be eligible for the charitable contribution deduction this year?

There is a way to meet the wealthy taxpayer's objectives. He can make his contribution to a "donor-advised fund." Such funds are components of a qualified charitable organization.

To receive this favorable treatment, however, certain statutory and administrative requirements must be met. Even though the donor may advise as to how the funds are to be used, the charitable organization must have ultimate control over their distribution. For any contributions to donor-advised funds made after February 13, 2007, the donor must obtain written acknowledgment from the charitable organization that it has exclusive legal control over the contributed assets.

Recognizing the potential for abuse in this area, both the Senate Finance Committee and the House Ways and Means Committee have identified donor-advised funds as a potential topic for additional legislation.

$5,000 is counted as support. Thus, the total countable support is $30,000 ($20,000 from the general public + $5,000 + $5,000), and Lion fails the test for the taxable year ($30,000/$100,000 = 30%; need > 33.3%). The $15,000 received from disqualified persons is excluded from the numerator but is included in the denominator.

External Support Test	
Governmental unit A for services rendered	$ 5,000
Governmental unit B for services rendered	5,000
General public for services rendered	20,000
Total countable support	$30,000

$$\frac{\$30{,}000}{\$100{,}000} = 30\% \quad \text{Fails external support test}$$

In calculating the *internal support test*, only the gross investment income of $15,000 is included in the numerator. Thus, the test is satisfied ($15,000/$100,000 = 15%; cannot > 33%) for the taxable year.

Internal Support Test	
Gross investment income	$15,000
Unrelated business taxable income	–0–
Total countable support	$15,000

$$\frac{\$15{,}000}{\$100{,}000} = 15\% \quad \text{Passes internal support test}$$

Since Lion did not satisfy both tests, it does not qualify as an organization that is broadly supported. ■

The intent of the two tests is to exclude from private foundation status those § 501(c)(3) organizations that are responsive to the general public rather than to the private interests of a limited number of donors or other persons.

Examples of § 501(c)(3) organizations that would be classified as private foundations, except that they receive broad public support, include the United Fund, the Girl Scouts, university alumni associations, and symphony orchestras.

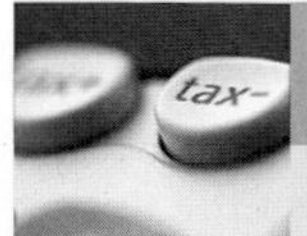

CONCEPT SUMMARY 15.3

Taxes Imposed on Private Foundations

Type of Tax	Code Section	Purpose	Private Foundation Initial Tax	Private Foundation Additional Tax	Foundation Manager Initial Tax	Foundation Manager Additional Tax
On investment income	§ 4940	Audit fee to defray IRS expenses.	2%*			
On self-dealing	§ 4941	Engaging in transactions with disqualified persons.	5%**	200%**	2.5%†	50%†
On failure to distribute income	§ 4942	Failing to distribute adequate amount of income for exempt purposes.	15%	100%		
On excess business holdings	§ 4943	Investments that enable the private foundation to control unrelated businesses.	5%	200%		
On jeopardizing investments	§ 4944	Speculative investments that put the private foundation's assets at risk.	5%	25%	5%††	5%†
On taxable expenditures	§ 4945	Expenditures that should not be made by private foundations.	10%	100%	2.5%††	50%†

*May be possible to reduce the tax rate to 1%. In addition, an exempt operating foundation [see §§ 4940 (d)(2) and 4942 (j)(3)] is not subject to the tax.
**Imposed on the disqualified person rather than the foundation.
†Subject to a statutory ceiling of $10,000.
††Subject to a statutory ceiling of $5,000.

TAXES IMPOSED ON PRIVATE FOUNDATIONS

LO.5

Recognize the taxes imposed on private foundations and calculate the related initial tax and additional tax amounts.

In general, a private foundation is exempt from Federal income tax. However, because a private foundation is usually not a broadly, publicly supported organization, it may be subject to the following taxes.[26]

- Tax based on investment income.
- Tax on self-dealing.
- Tax on failure to distribute income.
- Tax on excess business holdings.
- Tax on investments that jeopardize charitable purposes.
- Tax on taxable expenditures.

These taxes restrict the permitted activities of private foundations. Two levels of tax may be imposed on the private foundation and the foundation manager: an initial tax and an additional tax. The initial taxes (first-level), with the exception of the tax based on investment income, are imposed because the private foundation engages in so-called *prohibited transactions.* The additional taxes (second-level) are imposed only if the prohibited transactions are not corrected within a statutory time period.[27] See Concept Summary 15.3 for additional details.

The tax on a failure to distribute income will be used to illustrate how expensive these taxes can be and the related importance of avoiding their imposition. Both an initial (first-level) tax and an additional (second-level) tax may be imposed on a private

[26]§§ 4940–4945.

[27]§ 4961.

nonoperating foundation for failure to distribute a sufficient portion of its income. The initial tax is imposed at a rate of 15 percent on the undistributed income for the taxable year that is not distributed by the end of the following taxable year. The initial tax is imposed on such undistributed income for each year until the IRS assesses the tax.

The additional tax is imposed at a rate of 100 percent on the amount of the inadequate distribution that is not distributed by the assessment date. The additional tax is effectively waived if the undistributed income is distributed within 90 days after the mailing of the deficiency notice for the additional tax. Extensions of this period may be obtained.

Undistributed income is the excess of the distributable amount (in effect, the amount that should have been distributed) over qualifying distributions made by the entity. The distributable amount is the excess of the minimum investment return over the sum of (1) the unrelated business income tax and (2) the excise tax based on net investment income.[28] The minimum investment return is 5 percent of the excess of the fair market value of the foundation's assets over the unpaid debt associated with acquiring or improving these assets. The foundation's assets employed directly in carrying on the foundation's exempt purpose are not used in making this calculation.

EXAMPLE 4

Gold, Inc., a private foundation, has undistributed income of $80,000 for the taxable year 2008. It distributes $15,000 of this amount during 2009 and an additional $45,000 during 2010. An IRS deficiency notice is mailed to Gold on August 5, 2011. The initial tax is $12,750 [($65,000 × 15%) + ($20,000 × 15%)].

At the date of the deficiency notice, no additional distributions have been made from the 2008 undistributed income. Therefore, since the remaining undistributed income of $20,000 has not been distributed by August 5, 2011, an additional tax of $20,000 ($20,000 × 100%) is imposed.

If Gold distributes the $20,000 of undistributed income for 2008 within 90 days of the deficiency notice, the additional tax is waived. Without this distribution, however, the foundation will owe $32,750 in taxes. ■

Exhibit 15.2 shows the classifications of exempt organizations and indicates the potential negative consequences of classification as a private foundation.

15.5 Unrelated Business Income Tax

LO.6

Determine when an exempt organization is subject to the unrelated business income tax and calculate the amount of the tax.

As explained in the previous section, private foundations are subject to excise taxes for certain actions. One of these excise taxes penalizes the private foundation for using the foundation to gain control of unrelated businesses (tax on excess business holdings). However, *unrelated business* has different meanings for purposes of that excise tax and for the unrelated business income tax.

The **unrelated business income tax (UBIT)** is designed to treat the entity as if it were subject to the corporate income tax. Thus, the rates that are used are those applicable to a corporate taxpayer.[29]

In general, **unrelated business income (UBI)** is derived from activities not related to the exempt purpose of the exempt organization. The tax is levied because the organization is engaging in substantial commercial activities.[30] Without such a tax, nonexempt organizations (regular taxable business entities) would be at a substantial disadvantage when trying to compete with the exempt organization. Thus, the UBIT is intended to neutralize the exempt entity's tax advantage.[31]

It is the source of the business profits that triggers the UBIT, and not their use. UBI that is employed for the entity's exempt purpose still is subject to the tax.

[28] § 4940.
[29] § 511(a)(1).
[30] § 512(a)(1).
[31] Reg. § 1.513–1(b).

EXHIBIT 15.2 Exempt Organizations: Classification

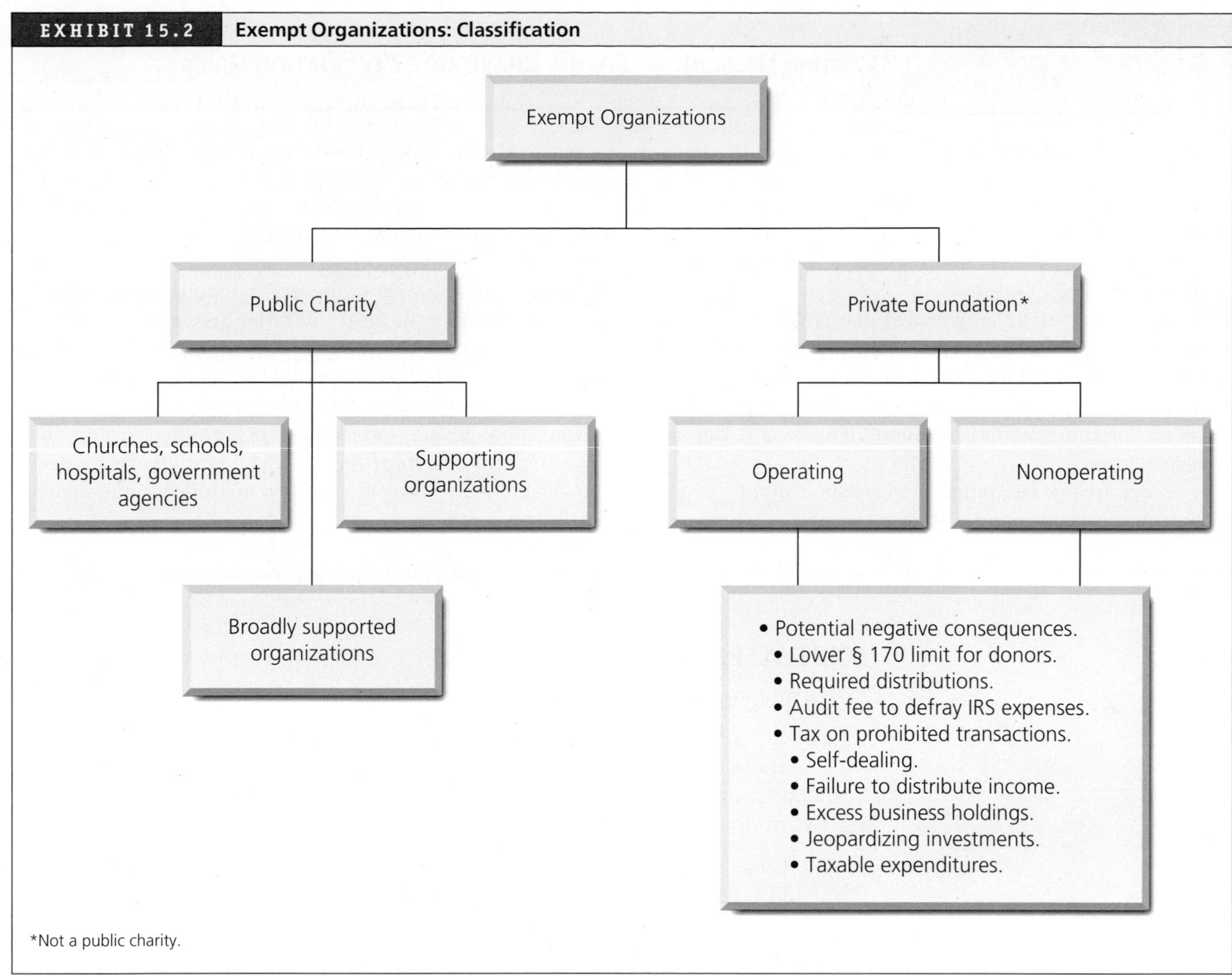

*Not a public charity.

EXAMPLE 5
THE BIG PICTURE

Return to the facts of *The Big Picture* on p. 15–2. Recall that Hopeful, Inc., an exempt organization under § 501(c)(3), has received Taste Good Ice Cream, a chain of gourmet ice cream shops, as a bequest. Assume that Hopeful has decided to operate Taste Good as a division. Although the income from Taste Good's shops will be used to support Hopeful's exempt purpose of providing temporary lodging and psychological services to abused women, the net revenue constitutes unrelated business income, and therefore it is subject to the UBIT. ■

The UBIT applies to all organizations that are exempt from Federal income tax under § 501(c), except Federal agencies. In addition, the tax applies to state colleges and universities.[32]

A materiality exception generally exempts an entity from being subject to the UBIT if such income is insignificant. See the later discussion of the $1,000 statutory deduction generally available to all exempt organizations.

[32] § 511(a)(2) and Reg. § 1.511–2(a)(2).

TAX *in the NEWS*

Getting Back More Than a Charitable Foundation Gives

Charitable foundations typically give away money in carrying out their tax-exempt mission. Unless they are educational institutions, private foundations must distribute 5 percent of their investment assets every year for charitable purposes. Generally, private foundations meet this requirement by making grants.

However, there is another way that private foundations can satisfy this 5 percent requirement and at the same time create the potential for receiving back more from the recipient than the amount initially disbursed. This opportunity is called "program-related investing" (PRI), which can take several forms.

In one type of PRI, rather than making a grant to the recipient, a private foundation loans money to what would otherwise be the recipient and then collects interest (usually at a below-market interest rate) on the loan. In other forms of PRI, a private foundation makes an equity investment in the recipient or guarantees a loan that the recipient obtains from a conventional source.

PRI provides a way for a private foundation to conserve its assets, leverage its asset utilization (i.e., money potentially can be recycled to multiple recipients), and at the same time carry out its tax-exempt mission (i.e., a key requirement for PRI under the tax law). In addition, many of those involved in private foundations believe that expecting investment returns from the PRI recipient results in a greater buy-in, more accountability, and greater effort on the part of the recipient.

UNRELATED TRADE OR BUSINESS

An exempt organization may be subject to the UBIT in the following circumstances.[33]

- The organization conducts a trade or business.
- The trade or business is not substantially related to the exempt purpose of the organization.
- The trade or business is regularly carried on by the organization.

The Code specifically exempts the following activities from classification as an unrelated trade or business. Thus, even if all of the above factors are present, the activity is not classified as an unrelated trade or business.

- The individuals performing substantially all the work of the trade or business do so without compensation (e.g., an orphanage operates a retail store for sales to the general public, and all the work is done by volunteers).
- The trade or business consists of selling merchandise, and substantially all of the merchandise has been received as gifts or contributions (e.g., thrift shops).
- For § 501(c)(3) organizations and for state colleges or universities, the trade or business is conducted primarily for the convenience of the organization's members, students, patients, officers, or employees (e.g., a laundry operated by the college for laundering dormitory linens and students' clothing, a college bookstore).
- For most employee unions, the trade or business consists of selling to members, at their usual place of employment, work-related clothing and equipment and items normally sold through vending machines, snack bars, or food-dispensing facilities.

Definition of Trade or Business

Trade or business, for this purpose, is broadly defined. It includes any activity conducted for the production of income through the sale of merchandise or the performance of services. An activity need not generate a profit to be treated as a trade or business. The activity may be part of a larger set of activities conducted by the

[33] § 513(a) and Reg. § 1.513–2(a).

organization, some of which may be related to the exempt purpose. Being included in a larger set does not cause the activity to lose its identity as an unrelated trade or business.[34]

EXAMPLE 6

Health, Inc., is an exempt hospital that operates a pharmacy. The pharmacy provides medicines and supplies to the patients in the hospital (i.e., it contributes to the conduct of the hospital's exempt purpose). In addition, the pharmacy sells medicines and supplies to the general public. The activity of selling to the general public constitutes a trade or business for purposes of the UBIT. ■

Not Substantially Related to the Exempt Purpose

Exempt organizations frequently conduct unrelated trades or businesses to provide income to help defray the costs of conducting the exempt purpose (like the ice cream shops in Example 5). Providing financial support for the exempt purpose will not prevent an activity from being classified as an unrelated trade or business and thereby being subject to the UBIT.

To be related to the accomplishment of the exempt purpose, the conduct of the business activities must be causally related and contribute importantly to the exempt purpose. Whether a causal relationship exists and the degree of its importance are determined by examining the facts and circumstances. One must consider the size and extent of the activities in relation to the nature and extent of the exempt function that the activities serve.[35]

EXAMPLE 7

Art, Inc., an exempt organization, operates a school for training children in the performing arts. As an essential part of that training, the children perform for the general public. The children are paid at the minimum wage for the performances, and Art derives gross income by charging admission to the performances.

The income from admissions is not income from an unrelated trade or business, because the performances by the children contribute importantly to the accomplishment of the exempt purpose of providing training in the performing arts. ■

EXAMPLE 8

Assume the facts are the same as in Example 7, except that four performances are conducted each weekend of the year. Assume that this number of performances far exceeds that required for training the children. Thus, the part of the income derived from admissions for these excess performances is income from an unrelated trade or business. ■

The trade or business may sell merchandise that has been produced as part of the accomplishment of the exempt purpose. The sale of such merchandise is normally treated as related to the exempt purpose. However, if the merchandise is not sold in substantially the same state it was in at the completion of the exempt purpose, the gross income subsequently derived from the sale of the merchandise is income from an unrelated trade or business.[36]

EXAMPLE 9

Help-Self, Inc., an exempt organization, conducts programs for the rehabilitation of the handicapped. One of the programs includes training in radio and television repair. Help-Self derives gross income by selling the repaired items. The income is substantially related to the accomplishment of the exempt purpose. ■

[34]Reg. § 1.513–1(b).

[35]Reg. § 1.513–1(d).

[36]Reg. § 1.513–1(d)(4)(ii).

An asset or facility used in the exempt purpose may also be used in a nonexempt purpose. Income derived from use for a nonexempt purpose is income from an unrelated trade or business.[37]

EXAMPLE 10

Civil, Inc., an exempt organization, operates a museum. As part of the exempt purpose of the museum, educational lectures are given in the museum's theater during the operating hours of the museum. In the evening, when the museum is closed, the theater is leased to an individual who operates a movie theater. The lease income received from the individual who operates the movie theater is income from an unrelated trade or business. ■

Unrelated Business Income Tax: Substantially Related

Mops and More, a § 501(c)(3) organization, makes mops and brooms that it sells to the general public. The exempt organization's mission is to provide short-term employment opportunities and temporary housing for recovering drug addicts during the two-month period they are at a halfway house. Profits from the sales of the mops and brooms are used to support the halfway house. The laborers are paid the minimum wage, with half of this amount going toward their room and board at the halfway house. In prior years, approximately 90 percent of the laborers involved in the production of the mops and brooms were recovering addicts staying at the halfway house. The remaining 10 percent were permanent employees who trained and supervised the recovering addicts.

In prior years, Mops and More has not filed a Form 990–T (Exempt Organization Business Income Tax Return). The treasurer of Mops and More believes that the sale of the mops and brooms does not constitute unrelated business income, because the production of the items is substantially related to the mission of the exempt organization.

For the current tax year, there is a substantial drop in the number of recovering addicts who stay at the halfway house. To meet production quotas, the organization hires foreign workers who are legally in this country on temporary visas. They account for 70 percent of the labor force in the current year.

The treasurer believes that this shift from recovering addicts to foreign workers is temporary in nature. So she does not believe that it is necessary to file a Form 990–T. Has she acted appropriately?

Special Rule for Corporate Sponsorship Payments

The term *unrelated trade or business* does not include the soliciting and receiving of qualified sponsorship payments.[38]

A payment qualifies as a qualified sponsorship payment if it meets the following requirements.

- There is no arrangement or expectation that the trade or business making the payment will receive any substantial benefit other than the use or acknowledgment of its name, logo, or product lines in connection with the activities of the exempt organization.
- Such use or acknowledgment does not include advertising the payor's products or services.
- The payment does not include any payment for which the amount is contingent upon the level of attendance at one or more events, broadcast ratings, or other factors indicating the degree of public exposure to one or more events.

EXAMPLE 11

Pets, Inc., a manufacturer of cat food, contributes $25,000 to Feline Care, Inc., an exempt organization that cares for abandoned cats. In return for the contribution,

[37] Reg. § 1.513–1(d)(4)(iii) addresses the allocation of expenses to exempt and nonexempt activities.

[38] § 513(i).

TAX *in* the NEWS

Bingo Halls: Legal or Not?

If bingo games are legal under both state and local law, holding bingo games is not an unrelated trade or business for an exempt organization, if for-profit bingo games ordinarily are not permitted in the area. Sometimes, though, there are different rules—and a different related tax result—depending on how the games are played, as some bingo halls in Jefferson County, Alabama, discovered.

Recently, the Alabama Bureau of Investigation raided five bingo halls and confiscated several electronic bingo machines. The halls previously had been warned that the use of slot-style electronic bingo machines was illegal. Apparently, how a bingo game is conducted does matter.

Source: Adapted from Associated Press, "Five Bingo Halls Raided," *Wall Street Journal*, April 8, 2010, p. A9.

Feline agrees to put Pets' corporate logo in its monthly newsletter to donors. Under these circumstances, the $25,000 payment is a qualified sponsorship payment and is not subject to the UBIT. ■

EXAMPLE 12

Assume the same facts as in Example 11, except that Feline agrees to endorse Pets' cat food in its monthly newsletter by stating that it feeds only Pets' cat food to its cats. The $25,000 is not a qualified sponsorship payment and is subject to the UBIT. ■

Special Rule for Bingo Games

A special provision applies in determining whether income from bingo games is from an unrelated trade or business. Under this provision, a *qualified bingo game* is not an unrelated trade or business if both of the following requirements are satisfied.[39]

- The bingo game is legal under both state and local law.
- Commercial bingo games (conducted for a profit motive) ordinarily are not permitted in the jurisdiction.

EXAMPLE 13

Play, Inc., an exempt organization, conducts weekly bingo games. The laws of the state and municipality in which Play conducts the games expressly provide that exempt organizations may conduct bingo games, but do not permit profit-oriented entities to do so. Since both of the requirements for bingo games are satisfied, the bingo games conducted by Play are not an unrelated trade or business. ■

EXAMPLE 14

Game, Inc., an exempt organization, conducts weekly bingo games in City X and City Y. State law expressly permits exempt organizations to conduct bingo games. State law also provides that profit-oriented entities may conduct bingo games in X, which is a resort community. Several businesses regularly conduct bingo games there.

The bingo games conducted by Game in Y are not an unrelated trade or business. However, the bingo games that Game conducts in X are an unrelated trade or business, because commercial bingo games are regularly permitted to be conducted there. ■

Special Rule for Distribution of Low-Cost Articles

If an exempt organization distributes low-cost items as an incidental part of its solicitation for charitable contributions, the distributions may not be considered an unrelated trade or business. A low-cost article is one that costs $9.70 (indexed annually) or less for 2011. Examples of such items are pens, stamps, stickers, stationery, and

[39] § 513(f).

address labels. If more than one item is distributed to a person during the calendar year, the costs of the items are combined.[40]

Special Rule for Rental or Exchange of Membership Lists

If an exempt organization conducts a trade or business that consists of either exchanging with or renting to other exempt organizations the organization's donor or membership list (mailing lists), the activity is not an unrelated trade or business.[41]

Other Special Rules

Other special rules are used in determining whether each of the following activities is an unrelated trade or business.[42]

- Qualified public entertainment activities (e.g., a state fair).
- Qualified convention and trade show activities.
- Certain services provided at cost or less by a hospital to other small hospitals.
- Certain pole rentals by telephone or electric companies.

UNRELATED BUSINESS INCOME

Even when an exempt organization conducts an unrelated trade or business, a tax is assessed only if the exempt organization regularly conducts the activity and the business produces unrelated business income.

Regularly Carried on by the Organization

An activity is classified as unrelated business income only if it is regularly carried on by the exempt organization. This provision assures that only activities that are actually competing with taxable organizations are subject to the UBIT. Accordingly, factors to be considered in applying the *regularly carried on* test include the frequency of the activity, the continuity of the activity, and the manner in which the activity is pursued.[43]

EXAMPLE 15

Silver, Inc., an exempt organization, owns land that is located next to the state fairgrounds. During the 10 days of the state fair, Silver uses the land as a parking lot and charges individuals attending the state fair for parking there. The activity is not regularly carried on. ■

EXAMPLE 16

Black, Inc., an exempt organization, has its offices in the downtown area. It owns a parking lot adjacent to its offices on which its employees park during the week. On Saturdays, it rents the spaces in the parking lot to individuals shopping or working in the downtown area. Black is conducting a business activity on a year-round basis, even though it is only for one day per week. Thus, an activity is regularly being carried on. ■

Unrelated Business Income Defined

Unrelated business income is generally that derived from the unrelated trade or business, reduced by the deductions directly connected with the conduct of the unrelated trade or business.[44]

UNRELATED BUSINESS TAXABLE INCOME

General Tax Model

The model for unrelated business taxable income (UBTI) appears in Figure 15.2.

Positive adjustments[45]

[40] § 513(h)(1)(A).
[41] § 513(h)(1)(B).
[42] §§ 513(d), (e), and (g).
[43] § 512(a)(1) and Reg. § 1.513–1(c).
[44] § 512(a)(1).
[45] §§ 512(a)(1) and (b) and Reg. § 1.512(b)–1.

TAX *in* the NEWS

SHOULD THE NCAA BE TAX-EXEMPT?

The National Collegiate Athletic Association (NCAA) is a tax-exempt organization. Although donors cannot deduct contributions to the NCAA as charitable contributions, the NCAA itself does not pay taxes on its revenues.

Several members of Congress have questioned whether the NCAA should be tax-exempt. Among them is former Congressman Bill Thomas (served as chairman of the House Ways and Means Committee), who suggested that the NCAA's tax-exempt status amounts to a government subsidy from the taxpayers. Another concern is that the NCAA's member educational institutions may be using their tax-exempt status to help pay for escalating athletic program costs, including coaches' multimillion-dollar salaries, chartered travel, and state-of-the-art athletic facilities.

1. A charitable contribution deduction is permitted without regard to whether the gift is associated with the unrelated trade or business. However, to the extent the charitable contributions deducted in calculating net unrelated business income (see Figure 15.2) exceed 10 percent of UBTI (without regard to the charitable contribution deduction), the excess amount is disallowed, i.e., a positive adjustment results.

EXAMPLE 17

Brown, Inc., an exempt organization, has UBTI of $100,000 (excluding any modifications associated with charitable contributions). Total charitable contributions (all associated with the unrelated trade or business) are $13,000. Assuming that the $13,000 is deducted in calculating net unrelated business income, the excess of $3,000 [$13,000 – 10%($100,000)] is a positive adjustment in calculating UBTI. ■

2. Unrelated debt-financed income net of the unrelated debt-financed deductions (see the subsequent discussion of Unrelated Debt-Financed Income).
3. Certain net interest, annuity, royalty, and rent income received by the exempt organization from an organization it controls (80 percent test). This provision overrides the modifications for these types of income (negative adjustment 3).

Negative adjustments

1. Income from dividends, interest, and annuities, net of all deductions directly related to producing such income.
2. Royalty income, regardless of whether it is measured by production, gross income, or taxable income from the property, net of all deductions directly related to producing such income.
3. Rent income from real property and from certain personal property net of all deductions directly related to producing such income. Personal property rents are included in the negative adjustment only if the personal property is leased with the real property. In addition, the personal property rent income must be incidental (does not exceed 10 percent of

FIGURE 15.2 **Tax Formula for Unrelated Business Taxable Income**

Gross unrelated business income
– Deductions
= Net unrelated business income
± Modifications
= Unrelated business taxable income

the gross rent income under the lease) to be used in computing the negative adjustment. In both of the following cases, however, none of the rent income is treated as a negative adjustment.

- More than 50 percent of the rent income under the lease is from personal property.
- Rent income is calculated using the tenant's profits.

EXAMPLE 18

Beaver, Inc., an exempt organization, leases land and a building (realty) and computers (personalty) housed in the building. Under the lease, $46,000 of the rent is for the land and building, and $4,000 is for the computers. Expenses incurred for the land and building are $10,000. The net rent income from the land and building of $36,000 ($46,000 – $10,000) and the income from the computers of $4,000 are negative adjustments. ■

EXAMPLE 19

Assume the same facts as in Example 18, except that the rent income is $35,000 from the land and building and $15,000 from the computers. Since the rent income from the computers exceeds $5,000 (10% × $50,000) and is not incidental, it is not a negative adjustment. ■

EXAMPLE 20

Assume the same facts as in Example 18, except that the rent income is $20,000 from the land and building and $30,000 from the computers. Since more than 50% of the rent income under the lease is from the computers, neither the rent income from the land and building nor that from the computers is a negative adjustment. ■

If the lessor of real property provides significant services to the lessee, such income, for this purpose, is not rent income.

4. Gains and losses from the sale, exchange, or other disposition of property *except for* inventory.

EXAMPLE 21

Beaver, the owner of the land, building, and computers in Example 18, sells these assets for $450,000. Their adjusted basis is $300,000. Beaver's recognized gain of $150,000 is a negative adjustment. ■

5. Certain research income net of all deductions directly related to producing that income.
6. The charitable contribution deduction is permitted without regard to whether the gift is associated with the unrelated trade or business. Therefore, to the extent that the charitable contributions exceed those deducted in calculating net unrelated business income (see Figure 15.2), the excess is a negative adjustment in calculating UBTI. In making this calculation, though, the 10 percent of UBTI (without regard to the charitable contribution deduction) limit still applies (see positive adjustment 1).

EXAMPLE 22

Canine, Inc., an exempt organization, has UBTI of $100,000 (excluding any modifications associated with charitable contributions). The total charitable contributions are $9,000, of which $7,000 (those associated with the unrelated trade or business) has been deducted in calculating net unrelated business income. Therefore, the remaining $2,000 of charitable contributions make up a negative adjustment in calculating UBTI. ■

7. A "standard deduction" of $1,000 is allowed.

EXAMPLE 23

Petit Care, Inc., an exempt organization, reports net unrelated business income of $800. Since Petit claims a $1,000 statutory deduction, its UBTI is $0. Therefore, its income tax liability is $0. ■

After UBTI is determined, that amount is subject to tax using the regular corporate tax rates.

EXAMPLE 24

Patient, Inc., an exempt organization, has UBTI of $500,000. Patient's income tax liability is $170,000 ($500,000 UBTI × 34% corporate tax rate). ■

UNRELATED DEBT-FINANCED INCOME

In the formula for calculating UBTI (see Figure 15.2), unrelated debt-financed income is one of the positive adjustments. Examples of income from debt-financed property include rent income from real estate or tangible personal property, dividends from corporate stock, and gains from the disposition of debt-financed property. Gains from unrelated business income property are also included to the extent the gains are not otherwise treated as unrelated business income.

In terms of the UBIT, the positive adjustment for unrelated debt-financed income is a significant one. Without this provision, a tax-exempt organization could use borrowed funds to acquire unrelated business or investment property and use the untaxed (i.e., exempt) earnings from the acquisition to pay for the property.

Definition of Debt-Financed Income

Debt-financed income is the gross income generated from debt-financed property. *Debt-financed property* is all property of the exempt organization that is held to produce income and on which there is acquisition indebtedness, *except* for the following.[46]

- Property where substantially all (at least 85 percent) of the use is for the achievement of the exempt purpose of the exempt organization.[47]
- Property whose gross income is otherwise treated as unrelated business income.
- Property whose gross income is from the following sources and is not otherwise treated as unrelated business income.
  - *Income from research performed for the United States or a Federal governmental agency, or a state or a political subdivision thereof.*
  - *For a college, university, or hospital, income from research.*
  - *For an organization that performs fundamental (i.e., not applied) research for the benefit of the general public, income from research.*
- Property used in an activity that is not an unrelated trade or business.

If the 85 percent test is not satisfied, only the portion of the property that is *not* used for the exempt purpose is debt-financed property.

EXAMPLE 25

Deer, Inc., an exempt organization, owns a five-story office building on which there is acquisition indebtedness. Three of the floors are used for Deer's exempt purpose. The two other floors are leased to Purple Corporation. In this case, the *substantially all* test is not satisfied. Therefore, 40% of the office building is debt-financed property, and 60% is not. ■

Certain land that is acquired by an exempt organization for later exempt use is excluded from debt-financed property if the following requirements are satisfied.[48]

- The principal purpose of acquiring the land is for use (substantially all) in achieving the organization's exempt purpose.
- This use will begin within 10 years of the acquisition date.
- At the date when the land is acquired, it is located in the *neighborhood* of other property of the organization for which substantially all the use is for achieving the organization's exempt purpose.

Even if the third requirement is not satisfied, the land still is excluded from debt-financed property if it is converted to use for achieving the organization's exempt purpose within the 10-year period. Qualification under this provision will result in a

[46] § 514(b).

[47] Reg. § 1.514(b)–1(b)(1)(ii).

[48] § 514(b)(3).

refund of taxes previously paid. If the exempt organization is a church, the 10-year period becomes a 15-year period, and the neighborhood requirement is waived.

Definition of Acquisition Indebtedness

Acquisition indebtedness is debt sustained by the exempt organization in association with the acquisition of property. More precisely, *acquisition indebtedness* consists of the unpaid amounts of the following for debt-financed property.[49]

- Debt incurred in acquiring or improving the property.
- Debt incurred before the property was acquired or improved, but which would not have been incurred without the acquisition or improvement.
- Debt incurred after the property was acquired or improved, but which would not have been incurred without the acquisition or improvement.

EXAMPLE 26

Red, Inc., an exempt organization, acquires land for $100,000. To finance the acquisition, Red mortgages the land and receives loan proceeds of $80,000. Red leases the land to Duck Corporation. The mortgage is acquisition indebtedness. ■

EXAMPLE 27

Rose, Inc., an exempt organization, makes improvements to an office building that it rents to Bird Corporation. Excess working capital funds are used to finance the improvements. Rose is later required to mortgage its laboratory building, which it uses for its exempt purpose, to replenish working capital. The mortgage is acquisition indebtedness. ■

Portion of Debt-Financed Income and Deductions Treated as Unrelated Business Taxable Income

Once the amount of the debt-financed income and deductions is determined, one must ascertain what portion thereof constitutes unrelated debt-financed income and deductions. Unrelated debt-financed income increases UBTI, and unrelated debt-financed deductions decrease UBTI.

The calculation is made for each debt-financed asset. The gross income from the property is multiplied by the following percentage.[50]

$$\frac{\text{Average acquisition indebtedness for the property}}{\text{Average adjusted basis of the property}} = \text{Debt/basis percentage}$$

This percentage cannot exceed 100. If debt-financed property is disposed of during the taxable year at a gain, average acquisition indebtedness in the formula is replaced with highest acquisition indebtedness. *Highest acquisition indebtedness* is the largest amount of acquisition indebtedness for the property during the 12-month period preceding the date of disposition.[51]

Deductions are allowed for expenses directly related to the debt-financed property and the income from it. Cost recovery deductions must apply the straight-line method. Once allowable deductions are determined, this amount is multiplied by the debt/basis percentage.[52]

EXAMPLE 28

White, Inc., an exempt organization, owns an office building that it leases to Squirrel Corporation for $120,000 per year. The average acquisition indebtedness is $300,000, and the average adjusted basis is $500,000. Since the office building is debt-financed property, the gross unrelated debt-financed income is:

$$\frac{\$300{,}000}{\$500{,}000} \times \$120{,}000 = \$72{,}000.$$

[49] § 514(c)(1). Educational organizations can exclude certain debt incurred for real property acquisitions from classification as acquisition indebtedness.

[50] § 514(a)(1).

[51] § 514(c)(7).

[52] § 514(a)(3).

If White's expenses associated with the office building lease (including straight-line cost recovery) equal $50,000, then allowable deductions are:

$$\frac{\$300{,}000}{\$500{,}000} \times \$50{,}000 = \$30{,}000.$$

Thus, White's net unrelated debt-financed income is $42,000 ($72,000 – $30,000). ■

Average Acquisition Indebtedness

The *average acquisition indebtedness* for debt-financed property is the average amount of the outstanding debt for the taxable year (ignoring interest) during the portion of the year the property is held by the exempt organization. This amount is calculated by summing the outstanding debt on the first day of each calendar month the property is held by the exempt organization. Then this total is divided by the number of months the property is held by the organization.[53]

EXAMPLE 29

On August 12, Yellow, Inc., an exempt organization, acquires an office building that is debt-financed property for $500,000. The initial mortgage on the property is $400,000. The principal amount of the debt on August 12 and on the first of each subsequent month is as follows.

Month	Principal Amount
August 12	$ 400,000
September 1	380,000
October 1	360,000
November 1	340,000
December 1	320,000
Total	$1,800,000

Average acquisition indebtedness is $360,000 ($1,800,000 ÷ 5 months). August is treated as a full month. ■

Average Adjusted Basis

The *average adjusted basis* of debt-financed property is calculated by summing the adjusted bases of the property on the first and last days during the taxable year the property is held by the exempt organization and then dividing by two.[54]

EXAMPLE 30

Assume the facts are the same as in Example 29. In addition, during the taxable year, depreciation of $5,900 is deducted. The average adjusted basis is $497,050 [($500,000 + $494,100) ÷ 2]. ■

Concept Summary 15.4 presents the rules concerning the UBIT.

15.6 Reporting Requirements

OBTAINING EXEMPT ORGANIZATION STATUS

LO.7

List the reports exempt organizations must file with the IRS and the related due dates.

Not all exempt organizations are required to obtain IRS approval for their exempt status. Among those required by statute to do so are organizations exempt under §§ 501(c)(3), 501(c)(9), and 501(c)(20).[55] Even in these cases, exceptions are provided (e.g., churches).

Even when not required to obtain IRS approval, most exempt organizations do apply for exempt status. Typically, an organization does not want to assume that it qualifies for exempt status and describe itself in that way to the public, only to have

[53] § 514(c)(7) and Reg. § 1.514(a)–1(a)(3). A partial month is treated as a full month.

[54] § 514(a)(1) and Reg. § 1.514(a)–1(a)(2).

[55] §§ 505(c), 508(a), and 508(c).

CONCEPT SUMMARY 15.4

Unrelated Business Income Tax

Purpose	To tax the entity on unrelated business income as if it were subject to the corporate income tax.
Applicable tax rates	Corporate tax rates.
Exempt organizations to which applicable	All organizations exempt under § 501(c), except Federal agencies.
Entities subject to the tax	The organization conducts a trade or business; the trade or business is not substantially related to the exempt purpose of the organization; and the trade or business is regularly carried on by the organization.
Exceptions to the tax	• All the work is performed by volunteers. • Substantially all of the merchandise being sold has been received by gift. • For § 501(c)(3) organizations, the business is conducted primarily for the benefit of the organization's members, students, patients, officers, or employees. • For most employee unions, the trade or business consists of selling to members work-related clothing and equipment and items normally sold through vending machines, snack bars, or food-dispensing facilities.
$1,000 provision	If the gross income from an unrelated trade or business is less than $1,000, it is not necessary to file a return associated with the unrelated business income tax.

the IRS rule later that it does not qualify. Organizations exempt under § 501(c)(3) use Form 1023 [Application for Recognition of Exemption under Section 501(c)(3)]. Form 1024 [Application for Recognition of Exemption under Section 501(a)] is used by most other types of exempt organizations.

If an organization is required to obtain IRS approval for its exempt status and does not do so, it does not qualify as an exempt organization.

ANNUAL FILING REQUIREMENTS

Most exempt organizations are required to file an annual information return.[56] The return is filed on Form 990 (Return of Organization Exempt from Income Tax). Religious groups and Federal agencies need not file Form 990.[57]

An exempt organization whose annual gross receipts normally are $50,000 or less must file a Form 990–N, an online form known as the e-Postcard.[58] The e-Postcard is designed to be a simpler version of the full Form 990, to be used by small exempt entities. Supporting organizations and private foundations cannot use the Form 990–N.

The Form 990–EZ can be used by exempt organizations with gross receipts less than $200,000 and total assets less than $500,000.

Private foundations must file Form 990–PF (Return of Private Foundation). Form 990–PF requires more information than Form 990. Form 4720 (Return of Certain Excise Taxes on Charities and Other Persons) is used to compute any excise tax liabilities of the private foundation. The return is filed with the private foundation's Form 990–PF.

The due date for Form 990 or Form 990–PF is the fifteenth day of the fifth month after the end of the taxable year. These returns are filed with the appropriate IRS Service

[56] § 6033(a)(1).
[57] § 6033(a)(3).
[58] Rev.Proc. 2011–15, 2011–3 I.R.B. 322.

TAX *in the NEWS*

THE E-POSTCARD: FORM 990–N

The new Form 990 (Return of Organization Exempt from Income Tax) requires more information than the old version of the form. But there now is a simplified form required of tax-exempts: Form 990–N, the e-Postcard. Hundreds of thousands of small tax-exempts that previously were exempt from an annual filing now must file electronically using the e-Postcard.

Information that must be disclosed on the e-Postcard includes the following.

- The organization's legal name.
- Any name under which the organization operates or does business.
- The organization's mailing address and website address (if any).
- The organization's taxpayer identification number.
- The name and address of a principal officer.
- A statement confirming that the organization's annual gross receipts normally are not greater than $50,000.

What happens if an organization fails to file Form 990–N? There is no monetary penalty, but if the form is not filed for three consecutive years, the organization's tax-exempt status is revoked. To have its tax-exempt status reinstated, the organization must file a new exemption application and pay the related fee.

A substantial number of small tax-exempts failed to file their first Form 990–N on time (i.e., by May 17, 2010). Since they were unaware of the filing requirement and/or that tax-exempt status could be lost, the IRS provided a filing extension until October 15, 2010. Most likely, this extension represented a one-time relief only.

Center based on the location of the exempt organization's principal office. Requests for extensions on filing are made by filing Form 2758 (Applications for Extension of Time).

EXAMPLE 31

Green, Inc., a § 501(c)(3) organization, has a fiscal year that ends June 30, 2011. The due date for the annual return is November 15, 2011. If Green were a calendar year entity, the due date for the 2011 annual return would be May 15, 2012. ■

Exempt organizations incurring the UBIT file Form 990–T (Exempt Organization Business Income Tax Return). The return must be filed if the organization has gross income of at least $1,000 from an unrelated trade or business.

EXAMPLE 32

During the year, the First Church of Kentwood receives parishioner contributions of $450,000. Of this amount, $125,000 is designated for the church building fund. None of its receipts constitute unrelated business income. First Church is not required to file an annual return (Form 990) because churches are exempt from doing so. In addition, it is not required to file Form 990–T.

Colonial, Inc., is a private foundation. Gross receipts for the year total $800,000, of which 40% is from admission fees paid by members of the general public who visit Colonial's museum of eighteenth-century life. The balance is endowment income and contributions from the founding donor. Because Colonial is a private foundation, it must file Form 990–PF.

Orange, Inc., is an exempt organization and is not a private foundation. Gross receipts for the year are $20,000. None of this amount is unrelated business income. Orange is not required to file Form 990 because its annual gross receipts do not exceed $50,000. However, it must file an e-Postcard, Form 990–N.

Restoration, Inc., is an exempt organization. Gross receipts for the year are $100,000. None of this amount is unrelated business income. Restoration files Form 990–EZ because of its level of gross receipts.

During the year, the Second Church of Port Allen receives parishioner contributions of $300,000. In addition, the church has unrelated business income of $5,000. Second Church is not required to file Form 990 because churches are exempt from doing so. Form 990–T must be filed, however, because churches are not exempt from the UBIT and Second Church has exceeded the $1,000 floor. ■

TAX in the NEWS

Specific Identity of a Donor

The College of William and Mary, a public university, received generous donations from two of its alumni that are enabling it to build with private funds a world-class building (Miller Hall) for its Mason School of Business. Both of the donors, Raymond A. "Chip" Mason and Alan B. Miller, have long supported the college with their talents and financial resources.

Legendary investor Warren Buffett has begun the process of giving away much of his fortune in stock, valued at over $40 billion at the time of the announcement. Principal charitable recipients are the Bill and Melinda Gates Foundation, Susan A. Buffett Foundation, Howard G. Buffett Thomson Foundation, Susan Thomson Buffett Foundation, and NOVO Foundation.

Chip Mason, Alan Miller, and Warren Buffett all have permitted their names to be associated with their charitable gifts. Such identified donors likely have encouraged others to increase their giving.

An increasing number of donors, however, prefer not to have their identity made public when they make substantial gifts to charity. In 2007, for example, philanthropists made 37 gifts of $5 million or more without publicly revealing their names. Some donors make anonymous gifts because their religion regards such gifts as more sincere. Others want to avoid being deluged with fund-raising pitches or fear that their own personal safety or that of family members may be threatened if their wealth becomes public knowledge.

As calls for greater transparency increase throughout society, it is becoming more difficult for major donors to remain anonymous. Opponents of anonymity, who include both consumer groups and lawmakers, argue that secret gifts can be used to exert undue influence over the charity. On the other side, some state lawmakers are pushing to protect donor privacy. They feel that too much disclosure could dampen charitable giving.

Source: Adapted from Sally Beatty, "Why Donating Millions Is Hard to Keep Secret," *Wall Street Journal*, January 9, 2008, p. D1.

DISCLOSURE REQUIREMENTS

As a result of recent consumer-friendly rules, exempt entities must make more information readily available to the general public.[59] Prior to the issuance of these rules, the disclosure requirements could be satisfied by making the information available for public inspection during regular business hours at the principal office of the exempt entity.

Copies of the following now must be made available to the general public.[60]

- Form 990.
- Form 1023 (or Form 1024).

Copies of the three most recent returns of the Form 990 must be made available. Private foundations must make Form 990–PF available for public inspection.

If an individual requests the entity's tax form in person, the exempt entity must provide a copy immediately. If the request is received in writing or by e-mail or fax, the copy must be provided within 30 days. The copy must be provided without charge, except for a reasonable fee for reproduction and mailing costs.

If the exempt entity has made the forms widely available to the general public, it is not required to fill individual requests. One technique for making the forms widely available is to put them on the Internet. Individual requests can also be disregarded if the exempt entity can show the request is part of a harassment campaign.

TAX PLANNING:

15.7 General Considerations

LO.8

Identify tax planning opportunities for exempt organizations.

Exempt organization status provides at least two potential tax benefits. First, the entity may be exempt from Federal income tax. Second, contributions to the entity may be deductible by the donor.

An organization that qualifies as an exempt organization may still be subject to certain types of Federal income tax, including the following.

[59] § 6104(d), Reg. § 301.6104(d), and T.D. 8818 (April 1999).

[60] An Internet source of Forms 990 and 990–PF and other relevant materials on exempt entities is **www2.guidestar.org**.

TAX *in the NEWS*

Revised Form 990 to Provide Better Disclosure

Form 990 has undergone a comprehensive revision. The form had not been substantially revised since 1979 and had failed to keep pace with changes in the tax law and with the increasing size, diversity, and complexity of the exempt sector. In redesigning Form 990, the guiding principles were to enhance transparency, promote tax compliance, and minimize the burden for the filing organization. Aiding in the redesign were nearly 700 public comment letters and advice provided by nonprofit experts, nonprofit sector leaders, and state regulators.

Among the many improvements in the revised Form 990 and the related instructions are the following.

- Now the exempt organization can "tell its story" before reporting other information in terms of location on the form.
- There is more space for comments by the entity, so narrative information can be provided in close proximity to the related question.
- Measures of percentages and ratios from the summary page have been eliminated.
- Reporting by expense type replaces reporting by functional classifications.
- The governance section has been divided into three parts: governing body, policies, and disclosures.
- Exempt organizations are allowed to report financial information on a GAAP basis, but are not required to do so.
- Various schedules and thresholds have been revised to reduce the reporting burden of the exempt organization.

- Tax on prohibited transactions.
- Tax on feeder organizations.
- Tax on private foundations.
- Tax on unrelated business income.

Therefore, classification as an exempt organization should not be interpreted to mean that the organization need not be concerned with any Federal income tax. Such a belief can result in the organization engaging in transactions that produce a substantial tax liability.

An organization is exempt from taxation only if it fits into one of the categories enumerated in the Code. Thus, particular attention must be given to the qualification requirements. These requirements must continue to be satisfied to avoid termination of exempt status (in effect they are now maintenance requirements).

15.8 Maintaining Exempt Status

To maintain exempt status, the organization must satisfy both an organizational test and an operational test. The organizational test requires that the entity satisfy the statutory requirements for exempt status on paper. The operational test ensures that the entity does, in fact, satisfy the statutory requirements for exempt status.

King Shipping Consum., Inc. (Zion Coptic Church, Inc.) illustrates that it is usually much easier to satisfy the organizational test than the operational test.[61] Zion's stated purpose was to engage in activities usually and normally associated with churches. Based on this, the IRS approved Zion's exempt status as a § 501(c)(3) organization.

Zion's real intent, however, was to smuggle illegal drugs into the country and to distribute them for profit. The church's justification for the drugs was that it used marijuana in its sacrament. During a four-month period, however, the police confiscated 33 tons of marijuana from church members. The IRS calculated that, even assuming the maximum alleged church membership of several thousand, each member would have had to smoke over 33 pounds of marijuana during the four-month confiscation period.

The court concluded that Zion's real purpose was to cloak a large commercial drug smuggling operation. Since this activity was inconsistent with the religious purpose for exempt status, the court upheld the IRS's revocation of Zion's exempt status and the deficiency assessment of approximately $1.6 million.

[61] 58 TCM 574, T.C.Memo. 1989–593.

15.9 Private Foundation Status

Exempt organizations that can qualify as public charities receive more beneficial tax treatment than do those that qualify as private foundations. Thus, if possible, the organization should be structured to qualify as a public charity. The following can result when an exempt organization is classified as a private foundation.

- Taxes may be imposed on the private foundation.
  - *Tax based on investment income.*
  - *Tax on self-dealing.*
  - *Tax on failure to distribute income.*
  - *Tax on excess business holdings.*
  - *Tax on investments that jeopardize charitable purposes.*
  - *Tax on taxable expenditures.*
- Donors may receive less favorable tax deduction treatment under § 170 than they would if the exempt organization were not a private foundation.

EXAMPLE 33

David has undeveloped land ($25,000 adjusted basis, $100,000 fair market value) that he is going to contribute to one of the following exempt organizations: Blue, Inc., a public charity, or Teal, Inc., a private nonoperating foundation. David has owned the land for five years.

David asks the manager of each organization to describe the tax benefits of contributing to that organization. He tells them he is in the 35% tax bracket and his AGI exceeds $500,000.

Based on the data provided by the managers, David decides to contribute the land to Blue, Inc. He calculates the amount of the charitable contribution under each option as follows.[62]

Donee	Contribution Deduction	Tax Rate	Contribution Borne by U.S. Government
Blue	$100,000	35%	$35,000
Teal	25,000 ($100,000 – $75,000)	35%	8,750

■

One method of avoiding private foundation status is to have a tax-exempt purpose that results in the organization not being classified as a private foundation (the *organization* approach). If this is not feasible, it may be possible to operate the organization so that it receives broad public support and thereby avoids private foundation status (the *operational* approach).

If the organization is a private foundation, care must be exercised to avoid the assessment of a tax liability on prohibited transactions. This objective can best be achieved by establishing controls that prevent the private foundation from engaging in transactions that trigger the imposition of the taxes. If an initial tax is assessed, corrective actions should be implemented to avoid the assessment of an additional tax. See Concept Summary 15.5.

15.10 Unrelated Business Income Tax

If the exempt organization conducts an unrelated trade or business, it may be subject to tax on the unrelated business income. Worse yet, the unrelated trade or business could result in the loss of exempt status if the IRS determines that the activity is the primary purpose of the organization. Thus, caution and planning should be used to eliminate the latter possibility and to minimize the former.

One approach that can be used to avoid the imposition of the UBIT is to establish a taxable subsidiary to conduct the unrelated trade or business. With a subsidiary, the revenues and expenses of the exempt organization can be separated from those of the unrelated trade or business. When the subsidiary remits its after-tax profits to the exempt

[62]See Chapter 2 of this text and Chapter 10 in *South-Western Federal Taxation: Individual Income Taxes.*

CONCEPT SUMMARY 15.5

Private Foundation Status

	Exempt Organization Is	
	A Private Foundation	**Not a Private Foundation**
Reason for classification	Does not serve the common good because it lacks an approved exempt purpose or does not receive broad public financial support.	Serves the common good
Eligible for exempt status?	Yes	Yes
Most beneficial charitable contribution deduction treatment available to donors?	Depends. No, if the private foundation is classified as a private *nonoperating* foundation.	Yes
Subject to excise taxes levied on prohibited transactions?	Yes	No
Subject to tax on unrelated business income?	Yes	Yes

organization in the form of dividends, the dividends will not be taxable to the exempt organization. In addition, having a taxable subsidiary conduct the unrelated trade or business avoids the possibility that the IRS will consider the unrelated business income to be an excessive percentage of the total revenues of the exempt organization. Such a view can lead to the IRS's questioning the exempt organization's right to retain its exempt status.

Another approach to avoiding the UBIT is to fail the definition of an unrelated trade or business. This is accomplished by *not* satisfying at least one of the following requirements.

- The organization conducts a trade or business.
- The trade or business is not substantially related to the exempt purpose of the organization.
- The trade or business is regularly carried on by the organization.

Even if the definitional requirements for an unrelated trade or business appear to be satisfied, the negative adjustments in calculating unrelated business taxable income (see Figure 15.2) can be used to minimize the tax liability.

Rental activities best illustrate the necessity of careful planning to avoid including the income from the activity in calculating unrelated business taxable income. The income from the rental of real property by an exempt organization is not part of unrelated business taxable income. However, leases must be drafted so as to preserve the negative adjustment and avoid the UBIT prevalent in the following circumstances.

- If personal property is leased with real property and more than 50 percent of the rent income under the lease is from personal property, all the rent income is included in calculating unrelated business taxable income.
- If rent income from real property is calculated completely, or in part, based on the profits of the lessee (unless the calculation is based on a fixed percentage of sales or receipts), the rent income is included in calculating unrelated business taxable income.
- If the lessor of real property provides significant services to the lessee, the income is not treated as rent income and thus is included in the computation of unrelated business taxable income.
- If the rent income is received from an organization that the exempt organization controls (80 percent), the income is included in calculating unrelated business taxable income.
- To the extent the rent income is classified as unrelated debt-financed income, it is included in calculating unrelated business taxable income.

REFOCUS ON THE BIG PICTURE

EFFECT OF A FOR-PROFIT BUSINESS ON A TAX-EXEMPT ENTITY

A § 501(c)(3) entity is exempt from Federal income tax only on the conduct of its charitable activities. However, if an exempt entity generates income from the conduct of a trade or business that is not related to the organization's exempt purpose, this income generally is subject to Federal income tax. These principles can be used in analyzing Hopeful's options for the ice cream business it has inherited.

- *Sale of the stock of Taste Good Ice Cream.* A sale of the Taste Good Ice Cream stock is unlikely to result in much realized gain because the fair market value probably has not changed very much in the limited time between the date of Betty's death and the present. In any case, this amount is not relevant because any realized gain on the sale of the stock is tax-exempt under § 501(c)(3).
- *Conduct the ice cream business as a division of Hopeful.* Under this option, the taxable income of the ice cream chain is classified as unrelated business income. Since the ice cream division is competing with for-profit entities, it is subject to the Federal income tax that applies to corporate entities. In essence, the tax is levied because the exempt organization is engaging in substantial commercial activities.
- *Conduct the ice cream business as a wholly owned subsidiary of Hopeful.* Under this option, the ice cream chain subsidiary is classified as a feeder organization (i.e., carries on a trade or business for the benefit of an exempt organization and remits its profits to that entity). The Federal income tax consequences are the same as those under the prior option.

So, Hopeful's board of directors must decide whether they want Hopeful to be involved in the pursuit of a for-profit business and whether selling or operating the business can provide a greater economic benefit for Hopeful.

KEY TERMS

Debt-financed income, 15–25
Excess lobbying expenditures, 15–9
Exempt organizations, 15–2
Feeder organization, 15–11
Grass roots expenditures, 15–9
Intermediate sanctions, 15–10
Lobbying expenditures, 15–9
Private foundations, 15–12
Unrelated business income (UBI), 15–16
Unrelated business income tax (UBIT), 15–16

DISCUSSION QUESTIONS

1. **LO.1, 6** Eggshell, Inc., a C corporation, operates a rental clothing store, and its profits are subject to double taxation. First Church of the States operates a retail gift and book shop and is not subject to taxation. What is the explanation for this difference in Federal income tax treatment?

2. **LO.1** Why are certain organizations either partially or completely exempt from Federal income tax?

3. **LO.1** Which of the following organizations qualify for exempt status?
   a. Tulane University (a private university).
   b. Virginia Qualified Tuition Program.
   c. Red Cross.
   d. Disneyland.

e. Ford Foundation.
f. Jacksonville Chamber of Commerce.
g. Colonial Williamsburg Foundation.
h. Professional Golfers Association (PGA) Tour.
i. Green Bay Packers.
j. Cleveland Indians.
k. Louisiana State University (a public university).

4. **LO.1** Identify the statutory authority under which each of the following is exempt from Federal income tax.
   a. Kingsmill Country Club.
   b. Shady Lawn Cemetery.
   c. Amber Credit Union.
   d. Veterans of Foreign Wars.
   e. Boy Scouts of America.
   f. United Fund.
   g. Federal Deposit Insurance Corporation.
   h. Bruton Parish Episcopal Church.
   i. PTA.
   j. National Press Club.
   k. Brown University (a private university).

5. **LO.2** What are the common characteristics shared by many exempt organizations?

6. **LO.3** Robert contributes $5,000 to an exempt organization. Addie contributes $5,000 to a different exempt organization. Why might Addie be permitted a $5,000 charitable contribution deduction in calculating her itemized deductions when Robert is not?

7. **LO.3** What negative tax consequences may be associated with an exempt organization engaging in § 503 prohibited transactions?

8. **LO.3** Rex is the chief executive officer of Helping People, Inc., a § 501(c)(3) exempt organization located in Mobile, Alabama. He and the organization's board of directors are concerned about the effect that proposed legislation would have on the organization's budget and its ability to carry out its mission. They are discussing a proposal to have a law firm in Washington, D.C., aid in opposing the legislation. **ISSUE ID**
   a. What tax issues are relevant to Helping People, Inc., as it makes this decision?
   b. Would your answer in (a) change if Helping People, Inc., planned to hire the law firm to lobby for the passage of the proposed legislation?

9. **LO.3** An exempt organization appropriately makes the § 501(h) election to lobby on a limited basis. The amount of its lobbying expenditures is less than its lobbying expenditures ceiling, yet it is subject to a tax at a 25% rate. Explain.

10. **LO.3** Under what circumstances can an exempt organization engage in lobbying activities? What types of exempt organizations are eligible for this treatment?

11. **LO.3** The IRS can impose *intermediate sanctions* on a public charity if its gross unrelated business income exceeds 50% of its gross income, or if less than two-thirds of its net unrelated business income is used in carrying out its tax-exempt mission. Evaluate this statement.

12. **LO.3** Service, Inc., an exempt organization, owns all of the stock of Blue, Inc., a retailer of boating supplies. Blue remits all of its profits to Service. According to a policy adopted by Service's board, 60% of the amount received from Blue is to be spent annually in carrying out Service's tax-exempt mission, and 40% is to be invested in Service's endowment fund.
    a. What are the tax consequences to Service and to Blue?
    b. Would your answer in (a) change if 100% of the amount received from Blue was spent annually in carrying out Service's tax-exempt mission?

13. **LO.3** Which of the following activities are *not* subject to the tax imposed on feeder organizations?
    a. Substantially all of the work is performed by volunteers.
    b. Substantially all of the services are performed by paid employees of the exempt organization.
    c. Substantially all of the merchandise being sold is used property.
    d. Substantially all of the merchandise being sold was received as contributions or gifts.

e. A building is rented to a tenant who uses the building as a warehouse for her business.
f. All of the earnings of a for-profit corporate entity are distributed annually to its tax-exempt parent.

14. **LO.4, 5** What is a private foundation, and what are the disadvantages of an exempt organization being classified as a private foundation?

15. **LO.4** Which of the following exempt organizations could be private foundations?
    a. Bruton Parish Episcopal Church.
    b. Our Lady Catholic Church.
    c. Kentwood Community Hospital.
    d. National Football League (NFL).
    e. Southeastern Louisiana University Alumni Association.
    f. United Fund.
    g. Burr's Foundation.
    h. Rice University (a private university).

16. **LO.4** Describe the external support test and the internal support test for a private foundation.

17. **LO.5** What types of taxes may be levied on a private foundation? Why are the taxes levied?

18. **LO.5** Sunset, Inc., a § 501(c)(3) exempt organization that is classified as a private foundation, generates investment income of $485,000 for the current tax year. This amount represents 18% of Sunset's total income.
    a. What type of tax is imposed on Sunset associated with its investment income?
    b. Is the receipt of this investment income likely to result in Sunset losing its exempt status?

19. **LO.5** At the end of the tax year, Amethyst, Inc., a private foundation, has excess business holdings of $450,000. This is the first year that Amethyst has had any excess business holdings.
    a. What are the tax consequences to Amethyst?
    b. Would your answer in (a) change if this was the third consecutive year that Amethyst had excess business holdings?

20. **LO.5** During the tax year, Matte, Inc., a private foundation, makes speculative investments of $675,000 that are classified as jeopardizing investments. What are the tax consequences to Matte?

21. **LO.5** Shining Day, Inc., a private foundation, has taxable expenditures of $800,000. What are the tax consequences to Shining Day?

ISSUE ID

22. **LO.4, 5** Really Welcome, Inc., a tax-exempt organization, receives 30% of its support from disqualified persons. Another disqualified person has agreed to match this support if Really Welcome will appoint him to the organization's board of directors. What tax issues are relevant to Really Welcome as it makes this decision?

23. **LO.6** Bob recently became the treasurer of Kind, Inc., a § 501(c)(3) organization that feeds the homeless. One of the entity's directors has proposed that Kind purchase and operate a fast-food franchise as part of Kind, Inc., to raise additional revenue (an increase of 35%) to carry out its tax-exempt mission. Since the earnings generated by the fast-food franchise would be tax-exempt, substantial additional revenue would be provided. How should Bob respond?

24. **LO.6** Less, Inc., a § 501(c)(3) organization, has unrelated business taxable income of $600,000 and total earnings of $1 million. Why is only the $600,000 subject to Federal income tax? What is the Federal income tax liability?

25. **LO.6** What type of activity by a church is likely to be subject to the unrelated business income tax? What factors must be present for this activity to be classified as an unrelated trade or business?

26. **LO.6** An exempt municipal hospital operates a pharmacy that is staffed by a pharmacist 24 hours per day. The pharmacy serves only hospital patients. Is the pharmacy an unrelated trade or business?

DECISION MAKING

27. **LO.6, 8** Second Church is going to operate a gift and book shop that will include only religious articles in its inventory. The shop will be staffed by employees who are not church

members. Under consideration are two options: (1) organizing the shop as a wholly owned corporate subsidiary and (2) including it within the organizational structure of Second Church. The projected annual profits of $100,000 are to be used in the church's outreach mission. What are the tax consequences of each option? Which should Second Church select?

28. **LO.1, 6** To which of the following tax-exempt organizations may the UBIT apply?
    a. Red Cross.
    b. Salvation Army.
    c. United Fund.
    d. College of William and Mary.
    e. Rainbow, Inc., a private foundation.
    f. Louisiana State University.
    g. Colonial Williamsburg Foundation.
    h. Federal Land Bank.
    i. University of Virginia Hospital.

29. **LO.6** Sight, Inc., a tax-exempt organization that trains the visually impaired to restore and tune pianos, receives pianos as contributions. When the number of pianos on hand exceeds 15, Sight sells the excess; the pianos used in the training program the longest are sold first. Is the revenue from the sale of the excess pianos subject to the UBIT?

30. **LO.6** An exempt organization is considering conducting bingo games on Thursday nights as a way of generating additional revenue to support its exempt purpose. Before doing so, however, the president of the organization has come to you for advice regarding the effect on the organization's exempt status and whether the net income from the bingo games will be taxable. Identify the relevant tax issues. **ISSUE ID**

31. **LO.6** When an exempt organization acquires land for later exempt use and there is acquisition indebtedness on the land, what requirements must be satisfied for the land to be excluded from classification as debt-financed property?

32. **LO.1, 7** Tom is the treasurer of the City Garden Club, a new garden club. A friend, who is the treasurer of the garden club in a neighboring community, tells Tom that it is not necessary for the garden club to file a request for exempt status with the IRS. Has Tom received correct advice?

33. **LO.1, 7** Abby Sue recently became the treasurer of First Point Church. The church has been in existence for three years and has never filed anything with the IRS. **ISSUE ID**
    a. Identify any reporting responsibilities Abby Sue might have as church treasurer.
    b. Would your answer in (a) change if First Point Church has been in existence for more than 10 years?

34. **LO.7** Robin, Inc., a private foundation, generated $22,000 of gross receipts this year.
    a. Must Robin file an annual information return? If so, what form should be used?
    b. Assume instead that Robin is a § 501(c)(3) organization that is not classified as a private foundation. How would your answer in (a) change?

35. **LO.7** Shane and Brittany are treasurers for § 501(c)(3) exempt organizations. Neither exempt organization is a church. Each year Shane's exempt organization files a Form 990 while Brittany's exempt organization files a Form 990–PF. Discuss the public disclosure requirements for each exempt organization.

PROBLEMS

36. **LO.1** Match the following exempt organizations with the statutory authority under which exempt status is granted. The statutory authority may apply to more than one exempt organization.

Exempt Organizations	Statutory Authority
Girl Scouts	§ 501(c)(1)
Catholic Church	§ 501(c)(2)
National Football League (NFL)	§ 501(c)(3)
American Red Cross	§ 501(c)(4)

Exempt Organizations	Statutory Authority
Salvation Army	§ 501(c)(5)
United Fund	§ 501(c)(6)
Bill and Melinda Gates Foundation	§ 501(c)(7)
University of Richmond	§ 501(c)(8)
Underwriters Laboratories (UL)	§ 501(c)(9)
PGA Tour	§ 501(c)(10)
Veterans of Foreign Wars (VFW)	§ 501(c)(11)
Dallas Rodeo Club	§ 501(c)(12)
PTA	§ 501(c)(13)
Toano Cemetery Association	§ 501(c)(14)
Alpha Chi Omega Sorority	§ 501(c)(15)
Green, Inc., Legal Services Plan	§ 501(c)(16)
National Press Club	§ 501(c)(19)
Federal Deposit Insurance Corporation (FDIC)	§ 501(c)(20)
League of Women Voters	§ 501(d)

DECISION MAKING

37. **LO.2, 3** Innovation, Inc., a § 501(c)(3) medical research organization, makes lobbying expenditures of $1.1 million. Innovation incurs exempt purpose expenditures of $15 million in carrying out its medical research mission.
    a. Determine the tax consequences for Innovation if it does not elect to be eligible to participate in lobbying activities on a limited basis.
    b. Determine the tax consequences for Innovation if it does elect to be eligible to participate in lobbying activities on a limited basis.
    c. In light of pending health care legislation, Innovation is considering increasing its lobbying expenditures by 50% annually. Advise Innovation whether this is a wise thing to do from an after-tax perspective.

38. **LO.3** Choice, Inc., a § 501(c)(3) organization, pays unreasonable compensation to Kayla, the treasurer of Choice. Kayla's compensation is $750,000. Assume reasonable compensation would be $600,000.
    a. Determine any adverse tax consequences for Choice, Inc.
    b. Determine any adverse tax consequences for Kayla.

DECISION MAKING

COMMUNICATIONS

39. **LO.3, 6, 8** Roadrunner, Inc., is an exempt medical organization. Quail, Inc., a sporting goods retailer, is a wholly owned subsidiary of Roadrunner. Roadrunner inherited the Quail stock last year from a major benefactor of the medical organization. Quail's taxable income is $550,000. Quail will remit all of its earnings, net of any taxes, to Roadrunner to support the exempt purpose of the parent.
    a. Is Quail subject to Federal income tax? If so, calculate the liability.
    b. Arthur Morgan, the treasurer of Roadrunner, has contacted you regarding minimizing or eliminating Quail's tax liability. He would like to know if the tax consequences would be better if Quail were liquidated into Roadrunner. Write a letter to Morgan that contains your advice. Roadrunner's address is 500 Rouse Tower, Rochester, NY 14627.
    c. Would your answer in (a) change if Roadrunner had acquired the Quail stock by purchase or gift rather than by inheritance? Discuss.
    d. How would the tax consequences change if Quail's taxable income was only $100,000 and it remitted only 75% of its earnings, net of taxes, to Roadrunner?

40. **LO.3** Respond, Inc., a § 501(c)(3) organization, receives the following revenues and incurs the following expenses.

Grant from Gates Foundation	$ 50,000
Charitable contributions received	625,000
Expenses in carrying out its exempt mission	725,000
Net income before taxes of Landscaping, Inc., a wholly owned for-profit subsidiary	350,000

Landscaping, Inc., remits all of its after-tax profits each year to Respond. Calculate the amount of the Federal income tax, if any, for Respond and for Landscaping.

41. **LO.4** Pigeon, Inc., a § 501(c)(3) organization, received support from the following sources. COMMUNICATIONS

Governmental unit A for services rendered	$ 6,300
Governmental unit B for services rendered	4,500
Fees from the general public for services rendered (Each payment was of $100)	75,000
Gross investment income	39,000
Contributions from disqualified persons	26,000
Contributions from other than disqualified persons (Each gift was of $50)	160,000
Total support	$310,800

a. Does Pigeon satisfy the test for receiving broad public support?
b. Is Pigeon a private foundation?
c. Arnold Horn, Pigeon's treasurer, has asked you to advise him on whether Pigeon is a private foundation. Write a letter to him in which you address the issue. His address is 250 Bristol Road, Charlottesville, VA 22903.

42. **LO.5** Gray, Inc., a private foundation, has the following items of income and deductions.

Interest income	$ 29,000
Rent income	61,000
Dividend income	15,000
Royalty income	22,000
Unrelated business income	80,000
Rent expenses	(26,000)
Unrelated business expenses	(12,000)

Gray is not an exempt operating foundation and is not eligible for the 1% tax rate.
a. Calculate the net investment income.
b. Calculate the tax on net investment income.
c. What is the purpose of the tax on net investment income?

43. **LO.5** Egret, Inc., a private foundation, has been in existence for 10 years. During this period, Egret has been unable to satisfy the requirements for classification as a private operating foundation. At the end of 2010, it had undistributed income of $320,000. Of this amount, $170,000 was distributed in 2011, and $150,000 was distributed during the first quarter of 2012. The IRS deficiency notice was mailed on August 1, 2013.
a. Calculate the initial tax for 2010, 2011, and 2012.
b. Calculate the additional tax for 2013.

44. **LO.5, 8** Otis is the CEO of Rectify, Inc., a private foundation. Otis invests $500,000 (80%) of the foundation's investment portfolio in derivatives. Previously, the $500,000 had been invested in corporate bonds with an AA rating that earned 7% per annum. If the derivatives investment works as Otis's investment adviser claims, the annual earnings could be as high as 20%. DECISION MAKING
a. Determine if Rectify is subject to any of the taxes imposed on private foundations.
b. If so, calculate the amount of the initial tax.
c. If so, calculate the amount of the additional tax if the act causing the imposition of the tax is not addressed within the correction period.
d. Are Otis and the foundation better off financially if the prohibited transaction, if any, is addressed within the correction period?

45. **LO.5** The board of directors of Black Pearl, Inc., a private foundation, consists of Alice, Beth, and Carlos. They vote unanimously to provide a $250,000 grant to Mark, their business associate. The grant is to be used for travel and education and does not qualify as a permitted grant to individuals (i.e., it is a taxable expenditure under § 4945). Each director knows that Mark was selected for the grant because he is a friend of the organization and that the grant is a taxable expenditure.
a. Calculate the initial tax imposed on Black Pearl.
b. Calculate the initial tax imposed on the foundation manager (i.e., board of directors).

46. **LO.6** The Open Museum is an exempt organization that operates a gift shop. The museum's annual operations budget is $3.2 million. Gift shop sales generate a profit of $900,000. COMMUNICATIONS

Another $600,000 of endowment income is generated. Both the income from the gift shop and the endowment income are used to support the exempt purpose of the museum. The balance of $1.7 million required for annual operations is provided through admission fees.

Wayne Davis, a new board member, does not understand why the museum is subject to tax at all, particularly since the profits are used in carrying out the mission of the museum. The museum's address is 250 Oak Avenue, Peoria, IL 61625.

a. Calculate the amount of unrelated business income.

b. Assume that the endowment income is reinvested in the endowment fund, rather than being used to support annual operations. Calculate the amount of unrelated business income.

c. As the museum treasurer, write a letter to Wayne explaining the reason for the tax consequences. Mr. Davis's address is 45 Pine Avenue, Peoria, IL 61625.

47. **LO.6** Upward, Inc., a § 501(c)(3) organization that provides training programs for welfare recipients, reports the following income and expenses from the sale of products associated with the training program.

Gross income from sales	$800,000
Cost of goods sold	190,000
Advertising and selling expenses	50,000
Administrative expenses	200,000

Calculate Upward's UBIT:

a. If the sale of the training program products is substantially related to Upward's exempt purpose.

b. If the sale of the training program products is not substantially related to Upward's exempt purpose.

COMMUNICATIONS

48. **LO.6** Perch, Inc., an exempt organization, has unrelated business taxable income of $4 million.

a. Calculate Perch's UBIT.

b. Prepare an outline of a presentation you are going to give to the new members of Perch's board on why Perch is subject to the UBIT even though it is an exempt organization.

49. **LO.6** For each of the following organizations, determine its UBTI and any related UBIT.

a. AIDS, Inc., an exempt charitable organization that provides support for individuals with AIDS, operates a retail medical supply store open to the general public. The net income of the store, before any Federal income taxes, is $305,000.

b. The local Episcopal Church operates a retail gift shop. The inventory consists of the typical items sold by commercial gift shops in the city. The director of the gift shop estimates that 80% of the gift shop sales are to tourists and 20% are to church members. The net income of the gift shop, before the salaries of the three gift shop employees and any Federal income taxes, is $300,000. The salaries of the employees total $80,000.

c. Education, Inc., a private university, has vending machines in the student dormitories and academic buildings on campus. In recognition of recent tuition increases, the university has adopted a policy of merely trying to recover its costs associated with the vending machine activity. For the current year, however, the net income of the activity, before any Federal income taxes, is $75,000.

d. Worn, Inc., an exempt organization, provides food for the homeless. It operates a thrift store that sells used clothing to the general public. The thrift shop is staffed by four salaried employees. All of the clothes it sells are received as contributions. The $100,000 profit generated for the year by the thrift shop is used in Worn's mission of providing food to the homeless.

e. Small, Inc., an exempt organization, has gross unrelated business income of $900 and unrelated business expenses of $400.

f. In Care, Inc., is a § 501(c)(3) exempt organization. It owns a convenience store and gas pumps, which it received as a bequest from a patron. The store/gas pumps entity is organized as StopBy, a C corporation. Because StopBy is profitable, In Care hires a manager and several employees to run the entity. For the current year, StopBy's profit is $640,000. All of this amount is distributed by StopBy to In Care, to use in carrying out its exempt mission.

50. **LO.6** Ongoing, Inc., an exempt organization, has gross unrelated business income of $22,000 and unrelated business expenses of $8,000. Calculate the amount of any UBIT.

51. **LO.6** Falcon Basketball League, an exempt organization, is a youth basketball league for children ages 12 through 14. The league has been in existence for 30 years. In the past, revenue for operations has been provided through community fund-raising and the sale of snacks at the games by the parents. Due to a projected revenue shortfall of approximately $5,000, the governing board has decided to charge admission to the basketball games of $1.00 for adults and $0.50 for children. COMMUNICATIONS
   a. Will the admission charge affect Falcon's exempt status?
   b. What are the tax consequences to Falcon of the net income from snack sales and the new admission fee?
   c. As the volunteer treasurer of the Falcon League, prepare a memo for the board in which you explain the effect, if any, of the admission fee policy on Falcon's exempt status.

52. **LO.6** Onward, Inc., is an exempt organization that assists disabled individuals by training them in digital TV repair. Used digital TVs are donated to Onward, Inc., by both organizations and individuals. Some of the donated digital TVs are operational, but others are not. After being used in the training program, the digital TVs, all of which are now operational, are sold to the general public. Onward's revenues and expenses for the current period are as follows.

Contributions	$ 700,000
Revenues from digital TV sales	3,600,000
Administrative expenses	500,000
Materials and supplies for digital TV repairs	800,000
Utilities	25,000
Wages paid to disabled individuals in the training program (at minimum-wage rate)	1,200,000
Rent for building and equipment	250,000

Any revenues not expended during the current period are deposited in a reserve fund to finance future activities.
   a. Is the digital TV repair and sales activity an unrelated trade or business?
   b. Calculate the net income of Onward, Inc., and the related Federal income tax liability, if any.

53. **LO.6** Save the Squirrels, Inc., a § 501(c)(3) organization that feeds the squirrels in municipal parks, receives a $250,000 contribution from Animal Feed, Inc., a corporation that sells animal feed. In exchange for the contribution, Save the Squirrels will identify Animal Feed as a major supporter in its monthly newsletter. Determine Save the Squirrels's UBTI and any related UBIT, under the following independent assumptions:
   a. Save the Squirrels receives no other similar payments.
   b. Save the Squirrels agrees to identify Animal Feed as a major supporter and to include a half-page advertisement for Animal Feed products in its monthly newsletter as a result of the contribution.

54. **LO.6** Faith Church is exempt from Federal income taxation under § 501(c)(3). To supplement its contribution revenue, it holds bingo games on Saturday nights. It has the licenses and permits required to do so. The net income from the bingo games is $90,000. Of these funds, $60,000 are used to support the ministry of the church. The balance of $30,000 is invested in Faith's endowment fund for church music. Faith Church is located in a resort city where bingo games can be conducted by churches, charities, and for-profit entities.
   a. Will conducting the bingo games affect the exempt status of Faith Church?
   b. Calculate the Federal tax liability, if any, associated with the bingo games.

55. **LO.6** Fish, Inc., an exempt organization, reports unrelated business taxable income of $400,000 (excluding the deduction for charitable contributions). During the year, Fish makes charitable contributions of $45,000, of which $38,000 are associated with the unrelated trade or business.
   a. Calculate Fish's unrelated business taxable income (UBTI).
   b. Assume that the charitable contributions are $39,000, of which $38,000 are associated with the unrelated trade or business. Calculate the UBTI.

56. **LO.3, 6** Comfort, Inc., an exempt hospital, is going to operate a pharmacy that will be classified as an unrelated trade or business. Comfort establishes the pharmacy as a wholly owned subsidiary. During the current year, the subsidiary generates taxable income of $280,000 and pays dividends of $200,000 to Comfort.
    a. What are the tax consequences to the subsidiary?
    b. What are the tax consequences to Comfort?

57. **LO.6** Tranquility, Inc., an exempt organization, leases factory equipment to Blouses, Inc. Blouses is a taxable entity that manufactures women's clothing for distribution through upscale department stores. Blouses owns the land and building where it conducts its manufacturing operations. The original cost of the building to Blouses was $800,000, and the cost recovery deduction for the current year is $20,512. Rent income to Tranquility for the factory's equipment is $300,000, and the related expenses are $170,000. Calculate the effect of the equipment lease on Tranquility's unrelated business taxable income.

58. **LO.6** Kind, Inc., an exempt organization, leases land, a building, and factory equipment to Shirts, Inc. Shirts is a taxable entity that manufactures shirts for distribution through its factory outlet stores. The rent income and the related expenses for Kind are as follows.

	Rent Income	Rent Expenses
Land and building	$100,000	$40,000
Factory equipment	125,000	25,000

a. Calculate the amount of Kind's unrelated business taxable income.
b. Assume instead that Kind's rent income and expenses are as follows.

	Rent Income	Rent Expenses
Land and building	$100,000	$20,000
Factory equipment	125,000	50,000

Calculate the amount of Kind's unrelated business taxable income.

59. **LO.6** Education, Inc., an exempt organization that provides educational services, reports the following gains and losses from property transactions.

- $42,000 loss on the sale of land and a building. The building had been used in carrying out Education's exempt purpose, but the building no longer was needed due to a decline in the population in the geographic area that Education serves.
- $185,000 gain on the sale of land and a building. The building initially had been acquired to lease to a national retailer. Due to a reduction in the number of its stores, the national retailer canceled the lease at the end of last year.
- $45,000 loss on the sale of investment land.
- $20,000 loss on the sale of computers. The computers had been leased to Teachers, Inc., an unrelated exempt organization. Prior to leasing the computers, Education had used them in carrying out its own exempt purpose.

Determine the effect of these transactions on Education's unrelated business taxable income.

60. **LO.6** Medical, Inc., an exempt organization, has unrelated business taxable income of $450,000 (excluding any modifications associated with charitable contributions). Of total charitable contributions of $44,000 made by Medical, $40,000 are associated with its unrelated trade or business. Determine the effect of the charitable contributions on Medical's unrelated business taxable income.

61. **LO.6** Crow, Inc., an exempt organization, owns a building that cost $800,000. Depreciation of $300,000 has been deducted. The building is mortgaged for $600,000. The mortgage was incurred at the acquisition date. The building contains 10,000 square feet of floor space. Crow uses 8,000 square feet of the building in carrying on its exempt purpose and leases the remaining 2,000 square feet to Uranium Corporation. Is the building debt-financed property?

62. **LO.6** Benevolent, Inc., an exempt organization, owns the following properties. Calculate the adjusted basis to Benevolent of its debt-financed property.

Property	Basis	Acquisition Indebtedness	% Used in Exempt Purpose
Building A	$400,000	$300,000	100%
Building B	450,000	–0–	90
Building C	600,000	200,000	85
Building D	900,000	500,000	70

63. **LO.7** Rodeo, Inc., is a social club that is exempt under § 501(c)(7). Its annual gross receipts are $321,000. Of this amount, $23,000 is from an unrelated trade or business. Rodeo's fiscal year ends on May 31.
    a. Is Rodeo required to file an annual information return? If so, what form should be used?
    b. Is Rodeo subject to the UBIT? If so, what form should be used?
    c. If tax returns must be filed, what is the due date?

64. **LO.7** Education, Inc., a § 501(c)(3) organization, is a private foundation with a tax year that ends on May 31, 2011. Gross receipts for the fiscal year are $180,000, and the related expenses are $160,000.
    a. Is Education required to file an annual information return?
    b. If so, what form is used?
    c. If so, what is the due date?
    d. How would your answers in (a), (b), and (c) change if Education is an exempt organization that is not a private foundation?

65. **LO.8** Historic Burg is an exempt organization that operates a museum depicting eighteenth-century life. Sally gives the museum an eighteenth-century chest that she has owned for 10 years. Her adjusted basis is $55,000, and the chest's appraised value is $100,000. Sally's adjusted gross income is $300,000. Calculate Sally's charitable contribution deduction if Historic Burg is:
    a. A private operating foundation (deduct FMV, 30% AGI limit).
    b. A private nonoperating foundation (deduct basis, 50% AGI limit).

RESEARCH PROBLEMS

Note: Solutions to Research Problems can be prepared by using the **Checkpoint® Student Edition** online research product, which is available to accompany this text. It is also possible to prepare solutions to the Research Problems by using tax research materials found in a standard tax library.

THOMSON REUTERS
Checkpoint® Student Edition

Research Problem 1. Allied Fund, a charitable organization exempt under § 501(c)(3), has branches located in each of the 50 states. Allied is not a private foundation. Rather than having each of the state units file an annual return with the IRS, Allied would like to file a single return that reports the activities of all of its branches. Is this permissible? What is the due date of the return?

Partial list of research aids:
§ 6033.
§ 6072.
Reg. § 1.6033–2(d).

Research Problem 2. Heal, Inc., a tax-exempt hospital, was sold to its shareholders for $6.6 million. The IRS determined that the fair market value of the hospital was $7.8 million. An IRS agent is proposing that the tax-exempt status of the hospital be revoked because the sale of the hospital to the shareholders for less than the fair market value resulted in "private inurement" to them. Evaluate the IRS's proposal in a memo to the research file.

COMMUNICATIONS

Research Problem 3. City University has operated KTAX, a television station, since 1960. KTAX operates under a commercial license and is an affiliate of CBS. In addition to

regular network programming, KTAX broadcasts educational programming in the form of in-school classroom instruction, educational extension programming, and closed-circuit educational programming. The station also is used in training students who are enrolled in degree programs as preparation for careers in the television industry.

City University maintains that KTAX is substantially related to the purpose for which the university was granted exempt status under § 501(c)(3). The only purpose for operating the station is to contribute to the achievement of the educational goals of the university.

Determine if KTAX has generated any unrelated business income.

COMMUNICATIONS

Research Problem 4. City Hospital, a tax-exempt hospital, has purchased a sports and fitness center located about three miles from the hospital. It is a state-of-the-art fitness center that includes an open fitness room with cardiovascular and strength equipment, an indoor track, exercise rooms, racquetball and tennis courts, an aquatic area with two pools, a nutrition center/juice bar, and tanning beds. The hospital's overall goals for the center are to enhance cardiovascular, physical, and psychosocial function, reduce morbidity and mortality, improve quality of life, and promote compliance with a lifelong prevention program.

The membership of the center will consist of three segments of the community: the general public, employees, and former rehabilitation patients. Each group will be charged a monthly fee and an initiation fee with a reduced fee provided for employees. Within each category, the fees vary depending on the member's age and restrictions on availability of the facilities during specific hours. The hospital hired a professional consulting firm to conduct a survey of the community to ensure that the fee structure would achieve its goal of making the center facilities available to an economic cross section of the community.

You have been contacted by Anne Dexter, the chief financial officer for the hospital. She is concerned that some or perhaps all of the revenue from the sports and fitness center will be classified as unrelated business income and therefore be subject to the UBIT. Write a letter to Ms. Dexter that contains your findings, and prepare a memo for the tax files. City Hospital's address is 1000 Board Street, Billings, MT 59101.

Research Problem 5. The American Accounting Association holds its regional meetings at seven locations in the spring and its national meeting in August of each year. The meetings include the formal presentation of papers, panel discussions, business sessions, and various committee meetings. In addition, textbook publishers are permitted to display their wares in a publisher's exhibit hall. The book exhibitors must pay a fee to the AAA for the right to do so. Are these fees unrelated business income?

Research Problem 6. A volunteer fire department located in Green County holds tax-exempt status. As a way of raising funds to support its firefighting activities, the department obtained the permission of the owners of three taverns located in Green County to place "tip jars" in the taverns. A tip jar is a gambling device from which patrons purchase sealed pieces of paper containing numbers, series of numbers, or symbols that may entitle the patron to cash or other prizes. The tip jars are legal under state law and under the county ordinance for tax-exempt organizations.

Under the county ordinance, the tax-exempt organization must receive at least 70% of the net proceeds after the winnings are paid, and the business where the tip jar is located must receive no more than 30%. Under the arrangement with the three taverns, the volunteer fire department received 80%.

The three taverns included the 20% they received in their gross income in calculating their taxable income. Since the volunteer fire department is tax-exempt, it did not pay Federal income taxes on the 80% it received.

The IRS determines that the tip jar income received by the volunteer fire department is unrelated business income and issues a deficiency notice. Evaluate the position of the IRS.

COMMUNICATIONS

Research Problem 7. Roger is the pastor at the Third Ecumenical Church in Atlanta. Over lunch with Priscilla, the pastor at another church with whom Roger went to seminary, he learns that another friend's church recently had its tax-exempt status revoked for engaging in political activities. From time to time, certain political figures "give testimony" at Roger's church. Being concerned about his own church's tax-exempt status, he asks you to provide him with the types of activities his church should not engage in or permit.

Locate a recent Revenue Ruling that you can use to provide Roger with the desired information. Summarize the ruling with two PowerPoint slides.

Use the tax resources of the Internet to address the following questions. Do not restrict your search to the Web, but include a review of newsgroups and general reference materials, practitioner sites and resources, primary sources of the tax law, chat rooms and discussion groups, and other opportunities.

COMMUNICATIONS

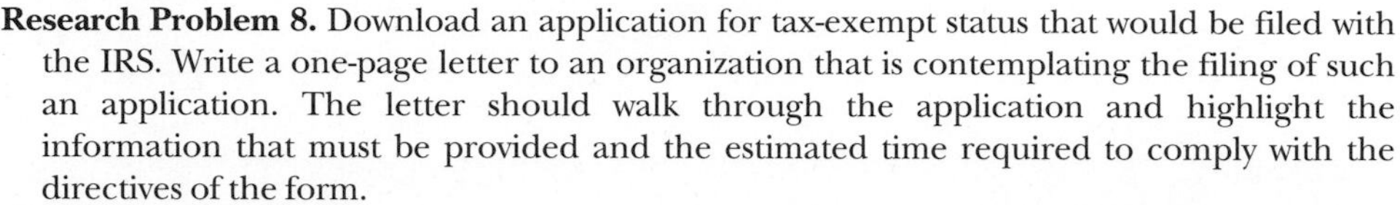

Research Problem 8. Download an application for tax-exempt status that would be filed with the IRS. Write a one-page letter to an organization that is contemplating the filing of such an application. The letter should walk through the application and highlight the information that must be provided and the estimated time required to comply with the directives of the form.

Research Problem 9. Determine if the Kellogg Foundation is a private foundation. Print a copy of its Form 990 or Form 990–PF.

COMMUNICATIONS

Research Problem 10. Verify the exempt status of the symphony orchestra that performs closest to your home. Who are its three highest-paid associates? Send an e-mail to your instructor explaining how you found this information.

Research Problem 11. Use **www2.guidestar.org** to obtain the following information on the Jamestown Yorktown Foundation, Inc., which is located in Williamsburg, Virginia.

- Locate the foundation's website.
- Under what paragraph of § 501(c) is the organization exempt from Federal income tax?
- Use the Form 990 to determine the amount of compensation paid to officers and directors.

CHAPTER 16

Multistate Corporate Taxation

LEARNING OBJECTIVES

After completing Chapter 16, you should be able to:

LO.1 Illustrate the computation of a multistate corporation's state tax liability.

LO.2 Define nexus and explain its role in state income taxation.

LO.3 Distinguish between allocation and apportionment of a multistate corporation's taxable income.

LO.4 Describe the nature and treatment of business and nonbusiness income.

LO.5 Discuss the sales, payroll, and property apportionment factors.

LO.6 Apply the unitary method of state income taxation.

LO.7 Discuss the states' income tax treatment of S corporations, partnerships, and LLCs.

LO.8 Describe other commonly encountered state and local taxes on businesses.

LO.9 Recognize tax planning opportunities available to minimize a corporation's state and local tax liability.

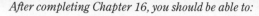

OUTLINE

For the latest in changes to tax legislation, visit **www.cengage.com/taxation/swft.**

THE BIG PICTURE **Tax Solutions for the Real World**

MAKING A LOCATION DECISION IN A MULTISTATE TAX ENVIRONMENT

LocalCo has customers in most U.S. states. It does not employ a traditional sales force. Instead, it sells its products exclusively through Internet solicitations and its elaborate website.

LocalCo has two product lines: cell phone accessories, which it manufactures in Alabama, and various sports-themed apparel items, all of which are produced in California. LocalCo has been quite profitable in the past, and it holds a sizable investment portfolio, made up chiefly of U.S. Treasury securities. Banking, payroll, and other administrative operations are located in rural New York State, where the entity is incorporated. LocalCo's rank and file employees receive compensation packages that are below the national median, but its top 10 executives are very highly paid.

In an effort to "go green," LocalCo wants to hold down its costs for shipping raw materials to its manufacturing facilities and for sending its sold goods to customers. Thus, it is considering the construction of a sizable new multifunction building. Ideally, the new facility would have access to both interstate highways and a reliable airport with excess capacity for freight operations.

How will LocalCo's expansion decision be affected by state and local tax considerations? **Read the chapter and formulate your response.**

Although most of this text concentrates on the effects of the Federal income tax law upon the computation of a taxpayer's annual tax liability, a variety of tax bases apply to most business taxpayers. For instance, a multinational corporation may be subject to tax in a number of different countries (see Chapter 9). Similarly, the taxpayer may be subject to a county-level wheel tax on its business vehicles, a state sales or use tax on many of its asset purchases, and state and local income or franchise taxes on its net income or on the privilege of doing business in the taxing jurisdiction. Indeed, estimates are that about 40 percent of the tax dollars paid by business taxpayers go to state and local authorities.

Businesses operate in a multistate environment for a variety of reasons. For the most part, nontax motivations drive such location decisions as where to build new plants or distribution centers or whether to move communications and data processing facilities and corporate headquarters. For instance, a business typically wants to be close to its largest markets and to operate in a positive private- and public-sector business climate, where it has access to well-trained and reasonably priced labor, suppliers and support operations, sources of natural resources, communication facilities, and transportation networks.

Many location decisions, though, are motivated by multistate tax considerations.

- The taxpayer's manufacturing, wholesaling, sales, retailing, and credit operations each may be centered in a different state to take advantage of various economic development incentives created by politicians. Several states are making highly visible efforts to attract movie and television projects by granting a refundable credit (often at 25 to 35 percent of in-state expenditures) to film production companies. Such credits are offered by New York and California to retain film production work and by Mississippi and Illinois to attract it.
- In addition to flying over virtually the entire country, the major airlines depart from and land in the majority of the states. Which state's income tax should apply to the ticket income? Should sales or income tax apply to sales of movies or liquor while the plane is airborne?
- Local political concerns lead to a multiplicity of tax rules as politicians attempt to serve their constituents by introducing a variety of special tax incentives. This variety can be confusing, however. Taxpayers may have difficulty determining whether they qualify for energy or enterprise zone credits, S corporation status, exemptions from sales tax liability or income tax withholding, or gasoline tax relief at the local level.

TAX *in* the NEWS

Paying the States' Bills

For 2009, the states collected more than $700 billion in taxes (i.e., more than $2,000 per person). The corporate income tax accounts for only a small portion of the states' revenues—6 percent in 2009. This percentage is even less than the contribution of the Federal corporate tax to the U.S. government's revenues. Most of the states' property tax collections (2 percent of the total) are received by counties and smaller taxing jurisdictions.

The States' Tax Revenue Sources, 2009

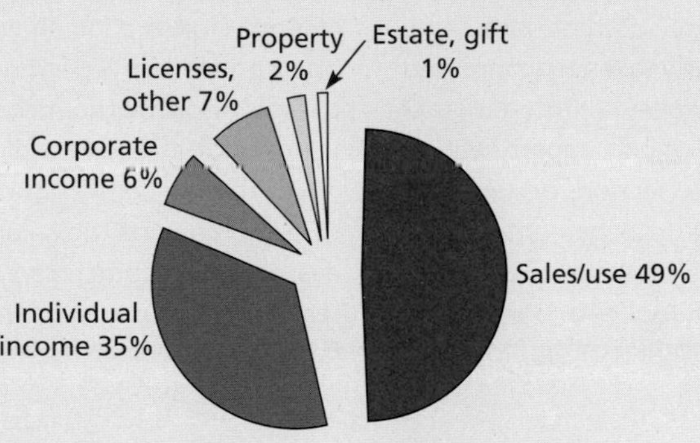

Source: U.S. Census.

- Politicians have a strong incentive to impose new tax burdens on visitors and others who have no direct say in their reelection. Thus, it is increasingly common to see tourist and hotel-bed taxes on convention delegates, often approaching a rate of 20 percent; city payroll taxes on commuters; and the use of obscure tax formulas that otherwise discriminate against those with limited contact in the area.
- Each jurisdiction in which the entity is subject to tax represents a geometrical increase in compliance responsibilities. For instance, how many tax returns must be filed by a three-shareholder S corporation operating in 15 states?
- Various states and localities have adopted revenue-raising statutes that vary in sophistication and operate on different time schedules. For instance, only a few states have adopted an alternative minimum tax, and states that impose the tax have tended to select different bases. In addition, the aggressiveness with which departments of revenue enforce their tax statutes varies greatly from state to state, even in a context of ongoing pressure to enhance revenues. Accordingly, the taxpayer must deal with a patchwork of germane taxing and enforcement provisions in an environment that is often uncertain.

This chapter reviews the basic tax concepts that are predominant among most states that impose a tax based on net income, and it discusses the major areas in which tax planning can reduce a corporation's overall state tax burden.

Most of this chapter is devoted to a discussion of state taxes that are based on income. Each state is free to identify its corporate tax by a different term. Not all of the states that impose a tax on corporate income call the tax an "income tax." Rather, some states refer to their tax on corporate income as a franchise tax,[1] a business tax, a license tax, or a business profits tax.

[1]Although a franchise tax in some states is a business privilege tax based on a corporation's capital stock or net worth, several states use that term for the tax that they impose on a corporation's net income.

TAX in the NEWS

As the Economy Goes, So Go Local Tax Collections

City and county governments depend heavily on sales, property, and payroll taxes as stable and productive sources of revenue. But in a "down" economy, the risk of this taxing strategy becomes clear. One of the effects of an economic downturn, for instance, is a sharp decline in sales/use tax revenues. Other tax collections are affected as well.

The burst of the housing bubble has reduced the value of residences and commercial real estate, in some locales by more than 20 percent. Although property taxes are computed using various formulas, most jurisdictions levy a tax of about 2 percent of current value. Therefore, when property values fall, a proportionate reduction in tax collections occurs.

Several large cities levy taxes of 1 to 3 percent on the wages of those who work in the city. These taxes are justified as a way to recoup the costs of the police and transportation services that commuters enjoy. When unemployment increases and pay raises are few and far between, these payroll tax collections drop significantly.

Economists describe the current situation as a "jobless recovery," meaning that inventory sales and stock prices are showing signs of bouncing back, but few new, high-paying, full-time jobs have yet been created. That is not a good sign for an increase in future payroll tax collections.

Some jurisdictions have tried to make up for their revenue shortfalls by creating new fees, raising the amounts charged for traffic tickets and garbage collection, and increasing tax audits and other enforcement measures.

As the majority of state and local government expenditures go toward the salaries and benefits of their employees, a revenue pinch can create further problems. Expected results are cuts in government services and personnel layoffs.

16.1 Overview of Corporate State Income Taxation

Forty-six states and the District of Columbia impose a tax based on a corporation's taxable income. Since each state is free to create its own tax provisions, the tax practitioner could be faced with 47 entirely different state tax provisions.[2] Fortunately, however, to simplify the filing of tax returns and increase compliance with state tax laws, the majority of states "piggyback" onto the Federal income tax base. This means they have adopted *en masse* part or all of the Federal provisions governing the definition of income and the allowance of various exemptions, exclusions, and deductions. None of the states, however, has piggybacked its tax collections with the IRS.

Computing State Income Tax

LO.1

Illustrate the computation of a multistate corporation's state tax liability.

In more than 40 of the states that impose a corporate income tax, the starting point in computing the tax base is taxable income as reflected on the Federal corporate income tax return (Form 1120). Those states whose computation of state taxable income is not coupled to the Federal tax return have their own state-specific definitions of gross and taxable income. Nonetheless, even these states typically adopt most Federal income and deduction provisions.

Although Federal tax law plays a significant role in the computation of state taxable income, there is a wide disparity in both the methods used to determine a state's taxable income and the tax rates imposed on that income. As only a few states apply more than one or two tax rates to taxable income, there is little progressivity to these tax systems. State tax credits typically are designed to encourage increased hiring and investment in local facilities. Cities and states often use targeted tax credits to entice businesses to expand within their borders. For instance, a state might offer a

[2] The District of Columbia operates in much the same manner as a state and imposes a tax based on income. Four states impose no corporate income tax at all: Nevada, South Dakota, Washington, and Wyoming. Corporations, however, are subject to a business and occupation tax in Washington. Several states base the tax on the entity's gross receipts.

FIGURE 16.1 **Computing Corporate State Income Tax Liability**

	Starting point in computing taxable income*
±	State modification items
	State tax base
±	Total net allocable income/(loss) *(nonbusiness income)*
	Total apportionable income/(loss) *(business income)*
×	State's apportionment percentage
	Income apportioned to the state
±	Income/(loss) allocated to the state
	State taxable income/(loss)
×	State tax rate
	Gross income tax liability for state
–	State's tax credits
	Net income tax liability for the state

*Most states use either line 28 or line 30 of the Federal corporate income tax return (Form 1120). In other states, the corporation is required to identify and report each element of income and deduction on the state return.

$10,000 credit for each new job created by the taxpayer or a 15 percent credit for taxpayers who purchase automobiles that were assembled in the state.

The formula used by a multistate corporation to determine its tax liability in a typical state is illustrated in Figure 16.1.

OPERATIONAL IMPLICATIONS

Generally, the accounting period and methods used by a corporation for state tax purposes must be consistent with those used on the Federal return. States often apply different rules, however, in identifying the members of a group filing a consolidated return and the income of each group member that is subject to tax.

As the starting point for computing state taxable income often is directly related to the Federal taxable income amount, most states also piggyback onto the IRS's audit process. Consequently, virtually all of the states that levy an income tax require notification of the final settlement of a Federal income tax audit. State authorities then adjust the originally calculated state tax liability appropriately.

STATE MODIFICATIONS

Federal taxable income generally is used as the starting point in computing the state's income tax base, but numerous state adjustments or modifications are often made to Federal taxable income to:

- Reflect differences between state and Federal tax statutes.
- Remove income that a state is constitutionally prohibited from taxing.

The required modifications to Federal taxable income vary significantly among the states. Accordingly, this discussion is limited to the most common additions and subtractions that the states require. Exhibit 16.1 lists the most frequently encountered modifications. In computing the taxable income for a given state, only a selected number of these modifications may be applicable.

EXAMPLE 1

Blue Corporation is subject to tax only in State A. The starting point in computing A taxable income is Federal taxable income. Modifications then are made to reflect, among other provisions, the exempt status of interest on A obligations, all dividends received from other U.S. corporations, and the disallowance of a deduction for state income taxes. Blue generated the following income and deductions this year.

EXHIBIT 16.1 Common State Modifications

Addition Modifications

* * Interest income received on state and municipal obligations and any other interest income that is exempt from Federal income tax. For this purpose, some states exempt interest earned on their own obligations.
* * Expenses deducted in computing Federal taxable income that are directly or indirectly related to U.S. obligations.
* * Income-based franchise and income taxes imposed by any state and the District of Columbia that were deducted in computing Federal taxable income.
* * The amount by which the Federal deductions for depreciation, amortization, or depletion exceed those permitted by the state.
* * The amount by which the state gain or loss from the disposal of assets differs from the Federal gain or loss. Due to the difference in permitted depreciation methods and other adjustments, a corporation's assets may have different Federal and state tax bases. This adjustment is not necessary if the state and Federal basis provisions are identical.

Adjustments required as a result of different elections being made for state and Federal purposes. Examples of such elections include the methods under which income from installment sales or long-term contracts is determined.

Federal net operating loss deduction, if the starting point in the computation of taxable income is Federal taxable income after special deductions.

Subtraction Modifications

* * Interest on U.S. obligations or obligations of Federal agencies to the extent included in Federal taxable income but exempt from state income taxes under U.S. law.
* * Expenses that are directly or indirectly related to the state and municipal interest that is taxable for state purposes.
* * Refunds of franchise and income taxes imposed by any state and the District of Columbia, to the extent included in Federal taxable income.
* * The amount by which the state deductions for depreciation, amortization, or depletion exceed the deductions permitted for Federal tax purposes.

Adjustments required as a result of different elections being made for state and Federal purposes, as above.

Dividends received from other U.S. corporations, to the extent included in Federal taxable income.

Net operating loss deduction as determined for state tax purposes.

Federal income tax paid.

*Required by most states.

Sales	$1,500,000
Interest on Federal obligations	50,000
Interest on municipal obligations of State B	100,000
Dividends received from 50%-owned U.S. corporations	200,000
Total income	$1,850,000
Expenses related to Federal obligations	$ 1,000
Expenses related to municipal obligations	5,000
State income tax expense	50,000
Depreciation allowed for Federal tax purposes (the deduction allowed for state purposes is $300,000)	400,000
Other allowable deductions	1,000,000
Total deductions	$1,456,000

Blue's taxable income for Federal and state purposes is $139,000 and $295,000, respectively.

Federal Taxable Income	
Sales	$1,500,000
Interest on Federal obligations	50,000
Dividends received from U.S. corporations	200,000
Total income	$1,750,000
Expenses related to Federal obligations	$ 1,000
State income tax expense	50,000
Depreciation	400,000
Other allowable deductions	1,000,000
Total deductions	$1,451,000
Taxable income before special deductions	$ 299,000
Less: Dividends received deduction (80% × $200,000)	160,000
Federal taxable income	$ 139,000

State A Taxable Income	
Federal taxable income	$139,000
Addition Modifications	
Interest on State B obligations	100,000
State income tax expense	50,000
Excess depreciation deduction allowed for Federal purposes ($400,000 − $300,000)	100,000
Expenses related to Federal obligations	1,000
Subtraction Modifications	
Expenses related to State B obligations	(5,000)
Dividends from other corporations, to extent included in Federal taxable income ($200,000 − $160,000)	(40,000)
Interest on Federal obligations	(50,000)
State A taxable income	$295,000

■

EXAMPLE 2

Continue with the facts of Example 1, except that the $100,000 of municipal bond interest was generated from State A obligations. The computation of Federal taxable income is unaffected by this change. Since A exempts interest on its own obligations from taxation, Blue's A taxable income is $200,000.

State A Taxable Income	
Federal taxable income	$139,000
Addition Modifications	
State income tax expense	50,000
Excess depreciation deduction allowed for Federal purposes ($400,000 − $300,000)	100,000
Expenses related to Federal obligations	1,000
Subtraction Modifications	
Dividends from other U.S. corporations, to extent included in Federal taxable income ($200,000 − $160,000)	(40,000)
Interest on Federal obligations	(50,000)
State A taxable income	$200,000

■

THE UDITPA AND THE MULTISTATE TAX COMMISSION

The Uniform Division of Income for Tax Purposes Act (**UDITPA**) is a model law relating to the assignment of income among the states for corporations that maintain

FINANCIAL DISCLOSURE *Insights*

State/Local Taxes and the Effective Tax Rate

In applying GAAP principles for a business entity, state and local tax expenses are found in several places in the taxpayer's financial reports. In the tax footnote, the state/local tax costs often are reported in dollar and/or percentage terms, in both current and deferred components. The following are examples of state/local tax expenses that were reported in a recent year.

	Current State/ Local Tax Expense ($000)	Deferred State/ Local Tax Expenses ($000)
Eli Lilly	49	(1)
Ryder Systems	6	3
Ford Motor	7	(59)

Corporations also report permanent book/tax differences in determining the effective tax rate for the reporting period. In a recent year, Berkshire Hathaway reported that state/local permanent book/tax differences reduced its effective income tax rate by about 1.5 percentage points. Ford Motor reported a similar rate reduction, but Ryder Systems' effective tax rate increased by about 6 percentage points for the year due to such permanent book/tax differences.

operations in more than one state (multistate corporations). Many states have adopted the provisions of the UDITPA, either by joining the Multistate Tax Compact or by modeling their laws after the provisions of the UDITPA.

The **Multistate Tax Commission (MTC)** writes regulations and other rules that interpret the UDITPA. When a new MTC rule or regulation is created, the member states propose its adoption to their respective legislatures. The majority of member states adopt the regulations with no exceptions or only minor changes.[3]

LO.2

Define nexus and explain its role in state income taxation.

JURISDICTION TO IMPOSE TAX: NEXUS AND PUBLIC LAW 86–272

The state in which a business is incorporated has the jurisdiction to tax the corporation, regardless of the volume of its business activity within the state. Whether a state can tax the income of a business that is incorporated in another state usually depends on the relationship between the state and the corporation.

Nexus describes the degree of business activity that must be present before a taxing jurisdiction has the right to impose a tax on an out-of-state entity's income. State law defines the measure of the relationship that is necessary to create nexus. Typically, sufficient nexus is present when a corporation derives income from sources within the state, owns or leases property in the state, employs personnel in the state, or has physical or financial capital there. **Public Law 86–272** limits the states' right to impose an income tax on certain interstate activities.[4] This Federal law prohibits a state from taxing a business whose only connection with the state is to solicit orders for sales of tangible personal property that is sent outside the state for approval or rejection. If approved, the orders must be filled and shipped by the business from a point outside the state.

Only the sales of tangible personal property are immune from taxation under the law, however. Leases, rentals, and other dispositions of tangible personal property are not protected activities. Moreover, dispositions of real property and intangible property, as well as sales of services, are not protected by Public Law 86–272. In this regard, each state constructs its own definition of tangible and intangible property. Thus, since property ownership is not a protected activity, providing company-owned

[3]Many of the states that are not members of the Multistate Tax Compact also model their laws after the UDITPA and the MTC regulations.

[4]15 U.S.C. 381–385.

EXHIBIT 16.2 **Common Nexus Definitions under Public Law 86–272**

General rule: P.L. 86–272 immunity from nexus applies where the sales representative's activities are ancillary to the order-solicitation process.

Activities That Usually Do Not Create Nexus

- Advertising campaigns.
- Carrying free samples only for display or distribution.
- Owning or furnishing automobiles to salespersons.
- Passing inquiries or complaints on to the home office.
- Checking customers' inventories for reorder.
- Maintaining a sample or display room for two weeks or less during the year.
- Maintaining an office for an employee, including an office in the home.

Activities Usually Sufficient to Establish Nexus

- Making repairs or providing maintenance.
- Collecting delinquent accounts; investigating creditworthiness.
- Installation or supervision of installation.
- Conducting training classes, seminars, or lectures for persons other than sales personnel.
- Approving or accepting orders.
- Picking up or replacing damaged or returned property.
- Hiring, training, or supervising personnel other than sales employees.
- Providing shipping information and coordinating deliveries.
- Carrying samples for sale, exchange, or distribution in any manner for consideration or other value.
- Owning, leasing, maintaining, or otherwise using any of the following facilities or property in the state.
  - *Real estate*
  - *Repair shop*
  - *Parts department*
  - *Employment office*
  - *Purchasing office*
  - *Warehouse*
  - *Meeting place for directors, officers, or employees*
  - *Stock of goods*
  - *Call center*
  - *Mobile retailing (e.g., trucks with driver-salespersons)*

communications, document processing, or computer equipment to an out-of-state salesperson may create nexus with a state, even though the salesperson merely solicits sales orders there.

An activity that consists merely of solicitation is immune from taxation. The statute does not define the term *solicitation*, but the Supreme Court has held that *solicitation of orders* includes any explicit verbal request for orders and any speech or conduct that implicitly invites an order.[5] The Court also created a *de minimis* rule, allowing immunity from nexus where a limited amount of solicitation occurs.

Exhibit 16.2 summarizes the activities that the MTC has identified as being directly related to solicitation (protected activities) and activities unrelated to solicitation (which establish income tax nexus for the entity).

Independent Contractors

Public Law 86–272 extends immunity to certain in-state activities conducted by an independent contractor that would not be permitted if performed directly by the taxpayer. Generally, an independent contractor may engage in the following limited activities without establishing income tax nexus for the principal: (1) soliciting sales, (2) making sales, and (3) maintaining a sales office.

[5] *Wisconsin Department of Revenue v. William Wrigley, Jr., Co.*, 112 S.Ct. 2447 (1992).

TAX in the NEWS

SO WHERE DID YOU WORK TODAY?

It is the dream of many intellectual-property employees to work at home with the employer's computer and communications equipment. Not only is the dress code based on the worker's comfort, but the employee can avoid the time and cost of commuting. The employer saves by not having to provide office space.

But what are the tax effects when the employee or independent contractor submits work to an employer located in a different state? The general rule has been that state income taxes fall in full in the state where the work is done. Is this still the rule, or must the employee apportion the hours of the day among the various states that receive the work product? If so, on what basis should such apportionment be made? Furthermore, how will the worker avoid potential taxation of the same income by more than one state?

A few states and cities, most notably in New York, are aggressively trying to impose income taxes on the work of telecommuters that enters the state. In these situations, enough nexus purportedly exists to permit the levying of income taxes on telecommuters based in other states. The finding of nexus with New York (both the city and the state) can be an expensive proposition for the worker and employer.

For now, it will be up to the states considering this form of taxation to decide if the additional revenue is worth the risk of angering the desirable high-tech, information workers who play a large role in our economy.

16.2 ALLOCATION AND APPORTIONMENT OF INCOME

LO.3

Distinguish between allocation and apportionment of a multistate corporation's taxable income.

A corporation that conducts business activities in more than one state must determine the portion of its net income that is subject to tax by each state. A corporation that has established sufficient nexus with another state generally must both **allocate** and **apportion** its income.

Apportionment is a means by which a corporation's business income is divided among the states in which it conducts business. Under an apportionment procedure, a corporation determines allowable income and deductions for the company as a whole and then apportions some of its net income to a given state, according to an approved formula.

Allocation is a method under which specific components of a corporation's income, net of related expenses, are directly assigned to a certain state. Allocation differs from apportionment in that allocable income is assigned to one state, whereas apportionable income is divided among several states. Nonapportionable (nonbusiness) income generally includes:

- Income or losses derived from the sale of nonbusiness real or tangible property, or
- Income or losses derived from rentals and royalties from nonbusiness real or tangible personal property.

This income is allocated to the state where the property that generated the income or loss is located.

As Figure 16.1 indicated, total allocable (nonapportionable) income or loss typically is removed from corporate net income before the state's apportionment percentage is applied. The nonapportionable income or loss assigned to a state then is combined with the income apportionable to that state to arrive at total income subject to tax in the state.

EXAMPLE 3

Green Corporation conducts business in States N, O, P, and Q. Green's $900,000 taxable income consists of $800,000 apportionable income and $100,000 allocable income generated from transactions conducted in State Q. Green's sales, property, and payroll are evenly divided among the four states, and the states all employ an identical apportionment formula. Accordingly, $200,000 of Green's income is taxable in each of States N, O, and P. Green is subject to income tax on $300,000 of income in State Q.

Apportionable income	$800,000
Apportionment percentage (apportionable income is divided equally among the four states)	× 25%
Income apportioned to each state	$200,000

	State N	State O	State P	State Q
Income apportioned	$200,000	$200,000	$200,000	$200,000
Income allocated	–0–	–0–	–0–	100,000
Taxable income	$200,000	$200,000	$200,000	$300,000

■

THE APPORTIONMENT PROCEDURE

Apportionment assumes that the production of business income is linked to business activity, and the laws of each state define a number of factors believed to indicate the amount of corporate activity conducted within the state. However, apportionment often does not provide a uniform division of an organization's income based on its business activity, because each state is free to choose the type and number of factors that it believes are indicative of the business activity conducted within its borders. Therefore, a corporation may be subject to state income tax on more or less than 100 percent of its income.

An equally incongruous consequence of apportionment may occur when the operations in a state result in a loss.

EXAMPLE 4

Red Corporation's operations include two manufacturing facilities, located in States A and B, respectively. The plant located in A generated $500,000 of income, and the plant located in B generated a loss of $200,000. Therefore, Red's total taxable income is $300,000.

By applying the statutes of each state, Red determines that its apportionment factors for A and B are .65 and .35, respectively. Accordingly, Red's income is apportioned to the states as follows.

Income apportioned to State A: .65 × $300,000 = $195,000

Income apportioned to State B: .35 × $300,000 = $105,000

Red is subject to tax in B on $105,000 of income, even though the operations conducted in that state resulted in a loss. ■

BUSINESS AND NONBUSINESS INCOME

LO.4

Describe the nature and treatment of business and nonbusiness income.

Business income is assigned among the states by using an apportionment formula. In contrast, *nonbusiness income* is either apportioned or allocated to the state in which the income-producing asset is located. For instance, income derived from the rental of nonbusiness real property generally is allocated to the state in which the property is located.

EXAMPLE 5

TNT Corporation, a manufacturer of explosive devices, is a multistate taxpayer that has nexus with States P and Q. During the taxable year, TNT's net sales of explosive devices were $900,000; $600,000 of these sales were made in P and $300,000 were made in Q. The corporation also received $90,000 from the rental of nonbusiness real property located in P.

Both states employ a three-factor apportionment formula under which sales, property, and payroll are equally weighted. However, the states do not agree on the definition of apportionable income. Under P's tax provisions, nonbusiness rent income is allocable and business income is apportionable, while Q requires a corporation to apportion all of its (business and nonbusiness) income. The sales factor (the ratio of in-state sales to total sales) for each of the states is computed as follows.

$$\text{State P: } \frac{\$600{,}000 \text{ (sales in State P)}}{\$900{,}000 \text{ (total sales)}} = 66.67\%$$

$$\text{State Q: } \frac{\$300{,}000 \text{ (sales in State Q)}}{\$990{,}000 \text{ (total sales)*}} = 30.30\%$$

*Since rent income is treated as business income, rents are included in the denominator of the sales factor. ■

EXAMPLE 6

Continue with the facts of Example 5, except that the rent income was generated from property located in Q, rather than from property located in P. Although the sales factor for P remains the same, the sales factor for Q changes.

$$\text{State P: } \frac{\$600{,}000 \text{ (sales in State P)}}{\$900{,}000 \text{ (total sales)}} = 66.67\%$$

$$\text{State Q: } \frac{\$390{,}000 \text{ (sales in State Q)}}{\$990{,}000 \text{ (total sales)}} = 39.39\%$$

Due to the composition of the sales factor in the two states, TNT's income never is perfectly apportioned: the aggregate of the sales factors is either more or less than 100%. ■

Business income arises from the taxpayer's regular course of business or constitutes an integral part of the taxpayer's regular business.[6] In determining whether an item of income is (apportionable) business income, state courts have developed a variety of approaches to determine what constitutes a taxpayer's "regular course of business."[7]

A few states, including Connecticut and Rhode Island, fail to distinguish between business and nonbusiness income. In these states, all of a corporation's income is deemed to be business income and subject to apportionment.

EXAMPLE 7

Scarlet Corporation is subject to income tax in several states. Scarlet earned $2.5 million from the sales of its products and $1 million from the sale of assets that were unrelated to its regular business operations.

In the states that distinguish between business and nonbusiness income, $2.5 million of Scarlet's income is apportioned to the state according to the state's apportionment formula. The gain on the sale of the nonbusiness assets is allocated to the state in which the assets were located. In the states that subject a corporation's entire income to apportionment, $3.5 million ($2,500,000 + $1,000,000) is apportioned to the states in which the taxpayer conducts business. ■

Nonbusiness income is "all income other than business income."[8] Usually, nonbusiness income comprises passive and portfolio income, such as dividends, interest, rents, royalties, and certain capital gains. However, passive or portfolio income may be classified as business income when the acquisition, management, and disposition of the underlying property constitute an integral part of the taxpayer's regular business operation.

EXAMPLE 8

Gray Corporation owns and operates two manufacturing facilities, one in State A and the other in State B. Due to a temporary decline in sales, Gray has rented 10% of its A facility to an unaffiliated corporation. Gray generated $100,000 net rent income and $900,000 income from manufacturing.

[6]MTC Reg. IV.1.(a).

[7]*Atlantic Richfield Co. v. State of Colorado and Joseph F. Dolan*, 601 P.2d 628 (Colo.S.Ct., 1979); *Appeal of A. Epstein and Sons, Inc.* (Cal.State Bd. of Equalization, 1984).

[8]UDITPA § 1(e).

Both A and B classify such rent income as allocable nonbusiness income. By applying the statutes of each state, as discussed in the next section, Gray determines that its apportionment factors are 0.40 for A and 0.60 for B.

Income Subject to Tax in State A	
Taxable income	$1,000,000
Less: Allocable income	(100,000)
Apportionable income	$ 900,000
Times: Apportionment factor	× 40%
Income apportioned to State A	$ 360,000
Plus: Income allocated to State A	100,000
Income subject to tax in State A	$ 460,000

Income Subject to Tax in State B	
Taxable income	$1,000,000
Less: Allocable income	(100,000)
Apportionable income	$ 900,000
Times: Apportionment factor	× 60%
Income apportioned to State B	$ 540,000
Plus: Income allocated to State B	-0-
Income subject to tax in State B	$ 540,000

■

EXAMPLE 9

Continue with the facts of Example 8, but assume that B does not distinguish between business and nonbusiness income. Thus, all of Gray's income is apportionable.

Gray properly determines that its apportionment factors are 0.40 for A and 0.58 for B. Since the apportionment factors used by the two states are derived differently, Gray's income that is subject to tax does not equal 100%.

Income Subject to Tax in State A	$ 460,000

Income Subject to Tax in State B	
Apportionable income	$1,000,000
Times: Apportionment factor	× 58%
Income apportioned to State B	$ 580,000

Due to differences in the states' definitions of apportionable and allocable income, $1.04 million of Gray's $1 million Federal taxable income is subject to state income taxation. ■

APPORTIONMENT FACTORS: ELEMENTS AND PLANNING

LO.5

Discuss the sales, payroll, and property apportionment factors.

Business income is apportioned among the states by determining the appropriate apportionment percentage for each state that has a right to tax the entity. To determine the apportionment percentage for each state, a ratio is established for each of the factors included in the state's apportionment formula. Each ratio is calculated by comparing the level of a specific business activity within a state to the total corporate activity of that type. The ratios then are summed, averaged, and appropriately weighted (if required) to determine the corporation's apportionment percentage for a specific state.

Although apportionment formulas vary among jurisdictions, the traditional three-factor formula equally weights sales, property, and payroll.[9] However, most of

[9]Certain industries, such as financial services institutions, insurance companies, air and motor carriers, pipeline companies, and communications providers, typically are required to use special apportionment formulas.

the states now use a modified three-factor formula, where the sales factor receives more than a one-third weight. The use of a higher-weighted sales factor tends to pull a larger percentage of an out-of-state corporation's income into the taxing jurisdiction of the state, because the corporation's major activity within the state—the sales of its products—is weighted more heavily than are its payroll and property activities. Overweighting the sales factor, however, provides tax relief for corporations that are domiciled in the state. Those corporations generally own significantly more property and incur more payroll costs (factors that are given less weight in the apportionment formula) within the state than do out-of-state corporations.

EXAMPLE 10

Musk Corporation realized $500,000 of taxable income from the sales of its products in States A and B. Musk's activities in both states establish nexus for income tax purposes. Musk's sales, payroll, and property in the states include the following.

	State A	State B	Total
Sales	$1,250,000	$750,000	$2,000,000
Property	2,500,000	–0–	2,500,000
Payroll	1,500,000	–0–	1,500,000

If State B uses an equally weighted three-factor apportionment formula, $62,500 of Musk's taxable income is apportioned to B.

Sales ($750,000/$2,000,000)	=	37.5%
Property ($0/$2,500,000)	=	–0–
Payroll ($0/$1,500,000)	=	–0–
Sum of apportionment factors		37.5%
Average	÷	3
Apportionment factor for State B		12.5%
Taxable income	×	$500,000
Income apportioned to State B		$ 62,500

If State B uses a double-weighted sales factor in its three-factor apportionment formula, $93,750 of Musk's taxable income is apportioned to B.

Sales ($750,000/$2,000,000)	= 37.5% × 2 =		75%
Property ($0/$2,500,000)	=		–0–
Payroll ($0/$1,500,000)	=		–0–
Sum of apportionment factors			75%
Average		÷	4
Apportionment factor for State B			18.75%
Taxable income		×	$500,000
Income apportioned to State B			$ 93,750

When a state uses a double-weighted sales factor, typically a larger percentage of an out-of-state corporation's income is subject to tax in the state. Here, an additional $31,250 ($93,750 – $62,500) of Musk's income is subject to tax in B. ■

A single-factor apportionment formula consisting solely of a sales factor is even more detrimental to an out-of-state corporation than an apportionment factor that double weights the sales factor.[10]

EXAMPLE 11

PPR Corporation, a retailer of paper products, owns retail stores in States A, B, and C. A uses a three-factor apportionment formula under which the sales, property, and payroll factors are equally weighted. B uses a three-factor apportionment formula under

[10]Currently, Colorado, Georgia, Illinois, Iowa, Maine, Michigan, Nebraska, New York, Oregon, Texas, and Wisconsin require the use of a single-factor apportionment formula for all taxpayers.

which sales are double weighted. C employs a single-factor apportionment factor, based solely on sales.

PPR's operations generated $800,000 of apportionable income, and its sales, payroll activity, and average property owned in each of the three states are as follows.

	State A	State B	State C	Total
Sales	$500,000	$400,000	$300,000	$1,200,000
Payroll	100,000	125,000	75,000	300,000
Property	150,000	250,000	100,000	500,000

$280,000 of PPR's apportionable income is assigned to A.

Sales ($500,000/$1,200,000)	=	41.67%
Payroll ($100,000/$300,000)	=	33.33%
Property ($150,000/$500,000)	=	30.00%
Sum of apportionment factors		105.00%
Average	÷	3
Apportionment factor for State A		35.00%
Apportionable income	×	$800,000
Income apportioned to State A		$280,000

$316,640 of PPR's apportionable income is assigned to B.

Sales ($400,000/$1,200,000)	= 33.33% × 2	=	66.66%
Payroll ($125,000/$300,000)		=	41.67%
Property ($250,000/$500,000)		=	50.00%
Sum of apportionment factors			158.33%
Average		÷	4
Apportionment factor for State B			39.58%
Apportionable income		×	$800,000
Income apportioned to State B			$316,640

$200,000 of PPR's apportionable income is assigned to C.

Sales ($300,000/$1,200,000)	=	25.00%
Sum of apportionment factors		25.00%
Average	÷	1
Apportionment factor for State C		25.00%
Apportionable income	×	$800,000
Income apportioned to State C		$200,000

Summary	
Income apportioned to State A	$280,000
Income apportioned to State B	316,640
Income apportioned to State C	200,000
Total income apportioned	$796,640

Due to the variations in the apportionment formulas employed by the various states, only 99.58% ($796,640/$800,000) of PPR's income is apportioned to the states in which it is subject to tax. ■

THE SALES FACTOR

The **sales factor** is a fraction, whose numerator is the corporation's total sales in the state during the tax period. The denominator is the corporation's total sales everywhere during the tax period. Gross sales for this purpose generally are net of returns, allowances, and discounts. Moreover, interest income, service charges, and carrying charges are included in the sales factor. Federal and state excise taxes and state sales taxes are included in the factor if these taxes are either passed on to the buyer or included in the selling price of the goods.

Since the sales factor is a component in the formula used to apportion a corporation's business income to a state, only sales that generate business income are includible in the fraction. The "sales" factor actually resembles a "receipts" factor in most states, since it also generally includes business income from the sale of inventory or services, interest, dividends, rentals, royalties, sales of assets, and other business income. Income on Federal obligations, however, is not included in the sales factor.

When the sale involves capital assets, some states require that the gross proceeds, rather than the net gain or loss, be included in the fraction. Most states allow incidental or occasional asset sales and sales of certain intangible assets to be excluded from gross receipts.[11]

In determining the numerator of the sales factor, most states follow the UDITPA's "ultimate destination concept," under which tangible asset sales are assumed to take place at the point of delivery, not at the location at which the shipment originates.

EXAMPLE 12

Olive Corporation, whose only manufacturing plant is located in State A, sells its products to residents of A through its local retail store. Olive also ships its products to customers in States B and C. The products that are sold to residents of A are assigned to A, while the products that are delivered to B and C are assigned to B and C, respectively. ■

Dock Sales

Dock sales occur where a purchaser uses its owned or rented vehicles, or a common carrier with which it has made arrangements, to take delivery of the product at the seller's shipping dock. Most states apply the destination test to dock sales in the same manner as it is applied to other sales. Thus, if the seller makes dock sales to a purchaser that has an out-of-state location to which it returns with the product, the sale is assigned to the purchaser's state.

Throwback Rule

Out-of-state sales that are not subject to tax in the destination state are pulled back into the origination state if that state has adopted a **throwback rule**. About half of the states apply this exception to the destination test.

The throwback rule provides that, when a corporation is not subject to tax in the destination state or the purchaser is the U.S. government, the sales are treated as in-state sales of the origination state, and the actual destination of the product is disregarded. Consequently, when the seller is immune from tax in the destination state under Public Law 86–272, the sales are considered to be in-state sales of the origination state if that state has a throwback provision.

The throwback rule seems inappropriate when the sale is made to a purchaser in another country, where the transaction is subject to a value-added or gross receipts tax (but no income tax). In these cases, the taxpayer truly is subject to double taxation, as state taxes increase but no Federal foreign tax credit is available. Nonetheless, most of the throwback states fail to distinguish between U.S. and overseas throwback sales.

EXAMPLE 13

Braun Corporation's entire operations are located in State A. Seventy percent ($700,000) of Braun's sales are made in A, and the remaining 30% ($300,000) are made in State B. Braun's solicitation of sales in B is limited to mailing a monthly catalog to its customers in that state. However, Braun employees do pick up and replace damaged merchandise in State B.

The pickup and replacement of damaged goods establish nexus with A. Braun's activities in B are sufficient (as determined by A's law) to subject Braun to a positive tax, based on its income. Therefore, Braun is permitted to apportion its income between A and B. However, B's definition of activities necessary to create nexus is less

[11] MTC Reg. IV.18.(c).

strict than that imposed by A; in B, the mere pickup and replacement of damaged goods do not subject a corporation's income to tax.

Braun's taxable income is $900,000. Both A and B impose a 10% corporate income tax and include only the sales factor in their apportionment formulas. If A has not adopted a throwback rule, Braun's effective state income tax rate is 7%.

	Apportionment Factors	Net Income	Tax Rate	Tax
State A	70%	$900,000	10%	$63,000
State B	*	900,000	10%	–0–
Total tax liability				$63,000
Effective state income tax rate: $63,000/$900,000 =				7%

*As determined under B's laws, Braun's income is not apportionable to State B, because of insufficient nexus.

If A has adopted a throwback rule, Braun does not benefit from its lack of nexus with B, because the sales in B are considered to be in-state sales of A. Thus, Braun's effective tax rate is 10%.

	Apportionment Factors	Net Income	Tax Rate	Tax
State A	100%	$900,000	10%	$90,000
State B	–0–	900,000	10%	–0–
Total tax liability				$90,000
Effective state income tax rate: $90,000/$900,000 =				10%
Tax increase due to throwback provision ($90,000 – $63,000)				$27,000

■

THE PAYROLL FACTOR

The **payroll factor** is determined by comparing the compensation paid for services rendered within a state to the total compensation paid by the corporation. Generally, the payroll factor is a fraction, whose numerator is the total amount that a corporation paid or accrued for compensation in a state during the tax period. The denominator is the total amount paid or accrued by the corporation for compensation during the tax period. For purposes of the payroll factor, compensation includes wages, salaries, commissions, and any other form of remuneration paid or accrued to employees for personal services. Compensation may also include the value of board, rent, housing, lodging, and other benefits or services furnished to employees by the taxpayer in return for personal services, if these amounts constitute Federal gross income.

Payments made to an independent contractor or any other person who is not properly classifiable as an employee generally are excluded from the numerator and denominator of the payroll factor. Some states, including Delaware and North Carolina, exclude from the payroll factor the compensation paid to corporate officers.

More than half of the states provide that earnings paid to a cash or deferred compensation plan, excluded from Federal gross income under § 401(k), are to be included in the numerator and the denominator of the payroll factor. Accordingly, the total compensation that is included in the denominator of a corporation's payroll factor may vary among the states in which the corporation's income is apportioned.

EXAMPLE 14

Mice Corporation's sales office and manufacturing plant are located in State A. Mice also maintains a manufacturing plant and sales office in State C. For purposes of apportionment, A defines payroll as all compensation paid to employees, including contributions to § 401(k) deferred compensation plans. Under the statutes of C, neither compensation paid to officers nor contributions to § 401(k) plans are included in the payroll factor. Mice incurred the following personnel costs.

	State A	State C	Total
Wages and salaries for employees other than officers	$350,000	$250,000	$600,000
Salaries for officers	150,000	100,000	250,000
Contributions to § 401(k) plans	30,000	20,000	50,000
Total	$530,000	$370,000	$900,000

The payroll factor for State A is computed as follows.

$$\frac{\$530,000}{\$900,000} = 58.89\%$$

Since C excludes from the payroll factor any compensation paid to officers and contributions to § 401(k) plans, C's factor is computed as follows.

$$\frac{\$250,000}{\$600,000} = 41.67\%$$

The aggregate of Mice's payroll factors is 100.56% (58.89% + 41.67%). In certain cases, the sum of a corporation's payroll factors may be significantly more or less than 100%. ■

The compensation of an employee normally is not split between two or more states during the year, unless he or she is transferred or changes positions during the year. Instead, each employee's compensation is allocated to only one state. Under the UDITPA, compensation is treated as being paid in the state (it is included in the numerator of the payroll factor) in which the services primarily are performed.

When an employee's services are performed in more than one state, his or her compensation is attributed to the employee's base of operations or, if there is no base of operations in any state in which some part of the service is performed, to the place from which the services are directed or controlled. When no services are performed in the state that serves as the base of operations or the place from which the services are directed, the employee's compensation is attributed to his or her state of residency.[12]

EXAMPLE 15

Geese Corporation has its headquarters and a manufacturing plant in State A. Reggie, a resident of State Y, works at the A manufacturing plant. His compensation is included in the numerator of A's payroll factor, as the service is performed entirely in A. ■

Only compensation that is related to the production of apportionable income is included in the payroll factor. Accordingly, in those states that distinguish between business and nonbusiness income, compensation related to the operation, maintenance, protection, or supervision of nonbusiness income is not includible in the payroll factor.

EXAMPLE 16

Dog Corporation, a manufacturer of automobile parts, is subject to tax in States X and Y. Dog incurred the following payroll costs.

	State X	State Y	Total
Wages and salaries for officers and personnel of manufacturing facilities	$450,000	$350,000	$800,000
Wages and salaries for personnel involved in nonbusiness rental activities	50,000	–0–	50,000

If both states distinguish between business and nonbusiness income in determining apportionable income and include officers' compensation in the payroll factor, Dog's payroll factors are computed as follows.

Payroll factor for State X: $450,000/$800,000 = 56.25%

Payroll factor for State Y: $350,000/$800,000 = 43.75% ■

[12] UDITPA § 14.

EXAMPLE 17

Continue with the facts of Example 16, but assume that Y defines apportionable income as the corporation's total income (business and nonbusiness income). Dog's payroll factor for X remains unchanged, but its payroll factor for Y is reduced.

Payroll factor for State X: $450,000/$800,000 = 56.25%

Payroll factor for State Y: $350,000/$850,000* = 41.18%

*$800,000 (compensation related to business income) + $50,000 (compensation related to nonbusiness income). ■

In deriving the payroll factors, compensation is prorated between business and nonbusiness sources.

EXAMPLE 18

Tall Corporation, a manufacturer of paper products, operates paper mills in States A and B. In addition, the corporation owns nonbusiness rental real property in A. Tall incurred the following compensation expenses.

	State A	State B	Total
Wages and salaries for mill employees	$1,200,000	$1,500,000	$2,700,000
Wages and salaries for administrative staff	600,000	500,000	1,100,000
Compensation of officers	800,000	400,000	1,200,000

Ten percent of the time spent by the administrative staff located in A and 5% of the time spent by officers located in A are devoted to the operation, maintenance, and supervision of the nonbusiness rental property. Both states exclude such rent income from the definition of apportionable income.

Payroll factor for State A

$$\frac{[\$1{,}200{,}000 + 90\%(\$600{,}000) + 95\%(\$800{,}000)]}{[\$2{,}700{,}000 + 90\%(\$600{,}000) + \$500{,}000 + 95\%(\$800{,}000) + \$400{,}000]} = \frac{\$2{,}500{,}000}{\$4{,}900{,}000} = 51.02\%$$

Payroll factor for State B

$$\frac{(\$1{,}500{,}000 + \$500{,}000 + \$400{,}000)}{[\$2{,}700{,}000 + 90\%(\$600{,}000) + \$500{,}000 + 95\%(\$800{,}000) + \$400{,}000]} = \frac{\$2{,}400{,}000}{\$4{,}900{,}000} = 48.98\%$$

■

THE PROPERTY FACTOR

The **property factor** generally is a fraction, whose numerator is the average value of the corporation's real property and its tangible personal property owned and used or rented and used in the state during the taxable year. The denominator is the average value of all of the corporation's real property and its tangible personal property owned or rented and used during the taxable year, wherever it is located. In this manner, a state's property factor reflects the extent of total property usage by the taxpayer in the state.

For this purpose, property includes land, buildings, machinery, inventory, equipment, and other real and tangible personal property, other than coins or currency.[13] Other types of property that may be included in the factor are offshore property, outer space property (satellites), and partnership property.

In the case of property that is in transit between locations of the taxpayer or between a buyer and seller, the assets are included in the numerator of the destination state. With respect to mobile or movable property, such as construction equipment, trucks, and leased equipment, which is both in- and outside the state during the tax period, the numerator of a state's property factor generally is determined on the basis of the total time that the property was within the state.

[13] MTC Reg. IV.10.(a).

Property owned by the corporation typically is valued at its average original or historical cost plus the cost of additions and improvements, but without adjusting for depreciation. Some states allow property to be included at net book value or adjusted tax basis. The value of the property usually is determined by averaging the values at the beginning and end of the tax period. Alternatively, some states allow or require the amount to be calculated on a monthly basis if annual computation results in or requires substantial distortions.

EXAMPLE 19

Blond Corporation, a calendar year taxpayer, owns property in States A and B. Both A and B require that the average value of assets be included in the property factor. A requires that the property be valued at its historical cost, and B requires that the property be included in the property factor at its net book value.

Account Balances at January 1

	State A	State B	Total
Inventories	$ 150,000	$ 100,000	$ 250,000
Building and machinery (cost)	200,000	400,000	600,000
Accumulated depreciation for building and machinery	(150,000)	(50,000)	(200,000)
Land	50,000	100,000	150,000
Total	$ 250,000	$ 550,000	$ 800,000

Account Balances at December 31

	State A	State B	Total
Inventories	$ 250,000	$ 200,000	$ 450,000
Building and machinery (cost)	200,000	400,000	600,000
Accumulated depreciation for building and machinery	(175,000)	(100,000)	(275,000)
Land	50,000	100,000	150,000
Total	$ 325,000	$ 600,000	$ 925,000

State A Property Factor

Historical Cost	January 1	December 31	Average
Property in State A	$ 400,000*	$ 500,000**	$ 450,000
Total property	1,000,000†	1,200,000††	1,100,000

*$150,000 + $200,000 + $50,000.
**$250,000 + $200,000 + $50,000.
†$250,000 + $600,000 + $150,000.
††$450,000 + $600,000 + $150,000.

$$\text{Property factor for State A: } \frac{\$450{,}000}{\$1{,}100{,}000} = 40.91\%$$

State B Property Factor

Net Book Value	January 1	December 31	Average
Property in State B	$550,000	$600,000	$575,000
Total property	800,000	925,000	862,500

$$\text{Property factor for State B: } \frac{\$575{,}000}{\$862{,}500} = 66.67\%$$

Due to the variations in the property factors, the aggregate of Blond's property factors equals 107.58%. ■

Leased property, when included in the property factor, is valued at eight times its annual rental. Annual rentals may include payments, such as real estate taxes and insurance, made by the lessee in lieu of rent.

EXAMPLE 20

Jasper Corporation is subject to tax in States D and G. Both states require that leased or rented property be included in the property factor at eight times the annual rental costs, and that the average historical cost be used for other assets. Information regarding Jasper's property and rental expenses follows.

Average Historical Cost	
Property located in State D	$ 750,000
Property located in State G	450,000
Total property	$1,200,000

Lease and Rental Expenses	
State D	$ 50,000
State G	150,000
Total	$200,000

Property factor for State D

$$\frac{[\$750{,}000 + 8(\$50{,}000)]}{[\$1{,}200{,}000 + 8(\$200{,}000)]} = \frac{\$1{,}150{,}000}{\$2{,}800{,}000} = 41.07\%$$

Property factor for State G

$$\frac{[\$450{,}000 + 8(\$150{,}000)]}{[\$1{,}200{,}000 + 8(\$200{,}000)]} = \frac{\$1{,}650{,}000}{\$2{,}800{,}000} = 58.93\%$$

■

Only property that is used in the production of apportionable income is includible in the numerator and denominator of the property factor. In this regard, idle property and property that is used in producing nonapportionable income generally are excluded. However, property that is temporarily idle or unused generally remains in the property factor.

16.3 The Unitary Theory

LO.6

Apply the unitary method of state income taxation.

The **unitary theory** developed in response to the early problems that states faced in attributing the income of a multistate business among the states in which the business was conducted. Originally, this theory was applied to justify apportionment of the income of multiple operating divisions within a single company. Over the years, however, the concept has been extended to require the combined reporting of certain affiliated corporations, including those outside the United States.

When two affiliated corporations are subject to tax in different states, each entity must file a return and report its income in the state in which it conducts business. Each entity reports its income separately from that of its affiliated corporations. In an effort to minimize overall state income tax, multistate entities have attempted to separate the parts of the business that are carried on in the various states.

EXAMPLE 21

Arts Corporation owns a chain of retail stores located in several states. To enable each store to file and report the income earned only in that state, each store was organized as a separate subsidiary in the state in which it did business. In this manner, each store is separately subject to tax only in the state in which it is located. ■

Most states attempt to assign as much of an entity's income to in-state sources as possible, so the *unitary* approach to computing state taxable income is attractive to them. Under this method, a corporation is required to file a **combined return** that includes the results from all of the operations of the related corporations, not just from those that transacted business in the state. In this manner, the unitary method allows a state to apply the apportionment formula to a firm's nationwide or worldwide unitary income. To include the activities of the corporation's subsidiaries in the apportionment formula, the state must determine that the subsidiaries' activities are an integral part of a unitary business and, as a result, are subject to apportionment.

WHAT IS A UNITARY BUSINESS?

A unitary business operates as a unit and cannot be segregated into independently operating divisions. The operations are integrated, and each division depends on or contributes to the operation of the business as a whole. It is not necessary that each unit operating within a state contribute to the activities of all divisions outside the state.

The unitary theory ignores the separate legal existence of the entities and focuses instead on practical business realities. Accordingly, the separate entities are treated as a single business for state income tax purposes, and the apportionment formula is applied to the combined income of the unitary business.

EXAMPLE 22

Continue with the facts of Example 21. Arts manufactured no goods, but conducted central management, purchasing, distributing, advertising, and administrative departments. The subsidiaries carried on a purely intrastate business, and they paid for the goods and services received at the parent company's cost, plus overhead. Arts and the subsidiaries constitute a unitary business due to their unitary operations (purchasing, distributing, advertising, and administrative functions). Accordingly, in states that have adopted the unitary method, the income and apportionment factors of the entire unitary group are combined and apportioned to the states in which at least one member of the group has nexus. ■

EXAMPLE 23

Crafts Corporation organized its departments as separate corporations on the basis of function: mining copper ore, refining the ore, and fabricating the refined copper into consumer products. Even though the various steps in the process are operated substantially independently of each other with only general supervision from Crafts' executive offices, Crafts is engaged in a single unitary business. Its various divisions are part of a large, vertically structured enterprise, in which each business segment needs the products or raw materials provided by another. The flow of products among the affiliates also provides evidence of functional integration, which generally requires some form of central decision or policy making, another characteristic of a unitary business. ■

Notice that the application of the unitary theory is based on a series of subjective observations about the organization and operation of the taxpayer's businesses, whereas the availability of Federal controlled and affiliated group status (see Chapter 8) is based on objective, mechanical ownership tests. More than half of the states require or allow unitary reporting.

TAX EFFECTS OF THE UNITARY THEORY

Use of the unitary approach by a state eliminates several of the planning techniques that could be used to shift income between corporate segments to avoid or minimize state taxes. In addition, the unitary approach usually results in a larger portion of the corporation's income being taxable in states where the compensation, property values, and sales prices are high relative to other states. This occurs because the larger in-state costs (numerators in the apportionment formula) include in the tax base a larger portion of the taxable income within the state's taxing jurisdiction. This has an adverse effect upon the corporation's overall state tax burden if the states in which the larger portions are allocated impose a high tax rate relative to the other states in which the business is conducted.

The presence of a unitary business is favorable when losses of unprofitable affiliates may be offset against the earnings of profitable affiliates. It also is favorable when income earned in a high-tax state may be shifted to low-tax states due to the use of combined apportionment factors.

EXAMPLE 24

Rita Corporation owns two subsidiaries, Arts and Crafts. Arts, located in State K, generated taxable income of $700,000. During this same period, Crafts, located in State M, generated a loss of $400,000. If the subsidiaries are independent corporations, Arts is required to pay K tax on $700,000 of income. However, if the corporations constitute a unitary business, the incomes, as well as the apportionment factors, of the two entities are combined. As a result, the combined income of $300,000 ($700,000 – $400,000) is apportioned to unitary states K and M. ■

EXAMPLE 25

Eve Corporation, a wholly owned subsidiary of Dan Corporation, generated $1 million taxable income. Eve's activities and sales are restricted to State P, which imposes a 10% income tax. Dan's income for the taxable period is $1.5 million. Dan's activities and sales are restricted to State Q, which imposes a 5% income tax. Both states use a three-factor apportionment formula that equally weights sales, payroll, and property. Sales, payroll, and average property for each of the corporations are as follows.

	Eve Corporation	Dan Corporation	Total
Sales	$3,000,000	$7,000,000	$10,000,000
Payroll	2,000,000	3,500,000	5,500,000
Property	2,500,000	4,500,000	7,000,000

If the corporations are independent entities, the overall state income tax liability is $175,000.

State P (10% × $1,000,000)	=	$100,000
State Q (5% × $1,500,000)	=	75,000
Total state income tax		$175,000

If the corporations are members of a unitary business, the income and apportionment factors are combined in determining the income tax liability in unitary states P and Q. As a result of the combined reporting, the overall state income tax liability is reduced.

State P Income Tax				
Total apportionable income			$2,500,000	
Apportionment formula				
Sales ($3,000,000/$10,000,000)	=	30.00%		
Payroll ($2,000,000/$5,500,000)	=	36.36%		
Property ($2,500,000/$7,000,000)	=	35.71%		
Total		102.07%		
Average (102.07% ÷ 3)			× 34.02%	
State P taxable income			$ 850,500	
Tax rate			× 10%	
State P tax liability				$ 85,050

GLOBAL Tax Issues

WATER'S EDGE IS NOT A DAY AT THE BEACH

As a result of pressure from the business community, the Federal government, and foreign countries, most of the states that impose an income tax on a unitary business's worldwide operations permit a multinational business to elect **water's edge** unitary reporting as an alternative to worldwide unitary filing.

The water's edge provision permits a multinational corporation to elect to limit the reach of the state's taxing jurisdiction over out-of-state affiliates to activities occurring within the boundaries of the United States. The decision to make a water's edge election may have a substantial effect on the tax liability of a multinational corporation. For instance, a water's edge election usually cannot be revoked for a number of years without permission from the appropriate tax authority.

Moreover, corporations making this election may be assessed an additional tax or fee for the privilege of excluding out-of-state entities from the combined report.

State Q Income Tax				
Total apportionable income			$2,500,000	
Apportionment formula				
Sales ($7,000,000/$10,000,000)	=	70.00%		
Payroll ($3,500,000/$5,500,000)	=	63.64%		
Property ($4,500,000/$7,000,000)	=	64.29%		
Total		197.93%		
Average (197.93% ÷ 3)			× 65.98%	
State Q taxable income			$1,649,500	
Tax rate			× 5%	
State Q tax liability				$ 82,475
Total state income tax, if unitary				$167,525
Total state income tax, if nonunitary				175,000
Tax reduction from unitary combined reporting				$ 7,475

The results of unitary reporting would have been detrimental if Q had imposed a higher rate of tax than P, because a larger percentage of the corporation's income is attributable to Q when the apportionment factors are combined. ■

CONSOLIDATED AND COMBINED RETURNS

As discussed in Chapter 8, an affiliated group of corporations may file a consolidated return if all members of the group consent. Once such a return has been filed, the group must continue to file on a consolidated basis as long as it remains in existence, or until permission to file separate returns has been obtained. The consolidated return essentially treats the controlled corporations as a single taxable entity. Thus, the affiliated group pays only one tax, based upon the combined income of its members after certain adjustments (e.g., net operating losses) and eliminations (e.g., intercompany dividends and inventory profits).

Several states permit affiliated corporations to file a consolidated return if such a return has been filed for Federal purposes. The filing of a consolidated return is mandatory in only a few states.

Usually, only corporations that are subject to tax in the state can be included in a consolidated return unless specific requirements are met or the state permits the inclusion of corporations without nexus.

Do not confuse elective consolidated returns with required combined returns in unitary states. A combined return is filed in every unitary state in which one or more

CONCEPT SUMMARY 16.1

Principles of Multistate Corporate Income Taxation

1. Taxability of an organization's income in a state other than the one in which it is incorporated depends on the laws, regulations, and judicial interpretations of the other state; the nature and level of the corporation's activity in, or contacts with, that state; and, to a limited extent, the application of P.L. 86–272.
2. Each state has adopted its own multistate income tax laws, regulations, methods, and judicial interpretations; consequently, the nonuniformity of state income taxing provisions provides a multitude of planning techniques that allow a multistate corporation to reduce its overall state tax liability legally.
3. The apportionment procedure is used to assign the income of a multistate taxpayer to the various states in which business is conducted. Generally, nonbusiness income is allocated, rather than apportioned, directly to the state in which the nonbusiness income-generating assets are located.
4. The various state apportionment factors and formulas offer planning opportunities in that more or less than 100% of the taxpayer's income may be subjected to state income tax.
5. Most states employ an equally weighted three-factor apportionment formula. In some states, the sales factor is doubled, and in a few states, only the sales factor is used in apportioning multistate taxable income. Generally, the greater the relative weight assigned to the sales factor, the greater the tax burden on out-of-state taxpayers.
6. The sales factor is based upon the destination concept except where a throwback rule applies. The payroll factor generally includes compensation that is included in Federal gross income, but some states include excludible fringe benefits. An employee's compensation usually is not divided among states. The property factor is derived using the average undepreciated historical costs for the assets and eight times the rental value of the assets.
7. The unitary theory may require the taxpayer to include worldwide activities and holdings in the apportionment factors. A water's edge election can limit these amounts to U.S. transactions.

unitary members have nexus. The computations reflect apportioned and allocated income of the unitary members, resulting in a summary of the taxable income of the entities in each state. The combined method chiefly permits the unitary taxpayer to develop the summary of assigned taxable incomes, which is accepted by (and disclosed to) all of the states.

16.4 Taxation of S Corporations

LO.7

Discuss the states' income tax treatment of S corporations, partnerships, and LLCs.

The majority of the 46 states that impose a corporate income tax have special provisions, similar to the Federal law, that govern the taxation of S corporations. As of 2011, only a few states—including Tennessee and Texas—and the District of Columbia do not provide special (no corporate-level tax) treatment for Federal S corporations. In addition, Massachusetts imposes a corporate-level tax on S corporations that have gross receipts in excess of $6 million. Some states, including Illinois, Texas, and California, apply a corporate-level tax, at special rates, on an S corporation.

In the non-S election states, a Federal S corporation generally is subject to tax in the same manner as a regular C corporation. Accordingly, if a multistate S corporation operates in any of these states, it is subject to state income tax and does not realize one of the primary benefits of S status—the avoidance of double taxation. Other potential tax-related benefits of the S election, including the pass-through of net operating losses and the reduction in the rate of tax imposed on individual and corporate taxpayers, may be curtailed.

EXAMPLE 26

Bryan, an S corporation, has established nexus in States A and B. A recognizes S status, while B does not. Bryan generated $600,000 of ordinary business income and $100,000 of dividends that were received from corporations in which Bryan owns 50% of the stock. Bryan's State B apportionment percentage is 50%.

For B tax purposes, Bryan first computes its income as though it were a C corporation. It then apportions the resulting income to B. Assuming that B has adopted the Federal provisions governing the dividends received deduction, Bryan's income, determined as though it were a C corporation, is $620,000 [$600,000 + (100% − 80%) × $100,000]. Accordingly, Bryan may be subject to B corporate income tax on $310,000 ($620,000 × 50% apportionment percentage) of taxable income. ■

ELIGIBILITY

All of the states that recognize S status permit a corporation to be treated as an S corporation for state purposes only if the corporation has a valid Federal S election in place. Generally, the filing of a Federal S election is sufficient to render the corporation an S corporation for state tax purposes. In most states, an entity that is an S corporation for Federal tax purposes automatically is treated as an S corporation for state tax purposes. Wisconsin allows the entity to *elect out* of its S status for state purposes.

CORPORATE-LEVEL TAX

Although S corporations generally are not taxable entities, Federal income tax liability may arise if the corporation has excess passive investment income or recognized built-in gains (see Chapter 12). Several states have adopted similar provisions, and, therefore, an S corporation is exempt from the related state income tax only to the extent that it is exempt from corresponding Federal income taxes. In the majority of these states, the imposition of Federal income taxes generates a corporate-level tax for state purposes to the extent that corporate income is allocated or apportioned to the state.

EXAMPLE 27

Amp, an S corporation, has nexus with States X and Y, both of which recognize S status. X imposes a corporate-level tax on S corporations to the extent that the corresponding Federal tax applies. Amp is subject to the § 1374 tax. This year, its Federal excessive passive income is $60,000. The amount of income subject to tax in X depends on Amp's apportionment percentage for X.

If Amp's State X apportionment percentage is 50%, Amp is subject to a corporate-level tax in X on $30,000 of passive income ($60,000 × 50%). ■

A few states deviate from the Federal S corporation provisions and provide that an S corporation is entirely exempt from state income tax only if all of its shareholders are residents of the state. In these states, an S corporation is taxed on the portion of its income that is attributable to nonresident shareholders. Some of these states permit the S corporation to escape corporate-level tax on this income if its nonresident shareholders sign a form, agreeing to pay state tax on their share of the corporation's income. Moreover, about half of the states require the corporation to withhold taxes on the nonresident shareholders' portions of the entity's income.

EXAMPLE 28

ARGO, an S corporation, is subject to income tax only in Vermont. On the last day of its taxable year, 40% of ARGO's stock is held by nonresident shareholders. To the extent that ARGO's stock is held by resident shareholders, the corporation is not subject to income tax. Accordingly, ARGO is not subject to tax on 60% of its income.

The corporation *is* subject to tax on the remaining 40% of its income. ARGO may be able to avoid this corporate-level tax by withholding Vermont income tax for its nonresident shareholders. ■

In an effort to decrease compliance burdens and simplify the filing process for nonresident shareholders of S corporations, several states allow an S corporation to file a single income tax return and pay the resulting tax on behalf of some or all of its nonresident shareholders. State requirements for the filing of a "block" or **composite return** vary substantially.

TAX *in* the NEWS — **What Are You Taxing?**

Taxware.com, an observer of the state and local tax scene, has identified several of the most unusual sales and use tax laws that remain on the books of various states.

- Kentucky horse breeders pay sales tax on "stud fees" related to the breeding of Thoroughbred horses.
- North Carolina is a "tax-free zone" for motor sport racing teams. This includes a refund for the sales tax allocated to the fuel used by the aircraft that transport team members to the state.
- Cloth diapers are exempt from sales tax in Wisconsin, but disposables are taxable.
- Ohioans receive a tax break when they die. Makeup applications are exempt from sales tax when they are applied in a mortuary, but not when they occur in a beauty salon.
- Pennsylvania taxes air, in the form of a fee for the vacuum cleaner used at a car wash. No tax applies, though, for air used to inflate tires by a similar machine.

16.5 Taxation of Partnerships and LLCs

Most states apply income tax provisions to partnerships, limited liability companies (LLCs), and limited liability partnerships (LLPs) in a manner that parallels Federal treatment. The entity is a tax-reporting, not a taxpaying, entity. Income, loss, and credit items are allocated and apportioned among the partners according to the terms of the partnership agreement and state income tax law.

Some states require that the entity make estimated tax payments on behalf of out-of-state partners. This approach helps to assure that nonresident partners file appropriate forms and pay any resulting tax to the state. A few states, including Michigan for partnerships and Texas for LLCs, apply an entity-level tax on operating income. As is the case with S corporations, some states allow composite returns to be filed relative to out-of-state partners.

Generally, an in-state partner computes the income tax resulting from all of the flow-through income from the entity. The partner then is allowed a credit for income taxes paid to other states on this income.

Key issues facing partnerships doing business in multiple states include those listed here. Applicable law varies from state to state, and more complex transactions may not yet be addressed by existing law.

- Whether the partnership automatically has nexus with every state in which a partner resides.
- Whether a partner is deemed to have nexus with every state in which the partnership does business.
- How to assign the income/loss of a partner upon retirement or when a liquidating distribution is received.

16.6 Other State and Local Taxes

LO.8

Describe other commonly encountered state and local taxes on businesses.

STATE AND LOCAL SALES AND USE TAXES

Forty-five states and the District of Columbia impose a consumers' sales tax on retail sales of tangible personal property for use or consumption. In many of these states, in-state localities, including cities, towns, school districts, or counties, also have the power to levy a sales tax. A consumers' sales tax is a tax imposed directly on the purchaser who acquires the asset at retail; the tax is measured by the price of the sale. The vendor or retailer merely acts as a collection agent for the state.

A use tax is designed to complement the sales tax. The use tax has two purposes: to prevent consumers from evading sales tax by purchasing goods outside the state for in-state use, and to provide an equitable sales environment between in-state and out-of-state retailers.

Generally, sales of tangible personal property are subject to tax. In several states, selected services are subject to tax.

Each jurisdiction that applies a sales/use tax defines its own tax base (i.e., which items are taxable and to whom). For a multistate business, complying with the thousands of sets of sales/use tax statutes and regulations can be a difficult burden. In an effort to ease this confusion, state and local government officials and the MTC developed the Streamlined Sales Tax Project (SSTP). Members working in conjunction with the SSTP write model laws for taxing jurisdictions to adopt, thereby allowing for a more uniform application of the rules and for a more efficient exchange of information among revenue agencies.

To date, the most popular SSTP rules are those defining which products and services are subject to sales/use tax. For instance, SSTP rules set out the items of clothing that would be subject to tax, but each jurisdiction decides on its own whether to include clothing in the tax base and whether to allow "back to school" clothing amnesties during specific weeks of the year. However, little interest has been shown in having identical sales/use tax rates among the jurisdictions.

Almost all of the states that have adopted a sales/use tax are members of the SSTP, but only about half of them automatically adopt model SSTP laws.

Sales/Use Tax Exemptions

A majority of the states exempt sales of certain items from the sales/use tax base. The most common exemptions and exclusions include the following.

- *Sales for resale* are exempt because the purchaser is not the ultimate user of the sold property. For instance, meat purchased by a grocer and a garment purchased by a retailer are not subject to sales/use tax under the resale rule.
- *Casual or occasional sales* that occur infrequently are exempt from the sales/use tax base chiefly for administrative convenience. Most states exclude rummage sales, the transfer of an entire business, sales of used autos, and the like under this rule.
- Most *purchases by exempt organizations* are excluded from taxable sales. Charities, governments and their agencies, and other organizations qualifying for Federal income tax exemption are relieved of sales/use tax liabilities in all of the states.
- *Sales of targeted items* can be exempt to improve the equity of the sales/use tax system. Sales of groceries, medical prescriptions and equipment, and school clothes can fall into this category and become nontaxable. Special exemptions for sales of farm, industrial, and computing equipment might also qualify under this type of exclusion.
- Certain *sales to manufacturers, producers, and processors* may also be exempt. Exemptions usually include one or more of the following.
  - *Containers and other packing, packaging, and shipping materials actually used to transfer merchandise to customers of the purchaser.*
  - *Machines and specific processing equipment and repair parts or replacements exclusively and directly used in manufacturing tangible personal property.*

Taxing Clicks and Bricks

The states' enforcement efforts tend to be lax concerning sales/use tax collections for sales conducted on the Internet. But does this audit-deployment decision give Internet retailers an unfair advantage over "bricks and mortar" businesses that must collect sales tax on the sales that they make? Local retailers have invested in physical stores and merchandise and make up most downtown and shopping mall areas. Why should the law effectively allow a tax holiday for "clicks and mortar" Internet sellers, which have invested in just-in-time inventories and intangible assets like e-commerce web software? Do Internet retailers carry more political clout than those with stores or other physical presence in the state?

Comment on the equity of the current situation regarding Internet sales and the sales/use tax.

TAX *in* *the NEWS*

Collecting Those Sales/Use Tax Revenues

Today, state and local tax administrators face a major problem: How can governments get their sales/use tax revenues from mail-order, phone, and Internet sales? The problem is that the governments must rely on the seller to collect sales and use taxes, rather than collecting them directly from the purchaser. Consequently, a seller conceivably must deal with thousands of different sales/use taxing jurisdictions, each with its own forms and filing deadlines, rates of applicable tax, and definitions of what is taxable or exempt. Examples of issues on which jurisdictions may disagree include:

- Are snack foods exempt groceries or taxable candy?
- Are therapeutic stockings exempt medical supplies or taxable clothing?
- Which types of software are subject to tax?

Large retailers such as Wal-Mart, Amazon, and Radio Shack can develop software to handle these problems, but smaller businesses cannot afford to create their own software or to purchase someone else's. The result has been a very low level of compliance by sellers with respect to out-of-state sales transactions.

Governments meanwhile have limited resources to enforce tax rules that have long been on the books. Many states ask individuals and businesses to include the unpaid use taxes for Internet, phone, and mail-order purchases on their annual income tax returns, but the number of taxpayers complying is insignificant. This is not a matter of "increasing the taxes on the Internet economy," but rather of collecting revenues that already are due and are desperately needed to balance state budgets.

Sales/Use Tax Nexus

A separate set of nexus rules applies in determining whether a seller must collect a sales/use tax from a customer. Strictly, the tax must be collected only if the seller has a *physical presence* (e.g., a store building but not a web page) in the state.

The regular solicitation of sales by independent brokers establishes sufficient nexus to require a nonresident seller to register and collect the use tax, even though the seller does not have regular employees, agents, and an office or other place of business in the state.[14] As a result, a corporation may be required to collect sales and use taxes in a state even though it is immune from the imposition of an income tax.

Sales/Use Tax on Services

Most sales/use tax laws were developed 50 or more years ago, when the U.S. economy was based on manufacturing and merchandising. Today, with perhaps two-thirds of all retail transactions in the United States consisting at some level of the rendering of services, the sales/use tax may be considered inadequate at generating revenues for the taxing jurisdictions. Consequently, some states have been adding specific service transactions to the sales/use tax base.

The services most commonly being subjected to tax include transactions involving hotels and restaurants, hair and beauty salons, entertainment events, cable and satellite television subscriptions, and lawn care. To date, taxation of legal/accounting, medical, education, and advertising services has been blocked by the professional associations of the providers of these services. Revenue shortfalls at the state and local level, however, may force legislatures to expand the sales/use tax base to include a broader array of services in the future.

LOCAL PROPERTY TAXES

Property taxes, a major source of revenue at the city and county level, often are designated as *ad valorem* taxes because they are based on the value of property that is located in the state on a specific date. Generally, that date fixes taxable ownership, situs (location), and the valuation of the property. Nonetheless, to avoid tax evasion, personal property that is temporarily outside the state may be taxed at the domicile of the owner.

[14] *Quill Corp. v. North Dakota*, 112 S.Ct. 1904 (1992); *Scripto, Inc. v. Carson*, 80 S.Ct. 619 (1960).

TAX *in the NEWS*

THE AMAZON TAX

To counter the loss of significant sales/use tax revenues on Internet transactions due to inadequate collection methods, New York and a few other states have found nexus through a vendor's use of sales, distribution, and marketing affiliates. For instance, suppose that a consumer clicks on a link on an Amazon.com page to Overstock.com, Target.com, or some other retailer and then purchases goods from the vendor. These states contend that Amazon has sales/use tax nexus because of the physical presence established in-state *by use of the affiliate*, even though Amazon itself has no such presence.

This so-called Amazon tax has been supported by most lower-level courts that have reviewed the issue. The taxpayers are appealing those holdings—not surprisingly, given that most of Amazon's affiliates (e.g., Target) have outlets in nearly every U.S. state and that considerable sales/use tax revenue is at stake.

Amazon long has enjoyed its no-nexus status as a strictly virtual seller, collecting sales/use taxes only in its headquarters state of Washington and in the three states with Amazon distribution centers. But any version of the Amazon tax will bring significant changes to the way that online commerce is conducted in other sales/use tax states.

Property taxes can take the form of either real property taxes or personal property taxes. States apply different tax rates and means of assessment to the two classes of property. The methods of assessing the value of the real and tangible property also vary in different taxing jurisdictions.

Although a personal property tax may be imposed on both intangible and tangible property, most states limit the tax to tangible property. The distinction between the various items of personal property is important because special rates, computations, or exemptions apply to certain types of property. For instance, inventory constitutes tangible personal property, but is exempt from taxation in most states.

OTHER TAXES

States may impose a variety of other state and local taxes on corporations, including incorporation or entrance fees or taxes, gross receipt taxes, stock transfer taxes, realty transfer and mortgage recording taxes, license taxes, and franchise taxes based on net worth or capital stock outstanding.

An *incorporation tax* is an excise tax for the corporate privilege conferred on the business. At the time the business is incorporated, the state generally imposes a fee or tax for the privilege of conducting business within the state as a corporation. Similarly, an out-of-state corporation usually must pay an entrance fee or tax before it can transact business in a state other than its state of incorporation.

Some states base the incorporation tax on the par value of the authorized stock. To prevent tax evasion, a few of these states impose a similar fee or tax on subsequent increases in the corporation's authorized stock. Where the incorporation fee or tax is based on the amount of authorized stock, the tax may be based on the total amount of the stock, even though the corporation conducts business in several states.

A *license tax* is an excise tax on the privilege of engaging in a certain business, occupation, or profession. A jurisdiction may impose business, occupational, or professional license taxes as a means of generating revenue or regulating the activities of the business, occupation, or profession for the public welfare.

Stock and realty transfer and mortgage recording taxes are nonrecurring taxes that are imposed at the time of recording or transfer. *Stock transfer taxes* are imposed on the transfer of shares or certificates of stock of domestic and foreign corporations. The tax typically is based on the number of shares transferred and the par or market value of the stock. Generally, the following stock transfers are exempt from the transfer tax: original issues, deposits of stock as security for a loan, and transfers to a broker for sale or purchase.

The base of the *realty transfer tax* usually is measured by the consideration paid or to be paid for the realty. The *mortgage recording tax* may be based on the actual consideration given, the value of the property, or the debt to be secured by the instrument.

Typically, a *capital stock tax* is an excise tax imposed on a domestic corporation for the privilege of existing as a corporation or imposed on an out-of-state corporation, either for the privilege of doing business or for the actual transaction of business within the state. This annual tax usually is based on the book value of the corporation's net worth, including capital, surplus, and retained earnings. In a few states, a corporation is subject to a *franchise tax* only to the extent that the tax exceeds the corporate income tax, but in the majority of states, the entity is subject to both taxes.

The majority of capital stock taxes are apportioned if the corporation does business or maintains an office in another state. In some states, however, the tax is levied on the entire authorized or issued capital stock of a domestic corporation, even though the corporation may be engaged in business in other states. For corporations based in other states, the tax is imposed only on the capital that is employed in the state as determined by an apportionment formula.

EXAMPLE 29

The balance sheet of Bull, a domestic corporation of State A, at the end of its taxable year is as follows.

Cash	$100,000
Equipment (net of $50,000 accumulated depreciation)	150,000
Building (net of $75,000 accumulated depreciation)	225,000
Land	125,000
Total assets	$600,000
Accounts payable and other short-term liabilities	$100,000
Long-term liabilities	200,000
Capital stock	50,000
Paid-in capital in excess of par value	50,000
Retained earnings	200,000
Total liabilities and equity	$600,000

A imposes a 2% franchise tax based on the entire net worth of a domestic corporation. Bull is subject to a franchise tax in A of $6,000 ($600,000 assets − $300,000 liabilities = $300,000 net worth × 2% rate). ■

EXAMPLE 30

Continue with the facts of Example 29, except that A subjects a domestic corporation to tax only on the capital that is employed in the state. Bull properly determines its A apportionment percentage as 20%. In this case, Bull's A franchise tax liability is $1,200 ($300,000 net worth × 20% apportionment percentage = $60,000 capital employed in A × 2% rate). ■

Encouraging Economic Development through Tax Concessions

The tax professional occasionally is in a position to negotiate with a state or city taxing jurisdiction to garner tax relief for a client as an incentive to locate a plant or distribution center in that geographic area. In times when construction budgets are high and interstate competition is fierce, such tax concessions can be significant.

For instance, to encourage a business to build a large distribution center in the area, community leaders might be agreeable to (1) paying for roads, sewer, water, and other improvements through taxpayer bonds; (2) reducing property taxes by 50 percent for the first 10 years of the center's operations; and (3) permanently excluding any distribution-related vehicles and equipment from the personal property tax.

An incentive-granting community provides the concessions even though the influx of new workers will place a great strain on public school facilities and likely necessitate improvements in traffic patterns and other infrastructure. Local residents, even those who obtain jobs at the new facility, and the tax adviser may wonder whether the tax concessions are supportable in light of these changes in the community's quality of life.

Take the position of a large employer that has been located in the area for more than 50 years. By how much should it be willing to absorb the tax increases that result when economic development concessions are used to attract new, perhaps temporary, businesses to the area? Should the employer challenge the constitutionality of the grant of such sizable tax breaks to some, but not all, business taxpayers in the jurisdiction?

Should higher "impact fees" be assessed on new developments? Does your analysis change if the new business competes with the longtime resident for sales? For employees? For political power?

TAX PLANNING:

LO.9

Recognize tax planning opportunities available to minimize a corporation's state and local tax liability.

The inconsistencies in the tax laws and rates among the states not only complicate state tax planning, but also provide the nucleus of pertinent planning opportunities. Although several tax planning devices are available to a corporation that does business in only one state, most planning techniques are directed toward corporations that do business or maintain property in more than one state. All suggested tax planning strategies should be reviewed in light of practical business considerations and the additional administrative and other costs that may be incurred, because simply minimizing state taxes may not be prudent from a business perspective.

16.7 Selecting the Optimal State in Which to Operate

Because the states employ different definitions of the amount and type of activity necessary to establish nexus, a company has some latitude in selecting the states by which it will be taxed. When a corporation has only a limited connection with a high-tax state, it may abandon that activity by electing an alternative means of accomplishing the same result. For example, if providing a sales representative with a company-owned BlackBerry constitutes nexus in an undesired state, the company could eliminate its connection with that state by reimbursing sales personnel for equipment expenses, instead of providing a company communications device. Similarly, when nexus is caused by conducting customer training sessions or seminars in the state, the corporation could bypass this connection. This can be done by sending the personnel to a nearby state in which nexus clearly has been established or in which the activity would not constitute nexus.

In addition, when sufficient activity originates from the repair and maintenance of the corporation's products or the activities performed by the sales representatives within the state, the organization could incorporate the service or sales divisions. This would invalidate a nonunitary state's right to tax the parent corporation's income; only the income of the service or sales divisions would be subject to tax. However, this technique is successful only if the incorporated division is a *bona fide* business operation. Therefore, the pricing of any sales or services between the new subsidiary and the parent corporation must be at arm's length, and the operations of the new corporation preferably should result in a profit.

Although planning techniques often are employed to disconnect a corporation's activities from an undesirable state, they can also be utilized to create nexus in a desirable state. For example, when the presence of a company-owned computer creates nexus in a desirable state, the corporation could provide its sales representatives in that state with company-owned equipment, rather than reimbursing or providing increased compensation for equipment costs.

Establishing nexus in a state is advantageous, for instance, when that state has a lower tax rate than the state in which the income currently is taxed, or when losses or credits become available to reduce tax liabilities in the state.

EXAMPLE 31

Bird Corporation generates $500,000 of taxable income from selling goods; specifically, 40% of its product is sold in State A and 60% in State B. Both states levy a corporate income tax and include only the sales factor in their apportionment formulas. The tax rate in A is 10%; B's rate is only 3%. Bird's manufacturing operation is located in A; therefore, the corporation's income is subject to tax in that state. Currently, Bird is immune from tax under Public Law 86–272 in B. Since A has adopted a throwback provision, Bird incurs $50,000 of state income taxes.

	Apportionment Formula	Net Income	Tax Rate	Tax
State A	100/100	$500,000	10%	$50,000
State B	0/100	500,000	3%	–0–
Total tax liability				$50,000

Because B imposes a lower tax rate than A, Bird substantially reduces its state tax liability if sufficient nexus is created with B.

	Apportionment Formula	Net Income	Tax Rate	Tax
State A	40/100	$500,000	10%	$20,000
State B	60/100	500,000	3%	9,000
Total tax liability				$29,000

A corporation may benefit by storing inventory in a low- or no-tax state because the average property value in the state in which the manufacturing operation is located is reduced significantly. When the manufacturing operation is located in a high-tax state, the establishment of a distribution center in a low- or no-tax state may reduce the overall state tax liability.

EXAMPLE 32

Trill Corporation realized $200,000 of taxable income from selling its product in States A and B. Trill's manufacturing plant, product distribution center, and warehouses are located in A. The corporation's activities within the two states are as follows.

	State A	State B	Total
Sales	$500,000	$200,000	$700,000
Property	300,000	50,000	350,000
Payroll	100,000	10,000	110,000

Trill is subject to tax in A and B. Both states utilize a three-factor apportionment formula that equally weights sales, property, and payroll; however, A imposes a 10% corporate income tax, while B levies a 3% tax. Trill incurs a total income tax liability of $17,575.

	Apportionment Formulas					
	State A			State B		
Sales	$500,000/$700,000	=	71.43%	$200,000/$700,000	=	28.57%
Property	$300,000/$350,000	=	85.71%	$50,000/$350,000	=	14.29%
Payroll	$100,000/$110,000	=	90.91%	$10,000/$110,000	=	9.09%
Total			248.05%			51.95%
Apportionment factor (totals/3)			82.68%			17.32%
Income apportioned to the state ($200,000 × apportionment factor)			$165,360			$34,640
Tax rate			× 10%			× 3%
Tax liability			$ 16,536			$ 1,039
Total tax liability				$17,575		

EXAMPLE 33

Continue with the facts of Example 32, and further assume that Trill's product distribution center and warehouse operations were acquired for $200,000 and the payroll of these operations is $20,000. Ignoring all nontax considerations, Trill could reduce its tax liability by $3,514 (a 20% reduction) by moving its distribution center, warehouses, and applicable personnel to B.

	State A	State B	Total
Sales	$500,000	$200,000	$700,000
Property	100,000	250,000	350,000
Payroll	80,000	30,000	110,000

Apportionment Formulas

	State A			State B		
Sales	$500,000/$700,000	=	71.43%	$200,000/$700,000	=	28.57%
Property	$100,000/$350,000	=	28.57%	$250,000/$350,000	=	71.43%
Payroll	$80,000/$110,000	=	72.73%	$30,000/$110,000	=	27.27%
Total			172.73%			127.27%
Apportionment factor (totals/3)			57.58%			42.42%
Income apportioned to the state ($200,000 × apportionment factor)			$115,160			$ 84,840
Tax rate			× 10%			× 3%
Tax liability			$ 11,516			$ 2,545
Total tax liability				$14,061		
Tax imposed before move to State B				17,575		
Tax reduction due to move				$ 3,514		

■

16.8 Restructuring Corporate Entities

One of the major objectives of state tax planning is to design the proper mix of corporate entities. An optimal mix of entities often generates the lowest combined state income tax for the corporation. Ideally, the income from all of the entities will be subject to a low tax rate or no tax at all. However, this generally is not possible. Consequently, the goal of designing a good corporate combination often is to situate the highly profitable entities in states that impose a low (or no) income tax.

MATCHING TAX RATES AND CORPORATE INCOME

When the corporation must operate in a high-tax state, divisions that generate losses also should be located there. Alternatively, unprofitable or less profitable operations can be merged into profitable operations to reduce the overall income subject to tax in the state. An ideal candidate for this type of merger may be a research and development subsidiary that is only marginally profitable but is vital to the parent corporation's strategic goals. By using computer simulation models, a variety of different combinations can be tested to determine the optimal corporate structure.

UNITARY OPERATIONS

By identifying the states that have adopted the unitary method and the criteria under which a particular state defines a unitary business, a taxpayer may reduce its overall state tax by restructuring its corporate relationships to create or guard against a unitary relationship. For instance, an independent business enterprise can be made unitary by exercising day-to-day operational control and by centralizing functions, such as marketing, financing, accounting, and legal services.

EXAMPLE 34
THE BIG PICTURE

Return to the facts of *The Big Picture* on p. 16-2. LocalCo already operates in both unitary and nonunitary states. Application of unitary corporate income tax rules can make tax planning more difficult. Subjecting certain LocalCo activities to the unitary theory could either increase or decrease the combined Federal corporate income tax liability of the affiliates, depending especially on the apportionment formulas applied in the unitary states.

LocalCo needs to make projections of the profitability of its operations in the new multifunction building. Then LocalCo should determine the income tax effects of expanding its operations into several target states, including both unitary and nonunitary jurisdictions, and compare how the unitary rules (and all associated compliance costs) affect its after-tax profits. ■

PASSIVE INVESTMENT COMPANIES

The creation of a **passive investment company** is another restructuring technique utilized to minimize a corporation's state tax burden. Nonbusiness or passive income generally is allocated to the state in which the income-producing asset is located, rather than apportioned among the states in which the corporation does business. Therefore, significant tax savings may be realized when nonbusiness assets are located in a state that either does not levy an income tax or provides favorable tax treatment for passive income. The corporation need not be domiciled in the state to benefit from these favorable provisions. Instead, the tax savings can be realized by forming a passive investment subsidiary to hold the intangible assets and handle the corporation's investment activities. The passive investment subsidiary technique usually produces the desired result in any no-tax state. Delaware, however, often is selected for this purpose due to its other corporate statutory provisions and favorable political, business, and legal climate.

Delaware does not impose an income tax upon a corporation whose only activity within the state is the maintenance and management of intangible investments and the collection and distribution of income from such investments or from tangible property physically located in another state. Consequently, trademarks, patents, stock, and other intangible property can be transferred to a Delaware corporation whose activity is limited to collecting passive income. The assets can be transferred to the subsidiary without incurring a Federal income tax under § 351 (see Chapter 4).

However, to receive the desired preferential state tax treatment, the holding company's activities within the state must be sufficient to establish income tax nexus in the state. The passive investment company should avoid performing any activity outside the state that may result in establishing nexus with another state. In addition, the formation of the subsidiary must be properly implemented to assure the legal substance of the operation. The passive investment company must have a physical office, and it must function as an independent operation. Ensuring nexus and proper formation is not difficult since numerous consulting organizations are available to furnish new passive investment companies with all of the elements necessary to fulfill these requirements.

Because the subsidiary's activities are confined to Delaware (or some other no- or low-tax state), and its operations generate only passive income, its income will not be taxed in any nonunitary state. Moreover, most states exclude dividends from taxation or otherwise treat them favorably; therefore, the earnings of a passive investment subsidiary can be distributed as a dividend to the parent at a minimal tax cost. If the state in which the parent is located does not levy the full income tax on dividends received, the entire measure of passive income may escape taxation.

Formation of a passive investment subsidiary also may favorably affect the parent corporation's apportionment formula in nonunitary states because the passive income earned by the subsidiary is excluded from the numerator of its sales factor.

EXAMPLE 35

Purple Corporation generates $800,000 of taxable income; $600,000 is income from its manufacturing operations, and $200,000 is dividend income from passive investments. All of Purple's sales are made, and assets are kept, in State A, which imposes a 10% corporate income tax and permits a 100% deduction for dividends received from subsidiaries. The corporation is not subject to tax in any other state. Consequently, Purple incurs $80,000 of income tax (tax base $800,000 × tax rate 10%).

If Purple creates a passive investment subsidiary in State B, which does not impose an income tax upon a corporation whose only activity within the state is the maintenance and management of passive investments, Purple's tax liability is reduced by $20,000 (a 25% decrease). Since passive income is nonbusiness income (which is allocated for state tax purposes to the state in which it is located), the income earned from its passive investments is not subject to tax in A.

	State A (Purple Corporation)	State B (Passive Investment Company)
Taxable income	$600,000	$200,000
Tax rate	× 10%	× -0-*
Tax liability	$ 60,000	$ -0-
Total tax liability		$ 60,000
Tax imposed without restructuring		80,000
Tax reduction due to use of subsidiary		$ 20,000

*B does not impose an income tax on a passive investment corporation.

The income earned by the subsidiary from its passive investments can be distributed to Purple as a dividend without incurring a tax liability because A allows a 100% deduction for dividends that are received from subsidiary corporations. ■

These desired results, however, will not be fully available in states that view the entire corporate operation as being unitary. Since those states require combined reporting, the income earned by the passive investment subsidiary is included in the corporation's apportionable or allocable income.

16.9 Subjecting the Corporation's Income to Apportionment

When a multistate organization is domiciled in a high-tax state, some of its apportionable income is eliminated from the tax base in that state. In light of the high tax rate, this may result in significant tax savings. Apportioning income will be especially effective where the income that is attributed to the other states is not subject to income tax. The income removed from the taxing jurisdiction of the domicile state entirely escapes state income taxation when the state to which the income is attributed (1) does not levy a corporate income tax; (2) requires a higher level of activity necessary to subject an out-of-state company to taxation than that adopted by the state of domicile; or (3) is prohibited under Public Law 86–272 from taxing the income (assuming that the domicile state has not adopted a throwback provision). Thus, the right to apportion income may provide substantial benefits because the out-of-state sales are excluded from the numerator of the sales factor and may not be taxed in another state.

However, to acquire the right to apportion its income, the organization must have sufficient activities in, or contacts with, one or more other states. Whether the type and amount of activities and/or contacts are considered adequate is determined by the

TAX *in the NEWS*

Leave That Giraffe at Home!

Passive investment subsidiaries make some states very angry. Revenue departments complain that millions of dollars of taxable income are fleeing to Delaware or Nevada. Industrial states like Ohio and Michigan regard the device as a means of creating a tax haven within the United States, in much the same way as the Cayman Islands serve as a haven from the Federal income tax. Somewhat ironically, even the revenue authorities of Switzerland have criticized the United States for allowing such a technique to flourish, and some countries characterize the United States as a tax haven when the device is used.

One of the means by which the states have attacked the use of passive investment subsidiaries is the *Geoffrey* rule. The device is named after Geoffrey the Giraffe, the mascot of Toys 'R Us. Over a decade ago, the Supreme Court of South Carolina held that the presence of intangible assets, including corporate logos and mascots such as Geoffrey, created nexus with the state. Thus, some taxable income could be apportioned to a state where the intangible asset is used. The *Geoffrey* decision came as a surprise to many tax advisers, and the rule now limits some of the planning opportunities formerly available to those operating in nonunitary jurisdictions.

About one-half of the states have attempted, usually through administrative rules, to adopt the *Geoffrey* approach. Other states either have not addressed the issue or purposely have ignored the rule to avoid the appearance of a hostile tax climate that could impede the recruitment of new businesses. Many states want to close this loophole but without seeming unfriendly to business.

The other popular approach used by the states to attack passive investment subsidiaries is to require combined reporting under the unitary theory. Almost a dozen states have adopted required combined reporting, or are considering legislation to do so, in the last few years. These states include New York, Pennsylvania, and Maryland. The unitary tax movement no longer is only a western states phenomenon.

Because the taxes of some taxpayers go up under combined reporting, while the taxes of others decrease, there often is no political force to block the adoption of unitary taxation. In fact, pressure for states to "go unitary" may be fueled by media reports of how well multistate tax planning can work (e.g., how Wal-Mart saves billions in taxes by paying rent for the use of property owned by its affiliates).

Some now are touting unitary tax theories on the basis of fairness. They say that the corporate income tax may be assessed more equitably in today's economy by using the broadest tax base and apportionment data possible.

domicile state's nexus rules. Therefore, a corporation should analyze its current activities in, and contacts with, other states to determine which, if any, activities or contacts could be redirected so that the corporation gains the right to apportion its income.

EXAMPLE 36
THE BIG PICTURE

Return to the facts of *The Big Picture* on p. 16-2. Most corporate taxpayers consist of a parent corporation and perhaps one or more existing subsidiaries. Given its expansion plans, LocalCo has the opportunity to determine "from scratch" in which states it wants to create nexus for the operations in the multifunction building.

The tax professional needs to offer advice to LocalCo's board of directors as to where the building might be situated and how the operations of any related sales and administrative personnel might be structured in an effort to provide optimal tax consequences. Nexus issues to be considered include the following.

- Is income tax nexus created with the target state?
- Is sales/use tax nexus created with the target state?
- How are the income tax apportionment factors affected by the expansion plans (e.g., whether the target state uses a property factor in the apportionment formula and, if so, how it is weighted)?
- Would a building like that planned by LocalCo receive any special computational treatment for the target state's property factor (e.g., in averaging the building's costs or applying accumulated depreciation)? ■

Can You Be a Nowhere Adviser?

The intent of much of today's multistate income tax planning is to create so-called *nowhere sales,* such that the income from the transaction is not subject to tax in any state. Suppose, for instance, that a sale is made from Georgia (a state with no throwback rule) into Nevada (the place of ultimate destination, but a state with no income tax). No state-level income tax liability is generated.

Is it ethical for a tax adviser to suggest such a strategy? Could you ethically propose the establishment of a sales office in a nonthrowback state, thereby avoiding state income tax on a transaction that is fully taxable under Federal rules?

16.10 Planning with Apportionment Factors

SALES FACTOR

The sales factor often yields the greatest planning opportunities for a multistate corporation. In-state sales include those to purchasers with a destination point in that state; sales delivered to out-of-state purchasers are included in the numerator of the sales factor of the destination state. However, to be permitted to exclude out-of-state sales from the sales factor of the origination state, the seller generally must substantiate the shipment of goods to an out-of-state location. Therefore, the destinations of sales that a corporation makes and the means by which the goods are shipped must be carefully reviewed. The corporation's overall state tax possibly can be reduced by establishing a better record-keeping system or by manipulating the numerator of the sales factor by changing the delivery location or method.

For example, a corporation may substantially reduce its state tax if the delivery location of its sales is changed from a state in which the company is taxed to one in which it is not. This technique may not benefit the corporation if the state in which the sales originate has adopted the throwback rule.

PROPERTY FACTOR

Because most fixed assets are physically stationary in nature, the property factor is not so easily manipulated. Nonetheless, significant tax savings can be realized by establishing a leasing subsidiary in a low- or no-tax state. If the property is located in a state that does not include leased assets in the property factor, the establishment of a subsidiary from which to lease the property eliminates the assets from the property factor in the parent's state.

Permanently idle property generally is excluded from the property factor. Accordingly, a corporation should identify and remove such assets from the property factor to ensure that the factor is not distorted. It is equally important to identify and remove nonbusiness assets from the property factor in states that distinguish between business and nonbusiness income.

EXAMPLE 37

The property factor valuations of Quake Corporation's holdings are as follows.

	State A	Total
Equipment (average historical cost)	$1,200,000	$2,000,000
Accumulated depreciation (average)	800,000	1,000,000

Twenty percent of the equipment in State A is fully depreciated and is idle. Assuming that A includes property in the factor at historical cost, Quake's property factor is 54.55% [($1,200,000 – $240,000 idle property)/($2,000,000 – $240,000)]. If the idle property is not removed from the property factor, Quake's property factor in A is incorrectly computed as 60% ($1,200,000/$2,000,000). ■

PAYROLL FACTOR

The payroll factor provides planning potential where several corporate employees spend substantial periods of time outside their state of employment, or the corporation is able to relocate highly paid employees to low- or no-tax states.

Use of an independent contractor who works for more than one principal can be beneficial under certain circumstances. Since the commissions paid to independent contractors are excluded from the payroll factor, the taxpayer may reduce its payroll factor in a high-tax state.

EXAMPLE 38

Yellow Corporation's total payroll costs are $1.4 million. Of this amount, $1 million was attributable to State A, a high-tax state. Yellow's payroll factor in A is 71.43% ($1,000,000/$1,400,000).

Assuming that $200,000 of the A compensation had been paid to sales representatives and that Yellow replaced its sales force with independent contractors, Yellow's payroll factor in A would be reduced to 66.67% [($1,000,000 – $200,000)/($1,400,000 – $200,000)]. ■

16.11 Sales/Use Taxes on Capital Changes

The tax adviser must be aware of the effects that sales and use taxes may have on a transaction that might otherwise be free from income tax. For example, although the transfer of property to a controlled corporation in exchange for its stock generally is not subject to corporate income taxes, several states provide that such transfers constitute taxable sales for sales and use tax purposes. Similarly, a corporate reorganization may be structured to avoid the imposition of income taxes, but under the statutes of several states, such transfers are considered to be taxable sales and, accordingly, are subject to sales and use taxes.

16.12 Capital Stock Taxation

Capital stock tax liabilities can be significant for capital-intensive taxpayers to the extent that they reinvest a large portion of retained earnings (the tax base) in productive assets. If all nontax factors are equal, a taxpayer with sizable exposure to a capital stock tax should consider the following techniques.

- Funding expansion with debt, rather than retained earnings.
- Funding subsidiary operations with debt, rather than direct capital contributions.
- Regularly paying dividends to parent companies that are domiciled in tax-favored states, such as Delaware and Nevada.

REFOCUS ON THE BIG PICTURE

MAKING A LOCATION DECISION IN A MULTISTATE TAX ENVIRONMENT

LocalCo holds a competitive advantage with the states and localities in negotiating where its new facility should be located. Politicians like to attract new facilities to their jurisdictions as a way to create construction jobs and to expand the income and sales/use tax base. LocalCo's top management should work with the governors and development executives of the states that are final candidates for the location of the proposed new building.

LocalCo's agenda for these negotiations should include the following items.

- Many states offer targeted tax incentives to attract and retain "clean" businesses like LocalCo. Such incentives might include property tax abatements, research and investment credits, and tax waivers for the state and local income and payroll taxes on new jobs. The company should determine whether it qualifies for any existing incentives. If a state does not currently offer incentives, perhaps its tax law could be amended to provide them.
- LocalCo should also ascertain how the potential locations apply income and sales/use taxes to Internet sales. How aggressive are these tax laws at the present time (e.g., as to the application of P.L. 86–272 and other nexus rules)? What is the level of projected state budget deficits and cash-flow needs, and what are the chances that the laws of the target states will be modified in the near future?
- Currently, LocalCo's manufacturing operations are split between a very low-tax state (Alabama) and a very high-tax state (California). Under a relocation plan that makes good business sense, nexus might be eliminated with California and shifted to a low-tax jurisdiction. Nevada is a good candidate, given its proximity to the current sportswear location.
- California applies the unitary theory of income taxation. LocalCo should determine whether unitary rules increase or decrease its total tax burden.
- Corporate headquarters currently are located in New York, another high-tax jurisdiction. If the new facility is located in a corporation-favorable, low-tax state, the company should consider moving its headquarters there.
- Relocating the corporate headquarters would also benefit the entity's highly paid executives. The individual income and sales/use tax burden of employees should be a factor in LocalCo's decision.
- In any event, shifting the entity's investment income to a low-tax jurisdiction appears advisable. Use of a passive investment company will carry out this tax planning objective.
- States often assess special taxes on trucking and airport functions and might even apply different income tax apportionment formulas to these operations. LocalCo's tax department and its outside advisers should research these features of the various relevant tax systems to avoid any unexpected surprises.

What If?

If LocalCo did not have a history of strong profitability, some of these state and local tax recommendations might be different. In that case, the company would consider such issues as how a state applies loss and credit carryovers. In addition, if there is no state income tax liability to pay, income tax credits and deductions would be less attractive, so the negotiations might focus on property and payroll taxes instead.

KEY TERMS

Allocate, 16–10
Apportion, 16–10
Combined return, 16–21
Composite return, 16–26
Dock sales, 16–16
Multistate Tax Commission (MTC), 16–8
Nexus, 16–8
Passive investment company, 16–35
Payroll factor, 16–17
Property factor, 16–19
Public Law 86–272, 16–8
Sales factor, 16–15
Throwback rule, 16–16
UDITPA, 16–7
Unitary theory, 16–21
Water's edge, 16–24

DISCUSSION QUESTIONS

1. **LO.1** You are working with the top management of one of your clients in selecting the U.S. location for a new manufacturing operation. Craft a plan for the CEO to use in discussions with the economic development representatives of several candidate states. In no more than two PowerPoint slides, list some of the tax incentives the CEO should request from a particular state during the negotiations. Be both creative and aggressive in the requests. **ISSUE ID** **COMMUNICATIONS**

2. **LO.1** Complete the following chart by indicating whether each item is true or false. Explain your answers by reference to the overlap of rules appearing in Federal and most state income tax laws.

	Item	True or False
a.	All of the states and the District of Columbia assess an income tax on entities doing business within the jurisdiction.	________
b.	Federal tax accounting methods, such as LIFO inventory and specific write-off of bad debts, are followed for state income tax purposes.	________
c.	State rules as to which entities can join in a consolidated return match those of Federal law.	________
d.	Some states use Federal taxable income as their income tax base, while others modify this amount or create their own state taxable income.	________
e.	A typical state income tax credit would equal 10% of the costs incurred to purchase and install solar energy panels for an existing factory.	________
f.	The corporate income tax systems of most states can be described as having progressive rate structures.	________
g.	A state that "piggybacks" onto the Federal income tax likely allows the IRS to collect the state corporate income tax on the Federal Form 1120.	________

3. **LO.1** In designing and drafting corporate income tax statutes and regulations, is each of the U.S. states "on its own"? (*Hint*: Use the terms *Multistate Tax Commission*, *MTC*, and *UDITPA* in your answer.)

4. **LO.1** Many states "outsource" their responsibility to write income tax rules to the MTC. Evaluate this statement.

5. **LO.2** In no more than three PowerPoint slides, list some general guidelines that a taxpayer can use to determine if it has an obligation to file an income or sales/use tax return with a particular state. Address the rules for in-state and out-of-state businesses. **COMMUNICATIONS**

6. **LO.2** Josie is a sales representative for Talk2Me, a communications retailer based in Fort Smith, Arkansas. Josie's sales territory is Oklahoma, and she regularly takes day trips into Tulsa to meet with customers. During a typical sales call, Josie takes the customers'

current orders and, using her wireless phone, sends the orders to headquarters in Fort Smith for immediate action. Approved orders are shipped from the Little Rock warehouse. Are Josie's sales subject to the Oklahoma corporate income tax?

7. **LO.2** Continue with the facts of Question 6. One of Josie's customers who is facing tight cash flow problems wants to return some defective cell phones. Talk2Me tells Josie to bring the phones back to headquarters. Fearing that she will lose a customer if she does not comply with the request, Josie says, "Let me save you the time and cost of packing and shipping the defective phones. Put them in the trunk of my car and I'll take them back." Does Josie's action change the answer to Question 6?

8. **LO.3** Describe the key concepts of *allocation* and *apportionment* in the taxation of the net income of a multistate business.

9. **LO.3** Indicate whether each of the following items should be *allocated* or *apportioned* by the taxpayer in computing state corporate taxable income. Assume the state follows the general rules of UDITPA.
   a. Profits from sales activities.
   b. Gain on the sale of a plot of land held by a real estate developer.
   c. Gain on the sale of a plot of land held by a manufacturer, on which it may expand its factory.
   d. Rent income received by a manufacturer from the leasing of space to a supplier.
   e. Profits from consulting and other service activities.

10. **LO.3** Regarding the apportionment formula used to compute state taxable income, does each of the following independent characterizations describe a taxpayer that is based in-state or out-of-state?
    a. The sales factor is positively correlated with the payroll, but not the property, factor.
    b. The sales factor is much higher than the property and payroll factors.
    c. The property and payroll factors are much higher than those for other nexus states.
    d. The sales and payroll factors are low, but the property factor is very high.

ISSUE ID

11. **LO.3** The traditional income apportionment formula applied three factors, equally weighted, in determining the taxable income of a business in the state. Now a majority of the states employ a formula in which the sales factor is assigned a greater than one-third weight. Why is such a formula attractive to a state?

12. **LO.5** In computing the corporate income taxes for Iowa-based SpillCo, should a single large sale in August, in which merchandise was shipped to a customer in Kentucky, be included in the Iowa sales factor?

13. **LO.5** Continue with the facts of Question 12. Another large shipment was made in May to a customer in South Dakota, a state that does not impose any corporate income tax. Is this sale to be included in SpillCo's Iowa sales factor?

14. **LO.5** Megan is a telecommuter and works most days from her home in Tennessee. Twice a month she travels to Georgia for a staff meeting at the Atlanta headquarters. In which state's payroll factor should Megan's compensation be included if:
    a. Megan is an employee and is covered by the qualified retirement plan of her Atlanta employer?
    b. Megan works as an independent contractor for several clients, including the Atlanta-based firm?

ISSUE ID

15. **LO.5** You are preparing an analysis of a state's apportionment formula. List at least five questions that you should ask in determining whether an asset that is owned by the taxpayer is to be included in the state's property factor numerator.

16. **LO.6** About 20 states apply a unitary system of business income taxation.
    a. Explain why these states are attracted to the unitary theory and a combined reporting scheme of multistate income taxation.
    b. Is the application of the unitary theory a help or a detriment to the taxpayer?

ISSUE ID

17. **LO.6** State A enjoys a prosperous economy, with high real estate values and compensation levels. State B's economy has seen better days—property values are depressed, and unemployment is higher than in other states. Most consumer goods are priced at about 10% less in B than in A. Both A and B apply unitary income taxation to

businesses that operate within the state. Does unitary taxation distort the assignment of taxable income between A and B? Explain.

18. **LO.6** Your client makes the comment, "Unitary corporate income taxation is a bad idea for the business community." Is her characterization correct? Elaborate.

19. **LO.6** Carmina operates a multinational business from Colorado, a state that applies the unitary theory and requires combined state income tax reporting. Most of her off-shore customers are located in the United Kingdom and Germany, where sales prices and property valuations are relatively high. Make a recommendation as to how Carmina might reduce her Colorado income tax liabilities. (*Hint*: There is an attractive unitary tax election that Carmina should consider).

20. **LO.7** Chip and Dale are the only shareholders of VisitTime, a medical transportation firm that is organized as an S corporation. VisitTime makes quarterly estimated income tax payments, related to Chip's stock ownership, to State Q, its headquarters state. Explain.

21. **LO.7** Evaluate this statement: An S corporation can facilitate the meeting of its state income tax filing obligations by developing a common spreadsheet that allocates and apportions income among the states with which it has nexus. This spreadsheet is attached to each of the state returns to be filed. (*Hint*: Use the term *composite return* in your answer.)

22. **LO.7** The Quail LLC operates solely in State W. As a pass-through entity, Quail does not pay any W taxes. Evaluate this statement.

23. **LO.8** HernandezCo wants to avoid the creation of sales/use tax nexus with State G. The HernandezCo sales representatives believe that they will lose customers because of an increase in their products' prices, as the company would need to cover its new tax obligations. Are the sales representatives correct to be concerned about their employer's new tax issue? ISSUE ID

24. **LO.8** Create a PowerPoint outline describing the major exemptions and exclusions from the sales/use tax base of most states. Use your slides to discuss this topic with your accounting students' club. COMMUNICATIONS

25. **LO.8** What is the Streamlined Sales Tax Project? What tax problems does it address?

26. **LO.8** List three or more taxes, other than the income and sales/use tax, that a state or local jurisdiction might levy.

27. **LO.2, 9** Your client, Ecru Limited, is considering an expansion of its sales operations, but it fears adverse resulting tax consequences. Write a memo for the tax research file identifying the planning opportunities presented by the ability of a corporation to terminate or create income tax nexus. Be certain to discuss the *Wrigley* case in your analysis. COMMUNICATIONS

28. **LO.9** Your client, Royal Corporation, generates significant interest income from its working capital liquid investments. Write a memo for the tax research file discussing the planning opportunities presented by establishing a passive investment company. Support your memo with a diagram of the resulting flow of assets and income. COMMUNICATIONS

29. **LO.9** Sherri has acquired a franchise to operate a QuickClip hair salon in her home state Y. QuickClip's corporate offices are located in State Z, and all financial transactions of the franchisees use QuickClip's Z banks exclusively. The franchise agreement allows Sherri to purchase and use QuickClip branded supplies and to join in national advertising campaigns, as they are crafted and carried out from Z. QuickClip (not Sherri personally) is the tenant on all of Sherri's leased salon space and other property.

    A Y tax auditor maintains that Sherri's profits are subject to that state's tax on business income. Explain to Sherri whether she has income tax nexus with Y. (*Hint*: Include the *Geoffrey* case in your explanation).

30. **LO.9** As the director of the multistate tax planning department of a consulting firm, you are developing a brochure to highlight the services it can provide. Part of the brochure is a list of five or so key techniques that clients can use to reduce state income tax liabilities. Develop this list for the brochure. COMMUNICATIONS

31. **LO.9** Continuing with Problem 30, provide two or three bullet points containing planning ideas relating to a client's liability for a capital stock tax. COMMUNICATIONS

PROBLEMS

32. **LO.1** Use Figure 16.1 to compute Beta Corporation's State F taxable income for the year.

Addition modifications	$19,000
Allocated income (total)	$15,000
Allocated income (State F)	$3,000
Allocated income (State G)	$12,000
Apportionment percentage	40%
Credits	$80
Federal taxable income	$90,000
Subtraction modifications	$15,000
Tax rate	5%

33. **LO.1** Use Figure 16.1 to provide the required information for Warbler Corporation, whose Federal taxable income totals $10 million.

    Warbler apportions 60% of its business income to State C. Warbler generates $3 million of nonbusiness income each year, and 20% of that income is allocated to C. Applying the state income tax modifications, Warbler's total business income this year is $9 million.

    a. How much of Warbler's business income does State C tax?
    b. How much of Warbler's nonbusiness income does State C tax?
    c. Explain your results.

34. **LO.1** For each of the following independent cases, indicate whether the circumstances call for an addition modification (*A*), a subtraction modification (*S*), or no modification (*N*) in computing state taxable income. Then indicate the amount of any modification. The starting point in computing State Q taxable income is the year's Federal taxable income, before any deduction for net operating losses.

    a. Federal cost recovery = $10,000, and Q cost recovery = $15,000.
    b. Federal cost recovery = $15,000, and Q cost recovery = $10,000.
    c. Federal income taxes paid = $30,000.
    d. Refund received from last year's Q income taxes = $3,000.
    e. Local property taxes, deducted on the Federal return as a business expense = $7,000.
    f. Interest income from holding U.S. Treasury bonds = $20,000.
    g. Interest income from holding Q revenue anticipation bonds = $3,000.
    h. An asset was sold for $18,000; its purchase price was $20,000. Accumulated Federal cost recovery = $11,000, and accumulated Q cost recovery = $8,000.
    i. Dividend income received from State R corporation = $10,000, subject to a Federal dividends received deduction of 70%.

35. **LO.1** Perk Corporation is subject to tax only in State A. Perk generated the following income and deductions.

Federal taxable income	$200,000
State A income tax expense	10,000
Refund of State A income tax	3,000
Depreciation allowed for Federal tax purposes	300,000
Depreciation allowed for state tax purposes	120,000

    Federal taxable income is the starting point in computing A taxable income. State income taxes are not deductible for A tax purposes. Determine Perk's A taxable income.

36. **LO.1** Flip Corporation is subject to tax only in State X. Flip generated the following income and deductions. State income taxes are not deductible for X income tax purposes.

Sales	$4,000,000
Cost of sales	2,800,000
State X income tax expense	200,000
Depreciation allowed for Federal tax purposes	400,000
Depreciation allowed for state tax purposes	300,000
Interest income on Federal obligations	50,000
Interest income on X obligations	30,000
Expenses related to carrying X obligations	10,000

a. The starting point in computing the X income tax base is Federal taxable income. Derive this amount.
b. Determine Flip's X taxable income, assuming that interest on X obligations is exempt from X income tax.
c. Determine Flip's X taxable income, assuming that interest on X obligations is subject to X income tax.

37. **LO.4, 5** Jest Corporation owns and operates two facilities that manufacture paper products. One of the facilities is located in State D, and the other is located in State E. Jest generated $2.8 million of taxable income, consisting of $2 million of income from its manufacturing facilities and an $800,000 gain from the sale of nonbusiness property, located in E. E does not distinguish between business and nonbusiness income, but D apportions only business income. Jest's activities within the two states are outlined below.

	State D	State E	Total
Sales of paper products	$3,000,000	$7,000,000	$10,000,000
Property	600,000	1,500,000	2,100,000
Payroll	1,200,000	1,800,000	3,000,000

Both D and E utilize a three-factor apportionment formula, under which sales, property, and payroll are equally weighted. Determine the amount of Jest's income that is subject to income tax by each state.

38. **LO.4, 5** Assume the same facts as Problem 37, except that, under the statutes of both D and E, only business income is subject to apportionment.

39. **LO.5** Dillman Corporation has nexus in States A and B. Dillman's activities for the year are summarized below.

	State A	State B	Total
Sales	$1,000,000	$ 600,000	$1,600,000
Property			
Average cost	500,000	300,000	800,000
Average accumulated depreciation	(300,000)	(100,000)	(400,000)
Payroll	2,500,000	500,000	3,000,000
Rent expense	10,000	25,000	35,000

Determine the apportionment factors for A and B, assuming that A uses a three-factor apportionment formula under which sales, property (net depreciated basis), and payroll are equally weighted, and B employs a single-factor formula that consists solely of sales. State A has adopted the UDITPA with respect to the inclusion of rent payments in the property factor.

40. **LO.5** Assume the facts of Problem 39, except that A uses a single-factor apportionment formula that consists solely of sales, and B uses a three-factor apportionment formula that equally weights sales, property (at historical cost), and payroll. State B does not include rent payments in the property factor.

41. **LO.5** Assume the facts of Problem 39, except that both states employ a three-factor formula, under which sales are double weighted. The basis of the property factor in A is historical cost, while the basis of this factor in B is the net depreciated basis. Neither A nor B includes rent payments in the property factor.

42. **LO.5** McKay Corporation operates in two states, as indicated below. This year's operations generated $300,000 of apportionable income.

	State A	State B	Total
Sales	$600,000	$400,000	$1,000,000
Property	300,000	300,000	600,000
Payroll	200,000	50,000	250,000

Compute McKay's State A taxable income, assuming that State A apportions income based on a:

a. Three-factor formula, equally weighted.
b. Double-weighted sales factor.
c. Sales factor only.

43. **LO.5** Tootie Corporation operates in two states, as indicated below. All goods are manufactured in State A. Determine the sales to be assigned to both states in computing Tootie's sales factor for the year. Both states follow the UDITPA and the MTC regulations in this regard.

Sales shipped to A locations	$300,000
Sales shipped to B locations	500,000
Interest income from Tootie's B business checking accounts	5,000
Rent income from excess space in A warehouse	40,000
Interest income from Treasury bills in Tootie's B brokerage account, holding only idle cash from operations	65,000
One-time sale of display equipment to B purchaser (tax basis $90,000)	75,000
Royalty received from holding patent, licensed to B user	90,000

DECISION MAKING

44. **LO.5, 9** State E applies a throwback rule to sales, while State F does not. State G has not adopted an income tax to date. Orange Corporation, headquartered in E, reported the following sales for the year. All of the goods were shipped from Orange's E manufacturing facilities. Determine its sales factor in those states. Comment on Orange's location strategy, using only your tax computations.

Customer	Customer's Location	This Year's Sales
ShellTell, Inc.	E	$ 75,000,000
Tourists, Ltd.	F	40,000,000
PageToo Corp.	G	100,000,000
U.S. Department of Interior	All 50 states	35,000,000
Total		$250,000,000

DECISION MAKING

45. **LO.5, 9** Quinn Corporation is subject to tax in States G, H, and I. Quinn's compensation expense includes the following.

	State G	State H	State I	Total
Salaries and wages for nonofficers	$200,000	$400,000	$100,000	$ 700,000
Officers' salaries	–0–	–0–	500,000	500,000
Total				$1,200,000

Officers' salaries are included in the payroll factor for G and I, but not for H. Compute Quinn's payroll factors for G, H, and I. Comment on your results.

46. **LO.5** Judy, a regional sales manager, has her office in State U. Her region includes several states, as indicated in the sales report below. Judy is compensated through straight commissions on the sales in her region and a fully excludible cafeteria plan conveying various fringe benefits to her. Determine how much of Judy's $650,000 commissions and $75,000 fringe benefit package is assigned to the payroll factor of State U.

State	Sales Generated	Judy's Time Spent There
U	$3,000,000	30%
V	4,000,000	50%
X	5,000,000	20%

47. **LO.5** Justine Corporation operates manufacturing facilities in State G and State H. In addition, the corporation owns nonbusiness rental property in H. Justine incurred the following compensation expenses.

	State G	State H	Total
Manufacturing wages	$500,000	$200,000	$700,000
Administrative wages	200,000	70,000	270,000
Officers' salaries	200,000	50,000	250,000

Thirty percent of the time spent by the administrative staff located in H and 20% of the time spent by officers located in H are devoted to the operation, maintenance, and supervision of the rental property. G includes all income in the definition of apportionable income, while H excludes nonbusiness income from apportionable income. Only G includes officers' compensation in the payroll factor numerator.

Determine Justine's payroll factors for G and H.

48. **LO.5** Kim Corporation, a calendar year taxpayer, has manufacturing facilities in States A and B. A summary of Kim's property holdings follows.

		Beginning of Year	
	State A	State B	Total
Inventory	$ 300,000	$ 200,000	$ 500,000
Plant and equipment	2,500,000	1,500,000	4,000,000
Accumulated depreciation: plant and equipment	(1,000,000)	(600,000)	(1,600,000)
Land	600,000	1,000,000	1,600,000
Rental property*	900,000	300,000	1,200,000
Accumulated depreciation: rental property	(200,000)	(90,000)	(290,000)

		End of Year	
	State A	State B	Total
Inventory	$ 400,000	$ 150,000	$ 550,000
Plant and equipment	2,500,000	1,200,000	3,700,000
Accumulated depreciation: plant and equipment	(1,200,000)	(650,000)	(1,850,000)
Land	600,000	1,200,000	1,800,000
Rental property*	950,000	300,000	1,250,000
Accumulated depreciation: rental property	(250,000)	(100,000)	(350,000)

*Unrelated to regular business operations.

Determine Kim's property factors for the two states, assuming that the statutes of both A and B provide that average historical cost of business property is to be included in the property factor.

49. **LO.5** Assume the facts of Problem 48, except that nonbusiness income is apportionable in B.

50. **LO.5, 9** Crate Corporation, a calendar year taxpayer, has established nexus with numerous states. On December 3, Crate sold one of its two facilities in State X. The cost of this facility was $800,000. **DECISION MAKING**

On January 1, Crate owned property with a cost of $3 million, $1.5 million of which was located in X. On December 31, Crate owned property with a cost of $2.5 million, $700,000 of which was located in X.

X law allows the use of average annual or monthly cost amounts in determining the property factor. If Crate wants to minimize the property factor in X, which method should be used to determine the property factor there?

DECISION MAKING

COMMUNICATIONS

51. **LO.6, 9** True Corporation, a wholly owned subsidiary of Trumaine Corporation, generated a $400,000 taxable loss in its first year of operations. True's activities and sales are restricted to State A, which imposes an 8% income tax. In the same year, Trumaine's taxable income is $1 million. Trumaine's activities and sales are restricted to State B, which imposes an 11% income tax. Both states use a three-factor apportionment formula that equally weights sales, payroll, and property, and both require a unitary group to file on a combined basis. Sales, payroll, and average property for each corporation are as follows.

	True Corporation	Trumaine Corporation	Total
Sales	$2,500,000	$4,000,000	$6,500,000
Property	1,000,000	2,500,000	3,500,000
Payroll	500,000	1,500,000	2,000,000

True and Trumaine have been found to be members of a unitary business.

a. Determine the overall state income tax for the unitary group.
b. Determine aggregate state income tax for the entities if they were nonunitary.
c. Incorporate this analysis in a letter to Trumaine's board of directors. Corporate offices are located at 1234 Mulberry Lane, Chartown, AL 35298.

52. **LO.6** Chang Corporation is part of a three-corporation unitary business. The group has a water's edge election in effect with respect to unitary State Q. State B does not apply the unitary concept with respect to its corporate income tax laws. Nor does Despina, a European country to which Saldez paid a $4 million value added tax this year.

Saldez was organized in Despina and conducts all of its business there. Given the summary of operations that follows, determine Chang's and Elena's sales factors in B and Q.

Corporation	Customer's Location	Sales
Chang	B	$20,000,000
	Q	60,000,000
Elena	Q	20,000,000
Saldez	Despina	40,000,000

COMMUNICATIONS

53. **LO.7** Hernandez, which has been an S corporation since inception, is subject to tax in States Y and Z. On Schedule K of its Federal Form 1120S, Hernandez reported ordinary income of $500,000 from its business, taxable interest income of $10,000, capital loss of $30,000, and $40,000 of dividend income from a corporation in which it owns 30%.

Both states apportion income by use of a three-factor formula that equally weights sales, payroll, and the average cost of property; both states treat interest and dividends as business income. In addition, both Y and Z follow Federal provisions with respect to the determination of taxable income for a corporation. Y recognizes S status, but Z does not. Based on the following information, write a memo to the shareholders of Hernandez, detailing the amount of taxable income on which Hernandez will pay tax in Y and Z. Hernandez corporate offices are located at 5678 Alabaster Circle, Koopville, KY 47697.

	State Y	State Z
Sales	$1,000,000	$800,000
Property (average cost)	500,000	100,000
Payroll	800,000	200,000

54. **LO.8** Using the following information from the books and records of Grande Corporation, determine Grande's total sales that are subject to State C's sales tax. Grande operates a retail hardware store.

Sales to C consumers, general merchandise	$1,100,000
Sales to C consumers, crutches and other medical supplies	245,000
Sales to consumers in State D, via mail order	80,000
Purchases from suppliers	55,000

55. **LO.8** As a retailer, Granite Corporation sells software programs manufactured and packaged by other parties. Granite also purchases computer parts, assembles them as specified by a customer in a purchase order, and sells them as operating stand-alone computers. All of Granite's operations take place in State F, which levies a 9% sales tax. Results for the current year are as follows.

Sales of software	$2,500,000
Purchases of computer parts	1,300,000
Sales of computer systems	8,500,000
Purchases of office supplies	60,000
Purchases of packaging materials for the computer systems	30,000
Purchases of tools used by computer assemblers	50,000

a. What is Granite's own sales tax expense for the year?
b. How much F sales tax must Granite collect and pay over to the state on behalf of other taxpayers subject to the tax?

56. **LO.8** Indicate for each transaction whether a sales (*S*) or use (*U*) tax applies or whether the transaction is nontaxable (*N*). Where the laws vary among states, assume that the most common rules apply. All taxpayers are individuals.
a. A resident of State A purchases an automobile in A.
b. A resident of State A purchases groceries in A.
c. A resident of State B purchases an automobile in A.
d. A charity purchases office supplies in A.
e. An A resident purchases in B an item that will be in the inventory of her business.

57. **LO.8** Wayne Corporation is subject to State A's franchise tax. The tax is imposed at a rate of 1.2% of the corporation's net worth that is apportioned to the state by use of a two-factor formula (sales and property factors, equally weighted). The property factor includes real and tangible personal property, valued at historical cost as of the end of the taxable year.

Forty percent of Wayne's sales are attributable to A, and $600,000 of the cost of Wayne's tangible personal property is located in A.

Determine the A franchise tax payable by Wayne this year, given the following end-of-the-year balance sheet.

Cash		$ 200,000
Equipment	$1,000,000	
Accumulated depreciation	(300,000)	700,000
Furniture and fixtures	$ 800,000	
Accumulated depreciation	(50,000)	750,000
Intangible assets		450,000
Total assets		$2,100,000
Accounts and taxes payable		$ 600,000
Long-term debt		750,000
Common stock		1,000
Additional paid-in capital		249,000
Retained earnings		500,000
Total liabilities and equity		$2,100,000

58. **LO.5, 9** Dread Corporation operates in a high-tax state. The firm asks you for advice on a plan to outsource administrative work done in its home state to independent contractors. **DECISION MAKING**

This work now costs the company $750,000 in wages and benefits. Dread's total payroll for the year is $5 million, of which $4 million is for work currently done in the home state.

ISSUE ID

COMMUNICATIONS

59. **LO.9** Prepare a PowerPoint presentation (maximum of six slides) entitled "Planning Principles for Our Multistate Clients." The slides will be used to lead a 20-minute discussion with colleagues in the corporate tax department. Keep the outline general, but assume that your colleagues have clients operating in at least 15 states. Address only income tax issues.

RESEARCH PROBLEMS

INTERNET *activity*

Use the tax resources of the Internet to address the following questions. Do not restrict your search to the Web, but include a review of newsgroups and general reference materials, practitioner sites and resources, primary sources of the tax law, chat rooms and discussion groups, and other opportunities.

COMMUNICATIONS

Research Problem 1. Send an e-mail message to the secretary of revenue for your home state, proposing adoption of one of the following provisions that does not currently exist in your state.

a. Increase the apportionment weight for the sales factor.
b. Exempt computer and communications technology from the apportionment weight for the property factor.
c. Adopt a throwback rule for the sales factor.
d. Subject advertising expenditures to the sales/use tax.
e. Allow an income tax credit for 20% of the cost of in-state construction projects that are substantially completed within the next 18 months.
f. Tax the income of a passive investment company set up by a domestic taxpayer.
g. Add a "nexus team" to find the taxpayers operating in your state, but based in Ohio, Illinois, or Arizona.
h. Adopt the definitions and other rules of the Streamlined Sales Tax Project.
i. Allow an income tax credit for film and television producers equal to 30% of in-state expenditures.
j. Apply a tax on S corporations operating in the state, equal to 2% of the entity's hypothetical Subchapter C taxable income.
k. Convert the corporate income tax to a tax on gross receipts, in an effort to tax the profits of passive investment companies owned by in-state parent entities.

COMMUNICATIONS

Research Problem 2. For your state and one of its neighbors, determine the following. Place your data in a chart and e-mail your findings to your professor.

a. To what extent does each state follow the rulings of the Multistate Tax Commission?
b. What is each state's apportionment formula, with factors and weightings?
c. Does the state adopt pertinent changes to the Internal Revenue Code? As of what date?
d. Has the state joined the Streamlined Sales Tax Project? Which of the project's rules has the state adopted? What is the effective date?
e. How does the state apply income tax nexus rules to profits from intangible assets? Is the tax-effectiveness of a passive investment company limited in some way? Has the state adopted the *Geoffrey* approach to the taxation of income from intangibles?
f. Does the state apply entity-level income taxes for S corporations, partnerships, and LLCs? What are the terms of those taxes?
g. What are the requirements for the occasional-sale rule as an exception to the sales/use tax? Who can use this rule?
h. Describe any exemptions from the sales/use tax base that are allowed for transactions involving groceries, school clothing and supplies, religious goods, and legal services.
i. What is the discount allowed, if any, when a vendor remits sales/use tax to the state in a timely manner?
j. Does the state levy a "minimum tax" or "alternative minimum tax"? If so, what are the terms and rates for the tax?

Research Problem 3. Does Walmart.com collect use tax when it ships an order into your state? Does Dell.com? Gateway.com? Amazon.com? Crateandbarrel.com? SamGoody.com? (If your state does not have a sales tax law, answer for a neighboring state.)

Research Problem 4. Read the "tax footnote" of five publicly traded U.S. corporations. Find the effective state/local income tax rates of each. Create a PowerPoint presentation (maximum of five slides) for your instructor, summarizing the search and reporting the findings.

COMMUNICATIONS

Research Problem 5. Use **taxsites.com** or some other index to find a state/local tax organization (e.g., the Committee on State Taxation). Read its current newsletter. In an e-mail to your instructor, summarize a major article at the site. Look especially for articles on one of these topics.

COMMUNICATIONS

- Judicial and legislative developments concerning the income taxation of intangible income (e.g., trademark royalties).
- Legislation applying a physical-presence test as the exclusive definition of nexus at the Federal level or for your state's income or sales/use tax.
- Responses by the states to the economic downturn (e.g., more aggressive enforcement, new taxes and fees, installment options for the late payment of taxes and penalties).
- Incidence of state/local tax payments (i.e., how much of the total tax collections are paid by individuals, corporations, out-of-state businesses).
- The positive or negative "business tax climate" of your state and its neighbors, as measured by two or more policy centers or think tanks, and any measurable trends in the climate over the last 20 years.
- Attempts by the legislatures of your state and its neighbors to add advertising services to the sales/use tax base.
- Limitations on the taxpayer's ability to carry back net operating losses in computing your state's corporate taxable income.

Research Problem 6. Many states offer a tax credit for expenditures made in-state for new computing and energy-saving equipment. For your state and one of its neighbors, summarize in a table three of the tax incentives offered through the income, sales, or property tax structure. In your table, list at least the following. E-mail your table to the others in your course.

COMMUNICATIONS

- Name of the credit, deduction, exemption, etc.
- Who qualifies for the incentive (e.g., corporations, individuals, partnerships).
- Computational base for the incentive (e.g., dollars spent).
- Rate of the credit or deduction.
- Minimums, maximums, and other limitations that apply to the incentive amount.

CHAPTER

17

Tax Practice and Ethics

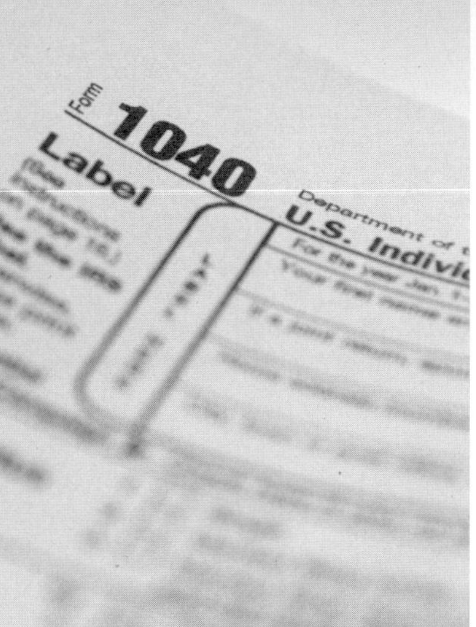

LEARNING OBJECTIVES

After completing Chapter 17, you should be able to:

LO.1

Describe the organization and structure of the IRS.

LO.2

Identify the various administrative pronouncements issued by the IRS and explain how they can be used in tax practice.

LO.3

Describe the audit process, including how returns are selected for audit and the various types of audits.

LO.4

Explain the taxpayer appeal process, including various settlement options available.

LO.5

Determine the amount of interest on a deficiency or a refund and when it is due.

LO.6

Discuss the various penalties that can be imposed on acts of noncompliance by taxpayers and return preparers.

LO.7

Understand the rules governing the statute of limitations on assessments and on refunds.

LO.8

Summarize the legal and ethical guidelines that apply to those engaged in tax practice.

OUTLINE

THE BIG PICTURE **Tax Solutions for the Real World**

A TAX ADVISER'S DILEMMA

Campbell Corporation is preparing its Form 1120 for the tax year. The entity develops and manufactures a number of electronic products, including a line of GPS applications that are downloaded onto cell phones. Campbell's research department needs to work with the U.S. government on this line of software because of the potential for security breaches when the software is used in sensitive parts of the world. Other efforts of the research department include traditional software architecture and development. Projections show that the GPS products will be highly profitable, with sales concentrated among various commercial and governmental communications providers around the world.

Some of the research department's work on the GPS products clearly qualifies for the Federal income tax credit for incremental research expenditures, but for some other items the availability of the credit is not so certain. Either the language of the pertinent Regulations is unclear in Campbell's setting, or, because of the innovative aspects of the products under development, the law is silent as to whether Campbell can claim the credit.

You are Campbell's tax adviser. This situation presents you with several levels of difficulty. How aggressive should you advise Campbell to be in reporting items on the Form 1120 that qualify for the incremental research credit? Will Campbell's taking an overly aggressive position on the credit trigger a tax preparer penalty for your consulting firm? What level of diligence should you exercise in advising Campbell as to whether specific expenditures qualify for the credit, given that your expertise with GPS software is limited to using the unit in your personal auto? **Read the chapter and formulate your response.**

Few events arouse so much fear in the typical individual or corporation as the receipt of a letter from the Internal Revenue Service (IRS), notifying the taxpayer that prior years' tax returns are to be the subject of an audit. Almost immediately, calls are made to the tax adviser. Advice is sought as to what to reveal (or not reveal) in the course of the audit, how to delay or avoid the audit, and how friendly one should be with the auditor when he or she ultimately arrives.

Indeed, many tax practitioners' reputations with their clients have been made or broken by the way they are observed to behave under the pressure of an audit situation. The strategy and tactics of audits—including such seemingly unimportant issues as whether the tax adviser brings donuts or other refreshments to the audit session, the color of his or her clothes, and the most effective negotiation techniques—are the subject of both cocktail party banter and scholarly review.

In actuality, the tax professional can render valuable services to the taxpayer in an audit context, thereby assuring that tax payments for the disputed years are neither under- nor over-reported, as part of an ongoing tax practice. In this regard, the adviser must appreciate the following.

- The elements of the Treasury's tax administration process and opportunities for appeal within the structure of the IRS.
- The extent of the negative sanctions that can be brought to bear against taxpayers whose returns are found to have been inaccurate.
- The ethical and professional constraints on the advice tax advisers can give and the actions they can take on behalf of their clients, within the context of an adversarial relationship with the IRS.

TAX *in the NEWS*

How Big Is the Tax Gap?

Every year the IRS estimates the size of the Federal income "tax gap"—the difference between how much tax *is* collected and how much *should be* collected. The tax gap reflects the taxes not paid by nonfilers, tax cheats, delinquents, and those who interpret or apply the tax laws incorrectly, whether deliberately or innocently.

According to the most recent analysis, the tax gap is a net amount of almost $300 billion annually. More specifically, the underpayments total about $345 billion per year but are offset by $55 billion obtained through IRS enforcement efforts (audits, collection procedures, etc.).

The IRS maintains that only 84 percent of taxpayers report the "correct" amount of tax under the existing system of voluntary compliance. The main sources of the tax gap are:

- Underreporting net taxable income (82 percent of the tax gap).
- Underpayment of tax (10 percent of the tax gap).
- Nonfiling (8 percent of the tax gap).

If, by some miracle, the entire tax gap were collected each year, the current Federal budget deficit would be cut significantly. A complete elimination of the tax gap is unlikely to occur, however, for several reasons.

- Citizens are not likely to tolerate the increased audit activity and data collection necessary for the Treasury to collect all of the tax owed.
- Citizens who are so inclined will continue to commit tax fraud, even if statutory and administrative changes are made to the system to identify them. Tax cheats are always "one step ahead" of the government in this regard.
- Congress is not likely to adopt the sweeping simplification of the tax law needed to alleviate its complexity, which many see as the underlying cause of the tax gap. Taxpayers who have difficulty understanding the tax law cannot be expected to fully comply with its provisions.

17.1 Tax Administration

The Treasury has delegated the administration and enforcement of the tax laws to its subsidiary agency, the IRS. In this process, the Service is responsible for providing adequate information, in the form of publications and forms with instructions, to taxpayers so that they can comply with the laws in an appropriate manner. The IRS also identifies delinquent tax payments and carries out assessment and collection procedures under the restrictions of due process and other constitutional guarantees.

The IRS is one of the largest Federal agencies. It employs about 87,500 staff members, and the total agency budget exceeds $12 billion. In meeting its responsibilities, the Service conducts audits of selected tax returns. About 1 percent of all individual tax returns are subjected to audit in a given tax year. However, certain types of both taxpayers and income—including, for instance, high-income individuals (about 4 percent for those with income exceeding $100,000, and over 9 percent for those with income exceeding $1 million), cash-oriented businesses, real estate transactions, and estate- and gift-taxable transfers (as high as 20 percent)—are subject to much higher probabilities of audit.

The audit rate for corporations with at least $250 million in assets is about 27.5 percent, but the rate drops to about 2 percent for businesses with less than $10 million in assets. In the past few years, the IRS has stepped up its audit and enforcement activities and is targeting narrower issues that are projected to produce more revenue for the time spent. Thus, audit rates for large corporations have decreased although the dollars collected from such audits continue to increase.

Recently, much of the IRS's effort has been devoted to developing statutory and administrative requirements relative to information reporting and document matching. For instance, when a taxpayer engages in a like-kind exchange or sells a personal residence, various parties to the transaction are required to report the nature and magnitude of the transaction to the IRS. Later the Treasury's computers determine whether the transaction has been reported properly by comparing the information reported by the third parties with the events included on the relevant taxpayers' returns for the year.

FIGURE 17.1 IRS National Office Organization

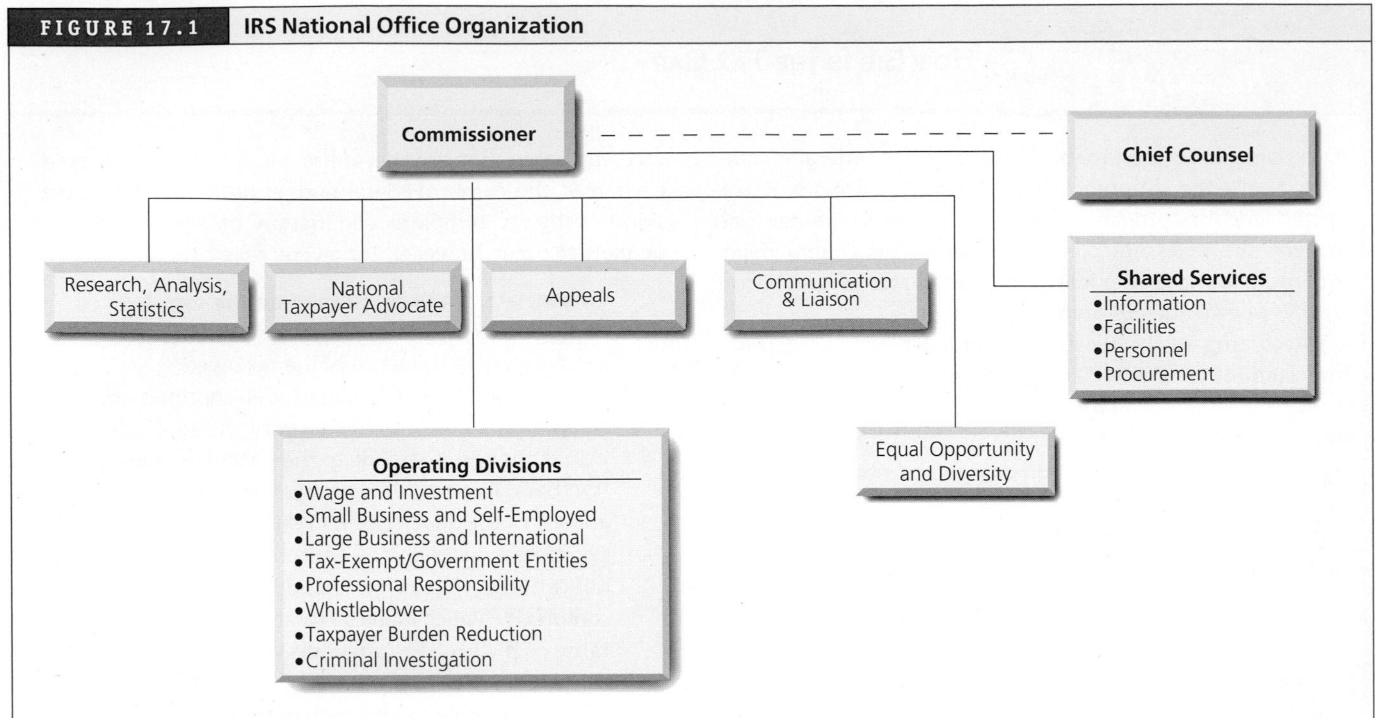

In addition, the IRS has been placing increasing pressure on the community of tax advisers. Severe penalties may be assessed on those who have prepared the appropriate return when the Service's interpretation of applicable law conflicts with that of the preparer.

The IRS processes about 145 million individual income tax returns every year, almost 95 million of which are filed electronically (i.e., known as **e-filing**). It collects about $2.5 trillion in annual tax revenues and pays refunds to about 100 million individual taxpayers every year. The average refund exceeds $3,000.

> **LO.1**
> Describe the organization and structure of the IRS.

ORGANIZATIONAL STRUCTURE OF THE IRS

The structure of the IRS is moving toward that illustrated in Figure 17.1. The IRS Commissioner, a presidential appointee, has organized the day-to-day operations of the agency into four divisions, based on the type of tax returns to be processed. Administrative functions, such as those relating to personnel and computer issues, are organized on a shared-services model, managed from the national office. Broader functions, such as litigation, investigations, and taxpayer relations, are managed at the national level as well.

The Chief Counsel, another presidential appointee, is the head legal officer of the IRS. The Chief Counsel's office provides legal advice to the IRS and guidance to the public on matters pertaining to the administration and enforcement of the tax laws. For instance, the Chief Counsel's duties include establishing uniform nationwide interpretive positions on the law, drafting tax guide material for taxpayers and IRS personnel, issuing technical rulings to taxpayers, and providing advice and technical assistance to IRS personnel. The Chief Counsel represents the IRS in all litigation before the Tax Court.

> **LO.2**
> Identify the various administrative pronouncements issued by the IRS and explain how they can be used in tax practice.

IRS PROCEDURE—LETTER RULINGS

When a tax issue is controversial or a transaction involves considerable tax dollars, the taxpayer often wishes to obtain either assurance or direction from the IRS as to the treatment of the event. The **letter ruling** process is an effective means of dealing directly with the IRS while in the planning stages of a large or otherwise important transaction.

Rulings issued by the National Office provide a written statement of the position of the IRS concerning the tax consequences of a course of action contemplated by the taxpayer. Letter rulings do not have the force and effect of law, but they do provide

TAX *in the NEWS*

IRS Audit Initiatives

The IRS's current audit initiatives seem to be aimed at chronic and high-risk noncompliance. In an age of shrinking real budget dollars for the Service, this "biggest bang for the buck" strategy may be appropriate. The Service seems to be hunting for annuities of tax dollars, rather than just maximizing current collections. For example, permanently adding a noncompliant taxpayer to the tax rolls can optimize the present value of revenue collections tied to the IRS's efforts.

Announced priority areas for the IRS audit staff include the following.

- Offshore credit card users.
- High-risk, high-income taxpayers.
- Tax shelters, abusive schemes, and their promoters.
- High-income nonfilers.
- Unreported income.
- Transfer pricing involving transactions between U.S. companies and their foreign affiliates.
- Employment taxes.
- Transfers of intangible assets to offshore affiliated companies.
- Executive compensation (particularly stock option transactions).
- Claims of the research credit.
- Abuse of the rules for tax-exempt entities.
- Further research as to audit initiatives.

The agency has stated that it is revising its training materials and case studies to reflect the revised priorities. "Hardball" techniques apparently will be used to deal with the priority issues. Such techniques include issuing summonses, obtaining injunctions, initiating civil audits for shelter participants, and pursuing criminal investigations of shelter promoters.

guidance and support for taxpayers in similar transactions. The IRS issues rulings only on uncompleted, actual (rather than hypothetical) transactions or on transactions that have been completed before the filing of the tax return for the year in question.

In certain circumstances, the IRS will not issue a ruling. It ordinarily will not rule in cases that essentially involve a question of fact.[1] For example, no ruling will be issued to determine whether compensation paid to employees is reasonable in amount and therefore allowable as a deduction.[2]

A letter ruling represents the current opinion of the IRS on the tax consequences of a transaction with a given set of facts. IRS rulings are not unchangeable. They frequently are declared obsolete or are superseded by new rulings in response to tax law changes. However, revocation or modification of a ruling usually is not applied retroactively to the taxpayer who received the ruling, if it was relied on in good faith and if the facts in the ruling request were in agreement with the completed transaction. The IRS may revoke any ruling if, upon subsequent audit, the agent finds a misstatement or omission of facts or substantial discrepancies between the facts in the ruling request and the actual situation.

A ruling may be relied upon only by the taxpayer who requested and received it. It must be attached to the tax return for the year in question.

Letter rulings benefit both the IRS and the taxpayer. Not only do they help promote a uniform application of the tax laws, but they may also reduce the potential for litigation or disputes with IRS agents. In addition, they make the IRS aware of significant transactions being consummated by taxpayers. A fee of $11,500 is charged for processing a ruling request; the fee is reduced to $625 if the taxpayer's income is less than $250,000.

IRS PROCEDURE—OTHER ISSUANCES

In addition to issuing unpublished letter rulings and published rulings and procedures, the IRS issues determination letters and technical advice memoranda.

A **determination letter** relates to a completed transaction when the issue involved is covered by judicial or statutory authority, Regulations, or rulings. Determination letters are issued for various estate, gift, income, excise, and employment tax matters.

[1] Rev.Proc. 2011–1, I.R.B. No. 1, 14.

[2] Rev.Proc. 2011–3, I.R.B. No. 1, 113.

EXAMPLE 1

True Corporation recently opened an auto care clinic and has employed numerous mechanics. The corporation is not certain whether its educational reimbursement plan is nondiscriminatory. True may request a determination letter. ■

EXAMPLE 2

Assume the same facts as in Example 1. True would like to establish a pension plan that qualifies for the tax advantages of § 401(k). To determine whether the plan qualifies, True should request and obtain a determination letter from the IRS. ■

EXAMPLE 3

A group of physicians plans to form an association to construct and operate a hospital. The determination letter procedure is appropriate to ascertain whether the group is subject to the Federal income tax or is tax-exempt. ■

A **technical advice memorandum (TAM)** is issued by the National Office to IRS personnel in response to a specific request by an agent, Appellate Conferee, or IRS executive. The taxpayer may request a TAM if an issue in dispute is not treated by the law or precedent and/or published rulings or Regulations. TAMs also are appropriate when there is reason to believe that the IRS is not administering the tax law consistently. For example, a taxpayer may inquire why an agent proposes to disallow a certain expenditure when agents in other parts of the country permit the deduction. Technical advice requests arise from the audit process, whereas ruling requests are issued before any IRS audit.

A technical expedited advice memorandum (TEAM) can be used during an office or field audit. The TEAM is designed to reflect the position of the IRS in a shorter time than a TAM otherwise would take. This quicker response time is possible because the following occur before a TEAM request is submitted.

- The taxpayer and the IRS agree to a set of facts for the case.
- The parties conduct a presubmission conference, with attorneys for both sides in attendance.
- Technology, including e-mails and faxes, is used to gather facts as part of the process.
- The IRS holds an internal strategic planning meeting, discussing potential responses to various holdings that could be issued as part of the TEAM.

ADMINISTRATIVE POWERS OF THE IRS

Examination of Records

The IRS can examine the taxpayer's books and records as part of the process of determining the correct amount of tax due. The IRS can also require the persons responsible for the return to appear and to produce any necessary books and records.[3] Taxpayers are required to maintain certain record-keeping procedures and retain the records necessary to facilitate the audit.

Burden of Proof

If the taxpayer meets the record-keeping requirement and substantiates income and deductions properly, the IRS bears the burden of proof in establishing a tax deficiency during litigation. The taxpayer must have cooperated with the IRS regarding reasonable requests for information, documents, meetings, and interviews. For individual taxpayers, the IRS's burden of proof extends to penalties and interest amounts that it assesses in a court proceeding with the taxpayer.[4]

Assessment and Demand

The Code permits the IRS to assess a deficiency and to demand payment for the tax. However, no assessment or effort to collect the tax may be made until 90 days after a statutory notice of a deficiency (a *90-day letter*) is issued. The taxpayer therefore has

[3] § 7602.

[4] §§ 7491(a)(1), (a)(2)(B), and (c).

TAX in the NEWS

Tax Preparation by the Numbers

The community of taxpayers and their tax preparers is extensive and increasingly is using electronic means to meet current filing requirements. The following summary is based on recent estimates.

Number of individuals who prepare Federal tax returns for a fee	**1 million**
Percentage of all Federal tax returns that were filed using computer software and/or a paid tax preparer	**80%**
Number of Federal tax returns filed by paid preparers using tax filing software	**62 million**
Number of self-prepared Federal tax returns filed by taxpayers using tax filing software	**32 million**
Number of unpaid volunteers who registered with the IRS to assist taxpayers with filing requirements	**80,000**

90 days to file a petition to the U.S. Tax Court, effectively preventing the deficiency from being assessed or collected pending the outcome of the case.[5]

Following assessment of the tax, the IRS issues a notice and demand for payment. The taxpayer is usually given 30 days after the notice and demand for payment to pay the tax.

If the IRS believes the assessment or collection of a deficiency is in jeopardy, it may assess the deficiency and demand immediate payment.[6] The taxpayer can avoid (*stay*) the collection of the jeopardy assessment by filing a bond for the amount of the tax and interest. This action prevents the IRS from selling any property it has seized.

Collection

If the taxpayer neglects or refuses to pay the tax after receiving the demand for payment, a lien in favor of the IRS is placed on all property (realty and personalty, tangible and intangible) belonging to the taxpayer.

The levy power of the IRS is very broad. It allows the IRS to garnish (*attach*) wages and salary and to seize and sell all nonexempt property by any means. After a 30-day notice period, the IRS can make successive seizures on any property owned by the taxpayer until the levy is satisfied.[7] A taxpayer's principal residence is exempt from the levy process, unless the disputed tax, interest, and penalty exceed $5,000 and a U.S. District Court judge approves of the seizure.[8]

THE AUDIT PROCESS

LO.3

Describe the audit process, including how returns are selected for audit and the various types of audits.

Selection of Returns for Audit

The IRS utilizes mathematical formulas to select tax returns that are most likely to contain errors and yield substantial amounts of additional tax revenues upon audit. The IRS does not disclose all of its audit selection techniques. However, some observations can be made regarding the probability of a return's selection for audit.

- Certain groups of taxpayers are subject to audit more frequently than others. These groups include individuals with gross income in excess of $100,000, self-employed individuals with substantial business income and deductions, and cash businesses where the potential for tax evasion is high.

EXAMPLE 4

Tracey owns and operates a liquor store. As nearly all of her sales are for cash, Tracey might be a prime candidate for an audit by the IRS. Cash transactions are easier to conceal than those made on credit. ■

- If a taxpayer has been audited in a past year and the audit led to the assessment of a substantial deficiency, the IRS often makes a return visit.

[5]§§ 6212 and 6213.

[6]§ 6861. A jeopardy assessment is appropriate, for instance, when the IRS fears that the taxpayer will flee the country or destroy valuable property.

[7]The taxpayer can keep certain personal and business property and a minimal amount of his or her income as a subsistence allowance, even if a lien is outstanding. § 6334.

[8]§§ 6334(a)(13)(A) and (e)(1).

- An audit might materialize if information returns (e.g., Form W–2, Form 1099) are not in substantial agreement with the income reported on the taxpayer's return. Obvious discrepancies do not necessitate formal audits and usually can be handled by correspondence with the taxpayer.
- If an individual's itemized deductions are in excess of norms established for various income levels, the probability of an audit increases. Certain deductions (e.g., casualty and theft losses, business use of the home, tax-sheltered investments) are sensitive areas, as the IRS realizes that many taxpayers determine the amount of the deduction incorrectly or may not be entitled to the deduction at all.
- The filing of a refund claim by the taxpayer may prompt an audit of the return.
- Some returns are selected because the IRS has targeted a specific industry or type of tax return for in-depth review. This enables examiners to develop special skills and interests applicable to those returns. In the Industry Specialization Program (ISP), returns might be selected from retailers, energy developers, or health care operations for special review. In the Market Segment Specialization Program (MSSP), specialized auditors focus on returns that show passive losses, involve construction activities, or include legal or consulting income.
- Information often is obtained from other sources (e.g., other government agencies, news items, informants). The IRS then applies its own judgment and experience, and it may audit the return to address such questions as: Why did dividend income increase so much this year? Why did mortgage interest payments decrease? How did the taxpayer pay for such a large vacation home, sold this year?

Many individual taxpayers mistakenly assume that if they do not hear from the IRS within a few weeks after filing their return or if they receive a refund check, no audit will be forthcoming. As a practical matter, most individual returns are examined about two years from the date of filing. If not, they generally remain unaudited. All large corporations, however, are subject to annual audits.

The IRS can pay rewards to persons who provide information that leads to the detection and punishment of those who violate the tax laws. The rewards are paid at the discretion of the IRS. Such a payment usually cannot exceed 15 percent of the taxes, fines, and penalties recovered as a result of such information.[9] About 500 rewards are paid in the typical year. The average reward paid is about $4,500.

Another IRS office, through the so-called **Whistleblower Program**, offers special rewards to informants who provide information concerning businesses or high-income (gross income exceeds $200,000) individuals, when more than $2 million of tax, penalty, and interest is at stake. Some informants claim that hundreds of millions of dollars of tax, penalty, and interest are due from allegedly noncompliant taxpayers. The reward can reach 30 percent of the amount collected by the Treasury and traceable to the whistleblower's information. The reward can be reduced if the whistleblower participated in the original understatement of tax. About 500 cases are initiated every year as a result of tips from whistleblowers.

The rewards are paid out of the taxes recovered under the informant and whistleblower programs. To claim a reward of this sort, an informant must file Form 211 with the IRS.

EXAMPLE 5

Phil reports to the police that burglars broke into his home while he was out of town and took a shoe box containing $25,000 in cash, among other things. A representative of the IRS reading the newspaper account of the burglary might wonder why Phil kept such a large amount of cash in a shoe box at home. ■

EXAMPLE 6

After 15 years, Betty is discharged by her employer, Dr. Franklin. Shortly thereafter, the IRS receives a letter from Betty stating that Franklin keeps two sets of books, one of which substantially understates his cash receipts. ■

[9] § 7623 and Reg. § 301.7623–1.

TAX *in the NEWS*

E-Filing the Form 1040

Roughly 70 percent of all Forms 1040 are filed electronically. Most of the e-filed returns are submitted by tax professionals, who often charge a processing fee of about $25 per return, or by individuals who use commercial or IRS software programs to submit the return.

The IRS encourages e-filing because the filing software eliminates math errors and clarifies ambiguous disclosures by the taxpayer. However, the labor unions that represent IRS employees maintain that paperless tax filing is putting their members' jobs at risk. In fact, the number of IRS personnel has shrunk by more than 10 percent in the last decade, and data processing centers have been downsized. Yet no government official admits that the growth of e-filing has contributed to this contraction.

Taxpayers like e-filing because the IRS processes their returns in less than half the time needed for traditional paper-based forms. Also, e-filing presents a "green" alternative, in that less paper, ink, and toner may be required. The taxpayer also avoids postage costs and the time spent waiting in line at the post office. By use of the direct deposit system for refunds, the taxpayer has quicker access to the funds. If the taxpayer owes taxes, most e-filing software also allows for a direct debit process.

Large C corporations have been required to e-file for many years, and electronic processing has been phased in for smaller businesses, trusts, and tax-exempt entities. The IRS is pressuring tax practitioners to eliminate their fees for filing tax returns electronically, especially for low-income taxpayers, and may soon provide its own filing portal to facilitate "free filing." Growth in the number of e-filed returns may come from those 40 million individuals who use preparation software and then mail the printed return to the IRS. Also, a new rule requiring all tax preparers who file more than 10 returns annually to use e-filing may result in about 15 million more e-filed returns.

The statistical models used by the IRS to select individual tax returns for audit come from random audits of a small number of taxpayers, who are required to document every entry that they made on the Form 1040. The latest round of these National Research Program (NRP) audits resulted in the construction of new Discriminant Function (DIF) scores that project the amount of revenue that the IRS will gain from pursuing tax returns with various statistical profiles. The higher the DIF score, the better the return to the IRS from pursuing the audit, and the higher the probability of selection for an examination.

These data-seeking audits are controversial and have led to taxpayer complaints to Congress about the stress that they create.[10] But the data from older DIF models no longer reflected the U.S. service-based, information-powered economy. Consequently, the underlying models require a more frequent updating for effective enforcement of the tax laws. The IRS believes that, by constantly updating the NRP data through a diligent review of randomly selected tax returns, changes in tax avoidance behaviors will be detected and fewer routine audits will be required.

Can the IRS Pretend to Be Your Friend?

Should IRS agents be allowed to identify audit subjects by reading the society page of the newspaper looking for indicators of wealth? What if the agency subscribes to Facebook and seeks comments from its "friends" as to income windfalls and stock market dealings? In the past, some state and local taxing agencies have used social networking sites for audit selection purposes. State and local revenue agents have used the sites to find self-employed individuals who advertise their business and report about upcoming income-producing events. The sites also have been used to determine whether a taxpayer who has requested an extension of time to pay a delinquent tax actually is strapped for cash.

Some state tax officials claim that looking for a taxpayer's self-declarations on a website is a much more efficient way to find income understatements than searching through most other sources of nonstatistical data. Should taxing agencies be using Google, Facebook, and other public-domain online sources of taxpayer information to help identify tax returns for audit?

[10]On average, the total annual NRP audit sample consists of 13,000 returns. Some of these returns are analyzed without contacting the taxpayer, and other taxpayers are contacted only by mail with queries about one or two items. Only a few returns are subjected to "line-by-line" review. Most of the returns are reviewed for a period of three tax years.

TABLE 17.1 IRS Audit Information by Type

	Conducted (Number)	Conducted (Percent)
Correspondence audit	1,125,000	69%
Office audit	50,000	3%
Field audit	450,000	28%

Verification and Audit Procedures

The filed tax return immediately is reviewed for mathematical accuracy. A check is also made for deductions, exclusions, etc., that are clearly erroneous. One obvious error would be the failure to comply with the 7.5 percent limitation on the deduction for medical expenses.

About 2 percent of all paper-filed individual returns show a math error. The math error rate for e-filed returns is only 0.1 percent. When a math or clerical error occurs, the Service Center merely sends the taxpayer revised computations and a bill or refund as appropriate.

Taxpayers usually are able to settle routine tax disputes (e.g., queries involving the documentation of deductions) through a by-mail-only *correspondence audit* with the IRS, without the necessity of a formal meeting.

Office audits are conducted in an office of the IRS. Individual returns with few or no items of business income are usually handled through the office audit procedure. In most instances, the taxpayer is required merely to substantiate a deduction, credit, or item of income that appears on the return. The taxpayer presents documentation in the form of canceled checks, invoices, etc., for the items in question.

The *field audit* procedure is commonly used for corporate returns and for returns of individuals engaged in business or professional activities. This type of audit generally involves a more complete examination of a taxpayer's transactions.

A field audit is conducted by IRS agents at the office or home of the taxpayer or at the office of the taxpayer's representative. The agent's work may be facilitated by a review of certain tax workpapers and discussions with the taxpayer's representative about items appearing on the tax return. Table 17.1 summarizes key audit information.

Prior to or at the initial interview, the IRS must provide the taxpayer with an explanation of the audit process that is the subject of the interview and describe the taxpayer's rights under that process. If the taxpayer clearly states at any time during the interview the desire to consult with an attorney, CPA, or enrolled agent or any other person permitted to represent the taxpayer before the IRS, then the IRS representative must suspend the interview.[11]

Any officer or employee of the IRS must, upon advance request, allow a taxpayer to make an audio recording of any in-person interview with the officer or employee concerning the determination and collection of any tax.[12]

Settlement with the Revenue Agent

Following an audit, the IRS agent may either accept the return as filed or recommend certain adjustments. The **Revenue Agent's Report (RAR)** is reviewed within the IRS. In most instances, the agent's proposed adjustments are approved.

Agents must adhere strictly to IRS policy as reflected in published rulings, Regulations, and other releases. The agent cannot settle an unresolved issue based upon the probability of winning the case in court. Usually, issues involving factual questions

[11] § 7521(b).

[12] § 7521(a).

can be settled at the agent level, and it may be advantageous for both the taxpayer and the IRS to reach agreement at the earliest point in the settlement process. For example, it may be to the taxpayer's advantage to reach agreement at the agent level and avoid any further opportunity for the IRS to raise new issues.

If agreement is reached upon the proposed deficiency, the taxpayer signs Form 870 (Waiver of Restrictions on Assessment and Collection of Deficiency in Tax). One advantage to the taxpayer of signing Form 870 at this point is that interest stops accumulating on the deficiency 30 days after the form is filed.[13] When this form is signed, the taxpayer effectively waives the right to receive a statutory notice of deficiency (90-day letter) and to subsequently petition the Tax Court. In addition, it is no longer possible for the taxpayer later to go to the IRS Appeals Division. The signing of Form 870 at the agent level generally closes the case. However, the IRS is not restricted by Form 870 and may assess additional deficiencies if deemed necessary.

THE TAXPAYER APPEAL PROCESS

LO.4

Explain the taxpayer appeal process, including various settlement options available.

If agreement cannot be reached at the agent level, the taxpayer receives a copy of the Revenue Agent's Report and a **30-day letter**. The taxpayer has 30 days to request an administrative appeal. If an appeal is not requested, a **90-day letter** is issued. Figure 17.2 illustrates the taxpayer's alternatives when a disagreement with the IRS persists.

A taxpayer who wishes to appeal must make an appropriate request to the Appeals Division. The request must be accompanied by a written protest except in the following cases.

- The proposed tax deficiency does not exceed $10,000 for any of the tax periods involved in the audit.
- The deficiency resulted from a correspondence or office audit (i.e., not as a result of a field audit).

The Appeals Division is authorized to settle all tax disputes based on the hazards of litigation (the chances of winning in court). Since the Appeals Division has final settlement authority until a 90-day letter has been issued, the taxpayer may be able to negotiate a settlement. In addition, an overall favorable settlement may be reached by "trading" disputed issues. The Appeals Division occasionally may raise new issues if the grounds are substantial and of significant tax impact.

Both the Appeals Division and the taxpayer have the right to request technical advice memoranda from the National Office of the IRS. A TAM that is favorable to the taxpayer is binding on the Appeals Division. Even if the TAM is favorable to the IRS, the Appeals Division may nevertheless settle the case based on the hazards of litigation.

EXAMPLE 7

At the time Terri is audited, the corporation that she controls had advances outstanding to her in the amount of $80,000. The IRS field agent held that these advances were constructive dividends to her (refer to the discussion in Chapter 5). Some facts point toward this result (e.g., the corporation is closely held, Terri has made no repayments, and the loan balance has increased over several years). Other facts, however, appear to indicate that these advances are bona fide loans (e.g., a written instrument provides for interest, Terri has the independent means of repayment, and the corporation has a good dividend-paying record).

The Appeals Division and Terri's representative assess the hazards of litigation as being 50% for each side. Thus, if Terri chooses to take the issue to court, she would have an even chance of winning or losing her case. Based on this assessment, both sides agree to treat $40,000 of the advance as a dividend and $40,000 as a bona fide loan. The agreement enables Terri to avoid $40,000 of dividend income (the loan portion) and saves her the cost of litigating the issue.

Thus, by going to the Appeals Division, Terri obtained a satisfactory settlement otherwise unobtainable from the agent. ■

[13] § 6601(c).

FIGURE 17.2 Income Tax Appeal Procedure

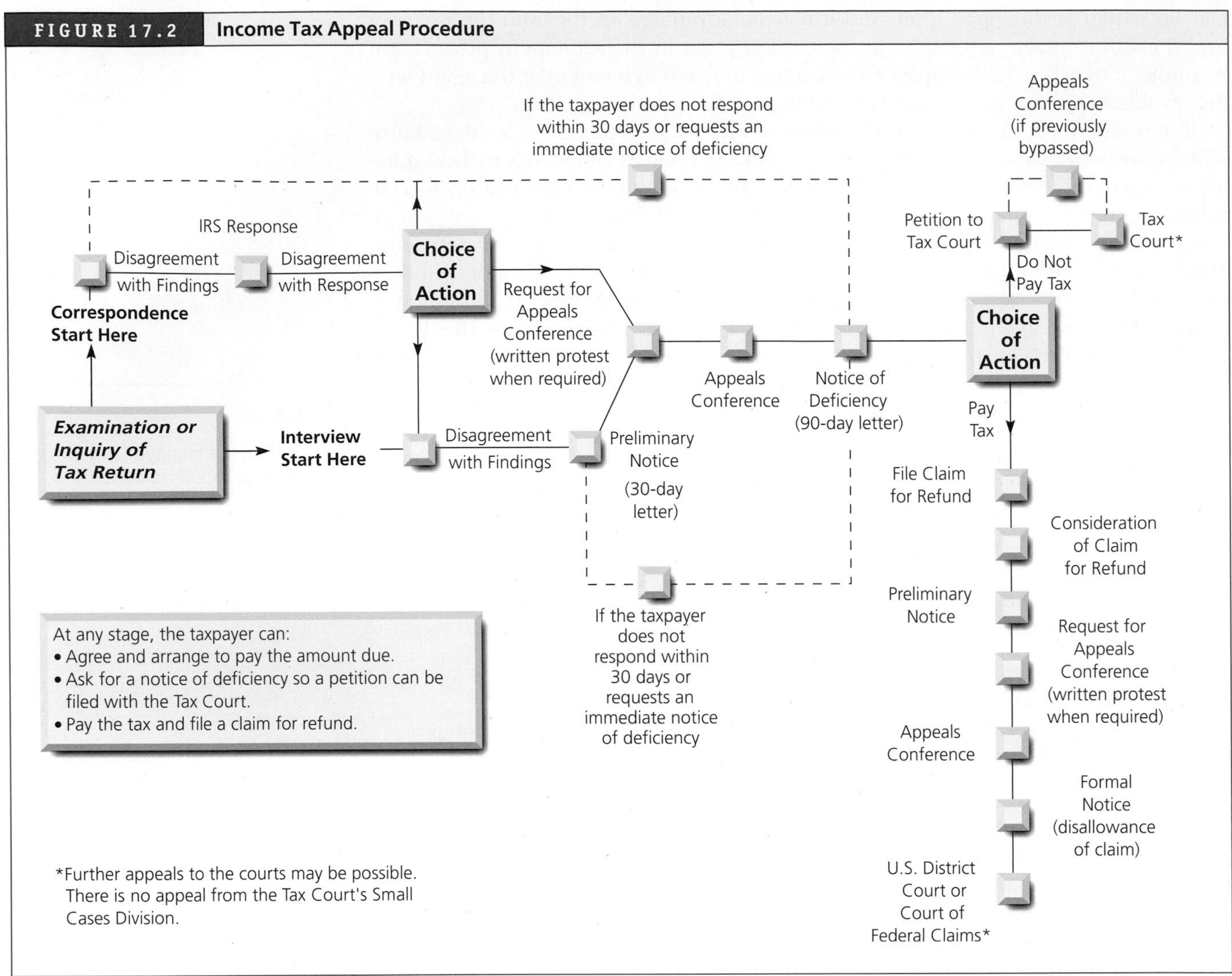

Taxpayers who file a petition with the U.S. Tax Court have the option of having the case heard before the more informal Small Cases Division if the amount of tax in dispute does not exceed $50,000.[14] If the Small Cases Division is used, neither party may appeal the case.

The economic costs of a settlement offer from the Appeals Division should be weighed against the costs of litigation and the probability of winning the case. The taxpayer also should consider the impact of the settlement upon the tax liability for future periods in addition to the years under audit.

If a settlement is reached with the Appeals Division, the taxpayer is required to sign Form 870–AD. Interest stops running on the deficiency when the Appeals Division accepts the Form 870–AD. According to the IRS, this settlement is binding upon both parties unless fraud, malfeasance, concealment, or misrepresentation of material fact has occurred.

OFFERS IN COMPROMISE AND CLOSING AGREEMENTS

The IRS can negotiate a compromise if the taxpayer's ability to pay the tax is doubtful. If the taxpayer is financially unable to pay the total amount of the tax, a Form 656 (Offer in Compromise) is filed. An **offer in compromise** is appropriate in the following circumstances.[15]

[14] § 7463(a).

[15] § 7122 and Reg. § 301.7122–1(b).

Our Taxing System of Self-Assessment

The United States is a large country of diverse taxpayers and businesses. Perhaps the only way that the massive dollar amounts of Federal income taxes can be collected on a timely basis is through a *self-assessment* process, whereby the taxpayer is charged with disclosing a full picture of the tax year's results and the corresponding computation of taxable income. But a system of self-assessment depends heavily on the honesty and integrity of the taxpayers, and their ability to know and comply with the pertinent tax rules.

A recent survey of taxpayer attitudes by the IRS Oversight Board revealed the following results.

Why Do You Report and Pay Your Taxes Honestly? (more than one answer allowed)

Taxpayer Responses	Taxpayers Mentioning This Reason (Percent)
My own personal integrity	81%
A third party reported my information to the IRS (e.g., through a Form W–2 or 1099), so I must match that amount in my tax form	40%
Fear of an audit	36%
My neighbors report and pay their taxes honestly, so I will too	23%

What Is an Acceptable Amount by Which to Cheat on Your Income Taxes?

	Taxpayers Responding (Percent)
Not at all	89%
A little here and a little there	6%
As much as possible	3%
Other answers	3%

Given the results of this survey, do you think the current self-assessment system is satisfactory? If not, should Congress create additional enforcement procedures to ensure taxpayer compliance? What sort of new reporting rules might be useful?

Source: *2008 Taxpayer Attitude Survey* (February 2009), at **www.ustreas.gov/irsob/reports/2009/IRSOB_2008-TAS.pdf**.

- There is doubt as to the taxpayer's liability for the tax (i.e., disputed issues still exist).
- There is doubt as to the collectibility of the tax (i.e., the taxpayer's net worth and earnings capacity are low).
- Payment of the disputed amount would constitute an economic hardship for the taxpayer. For instance, the taxpayer is incapable of earning a living because of a long-term illness or disability, or liquidation of the taxpayer's assets to pay the amount due would leave the taxpayer unable to meet basic living expenses.

The IRS investigates the offer by evaluating the taxpayer's financial ability to pay the tax. In some instances, the compromise settlement includes an agreement for final settlement of the tax through payments of a specified percentage of the taxpayer's future earnings. This settlement procedure usually entails lengthy negotiations with the IRS, but the presumption is that the agency will find terms upon which to enter into a compromise with the taxpayer. A 20 percent nonrefundable current payment is required to set up the compromise offer, and a $150 filing fee is required. Low-income individuals can apply for a waiver of the fee and of the 20 percent down payment.[16]

The IRS can agree to allow taxes to be paid on an installment basis if that arrangement facilitates the tax collection. An individual who has filed timely tax returns for five years is guaranteed the right to use an installment agreement when the amount in dispute does not exceed $10,000. The taxpayer uses Form 9465 to initiate an installment plan.

[16]Reg. § 300.3(b)(1)(ii). "Low-income" is defined as less than 250% of the Federal poverty level.

TAX *in* the NEWS

Late-Night Tax Advice

What are those people on late-night TV commercials talking about when they offer to handle your back taxes with the IRS or reduce your tax bill by half?

Most of these commercials that are trying to grab your attention are promoting tax resolution firms that will put together an offer in compromise for submission to the IRS. For a sometimes sizable up-front fee, a firm will carry out the filing process for an offer in compromise and suggest terms that may be acceptable to the IRS. Because the firm has experience with these arrangements, it can likely reach an agreement on the offer in a shorter time than a typical individual would require. Although tax resolution firms may be helpful in certain situations, the IRS has warned that some firms engage in poor business practices.

Rather than pursue an offer in compromise, a taxpayer might request an installment payment schedule from the IRS. The installment approach does not avoid taxes and interest, but it does buy time for the taxpayer by allowing affordable payments over an agreed-on period of time. Moreover, it avoids the sizable up-front fees that a tax resolution firm would charge for often unsatisfactory service.

The IRS provides an annual statement accounting for the status of the agreement. The agreement may later be modified or terminated because of (1) inadequate information, (2) subsequent change in financial condition, or (3) failure to pay an installment when due or to provide requested information.[17]

Every year, the IRS accepts about 10,000 offers in compromise, involving about $150 million in unpaid taxes, interest, and penalties.

A **closing agreement** is binding on both the taxpayer and the IRS except upon a subsequent showing of fraud, malfeasance, or misrepresentation of a material fact.[18] The closing agreement may be used when disputed issues carry over to future years. It may also be employed to dispose of a dispute involving a specific issue for a prior year or a proposed transaction involving future years. If, for example, the IRS is willing to make substantial concessions in the valuation of assets for death tax purposes, it may require a closing agreement from the recipient of the property to establish the income tax basis of the assets.

LO.5

Determine the amount of interest on a deficiency or a refund and when it is due.

INTEREST

Determination of the Interest Rate

Congress sets the interest rates applicable to Federal tax underpayments (deficiencies) and overpayments (refunds) close to the rates available in financial markets. The Code provides for the rates to be determined quarterly.[19] Thus, the rates that are determined during March are effective for the following April through June.

IRS interest is based on the Federal short-term rates published periodically by the IRS in Revenue Rulings. They are based on the average market yield on outstanding marketable obligations of the United States with remaining maturity of three years or less.

For noncorporate taxpayers, the interest rate applicable to *both* overpayments and underpayments is 3 percent for the first quarter of 2011. For most corporate taxpayers, the rate is 2 percent for overpayments and 3 percent for underpayments. Corporations with large overpayments or underpayments are subject to different rates.

Computation of the Amount of Interest

Interest is compounded daily.[20] Depending on the applicable interest rate, daily compounding can double the payable amount over a period of five to eight years.

Tables for determining the daily compounded amount are available from the IRS and on the Internet. The tables ease the burden of those who prepare late returns where additional taxes are due.[21]

[17] § 6159.
[18] § 7121(b).
[19] § 6621.
[20] § 6622.
[21] Rev.Proc. 95–17, 1995–1 C.B. 556.

IRS Deficiency Assessments

Interest usually accrues from the unextended due date of the return until 30 days after the taxpayer agrees to the deficiency by signing Form 870. If the taxpayer does not pay the amount shown on the IRS's notice and demand (tax bill) within 30 days, interest again accrues on the deficiency.

Refund of Taxpayer's Overpayments

If an overpayment is refunded to the taxpayer within 45 days after the date the return is filed or is due, no interest is allowed. When the taxpayer files an amended return or makes a claim for refund of a prior year's tax (e.g., when net operating loss carrybacks result in refunds of a prior year's tax payments), however, interest is authorized from the original due date of the return through the date when the amended return is filed. In general, taxpayers applying for refunds receive interest as follows.

- When a return is filed after the due date, interest on any overpayment accrues from the date of filing. However, no interest is due if the IRS makes the refund within 45 days of the date of filing.

EXAMPLE 8

Naomi, a calendar year taxpayer, files her 2010 return on December 1, 2011. The return reflects an overwithholding of $2,500. On June 8, 2012, Naomi receives a refund of her 2010 overpayment. Interest on the refund began to accrue on December 1, 2011 (not April 15, 2011). ■

EXAMPLE 9

Assume the same facts as in Example 8, except that the refund is paid to Naomi on January 5, 2012 (rather than June 8, 2012). No interest is payable by the IRS, since the refund was made within 45 days of the filing of the return. ■

- In no event will interest accrue on an overpayment unless the return that is filed is in "processible form." Generally, this means that the return must contain enough information in a readable format to enable the IRS to identify the taxpayer and to determine the tax (and overpayment) involved.
- In the case of a carryback (e.g., net operating loss, capital loss, tax credit), interest on any refund begins to accrue on the due date of the return (disregarding extensions) for the year in which the carryback arises. Even then, however, no interest accrues until a return is filed or, if the return has been filed, if the IRS pays the refund within 45 days.

EXAMPLE 10

Top Corporation, a calendar year taxpayer, incurs a net operating loss during 2010 that it can carry back to tax year 2008 and obtain a refund. On December 28, 2011, Top files a claim for refund. The earliest that interest can begin to accrue in this situation is March 16, 2011, but since the return was not filed until December 28, 2011, the later date controls. If, however, the IRS pays the refund within 45 days of December 28, 2011, no interest need be paid. ■

TAXPAYER PENALTIES

LO.6

Discuss the various penalties that can be imposed on acts of noncompliance by taxpayers and return preparers.

To promote and enforce taxpayer compliance with the U.S. voluntary self-assessment system of taxation, Congress has enacted a comprehensive array of penalties.

Tax penalties may involve both criminal and civil offenses. Criminal tax penalties are imposed only after the usual criminal process, in which the taxpayer is entitled to the same constitutional guarantees as nontax criminal defendants. Normally, a criminal penalty provides for imprisonment. Civil tax penalties are collected in the same manner as other taxes and usually provide only for monetary fines. Criminal and civil penalties are not mutually exclusive; therefore, both types of sanctions may be imposed on a taxpayer.

The Code characterizes tax penalties as additions to tax; thus, they cannot subsequently be deducted by the taxpayer.

Ad valorem penalties are additions to tax that are based upon a percentage of the owed tax. *Assessable penalties,* on the other hand, typically include a flat dollar amount. Assessable penalties are not subject to review by the Tax Court, but ad valorem penalties are subject to the same deficiency procedures that apply to the underlying tax.

Failure to File and Failure to Pay

For a failure to file a tax return by the due date (including extensions), a penalty of 5 percent per month (up to a maximum of 25 percent) is imposed on the amount of tax shown as due on the return, with a minimum penalty amount of $135.[22] If the failure to file is attributable to fraud, the penalty becomes 15 percent per month, to a maximum of 75 percent of the tax.[23]

For a failure to pay the tax due as shown on the return, a penalty of 0.5 percent per month (up to a maximum of 25 percent) is imposed on the amount of the tax. The penalty is doubled if the taxpayer fails to pay the tax after receiving a deficiency assessment.

In all of these cases, a fraction of a month counts as a full month. These penalties relate to the net amount of the tax due.

Obtaining an extension for filing a tax return does not by itself extend the date by which the taxes due must be paid. Thus, an application for an extended due date for a tax return almost always is accompanied by a payment by the taxpayer of a good faith estimate of the taxes that will be owed with the return when it is filed by the extended due date. If the taxpayer does not make such a good faith estimate and payment, the extension itself may be voided by the IRS (e.g., when the return is filed by the extended due date with a much larger amount due than had been estimated).

EXAMPLE 11

Conchita uses an automatic six-month extension for the filing of her 2011 tax return. Thus, the return is due on October 15, 2012, not on April 15. Conchita's application for the extension includes a $5,000 check, the amount that she estimates her 2011 return will show as owing for the year when she files it in October. ■

During any month in which both the failure to file penalty and the failure to pay penalty apply, the failure to file penalty is reduced by the amount of the failure to pay penalty.

EXAMPLE 12

Jason files his tax return 10 days after the due date. Along with the return, he remits a check for $4,000, which is the balance of the tax he owes. Disregarding any interest liabilities, Jason's total penalties are as follows.

Failure to pay penalty (0.5% × $4,000)		$ 20
Failure to file penalty (5% × $4,000)	$200	
Less: Failure to pay penalty for the same period	20	
Failure to file penalty		180
Total penalties		$200

The penalties for one full month are imposed even though Jason was delinquent by only 10 days. Unlike the method used to compute interest, any part of a month is treated as a whole month. ■

These penalties can be avoided if the taxpayer shows that the failure to file and/or failure to pay was due to reasonable cause and not due to willful neglect. The

[22]§ 6651(a). The minimum penalty cannot exceed the amount of tax due on the return.

[23]§ 6651(f).

Code is silent as to what constitutes reasonable cause, and the Regulations do little to clarify this important concept.[24] Reasonable cause for failure to pay is presumed under the automatic six-month extension (Form 4868) when the additional tax due is not more than 10 percent of the tax liability shown on the return. In addition, the courts have ruled on some aspects of **reasonable cause**.

- Reasonable cause was found where the taxpayer relied on the advice of a competent tax adviser given in good faith, the facts were fully disclosed to the adviser, and he or she considered that the specific question represented reasonable cause.[25] No reasonable cause was found, however, where the taxpayer delegated the filing task to another, even when that person was an accountant or an attorney.[26]
- Among the reasons not qualifying as reasonable cause were lack of information on the due date of the return,[27] illness that did not incapacitate a taxpayer from completing a return,[28] refusal of the taxpayer's spouse to cooperate for a joint return,[29] and ignorance or misunderstanding of the tax law.[30]

Accuracy-Related Penalties

Major civil penalties relating to the accuracy of tax return data, including misstatements stemming from taxpayer negligence and improper valuation of income and deductions, are coordinated under the umbrella term **accuracy-related penalties.**[31] This consolidation of related penalties into a single levy eliminates the possibility that multiple penalties will apply to a single understatement of tax.

The accuracy-related penalties each amount to 20 percent of the portion of the tax underpayment that is attributable to one or more of the following infractions.

- Negligence or disregard of rules and regulations.
- Substantial understatement of tax liability.
- Substantial valuation overstatement.
- Substantial valuation understatement.

The penalties apply only where the taxpayer fails to show a *reasonable basis* for the position taken on the return.[32]

Negligence

For purposes of this accuracy-related penalty, **negligence** includes any failure to make a reasonable attempt to comply with the provisions of the tax law. The penalty also applies to any disregard (whether careless, reckless, or intentional) of rules and regulations.[33] The penalty can be avoided upon a showing of reasonable cause and that the taxpayer acted in good faith.[34]

The negligence penalty applies to *all* taxes, except when fraud is involved. A negligence penalty may be assessed when the taxpayer fails to report gross income, overstates deductions, or fails to keep adequate records. When the taxpayer takes a nonnegligent position on the return that is contrary to a judicial precedent or published pronouncement of the IRS, the penalty is waived if the taxpayer has a

---

[24] Reg. § 301.6651–1(c)(1) likens reasonable cause to the exercise of "ordinary business care and prudence" on the part of the taxpayer.

[25] *Estate of Norma S. Bradley*, 33 TCM 70, T.C.Memo. 1974–17.

[26] *U.S. v. Boyle*, 85–1 USTC ¶13,602, 55 AFTR 2d 85–1535, 105 S.Ct. 687 (USSC, 1985). This rule appears to apply to electronic as well as paper-based return filings, to employment as well as income taxes, and to returns where the tax preparer himself or herself commits a fraudulent act. *Brandon R. Ballantyne*, 99 TCM 1523, T.C.Memo. 2010–125; *McNair Eye Center, Inc.*, 99 TCM 1345, T.C.Memo. 2010–81. Knowledgeable taxpayers, like a tax attorney, are held to a higher standard in determining negligence. *Pelton & Gunther P.C.*, 78 TCM 578, T.C.Memo. 1999–339. A taxpayer might be negligent if, when a complicated tax issue is involved, a tax expert is *not* consulted. *Zmuda v. Comm.*, 84-1 USTC ¶9,442, 53 AFTR 2d 84–1269, 731 F.2d 1417 (CA–9, 1984).

[27] *Beck Chemical Equipment Co.*, 27 T.C. 840 (1957).

[28] *Alex and Tonya Oria*, 94 TCM 170, T.C.Memo. 2007–276, and *Babetta Schmidt*, 28 T.C. 367 (1957). Compare *Estate of Kirchner*, 46 B.T.A. 578 (1942).

[29] *Electric and Neon, Inc.*, 56 T.C. 1324 (1971).

[30] *Stevens Brothers Foundation, Inc.*, 39 T.C. 93 (1965).

[31] § 6662.

[32] Reg. § 1.6662–3(b)(3). Most tax professionals measure this standard as a 20% probability of prevailing in court.

[33] § 6662(c). There can be no intentional disregard of the rules where the underlying law is unclear, complex, or subject to disagreement. *James J. Freeland*, 51 TCM 253, T.C.Memo. 1986–10, and *Lansdown v. Comm.*, 96–1 USTC ¶50,025, 77 AFTR 2d 96–491, 73 F.3d 373 (CA–10, 1996).

[34] § 6664(c)(1).

reasonable basis for the interpretation and has disclosed the disputed position on Form 8275.

Substantial Understatement of Tax Liability

The understatement penalty is designed to strike at middle- and high-income taxpayers who are tempted to play the so-called audit lottery.[35] Some taxpayers take questionable and undisclosed positions on their tax returns in the hope that the return will not be selected for audit. Disclosing the positions would have called attention to the return and increased the probability of audit.

A substantial understatement of a tax liability transpires when the understatement exceeds the larger of 10 percent of the tax due or $5,000. For a C corporation, a substantial understatement is the lesser of the following.[36]

- 10 percent of the tax due, but at least $10,000.
- $10 million.

The understatement to which the penalty applies is the difference between the amount of tax required to be shown on the return and the amount of tax actually shown on the return.

The penalty is avoided under any of the following circumstances.[37]

- The taxpayer has **substantial authority** for the treatment.
- There is a *reasonable basis* for the tax return position, which is adequately disclosed in the return by attaching Form 8275.

Penalty for Overvaluation

The objective of the overvaluation penalty is to deter taxpayers from inflating values (or basis), usually of charitable contributions of property, to reduce income taxes.[38]

- The penalty is 20 percent of the additional tax that would have been paid had the correct valuation (or basis) been used.
- The penalty applies only when the valuation (or basis) used by the taxpayer is 150 percent or more of the correct valuation (or basis). The penalty is doubled if the valuation error is *gross* (overstated by 200 percent or more).
- The penalty applies only when the resulting income tax underpayment exceeds $5,000 ($10,000 for C corporations).

EXAMPLE 13

Gretchen (a calendar year taxpayer) purchased a painting for $10,000. When the painting is worth $18,000 (as later determined by the IRS), Gretchen donates the painting to an art museum. Based on the appraisal of a cousin who is an amateur artist, she deducts $40,000 for the donation. Since Gretchen was in the 30% tax bracket, overstating the deduction by $22,000 results in a tax underpayment of $6,600.

Gretchen's penalty for overvaluation is $2,640, or *double* the regular penalty of $1,320 (20% × $6,600 underpayment). ■

The substantial valuation overstatement penalty is avoided if the taxpayer can show reasonable cause and good faith. However, when the overvaluation involves *charitable deduction property*, the taxpayer must substantiate both of the following.

- The claimed value of the property is based on a qualified appraisal made by a qualified appraiser.
- The taxpayer made a good faith investigation of the value of the contributed property.[39]

[35] § 6662(b)(2).

[36] § 6662(d)(1).

[37] § 6662(d)(2)(B). Substantial authority is measured as of either the last day of the tax year to which the return relates or the date that the return was filed. Reg. § 1.6662–4(d)(3)(iv)(C).

[38] §§ 6662(b)(3), (e), and (h).

[39] §§ 6664(c)(2) and (3).

Based on these criteria, Gretchen in Example 13 would find it difficult to avoid the penalty. A cousin who is an amateur artist does not meet the definition of a qualified appraiser. Likewise, Gretchen apparently has not made her own good faith investigation of the value of the contributed property.

Penalty for Undervaluation

When attempting to minimize the income tax, it is to the benefit of taxpayers to *overvalue* deductions. When attempting to minimize transfer taxes (estate and gift taxes), however, executors and donors may be inclined to *undervalue* the assets transferred. A lower valuation reduces estate and gift taxes. An accuracy-related penalty is imposed for substantial estate or gift tax valuation understatements.[40] As with other accuracy-related penalties, reasonable cause and good faith on the part of the taxpayer are a defense.

- The penalty is 20 percent of the additional transfer tax that would have been due had the correct valuation been used on Form 706 (estate tax return) or Form 709 (gift and generation-skipping tax return).
- The penalty applies only if the value of the property claimed on the return is 65 percent or less than the amount determined to be correct. The penalty is doubled if the reported valuation error is *gross* (reported value is 40 percent or less than the correct determination).
- The penalty applies only to an additional transfer tax liability in excess of $5,000.

GOOD FAITH VALUATIONS

When dealing with the undervaluation penalty, the tax adviser may shift from being in adversarial alliance with the taxpayer to being a mediator for the court. Good faith value estimates, especially for family-owned businesses, can easily vary by as much as the 65 percentage points specified for the penalty. Even a gross undervaluation can occur when someone in the business other than the donor or decedent is a particularly talented entrepreneur, an effective sales representative, and/or the founder of the company; similarly, a business may be substantially undervalued when a minority equity interest is involved, or an intangible asset conveys a sizable nominal amount of goodwill to the valuation.

Because most taxpayers are highly averse to incurring any nondeductible penalties, the client may be tempted to compromise on the business valuation "too soon" (i.e., when the return is filed), eliminating any possibility of a more favorable valuation being presented before the Appeals Division or a court. Keeping in mind all of the potential taxpayer and preparer penalties that might apply, the tax professional should stick with a good faith appraisal of the business value, no matter what its nominal amount.

How would you react if your client, a composer, wanted to deduct $100,000 for the contribution of an obscure manuscript to the Symphony Society? What if your (first) appraiser placed the value of the manuscript at $15,000? What course of action would you propose to the client concerning the deduction? Any consequent penalties?

Appraiser's Penalty

When a valuation penalty arises because of the taxpayer's reliance on an appraisal, a further penalty can apply.[41] If the appraiser knew or reasonably should have known that the appraisal would be used as part of a tax or refund computation and that the appraised value more likely than not was improper, then the appraiser pays a penalty equal to the lesser of:

- 10 percent of the tax understatement, but at least $1,000, or
- 125 percent of the gross income received by the appraiser from the engagement (e.g., the appraisal fee collected).

This amount is in addition to the taxpayer's valuation penalty as discussed above.

[40] §§ 6662(b)(5), (g), and (h).

[41] § 6695A.

Penalty for Improper Refund Claim

Whenever a taxpayer files a claim for a tax refund and the refund claim later is found to exceed the final amount allowed by the IRS or a court, a penalty of 20 percent of the disallowed refund results.[42] The penalty is waived if the taxpayer can show a *reasonable basis* for the refund claim (i.e., probably a 20 percent chance that a court would allow the refund). This penalty is meant to discourage the taxpayer from overstating the amount of the refund requested from the IRS. It does not apply to claims for the earned income tax credit.

Civil Fraud Penalty

A 75 percent civil penalty is imposed on any underpayment resulting from **fraud** by the taxpayer who has filed a return.[43] For this penalty, the burden of proof *is on the IRS* to show by a preponderance of the evidence that the taxpayer had a specific intent to evade a tax.

Once the IRS initially has established that fraud has occurred, the taxpayer then bears the burden of proof to show by a preponderance of the evidence the portion of the underpayment that is not attributable to fraud.

Although the Code and Regulations do not provide any assistance in ascertaining what constitutes civil fraud, it is clear that mere negligence on the part of the taxpayer (however great) will not suffice. Fraud has been found in cases of manipulations of the books, substantial omissions from income, and erroneous deductions.[44]

EXAMPLE 14

Frank underpaid his income tax by $90,000. The IRS can prove that $60,000 of the underpayment was due to fraud. Frank responds by a preponderance of the evidence that $30,000 of the underpayment was not due to fraud. The civil fraud penalty is $45,000 (75% × $60,000). ■

If the underpayment of tax is partially attributable to negligence and partially attributable to fraud, the fraud penalty is applied first.

Failure to Pay Estimated Taxes

A penalty is imposed for a failure to pay estimated income taxes. The penalty applies to individuals and corporations and is based on the rate of interest in effect for deficiency assessments.[45] The penalty also applies to trusts and certain estates that are required to make estimated tax payments. The penalty is not imposed if the tax due for the year (less amounts withheld and credits) is less than $500 for corporations, $1,000 for all others. For employees, an equal part of withholding is deemed paid on each due date.

Quarterly payments are to be made on or before the fifteenth day of the fourth month (April 15 for a calendar year taxpayer), sixth month, ninth month, and the first month of the following year. Corporations must make the last quarterly payment by the twelfth month of the same year.

An individual's underpayment of estimated tax is the difference between the estimates that were paid and the least of:

- 90 percent of the current-year tax,
- 100 percent of the prior-year tax (the tax year must have been a full 12 months, and a return must have been filed), and
- 90 percent of the tax that would be due on an annualized income computation for the period running through the end of the quarter.

If the taxpayer's prior-year AGI exceeds $150,000, the 100 percent requirement becomes 110 percent.

[42] § 6676.

[43] § 6663. As noted later in the chapter, underpayments traceable to fraudulent acts are not subject to a statute of limitations.

[44] *Dogget v. Comm.*, 60–1 USTC ¶9342, 5 AFTR 2d 1034, 275 F.2d 823 (CA–4, 1960); *Harvey Brodsky*, 21 TCM 578, T.C.Memo. 1962–105; and *Lash v. Comm.*, 57–2 USTC ¶9725, 51 AFTR 492, 245 F.2d 20 (CA–1, 1957).

[45] §§ 6655 (corporations) and 6654 (other taxpayers). Other computations can avoid the penalty. See §§ 6654(d)(2) and (k), 6655(e) and (i).

A corporation's underpayment of estimated tax is the difference between the estimates that were paid and the least of (1) the current-year tax, (2) the prior-year tax, and (3) the tax on an annualized income computation using one of three methods of computation sanctioned by the Code. For the prior-year alternative, (1) the prior tax year must have been a full 12 months, (2) a nonzero tax amount must have been generated for that year, and (3) large corporations (taxable income of $1 million or more in any of the three immediately preceding tax years) can use the alternative only for the first installment of a year.

In computing the penalty, Form 2210 (Underpayment of Estimated Tax by Individuals) or Form 2220 (Underpayment of Estimated Tax by Corporations) is used.

False Information with Respect to Withholding

Withholding from wages is an important element of the Federal income tax system, which is based on a pay-as-you-go approach. One way employees might hope to avoid this withholding would be to falsify the information provided to the employer on Form W–4 (Employee Withholding Allowance Certificate). For example, by overstating the number of exemptions, income tax withholdings could be reduced or completely eliminated.

To encourage compliance, a civil penalty of $500 applies when a taxpayer claims withholding allowances based on false information. The criminal penalty for willfully failing to supply information or for willfully supplying false or fraudulent information in connection with wage withholding is an additional fine of up to $1,000 and/or up to one year of imprisonment.[46]

Failure to Make Deposits of Taxes and Overstatements of Deposits

When a business is not doing well or cash-flow problems develop, employers have a great temptation to "borrow" from Uncle Sam. One way this can be done is to fail to pay to the IRS the amounts that have been withheld from the wages of employees for FICA and income tax purposes. The IRS does not appreciate being denied the use of these funds and has a number of weapons at its disposal to discourage the practice.

- A penalty of up to 15 percent of any underdeposited amount not paid, unless the employer can show that the failure is due to reasonable cause and not to willful neglect.[47]
- Various criminal penalties.[48]
- A 100 percent penalty if the employer's actions are willful.[49] The penalty is based on the amount of the tax evaded (i.e., not collected, or not accounted for or paid over). Since the penalty is assessable against the "responsible person" of the business, more than one party may be vulnerable (e.g., the president and treasurer of a corporation). Although the IRS may assess the penalty against several persons, it cannot collect more than the 100 percent due.
- In addition to these penalties, the actual tax due must be remitted. For instance, an employer remains liable for the employees' income and payroll taxes that should have been paid.

Failure to Provide Information Regarding Tax Shelters

The IRS has identified over two dozen transactions that it regards as "tax shelters." These arrangements, often involving leveraged financing and accelerated interest and cost recovery deductions, allegedly are motivated solely by the desire to reduce taxes and have no business or profit-seeking goals. Over the last two decades, the IRS has struggled with numerous means of identifying taxpayers who use such tax shelters.

[46] §§ 6682 and 7205.

[47] § 6656.

[48] See, for example, § 7202 (willful failure to collect or pay over a tax).

[49] § 6672.

A tax shelter organizer must register the shelter with the IRS before any sales are made to investors.[50] A penalty of up to $10,000 is assessed if the required information is not filed with the Service. This includes a description of the shelter and the tax benefits that are being used to attract investors. The shelter organizer must maintain a list of identifying information of all its investors. Failure to fully and truthfully maintain the list can result in a penalty of up to $100,000 per investment.

Criminal Penalties

In addition to civil fraud penalties, the Code contains numerous criminal sanctions that carry various monetary fines and/or imprisonment. The difference between civil and criminal fraud is often one of degree. Thus, § 7201, dealing with attempts to evade or defeat a tax, contains the following language.

> Any person who *willfully* attempts in any manner to evade or defeat any tax imposed by this title or the payment thereof shall, in addition to other penalties provided by law, be guilty of a felony and, upon conviction thereof, shall be fined not more than $100,000 ($500,000 in the case of a corporation), or imprisoned not more than five years, or both, together with the costs of prosecution. [Emphasis added.]

As to the burden of proof, the IRS must show that the taxpayer was guilty of willful evasion "beyond the shadow of any reasonable doubt." Thus, to avoid a criminal tax penalty, the taxpayer needs to create a degree of reasonable doubt as to guilt. To do so, the taxpayer might assert that he or she was confused or ignorant about the application of the tax law or relied on the erroneous advice of a competent tax adviser. Another defense against a criminal tax penalty is the lack of capacity to plan and carry out tax evasion (e.g., mental disease or other medical disorder).

Violations of the Federal criminal code in the context of filing tax returns also may arise from other crimes that are not provided for in the Internal Revenue Code. Examples include:

- Making a false claim against the Federal government.
- Participating in a conspiracy to evade Federal taxes (i.e., in addition to the tax understatement).
- Making a false statement to the Federal government or filing a false document (i.e., perjury).

LO.7

Understand the rules governing the statute of limitations on assessments and on refunds.

STATUTES OF LIMITATIONS

A **statute of limitations** defines the period of time during which one party may pursue against another party a cause of action or other suit allowed under the governing law. Failure to satisfy any requirement provides the other party with an absolute defense should the statute be invoked. Inequity would result if no limits were placed on such suits. Permitting an extended period of time to elapse between the initiation of a claim and its pursuit could place the defense at a serious disadvantage. Witnesses may have died or disappeared; records or other evidence may have been discarded or destroyed.

Assessment and the Statute of Limitations

In general, any tax that is imposed must be assessed within three years of the filing of the return (or, if later, the unextended due date of the return).[51] Some exceptions to this three-year limitation exist.

- If no return is filed or a fraudulent return is filed, assessments can be made at any time. There is, in effect, no statute of limitations in these cases.
- If a taxpayer omits an amount of gross income in excess of 25 percent of the gross income stated on the return, the statute of limitations is increased to six years. The courts have interpreted this rule as including only items affecting income and not the omission of items affecting deductions,

[50] § 6111.

[51] §§ 6501(a) and (b)(1).

operating losses, or cost of sales.[52] *Gross income* here includes capital gains, but not reduced by capital losses.

EXAMPLE 15

During 2006, Jerry had the following income transactions (all of which were duly reported on his timely filed return).

Gross receipts		$ 480,000
Cost of sales		(400,000)
Net business income		$ 80,000
Capital gains and losses		
Capital gain	$ 36,000	
Capital loss	(12,000)	24,000
Total income		$ 104,000

Jerry retains your services in 2011 as a tax consultant. It seems that he inadvertently omitted some income on his 2006 return and he wishes to know if he is "safe" under the statute of limitations. The six-year statute of limitations would apply, putting Jerry in a vulnerable position only if he omitted more than $129,000 on his 2006 return [($480,000 + $36,000) × 25%]. ■

- The statute of limitations may be extended for a fixed period of time by mutual consent of the IRS and the taxpayer. This extension covers a definite period and is made by signing Form 872 (Consent to Extend the Time to Assess Tax). The extension is frequently requested by the IRS when the lapse of the statutory period is imminent and the audit has not been completed. This practice often is applied to audits of corporate taxpayers and explains why many corporations have more than three "open years."

Special rules relating to assessment are applicable in the following situations.

- Taxpayers may request a prompt assessment of the tax, forcing the IRS to examine a return.
- The assessment period for capital loss and net operating loss carrybacks generally relates to the determination of tax in the year of the loss or unused credit rather than in the carryback years.

If the IRS issues a statutory notice of deficiency to the taxpayer, who then files a Tax Court petition, the statute is suspended on both the deficiency assessment and the period of collection until 60 days after the decision of the Tax Court becomes final. The statute also is suspended when the taxpayer is "financially disabled"; that is, the taxpayer has been rendered unable to manage his or her financial affairs by a physical or mental impairment that is likely to last for a year or more or to cause the taxpayer's death. The statute continues to run if another party is authorized to act for the taxpayer in financial matters.[53]

Refund Claims and the Statute of Limitations

To receive a tax refund, the taxpayer is required to file a valid refund claim. The official form for filing a claim is Form 1040X for individuals and Form 1120X for corporations. If the refund claim does not meet certain procedural requirements, the IRS may reject the claim with no consideration of its merit.

- A separate claim must be filed for each taxable period.
- The grounds for the claim must be stated in sufficient detail.
- The statement of facts must be sufficient to permit the IRS to evaluate the merits of the claim.

[52] *The Colony, Inc. v. Comm.*, 58–2 USTC ¶9593, 1 AFTR 2d 1894, 78 S.Ct. 1033 (USSC, 1958).

[53] Suspension of the statute of limitations has been allowed by some courts when attributable to a taxpayer disability or IRS misconduct. See *Brockamp v. Comm.*, 97–1 USTC ¶50,216, 79 AFTR 2d 97–986, 117 S.Ct. 849 (USSC, 1997). §§ 6501(c)(4) and 6511(h).

The refund claim must be filed within three years of the filing of the tax return or within two years following the payment of the tax if this period expires on a later date.[54]

EXAMPLE 16

On March 10, 2009, Louise filed her 2008 income tax return reflecting a tax of $10,500. On July 11, 2010, she filed an amended 2008 return showing an additional $3,000 of tax that was then paid. On May 19, 2012, she filed a claim for refund of $4,500.

Assuming that Louise is correct in claiming a refund, how much tax can she recover? The answer is only $3,000. Because the claim was not filed within the three-year statute of limitations period, Louise is limited to the amount she actually paid during the last two years. ■

Special rules are available for claims relating to bad debts and worthless securities. A seven-year period of limitations applies in lieu of the normal three-year rule.[55] The extended period is provided in recognition of the inherent difficulty of identifying the exact year in which a bad debt or security becomes worthless.

17.2 The Tax Profession and Tax Ethics

LO.8

Summarize the legal and ethical guidelines that apply to those engaged in tax practice.

Society and its governments expect taxpayers to comply with the letter and the spirit of the tax laws. Tax audits and penalties encourage a high degree of technical tax conformity, but the proper functioning of a voluntary tax compliance system also depends on the ethics of the taxpayer and the tax adviser.

The Treasury and various professional organizations have issued ethical guidelines that are relevant to the tax profession. Professional licensing agencies also are likely to require tax professionals to receive training in ethics to obtain initial certification and to remain in good standing over time.

THE TAX PROFESSIONAL

Who is a tax practitioner? What services does the practitioner perform? A number of different groups apply constraints on the way that a tax professional conducts his or her practice.

To begin defining the term *tax practitioner*, one should consider whether the individual is qualified to practice before the IRS. Generally, practice before the IRS is limited to CPAs, attorneys, and persons who have been enrolled to practice before the IRS (**enrolled agents [EAs]**). In most cases, EAs are admitted to practice only if they pass an examination administered by the IRS. CPAs and attorneys are not required to take this examination and are automatically admitted to practice if they are in good standing with the appropriate licensing board regulating their profession.

Persons other than CPAs, attorneys, and EAs may be allowed to practice before the IRS in limited situations. **Circular 230** ("Rules Governing the Practice of Attorneys and Agents Before the Internal Revenue Service") issued by the Treasury Department permits certain notable exceptions.

- A taxpayer may always represent himself or herself. A person may also represent a member of the immediate family if no compensation is received for such services.
- Regular full-time employees may represent their employers.
- Corporations may be represented by any of their bona fide officers.
- Partnerships may be represented by any of the partners.
- Trusts, receiverships, guardianships, or estates may be represented by their trustees, receivers, guardians, or administrators or executors.

[54]§§ 6511(a) and 6513(a).

[55]§ 6511(d)(1).

- A taxpayer may be represented by whoever prepared the return for the year in question. However, such representation cannot proceed beyond the agent level.

EXAMPLE 17

Joel is currently undergoing audit by the IRS for tax years 2010 and 2011. He prepared the 2010 return himself but paid AddCo, a bookkeeping service, to prepare the 2011 return. AddCo may represent Joel only in matters concerning 2011. However, even for 2011, AddCo would be unable to represent Joel at an Appeals Division proceeding. Joel could, of course, represent himself, or he could retain a CPA, attorney, or EA to represent him in matters concerning both years under examination. ■

All nonattorney tax practitioners should avoid becoming engaged in activities that constitute the *unauthorized practice of law*. If they engage in this practice (e.g., by drafting legal documents for a third party), action could be instituted against them in the appropriate state court by the local or state bar association. What actions constitute the unauthorized practice of law is largely undefined, though, and such charges are filed only rarely today.

LICENSING TAX PREPARERS

There are no minimum education or experience requirements for those who file Federal tax returns for others. But the IRS does require that all paid tax return preparers, including CPAs and attorneys, obtain a Preparer Tax Identification Number (PTIN) before they assist taxpayers with returns for a new filing season.

For most preparers, the fee to obtain PTINs is about $65 per year. This amount is in addition to any other professional, certification, or licensing fee that the preparer might be required to pay (e.g., annual dues to maintain a CPA certificate).

Preparers (other than CPAs, attorneys, and enrolled agents) must pass an annual qualifying exam, designed to evaluate their familiarity with new tax laws and filing requirements that will apply for the filing season.

Efforts to "register" or "certify" tax preparers have been advocated for at least three decades, but to no avail. Increased regulation developed to govern other aspects of financial and consumer affairs led to the PTIN system effective for the 2011 filing season. The year's PTIN usually is obtained online, and confirmation of the preparer's identity, prior registrations, and testing status is needed before the PTIN is issued or renewed.

The IRS may use PTIN data to identify preparers who commit a pattern of errors or who participate in fraudulent actions. With more than 1 million paid preparers at work in any filing season, the IRS must use an outside consultant to manage the registration and testing functions.

IRS RULES GOVERNING TAX PRACTICE

Circular 230 prescribes the rules governing practice before the IRS. The following are some of the most important rules imposed on CPAs, attorneys, EAs, and all others who prepare tax returns for compensation.

- A prohibition against taking a position on a tax return unless there is a *realistic possibility* of the position being sustained on its merits. Generally, the realistic possibility standard is met when a person knowledgeable in the tax law would conclude that the position has at least a one-in-three probability of prevailing in the court of final jurisdiction.
- A prohibition against taking frivolous tax return positions. A **frivolous return** is one with a less than 5 percent chance of being sustained by the court of final jurisdiction.
- A requirement that nonfrivolous tax return positions that fail the realistic possibility standard be disclosed in the return (i.e., using Form 8275).

EXAMPLE 18
THE BIG PICTURE

Return to the facts of *The Big Picture* on p. 17–2. Campbell wants to claim the research credit for a testing program that it has developed, to be used by its in-house engineers before a new GPS app is released to the public. Based on their tax research on this issue, the members of your firm's tax department have severe doubts about taking the credit for this program. Your firm's position is that there is a one-in-four chance that the courts would allow Campbell's credit.

Claiming the credit fails the realistic possibility standard of Circular 230. Therefore, if Campbell claims the credit, you must insist that its Form 1120 include a separate disclosure on the return, probably using Form 8275. ■

- A requirement to inform clients of penalties likely to apply to return positions and of ways such penalties can be avoided.
- A requirement to make known to a client any error or omission the client may have made on any return or other document submitted to the IRS.
- A duty to submit, in a timely fashion, records or information lawfully requested by the IRS.
- An obligation to exercise *due diligence* and to use the *best practices* of the tax profession in preparing, reviewing, and filing tax returns accurately. Best practices include, for instance, the tax professional's use of appropriate software, a thorough office procedure for receiving and processing client tax returns, and the execution of a plan for continuing education in technical tax matters.
- A restriction against unreasonably delaying the prompt disposition of any matter before the IRS.
- A restriction against charging the client a contingent fee for preparing an original return, although such a fee can be charged when the tax professional deals with an audited or amended return.
- A restriction against charging the client "an unconscionable fee" for representation before the IRS.
- A restriction against representing clients with conflicting interests.

Nothing prevents the "unlicensed" tax practitioner from advertising his or her specialty, directly soliciting clients, or engaging in other actions that are regulated by the standards of conduct controlling CPAs, attorneys, and EAs. Nevertheless, some constraints do govern all parties engaged in rendering tax returns for the general public.

- A person who holds himself or herself out to the general public as possessing tax expertise could be liable to the client if services are performed in a negligent manner. At a minimum, the practitioner is liable for any interest and penalties the client incurs because of the practitioner's failure to exercise due professional care.
- If a practitioner agrees to perform a service (e.g., prepare a tax return) and subsequently fails to do so, the aggrieved party may be in a position to obtain damages for breach of contract.
- All persons who prepare tax returns or refund claims for a fee must sign as preparer of the return.[56] Failure to comply with this requirement could result in a penalty assessment against the preparer.
- The Code prescribes various penalties for the deliberate filing of false or fraudulent returns. These felonies apply to a tax practitioner who either was aware of the situation or actually perpetrated the false information or the fraud.[57]

[56]Reg. § 1.6065–1(b)(1). Rev.Rul. 84–3, 1984–1 C.B. 264, contains a series of examples illustrating when a person is deemed to be a preparer of the return.

[57]§ 7206.

TAX *in* *the NEWS*

Have You Been Drafted by the IRS?

With the accumulation of tax preparer penalties over the years, many tax professionals now feel that they have been "deputized" by the IRS and that, as a consequence, their ability to advise and represent their clients in an aggressive manner is limited. Has the potential for providing effective tax planning diminished as a result of the increased regulation of the tax and accounting profession, the additional disclosures that the tax practitioner must make to the client and to the government, and the severity of preparer penalties?

Not so, according to the IRS. Its objective is to "ensure that attorneys, accountants, and other tax practitioners adhere to professional standards and follow the law." Here are some specific items from the IRS's plan to raise the level of tax ethics found in tax practice today.

- Strengthen ties with practitioners to achieve the highest level of professional integrity and improve tax compliance.
- Establish and communicate clear, robust, current, and meaningful standards of conduct for tax practitioners.
- Establish and maintain a vigorous, targeted, and effective system of practitioner oversight.
- Establish and administer a fair, diligent, and effective system of sanctions for practitioners who fail to observe standards of conduct.

- Penalties are prescribed for tax practitioners who disclose to third parties information they have received from clients in connection with the preparation of tax returns or the rendering of tax advice.[58]

EXAMPLE 19

Sarah operates a tax return preparation service. Her brother-in-law, Butch, has just taken a job as a life insurance salesman. To help Butch find contacts, Sarah furnishes him with a list of the names and addresses of all of her clients who report AGI of $50,000 or more. Sarah is subject to the disclosure penalty. ■

PREPARER PENALTIES

The Code provides penalties to discourage improper actions by tax practitioners. **Tax preparer** penalties are assessed on any person who prepares for compensation, or engages employees to prepare, a substantial portion of any Federal tax return or refund claim. The following individuals are exempt from the preparer penalties.

- An IRS employee.
- A volunteer who prepares tax returns in a government assistance effort such as Tax Counseling for the Elderly (TCE) or the Volunteer Income Tax Assistance (VITA) program.
- An employee preparing a return for the employer.
- A fiduciary preparing a return for a trust or estate.
- An individual who provides only data processing, typing, reproduction, or other assistance in preparing a return.

The preparer penalties are applied on a "one preparer per firm, per filing position" basis, so penalty dollars can compound quickly within the tax practice. Some of the most important tax preparer penalties include the following.

1. A penalty for understatements due to taking an **unreasonable position** on a tax return.[59] The penalty is imposed if the tax position:

[58] § 7216.

[59] § 6694(a). For the most part, these standards match those that apply to the taxpayer penalties of § 6662(d). Stricter disclosure standards apply for tax shelter items and reportable transactions. § 6662A.

- Is not disclosed on the return and there was no *substantial authority* (i.e., a greater than 40 percent chance) that the tax position would be sustained by its merits on a final court review; or
- Is disclosed on the return and there was not a *reasonable basis* (i.e., probably a 20 percent chance) for the position.

The penalty is computed as the greater of $1,000 or one-half of the income of the practitioner that is attributable to the return or claim that violated the conduct standard. The penalty can be avoided by showing reasonable cause and by showing that the preparer acted in good faith.

EXAMPLE 20

Josie is the tax return preparer for Hal's Form 1040. The return includes a deduction that has a 60% chance of being sustained on its merits because it is contrary to an applicable tax Regulation. If a court denies the deduction, Josie is not assessed a § 6694 penalty.

Now assume that Hal's deduction has a 30% chance of being sustained on its merits. If a court denies the deduction, Josie is assessed a § 6694 penalty (unless the disputed position was disclosed on the return with a Form 8275–R). The amount of the penalty is the greater of $1,000 or one-half of Josie's fees for preparing Hal's Form 1040.

What if Hal's deduction has a 15% chance of being sustained on its merits? If a court denies the deduction, Josie is assessed a § 6694 penalty (even if the disputed position was disclosed on the return with a Form 8275–R). The amount of the penalty is the greater of $1,000 or one-half of Josie's fees for preparing Hal's Form 1040. ■

2. A penalty for willful and reckless conduct.[60] The penalty applies if any part of the understatement of a taxpayer's liability on a return or claim for refund is due to:

   - The preparer's willful attempt to understate the taxpayer's tax liability in any manner.
   - Any reckless or intentional disregard of IRS rules or regulations by the preparer.

   The penalty is computed as the greater of $5,000 or one-half of the income of the practitioner that is attributable to the return or claim that violated the conduct standard. Adequate disclosure can avoid the penalty. If both this penalty and the unreasonable position penalty (see item 1 above) apply to the same return, the reckless conduct penalty is reduced by the amount of the penalty for unreasonable positions.
3. A $1,000 ($10,000 for the tax returns of corporations) penalty per return or document is imposed against persons who aid in the preparation of returns or other documents that they know (or have reason to believe) would result in an understatement of the tax liability of another person.[61] Thus, this penalty also applies to those other than the preparer of the actual tax return (e.g., unpaid advisers, attorneys, corporate officers and executives, and tax shelter promoters). Clerical assistance in the return preparation process does not incur the penalty.

   If this penalty applies, neither the unreasonable position penalty (item 1) nor the willful and reckless conduct penalty (item 2) is assessed.
4. A $50 penalty is assessed against the preparer for failure to sign a return or furnish the preparer's PTIN.[62]
5. A $50 penalty is assessed if the preparer fails to furnish a copy of the return or claim for refund to the taxpayer.
6. A $500 penalty may be assessed if a preparer endorses or otherwise negotiates a check for refund of tax issued to the taxpayer.

[60] § 6694(b).

[61] § 6701.

[62] § 6695.

PRIVILEGED COMMUNICATIONS

Communications between an attorney and client have long been protected from disclosure to other parties (such as the IRS and the tax courts). A similar privilege of confidentiality extends to tax advice between a taxpayer and tax practitioner, as we used that term above. The privilege is not available for matters involving criminal charges or questions brought by other agencies, such as the Securities and Exchange Commission.[63] Nor is it allowed in matters involving promoting or participating in tax shelters.

A taxpayer likely will want to protect documents such as the tax adviser's research memo detailing the strengths and weaknesses of a tax return position or a conversation about an appeals strategy. The confidentiality privilege should be interpreted in the following manner.

- The privilege often is available when an attorney or CPA completes a tax return for the taxpayer. But some courts have restricted the attorney's privilege in this context on the grounds that the tax professional is conducting accounting work, not offering legal advice. Others assert that the confidentiality privilege is waived when the taxpayer discloses financial data on the tax return. To the contrary, if the tax professional is providing traditional legal advice to help the client decide what to disclose on a tax return, the privilege should be available.
- The privilege for CPAs applies only to tax advice. Attorneys still can exercise the privilege concerning advice rendered as a business consultant, estate/financial planner, and so on.
- About a third of the states offer a similar confidentiality privilege for CPAs, but outside the Federal tax appeals process, protection is not yet the norm.
- The privilege is not available for tax accrual workpapers prepared as part of an independent financial audit.

Thus, the CPA needs to exercise care to ensure that the privilege of confidentiality will apply to his or her tax work. Taking the following steps can help.

- Segregate the time spent and documents produced in rendering services for tax compliance from the time and documents devoted to tax advice. Doing this will protect the privilege from being waived as to the tax advice.
- Explain the extent of the privilege to the client—specify what will and will not be protected from the IRS in a dispute.
- Do not inadvertently waive the privilege, say, by telling "too much" to the IRS or to a third party who is not protected by the privilege.
- Indemnify the CPA for time spent protecting and enforcing the privilege once it is challenged.

AICPA STATEMENTS ON STANDARDS FOR TAX SERVICES

Tax practitioners who are CPAs, attorneys, or EAs must abide by the codes or canons of professional ethics applicable to their respective professions. The various codes and canons have much in common with and parallel the standards of conduct set forth in Circular 230.[64]

The AICPA has issued a series of Statements on Standards for Tax Services (SSTSs). The Statements are enforceable standards of professional practice for AICPA members working in state or Federal tax practice. The SSTSs comprise part of the AICPA's Code of Professional Conduct. Together with the provisions of Circular 230 and the penalty provisions of the Code, the SSTSs make up a set of guidelines for the conduct of the tax practitioner who is also a CPA. Other sources of

[63] § 7525(a)(1).

[64] For an additional discussion of tax ethics, see Raabe, Whittenburg, Sanders, and Sawyers, *Federal Tax Research*, 9th ed. (Cengage Learning/South-Western, 2012), especially Chapters 1 and 14.

Where Does My Cost Saving Go?

As is the case in many other U.S. industries, tax return preparers have been outsourcing some of their operations to lower-cost locations overseas. By some estimates, almost a million state and Federal tax returns are completed in India alone, and all such estimates are probably understated because of a lack of disclosure by tax practitioners.

Circular 230 does not prohibit outsourcing, and the IRS does not even require a disclosure by the tax preparer when it occurs. Tax and consulting firms defend the practice as a cost-saving measure and contend that the confidentiality of taxpayer data is not compromised.

AICPA ethics rules (applying both to tax return preparation and other work) require:

- Notice to the taxpayer before any data are shared with a third-party service provider.
- Acceptance by the practitioner of full responsibility for the third party's work (i.e., as to quality and security).

Should any cost saving that outsourcing provides be passed on to the client in the form of lower fees? Do you expect this will occur?

descriptions of professional ethics are issued by state bar associations and CPA societies, the American Bar Association, and the associations of enrolled agents.

Key provisions of some of the SSTSs are presented below.

Statement No. 1: Tax Return Positions

Under certain circumstances, a CPA may take a position that is contrary to that taken by the IRS. To do so, however, the CPA must have a good faith belief that the position has a realistic possibility (i.e., probably a one-in-three chance) of being sustained administratively or judicially on its merits if challenged. If the taxing authority (say, a state revenue statute) uses a lower standard than that of a *realistic possibility*, this higher standard still applies.

The client should be fully advised of the risks involved and the penalties that may result if the position taken on the tax return is not successful. The client should also be informed that disclosure on the return may avoid some or all of these penalties.

In no case, though, should the CPA exploit the audit lottery. That is, the CPA should not take a questionable position based on the probabilities that the client's return will not be chosen by the IRS for audit. Furthermore, the CPA should not "load" the return with questionable items in the hope that they might aid the client in a later settlement negotiation with the IRS.

EXAMPLE 21
THE BIG PICTURE

Return to the facts of *The Big Picture* on p. 17-2. Campbell's new marketing program solicits the opinions of a virtual focus group to test ideas for new products. Based on your tax research, you believe that because the program relies on innovative algorithms that use online contacts to carry out the focus group activities, the program might qualify for the Federal income tax research credit even though it involves marketing research that is excluded from the credit under § 41(d)(4). Still, you believe that there is only a 30% chance that the courts would allow the credit.

You meet with Shelly Watkins, Campbell's tax director, to convey the results of your research. Watkins agrees that the research credit would be turned down by an IRS auditor, but she says that Campbell never has been audited and that it is not likely to be audited as long as its legal structure and income levels do not significantly change. Watkins believes that Campbell's corporate officers will sign off on the credit, given both the firm's weak cash position and the low chances that the item will be discovered.

As a CPA, you must inform Campbell that claiming the credit for this activity does not have a realistic possibility of being sustained on its merits, and that certain penalties will be assessed if the credit is claimed and not further disclosed on the return.

Whether the credit is claimed is the decision of your client, the taxpayer. But if Campbell wants to claim the credit without the required additional disclosures, you must terminate your engagement with Campbell, under the SSTS and other AICPA provisions. ■

Statement No. 2: Questions on Returns

A CPA should make a reasonable effort to obtain from the client, and provide, appropriate answers to all questions on a tax return before signing as preparer. Reasonable grounds may exist for omitting an answer.

- The information is not readily available, and the answer is not significant in amount in computing the tax.
- The meaning of the question as it applies to a particular situation is genuinely uncertain.
- The answer to the question is voluminous.

The fact that an answer to a question could prove disadvantageous to the client does not justify omitting the answer.

Statement No. 3: Procedural Aspects of Preparing Returns

In preparing a return, a CPA may in good faith rely without verification on information furnished by the client or by third parties. However, the CPA should make reasonable inquiries if the information appears to be incorrect, incomplete, or inconsistent. In this regard, the CPA should refer to the client's returns for prior years whenever appropriate.

EXAMPLE 22

A CPA normally can take a client's word for the validity of dependency exemptions. But suppose a recently divorced client wants to claim his three children as dependents when he does not have custody. You must act in accordance with § 152(e)(2) in preparing the return, and this will require evidence of a waiver by the custodial parent. Without this waiver, you should not claim the dependency exemptions on your client's tax return. ■

EXAMPLE 23

While preparing Sunni's income tax return for 2011, you review her income tax return for 2010. In comparing the dividend income reported on the 2010 Schedule B with that received in 2011, you note a significant decrease. Further investigation reveals the variation is due to a stock sale in 2011 that was unknown to you until now. Thus, the review of the 2010 return has unearthed a transaction that should be reported on the 2011 return. ■

If the Code or Regulations require certain types of verification (as is the case with travel and entertainment expenditures), the CPA must advise the client of these rules. Further, inquiry must be made to ascertain whether the client has complied with the verification requirements.

Statement No. 4: Estimates

A CPA may prepare a tax return using estimates received from a taxpayer if it is impracticable to obtain exact data. The estimates must be reasonable under the facts and circumstances as known to the CPA. When estimates are used, they should be presented in such a manner as to avoid the implication of greater accuracy than exists.

Statement No. 5: Recognition of Administrative Proceeding or Court Decision

As facts may vary from year to year, so may the position taken by a CPA. In these types of situations, the CPA is not bound by an administrative or judicial proceeding involving a prior year.

EXAMPLE 24

Upon audit of Ramon Corporation's income tax return for 2009, the IRS disallowed $78,000 of the $600,000 salary paid to its president and sole shareholder on the grounds that it is unreasonable. You are the CPA who has been engaged to prepare Ramon's income tax return for 2011. Again the corporation paid its president a salary of $600,000 and chose to deduct this amount. Because you are not bound for 2011 by what the IRS deemed reasonable for 2009, the full $600,000 can be claimed as a salary deduction. ■

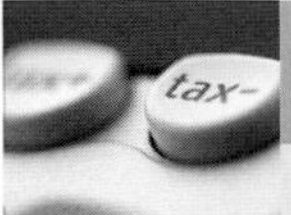

CONCEPT SUMMARY 17.1

Tax Profession and Ethics

1. The Internal Revenue Service (IRS) enforces the tax laws of the United States. Its size and form of organization reflect its various responsibilities relative to taxpayer interaction, litigation, and collection, as well as its internal functions.
2. The IRS issues various pronouncements in communicating its position on certain tax issues. These pronouncements promote the uniform enforcement of the tax law among taxpayers and among the internal divisions of the IRS. Taxpayers should seek such rulings and memoranda when the nature or magnitude of a pending transaction requires a high degree of certainty in the planning process.
3. IRS audits can take several forms. Taxpayers are selected for audit based on the probable net dollar return to the Treasury from the process. Offers in compromise and closing agreements can be a useful means of completing an audit without resorting to litigation.
4. Certain IRS personnel are empowered to consider the hazards of litigation in developing a settlement with the taxpayer during the audit process.
5. The IRS pays interest to taxpayers on overpaid taxes, starting essentially 45 days after the due date of the return, in amounts tied to the Federal short-term rate. Interest paid to the IRS on underpayments is similarly based on the Federal rate, starting essentially on the due date of the return. Interest for both purposes is compounded daily.
6. The Treasury assesses penalties when the taxpayer fails to file a required tax return or pay a tax. Penalties also are assessed when an inaccurate return is filed due to negligence or other disregard of IRS rules. Tax preparers are subject to penalties for assisting a taxpayer in filing an inaccurate return, failing to follow IRS rules in an appropriate manner, or mishandling taxpayer data or funds.
7. Statutes of limitations place outer boundaries on the timing and amounts of proposed amendments to completed tax returns that can be made by the taxpayer or the IRS.
8. Tax practitioners must operate under constraints imposed on them by codes of ethics or pertinent professional societies and by Treasury Circular 230. These rules also define the parties who can represent others in an IRS proceeding.
9. A limited privilege of confidentiality exists between the taxpayer and tax preparer.

Statement No. 6: Knowledge of Error

A CPA should promptly advise a client upon learning of an error in a previously filed return or upon learning of a client's failure to file a required return. The advice can be oral or written and should include a recommendation of the corrective measures, if any, to be taken. The error or other omission should not be disclosed to the IRS without the client's consent.

If the past error is material and is not corrected by the client, the CPA may be unable to prepare the current year's tax return. This situation might occur if the error has a carryover effect that prevents the CPA from determining the correct tax liability for the current year.

EXAMPLE 25

In preparing a client's 2011 income tax return, you discover that final inventory for 2010 was materially understated. First, you should advise the client to file an amended return for 2010 reflecting the correct amount in final inventory. Second, if the client refuses to make this adjustment, you should consider whether the error will preclude you from preparing a substantially correct return for 2011. Because this will probably be the case (the final inventory for 2010 becomes the beginning inventory for 2011), you should withdraw from the engagement.

If the client corrects the error, you may proceed with the preparation of the tax return for 2011. You must assure yourself that the error is not repeated. ■

Statement No. 7: Advice to Clients

In providing tax advice to a client, the CPA must use judgment to assure that the advice reflects professional competence and appropriately serves the client's needs.

No standard format or guidelines can be established to cover all situations and circumstances involving written or oral advice by the CPA.

The CPA may communicate with the client when subsequent developments affect previous advice on significant matters. However, the CPA cannot be expected to assume responsibility for initiating the communication, unless he or she is assisting a client in implementing procedures or plans associated with the advice. The CPA may undertake this obligation by specific agreement with the client.

TAX PLANNING:
17.3 Strategies in Seeking an Administrative Ruling

DETERMINATION LETTERS

In many instances, the request for an advance ruling or a determination letter from the IRS is a necessary or desirable planning strategy. The receipt of a favorable ruling or determination reduces the risk associated with a transaction when the tax results are in doubt. For example, the initiation or amendment of a qualified pension or profit sharing plan should be accompanied by a determination letter. Otherwise, on subsequent IRS review, the plan may not qualify, and the tax deductibility of contributions to the plan will be disallowed. In some instances, the potential tax effects of a transaction are so numerous and of such consequence that proceeding without a ruling is unwise.

LETTER RULINGS

In some cases, it may not be necessary or desirable to request an advance ruling. For example, it generally is not desirable to request a ruling if the tax results are doubtful and the company is committed to complete the transaction in any event. If a ruling is requested and negotiations with the IRS indicate that an adverse determination will be forthcoming, it is usually possible to have the ruling request withdrawn. However, the National Office of the IRS may forward its findings, along with a copy of the ruling request, to local IRS personnel. In determining the advisability of a ruling request, the taxpayer should consider the potential exposure of other items in the tax returns of all "open years."

A ruling request may delay the consummation of a transaction if the issues are novel or complex. Frequently, a ruling can be processed within six months, although in some instances a delay of a year or more may be encountered.

TECHNICAL ADVICE MEMORANDA

A taxpayer in the process of contesting a proposed deficiency with the Appeals Division should consider requesting a technical advice memorandum from the IRS. If the memorandum is favorable to the taxpayer, it is binding on the Appeals Division. The request may be particularly appropriate when the practitioner feels that the agent or Appeals Division has been too literal in interpreting an IRS ruling.

17.4 Considerations in Handling an IRS Audit

As a general rule, a taxpayer should attempt to settle disputes at the earliest possible stage of the administrative appeal process. It usually is possible to limit the scope of the examination by furnishing pertinent information requested by the agent.

Extraneous information or fortuitous comments may result in the opening of new issues and should be avoided. Agents usually appreciate prompt and efficient responses to inquiries, since their performance may in part be judged by their ability to close or settle assigned cases.

To the extent possible, it is advisable to conduct the investigation of field audits in the practitioner's office, rather than the client's office. This procedure permits greater control over the audit investigation and facilitates the agent's review and prompt closure of the case.

Many practitioners feel that it is generally not advisable to have clients present at the scheduled conferences with the agent, since the client may give emotional or gratuitous comments that impair prompt settlement. If the client is not present, however, he or she should be advised of the status of negotiations. The client makes the final decision on any proposed settlement.

SHOULD THE CLIENT ATTEND AN AUDIT?

Whether the client should be present during an audit is a matter of some debate. Certainly, the client's absence tends to slow down the negotiating process because the taxpayer must make all final decisions on settlement terms and is the best source of information for open questions of fact. Nevertheless, most practitioners discourage their clients from attending audits or conferences with the Appeals Division involving an income tax dispute. Ignorance of the law and of the conventions of the audit process can make the taxpayer a "loose cannon" that can do more harm than good if unchecked. All too often, a client will "say too much" in the presence of a government official.

In reality, though, by discouraging clients from attending the audit, practitioners may be interfering with the IRS's function of gathering evidence, depending on what precisely the taxpayer is being prevented from saying. To many practitioners, a "wrong" answer is one that increases taxes, not one that misrepresents the truth. A popular saying among tax advisers is "Don't tell me more than I want to know." Although this philosophy is supportable under various professional codes of conduct, it is hardly defensible in the larger scheme of things.

In your opinion, under what circumstances should the client attend such a session? To what degree should the tax professional "coach" the client as to how to behave in that setting? Or do a taxpayer's rights include the right to increase his or her own tax liability?

PREPARING FOR THE AUDIT

The tax professional must prepare thoroughly for the audit or Appeals proceeding. Practitioners often cite the following steps as critical to such preparations. Carrying out a level of due diligence in preparing for the proceeding is part of the tax professional's responsibility in representing the client.

- Make certain that both sides agree on the issues to be resolved in the audit. The goal here is to limit the agent's list of open issues.
- Identify all of the facts underlying the issues in dispute, including those favorable to the IRS. Gather evidence to support the taxpayer's position, and evaluate the evidence supporting the other side.
- Research current tax law authorities as they bear on the facts and open issues. Remember that the IRS agent is bound only by Supreme Court cases and IRS pronouncements. Determine the degree of discretion that the IRS is likely to have in disposing of the case.
- Prepare a list of points supporting and contradicting the taxpayer's case. Include both minor points bearing little weight and core principles. Short research memos also will be useful in the discussion with the agent. Points favoring the taxpayer should be mentioned during the discussion and "entered into the record."
- Prepare tax and interest computations showing the effects of points that are in dispute, so that the consequences of closing or compromising an issue can be readily determined.

- Determine a "litigation point" (i.e., at which the taxpayer will withdraw from further audit negotiation and pursue the case in the courts). This position should be based on the dollars of tax, interest, and penalty involved, the chances of prevailing in various trial-level courts, and other strategies discussed with the taxpayer. One must have an "end game" strategy for the audit, and thorough tax research is critical in developing that position in this context.

OFFERS IN COMPROMISE

Both parties to a tax dispute may find a compromise offer useful because it conclusively settles all of the issues covered by the agreement and may include a favorable payment schedule for the taxpayer.

On the other hand, several attributes of an offer in compromise may work to the detriment of the taxpayer. Just as the IRS no longer can raise new issues as part of the audit proceedings against the taxpayer, he or she cannot contest or appeal any such agreement. As part of the offer process, the taxpayer must disclose all relevant finances and resources, including details he or she might not want the government to know, and an up-front down payment will be due. Furthermore, both parties are bound to the filing positions established by the compromise for five tax years, a level of inflexibility that may work against a taxpayer whose circumstances change over time.

DOCUMENTATION ISSUES

The tax practitioner's workpapers should include all research memoranda, and a list of resolved and unresolved issues should be continually updated during the course of the IRS audit. Occasionally, agents request access to excessive amounts of accounting data in order to engage in a so-called fishing expedition. Providing blanket access to working papers should be avoided. Workpapers should be reviewed carefully to minimize opportunities for the agent to raise new issues not otherwise apparent. It is generally advisable to provide the agent with copies of specific workpapers upon request.

In unusual situations, a Special Agent may appear to gather evidence in the investigation of possible criminal fraud. When this occurs, the taxpayer should be advised to seek legal counsel to determine the extent of his or her cooperation in providing information to the agent. Further, it is frequently desirable for the tax adviser to consult his or her own personal legal counsel in such situations. If the taxpayer receives a Revenue Agent's Report, it generally indicates that the IRS has decided not to initiate criminal proceedings. The IRS usually does not take any action on a tax deficiency until the criminal matter has been resolved. If, for whatever reasons, the criminal action is dropped, the 75 percent civil fraud penalty still can be assessed.

17.5 Statute of Limitations

EXTENDING THE STATUTE

The IRS requests an extension of the statute of limitations when it finds that there is insufficient time to complete an audit or appellate review. The taxpayer is not compelled to agree to the extension request and may be averse to giving the IRS more time. But adverse consequences can result if the taxpayer denies the IRS request.

EXAMPLE 26

Although the statute of limitations governing Thornton's tax return is scheduled to expire in 15 days, the IRS has requested an extension for another 60 days. It wants to complete a more thorough investigation into a disputed $50,000 deduction. If Thornton refuses to agree to the extension, the IRS likely will disallow the entire deduction. However, if Thornton agrees to the extension, all or part of the deduction may be salvaged. ■

A disadvantage of extending the statute is that the IRS sometimes can raise new issues during the extension period. However, the taxpayer can take the following protective measures as a condition to agreeing to the extension.

- Shorten the extension period requested before signing the Form 872. This will reduce the chance that the IRS will find and investigate new issues.
- Restrict the scope of the issues covered by the extension (e.g., extend the period only as to the computation of cost of goods sold).
- Instead of Form 872, use a Form 872–A. This allows for an open-ended termination date of the extension. Consequently, when the examination of a disputed issue is completed, the taxpayer can request that the IRS close off the extension. This reduces the chances that the IRS will find and pursue any new issues.

PROMPT ASSESSMENT

The "prompt assessment" approach forces the IRS to conduct some sort of an examination of a return. Although most taxpayers are unlikely to volunteer for an audit, the procedure is attractive in several circumstances.

- An estate or trust (Chapters 18–20) is being terminated, and the executor or trustee needs some assurance that the entity's tax affairs are in order.
- A corporation is being liquidated, and the trustee of the liquidating trust wants to protect itself from unanticipated future income tax assessments by the IRS on years open under the statute of limitations.

A request for a prompt assessment is made by filing Form 4810. The IRS has 18 months to complete its review once the taxpayer files the request.[65]

17.6 Litigation Considerations

During the process of settlement with the IRS, the taxpayer must assess the economic consequences of possible litigation. Specifically, the probability of winning in court should be weighed against the costs of litigating the dispute (legal, support, and court costs). In some instances, taxpayers become overly emotional and do not adequately consider the economic and psychological costs of litigation.

Signing Form 870 or Form 870–AD precludes the use of the Tax Court as a forum for future litigation. In that event, the taxpayer's only recourse is to pay the taxes and sue for a refund in a different court. The Tax Court was established to provide taxpayers an opportunity to litigate issues without first paying the tax on the deficiency. Some taxpayers, however, prefer to litigate the case in a Federal District Court or the Court of Federal Claims, since the payment of tax effectively stops the running of interest on the deficiency.

In selecting a proper tax forum, consideration should be given to the decisions of the various courts in related cases. The Tax Court follows the decisions of U.S. Courts of Appeals if the court is one to which the taxpayer may appeal.[66] For example, if an individual is in the jurisdiction of the Fifth Circuit Court of Appeals and that court has issued a favorable opinion on the same issue that currently confronts the taxpayer, the Tax Court will follow this opinion in deciding the taxpayer's case, even if previous Tax Court decisions have been adverse.

If the issue involves a question in which equity is needed, strategy may dictate the choice of the Court of Federal Claims, which has frequently given greater weight to equity considerations than to strict legal precedent, or of a Federal District Court, where a jury trial is available.

[65] § 6501(d).

[66] *Jack E. Golsen*, 54 T.C. 742 (1970).

17.7 Penalties

Penalties are imposed upon a taxpayer's failure to file a return or pay a tax when due. These penalties can be avoided if the failure is due to reasonable cause and not due to willful neglect. Reasonable cause, however, has not been liberally interpreted by the courts and should not be relied upon in the routine situation.[67] A safer way to avoid the failure to file penalty is to obtain from the IRS an extension of time for filing the return.

The penalty for failure to pay estimated taxes can become quite severe. Often trapped by the provision are employed taxpayers with outside income. They may forget about the outside income and assume the amount withheld from wages and salaries is adequate to cover their liability. Not only does April 15 provide a real shock (in terms of the additional tax owed) for these persons, but a penalty situation may have evolved. One way for an employee to mitigate this problem (presuming the employer is willing to cooperate) is described in the following example.

EXAMPLE 27

Patty, a calendar year taxpayer, is employed by Finn Corporation and earns (after withholding) a monthly salary of $4,000 payable at the end of each month. Patty also receives income from outside sources (interest, dividends, and consulting fees). After some quick calculations in early October, Patty determines that she has underestimated her tax liability by $7,500 and will be subject to the penalty for the first two quarters of the year and part of the third quarter. Patty, therefore, completes a new Form W–4 in which she arbitrarily raises her income tax withholding by $2,500 a month. Finn accepts the Form W–4, and as a result, an extra $7,500 is paid to the IRS on Patty's account for the payroll period from October through December.

Patty avoids penalties for the underpayment for the first three quarters because withholding of taxes is allocated pro rata over the year involved. Thus, a portion of the additional $7,500 withheld in October–December is assigned to the January 1–April 15 period, the April 16–June 15 period, etc. Had Patty merely paid the IRS an additional $7,500 in October, the penalty would still have been assessed for the earlier quarters. ■

To avoid tax preparer penalties, the tax professional must carry out a number of quality control measures within the context of his or her firm.

- Adopt a "tone at the top" that stresses ethical tax practice, emphasizing at all times the importance of integrity and objectivity in the context of client advocacy.
- Establish and follow ethical guidelines with respect to all forms of client communication and documentation, including tax returns and written, spoken, and electronic tax advice.
- Apply ethical standards even before an engagement letter is prepared for a potential client. The client should be aware of, and participate in, this dedication to ethical behavior.
- Keep current on changes to penalties, ethical guidelines, and Circular 230 provisions through an ongoing educational effort that communicates rule changes and the firm's best practices to all who handle tax return data.
- Monitor the compliance of all members of the firm with the established ethical guidelines. Use a peer review process periodically to confirm that the system is working as designed and to bring third-party suggestions into the process.

[67] *Dustin v. Comm.*, 72–2 USTC ¶9610, 30 AFTR 2d 72–5313, 467 F.2d 47 (CA–9, 1972), *aff'g* 53 T.C. 491 (1969).

REFOCUS ON THE BIG PICTURE

A TAX ADVISER'S DILEMMA

Your work with Campbell Corporation and its incremental research credit may prove troublesome. To avoid the taxpayer and tax preparer penalties, substantial authority must exist for claiming the credit, but the tax cases and Regulations do not appear to provide much guidance with respect to research expenditures of this sort. How does one craft a tax return position when the tax law largely is silent as to the particulars of the facts of the taxpayer's situation? How much risk of incurring a tax penalty are the taxpayer and your firm willing to assume in deciding how and whether to report these expenditures?

Beyond the monetary effects of claiming the credit, you and the client must consider the publicity aspects of taking this issue to court: Does Campbell want to be the "test case" in the Tax Court on this matter? What would be the effects on your consulting firm if a preparer penalty or even loss of professional certification were to result? If the credit is to be claimed, what degree of "disclosure" does the law require?

At a minimum, your firm and Campbell's tax department must conduct thorough research of analogous situations in the law in which the incremental research credit was and was not allowed for the taxpayer. Due diligence in this regard would require that you examine how other software applications and similar technological innovations, probably having nothing to do with GPS software and national security concerns, were treated for tax credit purposes. Constrained only by the budget dollars that Campbell is willing to dedicate to this task, your research is likely to be both interesting and frustrating, as no "on point" resolution is likely to be found prior to a later audit of the Form 1120 and its disclosures.

What If?

The risk profiles of the tax adviser and a client seldom are identical. What position should your firm take if Campbell's tax department decides to claim the full incremental research credit for an item on which the tax law is silent or unclear, but your firm recommends that a special disclosure be made on the return concerning the item? A disclosure of this sort would protect the parties from later assessment of tax penalties, but Campbell believes that drawing attention to the credit item would increase the likelihood of a targeted audit of the expenditures by the IRS.

Although you are certain that tax fraud is not a problem on the Campbell return, you are concerned about the ramifications of Campbell's desire to omit the recommended disclosure. Your firm might decide to leave the Campbell engagement altogether if it is especially sensitive to exposure to penalties, or if it is not certain that adequate research has been done to support the tax return position. Charges of a lack of due diligence by your firm might be brought by the IRS, the firm's professional ethics or certification bodies, or the issuer of its malpractice insurance. Clearly, none of these results is attractive to your firm.

KEY TERMS

Accuracy-related penalties, 17–17
Circular 230, 17–24
Closing agreement, 17–14
Determination letter, 17–5
E-filing, 17–4
Enrolled agents (EAs), 17–24
Fraud, 17–20
Frivolous return, 17–25
Letter ruling, 17–4
Negligence, 17–17
Ninety day letter, 17–11
Offer in compromise, 17–12
Reasonable cause, 17–17
Revenue Agent's Report (RAR), 17–10
Statute of limitations, 17–22
Substantial authority, 17–18
Tax preparer, 17–27
Technical advice memorandum (TAM), 17–6
Thirty day letter, 17–11
Unreasonable position, 17–27
Whistleblower Program, 17–8

DISCUSSION QUESTIONS

1. **LO.1** Tax professionals should show an interest in the organizational structure of the IRS and in the various processes that are necessary to work with the agency. What is the payback to the tax professional and his or her clients for this investment of time in discerning how the IRS works?

2. **LO.1** Where does the IRS "fit" in the operations of the Federal government? Summarize its responsibilities to the government and to the taxpayers.

3. **LO.1** An article in *USA Today* refers to the "audit lottery" and how one's chances of being audited are higher under the current IRS leadership. What is the audit lottery, and how should a tax professional view the statistics about a taxpayer's audit likelihood?

4. **LO.1** Recently, a politician was interviewed about fiscal policy, and she mentioned reducing the "tax gap." Explain what this term means. What are some of the pertinent political and economic issues relative to the tax gap? **ISSUE ID**

5. **LO.1** Review Figure 17.1 and identify the following.
   a. The title of the IRS's chief executive officer.
   b. The title of the "IRS's attorney."
   c. The names of the four major operating divisions of the IRS.

6. **LO.1** Identify three or more of the duties of the IRS's Chief Counsel.

7. **LO.2** Your tax research has located a Tax Court case that supports the claiming of a deduction by a client, while an IRS letter ruling holds to the contrary. The pertinent facts of both the case and the ruling match those of the client. Which holding should be followed in preparing the client's tax return? Summarize your findings in a memo to the tax research file. **COMMUNICATIONS**

8. **LO.2** Your client is litigating in the Tax Court concerning a tax credit that she claimed and the IRS has denied. Who bears the burden of proof regarding the litigation?

9. **LO.2** Describe the process that the IRS uses to collect the tax that is found to be due after an audit is completed. Assume that the IRS findings are not appealed but that the taxpayer does not pay the amount due as determined by the audit. Illustrate the process with no more than four PowerPoint slides. **COMMUNICATIONS**

10. **LO.3** Gloria and Maria work together in an insurance office. Gloria's Form 1040 seems to be audited two out of every three years, while Maria never has been audited. How does the IRS select tax returns for audit? List some of the factors that might result in the different treatment of Gloria's and Maria's returns.

11. **LO.3** When can an individual taxpayer feel certain that his or her tax return will not be audited by the IRS? One year after it is filed? Two years? Five years? Explain.

12. **LO.3, 4** Lori wants to establish that her niece Suzette actually qualifies for a dependency exemption. After the issue is raised by the IRS on audit, Lori could argue the matter with the agent, an IRS Appeals officer, or the Tax Court. Give Lori advice about how to handle her tax dispute.

13. **LO.3** Describe the three broad types of IRS audits. Give an example of an issue that each type of audit might address, and indicate how frequently such audits are conducted by the IRS. **ISSUE ID**

14. **LO.4** Which taxpayers should try to settle tax disputes with the Small Cases Division of the U.S. Tax Court? What is the precedential value of a Small Cases decision?

15. **LO.4** Under what circumstances will the IRS consider a request from the taxpayer for an offer in compromise?

16. **LO.5** Explain how the interest rates that apply to Federal income tax underpayments and overpayments are determined. If a taxpayer owes additional taxes, when does interest begin to accrue?

17. **LO.6** Define the following terms in the context of tax law enforcement.
    a. Civil penalty.
    b. Criminal penalty.
    c. *Ad valorem* penalty.
    d. *Assessable* penalty.
    e. Deductible penalty.

18. **LO.6** Which of the valuation penalties is likely to arise when an aggressive taxpayer reports:
    a. A charitable contribution?
    b. A business deduction?
    c. A decedent's taxable estate?

19. **LO.6** Describe how the valuation penalties work. What is the rate of the penalty, and on which amount is it imposed?

20. **LO.6** Yonkers Corporation recomputes its research credit for the prior tax year and, as a result, claims a $100,000 refund. The IRS reviews the claim and allows only $20,000 of the requested refund. If Yonkers does not appeal, is this matter finished? Is Yonkers certain to receive the full $20,000 refund allowed?

ISSUE ID

21. **LO.6** On October 30, Cameron determines that his tax for the year will total $10,000. If his employer is scheduled to withhold only $6,500 in Federal income taxes, what can Cameron do to avoid any underpayment penalty?

22. **LO.4, 5, 7** Indicate whether each of the following statements is true or false.
    a. The government never pays a taxpayer interest on an overpayment of tax.
    b. The IRS can compromise on the amount of tax liability if there is doubt as to the taxpayer's ability to pay.
    c. The statute of limitations for assessing a tax can extend beyond three years from the filing of a return.
    d. For a tax return that has not been filed, the statute of limitations is extended to five years from the original due date of the return.

23. **LO.4, 6** In each of the following cases, distinguish between the terms.
    a. Offer in compromise and closing agreement.
    b. Failure to file and failure to pay.
    c. Ninety-day letter and thirty-day letter.
    d. Negligence and fraud.
    e. Criminal and civil tax fraud.

24. **LO.6** Describe at least two civil tax penalties that could apply when there is a violation of the rules involving the withholding of taxes from wages and salaries. Be specific.

ISSUE ID

25. **LO.7** Why should the taxpayer be "let off the hook" and no longer be subject to audit exposure once the applicable statute of limitations has expired? Do statutes of limitations protect the government? Other taxpayers?

ISSUE ID

26. **LO.8** The disclosures about Enron, Tyco, and WorldCom changed the regulation of the accounting profession. Who regulates the behavior of tax return preparers? What documents provide the major constraints on the conduct of the tax profession?

27. **LO.8** Give the Circular 230 position concerning each of the following situations sometimes encountered in the tax profession.
    a. Taking an aggressive pro-taxpayer position on a tax return.
    b. Not having a quality review process for a return completed by a partner of the tax firm.
    c. Purposely delaying compliance with a document request received from the IRS.
    d. Not keeping up with changes in the tax law.
    e. Charging $1,500 to complete a Form 1040-EZ.
    f. When representing a taxpayer in a Federal income tax audit, charging a fee equal to one-third of the reduction of the tax proposed by the IRS agent.
    g. Representing both the grantor and the beneficiaries of a trust that is being created.

28. **LO.8** Indicate whether each of the following parties could be subject to the tax preparer penalties.
    a. Tom prepared Sally's return for $250.
    b. Theresa prepared her grandmother's return for no charge.

c. Georgia prepared her church's return for $500 (she would have charged an unrelated party $3,000 for the same work).
d. Geoff prepared returns for low-income taxpayers under his college's VITA program.
e. Hildy prepared the return of her corporate employer.
f. Heejeo, an administrative assistant for an accounting firm, processed a client's return through TurboTax.

29. **LO.6, 8** In no more than three PowerPoint slides, list at least four of the Code's penalties that could be assessed against paid preparers of tax returns. Name the violation that triggers the penalty, and explain how the dollar amount of the penalty is determined. **COMMUNICATIONS**

30. **LO.8** Indicate which codes, canons, and other bodies of ethical statements apply to each of the following tax practitioners.
a. CPAs who are members of the AICPA.
b. CPAs who are not members of the AICPA.
c. Attorneys.
d. Enrolled agents.
e. Tax preparers who are not CPAs, EAs, or attorneys.

PROBLEMS

31. **LO.5** Gordon paid the $10,000 balance of his Federal income tax three months late. Ignore daily compounding of interest. Determine the interest rate that applies relative to this amount, assuming that:
a. Gordon is an individual.
b. Gordon is a C corporation.
c. The $10,000 is not a tax that is due but is a refund payable by the IRS to Gordon (an individual).
d. The $10,000 is not a tax that is due but is a refund payable by the IRS to Gordon (a C corporation).

32. **LO.6** Rita forgot to pay her Federal income tax on time. When she actually filed, she reported a balance due. Compute Rita's failure to file penalty in each of the following cases.
a. Two months late, $1,000 additional tax due.
b. Five months late, $3,000 additional tax due.
c. Eight months late, $4,000 additional tax due.
d. Two and a half months late, $3,000 additional tax due.
e. Five months late due to fraud by Rita, $4,000 additional tax due.
f. Ten months late due to fraud by Rita, $15,000 additional tax due.

33. **LO.6** Tom filed his Federal income tax return on time but did not remit the balance due. Compute Tom's failure to pay penalty in each of the following cases. The IRS has not issued a deficiency notice.
a. Four months late, $3,000 additional tax due.
b. Ten months late, $4,000 additional tax due.
c. Five years late, $5,000 additional tax due.

34. **LO.6** Compute the failure to pay and failure to file penalties for John, who filed his 2010 income tax return on October 20, 2011, paying the $30,000 amount due at that time. On April 1, 2011, John had received a six-month extension of time in which to file his return. He has no reasonable cause for failing to file his return by October 15 or for failing to pay the tax that was due on April 15, 2011. John's failure to comply with the tax laws was not fraudulent.

35. **LO.6** Olivia, a calendar year taxpayer, does not file her 2010 return until December 12, 2011. At this point, she pays the $40,000 balance due on her 2010 tax liability of $70,000. Olivia did not apply for and obtain any extension of time for filing the 2010 return. When questioned by the IRS on her delinquency, Olivia asserts: "If I was too busy to file my regular tax return, I was too busy to request an extension."
a. Is Olivia liable for any penalties for failure to file and for failure to pay?
b. If so, compute the penalty amounts.

36. **LO.6** Orville, a cash basis, calendar year taxpayer, filed his income tax return 70 days after the due date. Orville never extended his return, and he paid the taxes that were due when he filed the return. What penalty will Orville incur, and how much will he have to pay if his additional tax is $6,000? Disregard any interest he must pay.

37. **LO.6** Rhoda, a calendar year individual taxpayer, files her 2010 return on November 4, 2012. She did not obtain an extension for filing her return, and the return reflects additional income tax due of $25,000.
    a. What are Rhoda's penalties for failure to file and to pay?
    b. Would your answer to (a) change if Rhoda, before the due date of the return, had retained a CPA to prepare the return and it was the CPA's negligence that caused the delay?

38. **LO.6** Dana underpaid her taxes by $250,000. A portion of the underpayment was shown to be attributable to Dana's negligence ($200,000). A court found that a portion of that deficiency constituted civil fraud ($50,000). Compute the total fraud and negligence penalties incurred.

39. **LO.6** Compute the overvaluation penalty for each of the following independent cases involving the fair market value of charitable contribution property. In each case, assume a marginal income tax rate of 35%.

	Taxpayer	Corrected IRS Value	Reported Valuation
a.	Individual	$ 40,000	$ 50,000
b.	C corporation	30,000	50,000
c.	S corporation	40,000	50,000
d.	Individual	150,000	200,000
e.	Individual	150,000	250,000
f.	C corporation	150,000	750,000

40. **LO.6** Compute the undervaluation penalty for each of the following independent cases involving the value of a closely held business in the decedent's gross estate. In each case, assume a marginal estate tax rate of 35%.

	Reported Value	Corrected IRS Valuation
a.	$ 20,000	$ 25,000
b.	100,000	150,000
c.	150,000	250,000
d.	150,000	500,000

41. **LO.6** Singh, a qualified appraiser of fine art and other collectibles, was advising Colleen when she was determining the amount of the charitable contribution deduction for a gift of sculpture to a museum. Singh sanctioned an $800,000 appraisal, even though he knew that the market value of the piece was only $300,000. Colleen assured Singh that she had never been audited by the IRS and that the risk of the government questioning his appraisal was negligible.

    But Colleen was wrong and her return was audited. The IRS used its own appraisers to set the value of the sculpture at $400,000. Colleen is in the 30% Federal income tax bracket while Singh's fee for preparing the appraisal was $50,000.
    a. Compute the penalty that the IRS can assess against Singh. (Do not consider the valuation penalty as to Colleen's return.)
    b. What is the penalty if Singh's appraisal fee was $5,000 (not $50,000)?

42. **LO.6** The Eggers Corporation filed an amended Form 1120, claiming an additional $400,000 deduction for payments to a contractor for a prior tax year. The amended return was based on the entity's interpretation of a Regulation that defined deductible advance payment expenditures. The nature of Eggers's activity with the contractor did not exactly fit the language of the Regulation. Nevertheless, because so much tax was at stake, Eggers's tax department decided to broaden its interpretation and claim the deduction.

Eggers's tax department estimated that there was only a 15% chance that Eggers's interpretation would stand up to a Tax Court review.

a. What is the amount of tax penalty that Eggers is risking by taking this position?
b. What would be the result if there was a 45% chance that Eggers's interpretation of the Regulation was correct?

43. **LO.6** Moose, a former professional athlete, now supplements his income by signing autographs at collectors' shows. Unfortunately, Moose has not been conscientious about reporting all of this income on his tax return. Now the IRS has charged him with additional taxes of $100,000 due to negligence in his record keeping and $20,000 due to an intent to defraud the U.S. government of income taxes. No criminal fraud charges are brought against Moose. The District Court finds by a preponderance of the evidence that only half of the $20,000 underpayment was due to Moose's fraudulent action; the remainder was due to mere negligence. Compute the accuracy-related and civil fraud penalties in this matter.

44. **LO.6** Trudy's AGI last year was $200,000. Her Federal income tax came to $65,000, which she paid through a combination of withholding and estimated payments. This year, her AGI will be $300,000, with a projected tax liability of $45,000, all to be paid through estimates.
    a. Ignore the annualized income method. Compute Trudy's quarterly estimated tax payment schedule for this year.
    b. Assume instead that Trudy's AGI last year was $100,000 and resulted in a Federal income tax of $20,000. Determine her quarterly estimated tax payment schedule for this year.

45. **LO.6** Kold Services Corporation estimates that its 2012 taxable income will be $500,000. Thus, it is subject to a flat 34% income tax rate and incurs a $170,000 liability. For each of the following independent cases, compute Kold's minimum quarterly estimated tax payments that will avoid an underpayment penalty.
    a. For 2011, taxable income was ($200,000). Kold carried back all of this loss to prior years and exhausted the entire net operating loss in creating a zero 2011 liability.
    b. For 2011, taxable income was $450,000, and tax liability was $153,000.
    c. For 2010, taxable income was $2 million, and tax liability was $680,000. For 2011, taxable income was $400,000, and tax liability was $136,000.

46. **LO.6** The Scooter Company, owned equally by Julie (chair of the board of directors) and Jeff (company president), is in very difficult financial straits. Last month, Jeff used the $100,000 withheld from employee paychecks for Federal payroll and income taxes to pay off a creditor who threatened to cut off all supplies. To keep the company afloat, Jeff used these government funds willfully for the operations of the business, but even that effort was not enough. The company missed the next two payrolls, and today other creditors took action to shut down Scooter altogether. How much will the IRS assess in taxes and penalties in this matter, and from whom? How can you as a tax professional best offer service to Julie, Jeff, and Scooter? Address these matters in a memo for the tax research file. DECISION MAKING COMMUNICATIONS

47. **LO.7** What is the applicable statute of limitations in each of the following independent situations?
    a. No return was filed by the taxpayer.
    b. The taxpayer incurred a bad debt loss that she failed to claim.
    c. A taxpayer inadvertently omitted a large amount of gross income.
    d. Same as (c), except that the omission was deliberate.
    e. A taxpayer innocently overstated her deductions by a large amount.

48. **LO.7** Suzanne (a calendar year taxpayer) had the following transactions, all of which were properly reported on a timely filed return.

Gross receipts		$ 975,000
Cost of sales		(850,000)
Gross profit		$ 125,000
Capital gain	$ 90,000	
Capital loss	(25,000)	65,000
Total income		$ 190,000

a. Presuming the absence of fraud, how much of an omission from gross income is required before the six-year statute of limitations applies?
b. Would it matter if cost of sales had been inadvertently overstated by $100,000?
c. How does the situation change in the context of fraud by Suzanne?

DECISION MAKING

49. **LO.5, 7** On April 3, 2008, Mark filed his 2007 income tax return, which showed a tax due of $80,000. On June 1, 2010, he filed an amended return for 2007 that showed an additional tax of $10,000. Mark paid the additional amount. On May 18, 2011, Mark filed a claim for a 2007 refund of $45,000.
a. If Mark's claim for a refund is correct in amount, how much tax will he recover?
b. What is the period that government-paid interest runs with respect to Mark's claim for a refund?
c. How would you have advised him differently?

COMMUNICATIONS

50. **LO.7** Carol owed $4,000 in Federal income tax when she filed her Form 1040 for 2011. She attached a Post-It note to the 1040 saying, "My inventory computations on last year's (2010) return were wrong, so I paid $1,000 too much in tax." Carol then included a check for $3,000 with the Form 1040 for 2011. Write a memo to the tax research file commenting on Carol's actions.

51. **LO.8** Rod's Federal income tax returns (Form 1040) for the indicated three years were prepared by the following persons.

Year	Preparer
2009	Rod
2010	Ann
2011	Cheryl

Ann is Rod's next-door neighbor and owns and operates a pharmacy. Cheryl is a licensed CPA and is engaged in private practice. In the event Rod is audited and all three returns are examined, who may represent him before the IRS at the agent level? Who may represent Rod before the Appeals Division?

52. **LO.8** Lois is the preparer of the Form 1120 for Yostern Corporation. On the return, Yostern claimed a deduction that the IRS later disallowed on audit. Compute the tax preparer penalty that could be assessed against Lois in each of the following independent situations.

	Form 8275 Disclosure on the Return of the Disputed Deduction?	Tax Reduction Resulting from the Deduction	Probability That the Courts Would Approve the Deduction	Lois's Fee to Complete Yostern's Return
a.	No	$50,000	65%	$10,000
b.	No	50,000	35	10,000
c.	No	50,000	35	1,500
d.	Yes	50,000	35	10,000
e.	Yes	50,000	15	5,000

53. **LO.8** Discuss which penalties, if any, might be imposed on the tax adviser in each of the following independent circumstances. In this regard, assume that the tax adviser:
a. Suggested to the client various means by which to acquire excludible income.
b. Suggested to the client various means by which to conceal cash receipts from gross income.
c. Suggested to the client means by which to improve her cash flow by delaying for six months or more the deposit of the employees' share of Federal employment taxes.
d. Failed, because of pressing time conflicts, to conduct the usual review of the client's tax return. The IRS later discovered that the return included fraudulent data.
e. Failed, because of pressing time conflicts, to conduct the usual review of the client's tax return. The IRS later discovered a mathematical error in the computation of the personal exemption.

54. **LO.8** Compute the preparer penalty that the IRS could assess on Gerry in each of the following independent cases.
    a. On March 21, the copy machine was not working, so Gerry gave original returns to her 20 clients that day without providing any duplicates for them. Copies for Gerry's files and for use in preparing state tax returns had been made on March 20.
    b. Because Gerry extended her vacation a few days, she missed the Annual Tax Update seminar that she usually attends. As a result, she was unaware that Congress had changed a law affecting limited partnerships. The change affected the transactions of 25 of Gerry's clients, all of whom understated their tax as a result.
    c. Gerry heard that the IRS was increasing its audits of corporations that hold assets in a foreign trust. As a result, Gerry instructed the intern who prepared the initial drafts of the returns for five corporate clients to leave blank the question about such trusts. Not wanting to lose his position, the intern, a senior accounting major at State University, complied with Gerry's instructions.

55. **LO.8** You are the chair of the Ethics Committee of your state's CPA Licensing Commission. Interpret controlling AICPA authority in addressing the following assertions by your membership.

    DECISION MAKING

    a. When a CPA has reasonable grounds for not answering an applicable question on a client's return, a brief explanation of the reason for the omission should not be provided, because it would flag the return for audit by the IRS.
    b. If a CPA discovers during an IRS audit that the client has a material error in the return under examination, he should immediately withdraw from the engagement.
    c. If the client tells you that she paid $500 for office supplies, but has lost the receipts, you should deduct an odd amount on her return (e.g., $499), because an even amount ($500) would indicate to the IRS that her deduction was based on an estimate.
    d. If a CPA knows that the client has a material error in a prior year's return, he should not, without the client's consent, disclose the error to the IRS.
    e. If a CPA's client will not correct a material error in a prior year's return, the CPA should not prepare the current year's return for the client.

RESEARCH PROBLEMS

Note: Solutions to Research Problems can be prepared by using the **Checkpoint® Student Edition** online research product, which is available to accompany this text. It is also possible to prepare solutions to the Research Problems by using tax research materials found in a standard tax library.

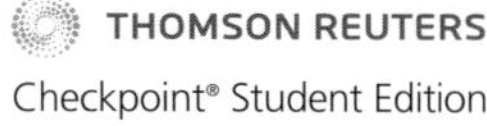

Checkpoint® Student Edition

COMMUNICATIONS

Research Problem 1. Lopez always had taken his Form 1040 data to the franchise tax preparers in a local mall, but this year his friend Cheryl asked to prepare his return. Cheryl quoted a reasonable fee, and Lopez reasoned that, with finances especially tight in Cheryl's household, she could use the money.

Lopez delivered his Forms W–2, 1099, and other documentation and said, "I'll pick up the finished return from you on Monday." Cheryl completed the return by that deadline, and without signing and reviewing the forms, Lopez allowed Cheryl to e-file it that day. The arrangement was that Cheryl would receive the refund through a special bank account and write Lopez a check for that amount, less her fee. When the refund came through about three weeks later, Cheryl wrote Lopez a check for $2,400, and all parties were satisfied. Lopez gladly used Cheryl to e-file the next year's return using the same procedures.

To his surprise, Lopez received a letter from the IRS about 18 months later. The auditor had found that the return Cheryl had e-filed vastly overstated deductions, created false dependency exemptions (using Social Security numbers that did not exist), and wrongly calculated the earned income tax credit. According to the audit report, the refund issued was $4,500—Cheryl had pocketed the difference. Thus, the corrected tax liability meant that Lopez now owed $7,000 in tax, before considering interest and penalties.

Lopez contends that he relied on Cheryl's expertise in the tax law and e-filing procedures. Consequently, there was reasonable cause for the underpayment of tax, and the IRS should waive the understatement and negligence penalties. The IRS has expressed sympathy for Lopez's position, but it maintains that the penalty should stand. What do you think? Summarize your findings in a memo to the tax research file.

Research Problem 2. In 2007, Gupta sold some shares of Wingo, a private U.S. corporation, for $40 million. On his Form 1040 Schedule D for 2007, Gupta showed the basis of the stock as $11 million, thereby reporting a $29 million capital gain. Gupta filed his return on October 1, 2008, after properly receiving an extension of the filing due date. Other income and deductions on the 2007 return netted to zero.

On March 1, 2012, while auditing the tax return of one of the purchasers of Gupta's Wingo shares, the IRS found that the basis for the shares actually was $3 million. Thus, Gupta's capital gain should have been $37 million and not $29 million.

Upon audit of Gupta's 2007 return, the IRS maintains that it can collect the underpaid taxes, plus interest and penalties, because the six-year statute of limitations applies (i.e., Gupta's return showed a substantial understatement of gross income). Gupta has asked you for tax advice on this matter. Did the statute of limitations expire on October 1, 2011, so that the IRS no longer can pursue the matter? Explain.

COMMUNICATIONS

Research Problem 3. Blanche Creek (111 Elm Avenue, Patriotville, IN 40123) has engaged your firm because she has been charged with failure to file her 2009 Federal Form 1040. Blanche maintains that the "reasonable cause" exception should apply. During the entire tax filing season in 2010, she was under a great deal of stress at work and in her personal life. As a result, Blanche developed a sleep disorder, which was treated through a combination of pills and counseling.

Your firm ultimately prepared the 2009 tax return for Blanche, but it was filed far beyond the due date. Blanche is willing to pay the delinquent tax and related interest. However, she feels that the failure to pay penalty is unfair as she was ill. Consequently, she could not be expected to keep to the usual deadlines for filing.

Write a letter to Blanche concerning these matters.

COMMUNICATIONS

Research Problem 4. Dick Whitman retired as a partner from the Sterling Company consulting firm two years ago. He continues to furnish services for the partnership by providing high-level tax advice for clients who are considering large investments or other transactions with substantial income tax consequences. Whitman's compensation for these services is a flat fee based on his previous billing rate of $1,000 per hour.

Since Sterling's malpractice insurance no longer fully covers Whitman, he is concerned about the preparer penalties that could result from his tax advice. He is particularly alarmed by the expansion of the § 6694 penalty for taking unreasonable tax return positions.

As an associate in Sterling's tax department, prepare a memo to the research file addressing Whitman's concerns. Hint: Most of your research should deal with the income tax Regulations.

Research Problem 5. You have just rendered service for a taxpayer as an expert witness in a case heard by the U.S. Tax Court. The taxpayer is requesting reimbursement for your fees and for those amounts paid to her attorney in presenting the case. Your billing rate for this type of engagement is $500 per hour, the market rate for such services in your city, plus out-of-pocket expenses (e.g., auto mileage, computer charges). How much of your fee will the taxpayer recover?

Use the tax resources of the Internet to address the following questions. Do not restrict your search to the Web, but include a review of newsgroups and general reference materials, practitioner sites and resources, primary sources of the tax law, chat rooms and discussion groups, and other opportunities.

COMMUNICATIONS

Research Problem 6. Find an article in which a tax professional describes the confidentiality privilege available under the Code for a CPA tax adviser. Then construct a list of "Confidentiality Dos and Don'ts for the CPA." Summarize the article in an e-mail to your professor.

Research Problem 7. Corporations with large estimated tax overpayments and underpayments are subject to special interest rates.

a. Find in the Code how these rates are determined.
b. List the rates that have been in effect for the last six calendar quarters.
c. Find and subscribe to a feed that automatically will alert you when the interest rate changes.

COMMUNICATIONS

Research Problem 8. Prepare a graph illustrating the trends in IRS audit activity over the past decade, and submit it to your instructor. First decide whether you are measuring audited returns, tax dollars recovered by audit, or budget resources dedicated to audit activities. Next decide which types of taxpayers and returns you will be graphing. Then find your data at **www.irs.gov**.

Research Problem 9. In a PowerPoint presentation for your classmates, describe how the IRS targets certain tax issues, taxpayers, and transactions in the audit process. Give examples of high- and low-priority audit issues for the current year. (*Hint*: Search using terms like Tier I and Tier II.)

COMMUNICATIONS

Research Problem 10. Every year toward the end of the Form 1040 filing season, newspapers and blogs run articles about how to pay your taxes if you lack the funds to do so. The articles promote filing extensions, installment plans, and credit card payments. Find two articles of this sort that were published in the last 12 months. Summarize the articles, and develop a speech outline and no more than four PowerPoint slides for a presentation you will make to your town's Young Executives Club.

COMMUNICATIONS

Research Problem 11. Find a website that lists suggestions on how to deal with an IRS auditor during the first meeting with him or her. Summarize and evaluate each of the key points in an e-mail to your instructor.

COMMUNICATIONS

Research Problem 12. You have been assigned the task of preparing a letter ruling request on behalf of one of the firm's clients. As the firm has not prepared a ruling request before, you are to outline the IRS's procedure for receiving and processing such a request. Summarize the more significant points in a memo to the tax file. Provide Code and other citations as needed.

COMMUNICATIONS

Part 5

Family Tax Planning

Family tax planning has as its objective the minimization of all taxes imposed on the family unit. Carrying out this objective requires familiarity with the rules applicable to transfers by gift and by death. These rules must then be applied to reduce the transfer tax burden. Also to be considered are the income tax consequences of the transfers made. Specifically, entities created as a result of these transfers (trusts and estates) are subject to unique income tax rules.

CHAPTER 18

The Federal Gift and Estate Taxes

LEARNING OBJECTIVES

After completing Chapter 18, you should be able to:

LO.1
Explain the nature of the Federal gift and estate taxes.

LO.2
Analyze the Federal gift tax formula.

LO.3
Analyze the Federal estate tax formula.

LO.4
Discuss the operation of the Federal gift tax.

LO.5
Calculate the Federal gift tax.

LO.6
Identify the components of the gross estate.

LO.7
Describe the components of the taxable estate.

LO.8
Calculate the Federal estate tax liability.

LO.9
Demonstrate the role of the generation-skipping transfer tax.

OUTLINE

For the latest in changes to tax legislation, visit **www.cengage.com/taxation/swft.**

THE BIG PICTURE **Tax Solutions for the Real World**

AN EVENTFUL AND FINAL YEAR

Over his lifetime, Peter Hood started and purchased numerous automobile dealerships that he eventually transferred to a newly formed entity, Hood Corporation. Upon his death in 2000, the stock in Hood Corporation passed in equal shares to Peter's surviving spouse, Martha, and their adult children, John and Helen.

For John Hood, 2011 proved to be an eventful and final tax year. Among the major happenings were the following.

- In January, John's divorce from his first wife, Hannah, became final.
- In February, he married Ashley, the manager of one of the Hood car dealerships.
- He made various gifts to family members.
- In July, his mother died of a heart condition, and John served as executor of her estate.
- In late November, he was seriously injured in a car accident (caused by another motorist).
- In early December, he carried out some predeath planning.
- John died of his injuries in mid-December.

What are some of the tax problems (i.e., income, gift, and estate taxes) that might be encountered as a result of these events? **Read the chapter and formulate your response.**

18.1 Transfer Taxes—In General

Until now, this text has dealt primarily with the various applications of the Federal income tax. Also important in the Federal tax structure are various excise taxes that cover transfers of property. Sometimes called transaction taxes, excise taxes are based on the value of the property transferred, not on the income derived from the property. Two such taxes—the Federal gift tax and the Federal estate tax—are the central focus of Chapters 18 and 19.

LO.1

Explain the nature of the Federal gift and estate taxes.

NATURE OF THE TAXES

Historical Background

Federal tax law imposes a tax on the gratuitous transfer of property in one of two ways. If the transfer occurs during the owner's life, it is subject to the Federal gift tax. If the property passes by virtue of the death of the owner, the Federal estate tax applies. Originally, the two taxes were governed by different rules including separate sets of tax rates. As Congress felt that lifetime transfers of wealth should be encouraged, the gift tax rates were 25 percentage points lower than the estate tax rates.[1]

The Tax Reform Act of 1976 significantly changed the approach taken by the Federal gift and estate taxes. Recognizing that prior rules had not significantly stimulated a preference for lifetime over death transfers, Congress decided that all transfers should be taxed the same way. Consequently, much of the distinction between life and death transfers was eliminated. Instead of subjecting these transfers to two separate tax rate schedules, the Act substituted a **unified transfer tax** that covered all gratuitous transfers. Thus, gifts were subject to a gift tax at the same rates as those applicable to transfers at death.

[1]The estate tax was enacted in 1916. Because the estate tax could be avoided by making transfers just prior to dying (i.e., "deathbed gifts"), a gift tax was added in 1932.

The Economic Growth and Tax Relief Reconciliation Act of 2001 (EGTRRA) made further changes. Reacting to general public sentiment, Congress concluded that the Federal estate tax was objectionable because it leads to the breakup of family farms and other closely held businesses. Thus, by scheduled increases in the unified tax credit applicable to estates, the estate tax would be eliminated by the year 2010, but the gift tax would be retained. For budget reasons, under "sunset provisions," all changes made by EGTRRA were to be eliminated after December 31, 2010. At the last minute, however, Congress enacted the Tax Relief Act of 2010 (TRA). Under TRA, the sunset provisions are postponed (until after 2012), and the legislation added some generous estate and gift tax provisions (maximum rate of 35 percent and a credit of $5 million). TRA is effective for 2011 and 2012. If the sunset provisions come into play after 2012, the rates will increase to a maximum of 55 percent, and the credit will decrease to $1 million.

Clearly, Congress has not been consistent in its treatment of lifetime (i.e., gift tax) and death (i.e., estate tax) transfers.

Persons Subject to the Tax

The Federal gift tax is imposed on the right to transfer property by one person (the donor) to another (the donee) for less than full and adequate consideration. The tax is payable by the donor.[2] If the donor fails to pay the tax when due, the donee may be held liable for the tax to the extent of the value of the property received.[3]

A gift by a corporation is considered a gift by the individual shareholders. A gift to a corporation is generally considered a gift to the individual shareholders. In certain cases, however, a gift to a charitable, public, political, or similar organization may be regarded as a gift to the organization as a single entity.[4]

Upon the death of an individual, the Federal estate tax is imposed on the entire estate.[5] The executor (or administrator) of the estate has the obligation to pay any estate tax that may be due.

If the transferor is a resident or citizen of the United States, then the location of the property transferred is immaterial. Thus, a gift by a U.S. resident of property located in Honduras is subject to the Federal gift tax. For a U.S. citizen, the place of residence at the time of the transfer is not relevant. For these purposes, "United States" includes only the 50 states and the District of Columbia and does not include U.S. possessions or territories.[6]

For individuals who are neither residents nor citizens of the United States (i.e., nonresident aliens or NRAs), the Federal gift tax applies only to gifts of property situated within the United States. Exempted, however, are gifts of intangibles, such as stocks and bonds.[7]

For decedents who are NRAs, the Federal estate tax is imposed on the value of property located within the United States. Unlike the gift tax, however, the estate tax applies to stock in U.S. corporations.[8] Special reporting procedures apply to the estate taxation of NRAs.[9]

Types of Tax at Death

Taxes payable by virtue of a person's death fall into two categories: estate and inheritance. The U.S. government, some states, and several foreign countries impose estate taxes. Inheritance taxes are imposed by some states and other countries. Some states and countries use both types of taxes.

[2] § 2502(c).

[3] § 6324(b). Known as the doctrine of transferee liability, this rule also operates to enable the IRS to enforce the collection of other taxes (e.g., income tax, estate tax).

[4] Reg. §§ 25.0–1(b) and 25.2511–1(h)(1). But note the exemption from the Federal gift tax for certain transfers to political organizations discussed later.

[5] § 2001(a). Subchapter A (§§ 2001 through 2058) covers the estate tax treatment of those who are either residents or citizens.

[6] § 7701(a)(9).

[7] §§ 2501(a)(2) and (3) and 2511(a).

[8] Subchapter B (§§ 2101 through 2108) covers the estate tax rules applicable to NRAs.

[9] See the instructions to Form 706NA (U.S. Estate Tax Return of Nonresident Not a Citizen of the U.S.).

The Federal estate tax differs in several respects from the typical *inheritance tax.* First, the Federal estate tax is levied on the decedent's entire estate. It is a tax on the right to pass property at death. Inheritance taxes apply to the right to receive property at death and are therefore levied on the heirs. Second, the relationship of the heirs to the decedent usually has a direct bearing on the amount of the inheritance tax. In general, the more closely related the parties, the larger the exemptions and the lower the applicable rates.[10] Except for transfers to surviving spouses that may result in a marital deduction, the relationship of the heirs to the decedent has no effect on the Federal estate tax.

LO.2

Analyze the Federal gift tax formula.

Formula for the Gift Tax

Like the income tax, which uses taxable income (not gross income) as a tax base, the gift tax usually does not apply to the full amount of the gift. Deductions and the annual exclusion may be allowed to arrive at an amount called the **taxable gift.** However, unlike the income tax, which does not consider taxable income from prior years, *prior taxable gifts* must be added in arriving at the tax base to which the unified transfer tax rate is applied. Otherwise, the donor could start over again each year with a new set of progressive rates.

EXAMPLE 1

Don makes taxable gifts of $1 million in 1986 and $1 million in 2009. Presuming no other taxable gifts and *before applying the unified tax credit,* Don must pay a tax of $345,800 (see Appendix A, p. A–4) on the 1986 transfer and a tax of $780,800 (see Appendix A, p. A–7) on the 2009 transfer (using a tax base of $2 million). If the 1986 taxable gift had not been included in the tax base for the 2009 gift, the tax would have been $345,800. The correct tax liability of $780,800 is more than twice $345,800! ■

Because the gift tax is cumulative in effect, a credit is allowed against the gift taxes paid (or deemed paid) on prior taxable gifts included in the tax base. The deemed paid credit is explained later in the chapter.

EXAMPLE 2

Assume the same facts as in Example 1. Don will be allowed a credit of $345,800 against the gift tax of $780,800. Thus, his gift tax liability for 2009 becomes $435,000 ($780,800 – $345,800). ■

Because Congress did not intend for the gift tax to apply to smaller transfers, it provided for an annual exclusion. Originally set at $3,000, the amount allowed is periodically adjusted for *significant* inflation. For 2009 through 2011, the amount allowed is $13,000 (for the period 2006–2008, the exclusion was $12,000).[11]

The formula for the gift tax is summarized in Figure 18.1.

LO.3

Analyze the Federal estate tax formula.

Formula for the Federal Estate Tax

The Federal unified transfer tax at death, commonly known as the Federal estate tax, is summarized in Figure 18.2.

The gross estate includes all of the property a decedent owns at the time of death. The inclusion may even extend to property that the decedent no longer owns—see the later discussion of gifts made within three years of death (§ 2035) and certain incomplete transfers (§§ 2036–2038). Moreover, the gross estate is to be distinguished from the probate estate, which is property that is subject to administration by the executor. (The probate estate is discussed further later in the chapter.)

Deductions from the gross estate to arrive at the taxable estate are quite extensive. In addition to the debts of the decedent (e.g., mortgages, credit card accounts, unpaid medical bills), they even include current and past income taxes (both

[10] For example, one state's inheritance tax provides an unlimited exemption for a surviving spouse and charities, $100,000 for Class A heirs (lineal descendants and ascendants), $500 for Class B heirs (collateral heirs), and $100 for Class C (other relatives and strangers). Beginning tax rates applicable to the nonexempt portion range from 2% to 10%, with the top rate applicable to Class C heirs reaching 20%.

[11] § 2503(b)(2).

FIGURE 18.1 Formula for the Federal Gift Tax

Determine whether the transfers are considered gifts by referring to §§ 2511 through 2519; list the fair market value of only the covered transfers		$xxx,xxx
Claim the annual exclusion (per donee) as available	$13,000 each	
Determine the charitable and marital deductions	xx,xxx	xx,xxx
Taxable gifts [as defined by § 2503(a)] for the current period		$ xx,xxx
Add: Taxable gifts from prior years		xx,xxx
Total of current and past taxable gifts		$ xx,xxx
Compute the gift tax on the total of current and past taxable gifts by using the rates in Appendix A		$ x,xxx
Subtract: Gift tax paid or deemed paid on past taxable gifts and the unified tax credit		xxx
Gift tax due on transfers during the current period		$ xxx

Federal and state). As in the case of the Federal gift tax, transfers to charity and to a spouse are deductible.

Note that the taxable estate must be adjusted further to arrive at a tax base before a tentative estate tax can be determined. The further adjustment requires the consideration of prior taxable gifts. The reason that post-1976 taxable gifts are added to the taxable estate to arrive at the tax base goes back to the scheme of the unified transfer tax. Starting in 1977, all transfers, whether lifetime or by death, were to be treated the same. Consequently, taxable gifts made after 1976 must be accounted for upon the death of the donor. Any possible double tax effect of including these gifts is mitigated by allowing a credit against the estate tax for the gift taxes previously paid or deemed paid.

Role of the Unified Tax Credit

The purpose of the **unified tax credit** is to allow donors and decedents to transfer modest amounts of wealth without being subject to the gift and estate taxes.

Table 18.1 shows the unified tax credit applicable to transfers by gift and by death from 2000 through 2013.[12]

FIGURE 18.2 Formula for the Federal Estate Tax

Gross estate (§§ 2031–2046)		$xxx,xxx
Subtract:		
Expenses, indebtedness, and taxes (§ 2053)	$xx	
Losses (§ 2054)	xx	
Charitable bequests (§ 2055)	xx	
Marital deduction (§§ 2056 and 2056A)	xx	
State death taxes (§ 2058)	xx	x,xxx
Taxable estate (§ 2051)		$ xx,xxx
Add: Post-1976 taxable gifts [§ 2001(b)]		x,xxx
Tax base		$xxx,xxx
Tentative tax on tax base [§ 2001(c)]		$ xx,xxx
Subtract:		
Unified transfer tax on post-1976 taxable gifts (gift taxes paid or deemed paid)	$xx	
Tax credits (including the unified tax credit) (§§ 2010–2016)	xx	x,xxx
Estate tax due		$ xxx

[12]The unified tax credits prior to 2000 can be found in §§ 2010 and 2505.

TABLE 18.1 Partial List of Unified Tax Credits

	Gift Tax		Estate Tax	
Year of Transfer	Credit	Exclusion Amount	Credit	Exclusion Amount
2000 and 2001	$ 220,550	$ 675,000	$ 220,550	$ 675,000
2002 and 2003	345,800	1,000,000	345,800	1,000,000
2004 and 2005	345,800	1,000,000	555,800	1,500,000
2006, 2007, and 2008	345,800	1,000,000	780,800	2,000,000
2009	345,800	1,000,000	1,455,800	3,500,000
2010	330,800*	1,000,000	–0–	–0–
2011 and 2012	1,730,800	5,000,000	1,730,800	5,000,000
2013	345,800	1,000,000	345,800	1,000,000

* Maximum gift tax rate drops to 35%.

The **exclusion amount** (also termed the **exemption equivalent** and the **bypass amount**) is the amount of the transfer that will pass free of the gift or estate tax by virtue of the credit.

EXAMPLE 3

In 2011, Janet makes a taxable gift of $5 million. Presuming she has made no prior taxable gifts, Janet will not owe any gift tax. Under the tax rate schedules (see Appendix A, p. A–8), the tax on $5 million is $1,730,800, which is the exact amount of the credit allowed.[13] ■

VALUATION FOR ESTATE AND GIFT TAX PURPOSES (§ 2032)

The value of the property on the date of its transfer generally determines the amount that is subject to the gift tax or the estate tax. Under certain conditions, however, an executor can elect to value estate assets on the **alternate valuation date**. The election is made by the executor of the estate and is irrevocable.

The alternate valuation date election was designed as a relief provision to ease the economic hardship that could result when estate assets decline in value over the six months after the date of death. If the election is made, all assets of the estate are valued six months after death *or* on the date of disposition if this occurs earlier.[14] The election covers *all* assets in the gross estate and cannot be applied to only a portion of the property.

EXAMPLE 4

In 2011, Robert's gross estate consists of the following property.

	Value on Date of Death	Value Six Months Later
Land	$4,800,000	$4,840,000
Stock in Brown Corporation	900,000	700,000
Stock in Green Corporation	500,000	460,000
Total	$6,200,000	$6,000,000

If Robert's executor elects the alternate valuation date, the estate must be valued at $6 million. It is not permissible to value the land at its date of death value ($4.8 million) and choose the alternate valuation date for the rest of the gross estate. ■

[13] The rate schedules are contained in § 2001(c), and *some* are reproduced in Appendix A of this text. The credits are subject to indexation for inflation for 2012, but the rate schedules are not.

[14] § 2032(a)(1). For this purpose, the term "disposition" is broadly defined. It includes the transfer of property to an heir to satisfy a bequest and the use of property to fund a testamentary trust. Reg. § 20.2032–1(c).

TAX *in the NEWS* — Estate Planning in Perspective

The future of the Federal estate and gift taxes is quite uncertain. For example, the generous provisions of TRA of 2010 (i.e., maximum rate of 35 percent and a credit of $5 million) are unlikely to be made permanent. It is also unlikely that the sunset provisions (i.e., maximum rate of 55 percent and a credit of $1 million) will be allowed to take effect in 2013—see Table 18.1. All of this uncertainty is unfortunate as one of the keys to effective tax planning is the ability to rely on the stability of the tax law.

Wealth transfers entail long-term projections that are dependent on assumptions that the relevant tax law will remain largely constant. Once an estate plan is established, practitioners and their clients generally do not anticipate the need for frequent modifications.

The somewhat drastic changes in the estate and gift tax provisions have made this traditional long-term approach impossible. Consequently, the validity of an estate plan may need to be reevaluated every time that Congress meets! This legislative instability adds to compliance costs and places an unnecessary burden on both taxpayers and their practitioners.

EXAMPLE 5

Assume the same facts as in Example 4, except that the executor sells the stock in Green Corporation for $480,000 four months after Robert's death. If the alternate valuation date is elected, the estate must be valued at $6,020,000 ($4,840,000 + $700,000 + $480,000). As to the Green stock, the value on its date of disposition controls because that date occurred prior to the six months' alternate valuation date. ■

The alternate valuation date election is not available unless the estate must file a Form 706 (Estate Tax Return). When an estate is required to file a Form 706 is discussed later in this chapter.

The election of the alternate valuation date must decrease the value of the gross estate *and* decrease the estate tax liability. The reason for this last requirement is that the income tax basis of property acquired from a decedent will be the value used for estate tax purposes (discussed further in Chapter 19). Without a special limitation, the alternate valuation date could be elected solely to add to income tax basis.

EXAMPLE 6

Al's gross estate consists of assets with a date of death value of $6 million and an alternate valuation date value of $6.1 million. Under Al's will, all of his property passes outright to Jean (Al's wife). Because of the marital deduction, no estate tax results regardless of which value is used. But if the alternate valuation date could be elected, Jean would have an income tax basis of $6.1 million in the property acquired from Al. ■

The alternate valuation date cannot be elected in Example 6 for two reasons, either of which would suffice. First, the alternate valuation date will not decrease Al's gross estate. Second, the election will not decrease Al's estate tax liability. Thus, his estate must use the date of death valuation of $6 million. As a result, Jean's income tax basis in the property received from Al is $6 million.

The election of the alternate valuation date does not take into account any postdeath income earned by the property. Any accrued income, therefore, is limited to that existing as of the date of death.

EXAMPLE 7

At the time of her death, Emma owned, *among other assets*, an apartment building with a value of $800,000 on which $40,000 of rents had accrued. On the alternate valuation date, the property had a value of $780,000 and accrued rents were $30,000. If the § 2032 election is made, $820,000 ($780,000 + $40,000) as to this property is included in Emma's gross estate. The $30,000 of postdeath income is not part of her gross estate. ■

Another valuation option available for estate tax purposes is the special use valuation method. Election of this method is limited to certain situations involving interests in closely held businesses (usually farms). Special use valuation is discussed in Chapter 19.

KEY PROPERTY CONCEPTS

When property is transferred either by gift or by death, the form of ownership can have a direct bearing on any transfer tax consequences. Understanding the different forms of ownership is necessary for working with Federal gift and estate taxes.

Undivided Ownership

Assume Dan and Vicky own an undivided but equal interest in a tract of land. Such ownership can fall into any of four categories: joint tenancy, tenancy by the entirety, tenancy in common, or community property.

If Dan and Vicky hold ownership as **joint tenants** or **tenants by the entirety**, the right of survivorship exists. This means that the last tenant to survive receives full ownership of the property. Thus, if Dan predeceases Vicky, the land belongs entirely to Vicky. None of the land will pass to Dan's heirs or will be subject to administration by Dan's executor. A tenancy by the entirety is a joint tenancy between husband and wife.

If Dan and Vicky hold ownership as **tenants in common** or as community property, death does not defeat an owner's interest. Thus, if Dan predeceases Vicky, Dan's one-half interest in the land will pass to his estate or heirs.

Community property interests arise from the marital relationship. Normally, all property acquired after marriage, except by gift or inheritance, by husband and wife residing in a community property state becomes part of the community. The following states have the community property system in effect: Louisiana, Texas, New Mexico, Arizona, California, Washington, Idaho, Nevada, Wisconsin, and (by election of the spouses) Alaska. All other states follow the common law system of ascertaining a spouse's rights to property acquired after marriage.

Partial Interests

Interests in assets can be divided in terms of rights to income and principal. Particularly when property is placed in trust, it is not uncommon to carve out various income interests that must be accounted for separately from the ultimate disposition of the property itself.

EXAMPLE 8

Under Bill's will, a ranch is to be placed in trust, life estate to Sam, Bill's son, with remainder to Sam's children (Bill's grandchildren). Under this arrangement, Sam is the life tenant and, as such, is entitled to the use of the ranch (including any income) during his life. Upon Sam's death, the trust terminates, and its principal passes to his children. Thus, Sam's children receive outright ownership in the ranch when Sam dies. ■

18.2 The Federal Gift Tax

LO.4

Discuss the operation of the Federal gift tax.

GENERAL CONSIDERATIONS

In working with the gift tax, it is first necessary to determine whether a gift has in fact taken place. In addition, some transfers are excluded from the gift tax.

Requirements for a Gift

For a gift to be complete under state law, the following elements must be present.

- A donor competent to make the gift.
- A donee capable of receiving and possessing the property.
- Donative intent on behalf of the donor.
- Actual or constructive delivery of the property to the donee or the donee's representative.
- Acceptance of the gift by the donee.

Incomplete Transfers

The Federal gift tax does not apply to transfers that are incomplete. Thus, if the transferor retains the right to reclaim the property or has not really parted with the possession of the property, a taxable event has not taken place.

EXAMPLE 9

Lesly creates a trust, income payable to Mary for life, remainder to Paul. Under the terms of the trust instrument, Lesly can revoke the trust at any time and repossess the trust principal and the income earned. No gift takes place on the creation of the trust; Lesly has not ceased to have dominion and control over the property. ■

EXAMPLE 10

Assume the same facts as in Example 9, except that one year after the transfer, Lesly relinquishes his right to terminate the trust. At this point, the transfer becomes complete, and the Federal gift tax applies. ■

Business versus Personal Setting

In a business setting, full and adequate consideration is apt to exist. If the parties are acting in a personal setting, however, a gift usually is the result.

EXAMPLE 11

Grace loans money to Debby in connection with a business venture. About a year later, Grace forgives part of the loan. Grace probably has not made a gift to Debby if she and Debby are unrelated parties.[15] ■

EXAMPLE 12

Assume the same facts as in Example 11, except that Grace and Debby are mother and daughter and no business venture is involved. If the loan itself was not actually a disguised gift, the later forgiveness is probably a gift. ■

It is the position of the IRS that valuable consideration (such as would preclude a gift result) does not include a payment or transfer based on "love and affection . . . promise of marriage, etc."[16] Consequently, property settlements in consideration of marriage (i.e., pre- or antenuptial agreements) are regarded as gifts.

IT'S THE THOUGHT THAT COUNTS

Joe (age 86) and Nicole (age 22) are married. Two days later they exchange wedding gifts. Joe's gift to Nicole is stock in IBM (valued at $2 million), while Nicole's gift to Joe is a bottle of cologne (value of $32). What tax goals are they trying to accomplish? Will their plan work?

Do not conclude that the presence of *some* consideration is enough to preclude Federal gift tax consequences. Again, the answer may rest on whether the transfer occurred in a business setting.

EXAMPLE 13

Peter sells Bob some real estate for $40,000. Unknown to Peter, the property contains valuable mineral deposits and is really worth $200,000. Peter may have made a bad business deal, but he has not made a gift of $160,000 to Bob. ■

EXAMPLE 14

Assume the same facts as in Example 13, except that Peter and Bob are father and son. In addition, Peter is very much aware that the property is worth $200,000. Peter has made a gift of $160,000 to Bob. ■

Certain Excluded Transfers

Transfers to political organizations are exempt from the application of the Federal gift tax.[17] This provision in the Code made unnecessary the previous practice whereby candidates for public office established multiple campaign committees to maximize the number of annual exclusions available to their contributors. As noted later, an annual exclusion of $13,000 for each donee passes free of the Federal gift tax.

[15]The forgiveness could result in taxable income to Debby under § 61(a)(12).

[16]Reg. § 25.2512–8.

[17]§ 2501(a)(5).

The Federal gift tax does not apply to tuition payments made to an educational organization (e.g., a college) on another's behalf. Nor does it apply to amounts paid on another's behalf for medical care.[18] In this regard, the law is realistic since it is unlikely that most donors would recognize these items as transfers subject to the gift tax. The payments, however, must be made directly to the provider (e.g., physician, hospital, college). There is no requirement that the beneficiary of the service (e.g., patient, student) qualify as a dependent of the person making the payment.

EXAMPLE 15
THE BIG PICTURE

Return to the facts of *The Big Picture* on p. 18-2. After Peter died in 2000, his widow, Martha, continued to live in the family home and refused to move in with either of her children (John or Helen). As Martha's health and mental condition deteriorated, her children did everything possible to keep the family housekeeper from quitting. In fact, Helen paid for the housekeeper's gallbladder operation, and John paid the college tuition of her oldest son.

Neither Helen nor John has made gifts to the housekeeper or her son. Gifts would have occurred, however, if Helen and John had reimbursed the housekeeper for the amounts involved, instead of paying the providers (i.e., physician, hospital, college) directly. ■

Satisfying an obligation of support is not subject to the gift tax. Thus, no gift takes place when parents pay for their children's education because one of the obligations of parents is to educate their children. What constitutes an obligation of support is determined by applicable state law. In many states, for example, adult children may have an obligation of support with respect to providing for indigent parents.

WHAT CONSTITUTES SUPPORT?

When Earl's daughter, Clara, turns 40, he gives her a Mercedes convertible as a birthday present. Clara is married and has a family of her own. She is a licensed orthopedic surgeon and maintains a successful practice in the field of sports medicine.

Earl does not regard the transfer as being subject to the gift tax. As a parent, he is merely satisfying his obligation of support. Such obligation includes providing your child with transportation. Is Earl's reasoning sound?

Lifetime versus Death Transfers

Be careful to distinguish between lifetime *(inter vivos)* and death (testamentary) transfers.

EXAMPLE 16

Dudley buys a 12-month certificate of deposit (CD) from State Bank and lists ownership as follows: "Dudley, payable on proof of death to Faye." Nine months later, Dudley dies. When the CD matures, Faye collects the proceeds from State Bank. No gift takes place when Dudley invests in the CD; Faye has received a mere expectancy (i.e., to obtain ownership of the CD upon Dudley's death). At any time before his death, Dudley may withdraw the funds or delete Faye's name from the account, thereby cutting off her expectancy. Furthermore, no gift occurs upon Dudley's death as the CD passes to Faye by testamentary disposition. As noted later, the CD will be included in Dudley's gross estate as property in which the decedent had an interest (§ 2033). ■

The payable on death (POD) designation used in Example 16 is a form of ownership frequently used in a family setting when investments are involved (e.g., stocks and bonds, savings accounts). It is very similar in effect to a revocable trust (see Example 9 above). Both carry the advantage of avoiding the probate estate (see Chapter 19). The POD designation, however, is simpler to use in the case of bank accounts and securities, and it avoids the need of having to create a formal trust.

[18]§ 2503(e).

TRANSFERS SUBJECT TO THE GIFT TAX

Whether a transfer is subject to the Federal gift tax depends upon the application of §§ 2511 through 2519 and the applicable Regulations.

Gift Loans

Loans between related parties are quite common. Such loans are frequently made to help pay for a college education or to finance a new business owned by a family member. Presuming that the advance is a bona fide loan at the outset (i.e., a gift is not intended), the absence of a provision for adequate interest can generate a multitude of tax consequences.

EXAMPLE 17

Harold lends his daughter Venetia $400,000 to start a dental practice. The loan is payable on demand, and no interest is provided for. Assuming a Federal interest rate of 10%, *each year* the loan is outstanding, the following tax consequences ensue.

- *Gift tax.* Harold makes a gift to Venetia of $40,000 (10% × $400,000). The annual exclusion is available to offset part of this transfer.
- *Income tax.* Harold has interest income of $40,000, and Venetia has an interest deduction of a like amount.[19] Because it relates to her trade or business, Venetia has a deduction *for* adjusted gross income. ■

The Code defines a gift loan as "any below-market loan where the foregoing [sic] of interest is in the nature of a gift."[20] Unless tax avoidance was one of the principal purposes of the loan, special limitations apply if the gift loan does not exceed $100,000. In such a case, the interest element may not exceed the borrower's net investment income.[21] Furthermore, if the net investment income does not exceed $1,000, it is treated as zero. Under a $1,000 *de minimis* rule, the interest element is disregarded.

Certain Property Settlements (§ 2516)

Normally, the settlement of certain marital rights is not regarded as being for consideration and is subject to the Federal gift tax.[22] As a special exception to this general approach, Congress enacted § 2516. By this provision, transfers of property interests made under the terms of a written agreement between spouses in settlement of their marital or property rights are deemed to be for adequate consideration. These transfers are exempt from the Federal gift tax if a final decree of divorce is obtained within the three-year period beginning on the date one year before the parties entered into the agreement. Likewise excluded are transfers to provide a reasonable allowance for the support of minor children (including legally adopted children) of a marriage. The agreement need not be approved by the divorce decree.

EXAMPLE 18
THE BIG PICTURE

Return to the facts of *The Big Picture* on p. 18-2. Recall that John and Hannah's divorce became final in January 2011. After extended but amicable negotiations, in September 2010 John and Hannah had agreed on a property settlement. In return for the receipt of $200,000 and title to their home, Hannah released all of her marital rights. Shortly thereafter, John made the transfer. Under § 2516, the property settlement resulted in no gift tax consequences to John. ■

Disclaimers (§ 2518)

A **disclaimer** is a refusal by a person to accept property that is designated to pass to him or her. The effect of the disclaimer is to pass the property to someone else.

[19] Example 20 in Chapter 1 deals with a similar situation and also covers any nonbusiness bad debt deduction the creditor might have if the loan is not repaid.

[20] § 7872(f)(3).

[21] Net investment income has the same meaning given to the term by § 163(d). Generally, net investment income is investment income (e.g., interest, dividends) less related expenses.

[22] Reg. § 25.2512–8.

EXAMPLE 19
THE BIG PICTURE

Return to the facts of *The Big Picture* on p. 18-2. Recall that Martha died in July of a heart condition. Under her will, her estate passes in equal parts to her son and daughter or, if they disclaim, to their children. (Under a buy-sell agreement—see Chapter 19—her stock in Hood Corporation is redeemed by the corporation with the insurance proceeds from a policy it took out on her life.) Helen disclaims her share of the inheritance, and the assets pass to her children. ■

Why might Helen disclaim her inheritance and have the property pass directly from Martha to the children? By doing so, an extra transfer tax may be avoided. If the disclaimer does not take place (i.e., Helen accepts the inheritance) and the property eventually passes to the children (either by gift or by death), the later transfer is subject to the application of either the gift tax or the estate tax.

The Federal gift tax can also be avoided in cases of a partial disclaimer of an undivided interest.

EXAMPLE 20
THE BIG PICTURE

Assume the same facts as in Example 19. John's share of his inheritance from Martha also includes the family hunting lodge. Except for the hunting lodge, John disclaims his share of the inheritance, and the remaining assets pass to his children. ■

To be effective, the disclaimer must be in writing and timely made. Generally, this means no later than nine months after the right to the property arose. Furthermore, the person making the disclaimer must not have accepted any benefits or interest in the property.

Other Transfers Subject to Gift Tax

Other transfers that may carry gift tax consequences (e.g., the exercise of a power of appointment, the creation of joint ownership) are discussed and illustrated in connection with the Federal estate tax.

Income Tax Considerations

Generally, a donor has no income tax consequences on making a gift.[23] A donee recognizes no income on the receipt of a gift.[24] A donee's income tax basis in the property received depends on a number of factors (e.g., donor's basis, year of gift, gift tax incurred by donor) and is discussed elsewhere in this text.[25]

ANNUAL EXCLUSION

In General

The first $13,000 of gifts made to any one person during any calendar year (except gifts of future interests in property) is excluded in determining the total amount of gifts for the year.[26] The **annual exclusion** applies to all gifts of a present interest made during the calendar year in the order in which they are made until the $13,000 exclusion per donee is exhausted. For a gift in trust, each beneficiary of the trust is treated as a separate person for purposes of the exclusion.

A **future interest** is defined as one that will come into being (as to use, possession, or enjoyment) at some future date. Examples of future interests include such rights as remainder interests that are commonly encountered when property is transferred to a trust. A *present interest* is an unrestricted right to the immediate use, possession, or enjoyment of property or of the income.

EXAMPLE 21

During 2011, Laura makes the following cash gifts: $8,000 to Rita and $14,000 to Maureen. Laura may claim an annual exclusion of $8,000 with respect to Rita and $13,000 with respect to Maureen. ■

[23]For situations where recognition can occur, see Chapter 19, Example 34.
[24]Both gifts and inheritances are excluded from income under § 103.
[25]Section 1015 is discussed and illustrated in Chapter 19, Examples 17 and 18.
[26]§ 2503(b).

EXAMPLE 22

By a lifetime gift, Ron transfers property to a trust with a life estate (with income payable annually) to June and remainder upon June's death to Albert. Ron has made two gifts: one to June of a life estate and one to Albert of a remainder interest. (The valuation of each of these gifts is discussed in Chapter 19.) The life estate is a present interest and qualifies for the annual exclusion. The remainder interest granted to Albert is a future interest and does not qualify for the exclusion. Note that Albert's interest does not come into being until some future date (on the death of June). ■

Although Example 22 indicates that the gift of an income interest is a present interest, this is not always the case. If a possibility exists that the income beneficiary may not receive the immediate enjoyment of the property, the transfer is of a future interest.

EXAMPLE 23

Assume the same facts as in Example 22, except that the income from the trust need not be payable annually to June. It may, at the trustee's discretion, be accumulated and added to the principal. Since June's right to receive the income from the trust is conditioned on the trustee's discretion, it is not a present interest. No annual exclusion is allowed. The mere possibility of diversion is enough. It would not matter if the trustee never exercised the discretion to accumulate and did, in fact, distribute the trust income to June annually. ■

Trust for Minors

Section 2503(c) offers an important exception to the future interest rules just discussed. Under this provision, a transfer for the benefit of a person who has not attained the age of 21 years on the date of the gift may be considered a gift of a present interest. This is true even though the minor is not given the unrestricted right to the immediate use, possession, or enjoyment of the property. For the exception to apply, the following conditions must be satisfied.

- Both the property and its income may be expended by or for the benefit of the minor before the minor attains the age of 21.
- Any portion of the property or its income not expended by the time the minor reaches the age of 21 shall pass to the minor at that time.
- If the minor dies before attaining the age of 21, the property and its income will be payable either to the minor's estate or as the minor may designate under a general power of appointment (discussed later in the chapter).

The exception allows a trustee to accumulate income on behalf of a minor beneficiary without converting the income interest to a future interest.

Contributions to Qualified Tuition Programs

For income tax purposes, § 529 plans have become the best of all possible worlds. Although no up-front deduction is allowed,[27] income earned by the fund accumulates free of income tax, and distributions are not taxed if they are used for higher education purposes. A special provision allows a donor to enjoy a gift tax advantage by using five years of annual exclusions.[28]

EXAMPLE 24

Trevor and Audrey would like to start building a college education fund for their 10-year-old granddaughter, Loni. In 2011, Trevor contributes $130,000 to the designated carrier of their state's § 529 plan. By electing to split the gift and using five annual exclusions [2 (number of donors) × $13,000 (annual exclusion) × 5 years = $130,000], no taxable gift results. (The gift-splitting election is discussed in detail later in this chapter.) Making the five-year election precludes Trevor and Audrey from using any annual exclusion on gifts to Loni for the next four years.[29] ■

[27] Depending on the taxpayer's home state, some (or all) of the deduction may be allowed for *state* income tax purposes.

[28] Section 529(c)(2)(A) protects against future interest treatment.

[29] Trevor and Audrey could resort to § 2503(e)(2)(A) to avoid any gift at all. As mentioned earlier, a *direct* payment of tuition to certain educational institutions is exempt from the gift tax. But this rule does not help to build an education fund for future use, as § 529 does. Recall that Loni, the granddaughter, is 10 years old.

Section 529(c)(4) provides that these college plans are not to be included in the gross estate of the transferor. This preferential treatment is needed because § 529 plans are incomplete transfers (some or all of the funds may be returned if college is not attended). As noted later, incomplete transfers are invariably subject to the estate tax.

DEDUCTIONS

In arriving at taxable gifts, a deduction is allowed for transfers to certain qualified charitable organizations. On transfers between spouses, a marital deduction may be available. Since both the charitable and marital deductions apply in determining the Federal estate tax, these deductions are discussed later in the chapter.

COMPUTING THE FEDERAL GIFT TAX

LO.5

Calculate the Federal gift tax.

The Unified Transfer Tax Rate Schedule

The top rates of the unified transfer tax rate schedule originally reached as high as 70 percent. Over the years, these top rates were reduced to 55 percent and then to 45 percent for 2007.[30] Effective for 2011 and 2012, the top rate is 35 percent for both the gift tax and the estate tax. (The 35 percent rate is the lowest since the Hoover administration.) Keep in mind that the unified transfer tax rate schedule applies to all transfers (by gift or death) after 1976. Different rate schedules apply for pre-1977 gifts and pre-1977 deaths.

The Deemed Paid Adjustment

As noted earlier, the gift tax is cumulative in effect (see Example 1). Since this means prior transfers will again be subject to tax, a credit is allowed for the taxes previously incurred (see Example 2). However, the amount of the credit allowed is based on the rates currently in effect. Called the *deemed paid* credit, it could be the same as, less than, or more than the tax actually paid. The difference between the deemed paid taxes and those actually paid is attributable to the change in the tax rate schedule that has taken place over the years. For example, see the variation in rates in Appendix A, pp. A–4 through A–7.

The Election to Split Gifts by Married Persons

To understand the reason for the gift-splitting election of § 2513, consider the following situations:

EXAMPLE 25

Dick and Margaret are husband and wife and reside in Michigan, a common law state. Dick has been the only breadwinner in the family, and Margaret has no significant property of her own. Neither has made any prior taxable gifts. In 2011, Dick makes a gift to Leslie of $6,026,000. Presuming the election to split gifts did not exist, Dick's gift tax is as follows.

Amount of gift	$ 6,026,000
Subtract: Annual exclusion	(13,000)
Taxable gift	$ 6,013,000
Gift tax on $6,013,000 per Appendix A, p. A–8 [$155,800 + 35% ($6,013,000 – $500,000)]	$ 2,085,350
Subtract: Unified transfer tax credit for 2011	(1,730,800)
Gift tax due on the 2011 taxable gift	$ 354,550

■

[30] § 2001(c)(2)(B). Note the drop in the top rate from 50% to 45% in the rate schedules for 2002 through 2007, reproduced in Appendix A. The rates for 2011 and 2012 are on p. A–8 and on the inside back cover of the text.

EXAMPLE 26

Assume the same facts as in Example 25, except that Dick and Margaret always have resided in California (a community property state). Even though Dick is the sole breadwinner, income from personal services generally is community property. Consequently, the gift to Leslie probably involves community property. If this is the case, the gift tax is as follows.

	Dick	Margaret
Amount of gift	$3,013,000	$3,013,000
Subtract: Annual exclusion	(13,000)	(13,000)
Taxable gift	$3,000,000	$3,000,000
Gift tax on $3,000,000 per Appendix A, p. A-8	$1,030,800	1,030,800
Subtract: Unified transfer tax credit for 2011	(1,730,800)	(1,730,800)
Gift tax due on the 2011 taxable gift	$ -0-	$ -0-

■

As the results of Examples 25 and 26 indicate, married donors residing in community property jurisdictions possessed a significant gift tax advantage over those residing in common law states. To rectify this inequity, the Revenue Act of 1948 incorporated into the Code the predecessor to § 2513. Under this provision, a gift made by a person to someone other than his or her spouse may be considered, for Federal gift tax purposes, as having been made one-half by each spouse. Returning to Example 25, Dick and Margaret could treat the gift passing to Leslie as being made one-half by each of them. They may do this even though the cash belonged to Dick. As a result, the parties are able to achieve the same tax consequence as in Example 26. As is the case with the owner spouse, any past taxable gifts of the non-owner spouse must be taken into account in determining the current gift tax.

To split gifts, the spouses must be legally married to each other at the time of the gift. If they are divorced later in the calendar year, they may still split the gift if neither marries anyone else during that year. They both must indicate on their separate gift tax returns their consent to have all gifts made in that calendar year split between them. In addition, both must be citizens or residents of the United States on the date of the gift. A gift from one spouse to the other spouse cannot be split. Such a gift might, however, be eligible for the marital deduction.

The election to split gifts is not necessary when husband and wife transfer jointly owned or community property to a third party. It is available, however, if the gift consists of the separate property of one of the spouses. Community property rules generally define separate property as property acquired before marriage and property acquired after marriage by gift or inheritance. The election, then, is not limited to residents of common law states.

Special Rule for Gifts Made in 2010

In addition to eliminating the estate tax for 2010, EGTRRA of 2001 provided special rules for gifts made in 2010.

- The maximum tax rate was reduced to 35 percent—see Appendix A, p. A-7.
- Although the exclusion amount remains at $1 million, the credit allowed drops to $330,800—see Table 18.1.

As previously noted, after 2010 the exclusion amounts for both the gift tax and the estate tax are the same (i.e., unified) and rise to $5 million.

PROCEDURAL MATTERS

Having determined which transfers are subject to the Federal gift tax and the various deductions and exclusions available to the donor, the procedural aspects of the tax should be considered. The following section discusses the return itself, the due dates for filing and paying the tax, and other related matters.

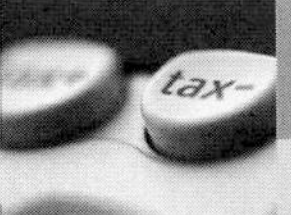

CONCEPT SUMMARY 18.1

Federal Gift Tax Provisions

1. The Federal gift tax applies to all gratuitous transfers of property made by U.S. citizens or residents. In this regard, it does not matter where the property is located.
2. In the eyes of the IRS, a gratuitous transfer is one not supported by full and adequate consideration. If the parties are acting in a business setting, such consideration usually exists. If, however, purported sales are between family members, a gift element may be suspected.
3. If one party lends money to another and intends some or all of the interest element to be a gift, the arrangement is categorized as a gift loan. To the extent that the interest provided for is less than the market rate, three tax consequences result. First, a gift has taken place between the lender and the borrower as to the interest element. Second, income may result to the lender. Third, an income tax deduction may be available to the borrower.
4. Property settlements can escape the gift tax if a divorce occurs within a prescribed period of time.
5. A disclaimer is a refusal by a person to accept property designated to pass to that person. The effect of a disclaimer is to pass the property to someone else. If certain conditions are satisfied, the issuance of a disclaimer will not be subject to the Federal gift tax.
6. Except for gifts of future interests, a donor is allowed an annual exclusion of $13,000. The future interest limitation does not apply to certain trusts created for minors.
7. The election to split a gift enables a married couple to be treated as two donors. The election doubles the annual exclusion and makes the nonowner spouse's unified tax credit available to the owner spouse.
8. The election to split gifts is not necessary if the property is jointly owned by the spouses. That is the case when the property is part of the couple's community.
9. In determining the tax base for computing the gift tax, all prior taxable gifts must be added to current taxable gifts. Thus, the gift tax is cumulative in nature.
10. Gifts are reported on Form 709. The return is due on April 15 following the year of the gift.

The Federal Gift Tax Return

For transfers by gift, a Form 709 (U.S. Gift Tax Return) must be filed whenever the gifts for any one calendar year exceed the annual exclusion or involve a gift of a future interest. A Form 709 need not be filed, however, for transfers between spouses that are offset by the unlimited marital deduction regardless of the amount of the transfer.[31]

EXAMPLE 27

In 2011, Larry makes five gifts, each in the amount of $13,000, to his five children. If the gifts do not involve future interests, a Form 709 need not be filed to report the transfers. ■

EXAMPLE 28

During 2011, Esther makes a gift of $26,000 cash of her separate property to her daughter. To double the amount of the annual exclusion allowed, Jerry (Esther's husband) is willing to split the gift. Since the § 2513 election can be made only on a gift tax return, a Form 709 must be filed even though no gift tax will be due as a result of the transfer. ■

In Example 28, no gift tax return would be necessary if the transfer consisted of community property. Since two donors are now involved, the cap for filing becomes more than $26,000, rather than more than $13,000.

Presuming a gift tax return is due, it must be filed on or before the fifteenth day of April following the year of the gift.[32] As is the case with other Federal taxes, when the due date falls on Saturday, Sunday, or a legal holiday, the date for filing the return is the next business day. Note that the filing requirements for Form 709 have no correlation to the accounting year used by a donor for Federal income tax purposes. Thus, a fiscal year taxpayer must follow the April 15 rule for any reportable gifts. If sufficient reason is shown, the IRS is authorized to grant reasonable extensions of time for filing the return.[33]

[31] § 6019(a)(2).

[32] § 6075(b)(1).

[33] § 6081. Under § 6075(b)(2), an extension of time granted to a calendar year taxpayer for filing an income tax return automatically extends the due date of a gift tax return.

18.3 The Federal Estate Tax

The following discussion of the estate tax coincides with the formula that appeared earlier in the chapter in Figure 18.2. The key components in the formula are the gross estate, the taxable estate, the tax base, and the credits allowed against the tentative tax. This formula can be summarized as follows:

GROSS ESTATE

LO.6

Identify the components of the gross estate.

Simply stated, the **gross estate** includes all property subject to the Federal estate tax. This depends on the provisions of the Internal Revenue Code as supplemented by IRS pronouncements and the judicial interpretations of Federal courts.

In contrast to the gross estate, the **probate estate** is controlled by state (rather than Federal) law. The probate estate consists of all of a decedent's property subject to administration by the executor or administrator of the estate. The administration is supervised by a local court of appropriate jurisdiction (usually designated as a probate court). An executor is the decedent's personal representative appointed under the decedent's will. When a decedent dies without a will or fails to name an executor in the will (or that person refuses to serve), the local probate court appoints an administrator.

The probate estate is frequently smaller than the gross estate. It contains only property owned by the decedent at the time of death and passing to heirs under a will or under the law of intestacy (the order of distribution for those dying without a will). As noted later, such items as the proceeds of many life insurance policies and distributions from retirement plans become part of the gross estate but are not included in the probate estate.

All states provide for an order of distribution in the event someone dies *intestate* (i.e., without a will). After the surviving spouse, who receives some or all of the estate, the preference is usually in the following order: down to lineal descendants (e.g., children, grandchildren), up to lineal ascendants (e.g., parents, grandparents), and out to collateral relations (e.g., brothers, sisters, aunts, and uncles).

Property Owned by the Decedent (§ 2033)

Property owned by the decedent at the time of death is included in the gross estate. The nature of the property or the use to which it was put during the decedent-owner's lifetime has no significance as far as the estate tax is concerned. Thus, personal effects (such as clothing), stocks, bonds, mutual funds, furniture, jewelry, bank accounts, and certificates of deposit are all included in the deceased owner's gross estate. No distinction is made between tangible and intangible, depreciable and nondepreciable, business and personal assets. However, a deceased spouse's gross estate does not include the surviving spouse's share of the community property.

The application of § 2033 is illustrated as follows:

EXAMPLE 29

Irma dies owning some City of Denver bonds. The fair market value of the bonds plus any interest accrued to the date of Irma's death is included in her gross estate. Although interest on municipals normally is not taxable under the Federal income tax, it is property owned by Irma at the time of death. However, any interest accrued after death is not part of Irma's gross estate. ■

GLOBAL Tax Issues

FOREIGN TRANSFER TAXES—A MIXED BAG

Of the 30 countries that are members of the Organization for Economic Cooperation and Development (OECD), only the United States and the United Kingdom assess gift and estate taxes that apply to transfers during life *and* at death. The majority of OECD countries impose inheritance taxes. Six countries—Australia, Canada, Mexico, New Zealand, the Slovak Republic, and Sweden—impose neither inheritance nor estate taxes. In Canada, however, the transfer of a capital asset at death is treated as a sale, and any gain must be recognized. Although no sale occurs, in Australia and Mexico the decedent's income tax basis carries over to the heir. New Zealand does not have an estate tax, but it imposes a form of gift tax for annual lifetime transfers beyond a certain amount.

Source: Adapted from Joint Committee on Taxation, "Description and Analysis of Alternative Wealth Transfer Tax Systems," March 10, 2008, p. 3.

EXAMPLE 30

Sharon dies on April 7, 2011, at a time when she owns stock in Robin Corporation and Wren Corporation. On March 3 of this year, both corporations authorized a cash dividend payable on May 5. Robin's dividend is payable to shareholders of record as of April 1. Wren's date of record is April 8. Sharon's gross estate includes the following: the stock in Robin Corporation, the stock in Wren Corporation, and the dividend on the Robin stock. It does not include the dividend on the Wren stock. ■

EXAMPLE 31

Ray dies holding some promissory notes issued to him by his son. In his will, Ray forgives these notes, relieving the son of the obligation to make any payments. The fair market value of these notes is included in Ray's gross estate. ■

EXAMPLE 32
THE BIG PICTURE

Return to the facts of *The Big Picture* on p. 18-2. At the time of his death, John was the president of Hood Corporation. John's estate receives a distribution from Hood's qualified pension plan of $1.1 million consisting of the following:

Hood's contributions	$450,000
John's after-tax contributions	350,000
Income earned by the plan	300,000

John's estate also receives $150,000 from Hawk Insurance Company. The payment represents the maturity value of term life insurance from a group plan Hood maintains for its employees. As to these amounts, John's gross estate includes $1,250,000 ($1,100,000 + $150,000). For income tax purposes, however, $750,000 ($450,000 + $300,000) is subject to tax, while $500,000 ($350,000 + $150,000) is not. ■

Regarding the result reached in Example 32, retirement plan benefits are invariably subject to estate tax. Besides the conventional qualified pension and profit-sharing plans involved in Example 32, retirement plans include those under § 401(k), § 403(b) for teachers, § 457 for government employees, Keogh (H.R. 10) for self-employed persons, and IRAs—both traditional and Roth. Inclusion in the gross estate occurs irrespective of income tax consequences. Thus, a benefit paid under a Roth IRA is fully subject to the estate tax even though it may not be taxable as income to the beneficiary. The possibility of an income tax deduction for estate taxes paid is covered in Chapter 20 in connection with the discussion of income in respect of a decedent.

In addition to the items noted above, § 2033 operates to include in the gross estate many assets that can be of significant value. Examples include:

- Real estate holdings (but see § 2040 for jointly owned property).
- Present value of future royalty rights (e.g., patents, copyrights, mineral interests).

- Interests in a business (i.e., sole proprietorship, partnership).
- Collectibles (e.g., works of art, coin collections).
- Renewal value of leasehold interests.
- Terminable interests (e.g., life estates in realty or trusts) held by a surviving spouse as to which a deceased spouse's estate has made a QTIP election (discussed later in this chapter).
- Unmatured insurance policies on the lives of others.
- Proceeds from casualty and life insurance policies payable to the estate.
- Present value of pending and potential lawsuits or past judgments rendered.

EXAMPLE 33
THE BIG PICTURE

Return to the facts of *The Big Picture* on p. 18-2. Recall that John's death ultimately resulted from injuries suffered in a car accident caused by another motorist. In addition, John's auto was destroyed in the accident. Presuming the other driver is solvent or carries casualty insurance, John's gross estate should include the present value of any expected settlement that could result from possible legal action. At the least, his estate must include the recovery expected from his own casualty policy. ■

Dower and Curtesy Interests (§ 2034)

In its common law (nonstatutory) form, dower generally gave a surviving widow a life estate in a portion of her husband's estate (usually the real estate he owned) with the remainder passing to their children. Most states have modified and codified these common law rules, and the resulting statutes often vary between jurisdictions. Curtesy is a similar right held by the husband in his wife's property that takes effect in the event he survives her.

Dower and curtesy rights are incomplete interests and may never materialize. Thus, if a wife predeceases her husband, the dower interest in her husband's property is lost.

EXAMPLE 34

Martin dies without a will, leaving an estate of $6.9 million. Under state law, Belinda (Martin's widow) is entitled to one-third of his property. The $2.3 million Belinda receives is included in Martin's gross estate. Depending on the nature of the interest Belinda receives in the $2.3 million, this amount could qualify Martin's estate for a marital deduction. (This possibility is discussed at greater length later in the chapter. For the time being, however, the focus is on what is or is not included as part of the decedent's gross estate.) ■

Adjustments for Gifts Made within Three Years of Death (§ 2035)

At one time, all taxable gifts made within three years of death were included in the donor's gross estate unless it could be shown that the gifts were not made in contemplation of death. The special three-year rule for "deathbed gifts" was needed because the gift and estate taxes had not yet been merged into a unified tax. Making such gifts prior to death was advantageous then, as the lower tax rates of the separate gift tax applied.

With the adoption of the unified transfer tax system, post-1976 taxable gifts are added to the taxable estate in arriving at the tax base for determining the estate tax liability—see Figure 18.2 earlier in the chapter. Nevertheless, the three-year rule for inclusion in the gross estate has been retained for the following items.

- Inclusion in the gross estate of any gift tax paid on gifts made within three years of death. Called the *gross-up* procedure, it prevents the gift tax amount from escaping the estate tax.
- Any property interests transferred by gift within three years of death that would have been included in the gross estate and consist of transfers with a retained life estate (§ 2036), transfers taking effect at death (§ 2037), revocable transfers (§ 2038), and proceeds of life insurance (§ 2042). All except transfers taking effect at death (§ 2037) are discussed later in the chapter.

EXAMPLE 35

Before her death in 2011, Jennifer made the following taxable gifts.

Year of Gift	Nature of the Asset	Fair Market Value: Date of Gift	Fair Market Value: Date of Death	Gift Tax Paid
1992	Hawk Corporation stock	$200,000	$1,300,000	$ –0–
2009	Policy on Jennifer's life	80,000 (cash value)	1,000,000 (face value)	–0–
2010	Land	800,000	810,000	16,000

Jennifer's *gross estate* includes $1,016,000 [$1,000,000 (life insurance proceeds) + $16,000 (gross-up for the gift tax on the 2010 taxable gift)] as to these transfers. Referring to the formula for the estate tax (see Figure 18.2), the other post-1976 taxable gifts are added to the *taxable estate* (at the fair market value on the date of the gift) in arriving at the tax base. In the case of the Hawk stock, notice the substantial saving in transfer taxes that will occur. The gift tax (although none resulted) is based on $200,000, whereas an estate tax would have applied to $1.3 million. Thus, the appreciation of $1.1 million has escaped any transfer tax. Jennifer's estate is allowed a credit for the gift tax paid (or deemed paid) on the 2010 transfer. ■

The three-year rule also applies in testing for qualification under § 303 (stock redemptions to pay death taxes and administration expenses), § 2032A (special valuation procedures), and § 6166 (extensions of time to pay Federal estate taxes).[34] These provisions are discussed in Chapters 6 and 19.

Transfers with a Retained Life Estate (§ 2036)

Code §§ 2036 through 2038 were enacted on the premise that the estate tax can be avoided on lifetime transfers only if the decedent does not retain control over the property. The logic of this approach is somewhat difficult to dispute. One should not be able to escape the tax consequences of property transfers at death while remaining in a position to enjoy some or all of the fruits of ownership during life.

Under § 2036, the value of any property transferred by the deceased during lifetime for less than adequate consideration must be included if either of the following was retained:

- The possession or enjoyment of, or the right to the income from, the property.
- The right, either alone or in conjunction with any person, to designate the persons who shall possess or enjoy the property or the income.

The decedent is considered to have retained the right to the income from the property to the extent that such income is to be applied toward the discharge of his or her legal obligations.[35]

EXAMPLE 36
THE BIG PICTURE

Return to the facts of *The Big Picture* on p. 18-2. Before Peter Hood died in 2000, he established several trusts. One trust grants John an income interest for life (i.e., a life estate), and upon his death, the trust passes to his children (i.e., remainder interest). On John's death, none of the trust property is included in his gross estate. Although he held a life estate, he was not the transferor (Peter was) of the property placed in trust. ■

EXAMPLE 37
THE BIG PICTURE

Return to the facts of *The Big Picture* on p. 18-2. Immediately after inheriting the family hunting lodge from his mother (see Example 20), John transfers it to a newly created trust. Under the terms of the trust instrument, he retains a life estate, remainder to his children and Helen (John's sister). Upon John's death, the property in the trust will be included in his gross estate under § 2036. ■

[34] §§ 2035(c)(1) and (2).

[35] § 2036(a)(1).

In both of the preceding examples, a gift occurred when the trusts were created. In Example 36, Peter made a gift of the entire amount placed in trust. In Example 37, John made a gift of only the remainder interest—see Chapter 19 for how the value of a remainder interest is determined.

Revocable Transfers (§ 2038)

Another type of lifetime transfer that is drawn into a decedent's gross estate is covered by § 2038. The gross estate includes the value of property interests transferred by the decedent (except to the extent that the transfer was made for full consideration) if the enjoyment of the property transferred was subject, at the date of the decedent's death, to any power of the decedent to *alter, amend, revoke, or terminate* the transfer. This includes the power to change the beneficiaries or the power to accelerate or increase any beneficiary's enjoyment of the property.

The Code and the Regulations make it clear that one cannot avoid inclusion in the gross estate under § 2038 by relinquishing a power within three years of death.[36] Recall that § 2038 is one of several types of situations listed as exceptions to the usual rule excluding gifts made within three years of death from the gross estate.

The classic § 2038 situation results from the use of a revocable trust. Example 9 (earlier in this chapter) illustrates the use of a revocable trust. Example 10 shows what happens when the right of revocation is relinquished during the life of the creator of the trust. When the right of revocation is relinquished within three years of death, the trust is included in the creator's gross estate.

Annuities (§ 2039)

Annuities can be divided by their origin into commercial and noncommercial contracts. Noncommercial annuities are issued by private parties and, in some cases, charitable organizations that do not regularly issue annuities. The two varieties have much in common, but noncommercial annuities present special income tax problems and are not treated further in this discussion.

An annuity is one or more payments extending over any period of time. The payments may be equal or unequal, conditional or unconditional, periodic or sporadic. Annuity contracts that terminate upon the death of the person covered (i.e., annuitant) are designated as straight-life annuities. Other contracts provide for a survivorship feature (e.g., reduced payments to a surviving spouse).

In the case of a straight-life annuity, nothing is included in the gross estate of the annuitant at death. Section 2033 (property in which the decedent had an interest) does not apply because the annuitant's interest in the contract is terminated by death. Section 2036 (transfers with a retained life estate) does not cover the situation; a transfer made for full consideration is specifically excluded from § 2036 treatment. A commercial annuity is presumed to have been purchased for full consideration unless some evidence exists to indicate that the parties were not acting at arm's length.

EXAMPLE 38

Arnold purchases a straight-life annuity that will pay him $24,000 a month when he reaches age 65. Arnold dies at age 70. Except for the payments he received before his death, nothing relating to this annuity affects Arnold's gross estate. ■

In the case of a survivorship annuity, the estate tax consequences under § 2039(a) are usually triggered by the death of the first annuitant. The amount included in the gross estate is the cost from the same company of a comparable annuity covering the survivor at his or her attained age on the date of the deceased annuitant's death.

EXAMPLE 39

Assume the same facts as in Example 38, except that the annuity contract provides for Veronica to be paid $12,000 a month for life as a survivorship feature. Veronica is 62 years of age when Arnold dies. Under these circumstances, Arnold's gross estate

[36] § 2038(a)(1) and Reg. § 20.2038–1(e)(1).

includes the cost of a comparable contract that provides an annuity of $12,000 per month for the life of a female, age 62. ■

Full inclusion of the survivorship element in the gross estate is subject to an exception under § 2039(b). The amount includible is to be based on the proportion of the deceased annuitant's contribution to the total cost of the contract. This is expressed by the following formula:

$$\frac{\text{Decedent's contribution to purchase price}}{\text{Total purchase price of the annuity}} \times \text{Value of the annuity (or refund) at decedent's death} = \text{Amount includible in the deceased annuitant's gross estate}$$

EXAMPLE 40

Assume the same facts as in Example 39, except that Arnold and Veronica are husband and wife and have always lived in a community property state. The premiums on the contract were paid with community funds. Since Veronica contributed half of the cost of the contract, only half of the amount determined under Example 39 is included in Arnold's gross estate. ■

The result reached in Example 40 is not unique to community property jurisdictions. The outcome would have been the same in a noncommunity property state if Veronica had furnished half of the consideration from her own funds.

In determining a decedent's contribution to an annuity contract, a special rule applies to employment-related retirement plans. In these cases, the employer's contribution to the plan is treated as having been made by the employee.

EXAMPLE 41

Under a noncontributory qualified retirement plan funded by his employer, Jim is entitled to an annuity for life. The plan also provides for a survivorship annuity for Jim's wife, Ellen, in the event he predeceases her. Upon Jim's prior death, the value of the survivorship annuity is included in his gross estate. Jim did not actually contribute to the cost of the annuity, but his employer's contributions are attributed to him. ■

Joint Interests (§§ 2040 and 2511)

Recall that joint tenancies and tenancies by the entirety are characterized by the right of survivorship. Thus, upon the death of a joint tenant, title to the property passes to the surviving tenant. None of the property is included in the *probate* estate of the deceased tenant. In the case of tenancies in common and community property, death does not defeat an ownership interest. Further, the deceased owner's interest is part of the probate estate.

The Federal *estate tax treatment* of tenancies in common or of community property follows the logical approach of taxing only the portion of the property included in the deceased owner's probate estate.

EXAMPLE 42

Homer, Wilma, and Thelma acquire a tract of land, ownership listed as tenants in common, each party furnishing $200,000 of the $600,000 purchase price. When the property is worth $900,000, Homer dies. If Homer's undivided interest in the property is $33\frac{1}{3}$%, the gross estate *and* probate estate each include $300,000. This one-third interest is also the same amount that passes to Homer's heirs. ■

Unless the parties have provided otherwise, each tenant is deemed to own an interest equal to the portion of the original consideration he or she furnished. The parties in Example 42 could have provided that Homer would receive an undivided half interest in the property although he contributed only one-third of the purchase price. In that case, Wilma and Thelma have made a gift to Homer when the tenancy was created, and Homer's gross estate and probate estate each include $450,000.

For certain joint tenancies, the tax consequences are different. All of the property is included in the deceased co-owner's gross estate unless it can be proved that the surviving co-owners contributed to the cost of the property.[37] If a contribution can be shown, the amount to be *excluded* is calculated by the following formula:

$$\frac{\text{Surviving co-owner's contribution}}{\text{Total cost of the property}} \times \text{Fair market value of the property}$$

In computing a survivor's contribution, any funds received as a gift *from the deceased co-owner* and applied to the cost of the property cannot be counted. However, income or gain from gift assets can be counted.

EXAMPLE 43

Keith and Steve (father and son) acquire a tract of land, ownership listed as joint tenancy with right of survivorship. Keith furnished $400,000 and Steve $200,000 of the $600,000 purchase price. Of the $200,000 provided by Steve, $100,000 had previously been received as a gift from Keith. When the property is worth $900,000, Keith dies. Because only $100,000 of Steve's contribution can be counted (the other $100,000 was received as a gift from Keith), Steve has furnished only one-sixth ($100,000/$600,000) of the cost. Thus, Keith's gross estate must include five-sixths of $900,000, or $750,000. This presumes Steve can prove that he did in fact make the $100,000 contribution. In the absence of such proof, the full value of the property is included in Keith's gross estate. Keith's death makes Steve the immediate owner of the property by virtue of the right of survivorship. None of the property is part of Keith's probate estate. ■

If the co-owners receive the property as a gift or bequest *from another*, each owner is deemed to have contributed to the cost (or value on date of death) of his or her own interest.

EXAMPLE 44
THE BIG PICTURE

Return to the facts of *The Big Picture* on p. 18-2. During his lifetime, Peter Hood purchased timberland listing title as follows: "John and Helen Hood as equal tenants in common." John's basis in the property is one-half of Peter's cost. Upon John's death, one-half of the value of the timberland is included in his gross estate. ■

EXAMPLE 45
THE BIG PICTURE

Return to the facts of *The Big Picture* on p. 18-2. In her will, Martha leaves the Hood family residence to her children (John and Helen) as joint tenants with right of survivorship. John's income tax basis is one-half of the value on Martha's death. On John's later death, one-half of the value at that time will be included in his gross estate. Keep in mind that under the right of survivorship, outright ownership goes to Helen and none of the property passes to John's heirs. ■

To simplify the joint ownership rules for *married persons*, § 2040(b) provides for an automatic inclusion rule upon the death of the first joint-owner spouse to die. Regardless of the amount contributed by each spouse, one-half of the value of the property is included in the gross estate of the spouse who dies first. The special rule eliminates the need to trace the source of contributions and recognizes that any inclusion in the gross estate is neutralized by the marital deduction.

[37] § 2040(a).

EXAMPLE 46
THE BIG PICTURE

Return to the facts of *The Big Picture* on p. 18-2. Recall that after his divorce from Hannah, John married Ashley. Since Hannah kept his prior home as part of the property settlement (see Example 18), John purchased a new residence. He listed title to the property as "John and Ashley Hood, tenancy by the entirety with right of survivorship." Upon John's death, only one-half of the value of the property is included in his gross estate.

If Ashley had died first, one-half of the value of the residence would have been included in her gross estate even though she made no contribution to its cost. ■

In Example 46, inclusion in the gross estate of the first spouse to die is neutralized by the unlimited marital deduction allowed for estate tax purposes (see the discussion of § 2056 later in the chapter). Under the right of survivorship, the surviving joint tenant obtains full ownership of the property. The marital deduction generally is allowed for property passing from one spouse to another.

Whether a *gift* results when property is transferred into some form of joint ownership depends on the consideration furnished by each of the contributing parties for the ownership interest acquired.

EXAMPLE 47

Brenda and Sarah purchase real estate as tenants in common. Of the $800,000 purchase price, Brenda furnishes $600,000 and Sarah furnishes only $200,000. If each is an equal owner in the property, Brenda has made a gift to Sarah of $200,000. ■

EXAMPLE 48

Martha purchases real estate for $900,000, the title to the property being listed as follows: "Martha, Sylvia, and Dan as joint tenants with the right of survivorship." If under state law the mother (Martha), the daughter (Sylvia), and the son (Dan) are deemed to be equal owners in the property, Martha is treated as having made gifts of $300,000 to Sylvia and $300,000 to Dan. ■

Several important *exceptions* exist to the general rule that gift treatment is triggered by the creation of a joint ownership with disproportionate interests resulting from unequal consideration. First, if the transfer involves a joint bank account, there is no gift at the time of the contribution. If a gift occurs, it is when the noncontributing party withdraws the funds provided by the other joint tenant. Second, the same rule applies to the purchase of U.S. savings bonds.[38] Again, any gift tax consequences are postponed until the noncontributing party appropriates some or all of the proceeds for his or her individual use.

EXAMPLE 49

Cynthia deposits $400,000 in a bank account under the names of Cynthia and Carla as joint tenants. Both Cynthia and Carla have the right to withdraw funds from the account without the other's consent. Cynthia has not made a gift to Carla when the account is established. ■

EXAMPLE 50

Assume the same facts as in Example 49. At some later date, Carla withdraws $100,000 from the account for her own use. At this point, Cynthia has made a gift to Carla of $100,000. ■

EXAMPLE 51

Wesley purchases a U.S. savings bond that he registers in the names of Wesley and Harriet. After Wesley dies, Harriet redeems the bond. No gift takes place when Wesley buys the bond. In addition, Harriet's redemption is not treated as a gift since the bond passed to her by testamentary disposition (Harriet acquired the bond by virtue of surviving Wesley) and not through a lifetime transfer. However, the fair market value of the bond is included in Wesley's gross estate under § 2040. ■

[38] Reg. § 25.2511–1(h)(4).

TAX *in* the NEWS — **What Did That Decedent Own?**

Recent IRS data examining Forms 706 offer insights into the investment portfolios and other asset holdings of decedents who filed Federal estate tax returns.

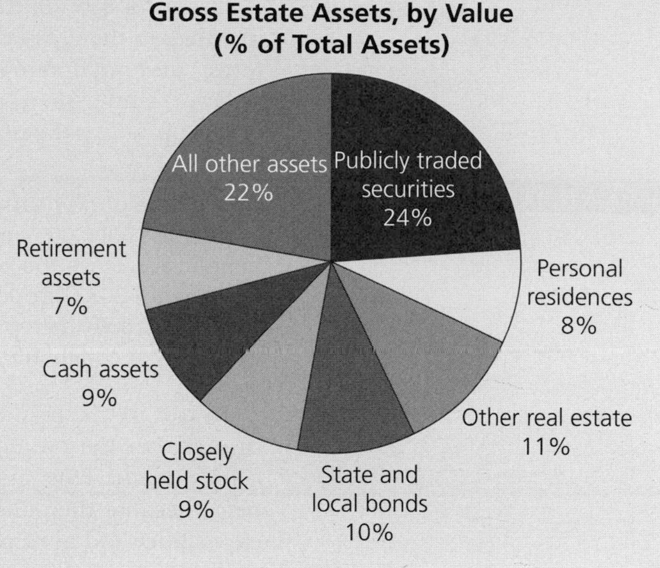

Powers of Appointment (§§ 2041 and 2514)

A **power of appointment** is a power to determine who shall own or enjoy, at the present or in the future, the property subject to the power. It must be created by another and does not include a power created or retained by the decedent when he or she transferred his or her own property.

Powers of appointment fall into one of two classifications: *general* and *special*. A general power of appointment is one in which the decedent could have appointed himself, his creditors, his estate, or the creditors of his estate. In contrast, a special power enables the holder to appoint to others but *not* to herself, her creditors, her estate, or the creditors of her estate. Assume, for example, that Don has the power to designate how the principal of the trust will be distributed among Edie, Frank, and Georgia. At this point, Don's power is only a special power of appointment. If Don is given the further right to appoint the principal to himself, what was a special power of appointment becomes a general power.

Three things can happen to a power of appointment: exercise, lapse, and release. Exercising the power involves appointing the property to one or all of the parties designated. A lapse occurs upon failure to exercise a power. Thus, if Don fails to indicate how the principal of a trust will be distributed among Edie, Frank, and Georgia, Don's power of appointment will lapse, and the principal will pass in accordance with the terms of the trust instrument. A release occurs if the holder relinquishes a power of appointment.

Powers of appointment have the following transfer tax consequences.

1. No tax implications result from the exercise, lapse, or release of a special power of appointment.
2. A gift or inclusion in the gross estate results from the exercise, lapse, or release of a general power of appointment.

EXAMPLE 52

Justin, Monica's father, leaves his property in trust, life estate to Monica and remainder to whichever of Monica's children she decides to appoint in her will. Monica's power is not a general power of appointment because she cannot exercise it in favor of herself. Thus, regardless of whether Monica exercises the power or not, none of the trust property subject to the power is included in her gross estate. ■

Life Insurance (§ 2042)

Under § 2042, the gross estate includes the proceeds of life insurance on the decedent's life if (1) they are receivable by the estate, (2) they are receivable by another for the benefit of the estate, or (3) the decedent possessed an incident of ownership in the policy.

Life insurance on the life of another owned by a decedent at the time of death is included in the gross estate under § 2033 (property in which the decedent had an interest) and not under § 2042. The amount includible is the replacement value of the policy.[39] Under these circumstances, inclusion of the face amount of the policy is inappropriate as the policy has not yet matured.

EXAMPLE 53

At the time of his death, Luigi owned a life insurance policy on the life of Benito, face amount of $500,000 and replacement value of $50,000, with Sofia as the designated beneficiary. Since the policy has not matured at Luigi's death, § 2042 is inapplicable. However, § 2033 (property in which the decedent had an interest) compels the inclusion of $50,000 (the replacement value) in Luigi's gross estate. If Luigi and Sofia owned the policy as community property, only $25,000 is included in Luigi's gross estate. ■

In the frequent situation where the beneficiary of the insurance is neither the insured nor the owner of the policy, no tax consequences ensue upon the beneficiary's death. Thus, in Example 53, if Sofia predeceases Benito, no transfer takes place because the policy has not matured. Sofia's interest as a beneficiary is a mere expectancy and not a property interest possessing any value.

The term *life insurance* includes whole life policies, term insurance, group life insurance, travel and accident insurance, endowment contracts (before being paid up), and death benefits paid by fraternal societies operating under the lodge system.[40]

As just noted, proceeds of insurance on the life of the decedent receivable by the executor or administrator or payable to the decedent's estate are included in the gross estate. The estate need not be specifically named as the beneficiary. Assume, for example, that the proceeds of the policy are receivable by an individual beneficiary and are subject to an obligation, legally binding upon the beneficiary, to pay taxes, debts, and other charges enforceable against the estate. The proceeds are included in the decedent's gross estate to the extent of the beneficiary's obligation. If the proceeds of an insurance policy made payable to a decedent's estate are community assets and, under state law, one-half belongs to the surviving spouse, only one-half of the proceeds will be considered as receivable by or for the benefit of the decedent's estate.

Proceeds of insurance on the life of the decedent not receivable by or for the benefit of the estate are includible if the decedent at death possessed any of the incidents of ownership in the policy. In this connection, the term *incidents of ownership* means not only the ownership of the policy in a technical legal sense but also, generally speaking, the right of the insured or his or her estate to the economic benefits of the policy. Thus, it also includes the power to change beneficiaries, revoke an assignment, pledge the policy for a loan, or surrender or cancel the policy.[41]

EXAMPLE 54

At the time of death, Broderick was the insured under a policy (face amount of $1 million) owned by Gregory with Demi as the designated beneficiary. Broderick took out the policy five years ago and immediately transferred it as a gift to Gregory. Under the assignment, Broderick transferred all rights in the policy except the right to change beneficiaries. Broderick died without having exercised this right, and the policy proceeds are paid to Demi. Under § 2042(2), Broderick's retention of an incident of ownership in the policy (i.e., the right to change beneficiaries) causes $1 million to be included in his gross estate. ■

Assuming that the deceased-insured holds the incidents of ownership in a policy, how much is included in the gross estate if the insurance policy is a community asset? Only one-half of the proceeds becomes part of the deceased spouse's gross estate.

[39] Reg. § 20.2031–8(a)(1).

[40] Reg. § 20.2042–1(a)(1). As to travel and accident insurance, see *Comm. v. Estate of Noel*, 65–1 USTC ¶12,311, 15 AFTR 2d 1397, 85 S.Ct. 1238 (USSC, 1965). As to employer-sponsored group term life insurance, see Example 32 earlier in this chapter.

[41] Reg. § 20.2042–1(c)(2).

CONCEPT SUMMARY 18.2

Federal Estate Tax Provisions—Gross Estate

1. The starting point for applying the Federal estate tax is to determine which assets are subject to tax. Such assets comprise a decedent's gross estate.
2. The gross estate generally will not include any gifts made by the decedent within three years of death. It does include any gift tax paid on these transfers.
3. Based on the premise that one should not continue to enjoy or control property and not have it subject to the estate tax, certain incomplete transfers are included in the gross estate.
4. Upon the death of a joint tenant, the full value of the property is included in the gross estate unless the survivor(s) made a contribution toward the cost of the property. Spouses are subject to a special rule that calls for automatic inclusion of half of the value of the property in the gross estate of the first tenant to die. The creation of joint ownership is subject to the gift tax when a tenant receives a lesser interest in the property than is warranted by the consideration furnished.
5. A power of appointment is the right to determine who shall own or enjoy, at the present or in the future, the property subject to the power. The exercise, lapse, or release of a general power of appointment during the life of the holder is subject to the gift tax. If the exercise, lapse, or release occurs at death, the property subject to the power is included in the holder's gross estate. If, however, a special power of appointment is involved, no gift or estate tax consequences result.
6. If the decedent is the insured, life insurance proceeds are included in the gross estate if either of two conditions is satisfied. First, the proceeds are paid to the estate or for the benefit of the estate. Second, the decedent possessed incidents of ownership (e.g., the right to change beneficiaries) over the policy.

Merely purchasing a life insurance contract with someone else designated as the beneficiary does not constitute a *gift*. As long as the purchaser still owns the policy, nothing has really passed to the beneficiary. Even on the death of the insured-owner, no gift takes place. The proceeds paid to the beneficiary constitute a testamentary and not a lifetime transfer. But consider the following possibility.

EXAMPLE 55

Kurt purchases an insurance policy on his own life that he transfers to Olga. Kurt retains no interest in the policy (such as the power to change beneficiaries). In these circumstances, Kurt has made a gift to Olga. Furthermore, if Kurt continues to pay the premiums on the transferred policy, each payment constitutes a separate gift. ■

Under certain conditions, the death of the insured may constitute a gift to the beneficiary of part or all of the proceeds. This occurs when the owner of the policy is not the insured.

EXAMPLE 56

Randolph owns an insurance policy on the life of Frank, with Tracy as the designated beneficiary. Up until the time of Frank's death, Randolph retained the right to change the beneficiary of the policy. The proceeds paid to Tracy by the insurance company by reason of Frank's death constitute a gift from Randolph to Tracy.[42] ■

EXAMPLE 57

Hubert and Carrie live in a community property state. With community funds, Hubert purchases an insurance policy with a face amount of $1 million on his own life and designates Ann as the revocable beneficiary. On Hubert's death, the proceeds of the policy are paid to Ann. If under state law Hubert's death makes the transfer by Carrie complete, Carrie has made a gift to Ann of $500,000. Since the policy is community property, Carrie is the owner of only one-half of the policy. Furthermore, one-half of the proceeds of the policy ($500,000) is included in Hubert's gross estate under § 2042. ■

See Concept Summary 18.2 for a review of the components of the gross estate.

[42] *Goodman v. Comm.*, 46–1 USTC ¶10,275, 34 AFTR 1534, 156 F.2d 218 (CA–2, 1946).

LO.7

Describe the components of the taxable estate.

TAXABLE ESTATE

After the gross estate has been determined, the next step is to compute the taxable estate. By virtue of § 2051, the **taxable estate** is the gross estate less the following: expenses, indebtedness, and taxes (§ 2053); losses (§ 2054); charitable transfers (§ 2055); the marital deduction (§§ 2056 and 2056A); and the deduction for state death taxes (§ 2058). As previously noted, the charitable and marital deductions also have gift tax ramifications (§§ 2522 and 2523).

Expenses, Indebtedness, and Taxes (§ 2053)

A deduction is allowed for funeral expenses; expenses incurred in administering property; claims against the estate; and unpaid mortgages and other charges against property, whose value is included in the gross estate (without reduction for the mortgage or other indebtedness).

Expenses incurred in administering community property are deductible only in proportion to the deceased spouse's interest in the community.[43]

Administration expenses include commissions of the executor or administrator, attorney's fees of the estate, accountant's fees, court costs, and certain selling expenses for disposition of estate property.

Claims against the estate include property taxes accrued before the decedent's death, unpaid income taxes on income received by the decedent before he or she died, and unpaid gift taxes on gifts made by the decedent before death.

Amounts that may be deducted as claims against the estate are only for enforceable personal obligations of the decedent at the time of death. Deductions for claims founded on promises or agreements are limited to the extent that the liabilities were contracted in good faith and for adequate and full consideration. However, a pledge or subscription in favor of a public, charitable, religious, or educational organization is deductible to the extent that it would have constituted an allowable deduction had it been a bequest.[44]

Deductible funeral expenses include the cost of interment, the burial plot or vault, a gravestone, perpetual care of the grave site, and the transportation expense of the person bringing the body to the place of burial. No deduction is allowed for cemetery lots that the decedent acquired before death for himself or herself and family, but the lots are not included in the decedent's gross estate under § 2033 (property in which the decedent had an interest).

Losses (§ 2054)

Section 2054 permits an estate tax deduction for losses from casualty or theft incurred during the period when the estate is being settled. As is true with casualty or theft losses for income tax purposes, any anticipated insurance recovery must be taken into account in arriving at the amount of the deductible loss. Unlike the income tax, however, the deduction is not limited by a floor ($100) or a percentage amount (the excess of 10 percent of adjusted gross income). If the casualty occurs to property after it has been distributed to an heir, the loss belongs to the heir and not to the estate. If the casualty occurs before the decedent's death, it should be claimed on the appropriate Form 1040. The fair market value of the property (if any) on the date of death plus any insurance recovery is included in the gross estate.

As is true of certain administration expenses, a casualty or theft loss of estate property can be claimed as an income tax deduction on the fiduciary return of the estate (Form 1041). But a double deduction prohibition applies, and claiming the income tax deduction requires a waiver of the estate tax deduction.[45]

---

[43] *U.S. v. Stapf*, 63–2 USTC ¶12,192, 12 AFTR 2d 6326, 84 S.Ct. 248 (USSC, 1963).

[44] § 2053(c)(1)(A) and Reg. § 20.2053–5.

[45] § 642(g).

TAX *in the NEWS*

When Does the Cost of a Funeral Wake Become Nondeductible?

Due to a birth defect, Sarah died at the young age of 12. During her lifetime, she required constant medical care and treatment (e.g., special living accommodations, private teachers). To show their appreciation for those who helped her, Sarah's parents held a luncheon in her memory immediately after the funeral. The luncheon, which cost approximately $3,600, was attended by friends, relatives, and caregivers. Along with the usual expenses (e.g., priest, gravesite, flowers, published obituary), the executor of Sarah's estate deducted the $3,600 as a funeral expense.

Upon audit of the Form 706 filed for Sarah, the IRS disallowed the $3,600 deduction as being neither reasonable nor necessary to the funeral process. Reflecting a dearth of compassion, the Tax Court in *Estate of Sarah Davenport* (92 TCM 324, T.C.Memo. 2006–215) sustained the position of the IRS.

Does this mean that the cost of a wake celebrating the life of a decedent is always nondeductible? Hopefully not! A more modest function that is associated with the funeral service (e.g., held at the church meeting hall) might pass scrutiny by the IRS.

Transfers to Charity (§§ 2055 and 2522)

A deduction is allowed for the value of property in the decedent's gross estate that is transferred by the decedent through testamentary disposition to (or for the use of) any of the following.

- The United States or any of its political subdivisions.
- Any corporation or association organized and operated exclusively for religious, charitable, scientific, literary, or educational purposes.
- Various veterans' organizations.

The organizations just described are identical to those that qualify for the Federal gift tax deduction under § 2522. With the following exceptions, they are also the same organizations that qualify a donor for an income tax deduction under § 170.

- Certain nonprofit cemetery associations qualify for income tax but not estate and gift tax purposes.
- Foreign charities may qualify under the estate and gift tax but not under the income tax.

No deduction is allowed unless the charitable bequest is specified by a provision in the decedent's will or the transfer was made before death and the property is subsequently included in the gross estate. Generally speaking, a deduction does not materialize when an individual dies intestate (without a will). The amount of the bequest to charity must be mandatory and cannot be left to someone else's discretion. It is, however, permissible to allow another person—such as the executor of the estate—to choose which charity will receive the specified donation. Likewise, a bequest may be expressed as an alternative and still be effective if the noncharitable beneficiary disclaims (refuses) the intervening interest before the due date for the filing of the estate tax return (nine months after the decedent's death plus any extensions of time granted for filing).

EXAMPLE 58
THE BIG PICTURE

Return to the facts of *The Big Picture* on p. 18-2. After John's accident, he was in the intensive care unit at a local hospital. Although physically incapacitated, he was mentally alert. In early December, he reviewed his financial affairs with his attorney and CPA and executed a new will. His prior will, drawn up several years ago, contained a bequest to the Hood Scholarship Foundation (HSF), an organization created by Peter (John's father) to provide financial assistance to community college students. As HSF's qualified status had never been evaluated by the IRS, the attorney agreed to apply for a determination letter.

John's new will kept the bequest, but only if the IRS approved HSF's qualified status. John's CPA arranged to have all of John's medical expenses (e.g., hospital, physicians) paid as incurred. He also advised John to make a substantial payment on his property taxes and state income taxes. ■

Marital Deduction (§§ 2056, 2056A, and 2523)

The **marital deduction** originated with the Revenue Act of 1948 as part of the same legislation that permitted married persons to secure the income-splitting advantages of filing joint income tax returns. The purpose of these statutory changes was to eliminate the major tax variations that existed between taxpayers residing in community property and common law states. The marital deduction was designed to provide equity in the estate and gift tax areas.

In a community property state, for example, no marital deduction generally was allowed, since the surviving spouse already owned one-half of the community and that portion was not included in the deceased spouse's gross estate. In a common law state, however, most if not all of the assets often belonged to the breadwinner of the family. When that spouse died first, all of these assets were included in the gross estate. Recall that a dower or curtesy interest (regarding a surviving spouse's right to some of the deceased spouse's property) does not reduce the gross estate. To equalize the situation, therefore, a marital deduction, usually equal to one-half of all separate assets, was allowed upon the death of the first spouse.

Ultimately, Congress decided to dispense with these historical justifications and recognize husband and wife as a single economic unit. Consistent with the approach taken under the income tax, spouses are considered as one for transfer tax purposes. By making the marital deduction unlimited in amount, neither the gift tax nor the estate tax is imposed on outright interspousal transfers of property. The unlimited marital deduction even includes one spouse's share of the community property transferred to the other spouse.

Passing Requirement Under § 2056, the marital deduction is allowed only for property that is included in the deceased spouse's gross estate *and* that passes or has passed to the surviving spouse. In determining whether the parties are legally married, look to state law. In this regard, some foreign divorces may raise doubts as to the validity of a subsequent remarriage. Having an ex-spouse does not qualify the decedent for a marital deduction if, in fact, the divorce is valid and final.

EXAMPLE 59
THE BIG PICTURE

Return to the facts of *The Big Picture* on p. 18-2 and Example 58. In reviewing John's prior will, the parties discovered that one of the main beneficiaries was Hannah, John's first wife. The new will substituted Ashley (John's present wife) for Hannah, thereby salvaging a marital deduction. ■

Property that *passes* from the decedent to the surviving spouse includes any interest received as (1) the decedent's heir or donee; (2) the decedent's surviving tenant by the entirety or joint tenant; (3) the appointee under the decedent's exercise (or lapse or release) of a general power of appointment; or (4) the beneficiary of insurance on the life of the decedent.

EXAMPLE 60

At the time of his death in the current year, Matthew owned an insurance policy on his own life (face amount of $500,000) with Minerva (his wife) as the designated beneficiary. Matthew and Minerva also owned real estate (worth $600,000) as tenants by the entirety (Matthew had furnished all of the purchase price). As to these transfers, $800,000 ($500,000 + $300,000) is included in Matthew's gross estate, and this amount represents the property that passes to Minerva for purposes of the marital deduction.[46] ■

Disclaimers can affect the amount passing to the surviving spouse. If, for example, the surviving spouse is the remainderperson under the will of the deceased spouse, a disclaimer by another heir increases the amount passing to the surviving spouse.

[46]Inclusion in the gross estate falls under § 2042 (proceeds of life insurance) and § 2040 (joint interests). Although Matthew provided the full purchase price for the real estate, § 2040(b) requires inclusion of only one-half of the value of the property when one spouse predeceases the other.

This, in turn, will increase the amount of the marital deduction allowed to the estate of the deceased spouse.

A problem arises when a property interest passing to the surviving spouse is subject to a mortgage or other encumbrance. In this case, only the net value of the interest after reduction by the amount of the mortgage or other encumbrance qualifies for the marital deduction. To allow otherwise results in a double deduction since a decedent's liabilities are separately deductible under § 2053.

EXAMPLE 61

In his will, Oscar leaves real estate (fair market value of $500,000) to his wife. If the real estate is subject to a mortgage of $100,000 (upon which Oscar was personally liable), the marital deduction is limited to $400,000 ($500,000 − $100,000). The $100,000 mortgage is deductible under § 2053 as an obligation of the decedent (Oscar). ■

However, if the executor is required under the terms of the decedent's will or under local law to discharge the mortgage out of other assets of the estate or to reimburse the surviving spouse, the payment or reimbursement is an additional interest passing to the surviving spouse.

EXAMPLE 62

Assume the same facts as in Example 61, except that Oscar's will directs that the real estate is to pass to his wife free of any liabilities. Accordingly, Oscar's executor pays off the mortgage by using other estate assets and distributes the real estate to Oscar's wife. The marital deduction now becomes $500,000. ■

Federal estate taxes or other death taxes paid out of the surviving spouse's share of the gross estate are not included in the value of property passing to the surviving spouse. Therefore, it is usually preferable for the deceased spouse's will to provide that death taxes be paid out of the portion of the estate that does not qualify for the marital deduction.

Terminable Interest Limitation Certain interests in property passing from the deceased spouse to the surviving spouse are referred to as **terminable interests**. Such an interest will terminate or fail after the passage of time, upon the happening of some contingency, or upon the failure of some event to occur. Examples are life estates, annuities, estates for terms of years, and patents. A terminable interest will not qualify for the marital deduction if another interest in the same property passed from the deceased spouse to some other person. By reason of the passing, that other person or his or her heirs may enjoy part of the property after the termination of the surviving spouse's interest.[47]

EXAMPLE 63

Vicky's will places her property in trust, life estate to her husband, Brett, remainder to Andrew or his heirs. The interest passing from Vicky to Brett does not qualify for the marital deduction. It will terminate on Brett's death, and Andrew or his heirs will then possess or enjoy the property. ■

EXAMPLE 64

Assume the same facts as in Example 63, except that Vicky created the trust during her life. No marital deduction is available for gift tax purposes for the same reason as in Example 63.[48] ■

The justification for the terminable interest rule can be illustrated by examining the possible results of Examples 63 and 64. Without the rule, Vicky could have passed property to Brett at no cost because of the marital deduction. Yet, on Brett's death, none of the property would have been included in his gross estate. Section 2036 (transfers with a retained life estate) would not apply to Brett since he was not the original transferor of the property. The marital deduction should not be available in situations

[47]§§ 2056(b)(1) and 2523(b)(1).

[48]Both Examples 63 and 64 contain the potential for a qualified terminable interest property (QTIP) election discussed later in this section.

where the surviving spouse can enjoy the property and still pass it to another without tax consequences. The marital deduction merely postpones the transfer tax on the death of the first spouse and operates to shift any such tax to the surviving spouse.

The terminable interest rule can be avoided by use of a *power of appointment.*[49] Under this approach, a property interest passing from the deceased spouse to the surviving spouse qualifies for the marital deduction (and is not considered a terminable interest) if the surviving spouse is granted a general power of appointment over the property. Thus, the exercise, release, or lapse of the power during the survivor's life or at death will be subject to either the gift or the estate tax.[50] If Examples 63 and 64 are modified to satisfy this condition, the life estate passing from Vicky to Brett is not a terminable interest and will qualify for the marital deduction.

Consistent with the objective of the terminable interest rule, another approach offers an alternative means for obtaining the marital deduction. Under this provision, the marital deduction is allowed for transfers of **qualified terminable interest property** (commonly referred to as **QTIP**). This is defined as property that passes from one spouse to another by gift or at death and for which the transferee-spouse has a qualifying income interest for life.

For a donee or a surviving spouse, a qualifying income interest for life exists under the following conditions:

- The person is entitled for life to all of the income from the property (or a specific portion of it), payable at annual or more frequent intervals.
- No person (including the spouse) has a power to appoint any part of the property to any person other than the surviving spouse during his or her life.[51]

If these conditions are met, an election can be made to claim a marital deduction as to the QTIP. For estate tax purposes, the executor of the estate makes the election on Form 706 (the Federal estate tax return). For gift tax purposes, the donor spouse makes the election on Form 709 (the Federal gift tax return). The election is irrevocable.

If the election is made, a transfer tax is imposed upon the QTIP when the transferee-spouse disposes of it by gift or upon death. If the disposition occurs during life, the gift tax applies, measured by the fair market value of the property as of that time.[52] If no lifetime disposition takes place, the fair market value of the property on the date of death (or alternate valuation date if applicable) is included in the gross estate of the transferee-spouse.[53]

EXAMPLE 65

In 1990, Clyde dies and provides in his will that certain assets (fair market value of $2.1 million) are to be transferred to a trust under which Gertrude (Clyde's wife) is granted a life estate with the remainder passing to their children upon Gertrude's death. Presuming all of the preceding requirements are satisfied and Clyde's executor so elects, his estate receives a marital deduction of $2.1 million. ■

EXAMPLE 66

Assume the same facts as in Example 65, with the further stipulation that Gertrude dies in 2011 when the trust assets are worth $6.4 million. This amount is included in her gross estate. ■

Because the estate tax is imposed on assets not physically included in the probate estate, the law allows the liability for those assets to be shifted to the heirs. The amount to be shifted is determined by comparing the estate tax liability both with and without the inclusion of the QTIP. This right of recovery can be canceled by a provision in the deceased spouse's will.[54]

The major difference between the power of appointment and the QTIP exceptions to the terminable interest rules relates to the control the surviving spouse has over the principal of the trust. In the power of appointment situation, the surviving spouse can

[49] For the estate tax, see § 2056(b)(5). The gift tax counterpart is in § 2523(e).
[50] §§ 2514 and 2041.
[51] §§ 2523(f) and 2056(b)(7).
[52] § 2519.
[53] § 2044.
[54] § 2207A(a).

appoint the principal to himself or herself (or to his or her estate). Only if this power is not exercised will the property pass as specified in the deceased spouse's will. In the QTIP situation, however, the surviving spouse has no such control. If the QTIP election is made, the principal must pass as prescribed by the transferor (the donor in the case of a lifetime transfer or the decedent in the case of a death transfer).

Citizenship and Residency of Spouses In the case of a nonresident alien whose spouse is a U.S. citizen, the marital deduction is allowed for estate and gift tax purposes. Property passing to a surviving spouse who is not a U.S. citizen is not eligible for the estate tax marital deduction.[55] Similarly, no gift tax marital deduction is allowed where the spouse is not a U.S. citizen. However, the annual exclusion for these gift transfers is $136,000 for 2011 ($134,000 in 2010).[56]

For the estate tax, an exception exists for certain transfers to a surviving spouse who is not a U.S. citizen.[57] If the transfer is to a *qualified domestic trust,* the marital deduction is allowed.[58]

The requirements of a qualified domestic trust guarantee that the marital deduction property will not escape estate taxes on the death of the surviving spouse. This would be possible if the property and spouse are outside the jurisdiction of the U.S. tax laws.

State Death Taxes (§ 2058)

The purpose of the § 2058 deduction is to mitigate the effect of subjecting property to multiple death taxes (i.e., both Federal and state). In this regard, however, it provides less relief than was available with the § 2011 credit it replaced. A credit results in a dollar-for-dollar reduction in tax, whereas the benefit of a deduction is limited by the effective tax bracket of the estate.

COMPUTING THE FEDERAL ESTATE TAX

LO.8

Calculate the Federal estate tax liability.

Once the taxable estate has been determined, post-1976 taxable gifts are added to arrive at the tax base, and the estate tax can be computed.

EXAMPLE 67

Horton dies in 2011, leaving a taxable estate of $5.7 million. In 2002, he made a taxable gift of $100,000 upon which he paid no tax due to the availability of the unified tax credit. Horton's estate tax is $280,000, as determined below (see Figure 18.2).

Taxable estate	$ 5,700,000
Add: Post-1976 taxable gift	100,000
Tax base	$ 5,800,000
Tentative tax on tax base from tax rate schedule (Appendix A, p. A-8) [$155,800 + 35%($5,800,000 − $500,000)]	$ 2,010,800
Less: Unified tax credit for 2011	(1,730,800)
Estate tax due	$ 280,000

WATER UNDER THE BRIDGE

Amy, a recently deceased client, has named you as the executor of her estate. Upon examining some of her past financial affairs, you discover that she made taxable gifts in recent years. None of these gifts was reported on a Form 709. As far as you can tell without further investigation, none of these gifts resulted in a gift tax liability. When you suggest to Amy's heirs that gift tax returns should be filed reporting these transfers, they tell you not to bother as Amy's past actions are "water under the bridge" and irrelevant to your duties as executor. What should you do?

[55] § 2056(d)(1).
[56] § 2523(i).
[57] § 2056(d)(2).
[58] § 2056A.

TAX *in* the NEWS — CHOOSING THE RIGHT YEAR TO DIE

Assume three separate decedents—Tom, Jim, and Dave. Each is single and has a taxable estate of $6 million. Tom dies in 2009, Jim in 2010, and Dave in 2011. Assuming no prior taxable gifts and using the estate tax law in effect for the year of death, what is the result?

	Decedent		
	Tom	Jim	Dave
Estate tax due*	$1,125,000	$-0-	$350,000

* The estate tax was determined through the use of the credits in Table 18.1 and the tax rates in Appendix A (pp. A-7 and A-8) in the text.

Because no estate tax was imposed in 2010, Jim is the "lucky one"—if dying can ever be termed "lucky"! Besides Jim, such magnates as Dan Duncan (estate of $9 billion) and George Steinbrenner (estate of $1.15 billion) can also be considered lucky as they died in 2010. Thus, it pays to die in the right year!

ESTATE TAX CREDITS

Unified Tax Credit (§ 2010)

The role of the unified tax credit was discussed in connection with Example 3, and its application was illustrated in Example 67. The amount of the credit depends on the year the transfer occurred, and this information is contained in Table 18.1.

Credit for State Death Taxes (§ 2011)

The Code allowed a limited credit for the amount of any death tax actually paid to any state (or to the District of Columbia) attributable to any property included in the gross estate. Like the credit for foreign death taxes paid, this provision mitigated the harshness of subjecting the same property to multiple death taxes.

The credit allowed was limited to the lesser of the amount of tax actually paid or the amount provided for in a table contained in § 2011(b). About a dozen states still use the procedure and table set forth in § 2011 as a means of determining the *state* estate tax that each imposes.

The § 2011 credit was phased out completely by 2005. As previously noted, the *credit* for state death taxes paid has been replaced by a *deduction* under § 2058.[59]

Credit for Tax on Prior Transfers (§ 2013)

Suppose Nancy owns some property that she passes at death to Lisa. Shortly thereafter, Lisa dies and passes the property to Rita. Assuming both estates are subject to the Federal estate tax, the successive deaths result in a multiple effect. To mitigate the possible multiple taxation that might result, § 2013 provides relief in the form of a credit for Federal estate tax paid on prior transfers. In the preceding hypothetical case, Lisa's estate may be able to claim as an estate tax credit some of the taxes paid by Nancy's estate.

The credit is limited to the lesser of the following amounts:

1. The amount of the Federal estate tax attributable to the transferred property in the transferor's estate.
2. The amount of the Federal estate tax attributable to the transferred property in the decedent's estate.

[59]Section 2011 is to be reinstated as to decedents dying after 2012.

TABLE 18.2 Credit for Tax on Prior Transfers

Interval between Deaths	Credit Allowed
Within 2 years	100%
Within 3 to 4 years	80%
Within 5 to 6 years	60%
Within 7 to 8 years	40%
Within 9 to 10 years	20%

To apply the limitations, certain adjustments must be made that are not covered in this text.[60] However, it is not necessary for the transferred property to be identified in the present decedent's estate or for it to be in existence at the time of the present decedent's death. It is sufficient that the transfer of property was subjected to the Federal estate tax in the estate of the transferor and that the transferor died within the prescribed period of time. Table 18.2 shows the correlation between the credit allowed and the time interval between the two deaths.

EXAMPLE 68

Under Nancy's will, Lisa inherits property. One year later Lisa dies. Assume the estate tax attributable to the inclusion of the property in Nancy's gross estate was $150,000 and the estate tax attributable to the inclusion of the property in Lisa's gross estate is $120,000. Under these circumstances, Lisa's estate claims a credit against the estate tax of $120,000 (refer to limitation 2). ■

EXAMPLE 69

Assume the same facts as in Example 68, except that Lisa dies three years after Nancy. The applicable credit is now 80% of $120,000, or $96,000 (see Table 18.2). ■

Credit for Foreign Death Taxes (§ 2014)

A credit is allowed against the estate tax for any estate, inheritance, legacy, or succession tax actually paid to a foreign country. For purposes of this provision, the term *foreign country* means not only states in the international sense but also possessions or political subdivisions of foreign states and possessions of the United States.

The credit is allowed for death taxes paid with respect to (1) property situated within the foreign country to which the tax is paid, (2) property included in the decedent's gross estate, and (3) the decedent's taxable estate. No credit is allowed for interest or penalties paid in connection with foreign death taxes.

The credit is limited to the lesser of the following amounts:

1. The amount of the foreign death tax attributable to the property situated in the country imposing the tax and included in the decedent's gross estate for Federal estate tax purposes.
2. The amount of the Federal estate tax attributable to particular property situated in a foreign country, subject to death tax in that country, and included in the decedent's gross estate for Federal estate tax purposes.

Both of these limitations may require certain adjustments to arrive at the amount of the allowable credit. These adjustments are illustrated in the Regulations and are

[60] See the instructions to Form 706 and Reg. §§ 20.2013–2 and –3.

GLOBAL Tax Issues

TREATY RELIEF IS NOT ABUNDANT!

One means of mitigating double taxation at the international level is to take advantage of treaty provisions. A treaty will determine which country has primary taxing rights, and this may depend on such factors as the domicile of the decedent or the nature of the property involved (e.g., personalty or realty). Unfortunately, the United States has estate tax conventions with only 17 countries: Australia*, Austria*, Canada, Denmark*, Finland, France*, Germany*, Greece, Ireland, Italy, Japan*, the Netherlands, Norway, the Republic of South Africa, Sweden, Switzerland, and the United Kingdom*. In contrast, more than 50 countries have income tax treaties with the United States (see Exhibit 9.1 in Chapter 9). Thus, treaty relief in the estate tax area is not as widespread as with income tax situations.

*An asterisk indicates the existence of a gift tax treaty as well.

not discussed in this text.[61] In addition to the credit for foreign death taxes under the provisions of Federal estate tax law, similar credits are allowable under death tax conventions with a number of foreign countries. If a credit is allowed under either the provisions of law or the provisions of a convention, the credit that is most beneficial to the estate should be claimed.[62]

PROCEDURAL MATTERS

A Federal estate tax return, if required, is due nine months after the date of the decedent's death.[63] The time limit applies to all estates regardless of the nationality or residence of the decedent. Not infrequently, an executor will request and obtain from the IRS an extension of time for filing Form 706 (estate tax return).[64] Also available is an *automatic* six-month extension of time to file the estate tax return. To receive the extension, the executor must file Form 4768 [Application for Extension of Time to File a Return and/or Pay U.S. Estate (and Generation-Skipping Transfer) Taxes].

The filing requirements parallel the exclusion amounts of the unified tax credit available for each year (refer to Table 18.1). The filing requirements may be lower when the decedent has made taxable gifts after 1976.[65]

EXAMPLE 70

Carlos dies in 2011, leaving a gross estate of $5 million. If Carlos did not make any post-1976 taxable gifts, his estate need not file Form 706. But assume that Carlos made a taxable gift of $100,000 in 2002. Since the filing requirement now becomes $4.9 million [$5,000,000 (the regular filing requirement for 2011) – $100,000 (the post-1976 taxable gift)], Carlos's estate must file Form 706. ■

Concept Summary 18.3 highlights the major components in arriving at the taxable estate and the mechanics of determining the estate tax liability.

[61]Reg. § 20.2014–2 illustrates the foreign death tax limitation, and Reg. § 20.2014–3 covers that applicable to the U.S. estate tax. Also see the instructions to Schedule P of Form 706.

[62]Reg. § 20.2014–4 illustrates the selection process when both the § 2014 credit and an estate tax convention are involved.

[63]§ 6075(a).

[64]§ 6081.

[65]§ 6018(a)(3).

CONCEPT SUMMARY 18.3

Federal Estate Tax Provisions—Taxable Estate and Procedural Matters

1. In moving from the gross estate to the taxable estate, certain deductions are allowed.
2. Under § 2053, deductions are permitted for various administration expenses (e.g., executor's commissions), professional fees (appraisal, accounting, legal), debts of the decedent, certain unpaid taxes, and funeral expenses.
3. Casualty and theft losses occurring during the settlement of the estate and not compensated for by insurance can be deducted (§ 2054).
4. Charitable transfers are deductible if the designated organization holds qualified status with the IRS at the time of death (§ 2055). See Chapter 15.
5. Transfers to a surviving spouse yield a marital deduction if they do not violate the terminable interest rule (§ 2056). The terminable interest rule can be avoided by the use of a general power of appointment or by making a QTIP election.
6. A deduction is allowed for certain state and local death taxes paid (§ 2058).
7. The tax base for determining the estate tax is the taxable estate plus all post-1976 taxable gifts.
8. Using the unified transfer tax rates appearing in Appendix A, determine the tax on the tax base.
9. From the tax determined under item 8, subtract the credits allowed under §§ 2010–2016.
10. If required, a Federal estate tax return (Form 706) must be filed within nine months of the date of the decedent's death.

18.4 The Generation-Skipping Transfer Tax

LO.9

Demonstrate the role of the generation-skipping transfer tax.

In order to prevent partial avoidance of Federal gift and estate taxes on large transfers, the tax law imposes an additional generation-skipping transfer tax.

THE PROBLEM

Previously, by structuring the transaction carefully, it was possible to bypass a generation of transfer taxes.

EXAMPLE 71

Under his will, Edward creates a trust, life estate to Stephen (Edward's son) and remainder to Ava (Edward's granddaughter) upon Stephen's death. Edward is subject to the Federal estate tax, but no tax results on Stephen's death. Stephen held a life estate, but § 2036 does not apply because he was not the grantor of the trust. Nor does § 2033 (property owned by the decedent) come into play because Stephen's interest disappeared upon his death. The ultimate result is that the property in trust skips a generation of transfer taxes. ■

EXAMPLE 72

Joshua dies at age 89 and leaves all of his property to a trust. Under the terms of the trust instrument, trust income and corpus are to be distributed equally over a 10-year period to Amber and Ethan. Amber is Joshua's 22-year-old third wife, while Ethan is his 30-year-old grandson. As a result of this arrangement, the following tax consequences ensue: the estate tax applies on Joshua's death; income earned by the trust will be subject to income tax (see Chapter 20); and normally no transfer tax results when distributions of trust income and corpus occur. ■

EXAMPLE 73

Amy gives assets to Eric (her grandson). Called a direct skip, the gift would circumvent any transfer taxes that would have resulted had the assets been channeled through Eric's parents. ■

THE SOLUTION

The generation-skipping transfer tax (GSTT) is designed to preclude the avoidance of either the estate tax or the gift tax by making transfers that bypass the next lower generation. In the typical family setting, this involves transfers from grandparents to grandchildren. Such transfers, in effect, would skip any transfer tax that would result if the property were channeled through the children.

The GSTT is triggered by any of these three events: a taxable *termination* occurs; a taxable *distribution* takes place; or a *direct skip* is made.[66] Example 71 illustrates a termination event. Upon Stephen's death, the fair market value of the trust property that passes to Ava is subject to the GSTT (imposed on the trust). The GSTT will have the effect of reducing the amount Ava receives from the trust.

Example 72 illustrates a distribution event. When the trust makes a distribution to Ethan, the GSTT applies (imposed on Ethan). Any distribution to Amber is not subject to the GSTT because the spouse of the transferor (Joshua in this case) is deemed to be of the same generation.[67] The results reached in Example 72 show how ludicrous the application of the GSTT rules can be. Amber (age 22) is treated as being in the same generation as Joshua (age 89), while Ethan (age 30) is two generations removed!

Example 73 illustrates a lifetime version of the direct skip event.[68] In this situation, the GSTT is imposed upon Amy when the gift is made to Eric. Not only will Amy be subject to the GSTT but the amount of the tax represents an additional gift to Eric.[69]

The GSTT rate is the highest rate under the gift and estate tax schedule. Pursuant to transitional rules, these top rates are as follows: 35 percent (2011–2012), 45 percent (2007–2009), and 46 percent (2006). (The rates were 47 percent in 2005, 48 percent in 2004, and 49 percent in 2003.) To ameliorate the extra tax burden of the GSTT, an exemption is allowed equal to the exclusion amount applicable to the Federal estate tax (see Table 18.1).[70] For a donor who is married, the election to split the gift (under § 2513) will double the amount of the exemption.[71] For 2011, for example, the amount of the exemption could be \$10 million (\$5 million × 2). The exemption can be applied to whichever transfers the grantor (or personal representative of the grantor) chooses. Any appreciation attributable to the exempted portion of the transfer is not later subject to the GSTT.

Along with the estate tax, the GSTT was not applicable for 2010.

TAX PLANNING:

Tax planning for the Federal gift and estate tax is discussed in Chapter 19 in connection with family tax planning.

REFOCUS ON THE BIG PICTURE

AN EVENTFUL AND FINAL YEAR

By making use of § 2516, John was able to carry out a property settlement with Hannah without incurring any gift tax consequences (see Example 18). Both Helen and John acted wisely when they chose to disclaim most of their inheritance from their mother. By making the disclaimers, they were able to pass the property to their children without a transfer tax being imposed (see Examples 19 and 20).

Section 2033 operates to include in the gross estate not only John's retirement plan benefits but also any settlement from a potential lawsuit (see Examples 32 and 33). Section 2036 did not apply to the trust that John's father (Peter) created, but it did apply to the one John set up (see Examples 36 and 37). The difference in

CONTINUED

[66] § 2611.

[67] § 2651(c)(1).

[68] § 2612(c)(1). A direct skip can also take place in a testamentary transfer.

[69] § 2515.

[70] § 2631(c).

[71] § 2652(a)(2).

treatment occurs when it is the owner who retains an interest in the property, thereby making the transfer incomplete.

John's predeath planning was highly advantageous in several respects.

- By drawing up a new will, the loss of the charitable and marital deductions was avoided (see Examples 58 and 59).
- By prepaying state and local property and income taxes and staying current on medical expenses, John improved his Federal income tax position (see Example 58). He also avoided any estate taxes on the amounts used to pay these expenses.

KEY TERMS

Alternate valuation date, 18–6
Annual exclusion, 18–12
Bypass amount, 18–6
Disclaimer, 18–11
Exclusion amount, 18–6
Exemption equivalent, 18–6
Future interest, 18–12
Gross estate, 18–17
Joint tenants, 18–8
Marital deduction, 18–30
Power of appointment, 18–25
Probate estate, 18–17
Qualified terminable interest property (QTIP), 18–32
Taxable estate, 18–28
Taxable gift, 18–4
Tenants by the entirety, 18–8
Tenants in common, 18–8
Terminable interests, 18–31
Unified tax credit, 18–5
Unified transfer tax, 18–2

DISCUSSION QUESTIONS

1. **LO.1** Why can the unified transfer tax be categorized as an excise tax? In this regard, how does it differ from an income tax?

2. **LO.1** Over the years, the tax treatment of transfers by gift and by death has not been consistent. In this regard, what were the policy considerations supporting the original rules and the changes made?

3. **LO.1** In what manner does an inheritance tax differ from an estate tax?

4. **LO.1** Eight years ago, Alex made gifts of all of his assets to family and friends. Although the transfers would have generated gift taxes, none were paid, and no gift tax returns were filed. At present, no one knows where Alex is or even if he is still alive. The IRS has discovered that the gifts were made and is pursuing the donees for the gift tax due. Comment on the validity of the following defenses posed by the donees.
   a. The donor, not the donee, is responsible for the payment of any gift tax due.
   b. The assessment of any gift tax is barred by the statute of limitations.

5. **LO.1** Kim, a wealthy Korean national, is advised by his physicians to have an operation performed at the Mayo Clinic. Kim is hesitant to come to the United States because of the possible tax consequences. If the procedure is not successful, Kim does not want his wealth to be subject to the Federal estate tax. Are Kim's concerns justified? Explain. **ISSUE ID**

6. **LO.1** Carlos, a citizen and resident of Chile, would like to buy stock in General Electric and make gifts of the shares to his children. Will the Federal gift tax pose a problem for him? Explain.

7. **LO.1** To avoid both state and Federal transfer taxes (i.e., estate, inheritance, gift), Gary (a U.S. citizen) has moved to Costa Rica. Furthermore, he plans to limit his investments to non-U.S. assets (e.g., foreign stocks and bonds and real estate). Will Gary accomplish his objective? Explain.

COMMUNICATIONS

8. **LO.2** A new out-of-state client, Robert Ball, has asked you to prepare a Form 709 for a large gift he made in 2010. When you request copies of any prior gift tax returns he may have filed, he responds, "What do gifts in prior years have to do with 2010?" Send a letter to Robert at 4560 Walton Lane, Benton, AR 72015, clarifying this matter.

9. **LO.2, 4, 5** Regarding the formula for the Federal gift tax (see Figure 18.1 in the text), comment on the following observations.
   a. All prior gifts must be considered in determining the tax on a current gift.
   b. A credit is allowed for the gift taxes actually paid on prior gifts.
   c. A deduction for an annual exclusion might not be available.
   d. A gratuitous transfer might not be subject to the gift tax.

10. **LO.3** Regarding the formula for the Federal estate tax (see Figure 18.2 in the text), comment on the following.
    a. The gross estate may include property interests not owned by the decedent at the time of death.
    b. The gross estate may include assets that are not part of the probate estate (i.e., subject to administration by the executor of the estate).
    c. To arrive at the taxable estate, certain adjustments must be made to the gross estate.
    d. The role of prior taxable gifts in determining the tax base.
    e. Credits allowed in arriving at the estate tax due.

11. **LO.3** As to the alternate valuation date of § 2032, comment on the following.
    a. The justification for the election.
    b. A Form 706 need not be filed for the estate.
    c. The main heir prefers the date of death value.
    d. An estate asset is distributed to an heir three months after the decedent's death.
    e. Some estate assets have appreciated in value since the death of the decedent.
    f. Effect of the election on income tax basis.
    g. Treatment of income accruing from the property from the date of death to the alternate valuation date.

12. **LO.3** What type of ownership interest is appropriate in each of the following?
    a. A father desires to provide for his daughter during her life but wants to ensure that her younger husband (i.e., the son-in-law) does not inherit the property if he survives her.
    b. A married couple buys a home and wants to make sure that whoever survives obtains sole ownership of the property.
    c. Grandparents want to ensure that the family vacation home will be available for use by all of their children and grandchildren during their lifetimes.

13. **LO.4** Corinne wants to sell some valuable real estate to her son on an installment arrangement. Because related parties are involved, she fears that the IRS may question the selling price and contend that a portion of the transfer is a gift.
    a. Are Corinne's concerns realistic?
    b. How can Corinne protect herself from this contingency?

14. **LO.4** Addison provides all of the support of her dependent father, Walter, who lives with her. Because Walter is very proud and wants to appear independent, Addison gives him the money to pay his medical bills. Is Addison subject to the Federal gift tax as a result of these transfers? Explain.

ISSUE ID

15. **LO.4, 6** At a local bank, Jack purchases for $100,000 a five-year CD listing title as follows: "Meredith, payable on death to Briana." Four years later, Meredith dies, and Briana, Meredith's daughter, redeems the CD when it matures. Discuss the transfer tax consequences if Meredith is:
    a. Jack's wife.
    b. Jack's ex-wife.
    c. Jack's girlfriend.

ISSUE ID

16. **LO.4** Derek dies intestate (i.e., without a will) and is survived by a daughter, Ruth, and a grandson, Ted (Ruth's son). Derek's assets include a large portfolio of stocks and bonds and a beach house. Ruth has considerable wealth of her own, while Ted has just finished college and is unemployed. Under applicable state law, the order of priority as to heirship favors children followed by grandchildren.
    a. To minimize future transfer taxes, what action might Ruth take?
    b. What if Ruth wants only the beach house?

ISSUE ID

17. **LO.4** The Randalls have a married son and four grandchildren (ages 15, 17, 18, and 19). They establish a trust under which the income is to be paid annually to the grandchildren until the youngest reaches age 25. At that point, the trust terminates and the principal (corpus) is distributed to the son. What annual gift tax exclusions are allowed, if any, on the creation of the trust?

18. **LO.4** Qualified tuition programs under § 529 enjoy significant tax advantages. Describe these advantages with regard to the Federal:
    a. Income tax.
    b. Gift tax.
    c. Estate tax.

19. **LO.5** Regarding the gift-splitting provision of § 2513, comment on the following.
    a. What it was designed to accomplish.
    b. The treatment of any taxable gifts previously made by the nonowner spouse.
    c. How the election is made.
    d. The spouses are divorced during the year.
    e. The utility of the election in a community property jurisdiction.

20. **LO.5** In connection with the filing of a Federal gift tax return, comment on the following.
    a. No Federal gift tax is due.
    b. The gift is between spouses.
    c. The § 2513 election to split gifts is to be used.
    d. A gift of a future interest is involved.
    e. The donor uses a fiscal year for Federal income tax purposes.
    f. The donor obtained from the IRS an extension of time for filing his or her Federal income tax return.

21. **LO.4** In each of the following independent situations, indicate whether the transfer is subject to the Federal gift tax.
    a. Asa contributes to his mayor's reelection campaign fund. The mayor has promised to try to get some of Asa's property rezoned from residential to commercial use.
    b. Mary Ann inherits her father's collection of guns and mounted animals. Five months later, she disclaims any interest in the mounted animals.
    c. Same as (b). Ten months later, Mary Ann disclaims any interest in the guns.
    d. Haydon pays an orthodontist for the dental work performed on Michele, his dependent cousin.
    e. Same as (d), except that Michele is not Hayden's dependent.
    f. Marcus sells land to his mother, Marcie, for twice what it is worth.

22. **LO.4** In each of the following independent situations, indicate whether the transfer is subject to the Federal gift tax.
    a. Floyd creates a revocable trust with his children as the beneficiaries.
    b. In return for a premarital settlement of $1.2 million, Morgan (age 22) agrees to marry Errol (age 68). Errol transfers the funds *before* the marriage takes place.
    c. Same as (b), except that Errol makes the transfer *after* the marriage takes place.
    d. Florence purchases a U.S. savings bond listing herself and Taylor (her daughter) as joint owners.
    e. Same as (d). One year later, Taylor predeceases Florence.
    f. Same as (d). One year later, Florence predeceases Taylor.

23. **LO.3, 6, 8** Distinguish between the following.
    a. The gross estate and the taxable estate.
    b. The taxable estate and the tax base.
    c. The gross estate and the probate estate.

24. **LO.6** Discuss the estate tax treatment of each of the following. In all cases, assume that Mike is the decedent and that he died on July 5, 2011.
    a. Interest on State of South Dakota bonds paid on August 1, 2011.
    b. Cash dividend on Puce Corporation stock paid on August 10, 2011. Date of record was July 6, 2011.
    c. Same as (b). Declaration date was July 1, 2011.
    d. Distributions from traditional and Roth IRAs payable to Kirby (Mike's surviving spouse).

e. Same as (d), except that Kirby is Mike's surviving daughter (not his spouse).
f. Same as (d), except that the beneficiary is Mike's estate.

25. **LO.6** Discuss the estate tax treatment of each of the following. In all cases, assume that Rachel is the decedent and that she died on July 5, 2011.
    a. State income tax refund for 2010 received on July 7, 2011. Rachel claimed the standard deduction on her 2010 Federal income tax return.
    b. Federal income tax due for year 2010.
    c. Rachel held a life estate in a trust created by her husband. No QTIP election was made when the trust was created.
    d. Same as (c), except that a QTIP election was made.
    e. In 2010, Rachel gave an insurance policy on her life to her son, Jim, who was the beneficiary.
    f. Same as (e), except that the policy was on Jim's life (not Rachel's life).

26. **LO.6** At the time of Emile's death, he was a joint tenant with Colette in a parcel of real estate. With regard to the inclusion in Emile's gross estate under § 2040, comment on the following independent assumptions:
    a. Emile and Colette received the property as a gift from Douglas.
    b. Colette provided all of the purchase price of the property.
    c. Colette's contribution was received as a gift from Emile.
    d. Emile's contribution was derived from income generated by property he received as a gift from Colette.

27. **LO.6** With regard to "life insurance," comment on the following.
    a. What the term includes (i.e., types of policies).
    b. The meaning of "incidents of ownership."
    c. When a gift occurs upon maturity of the policy.
    d. The tax consequences when the owner of the policy predeceases the insured and the beneficiary.
    e. The tax consequences when the beneficiary of the policy predeceases the insured.

ISSUE ID

28. **LO.6, 7** Due to the negligence of the other driver, Adam's car is completely destroyed, and he is seriously injured. Two days later, Adam dies from injuries suffered in the accident.
    a. What, if any, are the estate tax consequences of these events?
    b. Are there any income tax consequences to Adam or his estate?

ISSUE ID

29. **LO.6, 7** Assume the same facts as in Question 28. Three months after Adam's death, his houseboat is destroyed by fire. Under Adam's will, the houseboat is bequeathed to a nephew.
    a. What, if any, are the estate tax consequences of this situation?
    b. The income tax consequences?

30. **LO.7** Troy predeceases his wife, Nell. Under his will, his estate is placed in trust, life estate to Nell, remainder to his children. Regarding any marital deduction allowed to Troy's estate, comment on the effect of the following independent cases.
    a. Nell is granted a power of appointment over the trust assets.
    b. Troy's executor makes a QTIP election.
    c. Nell issues a timely disclaimer that rejects her life estate.
    d. Nell elects to take against Troy's will and claim her dower interest. Under applicable state law, Nell's dower interest is outright ownership of one-third of Troy's property.

31. **LO.7** Steve and Pam are husband and wife. Steve predeceases Pam. Under Steve's will, all of his uncommitted estate passes to the children of his first marriage. Comment on any marital deduction allowed to Steve's estate in each of the following situations.
    a. Steve and Pam own real estate as tenants by the entirety.
    b. Steve and Pam own real estate as tenants in common.
    c. Steve owns an insurance policy on his life with Pam as the designated beneficiary.
    d. Pam owns an insurance policy on Steve's life with herself as the designated beneficiary.

e. Steve owns an annuity on his life. On Steve's prior death, the annuity pays Pam a reduced amount for her life.
f. Pam is the designated beneficiary of Steve's IRA.

32. **LO.7** Bernice dies and, under a will, passes real estate to her surviving husband. The real estate is subject to a mortgage. For estate tax purposes, how will any marital deduction be determined? Can Bernice's estate deduct the mortgage under § 2053? Explain.

33. **LO.7** Louis and Sonya are husband and wife. Louis dies first and leaves all of his property to Sonya. Comment on the availability of the marital deduction for estate tax purposes under the following circumstances.
   a. Louis was a nonresident alien, and Sonya is a U.S. citizen.
   b. Louis was a resident and citizen of the United States, and Sonya is a citizen of Sweden.
   c. What purpose might be served if Louis and Sonya set up a *qualified domestic trust* in part (b)?

ISSUE ID

34. **LO.8** Three unmarried and childless sisters live together. All are of advanced age and in poor health, and each owns a significant amount of wealth. Each has a will that passes her property to her surviving sister(s) or, if no survivor, to their church. Within a period of two years and on different dates, all three sisters die. Discuss the Federal estate tax consequences of these deaths.

35. **LO.4, 6** Using the legend provided, classify each of the following transactions.

Legend
NT = No transfer tax imposed
GT = Subject to the Federal gift tax
ET = Subject to the Federal estate tax

   a. Hal establishes a bank checking account listing ownership as "Hal and Darlene, joint tenants with right of survivorship."
   b. Same as (a). Six months later, Darlene withdraws all of the funds from the account.
   c. Dana purchases a certificate of deposit listing ownership as "Dana, payable on death to Ann." Dana and Ann are sisters.
   d. Same as (c). Six months later, Dana predeceases Ann.
   e. Same as (c) and (d), except that Dana and Ann are not sisters but husband and wife.
   f. Tim sends money to Robin College to pay for his daughter's room and board.
   g. Nick pays the doctor and hospital for his niece's reconstructive (i.e., plastic) surgery. The niece is Nick's dependent.
   h. Same as (g), except that the niece is not Nick's dependent.
   i. Pierce purchases land listing title as "Pierce and Stella, equal tenants in common." Pierce and Stella are brother and sister.
   j. Same as (i). Two years later, Stella predeceases Pierce.

36. **LO.8** Abby dies in the current year. In determining her Federal estate tax liability, comment on the relevance of each of the following.
   a. Abby made taxable gifts in 1975 and 2008.
   b. Abby held a life estate in a trust created by her late husband.
   c. State death taxes paid by Abby's estate.
   d. Abby's estate includes some assets inherited from a wealthy aunt several years ago.
   e. Abby's estate includes some assets located in foreign countries.
   f. At the time of her death, Abby was receiving payments from a straight-life annuity she purchased from an insurance company several years ago.

37. **LO.9** In terms of the generation-skipping transfer tax, comment on the following.
   a. A GSTT termination event and a GSTT distribution event look very similar.
   b. A direct skip can occur only in gift situations, not in testamentary situations.
   c. Spouses may be of different generations if there is enough disparity in their ages.
   d. How the election to split a gift by a married donor can help avoid the tax.

PROBLEMS

38. **LO.1, 3, 6, 7** Arlene's estate includes the following assets.

	Fair Market Value	
	Date of Death	**Six Months Later**
Apartment building	$4,400,000	$4,380,000
Stock in Red Corporation	1,200,000	1,300,000
Stock in Tan Corporation	900,000	700,000

Accrued rents on the apartment building are as follows: $70,000 (date of death) and $60,000 (six months later). In order to pay expenses, the executor of Arlene's estate sells the Tan stock for $600,000 eight months after her death.

a. If the § 2032 election is made, how much is included in Arlene's gross estate?
b. As to part (a), assume the Tan stock is sold for $600,000 five months (rather than eight months) after Arlene's death. How does this change your answer, if at all?
c. How much is included in the gross estate if the § 2032 election is not made?

39. **LO.3** In each of the following independent situations, indicate whether the alternate valuation date can be elected. Explain why or why not. Assume all deaths occur in 2011.

	Value of Gross Estate		Estate Tax Liability	
Decedent	**Date of Death**	**Six Months Later**	**Date of Death**	**Six Months Later**
Art	$6,000,000	$5,900,000	$240,000	$241,000
Maude	6,000,000	6,100,000	265,000	260,000
Bob	6,100,000	6,000,000	200,000	190,000
Bette	6,500,000	6,400,000	205,000	210,000

40. **LO.4** Carl made the following transfers during 2011.

- Transferred $900,000 in cash and securities to a revocable trust, life estate to himself and remainder interest to his three adult children by a former wife.
- In consideration of their upcoming marriage, gave Lindsey (age 21) a $90,000 convertible.
- Purchased a $100,000 certificate of deposit listing title as "Carl, payable on proof of death to Lindsey."
- Purchased for $80,000 a paid-up insurance policy on his life (maturity value of $500,000). Carl designated Lindsey as the beneficiary.

What are Carl's taxable gifs for 2011?

ISSUE ID

41. **LO.4, 7** In May 2010, Dudley and Eva enter into a property settlement preparatory to the dissolution of their marriage. Under the agreement, Dudley is to pay Eva $6 million in satisfaction of her marital rights. Of this amount, Dudley pays $2.5 million immediately, and the balance is due one year later. The parties are divorced in July. Dudley dies in December, and his estate pays Eva the remaining $3.5 million in May 2011. Discuss the tax ramifications of these transactions to the parties involved.

ISSUE ID

42. **LO.4** Jesse dies intestate (i.e., without a will) in May 2010. Jesse's major asset is a tract of land. Under applicable state law, Jesse's property will pass to Lorena, who is his only child. In December 2010, Lorena disclaims one-half of the property. In June 2011, Lorena disclaims the other half interest. Under state law, Lorena's disclaimer results in the property passing to Arnold (Lorena's only child). The value of the land (in its entirety) is as follows: $2 million in May 2010; $2.1 million in December 2010; and $2.2 million in June 2011. Discuss the transfer tax ramifications of these transactions.

43. **LO.5** Using property she inherited, Myrna makes a gift of $6.2 million to her adult daughter, Doris. The gift takes place in 2011. Neither Myrna nor her husband, Greg, have made any prior taxable gifts. Determine the gift tax liability if:
   a. The § 2513 election to split gifts is not made.
   b. The § 2513 election to split gifts is made.
   c. What are the tax savings from making the election?

44. **LO.6, 7** At the time of his death on September 2, 2011, Kenneth owned the following assets.

	Fair Market Value
City of Boston bonds	$1,500,000
Stock in Brown Corporation	800,000
Promissory note issued by Brad (Kenneth's son)	300,000

In October 2011, the executor of Kenneth's estate received the following: $90,000 interest on the City of Boston bonds ($20,000 accrued since September 2), and an $8,000 cash dividend on the Brown stock (date of record was September 1). The declaration date on the dividend was August 12. The $300,000 loan was made to Brad in late 2007, and he used the money to create a very successful business. The note was forgiven by Kenneth in his will. What are the estate tax consequences of these transactions?

45. **LO.6** At the time of her death on September 4, 2011, Alicia held the following assets.

	Fair Market Value
Bonds of Emerald Tool Corporation	$800,000
Stock in Drab Corporation	900,000
Insurance policy (face amount of $200,000) on the life of her father, Mitch	50,000*
Traditional IRAs	300,000

*Cash surrender value.

Alicia was also the life tenant of a trust (fair market value of $2 million) created by her late husband Brad. (The executor of Brad's estate had made a QTIP election.) In October, Alicia's estate received an interest payment of $12,000 ($10,000 accrued before September 4, 2011) paid by Emerald and a cash dividend of $9,000 from Drab. The Drab dividend was declared on August 19 and was payable to date of record shareholders on September 5, 2011. Although Mitch survives Alicia, she is the designated beneficiary of the policy. The IRAs are distributed to Alicia's children. What is the amount included in Alicia's gross estate?

46. **LO.6** Assume the same facts as in Problem 45 with the following modifications.

   - Mitch is killed by a rock slide while mountain climbing in November 2011, and the insurer pays Alicia's estate $200,000.
   - Brad's executor did not make a QTIP election.
   - Alicia's IRAs were the Roth type (not traditional).

   What is the amount included in Alicia's gross estate?

47. **LO.6, 7** At the time of Matthew's death, he was involved in the transactions described below.

   - Matthew was a participant in his employer's contributory qualified pension plan. The plan balance of $2 million is paid to Olivia, Matthew's daughter and beneficiary. The distribution consists of the following.

Employer contributions	$900,000
Matthew's after-tax contributions	600,000
Income earned by the plan	500,000

- Matthew was covered by his employer's group term life insurance plan for employees. The $200,000 proceeds are paid to Olivia, the designated beneficiary.

a. What are the estate tax consequences?
b. The income tax consequences?
c. Would the answer to part (a) change if Olivia was Matthew's surviving spouse (not his daughter)? Explain.

48. **LO.4, 6** Before her death in early 2011, Katie made the following transfers.

- In 2008, purchased stock in Green Corporation for $200,000 listing title as follows: "Katie, payable on proof of death to my son, Travis." Travis survives Katie, and the stock is worth $300,000 when Katie dies.
- In 2009, purchased an insurance policy on her life for $200,000 listing Paul, another of Katie's sons, as the designated beneficiary. The policy has a maturity value of $1 million and was immediately transferred to Paul as a gift.
- In 2010, made a gift of land (basis of $300,000; fair market value of $1.3 million) to Adriana, Katie's only daughter. As a result of the transfer, Katie paid a gift tax of $150,000. The value of the land is still $1.3 million at Katie's death.
- In 2009, established a savings account with $100,000 listing title as "Katie and Wilma, joint tenants with right of survivorship." Wilma, Katie's mother, died in 2010 when the account's balance was $102,000. At Katie's death, the balance was $104,000.

As to these transfers, how much is included in Katie's gross estate?

ISSUE ID

49. **LO.4, 6, 7** In 2004, using $2 million in community property, Warren creates a trust, life estate to his wife, Ava, and remainder to their children. Warren dies in 2008 when the trust is worth $3.4 million, and Ava dies in 2011 when the trust is worth $4.6 million.
a. Did Warren make a gift in 2004? Explain.
b. How much, if any, of the trust is included in Warren's gross estate in 2008?
c. How much, if any, of the trust is included in Ava's gross estate in 2011?
d. Would the answer to part (b) change if Warren had died in 2006 (rather than 2008)? Explain.

50. **LO.6, 9** At the time of his death, Garth was involved in the following arrangements.

- He held a life estate in the Myrtle Trust with the remainder passing to Garth's adult children. The trust was created by Myrtle (Garth's mother) in 1984 with securities worth $900,000. The Myrtle Trust had a value of $4.7 million when Garth died.
- Under the terms of the Myrtle Trust, Garth was given the power to provide for a disproportionate distribution of the remainder interest among his children. As Garth failed to exercise this power, the remainder interest is divided equally among the children.

Discuss the estate tax ramifications of these arrangements as to Garth.

51. **LO.6** In 2007, Peggy, a widow, places $3 million in trust, life estate to her children, remainder to her grandchildren, but retains the right to revoke the trust. In 2010, when the trust is worth $3.1 million, Peggy rescinds her right to revoke the trust. Peggy dies in 2011 when the trust is worth $3.2 million. What are Peggy's transfer tax consequences in:
a. 2007?
b. 2010?
c. 2011?

52. **LO.6, 7** In 2000, Alan purchases a commercial single premium annuity. Under the terms of the policy, Alan is to receive $120,000 annually for life. If Alan predeceases his wife, Katelyn, she is to receive $60,000 annually for life. Alan dies first at a time when the value of the survivorship feature is $900,000.
a. How much, if any, of the annuity is included in Alan's gross estate? Taxable estate?
b. Would the answers to part (a) change if the money Alan used to purchase the annuity was community property? Explain.
c. Would the answer to (a) change if one-half of the annuity purchase price had been furnished by Alan's employer?

53. **LO.6** At the time of his death on June 6, 2011, Keith was involved in the following real estate.

	Fair Market Value (on June 6, 2011)
Apartment building	$2,000,000
Tree farm	1,200,000
Pastureland	900,000
Residence	800,000

The apartment building was purchased by Emma, Keith's mother, and is owned in a joint tenancy with her. The tree farm and pastureland were gifts from Emma to Keith and his two sisters. The tree farm is held in joint tenancy, and the pastureland is owned as tenants in common. Keith purchased the residence and owns it with his wife as tenants by the entirety. How much is included in Keith's gross estate based on the following assumptions?

a. Keith dies first and is survived by Emma, his sisters, and his wife.
b. Keith dies after Emma, but before his sisters and his wife.
c. Keith dies after Emma and his sisters, but before his wife.
d. Keith dies last (i.e., he survives Emma, his sisters, and his wife).

54. **LO.4, 6, 7** In 2002, Gordon purchased real estate for $900,000 and listed title to the property as "Gordon and Fawn, joint tenants with right of survivorship." Gordon predeceases Fawn in 2011 when the real estate is worth $2.9 million. Gordon and Fawn are brother and sister.

a. Did a gift occur in 2002? Explain.
b. What, if any, are the estate tax consequences in 2011?
c. Under part (b), would your answer change if it was Fawn (not Gordon) who died in 2011? Explain.

55. **LO.4, 6, 7** Assume the same facts as in Problem 54, except that Gordon and Fawn are husband and wife (not brother and sister).

a. What are the gift tax consequences in 2002?
b. What are the estate tax consequences in 2011?
c. Under part (b), would your answer change if it was Fawn (not Gordon) who died in 2011? Explain.

56. **LO.6** In 2009, Jessica placed $250,000 in a savings account listing ownership as follows: "Jessica, Keri, and Jason, joint tenancy with the right of survivorship." Keri and Jason are Jessica's adult children. In 2010, Jason withdrew $50,000 from the account. In 2011, when the account had a balance of $210,000, Jessica predeceases her children. What are the transfer tax consequences of these transactions in:

a. 2009?
b. 2010?
c. 2011?

57. **LO.5, 6, 7** In each of the independent situations below, determine the transfer tax (i.e., estate and gift) consequences of what has occurred. (In all cases, assume Gene and Mary are married and that Ashley is their daughter.)

a. Mary purchases an insurance policy on Gene's life and designates Ashley as the beneficiary. Mary dies first, and under her will, the policy passes to Gene.
b. Gene purchases an insurance policy on his life and designates Ashley as the beneficiary. Gene gives the policy to Mary and continues to pay the premiums thereon. Two years after the gift, Gene dies first, and the policy proceeds are paid to Ashley.
c. Gene purchases an insurance policy on Mary's life and designates Ashley as the beneficiary. Ashley dies first one year later.
d. Assume the same facts as in part (c). Two years later, Mary dies. Because Gene has not designated a new beneficiary, the insurance proceeds are paid to him.
e. Gene purchases an insurance policy on his life and designates Mary as the beneficiary. Gene dies first, and the policy proceeds are paid to Mary.

58. **LO.7** While vacationing in Florida in November 2011, Sally was seriously injured in an automobile accident (she died several days later). How are the following transactions handled for tax purposes?

a. Bruce, Sally's son and executor, incurred $6,200 in travel expenses in flying to Florida, retrieving the body, and returning it to Frankfort (KY) for burial.

b. Early in 2011, Sally had pledged $50,000 to the building fund of her church. Bruce paid this pledge from the assets of the estate.
c. Prior to her death, Sally had promised to give her nephew, Gary, $20,000 when he passed the bar exam. Gary passed the exam in December 2011, and Bruce kept Sally's promise by paying him $20,000 from estate assets.
d. At the scene of the accident and before the ambulance arrived, someone took Sally's jewelry (i.e., Rolex watch, wedding ring) and money. The property (valued at $33,000) was not insured and was never recovered.
e. As a result of the accident, Sally's auto was totally destroyed. The auto had a basis of $52,000 and a fair market value of $28,000. In January 2012, the insurance company pays Sally's estate $27,000.

59. **LO.7** In 2011, Roy dies and is survived by his wife, Marge. Under Roy's will, all of his otherwise uncommitted assets pass to Marge. Based on the property interests listed below, determine the marital deduction allowed to Roy's estate.
 a. Timberland worth $1.2 million owned by Roy, Marge, and Amber (Marge's sister) as equal tenants in common. Roy furnished the original purchase price.
 b. Residence of Roy and Marge worth $900,000 owned by them as tenants by the entirety with right of survivorship. Marge provided the original purchase price.
 c. Insurance policy on Roy's life (maturity value of $500,000) owned by Marge and payable to her as the beneficiary.
 d. Insurance policy on Roy's life (maturity value of $1 million) owned by Roy with Marge as the designated beneficiary.
 e. Distribution from a qualified pension plan of $1.5 million (Roy matched his employer's contribution of $500,000) with Marge as the designated beneficiary.

60. **LO.8** Under Rowena's will, Mandy (Rowena's sister) inherits her property. One year later, Mandy dies. Based on the following independent assumptions, what is Mandy's credit for the tax on prior transfers?
 a. The estate tax attributable to the inclusion of the property in Rowena's gross estate is $700,000, and the estate tax attributable to the inclusion of the property in Mandy's gross estate is $800,000.
 b. The estate tax attributable to the inclusion of the property in Rowena's gross estate is $1.2 million, and the estate tax attributable to the inclusion of the property in Mandy's gross estate is $1.1 million.
 c. Would your answers to parts (a) and (b) change if Mandy died seven years (rather than one year) after Rowena?

61. **LO.9** In 2012, Loretta makes a taxable gift of $2 million to her granddaughter, Bertha. Presuming that Loretta used up both her unified transfer tax credit and her generation-skipping transfer tax credit, how much tax does Loretta owe as a result of the transfer?

62. **LO.9** In 2011, Marsha died, and her after-tax estate of $6 million passed to a trust. Under the terms of the trust, Wilma (Marsha's daughter) is granted a life estate with the remainder passing to Karl (Marsha's grandson) upon Wilma's death. The trustee elects to use $3 million of the generation-skipping transfer tax exemption. Wilma dies in 2012 when the trust is worth $9 million.
 a. Presuming the GSTT applies, is it caused by a termination event, a distribution event, or a direct skip?
 b. How much of the trust is subject to the GSTT?
 c. Who pays the tax?
 d. What is the GSTT rate that applies?

63. **LO.5, 8** In each of the following independent situations, determine the gift tax that was due and the decedent's final estate tax liability (net of any unified tax credit).

	Decedent		
	Dana	**Alice**	**Ken**
Year of death	2003	2004	2012
Taxable estate	$900,000	$1,700,000	$1,400,000
Post-1976 taxable gifts—			
Made in 2000	900,000	—	—
Made in 2001	—	800,000	—
Made in 2011	—	—	5,200,000

TAX RETURN PROBLEMS

1. Drew M. and Bernice B. Fleming (Social Security numbers 123–45–6789 and 123–45–6788) live at 324 Seawall Drive, Savannah, GA 31402. Drew and Bernice have been married for many years and own and operate a profitable real estate business. They have two children, Lauren (age 20) and Ned (age 22), both of whom attend college. During 2010, the Flemings made the following transfers.

Transfer	Donor: Drew	Donor: Bernice
Paid college expenses ($50,000 tuition + $12,000 room and board). To foster financial responsibility, these amounts were given directly to Lauren and Ned.	$ 62,000	
Reimbursed Greta (Lauren's aunt) for her kidney transplant. Greta is not a dependent of the Flemings.		$42,000
With the $150,000 in insurance proceeds he received on the death of his grandfather, Drew purchased land in DeKalb County listing title as "Drew, Lauren, and Ned Fleming, equal tenants in common."	150,000	
As a wedding anniversary present, purchased an RV for Drew's parents (Ben and Thelma)	55,000	55,000
Cash contribution to the reelection campaign of the mayor of Savannah	5,000	5,000

In creating several trusts in 2008, the Flemings made taxable gifts of $2 million. Consequently, no gift tax was due because of the specific exemption ($1 million for each donor spouse).

Prepare 2010 gift tax returns (Form 709) for the Flemings. As in the past, the Flemings make the § 2513 election to split the gifts.

2. Judith Dunn (Social Security Number 111–11–1111) is a widow who lives at 4021 Ash Road, Independence, MO 64050. During 2010, she made the following gifts to her two adult children.

   a. A tract of undeveloped land (basis of $100,000; fair market value of $600,000) in Greene County to her son, Harry Dunn.

   b. A rental duplex (basis of $320,000; fair market value of $500,000) in Kansas City (MO) to her daughter, Margaret Clay.

   Prepare a gift tax return (Form 709) for Judith. She has not made any prior taxable gifts.

RESEARCH PROBLEMS

Note: Solutions to Research Problems can be prepared by using the **Checkpoint® Student Edition** online research product, which is available to accompany this text. It is also possible to prepare solutions to the Research Problems by using tax research materials found in a standard tax library.

THOMSON REUTERS
Checkpoint® Student Edition

Research Problem 1. In 2000, June, a 75-year-old widow, creates an irrevocable trust naming her five adult grandchildren as the beneficiaries. The assets transferred in trust consist of marketable securities (worth $800,000) and June's personal residence (worth $400,000). Bob, June's younger brother and a practicing attorney, is designated as the trustee. Other provisions of the trust are noted below.

- Bob is given the discretion to distribute the income to the beneficiaries based on their need or add it to corpus. He is also given the power to change trust investments and to terminate the trust.

- The trust is to last for June's lifetime or, if sooner, until termination by Bob.
- Upon termination of the trust, the principal and any accumulated income are to be distributed to the beneficiaries (June's grandchildren).

For 2000, June files a Form 709 to report the transfer in trust and pays a gift tax based on value of $1.2 million ($800,000 + $400,000).

After the transfer in trust and up to the time of her death, June continues to occupy the residence. Although she pays no rent, she maintains the property and pays the yearly property taxes. June never discussed the matter of her continued occupancy of the residence with either Bob or the beneficiaries of the trust.

On June's death in 2008, the value of the trust is $2.3 million, broken down as follows: marketable securities and cash ($1.6 million) and residence ($700,000). Shortly thereafter, Bob sells the residence, liquidates the trust, and distributes the proceeds to the beneficiaries.

What are the estate tax consequences of these transactions to June?

Partial list of research aids:
§ 2036.
Guynn v. U.S., 71–1 USTC ¶12,742, 27 AFTR 2d 71–1653, 437 F.2d 1148 (CA–4, 1971).
Estate of Eleanor T. R. Trotter, 82 TCM 633, T.C.Memo. 2001–250.
Estate of Lorraine C. Disbrow, 91 TCM 794, T.C.Memo. 2006–34.

Research Problem 2. Grace Tipton, a widow of considerable means, dies in February 2004. One month later, her designated executor is appointed by the probate court of appropriate jurisdiction, and the administration of the Tipton estate is initiated. Among the bequests in Grace's will is one that passes $10 million to the Christian Assisted Living Foundation (CALF), but only if it is a qualified charity for purposes of § 2055. Because the status of CALF has never been evaluated by the IRS, the executor feels compelled to postpone the satisfaction of the bequest. Instead, he files the Form 706 and pays the estate tax based on the charitable deduction being allowed. Further, he requests a "closing letter" from the IRS on the Form 706 that is filed. Since the issuance of a closing letter means acceptance of the deduction, it forces the IRS to investigate the charitable nature of CALF.

After investigating the activities of CALF, the IRS finds it to be a qualified charity. Consequently, in October 2006 the IRS issues a closing letter approving the charitable deduction claimed and accepting the Form 706 as filed. Shortly thereafter, the executor transfers $11 million to CALF. The amount transferred represents $10 million for the satisfaction of the bequest and $1 million for statutory interest accrued. Under state law, interest must be paid on any bequest that is not satisfied within a one-year period after the initiation of administration. The probate court sanctions the determination and payment of the $1 million interest amount.

Subsequent to the $11 million CALF distribution, the executor files an amended Form 706. The amended return claims a refund for the estate taxes attributable to the additional $1 million paid as interest. On the amended return, the interest is classified as an administration expense under § 2053, thereby reducing the taxable estate and resulting estate tax liability. The IRS denies the claim for refund on the grounds that the interest incurred was not necessary to the administration of the estate. If the executor had satisfied the CALF bequest earlier, the accrual of interest would have been avoided. The executor counters that the delay was necessary in order to maintain fiduciary integrity in complying with the terms of the decedent's will. Who should prevail?

Partial list of research aids:
§ 2053(a)(2).
Reg. § 20.2053–3(a).
Pitner v. U.S., 68–1 USTC ¶12,499, 21 AFTR 2d 1571, 388 F.2d 651 (CA–5, 1967).
Turner v. U.S., 2004–1 USTC ¶60,478, 93 AFTR 2d 2004–686, 306 F.Supp.2d 668 (D.Ct.N.Tex., 2004).

Research Problem 3. Ralph Heard dies in 2008 leaving a large estate. After providing for specific bequests to friends and distant relatives, his will states, "I leave the residue of my estate to be divided between my wife and two children." Ralph's will also states, "Any estate tax is to be paid from the residue of my estate." Applicable state law contains an apportionment provision that precludes the allocation of estate taxes to assets that did not create or generate such taxes unless the decedent provided otherwise.

On the Form 706 Ralph's executor filed for the estate, the estate taxes were deducted solely from the children's portion of the residue. After audit by the IRS, the estate taxes were charged against the entire residue of the estate.

a. What difference does it make?
b. Is the IRS's position correct?

Partial list of research aids:
§ 2056(b)(4)(A).
John David McCoy, 97 TCM 1312, T.C.Memo. 2009–61.

Research Problem 4. Before her death in 2009, Lucy entered into the following transactions.

a. In 2007, she borrowed $300,000 from a bank and promptly loaned that sum to her controlled corporation. The executor of Lucy's estate prepaid the bank loan, but never attempted to collect the amount due Lucy from the corporation.
b. In 2001, Lucy promised her sister, Ida, a bequest of $800,000 if Ida would move in with her and care for her during an illness (which eventually proved to be terminal). Lucy never kept her promise, as her will was silent on any bequest to Ida. After Lucy's death, Ida sued the estate and eventually recovered $600,000 for breach of contract.
c. One of the assets in Lucy's estate was a palatial residence that passed to George under a specific provision of the will. George did not want the residence, preferring cash instead. Per George's instructions, the residence was sold. Expenses incurred in connection with the sale were claimed as § 2053 expenses on Form 706 filed by Lucy's estate.
d. Before her death, Lucy incurred and paid certain medical expenses but did not have the opportunity to file a claim for partial reimbursement from her insurance company. After her death, the claim was filed by Lucy's executor, and the reimbursement was paid to the estate.

Discuss the estate and income tax ramifications of each of these transactions.

Partial list of research aids:
§§ 61(a)(1) and (12), 111, 213, 691, 2033, and 2053.
Estate of Allie W. Pittard, 69 T.C. 391 (1977).
Joseph F. Kenefic, 36 TCM 1226, T.C.Memo. 1977–310.
Hibernia Bank v. U.S., 78–2 USTC ¶13,261, 42 AFTR 2d 78–6510, 581 F.2d 741 (CA–9, 1978).
Rev.Rul. 78–292, 1978–2 C.B. 233.

Use the tax resources of the Internet to address the following questions. Do not restrict your search to the Web, but include a review of newsgroups and general reference materials, practitioner sites and resources, primary sources of the tax law, chat rooms and discussion groups, and other opportunities.

Research Problem 5. What type of transfer tax, if any, does your home state impose? What about the state(s) contiguous to your home state? (For Alaska, use Washington; for Hawaii, use California.)

COMMUNICATIONS

Research Problem 6. A considerable amount of material (e.g., magazine and newspaper commentaries, journal articles, books) is available on why the Federal estate tax should be repealed. Identify three recent sources. Summarize them in an e-mail to your instructor, and include a list of citations.

Research Problem 7. Based on the most recent IRS data available, determine the following.

a. The number of estate tax returns (Form 706) filed in a year. What percentage of these returns did the IRS audit?
b. The number of estate tax returns filed that also included GSTT situations.
c. The number of gift tax returns (Form 709) filed in a year. What percentage of these returns did the IRS audit?

COMMUNICATIONS

Research Problem 8. Find the IRS forms noted below. List the title of each, prepare a short comment as to its purpose or use, and e-mail this information to your instructor.

a. Schedule U of Form 706.
b. Form 706-A.
c. Form 706-GS(D).
d. Form 706-QDT.

Research Problem 9. When completing Form 706, how does one make the QTIP election? Be specific.

COMMUNICATIONS

Research Problem 10. Based on the most recent IRS data available, determine the following.

a. On how many Forms 706 was a charitable contribution claimed?
b. What was the total dollar amount of the charitable contribution deductions that were claimed? What percentage of the adjusted gross estate does this represent?
c. Were deductible charitable contributions made proportionately by all decedents? Were wealthier decedents more or less generous to charity? Illustrate your findings on this point in a graph, and send your report to your instructor.

CHAPTER

19

Family Tax Planning

LEARNING OBJECTIVES

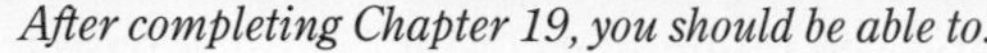

After completing Chapter 19, you should be able to:

LO.1 Describe various established concepts used in carrying out the valuation process.

LO.2 Apply the special use valuation method in appropriate situations.

LO.3 Identify problems involved in valuing an interest in a closely held business.

LO.4 Compare the income tax basis rules applying to property received by gift and by death.

LO.5 Explain how gifts can minimize gift taxes and avoid estate taxes.

LO.6 Evaluate how to make gifts so as to avoid income taxes for the donor.

LO.7 Assess how to reduce probate costs in the administration of an estate.

LO.8 Apply procedures that reduce estate tax consequences.

LO.9 Demonstrate procedures to obtain liquidity for an estate.

OUTLINE

For the latest in changes to tax legislation, visit **www.cengage.com/taxation/swft.**

THE BIG PICTURE **Tax Solutions for the Real World**

LIFETIME GIVING—THE GOOD AND THE BAD

Martin, age 75, is a wealthy widower who is considering making a lifetime gift of $500,000 to his only daughter, Francine. Among the assets that Martin can choose from, *each* worth $500,000, are the following.

- Farmland (current use value of $100,000).
- Partial interest in a closely held partnership.
- Insurance policy on Martin's life with a maturity value of $3 million.
- Marketable securities (adjusted basis to Martin of $900,000).
- Unimproved residential city lot (adjusted basis to Martin of $100,000).
- Ten annual installment notes from the sale of land (basis of $200,000) with a maturity value of $700,000.

In terms of present and future tax consequences, evaluate each choice. **Read the chapter and formulate your response.**

Broadly speaking, *family tax planning* involves the use of various procedures that minimize the effect of taxation on transfers within the family unit. As such, planning involves a consideration not only of transfer taxes (i.e., gift and estate) but also of the income tax ramifications to both the transferor (i.e., donor or decedent) and the transferees (i.e., donees or heirs).

The valuation of the transferred property also is an essential element of family tax planning. The gift tax is based on the fair market value of the property on the date of the transfer. For the Federal estate tax, the fair market value on the date of the owner's death or the alternate valuation date (if available and elected) controls.

19.1 Valuation Concepts

LO.1

Describe various established concepts used in carrying out the valuation process.

A major emphasis of this chapter concerns the valuation of property involved in transfers by gift and by death.

VALUATION IN GENERAL

The Internal Revenue Code refers to "value" and "fair market value," but does not discuss these terms at length.[1] Section 2031(b) comes closest to a definition when it treats the problem of stocks and securities for which no sales price information (the usual case with closely held corporations) is available. In such situations, "the value thereof shall be determined by taking into consideration, in addition to all other factors, the value of stock or securities of corporations engaged in the same or similar line of business which are listed on an exchange."

Regulation § 20.2031–1(b) is more specific in defining fair market value as "the price at which property would change hands between a willing buyer and a willing seller, neither being under any compulsion to buy or to sell and both having reasonable knowledge of relevant facts." The same Regulation makes clear that the fair market value of an item of property is not determined by a forced sale price. Nor is the fair market value determined by the sale price of the item in a market other than that in which the item is most commonly sold to the public. Sentiment should not play a part in the determination of value. Suppose, for example, the decedent's daughter is willing to pay $500 for a portrait of her mother. If the painting is really worth $200 (i.e., what the general public would pay), then that should be its value.

[1]See, for example, §§ 1001(b), 2031(a), and 2512(a). Sections 2032A(e)(7) and (8) set forth certain procedures for valuing farms and interests in closely held businesses.

The item's location must also be considered. Thus, the fair market value of property that generally is obtained by the public in a retail market is the price at which the property (or comparable items) would be sold at retail.

EXAMPLE 1

At the time of his death, Don owned three automobiles. The automobiles are included in Don's gross estate at their fair market value on the date of his death or on the alternate valuation date (if elected). The fair market value of the automobiles is determined by looking at the price a member of the general public would pay for automobiles of approximately the same description, make, model, age, condition, etc. The price a dealer in used cars would pay for these automobiles is inappropriate, because an automobile is an item obtainable by the public in a retail market. ■

If tangible personalty is sold as a result of an advertisement in the classified section of a newspaper and the property is of a type often sold in this manner, or if the property is sold at a public auction, the price for which it is sold is presumed to be the retail sales price of the item at the time of the sale. The retail sales price is also used if the sale is made within a reasonable period following the valuation date, and market conditions affecting the value of similar items have not changed substantially.[2] Tangible personalty includes all property except real estate and intangible property.

VALUATION OF SPECIFIC ASSETS

Stocks and Bonds

If there is a market for stocks and bonds on a stock exchange, in an over-the-counter market, or otherwise, the mean between the highest and lowest quoted selling prices on the valuation date is the fair market value per unit. A special rule applies if no sales occurred on the valuation date but did occur on dates within a reasonable period before and after the valuation date. The fair market value is the weighted average of the means between the highest and the lowest sales prices on the nearest date before and the nearest date after the valuation date. The average is weighted *inversely* by the respective number of trading days between the selling dates and the valuation date.[3]

EXAMPLE 2

Carla makes a gift to Antonio of shares of stock in Green Corporation. The transactions involving this stock that occurred closest to the date of the gift took place two trading days before the date of the gift at a mean selling price of $10 and three trading days after the gift at a mean selling price of $15. The $12 fair market value of each share of Green stock is determined as follows.

$$\frac{(3 \times \$10) + (2 \times \$15)}{5} = \$12$$

■

If no transactions occurred within a reasonable period before and after the valuation date, the fair market value is determined by taking a weighted average of the means between the bona fide bid and asked prices on the nearest trading dates before and after the valuation date. However, both dates must be within a reasonable period of time.

If no actual sales prices or bona fide bid and asked prices are available for dates within a reasonable period relative to the valuation date, the mean between the highest and lowest available sales prices or bid and asked prices on that date may be taken as the value.

In many instances, there are no established market prices for securities. This lack of information is typically the case with stock in closely held corporations. Problems

[2] Rev.Proc. 65–19, 1965–2 C.B. 1002.

[3] Reg. §§ 20.2031–2(b) and 25.2512–2(b).

unique to valuing interests in closely held businesses are discussed later in this chapter.

Notes Receivable

The fair market value of notes, secured or unsecured, is the amount of unpaid principal plus interest accrued to the valuation date, unless the parties (e.g., executor, donor) establish a lower value or prove the notes are worthless. Factors such as a low interest rate and a distant maturity date are relevant in showing that a note is worth less than its face amount. Crucial elements in proving that a note is entirely or partially worthless are the financial condition of the borrower and the absence of any value for the property pledged or mortgaged as security for the obligation.[4]

EXAMPLE 3

At the time of his death, Ira held a note (face amount of $50,000) issued by his son, Kevin. Although Kevin is solvent, he is relieved of the obligation because Ira forgives the note in his will. Presuming the note is payable on demand, it is included in Ira's gross estate at $50,000 plus accrued interest. If the note is not due immediately and/or the interest provided for is under the current rate, a discount may be in order, and the fair market value of the note would be less than $50,000. The burden of proof in supporting a discount for the note is on the executor. ■

ONE WAY TO HANDLE LOANS TO TROUBLESOME IN-LAWS

At the time of his death in 2011, Tim Landry held a note, payable on demand, in the amount of $40,000. The note had been issued by Roy Briggs, Tim's former brother-in-law, 10 years earlier. Roy used the funds to help pay the wedding and honeymoon expenses when he married Colleen Landry, Tim's sister. The couple have since separated, and Roy disappeared for parts unknown in 2005.

The executor of Tim's estate handled this matter as follows.

- Filed an amended income tax return for 2005 claiming a bad debt deduction. This set off a chain reaction, and several other amended returns had to be filed for years after 2005.
- Made no mention of the note on the Form 706 filed for Tim Landry's estate.

What, if any, could be the justification for the executor's actions? What caused the chain reaction? If an audit results, what position(s) might the IRS take?

Insurance Policies and Annuity Contracts

The value of a life insurance policy on the life of a person other than the decedent, or the value of an annuity contract issued by a company regularly engaged in selling annuities, is the cost of a comparable contract.[5]

EXAMPLE 4

Paul purchased a joint and survivor annuity contract from an insurance company (i.e., a commercial contract). Under the contract's terms, Paul is to receive payments of $120,000 per year for his life. Upon Paul's death, his wife (Kate) is to receive $90,000 annually for her life. Ten years after purchasing the annuity, when Kate is 40 years old, Paul dies. The value of the annuity contract on the date of Paul's death [and the amount includible in Paul's gross estate under § 2039(a)] is the amount the insurance company would charge in the year of Paul's death for an annuity that would pay $90,000 annually for the life of a female 40 years of age. ■

[4]Reg. §§ 20.2031–4 and 25.2512–4.

[5]Reg. §§ 20.2031–8(a)(1) and 25.2512–6(a).

EXAMPLE 5

At the time of her death, Lana owns an insurance policy (face amount of $500,000) on the life of her son, Sam. No further payments need be made on the policy (e.g., it is a single premium policy or a paid-up policy). The value of the policy on the date of Lana's death (and the amount includible in her gross estate under § 2033 as property owned by the decedent) is the amount the insurance company would charge in the year of her death for a single premium contract (face amount of $500,000) on the life of someone Sam's age. ■

Determining the value of an insurance policy by using the amount charged for a comparable policy is more difficult when, on the date of valuation, the contract has been in force for some time and further premium payments are to be made. In such a case, the value may be approximated by adding to the interpolated terminal reserve the proportionate part of the gross premium last paid before the valuation date that covers the period extending beyond that date.[6]

The valuation of annuities issued by parties *not regularly engaged in the sale of annuities* (i.e., noncommercial contracts) requires the use of special tables issued by the IRS.

Life Estates, Terms for Years, Reversions, and Remainders

As with noncommercial annuities, the valuation of life estates, income interests for a term of years, reversions, and remainders involves the use of tables.

Because life expectancies change, the IRS is required to issue new tables at least every 10 years.[7] The current tables were issued in 2009 and are effective for transfers beginning in May of that year.[8] The tables contain 50 different possible rates (ranging from 0.2 percent to 14 percent), but *only a portion of the tables is reproduced* in Appendix A.

The tables provide only the remainder factor. If the income interest (life estate) has also been transferred, the factor to be used is one minus the remainder factor.

EXAMPLE 6

Matt transfers $1 million in trust, specifying a life estate to Rita, remainder to Rick on Rita's death. The gift took place when Rita was age 35. Assume that the appropriate rate for the month of the gift is 4.4%. Using the table extract in Appendix A (Table S on p. A–10) for a person age 35 under the 4.4% column, the value of the remainder interest is $184,230 (.18423 × $1,000,000). The life estate factor is .81577 (1.00000 – .18423). Thus, Matt has made a gift to Rita of $815,770 and a gift to Rick of $184,230. ■

In computing the value of an income interest for a term of years, a different table is used. Again, the table furnishes the remainder factor. To compute the factor for the income interest, subtract the remainder factor from one. *Only a portion of the tables is reproduced* in Appendix A.

EXAMPLE 7

Julia transfers $400,000 by gift to a trust. Under the terms of the trust, income is payable to Paul for eight years. After the eight-year period, the trust terminates, and the trust principal passes to Sara. For the month in which the trust was created, the appropriate rate was 4.6%. The present worth of $1 due at the end of eight years is .697825 (Table B on p. A–12). Thus, Julia has made a gift to Sara of $279,130 (.697825 × $400,000). The factor for the income interest becomes .302175 (1.000000 – .697825), so the gift to Paul is $120,870 (.302175 × $400,000). ■

What is the significance of dividing a gift into several distinct parts? This is important in determining the applicability of the annual exclusion and the marital

[6] The terminal reserve value of a life insurance policy generally approximates the policy's cash surrender value. For an illustration on how to arrive at the interpolated terminal reserve value, see Reg. § 20.2031–8(a)(3) (Ex. 3).

[7] § 7520.

[8] The valuation factors in the tables represent 120% of whatever the Federal mid-term rate is for the month of the valuation date.

deduction. Under the facts of Example 6, an annual exclusion probably would be allowed for the gift to Rita but not for the interest passing to Rick (because of the future interest limitation). If Rita is Matt's wife, no marital deduction is allowed because the life estate is a terminable interest. As noted in Chapter 18, however, this problem could be cured with a qualified terminable interest property (QTIP) election.

Why might a trust be arranged so that the income interest is limited to a term of years rather than the life of a beneficiary (compare Example 7 with Example 6)? Suppose in Example 7 that Paul is the 13-year-old son of Sara, a single parent. Julia, the grandmother, establishes the trust to assure that Paul's support needs (e.g., medical, educational) will be provided for until he reaches the age of majority. Thereafter, the trust income will help maintain Sara. In this type of situation, however, caution is in order to avoid the possible application of the kiddie tax. Now applicable to children under the age of 19 (or under age 24 if the child is a full-time student, unless the child's earned income provides more than half of his or her support), the kiddie tax has the effect of taxing a child's net unearned income (i.e., unearned income in excess of $1,900) at the parents' income tax rate.

Can IRS Valuation Tables Be Disregarded?

Ted Lucas (age 50) is killed in an automobile accident. One of the provisions of Ted's will establishes a trust with $3 million in assets. Under the terms of the trust, a life estate is granted to Mel (age 75) with the remainder interest passing to Faye (age 45) on Mel's death. Mel is Ted's widower father and is suffering from cancer of the prostate. Faye is Ted's wife and is in good health. Under the applicable valuation tables, the life estate value in $3 million for a person age 75 is $1,031,640 (based on an interest rate of 4.2 percent).

If the Lucas estate valued Mel's estate in accordance with the IRS tables, this would reduce the marital deduction allowed for Faye's remainder interest to $1,968,360 ($3,000,000 – $1,031,640). Since Mel has cancer, however, his life estate is disregarded, and the full $3 million is claimed as a marital deduction. Is the estate correct in disregarding the valuation factor for a life estate in light of Mel's medical condition?

LO.2

Apply the special use valuation method in appropriate situations.

REAL ESTATE AND THE SPECIAL USE VALUATION METHOD

Proper valuation principles usually require that real estate be valued at its most suitable (i.e., "best" or "highest") use. Section 2032A, however, permits an executor to elect to value certain classes of real estate used in farming or in connection with a closely held business at its "current" use, rather than the most suitable use. The major objective of the **special use value** election is to provide a form of limited relief to protect the heirs against the possibility of having to sell a portion of the family farm to pay estate taxes.

EXAMPLE 8

At the time of his death, Rex owned a dairy farm on the outskirts of a large city. For farming purposes, the property's value is $1.5 million (the current use value).[9] As a potential site for a shopping center, however, the property is worth $2.2 million (the most suitable use value). The executor of Rex's estate can elect to include only $1.5 million in the gross estate. ■

The special use valuation procedure permits a reduction of no more than $1,020,000 in estate tax valuation in 2011 ($1 million in 2010). This amount is subject to indexation.

[9]Sections 2032A(e)(7) and (8) set forth various methods of valuation to be applied in arriving at current use value.

TAX *in the NEWS* — Should There Be an Unlimited Estate Tax Exemption for Farmland?

A bill introduced in Congress would exempt farmland from all Federal estate tax. The proposal immediately was criticized on several grounds.

- At least at current levels, the estate tax does not pose a serious problem for most farmers. Estate taxes can be minimized (or eliminated) by special use valuation, the extended payment procedures of § 6166 (see later in chapter), issuance of conservation easements, and various discounts for minority interests and lack of marketability.
- The exemption could hurt ordinary farmers by driving up the price of farmland. Wealthy taxpayers would shift their funds to large-scale farming in order to obtain exemption from the estate tax.

At least according to some, completely exempting farmland from estate taxes constitutes an overkill solution to a problem that is not that serious. It is extremely rare today that the survivors of a farmer must sell the land to pay off estate taxes.

Source: Adapted from Gillis Brunet and Chye-Ching Huang, "Unlimited Estate Tax Exemption for Farm Estates Is Unnecessary and Likely Harmful," Center on Budget and Policy Priorities, June 29, 2010.

EXAMPLE 9

At the time of her death in 2011, Wanda owned a farm with a most suitable use value of $3.5 million but a current use value of $2.3 million. Assuming the property qualifies under § 2032A and the special use valuation election is made, Wanda's gross estate must include $2,480,000 million. Only $1,020,000 can be excluded under § 2032A. ■

The special use valuation election is available if *all* of the following conditions are satisfied.

- At least 50 percent of the adjusted value of the gross estate consists of *real* or *personal* property devoted to a qualifying use (used for farming or in a closely held business) at the time of the owner's death.[10]
- The *real* property devoted to a qualifying use comprises at least 25 percent of the adjusted value of the gross estate.

  For purposes of satisfying both the 50 percent test (above) and the 25 percent test, the qualifying property is considered at its most suitable use value. Thus, in Example 8, the property would be treated as if it had a value of $2.2 million (not $1.5 million). The adjusted value of the gross estate is the gross estate less certain unpaid mortgages and other indebtedness.
- The qualifying property passes to a qualifying heir of the decedent. Qualifying heirs are certain family members as set forth in § 2032A(e)(2).
- The *real* property has been owned by the decedent or the decedent's family for five out of the eight years ending on the date of the decedent's death and was devoted to a qualifying use during that period.
- The decedent or a member of the decedent's family participated materially in the operation of the farm or business during the five-year period specified above.[11]

Any estate tax savings derived from the special use valuation method are recaptured from the heir if he or she disposes of the property or ceases to use it as qualifying use property within a period of 10 years from the date of the decedent's death.

EXAMPLE 10

Assume the same facts as in Example 9. Further assume that by electing § 2032A, Wanda's estate tax liability was reduced by $245,000. Three years after Wanda's death, Otis (the qualifying heir) leases the farm to an unrelated party. At this point, Otis must

[10] §§ 2032A(b)(1)(A) and (b)(2). For a definition of "farm" and "farming," see §§ 2032A(e)(4) and (5).

[11] § 2032A(b)(1)(C)(ii). "Material participation" is defined in § 2032A(e)(6).

pay the $245,000 additional estate tax liability that would have been imposed had § 2032A not been utilized. ■

In the event recapture occurs, the qualifying heir may *elect* to increase the income tax basis of the property by the amount of the recapture. If the election is made, however, interest on the additional estate tax due must be paid.[12]

In this regard, the Code gives the IRS security for compliance with the terms of § 2032A by placing a special lien on the qualifying property.[13]

LO.3

Identify problems involved in valuing an interest in a closely held business.

VALUATION PROBLEMS WITH A CLOSELY HELD BUSINESS

General Guidelines

Revenue Ruling 59–60 sets forth the approach, methods, and factors to be considered in valuing the shares of closely held corporations for gift and estate tax purposes.[14] The following factors, although not all-inclusive, are fundamental and require careful analysis in each case.

- The nature of the business and the history of the enterprise from its inception.
- The economic outlook in general and the condition and outlook of the specific industry in particular.
- The book value of the stock and the financial condition of the business.
- The earning capacity of the company.
- The company's dividend-paying capacity.
- Whether the enterprise has goodwill or other intangible value.
- The prices and number of shares of the stock sold previously and the size of the block of stock to be valued.
- The market price of stocks issued by corporations in the same or a similar line of business and actively traded in a free and open market, either on an exchange or over-the-counter.

Some of these factors are discussed in depth in the pages to follow.

Goodwill Aspects

If a closely held corporation's record of past earnings is higher than is usual for the industry, the IRS is apt to claim the presence of goodwill as a corporate asset.

EXAMPLE 11

Adam owned 70% of the stock of White Corporation, with the remaining 30% held by various family members. Over the past five years, White Corporation has generated average net profits of $200,000, and on the date of Adam's death, the book value of the corporation's stock was $500,000. If the IRS identifies 8% as an appropriate rate of return, one approach to the valuation of White stock would yield the following result.

Average net profit for the past five years	$ 200,000
8% of the $500,000 book value	40,000
Excess earnings over 8%	$ 160,000
Value of goodwill (5 × $160,000)	$ 800,000
Book value	500,000
Total value of the White stock	$1,300,000

■

Thus, the IRS might contend that the stock should be included in Adam's gross estate at 70 percent of $1,300,000, or $910,000. If the estate wishes to argue for a lower valuation, relevant factors might include any of the following.

[12] § 1016(c).

[13] § 6324B.

[14] 1959–1 C.B. 237. See also Reg. § 20.2031–2(f).

- The average net profit figure for the past five years ($200,000) may not be representative. Perhaps it includes some extraordinary gains that normally do not occur or are extraneous to the business conducted by the corporation. An example might be a windfall profit for a specific year because of an unusual market situation. The corporation may have recognized a large gain from an appreciated investment held for many years. The figure may fail to take into account certain expenses that normally would be incurred but for some justifiable reason have been deferred. In a family business during periods of expansion and development, it is not uncommon to find an unusually low salary structure. Profits might be considerably less if the owner-employees of the business were being paid the true worth of their services.
- The appropriate rate of return for this type of business may not be 8 percent. If it is higher, there would be less goodwill because the business is not as profitable as it seems.
- If Adam was a key person in the operation of White Corporation, could some or all of any goodwill developed by the business be attributed to his efforts? If so, is it not reasonable to assume that the goodwill might be seriously impaired by Adam's death?

Other Factors

Aside from the issue of goodwill, the valuation of closely held stock must take other factors into account. For example, consider the percentage of ownership involved. If the percentage represents a *minority interest* and the corporation has a poor dividend-paying record, a substantial discount is in order.[15] The justification for the discount is the general inability of the holder of the minority interest to affect corporate policy, particularly with respect to the distribution of dividends. At the other extreme is an interest large enough to represent control, either actual or effective. Considered alone, a controlling interest calls for valuation at a premium.[16]

A controlling interest may be so large, however, that the disposition of the stock within a reasonable period of time after the valuation date could have a negative effect on the market for such shares. The **blockage rule** recognizes what may happen to per-unit value when a large block of shares is marketed at one time.[17] Most often, the rule is applied to stock that has a recognized market. The rule permits a discount from the amount at which smaller lots are selling on or about the valuation date.[18] Although the blockage rule may have a bearing on the valuation of other assets, it is more frequently applied to stocks and securities.[19]

Because most stock in closely held corporations does not trade in a recognized market, a discount for *lack of marketability* may be in order. The discount recognizes the costs that would be incurred in creating a market for such shares to effect their orderly disposition.[20] The discount could be significant considering typical underwriting expenses and other costs involved in going public.

Closely related to the reasons that an asset's marketability might be impaired is the possibility of built-in income tax consequences. In one case, the value of stock in a holding company was significantly discounted because of the income tax that would ensue if the holding company distributed its major asset to its shareholders.[21]

[15]See, for example, *Jack D. Carr*, 49 TCM 507, T.C.Memo. 1985–19.

[16]*Helvering v. Safe Deposit and Trust Co. of Baltimore, Exr. (Estate of H. Walters)*, 38–1 USTC ¶9240, 21 AFTR 12, 95 F.2d 806 (CA–4, 1938), *aff'g* 35 B.T.A. 259 (1937).

[17]Reg. § 20.2031–2(e).

[18]See, for example, *Estate of Robert Damon*, 49 T.C. 108 (1967).

[19]In *Estate of David Smith*, 57 T.C. 650 (1972), the estate of a now-famous sculptor successfully argued for the application of the blockage rule to 425 sculptures included in the gross estate. See also *Estate of Georgia T. O'Keeffe*, 63 TCM 2699, T.C.Memo. 1992–210.

[20]See, for example, *Estate of Mark S. Gallo*, 50 TCM 470, T.C.Memo. 1985–363. In this case, the taxpayer also argued that a bad product image (i.e., the Thunderbird, Ripple, and Boone's Farm brands) would depress the value of the stock. Since the trend was toward better wines, association with cheaper products had a negative consumer impact. Not emphasized were the enormous profits that the sale of the cheap wines generated!

[21]*Estate of Artemus D. Davis*, 110 T.C. 530 (1998). The major asset held by the holding company was a considerable block of substantially appreciated stock in the Winn-Dixie supermarket chain.

Resolving the Valuation Problem for Stock in Closely Held Corporations

Since the valuation of closely held stock is subject to so many variables, planning should be directed toward bringing about some measure of certainty.

EXAMPLE 12

Polly wants to transfer some of her stock in Brown Corporation to a trust formed for her children. She would also like to make a substantial contribution to her alma mater, State University. At present, the Brown stock is owned entirely by Polly and has never been traded on any market or otherwise sold or exchanged. Brown's past operations have proved profitable, and Brown has established a respectable record of dividend distributions. Based on the best available information and taking into account various adjustments (e.g., discount for lack of marketability), Polly feels each share of Brown stock possesses a fair market value of $120. ■

If Polly makes a gift of some of the stock to the trust set up for the children and uses the $120 per share valuation, what assurance is there that the IRS will accept this figure? If the IRS is successful in increasing the fair market value per share, Polly could end up with additional gift tax liability.

Polly could hedge against any further gift tax liability. Concurrently with the gift of stock to the trust formed for the children, Polly could make an outright transfer of some of the shares to State University, thereby generating an income tax deduction. Polly would base the income tax deduction on the value used for gift tax purposes. If the IRS later raises the value and assesses more gift tax, Polly can file an amended income tax return, claim a larger charitable contribution deduction, and obtain an offsetting income tax refund. To carry out this hedge, Polly would derive the amount of her gift of Brown stock by comparing her prevailing gift tax and income tax brackets for the year of the transfers. By virtue of the charitable deduction allowed for gift tax purposes by § 2522 (discussed in Chapter 18), no gift tax liability is incurred for the stock transferred to State University.

The Buy-Sell Agreement and Valuation

The main objective of a **buy-sell agreement** is to effect the orderly disposition of a business interest without the risk of the interest falling into the hands of outsiders. Moreover, a buy-sell agreement can ease the problems of estate liquidity and valuation.

Two types of buy-sell agreements exist: **entity** and **cross-purchase** arrangements. Under the entity type, the business itself (partnership or corporation) agrees to buy out the interest of the withdrawing owner (partner or shareholder). For a corporation, this normally takes the form of a stock redemption plan set up to qualify for income tax purposes under either § 302(b) or § 303. By making use of these provisions, corporate distributions can qualify for sale or exchange treatment rather than being treated as dividends (see Chapter 6). Under a cross-purchase agreement, the surviving owners (partners or shareholders) agree to buy out the withdrawing owner. The structures of the most typical buy-sell agreements are illustrated in Figure 19.1.

EXAMPLE 13

Iris, Ned, and Hal are equal and unrelated shareholders in Blue Corporation, and all three share in Blue's management. All agree to turn in their stock to the corporation for redemption at $100 per share if any one of them withdraws (by death or otherwise) from the business. Shortly thereafter, Hal dies, and the estate redeems the Blue stock at the agreed-upon price of $100 per share. ■

EXAMPLE 14

Assume the same facts as in Example 13, except that the agreement is the cross-purchase type under which each shareholder promises to buy a portion of the withdrawing shareholder's interest. When Hal dies, the estate sells the Blue stock to Iris and Ned for $100 per share. ■

FIGURE 19.1 Structures of Typical Buy-Sell Agreements

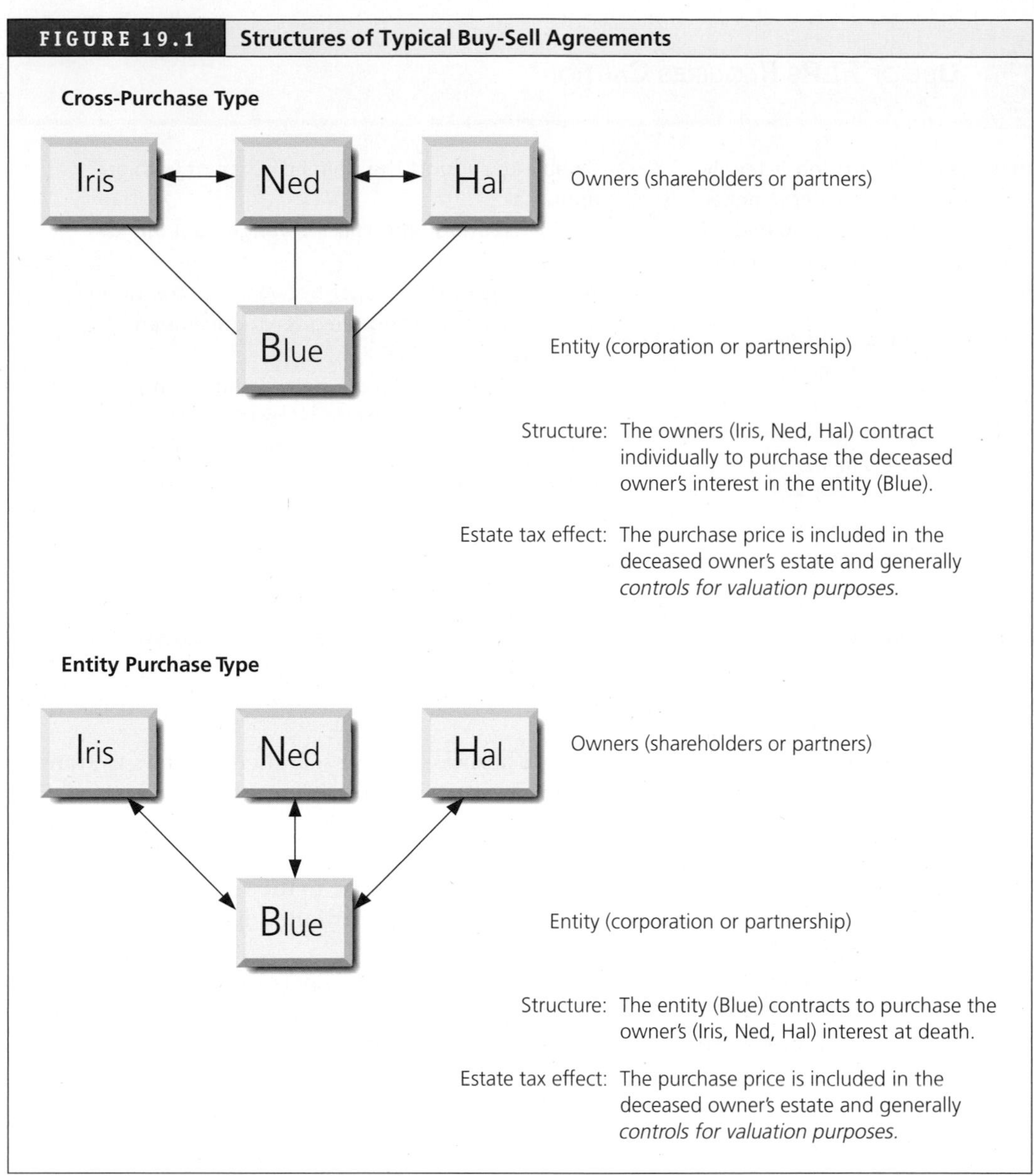
Cross-Purchase Type
Iris
Ned
Hal
Owners (shareholders or partners)
Blue
Entity (corporation or partnership)
Structure: The owners (Iris, Ned, Hal) contract individually to purchase the deceased owner's interest in the entity (Blue).
Estate tax effect: The purchase price is included in the deceased owner's estate and generally *controls for valuation purposes.*
Entity Purchase Type
Iris
Ned
Hal
Owners (shareholders or partners)
Blue
Entity (corporation or partnership)
Structure: The entity (Blue) contracts to purchase the owner's (Iris, Ned, Hal) interest at death.
Estate tax effect: The purchase price is included in the deceased owner's estate and generally *controls for valuation purposes.*

Will the $100 per share paid to Hal's estate determine the amount to be included in his gross estate? The answer is *yes,* subject to the following conditions.

- The price is the result of a bona fide business agreement.
- The agreement is not a device to transfer property to family members.
- The agreement is comparable to other arrangements entered into by persons dealing at arm's length.[22]

Life insurance often is used to provide some or all of the financing needed to carry out buy-sell agreements. Such financing can be particularly necessary in the early life of a business when cash-flow problems are critical. If insurance is used in the entity type of agreement, the corporation (or partnership) takes out a policy on the life of each owner. With the cross-purchase type, however, each owner must insure the life of every other owner, so more policies will be needed. In Example 14, full funding with insurance would require *nine* policies. By contrast, Example 13 requires only *three* policies.

[22] § 2703.

TAX *in* the NEWS

Use of FLPs Requires Caution

An estate planner must exercise care when using a family limited partnership (FLP). Considering the decidedly negative attitude of the IRS, the planner must be prepared to take a defensive posture in the event of challenge. The following guidelines may be helpful.

- Avoid the appearance that tax avoidance is the only motivation for using the FLP. For example, more efficient management of the property involved is a proper business justification.
- Depending on the nature of the assets involved, temper the amount of the discount claimed. For example, taking a discount of more than 30 percent for a partnership with marketable securities is inviting IRS scrutiny.
- Be able to support the claimed discount with an appraisal.
- Avoid creating the FLP arrangement in a "deathbed" setting.
- Allow some time to elapse between the creation of the partnership and the gifts of the limited interests.
- Try to avoid funding the partnership with personal use assets (e.g., personal residence).
- Recognize the existence of the arrangement. For example, do not continue to exercise unrestricted control over the transferred property and to enjoy the benefits of ownership.

Estate Freezes—Corporations

Over the years, owners of closely held businesses have searched for ways to transfer the major value of the business to their heirs while retaining some security interest. The typical approach with corporations has been for the owner to retain preferred stock and make gifts of common stock to the family. The approach freezes the amount that will be included in the owner's gross estate to the value of the preferred stock. Any post-gift appreciation in the business is attributed to the common stock and is *not* part of the owner's gross estate.

Under current law, some degree of the **estate freeze** is permitted.[23] Unfortunately, current law is designed to maximize the amount of the gift made by the donor upon the creation of the freeze. Generally, the retained interest is valued at zero, thereby resulting in the transfer of the *full* value of the business.

EXAMPLE 15

Quinn owns all of the stock in Robin Corporation valued as follows: $4 million common stock and $1 million preferred stock. The preferred stock is noncumulative, does not have a redemption date, and possesses no liquidation preference. Quinn gives the common stock to his adult children and retains the preferred stock. Quinn has made a gift to the children of $5 million. The $1 million worth of preferred stock Quinn retained is treated as having no value. ■

The estate freeze does, however, allow any post-transfer appreciation that develops to escape later estate taxation.

EXAMPLE 16

Assume the same facts as in Example 15. Quinn dies 10 years after the gift when the Robin Corporation common and preferred stock are worth $10 million and $1 million, respectively. Quinn's estate includes only $1 million for the preferred stock. The $6 million appreciation on the common stock ($10 million – $4 million) has escaped a transfer tax. ■

Estate Freezes—Partnerships

Due to the statutory limitations imposed on estate freezes using corporations, the adoption of a family limited partnership (FLP) to carry out an estate freeze has

[23]§ 2701.

CONCEPT SUMMARY 19.1

Valuation Concepts

1. Fair market value is "the price at which property would change hands between a willing buyer and a willing seller, neither being under any compulsion to buy or to sell and both having reasonable knowledge of relevant facts."
2. Special rules govern the valuation of life insurance policies and annuity contracts. In the case of unmatured life insurance policies, value depends on whether the policies are paid up or not. Use of the IRS valuation tables is necessary when the annuities are issued by parties not regularly engaged in selling annuities.
3. The IRS valuation tables must be used to value multiple interests in property. Such interests include income for a term of years, life estates, and remainders.
4. Section 2032A provides valuation relief for the estates of persons who hold real estate used in farming or in connection with a closely held business. If the requirements of the provision are met and if the executor elects, the property can be valued at its *current use* rather than its *most suitable use*.
5. Determining the value of the stock in a closely held corporation presents unique problems. The presence or absence of *goodwill* at the corporate level has a direct bearing on the stock being valued. A discount may be in order for any of the following: a minority interest, lack of marketability, and the application of the blockage rule. The IRS will contend that a premium attaches to an interest that represents control of the corporation.
6. A properly structured buy-sell agreement will control the value to be assigned a deceased owner's interest in a partnership or a corporation.
7. An estate tax freeze is useful in avoiding post-transfer appreciation that develops on the partnership or corporate interest involved. However, the donor must consider the gift tax consequences that result when the freeze is created.

become popular. A common scenario is for grandparents to form an FLP to hold a closely held business or other assets that can be expected to appreciate (e.g., real estate). The grandparents make themselves general partners and over a period of years make gifts of limited partnership interests to their children and grandchildren.

In valuing gifts of limited partnership interests, generous discounts (from 25 to 60 percent) are made for lack of marketability and a minority interest. As the grandparents are the general partners, they remain in control of the business (i.e., the FLP).

The overall expectation underlying the FLP approach is that a lesser value of the business can be transferred by gift than would be the case if everything is passed by death. The key to success, however, is the acceptability of the discounts used to value the gifts. Overly generous discount percentages could result in vulnerability to the penalty for undervaluation.[24]

In light of what happened to the estate freeze of corporate stock previously discussed, it is not unlikely that Congress may enact statutory limitations on the use of FLPs.[25]

Valuation concepts are reviewed in Concept Summary 19.1.

19.2 Income Tax Concepts

LO.4

Compare the income tax basis rules applying to property received by gift and by death.

Family tax planning also involves an assessment of the income tax positions of the transferor (the donor or decedent) and the transferee (the donee or heir).

BASIS OF PROPERTY ACQUIRED BY GIFT

The income tax basis of property acquired by gift depends on whether the donee sells the property for a gain or for a loss.

[24] § 6662(b)(5). See the discussion of accuracy-related penalties in Chapter 17.

[25] The current administration plans to seek legislation that will curtail the use of various discount procedures that reduce the value of businesses for transfer tax purposes. Department of the Treasury, *General Explanation of the Administration's Fiscal Year 2010 Revenue Proposals* (May 2009).

TAX *in* the NEWS

The Cost of Uncertainty

Uncertainty has become a permanent feature of the tax law. Every year Congress decides which tax provisions will be extended for another year—or sometimes two years. In some cases, provisions are added and others are dropped. Some sunset provisions are allowed to take effect (e.g., no estate tax in 2010), but others are revoked (e.g., a $1 million exemption and a 55 percent estate tax rate for 2011). Consequently, forecasting future tax consequences has become a matter of chance.

In this atmosphere of uncertainty, estate planning has evolved into an annual and expensive event. Estate planning involves professionals (i.e., attorneys, CPAs, appraisers) whose services can be costly. But many clients must either pay the price or risk losing the family business due to a change in the tax law that was enacted after their last visit to the estate planning team.

Source: Adapted from Emily Maltry, "For Family-Run Small Businesses, Estate-Tax Uncertainty Adds Cost," *Wall Street Journal*, December 16, 2010, p. B7.

- The donee's basis for gain is the donor's adjusted basis plus only the gift tax attributable to the appreciation of the property to the point of the gift (but not to exceed the fair market value on the date of the gift). For this purpose, use the *taxable gift* amount (i.e., gift less annual exclusion).[26]

EXAMPLE 17

In 2011, Norm receives stock as a gift from Lana. The stock cost Lana $20,000 and was worth $100,000 on the date of the gift. As a result of the transfer, Lana paid a gift tax of $10,000. In arriving at Norm's basis for gain, first compute the gift tax adjustment. Only the portion of the gift tax that is attributable to the appreciation is considered. This portion is determined as follows.

$$\frac{\$80{,}000 \text{ (appreciation)}}{\$87{,}000 \text{ (taxable gift)}} = 92\% \text{ (rounded)}$$

Consequently, Norm's income tax basis for gain is $29,200.

Lana's basis	$20,000
Allowable gift tax adjustment (92% × $10,000)	9,200
Basis for gain	$29,200

■

- The donee's basis for loss is the *lesser of* the basis for gain or the fair market value of the property on the date of the gift.

EXAMPLE 18

Connie receives stock as a gift from Trevor. The stock cost Trevor $100,000 and had a value of $20,000 on the date of the gift. No gift tax resulted from the transfer. Connie's basis for loss is $20,000—the lesser of $100,000 or $20,000. (Her basis for gain is $100,000—see Example 17.) ■

Because the donee usually assumes the donor's basis in the property, transfers by gifts are considered carryover situations. Consistent with this approach, the donee's holding period includes that of the donor.[27]

[26] §§ 1015(a) and (d). For gifts after 1920 and before 1977, the *full amount* of the gift tax is added (but not to exceed the fair market value on the date of the gift).

[27] § 1223(2).

BASIS OF PROPERTY ACQUIRED BY DEATH

General Rule

Except as otherwise noted in the following sections, the income tax basis of property acquired from a decedent is the fair market value on the date of death or, if elected, on the alternate valuation date. When property has appreciated in value between acquisition and date of death, the estate or heirs receive a **step-up in basis** for income tax purposes. In other words, the appreciation existing on the date of death escapes the Federal income tax. If, however, the property has declined in value, a **step-down in basis** occurs and built-in losses disappear.

EXAMPLE 19
THE BIG PICTURE

Return to the facts of *The Big Picture* on p. 19-2. Suppose that Martin is considering only the city lot and the marketable securities. A gift of either would make $500,000 subject to the Federal gift tax, and this would become Francine's income tax basis under § 1015. If instead these assets pass to Francine by Martin's death, under § 1014 she would receive a step-up in basis in the city lot (i.e., from $100,000 to $500,000) but a step-down in basis as to the marketable securities (from $900,000 to $500,000). Hence, Martin should sell the securities while he is alive, so as to benefit from the $400,000 built-in loss. ■

The holding period to the estate or heir of property acquired from a decedent is automatically treated as long term.[28]

If the property does not pass through a decedent's estate, there is no step-up (or step-down) in income tax basis.

EXAMPLE 20

In 1980, Aaron and Sandra (brother and sister) purchased land for $200,000, listing title as "joint tenants with the right of survivorship." Each furnished one-half of the purchase price. In 2011, when the land is worth $600,000, Aaron dies. Under § 2040 (see Chapter 18), Aaron's estate includes $300,000 as to the land. Sandra's income tax basis in the land is $400,000, determined as follows: $100,000 (Sandra's original cost basis) + $300,000 (amount passing through Aaron's estate). ■

Community Property

Although there is usually no change in basis for property that is not part of a decedent's gross estate (see Example 20 above), a special exception applies to community property. In such situations, the surviving spouse's half of the community takes the same basis as the half included in the deceased spouse's gross estate.[29] The following examples illustrate the reason for and the effect of this special rule.

EXAMPLE 21

Leif and Rosa were husband and wife and lived in a common law state. At the time of Leif's death, he owned assets (worth $1.6 million with a basis to him of $200,000), which he bequeathed to Rosa. Presuming the transfer qualifies under § 2056, Leif's estate is allowed a marital deduction of approximately $1.6 million. As the property passes through Leif's estate, Rosa receives a step-up in basis to $1.6 million. ■

EXAMPLE 22

Assume the same facts as in Example 21, except that Leif and Rosa had always lived in California (a community property state). If the $1.6 million of assets are community property, only one-half of this value is included in Leif's gross estate. Because the other half does not pass through Leif's estate (it already belongs to Rosa), is it fair to deny Rosa a new basis in it? Therefore, allowing the surviving spouse's share of the community to take on a basis equal to the half included in the deceased spouse's gross estate equalizes the income tax result generally achieved in common law states through the use of the marital deduction. By giving Rosa an income tax basis of $1.6 million

[28] § 1223(11).

[29] § 1014(b)(6).

($800,000 for Leif's half passing to her plus $800,000 for her half) and including only $800,000 in Leif's gross estate, the tax outcome is the same as in Example 21. ■

Effect of Valuation Elections

The election of the special use valuation method under § 2032A (discussed earlier in the chapter) and the alternate valuation date under § 2032 (see Chapter 18) will have a direct impact on income tax basis. Since the election of either of these provisions reduces the value of the property for estate tax purposes, a lower income tax basis results. Thus, any estate tax saving should be contrasted with the income tax consequences (i.e., higher gain or lower loss) when the property is sold.

When community property is involved, the election of special valuation provisions can carry a double income tax penalty. This double impact comes about because the surviving spouse's half of the community property takes on the same basis as the half included in the deceased spouse's gross estate (see Example 22 above).

EXAMPLE 23

Christopher and Samantha are husband and wife and have always lived in Arizona, a community property state. Samantha dies before Christopher. At the time of her death, their community includes assets (mainly stock) worth $6.4 million that decline in value to $6.2 million six months later. Under Samantha's will, her share of the stock passes to her children. ■

In Example 23, the election of § 2032 means that Samantha's estate includes only $3.1 million (50% of $6.2 million) as to the community property. But the estate tax saving on $100,000 [$3.2 million (date of death value) − $3.1 million (alternate valuation date)] must be compared with the $200,000 ($100,000 for the children + $100,000 for Christopher's share of the community property) loss in income tax basis.

AN EXECUTOR'S REVENGE

In 2011, Lindsey dies and is survived by Norman (Lindsey's second husband) and Brenda (Lindsey's daughter from her first marriage). Under Lindsey's will, her property, largely made up of marketable securities, is divided equally between Norman and Brenda, with all estate expenses and taxes assigned to Brenda's portion. The will designates Norman as the executor of the estate.

Lindsay's gross estate has a date of death value of $8 million and an alternate valuation date of $7.8 million. Although the use of the alternate valuation date would save $45,000 in estate taxes, the election is not made. Why did the executor not make the election? Was the failure to make the election improper?

Step-Up in Basis and the One-Year Rule

To understand the need for § 1014(e), consider the following situation.

EXAMPLE 24

Gary and Hazel are husband and wife and reside in a common law state. When the couple learns that Hazel has a terminal illness, Gary transfers property (basis of $100,000 and fair market value of $900,000) to her as a gift. Hazel dies shortly thereafter, and under the provisions of her will, the property returns to Gary. ■

If it were not for § 1014(e), what have the parties accomplished? No gift tax occurs on the transfer from Gary to Hazel because of the application of the marital deduction. Upon Hazel's death, her bequest to Gary does not generate any estate tax because the inclusion of the property in her gross estate is offset by the marital deduction. Through the application of the general rule of § 1014, Gary ends up with the same property, with its basis stepped up to $900,000. Thus, the procedure enables Gary to get a "free" increase in income tax basis of $800,000.

When applicable, § 1014(e) forces Gary (the original donor) to assume the property with the same basis it had to Hazel immediately before her death. Hazel's basis would have been determined under § 1015 (basis of property acquired by gift). The basis would have been $100,000 (donor's adjusted basis) plus any gift tax adjustment (none in this case) and any capital additions made by the donee (none in this case), or $100,000. If § 1014(e) applies to Example 24, Gary ends up where he started (with $100,000) in terms of income tax basis.

For § 1014(e) to be operative, the following conditions must be satisfied.

- The decedent must have received appreciated property as a gift during the one-year period ending with his or her death.
- The property is acquired from the decedent by the donor (or the donor's spouse).

Even if the hazards of § 1014(e) can be avoided, channeling property through the estate of a donee can carry other pitfalls. Unless a donee spouse is involved and the gift is neutralized by the marital deduction, a gift tax could be generated by the transfer. Also, shifting property to another's estate can add to or cause probate costs to be incurred. Lastly and despite assurances to the contrary, what is to prevent the donee from changing the testamentary arrangement (i.e., drawing up a new and different will) and designating someone else as the heir?

Special Rules for Deaths in 2010

Under legislation enacted in 2001, the estate tax was eliminated for year 2010. With the disappearance of the estate tax, Congress deemed a full step-up in income tax basis at death to be unnecessary. Therefore, the income tax basis of the decedent carries over in the noncash assets. The carryover basis rule, however, is modified by allowing a $1.3 million (plus an extra $3 million for a surviving spouse) addition to basis for asset appreciation. Except for the possibility noted below, TRA of 2010 repealed the carryover basis at death rules.

For a person dying in 2010, the estate has a choice of two options: (1) pay *no* estate tax and use the carryover basis rules of § 1022, or (2), pay an estate tax (using the rules in effect for 2011–2012) and use the regular step-up (step-down) in basis rules (see Example 19). The IRS is to provide the details and necessary forms for making the election.

In making the choice, an executor should consider the following.

- The resulting estate tax versus potential income tax consequences.
- The timing of income tax recognition—future sales of low-basis property are less troublesome than immediate sales.
- The nature of the income that will be recognized (i.e., capital gains or ordinary income).
- Potential discord that may be created among the heirs depending on how the executor allocates the allowable appreciation (i.e., $1.3 million) among qualifying estate assets.

Income in Respect of a Decedent

Income in respect of a decedent (IRD) is income earned by a decedent to the point of his or her death but not reportable on the final income tax return under the method of accounting used. IRD is most frequently applicable to decedents using the cash basis of accounting. IRD also occurs, for example, when a taxpayer at the time of death held installment notes receivable on which the gain has been deferred. For both cash and accrual taxpayers, IRD is increasingly including postdeath distributions from retirement plans [e.g., traditional IRA, § 401(k), H.R. 10 (Keogh), § 403(b)(1), qualified plan]. With the exception of Roth IRAs, distributions from retirement plans invariably contain an income component that has not yet been subject to income tax.

IRD is included in the gross estate at its fair market value on the appropriate valuation date. However, the income tax basis of the decedent transfers to the estate or heirs. Neither a step-up nor a step-down in basis is possible as is true of property received by death.[30] Furthermore, the recipient of IRD must classify it in the same manner (e.g., ordinary income, capital gain) as the decedent would have.[31]

[30]§ 1014(c).

[31]§ 691(a)(3). See Chapter 20 for a further discussion of IRD. Example 11 in Chapter 20 specifically deals with the IRD classification of distributions from retirement plans.

TAX *in* the NEWS

Keeping an IRA Alive after the Owner's Death

One sizable asset of interest to the tax planner is the traditional IRA. Plan accumulations are characterized as income in respect of a decedent (IRD) and are subject to income tax when distributed to the beneficiary. But does the beneficiary have any flexibility as to when the distributions occur?

Taking an immediate payout, the choice most frequently made, yields the worst result. Not only is the distribution fully taxable, but the bunching effect pushes the beneficiary into the top brackets. This horrendous tax result may occur because the parties involved are not aware that a more attractive tax alternative is available.

The deferral aspects of traditional IRAs need not terminate upon the owner's death. By following certain prescribed procedures, the distributions (and income recognition) can be "stretched" over the actuarial life expectancy of the beneficiary. The following rules apply to "inherited IRAs."

- Distributions to beneficiaries should be avoided. Any transfers between plans should be direct (i.e., from trustee to trustee) and not indirect (i.e., through beneficiaries).
- The IRA must be clearly designated as an inherited IRA. Records should indicate who the decedent was, who the beneficiary is, and that the IRA is to continue in effect.
- The beneficiary must begin taking annual distributions from the IRA based on the beneficiary's life expectancy. In the case of a surviving spouse, the distributions need not start until the survivor reaches age 70½.
- Except in the case of a surviving spouse, the inherited IRA cannot be rolled over, added to, or combined with others—it must be kept separate.
- An income tax deduction is available to the beneficiary for any estate tax attributable to the IRA distribution. [See the discussion of § 691(c) in Chapter 20.]

Although the income tax rules dealing with lifetime IRA distributions are fairly well known, those relating to inherited situations are not. Needless to say, the tax planner needs to be aware of the "inherited IRA" and its role in postdeath distributions.

How Conclusive Is the Value Used for Estate Tax Purposes?

Suppose a value is used for estate tax purposes and reflected on the estate tax return. At some future date, an heir to the property included in the gross estate believes the value used for estate tax purposes was incorrect. An heir might desire a change in value for countless reasons, including the following.

- The property is sold. Higher value leads to higher basis and less income tax gain.
- The property is depreciable. More basis means larger depreciation deductions.
- A home equity loan is obtained. With a higher value, a larger loan is allowed.
- If the heir is a charitable organization, higher value could improve its fundraising potential.

Is there any chance of success in arguing for a different value and thereby changing the income tax basis? The answer is yes, but with definite reservations.

If the statute of limitations has not lapsed for the estate tax return, the heir may try for a higher income tax basis by having the estate tax valuation raised. Any new valuation, however, requires both cooperation from the decedent's executor and acceptance by the IRS.

If the statute of limitations has lapsed for the estate tax return, the success of the heir's challenge depends on the following factors.

- The value reflected on the estate tax return and accepted by the IRS is presumed to be correct.[32] The heir must rebut the presumption.
- To rebut the presumption of correctness, it is important to determine by what means the property was originally valued. Did the valuation result

[32] Rev.Rul. 54–97, 1954–1 C.B. 113; *H. B. Levy*, 17 T.C. 728 (1951); and *Malcolm C. Davenport*, 6 T.C. 62 (1946).

CONCEPT SUMMARY 19.2

Income Tax Concepts

1. The income tax basis of property acquired by gift is the donor's basis with appropriate adjustment for any gift tax paid. With built-in loss situations, the income tax basis is the fair market value of the property on the date of the gift.
2. The income tax basis of property acquired through the death of the owner is its fair market value on the appropriate estate tax valuation date.
3. No step-up in basis is allowed if the property returns to the donor or donor's spouse within one year.
4. Items of income in respect of a decedent do not undergo a step-up or step-down in basis.
5. The value used for estate tax purposes is presumed to establish basis for income tax purposes. This presumption can be rebutted, but only with great difficulty.

from a unilateral determination by the IRS, or was it the result of a carefully considered compromise between the estate and the IRS? The presumption is more difficult for the heir to overcome in the latter instance.

- Did the heir have a hand in setting the original value? If so, allowing the value to be changed now would seem to give the heir an unfair advantage. The heir used or influenced the use of a lower value for estate tax purposes (thereby eliminating estate taxes) and now wants a higher value for income tax purposes (thereby reducing a recognized gain).[33]
- Even if no questions of fairness are raised because the heir was not involved in setting the original value, justification for a new value must be produced.

19.3 Gift Planning

LO.5

Explain how gifts can minimize gift taxes and avoid estate taxes.

One of the ways to carry out family tax planning is to start a program of lifetime giving. The objectives of such a program are to minimize transfer taxes while keeping income tax consequences in mind.

MINIMIZING GIFT TAXES

The Federal gift tax can be avoided through proper use of the annual exclusion. Because a new annual exclusion is available each year, spacing gifts over multiple years increases the amount that can be transferred free of gift tax.

EXAMPLE 25

Starting in 2002, Cora makes gifts in the amount of the annual exclusion to each of her five grandchildren. Taking into account the changes in the amount of the annual exclusion allowed, Cora will have transferred $595,000 through 2011 with no gift tax consequences.

Years		Amount of Exclusion
2002–2005	\$11,000 (annual exclusion) × 5 (number of donees) × 4 (number of years)	\$220,000
2006–2008	\$12,000 (annual exclusion) × 5 (number of donees) × 3 (number of years)	180,000
2009–2011	\$13,000 (annual exclusion) × 5 (number of donees) × 3 (number of years)	195,000

■

[33]In *William A. Beltzer*, 74–1 USTC ¶9373, 33 AFTR 2d 74–1173, 495 F.2d 211 (CA–8, 1974), *aff'g* 73–2 USTC ¶9512, 32 AFTR 2d 73–5250 (D.Ct.Neb., 1973), the concept of fairness was *invoked against the taxpayer* since, as the executor of the estate, he had been instrumental in setting the original value reported on the death tax return.

For married donors, the § 2513 election to split gifts can double the amount of a tax-free transfer. Referring to Example 25, if Cora is married and her husband makes the § 2513 election, $1,190,000 [$595,000 (amount allowed Cora) × 2 (number of donors)] can be transferred with no gift tax consequences.

From a practical standpoint, many donors who want to take advantage of the annual exclusion do not wish to give cash or near-cash assets (e.g., marketable securities). Where the value of the gift property substantially exceeds the amount of the annual exclusion, as is often the case with real estate, gifts of a partial interest are an attractive option.

EXAMPLE 26

Seth and Kate want to give a parcel of unimproved land to their three adult children and five grandchildren as equal owners. The land has an adjusted basis of $100,000, is held by Seth and Kate as community property, and has an appraised value of $416,000 as of December 17, 2010. On December 22, 2010, Seth and Kate convey a one-half undivided interest in the land to their children and grandchildren as tenants in common. This is followed by a transfer of the remaining one-half interest on January 5, 2011. Neither transfer causes gift tax because each is fully offset by annual exclusions of $208,000 [$26,000 (annual exclusion for two donors) × 8 (number of donees)]. Thus, in a period of two weeks, Seth and Kate transfer $416,000 in value free of any Federal tax consequences. ■

Further examination of Example 26 leads to the following observations.

- No income tax consequences ensue from the gift. However, had Seth and Kate first sold the land and made a gift of the cash proceeds, recognized gain of $316,000 [$416,000 (selling price) – $100,000 (adjusted basis)] would have resulted.
- The § 2513 election to split gifts is not necessary because the land was community property. If the land had been held by one of the spouses as separate property, the election would have been necessary to generate the same $416,000 of exclusions. The annual exclusion for 2011 is $13,000.
- Good tax planning generally dictates that sizable gifts of property be supported by reliable appraisals. In the case of successive gifts of partial interests in the same property, multiple appraisals should be obtained to cover each gift. This advice was not followed in Example 26 due to the short interval between gifts. Barring exceptional circumstances, the value of real estate will not change over a period of two weeks.

MINIMIZING ESTATE TAXES

Aside from the annual exclusion, do lifetime gifts offer any tax advantages over transfers at death? Someone familiar with the tax law applicable to asset transfers would answer "no" to this question. Under the unified transfer tax scheme, the tax rates are the same. However, as the following discussion shows, lifetime transfers may be preferable to those at death.

Avoiding a Transfer Tax on Future Appreciation

If property is expected to appreciate in value, a gift removes the appreciation from the donor's gross estate.

EXAMPLE 27
THE BIG PICTURE

Return to the facts of *The Big Picture* on p. 19-2. One of the assets Martin is considering giving to Francine is an insurance policy on his life. Although the policy has a current value of only $500,000, it has a maturity value of $3 million. Therefore, by making a gift of $500,000, Martin would save a future inclusion in his gross estate of $3 million. ■

Besides life insurance, other assets that often appreciate in value include real estate, art objects, and special collections (e.g., rare books, coins, and stamps).

In making these gifts, consider the financial status of the donee. Will the gift create an economic hardship for him or her? The recipient of the family vacation home will have upkeep expenses and property taxes to pay. The donee of an art collection can anticipate maintenance costs such as storage fees and provision for security of the property (e.g., insurance against fire and theft).

Unfortunately, the properties most likely to appreciate, and thus the subject of gifts to save on estate taxes, often are "dry assets" (i.e., those that do not generate income). It may be necessary, therefore, for a donor to plan to make follow-up gifts of cash to mitigate any financial strain placed on the donee by the original gift. Returning to the facts of Example 27, if Martin decides to give Francine the insurance policy, he may need to make annual gifts to her to enable her to pay the premiums required to keep the policy from lapsing.

Providing for the Education of Family Members

Several different approaches can be taken to meet the educational needs of loved ones and still avoid any transfer taxes. One possibility is to pay tuition directly to an educational institution. As noted in Chapter 18, such payments are treated as excluded transfers under § 2503(e) and are not subject to the gift tax. In a private letter ruling, the IRS has indicated that the same treatment is available when the payment involves multiple years. Thus, grandparents can make tuition payments to a private school on behalf of their grandchildren for not only the current year but future years as well. Besides avoiding any gift tax, such payments are not subject to the estate tax on the later death of the donor.

Another approach to meeting family educational needs involves contributions to qualified tuition programs (i.e., "§ 529 plans"). Although usually touted for their income tax advantages, these plans can be structured so as to avoid transfer taxes. Like direct tuition payments, the contributions are not included in the gross estate on the later death of the contributor. Unlike direct tuition payments, however, the gift tax can apply and must be circumvented. This is done by judicious use of the annual exclusion. Extending contributions over several years and making the § 2513 election to split gifts are just two ways to maximize the availability of the annual exclusion. Moreover, for impatient donors, it is even possible to accelerate five years of annual exclusions into the current year (see Example 24 in Chapter 18).

Preparing for the Special Use Valuation Method

The § 2032A election is not available for valuing transfers by gift. Yet, if its use is planned in estate tax situations, gifts of nonqualifying property may aid in meeting the requirements of § 2032A. Recall that one of the requirements of § 2032A is that qualified use property must constitute at least 50 percent of the adjusted value of the gross estate.

EXAMPLE 28

In 2007, Floyd's estate includes the following.

	Fair Market Value
Farm operated by Floyd with current use value of $500,000	$3,500,000
Stock in a local bank	2,400,000
Marketable securities and cash	1,700,000

At this point, Floyd's estate does not qualify for the § 2032A election. The qualifying property [$3,500,000 (farm)] does not equal or exceed 50% of the adjusted gross estate [$3,500,000 (farm) + $2,400,000 (bank stock) + $1,700,000 (marketable securities and cash)]. ■

EXAMPLE 29

Continuing with the facts of Example 28, Floyd makes a gift of one-half of the bank stock in 2007. He dies in 2011 with no change in asset values. Floyd's estate now qualifies for § 2032A treatment since $3.5 million (farm) is 50% or more of $6.4 million [$3,500,000 (farm) + $1,200,000 (bank stock) + $1,700,000 (marketable securities and cash)]. The election enables the estate to value the farm at current use. As a result, the estate tax on $1,020,000 in value is saved. ■

Care must be taken to avoid gifts of property within three years of death. Though such gifts usually are not included in the gross estate of the donor for estate tax purposes, they are counted when testing for the percentage requirements of § 303 (stock redemptions to pay estate taxes and administration expenses—refer to Chapter 6), § 2032A, and § 6166 (extension of time to pay estate taxes in installments—discussed later in this chapter).[34]

EXAMPLE 30

Assume the same facts as in Example 29, except that the gift occurs in 2009 (not 2007). Although only $1,200,000 of the bank stock is included in Floyd's gross estate for estate tax purposes, $2.4 million is used for the percentage requirements of the special use valuation provisions. As a result, the estate fails to qualify for the election. ■

Besides the unavailability of § 2032A for gift tax purposes, other reasons may exist for retaining special use property until death.

EXAMPLE 31
THE BIG PICTURE

Return to the facts of *The Big Picture* on p. 19-2. Making a gift of the farmland is probably unwise for two reasons. First, without further information on the other assets Martin owns (or is likely to acquire), it is impossible to ascertain how close he might be to meeting the percentage requirements of § 2032A. Second, even if the special use valuation election is not available, consider the substantial step-up in basis that occurs (i.e., $100,000 to $500,000) if the farmland is passed at death. ■

LO.6

Evaluate how to make gifts so as to avoid income taxes for the donor.

INCOME TAX CONSIDERATIONS

Income Shifting

One way to lower the overall tax burden on the family unit is to shift capital gain income from high-bracket taxpayers to lower-bracket family members. The maximum rates on dividends and net capital gain provide an excellent opportunity to take advantage of the 0 percent rate that normally would apply to certain younger donees. The maximum rate is 15%/0%, with the 0 percent rate being applicable to taxpayers below the 25 percent bracket (i.e., those in the 10 percent and 15 percent brackets).

The shifting is accomplished by giving capital assets (frequently securities) to others who make the sale and recognize the gain. If the donees are children, however, care must be taken to avoid the hazard of the kiddie tax. Under the kiddie tax, which currently applies to a child under age 19 (or to a full-time student under age 24 whose earned income is not more than 50 percent of his or her support), any gain is taxed at the parents' higher rate.[35]

[34] §§ 2035(c)(1) and (2).

[35] § 1(g)(2)(A). Children who are married and file a joint return are exempted.

EXAMPLE 32

The Millers have four daughters who are in graduate school. As each child reaches age 24, they give her enough appreciated stock to yield a gain of $30,000. The daughter sells the stock and uses the proceeds to pay for education loans. The daughter pays no tax on the recognized gain of $30,000 (0% × $30,000). Had the Millers sold the stock on their own instead of giving it, the tax would have been $4,500 (15% × $30,000). Thus, the Millers have saved $4,500 in capital gains taxes by making the transfer. If the same procedure is followed with the other three daughters, the total savings become $18,000 ($4,500 × 4). ■

In Example 32, note that the amount of the built-in gain transferred was controlled so as to keep the donee below the 25 percent income tax bracket (approximately $34,500 taxable income). Furthermore, no gift tax resulted from the transfer as the Millers are merely satisfying their obligation of support (providing an education for their child).

The procedure followed in Example 32 can be repeated with the same daughter in a later year with the same tax effect. It can also be used to shift capital gains to other family members. Furthermore, when the donees are not children, the kiddie tax problem will not be a hurdle.

If a gift of property is to shift income to the donee, the transfer must be *complete.*

EXAMPLE 33

Gloria, subject to a 35% marginal income tax rate, owns all of the stock in Orange, an S corporation. Gloria transfers by gift 60% of the Orange stock to her three married children. The children range in age from 24 to 28 years and are all in the 10% income tax bracket. After the transfer, Gloria continues to operate the business. No shareholder meetings are held. Except for reporting 60% of the pass-through of Orange's profits, Gloria's children have no contact with the business. Aside from the salary paid to Gloria, Orange makes no cash distributions to its shareholders. ■

The situation posed in Example 33 occurs frequently and is fraught with danger. If the purported gift by Gloria lacks economic reality and Gloria is the true economic owner of all of Orange's stock, the pass-through to the children is disregarded.[36] The profits are taxed to Gloria at her 35 percent rate rather than to the children at their 10 percent rates. Consequently, the transfer has not accomplished the intended shifting of income.

What can be done to make the transfer in Example 33 tax-effective? First, a distribution of dividends would provide some economic benefit to the children. As the transfer is currently constituted, all that the children have received as a result of the gift is an economic detriment, because they must pay income taxes on their share of Orange's pass-through of profits. Second, some steps should be taken to recognize and protect the interests of the children as donees. Shareholder meetings should be held and attendance encouraged. That the children do not actively participate in the business of Orange is of no consequence, as long as they are given the opportunity to do so.

Income Tax Consequences to the Donor

Generally, a gift of property results in no income tax consequences to the donor. Two important exceptions, however, involve installment notes receivable and U.S. savings bonds.

A gift of an installment note receivable is a taxable disposition, and the donor is treated as if the note had been sold for its fair market value.[37] As a result, the donor recognizes the deferred profit.

[36] *Donald O. Kirkpatrick,* 36 TCM 1122, T.C.Memo. 1977–281; *Michael F. Beirne,* 52 T.C. 210 (1969) and 61 T.C. 268 (1973).

[37] § 453B(a).

EXAMPLE 34
THE BIG PICTURE

Return to the facts of *The Big Picture* on p. 19-2. Recall that another asset that Martin is considering giving Francine is installment notes receivable. Although the notes have a face amount of $700,000, due to the extended payout period and possibly other factors (e.g., a low interest rate), their current value is only $500,000. Unfortunately, Martin's basis in the notes is $200,000. Thus, since the gift is treated as a sale, Martin would have a taxable gain of $300,000 ($500,000 − $200,000). ■

A gift of U.S. savings bonds is not effective unless the bonds are re-registered in the donee's name.[38] This forces the donor to recognize any deferred income accrued on the bonds. The result may surprise donors who expect to postpone the recognition of interest income until the bonds are redeemed. Thus, the donor who desires to avoid income tax consequences should avoid gifts of installment notes receivable and U.S. savings bonds.

For purposes of contrasting tax results, what happens if these properties are passed by death?

- Installment notes receivable are taxed to whoever collects the notes (the estate or heirs).[39] If the notes are forgiven or canceled by the decedent's will, the income is taxed to the estate.
- Deferred interest income on U.S. savings bonds is taxed to whoever redeems the bonds (the estate or heirs).
- Recapture potential disappears at death.[40] The estate or heirs take the property free of any recapture potential existing at the time of the owner's death.

Carryover Basis Situations

When considering the income tax effect of a transfer on the donee or heir, the basis rules of §§ 1014 and 1015 warrant close examination. When appreciated property is involved, receiving the property from a decedent is preferred to a lifetime transfer.

The situation may be different, however, when the property to be transferred has depreciated in value. Presuming the transferor cannot take advantage of the built-in loss (e.g., no existing or potential offsetting gains), should the transfer be made by gift or at death?

EXAMPLE 35
THE BIG PICTURE

Return to the facts of *The Big Picture* on p. 19-2. Assume that Martin is terminally ill and cannot take advantage of any more capital losses (e.g., he has excess capital loss carryovers from prior years). Is it preferable for Martin to give the marketable securities to Francine or for them to pass to her at his death?

If the property passes by a gift, she takes the securities with a basis for gain of $900,000 and a basis for loss of $500,000. If the property passes on account of a death, however, Francine's basis for *both* gain and loss steps down to $500,000. Thus, the gift result might protect Francine from later gain on the disposition of the securities. ■

19.4 ESTATE PLANNING

Estate planning considers the nontax and tax aspects of death. In the nontax area are the various steps that can be taken to reduce the costs of probating an estate. In

[38] Reg. § 25.2511–1(h)(4).

[39] The deferred gain element of an installment note is income in respect of a decedent (see the discussion earlier in this chapter and in Chapter 20) and does not receive a step-up in basis at death. § 453B(c).

[40] Contrast this result with what happens when § 1245 or § 1250 property is transferred by gift. Here, the recapture potential carries over to the donee. §§ 1245(b)(1) and 1250(d)(1).

the tax area, the focus is on controlling the amount of the gross estate and maximizing estate tax deductions.

PROBATE COSTS

LO.7

Assess how to reduce probate costs in the administration of an estate.

The probate estate consists of all properties subject to administration by an executor. The administration is conducted under the supervision of a local court, usually called a probate court. In certain states, probate functions are performed by county courts, surrogate courts, or orphan's courts.

Probate costs include attorney fees, accountant fees, appraisal and inventory fees, court costs, expenses incident to the disposition of assets and satisfaction of liabilities, litigation costs needed to resolve will contests, and charges for the preparation of tax returns. The total amount of probate costs cannot be accurately predicted because so many variables are involved. A conservative range might be from 5 to 15 percent of the amount of the probate estate.

Many procedures can be used to reduce the probate estate and thereby save probate costs, including the following.

- Owning property as joint tenants (or tenants by the entirety) with right of survivorship. Upon death, the property passes to the surviving tenant and generally is not subject to probate.
- Making life insurance payable to a beneficiary other than the estate.
- Utilizing a revocable trust. Upon the death of the creator, the trust becomes irrevocable and is not subject to probate. A revocable trust is often popularly referred to as a **living trust**.
- Listing bank accounts and title to securities by use of the payable on death arrangement. As noted in Chapter 18, the designation "payable on proof of death" passes title to the property if the listed beneficiary survives the owner. A payable on death arrangement has the same effect as a revocable trust but avoids the need to create a formal trust.

In some situations, the probate estate is increased because the parties have been careless.

EXAMPLE 36

When John dies, all of the primary and secondary beneficiaries named on his life insurance policies and pension plans have predeceased him. Therefore, under the terms of the policies and pension plans, the distributions are paid to his estate. John's failure to name new beneficiaries results in an unintended increase in the probate estate. ■

Another advantage of bypassing the probate estate is that the beneficiary can obtain immediate possession and enjoyment of the property. The probate process can become prolonged, and the heir may have to await the final settlement of the estate before getting the property.

In terms of probate costs, the ownership of out-of-state real estate can cause horrendous problems. Out-of-state ownership is not uncommon with decedents who have relocated after retirement or who maintain vacation homes.

EXAMPLE 37

After retirement and five years before his death, Ted moved from Nebraska to Arizona. At death, Ted still owns a rental house in Nebraska and a vacation home in Idaho. To clear title to these properties, Ted's executor must institute ancillary probate proceedings in Nebraska and Idaho. This will result in additional attorney fees and court costs. ■

The solution to the dilemma posed in Example 37 is to dispose of these properties before death. Although this may generate some legal fees, they will be far less than the cost of ancillary probate proceedings.

Avoiding State and Local Taxation at Death

Before he retired, Victor was the CEO of a major corporation and a resident of New York. After his retirement, he moves to Florida but continues to be on the board of directors of numerous multinational companies. For convenience, he still owns a condominium in New York City, valued at approximately $2 million.

When Victor learns that New York imposes an estate tax (with a maximum rate of 16 percent), he sells the condominium to one of his sons for its fair market value of $2 million. Six months later, Victor dies from a stroke. Did Victor act wisely prior to his death? (Note: Florida has no income, gift, estate, or inheritance tax.)

LO.8

Apply procedures that reduce estate tax consequences.

CONTROLLING THE AMOUNT OF THE GROSS ESTATE

Unlike the probate estate, the gross estate determines what property is subject to the Federal estate tax. In fact, many of the steps taken to reduce the probate estate will not have a similar effect on the gross estate—see the discussion of §§ 2036 and 2038 in Chapter 18.

Valuation procedures sometimes can be applied to control the amount of the gross estate. The special use valuation method of § 2032A can be elected when the estate consists of real estate used in farming or in connection with a closely held business. When the estate comprises assets that have declined in value shortly after death, the use of the alternate valuation date of § 2032 (see Chapter 18) is advised.

PROPER HANDLING OF ESTATE TAX DEDUCTIONS

Estate taxes can be reduced either by decreasing the size of the gross estate or by increasing the total allowable deductions. The lower the taxable estate, the less estate tax is generated. Planning with deductions involves the following considerations.

- Making proper use of the marital deduction.
- Working effectively with the charitable deduction.
- Taking advantage of the bypass amount.
- Optimizing other deductions and losses allowed under §§ 2053 and 2054.

Approaches to the Marital Deduction

When planning for the estate tax marital deduction, both tax and nontax factors are taken into account. Two major tax goals guide the planning. They are the *equalization* and *deferral* approaches.

- Attempt to equalize the estates of both spouses. Clearly, for example, the estate tax on $6 million is more than the estate tax on $5 million ($350,000 versus $0).
- Based on the time value of taxes deferred, try to postpone estate taxation as long as possible.

Barring certain circumstances, the deferral approach generally is preferable. By maximizing the marital deduction on the death of the first spouse to die, taxes are saved, and the surviving spouse can trim his or her future estate by entering into a program of lifetime giving. By making optimum use of the annual exclusion, considerable amounts can be shifted without incurring *any* transfer tax.

Tax planning must remain flexible and be tailored to the individual circumstances of the parties involved. The equalization approach may be most attractive in the following situations.

- Both spouses are of advanced age and/or in poor health, and neither is expected to survive the other for a prolonged period of time.

TAX *in the NEWS*

How to Save Taxes and Protect the Environment

What do Ted Turner, Robert Redford, Clint Eastwood, and James Baker (former secretary of state) have in common? Besides being celebrities and financially well-to-do, all have issued **conservation easements** in some or all of the real estate they own. By this means, any "scenic view" that currently exists is preserved. The owner is precluded from obstructing the view by further development of the property. Allegedly, the transfer of the easement is motivated by the owner's desire to "conserve the environment." Realistically, the transfer is largely tax motivated.

The steps involved in creating a conservation easement and the tax consequences that ensue are as follows.

- After the easement is drafted, the owner transfers it to a conservation trust. Usually, the trust is already in existence, having been created by an environmental group, and operates under the auspices of a local government agency.
- The owner obtains a generous appraisal as to the value of the easement transferred.
- The owner claims the value of the easement as an income tax deduction.
- The value of the property retained (e.g., residence, vacation home) is accordingly reduced by the value of the easement for ad valorem property tax purposes.
- Upon the owner's death, the gross estate includes the property at a discounted value due to the restrictions contained in the easement.

In summary, the conservation easement saves income, property, and estate taxes. The donor receives all of this plus the aura of being hailed as an environmentalist.[41]

- The spouse who is expected to survive has considerable assets of his or her own. Keep in mind that the transfer tax rate schedules are progressive in nature.
- Because of appreciation, property worth $5 million today when it passes to the surviving spouse may be worth $8 million five years later when the survivor dies.

Effectively Working with the Charitable Deduction

As a general guide to obtaining overall tax savings, lifetime charitable transfers are preferred over testamentary dispositions. For example, an individual who gives $20,000 to a qualified charity during his or her life secures an income tax deduction, avoids any gift tax, and reduces the gross estate by the amount of the gift. By way of contrast, if the $20,000 is willed to charity, no income tax deduction is available, and the amount of the gift is includible in the decedent's gross estate (though later deducted for estate tax purposes). In short, the lifetime transfer provides a double tax benefit (income tax deduction plus reduced estate taxes) at no gift tax cost (§ 2522). The testamentary transfer merely neutralizes the effect of the inclusion of the property in the gross estate (inclusion under § 2033 and then deduction under § 2055).

A lifetime transfer to charity, however, can have income tax implications when a bargain sale arrangement is involved. In a bargain sale, the taxpayer wants to make a charitable contribution as to the appreciation, while maintaining his or her investment in the property. The tax law treats these transactions as being part sale and part contribution.[42] Consequently, only a portion of the basis of the property can be utilized in determining the gain on the sale portion. This is calculated by applying the percentage resulting from dividing the sale price by the fair market value of the property.[43]

[41]If the contribution of the conservation easement occurs postmortem (i.e., after the death of the owner), the estate can claim a § 2055(f) charitable contribution. It then can elect, under § 2031(c), to *exclude* up to 40% of the value of the land subject to the easement. In computing the amount of the exclusion, the value of the land must be reduced by the charitable contribution allowed.

[42]§ 1011(b).

[43]Reg. § 1.170(A)–4(c)(2)(i).

Presuming that the transfer involves long-term capital gain property, the charitable deduction is the difference between its fair market value and the selling price.

EXAMPLE 38

Arthur transfers a tract of land to his church on which it will build a sanctuary. He acquired the land 20 years ago as an investment for $100,000, and it is currently worth $1 million. Because Arthur desires to recover his original investment, he sells the land to the church for $100,000. Arthur has a long-term capital gain of $90,000 [$100,000 (selling price) − $10,000 (allocated basis)] and a charitable contribution deduction of $900,000 [$1,000,000 (fair market value) − $100,000 (consideration received)]. ■

To ensure that an estate tax deduction is allowed for a charitable contribution, the designated recipient must fall within the classifications set forth in § 2055 (or § 2522). For estate tax purposes, this is the status of the organization on the date the transfer becomes effective and not the status on the date the will authorizing the transfer was executed.

EXAMPLE 39

In 2000, Lisa drew up and executed a will in which she provided for $500,000 to pass to the Rose Academy, a nonprofit educational organization described in § 2055(a)(2) and, at that time, approved by the IRS as a qualified recipient. In 2004, the qualified status of the academy was revoked for practicing racial discrimination in the enrollment of its student body.[44] Lisa dies in 2011, and the executor of her estate, being compelled to satisfy the provisions of the will, transfers $500,000 to the academy. ■

Even though Lisa may have been unaware of the action taken by the IRS in 2004, her estate is not allowed a charitable deduction. The recipient was no longer qualified on the date of Lisa's death. It may be that Lisa, even if she had known about the probable loss of the charitable deduction, would still have wished the bequest carried out as originally conceived. If not, it is easy to see that the error was of Lisa's own making because of her failure to review her estate planning situation.

One way to circumvent the quandary posed by Example 39 (other than changing Lisa's will before her death) is to express the charitable bequest in more flexible terms. The transfer to the academy could have been conditioned on the organization's continued status as a qualified recipient at the time of Lisa's death. Alternatively, Lisa's will may grant her executor the authority to substitute a different, but comparable, charitable organization *that is qualified* in the event of the disqualification of the named group.

On occasion, a charitable bequest depends on the issuance of a disclaimer by a noncharitable heir.[45] Such a situation frequently arises with special types of property or collections, which the decedent may feel a noncharitable heir should have a choice of receiving.

EXAMPLE 40

Megan specified in her will that her valuable art collection is to pass to her son or, if the son refuses, to a designated and qualified art museum. At the time the will was drawn, Megan knew that her son was not interested in owning the collection. If, after Megan's death, the son issues a timely disclaimer, the collection passes to the museum, and Megan's estate takes a charitable deduction for its estate tax value. ■

EXAMPLE 41

Dick's will specifies that one-half of his disposable estate is to pass to his wife and the remainder of his property to a specified qualified charitable organization. If the wife

[44]Most of the organizations that are qualified recipients (which will permit the donor a charitable deduction) are listed in IRS Publication 78. This compilation, revised and supplemented from time to time, addresses § 170 (income tax deduction) transfers. Publication 78, with the exceptions noted in Chapter 18, also applies to § 2055 (estate tax deduction) and § 2522 (gift tax deduction) transfers.

[45]As noted in Chapter 18, a disclaimer is a refusal to accept the property. If the disclaimer is timely made, the property is not treated as having passed through the person issuing the disclaimer, and a gift tax is avoided.

issues a timely disclaimer after Dick's death, all of the property passes to the charity and qualifies for the § 2055 charitable deduction. ■

Has the son in Example 40 acted wisely if he issues the disclaimer in favor of the museum? Although such a disclaimer will provide Megan's estate with a deduction for the value of the art collection, consider the income tax deduction alternative. If the son accepts the bequest, he can still dispose of the collection (and fulfill his mother's philanthropic objectives) through a lifetime donation to the museum. At the same time, he obtains an income tax deduction under § 170. Whether this saves taxes for the family depends on a comparison of the mother's estate tax bracket with the estimated income tax bracket of the son. If the value of the collection runs afoul of the percentage limitations of § 170(b)(1), the donations could be spread over more than one year. If this is done, and to protect against the contingency of the son's dying before the entire collection is donated, the son can neutralize any potential estate tax consequences by providing in his will for the undonated balance to pass to the museum.

The use of a disclaimer in Example 41 would be sheer folly. It would not reduce Dick's estate tax; it would merely substitute a charitable deduction for the marital deduction. Whether the wife issues a disclaimer or not, no estate taxes will be due. The wife should accept her bequest and, if she is so inclined, make lifetime gifts of it to a qualified charity. In so doing, she generates an income tax deduction for herself.

A recent provision permits, under very limited circumstances, a tax-free distribution from an IRA to a qualified charity. The provision does not generate a charitable deduction but allows the donor to avoid the recognition of income that normally results when a distribution occurs. An estate tax saving also takes place because the donor will no longer own the amount donated upon his or her later death.[46] For the provision to apply, the donor must be age 70½ or older. The exclusion is limited to $100,000 per year and is available for distributions made in 2006 through 2012.

Taking Advantage of the Bypass Amount

The bypass amount, also known as the exclusion amount or the exemption equivalent, is the amount that can pass free of a transfer tax due to the unified credit. For a credit of $1,730,800, which is available for estate tax purposes for 2011, the bypass amount is $5 million.

Spousal Transfers In the past, a bypass amount often was wasted upon the death of the first spouse. Human nature often compels a spouse to leave all of his or her assets to the survivor.

EXAMPLE 42

Ethan and Hope are married, and each has a net worth of $5 million. On Ethan's prior death, his will passes his $5 million to Hope. Although Ethan has avoided any estate tax due to the marital deduction, he has wasted his bypass amount and concentrated $10 million in Hope's potential estate. ■

Under TRA of 2010, the result reached in Example 42 was changed by making the bypass amount (designated the exclusion amount) "portable," meaning that a deceased spouse's unused exclusion amount (DSUEA) can be transferred to the surviving spouse.[47]

EXAMPLE 43

Assume the same facts as in Example 42. If Ethan died after 2010 and a proper election is made on his return, his DSUEA becomes available. As a result, Hope now has an

[46] § 408(d)(8).

[47] § 2010(c) as amended by TRA of 2010.

exclusion amount of $10 million [$5 million (DSUEA) + $5 million (her own basic exclusion amount)]. ■

If a surviving spouse is predeceased by more than one spouse, the DSUEA that is available for such a surviving spouse is limited to the *lesser of* $5 million or the unused exclusion of the last surviving spouse.

EXAMPLE 44

Continue with the facts of Example 43. After Ethan's death, Hope marries Michael who also predeceases her. Because he has used $2 million in making past taxable gifts, Michael has an unused exclusion of only $3 million at the time of his death. Hope now has an exclusion amount of $8 million [$3 million (DSUEA from Michael) + $5 million (Hope's basic exclusion amount)]. ■

Use of Disclaimers to Maximize the Benefits of the Bypass Amount In some cases, it may be possible to control the bypass amount by the judicious use of disclaimers.

EXAMPLE 45

Dylan dies in 2011 leaving an estate of $8 million. He is survived by his wife, Emma, and two adult children. His will passes $4 million to Emma and the remainder to the children. Emma disclaims $1 million of her inheritance. ■

EXAMPLE 46

Assume the same facts as in Example 45, except that Dylan's will passes $6 million to the children and the remainder to Emma. The children disclaim $1 million of their inheritance. ■

Both examples reflect the wise use of disclaimers. In Example 45, Emma's disclaimer has the effect of increasing the children's inheritance to $5 million, thereby optimizing the allowable bypass amount. In Example 46, the children avoid any estate tax on $1 million (the excess over the $5 million bypass amount) by shifting it to the remainderperson. Since the remainderperson is the surviving spouse, the $1 million is sheltered from estate tax by the marital deduction.

Proper Handling of Other Deductions and Losses under §§ 2053 and 2054

Many § 2053 and § 2054 deductions and losses may be claimed either as estate tax deductions or as income tax deductions by the estate on the fiduciary return (Form 1041), but not both.[48] The income tax deduction is not allowed unless the estate tax deduction is waived. It is possible for these deductions to be apportioned between the two returns.

In situations where the taxpayer is terminal (i.e., death is imminent), it may be possible to shift the upcoming § 2053 expenses to obtain a lifetime income tax benefit. Thus, such items as accrued medical expenses, property taxes, and interest on home equity loans can be paid prior to death if they will be deductible on the decedent's final income tax return. Although this forgoes the § 2053 deduction that would have been available if the expenses had been paid by the estate, the estate tax saving still exists. As the funds that were used to pay these expenses are not part of the gross estate, the taxable estate is correspondingly reduced. The net result is the same estate tax saving, but with the added advantage of an income tax deduction.

LO.9

Demonstrate procedures to obtain liquidity for an estate.

PROVIDING ESTATE LIQUIDITY

Recognizing the Problem

Even with effective predeath family tax planning directed toward a minimization of transfer taxes, the smooth administration of an estate necessitates a certain degree of liquidity. After all, probate costs will be incurred, and most important of all, estate

[48] § 642(g) and Reg. § 20.2053–1(d).

taxes must be satisfied. In the meantime, the surviving spouse and dependent beneficiaries may need financial support. Without funds to satisfy these claims, estate assets may have to be sold at sacrifice prices, and most likely, the decedent's scheme of testamentary disposition will be defeated.

EXAMPLE 47

At the time of Myrtle's death, her estate was made up almost entirely of a large ranch currently being operated by Jim, one of Myrtle's two sons. Because the ranch had been in the family for several generations and was a successful economic unit, Myrtle hoped that Jim would continue its operation and share the profits with Bob, her other son. Unfortunately, Bob, on learning that his mother had died without a will, demanded and obtained a partition and sale of his share of the property. Additional land was sold to pay for administration expenses and estate taxes. After all of the sales had taken place, the portion remaining for Jim could not be operated profitably, and he was forced to give up the family ranch activity. ■

What type of predeath planning might have avoided the result reached in Example 47? Certainly, Myrtle should have recognized and provided for the cash needs of the estate. Life insurance payable to her estate, although it adds to the estate tax liability, could have eased or solved the problem. This presumes that Myrtle was insurable or that the cost of the insurance would not be prohibitive. Furthermore, Myrtle made a serious error in dying without a will. A carefully drawn will could have precluded Bob's later course of action and perhaps kept much more of the ranch property intact. The ranch could have been placed in trust, life estate to Jim and Bob, remainder to their children. With such an arrangement, Bob would have been unable to sell the principal (the ranch).

Being able to defer the payment of estate taxes may be an invaluable option for an estate that lacks cash or near-cash assets (e.g., marketable securities). In this connection, two major possibilities exist.

- The discretionary extension of time (§ 6161).
- The extension of time when the estate consists largely of an interest in a closely held business (§ 6166).

Discretionary Extension of Time to Pay Estate Taxes—§ 6161

Currently, an executor or administrator may request an extension of time for paying the estate tax for a period not to exceed 10 years from the date fixed for the payment. The IRS grants such requests whenever there is "reasonable cause." Reasonable cause is not limited to a showing of undue hardship. It includes cases in which the executor or administrator is unable to marshal liquid assets readily because they are located in several jurisdictions. It also includes situations where the estate is largely made up of assets in the form of payments to be received in the future (e.g., annuities, copyright royalties, contingent fees, or accounts receivable), or where the assets that must be liquidated to pay the estate tax must be sold at a sacrifice or in a depressed market.

Extension of Time When the Estate Consists Largely of an Interest in a Closely Held Business—§ 6166

Congress always has been sympathetic to the plight of an estate that consists of an interest in a closely held business. The immediate imposition of the estate tax in such a situation may force the liquidation of the business at distress prices or cause the interest to be sold to outside parties.

A possible resolution of the problem is to use § 6166, which requires the IRS to accept a 15-payment procedure (5 interest-only payments, followed by 10 installment payments of the estate tax). This delay can enable the business to generate enough income to buy out the deceased owner's interest without disruption of operations or other financial sacrifice.

CONCEPT SUMMARY 19.3

Estate and Gift Planning

1. In reducing (or eliminating) gift taxes, one can take advantage of the annual exclusion and the election to split gifts. In the case of a single asset with high value (e.g., land), annual gifts of partial interests should be considered.
2. Gifts can reduce later estate taxes. This is accomplished by giving away assets that will appreciate in value (e.g., life insurance policies, art works, rare collections).
3. Timely gifts can help an estate qualify for § 2032A (special use valuation method), § 6166 (15-year payout of estate taxes), and § 303 (stock redemptions to pay estate taxes). To be effective, the gift must avoid the three-year rule of § 2035.
4. Gifts can relieve the income tax burden on the family unit. This objective is accomplished by shifting the income from the gift property to family members who are in a lower income tax bracket. In this regard, make sure the gift is *complete* and circumvents kiddie tax treatment.
5. Avoid gifts of property that result in income tax consequences to the donor.
6. Potential *probate costs* can be an important consideration in meaningful estate planning. Some procedures that reduce these costs include joint tenancies with the right of survivorship, living trusts, and predeath dispositions of out-of-state real estate. Keep in mind that most of these procedures *do not reduce* estate taxes.
7. A program of lifetime gifts and proper use of valuation techniques will reduce a decedent's *gross* estate. Further planning can reduce the *taxable* estate by proper handling of estate tax deductions.
8. For a married decedent, the most important deduction is the *marital deduction*. The two major approaches to the marital deduction are the *equalization* and *deferral* approaches.
9. Whether the equalization approach or the deferral approach is emphasized, make use of the *bypass amount*.
10. Lifetime charitable contributions are preferable to transfers by death. The lifetime contributions provide the donor with an income tax deduction, and the amount donated is not included in the gross estate.
11. The *disclaimer* procedure can be used to control (either lower or raise) the amount of the marital deduction and to increase the amount of the charitable deduction. Disclaimers can also be effective in taking full advantage of the available bypass amount.
12. Portability provisions allow both spouses to make full use of their bypass (exclusion) amounts. After the death of one spouse, for example, the surviving spouse can add to the basic exclusion amount the deceased spouse's unused exclusion amount (DSUEA).
13. Gift planning can help ease potential *estate liquidity* problems (see item 3 above). After death, § 6166 can be useful if the estate qualifies. The provision allows installment payments of deferred estate taxes over an extended period of time.

To meet the requirements of § 6166, the decedent's interest in a farm or other closely held business must exceed 35 percent of the decedent's adjusted gross estate.[49] The adjusted gross estate is the gross estate less the sum allowable as deductions under § 2053 (expenses, indebtedness, and taxes) and § 2054 (casualty and theft losses during the administration of an estate).

An interest in a closely held business includes the following.[50]

- Any sole proprietorship.
- An interest in a partnership carrying on a trade or business, if 20 percent of the capital interest in the partnership is included in the gross estate *or* the partnership has 45 or fewer partners.
- Stock in a corporation carrying on a trade or business, if 20 percent or more of the value of the voting stock of the corporation is included in the gross estate *or* the corporation has 45 or fewer shareholders.

[49] § 6166(a)(1).

[50] § 6166(b)(1).

In meeting the preceding requirements, a decedent and his or her surviving spouse are treated as one owner (shareholder or partner) if the interest is held as community property, tenants in common, joint tenants, or tenants by the entirety. Attribution from family members is allowed.[51]

EXAMPLE 48

Decedent Bonnie held a 15% capital interest in the Wren Partnership. Her son holds another 10%. Wren had 46 partners including Bonnie and her son. Since the son's interest is attributed to Bonnie, the estate is deemed to hold a 25% interest, and Wren (for purposes of § 6166) has only 45 partners. ■

In satisfying the more-than-35 percent test for qualification under § 6166, interests in more than one closely held business are aggregated when the decedent's gross estate includes 20 percent or more of the value of each such business.[52]

EXAMPLE 49

Henry's estate includes stock in Green Corporation and Brown Corporation, each of which qualifies as a closely held business. If the stock held in each entity represents 20% or more of the total value outstanding, the stocks can be combined for purposes of the more-than-35% test. ■

If the conditions of § 6166 are satisfied and the provision is elected, the following results transpire.

- No payments on the estate tax attributable to the inclusion of the interest in a closely held business in the gross estate need be made with the first five payments. Then, annual installments are made over a period not longer than 10 years.
- From the outset, interest at the rate of 2 percent is paid.[53] Originally, the 2 percent rate of interest applied only to the first $1 million of estate tax value. Since the estate tax value amount has been indexed for inflation, for 2011 it is $1.36 million.
- Acceleration of deferred payments may be triggered upon the disposition of the interest or failure to make scheduled principal or interest payments.[54]

Is It Too Late?

Donald, who is suffering from a terminal illness, is advised by his CPA that his current estate needs an additional $180,000 in stock of Hawk Corporation to qualify for § 6166. Immediately thereafter, Donald purchases the stock. Upon Donald's death two months later, his executor elects to come under the provisions of § 6166. Presuming the percentage requirements are satisfied, is the election proper?

In qualifying for § 6166, prune the potential estate of assets that may cause the 35 percent test to be failed. In this regard, lifetime gifts of such assets as marketable securities and life insurance should be considered.[55]

Some of the estate planning procedures covered in the last part of this chapter appear in Concept Summary 19.3 on the previous page.

[51] As described in § 267(c)(4).
[52] § 6166(c).
[53] § 6601(j)(1).
[54] § 6166(g).
[55] A gift within three years of death is not effective for this purpose. § 2035(c)(2).

REFOCUS ON THE BIG PICTURE

LIFETIME GIVING—THE GOOD AND THE BAD

Is Martin's potential estate a possible candidate for a § 2032A election (i.e., special use valuation method)? If so, a gift of the farmland could make it hard to meet the percentage qualification requirements of § 2032A. Barring certain limitations, qualifying under § 2032A would allow the farmland to be valued at $100,000 (rather than $500,000) for estate tax purposes (see Example 31).

Is it possible that Martin's potential estate would use the deferred payment procedure of § 6166? If so, the gift of the partnership interest could impair the closely held business qualification requirement for the § 6166 election.

The gift of the life insurance policy is very attractive. By making a gift of $500,000, Martin avoids $3 million being subject to the estate tax (see Example 27). (This assumes that Martin's estate avoids the three-year trap of § 2035.)

The marketable securities might better be sold to enable Martin to recognize an income tax loss of $400,000. However, a gift could preserve some of the built-in loss for the donee (see Example 35). Otherwise, there will be a step-down in income tax basis if Martin dies with these securities.

Under the circumstances, the gift of the city lot shifts to the donee a built-in gain of $400,000. Moreover, if this property passes by death, it receives a step-up in basis (see Example 19), and the gain component disappears. In either case (i.e., gift or inheritance), the amount subject to a transfer tax is $500,000.

The installment notes receivable present a "no win" situation. If Martin transfers them by gift, he must recognize income on the transfer (see Example 34). If they pass by death, however, either the estate or the heirs will recognize the deferred gain. As the gain is income in respect of a decedent, there is no step-up in basis due to Martin's death.

KEY TERMS

Blockage rule, 19–9
Buy-sell agreement, 19–10
Conservation easements, 19–27
Cross-purchase buy-sell agreement, 19–10
Entity buy-sell agreement, 19–10
Estate freeze, 19–12
Living trust, 19–25
Probate costs, 19–25
Special use value, 19–6
Step-down in basis, 19–15
Step-up in basis, 19–15

DISCUSSION QUESTIONS

1. **LO.1** Discuss the relevance of the following in defining "fair market value" for Federal gift and estate tax purposes.
   a. § 2031(b).
   b. The definition contained in Reg. § 20.2031–1(b).
   c. The sentimental value of the property being valued.
   d. Tangible personalty sold as a result of an advertisement in the classified section of a newspaper.
   e. Sporadic sales (occuring on other than the valuation date) of stocks traded in an over-the-counter stock exchange.

2. **LO.1** At the time of his death from a terminal illness, Hugo owned the following major assets.

   - A 3,400-square-foot condominium located in Kansas City, Kansas.
   - An antique car collection.

   In terms of valuing these assets for estate tax purposes, comment on these additional factors.

a. A similar condominium (same architect, same builder, same square footage) recently sold in midtown Manhattan (NYC) for $20 million.
b. To avoid bankruptcy and to provide immediate cash for the estate, Hugo's executor sold the antique car collection to the first wholesale dealer who made an offer.

3. **LO.1** Marvin's daughter Carol was a student at an exclusive private women's college. Each year that she attended, Marvin had Carol sign a note for $40,000 to cover books, tuition, and room and board. Ten years after Carol graduated, Marvin dies without a will. The notes are found in his safe deposit box. Although Carol has become a successful business executive, Marvin never discussed the notes with her or made any attempts at collection. What are the pertinent tax issues? (Note: In answering this question, a review of the earlier part of Chapter 18 might prove useful.) **ISSUE ID**

4. **LO.1** Comment on the valuation of each of the following items.
   a. An annuity contract issued by a party not regularly engaged in issuing such contracts.
   b. An annuity contract issued by an insurance company.
   c. A single premium life insurance policy.
   d. A life insurance policy, not recently issued, on which future premiums need to be made.

5. **LO.1** Brian creates a trust, life estate to Freda, remainder on Freda's death to Daniel.
   a. Presuming the trust is irrevocable, how is the value of each gift determined?
   b. Which gift, if any, qualifies for the annual exclusion?
   c. If Freda is Brian's wife, does this transfer qualify Brian for a marital deduction?

6. **LO.1** Sophie creates an irrevocable trust, income interest to her granddaughter, Brandi, for six years. After six years, the remainder interest in the trust is to go to Hailey, Sophie's divorced daughter (Brandi's mother).
   a. How is the value of this transfer by gift determined?
   b. Is the annual exclusion available?
   c. What might be the justification for such an arrangement?

7. **LO.2** In connection with § 2032A, comment on the following.
   a. The reason for the provision.
   b. Distinguish between "most suitable" and "special" use. Where do "best," "current," and "highest" use fit in?
   c. Who makes the election.
   d. The amount of valuation that can be excluded under this provision.
   e. Satisfying the percentage requirements as to qualified use property.
   f. The relevance of material participation.

8. **LO.2** Miles recently inherited farmland from his father that qualifies for § 2032A. Nevertheless, he is hesitant about making the election because of its effect on income tax basis. Explain Miles's concern. **ISSUE ID**

9. **LO.3** In determining the value of goodwill attributable to stock in a closely held corporation, comment on the following factors.
   a. The corporation's average profit figure includes large gains from the sale of assets not related to the business conducted.
   b. The operations of the corporation are largely financed with loans from its shareholders (rather than from outsiders).
   c. The rate of return used by the IRS for this type of business is too low.
   d. The deceased owner was active in the operation of the business.

10. **LO.3** What effect, if any, will each of the following factors have on the valuation of stock in a closely held corporation?
    a. A minority interest is involved.
    b. A majority interest is involved.
    c. The "blockage rule."
    d. The cost the corporation would incur in going public.

11. **LO.3** One of the major assets in John's estate is stock in Falcon Corporation, a closely held investment company. Falcon has a large portfolio of ExxonMobil stock, acquired when crude oil was selling for under $20 a barrel. In valuing the Falcon stock for estate tax purposes, what would be an important consideration? **ISSUE ID**

ISSUE ID

12. **LO.3** During the same year, a donor gives stock in a closely held corporation to family members and to a qualified charitable organization. In terms of tax planning, what might such a procedure accomplish?

13. **LO.3** The Sullivan family has developed a profitable business in which all adult members participate. They would like to make sure that the business stays in the family in the event of any future disruption (e.g., death, divorce, other discord).
    a. What do you suggest?
    b. Does it matter whether the business is conducted as a corporation or a partnership? Explain.

14. **LO.3** Buy-sell agreements for a closely held business are sometimes funded with life insurance policies. Explain how such an arrangement would be set up for:
    a. A cross-purchase type.
    b. An entity type.

15. **LO.4** What is the income tax basis to the donee if property received by gift is later sold for a:
    a. Gain?
    b. Loss?

16. **LO.4** When her grandmother (Hannah) died, Tracy was her sole heir. Some of the assets inherited by Tracy received a "step-up" in basis, while others received a "step-down" in basis. Explain.

17. **LO.4** In a community property jurisdiction, how does the death of one spouse affect the income tax basis in the survivor's share of the community?

ISSUE ID

18. **LO.4** Before electing certain valuation provisions such as § 2032 (alternate valuation date) and § 2032A (special use valuation), income tax consequences should be taken into account.
    a. Explain this statement.
    b. What is the impact, if any, if the parties involved (i.e., decedent and heirs) reside in a community property state?

19. **LO.4** When Brent learns that his mother, Della, is terminally ill, he gives her a valuable art collection. In her will, Della leaves the collection to Melody, Brent's wife.
    a. For income tax purposes, what was Brent trying to accomplish? Will it work?
    b. What are some of the nontax pitfalls of this procedure?

COMMUNICATIONS

20. **LO.4** Jonathan Rand is distressed about the basis of some land he inherited five years ago and recently sold for a large gain. He feels that the value placed on the property is too low. Consequently, he requests your advice as to whether he is bound by this value.
    a. Write a letter to Jonathan regarding this matter. Jonathan's address is 326 Wisteria Avenue, Charlotte, NC 28223.
    b. Include in the letter a list of further information you will need before you can assess the probability of success in challenging the value used by the estate.

COMMUNICATIONS

21. **LO.6** Cynthia and Norton Enright own all of the stock in Ibis Company, an S corporation. The Enrights are considering making gifts of some of the stock to their children (Addison, Tracy, Jordan, and Kirby) so as to shift income to them. Addison (age 20) is a high school graduate and does not intend to go to college. Tracy (age 21) is married and files a joint return with her husband. Jordan (age 23) and Kirby (age 24) are full-time college students. The Enrights request your advice on how to make these gifts effectively for tax purposes.
    a. Write a letter to the Enrights on this matter. Their address is 1486 Garden Park, Elizabeth, NJ 07207.
    b. Prepare a memo for your firm's tax research files.

22. **LO.5** Making gifts can save on estate taxes. Comment on the relevance of this statement to each of the following.
    a. The amount of the annual exclusion utilized.
    b. Subsequent appreciation of the property given.
    c. Contributions to § 529 plans on behalf of family members.
    d. The amount of gift tax actually paid.

23. **LO.2, 5** A program of lifetime giving can help an estate qualify for the special use election of § 2032A.
    a. Explain how this objective can be achieved.
    b. What could go wrong?

24. **LO.5** In choosing assets with which to make gifts, what is the importance of considering whether "dry" or income-producing assets are selected?

25. **LO.4, 6** For income tax purposes, what difference does it make to the parties (i.e., transferor and transferee) whether the following assets are transferred by gift or by death?
    a. Installment notes receivable.
    b. U.S. savings bonds.
    c. Property with depreciation recapture potential.

DECISION MAKING

COMMUNICATIONS

26. **LO.6** Charles Horn wants his daughter Sharon to get stock that he owns in Crimson Corporation. He acquired the stock two years ago at a cost of $800,000, and it currently has a fair market value of $650,000. Charles has made prior taxable gifts and is in poor health. He seeks your advice as to whether he should gift the stock to Sharon or pass it to her under his will. Charles has a large capital loss carryover and has no prospect for any capital gains.
    a. Write a letter to Charles regarding the tax implications of the alternatives he has suggested. His address is 648 Scenic Drive, Chattanooga, TN 37403.
    b. Prepare a memo for your firm's files on this matter.

27. **LO.7** Two years ago, after his wife Esther died, Frank took early retirement. He moved from New York to New Mexico to be near his only daughter, Pamela, and her family. Although he still owns his personal residence in New York—it has been converted to rental property—he plans to buy a condo in New Mexico. Other information regarding Frank's affairs is summarized below.

    - Several policies on his life list Esther as the beneficiary.
    - His § 401(k) plans and traditional IRAs do not name secondary beneficiaries.
    - Ownership of numerous, sizable CDs is listed as joint tenancy with Esther.
    - Frank and Esther executed New York wills naming the survivor as the sole heir.
    - Title to the family hunting lodge in Idaho is in Frank's name.

    a. In terms of reducing Frank's future *probate* estate, what changes can be made? (Assume Frank desires that all of his property will pass to Pamela.)
    b. Suppose Frank wants to retain the income stream from the New York rental property (i.e., his former residence). What do you suggest?

28. **LO.8** In deciding between the *deferral* and the *equalization* approaches to the marital deduction, comment on the following variables. In each case, the wife is expected to survive her husband's earlier death.
    a. The wife has little wealth of her own.
    b. The wife just won the championship (senior women's division) at her tennis club.
    c. The wife is scheduled to undergo a triple bypass heart operation.
    d. The wife is nine years older than her husband.
    e. Most of the property that will pass to the wife is expected to appreciate significantly in value.

29. **LO.8** In terms of Federal tax consequences, why are lifetime transfers to charity preferable to testamentary transfers?

30. **LO.8** What is the *bypass amount*? How can it be utilized effectively through the use of disclaimers in the case of:
    a. A surviving spouse?
    b. Nonspousal heirs?

ISSUE ID

31. **LO.9** The estate of Janet, currently still alive, almost qualifies for an election under § 6166. Janet is not concerned, however, because she plans on giving away her life insurance policy before her death. This, she believes, will allow her estate to meet the requirements of § 6166. Any comment?

PROBLEMS

32. **LO.1** When Wanda died in 2011, she owned 2,000 shares of Kite Corporation. The stock is traded in an over-the-counter market. The nearest trades before and after the date of Wanda's death are as follows.

	Per Share Mean Selling Price
Eight days before Wanda's death	$400
Five days after Wanda's death	460

Assuming the alternate valuation date is not elected, at what value should the Kite stock be included in Wanda's gross estate?

33. **LO.1** Barry creates a trust with property valued at $6 million. Under the terms of the trust instrument, Michelle (age 52) receives a life estate, while Terry (age 25) receives the remainder interest. In the month the trust is created, the interest rate is 4.2%. Determine the value of Barry's gifts.

34. **LO.1** Arlene creates a trust with assets worth $1 million. Under the terms of the trust, Tracy (age 17) receives the income for eight years, remainder to Dawn (age 35). In the month the trust is created, the interest rate is 4.4%. Determine the value of Arlene's gifts.

35. **LO.1** In 2011, Dale (age 72) creates a trust with assets worth $5 million. Under the terms of the trust, Dale retains a life estate with the remainder passing to Nicole (age 33) upon his death. In the month the trust is created, the interest rate is 4.6%.
    a. Determine the amount of Dale's gift. Of his taxable gift.
    b. Does the answer in part (a) change if Nicole is Dale's wife? (Refer to Chapter 18, if necessary.)

36. **LO.1** Assume the same facts as in Problem 35. Dale dies four year later when the trust is worth $5.7 million. Nicole is 37, and the applicable interest rate is 4.8%
    a. How much as to the trust is included in Dale's gross estate?
    b. Does the answer change in part (a) if Nicole is Dale's wife? (Refer to Chapter 18, if necessary.)

37. **LO.2** In each of the following independent situations occurring in 2011, determine the valuation to be used for estate tax purposes if § 2032A is elected.

Decedent	Most Suitable Use Value	Special Use Value
Perry	$3,000,000	$3,500,000
Hopkins	3,000,000	1,500,000
Morris	5,000,000	2,000,000
Allen	5,000,000	4,200,000

38. **LO.3** At her death, Inez owned 60% of the stock in Taupe Corporation, with the balance held by family members. In the past five years, Taupe has earned average net profits of $1.5 million, and on the date of Inez's death, the book value of its stock is $3.9 million. An appropriate rate of return for the type of business Taupe is in is 8%.
    a. Assuming goodwill exists, what is the value of the Taupe stock?
    b. What factors could be present to reduce the value of such goodwill?

39. **LO.3** Kyle owns all of the stock of Blanco Corporation. The stock has a value of $4 million for the common and $900,000 for the preferred. The preferred is noncumulative, has no redemption value, and carries no preference as to liquidation. Kyle gives the common stock to his children and retains the preferred stock. What are the tax consequences?

40. **LO.3** Assume the same facts as in Problem 39. Eight years after the gift, Kyle dies. At that time, the Blanco stock is worth $5 million for the common and $1 million for the preferred. What are Kyle's tax consequences?

41. **LO.4** Olivia gives real estate (basis of $400,000 and fair market value of $1million) to Ray. Determine Ray's income tax basis if the gift occurred in 2011 and Olivia paid a gift tax of $100,000.

42. **LO.4** Jacob gives stock (basis of $400,000 and fair market value of $1.2 million) to Mandy. As a result of the transfer in 2011, Jacob paid a gift tax of $60,000. Determine Mandy's gain or loss if she later sells the stock for $1.3 million.

43. **LO.4** Clinton gives stock (basis of $600,000 and fair market value of $500,000) to Morgan in 2011. As a result of the transfer, Clinton paid a gift tax of $40,000. Compute Morgan's gain or loss if she later sells the stock for:
   a. $650,000.
   b. $550,000.
   c. $480,000.

44. **LO.4, 5, 6** Ted and Marge Dean are married and have always lived in a community property state. Ted (age 92) suffers from numerous disorders and is frequently ill, while Marge (age 70) is in good health. The Deans currently need $500,000 to meet living expenses, make debt payments, and pay Ted's backlog of medical expenses. They are willing to sell any one of the following assets:

DECISION MAKING

COMMUNICATIONS

	Adjusted Basis	Fair Market Value
Wren Corporation stock	$200,000	$500,000
Gull Corporation stock	600,000	500,000
Unimproved land	650,000	500,000

The stock investments are part of the Deans' community property, while the land is Ted's separate property that he inherited from his mother. If the land is not sold, Ted is considering making a gift of it to Marge.
   a. Write a letter to the Deans advising them on these matters. Their address is 290 Cedar Road, Carson, CA 90747.
   b. Prepare a memo on this matter for your firm's client files.

45. **LO.4** In June 2010, Reba gives Julius a house (basis of $150,000; fair market value of $450,000) to be used as his personal residence. Before his death in May 2011, Julius installs a tennis court in the backyard at a cost of $25,000. The residence has a value of $465,000 when Julius dies. Determine the income tax basis of the property to the heir based on the following independent assumptions.
   a. The residence passes to Reba.
   b. The residence passes to Burl (Reba's husband).
   c. The residence passes to Tina (Reba's daughter).

46. **LO.5** Nolan and Sarah are husband and wife with six married children and ten grandchildren. Commencing in December 2010, they would like to transfer a tract of land (worth $1,144,000) equally to their children (including spouses) and grandchildren as quickly as possible and without making a taxable gift. What do you suggest?

DECISION MAKING

47. **LO.2, 5** At the time of her death in 2011, Abigail has an adjusted gross estate of $6.5 million. Her estate includes the family farm, with a most suitable use value of $3.3 million and a current use value of $2.3 million. The farm is inherited by Jim, Abigail's son, who has worked it for her since 1985. Jim plans to continue farming indefinitely.
   a. Based on the information given, is the § 2032A election available to Abigail's estate?
   b. If so, what value must be used for the farm?
   c. Suppose Abigail had made a gift of securities (fair market value of $500,000) to her cousin six months before her death. Does this fact affect your analysis? Explain.

48. **LO.6** Last year, Henry sold real estate (basis of $450,000) to Bill (an unrelated party) for $1.8 million, receiving $300,000 in cash and notes for the balance. The notes carry an 8.5% rate of interest and mature annually at $500,000 each over three years. Henry did not elect out of the installment method of reporting the gain. Before any of the notes mature and when they have a fair market value of $1.3 million, Henry gives them to Jean.
   a. Disregarding the interest element, what are the tax consequences of the gift?

b. Suppose that instead of making the gift, Henry died. The notes passed to his estate and were later sold by the executor. What is the tax result?

49. **LO.7** At the time of her death in 2011, Monica held the following assets.

	Fair Market Value
Personal residence (title listed as "Monica and Peter, tenants by the entirety with right of survivorship")	$800,000
Savings account (listed as "Monica and Rex, joint tenants with right of survivorship") with funds provided by Rex	40,000
Certificate of deposit (listed as "Monica, payable on proof of death to Rex") with funds provided by Monica	100,000
Unimproved real estate (title listed as "Monica and Rex, equal tenants in common")	400,000
Insurance policy on Monica's life, issued by Lavender Company (Monica's estate is the designated beneficiary)	300,000
Insurance policy on Monica's life, issued by Crimson Company (Rex is the designated beneficiary)	400,000
Living trust created by Monica five years ago (life estate to Peter, remainder to Rex)	700,000

Assuming Peter and Rex survive Monica, how much is included in Monica's *probate estate?* Monica's *gross estate*? (Refer to Chapter 18 if needed.)

DECISION MAKING

50. **LO.8** Logan, a widower, is 80 years of age and in poor health. He would like to donate unimproved land to his church. The land cost Logan $20,000 and is currently worth $100,000. In carrying out the donation, Logan wants to regain his original capital investment of $20,000. In this regard evaluate the following options.

- An immediate donation of an 80% undivided interest in the land to the church.
- A sale of *all* of the land to the church for $20,000.
- A provision in his will passing an 80% undivided interest in the land to the church.

51. **LO.8** In terms of tax ramifications, comment on what is accomplished in the following disclaimer situations occurring in 2011.
   a. Lester dies intestate and is survived by a daughter, Nora, and a grandson, Nick. The major asset in Lester's estate is stock worth $3.5 million. Under the applicable state law of descent and distribution, children precede grandchildren in order of inheritance. As Nora is already well off and in ill health, she disclaims Lester's property.
   b. Under her will, Audrey's estate is to pass $6 million to her son, Raymond, and the $3 million remainder to her husband, George. Raymond disclaims $1 million of his inheritance.
   c. Under Isaac's will, $4 million is to pass to his wife, Brenda, and the $4.5 million remainder to his daughter, Sybil. Brenda disclaims $500,000 of her inheritance.
   d. Under Tricia's will, her $3 million cubist art collection is to pass to her husband, Leroy. If Leroy declines, the collection is to pass to the San Francisco Museum of Modern Art. Leroy neither understands nor admires this type of art.

52. **LO.8** In each of the following *independent situations*, what bypass (exclusion) amount is available to Ava's estate when she dies in 2012? Assume that any appropriate procedures are followed, and that elections are made to transfer to Ava any DSUEA of Al, the deceased husband.
   a. Al died in 2009 and never used any of his bypass amount.
   b. Al died in early 2011 and did not use any of his bypass amount.
   c. Same as part (b). Ava remarried in late 2011, and Andy, her second husband, had used $1 million of his bypass amount in making past taxable gifts. Andy predeceases Ava in early 2012.

53. **LO.9** At the time of his death in 2011, Clint had an adjusted gross estate of $6.2 million. Included in the estate is a 15% capital interest in a partnership valued at $2.6 million. Except for Clint's daughter Phoebe, none of the other 48 partners are related to him. Phoebe holds a 10% capital interest.
   a. Does Clint's estate qualify for the § 6166 election?
   b. Suppose that one year prior to his death, Clint gave $1.5 million in cash and securities to Phoebe. Does this change your analysis?

54. **LO.9** At the time of her death in 2011, June had an adjusted gross estate of $6 million. Included in the estate were the following business interests.

	Fair Market Value
A 30% capital interest in the JZ Partnership	$700,000
A 25% interest (i.e., 250 shares out of 1,000) in Silver Corporation	500,000
A catering service operated as a sole proprietorship	950,000

The JZ Partnership has 32 partners while Silver Corporation has a total of 30 shareholders. None of the other partners or shareholders are related to June. Can June's estate qualify for an election under § 6166? Explain.

RESEARCH PROBLEMS

Note: Solutions to Research Problems can be prepared by using the **Checkpoint®** **Student Edition** online research product, which is available to accompany this text. It is also possible to prepare solutions to the Research Problems by using tax research materials found in a standard tax library.

THOMSON REUTERS
Checkpoint® Student Edition

Research Problem 1. On June 1, 2009, Mario entered into a contract to sell real estate for $1 million (adjusted basis $200,000). The sale was conditioned on a rezoning of the property for commercial use. A $50,000 deposit placed in escrow by the purchaser was refundable in the event the rezoning was not accomplished.

After considerable controversy, the application was approved on November 10, and two days later, the sum of $950,000 was paid to Mario's estate in full satisfaction of the purchase price. Mario had died unexpectedly on November 1. Discuss the estate and income tax consequences of this set of facts if it is assumed that the sale of the real estate occurred:

a. After Mario's death.
b. Before Mario's death.
c. When do you think the sale occurred? Why?

Partial list of research aids:
§§ 691 and 1014.
George W. Keck, 49 T.C. 313 (1968), *rev'd* 69–2 USTC ¶9626, 24 AFTR 2d 69–5554, 415 F.2d 531 (CA–6, 1969).
Trust Company of Georgia v. Ross, 68–1 USTC ¶9133, 21 AFTR 2d 311, 392 F.2d 694 (CA–5, 1967).

Research Problem 2. In 2007, Troy wins the Connecticut LOTTO grand prize of $15 million. The LOTTO contest is governed by the following rules.

- The prize money is to be paid in 20 equal annual installments (in this case, $750,000 per year) with no interest provided for.
- The rights to the prize award are not assignable. If a winner dies during the payout period, however, the remaining installment payments are to be made to the winner's duly appointed executor.
- The prize award is not specifically funded or guaranteed by any state agency. It constitutes a general obligation of the state of Connecticut.

Troy dies in 2009 after having received two payments of $750,000 each. Troy's estate includes the present value of the remaining $13.5 million prize award in the estate at $4.86 million. This is determined by using the IRS table amount of $6.75 million and discounting it for absence of security (i.e., no separate funding or guarantee of payment by a state agency) and lack of marketability (i.e., the award cannot be assigned). The table used is that issued by the IRS in Reg. § 20.2031–7 under the authority of § 7520. The table is to be used in valuing, among other income interests, private (i.e., noncommercial) annuity contracts.

Upon audit of the estate tax return, the IRS disputes the deviation from the table amount. The IRS argues that the absence-of-security discount is inappropriate because the state of Connecticut has never defaulted on any of its LOTTO obligations. Furthermore, the lack-of-marketability discount is inappropriately applied to annuity-type situations. Unlike stocks and bonds and other ownership interests, private annuities are not subject to marketplace valuation procedures.

Who should prevail? The taxpayer or the IRS?

Partial list of research aids:
§§ 2039 and 7520.
Reg. § 20.7520–3(b).
O'Reilly v. Comm., 92–2 USTC ¶60,111, 70 AFTR 2d 92–6211, 973 F.2d 1403 (CA–8, 1992).
Shackleford v. U.S., 99–2 USTC ¶60,356, 84 AFTR 2d 99–5902 (D.Ct.Cal., 1999), *aff'd* in 88 AFTR 2d 2001–5658, 262 F.3d 1028 (CA–9, 2001).
Estate of Gribauskas, 116 T.C. 142 (2001), *rev'd* in 2003–2 USTC ¶60,466, 92 AFTR 2d 2003–5914, 342 F.3d 85 (CA–2, 2003).
Estate of Donovan v. U.S., 2005–1 USTC ¶50,322, 95 AFTR 2d 2005–2131 (D.Ct.Mass., 2005).

Research Problem 3. In late 2008, Gordon Clay unexpectedly suffered a stroke, and he died shortly thereafter. In his will, Gordon designated his sister, Loretta, as executor of his estate. Loretta was duly appointed executor, administered the estate, rendered a final accounting, and was discharged by the probate court in June 2009.

During the administration of the estate, Loretta satisfied a claim for $200,000 submitted by Raymond Clay, Gordon's older brother. Several years ago, Gordon had borrowed this amount from Raymond on open account. No note was issued or interest provided for. The loan was not a secret, and everyone in the immediate family was aware that it had been made and not repaid. When completing the Form 706 for Gordon's estate, Loretta deducted the $200,000 as a § 2053(a)(3) claim against the estate. Upon audit by the IRS, the deduction was disallowed on two grounds. First, the existence of the debt was not proved. Second, if the debt existed, it was barred by the statute of limitations.

The estate countered that the note existed and that its payment was sanctioned by the probate court. Further, the running of the statute of limitations does not invalidate a claim—it merely provides the debtor with a defense that may or may not be invoked. In the interest of family harmony, therefore, Loretta chose not to invoke the statute and bar a claim that was rightfully due and should be paid.

a. Who will prevail?
b. Has Loretta acted wisely? Answer also from the perspective of the remainderperson under Gordon's will.

Partial list of research aids:
Prop.Reg. §§ 20.2053–4(b)(4) and 4(d), Example 7. [Reg. § 143316–03 published in I.R.B. No. 21, 1292 (May 21, 2007.)]

Research Problem 4. Garth dies in 2009 and is survived by his wife Daisy and four adult children. Among the items included in his gross estate are the following.

	Fair Market Value
Apartment building	$2,900,000
Marketable securities	600,000
Insurance policy on Daisy's life (maturity value of $600,000)	60,000
Lake cottage	300,000
Cabin cruiser	240,000

Garth's will grants Daisy a life estate in the apartment building with the remainder passing to the children. Under the IRS valuation tables, the life estate is worth $1.8 million, and the remainder is worth $1.1 million. Garth's executor does not make a QTIP election as to the life estate. Under Garth's will, the rest of his property goes to Daisy. By applicable state law, whatever Daisy disclaims passes to the children. Daisy has considerable assets of her own, and the children are self-supporting.

a. What needs to be done to maximize the bypass amount?
b. How can Daisy's potential estate tax consequences be minimized?

Use the tax resources of the Internet to address the following questions. Do not restrict your search to the Web, but include a review of newsgroups and general reference materials, practitioner sites and resources, primary sources of the tax law, chat rooms and discussion groups, and other opportunities.

COMMUNICATIONS

Research Problem 5. Identify the following forms issued by the IRS: Forms 706–NA, 706–CE, 712, 4768, and 4808. What purpose does each serve? Summarize your comments in an e-mail to your professor.

COMMUNICATIONS

Research Problem 6. In your state, what is the designation of the court that handles the administration of an estate? What are the statutory guidelines on fees that an executor is allowed for probating an estate? Summarize your findings in a short PowerPoint presentation.

Research Problem 7. What procedures has the IRS recommended that a surviving spouse use to take advantage of a DSUEA?

Research Problem 8. Cecil inherits a farm from his father and, as executor of the estate, makes a § 2032A special use valuation election. Five years later, the farm is disposed of.

a. How is the disposition reported to the IRS?
b. Suppose that the disposition occurred due to condemnation by a public authority (i.e., an involuntary conversion took place) and Cecil reinvested some of the award in other farmland. How would your answer to part (a) change?

Research Problem 9. The Treasury Department's *General Explanation of the Administration's Fiscal Year 2010 Revenue Proposals* (also known as the "Green Book") describes the administration's tax agenda including changes in the estate and gift taxes. In this regard, comment on the following items.

a. Consistency in the value used for transfer tax and income tax purposes.
b. Requirement of certain reporting procedures by executors and donors.
c. Restrictions to be placed on the use of certain valuation procedures to reduce transfer taxes.
d. The maximum unified transfer tax rate and exclusion amount that should apply.

Research Problem 10. Refer to part (d) of Research Problem 9. Is the result reached in TRA of 2010 consistent among the Federal transfer taxes?

CHAPTER 20

Income Taxation of Trusts and Estates

LEARNING OBJECTIVES

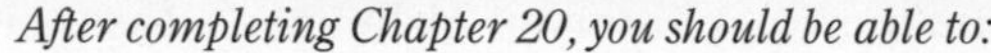

After completing Chapter 20, you should be able to:

LO.1 Use working definitions with respect to trusts, estates, beneficiaries, and other parties.

LO.2 Identify the steps in determining the accounting and taxable income of a trust or estate and the related taxable income of the beneficiaries.

LO.3 Illustrate the uses and implications of distributable net income.

LO.4 Use the special rules that apply to trusts where the creator (grantor) of the trust retains certain rights.

LO.5 Apply the Subchapter J rules in a manner that minimizes the income taxation of trusts and estates and still accomplishes the intended objectives of the grantor or decedent.

OUTLINE

For the latest in changes to tax legislation, visit **www.cengage.com/taxation/swft.**

THE BIG PICTURE **Tax Solutions for the Real World**

SETTING UP A TRUST TO PROTECT A FAMILY

Anna Jiang is the main breadwinner in her family, which includes her husband Tom, a social worker, and two children, Bobby, age 8, and Sally, age 13. Anna has accumulated about $2 million in after-tax investment accounts, largely made up of growth stocks that do not regularly pay dividends. Anna has addressed the problem of probate costs through joint property ownership, life insurance policies, and beneficiary arrangements for her retirement plans. She and Tom update their wills every five years or so.

Because there is a history of Alzheimer's disease in her family, Anna Jiang wants to make certain that, if she becomes unable to work and cannot manage her financial assets, Tom and the children will have adequate cash flow from the $2 million of investment assets. One of Anna's colleagues at the office suggests that Anna should set up a trust to take care of her family in case a medical problem ever arises. **Read the chapter and formulate your response.**

20.1 An Overview of Subchapter J

Taxpayers create trusts for a variety of reasons. Some trusts are established primarily for tax purposes, but most are designed to accomplish a specific financial goal or to provide for the orderly management of assets in case of emergency.

Because a trust is a separate tax entity, its gross income and deductions must be measured, and an annual tax return must be filed. Similarly, when an individual dies, a legal entity is created in the form of his or her estate. This chapter examines the rules related to the income taxation of trusts and estates.

Table 20.1 lists some of the more common reasons for creating a trust, and Figure 20.1 illustrates the structure of a typical trust and estate.

The income taxation of trusts and estates is governed by Subchapter J of the Internal Revenue Code, §§ 641 through 692. Certain similarities are apparent between Subchapter J and the income taxation of individuals (e.g., the definitions of gross income and deductible expenditures), partnerships and limited liability entities (e.g., the pass-through principle), and S corporations (e.g., the pass-through principle and the trust or estate as a separate taxable entity). Trusts also involve several important new concepts, however, including the determination of *distributable net income* and the *tier system* of distributions to beneficiaries.

WHAT IS A TRUST?

LO.1

Use working definitions with respect to trusts, estates, beneficiaries, and other parties.

The Code does not contain a definition of a trust. However, the term usually refers to an arrangement created by a will or by an *inter vivos* (lifetime) declaration through which trustees take title to property for the purpose of protecting or conserving it for the beneficiaries.[1] Usually, trust operations are controlled by the trust document and by the fiduciary laws of the state in which the trust documents are executed.

Typically, the creation of a trust involves at least three parties: (1) The **grantor** (sometimes referred to as the settlor or donor) transfers selected assets to the trust entity. (2) The trustee, who usually is either an individual or a corporation, is charged with the fiduciary duties associated with the trust. (3) The beneficiary is designated to receive income or property from the trust.

In some situations, fewer than three persons may be involved, as specified by the trust agreement. For instance, an elderly individual who no longer can manage his or her own property (e.g., because of ill health) may create a trust under which he

[1] Reg. § 301.7701–4(a).

TABLE 20.1 Common Motivations for Creating a Trust

Type of Trust	Financial and Other Goals
Life insurance trust	Holds life insurance policies on the insured, removes the proceeds of the policies from the gross estate (if an irrevocable trust), and safeguards against receipt of the proceeds by a young or inexperienced beneficiary.
"Living" (revocable) trust	Manages assets, reduces probate costs, provides privacy for asset disposition, protects against medical or other emergencies, and provides relief from the necessity of day-to-day management of the underlying assets.
Trust for minors	Provides funds for a college education, shifts income to other taxpayers, and transfers accumulated income without permanently parting with the underlying assets.
"Blind" trust	Holds and manages the assets of the grantor without his/her input or influence (e.g., while the grantor holds political office or some other sensitive position).
Retirement trust	Manages asset contributions as dictated by the terms of a qualified retirement plan.
Divorce trust	Manages the assets of an ex-spouse and assures they are distributed in a timely fashion to specified beneficiaries (e.g., as alimony or child support).
Liquidation trust	Collects and distributes the remaining assets of a corporation that is undergoing a complete liquidation.

or she is both the grantor and the beneficiary. In this case, a family member or corporate trustee is charged with the management of the grantor's assets.

In another situation, the grantor might designate himself or herself as the trustee of the trust assets. For example, someone who wants to transfer selected assets to a minor child or elderly parent could use a trust entity to assure that the beneficiary does not waste the property. By naming himself or herself as the trustee, the grantor retains virtual control over the property that is transferred.

Under the general rules of Subchapter J, the **grantor trusts** just described are not recognized for income tax purposes. Similarly, when only one party is involved (when the same individual is grantor, trustee, and sole beneficiary of the trust), Subchapter J rules do not apply, and the entity is ignored for income tax purposes.

Other Definitions

When the grantor transfers title of selected assets to a trust, those assets become the **corpus** (body), or principal, of the trust. Trust corpus, in most situations, earns *income*, which may be distributed to the beneficiaries or accumulated for the future by the trustee, as the trust instrument directs.

In the typical trust, the grantor creates two types of beneficiaries: one who receives the accounting income of the trust and one who receives the trust corpus that remains at the termination of the trust entity. Beneficiaries in the former category hold an *income interest* in the trust, and those in the latter category hold a *remainder interest* in the trust's assets. If the grantor retains the remainder interest, the interest is known as a **reversionary interest** (corpus reverts to the grantor when the trust entity terminates).

FIGURE 20.1 Structure of a Typical Trust and Estate

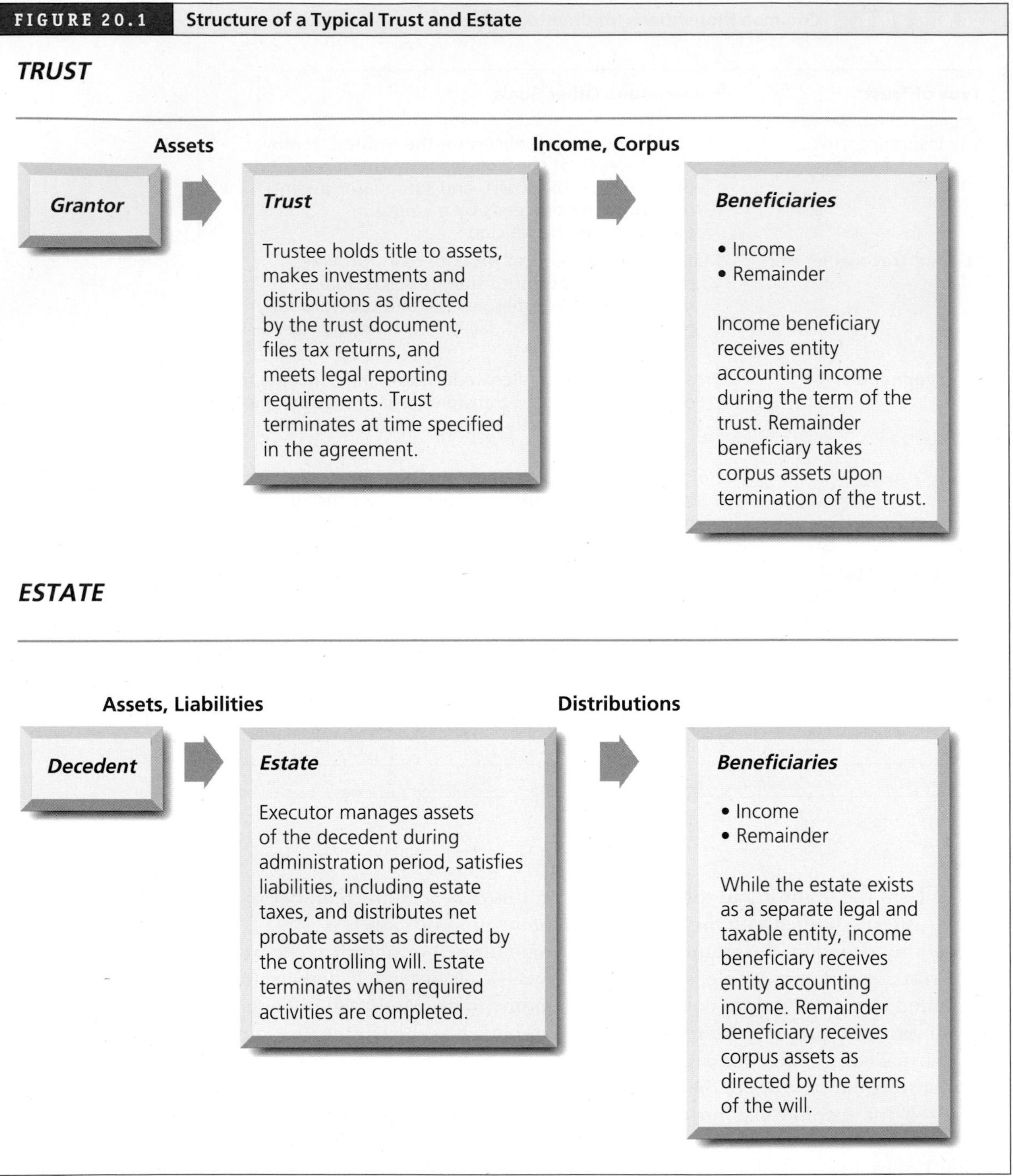

The trust document establishes the term of the trust. The term may be for a specific number of years (*term certain*) or until the occurrence of a specified event. For instance, a trust might exist (1) for the life of the income beneficiary, in which case the income beneficiary is known as a *life tenant* in the trust corpus; (2) for the life of some other individual; (3) until the income or remainder beneficiary reaches the age of majority; or (4) until the beneficiary, or another individual, marries, receives a promotion, or reaches some specified age.

The trustee may be required to distribute the accounting income of the entity according to a distribution schedule specified in the agreement. Sometimes, however, the trustee is given more discretion with respect to the timing and nature of the distributions. If the trustee can determine, within guidelines that may be included in the trust document, either the timing of the income or corpus

TAX *in the NEWS*

MUST A TRUST BENEFICIARY EVEN BE HUMAN?

Humane societies encourage the general public to care for their pets and to adopt those who need owners. But sometimes people carry this compassion even further. It is not uncommon to find provisions in a will to establish endowments to care for pets that the deceased leaves behind. Two prominent, eccentric investors recently established trusts dedicating significant funds to provide for a favorite dog, and the surviving (human) family did not take well to the idea.

- Leona Helmsley was an investor who favored building and decorating luxury hotels. When Helmsley died, her will left very little of her multibillion-dollar estate to her friends and family, perhaps not surprising for someone whose temperament had earned her the nickname "The Queen of Mean." But Helmsley's dog Trouble made out very well. The will established a $12 million trust, with income distributions to be used for Trouble's five-star kennels, dog sitters and manicurists, and other general care. With an annual income allowance averaging $600,000, Trouble could afford accommodations rivaling those available for guests at Helmsley's opulent hotels. After challenges from Helmsley's family, a judge reduced the endowment to benefit Trouble to $2 million and directed the trustee to contribute the rest of trust corpus to charity.
- Gail Posner's will created a $3 million trust to support her Chihuahua Conchita and two other dogs. The dogs received the right to continue to live in Posner's $8 million Miami Beach mansion. Posner's caretakers (e.g., bodyguards and housekeepers) inherited about $26 million in cash, and some of them were directed to live rent-free in the mansion to continue to care for the pets. Conchita owns a $15,000 diamond necklace and took over Posner's Cadillac Escalade when Posner acquired a new car. Posner's family is challenging the terms of the will, claiming that Posner was unduly influenced by the caretakers, and that Conchita's needs should not prevail over those of the relatives.

distributions or the specific beneficiaries who will receive them (from among those identified in the agreement), the trust is called a discretionary or **sprinkling trust**. Here, the trustee can "sprinkle" the distributions among the various beneficiaries. As discussed in Chapters 18 and 19, family-wide income taxes can be reduced by directing income to those who are subject to lower marginal tax rates. Thus, by giving the trustee a sprinkling power, the income tax liability of the family unit can be manipulated by applying the terms of the trust agreement.

For purposes of certain provisions of Subchapter J, a trust must be classified as either a **simple trust** or a **complex trust**. A simple trust (1) is required to distribute its entire accounting income to designated beneficiaries every year, (2) has no beneficiaries that are qualifying charitable organizations, and (3) makes no distributions of trust corpus during the year. A complex trust is any trust that is not a simple trust.[2] These criteria are applied to the trust every year. Thus, every trust is classified as a complex trust in the year in which it terminates (because it distributes all of its corpus during that year).

WHAT IS AN ESTATE?

An estate is created upon the death of every individual. The entity is charged with collecting and conserving all of the individual's assets, satisfying all liabilities, and distributing the remaining assets to the heirs identified by state law or the will.

Typically, the creation of an estate involves at least three parties: the decedent, all of whose probate assets are transferred to the estate for disposition; the executor, who is appointed under the decedent's valid will (or the administrator, if no valid will exists); and the beneficiaries of the estate, who are to receive assets or income from the entity, as the decedent has indicated in the will. An estate's operations are controlled by the probate laws of the decedent's state of residence and by the terms of the will as interpreted by the probate court.

[2]Reg. § 1.651(a)–1.

Recall that the assets that make up the probate estate are not identical to those that constitute the gross estate for transfer tax purposes (refer to Chapter 19). Many gross estate assets are not a part of the probate estate and thus are not subject to disposition by the executor or administrator. For instance, property held by the decedent as a joint tenant passes to the survivor(s) by operation of the applicable state's property law rather than through the probate estate. Proceeds of insurance policies on the life of the decedent, over which the decedent held the incidents of ownership, are not under the control of the executor or administrator. The designated beneficiaries of the policy receive the proceeds outright under the insurance contract.

An estate is a separate taxable entity. The termination date of the estate is somewhat discretionary, as it occurs when all of the assets and income of the decedent have been distributed, all estate and decedent liabilities have been satisfied, and all other business of the entity is completed. Thus, there may be an incentive to use the estate as part of an income-shifting strategy (e.g., where the income beneficiaries are subject to low marginal tax rates).

EXAMPLE 1

Maria dies, and her estate holds a high-yield investment portfolio. Paulo, the income beneficiary, is subject to a 15% marginal state and Federal income tax rate, while Julia, the remainder beneficiary, is subject to a 30% marginal rate. The tax adviser might suggest that Maria's estate delay its final distribution of assets by a year or more, to take advantage of the income tax reduction that is available before the entity terminates. ■

If an estate's existence is unduly prolonged, however, the IRS can terminate it for Federal income tax purposes after the expiration of a reasonable period for completing the duties of administration.[3]

20.2 Nature of Trust and Estate Taxation

In general, the taxable income of a trust or estate is taxed to the entity or to its beneficiaries to the extent that each has received the accounting income of the entity. Thus, Subchapter J creates a modified pass-through principle relative to the income taxation of trusts, estates, and their beneficiaries. Whoever receives the accounting income of the entity, or some portion of it, is liable for the income tax that results.

Subchapter J produces a significant amount of income tax revenue. About 3 million Forms 1041 are filed every year, and these returns reflect the following approximate amounts.

- Gross income of $200 billion.
- Taxable income of $110 billion.
- Tax liability of $25 billion.

EXAMPLE 2

Adam receives 80% of the accounting income of the Zero Trust. The trustee accumulated the other 20% of the income at her discretion under the trust agreement and added it to trust corpus. Adam is liable for income tax only on the amount of the distribution, while Zero is liable for the income tax on the accumulated portion of the income. ■

Table 20.2 summarizes the major similarities and differences between the taxation of trusts and estates and that of other pass-through entities—partnerships, limited liability entities, and S corporations.

TAX ACCOUNTING PERIODS AND METHODS

An estate or trust may use many of the tax accounting methods available to individuals. The method of accounting used by the grantor of a trust or the decedent of an estate need not carry over to the entity.

[3]Reg. § 1.641(b)–3(a).

TABLE 20.2 Tax Characteristics of Major Pass-Through Entities

Tax Treatment	Subchapter K (Partnerships, LLCs)	Subchapter S (S Corporations)	Subchapter J (Trusts, Estates)
Taxing structure	Pure pass-through, only one level of Federal income tax.	Chiefly pass-through, usually one level of Federal income tax.	Modified pass-through, Federal income tax falls on the recipient(s) of entity accounting income.
Entity-level Federal income tax?	Never.	Rarely. See Chapter 12.	Yes, if the entity retains any accounting income amounts.
Form for reporting income and expense pass-through	Schedules K and K–1, Form 1065.	Schedules K and K–1, Form 1120S.	Schedules K and K–1, Form 1041.
Subject to entity-level AMT?	No, but preferences and adjustments pass through to owners.	No, but preferences and adjustments pass through to owners.	Yes, if the entity retains any AMT-related accounting income amounts.
Controlling documents	Partnership agreement, LLC charter.	Corporate charter and bylaws.	Trust document or will, state fiduciary or probate law.

An estate has the same options for choosing a tax year as any new taxpayer. Thus, the estate of a calendar year decedent dying on March 3 can select any fiscal year or report on a calendar year basis. If the latter is selected, the estate's first taxable year will include the period from March 3 to December 31. If the first or last tax years are short years (less than one calendar year), income for those years need not be annualized.

To eliminate the possibility of deferring the taxation of fiduciary-source income simply by using a fiscal tax year, virtually all trusts (other than tax-exempt trusts) are required to use a calendar tax year.[4]

TAX RATES AND PERSONAL EXEMPTION

Congress's desire to stop trusts from being used as income-shifting devices has made the fiduciary entity the highest-taxed taxpayer in the Code. The entity reaches the 35 percent marginal rate with only $11,350 of 2011 taxable income, so the grantor's ability to shift income in a tax-effective manner is nearly eliminated. Table 20.3, which lists the 2011 taxes paid by various entities on taxable income of $50,000, shows how expensive the accumulation of income within an estate or trust can be. Proper income shifting might move assets *out of* the estate or trust and into the hands of the grantor or beneficiary.

A fiduciary's dividend income and net long-term capital gain usually is taxed at a nominal rate of no more than 15 percent. In addition to the regular income tax, an estate or trust may be subject to the alternative minimum tax, as discussed below.[5]

Both trusts and estates are allowed a personal exemption in computing the fiduciary tax liability. All estates are allowed a personal exemption of $600. The exemption available to a trust depends upon the type of trust involved. A trust that is required to distribute all of its income currently is allowed an exemption of $300. All other trusts are allowed an exemption of $100 per year.[6]

The classification of trusts as to the appropriate personal exemption is similar but not identical to the distinction between simple and complex trusts. The classification as a simple trust is more stringent.

[4]§ 645.
[5]§ 55.
[6]§ 642(b).

TABLE 20.3 Comparative Tax Liabilities

Filing Status/Entity	Taxable Income	Marginal Income Tax Rate (%)	2011 Tax Liability
Single	$50,000	25	$ 8,625
Married, filing jointly	50,000	15	6,650
C corporation	50,000	15	7,500
Trust or estate	50,000	35	16,465

EXAMPLE 3

Three trusts appear to operate in a similar fashion, but they are subject to different Subchapter J classifications and exemptions.

Trust Alpha is required to distribute all of its current accounting income to Susan. Thus, it is allowed a $300 personal exemption. No corpus distributions or charitable contributions are made during the year. Accordingly, Alpha is a simple trust.

Trust Beta is required to distribute all of its current accounting income; it is allowed a $300 personal exemption. The beneficiaries of these distributions are specified in the trust instrument: one-half of accounting income is to be distributed to Tyrone, and one-half is to be distributed to State University, a qualifying charitable organization. Since Beta has made a charitable distribution for the tax year, it is a complex trust.

The trustee of Trust Gamma can, at her discretion, distribute the current-year accounting income or corpus of the trust to Dr. Chapman. As the trustee is not required to distribute current accounting income, only a $100 personal exemption is allowed. During the current year, the trustee distributed all of the accounting income of the entity to Dr. Chapman, but made no corpus or charitable distributions. Nonetheless, because it lacks the current-year income distribution requirement, Gamma is a complex trust. ■

ALTERNATIVE MINIMUM TAX

The alternative minimum tax (AMT) may apply to a trust or estate in any tax year. Given the nature and magnitude of the tax preferences, adjustments, and exemptions that determine alternative minimum taxable income (AMTI), however, most trusts and estates are unlikely to incur the tax. Nevertheless, they could be vulnerable, for example, if they are actively engaged in cashing out the stock options of a donor/decedent who was a corporate executive.

In general, derivation of AMTI for the entity follows the rules that apply to individual taxpayers. Thus, the corporate ACE adjustment does not apply to fiduciary entities, but AMTI may be created through the application of most of the other AMT preference and adjustment items discussed in Chapter 3.

The fiduciary's AMT is computed using Schedule I of Form 1041. Two full pages of the Form 1041 are dedicated to the computation of taxable income and other items when the AMT applies to the trust or estate. A minimum tax credit might be available in future years through these computations.

The entity has a $22,500 annual AMT exemption. The exemption phases out at a rate of one-fourth of the amount by which AMTI exceeds $75,000.

A 26 percent AMT rate is applied to AMTI, increasing to 28 percent when AMTI in excess of the exemption reaches $175,000. In addition, estimated tax payments for the entity must include any applicable AMT liability.

LO.2

Identify the steps in determining the accounting and taxable income of a trust or estate and the related taxable income of the beneficiaries.

20.3 Taxable Income of Trusts and Estates

Generally, the taxable income of an estate or trust is computed similarly to that for an individual. Subchapter J does, however, include several important exceptions and provisions that make it necessary to use a systematic approach to calculating the taxable

FIGURE 20.2 **Accounting Income, Distributable Net Income, and Taxable Income of the Entity and Its Beneficiaries—The Five-Step Procedure**

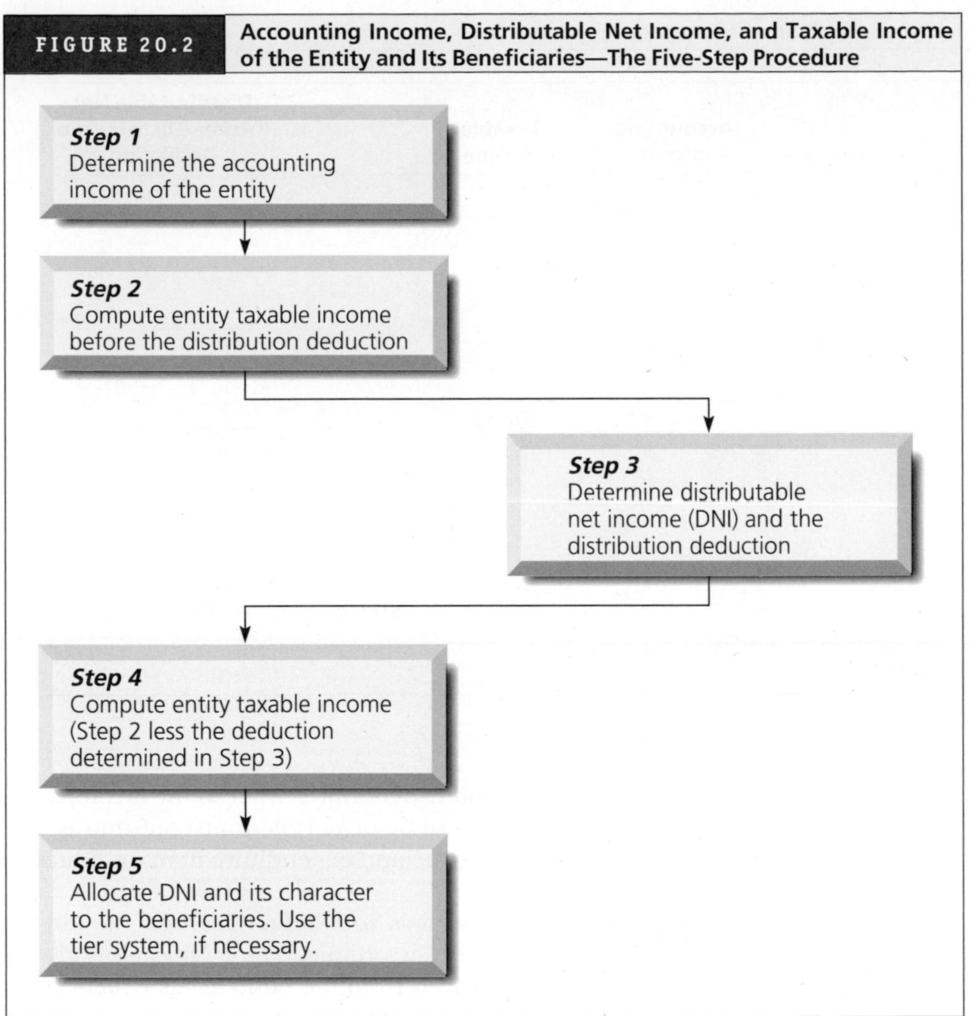
Step 1
Determine the accounting income of the entity
Step 2
Compute entity taxable income before the distribution deduction
Step 3
Determine distributable net income (DNI) and the distribution deduction
Step 4
Compute entity taxable income (Step 2 less the deduction determined in Step 3)
Step 5
Allocate DNI and its character to the beneficiaries. Use the tier system, if necessary.

income of these entities. Figure 20.2 illustrates the procedure implied by the Code, and Figure 20.3 presents a systematic computation method to be followed in this chapter.

ENTITY ACCOUNTING INCOME

The first step in determining the taxable income of a trust or estate is to compute the entity's accounting income for the period. Although this prerequisite is not apparent from a cursory reading of Subchapter J, a closer look at the Code reveals a number of references to the *income* of the entity.[7] Wherever the term *income* is used in Subchapter J without some modifier (e.g., *gross* income or *taxable* income), the statute is referring to the accounting income of the trust or estate for the tax year.

A definition of entity accounting income is critical to understanding the Subchapter J computation of fiduciary taxable income. Under state law, entity accounting income is the amount that the income beneficiary of the trust or estate is eligible to receive from the entity. More importantly, the calculation of accounting income is virtually under the control of the grantor or decedent (through a properly drafted trust agreement or will). If the document has been drafted at arm's length, a court will enforce a fiduciary's good faith efforts to carry out the specified computation of accounting income.

Entity accounting income generally is defined by state laws that are derived from the Uniform Principal and Income Act (latest major revision issued in 1997). Most states have adopted some form of the Uniform Act, which essentially constitutes generally accepted accounting principles (GAAP) in the fiduciary tax setting.

[7]For example, see §§ 651(a)(1), 652(a), and 661(a)(1).

FIGURE 20.3 Computational Template Applying the Five-Step Procedure

Item	Totals	Accounting Income	Taxable Income		Distributable Net Income/Distribution Deduction
Income	____	____	____		
Income	____	____	____		
Expense	____	____	____		
Expense	____	____	____		
Personal exemption			____		
Accounting income/taxable income before the distribution deduction		____	____		
Exemption		*Step 1*	*Step 2*		
Corpus capital gain/loss					____
Net exempt income					____
Distributable net income					____
Distribution deduction			____	*Step 3*	
Entity taxable income			____	*Step 4*	

Beneficiary taxable income is addressed in ***Step 5.***

By allocating specific items of income and expenditure either to the income beneficiaries or to corpus, the desires of the grantor or decedent are put into effect. Table 20.4 shows typical assignments of revenue and expenditure items to fiduciary income or corpus.

Where the controlling document is silent as to whether an item should be assigned to income or corpus, state fiduciary law prevails. These allocations are an important determinant of the benefits received from the entity by its beneficiaries and the timing of those benefits.

EXAMPLE 4

The Arnold Trust is a simple trust. Mrs. Bennett is its sole beneficiary. In the current year, the trust earns $20,000 in taxable interest and $15,000 in tax-exempt interest. In addition, the trust recognizes an $8,000 long-term capital gain. The trustee assesses a fee of $11,000 for the year. If the trust agreement allocates fees and capital gains to corpus, trust accounting income is $35,000, and Mrs. Bennett receives that amount. Thus, the income beneficiary receives no immediate benefit from the trust's capital gain, and she bears none of the financial burden of the fiduciary's fees.

Interest income	$35,000
Long-term capital gain	± –0–*
Fiduciary's fees	± –0–*
Trust accounting income	$35,000

*Allocable to corpus. ■

EXAMPLE 5

Assume the same facts as in Example 4, except that the trust agreement allocates the fiduciary's fees to income. The trust accounting income is $24,000, and Mrs. Bennett receives that amount.

Interest income	$35,000
Long-term capital gain	± –0–*
Fiduciary's fees	–11,000
Trust accounting income	$24,000

*Allocable to corpus. ■

TABLE 20.4 Common Allocations of Items to Income or Corpus

Allocable to Income	Allocable to Corpus
Ordinary and operating net income from trust assets	Depreciation on business assets
Interest, dividend, rent, and royalty income	Casualty gain/loss on income-producing assets
Stock dividends	Insurance recoveries on income-producing assets
One-half of fiduciary fees/commissions	Capital gain/loss on investment assets
	Stock splits
	One-half of fiduciary fees/commissions

EXAMPLE 6

Assume the same facts as in Example 4, except that the trust agreement allocates to income all capital gains and losses and one-half of the trustee's commissions. The trust accounting income is $37,500, and Mrs. Bennett receives that amount.

Interest income	$35,000
Long-term capital gain	+8,000
Fiduciary's fees	−5,500*
Trust accounting income	$37,500

*One-half allocable to corpus. ■

GROSS INCOME

The gross income of an estate or trust is similar to that of an individual. In determining the gain or loss to be recognized by an estate or trust upon the sale or other taxable disposition of assets, the rules for basis determination are similar to those applicable to other taxpayers. Thus, an estate's basis for property received from a decedent is stepped up or stepped down to the gross estate valuation (refer to Chapter 19 for a more detailed discussion). Property received as a gift (the usual case in trust arrangements) usually takes the donor's basis. Property purchased by the trust from a third party is assigned a basis equal to the purchase price.

Property Distributions

In general, the entity does not recognize gain or loss upon its distribution of property to a beneficiary under the provisions of the will or trust document. The distributed property has the same basis to the beneficiary of the distribution as it did to the estate or trust. Moreover, the distribution absorbs distributable net income (DNI) and qualifies for a distribution deduction (both of which are explained later in this chapter) to the extent of the lesser of the distributed asset's basis to the beneficiary or the asset's fair market value as of the distribution date.[8]

EXAMPLE 7
THE BIG PICTURE

Return to the facts of *The Big Picture* on p. 20-2. Assume that Anna has established the Jiang Family Trust. The trust distributes a painting, basis of $40,000 and fair market value of $90,000, to beneficiary Sally. Sally's basis in the painting is $40,000. The distribution absorbs $40,000 of the Jiang Trust's DNI, and the trust claims a $40,000 distribution deduction relative to the transaction. ■

[8] § 643(e).

EXAMPLE 8
THE BIG PICTURE

Assume the same facts as in Example 7, except that the Jiang Trust's basis in the painting is $100,000. Sally's basis in the painting is $100,000. The distribution absorbs $90,000 of the Jiang Trust's DNI, and the trust claims a $90,000 distribution deduction. ■

A trustee or executor can elect to recognize gain or loss with respect to all of its in-kind property distributions for the year. If the election is made, the beneficiary's basis in the asset is equal to the asset's fair market value as of the distribution date. The distribution absorbs DNI and qualifies for a distribution deduction to the extent of the asset's fair market value. However, the related-party rules can restrict an estate's or trust's deduction for such losses. Generally, related parties include a trust, its trustee, its grantor, and its beneficiaries, as well as an estate, its executor, and its beneficiaries.

EXAMPLE 9

The Green Estate distributes an antique piano, basis to Green of $10,000 and fair market value of $15,000, to beneficiary Kyle. The executor elects that Green recognize the related $5,000 gain on the distribution. Accordingly, Kyle's basis in the piano is $15,000 ($10,000 basis to Green + $5,000 gain recognized). Without the election, Green would not recognize any gain, and Kyle's basis in the piano would be $10,000. ■

EXAMPLE 10

Assume the same facts as in Example 9, except that Green's basis in the piano is $18,000. The executor elects that Green recognize the related $3,000 loss on the distribution. Accordingly, Kyle's basis in the piano is $15,000 ($18,000 − $3,000). Without the election, Green would not recognize any loss, and Kyle's basis in the piano would be $18,000.

The estate cannot deduct this loss, however. Because an estate and its beneficiaries are related parties, realized losses cannot be recognized immediately.[9] The loss could be recognized if Kyle later sells the piano to a stranger. ■

Income in Respect of a Decedent

The gross income of a trust or estate includes **income in respect of a decedent (IRD)** that the entity received.[10] For a cash basis decedent, IRD includes accrued salary, interest, rent, and other income items that were not constructively received before death. For both cash and accrual basis decedents, IRD includes, for instance, death benefits from qualified retirement plans and deferred compensation contracts.

The tax consequences of IRD can be summarized as follows.

- The fair market value of the right to IRD on the appropriate valuation date is included in the decedent's gross estate. Thus, it is subject to the Federal estate tax.[11]
- The decedent's basis in the property carries over to the recipient (the estate or heirs). There is no step-up or step-down in the basis of IRD items.
- The recipient of the income recognizes gain or loss, measured by the difference between the amount realized and the adjusted basis of the IRD in the hands of the decedent. The character of the gain or loss depends upon the treatment that it would have received had it been realized by the decedent before death. Thus, if the decedent would have realized capital gain, the recipient must do likewise.
- Expenses related to the IRD (such as interest, taxes, and depletion) that properly were not reported on the final income tax return of the decedent may be claimed by the recipient. These items are known as **expenses in respect of a decedent**.

[9] § 267(b)(13).

[10] § 691 and the Regulations thereunder. The concept of IRD was introduced in Chapter 19.

[11] To mitigate the effect of double taxation (imposition of both the estate tax and the income tax), § 691(c) allows the recipient an income tax deduction for the incremental estate tax attributable to the net IRD. For individual recipients, this is an itemized deduction, not subject to the 2%-of-AGI floor.

TAX *in* *the NEWS*

A Trend toward Dynasty Trusts

In a continuing attempt to discourage tax-motivated income shifting among family members, steep income tax rates on estates and trusts are also being seen at the state level. Although a few states (e.g., Alaska, Nevada, Texas, and Washington) do not impose any income tax on fiduciary entities, those that do are tending to increase their rates as part of their efforts to solve budget deficit woes.

Other states, however, have relaxed some of the rules that affect trusts. In such cases the objectives are to attract dollars to the state and to expand opportunities for attorneys, tax advisers, and other professionals who create and administer the entities.

One current development might be traced to the existence of the generation-skipping tax (GST), discussed in Chapter 18. After that tax was enacted, wealthy individuals and their advisers convinced about half of the states to allow a trust to survive for hundreds of years or indefinitely, by modifying the time-honored limitation of the "rule against perpetuities" (i.e., a life in being plus 21 years).

If a trust can survive for a long period of time, without making distributions or terminations that cause the GST, trust corpus can grow in a steady and tax-free manner. Wealthy individuals use these "dynasty trusts" as a form of inheritance, and many states also allow the trust assets to be protected from claims of the grantor's creditors.

Dynasty trusts operate like growth stocks. They minimize income distributions by investing profits and new capital in the family businesses, artwork, and multiple homes for the beneficiaries. The trust holds the title to these hard assets so that there is no income, gift, generation-skipping, or estate tax when younger generations take possession.

Some wealthy individuals do not want their children to have access to so much wealth that they never will need to work. Dynasty trusts can be used to accomplish this result.

Typically, such expenses also include fiduciary fees, commissions paid to dispose of estate assets, and state income taxes payable. They are deductible for both Federal estate and income tax purposes, *for* or *from* adjusted gross income (AGI) as would have been the case for the decedent.

- If the IRD item would have created an AMT preference or adjustment for the decedent (e.g., with respect to the collection of certain tax-exempt interest by the entity), an identical AMT item is created for the recipient.

EXAMPLE 11

Amanda died on July 13 of the current year. On August 2, the estate received a check (before deductions) for $1,200 from Amanda's former employer; this was Amanda's compensation for the last pay period of her life. On November 23, the estate received a $45,000 distribution from the qualified profit sharing plan of Amanda's employer, the full amount to which Amanda was entitled under the plan. Both Amanda and the estate are calendar year, cash basis taxpayers.

The last salary payment and the profit sharing plan distribution constitute IRD to the estate. Amanda had earned these items during her lifetime, and the estate had an enforceable right to receive each of them after Amanda's death. Consequently, the gross estate includes $46,200 with respect to these two items. However, the income tax basis to the estate for these items is not stepped up (from zero to $1,200 and $45,000, respectively) upon distribution to the estate.

The estate must report gross income of $46,200 for the current tax year with respect to the IRD items. The gain recognized upon the receipt of the IRD is $46,200 [$1,200 + $45,000 (amounts realized) − $0 (adjusted bases)]. ■

Including the IRD in both the taxpayer's gross estate and the gross income of the estate may seem harsh. Nevertheless, the tax consequences of IRD are similar to the treatment that applies to all of a taxpayer's earned income. The item is subject to income tax upon receipt, and to the extent that it is not consumed by the taxpayer before death, it is included in the gross estate.

EXAMPLE 12

Assume the same facts as in Example 11, except that Amanda is an accrual basis taxpayer. IRD now includes only the $45,000 distribution from the qualified retirement plan. Amanda's last paycheck is included in the gross income of her own last return (January 1 through date of death). The $1,200 salary is already properly recognized

TAX in the NEWS

COORDINATE YOUR DEDUCTIONS

The deduction under § 691(c) may be one of the more obscure provisions of the tax law, but its benefits can add up fast. The deduction is allowed on the tax return of the recipient of income in respect of a decedent (IRD). IRD often is received by the estate of the decedent or a trust that he or she created under the will or during lifetime. The deduction is for the Federal estate tax attributable to the IRD item. For an individual, it is a miscellaneous itemized deduction *not* subject to the 2 percent-of-AGI floor.

Because IRD often includes the value of the survivorship feature on pensions and other retirement plans and assets, the amount subject to the estate tax can be quite high. Thus, when computing the current-year income tax for the IRD recipient, the § 691(c) deduction can be extremely valuable in offsetting the IRD received.

For instance, suppose that a decedent's IRA balance generates $450,000 in attributable estate tax. If the recipient of the IRA takes the net-of-tax distribution in one year, the § 691(c) deduction shelters $450,000 in gross income and may be worth over $150,000 in Federal income taxes saved.

But taking the § 691(c) deduction is more complex than it looks. Because different tax advisers often prepare the Form 706 for the estate and the Form 1040 or 1041 for the IRD recipient, the § 691(c) deduction can get lost altogether or at least be miscomputed. When the IRD is paid out over several years, computing the § 691(c) deduction can become complex. And some tax professionals do not know the law well enough to track down the deduction, while tax software and IRS forms and publications say relatively little about it.

under Amanda's usual method of tax accounting. It does not constitute IRD and is not gross income when received by the executor. ■

EXAMPLE 13

Assume the same facts as in Example 11. Amanda's last paycheck was reduced by $165 for state income taxes that were withheld by the employer. The $165 tax payment is an expense in respect of a decedent and is allowed as a deduction on *both* Amanda's estate tax return *and* the estate's income tax return. ■

ORDINARY DEDUCTIONS

As a general rule, the taxable income of an estate or trust is similar to that of an individual.[12] Deductions are allowed for ordinary and necessary expenses paid or incurred in carrying on a trade or business; for the production or collection of income; for the management, conservation, or maintenance of property; and in connection with the determination, collection, or refund of any tax.[13] Reasonable administration expenses, including fiduciary fees and litigation costs in connection with the duties of administration, also can be deductible.

Expenses attributable to the production or collection of tax-exempt income are not deductible.[14] The amount of the disallowed deduction is found by using a formula based upon the composition of the income elements of entity accounting income for the year of the deduction. The § 212 deduction is apportioned without regard to the accounting income allocation of such expenses to income or to corpus. The deductibility of the fees is determined strictly by the Code (under §§ 212 and 265), and the allocation of expenditures to income and to corpus is controlled by the trust agreement or will or by state law.

EXAMPLE 14

The Silver Trust operates a business and invests idle cash in marketable securities. Its sales proceeds for the current year are $180,000. Expenses for wages, cost of sales, and office administration are $80,000. Interest income recognized is $20,000 from taxable bonds and $50,000 from tax-exempt bonds. The trustee claims a $35,000 fee for its activities. According to the trust agreement, $30,000 of this amount is allocated to the income beneficiaries and $5,000 is allocated to corpus.

[12] § 641(b).

[13] §§ 162 and 212.

[14] § 265.

Sales income	$180,000
Cost of sales	−80,000
Interest income ($50,000 is exempt)	+70,000
Fiduciary's fees, as allocated	−30,000
Trust accounting income	$140,000

The sales proceeds are included in the gross income of the trust under § 61. The costs associated with the business are deductible in full under § 162. The taxable income is included in Silver's gross income under § 61, but the tax-exempt income is excluded under § 103. The fiduciary's fees are deductible by Silver under § 212, but a portion of the deduction is lost because § 265 prohibits deductions for expenses incurred in the generation of tax-exempt income.

Specifically, 50/250 of the fees of $35,000 can be traced to tax-exempt income, so $7,000 of the fees is nondeductible. For purposes of the computation, only the income elements of the year's trust accounting income are included in the denominator. Moreover, the allocation of portions of the fees to income and to corpus is irrelevant in the calculation. The disallowed deduction for fiduciary's fees is computed in the following manner.

$$\$35{,}000^{*}\text{(total fees paid)} \times \frac{\$50{,}000^{**}\ (\textit{exempt}\text{ income elements of trust accounting income})}{\$250{,}000^{**}\ (\textit{all}\text{ income elements of trust accounting income})}$$

$$= \$7{,}000 \text{ (amount disallowed)}$$

*All of the fees, and not just those that are allocated to income, are deductible by the trust under § 212.

The numerator and denominator of this fraction are ***not* reduced by expense items allocable to income (e.g., cost of sales). ■

Under § 642(g), amounts deductible as administration expenses or losses for estate tax purposes (under §§ 2053 and 2054) cannot be claimed by the estate for income tax purposes, unless the estate files a waiver of the estate tax deduction. Although these expenses cannot be deducted twice, they may be allocated as the fiduciary sees fit between Forms 706 and 1041; they need not be claimed in their entirety on either return.[15] As discussed earlier, the prohibition against double deductions does not extend to expenses in respect of a decedent.

Trusts and estates are allowed cost recovery deductions. However, such deductions are assigned proportionately among the recipients of the entity accounting income.[16]

EXAMPLE 15

Lisa and Martin are the equal income beneficiaries of the Needle Trust. Under the terms of the trust agreement, the trustee has complete discretion as to the timing of the distributions from Needle's current accounting income. The trust agreement allocates all depreciation expense to income. In the current year, the trustee distributes 40% of the current trust accounting income to Lisa and 40% to Martin; thus, 20% of the income is accumulated. The depreciation deduction allowable to Needle is $100,000. This deduction is allocated among the trust and its beneficiaries on the basis of the distribution of current accounting income: Lisa and Martin each can claim a $40,000 deduction, and the trust can deduct $20,000. ■

EXAMPLE 16

Assume the same facts as in Example 15, except that the trust agreement allocates all depreciation expense to corpus. Lisa and Martin both still claim a $40,000 depreciation deduction, and Needle retains its $20,000 deduction. The Code assigns the depreciation deduction proportionately to the recipients of entity accounting income. Allocation of

[15] Reg. § 1.642(g)–2.

[16] §§ 167(h) and 611(b)(3) and (4).

depreciation to income or to corpus is irrelevant in determining which party can properly claim the deduction. ■

When a trust sells property received by transfer from the grantor, the amount of depreciation subject to recapture includes the depreciation claimed by the grantor before the transfer of the property to the trust. However, depreciation recapture potential disappears at death.

EXAMPLE 17

Jaime transferred an asset to the Shoulder Trust via a lifetime gift. The asset's total depreciation recapture potential was $40,000. If Shoulder sells the asset at a gain, ordinary income not to exceed $40,000 is recognized by the trust. Had Jaime transferred the asset after his death to his estate through a bequest, the $40,000 recapture potential would have disappeared. ■

If a trust or estate operates a trade or business, the entity may be eligible for the domestic production activities deduction (DPAD).[17] Computation of qualified production activities income (QPAI) is made at the entity level. Each beneficiary receives, as a pass-through from the entity, his or her share of QPAI and the W–2 wages paid, based on the proportion of entity accounting income received. The DPAD then can be claimed at the beneficiary level. In the case of an individual beneficiary, the DPAD is subject to the modified AGI limitation. See Chapter 3 for further discussion of the DPAD.

DEDUCTIONS FOR LOSSES

An estate or trust is allowed a deduction for casualty or theft losses that are not covered by insurance or other arrangements. Such losses may also be deductible by an estate for Federal tax purposes under § 2054. As a result, an estate is not allowed an income tax deduction unless the estate tax deduction is waived.[18]

The net operating loss (NOL) deduction is available for estates and trusts (i.e., where trade or business income is generated). The carryback of an NOL may reduce the distributable net income of the trust or estate for the carryback year and therefore affect the amount taxed to the beneficiaries for that year.

Except for the possibility of unused losses in the year of termination (discussed later in the chapter), the net capital losses of an estate or trust are used only on the fiduciary income tax return. The tax treatment of these losses is the same as for individual taxpayers.

CHARITABLE CONTRIBUTIONS

An estate or complex trust is allowed a deduction for contributions to charitable organizations under certain conditions.

- The contribution is made pursuant to the will or trust instrument, and its amount is determinable using the language of that document.
- The recipient is a qualified organization. For this purpose, qualified organizations include the same charities for which individual and corporate donors are allowed deductions, except that estates and trusts are permitted a deduction for contributions to certain foreign charitable organizations.
- Generally, the contribution is claimed in the tax year it is paid, but a fiduciary can treat amounts paid in the year immediately following as a deduction for the preceding year.[19] Under this rule, estates and complex trusts receive more liberal treatment than individuals or C corporations.

[17]§ 199(d)(1).

[18]See Reg. § 1.642(g)–1 for requirements as to the statement waiving the estate tax deduction. In addition, see Reg. §§ 1.165–7(c) and 1.165–8(b), requiring that a statement be filed to allow an income tax deduction for such losses.

[19]§ 642(c)(1) and Reg. § 1.642(c)–1(b).

Unlike the charitable contribution deductions of individuals and corporations, the deductions of estates and complex trusts are not limited (e.g., to a percentage of taxable or adjusted gross income). Nonetheless, an entity's charitable contribution may not be fully deductible. Specifically, the deduction is limited to amounts included in the gross income of the entity in the year of the contribution.[20] A contribution is deemed to have been made proportionately from each of the income elements of entity accounting income. However, if the will or trust agreement requires that the contribution be made from a specific type of income or from the current income from a specified asset, the allocation of the contribution to taxable and tax-exempt income will not be required.

EXAMPLE 18
THE BIG PICTURE

Return to the facts of *The Big Picture* on p. 20-2. Again assume that Anna has established the Jiang Family Trust. The trust has 2011 gross rent income of $80,000, expenses attributable to the rents of $60,000, and tax-exempt interest from state bonds of $20,000. Under the trust agreement, the trustee is to pay 30% of the annual trust accounting income to the United Way, a qualifying organization. Accordingly, the trustee pays $12,000 to the charity in 2012 (i.e., 30% × $40,000). The charitable contribution deduction allowed for 2011 is $9,600 [($80,000/$100,000) × $12,000]. ■

EXAMPLE 19
THE BIG PICTURE

Assume the same facts as in Example 18, except that the trust instrument also requires that the contribution be paid from the net rent income. The agreement controls, and the allocation formula need not be applied. The entire $12,000 is allowed as a charitable deduction. ■

DEDUCTION FOR DISTRIBUTIONS TO BENEFICIARIES

LO.3

Illustrate the uses and implications of distributable net income.

The modified pass-through approach of Subchapter J is embodied in the deduction allowed to trusts and estates for the distributions made to beneficiaries during the year. Some portion of any distribution that a beneficiary receives from a trust may be subject to income tax on the beneficiary's own return. At the same time, the distributing entity is allowed a deduction for some or all of the distribution. Consequently, the modified pass-through principle of Subchapter J is implemented. A good analogy is to the taxability of corporate profits distributed to employees as taxable wages. The corporation is allowed a deduction for the payment, but the employee receives gross income in the form of compensation.

A critical value that is used in computing the amount of the entity's distribution deduction is **distributable net income (DNI)**. As it is defined in Subchapter J, DNI serves several functions.

- DNI is the maximum amount of the distribution on which the beneficiaries can be taxed.[21]
- DNI is the maximum amount that the entity can use as a distribution deduction for the year.[22]
- The makeup of DNI carries over to the beneficiaries (the items of income and expenses retain their DNI character in the hands of the distributees).[23]

Subchapter J defines DNI in a circular manner, however. The DNI value is necessary to determine the entity's distribution deduction and therefore its taxable income for the year. Nonetheless, the Code defines DNI as a modification of the entity's taxable income itself. Using the systematic approach to determining the taxable income of the entity and its beneficiaries, as shown earlier in Figure 20.2, first

[20] Reg. §§ 1.642(c)–3(b) and (c).
[21] §§ 652(a) and 662(a).
[22] §§ 651(b) and 661(c).
[23] §§ 652(b) and 662(b).

compute *taxable income before the distribution deduction,* modify that amount to determine DNI and the distribution deduction, return to the calculation of *taxable income,* and apply the deduction that has resulted.

Taxable income before the distribution deduction includes all of the entity's items of gross income, deductions, gains, losses, and exemptions for the year. Therefore, to compute this amount, (1) determine the appropriate personal exemption for the year and (2) account for all of the other gross income and deductions of the entity.

The next step in Figure 20.2 is the determination of *distributable net income,* computed by making the following adjustments to the entity's *taxable income before the distribution deduction.*[24]

- Add back the personal exemption.
- Add back *net* tax-exempt interest. To arrive at this amount, reduce the total tax-exempt interest by charitable contributions and by related expenses not deductible under § 265.
- Add back the entity's net capital losses.
- Subtract any net capital gains allocable to corpus. In other words, the only net capital gains included in DNI are those attributable to income beneficiaries or to charitable contributions.

Since taxable income before the distribution deduction is computed by deducting all of the expenses of the entity (whether they were allocated to income or to corpus), DNI is reduced by expenses that are allocated to corpus. The effect is to reduce the taxable income of the income beneficiaries. The actual distributions to the beneficiaries exceed DNI because the distributions are not reduced by expenses allocated to corpus. Aside from this shortcoming of Subchapter J, DNI offers a good approximation of the current-year economic income available for distribution to the entity's income beneficiaries.

DNI includes the net tax-exempt interest income of the entity, so that amount must be removed from DNI in computing the distribution deduction. Moreover, for estates and complex trusts, the amount actually distributed during the year may include discretionary distributions of income and distributions of corpus permissible under the will or trust instrument. Thus, the distribution deduction for estates and complex trusts is computed as the lesser of (1) the deductible portion of DNI or (2) the taxable amount actually distributed to the beneficiaries during the year. For a simple trust, however, full distribution is always assumed, relative to both the entity and its beneficiaries, in a manner similar to the pass-through entities.

EXAMPLE 20

The Zinc Trust is a simple trust. Because of severe liquidity problems, its 2011 accounting income is not distributed to its sole beneficiary, Mark, until early in 2012. Zinc still is allowed a full distribution deduction for, and Mark still is taxable upon, the entity's 2011 income in 2011. ■

EXAMPLE 21

The Pork Trust is required to distribute its current accounting income annually to its sole income beneficiary, Barbara. Capital gains and losses and all other expenses are allocable to corpus. In the current year, Pork incurs the following items.

Dividend income	$25,000
Taxable interest income	15,000
Tax-exempt interest income	20,000
Net long-term capital gains	10,000
Fiduciary's fees	6,000

[24]These and other (less common) adjustments are detailed in § 643.

Item	**Totals**	**Accounting Income**		**Taxable Income**	**Distributable Net Income/ Distribution Deduction**
Dividend income	$25,000	$25,000		$ 25,000	
Taxable interest income	15,000	15,000		15,000	
Exempt interest income	20,000	20,000			
Net long-term capital gain	10,000			10,000	
Fiduciary fees	6,000			(4,000)	
Personal exemption				(300)	
Accounting income/ taxable income before the distribution deduction		$60,000		$ 45,700	$ 45,700
		Step 1		*Step 2*	
Exemption					300
Corpus capital gain/loss					(10,000)
Net exempt income					18,000
Distributable net income					$ 54,000
Distribution deduction			*Step 3*	(36,000)	
Entity taxable income			*Step 4*	$ 9,700	

Step 1. Trust accounting income is $60,000; this includes the tax-exempt interest income, but not the fees or the capital gains, pursuant to the trust document. Barbara receives $60,000 from the trust for the current year.

Step 2. Taxable income before the distribution deduction is computed as directed by the Code. The tax-exempt interest is excluded under § 103. Only a portion of the fees is deductible because some of the fees are traceable to the tax-exempt income. The trust claims a $300 personal exemption as it is required to distribute its annual trust accounting income.

Step 3. DNI and the distribution deduction reflect the required adjustments. The distribution deduction is the lesser of the distributed amount ($60,000) or the deductible portion of DNI ($54,000 – $18,000 net exempt income).

Step 4. Finally, return to the computation of the taxable income of the Pork Trust. A simple test should be applied at this point to assure that the proper figure for the trust's taxable income has been determined. On what is Pork to be taxed? Pork has distributed to Barbara all of its gross income except the $10,000 net long-term capital gains. The $300 personal exemption reduces taxable income to $9,700. ■

EXAMPLE 22

The Quick Trust is required to distribute all of its current accounting income equally to its two beneficiaries, Faith and the Universal Church, a qualifying charitable organization. Capital gains and losses and depreciation expenses are allocable to income. Fiduciary fees are allocable to corpus. In the current year, Quick incurs various items as indicated.

Item	**Totals**	**Accounting Income**	**Taxable Income**	**Distributable Net Income/ Distribution Deduction**
Rent income	$100,000	$100,000	$100,000	
Expenses—rent income	30,000	(30,000)	(30,000)	
Depreciation—rent income	15,000	(15,000)		
Net long-term capital gain	20,000	20,000	20,000	
Charitable contribution			(37,500)	
Fiduciary fees	18,000		(18,000)	
Personal exemption			(300)	

Item	Totals	Accounting Income		Taxable Income	Distributable Net Income/ Distribution Deduction
Accounting income/taxable income before the distribution deduction		$ 75,000		$ 34,200	$34,200
		Step 1		*Step 2*	
Exemption					300
Corpus capital gain/loss					
Net exempt income					
Distributable net income					$34,500
Distribution deduction			*Step 3*	(34,500)	
Entity taxable income			*Step 4*	($ 300)	

Step 1. Trust accounting income of $75,000 reflects the indicated allocations of items to income and to corpus. Each income beneficiary receives $37,500.

Step 2. In the absence of tax-exempt income, a deduction is allowed for the full amount of the fiduciary's fees. Quick is a complex trust, but since it is required to distribute its full accounting income annually, a $300 exemption is allowed. The trust properly does not deduct any depreciation for the rental property. The depreciation deduction is available only to the recipients of the entity's accounting income for the period. Thus, the deduction is split equally between Faith and the church. The deduction probably is of no direct value to the church, a tax-exempt organization. The trust's charitable contribution deduction is based upon the $37,500 that the charity actually received (one-half of trust accounting income).

Step 3. As there is no tax-exempt income, the only adjustment needed to compute DNI is to add back the trust's personal exemption. Subchapter J requires no adjustment for the charitable contribution. DNI is computed only from the perspective of Faith, who also received $37,500 from the trust.

Step 4. Perform the simple test (referred to above) to assure that the proper taxable income for the Quick Trust has been computed. All of the trust's gross income has been distributed to Faith and the charity. As is the case with most trusts that distribute all of their accounting income, the Quick Trust "wastes" the personal exemption. ■

TAX CREDITS

An estate or trust may claim the foreign tax credit to the extent that it is not passed through to the beneficiaries.[25] Similarly, other credits are apportioned between the estate or trust and the beneficiaries on the basis of the entity accounting income allocable to each.

20.4 Taxation of Beneficiaries

The beneficiaries of an estate or trust receive taxable income from the entity under the modified pass-through principle of Subchapter J. Distributable net income determines the maximum amount that can be taxed to the beneficiaries for any tax year. The constitution of DNI also carries over to the beneficiaries (e.g., net long-term capital gains and dividends retain their character when they are distributed from the entity to the beneficiary).

[25] §§ 642(a)(1) and 901.

The timing of any tax consequences to the beneficiary of a trust or estate presents a problem only when the parties involved use different tax years. A beneficiary includes in gross income an amount based upon the DNI of the trust for any taxable year or years of the entity ending with or within his or her taxable year.[26]

EXAMPLE 23

An estate uses a fiscal year ending on March 31 for tax purposes. Its sole income beneficiary is a calendar year taxpayer. For calendar year 2011, the beneficiary reports the income assignable to her for the entity's fiscal year April 1, 2010, to March 31, 2011. If the estate is terminated by December 31, 2011, the beneficiary also includes any trust income assignable to her for the short year. This could result in a bunching of income in 2011. ■

DISTRIBUTIONS BY SIMPLE TRUSTS

The amount taxable to the beneficiaries of a simple trust is limited by the trust's DNI. However, since DNI includes net tax-exempt income, the amount included in the gross income of the beneficiaries could be less than DNI. When there is more than one income beneficiary, the elements of DNI are apportioned ratably according to the amount required to be distributed currently to each.

EXAMPLE 24

A simple trust has ordinary income of $40,000, a long-term capital gain of $15,000 (allocable to corpus), and a trustee commission expense of $4,000 (payable from corpus). The two income beneficiaries, Allie and Bart, are entitled to the trust's annual accounting income, based on shares of 75% and 25%, respectively.

Although Allie receives $30,000 as her share (75% × trust accounting income of $40,000), she is allocated DNI of only $27,000 (75% × $36,000). Likewise, Bart is entitled to receive $10,000 (25% × $40,000), but he is allocated DNI of only $9,000 (25% × $36,000). The $15,000 capital gain is taxed to the trust. ■

DISTRIBUTIONS BY ESTATES AND COMPLEX TRUSTS

Typically, an estate or complex trust makes only discretionary distributions. In those cases, the DNI is apportioned ratably according to the distributed amounts.

A computational problem arises with estates and complex trusts when more than one beneficiary receives a distribution from the entity and the controlling document does not require a distribution of the entire accounting income of the entity.

EXAMPLE 25

The trustee of the Wilson Trust has the discretion to distribute the income or corpus of the trust in any proportion between the two beneficiaries of the trust, Wong and Washington. Under the trust instrument, Wong must receive $15,000 from the trust every year. In the current year, the trust's accounting income is $50,000, and its DNI is $40,000. The trustee pays $15,000 to Wong and $25,000 to Washington. ■

How is Wilson's DNI to be divided between Wong and Washington? Several arbitrary methods of allocating DNI between the beneficiaries could be devised. Subchapter J resolves the problem by creating a two-tier system to govern the taxation of beneficiaries in such situations.[27] The tier system determines which distributions will be included in the gross income of the beneficiaries in full, which will be included in part, and which will not be included at all.

Income that is required to be distributed currently, whether or not it is distributed, is categorized as a *first-tier distribution.* All other amounts properly paid, credited, or required to be distributed are *second-tier distributions.*[28] A formula is used to

[26]§§ 652(c) and 662(c).
[27]§§ 662(a)(1) and (2).
[28]Reg. §§ 1.662(a)–2 and –3.

allocate DNI among the appropriate beneficiaries when only first-tier distributions are made and those amounts exceed DNI.

$$\frac{\text{First-tier distributions to the beneficiary}}{\text{First-tier distributions to all beneficiaries}} \times \text{Distributable net income} = \text{Beneficiary's share of distributable net income}$$

When both first-tier and second-tier distributions are made and the first-tier distributions exceed DNI, the above formula is applied to the first-tier distributions. In this case, none of the second-tier distributions are taxed, because all of the DNI has been allocated to the first-tier beneficiaries.

If both first-tier and second-tier distributions are made and the first-tier distributions do not exceed DNI, but the total of both first-tier and second-tier distributions does exceed DNI, the second-tier beneficiaries recognize income as shown below.

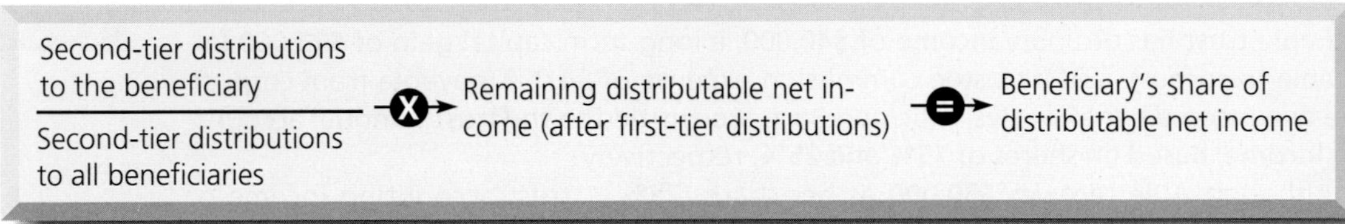

EXAMPLE 26

The trustee of the Gray Trust is required to distribute $10,000 per year to both Harriet and Wally, the two beneficiaries of the entity. In addition, he is empowered to distribute other amounts of trust income or corpus at his sole discretion. In the current year, the trust reports accounting income of $60,000 and DNI of $50,000. However, the trustee distributes only the required $10,000 each to Harriet and to Wally. The balance of the income is accumulated and added to trust corpus.

In this case, only first-tier distributions have been made, but the total amount of the distributions does not exceed DNI for the year. Although DNI is the maximum amount that is included by the beneficiaries for the year, they can include no more in gross income than is distributed by the entity. Thus, both Harriet and Wally may be subject to tax on $10,000 as their proportionate shares of DNI. ■

EXAMPLE 27

Assume the same facts as in Example 26, except that DNI is $12,000. Harriet and Wally each receive $10,000, but they cannot be taxed in total on more than DNI. Each is taxed on $6,000 [DNI $12,000 × ($10,000/$20,000 of the first-tier distributions)]. ■

EXAMPLE 28

Return to the facts in Example 25. Wong receives a first-tier distribution of $15,000. Second-tier distributions include $20,000 to Wong and $25,000 to Washington. Wilson's DNI is $40,000. The DNI is allocated between Wong and Washington as follows.

(1)	**First-tier distributions**	
	To Wong	$15,000 DNI
	To Washington	–0–
	Remaining DNI = $25,000	
(2)	**Second-tier distributions**	
	To Wong	$11,111 DNI [(20/45) × $25,000]
	To Washington	$13,889 DNI [(25/45) × $25,000]

■

EXAMPLE 29

Assume the same facts as in Example 28, except that accounting income is $80,000 and DNI is $70,000. DNI is allocated between Wong and Washington as follows.

(1)	**First-tier distributions**	
	To Wong	$15,000 DNI
	To Washington	–0–
	Remaining DNI = $55,000	
(2)	**Second-tier distributions**	
	To Wong	$20,000 DNI
	To Washington	$25,000 DNI ■

Separate Share Rule

For the sole purpose of determining the amount of DNI for a complex trust or estate with more than one beneficiary, the substantially separate and independent shares of different beneficiaries in the trust or estate are treated as *separate* trusts or estates.[29]

The separate share rule is designed to prevent the inequity that results if the corpus payments are treated under the regular rules applicable to second-tier beneficiaries. The rule also results in the availability of extra entity personal exemptions and in a greater use of lower entity tax brackets.

EXAMPLE 30

A trustee has the discretion to distribute or accumulate income on behalf of Greg and Hannah (in equal shares). The trustee also has the power to invade corpus for the benefit of either beneficiary to the extent of that beneficiary's one-half interest in the trust. For the current year, DNI is $10,000. Of this amount, $5,000 is distributed to Greg, and $5,000 is accumulated on behalf of Hannah. In addition, the trustee pays $20,000 from corpus to Greg.

Without the separate share rule, Greg is taxed on $10,000 (the full amount of the DNI). With the separate share rule, Greg is taxed on only $5,000 (his share of the DNI) and receives the $20,000 corpus distribution tax-free. The trust is taxed on Hannah's $5,000 share of the DNI that is accumulated. ■

CHARACTER OF INCOME

Consistent with the modified pass-through principle of Subchapter J, various classes of income (e.g., dividends, passive or portfolio gain and loss, AMT preferences, and tax-exempt interest) retain the same character for the beneficiaries that they had when they were received by the entity. If there are multiple beneficiaries *and* if all of the DNI is distributed, a problem arises in allocating the various classes of income among the beneficiaries.

Distributions are treated as consisting of the same proportion as the items that enter into the computation of DNI. This allocation does not apply, however, if local law or the governing instrument specifically allocates different classes of income to different beneficiaries.[30]

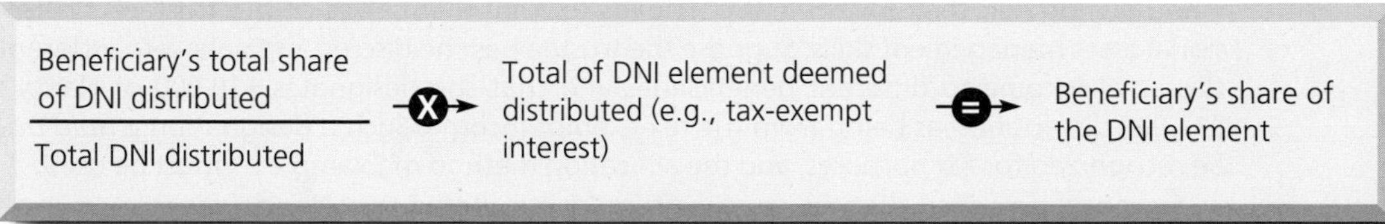

[29] § 663(c); Reg. § 1.663(c)–1(a).

[30] Reg. § 1.662(b)–1 seems to allow special allocations, but see *Harkness v. U.S.*, 72–2 USTC ¶9740, 30 AFTR 2d 72–5754, 469 F.2d 310 (Ct.Cls., 1972).

If the entity distributes only a part of its DNI, the amount of a specific class of DNI that is deemed distributed must first be determined.

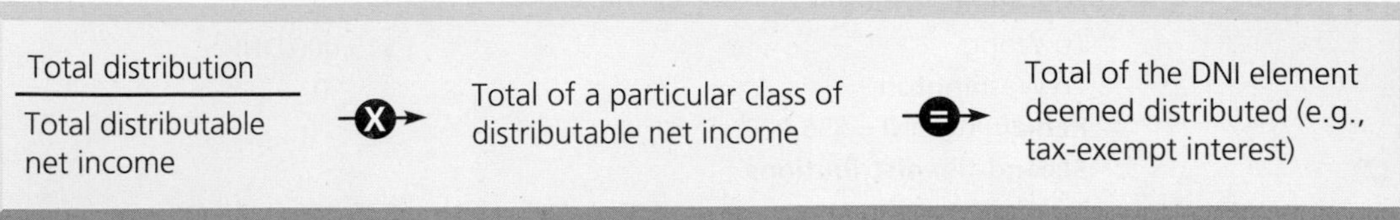

Total distribution
Total distributable net income
Total of a particular class of distributable net income
Total of the DNI element deemed distributed (e.g., tax-exempt interest)

EXAMPLE 31

The Baron Trust has DNI of $40,000, including the following: $10,000 of taxable interest, $10,000 of tax-exempt interest, and $20,000 of passive activity income. The trustee distributes, at her discretion, $8,000 to Mike and $12,000 to Nancy.

Beneficiary	Amount Received	Income Type: Taxable Interest	Exempt Interest	Passive Income
Mike	$ 8,000	$2,000*	$2,000	$4,000
Nancy	12,000	3,000	3,000	6,000

*$8,000 distribution/$40,000 total DNI × $10,000 taxable interest in DNI. ■

EXAMPLE 32

Continue with the facts of Example 31. The character of the income that flows through to Mike and Nancy is effective for all other tax purposes. For instance, the $2,000 exempt interest allocated to Mike is used in computing the taxable portion of any Social Security benefits Mike receives. If this exempt interest relates to bonds issued to fund nonessential activities of the issuing agency (and not issued during 2009 and 2010), Mike includes a $2,000 AMT preference on his current-year return.

The $4,000 passive activity income that is allocated to Mike is available for offset against passive losses that he has incurred from limited partnerships and rental activities for the year. Similarly, the $3,000 taxable interest income allocated to Nancy can be used to increase the amount of investment interest expense deductible by her in the year of the flow-through. The interest is treated as portfolio income to the same extent as that received directly by the taxpayer. ■

Special Allocations

Under limited circumstances, the parties may modify the character-of-income allocation method set forth above. A modification is permitted only to the extent that the allocation is required in the trust instrument and only to the extent that it has an economic effect independent of the cash-flow and income tax consequences of the allocation.[31]

EXAMPLE 33

Return to the facts in Example 31. Assume that the beneficiaries are elderly individuals who have pooled their investment portfolios to avail themselves of the trustee's professional asset management skills. Suppose the trustee has the discretion to allocate different classes of income to different beneficiaries and that she designates $10,000 of Nancy's $12,000 distribution as being from the tax-exempt income. Such a designation *would not be recognized* for tax purposes, and the allocation method of Example 31 must be used.

Suppose, however, that the trust instrument stipulated that Nancy was to receive all of the income from the tax-exempt securities because she alone contributed the exempt securities to trust corpus. Under this provision, the $10,000 of the nontaxable

[31] Reg. § 1.652(b)–2(b). This is similar to the § 704(b)(2) requirement for partnerships.

interest is paid to Nancy. This allocation *is recognized*, and $10,000 of Nancy's distribution is tax-exempt. ■

LOSSES IN THE TERMINATION YEAR

The ordinary net operating and capital losses of a trust or estate do not flow through to the entity's beneficiaries, as would such losses from a partnership or an S corporation. However, in the year in which an entity terminates its existence, the beneficiaries do receive a direct benefit from the loss carryovers of the trust or estate.[32]

Net operating losses and net capital losses are subject to the same carryover rules that otherwise apply to an individual. Consequently, NOLs can be carried back 2 years and then carried forward 20 years while net capital losses can be carried forward only, and for an indefinite period of time.

If the entity incurs a negative taxable income in the last year of its existence, the excess of deductions over the entity's gross income flows through directly to the beneficiaries. The net loss is available as a deduction *from* AGI in the beneficiary's tax year with or within which the entity's tax year ends. The amount allowed is in proportion to the relative amount of corpus assets that each beneficiary receives upon the termination of the entity, and it is subject to the 2-percent-of-AGI floor.

Any carryovers of the entity's other losses flow through to the beneficiaries in the year of termination in proportion to the relative amount of corpus assets that each beneficiary receives. The character of the loss carryover is retained by the beneficiary, except that a carryover of a net capital loss to a corporate beneficiary is always treated as short term. Beneficiaries who are individuals use these carryovers as deductions *for* AGI.

EXAMPLE 34

The Edgar Estate terminates on December 31, 2011. It had used a fiscal year ending July 31. For the termination year, the estate incurred a $15,000 negative taxable income. In addition, the estate had an unused NOL carryover of $23,000 from the year ending July 31, 2006, and an unused net long-term capital loss carryover of $10,000 from the year ending July 31, 2009. Dawn receives $60,000 of corpus upon termination, and Blue Corporation receives the remaining $40,000. Dawn and Blue are calendar year taxpayers.

Dawn can claim an itemized deduction of $9,000 [($60,000/$100,000) × $15,000] for the entity's negative taxable income in the year of termination. This deduction is subject to the 2%-of-AGI floor on her miscellaneous itemized deductions. In addition, Dawn can claim a $13,800 deduction *for* AGI in 2011 (60% × $23,000) for Edgar's NOL carryover, and she can use $6,000 of the estate's net long-term capital loss carryover with her other 2011 capital transactions.

Blue receives ordinary business deductions in 2011 for Edgar's NOLs: $6,000 for the loss in the year of termination and $9,200 for the carryover from fiscal 2006. Moreover, Blue can use the $4,000 carryover of Edgar's net capital losses to offset against its other 2011 capital transactions, although the loss must be treated as short term. ■

THE SIXTY-FIVE-DAY RULE

Amounts paid or credited to the beneficiaries in the first 65 days of the estate or trust's tax year may be treated as paid on the last day of the preceding taxable year.[33] This provision offers the trustee some flexibility in timing distributions so that entity-level accumulations can be avoided.

20.5 Grantor Trusts

LO.4

Use the special rules that apply to trusts where the creator (grantor) of the trust retains certain rights.

A series of special provisions applies when the grantor of the trust retains beneficial enjoyment or substantial control over the trust property or income.[34] In that event, the grantor is taxed on the trust income, and the trust is disregarded for income tax purposes. The person who is taxed on the income is allowed to claim, on his or her

[32] Reg. §§ 1.642(h)–1 and –2.

[33] See Reg. § 1.663(b)–2 for the manner and timing of the election.

[34] §§ 671–679.

TAX *in* *the NEWS*

Don't Trust Your Dictionary

Today, the middle and upper classes are often including trusts in their estate plans. Usually, the purpose of the trust is to spare the survivors the time and effort required to work through a state's probate proceedings.

But planning for death can sometimes lead to confusion about terminology, especially between a living trust and a living will. A "living trust" is typically created to hold the assets of the decedent-to-be, including investments, homestead, and household goods. Assets are retitled in the name of the trustee, who periodically files a Form 1041 for the new entity. The idea underlying the living trust is to reduce the probate estate. This, in turn, lowers the fees for carrying out the probate process. Such fees often total 5 percent or so of the date of death value of the probate assets.

The living trust accomplishes virtually no Federal tax savings. The trust assets are included in the decedent's gross estate, as the living trust is an incomplete transfer under §§ 2036 and 2038. For the most part, the entity is treated as a grantor trust. Because of the retained investment and distribution powers, the donor is still liable for taxes on the taxable income of the fiduciary.

A "living will," on the other hand, is a document that conveys powers to relatives and third parties to make medical and financial decisions when the decedent-to-be can no longer do so. More appropriately referred to as a "medical power of attorney," the document expresses the person's wishes as to how and when to reduce specified medical treatments (including directives for removing life support systems).

The proper use of these documents can become tricky under controlling state law when same-sex couples are involved. The adviser must assist the clients in determining whether a same-sex partner or spouse can qualify as the holder of a medical power of attorney, and whether special issues arise when a same-sex partner or spouse is named a trustee of a living trust.

own return, any deductions or credits attributable to the income. Such taxes restrict the grantor's ability to redirect the income recognized from trust corpus to the trust or its beneficiaries. The trustee still files a Form 1041, but no dollar amounts are included on the mostly "blank" return. All income and deduction items are reported on the grantor's Form 1040.

REVERSIONARY TRUSTS

Creation of virtually any new reversionary trust is subject to the Federal gift tax. If the grantor dies before the income interest expires, the present value of the reversionary interest is included in his or her gross estate; thus, a Federal estate tax could also result.

POWERS RETAINED BY THE GRANTOR

Other restrictions apply concerning the extent of the powers over the trust that the grantor can retain without incurring grantor trust status.[35] If any of these provisions is violated, the income of the trust is taxed to the grantor, and the usual Subchapter J rules do not apply to the trust.

The grantor is taxed on the income if he or she retains (1) the beneficial enjoyment of corpus or (2) the power to dispose of the trust income without the approval or consent of any adverse party. An *adverse party* is any person having a substantial beneficial interest in the trust who could be affected adversely by the power the grantor possesses over the trust assets.[36]

A number of important powers, including the following, will *not* cause such income to be taxed to the grantor.[37]

- To apply the income toward the support of the grantor's dependents (except to the extent that it actually is applied for this purpose).[38]

[35] §§ 674–677.

[36] §§ 672(a), (b), and 674. See Reg. § 1.672(a)–1 for examples of adverse party situations.

[37] § 674(b).

[38] § 677(b).

- To allocate trust income or corpus among charitable beneficiaries.
- To invade corpus on behalf of a designated beneficiary.
- To withhold income from a beneficiary during his or her minority or disability.
- To allocate receipts and disbursements between income and corpus.

The retention by the grantor or a nonadverse party of certain administrative powers over the trust causes the income to be taxed to the grantor. Such powers include those to deal with trust income or corpus for less than full and adequate consideration, and to borrow from the trust without providing adequate interest or security.[39]

The grantor of a trust is taxed on the trust's income if he or she (or a nonadverse party) possesses the power to revoke the trust.[40] In addition, a grantor is taxed on all or part of the income of a trust when, without the consent of any adverse party, the income is or, at the discretion of the grantor or a nonadverse party (or both), may be:

- Distributed to the grantor or the grantor's spouse.
- Held or accumulated for future distribution to the grantor or the grantor's spouse.
- Applied to the payment of premiums on insurance policies on the life of the grantor or the grantor's spouse.[41]

EXAMPLE 35

Frank creates an irrevocable trust for his children with a transfer of income-producing property and an insurance policy on the life of Marion, his wife. During the year, the trustee uses $3,000 of the trust income to pay the premiums on the policy covering Marion's life. Frank is taxed on $3,000 of the trust's income. ■

Moreover, trust income accumulated for the benefit of someone whom the grantor is *legally obligated* to support is taxed to the grantor but only to the extent that it is actually applied for that purpose.[42]

EXAMPLE 36

Melanie creates an irrevocable accumulation trust. Her son, Sean, is the life beneficiary, and the remainder goes to any grandchildren. During the year, the trust income of $8,000 is applied as follows: $5,000 toward Sean's college tuition and other related educational expenses and $3,000 accumulated on Sean's behalf. If, under state law, Melanie has an obligation to support Sean, and if this obligation includes providing a college education, Melanie is taxed on the $5,000 that is so applied. ■

20.6 Procedural Matters

The fiduciary is required to file a Form 1041 (U.S. Income Tax Return for Estates and Trusts) in the following situations.[43]

- For an estate that has gross income of $600 or more for the year.
- For a trust that either has any taxable income or, if there is no taxable income, has gross income of $600 or more.

The fiduciary return (and any related tax liability) is due, before extensions, no later than the fifteenth day of the fourth month following the close of the entity's

[39] See Reg. § 1.675–1(b) for a further discussion of this matter.

[40] § 676.

[41] § 677(a).

[42] § 677(b). The taxpayer's legal obligations vary according to state law, financial resources, and family expectations. See *Frederick C. Braun, Jr.*, 48 TCM 210, T.C.Memo. 1984–285, and *Cristopher Stone*, 54 TCM 462, T.C.Memo. 1987–454.

[43] §§ 6012(a)(3) and (4).

taxable year. The IRS encourages electronic filing of the Form 1041 and schedules. A paper return is filed with the Internal Revenue Service in Cincinnati or Ogden, Utah, depending on the location of the fiduciary's principal place of business.

Many fiduciary entities recognize capital gains during the year, through sales of assets that are part of corpus. In that event, a Schedule D is filed with the Form 1041, and the fiduciary entity or its beneficiaries can qualify for the favorable 15 percent (or lower) tax rate on long-term capital gains.

The pass-through of income and deduction items to the beneficiary is accomplished through Schedule K–1 to Form 1041. This form is similar in format and function to the Schedule K–1 for partners and S corporation shareholders (see Chapters 10 and 12). Since the fiduciary entity usually has only a few transactions during the year, the Schedule K–1 for Form 1041 is less detailed than those for Forms 1065 and 1120S. See the specimen Form 1041 and schedules in Appendix B to this text.

Trusts and estates are required to make estimated Federal income tax payments using the same quarterly schedule that applies to individual taxpayers. This requirement applies to estates and grantor trusts only for tax years that end two or more years after the date of the decedent's death. Charitable trusts and private foundations are exempt from estimated payment requirements altogether.[44]

The two-year estimated tax exception for estates recognizes the liquidity problems that an executor often faces during the early months of administering the estate. The exception does not assure, however, that an estate in existence less than 24 months will never be required to make an estimated tax payment.

EXAMPLE 37

Juanita died on March 15, 2011. Her executor elected a fiscal year ending on July 31 for the estate. Estimated tax payments will be required from the estate starting with the tax year that begins on August 1, 2012. ■

TAX PLANNING:

Many of the tax planning possibilities for estates and trusts were discussed in Chapter 19. However, several specific tax planning possibilities are available to help minimize the income tax effects on estates and trusts and their beneficiaries.

20.7 A Trust or Estate as an Income-Shifting Device

LO.5

Apply the Subchapter J rules in a manner that minimizes the income taxation of trusts and estates and still accomplishes the intended objectives of the grantor or decedent.

The compressed tax rate schedule applicable to Subchapter J entities may have reversed the traditional techniques by which families set aside funds for long-term activities, such as business startups, college education, and home purchases. When the tax rate schedules for trusts and estates were more accommodating, high-income individuals would shift income-producing assets to trusts to take advantage of the lower effective tax rate that would fall on the income accumulated within the trust. The target of the plan, usually a child, would receive the accumulated income (and, perhaps, trust corpus) at a designated age, and more funds would be available because a lower tax rate had been applied over the life of the investment in the trust.

Today, such an income shift would *deplete*, rather than shelter, the family's assets, as the rates falling on individuals are much more graduated than are those applicable to fiduciaries, and the kiddie tax also penalizes attempts to shift taxable income to children. Assuming that the objectives of the plan remain unchanged, possible strategies in view of these rate changes include the following.

[44]§ 6654(l).

CONCEPT SUMMARY 20.1

Principles of Fiduciary Taxation

1. Estates and trusts are temporary entities created to locate, maintain, and distribute assets and to satisfy liabilities according to the wishes of the decedent or grantor as expressed in the will or trust document.
2. Generally, the estate or trust acts as a conduit of the taxable income that it receives. To the extent that the income is distributed by the entity, it is taxed to the beneficiary. Taxable income retained by the entity is taxed to the entity itself.
3. The entity's accounting income must first be determined. Accounting conventions that are stated in the controlling document or, lacking such provisions, in state law allocate specific items of receipt and expenditure either to income or to corpus. Income beneficiaries typically receive payments from the entity that are equal to the accounting income.
4. The taxable income of the entity is computed using the scheme in Figure 20.2. The entity usually recognizes income in respect of a decedent. Deductions for fiduciary's fees and for charitable contributions may be reduced if the entity received any tax-exempt income during the year. Cost recovery deductions are assigned proportionately to the recipients of accounting income. Upon election, realized gain or loss on assets that properly are distributed in kind can be recognized by the entity.
5. A distribution deduction, computationally derived from distributable net income (DNI), is allowed to the entity. DNI is the maximum amount on which entity beneficiaries can be taxed. Moreover, the constitution of DNI is preserved for the recipients of the distributions.
6. Additional taxes are levied under Subchapter J to discourage the retention of excessive administrative powers by the grantor of a trust when the gross income is taxed to a lower-bracket beneficiary.

- Trust corpus should be invested in growth assets that are low on yield but high on appreciation, so that the trustee can determine the timing of the gain and somewhat control the effective tax rate that applies.
- Trust corpus should be invested in tax-exempt securities, such as municipal bonds and mutual funds that invest in them, to eliminate the tax costs associated with the investment. If this approach is taken, a trust might be unnecessary—the parent should simply retain full control over the assets and invest in the exempt securities in his or her own account.
- The grantor should retain high-yield assets, so that control over the assets is not surrendered when the tax cost is too high.
- Use of trust vehicles should be reserved for cases where professional management of the assets is necessary for portfolio growth and the additional tax costs can be justified.

20.8 Income Tax Planning for Estates

As a separate taxable entity, an estate can select its own tax year and accounting methods. The executor of an estate should consider selecting a fiscal year because this will determine when beneficiaries must include income distributions from the estate in their own tax returns. Beneficiaries must include the income for their tax year with or within which the estate's tax year ends. Proper selection of the estate's tax year can result in a smoothing out of income and a reduction of the income taxes for all parties involved.

Caution should be taken in determining when the estate is to be terminated. Selecting a fiscal year for the estate can result in a bunching of income to the beneficiaries in the year in which the estate is closed. Prolonging the termination of an estate can be effective income tax planning, but the IRS carefully examines the purpose of keeping the estate open. Since the unused losses of an estate pass through to the beneficiaries only in the termination year, the estate should be closed when the beneficiaries can enjoy the maximum tax benefit of the losses.

The timing and amounts of income distributions to the beneficiaries also present important tax planning opportunities. If the executor can make discretionary income distributions, he or she should evaluate the relative marginal income tax rates of the estate and its beneficiaries. By timing the distributions properly, the overall income tax liability can be minimized. Care should be taken, however, to time the distributions in light of the estate's DNI.

EXAMPLE 38

For several years before his death on March 7, Don had entered into annual deferred compensation agreements with his employer. These agreements collectively called for the payment of $200,000 six months after Don's retirement or death. To provide a maximum 12-month period within which to generate deductions to offset this large item of income in respect of a decedent, the executor or administrator of the estate should elect a fiscal year ending August 31. The election is made simply by filing the estate's first tax return for the short period of March 7 to August 31. ■

EXAMPLE 39

Carol, the sole beneficiary of an estate, is a calendar year, cash basis taxpayer. If the estate elects a fiscal year ending January 31, all distributions during the period of February 1 to December 31, 2011, are reported on Carol's tax return for calendar year 2012 (due April 15, 2013). Thus, assuming estimated tax requirements have otherwise been met, any income taxes that result from a $50,000 distribution made by the estate on February 20, 2011, may be deferred until April 15, 2013. ■

EXAMPLE 40

Assume the same facts as in Example 39. If the estate is closed on December 15, 2012, the DNI for both the fiscal year ending January 31, 2012, and the final tax year ending December 15, 2012, is included in Carol's tax return for the same calendar year. To avoid the effect of this bunching of income, the estate should not be closed until early in calendar year 2013. ■

EXAMPLE 41

Review Examples 28 and 29 carefully. Note, for instance, the flexibility that is available to the executor or administrator in timing the second-tier distributions of income and corpus of the estate. To illustrate, if Washington is subject to a high tax rate, distributions to him should be minimized except in years when DNI is low. In this manner, Washington's exposure to gross income from the distributions can be controlled so that most of the distributions he receives will be free of income tax. ■

In general, those beneficiaries who are subject to high income tax rates should be made beneficiaries of second-tier (but not IRD) distributions of the estate. Most likely, these individuals will have less need for an additional steady stream of (taxable) income while their income tax savings can be relatively large. Moreover, a special allocation of tax-favored types of income and expenses should be considered. For example, tax-exempt income can be directed more easily to beneficiaries in higher income tax brackets.

20.9 Income Tax Planning with Trusts

The great variety of trusts provides the grantor, trustee, and beneficiaries with excellent opportunities for tax planning. Many of the same tax planning opportunities available to the executor of an estate are available to the trustee. For instance, the distributions from a trust are taxable to the trust's beneficiaries to the extent of the trust's DNI. If income distributions are discretionary, the trustee can time the distributions to minimize the income tax consequences to all parties.

WHO SHOULD BE A TRUSTEE?

For decades, grantors have chosen a family member to be the trustee of the family savings, the children's education fund, or whatever other assets are placed into management by the trust. The relative chosen is often the most trusted but not always the one with the business sense. Now, however, as the financial work has become more complex, with wild stock market fluctuations, increased fiduciary standards, and potential conflicts of interest, some are questioning the wisdom of using a family member as the trustee.

Using a trust company or other financial institution as a trustee usually results in more stable investment returns, eliminating both the highs and the lows of the stock market cycle. Institutions can also bring other advantages.

- They do not die, run away, become mentally or physically incapacitated, or otherwise unexpectedly become unqualified for the position.
- They are not easily swayed by emotional appeals; nor do they react to family jealousies.
- They are prohibited by law from acting under a conflict of interest, such as might exist between family members when the related trustee is also a trust beneficiary.

On the negative side, human trustees often waive or discount their fiduciary fee, while institutions do not. Especially for trusts with a small corpus, institutional trustees can be prohibitively expensive. And the trust company most often is oriented toward expanding its customer base, rather than offering individual attention to existing clients.

How would you advise a client to address this delicate issue? Compromise solutions might be to:

- Appoint co-trustees. Aunt Grace or Uncle Roberto can provide the personal touch and ensure that trust decisions recognize family needs, while the trust company maximizes investment returns and furnishes professional management.
- Keep the family trustee, but hire professionals to provide advice only when needed, at an hourly rate. This approach avoids the fees based on asset values that trust companies usually charge.
- Use the advisory services of the mutual funds in which trust assets are invested, to manage and distribute the corpus and income.

20.10 DISTRIBUTIONS OF IN-KIND PROPERTY

The ability of the trustee or executor to elect to recognize the realized gain or loss relative to a distributed noncash asset allows the gain or loss to be allocated to the optimal taxpayer.

EXAMPLE 42

The Yorba Linda Estate distributed some inventory, basis of $40,000 and fair market value of $41,500, to beneficiary Larry. Yorba Linda is subject to a 15% marginal income tax rate, and Larry is subject to a 33% marginal rate. The executor of Yorba Linda should elect that the entity recognize the related $1,500 realized gain, thereby subjecting the gain to the estate's lower marginal tax rate.

Tax without election, at Larry's 33% rate	$495
Tax with election, at trust's 15% rate	225

■

20.11 DEDUCTIBILITY OF FIDUCIARY EXPENSES

Some deductions and losses may be claimed either on the estate tax return or as income tax deductions of the estate on the fiduciary return, at the taxpayer's choice.[45] In such a case, the deduction for income tax purposes is not allowed unless the estate tax deduction is waived. These deductions can be apportioned between the two returns.

[45] § 642(g) and Reg. § 20.2053–1(d).

EXAMPLE 43

Don's will named his surviving spouse, Donna, as the executor of his estate. The estate's assets total $10 million. The will includes bequests to pay various debts, make gifts to certain charities, and provide for the grandchildren through trusts. The will also allows for the payment of an executor's fee equal to 5% of the assets ($500,000).

Should Donna pay herself an executor's fee? If Donna is the estate's remainder beneficiary, a common occurrence, payment of the fee would result in the following.

- A deduction by the estate on the Form 706 (say, at the 35% marginal rate) or the estate's Form 1041 (at the 35% marginal rate).
- Gross income for services to Donna (say, at her individual 35% marginal tax rate).

If Donna waives the executor's fee, she will receive the $500,000 as the remainder beneficiary of the estate. Then the results would be:

- An increased marital deduction on the Form 706 (deductible at the 35% tax rate).
- No gross income to Donna, as the receipt of a bequest is nontaxable.

Almost certainly, a remainder beneficiary who is a surviving spouse would waive the fee.

If Donna is not the remainder beneficiary of the estate, the analysis becomes more difficult. Claiming the $500,000 as a fee will change the amounts that the charities and grandchildren receive, because the estate assets will have been reduced.

A surviving spouse, now perhaps the head of the family, will find this a difficult choice to make while fulfilling her executor duties. ■

An expense deductible for estate tax purposes may not qualify as an income tax deduction. Interest expense incurred to carry tax-exempt bonds is disallowed for income tax purposes. If this expense is not claimed for estate tax purposes, it is completely lost.

EXAMPLE 44

The executor of Dana's estate pays $5,000 in burial expenses (authorized under local law and approved by the probate court) from estate assets. The $5,000 expense should be claimed on the estate tax return, as it is not deductible at all for income tax purposes. ■

One of the duties of an estate's executor is to file the last income tax return of the decedent.[46] That Form 1040 is due on April 15 of the year following the date of death, regardless of when during the year death occurs.[47] The decedent's tax year ends on the date of death, but any personal and dependency exemptions, and standard deduction, are not reduced even though a short tax year results.

The final Form 1040 may be filed simply to claim a refund of the decedent's estimated tax payments or withholdings. However, it includes gross income and deductions to the point of death and can result in income tax being due. If the decedent was married on the date of death, a joint return can be filed, with signatures of both the executor and the surviving spouse.[48]

Medical expenses incurred by the decedent but unpaid at the time of the decedent's death are treated with a special rule. If paid by the estate during a one-year period beginning with the day after death, the expenses may be claimed as an income tax deduction in the year incurred or as an estate tax deduction, but not both.[49] The expenses may be divided in any way between the decedent's Form 1040 and his or her estate tax return.

[46] § 6012(b)(1).

[47] Reg. § 1.6072–1(b).

[48] § 6013(a). If an executor has not yet been appointed by the due date of a Form 1040, the surviving spouse signs for both taxpayers on a joint return. This also might occur for the prior year (when the spouse was alive) if the return for that year has not yet been filed.

[49] § 213(c).

REFOCUS ON THE BIG PICTURE

SETTING UP A TRUST TO PROTECT A FAMILY

Anna Jiang and her family should consider the creation of one or more trusts to provide security in case Anna is incapacitated by medical problems and unable to manage the family's finances. One suggestion for the family might be:

1. Anna transfers some or all of the $2 million assets to the Jiang Family Trust, with quarterly income payable to Tom and the children. Recipients would be designated by the trustee, but all of the entity's accounting income must be distributed. In this way, the income could be directed to the beneficiary most in need (e.g., to pay for education expenses or to start a new business). The children could be named first-tier beneficiaries, with Tom as a second-tier income beneficiary.
2. While Anna is still healthy and earning a regular salary, the trustee could accumulate the accounting income and allow the corpus to build up. Alternatively, the trustee could make gifts to charity or fund education plans for Bobby and Sally.
3. Anna should provide clear instructions to the trustee as to her preferences on how the trust corpus should be invested and specify which of Tom's and the children's expenses should and should not be covered.
4. The children should be named as remainder beneficiaries of the Jiang Family Trust. In case the trust corpus exceeds the estate tax bypass amount, other remainder beneficiaries could be named in order to avoid any generation-skipping tax (see Chapters 18 and 19).
5. Amendments to the trust document should be considered whenever Tom and Anna update their wills.

What If?

If Anna remains healthy, the Jiang Family Trust might be terminated when the children reach the age of majority, as the need for financial support will have diminished. However, if Tom is unable or unwilling to take over the management of the assets, the trust should continue. In this event, the trustee might shift the focus to funding long-term care for the couple, making charitable gifts, or financing the education needs of grandchildren.

The controlling trust document should be worded to provide flexibility as to the purposes and termination date of the trust. The trustee should be chosen from family members or business associates who know Anna and Tom well and are familiar with the couple's objectives.

KEY TERMS

Complex trust, 20–5
Corpus, 20–3
Distributable net income (DNI), 20–17
Expenses in respect of a decedent, 20–12
Grantor, 20–2
Grantor trusts, 20–3
Income in respect of a decedent (IRD), 20–12
Reversionary interest, 20–3
Simple trust, 20–5
Sprinkling trust, 20–5

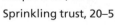

DISCUSSION QUESTIONS

COMMUNICATIONS

1. **LO.1** A local bank has asked you to speak at its Building Personal Wealth Conference on the topic of "What Should Your Trust Do for You?" Develop at least four PowerPoint slides, each one listing a function that a trust might be able to accomplish for an individual who has more than a modest level of financial resources.

2. **LO.1** Trusts and estates are known as *fiduciary* entities, in that a legal structure is formed to accomplish the financial and other goals of one or more individuals. List the parties who must be identified when a trust is created and describe the responsibilities of each. Do the same for an estate.

3. **LO.1** Define the following terms.
   a. Income interest.
   b. Remainder interest.
   c. Reversionary interest.
   d. Life tenant.
   e. Term certain.

4. **LO.1** Some fiduciary entities are known as *simple trusts*, while others are *complex trusts*. How does the tax professional know whether a trust is simple or complex? When is this determination made?

5. **LO.1** In general terms, describe how the following entities are subject to the Federal income tax. (Answer only for the entity, not for its owners, beneficiaries, etc.)
   a. C corporations (Subchapter C).
   b. Partnerships (Subchapter K).
   c. S corporations (Subchapter S).
   d. Trusts and estates (Subchapter J).

COMMUNICATIONS

6. **LO.1** Your college's accounting group has asked you to give a 10-minute speech, titled "Trusts, Estates, and the AMT." The audience will be students who have completed at least one course concerning Federal income taxation. Develop a brief outline for your remarks.

7. **LO.1** Create a fact pattern that illustrates each of the following tax situations. Be specific.
   a. A simple trust.
   b. A complex trust with a $300 personal exemption.
   c. A complex trust with a $100 personal exemption.

8. **LO.2** Using Figure 20.2 as a guide, describe the computation of a fiduciary entity's accounting income, taxable income, and distributable net income.

9. **LO.2** The Liu Trust is short of cash. It is required to distribute $100,000 to Yang every year, and that payment is due in six weeks. In its asset corpus, Liu holds a number of investments that are valued at $100,000. One of them has a tax basis to the trust of $60,000. Assuming that the trust agreement allows, what are the Federal income tax consequences if Liu distributes this stock to Yang?

DECISION MAKING

10. **LO.2** In its first tax year, the Wittmann Estate generated $50,000 of taxable interest income and $20,000 of tax-exempt interest income. It paid fiduciary fees of $7,000. The estate is subject to a 45% marginal estate tax rate and a 40% marginal income tax rate. How should the executor assign the deductions for the payment of the fees?

11. **LO.2** The Sterling Trust owns a business and generated $100,000 in depreciation deductions for the tax year. Mona is one of the income beneficiaries of the entity. Given the following information, can Mona deduct any of the Sterling depreciation on her Form 1040? If so, how much is her deduction?

Sterling's taxable income from the business	$ 800,000
Sterling's gross income from the business	2,000,000
Mona's share of trust accounting income	1,000,000
Total trust accounting income	2,500,000
Mona's share of distributable net income	200,000
Total distributable net income	600,000

12. **LO.2** In 2011, the Helpful Trust agreed to make a $90,000 contribution to Local Soup Kitchen, a charitable organization. Helpful's board agreed to the gift at a November 2011 meeting, but the check was not issued until February 20, 2012 (i.e., during the next tax year). Can the trust claim a charitable contribution deduction? If so, describe how Helpful should treat its gift.

13. **LO.3** One of the key concepts in fiduciary income taxation is that of *distributable net income* (DNI). List the major functions of DNI on one PowerPoint slide, with no more than five bullets, to present to your classmates as part of the discussion of this chapter of the text. Just review the uses of DNI in Subchapter J, and do not discuss its computation. **COMMUNICATIONS**

14. **LO.2, 3** Ivory Tower College, a charitable organization, is one of the income beneficiaries of the Campbell Trust. Was the selection of the college as an income beneficiary a wise decision by Campbell's grantor? Comment specifically concerning the tax effects of the trust's cost recovery deductions and of its potential business operating losses. **DECISION MAKING**

15. **LO.2, 3, 5** The Flan Trust is scheduled to terminate in two years, when Amy Flan reaches age 30. Several years ago, the trust operated a business that generated a sizable NOL carryforward that the trust has not been able to use. In addition, due to a bearish stock market, the value of the entity's investment portfolio has declined 15% from its purchase price. What issues must you consider in advising Amy and the corporate trustee? **ISSUE ID**

16. **LO.4** Harriet wants to transfer some assets to a trust this year; the income beneficiaries will be her two grandchildren. The trust income and assets will be used to pay the grandchildren's tuition to private high schools and universities. Upon the younger grandchild's graduation, the trust assets will return to Harriet's ownership. Identify tax issues related to Harriet's plan to use a temporary fiduciary entity. **ISSUE ID**

17. **LO.4** Carol has been promoted several times, and she may be named a partner next year. Thus, she will be subject to higher marginal income tax rates than in the past. Carol's colleague Isaiah has told her about a "college education trust" from which he pays tuition and fees for his children. He has implied that there are sizable tax advantages to setting up a trust for this purpose. Now Carol is considering establishing a similar trust to pay tuition for her own children. She believes that the trust will be able to deduct the tuition payments, something that she cannot currently do on her Form 1040. Write a memo to the tax research file addressing Carol's ideas. **DECISION MAKING** **COMMUNICATIONS**

18. **LO.1, 4** The Winter Trust must file a Form 1041 for the first time, because it has recognized about $5,000 of gross income. Corpus assets are transferred to the trust on April 30. Considering only the Federal income tax effects of the creation of Winter:
    a. What tax year should be used?
    b. Where should the completed Form 1041 be sent?

19. **LO.5** For tax planning purposes, should an estate adopt a calendar or a fiscal tax year? Why?

20. **LO.5** Comment on the following items relative to tax planning strategies of a fiduciary entity.
    a. To reduce taxes for a typical family, should income be shifted *to* a trust or *from* a trust? Why?
    b. To reduce overall taxes, should a high-income, wealthy beneficiary be assigned to the first or second tier of trust distributions? Why?
    c. To minimize taxes, how should a trust treat the distribution of an in-kind asset? Why?

PROBLEMS

21. **LO.1** Complete the following chart, indicating the comparative attributes of the typical simple trust and complex trust by answering yes/no or explaining the differences between the entities where appropriate.

Attribute	Simple Trust	Complex Trust
Trust could incur its own tax liability for the year	______	______
Trust generally distributes all of DNI	______	______
Trust can deduct its charitable contributions in the year of, or the year after, payment	______	______
Trust could claim a foreign tax credit	______	______
Maximum tax rate on net long-term capital gains = 15%	______	______
AMT preferences and adjustments flow through to beneficiaries ratably	______	______
Trust can adopt the FIFO method for its inventory assets; the grantor had been using lower of cost or market	______	______
Trust can use a tax year other than the calendar year	______	______
Amount of personal exemption	______	______

22. **LO.1** Compute the Federal income tax liability for the Kim Trust. The trustee reports the following transactions for the 2011 tax year. The trustee accumulates all accounting income for the year.

Operating income from a business	$400,000
Dividend income, all from U.S. corporations	70,000
Interest income, City of San Antonio bonds	40,000
Fiduciary fees, deductible portion	(20,000)
Net rental losses, passive activity	(100,000)

23. **LO.1** The Purple Trust incurred the following items this year.

Taxable interest income	$75,000
Tax-exempt interest income, not on private activity bonds	60,000
Tax-exempt interest income, on private activity bonds (not issued during 2009 or 2010)	25,000

Compute Purple's tentative minimum tax for the year. Purple does not have any credits available to reduce the AMT liability.

DECISION MAKING

24. **LO.2** The Grouper Trust will incur the following items next year, its first year of existence.

Interest income	$ 75,000
Rent income	100,000
Cost recovery deductions for the rental activity	15,000
Capital gain income	60,000
Fiduciary and tax preparation fees	11,000

Betty, the grantor of the trust, is working with you on the language in the trust instrument relative to the derivation of annual accounting income for the entity. She will name Shirley as the sole income beneficiary and Benny as the remainder beneficiary.

a. Suggest language to Betty that will maximize the annual income distribution to Shirley.
b. Suggest language to Betty that will minimize the annual distribution to Shirley and maximize the accumulation on Benny's behalf.

25. **LO.2** Complete the chart below, indicating the Calvet Trust's entity accounting income for each of the alternatives. For this purpose, use the following information.

Interest income, taxable	$300,000
Interest income, tax-exempt	30,000
Interest income, tax-exempt but AMT preference item	20,000
Long-term capital gain	25,000
Trustee fee	5,000

Trust Agreement Provisions	Trust Accounting Income
Fees and capital gains allocable to corpus	________
Capital gains allocable to corpus, one-half of fees allocable to income	________
Capital gains allocable to income, silent concerning allocation of fees	________
Fees and exempt income allocable to corpus, silent concerning allocation of capital gain/loss	________

26. **LO.1, 2, 3** Complete the following chart, indicating the comparative attributes of the typical trust and estate by answering yes/no or explaining the differences between the entities where appropriate.

Attribute	Estate	Trust
Separate income tax entity	________	________
Controlling document	________	________
Can have both income and remainder beneficiaries	________	________
Computes entity accounting income before determining entity taxable income	________	________
Termination date is determinable from controlling document	________	________
Legal owner of assets under fiduciary's control	________	________
Document identifies both income and remainder beneficiaries	________	________
Separate share rules apply	________	________
Generally must use calendar tax year	________	________

27. **LO.2** Roberto is one of the income beneficiaries of the Carol LeMans Estate. This year, as directed by the will, Roberto received all of the sales commissions that were earned and payable to Carol (cash basis) at her death, as well as one of three remaining installment payments. Compute Roberto's gross income attributable to Carol's activities for the current year, given the following financial data.

Sales commissions receivable	$60,000
Total ordinary gain on installment sale, two payments remaining after this year	50,000

28. **LO.2** Sanchez incurred the following items.

Business income	$120,000
Tax-exempt interest income	40,000
Payment to charity from 2011 income, paid 3/1/2012	20,000

Complete the following chart, indicating the charitable contributions deduction under the various assumptions.

Assumption	2011 Deduction for Contribution
Sanchez is a cash basis individual.	________
Sanchez is an accrual basis corporation.	________
Sanchez is a trust.	________

29. **LO.2** The Oliver Trust has generated $50,000 in depreciation deductions for the year. Its accounting income is $25,000. In computing this amount, pursuant to the trust document, depreciation was allocated to corpus. Accounting income was distributed at the trustee's discretion: $20,000 to Hernandez and $5,000 to Jackson.
    a. Compute the depreciation deductions that Hernandez, Jackson, and Oliver may claim.
    b. Same as (a), except that depreciation was allocated to income.
    c. Same as (a), except that the trustee distributed $10,000 each to Hernandez and to Jackson and retained the remaining accounting income.
    d. Same as (a), except that Oliver is an estate (and not a trust).

30. **LO.2, 3** The Ricardo Trust is a simple trust that correctly uses the calendar year for tax purposes. Its income beneficiaries (Lucy and Ethel) are entitled to the trust's annual accounting income in shares of one-half each. For the current calendar year, the trust generates ordinary income of $50,000, a long-term capital gain of $25,000 (allocable to corpus), and a trustee commission expense of $10,000 (allocable to corpus). Use the format of Figure 20.3 to address the following items.
    a. How much income is each beneficiary entitled to receive?
    b. What is the trust's DNI?
    c. What is the trust's taxable income?
    d. How much gross income is reported by each of the beneficiaries?

31. **LO.2, 3** Assume the same facts as in Problem 30, except that the trust instrument allocates the capital gain to income.
    a. How much income is each beneficiary entitled to receive?
    b. What is the trust's DNI?
    c. What is the trust's taxable income?
    d. How much gross income is reported by each of the beneficiaries?

32. **LO.3** Under the terms of the Lagos Trust instrument, the trustee has discretion to distribute or accumulate income on behalf of Willie, Sylvia, and Doris in equal shares. The trustee also can invade corpus for the benefit of any of the beneficiaries to the extent of each person's respective one-third interest in the trust.

    In the current year, the trust has DNI of $120,000. Distribution and accumulation amounts were as follows.

    - To Willie: $40,000 from DNI and $10,000 from corpus.
    - To Sylvia: $25,000. The remaining $15,000 DNI is accumulated.
    - To Doris: $0. The $40,000 DNI is accumulated.

    a. How much income is taxed to Willie? (*Hint*: Apply the separate share rule.)
    b. To Sylvia?
    c. To Doris?
    d. To Lagos?

33. **LO.3** The Putnam Sisters Trust is required to distribute $60,000 annually equally to its two income beneficiaries, Clare and David. If trust income is not sufficient to pay these amounts, the trustee can invade corpus to the extent necessary. During the current year, the trust generates only taxable interest income and has DNI of $150,000; the trustee distributes $30,000 to Clare and $130,000 to David.
    a. How much of the $130,000 distributed to David is included in his gross income?
    b. How much of the $30,000 distributed to Clare is included in her gross income?
    c. Are these distributions first-tier or second-tier distributions?

34. **LO.3** The Dailey Estate has $100,000 of DNI, composed of $40,000 in dividends, $20,000 in taxable interest, $15,000 of passive activity income, and $25,000 in tax-exempt interest. The entity's two noncharitable income beneficiaries, Brenda and Del, receive cash distributions of

$20,000 each. How much of each class of income is deemed to have been distributed to Brenda? To Del?

35. **LO.2, 3** The trustee of the Purple Trust can distribute any amount of accounting income and corpus to the trust's beneficiaries, Lydia and Kent. This year, the trust incurred the following.

Taxable interest income	$40,000
Tax-exempt interest income	60,000
Long-term capital gains—allocable to corpus	30,000
Fiduciary's fees—allocable to corpus	10,000

The trustee distributed $40,000 to Lydia and $20,000 to Kent.

a. What is Purple's trust accounting income?
b. What is Purple's DNI?
c. What is Purple's taxable income?
d. How much is taxed to each of the beneficiaries?

36. **LO.2** Each of the following items was incurred by José, the cash basis, calendar year decedent. Under the terms of the will, Dora took immediate ownership in all of José's assets, except the dividend-paying stock. The estate received José's final paycheck. DECISION MAKING

Applying the rules for income and deductions in respect of a decedent, indicate on which return each item should be reported: Dora's income tax return (Form 1040); the estate's first income tax return (Form 1041); or the estate's estate tax return (Form 706). More than one alternative may apply in some cases.

Item Incurred	Form(s) Reported on
a. Wages, last paycheck	__________
b. State income tax withheld on last paycheck	__________
c. Capital gain portion of installment payment received	__________
d. Ordinary income portion of installment payment received	__________
e. Dividend income, record date was two days prior to José's death	__________
f. Unrealized appreciation on a mutual fund investment	__________
g. Depreciation recapture accrued as of date of death	__________
h. Medical expenses of last illness	__________
i. Apartment building, rents accrued but not collected as of death	__________
j. Apartment building, property tax accrued and assessed but not paid as of death	__________

37. **LO.4** In each of the following independent cases, write a memo for the tax research file in preparation for a meeting with Gary. In each memo, explain whether the proposed plan meets his objective of shifting income and avoiding the grantor trust rules. DECISION MAKING COMMUNICATIONS

a. Gary transfers property in trust, income payable to Winnie (his wife) for life, remainder to his grandson. Gary's son is designated as the trustee.
b. Gary transfers income-producing assets and a life insurance policy to a trust, life estate to his children, remainder to his grandchildren. The policy is on Winnie's life, and the trustee (an independent trust company) is instructed to pay the premiums with income from the income-producing assets. The trust is designated as the beneficiary of the policy.
c. Gary transfers property in trust. The trust income is payable to Gary's grandchildren, as Winnie sees fit. Winnie and an independent trust company are designated as trustees.
d. Gary transfers property in trust, income payable to Winnie (Gary's ex-wife), remainder to Gary or his estate upon Winnie's death. The transfer was made in satisfaction of Gary's alimony obligation to Winnie. An independent trust company is designated as the trustee.

38. **LO.3** Determine the tax effects of the indicated losses for the Yellow Estate for both tax years. The estate holds a variety of investment assets, which it received from the decedent,

Mrs. Yellow. The estate's sole income and remainder beneficiary is Yellow, Jr. All taxpayers use a calendar tax year.

Tax Year	Loss Generated
2011 (first tax year)	Taxable income ($300) Capital loss ($15,000)
2012 (final tax year)	Taxable income, all classified as ordinary ($30,000)

DECISION MAKING

39. **LO.4** Woody wishes to transfer some of the income from his investment portfolio to his daughter Wendy, age 10. Woody wants the trust to be able to accumulate income on Wendy's behalf and to meet any excessive expenses associated with her chronic medical conditions. Furthermore, Woody wants the trust to protect Wendy against his own premature death without increasing his Federal gross estate. Thus, Woody provides the trustee with the powers to purchase insurance on his life and to meet any medical expenses that Wendy incurs.

    The trust is created in 2005. A whole life insurance policy with five annual premium payments is purchased during that year. The trustee spends $30,000 for Wendy's medical expenses in 2011 (but in no other year). Woody dies in 2013. Has the trust been tax-effective?

DECISION MAKING

COMMUNICATIONS

40. **LO.2, 3** Your client, Annie O'Toole (22 Beneficiary Lane, Bowling Green, KY 42101), has come to you for some advice regarding gifts of property. She has just learned that she must undergo major surgery, and she would like to make certain gifts before entering the hospital. On your earlier advice, she had established a plan of lifetime giving for four prior years.

    Build a spreadsheet, supplemented by a list of your assumptions, and write a cover letter to Annie, discussing each of the following assets that she is considering using as gifts to family and friends. In doing so, evaluate the income tax consequences of having such property pass through her estate to the designated heir.

    a. Annie plans to give a cottage to her son to fulfill a promise made many years ago. She has owned the cottage for the past 15 years and has a basis in it of $30,000 (fair market value of $20,000).
    b. Annie has $100,000 of long-term capital losses that she has been carrying forward for the past few years. Now she is considering making a gift of $200,000 in installment notes to her daughter. Her basis in the notes is $100,000, and the notes' current fair market value is $190,000.
    c. Annie has promised to make a special cash bequest of $25,000 to her grandson in her will. However, she does not anticipate having that much cash immediately available after her death. Annie requests your advice concerning the income tax consequences to the estate if the cash bequest is settled with some other property.

TAX RETURN PROBLEMS

1. Prepare the 2010 fiduciary income tax return (Form 1041) for the Blue Trust. In addition, determine the amount and character of the income and expense items that each beneficiary must report for 2010 and prepare a Schedule K–1 for Betty Blue. Omit all alternative minimum tax computations. The 2010 activities of the trust include the following.

Dividend income, all U.S. stocks	$20,000
Taxable interest income	30,000
Tax-exempt interest income	10,000
Fiduciary's fees	6,000

The trust and Betty both use the calendar tax year. Under the terms of the trust instrument, fiduciary's fees are allocated to income. The trustee must distribute all of the entity's accounting income to Betty Blue, by February 15 of the following year. The trustee followed this charge and made no other distributions during the year. Fiduciary's fees properly were assigned as an offset to taxable interest income.

The trust was created on July 8, 1990. There are no tax credits for the year, and none of the entity's income was derived from a personal services contract. The trust has no economic interest in any foreign trust. Its Federal identification number is 11–1111111.

The trustee, Hoover State Federal Bank, is located at 4959 Cold Harbor Boulevard, Mountain Brook, AL 35223. Its employer identification number is 98–7654321. Betty lives at 67671 Crestline Road, Birmingham, AL 35212. Her Social Security number is 123–45–6789.

2. Prepare the 2010 fiduciary income tax return (Form 1041) for the Green Trust. In addition, determine the amount and character of the income and expense items that each beneficiary must report for 2010 and prepare a Schedule K–1 for Marcus White. Omit all alternative minimum tax computations. The 2010 activities of the trust include the following. **H&R BLOCK** At Home

Dividend income, all qualified U.S. stocks	$10,000
Taxable interest income	50,000
Tax-exempt interest income	20,000
Net long-term capital gain, incurred 11/1/10	25,000
Fiduciary's fees	6,000

Under the terms of the trust instrument, cost recovery, net capital gains and losses, and fiduciary fees are allocable to corpus. The trustee is required to distribute $25,000 to Marcus every year. For 2010, the trustee distributed $40,000 to Marcus and $40,000 to Marcus's sister, Ellen Hayes. No other distributions were made.

In computing DNI, the trustee properly assigned all of the deductible fiduciary's fees to the taxable interest income.

The trustee paid $3,500 in estimated taxes for the year on behalf of the trust. Any 2010 refund is to be credited to 2011 estimates. The exempt income was not derived from private activity bonds.

The trust was created on December 14, 1953. It is not subject to any recapture taxes, nor does it have any tax credits. None of its income was derived under a personal services contract. The trust has no economic interest in any foreign trust. Its Federal identification number is 11–1111111.

The trustee, Wisconsin State National Bank, is located at 3100 East Wisconsin Avenue, Milwaukee, WI 53201. Its employer identification number is 11–1111111. Marcus lives at 9880 East North Avenue, Shorewood, WI 53211. His Social Security number is 123–45–6789. Ellen lives at 6772 East Oklahoma Avenue, St. Cecilia, WI 53204. Her Social Security number is 987–65–4321.

RESEARCH PROBLEMS

Note: Solutions to Research Problems can be prepared by using the **Checkpoint® Student Edition** online research product, which is available to accompany this text. It is also possible to prepare solutions to the Research Problems by using tax research materials found in a standard tax library.

Checkpoint® Student Edition

COMMUNICATIONS

Research Problem 1. Siri's revocable trust held title to a plot of investment land that she had acquired in 2003. On October 20, 2010, the trust entered into a sales contract with Hilltop Developers. A closing date of March 20, 2011, was set by the terms of the contract.

On February 3, 2011, Siri's engineers discovered that there was a natural gas pipeline under the land, a fact that was not previously known by the parties. To allow for changes in the terms of the contract that were needed because of this discovery, the closing date for the sale was delayed until June 1, 2011.

The trust's basis in the land is $1 million. The original sales price was set at $1.1 million, reflecting difficulties in finding a purchaser in a "down" real estate market. But after the terms of the sale were adjusted, on May 20, 2011, a new $1.5 million sales price was agreed to. The closing and title transfer occurred on June 1 of that year.

Siri died on May 3, 2011. Under § 2036, the land is included in Siri's gross estate. Is the $500,000 capital gain on the sale treated as income in respect of a decedent (IRD) to her as well? Remember that since neither party canceled the original deal, the sale was certain to occur under the contract. But Hilltop and the trust were renegotiating the terms of the contract when Siri died.

Identify the administrative and judicial precedents that are most pertinent for the parties. Cite and summarize your findings in an outline for a talk that you will deliver next week to your school's Accounting Club.

Research Problem 2. For three generations, the Dexter family has sent its children to Private University, preparing them for successful professional careers. The Edna Dexter Trust was established in the 1950s by LaKeisha's late grandmother and has accumulated a sizable corpus. It makes distributions to Edna's descendants rarely and only when they need large capital amounts. For example, two years ago, the trust distributed $500,000 to DuJuan Dexter to aid him in starting a practice in retirement and elder law. In most years, the trust's income is donated to a single charity.

Under the terms of the trust, Bigby Dexter, LaKeisha's uncle and legal guardian, can specify the trust beneficiaries and the amounts to be distributed to them. He can also replace the trustee and designate the charity that will receive the year's contribution. Accordingly, the trust falls under the grantor trust rules of § 678, and Bigby reports the trust's transactions on his own Form 1040.

LaKeisha wants to attend the prestigious local Academy High School, which will require a four-year expenditure for tuition and fees of $100,000, payable in advance. She approaches the Edna Dexter trustee and requests a current-year distribution of this amount, payable directly to the Academy. Under the laws of the state, the parent or guardian has the responsibility to provide a child with a public school education (no tuition charge) until age 16.

If the payment to the Academy is made, how is it treated under the Subchapter J rules: as a charitable contribution to the Academy, as a corpus distribution to LaKeisha, or in some other manner?

COMMUNICATIONS

Research Problem 3. You attended the local Tax Update conference and one of the speakers was promoting the use of a "divorce trust" as allowed by § 682. Outline the characteristics of a divorce trust in a memo for your tax partners, and highlight some of the potential advantages that the trust might bring to your clients.

Use the tax resources of the Internet to address the following questions. Do not restrict your search to the Web, but include a review of newsgroups and general reference materials, practitioner sites and resources, primary sources of the tax law, chat rooms and discussion groups, and other opportunities.

COMMUNICATIONS

Research Problem 4. How many estates filed a Form 1041 last year? Simple trusts? Complex trusts? Grantor trusts? How much Federal income tax has been collected on Forms 1041 over the last three tax years? Summarize your findings in a series of graphs to share with your classmates.

COMMUNICATIONS

Research Problem 5. Under the income tax laws of your state applicable to fiduciaries, how are the following items allocated among the entity and the beneficiaries? Put your findings in a PowerPoint presentation for your classmates.

- Capital gain.
- Cost recovery.
- Fiduciary fees.
- Exempt interest income.
- AMT adjustments.

COMMUNICATIONS

Research Problem 6. The IRS's list of abusive tax shelters includes a "family residence trust," which attempts to create deductions for personal items such as utilities, furniture purchases, and swimming pool maintenance. Search the Web for current definitions of these trusts and descriptions of how they operate. Summarize your findings, as well as the litigation strategy of the government to curtail the use of these trusts, in an e-mail to your instructor.

COMMUNICATIONS

Research Problem 7. Create no more than three PowerPoint slides, summarizing your state's definitions of and rules for using the following terms. *Hint*: Your state might not use these terms at all, or it might use a term that differs slightly, so make sure that your Internet research is broad enough to find the equivalent terminology.

- Living will.
- Living trust.
- Medical power of attorney.

Research Problem 8. Search the Internet to find sample language establishing a sprinkling trust. Using Word or Acrobat, mark up each specimen document with annotations highlighting how the terms of the trust make special allocations to certain income beneficiaries and how entity accounting income is defined. What powers does the trust document give to the trustee to change the definition of accounting income in later trust years?

Research Problem 9. Find the website of a law firm that seems to specialize in fiduciary entities, preferably a firm located in your state. Ask the firm to quote you a fee for (1) establishing a simple trust and (2) filing the annual Form 1041. Summarize your findings, and your communications with the firm, in an e-mail to your instructor. COMMUNICATIONS

Appendix A

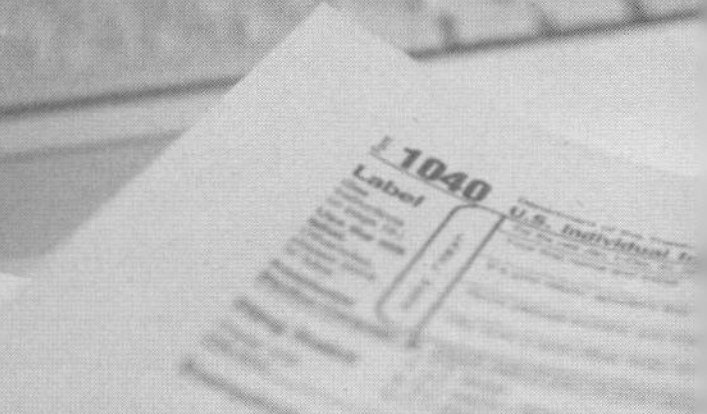

TAX RATE SCHEDULES AND TABLES

2010 Tax Rate Schedules

Single—Schedule X

If taxable income is: Over—	But not over—	The tax is:	of the amount over—
$ 0	$ 8,375	........10%	$ 0
8,375	34,000	$ 837.50 + 15%	8,375
34,000	82,400	4,681.25 + 25%	34,000
82,400	171,850	16,781.25 + 28%	82,400
171,850	373,650	41,827.25 + 33%	171,850
373,650	....	108,421.25 + 35%	373,650

Head of household—Schedule Z

If taxable income is: Over—	But not over—	The tax is:	of the amount over—
$ 0	$ 11,950	........10%	$ 0
11,950	45,550	$ 1,195.00 + 15%	11,950
45,550	117,650	6,235.00 + 25%	45,550
117,650	190,550	24,260.00 + 28%	117,650
190,550	373,650	44,672.00 + 33%	190,550
373,650	....	105,095.00 + 35%	373,650

Married filing jointly or Qualifying widow(er)—Schedule Y–1

If taxable income is: Over—	But not over—	The tax is:	of the amount over—
$ 0	$ 16,750	........10%	$ 0
16,750	68,000	$ 1,675.00 + 15%	16,750
68,000	137,300	9,362.50 + 25%	68,000
137,300	209,250	26,687.50 + 28%	137,300
209,250	373,650	46,833.50 + 33%	209,250
373,650	....	101,085.50 + 35%	373,650

Married filing separately—Schedule Y–2

If taxable income is: Over—	But not over—	The tax is:	of the amount over—
$ 0	$ 8,375	........10%	$ 0
8,375	34,000	$ 837.50 + 15%	8,375
34,000	68,650	4,681.25 + 25%	34,000
68,650	104,625	13,343.75 + 28%	68,650
104,625	186,825	23,416.75 + 33%	104,625
186,825	....	50,542.75 + 35%	186,825

2011 Tax Rate Schedules

Single—Schedule X

If taxable income is: Over—	But not over—	The tax is:	of the amount over—
$ 0	$ 8,500	........10%	$ 0
8,500	34,500	$ 850.00 + 15%	8,500
34,500	83,600	4,750.00 + 25%	34,500
83,600	174,400	17,025.00 + 28%	83,600
174,400	379,150	42,449.00 + 33%	174,400
379,150	....	110,016.50 + 35%	379,150

Head of household—Schedule Z

If taxable income is: Over—	But not over—	The tax is:	of the amount over—
$ 0	$ 12,150	........10%	$ 0
12,150	46,250	$ 1,215.00 + 15%	12,150
46,250	119,400	6,330.00 + 25%	46,250
119,400	193,350	24,617.50 + 28%	119,400
193,350	379,150	45,323.50 + 33%	193,350
379,150	....	106,637.50 + 35%	379,150

Married filing jointly or Qualifying widow(er)—Schedule Y–1

If taxable income is: Over—	But not over—	The tax is:	of the amount over—
$ 0	$ 17,000	........10%	$ 0
17,000	69,000	$ 1,700.00 + 15%	17,000
69,000	139,350	9,500.00 + 25%	69,000
139,350	212,300	27,087.50 + 28%	139,350
212,300	379,150	47,513.50 + 33%	212,300
379,150	....	102,574.00 + 35%	379,150

Married filing separately—Schedule Y–2

If taxable income is: Over—	But not over—	The tax is:	of the amount over—
$ 0	$ 8,500	........10%	$ 0
8,500	34,500	850.00 + 15%	8,500
34,500	69,675	4,750.00 + 25%	34,500
69,675	106,150	13,543.75 + 28%	69,675
106,150	189,575	23,756.75 + 33%	106,150
189,575	....	51,287.00 + 35%	189,575

Income Tax Rates—Estates and Trusts

Tax Year 2010

Taxable Income		The Tax Is:	
Over—	But not Over—		Of the Amount Over—
$ 0	$ 2,300	15%	$ 0
2,300	5,350	$ 345.00 + 25%	2,300
5,350	8,200	1,107.50 + 28%	5,350
8,200	11,200	1,905.50 + 33%	8,200
11,200	....	2,895.50 + 35%	11,200

Tax Year 2011

Taxable Income		The Tax Is:	
Over—	But not Over—		Of the Amount Over—
$ 0	$ 2,300	15%	$ 0
2,300	5,450	$ 345.00 + 25%	2,300
5,450	8,300	1,132.50 + 28%	5,450
8,300	11,350	1,930.50 + 33%	8,300
11,350	....	2,937.00 + 35%	11,350

Income Tax Rates—Corporations

Taxable Income		Tax Is:	
Over—	But not Over—		Of the Amount Over—
$ 0	$ 50,000	15%	$ 0
50,000	75,000	$ 7,500 + 25%	50,000
75,000	100,000	13,750 + 34%	75,000
100,000	335,000	22,250 + 39%	100,000
335,000	10,000,000	113,900 + 34%	335,000
10,000,000	15,000,000	3,400,000 + 35%	10,000,000
15,000,000	18,333,333	5,150,000 + 38%	15,000,000
18,333,333	....	35%	0

Unified Transfer Tax Rates

For Gifts Made and for Deaths After 1983 and Before 2002

If the Amount with Respect to Which the Tentative Tax to Be Computed Is:	The Tentative Tax Is:
Not over $10,000	18 percent of such amount.
Over $10,000 but not over $20,000	$1,800, plus 20 percent of the excess of such amount over $10,000.
Over $20,000 but not over $40,000	$3,800, plus 22 percent of the excess of such amount over $20,000.
Over $40,000 but not over $60,000	$8,200, plus 24 percent of the excess of such amount over $40,000.
Over $60,000 but not over $80,000	$13,000, plus 26 percent of the excess of such amount over $60,000.
Over $80,000 but not over $100,000	$18,200, plus 28 percent of the excess of such amount over $80,000.
Over $100,000 but not over $150,000	$23,800, plus 30 percent of the excess of such amount over $100,000.
Over $150,000 but not over $250,000	$38,800, plus 32 percent of the excess of such amount over $150,000.
Over $250,000 but not over $500,000	$70,800, plus 34 percent of the excess of such amount over $250,000.
Over $500,000 but not over $750,000	$155,800, plus 37 percent of the excess of such amount over $500,000.
Over $750,000 but not over $1,000,000	$248,300, plus 39 percent of the excess of such amount over $750,000.
Over $1,000,000 but not over $1,250,000	$345,800, plus 41 percent of the excess of such amount over $1,000,000.
Over $1,250,000 but not over $1,500,000	$448,300, plus 43 percent of the excess of such amount over $1,250,000.
Over $1,500,000 but not over $2,000,000	$555,800, plus 45 percent of the excess of such amount over $1,500,000.
Over $2,000,000 but not over $2,500,000	$780,800, plus 49 percent of the excess of such amount over $2,000,000.
Over $2,500,000 but not over $3,000,000	$1,025,800, plus 53 percent of the excess of such amount over $2,500,000.
Over $3,000,000*	$1,290,800, plus 55 percent of the excess of such amount over $3,000,000.

*For large taxable transfers (generally in excess of $10 million) there is a phaseout of the graduated rates and the unified tax credit.

Unified Transfer Tax Rates

For Gifts Made and for Deaths in 2002

If the Amount with Respect to Which the Tentative Tax to Be Computed Is:	The Tentative Tax Is:
Not over $10,000	18 percent of such amount.
Over $10,000 but not over $20,000	$1,800, plus 20 percent of the excess of such amount over $10,000.
Over $20,000 but not over $40,000	$3,800, plus 22 percent of the excess of such amount over $20,000.
Over $40,000 but not over $60,000	$8,200, plus 24 percent of the excess of such amount over $40,000.
Over $60,000 but not over $80,000	$13,000, plus 26 percent of the excess of such amount over $60,000.
Over $80,000 but not over $100,000	$18,200, plus 28 percent of the excess of such amount over $80,000.
Over $100,000 but not over $150,000	$23,800, plus 30 percent of the excess of such amount over $100,000.
Over $150,000 but not over $250,000	$38,800, plus 32 percent of the excess of such amount over $150,000.
Over $250,000 but not over $500,000	$70,800, plus 34 percent of the excess of such amount over $250,000.
Over $500,000 but not over $750,000	$155,800, plus 37 percent of the excess of such amount over $500,000.
Over $750,000 but not over $1,000,000	$248,300, plus 39 percent of the excess of such amount over $750,000.
Over $1,000,000 but not over $1,250,000	$345,800, plus 41 percent of the excess of such amount over $1,000,000.
Over $1,250,000 but not over $1,500,000	$448,300, plus 43 percent of the excess of such amount over $1,250,000.
Over $1,500,000 but not over $2,000,000	$555,800, plus 45 percent of the excess of such amount over $1,500,000.
Over $2,000,000 but not over $2,500,000	$780,800, plus 49 percent of the excess of such amount over $2,000,000.
Over $2,500,000	$1,025,800, plus 50 percent of the excess of such amount over $2,500,000.

Unified Transfer Tax Rates

For Gifts Made and for Deaths in 2003

If the Amount with Respect to Which the Tentative Tax to Be Computed Is:	The Tentative Tax Is:
Not over $10,000	18 percent of such amount.
Over $10,000 but not over $20,000	$1,800, plus 20 percent of the excess of such amount over $10,000.
Over $20,000 but not over $40,000	$3,800, plus 22 percent of the excess of such amount over $20,000.
Over $40,000 but not over $60,000	$8,200, plus 24 percent of the excess of such amount over $40,000.
Over $60,000 but not over $80,000	$13,000, plus 26 percent of the excess of such amount over $60,000.
Over $80,000 but not over $100,000	$18,200, plus 28 percent of the excess of such amount over $80,000.
Over $100,000 but not over $150,000	$23,800, plus 30 percent of the excess of such amount over $100,000.
Over $150,000 but not over $250,000	$38,800, plus 32 percent of the excess of such amount over $150,000.
Over $250,000 but not over $500,000	$70,800, plus 34 percent of the excess of such amount over $250,000.
Over $500,000 but not over $750,000	$155,800, plus 37 percent of the excess of such amount over $500,000.
Over $750,000 but not over $1,000,000	$248,300, plus 39 percent of the excess of such amount over $750,000.
Over $1,000,000 but not over $1,250,000	$345,800, plus 41 percent of the excess of such amount over $1,000,000.
Over $1,250,000 but not over $1,500,000	$448,300, plus 43 percent of the excess of such amount over $1,250,000.
Over $1,500,000 but not over $2,000,000	$555,800, plus 45 percent of the excess of such amount over $1,500,000.
Over $2,000,000	$780,800, plus 49 percent of the excess of such amount over $2,000,000.

For Gifts Made and for Deaths in 2004

(For amounts not over $2,000,000, see rates for 2003 above)	
Over $2,000,000	$780,800, plus 48 percent of the excess of such amount over $2,000,000.

For Gifts Made and for Deaths in 2005

(For amounts not over $2,000,000, see rates for 2003 above)	
Over $2,000,000	$780,800, plus 47 percent of the excess of such amount over $2,000,000.

For Gifts Made and for Deaths in 2006

(For amounts not over $2,000,000, see rates for 2003 above)	
Over $2,000,000	$780,800, plus 46 percent of the excess of such amount over $2,000,000.

Unified Transfer Tax Rates

For Gifts Made and for Deaths in 2007–2009

If the Amount with Respect to Which the Tentative Tax to Be Computed Is:	The Tentative Tax Is:
Not over $10,000	18 percent of such amount.
Over $10,000 but not over $20,000	$1,800, plus 20 percent of the excess of such amount over $10,000.
Over $20,000 but not over $40,000	$3,800, plus 22 percent of the excess of such amount over $20,000.
Over $40,000 but not over $60,000	$8,200, plus 24 percent of the excess of such amount over $40,000.
Over $60,000 but not over $80,000	$13,000, plus 26 percent of the excess of such amount over $60,000.
Over $80,000 but not over $100,000	$18,200, plus 28 percent of the excess of such amount over $80,000.
Over $100,000 but not over $150,000	$23,800, plus 30 percent of the excess of such amount over $100,000.
Over $150,000 but not over $250,000	$38,800, plus 32 percent of the excess of such amount over $150,000.
Over $250,000 but not over $500,000	$70,800, plus 34 percent of the excess of such amount over $250,000.
Over $500,000 but not over $750,000	$155,800, plus 37 percent of the excess of such amount over $500,000.
Over $750,000 but not over $1,000,000	$248,300, plus 39 percent of the excess of such amount over $750,000.
Over $1,000,000 but not over $1,250,000	$345,800, plus 41 percent of the excess of such amount over $1,000,000.
Over $1,250,000 but not over $1,500,000	$448,300, plus 43 percent of the excess of such amount over $1,250,000.
Over $1,500,000	$555,800, plus 45 percent of the excess of such amount over $1,500,000.

Gift Tax Rates

For Gifts Made Only in 2010

If the Amount with Respect to Which the Tentative Tax to Be Computed Is:	The Tentative Tax Is:
Not over $10,000	18 percent of such amount.
Over $10,000 but not over $20,000	$1,800, plus 20 percent of the excess of such amount over $10,000.
Over $20,000 but not over $40,000	$3,800, plus 22 percent of the excess of such amount over $20,000.
Over $40,000 but not over $60,000	$8,200, plus 24 percent of the excess of such amount over $40,000.
Over $60,000 but not over $80,000	$13,000, plus 26 percent of the excess of such amount over $60,000.
Over $80,000 but not over $100,000	$18,200, plus 28 percent of the excess of such amount over $80,000.
Over $100,000 but not over $150,000	$23,800, plus 30 percent of the excess of such amount over $100,000.
Over $150,000 but not over $250,000	$38,800, plus 32 percent of the excess of such amount over $150,000.
Over $250,000 but not over $500,000	$70,800, plus 34 percent of the excess of such amount over $250,000.
Over $500,000	$155,800, plus 35 percent of the excess of such amount over $500,000.

Unified Transfer Tax Rates

For Gifts Made and for Deaths in 2011–2012

If the Amount with Respect to Which the Tentative Tax to Be Computed Is:	The Tentative Tax Is:
Not over $10,000	18 percent of such amount.
Over $10,000 but not over $20,000	$1,800, plus 20 percent of the excess of such amount over $10,000.
Over $20,000 but not over $40,000	$3,800, plus 22 percent of the excess of such amount over $20,000.
Over $40,000 but not over $60,000	$8,200, plus 24 percent of the excess of such amount over $40,000.
Over $60,000 but not over $80,000	$13,000, plus 26 percent of the excess of such amount over $60,000.
Over $80,000 but not over $100,000	$18,200, plus 28 percent of the excess of such amount over $80,000.
Over $100,000 but not over $150,000	$23,800, plus 30 percent of the excess of such amount over $100,000.
Over $150,000 but not over $250,000	$38,800, plus 32 percent of the excess of such amount over $150,000.
Over $250,000 but not over $500,000	$70,800, plus 34 percent of the excess of such amount over $250,000.
Over $500,000	$155,800, plus 35 percent of the excess of such amount over $500,000.

Valuation Tables (On or After May 1, 2009)

Table S Single Life Remainder Factors Interest Rate

AGE	4.2%	4.4%	4.6%	4.8%	5.0%	5.2%	5.4%	5.6%
0	.06083	.05483	.04959	.04501	.04101	.03749	.03441	.03170
1	.05668	.05049	.04507	.04034	.03618	.03254	.02934	.02652
2	.05858	.05222	.04665	.04178	.03750	.03373	.03042	.02750
3	.06072	.05420	.04848	.04346	.03904	.03516	.03173	.02871
4	.06303	.05634	.05046	.04530	.04075	.03674	.03319	.03006
5	.06547	.05861	.05258	.04726	.04258	.03844	.03478	.03153
6	.06805	.06102	.05482	.04935	.04453	.04026	.03647	.03312
7	.07074	.06353	.05717	.05155	.04658	.04217	.03826	.03479
8	.07356	.06617	.05964	.05386	.04875	.04421	.04017	.03658
9	.07651	.06895	.06225	.05631	.05105	.04637	.04220	.03849
10	.07960	.07185	.06499	.05889	.05347	.04865	.04435	.04052
11	.08283	.07490	.06786	.06160	.05603	.05106	.04663	.04267
12	.08620	.07808	.07087	.06444	.05871	.05360	.04903	.04494
13	.08967	.08137	.07397	.06738	.06149	.05623	.05152	.04729
14	.09321	.08472	.07715	.07038	.06433	.05892	.05406	.04971
15	.09680	.08812	.08036	.07342	.06721	.06164	.05664	.05214
16	.10041	.09154	.08360	.07649	.07011	.06438	.05923	.05459
17	.10409	.09502	.08689	.07960	.07305	.06716	.06185	.05707
18	.10782	.09855	.09024	.08276	.07604	.06998	.06452	.05959
19	.11164	.10217	.09366	.08600	.07910	.07288	.06726	.06218
20	.11559	.10592	.09721	.08937	.08228	.07589	.07010	.06487
21	.11965	.10977	.10087	.09283	.08557	.07900	.07305	.06765
22	.12383	.11376	.10465	.09642	.08897	.08223	.07610	.07055
23	.12817	.11789	.10859	.10016	.09252	.08559	.07930	.07358
24	.13270	.12221	.11270	.10408	.09625	.08914	.08267	.07678
25	.13744	.12674	.11703	.10821	.10019	.09289	.08625	.08018
26	.14239	.13149	.12158	.11256	.10435	.09686	.09003	.08380
27	.14758	.13647	.12636	.11714	.10873	.10106	.09405	.08764
28	.15300	.14169	.13137	.12195	.11335	.10549	.09829	.09171
29	.15864	.14712	.13660	.12698	.11819	.11013	.10275	.09598
30	.16448	.15275	.14203	.13222	.12323	.11498	.10742	.10047
31	.17053	.15861	.14769	.13768	.12849	.12006	.11230	.10517
32	.17680	.16468	.15357	.14336	.13398	.12535	.11741	.11009
33	.18330	.17099	.15968	.14927	.13970	.13088	.12275	.11525
34	.19000	.17750	.16599	.15539	.14562	.13661	.12829	.12061

Valuation Tables (On or After May 1, 2009, *continued*)

Table S Single Life Remainder Factors Interest Rate

AGE	4.2%	4.4%	4.6%	4.8%	5.0%	5.2%	5.4%	5.6%
35	.19692	.18423	.17253	.16174	.15178	.14258	.13408	.12621
36	.20407	.19119	.17931	.16833	.15818	.14879	.14009	.13204
37	.21144	.19838	.18631	.17515	.16481	.15523	.14635	.13811
38	.21904	.20582	.19357	.18222	.17170	.16193	.15287	.14444
39	.22687	.21348	.20105	.18952	.17882	.16887	.15962	.15102
40	.23493	.22137	.20878	.19707	.18619	.17606	.16663	.15784
41	.24322	.22950	.21674	.20487	.19381	.18350	.17390	.16493
42	.25173	.23786	.22494	.21290	.20168	.19120	.18141	.17227
43	.26049	.24648	.23342	.22122	.20982	.19918	.18922	.17990
44	.26950	.25535	.24214	.22979	.21824	.20742	.19730	.18781
45	.27874	.26447	.25112	.23862	.22692	.21595	.20566	.19600
46	.28824	.27385	.26038	.24774	.23589	.22476	.21431	.20450
47	.29798	.28349	.26989	.25712	.24513	.23386	.22326	.21328
48	.30797	.29338	.27967	.26678	.25466	.24325	.23250	.22238
49	.31822	.30355	.28974	.27674	.26449	.25294	.24206	.23179
50	.32876	.31401	.30011	.28701	.27465	.26298	.25196	.24156
51	.33958	.32477	.31079	.29759	.28513	.27335	.26221	.25168
52	.35068	.33582	.32178	.30851	.29595	.28407	.27282	.26216
53	.36206	.34717	.33308	.31974	.30710	.29513	.28378	.27301
54	.37371	.35880	.34467	.33127	.31857	.30651	.29507	.28420
55	.38559	.37067	.35652	.34308	.33032	.31820	.30668	.29572
56	.39765	.38275	.36859	.35512	.34232	.33014	.31855	.30751
57	.40990	.39502	.38086	.36739	.35455	.34233	.33068	.31957
58	.42231	.40747	.39333	.37985	.36700	.35474	.34304	.33188
59	.43490	.42011	.40600	.39253	.37968	.36740	.35567	.34446
60	.44768	.43296	.41890	.40546	.39261	.38033	.36858	.35733
61	.46064	.44600	.43200	.41860	.40578	.39351	.38175	.37048
62	.47373	.45920	.44527	.43194	.41915	.40690	.39514	.38387
63	.48696	.47253	.45870	.44544	.43271	.42049	.40876	.39749
64	.50030	.48601	.47229	.45911	.44645	.43428	.42258	.41133
65	.51377	.49963	.48603	.47295	.46037	.44827	.43662	.42540
66	.52750	.51352	.50007	.48711	.47464	.46262	.45103	.43987
67	.54144	.52765	.51436	.50154	.48919	.47727	.46578	.45468
68	.55554	.54196	.52885	.51619	.50398	.49218	.48079	.46978
69	.56976	.55640	.54349	.53102	.51896	.50731	.49603	.48513

Valuation Tables (On or After May 1, 2009, *continued*)

Table S Single Life Remainder Factors Interest Rate

AGE	4.2%	4.4%	4.6%	4.8%	5.0%	5.2%	5.4%	5.6%
70	.58407	.57095	.55826	.54598	.53410	.52260	.51147	.50069
71	.59848	.58561	.57316	.56109	.54940	.53808	.52710	.51646
72	.61294	.60035	.58815	.57632	.56484	.55371	.54291	.53243
73	.62741	.61512	.60318	.59160	.58035	.56943	.55882	.54851
74	.64183	.62983	.61818	.60686	.59586	.58516	.57476	.56464
75	.65612	.64444	.63309	.62204	.61129	.60083	.59065	.58074
76	.67026	.65891	.64786	.63710	.62661	.61640	.60646	.59676
77	.68423	.67321	.66248	.65201	.64181	.63186	.62215	.61269
78	.69800	.68733	.67692	.66676	.65684	.64717	.63772	.62849
79	.71156	.70124	.69116	.68132	.67170	.66230	.65312	.64414
80	.72487	.71490	.70516	.69563	.68632	.67721	.66830	.65959
81	.73791	.72830	.71890	.70970	.70069	.69188	.68325	.67481
82	.75065	.74140	.73235	.72348	.71479	.70628	.69794	.68977
83	.76308	.75419	.74548	.73695	.72858	.72037	.71232	.70443
84	.77516	.76664	.75828	.75008	.74203	.73413	.72638	.71877
85	.78689	.77873	.77072	.76285	.75512	.74753	.74008	.73275
86	.79825	.79044	.78278	.77524	.76783	.76055	.75340	.74636
87	.80921	.80176	.79443	.78722	.78014	.77316	.76630	.75956
88	.81978	.81268	.80569	.79880	.79203	.78536	.77880	.77234
89	.82994	.82317	.81651	.80995	.80349	.79712	.79085	.78467
90	.83967	.83324	.82690	.82065	.81450	.80843	.80244	.79655
91	.84898	.84288	.83685	.83091	.82505	.81928	.81358	.80795
92	.85787	.85208	.84636	.84072	.83515	.82966	.82423	.81888
93	.86632	.86083	.85541	.85006	.84477	.83955	.83440	.82931
94	.87435	.86915	.86402	.85894	.85393	.84898	.84409	.83925
95	.88197	.87705	.87219	.86739	.86265	.85795	.85331	.84872
96	.88915	.88451	.87991	.87537	.87088	.86643	.86203	.85768
97	.89593	.89154	.88720	.88290	.87865	.87444	.87028	.86616
98	.90232	.89818	.89408	.89002	.88600	.88202	.87808	.87418
99	.90835	.90444	.90057	.89674	.89294	.88918	.88546	.88177
100	.91397	.91028	.90663	.90301	.89942	.89587	.89234	.88885
101	.91930	.91583	.91238	.90897	.90558	.90223	.89890	.89560
102	.92424	.92096	.91771	.91448	.91128	.90811	.90496	.90184
103	.92914	.92605	.92300	.91996	.91695	.91397	.91100	.90806
104	.93364	.93074	.92786	.92501	.92217	.91935	.91656	.91379
105	.93809	.93537	.93266	.92998	.92731	.92467	.92204	.91943
106	.94365	.94115	.93867	.93621	.93376	.93133	.92892	.92651
107	.94994	.94771	.94549	.94328	.94108	.93890	.93673	.93457
108	.96010	.95830	.95651	.95472	.95295	.95118	.94942	.94767
109	.97985	.97893	.97801	.97710	.97619	.97529	.97438	.97348

Valuation Tables (On or After May 1, 2009)

Table B Term Certain Remainder Factors Interest Rate

YEARS	4.2%	4.4%	4.6%	4.8%	5.0%	5.2%	5.4%	5.6%
1	.959693	.957854	.956023	.954198	.952381	.950570	.948767	.946970
2	.921010	.917485	.913980	.910495	.907029	.903584	.900158	.896752
3	.883887	.878817	.873786	.868793	.863838	.858920	.854040	.849197
4	.848260	.841779	.835359	.829001	.822702	.816464	.810285	.804163
5	.814069	.806302	.798623	.791031	.783526	.776106	.768771	.761518
6	.781257	.772320	.763501	.754801	.746215	.737744	.729384	.721135
7	.749766	.739770	.729925	.720230	.710681	.701277	.692015	.682893
8	.719545	.708592	.697825	.687242	.676839	.666613	.656561	.646679
9	.690543	.678728	.667137	.655765	.644609	.633663	.622923	.612385
10	.662709	.650122	.637798	.625730	.613913	.602341	.591009	.579910
11	.635997	.622722	.609750	.597071	.584679	.572568	.560729	.549157
12	.610362	.596477	.582935	.569724	.556837	.544266	.532001	.520035
13	.585760	.571339	.557299	.543630	.530321	.517363	.504745	.492458
14	.562150	.547259	.532790	.518731	.505068	.491790	.478885	.466343
15	.539491	.524195	.509360	.494972	.481017	.467481	.454350	.441612
16	.517746	.502102	.486960	.472302	.458112	.444374	.431072	.418194
17	.496877	.480941	.465545	.450670	.436297	.422408	.408987	.396017
18	.476849	.460671	.445071	.430028	.415521	.401529	.388033	.375016
19	.457629	.441256	.425498	.410332	.395734	.381681	.368153	.355129
20	.439183	.422659	.406786	.391538	.376889	.362815	.349291	.336296
21	.421481	.404846	.388897	.373605	.358942	.344881	.331396	.318462
22	.404492	.387783	.371794	.356494	.341850	.327834	.314417	.301574
23	.388188	.371440	.355444	.340166	.325571	.311629	.298309	.285581
24	.372542	.355785	.339813	.324586	.310068	.296225	.283025	.270437
25	.357526	.340791	.324869	.309719	.295303	.281583	.268525	.256096
26	.343115	.326428	.310582	.295533	.281241	.267664	.254768	.242515
27	.329285	.312670	.296923	.281998	.267848	.254434	.241715	.229654
28	.316012	.299493	.283866	.269082	.255094	.241857	.229331	.217475
29	.303275	.286870	.271382	.256757	.242946	.229902	.217582	.205943
30	.291051	.274780	.259447	.244997	.231377	.218538	.206434	.195021
31	.279319	.263199	.248038	.233776	.220359	.207736	.195858	.184679
32	.268061	.252106	.237130	.223069	.209866	.197468	.185823	.174886
33	.257256	.241481	.226702	.212852	.199873	.187707	.176303	.165612
34	.246887	.231304	.216732	.203103	.190355	.178429	.167270	.156829
35	.236935	.221556	.207201	.193801	.181290	.169609	.158701	.148512

Valuation Tables (On or After May 1, 2009, *continued*)

Table B Term Certain Remainder Factors Interest Rate

YEARS	4.2%	4.4%	4.6%	4.8%	5.0%	5.2%	5.4%	5.6%
36	.227385	.212218	.198089	.184924	.172657	.161225	.150570	.140637
37	.218220	.203274	.189377	.176454	.164436	.153256	.142856	.133179
38	.209424	.194707	.181049	.168373	.156605	.145681	.135537	.126116
39	.200983	.186501	.173087	.160661	.149148	.138480	.128593	.119428
40	.192882	.178641	.165475	.153302	.142046	.131635	.122004	.113095
41	.185107	.171112	.158198	.146281	.135282	.125128	.115754	.107098
42	.177646	.163900	.151241	.139581	.128840	.118943	.109823	.101418
43	.170486	.156992	.144590	.133188	.122704	.113064	.104197	.096040
44	.163614	.150376	.138231	.127088	.116861	.107475	.098858	.090947
45	.157019	.144038	.132152	.121267	.111297	.102163	.093793	.086124
46	.150690	.137968	.126340	.115713	.105997	.097113	.088988	.081557
47	.144616	.132153	.120784	.110413	.100949	.092312	.084429	.077232
48	.138787	.126583	.115473	.105356	.096142	.087749	.080103	.073136
49	.133193	.121248	.110395	.100530	.091564	.083412	.075999	.069258
50	.127824	.116138	.105540	.095926	.087204	.079289	.072106	.065585
51	.122672	.111243	.100898	.091532	.083051	.075370	.068411	.062107
52	.117728	.106555	.096461	.087340	.079096	.071644	.064907	.058813
53	.112982	.102064	.092219	.083340	.075330	.068103	.061581	.055695
54	.108428	.097763	.088164	.079523	.071743	.064737	.058426	.052741
55	.104058	.093642	.084286	.075880	.068326	.061537	.055433	.049944
56	.099864	.089696	.080580	.072405	.065073	.058495	.052593	.047296
57	.095839	.085916	.077036	.069089	.061974	.055604	.049898	.044787
58	.091976	.082295	.073648	.065924	.059023	.052855	.047342	.042412
59	.088268	.078826	.070409	.062905	.056212	.050243	.044916	.040163
60	.084710	.075504	.067313	.060024	.053536	.047759	.042615	.038033

Appendix B

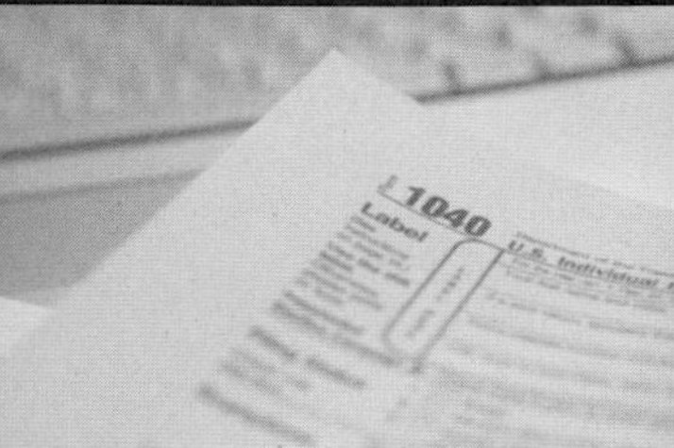

TAX FORMS

(Tax forms can be obtained from the IRS website: **http://www.irs.gov**)

Form **709**

Department of the Treasury
Internal Revenue Service

United States Gift (and Generation-Skipping Transfer) Tax Return

(For gifts made during calendar year 2010)

▶ **See separate instructions.**

OMB No. 1545-0020

2010

Part 1—General Information

1 Donor's first name and middle initial	2 Donor's last name	**3 Donor's social security number**
4 Address (number, street, and apartment number)		5 Legal residence (domicile)
6 City, state, and ZIP code		7 Citizenship (see instructions)

		Yes	No
8	If the donor died during the year, check here ▶ ☐ and enter date of death ______ , ______.		
9	If you extended the time to file this Form 709, check here ▶ ☐		
10	Enter the total number of donees listed on Schedule A. Count each person only once. ▶		
11a	Have you (the donor) previously filed a Form 709 (or 709-A) for any other year? If "No," skip line 11b		
b	If the answer to line 11a is "Yes," has your address changed since you last filed Form 709 (or 709-A)?		
12	**Gifts by husband or wife to third parties.** Do you consent to have the gifts (including generation-skipping transfers) made by you and by your spouse to third parties during the calendar year considered as made one-half by each of you? (See instructions.) (If the answer is "Yes," the following information must be furnished and your spouse must sign the consent shown below. **If the answer is "No," skip lines 13–18 and go to Schedule A.**)		
13	Name of consenting spouse — 14 SSN		
15	Were you married to one another during the entire calendar year? (see instructions)		
16	If 15 is "No," check whether ☐ married ☐ divorced or ☐ widowed/deceased, and give date (see instructions) ▶		
17	Will a gift tax return for this year be filed by your spouse? (If "Yes," mail both returns in the same envelope.)		
18	**Consent of Spouse.** I consent to have the gifts (and generation-skipping transfers) made by me and by my spouse to third parties during the calendar year considered as made one-half by each of us. We are both aware of the joint and several liability for tax created by the execution of this consent.		

Consenting spouse's signature ▶ **Date** ▶

Part 2—Tax Computation

1	Enter the amount from Schedule A, Part 4, line 11	1		
2	Enter the amount from Schedule B, line 3	2		
3	Total taxable gifts. Add lines 1 and 2	3		
4	Tax computed on amount on line 3 (see *Table for Computing Gift Tax* in separate instructions) . .	4		
5	Tax computed on amount on line 2 (see *Table for Computing Gift Tax* in separate instructions) . .	5		
6	Balance. Subtract line 5 from line 4	6		
7	Maximum unified credit (nonresident aliens, see instructions)	7	330,800	00
8	Enter the unified credit against tax allowable for all prior periods (from Sch. B, line 1, col. C) . .	8		
9	Balance. Subtract line 8 from line 7. Do not enter less than zero	9		
10	Enter 20% (.20) of the amount allowed as a specific exemption for gifts made after September 8, 1976, and before January 1, 1977 (see instructions)	10		
11	Balance. Subtract line 10 from line 9. Do not enter less than zero	11		
12	Unified credit. Enter the smaller of line 6 or line 11	12		
13	Credit for foreign gift taxes (see instructions)	13		
14	Total credits. Add lines 12 and 13	14		
15	Balance. Subtract line 14 from line 6. Do not enter less than zero	15		
16	Generation-skipping transfer taxes (from Schedule C, Part 3, col. H, Total)	16	0	00
17	Total tax. Add lines 15 and 16	17		
18	Gift and generation-skipping transfer taxes prepaid with extension of time to file	18		
19	If line 18 is less than line 17, enter **balance due** (see instructions)	19		
20	If line 18 is greater than line 17, enter **amount to be refunded**	20		

Attach check or money order here.

Sign Here

Under penalties of perjury, I declare that I have examined this return, including any accompanying schedules and statements, and to the best of my knowledge and belief, it is true, correct, and complete. Declaration of preparer (other than donor) is based on all information of which preparer has any knowledge.

May the IRS discuss this return with the preparer shown below (see instructions)? ☐ **Yes** ☐ **Nc**

▶ Signature of donor — Date

Paid Preparer Use Only

Print/Type preparer's name	Preparer's signature	Date	Check ☐ if self-employed	PTIN
Firm's name ▶			Firm's EIN ▶	
Firm's address ▶			Phone no.	

For Disclosure, Privacy Act, and Paperwork Reduction Act Notice, see the separate instructions for this form. Cat. No. 16783M Form 7(

Form 709 (2010) Page **2**

SCHEDULE A Computation of Taxable Gifts (Including transfers in trust) (see instructions)

A Does the value of any item listed on Schedule A reflect any valuation discount? If "Yes," attach explanation . . . . Yes ☐ No ☐

B ☐ ◄ Check here if you elect under section 529(c)(2)(B) to treat any transfers made this year to a qualified tuition program as made ratably over a 5-year period beginning this year. See instructions. Attach explanation.

Part 1—Gifts Subject Only to Gift Tax. Gifts less political organization, medical, and educational exclusions. (see instructions)

A Item number	B • Donee's name and address • Relationship to donor (if any) • Description of gift • If the gift was of securities, give CUSIP no. • If closely held entity, give EIN	C	D Donor's adjusted basis of gift	E Date of gift	F Value at date of gift	G For split gifts, enter 1/2 of column F	H Net transfer (subtract col. G from col. F)
Gifts made by spouse —*complete* ***only*** *if you are splitting gifts with your spouse and he/she also made gifts.*							
Total of Part 1. Add amounts from Part 1, column H . . . . ►							

Part 2—Direct Skips. Gifts that are direct skips and are subject to both gift tax and generation-skipping transfer tax. You must list the gifts in chronological order.

A Item number	B • Donee's name and address • Relationship to donor (if any) • Description of gift • If the gift was of securities, give CUSIP no. • If closely held entity, give EIN	C 2632(b) election out	D Donor's adjusted basis of gift	E Date of gift	F Value at date of gift	G For split gifts, enter 1/2 of column F	H Net transfer (subtract col. G from col. F)
Gifts made by spouse —*complete* ***only*** *if you are splitting gifts with your spouse and he/she also made gifts.*							
Total of Part 2. Add amounts from Part 2, column H . . . . ►							

Part 3—Indirect Skips. Gifts to trusts that are currently subject to gift tax and may later be subject to generation-skipping transfer tax. You must list these gifts in chronological order.

A Item number	B • Donee's name and address • Relationship to donor (if any) • Description of gift • If the gift was of securities, give CUSIP no. • If closely held entity, give EIN	C 2632(c) election	D Donor's adjusted basis of gift	E Date of gift	F Value at date of gift	G For split gifts, enter 1/2 of column F	H Net transfer (subtract col. G from col. F)
Gifts made by spouse —*complete* ***only*** *if you are splitting gifts with your spouse and he/she also made gifts.*							
Total of Part 3. Add amounts from Part 3, column H . . . . ►							

(If more space is needed, attach additional sheets of same size.) Form **709** (2010)

Form 709 (2010) Page **3**

Part 4—Taxable Gift Reconciliation

1	Total value of gifts of donor. Add totals from column H of Parts 1, 2, and 3		1		
2	Total annual exclusions for gifts listed on line 1 (see instructions)		2		
3	Total included amount of gifts. Subtract line 2 from line 1		3		
Deductions (see instructions)					
4	Gifts of interests to spouse for which a marital deduction will be claimed, based on item numbers ______ of Schedule A	4			
5	Exclusions attributable to gifts on line 4	5			
6	Marital deduction. Subtract line 5 from line 4	6			
7	Charitable deduction, based on item nos. ______ less exclusions	7			
8	Total deductions. Add lines 6 and 7		8		
9	Subtract line 8 from line 3		9		
10	Generation-skipping transfer taxes payable with this Form 709 (from Schedule C, Part 3, col. H, Total)		10	0	00
11	**Taxable gifts.** Add lines 9 and 10. Enter here and on page 1, Part 2—Tax Computation, line 1		11		

Terminable Interest (QTIP) Marital Deduction. (See instructions for Schedule A, Part 4, line 4.)

If a trust (or other property) meets the requirements of qualified terminable interest property under section 2523(f), and:

a. The trust (or other property) is listed on Schedule A, and

b. The value of the trust (or other property) is entered in whole or in part as a deduction on Schedule A, Part 4, line 4,

then the donor shall be deemed to have made an election to have such trust (or other property) treated as qualified terminable interest property under section 2523(f).

If less than the entire value of the trust (or other property) that the donor has included in Parts 1 and 3 of Schedule A is entered as a deduction on line 4, the donor shall be considered to have made an election only as to a fraction of the trust (or other property). The numerator of this fraction is equal to the amount of the trust (or other property) deducted on Schedule A, Part 4, line 6. The denominator is equal to the total value of the trust (or other property) listed in Parts 1 and 3 of Schedule A.

If you make the QTIP election, the terminable interest property involved will be included in your spouse's gross estate upon his or her death (section 2044). See instructions for line 4 of Schedule A. If your spouse disposes (by gift or otherwise) of all or part of the qualifying life income interest, he or she will be considered to have made a transfer of the entire property that is subject to the gift tax. See *Transfer of Certain Life Estates Received From Spouse* in the separate instructions.

12 Election Out of QTIP Treatment of Annuities

☐ ◀ Check here if you elect under section 2523(f)(6) **not** to treat as qualified terminable interest property any joint and survivor annuities that are reported on Schedule A and would otherwise be treated as qualified terminable interest property under section 2523(f). See instructions. Enter the item numbers from Schedule A for the annuities for which you are making this election ▶ ______

SCHEDULE B **Gifts From Prior Periods**

If you answered "Yes" on line 11a of page 1, Part 1, see the instructions for completing Schedule B. If you answered "No," skip to the Tax Computation on page 1 (or Schedule C, if applicable). See instructions for recalculation of the column C amounts. Attach calculations.

A Calendar year or calendar quarter (see instructions)	B Internal Revenue office where prior return was filed	C Amount of unified credit against gift tax for periods after December 31, 1976	D Amount of specific exemption for prior periods ending before January 1, 1977	E Amount of taxable gifts
1 Totals for prior periods	1			

2	Amount, if any, by which total specific exemption, line 1, column D is more than $30,000	2	
3	Total amount of taxable gifts for prior periods. Add amount on line 1, column E and amount, if any, on line 2. Enter here and on page 1, Part 2—Tax Computation, line 2	3	

(If more space is needed, attach additional sheets of same size.)

Form 709 (2010) Page **4**

SCHEDULE C Computation of Generation-Skipping Transfer Tax

Note. Inter vivos direct skips that are completely excluded by the GST exemption must still be fully reported (including value and exemptions claimed) on Schedule C.

Part 1—Generation-Skipping Transfers

A Item No. (from Schedule A, Part 2, col. A)	B Value (from Schedule A, Part 2, col. H)	C Nontaxable portion of transfer	D Net Transfer (subtract col. C from col. B)
Gifts made by spouse (for gift splitting only)			

Part 2—GST Exemption Reconciliation (Section 2631) and Section 2652(a)(3) Election

Check here ▶ ☐ if you are making a section 2652(a)(3) (special QTIP) election (see instructions)

Enter the item numbers from Schedule A of the gifts for which you are making this election ▶

1	Maximum allowable exemption (see instructions)	1	
2	Total exemption used for periods before filing this return	2	
3	Exemption available for this return. Subtract line 2 from line 1	3	
4	Exemption claimed on this return from Part 3, column C total, below	4	
5	Automatic allocation of exemption to transfers reported on Schedule A, Part 3 (see instructions)	5	
6	Exemption allocated to transfers not shown on line 4 or 5, above. **You must attach a "Notice of Allocation."** (see instructions)	6	
7	Add lines 4, 5, and 6	7	
8	Exemption available for future transfers. Subtract line 7 from line 3	8	

Part 3—Tax Computation

A Item No. (from Schedule C, Part 1)	B Net transfer (from Schedule C, Part 1, col. D)	C GST Exemption Allocated	D RESERVED	E RESERVED	F RESERVED	G Applicable Rate	H Generation-Skipping Transfer Tax (multiply col. B by col. G)
			Not applicable to transfers made in 2010			0	0
						0	0
						0	0
						0	0
						0	0
						0	0
Gifts made by spouse (for gift splitting only)							
			Not applicable to transfers made in 2010			0	0
						0	0
						0	0
						0	0
						0	0
						0	0
Total exemption claimed. Enter here and on Part 2, line 4, above. May not exceed Part 2, line 3, above			**Total generation-skipping transfer tax.** Enter here; on page 3, Schedule A, Part 4, line 10; and on page 1, Part 2—Tax Computation, line 16				

(If more space is needed, attach additional sheets of same size.)

Form **990-EZ**

Department of the Treasury
Internal Revenue Service

Short Form
Return of Organization Exempt From Income Tax

Under section 501(c), 527, or 4947(a)(1) of the Internal Revenue Code
(except black lung benefit trust or private foundation)

▶ Sponsoring organizations of donor advised funds, organizations that operate one or more hospital facilities, and certain controlling organizations as defined in section 512(b)(13) must file Form 990 (see instructions). All other organizations with gross receipts less than $200,000 and total assets less than $500,000 at the end of the year may use this form.

▶ *The organization may have to use a copy of this return to satisfy state reporting requirements.*

OMB No. 1545-1150

2010

Open to Public Inspection

A For the 2010 calendar year, or tax year beginning , 2010, and ending , 20

B Check if applicable:
- ☐ Address change
- ☐ Name change
- ☐ Initial return
- ☐ Terminated
- ☐ Amended return
- ☐ Application pending

C Name of organization

Number and street (or P.O. box, if mail is not delivered to street address) | Room/suite

City or town, state or country, and ZIP + 4

D Employer identification number

E Telephone number

F Group Exemption Number ▶

G Accounting Method: ☐ Cash ☐ Accrual Other (specify) ▶

H Check ▶ ☐ if the organization is **not** required to attach Schedule B (Form 990, 990-EZ, or 990-PF).

I Website: ▶

J Tax-exempt status (check only one) – ☐ 501(c)(3) ☐ 501(c) ( ) ◀ (insert no.) ☐ 4947(a)(1) or ☐ 527

K Check ▶ ☐ if the organization is not a section 509(a)(3) supporting organization **and** its gross receipts are normally **not** more than $50,000. A Form 990-EZ or Form 990 return is not required though Form 990-N (e-postcard) may be required (see instructions). But if the organization chooses to file a return, be sure to file a complete return.

L Add lines 5b, 6c, and 7b, to line 9 to determine gross receipts. If gross receipts are $200,000 or more, or if total assets (Part II, line 25, column (B) below) are $500,000 or more, file Form 990 instead of Form 990-EZ . . . . ▶ $

Part I **Revenue, Expenses, and Changes in Net Assets or Fund Balances** (see the instructions for Part I.)
Check if the organization used Schedule O to respond to any question in this Part I . . . . ☐

Revenue	1	Contributions, gifts, grants, and similar amounts received		1	
	2	Program service revenue including government fees and contracts		2	
	3	Membership dues and assessments		3	
	4	Investment income		4	
	5a	Gross amount from sale of assets other than inventory	5a		
	b	Less: cost or other basis and sales expenses	5b		
	c	Gain or (loss) from sale of assets other than inventory (Subtract line 5b from line 5a)		5c	
	6	Gaming and fundraising events			
	a	Gross income from gaming (attach Schedule G if greater than $15,000)	6a		
	b	Gross income from fundraising events (not including $ ______ of contributions from fundraising events reported on line 1) (attach Schedule G if the sum of such gross income and contributions exceeds $15,000)	6b		
	c	Less: direct expenses from gaming and fundraising events	6c		
	d	Net income or (loss) from gaming and fundraising events (add lines 6a and 6b and subtract line 6c)		6d	
	7a	Gross sales of inventory, less returns and allowances	7a		
	b	Less: cost of goods sold	7b		
	c	Gross profit or (loss) from sales of inventory (Subtract line 7b from line 7a)		7c	
	8	Other revenue (describe in Schedule O)		8	
	9	**Total revenue.** Add lines 1, 2, 3, 4, 5c, 6d, 7c, and 8 ▶		9	
Expenses	10	Grants and similar amounts paid (list in Schedule O)		10	
	11	Benefits paid to or for members		11	
	12	Salaries, other compensation, and employee benefits		12	
	13	Professional fees and other payments to independent contractors		13	
	14	Occupancy, rent, utilities, and maintenance		14	
	15	Printing, publications, postage, and shipping		15	
	16	Other expenses (describe in Schedule O)		16	
	17	**Total expenses.** Add lines 10 through 16 ▶		17	
Net Assets	18	Excess or (deficit) for the year (Subtract line 17 from line 9)		18	
	19	Net assets or fund balances at beginning of year (from line 27, column (A)) (must agree with end-of-year figure reported on prior year's return)		19	
	20	Other changes in net assets or fund balances (explain in Schedule O)		20	
	21	Net assets or fund balances at end of year. Combine lines 18 through 20 ▶		21	

For Paperwork Reduction Act Notice, see the separate instructions. Cat. No. 10642I Form **990-EZ** (2010)

Form 990-EZ (2009) Page **2**

Part III **Statement of Program Service Accomplishments** (See the instructions for Part III.)

What is the organization's primary exempt purpose?

Describe what was achieved in carrying out the organization's exempt purposes. In a clear and concise manner, describe the services provided, the number of persons benefited, and other relevant information for each program title.

Expenses (Required for section 501(c)(3) and 501(c)(4) organizations and section 4947(a)(1) trusts; optional for others.)

28	(Grants $) If this amount includes foreign grants, check here . . . . ▶ ☐	28a	
29	(Grants $) If this amount includes foreign grants, check here . . . . ▶ ☐	29a	
30	(Grants $) If this amount includes foreign grants, check here . . . . ▶ ☐	30a	
31	Other program services (attach schedule) . . . . (Grants $) If this amount includes foreign grants, check here . . . . ▶ ☐	31a	
32	**Total program service expenses** (add lines 28a through 31a) . . . . ▶	32	

Part IV **List of Officers, Directors, Trustees, and Key Employees.** List each one even if not compensated. (See the instructions for Part IV.)

(a) Name and address	**(b)** Title and average hours per week devoted to position	**(c)** Compensation **(If not paid, enter -0-.)**	**(d)** Contributions to employee benefit plans & deferred compensation	**(e)** Expense account and other allowances

Form **990-EZ** (2009)

Part V **Other Information** (Note the statement requirements in the instructions for Part V.)
Check if the organization used Schedule O to respond to any question in this Part V . . . . ☐

			Yes	No
33	Did the organization engage in any activity not previously reported to the IRS? If "Yes," provide a detailed description of each activity in Schedule O	33		
34	Were any significant changes made to the organizing or governing documents? If "Yes," attach a conformed copy of the amended documents if they reflect a change to the organization's name. Otherwise, explain the change on Schedule O (see instructions)	34		
35	If the organization had income from business activities, such as those reported on lines 2, 6a, and 7a (among others), but **not** reported on Form 990-T, explain in Schedule O why the organization did not report the income on Form 990-T.			
a	Did the organization have unrelated business gross income of $1,000 or more or was it a section 501(c)(4), 501(c)(5), or 501(c)(6) organization subject to section 6033(e) notice, reporting, and proxy tax requirements?	35a		
b	If "Yes," has it filed a tax return on **Form 990-T** for this year (see instructions)?	35b		
36	Did the organization undergo a liquidation, dissolution, termination, or significant disposition of net assets during the year? If "Yes," complete applicable parts of Schedule N	36		
37a	Enter amount of political expenditures, direct or indirect, as described in the instructions. ▶ 37a			
b	Did the organization file **Form 1120-POL** for this year?	37b		
38a	Did the organization borrow from, or make any loans to, any officer, director, trustee, or key employee **or** were any such loans made in a prior year and still outstanding at the end of the tax year covered by this return?	38a		
b	If "Yes," complete Schedule L, Part II and enter the total amount involved 38b			
39	Section 501(c)(7) organizations. Enter:			
a	Initiation fees and capital contributions included on line 9 . . . . 39a			
b	Gross receipts, included on line 9, for public use of club facilities 39b			
40a	Section 501(c)(3) organizations. Enter amount of tax imposed on the organization during the year under: section 4911 ▶ ______ ; section 4912 ▶ ______ ; section 4955 ▶ ______			
b	Section 501(c)(3) and 501(c)(4) organizations. Did the organization engage in any section 4958 excess benefit transaction during the year, or did it engage in an excess benefit transaction in a prior year that has not been reported on any of its prior Forms 990 or 990-EZ? If "Yes," complete Schedule L, Part I	40b		
c	Section 501(c)(3) and 501(c)(4) organizations. Enter amount of tax imposed on organization managers or disqualified persons during the year under sections 4912, 4955, and 4958 ▶ ______			
d	Section 501(c)(3) and 501(c)(4) organizations. Enter amount of tax on line 40c reimbursed by the organization ▶ ______			
e	All organizations. At any time during the tax year, was the organization a party to a prohibited tax shelter transaction? If "Yes," complete Form 8886-T.	40e		

41 List the states with which a copy of this return is filed. ▶ ______

42a The organization's books are in care of ▶ ______ Telephone no. ▶ ______
Located at ▶ ______ ZIP + 4 ▶ ______

			Yes	No
b	At any time during the calendar year, did the organization have an interest in or a signature or other authority over a financial account in a foreign country (such as a bank account, securities account, or other financial account)?	42b		
	If "Yes," enter the name of the foreign country: ▶ ______ See the instructions for exceptions and filing requirements for **Form TD F 90-22.1, Report of Foreign Bank and Financial Accounts.**			
c	At any time during the calendar year, did the organization maintain an office outside of the U.S.?	42c		
	If "Yes," enter the name of the foreign country: ▶ ______			

43 Section 4947(a)(1) nonexempt charitable trusts filing Form 990-EZ in lieu of **Form 1041—**Check here . . . . ▶ ☐
and enter the amount of tax-exempt interest received or accrued during the tax year . . . . . ▶ 43 ______

			Yes	No
44a	Did the organization maintain any donor advised funds during the year? If "Yes," Form 990 must be completed instead of Form 990-EZ	44a		
b	Did the organization operate one or more hospital facilities during the year? If "Yes," Form 990 must be completed instead of Form 990-EZ	44b		
c	Did the organization receive any payments for indoor tanning services during the year?	44c		
d	If "Yes" to line 44c, has the organization filed a Form 720 to report these payments? *If "No," provide an explanation in Schedule O*	44d		

Form 990-EZ (2010) Page **4**

			Yes	No
45	Is any related organization a controlled entity of the organization within the meaning of section 512(b)(13)?	**45**		
a	Did the organization receive any payment from or engage in any transaction with a controlled entity within the meaning of section 512(b)(13)? If "Yes," Form 990 and Schedule R may need to be completed instead of Form 990-EZ (see instructions)	**45a**		
46	Did the organization engage, directly or indirectly, in political campaign activities on behalf of or in opposition to candidates for public office? If "Yes," complete Schedule C, Part I	**46**		

Part VI **Section 501(c)(3) organizations and section 4947(a)(1) nonexempt charitable trusts only.** All section 501(c)(3) organizations and section 4947(a)(1) nonexempt charitable trusts must answer questions 47–49b and 52, and complete the tables for lines 50 and 51.

Check if the organization used Schedule O to respond to any question in this Part VI ☐

			Yes	No
47	Did the organization engage in lobbying activities? If "Yes," complete Schedule C, Part II	**47**		
48	Is the organization a school as described in section 170(b)(1)(A)(ii)? If "Yes," complete Schedule E	**48**		
49a	Did the organization make any transfers to an exempt non-charitable related organization?	**49a**		
b	If "Yes," was the related organization a section 527 organization?	**49b**		

50 Complete this table for the organization's five highest compensated employees (other than officers, directors, trustees and key employees) who each received more than $100,000 of compensation from the organization. If there is none, enter "None."

(a) Name and address of each employee paid more than $100,000	**(b)** Title and average hours per week devoted to position	**(c)** Compensation	**(d)** Contributions to employee benefit plans & deferred compensation	**(e)** Expense account and other allowances

f Total number of other employees paid over $100,000 ▶ ____________

51 Complete this table for the organization's five highest compensated independent contractors who each received more than $100,000 of compensation from the organization. If there is none, enter "None."

(a) Name and address of each independent contractor paid more than $100,000	**(b)** Type of service	**(c)** Compensation

d Total number of other independent contractors each receiving over $100,000 ▶ ____________

52 Did the organization complete Schedule A? **Note**: All section 501(c)(3) organizations and 4947(a)(1) nonexempt charitable trusts must attach a completed Schedule A ▶ ☐ **Yes** ☐ **No**

Under penalties of perjury, I declare that I have examined this return, including accompanying schedules and statements, and to the best of my knowledge and belief, it is true, correct, and complete. Declaration of preparer (other than officer) is based on all information of which preparer has any knowledge.

Sign Here

▶ Signature of officer — Date

▶ Type or print name and title

Paid Preparer Use Only

Print/Type preparer's name	Preparer's signature	Date	Check ☐ if self-employed	PTIN

Firm's name ▶ Firm's EIN ▶

Firm's address ▶ Phone no.

May the IRS discuss this return with the preparer shown above? See instructions ▶ ☐ **Yes** ☐ **No**

Form **990-T**

Department of the Treasury
Internal Revenue Service

Exempt Organization Business Income Tax Return
(and proxy tax under section 6033(e))

For calendar year 2010 or other tax year beginning ________, 2010, and ending ________, 20 ___ .
▶ See separate instructions.

OMB No. 1545-0687

2010

Open to Public Inspection for 501(c)(3) Organizations Only

A ☐ Check box if address changed

B Exempt under section
☐ 501( )( )
☐ 408(e) ☐ 220(e)
☐ 408A ☐ 530(a)
☐ 529(a)

C Book value of all assets at end of year

Print or Type

Name of organization (☐ Check box if name changed and see instructions.)

Number, street, and room or suite no. If a P.O. box, see instructions.

City or town, state, and ZIP code

D Employer identification number (Employees' trust, see instructions.)

E Unrelated business activity codes (See instructions.)

F Group exemption number (See instructions.) ▶

G Check organization type ▶ ☐ 501(c) corporation ☐ 501(c) trust ☐ 401(a) trust ☐ Other trust

H Describe the organization's primary unrelated business activity. ▶

I During the tax year, was the corporation a subsidiary in an affiliated group or a parent-subsidiary controlled group? . . ▶ ☐ Yes ☐ No
If "Yes," enter the name and identifying number of the parent corporation. ▶

J The books are in care of ▶ Telephone number ▶

Part I Unrelated Trade or Business Income

			(A) Income	(B) Expenses	(C) Net
1a	Gross receipts or sales				
b	Less returns and allowances ____ c Balance ▶	1c			
2	Cost of goods sold (Schedule A, line 7)	2			
3	Gross profit. Subtract line 2 from line 1c	3			
4a	Capital gain net income (attach Schedule D)	4a			
b	Net gain (loss) (Form 4797, Part II, line 17) (attach Form 4797)	4b			
c	Capital loss deduction for trusts	4c			
5	Income (loss) from partnerships and S corporations (attach statement)	5			
6	Rent income (Schedule C)	6			
7	Unrelated debt-financed income (Schedule E)	7			
8	Interest, annuities, royalties, and rents from controlled organizations (Schedule F)	8			
9	Investment income of a section 501(c)(7), (9), or (17) organization (Schedule G)	9			
10	Exploited exempt activity income (Schedule I)	10			
11	Advertising income (Schedule J)	11			
12	Other income (See instructions; attach schedule.)	12			
13	**Total.** Combine lines 3 through 12	13			

Part II Deductions Not Taken Elsewhere (See instructions for limitations on deductions.) (Except for contributions, deductions must be directly connected with the unrelated business income.)

14	Compensation of officers, directors, and trustees (Schedule K)	14	
15	Salaries and wages	15	
16	Repairs and maintenance	16	
17	Bad debts	17	
18	Interest (attach schedule)	18	
19	Taxes and licenses	19	
20	Charitable contributions (See instructions for limitation rules.)	20	
21	Depreciation (attach Form 4562) ____ 21		
22	Less depreciation claimed on Schedule A and elsewhere on return ____ 22a	22b	
23	Depletion	23	
24	Contributions to deferred compensation plans	24	
25	Employee benefit programs	25	
26	Excess exempt expenses (Schedule I)	26	
27	Excess readership costs (Schedule J)	27	
28	Other deductions (attach schedule)	28	
29	**Total deductions.** Add lines 14 through 28	29	
30	Unrelated business taxable income before net operating loss deduction. Subtract line 29 from line 13	30	
31	Net operating loss deduction (limited to the amount on line 30)	31	
32	Unrelated business taxable income before specific deduction. Subtract line 31 from line 30	32	
33	Specific deduction (Generally $1,000, but see line 33 instructions for exceptions.)	33	
34	**Unrelated business taxable income.** Subtract line 33 from line 32. If line 33 is greater than line 32, enter the smaller of zero or line 32	34	

For Paperwork Reduction Act Notice, see instructions. Cat. No. 11291J Form **990-T** (2010)

Form 990-T (2010) Page **2**

Part III Tax Computation

35 **Organizations Taxable as Corporations.** See instructions for tax computation. Controlled group members (sections 1561 and 1563) check here ▶ ☐ **See instructions** and:

a Enter your share of the $50,000, $25,000, and $9,925,000 taxable income brackets (in that order):
(1) $ **(2)** $ **(3)** $

b Enter organization's share of: **(1)** Additional 5% tax (not more than $11,750) $
(2) Additional 3% tax (not more than $100,000) $

c Income tax on the amount on line 34 ▶ **35c**

36 **Trusts Taxable at Trust Rates.** See instructions for tax computation. Income tax on the amount on line 34 from: ☐ Tax rate schedule or ☐ Schedule D (Form 1041) ▶ **36**

37 **Proxy tax.** See instructions ▶ **37**

38 Alternative minimum tax **38**

39 **Total.** Add lines 37 and 38 to line 35c or 36, whichever applies **39**

Part IV Tax and Payments

40a	Foreign tax credit (corporations attach Form 1118; trusts attach Form 1116)	40a	
b	Other credits (see instructions)	40b	
c	General business credit. Attach Form 3800	40c	
d	Credit for prior year minimum tax (attach Form 8801 or 8827)	40d	
e	**Total credits.** Add lines 40a through 40d		40e
41	Subtract line 40e from line 39		41
42	Other taxes. Check if from: ☐ Form 4255 ☐ Form 8611 ☐ Form 8697 ☐ Form 8866 ☐ Other (attach schedule)		42
43	**Total tax.** Add lines 41 and 42		43
44a	Payments: A 2009 overpayment credited to 2010	44a	
b	2010 estimated tax payments	44b	
c	Tax deposited with Form 8868	44c	
d	Foreign organizations: Tax paid or withheld at source (see instructions)	44d	
e	Backup withholding (see instructions)	44e	
f	Credit for small employer health insurance premiums (Attach Form 8941)	44f	
g	Other credits and payments: ☐ Form 2439 ______ ☐ Form 4136 ______ ☐ Other ______ Total ▶	44g	
45	**Total payments.** Add lines 44a through 44g		45
46	Estimated tax penalty (see instructions). Check if Form 2220 is attached ▶ ☐		46
47	**Tax due.** If line 45 is less than the total of lines 43 and 46, enter amount owed ▶		47
48	**Overpayment.** If line 45 is larger than the total of lines 43 and 46, enter amount overpaid ▶		48
49	Enter the amount of line 48 you want: **Credited to 2011 estimated tax** ▶ **Refunded** ▶		49

Part V Statements Regarding Certain Activities and Other Information (see instructions)

		Yes	No
1	At any time during the 2010 calendar year, did the organization have an interest in or a signature or other authority over a financial account (bank, securities, or other) in a foreign country? If YES, the organization may have to file Form TD F 90-22.1, Report of Foreign Bank and Financial Accounts. If YES, enter the name of the foreign country here ▶		
2	During the tax year, did the organization receive a distribution from, or was it the grantor of, or transferor to, a foreign trust? If YES, see instructions for other forms the organization may have to file.		
3	Enter the amount of tax-exempt interest received or accrued during the tax year ▶ $		

Schedule A—Cost of Goods Sold. Enter method of inventory valuation ▶

1	Inventory at beginning of year	1		6	Inventory at end of year	6	
2	Purchases	2		7	**Cost of goods sold.** Subtract line 6 from line 5. Enter here and in Part I, line 2	7	
3	Cost of labor	3					
4a	Additional section 263A costs (attach schedule)	4a		8	Do the rules of section 263A (with respect to property produced or acquired for resale) apply to the organization?	Yes	No
b	Other costs (attach schedule)	4b					
5	**Total.** Add lines 1 through 4b	5					

Sign Here

Under penalties of perjury, I declare that I have examined this return, including accompanying schedules and statements, and to the best of my knowledge and belief, it is true, correct, and complete. Declaration of preparer (other than taxpayer) is based on all information of which preparer has any knowledge.

▶ Signature of officer | Date | ▶ Title

May the IRS discuss this return with the preparer shown below (see instructions)? ☐ Yes ☐ No

Paid Preparer Use Only

Print/Type preparer's name	Preparer's signature	Date	Check ☐ if self-employed	PTIN
Firm's name ▶			Firm's EIN ▶	
Firm's address ▶			Phone no.	

Form **990-T** (2010)

Form 990-T (2010) Page **3**

Schedule C—Rent Income (From Real Property and Personal Property Leased With Real Property) (see instructions)

1. Description of property
(1)
(2)
(3)
(4)

2. Rent received or accrued		
(a) From personal property (if the percentage of rent for personal property is more than 10% but not more than 50%)	**(b)** From real and personal property (if the percentage of rent for personal property exceeds 50% or if the rent is based on profit or income)	**3(a)** Deductions directly connected with the income in columns 2(a) and 2(b) (attach schedule)
(1)		
(2)		
(3)		
(4)		
Total	Total	**(b) Total deductions.** Enter here and on page 1, Part I, line 6, column (B) ▶

(c) Total income. Add totals of columns 2(a) and 2(b). Enter here and on page 1, Part I, line 6, column (A) . . . ▶

Schedule E—Unrelated Debt-Financed Income (see instructions)

1. Description of debt-financed property	**2.** Gross income from or allocable to debt-financed property	**3.** Deductions directly connected with or allocable to debt-financed property	
		(a) Straight line depreciation (attach schedule)	**(b)** Other deductions (attach schedule)
(1)			
(2)			
(3)			
(4)			

4. Amount of average acquisition debt on or allocable to debt-financed property (attach schedule)	**5.** Average adjusted basis of or allocable to debt-financed property (attach schedule)	**6.** Column 4 divided by column 5	**7.** Gross income reportable (column 2 × column 6)	**8.** Allocable deductions (column 6 × total of columns 3(a) and 3(b))
(1)		%		
(2)		%		
(3)		%		
(4)		%		
Totals . . . . ▶			Enter here and on page 1, Part I, line 7, column (A).	Enter here and on page 1, Part I, line 7, column (B).

Total dividends-received deductions included in column 8 . . . . ▶

Schedule F—Interest, Annuities, Royalties, and Rents From Controlled Organizations (see instructions)

1. Name of controlled organization	**2.** Employer identification number	Exempt Controlled Organizations			
		3. Net unrelated income (loss) (see instructions)	**4.** Total of specified payments made	**5.** Part of column 4 that is included in the controlling organization's gross income	**6.** Deductions directly connected with income in column 5
(1)					
(2)					
(3)					
(4)					

Nonexempt Controlled Organizations

7. Taxable Income	**8.** Net unrelated income (loss) (see instructions)	**9.** Total of specified payments made	**10.** Part of column 9 that is included in the controlling organization's gross income	**11.** Deductions directly connected with income in column 10
(1)				
(2)				
(3)				
(4)				
Totals . . . . ▶			Add columns 5 and 10. Enter here and on page 1, Part I, line 8, column (A).	Add columns 6 and 11. Enter here and on page 1, Part I, line 8, column (B).

Form **1041** Department of the Treasury—Internal Revenue Service
U.S. Income Tax Return for Estates and Trusts 2010
OMB No. 1545-0092

A Type of entity (see instr.):
- ☐ Decedent's estate
- ☐ Simple trust
- ☐ Complex trust
- ☐ Qualified disability trust
- ☐ ESBT (S portion only)
- ☐ Grantor type trust
- ☐ Bankruptcy estate-Ch. 7
- ☐ Bankruptcy estate-Ch. 11
- ☐ Pooled income fund

For calendar year 2010 or fiscal year beginning , 2010, and ending , 20

Name of estate or trust (If a grantor type trust, see page 15 of the instructions.)

C Employer identification number

Name and title of fiduciary

D Date entity created

Number, street, and room or suite no. (If a P.O. box, see page 15 of the instructions.)

E Nonexempt charitable and split-interest trusts, check applicable boxes (see page 16 of the instr.):
- ☐ Described in section 4947(a)(1)
- ☐ Not a private foundation
- ☐ Described in section 4947(a)(2)

City or town, state, and ZIP code

B Number of Schedules K-1 attached (see instructions) ▶

F Check applicable boxes: ☐ Initial return ☐ Final return ☐ Amended return ☐ Change in trust's name ☐ Change in fiduciary ☐ Change in fiduciary's name ☐ Change in fiduciary's address

G Check here if the estate or filing trust made a section 645 election . . . . ▶☐

Income	1	Interest income	1	
	2a	Total ordinary dividends	2a	
	b	Qualified dividends allocable to: **(1)** Beneficiaries ______ **(2)** Estate or trust ______		
	3	Business income or (loss). Attach Schedule C or C-EZ (Form 1040)	3	
	4	Capital gain or (loss). Attach Schedule D (Form 1041)	4	
	5	Rents, royalties, partnerships, other estates and trusts, etc. Attach Schedule E (Form 1040)	5	
	6	Farm income or (loss). Attach Schedule F (Form 1040)	6	
	7	Ordinary gain or (loss). Attach Form 4797	7	
	8	Other income. List type and amount ______	8	
	9	**Total income.** Combine lines 1, 2a, and 3 through 8 ▶	9	
Deductions	10	Interest. Check if Form 4952 is attached ▶ ☐	10	
	11	Taxes	11	
	12	Fiduciary fees	12	
	13	Charitable deduction (from Schedule A, line 7)	13	
	14	Attorney, accountant, and return preparer fees	14	
	15a	Other deductions **not** subject to the 2% floor (attach schedule)	15a	
	b	Allowable miscellaneous itemized deductions subject to the 2% floor	15b	
	16	Add lines 10 through 15b ▶	16	
	17	Adjusted total income or (loss). Subtract line 16 from line 9 . . . 17		
	18	Income distribution deduction (from Schedule B, line 15). Attach Schedules K-1 (Form 1041)	18	
	19	Estate tax deduction including certain generation-skipping taxes (attach computation)	19	
	20	Exemption	20	
	21	Add lines 18 through 20 ▶	21	
Tax and Payments	22	Taxable income. Subtract line 21 from line 17. If a loss, see page 23 of the instructions	22	
	23	**Total tax** (from Schedule G, line 7)	23	
	24	**Payments: a** 2010 estimated tax payments and amount applied from 2009 return	24a	
	b	Estimated tax payments allocated to beneficiaries (from Form 1041-T)	24b	
	c	Subtract line 24b from line 24a	24c	
	d	Tax paid with Form 7004 (see page 24 of the instructions)	24d	
	e	Federal income tax withheld. If any is from Form(s) 1099, check ▶ ☐	24e	
		Other payments: **f** Form 2439 ______ ; **g** Form 4136 ______ ; Total ▶	24h	
	25	**Total payments.** Add lines 24c through 24e, and 24h ▶	25	
	26	Estimated tax penalty (see page 24 of the instructions)	26	
	27	**Tax due.** If line 25 is smaller than the total of lines 23 and 26, enter amount owed	27	
	28	**Overpayment.** If line 25 is larger than the total of lines 23 and 26, enter amount overpaid	28	
	29	Amount of line 28 to be: **a Credited to 2011 estimated tax ▶** ; **b Refunded ▶**	29	

Sign Here

Under penalties of perjury, I declare that I have examined this return, including accompanying schedules and statements, and to the best of my knowledge and belief, it is true, correct, and complete. Declaration of preparer (other than taxpayer) is based on all information of which preparer has any knowledge.

▶ Signature of fiduciary or officer representing fiduciary | Date | ▶ EIN of fiduciary if a financial institution

May the IRS discuss this return with the preparer shown below (see instr.)? ☐**Yes** ☐**No**

Paid Preparer Use Only

Print/Type preparer's name	Preparer's signature	Date	Check ☐ if self-employed	PTIN
Firm's name ▶			Firm's EIN ▶	
Firm's address ▶			Phone no.	

For Paperwork Reduction Act Notice, see the separate instructions. Cat. No. 11370H Form **1041** (2010)

Form 1041 (2010) Page **2**

Schedule A **Charitable Deduction.** Do not complete for a simple trust or a pooled income fund.

1	Amounts paid or permanently set aside for charitable purposes from gross income (see page 25)	1	
2	Tax-exempt income allocable to charitable contributions (see page 25 of the instructions)	2	
3	Subtract line 2 from line 1	3	
4	Capital gains for the tax year allocated to corpus and paid or permanently set aside for charitable purposes	4	
5	Add lines 3 and 4	5	
6	Section 1202 exclusion allocable to capital gains paid or permanently set aside for charitable purposes (see page 25 of the instructions)	6	
7	**Charitable deduction.** Subtract line 6 from line 5. Enter here and on page 1, line 13	7	

Schedule B **Income Distribution Deduction**

1	Adjusted total income (see page 25 of the instructions)	1	
2	Adjusted tax-exempt interest	2	
3	Total net gain from Schedule D (Form 1041), line 15, column (1) (see page 26 of the instructions)	3	
4	Enter amount from Schedule A, line 4 (minus any allocable section 1202 exclusion)	4	
5	Capital gains for the tax year included on Schedule A, line 1 (see page 26 of the instructions)	5	
6	Enter any gain from page 1, line 4, as a negative number. If page 1, line 4, is a loss, enter the loss as a positive number	6	
7	**Distributable net income.** Combine lines 1 through 6. If zero or less, enter -0-	7	
8	If a complex trust, enter accounting income for the tax year as determined under the governing instrument and applicable local law — 8		
9	Income required to be distributed currently	9	
10	Other amounts paid, credited, or otherwise required to be distributed	10	
11	Total distributions. Add lines 9 and 10. If greater than line 8, see page 26 of the instructions	11	
12	Enter the amount of tax-exempt income included on line 11	12	
13	Tentative income distribution deduction. Subtract line 12 from line 11	13	
14	Tentative income distribution deduction. Subtract line 2 from line 7. If zero or less, enter -0-	14	
15	**Income distribution deduction.** Enter the smaller of line 13 or line 14 here and on page 1, line 18	15	

Schedule G **Tax Computation** (see page 27 of the instructions)

1	**Tax: a** Tax on taxable income (see page 27 of the instructions)	1a			
	b Tax on lump-sum distributions. Attach Form 4972	1b			
	c Alternative minimum tax (from Schedule I (Form 1041), line 56)	1c			
	d **Total.** Add lines 1a through 1c ▶			1d	
2a	Foreign tax credit. Attach Form 1116	2a			
b	General business credit. Attach Form 3800	2b			
c	Credit for prior year minimum tax. Attach Form 8801	2c			
d	Bond credits. Attach Form 8912	2d			
3	**Total credits.** Add lines 2a through 2d ▶			3	
4	Subtract line 3 from line 1d. If zero or less, enter -0-			4	
5	Recapture taxes. Check if from: ☐ Form 4255 ☐ Form 8611			5	
6	Household employment taxes. Attach Schedule H (Form 1040)			6	
7	**Total tax.** Add lines 4 through 6. Enter here and on page 1, line 23 ▶			7	

	Other Information	**Yes**	**No**
1	Did the estate or trust receive tax-exempt income? If "Yes," attach a computation of the allocation of expenses Enter the amount of tax-exempt interest income and exempt-interest dividends ▶ $		
2	Did the estate or trust receive all or any part of the earnings (salary, wages, and other compensation) of any individual by reason of a contract assignment or similar arrangement?		
3	At any time during calendar year 2010, did the estate or trust have an interest in or a signature or other authority over a bank, securities, or other financial account in a foreign country? See page 29 of the instructions for exceptions and filing requirements for Form TD F 90-22.1. If "Yes," enter the name of the foreign country ▶		
4	During the tax year, did the estate or trust receive a distribution from, or was it the grantor of, or transferor to, a foreign trust? If "Yes," the estate or trust may have to file Form 3520. See page 29 of the instructions		
5	Did the estate or trust receive, or pay, any qualified residence interest on seller-provided financing? If "Yes," see page 29 for required attachment		
6	If this is an estate or a complex trust making the section 663(b) election, check here (see page 29) ▶ ☐		
7	To make a section 643(e)(3) election, attach Schedule D (Form 1041), and check here (see page 29) ▶ ☐		
8	If the decedent's estate has been open for more than 2 years, attach an explanation for the delay in closing the estate, and check here ▶ ☐		
9	Are any present or future trust beneficiaries skip persons? See page 29 of the instructions		

Form **1041** (2010)

661110

☐ Final K-1 ☐ Amended K-1 OMB No. 1545-0092

Schedule K-1 (Form 1041)
Department of the Treasury
Internal Revenue Service

2010

For calendar year 2010, or tax year beginning ________, 2010, and ending ________, 20 ____

Beneficiary's Share of Income, Deductions, Credits, etc.

▶ See back of form and instructions.

Part I Information About the Estate or Trust

A Estate's or trust's employer identification number

B Estate's or trust's name

C Fiduciary's name, address, city, state, and ZIP code

D ☐ Check if Form 1041-T was filed and enter the date it was filed ________

E ☐ Check if this is the final Form 1041 for the estate or trust

Part II Information About the Beneficiary

F Beneficiary's identifying number

G Beneficiary's name, address, city, state, and ZIP code

H ☐ Domestic beneficiary ☐ Foreign beneficiary

Part III Beneficiary's Share of Current Year Income, Deductions, Credits, and Other Items

1	Interest income	11	Final year deductions
2a	Ordinary dividends		
2b	Qualified dividends		
3	Net short-term capital gain		
4a	Net long-term capital gain		
4b	28% rate gain	12	Alternative minimum tax adjustment
4c	Unrecaptured section 1250 gain		
5	Other portfolio and nonbusiness income		
6	Ordinary business income		
7	Net rental real estate income	13	Credits and credit recapture
8	Other rental income		
9	Directly apportioned deductions		
		14	Other information
10	Estate tax deduction		

*See attached statement for additional information.

Note. A statement must be attached showing the beneficiary's share of income and directly apportioned deductions from each business, rental real estate, and other rental activity.

For IRS Use Only

For Paperwork Reduction Act Notice, see the Instructions for Form 1041. Cat. No. 11380D **Schedule K-1 (Form 1041) 2010**

Form **1065**
Department of the Treasury
Internal Revenue Service

U.S. Return of Partnership Income

For calendar year 2010, or tax year beginning ______________, 2010, ending ______________, 20 ________.
▶ See separate instructions.

OMB No. 1545-0099

2010

	Print or type.		
A Principal business activity		Name of partnership	D Employer identification number
B Principal product or service		Number, street, and room or suite no. If a P.O. box, see the instructions.	E Date business started
C Business code number		City or town, state, and ZIP code	F Total assets (see the instructions) $

G Check applicable boxes: (1) ☐ Initial return (2) ☐ Final return (3) ☐ Name change (4) ☐ Address change (5) ☐ Amended return
(6) ☐ Technical termination - also check (1) or (2)

H Check accounting method: (1) ☐ Cash (2) ☐ Accrual (3) ☐ Other (specify) ▶ ____________

I Number of Schedules K-1. Attach one for each person who was a partner at any time during the tax year ▶ ____________

J Check if Schedules C and M-3 are attached . . . . . ☐

Caution. *Include **only** trade or business income and expenses on lines 1a through 22 below. See the instructions for more information.*

Income	1a	Gross receipts or sales	1a		
	b	Less returns and allowances	1b	1c	
	2	Cost of goods sold (Schedule A, line 8)		2	
	3	Gross profit. Subtract line 2 from line 1c		3	
	4	Ordinary income (loss) from other partnerships, estates, and trusts *(attach statement)*		4	
	5	Net farm profit (loss) *(attach Schedule F (Form 1040))*		5	
	6	Net gain (loss) from Form 4797, Part II, line 17 *(attach Form 4797)*		6	
	7	Other income (loss) *(attach statement)*		7	
	8	**Total income (loss).** Combine lines 3 through 7		8	
Deductions (see the instructions for limitations)	9	Salaries and wages (other than to partners) (less employment credits)		9	
	10	Guaranteed payments to partners		10	
	11	Repairs and maintenance		11	
	12	Bad debts		12	
	13	Rent		13	
	14	Taxes and licenses		14	
	15	Interest		15	
	16a	Depreciation *(if required, attach Form 4562)*	16a		
	b	Less depreciation reported on Schedule A and elsewhere on return	16b	16c	
	17	Depletion **(Do not deduct oil and gas depletion.)**		17	
	18	Retirement plans, etc.		18	
	19	Employee benefit programs		19	
	20	Other deductions *(attach statement)*		20	
	21	**Total deductions.** Add the amounts shown in the far right column for lines 9 through 20		21	
	22	**Ordinary business income (loss).** Subtract line 21 from line 8		22	

Sign Here

Under penalties of perjury, I declare that I have examined this return, including accompanying schedules and statements, and to the best of my knowledge and belief, it is true, correct, and complete. Declaration of preparer (other than general partner or limited liability company member manager) is based on all information of which preparer has any knowledge.

▶ ______________________ Signature of general partner or limited liability company member manager ▶ __________ Date

May the IRS discuss this return with the preparer shown below (see instructions)? ☐ **Yes** ☐ **No**

Paid Preparer Use Only

Print/Type preparer's name	Preparer's signature	Date	Check ☐ if self- employed	PTIN
Firm's name ▶			Firm's EIN ▶	
Firm's address ▶			Phone no.	

Form 1065 (2010) Page **2**

Schedule A **Cost of Goods Sold** (see the instructions)

1	Inventory at beginning of year	1	
2	Purchases less cost of items withdrawn for personal use	2	
3	Cost of labor	3	
4	Additional section 263A costs (*attach statement*)	4	
5	Other costs (*attach statement*)	5	
6	**Total.** Add lines 1 through 5	6	
7	Inventory at end of year	7	
8	**Cost of goods sold.** Subtract line 7 from line 6. Enter here and on page 1, line 2	8	

9a Check all methods used for valuing closing inventory:

(i) ☐ Cost as described in Regulations section 1.471-3

(ii) ☐ Lower of cost or market as described in Regulations section 1.471-4

(iii) ☐ Other (specify method used and attach explanation) ▶

b Check this box if there was a writedown of "subnormal" goods as described in Regulations section 1.471-2(c) ▶ ☐

c Check this box if the LIFO inventory method was adopted this tax year for any goods (*if checked, attach Form 970*) ▶ ☐

d Do the rules of section 263A (for property produced or acquired for resale) apply to the partnership? ☐ **Yes** ☐ **No**

e Was there any change in determining quantities, cost, or valuations between opening and closing inventory? ☐ **Yes** ☐ **No**
If "Yes," attach explanation.

Schedule B **Other Information**

		Yes	No
1	What type of entity is filing this return? Check the applicable box: **a** ☐ Domestic general partnership **b** ☐ Domestic limited partnership **c** ☐ Domestic limited liability company **d** ☐ Domestic limited liability partnership **e** ☐ Foreign partnership **f** ☐ Other ▶		
2	At any time during the tax year, was any partner in the partnership a disregarded entity, a partnership (including an entity treated as a partnership), a trust, an S corporation, an estate (other than an estate of a deceased partner), or a nominee or similar person?		
3	At the end of the tax year:		
a	Did any foreign or domestic corporation, partnership (including any entity treated as a partnership), trust, or tax-exempt organization own, directly or indirectly, an interest of 50% or more in the profit, loss, or capital of the partnership? For rules of constructive ownership, see instructions. If "Yes," attach Schedule B-1, Information on Partners Owning 50% or More of the Partnership		
b	Did any individual or estate own, directly or indirectly, an interest of 50% or more in the profit, loss, or capital of the partnership? For rules of constructive ownership, see instructions. If "Yes," attach Schedule B-1, Information on Partners Owning 50% or More of the Partnership		
4	At the end of the tax year, did the partnership:		
a	Own directly 20% or more, or own, directly or indirectly, 50% or more of the total voting power of all classes of stock entitled to vote of any foreign or domestic corporation? For rules of constructive ownership, see instructions. If "Yes," complete (i) through (iv) below		

(i) Name of Corporation	**(ii)** Employer Identification Number (if any)	**(iii)** Country of Incorporation	**(iv)** Percentage Owned in Voting Stock

		Yes	No
b	Own directly an interest of 20% or more, or own, directly or indirectly, an interest of 50% or more in the profit, loss, or capital in any foreign or domestic partnership (including an entity treated as a partnership) or in the beneficial interest of a trust? For rules of constructive ownership, see instructions. If "Yes," complete (i) through (v) below		

(i) Name of Entity	**(ii)** Employer Identification Number (if any)	**(iii)** Type of Entity	**(iv)** Country of Organization	**(v)** Maximum Percentage Owned in Profit, Loss, or Capital

		Yes	No
5	Did the partnership file Form 8893, Election of Partnership Level Tax Treatment, or an election statement under section 6231(a)(1)(B)(ii) for partnership-level tax treatment, that is in effect for this tax year? See Form 8893 for more details . . .		
6	Does the partnership satisfy **all four** of the following conditions?		
a	The partnership's total receipts for the tax year were less than $250,000.		
b	The partnership's total assets at the end of the tax year were less than $1 million.		
c	Schedules K-1 are filed with the return and furnished to the partners on or before the due date (including extensions) for the partnership return.		
d	The partnership is not filing and is not required to file Schedule M-3 . . .		
	If "Yes," the partnership is not required to complete Schedules L, M-1, and M-2; Item F on page 1 of Form 1065; or Item L on Schedule K-1.		
7	Is this partnership a publicly traded partnership as defined in section 469(k)(2)? . . .		
8	During the tax year, did the partnership have any debt that was cancelled, was forgiven, or had the terms modified so as to reduce the principal amount of the debt? . . .		
9	Has this partnership filed, or is it required to file, Form 8918, Material Advisor Disclosure Statement, to provide information on any reportable transaction? . . .		
10	At any time during calendar year 2010, did the partnership have an interest in or a signature or other authority over a financial account in a foreign country (such as a bank account, securities account, or other financial account)? See the instructions for exceptions and filing requirements for Form TD F 90-22.1, Report of Foreign Bank and Financial Accounts. If "Yes," enter the name of the foreign country. ▶		
11	At any time during the tax year, did the partnership receive a distribution from, or was it the grantor of, or transferor to, a foreign trust? If "Yes," the partnership may have to file Form 3520, Annual Return To Report Transactions With Foreign Trusts and Receipt of Certain Foreign Gifts. See instructions . . .		
12a	Is the partnership making, or had it previously made (and not revoked), a section 754 election? . . .		
	See instructions for details regarding a section 754 election.		
b	Did the partnership make for this tax year an optional basis adjustment under section 743(b) or 734(b)? If "Yes," attach a statement showing the computation and allocation of the basis adjustment. See instructions . . .		
c	Is the partnership required to adjust the basis of partnership assets under section 743(b) or 734(b) because of a substantial built-in loss (as defined under section 743(d)) or substantial basis reduction (as defined under section 734(d))? If "Yes," attach a statement showing the computation and allocation of the basis adjustment. See instructions.		
13	Check this box if, during the current or prior tax year, the partnership distributed any property received in a like-kind exchange or contributed such property to another entity (other than entities wholly-owned by the partnership throughout the tax year) . . . ▶ ☐		
14	At any time during the tax year, did the partnership distribute to any partner a tenancy-in-common or other undivided interest in partnership property? . . .		
15	If the partnership is required to file Form 8858, Information Return of U.S. Persons With Respect To Foreign Disregarded Entities, enter the number of Forms 8858 attached. See instructions ▶		
16	Does the partnership have any foreign partners? If "Yes," enter the number of Forms 8805, Foreign Partner's Information Statement of Section 1446 Withholding Tax, filed for this partnership. ▶		
17	Enter the number of Forms 8865, Return of U.S. Persons With Respect to Certain Foreign Partnerships, attached to this return. ▶		

Designation of Tax Matters Partner (see instructions)

Enter below the general partner designated as the tax matters partner (TMP) for the tax year of this return:

Name of designated TMP ▶		Identifying number of TMP ▶	
If the TMP is an entity, name of TMP representative ▶		Phone number of TMP ▶	
Address of designated TMP ▶			

Form 1065 (2010) Page **4**

		Schedule K — Partners' Distributive Share Items		Total amount
Income (Loss)	1	Ordinary business income (loss) (page 1, line 22)		1
	2	Net rental real estate income (loss) (*attach Form 8825*)		2
	3a	Other gross rental income (loss)	3a	
	b	Expenses from other rental activities (*attach statement*)	3b	
	c	Other net rental income (loss). Subtract line 3b from line 3a		3c
	4	Guaranteed payments		4
	5	Interest income		5
	6	Dividends: a Ordinary dividends		6a
		b Qualified dividends	6b	
	7	Royalties		7
	8	Net short-term capital gain (loss) (*attach Schedule D (Form 1065)*)		8
	9a	Net long-term capital gain (loss) (*attach Schedule D (Form 1065)*)		9a
	b	Collectibles (28%) gain (loss)	9b	
	c	Unrecaptured section 1250 gain (*attach statement*)	9c	
	10	Net section 1231 gain (loss) (*attach Form 4797*)		10
	11	Other income (loss) (*see instructions*) Type ▶		11
Deductions	12	Section 179 deduction (*attach Form 4562*)		12
	13a	Contributions		13a
	b	Investment interest expense		13b
	c	Section 59(e)(2) expenditures: **(1)** Type ▶ **(2)** Amount ▶		13c(2)
	d	Other deductions (*see instructions*) Type ▶		13d
Self-Employment	14a	Net earnings (loss) from self-employment		14a
	b	Gross farming or fishing income		14b
	c	Gross nonfarm income		14c
Credits	15a	Low-income housing credit (section 42(j)(5))		15a
	b	Low-income housing credit (other)		15b
	c	Qualified rehabilitation expenditures (rental real estate) (*attach Form 3468*)		15c
	d	Other rental real estate credits (*see instructions*) Type ▶		15d
	e	Other rental credits (*see instructions*) Type ▶		15e
	f	Other credits (*see instructions*) Type ▶		15f
Foreign Transactions	16a	Name of country or U.S. possession ▶		
	b	Gross income from all sources		16b
	c	Gross income sourced at partner level		16c
		Foreign gross income sourced at partnership level		
	d	Passive category ▶ **e** General category ▶ **f** Other ▶		16f
		Deductions allocated and apportioned at partner level		
	g	Interest expense ▶ **h** Other ▶		16h
		Deductions allocated and apportioned at partnership level to foreign source income		
	i	Passive category ▶ **j** General category ▶ **k** Other ▶		16k
	l	Total foreign taxes (check one): ▶ Paid ☐ Accrued ☐		16l
	m	Reduction in taxes available for credit (*attach statement*)		16m
	n	Other foreign tax information (*attach statement*)		
Alternative Minimum Tax (AMT) Items	17a	Post-1986 depreciation adjustment		17a
	b	Adjusted gain or loss		17b
	c	Depletion (other than oil and gas)		17c
	d	Oil, gas, and geothermal properties—gross income		17d
	e	Oil, gas, and geothermal properties—deductions		17e
	f	Other AMT items (*attach statement*)		17f
Other Information	18a	Tax-exempt interest income		18a
	b	Other tax-exempt income		18b
	c	Nondeductible expenses		18c
	19a	Distributions of cash and marketable securities		19a
	b	Distributions of other property		19b
	20a	Investment income		20a
	b	Investment expenses		20b
	c	Other items and amounts (*attach statement*)		

Analysis of Net Income (Loss)

1	Net income (loss). Combine Schedule K, lines 1 through 11. From the result, subtract the sum of Schedule K, lines 12 through 13d, and 16l				**1**	
2 Analysis by partner type:	**(i)** Corporate	**(ii)** Individual (active)	**(iii)** Individual (passive)	**(iv)** Partnership	**(v)** Exempt organization	**(vi)** Nominee/Other
a General partners						
b Limited partners						

Schedule L Balance Sheets per Books

Assets	Beginning of tax year (a)	(b)	End of tax year (c)	(d)
1 Cash				
2a Trade notes and accounts receivable . . .				
b Less allowance for bad debts				
3 Inventories				
4 U.S. government obligations				
5 Tax-exempt securities				
6 Other current assets (*attach statement*) . .				
7 Mortgage and real estate loans				
8 Other investments (*attach statement*) . . .				
9a Buildings and other depreciable assets . .				
b Less accumulated depreciation				
10a Depletable assets				
b Less accumulated depletion				
11 Land (net of any amortization)				
12a Intangible assets (amortizable only) . . .				
b Less accumulated amortization				
13 Other assets (*attach statement*)				
14 Total assets				
Liabilities and Capital				
15 Accounts payable				
16 Mortgages, notes, bonds payable in less than 1 year				
17 Other current liabilities (*attach statement*) .				
18 All nonrecourse loans				
19 Mortgages, notes, bonds payable in 1 year or more				
20 Other liabilities (*attach statement*)				
21 Partners' capital accounts				
22 Total liabilities and capital				

Schedule M-1 Reconciliation of Income (Loss) per Books With Income (Loss) per Return

Note. Schedule M-3 may be required instead of Schedule M-1 (see instructions).

1 Net income (loss) per books		6 Income recorded on books this year not included on Schedule K, lines 1 through 11 (itemize):	
2 Income included on Schedule K, lines 1, 2, 3c, 5, 6a, 7, 8, 9a, 10, and 11, not recorded on books this year (itemize):		a Tax-exempt interest $	
3 Guaranteed payments (other than health insurance)		7 Deductions included on Schedule K, lines 1 through 13d, and 16l, not charged against book income this year (itemize):	
4 Expenses recorded on books this year not included on Schedule K, lines 1 through 13d, and 16l (itemize):		a Depreciation $	
a Depreciation $			
b Travel and entertainment $		8 Add lines 6 and 7	
		9 Income (loss) (Analysis of Net Income (Loss), line 1). Subtract line 8 from line 5 .	
5 Add lines 1 through 4			

Schedule M-2 Analysis of Partners' Capital Accounts

1 Balance at beginning of year . . .		6 Distributions: **a** Cash	
2 Capital contributed: **a** Cash . . .		**b** Property	
b Property . .		7 Other decreases (itemize):	
3 Net income (loss) per books			
4 Other increases (itemize):			
		8 Add lines 6 and 7	
5 Add lines 1 through 4		9 Balance at end of year. Subtract line 8 from line 5	

651110

☐ Final K-1 ☐ Amended K-1 OMB No. 1545-0099

Schedule K-1 (Form 1065) **2010**

Department of the Treasury
Internal Revenue Service

For calendar year 2010, or tax year beginning ____________, 2010 ending ____________, 20____

Partner's Share of Income, Deductions, Credits, etc.

► See back of form and separate instructions.

Part I Information About the Partnership

A Partnership's employer identification number

B Partnership's name, address, city, state, and ZIP code

C IRS Center where partnership filed return

D ☐ Check if this is a publicly traded partnership (PTP)

Part II Information About the Partner

E Partner's identifying number

F Partner's name, address, city, state, and ZIP code

G ☐ General partner or LLC member-manager ☐ Limited partner or other LLC member

H ☐ Domestic partner ☐ Foreign partner

I What type of entity is this partner? ____________

J Partner's share of profit, loss, and capital (see instructions):

	Beginning	Ending
Profit	%	%
Loss	%	%
Capital	%	%

K Partner's share of liabilities at year end:

Nonrecourse . . . . $ ____________
Qualified nonrecourse financing . $ ____________
Recourse . . . . $ ____________

L Partner's capital account analysis:

Beginning capital account . . . $ ____________
Capital contributed during the year $ ____________
Current year increase (decrease) . $ ____________
Withdrawals & distributions . . $ (____________)
Ending capital account . . . . $ ____________

☐ Tax basis ☐ GAAP ☐ Section 704(b) book
☐ Other (explain)

M Did the partner contribute property with a built-in gain or loss?
☐ Yes ☐ No
If "Yes", attach statement (see instructions)

Part III Partner's Share of Current Year Income, Deductions, Credits, and Other Items

1 Ordinary business income (loss)	**15** Credits
2 Net rental real estate income (loss)	
3 Other net rental income (loss)	**16** Foreign transactions
4 Guaranteed payments	
5 Interest income	
6a Ordinary dividends	
6b Qualified dividends	
7 Royalties	
8 Net short-term capital gain (loss)	
9a Net long-term capital gain (loss)	**17** Alternative minimum tax (AMT) items
9b Collectibles (28%) gain (loss)	
9c Unrecaptured section 1250 gain	
10 Net section 1231 gain (loss)	**18** Tax-exempt income and nondeductible expenses
11 Other income (loss)	
	19 Distributions
12 Section 179 deduction	
13 Other deductions	**20** Other information
14 Self-employment earnings (loss)	

*See attached statement for additional information.

For IRS Use Only

SCHEDULE M-3 (Form 1065)

Department of the Treasury
Internal Revenue Service

Net Income (Loss) Reconciliation for Certain Partnerships

▶ Attach to Form 1065 or Form 1065-B.
▶ See separate instructions.

OMB No. 1545-0099

2010

Name of partnership | **Employer identification number**

This Schedule M-3 is being filed because (check all that apply):

A ☐ The amount of the partnership's total assets at the end of the tax year is equal to $10 million or more.

B ☐ The amount of the partnership's adjusted total assets for the year is equal to $10 million or more. If box B is checked, enter the amount of adjusted total assets for the tax year ____________ .

C ☐ The amount of total receipts for the tax year is equal to $35 million or more. If box C is checked, enter the total receipts for the tax year ____________ .

D ☐ An entity that is a reportable entity partner with respect to the partnership owns or is deemed to own an interest of 50 percent or more in the partnership's capital, profit, or loss, on any day during the tax year of the partnership.

Name of Reportable Entity Partner	Identifying Number	Maximum Percentage Owned or Deemed Owned

E ☐ Voluntary Filer

Part I Financial Information and Net Income (Loss) Reconciliation

1a Did the partnership file SEC Form 10-K for its income statement period ending with or within this tax year?

☐ **Yes.** Skip lines 1b and 1c and complete lines 2 through 11 with respect to that SEC Form 10-K.

☐ **No.** Go to line 1b. See instructions if multiple non-tax-basis income statements are prepared.

b Did the partnership prepare a certified audited non-tax-basis income statement for that period?

☐ **Yes.** Skip line 1c and complete lines 2 through 11 with respect to that income statement.

☐ **No.** Go to line 1c.

c Did the partnership prepare a non-tax-basis income statement for that period?

☐ **Yes.** Complete lines 2 through 11 with respect to that income statement.

☐ **No.** Skip lines 2 through 3b and enter the partnership's net income (loss) per its books and records on line 4a.

2 Enter the income statement period: Beginning ____/____/____ Ending ____/____/____

3a Has the partnership's income statement been restated for the income statement period on line 2?

☐ **Yes.** (If "Yes," attach an explanation and the amount of each item restated.)

☐ **No.**

b Has the partnership's income statement been restated for any of the five income statement periods preceding the period on line 2?

☐ **Yes.** (If "Yes," attach an explanation and the amount of each item restated.)

☐ **No.**

4a	Worldwide consolidated net income (loss) from income statement source identified in Part I, line 1	**4a**	
b	Indicate accounting standard used for line 4a (see instructions): **1** ☐ GAAP **2** ☐ IFRS **3** ☐ 704(b) **4** ☐ Tax-basis **5** ☐ Other: (Specify) ▶ ____________		
5a	Net income from nonincludible foreign entities (attach schedule)	**5a**	( )
b	Net loss from nonincludible foreign entities (attach schedule and enter as a positive amount) . . .	**5b**	
6a	Net income from nonincludible U.S. entities (attach schedule)	**6a**	( )
b	Net loss from nonincludible U.S. entities (attach schedule and enter as a positive amount)	**6b**	
7a	Net income (loss) of other foreign disregarded entities (attach schedule)	**7a**	
b	Net income (loss) of other U.S. disregarded entities (attach schedule)	**7b**	
8	Adjustment to eliminations of transactions between includible entities and nonincludible entities (attach schedule)	**8**	
9	Adjustment to reconcile income statement period to tax year (attach schedule)	**9**	
10	Other adjustments to reconcile to amount on line 11 (attach schedule)	**10**	
11	**Net income (loss) per income statement of the partnership.** Combine lines 4 through 10 . . . **Note.** Part I, line 11, must equal the amount on Part II, line 26, column (a).	**11**	

12 Enter the total amount (not just the partnership's share) of the assets and liabilities of all entities included or removed on the following lines:

	Total Assets	Total Liabilities
a Included on Part I, line 4		
b Removed on Part I, line 5		
c Removed on Part I, line 6		
d Included on Part I, line 7		

For Paperwork Reduction Act Notice, see the Instructions for your return. Cat. No. 39669D **Schedule M-3 (Form 1065) 2010**

Schedule M-3 (Form 1065) 2010 Page **2**

Name of partnership	**Employer identification number**

Part II **Reconciliation of Net Income (Loss) per Income Statement of Partnership with Income (Loss) per Return**

	Income (Loss) Items	**(a)** Income (Loss) per Income Statement	**(b)** Temporary Difference	**(c)** Permanent Difference	**(d)** Income (Loss) per Tax Return
	(Attach schedules for lines 1 through 9)				
1	Income (loss) from equity method foreign corporations				
2	Gross foreign dividends not previously taxed . . .				
3	Subpart F, QEF, and similar income inclusions . .				
4	Gross foreign distributions previously taxed . . .				
5	Income (loss) from equity method U.S. corporations				
6	U.S. dividends				
7	Income (loss) from U.S. partnerships				
8	Income (loss) from foreign partnerships				
9	Income (loss) from other pass-through entities . .				
10	Items relating to reportable transactions (attach details)				
11	Interest income (attach Form 8916-A)				
12	Total accrual to cash adjustment				
13	Hedging transactions				
14	Mark-to-market income (loss)				
15	Cost of goods sold (attach Form 8916-A)	( )			( )
16	Sale versus lease (for sellers and/or lessors) . . .				
17	Section 481(a) adjustments				
18	Unearned/deferred revenue				
19	Income recognition from long-term contracts . . .				
20	Original issue discount and other imputed interest .				
21a	Income statement gain/loss on sale, exchange, abandonment, worthlessness, or other disposition of assets other than inventory and pass-through entities .				
b	Gross capital gains from Schedule D, excluding amounts from pass-through entities				
c	Gross capital losses from Schedule D, excluding amounts from pass-through entities, abandonment losses, and worthless stock losses				
d	Net gain/loss reported on Form 4797, line 17, excluding amounts from pass-through entities, abandonment losses, and worthless stock losses .				
e	Abandonment losses				
f	Worthless stock losses (attach details)				
g	Other gain/loss on disposition of assets other than inventory				
22	Other income (loss) items with differences (attach schedule)				
23	**Total income (loss) items.** Combine lines 1 through 22				
24	**Total expense/deduction items.** (from Part III, line 31) (see instructions)				
25	Other items with no differences				
26	**Reconciliation totals.** Combine lines 23 through 25				

Note. Line 26, column (a), must equal the amount on Part I, line 11, and column (d) must equal Form 1065, page 5, Analysis of Net Income (Loss), line 1.

Schedule M-3 (Form 1065) 2010 Page **3**

Name of partnership | **Employer identification number**

Part III Reconciliation of Net Income (Loss) per Income Statement of Partnership With Income (Loss) per Return—Expense/Deduction Items

	Expense/Deduction Items	(a) Expense per Income Statement	(b) Temporary Difference	(c) Permanent Difference	(d) Deduction per Tax Return
1	State and local current income tax expense				
2	State and local deferred income tax expense				
3	Foreign current income tax expense (other than foreign withholding taxes)				
4	Foreign deferred income tax expense				
5	Equity-based compensation				
6	Meals and entertainment				
7	Fines and penalties				
8	Judgments, damages, awards, and similar costs				
9	Guaranteed payments				
10	Pension and profit-sharing				
11	Other post-retirement benefits				
12	Deferred compensation				
13	Charitable contribution of cash and tangible property				
14	Charitable contribution of intangible property				
15	Organizational expenses as per Regulations section 1.709-2(a)				
16	Syndication expenses as per Regulations section 1.709-2(b)				
17	Current year acquisition/reorganization investment banking fees				
18	Current year acquisition/reorganization legal and accounting fees				
19	Amortization/impairment of goodwill				
20	Amortization of acquisition, reorganization, and start-up costs				
21	Other amortization or impairment write-offs				
22	Section 198 environmental remediation costs				
23a	Depletion—Oil & Gas				
b	Depletion—Other than Oil & Gas				
24	Intangible drilling & development costs				
25	Depreciation				
26	Bad debt expense				
27	Interest expense (attach Form 8916-A)				
28	Purchase versus lease (for purchasers and/or lessees)				
29	Research and development costs (attach schedule)				
30	Other expense/deduction items with differences (attach schedule)				
31	**Total expense/deduction items.** Combine lines 1 through 30. Enter here and on Part II, line 24, reporting positive amounts as negative and negative amounts as positive				

SCHEDULE C (Form 1065)

Department of the Treasury
Internal Revenue Service

Additional Information for Schedule M-3 Filers

► **Attach to Form 1065. See separate instructions.**

OMB No. 1545-0099

2010

Name of partnership	**Employer identification number**

		Yes	No
1	At any time during the tax year, were there any transfers between the partnership and its partners subject to the disclosure requirements of Regulations section 1.707-8?		
2	Do the amounts reported on Schedule M-3, Part II, lines 7 or 8, column (d), reflect allocations to this partnership from another partnership of income, gain, loss, deduction, or credit that are disproportionate to this partnership's share of capital in such partnership or its ratio for sharing other items of such partnership?		
3	At any time during the tax year, did the partnership sell, exchange, or transfer any interest in an intangible asset to a related person as defined in sections 267(b) and 707(b)(1)?		
4	At any time during the tax year, did the partnership acquire any interest in an intangible asset from a related person as defined in sections 267(b) and 707(b)(1)?		
5	At any time during the tax year, did the partnership make any change in accounting principle for financial accounting purposes? See instructions for a definition of change in accounting principle		
6	At any time during the tax year, did the partnership make any change in a method of accounting for U.S. income tax purposes?		

For Paperwork Reduction Act Notice, see the Instructions for Form 1065. Cat. No. 49945S **Schedule C (Form 1065) 2010**

Form **1118** (Rev. December 2009) Department of the Treasury Internal Revenue Service

Foreign Tax Credit—Corporations

▶See separate instructions.
▶ Attach to the corporation's tax return.

OMB No. 1545-0122

For calendar year 20 , or other tax year beginning , 20 , and ending , 20

Name of corporation | **Employer identification number**

Use a **separate** Form 1118 for each applicable category of income listed below. See **Categories of Income** in the instructions. Also, see **Specific Instructions**. Check only one box on each form.

☐ Passive Category Income ☐ Section 901(j) Income: Name of Sanctioned Country ▶ ______

☐ General Category Income ☐ Income Re-sourced by Treaty: Name of Country ▶ ______

Schedule A **Income or (Loss) Before Adjustments** *(Report all amounts in U.S. dollars. See **Specific Instructions**.)*

	1. Foreign Country or U.S. Possession (Enter two-letter code; see instructions. Use a separate line for each.) *	Gross Income or (Loss) From Sources Outside the United States (*INCLUDE* Foreign Branch Gross Income here *and* on Schedule F)								
		2. Deemed Dividends (see instructions)		**3.** Other Dividends		**4.** Interest	**5.** Gross Rents, Royalties, and License Fees	**6.** Gross Income From Performance of Services	**7.** Other (attach schedule)	**8.** Total (add columns 2(a) through 7)
		(a) Exclude gross-up	**(b)** Gross-up (sec. 78)	**(a)** Exclude gross-up	**(b)** Gross-up (sec. 78)					
A										
B										
C										
D										
E										
F										
Totals (add lines A through F)										

* For section 863(b) income, NOLs, income from RICs, and high-taxed income, use a single line (see instructions).

Deductions (*INCLUDE* Foreign Branch Deductions here *and* on Schedule F)

	9. Definitely Allocable Deductions					**10.** Apportioned Share of Deductions Not Definitely Allocable (enter amount from applicable line of Schedule H, Part II, column (d))	**11.** Net Operating Loss Deduction	**12.** Total Deductions (add columns 9(e) through 11)	**13.** Total Income or (Loss) Before Adjustments (subtract column 12 from column 8)
	Rental, Royalty, and Licensing Expenses		**(c)** Expenses Related to Gross Income From Performance of Services	**(d)** Other Definitely Allocable Deductions	**(e)** Total Definitely Allocable Deductions (add columns 9(a) through 9(d))				
	(a) Depreciation, Depletion, and Amortization	**(b)** Other Expenses							
A									
B									
C									
D									
E									
F									
Totals									

For Paperwork Reduction Act Notice, see separate instructions. Cat. No. 10900F Form **1118** (Rev. 12-2009)

Form 1118 (Rev. 12-2009) Page **2**

Schedule B Foreign Tax Credit *(Report all foreign tax amounts in U.S. dollars.)*

Part I—Foreign Taxes Paid, Accrued, and Deemed Paid *(see instructions)*

	1. Credit is Claimed for Taxes: ☐ Paid	☐ Accrued	**2.** Foreign Taxes Paid or Accrued (attach schedule showing amounts in foreign currency and conversion rate(s) used) — Tax Withheld at Source on:			Other Foreign Taxes Paid or Accrued on:					**3.** Tax Deemed Paid (from Schedule C—Part I, column 10, Part II, column 8(b), and Part III, column 8)
	Date Paid	Date Accrued	**(a)** Dividends	**(b)** Interest	**(c)** Rents, Royalties, and License Fees	**(d)** Section 863(b) Income	**(e)** Foreign Branch Income	**(f)** Services Income	**(g)** Other	**(h)** Total Foreign Taxes Paid or Accrued (add columns 2(a) through 2(g))	
A											
B											
C											
D											
E											
F											
Totals (add lines A through F)											

Part II—Separate Foreign Tax Credit *(Complete a **separate** Part II for **each** applicable category of income.)*

1 Total foreign taxes paid or accrued (total from Part I, column 2(h))

2 Total taxes deemed paid (total from Part I, column 3)

3 Reductions of taxes paid, accrued, or deemed paid (enter total from Schedule G) ( )

4 Taxes reclassified under high-tax kickout

5 Enter the sum of any carryover of foreign taxes (from Schedule K, line 3, column (xiv)) plus any carrybacks to the current tax year

6 Total foreign taxes (combine lines 1 through 5)

7 Enter the amount from the applicable column of Schedule J, Part I, line 11 (see instructions). If Schedule J is **not** required to be completed, enter the result from the "Totals" line of column 13 of the applicable Schedule A

8a Total taxable income from all sources (enter taxable income from the corporation's tax return)

b Adjustments to line 8a (see instructions)

c Subtract line 8b from line 8a

9 Divide line 7 by line 8c. Enter the resulting fraction as a decimal (see instructions). If line 7 is greater than line 8c, enter 1

10 Total U.S. income tax against which credit is allowed (regular tax liability (see section 26(b)) minus American Samoa economic development credit)

11 Credit limitation (multiply line 9 by line 10) (see instructions)

12 **Separate foreign tax credit** (enter the smaller of line 6 or line 11 here and on the appropriate line of Part III)

Part III—Summary of Separate Credits (Enter amounts from Part II, line 12 for **each** applicable category of income. **Do not** include taxes paid to sanctioned countries.)

1 Credit for taxes on passive category income

2 Credit for taxes on general category income

3 Credit for taxes on income re-sourced by treaty (combine all such credits on this line)

4 Total (add lines 1 through 3)

5 Reduction in credit for international boycott operations (see instructions)

6 **Total foreign tax credit** (subtract line 5 from line 4). Enter here and on the appropriate line of the corporation's tax return

Form **1118** (Rev. 12-2009)

Form **1120** Department of the Treasury Internal Revenue Service

U.S. Corporation Income Tax Return

For calendar year 2010 or tax year beginning ________, 2010, ending ________, 20 ___

▶ See separate instructions.

OMB No. 1545-0123

2010

A Check if:
1a Consolidated return (attach Form 851) ☐
b Life/nonlife consolidated return ☐
2 Personal holding co. (attach Sch. PH) ☐
3 Personal service corp. (see instructions) ☐
4 Schedule M-3 attached ☐

Print or type

Name

Number, street, and room or suite no. If a P.O. box, see instructions.

City or town, state, and ZIP code

B Employer identification number

C Date incorporated

D Total assets (see instructions) $

E Check if: **(1)** ☐ Initial return **(2)** ☐ Final return **(3)** ☐ Name change **(4)** ☐ Address change

Income	1a	Gross receipts or sales ____ **b** Less returns and allowances ____ **c** Bal ▶	1c	
	2	Cost of goods sold (Schedule A, line 8)	2	
	3	Gross profit. Subtract line 2 from line 1c	3	
	4	Dividends (Schedule C, line 19)	4	
	5	Interest	5	
	6	Gross rents	6	
	7	Gross royalties	7	
	8	Capital gain net income (attach Schedule D (Form 1120))	8	
	9	Net gain or (loss) from Form 4797, Part II, line 17 (attach Form 4797)	9	
	10	Other income (see instructions—attach schedule)	10	
	11	**Total income.** Add lines 3 through 10 ▶	11	
Deductions (See instructions for limitations on deductions.)	12	Compensation of officers (Schedule E, line 4) ▶	12	
	13	Salaries and wages (less employment credits)	13	
	14	Repairs and maintenance	14	
	15	Bad debts	15	
	16	Rents	16	
	17	Taxes and licenses	17	
	18	Interest	18	
	19	Charitable contributions	19	
	20	Depreciation from Form 4562 not claimed on Schedule A or elsewhere on return (attach Form 4562)	20	
	21	Depletion	21	
	22	Advertising	22	
	23	Pension, profit-sharing, etc., plans	23	
	24	Employee benefit programs	24	
	25	Domestic production activities deduction (attach Form 8903)	25	
	26	Other deductions (attach schedule)	26	
	27	**Total deductions.** Add lines 12 through 26 ▶	27	
	28	Taxable income before net operating loss deduction and special deductions. Subtract line 27 from line 11.	28	
	29	**Less: a** Net operating loss deduction (see instructions) — 29a		
		b Special deductions (Schedule C, line 20) — 29b	29c	
Tax, Refundable Credits, and Payments	30	**Taxable income.** Subtract line 29c from line 28 (see instructions)	30	
	31	**Total tax** (Schedule J, line 10)	31	
	32a	2009 overpayment credited to 2010 — 32a		
	b	2010 estimated tax payments — 32b		
	c	2010 refund applied for on Form 4466 — 32c ( ) **d Bal** ▶ 32d		
	e	Tax deposited with Form 7004 — 32e		
	f	Credits: **(1)** Form 2439 ____ **(2)** Form 4136 ____ — 32f		
	g	Refundable credits from Form 3800, line 19c, and Form 8827, line 8c — 32g	32h	
	33	Estimated tax penalty (see instructions). Check if Form 2220 is attached ▶ ☐	33	
	34	**Amount owed.** If line 32h is smaller than the total of lines 31 and 33, enter amount owed	34	
	35	**Overpayment.** If line 32h is larger than the total of lines 31 and 33, enter amount overpaid	35	
	36	Enter amount from line 35 you want: **Credited to 2011 estimated tax ▶** ____ **Refunded ▶**	36	

Sign Here

Under penalties of perjury, I declare that I have examined this return, including accompanying schedules and statements, and to the best of my knowledge and belief, it is true, correct, and complete. Declaration of preparer (other than taxpayer) is based on all information of which preparer has any knowledge.

▶ Signature of officer ____ Date ____ ▶ Title ____

May the IRS discuss this return with the preparer shown below (see instructions)? ☐ **Yes** ☐ **No**

Paid Preparer Use Only

Print/Type preparer's name	Preparer's signature	Date	Check ☐ if self-employed	PTIN
Firm's name ▶			Firm's EIN ▶	
Firm's address ▶			Phone no.	

For Paperwork Reduction Act Notice, see separate instructions. Cat. No. 11450Q Form **1120** (2010)

Form 1120 (2010) Page **2**

Schedule A — Cost of Goods Sold (see instructions)

1	Inventory at beginning of year	1	
2	Purchases	2	
3	Cost of labor	3	
4	Additional section 263A costs (attach schedule)	4	
5	Other costs (attach schedule)	5	
6	**Total.** Add lines 1 through 5	6	
7	Inventory at end of year	7	
8	**Cost of goods sold.** Subtract line 7 from line 6. Enter here and on page 1, line 2	8	

9a Check all methods used for valuing closing inventory:

(i) ☐ Cost

(ii) ☐ Lower of cost or market

(iii) ☐ Other (Specify method used and attach explanation.) ▶ ____________

b Check if there was a writedown of subnormal goods ▶ ☐

c Check if the LIFO inventory method was adopted this tax year for any goods (if checked, attach Form 970) ▶ ☐

d If the LIFO inventory method was used for this tax year, enter percentage (or amounts) of closing inventory computed under LIFO **9d** ____

e If property is produced or acquired for resale, do the rules of section 263A apply to the corporation? ☐ Yes ☐ No

f Was there any change in determining quantities, cost, or valuations between opening and closing inventory? If "Yes," attach explanation ☐ Yes ☐ No

Schedule C — Dividends and Special Deductions (see instructions)

		(a) Dividends received	(b) %	(c) Special deductions (a) × (b)
1	Dividends from less-than-20%-owned domestic corporations (other than debt-financed stock)		70	
2	Dividends from 20%-or-more-owned domestic corporations (other than debt-financed stock)		80	
3	Dividends on debt-financed stock of domestic and foreign corporations		see instructions	
4	Dividends on certain preferred stock of less-than-20%-owned public utilities		42	
5	Dividends on certain preferred stock of 20%-or-more-owned public utilities		48	
6	Dividends from less-than-20%-owned foreign corporations and certain FSCs		70	
7	Dividends from 20%-or-more-owned foreign corporations and certain FSCs		80	
8	Dividends from wholly owned foreign subsidiaries		100	
9	**Total.** Add lines 1 through 8. See instructions for limitation			
10	Dividends from domestic corporations received by a small business investment company operating under the Small Business Investment Act of 1958		100	
11	Dividends from affiliated group members		100	
12	Dividends from certain FSCs		100	
13	Dividends from foreign corporations not included on lines 3, 6, 7, 8, 11, or 12			
14	Income from controlled foreign corporations under subpart F (attach Form(s) 5471)			
15	Foreign dividend gross-up			
16	IC-DISC and former DISC dividends not included on lines 1, 2, or 3			
17	Other dividends			
18	Deduction for dividends paid on certain preferred stock of public utilities			
19	**Total dividends.** Add lines 1 through 17. Enter here and on page 1, line 4 ▶			
20	**Total special deductions.** Add lines 9, 10, 11, 12, and 18. Enter here and on page 1, line 29b ▶			

Schedule E — Compensation of Officers (see instructions for page 1, line 12)

Note: *Complete Schedule E only if total receipts (line 1a plus lines 4 through 10 on page 1) are $500,000 or more.*

	(a) Name of officer	(b) Social security number	(c) Percent of time devoted to business	Percent of corporation stock owned: (d) Common	Percent of corporation stock owned: (e) Preferred	(f) Amount of compensation
1			%	%	%	
			%	%	%	
			%	%	%	
			%	%	%	
			%	%	%	

2	Total compensation of officers	
3	Compensation of officers claimed on Schedule A and elsewhere on return	
4	Subtract line 3 from line 2. Enter the result here and on page 1, line 12	

Form 1120 (2010) Page **3**

Schedule J Tax Computation (see instructions)

1	Check if the corporation is a member of a controlled group (attach Schedule O (Form 1120)) . . . . ▶ ☐		
2	Income tax. Check if a qualified personal service corporation (see instructions) . . . . ▶ ☐	2	
3	Alternative minimum tax (attach Form 4626)	3	
4	Add lines 2 and 3	4	
5a	Foreign tax credit (attach Form 1118) . . . 5a		
b	Credit from Form 8834, line 29 . . . 5b		
c	General business credit (attach Form 3800) . . . 5c		
d	Credit for prior year minimum tax (attach Form 8827) . . . 5d		
e	Bond credits from Form 8912 . . . 5e		
6	**Total credits.** Add lines 5a through 5e	6	
7	Subtract line 6 from line 4	7	
8	Personal holding company tax (attach Schedule PH (Form 1120))	8	
9	Other taxes. Check if from: ☐ Form 4255 ☐ Form 8611 ☐ Form 8697 ☐ Form 8866 ☐ Form 8902 ☐ Other (attach schedule)	9	
10	**Total tax.** Add lines 7 through 9. Enter here and on page 1, line 31	10	

Schedule K Other Information (see instructions)

		Yes	No
1	Check accounting method: **a** ☐ Cash **b** ☐ Accrual **c** ☐ Other (specify) ▶		
2	See the instructions and enter the:		
a	Business activity code no. ▶		
b	Business activity ▶		
c	Product or service ▶		
3	Is the corporation a subsidiary in an affiliated group or a parent-subsidiary controlled group? If "Yes," enter name and EIN of the parent corporation ▶		
4	At the end of the tax year:		
a	Did any foreign or domestic corporation, partnership (including any entity treated as a partnership), trust, or tax-exempt organization own directly 20% or more, or own, directly or indirectly, 50% or more of the total voting power of all classes of the corporation's stock entitled to vote? If "Yes," complete Part I of Schedule G (Form 1120) (attach Schedule G)		
b	Did any individual or estate own directly 20% or more, or own, directly or indirectly, 50% or more of the total voting power of all classes of the corporation's stock entitled to vote? If "Yes," complete Part II of Schedule G (Form 1120) (attach Schedule G)		
5	At the end of the tax year, did the corporation:		
a	Own directly 20% or more, or own, directly or indirectly, 50% or more of the total voting power of all classes of stock entitled to vote of any foreign or domestic corporation not included on **Form 851,** Affiliations Schedule? For rules of constructive ownership, see instructions If "Yes," complete (i) through (iv).		

(i) Name of Corporation	**(ii)** Employer Identification Number (if any)	**(iii)** Country of Incorporation	**(iv)** Percentage Owned in Voting Stock

Form **1120** (2010)

Form 1120 (2010) Page **4**

Schedule K *Continued*

		Yes	No
b	Own directly an interest of 20% or more, or own, directly or indirectly, an interest of 50% or more in any foreign or domestic partnership (including an entity treated as a partnership) or in the beneficial interest of a trust? For rules of constructive ownership, see instructions If "Yes," complete (i) through (iv).		

(i) Name of Entity	**(ii)** Employer Identification Number (if any)	**(iii)** Country of Organization	**(iv)** Maximum Percentage Owned in Profit, Loss, or Capital

		Yes	No
6	During this tax year, did the corporation pay dividends (other than stock dividends and distributions in exchange for stock) in excess of the corporation's current and accumulated earnings and profits? (See sections 301 and 316.) . . . . If "Yes," file **Form 5452,** Corporate Report of Nondividend Distributions. If this is a consolidated return, answer here for the parent corporation and on Form 851 for each subsidiary.		
7	At any time during the tax year, did one foreign person own, directly or indirectly, at least 25% of **(a)** the total voting power of all classes of the corporation's stock entitled to vote or **(b)** the total value of all classes of the corporation's stock? . . . . For rules of attribution, see section 318. If "Yes," enter: **(i)** Percentage owned ▶ ________ and **(ii)** Owner's country ▶ ________ **(c)** The corporation may have to file **Form 5472,** Information Return of a 25% Foreign-Owned U.S. Corporation or a Foreign Corporation Engaged in a U.S. Trade or Business. Enter the number of Forms 5472 attached ▶ ________		
8	Check this box if the corporation issued publicly offered debt instruments with original issue discount . . . . . . ▶ ☐ If checked, the corporation may have to file **Form 8281,** Information Return for Publicly Offered Original Issue Discount Instruments.		
9	Enter the amount of tax-exempt interest received or accrued during the tax year ▶ $ ________		
10	Enter the number of shareholders at the end of the tax year (if 100 or fewer) ▶ ________		
11	If the corporation has an NOL for the tax year and is electing to forego the carryback period, check here . . . . . . ▶ ☐ If the corporation is filing a consolidated return, the statement required by Regulations section 1.1502-21(b)(3) must be attached or the election will not be valid.		
12	Enter the available NOL carryover from prior tax years (do not reduce it by any deduction on line 29a.) ▶ $ ________		
13	Are the corporation's total receipts (line 1a plus lines 4 through 10 on page 1) for the tax year **and** its total assets at the end of the tax year less than $250,000? . . . . If "Yes," the corporation is not required to complete Schedules L, M-1, and M-2 on page 5. Instead, enter the total amount of cash distributions and the book value of property distributions (other than cash) made during the tax year. ▶ $ ________		
14	Is the corporation required to file Schedule UTP (Form 1120), Uncertain Tax Position Statement (see instructions)? . . . . If "Yes," complete and attach Schedule UTP.		

Form **1120** (2010)

Form 1120 (2010) Page **5**

Schedule L **Balance Sheets per Books**

Assets	Beginning of tax year (a)	(b)	End of tax year (c)	(d)
1 Cash				
2a Trade notes and accounts receivable				
b Less allowance for bad debts	( )		( )	
3 Inventories				
4 U.S. government obligations				
5 Tax-exempt securities (see instructions)				
6 Other current assets (attach schedule)				
7 Loans to shareholders				
8 Mortgage and real estate loans				
9 Other investments (attach schedule)				
10a Buildings and other depreciable assets				
b Less accumulated depreciation	( )		( )	
11a Depletable assets				
b Less accumulated depletion	( )		( )	
12 Land (net of any amortization)				
13a Intangible assets (amortizable only)				
b Less accumulated amortization	( )		( )	
14 Other assets (attach schedule)				
15 Total assets				
Liabilities and Shareholders' Equity				
16 Accounts payable				
17 Mortgages, notes, bonds payable in less than 1 year				
18 Other current liabilities (attach schedule)				
19 Loans from shareholders				
20 Mortgages, notes, bonds payable in 1 year or more				
21 Other liabilities (attach schedule)				
22 Capital stock: **a** Preferred stock				
b Common stock				
23 Additional paid-in capital				
24 Retained earnings—Appropriated (attach schedule)				
25 Retained earnings—Unappropriated				
26 Adjustments to shareholders' equity (attach schedule)				
27 Less cost of treasury stock		( )		( )
28 Total liabilities and shareholders' equity				

Schedule M-1 **Reconciliation of Income (Loss) per Books With Income per Return**

Note: Schedule M-3 required instead of Schedule M-1 if total assets are $10 million or more—see instructions

1 Net income (loss) per books		7 Income recorded on books this year not included on this return (itemize): Tax-exempt interest $	
2 Federal income tax per books			
3 Excess of capital losses over capital gains			
4 Income subject to tax not recorded on books this year (itemize):		8 Deductions on this return not charged against book income this year (itemize):	
5 Expenses recorded on books this year not deducted on this return (itemize):		**a** Depreciation . . $	
a Depreciation . . . . $		**b** Charitable contributions $	
b Charitable contributions . $			
c Travel and entertainment . $			
		9 Add lines 7 and 8	
6 Add lines 1 through 5		10 Income (page 1, line 28)—line 6 less line 9	

Schedule M-2 **Analysis of Unappropriated Retained Earnings per Books (Line 25, Schedule L)**

1 Balance at beginning of year		5 Distributions: **a** Cash	
2 Net income (loss) per books		**b** Stock	
3 Other increases (itemize):		**c** Property	
		6 Other decreases (itemize):	
		7 Add lines 5 and 6	
4 Add lines 1, 2, and 3		8 Balance at end of year (line 4 less line 7)	

SCHEDULE M-3 (Form 1120)

Department of the Treasury Internal Revenue Service

Net Income (Loss) Reconciliation for Corporations With Total Assets of $10 Million or More

▶ Attach to Form 1120 or 1120-C.
▶ See separate instructions.

OMB No. 1545-0123

2010

Name of corporation (common parent, if consolidated return) | **Employer identification number**

Check applicable box(es): (1) ☐ Non-consolidated return (2) ☐ Consolidated return (Form 1120 only)
(3) ☐ Mixed 1120/L/PC group (4) ☐ Dormant subsidiaries schedule attached

Part I Financial Information and Net Income (Loss) Reconciliation (see instructions)

1a Did the corporation file SEC Form 10-K for its income statement period ending with or within this tax year?
☐ **Yes.** Skip lines 1b and 1c and complete lines 2a through 11 with respect to that SEC Form 10-K.
☐ **No.** Go to line 1b. See instructions if multiple non-tax-basis income statements are prepared.

b Did the corporation prepare a certified audited non-tax-basis income statement for that period?
☐ **Yes.** Skip line 1c and complete lines 2a through 11 with respect to that income statement.
☐ **No.** Go to line 1c.

c Did the corporation prepare a non-tax-basis income statement for that period?
☐ **Yes.** Complete lines 2a through 11 with respect to that income statement.
☐ **No.** Skip lines 2a through 3c and enter the corporation's net income (loss) per its books and records on line 4a.

2a Enter the income statement period: Beginning MM/DD/YYYY Ending MM/DD/YYYY

b Has the corporation's income statement been restated for the income statement period on line 2a?
☐ **Yes.** (If "Yes," attach an explanation and the amount of each item restated.)
☐ **No.**

c Has the corporation's income statement been restated for any of the five income statement periods preceding the period on line 2a?
☐ **Yes.** (If "Yes," attach an explanation and the amount of each item restated.)
☐ **No.**

3a Is any of the corporation's voting common stock publicly traded?
☐ **Yes.**
☐ **No.** If "No," go to line 4a.

b Enter the symbol of the corporation's primary U.S. publicly traded voting common stock . . . .

c Enter the nine-digit CUSIP number of the corporation's primary publicly traded voting common stock . . . .

4a	Worldwide consolidated net income (loss) from income statement source identified in Part I, line 1 . .	**4a**	
b	Indicate accounting standard used for line 4a (see instructions): (1) ☐ GAAP (2) ☐ IFRS (3) ☐ Statutory (4) ☐ Tax-basis (5) ☐ Other (specify) ________		
5a	Net income from nonincludible foreign entities (attach schedule)	**5a**	( )
b	Net loss from nonincludible foreign entities (attach schedule and enter as a positive amount)	**5b**	
6a	Net income from nonincludible U.S. entities (attach schedule)	**6a**	( )
b	Net loss from nonincludible U.S. entities (attach schedule and enter as a positive amount)	**6b**	
7a	Net income (loss) of other includible foreign disregarded entities (attach schedule)	**7a**	
b	Net income (loss) of other includible U.S. disregarded entities (attach schedule)	**7b**	
c	Net income (loss) of other includible entities (attach schedule)	**7c**	
8	Adjustment to eliminations of transactions between includible entities and nonincludible entities (attach schedule)	**8**	
9	Adjustment to reconcile income statement period to tax year (attach schedule)	**9**	
10a	Intercompany dividend adjustments to reconcile to line 11 (attach schedule)	**10a**	
b	Other statutory accounting adjustments to reconcile to line 11 (attach schedule)	**10b**	
c	Other adjustments to reconcile to amount on line 11 (attach schedule)	**10c**	
11	**Net income (loss) per income statement of includible corporations.** Combine lines 4 through 10 . . .	**11**	

Note. Part I, line 11, must equal the amount on Part II, line 30, column (a), and Schedule M-2, line 2.

12 Enter the total amount (not just the corporation's share) of the assets and liabilities of all entities included or removed on the following lines.

	Total Assets	Total Liabilities
a Included on Part I, line 4 . . . . ▶		
b Removed on Part I, line 5 . . . . ▶		
c Removed on Part I, line 6 . . . . ▶		
d Included on Part I, line 7 . . . . ▶		

Schedule M-3 (Form 1120) 2010 Page **2**

Name of corporation (common parent, if consolidated return)	**Employer identification number**

Check applicable box(es): **(1)** ☐ Consolidated group **(2)** ☐ Parent corp **(3)** ☐ Consolidated eliminations **(4)** ☐ Subsidiary corp **(5)** ☐ Mixed 1120/L/PC group

Check if a sub-consolidated: **(6)** ☐ 1120 group **(7)** ☐ 1120 eliminations

Name of subsidiary (if consolidated return)	**Employer identification number**

Part II Reconciliation of Net Income (Loss) per Income Statement of Includible Corporations With Taxable Income per Return (see instructions)

Income (Loss) Items (Attach schedules for lines 1 through 11)	**(a)** Income (Loss) per Income Statement	**(b)** Temporary Difference	**(c)** Permanent Difference	**(d)** Income (Loss) per Tax Return
1 Income (loss) from equity method foreign corporations				
2 Gross foreign dividends not previously taxed				
3 Subpart F, QEF, and similar income inclusions				
4 Section 78 gross-up				
5 Gross foreign distributions previously taxed				
6 Income (loss) from equity method U.S. corporations				
7 U.S. dividends not eliminated in tax consolidation				
8 Minority interest for includible corporations				
9 Income (loss) from U.S. partnerships				
10 Income (loss) from foreign partnerships				
11 Income (loss) from other pass-through entities				
12 Items relating to reportable transactions (attach details)				
13 Interest income (attach Form 8916-A)				
14 Total accrual to cash adjustment				
15 Hedging transactions				
16 Mark-to-market income (loss)				
17 Cost of goods sold (attach Form 8916-A)	( )			( )
18 Sale versus lease (for sellers and/or lessors)				
19 Section 481(a) adjustments				
20 Unearned/deferred revenue				
21 Income recognition from long-term contracts				
22 Original issue discount and other imputed interest				
23a Income statement gain/loss on sale, exchange, abandonment, worthlessness, or other disposition of assets other than inventory and pass-through entities				
b Gross capital gains from Schedule D, excluding amounts from pass-through entities				
c Gross capital losses from Schedule D, excluding amounts from pass-through entities, abandonment losses, and worthless stock losses				
d Net gain/loss reported on Form 4797, line 17, excluding amounts from pass-through entities, abandonment losses, and worthless stock losses				
e Abandonment losses				
f Worthless stock losses (attach details)				
g Other gain/loss on disposition of assets other than inventory				
24 Capital loss limitation and carryforward used				
25 Other income (loss) items with differences (attach schedule)				
26 **Total income (loss) items.** Combine lines 1 through 25				
27 **Total expense/deduction items** (from Part III, line 38)				
28 Other items with no differences				
29a Mixed groups, see instructions. All others, combine lines 26 through 28				
b PC insurance subgroup reconciliation totals				
c Life insurance subgroup reconciliation totals				
30 **Reconciliation totals.** Combine lines 29a through 29c				

Note. Line 30, column (a), must equal the amount on Part I, line 11, and column (d) must equal Form 1120, page 1, line 28.

Schedule M-3 (Form 1120) 2010

Schedule M-3 (Form 1120) 2010 Page **3**

Name of corporation (common parent, if consolidated return) | **Employer identification number**

Check applicable box(es): **(1)** ☐ Consolidated group **(2)** ☐ Parent corp **(3)** ☐ Consolidated eliminations **(4)** ☐ Subsidiary corp **(5)** ☐ Mixed 1120/L/PC group

Check if a sub-consolidated: **(6)** ☐ 1120 group **(7)** ☐ 1120 eliminations

Name of subsidiary (if consolidated return) | **Employer identification number**

Part III **Reconciliation of Net Income (Loss) per Income Statement of Includible Corporations With Taxable Income per Return—Expense/Deduction Items** (see instructions)

Expense/Deduction Items	**(a)** Expense per Income Statement	**(b)** Temporary Difference	**(c)** Permanent Difference	**(d)** Deduction per Tax Return
1 U.S. current income tax expense				
2 U.S. deferred income tax expense				
3 State and local current income tax expense				
4 State and local deferred income tax expense				
5 Foreign current income tax expense (other than foreign withholding taxes)				
6 Foreign deferred income tax expense				
7 Foreign withholding taxes				
8 Interest expense (attach Form 8916-A)				
9 Stock option expense				
10 Other equity-based compensation				
11 Meals and entertainment				
12 Fines and penalties				
13 Judgments, damages, awards, and similar costs				
14 Parachute payments				
15 Compensation with section 162(m) limitation				
16 Pension and profit-sharing				
17 Other post-retirement benefits				
18 Deferred compensation				
19 Charitable contribution of cash and tangible property				
20 Charitable contribution of intangible property				
21 Charitable contribution limitation/carryforward				
22 Domestic production activities deduction				
23 Current year acquisition or reorganization investment banking fees				
24 Current year acquisition or reorganization legal and accounting fees				
25 Current year acquisition/reorganization other costs				
26 Amortization/impairment of goodwill				
27 Amortization of acquisition, reorganization, and start-up costs				
28 Other amortization or impairment write-offs				
29 Section 198 environmental remediation costs				
30 Depletion				
31 Depreciation				
32 Bad debt expense				
33 Corporate owned life insurance premiums				
34 Purchase versus lease (for purchasers and/or lessees)				
35 Research and development costs (attach schedule)				
36 Section 118 exclusion (attach schedule)				
37 Other expense/deduction items with differences (attach schedule)				
38 **Total expense/deduction items.** Combine lines 1 through 37. Enter here and on Part II, line 27, reporting positive amounts as negative and negative amounts as positive				

Form **1120S** | **U.S. Income Tax Return for an S Corporation** | OMB No. 1545-0130

Department of the Treasury
Internal Revenue Service

▶ **Do not file this form unless the corporation has filed or is attaching Form 2553 to elect to be an S corporation.**

▶ **See separate instructions.**

2010

For calendar year 2010 or tax year beginning , 2010, ending , 20

	TYPE OR PRINT	
A S election effective date	Name	**D Employer identification number**
B Business activity code number *(see instructions)*	Number, street, and room or suite no. If a P.O. box, see instructions.	**E** Date incorporated
C Check if Sch. M-3 attached ☐	City or town, state, and ZIP code	**F** Total assets *(see instructions)* $

G Is the corporation electing to be an S corporation beginning with this tax year? ☐ Yes ☐ No If "Yes," attach Form 2553 if not already filed

H Check if: **(1)** ☐ Final return **(2)** ☐ Name change **(3)** ☐ Address change
(4) ☐ Amended return **(5)** ☐ S election termination or revocation

I Enter the number of shareholders who were shareholders during any part of the tax year . . . . ▶

Caution. *Include **only** trade or business income and expenses on lines 1a through 21. See the instructions for more information.*

Income	1a	Gross receipts or sales ___ **b** Less returns and allowances ___ **c** Bal ▶	1c	
	2	Cost of goods sold (Schedule A, line 8)	2	
	3	Gross profit. Subtract line 2 from line 1c	3	
	4	Net gain (loss) from Form 4797, Part II, line 17 *(attach Form 4797)*	4	
	5	Other income (loss) *(see instructions—attach statement)*	5	
	6	**Total income (loss).** Add lines 3 through 5 ▶	6	
Deductions (see instructions for limitations)	7	Compensation of officers	7	
	8	Salaries and wages (less employment credits)	8	
	9	Repairs and maintenance	9	
	10	Bad debts	10	
	11	Rents	11	
	12	Taxes and licenses	12	
	13	Interest	13	
	14	Depreciation not claimed on Schedule A or elsewhere on return (*attach Form 4562*)	14	
	15	Depletion **(Do not deduct oil and gas depletion.)**	15	
	16	Advertising	16	
	17	Pension, profit-sharing, etc., plans	17	
	18	Employee benefit programs	18	
	19	Other deductions (*attach statement*)	19	
	20	**Total deductions.** Add lines 7 through 19 ▶	20	
	21	**Ordinary business income (loss).** Subtract line 20 from line 6	21	
Tax and Payments	22a	Excess net passive income or LIFO recapture tax (*see instructions*) — 22a		
	b	Tax from Schedule D (Form 1120S) — 22b		
	c	Add lines 22a and 22b (*see instructions for additional taxes*)	22c	
	23a	2010 estimated tax payments and 2009 overpayment credited to 2010 — 23a		
	b	Tax deposited with Form 7004 — 23b		
	c	Credit for federal tax paid on fuels (*attach Form 4136*) — 23c		
	d	Add lines 23a through 23c	23d	
	24	Estimated tax penalty (*see instructions*). Check if Form 2220 is attached ▶ ☐	24	
	25	**Amount owed.** If line 23d is smaller than the total of lines 22c and 24, enter amount owed	25	
	26	**Overpayment.** If line 23d is larger than the total of lines 22c and 24, enter amount overpaid	26	
	27	Enter amount from line 26 **Credited to 2011 estimated tax** ▶ ___ **Refunded** ▶	27	

Sign Here

Under penalties of perjury, I declare that I have examined this return, including accompanying schedules and statements, and to the best of my knowledge and belief, it is true, correct, and complete. Declaration of preparer (other than taxpayer) is based on all information of which preparer has any knowledge.

▶ Signature of officer | Date | ▶ Title

May the IRS discuss this return with the preparer shown below (see instructions)? ☐ Yes ☐ No

Paid Preparer Use Only

Print/Type preparer's name	Preparer's signature	Date	Check ☐ if self-employed	PTIN
Firm's name ▶			Firm's EIN ▶	
Firm's address ▶			Phone no.	

Form 1120S (2010) Page **2**

Schedule A Cost of Goods Sold (see instructions)

1	Inventory at beginning of year	1	
2	Purchases	2	
3	Cost of labor	3	
4	Additional section 263A costs (*attach statement*)	4	
5	Other costs (*attach statement*)	5	
6	**Total.** Add lines 1 through 5	6	
7	Inventory at end of year	7	
8	**Cost of goods sold.** Subtract line 7 from line 6. Enter here and on page 1, line 2	8	

9a Check all methods used for valuing closing inventory: (*i*) ☐ Cost as described in Regulations section 1.471-3
(*ii*) ☐ Lower of cost or market as described in Regulations section 1.471-4
(*iii*) ☐ Other (Specify method used and attach explanation.) ▶

b Check if there was a writedown of subnormal goods as described in Regulations section 1.471-2(c) ▶ ☐

c Check if the LIFO inventory method was adopted this tax year for any goods (if checked, attach Form 970) ▶ ☐

d If the LIFO inventory method was used for this tax year, enter percentage (or amounts) of closing inventory computed under LIFO | 9d |

e If property is produced or acquired for resale, do the rules of section 263A apply to the corporation? ☐ Yes ☐ No

f Was there any change in determining quantities, cost, or valuations between opening and closing inventory? ☐ Yes ☐ No
If "Yes," attach explanation.

Schedule B Other Information (see instructions)

		Yes	No
1	Check accounting method: a ☐ Cash b ☐ Accrual c ☐ Other (specify) ▶		
2	See the instructions and enter the: a Business activity ▶ b Product or service ▶		
3	At the end of the tax year, did the corporation own, directly or indirectly, 50% or more of the voting stock of a domestic corporation? (For rules of attribution, see section 267(c).) If "Yes," attach a statement showing: **(a)** name and employer identification number (EIN), **(b)** percentage owned, and **(c)** if 100% owned, was a qualified subchapter S subsidiary election made?		
4	Has this corporation filed, or is it required to file, **Form 8918,** Material Advisor Disclosure Statement, to provide information on any reportable transaction?		
5	Check this box if the corporation issued publicly offered debt instruments with original issue discount ▶ ☐ If checked, the corporation may have to file **Form 8281,** Information Return for Publicly Offered Original Issue Discount Instruments.		
6	If the corporation: **(a)** was a C corporation before it elected to be an S corporation **or** the corporation acquired an asset with a basis determined by reference to the basis of the asset (or the basis of any other property) in the hands of a C corporation **and (b)** has net unrealized built-in gain in excess of the net recognized built-in gain from prior years, enter the net unrealized built-in gain reduced by net recognized built-in gain from prior years (*see instructions*) ▶ $		
7	Enter the accumulated earnings and profits of the corporation at the end of the tax year. $		
8	Are the corporation's total receipts (*see instructions*) for the tax year **and** its total assets at the end of the tax year less than $250,000? If "Yes," the corporation is not required to complete Schedules L and M-1		
9	During the tax year, was a qualified subchapter S subsidiary election terminated or revoked? If "Yes," see instructions		

Schedule K Shareholders' Pro Rata Share Items

					Total amount
Income (Loss)	1	Ordinary business income (loss) (page 1, line 21)		1	
	2	Net rental real estate income (loss) (*attach Form 8825*)		2	
	3a	Other gross rental income (loss)	3a		
	b	Expenses from other rental activities (*attach statement*)	3b		
	c	Other net rental income (loss). Subtract line 3b from line 3a		3c	
	4	Interest income		4	
	5	Dividends: **a** Ordinary dividends		5a	
		b Qualified dividends	5b		
	6	Royalties		6	
	7	Net short-term capital gain (loss) (*attach Schedule D (Form 1120S)*)		7	
	8a	Net long-term capital gain (loss) (*attach Schedule D (Form 1120S)*)		8a	
	b	Collectibles (28%) gain (loss)	8b		
	c	Unrecaptured section 1250 gain (*attach statement*)	8c		
	9	Net section 1231 gain (loss) (*attach Form 4797*)		9	
	10	Other income (loss) (*see instructions*) Type ▶		10	

Form **1120S** (2010)

Form 1120S (2010) Page **3**

Section		**Shareholders' Pro Rata Share Items** (continued)		**Total amount**
Deductions	**11**	Section 179 deduction (*attach Form 4562*)	**11**	
	12a	Contributions	**12a**	
	b	Investment interest expense	**12b**	
	c	Section 59(e)(2) expenditures **(1)** Type ▶ **(2)** Amount ▶	**12c(2)**	
	d	Other deductions *(see instructions)* Type ▶	**12d**	
Credits	**13a**	Low-income housing credit (section 42(j)(5))	**13a**	
	b	Low-income housing credit (other)	**13b**	
	c	Qualified rehabilitation expenditures (rental real estate) (*attach Form 3468*)	**13c**	
	d	Other rental real estate credits (*see instructions*) Type ▶	**13d**	
	e	Other rental credits (*see instructions*) Type ▶	**13e**	
	f	Alcohol and cellulosic biofuel fuels credit (*attach Form 6478*)	**13f**	
	g	Other credits (*see instructions*) Type ▶	**13g**	
Foreign Transactions	**14a**	Name of country or U.S. possession ▶		
	b	Gross income from all sources	**14b**	
	c	Gross income sourced at shareholder level	**14c**	
		Foreign gross income sourced at corporate level		
	d	Passive category	**14d**	
	e	General category	**14e**	
	f	Other (*attach statement*)	**14f**	
		Deductions allocated and apportioned at shareholder level		
	g	Interest expense	**14g**	
	h	Other	**14h**	
		Deductions allocated and apportioned at corporate level to foreign source income		
	i	Passive category	**14i**	
	j	General category	**14j**	
	k	Other (*attach statement*)	**14k**	
		Other information		
	l	Total foreign taxes (check one): ▶ ☐ Paid ☐ Accrued	**14l**	
	m	Reduction in taxes available for credit (*attach statement*)	**14m**	
	n	Other foreign tax information (*attach statement*)		
Alternative Minimum Tax (AMT) Items	**15a**	Post-1986 depreciation adjustment	**15a**	
	b	Adjusted gain or loss	**15b**	
	c	Depletion (other than oil and gas)	**15c**	
	d	Oil, gas, and geothermal properties—gross income	**15d**	
	e	Oil, gas, and geothermal properties—deductions	**15e**	
	f	Other AMT items (*attach statement*)	**15f**	
Items Affecting Shareholder Basis	**16a**	Tax-exempt interest income	**16a**	
	b	Other tax-exempt income	**16b**	
	c	Nondeductible expenses	**16c**	
	d	Distributions *(attach statement if required) (see instructions)*	**16d**	
	e	Repayment of loans from shareholders	**16e**	
Other Information	**17a**	Investment income	**17a**	
	b	Investment expenses	**17b**	
	c	Dividend distributions paid from accumulated earnings and profits	**17c**	
	d	Other items and amounts (*attach statement*)		
Recon- ciliation	**18**	**Income/loss reconciliation.** Combine the amounts on lines 1 through 10 in the far right column. From the result, subtract the sum of the amounts on lines 11 through 12d and 14l	**18**	

Form 1120S (2010) Page **4**

Schedule L **Balance Sheets per Books**

Assets		Beginning of tax year (a)	(b)	End of tax year (c)	(d)
1	Cash				
2a	Trade notes and accounts receivable				
b	Less allowance for bad debts	( )		( )	
3	Inventories				
4	U.S. government obligations				
5	Tax-exempt securities (*see instructions*)				
6	Other current assets (*attach statement*)				
7	Loans to shareholders				
8	Mortgage and real estate loans				
9	Other investments (*attach statement*)				
10a	Buildings and other depreciable assets				
b	Less accumulated depreciation	( )		( )	
11a	Depletable assets				
b	Less accumulated depletion	( )		( )	
12	Land (net of any amortization)				
13a	Intangible assets (amortizable only)				
b	Less accumulated amortization	( )		( )	
14	Other assets (*attach statement*)				
15	Total assets				
	Liabilities and Shareholders' Equity				
16	Accounts payable				
17	Mortgages, notes, bonds payable in less than 1 year				
18	Other current liabilities (*attach statement*)				
19	Loans from shareholders				
20	Mortgages, notes, bonds payable in 1 year or more				
21	Other liabilities (*attach statement*)				
22	Capital stock				
23	Additional paid-in capital				
24	Retained earnings				
25	Adjustments to shareholders' equity (*attach statement*)				
26	Less cost of treasury stock		( )		( )
27	Total liabilities and shareholders' equity				

Schedule M-1 **Reconciliation of Income (Loss) per Books With Income (Loss) per Return**

Note: Schedule M-3 required instead of Schedule M-1 if total assets are $10 million or more—see instructions

1	Net income (loss) per books		5	Income recorded on books this year not included on Schedule K, lines 1 through 10 (itemize): a Tax-exempt interest $	
2	Income included on Schedule K, lines 1, 2, 3c, 4, 5a, 6, 7, 8a, 9, and 10, not recorded on books this year (itemize):				
3	Expenses recorded on books this year not included on Schedule K, lines 1 through 12 and 14l (itemize): a Depreciation $ b Travel and entertainment $		6	Deductions included on Schedule K, lines 1 through 12 and 14l, not charged against book income this year (itemize): a Depreciation $	
			7	Add lines 5 and 6	
4	Add lines 1 through 3		8	Income (loss) (Schedule K, line 18). Line 4 less line 7	

Schedule M-2 **Analysis of Accumulated Adjustments Account, Other Adjustments Account, and Shareholders' Undistributed Taxable Income Previously Taxed** (see instructions)

		(a) Accumulated adjustments account	(b) Other adjustments account	(c) Shareholders' undistributed taxable income previously taxed
1	Balance at beginning of tax year			
2	Ordinary income from page 1, line 21			
3	Other additions			
4	Loss from page 1, line 21	( )		
5	Other reductions	( )	( )	
6	Combine lines 1 through 5			
7	Distributions other than dividend distributions			
8	Balance at end of tax year. Subtract line 7 from line 6			

Form **1120S** (2010)

671110

☐ Final K-1 ☐ Amended K-1 OMB No. 1545-0130

Schedule K-1 (Form 1120S) **2010**

Department of the Treasury
Internal Revenue Service

For calendar year 2010, or tax year beginning ____________, 2010 ending ____________, 20____

Shareholder's Share of Income, Deductions, Credits, etc.

► See back of form and separate instructions.

Part I Information About the Corporation

A Corporation's employer identification number

B Corporation's name, address, city, state, and ZIP code

C IRS Center where corporation filed return

Part II Information About the Shareholder

D Shareholder's identifying number

E Shareholder's name, address, city, state, and ZIP code

F Shareholder's percentage of stock ownership for tax year . . . . ____________ %

For IRS Use Only

Part III Shareholder's Share of Current Year Income, Deductions, Credits, and Other Items

1	Ordinary business income (loss)	**13**	Credits
2	Net rental real estate income (loss)		
3	Other net rental income (loss)		
4	Interest income		
5a	Ordinary dividends		
5b	Qualified dividends	**14**	Foreign transactions
6	Royalties		
7	Net short-term capital gain (loss)		
8a	Net long-term capital gain (loss)		
8b	Collectibles (28%) gain (loss)		
8c	Unrecaptured section 1250 gain		
9	Net section 1231 gain (loss)		
10	Other income (loss)	**15**	Alternative minimum tax (AMT) items
11	Section 179 deduction	**16**	Items affecting shareholder basis
12	Other deductions		
		17	Other information

* See attached statement for additional information.

SCHEDULE M-3 (Form 1120S)

Department of the Treasury
Internal Revenue Service

Net Income (Loss) Reconciliation for S Corporations With Total Assets of $10 Million or More

▶ Attach to Form 1120S.
▶ See separate instructions.

OMB No. 1545-0130

2010

Name of corporation

Employer identification number

Part I Financial Information and Net Income (Loss) Reconciliation (see instructions)

1a Did the corporation prepare a certified audited non-tax-basis income statement for the period ending with or within this tax year? (See instructions if multiple non-tax-basis income statements are prepared.)

☐ **Yes.** Skip line 1b and complete lines 2 through 11 with respect to that income statement.
☐ **No.** Go to line 1b.

b Did the corporation prepare a non-tax-basis income statement for that period?

☐ **Yes.** Complete lines 2 through 11 with respect to that income statement.
☐ **No.** Skip lines 2 through 3b and enter the corporation's net income (loss) per its books and records on line 4a.

2 Enter the income statement period: Beginning ____/____/____ Ending ____/____/____

3a Has the corporation's income statement been restated for the income statement period on line 2?

☐ **Yes.** (If "Yes," attach an explanation and the amount of each item restated.)
☐ **No.**

b Has the corporation's income statement been restated for any of the five income statement periods preceding the period on line 2?

☐ **Yes.** (If "Yes," attach an explanation and the amount of each item restated.)
☐ **No.**

4a	Worldwide consolidated net income (loss) from income statement source identified in Part I, line 1 .	**4a**	
b	Indicate accounting standard used for line 4a (see instructions): (1) ☐ GAAP (2) ☐ IFRS (3) ☐ Tax-basis (4) ☐ Other (specify) ______		
5a	Net income from nonincludible foreign entities (attach schedule)	**5a**	( )
b	Net loss from nonincludible foreign entities (attach schedule and enter as a positive amount) . . .	**5b**	
6a	Net income from nonincludible U.S. entities (attach schedule)	**6a**	( )
b	Net loss from nonincludible U.S. entities (attach schedule and enter as a positive amount)	**6b**	
7a	Net income (loss) of other foreign disregarded entities (attach schedule)	**7a**	
b	Net income (loss) of other U.S. disregarded entities (except qualified subchapter S subsidiaries) (attach schedule)	**7b**	
c	Net income (loss) of other qualified subchapter S subsidiaries (QSubs) (attach schedule)	**7c**	
8	Adjustment to eliminations of transactions between includible entities and nonincludible entities (attach schedule)	**8**	
9	Adjustment to reconcile income statement period to tax year (attach schedule)	**9**	
10	Other adjustments to reconcile to amount on line 11 (attach schedule)	**10**	
11	**Net income (loss) per income statement of the corporation.** Combine lines 4 through 10 . . . **Note.** Part I, line 11, must equal Part II, line 26, column (a).	**11**	

12 Enter the total amount (not just the corporation's share) of the assets and liabilities of all entities included or removed on the following lines:

	Total Assets	Total Liabilities
a Included on Part I, line 4		
b Removed on Part I, line 5		
c Removed on Part I, line 6		
d Included on Part I, line 7		

Schedule M-3 (Form 1120S) 2010 Page **2**

Name of corporation | **Employer identification number**

Part II Reconciliation of Net Income (Loss) per Income Statement of the Corporation With Total Income (Loss) per Return (see instructions)

	Income (Loss) Items	(a) Income (Loss) per Income Statement	(b) Temporary Difference	(c) Permanent Difference	(d) Income (Loss) per Tax Return
1	Income (loss) from equity method foreign corporations (attach schedule)				
2	Gross foreign dividends not previously taxed				
3	Subpart F, QEF, and similar income inclusions (attach schedule)				
4	Gross foreign distributions previously taxed (attach schedule)				
5	Income (loss) from equity method U.S. corporations (attach schedule)				
6	U.S. dividends not eliminated in tax consolidation				
7	Income (loss) from U.S. partnerships (attach schedule)				
8	Income (loss) from foreign partnerships (attach schedule)				
9	Income (loss) from other pass-through entities (attach schedule)				
10	Items relating to reportable transactions (attach details)				
11	Interest income (attach Form 8916-A)				
12	Total accrual to cash adjustment				
13	Hedging transactions				
14	Mark-to-market income (loss)				
15	Cost of goods sold (attach Form 8916-A)	( )			( )
16	Sale versus lease (for sellers and/or lessors)				
17	Section 481(a) adjustments				
18	Unearned/deferred revenue				
19	Income recognition from long-term contracts				
20	Original issue discount and other imputed interest				
21a	Income statement gain/loss on sale, exchange, abandonment, worthlessness, or other disposition of assets other than inventory and pass-through entities				
b	Gross capital gains from Schedule D, excluding amounts from pass-through entities				
c	Gross capital losses from Schedule D, excluding amounts from pass-through entities, abandonment losses, and worthless stock losses				
d	Net gain/loss reported on Form 4797, line 17, excluding amounts from pass-through entities, abandonment losses, and worthless stock losses				
e	Abandonment losses				
f	Worthless stock losses (attach details)				
g	Other gain/loss on disposition of assets other than inventory				
22	Other income (loss) items with differences (attach schedule)				
23	**Total income (loss) items.** Combine lines 1 through 22				
24	**Total expense/deduction items** (from Part III, line 32)				
25	Other items with no differences				
26	**Reconciliation totals.** Combine lines 23 through 25				

Note. Line 26, column (a), must equal the amount on Part I, line 11, and column (d) must equal Form 1120S, Schedule K, line 18.

Schedule M-3 (Form 1120S) 2010

Schedule M-3 (Form 1120S) 2010 Page **3**

Name of corporation	**Employer identification number**

Part III **Reconciliation of Net Income (Loss) per Income Statement of the Corporation With Total Income (Loss) per Return—Expense/Deduction Items** (see instructions)

	Expense/Deduction Items	(a) Expense per Income Statement	(b) Temporary Difference	(c) Permanent Difference	(d) Deduction per Tax Return
1	U.S. current income tax expense				
2	U.S. deferred income tax expense				
3	State and local current income tax expense				
4	State and local deferred income tax expense				
5	Foreign current income tax expense (other than foreign withholding taxes)				
6	Foreign deferred income tax expense				
7	Equity-based compensation				
8	Meals and entertainment				
9	Fines and penalties				
10	Judgments, damages, awards, and similar costs				
11	Pension and profit-sharing				
12	Other post-retirement benefits				
13	Deferred compensation				
14	Charitable contribution of cash and tangible property				
15	Charitable contribution of intangible property				
16	Current year acquisition or reorganization investment banking fees				
17	Current year acquisition or reorganization legal and accounting fees				
18	Current year acquisition/reorganization other costs				
19	Amortization/impairment of goodwill				
20	Amortization of acquisition, reorganization, and start-up costs				
21	Other amortization or impairment write-offs				
22	Section 198 environmental remediation costs				
23a	Depletion—Oil & Gas				
b	Depletion—Other than Oil & Gas				
24	Depreciation				
25	Bad debt expense				
26	Interest expense (attach Form 8916-A)				
27	Corporate owned life insurance premiums				
28	Purchase versus lease (for purchasers and/or lessees)				
29	Research and development costs (attach schedule)				
30	Section 118 exclusion (attach schedule)				
31	Other expense/deduction items with differences (attach schedule)				
32	**Total expense/deduction items.** Combine lines 1 through 31. Enter here and on Part II, line 24, reporting positive amounts as negative and negative amounts as positive				

Schedule M-3 (Form 1120S) 2010

Form **8916-A**

Department of the Treasury
Internal Revenue Service

Supplemental Attachment to Schedule M-3

► Attach to Schedule M-3 for Form 1065, 1120, 1120-L, 1120-PC, or 1120S.

OMB No. 1545-2061

2010

Name of common parent	**Employer identification number**
Name of subsidiary	**Employer identification number**

Part I Cost of Goods Sold

	Cost of Goods Sold Items	(a) Expense per Income Statement	(b) Temporary Difference	(c) Permanent Difference	(d) Deduction per Tax Return
1	Amounts attributable to cost flow assumptions .				
2	Amounts attributable to:				
a	Stock option expense				
b	Other equity based compensation				
c	Meals and entertainment				
d	Parachute payments				
e	Compensation with section 162(m) limitation . .				
f	Pension and profit sharing				
g	Other post-retirement benefits				
h	Deferred compensation				
i	Section 198 environmental remediation costs . .				
j	Amortization				
k	Depletion				
l	Depreciation				
m	Corporate owned life insurance premiums . . .				
n	Other section 263A costs				
3	Inventory shrinkage accruals.				
4	Excess inventory and obsolescence reserves . .				
5	Lower of cost or market write-downs				
6	Other items with differences (attach schedule) . .				
7	Other items with no differences				
8	**Total cost of goods sold.** Add lines 1 through 7, in columns a, b, c, and d				

For Paperwork Reduction Act Notice, see page 4. Cat. No. 48657X Form **8916-A** (2010)

Appendix C

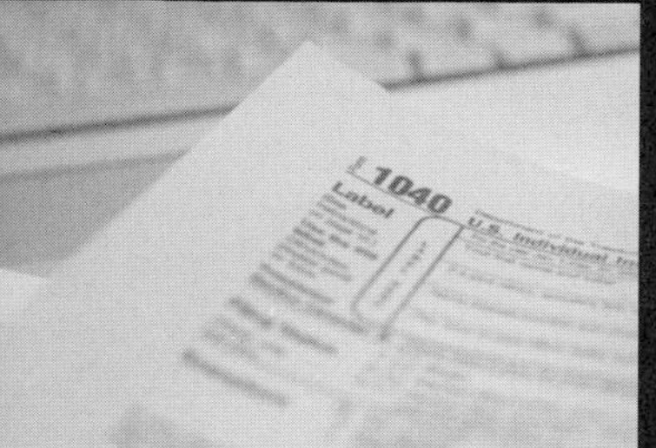

GLOSSARY

The words and phrases in this glossary have been defined to reflect their conventional use in the field of taxation. The definitions may therefore be incomplete for other purposes.

A

Accelerated cost recovery system (ACRS). A method in which the cost of tangible property is recovered over a prescribed period of time. The approach disregards salvage value, imposes a period of cost recovery that depends upon the classification of the asset into one of various recovery periods, and prescribes the applicable percentage of cost that can be deducted each year. The modified system is referred to as MACRS. § 168.

Accelerated depreciation. Various methods of *depreciation* that yield larger deductions in the earlier years of the life of an asset than the straight-line method. Examples include the double declining-balance and the sum-of-the-years' digits methods of depreciation.

Acceleration rule. Treatment of an intercompany transaction on a *consolidated return,* when a sold asset leaves the group.

Accounting method. The method under which income and expenses are determined for tax purposes. Important accounting methods include the *cash basis* and the *accrual basis.* Special methods are available for the reporting of gain on installment sales, recognition of income on construction projects (the *completed contract* and *percentage of completion* methods), and the valuation of inventories (last-in, first-out and first-in, first-out). §§ 446–474.

Accounting period. The period of time, usually a year, used by a taxpayer for the determination of tax liability. Unless a *fiscal year* is chosen, taxpayers must determine and pay their income tax liability by using the calendar year (January 1 through December 31) as the period of measurement. An example of a fiscal year is July 1 through June 30. A change in accounting periods (e.g., from a calendar year to a fiscal year) generally requires the consent of the IRS. Usually, taxpayers are free to select either an initial calendar or a fiscal year without the consent of the IRS. §§ 441–443. See also *annual accounting period concept.*

Accrual basis. A method of accounting that reflects expenses incurred and income earned for any one tax year. In contrast to the *cash basis* of accounting, expenses need not be paid to be deductible, nor need income be received to be taxable. *Unearned income* (e.g., prepaid interest and rent) generally is taxed in the year of receipt regardless of the method of accounting used by the taxpayer. § 446(c)(2). See also *accounting method.*

Accumulated adjustments account (AAA). An account that aggregates an *S corporation's* post-1982 income, loss, and deductions for the tax year (including nontaxable income and nondeductible losses and expenses). After the year-end income and expense adjustments are made, the account is reduced by distributions made during the tax year.

Accumulated earnings and profits. Net undistributed tax-basis earnings of a corporation aggregated from March 1, 1913, to the end of the prior tax year. Used to determine the amount of dividend income associated with a distribution to shareholders. See also *current earnings and profits* and *earnings and profits.* § 316 and Reg. § 1.316–2.

Accumulated earnings credit. A reduction allowed in arriving at *accumulated taxable income,* in determining the *accumulated earnings tax.*

Accumulated earnings tax. A special tax imposed on C corporations that accumulate (rather than distribute) their earnings beyond the *reasonable needs of the business.* The accumulated earnings tax and related interest are imposed on *accumulated taxable income* in addition to the corporate income tax. §§ 531–537.

Accumulated taxable income. The base upon which the *accumulated earnings tax* is imposed. Generally, it is the taxable income of the corporation as adjusted for certain items (e.g., the Federal income tax, excess charitable contributions, the *dividends received deduction*) less the *dividends paid deduction* and the *accumulated earnings credit.* § 535.

Accumulating trust. See *discretionary trust.*

Accuracy-related penalty. Major civil taxpayer penalties relating to the accuracy of tax return data, including misstatements stemming from taxpayer *negligence* and improper valuation of income and deductions, are coordinated under this umbrella term. The penalty usually equals 20 percent of the understated tax liability.

ACE adjustment. In calculating *alternative minimum taxable income (AMTI),* certain adjustments are added to or subtracted from *taxable income.* A *C corporation* subject to the *alternative minimum tax* computes the ACE adjustment as 75 percent of the excess of *adjusted current earnings (ACE)* over AMTI. The ACE adjustment can be negative in certain circumstances. ACE restricts/defers certain deductions and includes/accelerates certain income items, compared with AMTI.

Acquiescence. Agreement by the IRS on the results reached in some of the more significant decisions involving tax issues; sometimes abbreviated *Acq.* or *A.* See also *nonacquiescence.*

Acquisition. See *corporate acquisition.*

ACRS. See *accelerated cost recovery system.*

Ad valorem tax. A tax imposed on the value of property. The most common ad valorem tax is that imposed by states, counties, and cities on real estate. Ad valorem taxes can be imposed on personal property as well.

Adjusted basis. The cost or other basis of property reduced by *depreciation* allowed or allowable and increased by capital improvements. Other special adjustments are provided in § 1016 and the related Regulations. See also *basis.*

Adjusted current earnings (ACE). Used to determine an adjustment in computing corporate *alternative minimum taxable income* (AMTI). ACE reflects restrictions on the timing of certain recognition events. Exempt interest, *life insurance* proceeds, and other receipts that are included in *earnings and profits* but not in *taxable income* also increase ACE.

Adjusted gross estate. The *gross estate* of a *decedent* reduced by § 2053 expenses (e.g., administration, funeral) and § 2054 losses (e.g., casualty). Necessary in testing for the extension of time for installment payment of estate taxes under § 6166. See also *gross estate.*

Adjusted gross income (AGI). A tax determination peculiar to individual taxpayers. Generally, it represents the *gross income* of an individual, less business expenses and less any appropriate capital gain or loss adjustment.

Adjusted ordinary gross income (AOGI). A determination peculiar to the *personal holding company tax.* In ascertaining whether a corporation is a *personal holding company, personal holding company income* divided by adjusted ordinary gross income must equal 60 percent or more. Adjusted ordinary gross income is the corporation's *gross income* less net *capital gains, § 1231 gains,* and certain expenses. §§ 541 and 543(b)(2).

Administration. The supervision and winding up of an *estate.* The administration of an estate runs from the date of an individual's death until all assets have been distributed and liabilities paid.

Administrator. A person appointed by the court to administer (manage or take charge of) the assets and liabilities of a *decedent* (the deceased). See also *executor.*

Affiliate. A member of an *affiliated group.* See also *consolidated return.*

Affiliated group. A parent-subsidiary group of corporations that is eligible to elect to file on a consolidated basis. Eighty percent ownership of the voting power and value of all of the corporations must be achieved on every day of the tax year, and an identifiable parent corporation must exist (i.e., it must own at least 80 percent of another group member without applying *attribution* rules).

AFTR. *American Federal Tax Reports* contain Federal tax decisions issued by the U.S. *District Courts,* U.S. *Court of Federal Claims,* U.S. *Courts of Appeals,* and the *U.S. Supreme Court.*

AFTR 2d. The second series of the *American Federal Tax Reports,* dealing with 1954 and 1986 Code case law.

Aggregate concept. The theory of *partnership* taxation under which, in certain cases, a partnership is treated as a mere collection of the activities of each partner.

Alimony. Alimony deductions result from the payment of a legal obligation arising from the termination of a marital relationship. Payments designated as alimony generally are included in the *gross income* of the recipient and are deductible *for* AGI by the payor.

Allocable share of income. Certain entities receive conduit treatment under the Federal income tax law. This means the *earned income* or loss is not taxed to the entity, but is allocated to the owners or beneficiaries, regardless of the magnitude or timing of corresponding distributions. The portion of the entity's income that is taxed to the owner or *beneficiary* is the allocable share of the entity's income or loss for the period. The allocations are determined by (1) the *partnership agreement* for partners, (2) a weighted-average stock ownership computation for shareholders of an *S corporation,* and (3) the controlling will or trust instrument for the beneficiaries of an *estate* or *trust.*

Allocate. The assignment of income for various tax purposes. A *multistate corporation*'s nonbusiness income usually is allocated to the state where the nonbusiness assets are located; it is not *apportioned* with the rest of the entity's income. The income and expense items of an *estate* or *trust* are allocated between income and *corpus* components. Specific items of income, expense, gain, loss, and credit can be allocated to specific partners, if a substantial economic nontax purpose for the allocation is established. See also *apportion* and *substantial economic effect.*

Alternate valuation date. Property passing from a *decedent* by death may be valued for *estate tax* purposes as of the date of death or the alternate valuation date. The alternate valuation date is six months from the date of death or the date the property is disposed of by the estate, whichever comes first. To use the alternate valuation date, the *executor* or *administrator* of the estate must make an affirmative election. Election of the alternate valuation date is not available unless it decreases the amount of the *gross estate and* reduces the estate tax liability.

Alternative minimum tax (AMT). AMT is a fixed percentage of *alternative minimum taxable income* (AMTI). AMTI generally starts with the taxpayer's *adjusted gross income* (for individuals) or *taxable income* (for other taxpayers). To this amount, the taxpayer (1) adds designated preference items (e.g., interest income on private activity bonds), (2) makes other specified adjustments (e.g., to reflect a longer, straight-line *cost recovery* deduction), (3) subtracts certain AMT itemized deductions for individuals (e.g., interest incurred on housing but not taxes paid), and (4) subtracts an exemption amount (e.g., $40,000 on a C corporation's return). The taxpayer must pay the greater of the resulting AMT (reduced by only the foreign tax credit) or the regular income tax (reduced by all allowable tax credits). The AMT does not apply to certain small *C corporations. AMT preferences* and *adjustments* are assigned to partners, LLC members, and *S corporation* shareholders.

Alternative minimum taxable income (AMTI). The base for computing a taxpayer's *alternative minimum tax.* Generally, the taxable income for the year, modified for AMT adjustments, preferences, and exemptions.

Amortization. The tax deduction for the cost or other basis of an *intangible asset* over the asset's *estimated useful life.* Examples of amortizable intangibles include patents, copyrights, and leasehold interests. Most intangible assets are amortized over 15 years. § 195. For tangible assets, see *depreciation.* For natural resources, see *depletion.* See also *goodwill.*

Amount realized. The amount received by a taxpayer upon the sale or exchange of property. Amount realized is the sum of the cash and the *fair market value* of any property or services received by the taxpayer, plus any related debt assumed by the buyer. Determining the amount realized is the starting point for arriving at realized gain or loss. § 1001(b). See also *realized gain or loss* and *recognized gain or loss.*

AMT adjustments. In calculating *alternative minimum taxable income (AMTI),* certain adjustments are added to or subtracted from *taxable income.* AMT adjustments generally reflect timing differences, such as the use of slower *depreciation* deductions for the *alternative minimum tax (AMT).* A *C corporation* might be subject to the *ACE adjustment.*

AMT preferences. In calculating *alternative minimum taxable income (AMTI),* certain preference items are added to *taxable income.* AMT preferences generally reflect differences between the regular tax and the *alternative minimum tax (AMT)* computational bases. For instance, interest income from certain state and local bonds may be an AMT preference item.

Annual accounting period concept. In determining a taxpayer's income tax liability, only transactions taking place during a specified tax year are taken into consideration. For reporting and payment purposes, therefore, the tax life of taxpayers is divided into equal annual *accounting periods.* See also *mitigation of the annual accounting period concept.*

Annual exclusion. In computing the *taxable gifts* for the year, each *donor* excludes the first $13,000 of a gift to each *donee.* Usually, the annual exclusion is not available for gifts of *future interests.* § 2503(b). See also *gift splitting.*

Annuitant. The party entitled to receive payments from an *annuity* contract.

Annuity. A fixed sum of money payable to a person at specified times for a specified period of time or for life. If the party making the payment (i.e., the obligor) is regularly engaged in this type of business (e.g., an insurance company), the arrangement is classified as a commercial annuity. A so-called private annuity involves an obligor that is not regularly engaged in selling annuities (e.g., a charity or family member).

Anticipatory assignment of income. See *assignment of income.*

Appellate court. For Federal tax purposes, appellate courts include the U.S. *Courts of Appeals* and the U.S. *Supreme Court.* If the party losing in the trial (or lower) court is dissatisfied with the result, the dispute may be carried to the appropriate appellate court. See also *trial court.*

Apportion. The assignment of the business income of a *multistate corporation* to specific states for income taxation. Usually, the apportionment procedure accounts for the property, payroll, and sales activity levels of the various states, and a proportionate assignment of the entity's total income is made, using a three-factor apportionment formula. These activities indicate the commercial *domicile* of the corporation, relative to that income. Some states exclude *nonbusiness income* from the apportionment procedure; they *allocate* nonbusiness income to the states where the nonbusiness assets are located. See also *payroll factor, property factor,* and *sales factor.*

Appreciated inventory. In *partnership* taxation, appreciated inventory is a *hot asset,* and a *partner's* share of its ordinary income potential must be allocated. If a partner sells an interest in the partnership, ordinary income is recognized to the extent of the partner's share in the partnership's inventory and *unrealized receivables.* The definition of "inventory" is broad enough to include any accounts receivable, including unrealized receivables.

Arm's length concept. The standard under which unrelated parties would carry out a transaction. Suppose Bint Corporation sells property to its sole shareholder for $10,000. In determining whether $10,000 is an arm's length price, one would ascertain the amount for which the corporation could have sold the property to a disinterested third party.

Articles of incorporation. The legal document specifying a corporation's name, period of existence, purpose and powers, authorized number of shares, classes of stock, and other conditions for operation. The organizers of the corporation file the articles with the state of incorporation. If the articles are satisfactory and other conditions of the law are satisfied, the state will issue a charter recognizing the organization's status as a corporation.

ASC 450 (SFAS 5). Under *Generally Accepted Accounting Principles,* the rules for the financial reporting of contingent liabilities, including deferred taxes.

ASC 740 (SFAS 109). Under *Generally Accepted Accounting Principles,* the rules for the financial reporting of the tax expense of an enterprise. *Permanent differences* affect the enterprise's effective tax rate. *Temporary differences* create a *deferred tax asset* or a *deferred tax liability* on the balance sheet.

ASC 740-10 (FIN 48). Under *Generally Accepted Accounting Principles,* an interpretation of *ASC 740 (SFAS 109)* relating to when a tax benefit should be reported in an enterprise's financial statements. A tax benefit should be recorded for book purposes only if it is more likely than not that the taxpayer's filing position will be sustained after an audit, administrative appeal, and the highest applicable judicial review.

ASC 740-30 (APB 23). Under *Generally Accepted Accounting Principles,* the rules for the financial reporting of the tax expense relative to a U.S. corporation's non-U.S. subsidiary. If the parent documents that it is *permanently reinvesting* the non-U.S. earnings of a non-U.S. subsidiary, the parent does not record as an expense any U.S. income tax that the parent might pay on such earnings, i.e., the book tax expense is deferred until such earnings are (if ever) repatriated to the United States.

Assessment. The process whereby the IRS imposes a tax liability. If, for example, the IRS audits a taxpayer's income tax return and finds *gross income* understated or deductions overstated, it will assess a *deficiency* in the amount of the tax that should have been paid in light of the adjustments made.

Assignment of income. A taxpayer attempts to avoid the recognition of income by assigning to another the property that generates the income. Such a procedure will not avoid the recognition of income by the taxpayer making the assignment if the income was earned at the point of the transfer. In this case, the income is taxed to the person who earns it.

Assumption of liabilities. In a corporate formation, corporate takeover, or asset purchase, the new owner often takes assets and agrees to assume preexisting debt. Such actions do not create *boot* received on the transaction for the new shareholder, unless there is no *bona fide* business purpose for the exchange, or the principal purpose of the debt assumption is the avoidance of tax liabilities. Gain is recognized to the extent that liabilities assumed exceed the aggregated bases of the transferred assets. § 357.

At-risk amount. The taxpayer has an amount at risk in a business or investment venture to the extent that personal assets have been subjected to the risks of the business. Typically, the taxpayer's at-risk amount includes (1) the amount of money or other property that the investor contributed to the venture for the investment, (2) the amount of any of the entity's liabilities for which the taxpayer personally is liable and that relate to the investment, and (3) an allocable share of *nonrecourse debts* incurred by the venture from third parties in arm's length transactions for real estate investments.

At-risk limitation. Generally, a taxpayer can deduct losses related to a trade or business, *S corporation, partnership,* or investment asset only to the extent of the *at-risk amount.*

Attribution. Under certain circumstances, the tax law applies attribution rules to assign to one taxpayer the ownership interest of another taxpayer. If, for example, the stock of Tree Corporation is held 60 percent by Mary and 40 percent by Sam, Mary may be deemed to own 100 percent of Tree if Sam is her son. In that case, the stock owned by Sam is attributed to Mary. Stated differently, Mary has a 60 percent direct and a 40 percent indirect interest in Tree. It can also be said that Mary is the constructive owner of Sam's interest.

Audit. Inspection and verification of a taxpayer's return or other transactions possessing tax consequences. See also *correspondence audit, field audit,* and *office audit.*

Automobile expenses. Automobile expenses generally are deductible only to the extent the automobile is used in business or for the production of income. Personal commuting expenses are not deductible. The taxpayer may deduct actual out-of-pocket expenses (including depreciation and insurance), or a standard mileage rate for the tax year. For 2011, per-mile deduction amounts are 51 cents for business use of the auto, 14 cents if in support of charity, 19 cents for medical purposes, and 19 cents for a job-related move.

Avoidance. See *tax avoidance.*

B

Bailout. Various procedures whereby the owners of an entity can obtain the entity's profits with favorable tax consequences. With corporations, for example, the bailout of corporate profits might be accomplished by using fringe benefit plans, or by paying salaries or interest. The alternative of distributing the profits to the shareholders as dividends generally is less attractive since *dividend* payments are not deductible. See also *preferred stock bailout.*

Balance sheet approach. The process under *ASC 740 (SFAS 109)* by which an entity's *deferred tax expense* or *deferred tax benefit* is determined as a result of the reporting period's changes in the balance sheet's *deferred tax asset* and *deferred tax liability* accounts.

***Bardahl* formula.** A formula approved in a *Tax Court* memorandum decision, used in the context of the *accumulated earnings tax* to compute the reasonable business needs of the corporation for working capital. Most appropriate where the corporation holds inventory.

Bargain sale or purchase. A sale or purchase of property for less than fair market value. The difference between the sale or purchase price and the fair market value of the property may have tax consequences. If, for example, a corporation sells property worth $1,000 to one of its shareholders for $700, the $300 difference probably represents a *constructive dividend* to the shareholder. Suppose, instead, the shareholder sells the property (worth $1,000) to his or her corporation for $700. The $300 difference probably represents a contribution by the shareholder to the corporation's capital. Bargain sales and purchases among members of the same family may lead to *gift tax* consequences.

Basis. The acquisition cost assigned to an asset for income tax purposes. For assets acquired by purchase, basis is cost (§ 1012). Special rules govern the basis of property received by virtue of another's death (§ 1014) or by *gift* (§ 1015), the basis of stock received on a transfer of property to a controlled corporation (§ 358), the basis of the property transferred to the corporation (§ 362), and the basis of property received upon the *liquidation* of a corporation (§ 334). See also *adjusted basis.*

Basis in partnership interest. The acquisition cost of the partner's ownership interest in the *partnership.* Includes purchase price and associated debt acquired from other *partners* and in the course of the entity's trade or business.

Benchmarking. The tax professional's use of two or more entities' effective tax rates and deferred tax balance sheet accounts. Used chiefly to compare the effectiveness of the entities' tax planning techniques, and to suggest future tax-motivated courses of action.

Beneficiary. A party who will benefit from a transfer of property or other arrangement. Examples include the beneficiary of a *trust,* the beneficiary of a life insurance policy, and the beneficiary of an *estate.*

Bequest. A transfer of *personal property* by will. To bequeath is to leave such property by will. See also *devise.*

Blockage rule. A factor to be considered in valuing a large block of stock. Application of this rule generally justifies a discount in the fair market value since the disposition of a large amount of stock at any one time may depress the value of the shares in the marketplace.

Bona fide. In good faith, or real. In tax law, this term often is used in connection with a *business purpose* for carrying out a transaction. Thus, was there a bona fide business purpose for a shareholder's transfer of a liability to a controlled corporation? § 357(b)(1)(B). See also *business purpose.*

Book value. The net amount of an asset after reduction by a related reserve. The book value of machinery, for example, is the amount of the machinery less the reserve for *depreciation.*

Boot. Cash or property of a type not included in the definition of a nontaxable exchange. The receipt of boot causes an otherwise nontaxable transfer to become taxable to the extent of the lesser of the fair market value of the boot or the realized gain on the transfer. For example, see transfers to controlled corporations under § 351(b) and *like-kind exchanges* under § 1031(b). See also *realized gain or loss.*

Branch profits tax. A tax on the *effectively connected earnings* and profits of the U.S. branch of a *foreign corporation.* The tax is levied in addition to the usual § 11 tax, in an amount equal to 30 percent of the *dividend equivalent amount.* Treaties can override the tax or reduce the withholding percentage. Earnings reinvested in the U.S. operations of the entity are not subject to the tax until repatriation.

Bribes and illegal payments. Section 162 denies a deduction for bribes or kickbacks, fines, and penalties paid to a government official or employee for violation of law, and two-thirds of the treble damage payments made to claimants for violation of the antitrust law. Denial of a deduction for bribes and illegal payments is based upon the judicially established principle that allowing such payments would be contrary to public policy.

Brother-sister controlled group. More than one corporation owned by the same shareholders. If, for example, Clara and Dan each own one-half of the stock in Top Corporation and Bottom Corporation, then Top and Bottom form a brother-sister controlled group.

B.T.A. The Board of Tax Appeals was a trial court that considered Federal tax matters. This court is now the U.S. *Tax Court.*

Built-in gains tax. A penalty tax designed to discourage a shift of the incidence of taxation on unrealized gains from a *C corporation* to its shareholders, via an S election. Under this provision, any recognized gain during the first (5, 7, or) 10 years of S status generates a corporate-level tax on a base not to exceed the aggregate untaxed built-in gains brought into the *S corporation* upon its election from C corporation taxable years.

Built-in loss property. Property contributed to a corporation under § 351 or as a contribution to capital that has a basis in excess of its fair market value. An adjustment is necessary to step down the basis of the property to its fair market value. The adjustment prevents the corporation and the contributing shareholder from obtaining a double tax benefit. The corporation allocates the adjustment proportionately among the assets with the built-in loss. As an alternative to the corporate adjustment, the shareholder may elect to reduce the basis in the stock.

Burden of proof. The requirement in a lawsuit to show the weight of evidence and thereby gain a favorable decision. In cases of tax *fraud,* the burden of proof in a tax case is on the IRS.

Business bad debts. A tax deduction allowed for obligations obtained in connection with a *trade or business* that have become either partially or completely worthless. In contrast to *nonbusiness bad debts,* business bad debts are deductible as business expenses. § 166.

Business purpose. A justifiable business reason for carrying out a transaction. Mere tax avoidance is not an acceptable business purpose. The presence of a business purpose is crucial in the area of *corporate reorganizations* and certain *liquidations.* See also *bona fide.*

Buy-sell agreement. An arrangement, particularly appropriate in the case of a closely held corporation or a *partnership,* whereby the surviving owners (shareholders or *partners*) or the entity agrees to purchase the interest of a withdrawing owner. The buy-sell agreement provides for an orderly disposition of an interest in a business and may aid in setting the value of the interest for *estate tax* purposes. See also *cross-purchase buy-sell agreement* and *entity buy-sell agreement.*

Bypass amount. The amount that can be transferred by gift or death free of any unified transfer tax. For 2011, the by-pass amount is $5 million for *estate tax* and $5 million for *gift tax.* See also *exemption equivalent amount.*

Bypass election. In the context of a distribution by an *S corporation,* an election made by the entity to designate that the distribution is first from *accumulated earnings and profits,* and only then from the *accumulated adjustments account (AAA).*

C

C corporation. A separate taxable entity, subject to the rules of Subchapter C of the Code. This business form may create a double taxation effect relative to its shareholders. The entity is subject to the regular corporate tax and a number of penalty taxes at the Federal level.

Calendar year. See *accounting period.*

Capital account. The financial accounting analog of a partner's tax *basis* in the entity.

Capital asset. Broadly speaking, all assets are capital except those specifically excluded from that definition by the Code. Major categories of noncapital assets include property held for resale in the normal course of business (inventory), trade accounts and notes receivable, and depreciable property and real estate used in a *trade or business* (§ 1231 assets). § 1221. See also *capital gain* and *capital loss.*

Capital contribution. Various means by which a shareholder makes additional funds available to the corporation (placed at the risk of the business), sometimes without the receipt of additional stock. If no stock is received, the contributions are added to the *basis* of the shareholder's existing stock investment and do not generate *gross income* to the corporation. § 118.

Capital expenditure. An expenditure added to the *basis* of the property improved. For income tax purposes, this generally precludes a full deduction for the expenditure in the year paid or incurred. Cost recovery in the form of a tax deduction later comes in the form of *depreciation, depletion,* or *amortization.* § 263.

Capital gain. The gain from the sale or exchange of a *capital asset.*

Capital interest. Usually, the percentage of the entity's net assets that a *partner* would receive on liquidation. Typically determined by the partner's capital sharing ratio.

Capital loss. The loss from the sale or exchange of a *capital asset.*

Capital sharing ratio. A *partner's* percentage ownership of the entity's capital.

Capital stock tax. A state-level tax, usually imposed on out-of-state corporations for the privilege of doing business in the state. The tax may be based on the entity's apportionable income or payroll, or on its apportioned net worth as of a specified date.

Carryover basis. When a taxpayer exchanges one asset for another, many provisions in the tax law allow the basis assigned to the received asset to be precisely that of the traded asset. Thus, no step-up or -down of *basis* occurs as a result of the exchange. For instance, when an investor contributes an asset to a corporation or *partnership*, the entity generally takes a carryover basis in the property. § 723.

Cash basis. A method of accounting that reflects deductions as paid and income as received in any one tax year. However, deductions for prepaid expenses that benefit more than one tax year (e.g., prepaid rent and prepaid interest) usually are spread over the period benefited rather than deducted in the year paid. § 446(c)(1). See also *constructive receipt of income.*

Cash surrender value. The amount of money that an insurance policy would yield if cashed in with the insurance company that issued the policy.

CCH. Commerce Clearing House (CCH) is the publisher of a tax service and of Federal tax decisions (*USTC* series).

Cert. den. By denying the Writ of Certiorari, the U.S. *Supreme Court* refuses to accept an appeal from a U.S. *Court of Appeals.* The denial of *certiorari* does not, however, mean that the U.S. Supreme Court agrees with the result reached by the lower court.

Certiorari. Appeal from a U.S. *Court of Appeals* to the U.S. *Supreme Court* is by Writ of Certiorari. The Supreme Court need not accept the appeal, and it usually does not (*cert. den.*) unless a conflict exists among the lower courts that must be resolved or a constitutional issue is involved. See also *cert. den.*

Cf. Compare.

Charitable contributions. Contributions are deductible (subject to various restrictions and ceiling limitations) if made to qualified nonprofit charitable organizations. A cash basis taxpayer is entitled to a deduction solely in the year of payment. *Accrual basis* corporations may accrue contributions at year-end if payment is properly authorized before the end of the year and payment is made within two and one-half months after the end of the year. § 170.

Check-the-box Regulations. A business entity can elect to be taxed as a *partnership, S corporation,* or *C corporation* by indicating its preference on the tax return. Legal structure and operations are irrelevant in this regard. Thus, by using the check-the-box rules prudently, an entity can select the most attractive tax results offered by the Code, without being bound by legal forms. Not available if the entity is incorporated under state law.

Circular 230. A portion of the Federal tax *Regulations* that describes the levels of conduct at which a *tax preparer* must operate. Circular 230 dictates, for instance, that a tax preparer may not charge an unconscionable fee or delay the execution of a tax audit with inappropriate delays. Circular 230 requires that there be a *realistic possibility* that a tax return position be sustained upon review, and that no *frivolous returns* be filed.

Civil fraud. See *fraud.*

Closely held corporation. A corporation where stock ownership is not widely dispersed. Rather, a few shareholders are in control of corporate policy and are in a position to benefit personally from that policy.

Closing agreement. In a tax dispute, the parties sign a closing agreement to spell out the terms under which the matters are settled. The agreement is binding on both the IRS and the taxpayer.

Collapsing. To disregard a transaction or one of a series of steps leading to a result. See also *step transaction, substance vs. form concept,* and *telescoping.*

Combined return. In multistate taxation, a group of unitary corporations may elect or be required to file an income tax return that includes operating results for all of the *affiliates,* not just those with *nexus* in the state. Thus, apportionment data is reported for the group's worldwide or water's edge operations.

Commissioner of the IRS. The head of IRS operations, a presidential appointee.

Common law state. See *community property.*

Community property. Louisiana, Texas, New Mexico, Arizona, California, Washington, Idaho, Nevada, and Wisconsin have community property systems. The rest of the states are common law property jurisdictions. Alaska residents can elect community property status for assets. The difference between common law and community property systems centers around the property rights possessed by married persons. In a common law system, each spouse owns whatever he or she earns. Under a community property system, one-half of the earnings of each spouse is considered owned by the other spouse. Assume, for example, Hal and Wanda are husband and wife and their only income is the $50,000 annual salary Hal receives. If they live in New York (a common law state), the $50,000 salary belongs to Hal. If, however, they live in Texas (a community property state), the $50,000 salary is owned one-half each by Hal and Wanda. See also *separate property.*

Complete termination redemption. See *redemption (complete termination).*

Completed contract method. A method of reporting gain or loss on certain long-term contracts. Under this method of accounting, *gross income* and expenses are recognized in the tax year in which the contract is completed. Reg. § 1.451–3. See also *percentage of completion method.*

Complex trust. Not a *simple trust.* Such trusts may have charitable beneficiaries, accumulate income, and distribute corpus. §§ 661–663.

Composite return. In multistate taxation, an *S corporation* may be allowed to file a single income tax return that assigns pass-through items to resident and nonresident shareholders. The composite or "block" return allows the entity to remit any tax that is attributable to the nonresident shareholders.

Concur. To agree with the result reached by another, but not necessarily with the reasoning or the logic used in reaching the result. For example, Judge Ross agrees with Judges Smith and Tanaka (all being members of the same court) that the income is taxable but for a different reason. Judge Ross would issue a concurring opinion to the majority opinion issued by Judges Smith and Tanaka.

Condemnation. The taking of property by a public authority. The taking is by legal action, and the owner of the property is compensated by the public authority.

Conduit concept. An approach assumed by the tax law in the treatment of certain entities and their owners. Permits specified tax characteristics to pass through the entity without losing their identity. For example, long-term capital losses realized by a *limited liability company* are passed through as such to the individual members of the entity. Varying forms of the conduit concept apply for *partnerships, trusts, estates,* and *S corporations.* See also *aggregate concept.*

Consent dividend. For purposes of avoiding or reducing the penalty tax on the unreasonable accumulation of earnings or the *personal holding company tax,* a corporation may declare a consent dividend. No cash or property is distributed to the shareholders, although the corporation obtains a *dividends paid deduction.* The consent dividend is taxed to the shareholders and increases the *basis* in their stock investment. § 565.

Conservation easement. An interest in real property that maintains its natural or pristine condition. Most often it restricts the development of the property. Properly structured, the grant of such an easement can generate an income tax deduction for the donor. If the grant takes place after the owner's death, a § 2055 *charitable contribution deduction* results, and a portion of the property's value is excluded from the *gross estate.* § 2031(c).

Conservatism principle. The theory behind much of *Generally Accepted Accounting Principles,* under which assurance is provided that an entity's balance sheet assets are not overstated, nor liabilities understated. For instance, under *ASC 740 (SFAS 109),* a *deferred tax asset* is not recorded until it is more likely than not that the future tax benefit will be realized.

Consolidated return. A procedure whereby certain affiliated corporations may file a single return, combine the tax transactions of each corporation, and arrive at a single income tax liability for the group. The election to file a consolidated return usually is binding on future years. §§ 1501–1505 and related Regulations.

Consolidation. The combination of two or more corporations into a newly created corporation. Thus, Apt Corporation and Bye Corporation combine to form Cart Corporation. A consolidation may qualify as a nontaxable *reorganization* if certain conditions are satisfied. §§ 354 and 368(a)(1)(A).

Constructive dividend. A taxable benefit derived by a shareholder from his or her corporation that is not actually called a *dividend.* Examples include *unreasonable compensation,* excessive rent payments, bargain purchases of corporate property, and shareholder use of corporate property. Constructive dividends generally are found in *closely held corporations.* See also *bargain sale or purchase.*

Constructive liquidation scenario. The means by which *recourse debt* is shared among *partners* in *basis* determination.

Constructive ownership. See *attribution.*

Constructive receipt of income. If income is unqualifiedly available although not physically in the taxpayer's possession, it is subject to the income tax. An example is accrued interest on a savings account. Under the constructive receipt concept, the interest is taxed to a depositor in the year available, rather than the year actually withdrawn. The fact that the depositor uses the *cash basis* of accounting for tax purposes is irrelevant. See Reg. § 1.451–2.

Continuity of business enterprise. In a tax-favored *reorganization,* a shareholder or corporation that has substantially the same investment after an exchange as before should not be taxed on the transaction. Specifically, the transferee corporation must continue the historic business of the transferor or use a significant portion of the transferor's assets in the new business.

Continuity of interest test. In a tax-favored *reorganization,* a shareholder or corporation that has substantially the same investment after an exchange as before should not be taxed on the transaction. Specifically, the seller must acquire an equity interest in the purchasing corporation equal in value to at least 50 percent of all formerly outstanding stock of the acquired entity.

Continuity of life or existence. The death or other withdrawal of an owner of an entity does not terminate the existence of the entity. This is a characteristic of a corporation since the death or withdrawal of a shareholder does not affect the corporation's existence.

Contributions to the capital of a corporation. See *capital contribution.*

Contributory qualified pension or profit sharing plan. A plan funded with both employer and employee contributions. Since the employee's contributions to the plan are subject to income tax, a later distribution of the contributions to the employee generally is tax-free. See also *qualified pension or profit sharing plan.*

Control. Holding a specified level of stock ownership in a corporation. For § 351, the new shareholder(s) must hold at least 80 percent of the total combined voting power of all voting classes of stock. Other tax provisions require different levels of control to bring about desired effects, such as 50 or 100 percent.

Controlled foreign corporation (CFC). A non-U.S. corporation in which more than 50 percent of the total combined voting power of all classes of stock entitled to vote or the total value of the stock of the corporation is owned by "U.S. shareholders" on any day during the taxable year of the foreign corporation. For purposes of this definition, a U.S. shareholder is any U.S. person who owns, or is considered to own, 10 percent or more of the total combined voting power of all classes of voting stock of the foreign corporation. Stock owned directly, indirectly, and constructively is used in this measure.

Controlled group. A controlled group of corporations is required to share the lower-level corporate tax rates and various other tax benefits among the members of the group. A controlled group may be either a *brother-sister* or a *parent-subsidiary group.*

Corporate acquisition. The takeover of one corporation by another if both parties retain their legal existence after the transaction. An acquisition can be effected via a stock purchase or through a tax-free exchange of stock. See also *corporate reorganization* and *merger.*

Corporate liquidation. Occurs when a corporation distributes its net assets to its shareholders and ceases its legal existence. Generally, a shareholder recognizes capital gain or loss upon the liquidation of the entity, regardless of the corporation's balance in its *earnings and profits* account. However, the distributing corporation recognizes gain and loss on assets that it distributes to shareholders in kind.

Corporate reorganization. Occurs, among other instances, when one corporation acquires another in a *merger* or acquisition, a single corporation divides into two or more entities, a corporation makes a substantial change in its capital structure, or a corporation undertakes a change in its legal name or domicile. The exchange of stock and other securities in a corporate reorganization can be effected favorably for tax purposes if certain statutory requirements are followed strictly. Tax consequences include the nonrecognition of any gain that is realized by the shareholders except to the extent of *boot* received. See also *corporate acquisition.*

Corpus. The body or principal of a *trust.* Suppose, for example, George transfers an apartment building into a trust, income payable to Wanda for life, remainder to Sam upon Wanda's death. Corpus of the trust is the apartment building.

Correspondence audit. An *audit* conducted by the IRS by mail. Typically, the IRS writes to the taxpayer requesting the verification of a particular deduction or exemption. The completion of a special form or the remittance of copies of records or other support is all that is requested of the taxpayer. See also *field audit* and *office audit.*

Court of Appeals. Any of 13 Federal courts that consider tax matters appealed from the U.S. *Tax Court,* a U.S. *District Court,* or the U.S. *Court of Federal Claims.* Appeal from a U.S. Court of Appeals is to the *U.S. Supreme Court* by *Certiorari.* See also *appellate court* and *trial court.*

Court of Federal Claims. A *trial court* (court of original jurisdiction) that decides litigation involving Federal tax matters. Appeal is to the *Court of Appeals* for the Federal Circuit.

Credit for prior transfers. The *estate tax* credit for prior transfers applies when property is taxed in the estates of different *decedents* within a 10-year period. The credit is determined using a decreasing statutory percentage, with the magnitude of the credit decreasing as the length of time between the multiple deaths increases. § 2013.

Criminal fraud. See *fraud.*

Cross-purchase buy-sell agreement. Under this type of arrangement, the surviving owners of the business agree to buy out the withdrawing owner. Assume, for example, Ron and Sara are equal shareholders in Tip Corporation. Under a cross-purchase buy-sell agreement, Ron and Sara would contract to purchase the other's interest should that person decide to withdraw from the business. See also *buy-sell agreement* and *entity buy-sell agreement.*

Current earnings and profits. Net tax-basis earnings of a corporation aggregated during the current tax year. A corporate distribution is deemed to be first from the entity's current earnings and profits and then from accumulated earnings and profits. Shareholders recognize dividend income to the extent of the earnings and profits of the corporation. A *dividend* results to the extent of current earnings and profits, even if there is a larger negative balance in *accumulated earnings and profits.* § 316 and Reg. § 1.316–2.

Current tax expense. Under *ASC 740 (SFAS 109),* the book tax expense that relates to the current reporting period's net income and is actually payable (or creditable) to the appropriate governmental agencies for the current period. Also known as "cash tax" or "tax payable."

Current use valuation. See *special use value.*

Curtesy. A husband's right under state law to all or part of his wife's property upon her death. See also *dower.*

D

Death benefit. A payment made by an employer to the beneficiary or beneficiaries of a deceased employee on account of the death of the employee.

Debt-financed income. Included in computations of the *unrelated business income* of an *exempt organization,* the *gross income* generated from debt-financed property.

Decedent. An individual who has died.

Deduction. The Federal income tax is not imposed upon *gross income.* Rather, it is imposed upon *taxable income.* Congressionally identified deductions are subtracted from gross income to arrive at the tax base, taxable income.

Deductions in respect of a decedent. Deductions accrued at the moment of death but not recognizable on the final income tax return of a *decedent* because of the method of accounting used. Such items are allowed as deductions on the *estate tax* return and on the income tax return of the estate (Form 1041) or the heir (Form 1040). An example of a deduction in respect of a decedent is interest expense accrued to the date of death by a cash basis debtor.

Deferred compensation. Compensation that will be taxed when received and not when earned. An example is a contribution by an employer to a *qualified pension or profit sharing plan* on behalf of an employee. The contributions are not taxed to the employee until they are distributed (e.g., upon retirement).

Deferred tax asset. Under *ASC 740 (SFAS 109),* an item created on an enterprise's balance sheet by a temporary book-tax difference, such that a tax benefit is not recognized until a later date, although it already has been reported in the financial statements, e.g., the carryforward of a disallowed deduction.

Deferred tax benefit. Under *ASC 740 (SFAS 109),* a reduction in the book tax expense that relates to the current reporting period's net income but will not be realized until a future reporting period. Creates or adds to the entity's *deferred tax asset* balance sheet account. For instance, the carryforward of a *net operating loss* is a deferred tax benefit.

Deferred tax expense. Under *ASC 740 (SFAS 109),* a book tax expense that relates to the current reporting period's net income but will not be realized until a future reporting period. Creates or adds to the entity's *deferred tax liability* balance sheet account. For instance, a deferred tax expense is created when tax depreciation deductions for the period are "accelerated" and exceed the corresponding book depreciation expense.

Deferred tax liability. As determined under the rules of *ASC 740 (SFAS 109),* an item created on an enterprise's balance sheet by a temporary book-tax difference, such that a tax benefit is recognized earlier for tax purposes than it is in the financial accounting records, e.g., the use of an accelerated cost recovery deduction.

Deficiency. Additional tax liability owed by a taxpayer and assessed by the IRS. See also *assessment* and *statutory notice of deficiency.*

Deficiency dividend. Once the IRS has established a corporation's liability for the *personal holding company tax* in a prior year, the tax may be reduced or avoided by the issuance of a deficiency dividend under § 547. The deficiency dividend procedure does not avoid the usual penalties and interest applicable for failure to file a return or pay a tax.

Deficit. A negative balance, say, in the earnings and profits account.

Demand loan. A loan payable upon request by the creditor, rather than on a specific date.

Depletion. The process by which the cost or other *basis* of a natural resource (e.g., an oil or gas interest) is recovered upon extraction and sale of the resource. The two ways to determine the depletion allowance are the cost and percentage (or statutory) methods. Under cost depletion, each unit of production sold is assigned a portion of the cost or other basis of the interest. This is determined by dividing the cost or other basis by the total units expected to be recovered. Under percentage (or statutory) depletion, the tax law provides a special percentage factor for different types of minerals and other natural resources. This percentage is multiplied by the *gross income* from the interest to arrive at the depletion allowance. §§ 613 and 613A.

Depreciation. The deduction for the cost or other *basis* of a tangible asset over the asset's *estimated useful life.* Certain favorable Code provisions may allow the taxpayer to accelerate the depreciation deductions into earlier tax years. For intangible assets, see *amortization.* For natural resources, see *depletion.*

Depreciation recapture. Upon the disposition of depreciable property used in a *trade or business,* gain or loss is measured by the difference between the consideration received (the *amount realized*) and the *adjusted basis* of the property. The gain recognized could be *§ 1231 gain* and qualify for long-term capital gain treatment. The recapture provisions of the Code (e.g., §§ 291 and 1245) may operate to convert some or all of the previous § 1231 gain into ordinary income. The justification for depreciation recapture is that it prevents a taxpayer from converting a dollar of ordinary deduction (in the form of *depreciation*) into deferred tax-favored income (§ 1231 or long-term *capital gain*). The depreciation recapture rules do not apply when the property is disposed of at a loss or via a *gift.*

Determination letter. Upon the request of a taxpayer, the IRS will comment on the tax status of a completed transaction. Determination letters frequently are used to clarify employee status, determine whether a retirement or profit sharing plan qualifies under the Code, and determine the tax-exempt status of certain nonprofit organizations.

Devise. A transfer of real estate by will. See also *bequest.*

Disclaimers. Rejections, refusals, or renunciations of claims, powers, or property. Section 2518 sets forth the conditions required to avoid *gift tax* consequences as the result of a disclaimer.

Discretionary trust. A trust under which the *trustee* or another party has the right to accumulate (rather than distribute) the income for each year. Depending on the terms of the trust instrument, the income may be accumulated for future distributions to the *income beneficiaries* or added to *corpus* for the benefit of the remainder *beneficiary.*

Disguised sale. When a partner contributes property to the entity and soon thereafter receives a distribution from the partnership, the transactions are collapsed, and the distribution is seen as a purchase of the asset by the *partnership.* § 707(a)(2)(B).

Disproportionate. Not pro rata or ratable. Suppose, for example, Fin Corporation has two shareholders, Cal and Dot, each of whom owns 50 percent of its stock. If Fin distributes a cash dividend of $2,000 to Cal and only $1,000 to Dot, the distribution is disproportionate. The distribution would have been proportionate if Cal and Dot had received $1,500 each.

Disproportionate distribution. A distribution from a *partnership* to one or more of its partners in which at least one partner's interest in partnership *hot assets* is increased or decreased. For example, a distribution of cash to one *partner* and hot assets to another changes both partners' interest in hot assets and is *disproportionate.* The intent of rules for taxation of disproportionate distributions is to ensure each partner eventually recognizes his or her proportionate share of partnership ordinary income.

Disproportionate redemption. See *redemption (disproportionate).*

Dissent. To disagree with the majority. If, for example, Judge Bird disagrees with the result reached by Judges Crown and Dove (all of whom are members of the same court), Judge Bird could issue a dissenting opinion.

Distributable net income (DNI). The measure that determines the nature and amount of the distributions from *estates* and *trusts* that the *beneficiaries* must include in income. DNI also limits the amount that estates and trusts can claim as a deduction for such distributions. § 643(a).

Distribution deduction. Used to compute an *estate* or *trust's* taxable income for the year. The lesser of the amount distributed to *beneficiaries* from income, or the deductible portion of *distributable net income* for the period.

Distributions in kind. Transfers of property "as is." If, for example, a corporation distributes land to its shareholders, a distribution in kind has taken place. A sale of land followed by a distribution of the cash proceeds would not be a distribution in kind of the land.

District Court. A Federal District Court is a *trial court* for purposes of litigating Federal tax matters. It is the only trial court in which a jury trial can be obtained.

Dividend. A nondeductible distribution to the shareholders of a corporation. A dividend constitutes *gross income* to the recipient if it is from the *current* or *accumulated earnings and profits* of the corporation.

Dividend equivalent amount (DEA). The amount subject to the *branch profits tax,* it is equal to the *effectively connected earnings and profits* of the U.S. branch of a foreign corporation, reduced/(increased) by an increase/(reduction) in U.S. net equity.

Dividends paid deduction. Relative to the *accumulated earnings* and *personal holding company taxes,* reductions in the tax base are allowed to the extent that the corporation made *dividend* payments during the year. Thus, this adjustment reduces *accumulated taxable income* and *personal holding company income.*

Dividends received deduction. A deduction allowed a corporate shareholder for *dividends* received from a domestic corporation. The deduction usually is 70 percent of the dividends received, but it could be 80 or 100 percent depending upon the ownership percentage held by the payee corporation. §§ 243–246.

Divisive reorganization. A corporate division: some of the assets of one corporation are transferred to another corporation in exchange for control of the transferee. Then, in a *spinoff* or *split-off,* stock of the transferee is distributed to the transferor's shareholders.

Dock sale. A purchaser uses its owned or rented vehicles to take possession of the product at the seller's shipping dock. In most states, the sale is apportioned to the operating state of the purchaser, rather than the seller. See also *apportion* and *sales factor.*

Domestic corporation. A corporation created or organized in the United States or under the law of the United States or any state. § 7701(a)(4). Only *dividends* received from domestic corporations qualify for the *dividends received deduction* (§ 243). See also *foreign corporation.*

Domestic production activities deduction (DPAD). A deduction allowed to sole proprietors, *C corporations, partnerships, S corporations*, cooperatives, *estates*, and *trusts* for certain production activities. The deduction rate is 9 percent of *qualified production activities income.* The deduction cannot exceed 50 percent of *W–2 wages.* § 199.

Domestic production gross receipts (DPGR). A key component in computing the *domestic production activities deduction (DPAD).* Includes receipts from the sale and other disposition of qualified production property produced in significant part within the United States. § 199(c)(4).

Domicile. A person's legal home.

Donee. The recipient of a gift.

Donor. The maker of a gift.

Double-weighted apportionment formula. A means by which the total taxable income of a *multistate corporation* is assigned to a specific state. Usually, the payroll, property, and sales factors are equally treated, and the weighted average of these factors is used in the apportionment procedure. In some states, however, the sales factor may receive a double weight, or it may be the only factor considered. These latter formulas place a greater tax burden on the income of out-of-state corporations. See also *apportion, payroll factor, property factor, sales factor,* and *UDITPA.*

Dower. A wife's right to all or part of her deceased husband's property; unique to *common law* states as opposed to *community property* jurisdictions. See also *curtesy.*

E

Earned income. Income from personal services. Distinguished from passive, portfolio, and other *unearned income* (and sometimes referred to as "active" income). See §§ 469, 911, and the related Regulations.

Earnings and profits (E & P). Measures the economic capacity of a corporation to make a distribution to shareholders that is not a return of capital. Such a distribution results in *dividend* income to the shareholders to the extent of the corporation's current and accumulated *earnings and profits.*

Economic effect test. Requirements that must be met before a *special allocation* may be used by a *partnership.* The premise behind the test is that each *partner* who receives an allocation of income or loss from a partnership bears the economic benefit or burden of the allocation.

Effective tax rate. The financial statements for an entity include several footnotes, one of which reconciles the expected (statutory) income tax rate (e.g., 35 percent for a *C corporation*) with the effective tax rate, i.e., total tax expense as a percentage of book income. The reconciliation often is done in dollar and/or percentage terms.

Effectively connected income. Income of a *nonresident alien* or foreign corporation that is attributable to the operations of a U.S. trade or business under either the asset-use or the business-activities test.

E-filing. The process of submitting tax returns and other documents by the taxpayer to the IRS using a computer or other electronic equipment. Large businesses are required to file their income tax returns electronically, and the IRS has targeted that 80 percent of Forms 1040 use an e-filing option.

Employee stock ownership plan (ESOP). A type of qualified profit sharing plan that invests in securities of the employer. In a noncontributory ESOP, the employer usually contributes its shares to a trust and receives a deduction for the fair market value of the stock. Generally, the employee does not recognize income until the stock is sold after its distribution to him or her upon retirement or other separation from service. See also *qualified pension or profit sharing plan.*

En banc. The case was considered by the whole court. Typically, for example, only one of the judges of the U.S. *Tax Court* will hear and decide on a tax controversy. However, when the issues involved are unusually novel or of wide impact, the case will be heard and decided by the full court sitting *en banc.*

Energy tax credit–business property. Various tax credits are available to those who invest in certain energy property. The purpose of the credit is to create incentives for conservation and to develop alternative energy sources.

Enrolled agent (EA). A tax practitioner who has gained admission to practice before the IRS by passing an IRS examination.

Entity. An organization or being that possesses separate existence for tax purposes. Examples are *corporations, partnerships, estates,* and *trusts.*

Entity accounting income. Entity accounting income is not identical to the *taxable income* of a *trust* or *estate,* nor is it determined in the same manner as the entity's financial accounting income would be. The trust document or will determines whether certain income, expenses, gains, or losses are allocated to the corpus of the entity or to the entity's income beneficiaries. Only the items that are allocated to the income beneficiaries are included in entity accounting income.

Entity buy-sell agreement. An arrangement whereby the entity is to purchase a withdrawing owner's interest. When the entity is a corporation, the agreement generally involves a stock redemption on the part of the withdrawing shareholder. See also *buy-sell agreement* and *cross-purchase buy-sell agreement.*

Entity concept. Even in so-called flow-through entities, tax accounting elections are made (e.g., a tax year is adopted) and conventions are adopted (e.g., with respect to cost recovery methods) at the entity level. This may seem to violate the *conduit concept,* but such exceptions tend to ease the administration of such conduit taxpayers, especially in the context of a large number of shareholders/partners/members/beneficiaries.

Equity method. Under *Generally Accepted Accounting Principles,* the method of financial reporting for the operations of a subsidiary when the parent corporation owns between 20 and 50 percent of the subsidiary's stock. Creates a book-tax difference, as the two entities' operating results are combined for book purposes, but a Federal income tax *consolidated return* cannot be filed.

Equity structure shift. A tax-free reorganization other than a *divisive reorganization* or *recapitalization.* If there is a more than 50 percent change in the ownership of a loss corporation in an equity structure shift, § 382 limits the use of *net operating loss* carryovers of the loss corporation. Specifically, the annual net operating loss carryover deduction is limited to the value of the loss corporation immediately before the equity structure shift times the *long-term tax-exempt rate.*

Escrow. Money or other property placed with a third party as security for an existing or proposed obligation. Cyd, for example, agrees to purchase Don's stock in Rip Corporation but needs time to raise the necessary funds. Don places the stock with Ernie (the escrow agent), with instructions to deliver it to Cyd when the purchase price is paid.

Estate. An entity that locates, collects, distributes, and discharges the assets and liabilities of a *decedent.*

Estate freeze. Procedures directed toward fixing and stabilizing the value of an interest retained in a business, while transferring the growth portion to family members. In the case of a *closely held corporation,* the estate freeze usually involves keeping the preferred stock and giving away the common stock. The ultimate objective is to reduce estate value when the original owner-donor dies.

Estate tax. A tax imposed on the right to transfer property by death. Thus, an estate tax is levied on the *decedent's* estate and not on the heir receiving the property. See also *inheritance tax.*

Estimated useful life. The period over which an asset will be used by the taxpayer. Assets such as collectible artwork do not have an estimated useful life. The amount can be used in measuring the annual tax deduction for *depreciation* and *amortization.*

Estoppel. The process of being stopped from proving something (even if true) in court due to a prior inconsistent action. Estoppel usually is invoked as a matter of fairness to prevent one party (either the taxpayer or the IRS) from taking advantage of a prior error.

Evasion. See *tax evasion.*

Excess lobbying expenditure. An excise tax is applied on otherwise tax-exempt organizations with respect to the excess of total *lobbying expenditures* over *grass roots expenditures* for the year.

Excess loss account. When a subsidiary has generated more historical losses than its parent has invested in the entity, the parent's *basis* in the subsidiary is zero, and the parent records additional losses in an excess loss account. This treatment allows the parent to continue to deduct losses of the subsidiary, even where no basis reduction is possible, while avoiding the need to show a negative stock basis on various financial records. If the subsidiary stock is sold while an excess loss account exists, *capital gain* income usually is recognized to the extent of the balance in the account.

Excise tax. A tax on the manufacture, sale, or use of goods; on the carrying on of an occupation or activity; or on the transfer of property. Thus, the Federal estate and gift taxes are, theoretically, excise taxes.

Exclusion amount. The value of assets that is exempt from transfer tax, due to the credit allowed for gifts or transfers by death. For gifts and deaths in 2011, the exclusion amount is $5 million. An exclusion amount unused by a deceased spouse may be used by the surviving spouse. Often called the *exemption equivalent amount.* See also *bypass amount.*

Executor. A person designated by a will to administer (manage or take charge of) the assets and liabilities of a *decedent.* See also *administrator.*

Exempt organization. An organization that is either partially or completely exempt from Federal income taxation. § 501.

Exemption. An amount by which the tax base is reduced for all qualifying taxpayers. Individuals can receive personal and dependency exemptions, and taxpayers apply an exemption in computing their alternative minimum taxable income. Often, the exemption amount is phased out as the tax base becomes sizable.

Exemption equivalent. The maximum value of assets that can be transferred to another party without incurring any Federal *gift* or *estate tax* because of the application of the *unified tax credit.*

Exemption equivalent amount. The taxable amount (currently $5 million for *gift tax* and *estate tax*) that is the equivalent of the *unified transfer tax credit* allowed. See also *bypass amount.*

Expanded affiliated group (EAG). For purposes of the *domestic production activities deduction (DPAD),* all members of an expanded affiliated group (EAG) are treated as a single corporation. Thus, the activities of any member of the group are attributed to the other members. An EAG must meet the requirements for filing a *consolidated return* with ownership levels lowered to 50 percent. § 199(d)(4)(B).

Expenses in respect of a decedent. See *deductions in respect of a decedent.*

F

Fair market value. The amount at which property would change hands between a willing buyer and a willing seller, neither being under any compulsion to buy or to sell, and both having reasonable knowledge of the relevant facts. Reg. § 20.2031–1(b).

FAS 109. See *ASC 740 (SFAS 109).*

FASB. See *Generally accepted accounting principles (GAAP).*

Federal Register. The first place that the rules and regulations of U.S. administrative agencies (e.g., the U.S. Treasury Department) are published.

F.3d. An abbreviation for the third series of the *Federal Reporter,* the official series in which decisions of the U.S. *Court of Federal Claims* and the U.S. *Court of Appeals* are published. The second series is denoted F.2d.

F.Supp. The abbreviation for *Federal Supplement,* the official series in which the reported decisions of the U.S. Federal *District Courts* are published.

Feeder organization. An entity that carries on a trade or business for the benefit of an *exempt organization.* However, such a relationship does not result in the feeder organization itself being tax-exempt. § 502.

Fiduciary. A person who manages money or property for another and who must exercise a standard of care in the management activity imposed by law or contract. A *trustee,* for example, possesses a fiduciary responsibility to the *beneficiaries* of the *trust* to follow the terms of the trust and the requirements of applicable state law. A breach of fiduciary responsibility would make the trustee liable to the beneficiaries for any damage caused by the breach.

Field audit. An *audit* conducted by the IRS on the business premises of the taxpayer or in the office of the tax practitioner representing the taxpayer. See also *correspondence audit* and *office audit.*

FIN 48. See *ASC 740–10 (FIN 48).*

Financial Accounting Standards Board. See *Generally accepted accounting principles (GAAP).*

FIRPTA. Under the Foreign Investment in Real Property Tax Act, gains or losses realized by *nonresident aliens* and non-U.S. corporations on the disposition of U.S. real estate create U.S.-source income and are subject to U.S. income tax.

First-in, first-out (FIFO). An *accounting method* for determining the cost of inventories. Under this method, the inventory on hand is deemed to be the sum of the cost of the most recently acquired units. See also *last-in, first-out (LIFO).*

Fiscal year. See *accounting period.*

Flat tax. In its pure form, a flat tax would eliminate all exclusions, deductions, and credits and impose a one-rate tax on *gross income*.

Foreign corporation. A corporation that is not created in the United States or organized under the laws of one of the states of the United States. § 7701(a)(5). See also *domestic corporation*.

Foreign currency transaction. An exchange that could generate a foreign currency gain or loss for a U.S. taxpayer. For instance, if Avery contracts to purchase foreign goods, payable in a currency other than U.S. dollars, at a specified date in the future, any change in the exchange rate between the dollar and that currency generates a foreign currency gain or loss upon completion of the contract. This gain or loss is treated as separate from the underlying transaction; it may create ordinary or *capital gain* or loss.

Foreign earned income exclusion. The Code allows exclusions for earned income generated outside the United States to alleviate any tax base and rate disparities among countries. In addition, the exclusion is allowed for housing expenditures incurred by the taxpayer's employer with respect to the non-U.S. assignment, and self-employed individuals can deduct foreign housing expenses incurred in a trade or business.

Foreign sales corporation (FSC). An entity that qualified for a partial exemption of its gross export receipts from U.S. tax.

Foreign-source income. Income that is not sourced within the United States. Examples include earnings from the performance of a personal services contract outside the United States, interest received from a non-U.S. corporation, and income from the use of property outside the United States.

Foreign tax credit or deduction. A U.S. citizen or resident who incurs or pays income taxes to a foreign country on income subject to U.S. tax may be able to claim some of these taxes as a deduction or a credit against the U.S. income tax. §§ 27, 164, and 901–905.

Form 706. The U.S. Estate Tax Return. In certain cases, this form must be filed for a *decedent* who was a resident or citizen of the United States.

Form 709. The U.S. Gift Tax Return.

Form 870. The signing of Form 870 (Waiver of Restriction on Assessment and Collection of Deficiency in Tax and Acceptance of Overassessments) by a taxpayer permits the IRS to assess a proposed deficiency without issuing a *statutory notice of deficiency* (90-day letter). This means the taxpayer must pay the *deficiency* and cannot file a petition to the U.S. Tax Court. § 6213(d).

Form 872. The signing of this form by a taxpayer extends the applicable *statute of limitations*. § 6501(c)(4).

Form 1041. The U.S. Fiduciary Income Tax Return, required to be filed by *estates* and *trusts*. See Appendix B for a specimen form.

Form 1065. The U.S. Partnership Return of Income. See Appendix B for a specimen form.

Form 1120. The U.S. Corporation Income Tax Return. See Appendix B for a specimen form.

Form 1120–A. The U.S. Short-Form Corporation Income Tax Return.

Form 1120S. The U.S. Small Business Corporation Income Tax Return, required to be filed by *S corporations*. See Appendix B for a specimen form.

Fraud. Tax fraud falls into two categories: civil and criminal. Under civil fraud, the IRS may impose as a penalty an amount equal to as much as 75 percent of the underpayment [§ 6651(f)]. Fines and/or imprisonment are prescribed for conviction of various types of criminal tax fraud (§§ 7201–7207). Both civil and criminal fraud involve a specific intent on the part of the taxpayer to evade the tax; mere *negligence* is not enough. Criminal fraud requires the additional element of willfulness (i.e., done deliberately and with evil purpose). In practice, it becomes difficult to distinguish between the degree of intent necessary to support criminal, rather than civil, fraud. In either situation, the IRS has the burden of proving fraud. See also *burden of proof*.

Free transferability of interests. A corporation's shareholder usually can freely transfer the stock to others without the approval of the existing shareholders.

Fringe benefits. Compensation or other benefits received by an employee that are not in the form of cash. Some fringe benefits (e.g., accident and health plans, group term life insurance) may be excluded from the employee's *gross income* and thus are not subject to the Federal income tax.

Frivolous return. A tax return that included a position that has no more than a 5 percent chance of being sustained upon review. Taxpayer and *tax preparer* penalties are assessed if a frivolous position is included in a filed tax return.

Functional currency. The currency of the economic environment in which the taxpayer carries on most of its activities and transacts most of its business.

Future interest. An interest that will come into being at some future time. Distinguished from a *present interest*, which already exists. Assume that Dora transfers securities to a newly created *trust*. Under the terms of the trust instrument, income from the securities is to be paid each year to Nan for her life, with the securities passing to Steve upon Nan's death. Nan has a present interest in the trust since she is entitled to current income distributions. Steve has a future interest since he must wait for Nan's death to benefit from the trust. The *annual exclusion* of $13,000 is not allowed for a gift of a future interest. § 2503(b). See also *gift splitting*.

G

General business credit. The summation of various nonrefundable business credits, including the *energy credit*, alcohol fuels credit, and research activities credit. The amount of general business credit that can be used to reduce the tax liability is limited to the taxpayer's net income tax reduced by the greater of (1) the tentative minimum tax or (2) 25 percent of the net regular tax liability that exceeds $25,000. Unused general business credits can be carried back 1 year and forward 20 years. §§ 38 and 39.

General partner. A partner who is fully liable in an individual capacity for the debts of the *partnership* to third parties. A general partner's liability is not limited to the investment in the partnership. See also *limited partner*.

General partnership. A *partnership* that is owned by one or more *general partners*. Creditors of a general partnership can collect amounts owed them from both the partnership assets and the assets of the partners individually.

General power of appointment. See *power of appointment.*

Generally accepted accounting principles (GAAP). Guidelines relating to how to construct the financial statements of enterprises doing business in the United States. Promulgated chiefly by the Financial Accounting Standards Board (FASB).

Gift. A transfer of property for less than adequate consideration. Gifts usually occur in a personal setting (such as between members of the same family). They are excluded from the income tax base but may be subject to a *transfer tax.*

Gift splitting. A special election for Federal *gift tax* purposes under which husband and wife can treat a gift by one of them to a third party as being made one-half by each. If, for example, Hal (the husband) makes a gift of $26,000 to Sharon, Winnie (the wife) may elect to treat $13,000 of the gift as coming from her. The major advantage of the election is that it enables the parties to take advantage of the nonowner spouse's (Winnie in this case) *annual exclusion* and unified credit. § 2513.

Gift tax. A tax imposed on the transfer of property by *gift.* The tax is imposed upon the *donor* of a gift and is based on the *fair market value* of the property on the date of the gift.

Gifts within three years of death. Some *taxable gifts* automatically are included in the *gross estate* of the *donor* if death occurs within three years of the gift. § 2035.

Goodwill. The reputation and built-up business of a company. For accounting purposes, goodwill has no basis unless it is purchased. In the purchase of a business, goodwill generally is the difference between the purchase price and the value of the assets acquired. The intangible asset goodwill is amortized over 15 years. § 195. See also *amortization.*

Grantor. A transferor of property. The creator of a *trust* usually is referred to as the grantor of the entity.

Grantor trust. A *trust* under which the grantor retains control over the income or *corpus* (or both) to such an extent that he or she is treated as the owner of the property and its income for income tax purposes. Income from a grantor trust is taxable to the grantor, and not to the *beneficiary* who receives it. §§ 671–679. See also *reversionary interest.*

Grass roots expenditure. *Exempt organizations* are prohibited from engaging in political activities, but spending incurred to influence the opinions of the general public relative to specific legislation is permitted by the law. See also *excess lobbying expenditure.*

Green card test. Form I-551, received from a U.S. consul as a receipt showing that the holder has immigration status in the United States, and used to refute alien status for tax purposes.

Gross estate. The property owned or previously transferred by a *decedent* that is subject to the Federal *estate tax.* Distinguished from the *probate estate,* which is property actually subject to administration by the *administrator* or *executor* of an estate. §§ 2031–2046. See also *adjusted gross estate* and *taxable estate.*

Gross income. Income subject to the Federal income tax. Gross income does not include all economic income. That is, certain exclusions are allowed (e.g., interest on municipal bonds). For a manufacturing or merchandising business, gross income usually means gross profit (gross sales or gross receipts less cost of goods sold). § 61 and Reg. § 1.61– 3(a). See also *adjusted gross income* and *taxable income.*

Gross up. To add back to the value of the property or income received the amount of the tax that has been paid. For *gifts* made within three years of death, any *gift tax* paid on the transfer is added to the *gross estate.* § 2035.

Group term life insurance. Life insurance coverage provided by an employer for a group of employees. Such insurance is renewable on a year-to-year basis, and typically no *cash surrender value* is built up.

Guaranteed payment. Made by a *partnership* to a *partner* for services rendered or for the use of capital, to the extent that the payments are determined without regard to the income of the partnership. The payments are treated as though they were made to a nonpartner and thus are deducted by the entity.

Guardianship. A legal arrangement under which one person (a guardian) has the legal right and duty to care for another (the ward) and his or her property. A guardianship is established because the ward is unable to act legally on his or her own behalf (e.g., because of *minority* [he or she is not of age] or mental or physical incapacity).

H

Head of household. An unmarried individual who maintains a household for another and satisfies certain conditions set forth in § 2(b). This status enables the taxpayer to use a set of income tax rates that are lower than those applicable to other unmarried individuals but higher than those applicable to surviving spouses and married persons filing a joint return.

Heir. A person who inherits property from a *decedent.*

Hobby. An activity not engaged in for profit. The Code restricts the amount of losses that an individual can deduct for hobby activities so that these transactions cannot be used to offset income from other sources. § 183.

Holding period. The period of time during which property has been held for income tax purposes. The holding period is significant in determining whether gain or loss from the sale or exchange of a capital asset is long term or short term. § 1223.

Hot assets. *Unrealized receivables* and substantially appreciated inventory under § 751. When hot assets are present, the sale of a *partnership* interest or the disproportionate distribution of the assets can cause ordinary income to be recognized.

H.R. 10 plans. See *Keogh plans.*

I

Imputed interest. For certain long-term sales of property, the IRS can convert some of the gain from the sale into interest income if the contract does not provide for a minimum rate of interest to be paid by the purchaser. The seller recognizes less long-term *capital gain* and more ordinary income (interest income). § 483 and the related Regulations.

In kind. See *distributions in kind.*

Inbound taxation. U.S. tax effects when a non-U.S. person begins an investment or business activity in the United States.

Incident of ownership. An element of ownership or degree of control over a life insurance policy. The retention by an *insured* of an incident of ownership in a life insurance policy places the policy proceeds in the insured's *gross estate* upon death. § 2042(2) and Reg. § 20.2042–1(c).

Income beneficiary. The party entitled to income from property. In a typical *trust* situation, Art is to receive the income for life with *corpus* or principal passing to Bev upon Art's death. In this case, Art is the income beneficiary of the trust.

Income in respect of a decedent (IRD). Income earned by a *decedent* at the time of death but not reportable on the final income tax return because of the method of accounting that appropriately is utilized. Such income is included in the *gross estate* and is taxed to the eventual recipient (either the estate or heirs). The recipient is, however, allowed an income tax deduction for the estate tax attributable to the income. § 691.

Income interest. The right of a *beneficiary* to receive distributions from the fiduciary income of a *trust* or *estate.*

Income shifting. Occurs when an individual transfers some of his or her *gross income* to a taxpayer who is subject to a lower tax rate, thereby reducing the total income tax liability of the group. Income shifting produces a successful *assignment of income.* It can be accomplished by transferring income-producing property to the lower-bracket taxpayer or to an effective trust for his or her benefit, or by transferring ownership interests in a family *partnership* or in a *closely held corporation.*

Income tax provision. Under *ASC 740 (SFAS 109)*, a synonym for the book tax expense of an entity for the financial reporting period. Following the "matching principle," all book tax expense that relates to the net income for the reporting period is reported on that period's financial statements, including not only the *current tax expense,* but also any *deferred tax expense* and *deferred tax benefit.*

Incomplete transfer. A transfer made by a *decedent* during lifetime that, because of certain control or enjoyment retained by the transferor, is not considered complete for Federal *estate tax* purposes. Thus, some or all of the fair market value of the property transferred is included in the transferor's *gross estate.* §§ 2036–2038. See also *revocable transfer.*

Indexation. Various components of the tax formula are adjusted periodically for the effects of inflation, so that the effects of the formula are not eroded by price level changes. Tax rate schedules, exemption amounts, and the standard deduction, among other items, are indexed in this manner.

Individual retirement account (IRA). Individuals with *earned income* are permitted to set aside up to 100 percent of that income per year (usually not to exceed $5,000) for a retirement account. The amount so set aside can be deducted by the taxpayer and is subject to income tax only upon withdrawal. The Code limits the amount of this contribution that can be deducted *for* AGI depending upon the magnitude of the taxpayer's AGI before the IRA contribution is considered. No deduction is allowed for a contribution to a Roth IRA, but most Roth withdrawals are completely tax-free. § 219.

Inheritance tax. A tax imposed on the right to receive property from a *decedent.* Thus, theoretically, an inheritance tax is imposed on the *heir.* The Federal *estate tax* is imposed on the estate.

Inside basis. A *partnership's* basis in each of the assets it owns.

Installment method. A method of accounting enabling certain taxpayers to spread the recognition of gain on the sale of property over the collection period. Under this procedure, the seller arrives at the gain to be recognized by computing the gross profit percentage from the sale (the gain divided by the contract price) and applying it to each payment received. § 453.

Insured. A person whose life is the subject of an insurance policy. Upon the death of the insured, the *life insurance* policy matures, and the proceeds become payable to the designated *beneficiary.*

Intangible asset. Property that is a "right" rather than a physical object. Examples are patents, stocks and bonds, *goodwill,* trademarks, franchises, and copyrights. See also *amortization* and *tangible property.*

Inter vivos transfer. A transfer of property during the life of the owner. Distinguished from testamentary transfers, where the property passes at death.

Interest-free loans. Bona fide loans that charge no interest (or a below-market rate). If made in a nonbusiness setting, the *imputed interest* element is treated as a gift from the lender to the borrower. If made by a corporation to a shareholder, a *constructive dividend* could result. In either event, the lender may recognize interest income. § 7872.

Intermediate sanctions. The IRS can assess excise taxes on disqualified persons and organization managers associated with so-called public charities engaging in excess benefit transactions. An excess benefit transaction is one in which a disqualified person engages in a non-fair market value transaction with the *exempt organization* or receives *unreasonable compensation.* Prior to the idea of intermediate sanctions, the only option available to the IRS was to revoke the organization's exempt status.

Internal Revenue Code. The collected statutes that govern the taxation of income, property transfers, and other transactions in the United States and the enforcement of those provisions. Enacted by Congress, the Code is amended frequently, but it has not been reorganized since 1954. However, because of the extensive revisions to the statutes that occurred with the Tax Reform Act of 1986, Title 26 of the U.S. Code is known as the Internal Revenue Code of 1986.

Internal Revenue Service (IRS). The Federal agency, a division of the Department of the Treasury, charged with administering the U.S. revenue enforcement and collection provisions.

International Accounting Standards Board (IASB). The body that promulgates *International Financial Reporting Standards* (IFRS). Based in London, representing accounting standard setting bodies in over 100 countries, the IASB develops accounting standards that can serve as the basis for harmonizing conflicting reporting standards among nations.

International Financial Reporting Standards (IFRS). Produced by the *International Accounting Standards Board* (IASB), guidelines developed since 2001 as to revenue recognition, accounting for business combinations, and a conceptual framework for financial reporting. IFRS provisions are designed so that they can be used by all entities, regardless of where they are based or conduct business. IFRS have gained widespread acceptance throughout the world, and the SEC is considering how to require U.S. entities to use IFRS in addition to, or in lieu of, the accounting rules of the *Financial Accounting Standards Board.*

Interpolated terminal reserve. The measure used in valuing insurance policies for *gift* and *estate tax* purposes when the policies are not paid up at the time of their transfer. Reg. § 20.2031–8(a)(3), Ex. (3).

Intestate. The condition when no will exists at the time of death. In such cases, state law prescribes who will receive the *decedent's* property. The laws of intestate succession generally favor the surviving spouse, children, and grandchildren, and then parents and grandparents and brothers and sisters.

Investment income. Consisting of virtually the same elements as *portfolio income,* a measure by which to justify a deduction for interest on *investment indebtedness.*

Investment indebtedness. Debt incurred to carry or incur investments by the taxpayer in assets that will produce *portfolio income.* Limitations are placed upon interest deductions that are incurred in connection with the debt (generally to the corresponding amount of *investment income*).

Investor losses. Losses on stock and securities. If stocks and bonds are capital assets in the hands of the holder, a capital loss materializes as of the last day of the taxable year in which the stocks or bonds become worthless. Under certain circumstances involving stocks and bonds of affiliated corporations, an ordinary loss is permitted upon worthlessness.

Involuntary conversion. The loss or destruction of property through theft, casualty, or *condemnation.* Any gain realized on an involuntary conversion can, at the taxpayer's election, be deferred for Federal income tax purposes if the owner reinvests the proceeds within a prescribed period of time in property that is similar or related in service or use. § 1033.

IRA. See *individual retirement account.*

Itemized deductions. Personal and employee expenditures allowed by the Code as deductions from *adjusted gross income.* Examples include certain medical expenses, interest on home mortgages, and *charitable contributions.* Itemized deductions are reported on Schedule A of Form 1040. Certain miscellaneous itemized deductions are reduced by 2 percent of the taxpayer's adjusted gross income.

J

Jeopardy assessment. If the collection of a tax appears in question, the IRS may assess and collect the tax immediately without the usual formalities. The IRS can terminate a taxpayer's *tax year* before the usual date if it feels that the collection of the tax may be in peril because the taxpayer plans to leave the country. §§ 6851 and 6861–6864.

Joint and several liability. Permits the IRS to collect a tax from one or all of several taxpayers. A husband and wife who file a joint income tax return usually are collectively or individually liable for the full amount of the tax liability. The same rule applies to *consolidated return* partners. § 6013(d)(3).

Joint tenants. Two or more persons having undivided ownership of property with the right of survivorship. Right of survivorship gives the surviving owner full ownership of the property. Suppose Betty and Cheryl are joint tenants of a tract of land. Upon Betty's death, Cheryl becomes the sole owner of the property. For the *estate tax* consequences upon the death of a joint tenant, see § 2040. See also *tenants by the entirety* and *tenants in common.*

Joint venture. A one-time grouping of two or more persons in a business undertaking. Unlike a *partnership,* a joint venture does not entail a continuing relationship among the parties. A joint venture is treated like a partnership for Federal income tax purposes. § 7701(a)(2).

K

Keogh plans. Retirement plans available to self-employed taxpayers. They are also referred to as H.R. 10 plans. Under such plans, a taxpayer may deduct each year up to either 20 percent of net earnings from self-employment or $49,000 for 2011, whichever is less.

Kiddie tax. See *tax on unearned income of a child under age 19/24.*

L

Lapse. The expiration of a right either by the death of the holder or upon the expiration of a period of time. Thus, a *power of appointment* lapses upon the death of the holder if he or she has not exercised the power during life or at death (through a will).

Last-in, first-out (LIFO). An *accounting method* for valuing inventories for tax purposes. Under this method, it is assumed that the inventory on hand is valued at the cost of the earliest acquired units. § 472. See also *first-in, first-out (FIFO).*

Leaseback. The transferor of property later leases it back. In a sale-leaseback situation, for example, Ron sells property to Sal and subsequently leases the property from Sal. Thus, Ron becomes the lessee and Sal the lessor.

Least aggregate deferral rule. A test applied to determine the allowable fiscal year of a *partnership* or *S corporation.* Possible tax year-ends are tested, and the fiscal year allowed by the IRS is the one that offers the least amount of income deferral to the owners on an individual basis.

Legacy. A transfer of cash or other property by will.

Legal age. The age at which a person may enter into binding contracts or commit other legal acts. In most states, a minor reaches legal age or majority (comes of age) at age 18.

Legal representative. A person who oversees the legal affairs of another; for example, the *executor* or *administrator* of an *estate* or a court-appointed *guardian* of a minor or incompetent person.

Legatee. The recipient of property that is transferred under a will by the death of the owner.

Lessee. One who rents property from another. In the case of real estate, the lessee also is known as the tenant.

Lessor. One who rents property to another. In the case of real estate, the lessor also is known as the landlord.

Letter ruling. The written response of the IRS to a taxpayer's request for interpretation of the revenue laws with respect to a proposed transaction (e.g., concerning the tax-free status of a reorganization). Not to be relied on as precedent by other than the party who requested the ruling.

LEXIS. An online database system through which a tax researcher can obtain access to the Internal Revenue Code, Regulations, administrative rulings, and court case opinions.

Liabilities in excess of basis. On the contribution of capital to a corporation, an investor recognizes gain on the exchange to the extent that contributed assets carry liabilities with a face amount in excess of the tax basis of the contributed assets. This rule keeps the investor from holding the investment asset received with a negative basis. § 357(c).

Life estate. A legal arrangement under which the *beneficiary* (the life tenant) is entitled to the income from the property for his or her life. Upon the death of the life tenant, the property is transferred to the holder of the *remainder interest.* See also *income beneficiary.*

Life insurance. A contract between the holder of a policy and an insurance company (the carrier) under which the company agrees, in return for premium payments, to pay a specified sum (the face value or maturity value of the policy) to the designated beneficiary upon the death of the *insured.*

Like-kind exchange. An exchange of property held for productive use in a *trade or business* or for investment (except inventory and stocks and bonds) for other investment or trade or business property. Unless non-like-kind property (*boot*) is received, the exchange is fully tax-deferred. § 1031.

Limited liability. The liability of an entity and its owners to third parties is limited to the investment in the entity. This is a characteristic of a corporation, as shareholders generally are not responsible for the debts of the corporation and, at most, may lose the amount paid for the stock issued.

Limited liability company (LLC). A form of entity allowed by all of the states. The entity is taxed as a *partnership* in which all owners of the LLC are treated much like *limited partners.* There are no restrictions on ownership, all partners may participate in management, and none of the owners has personal liability for the entity's debts.

Limited liability limited partnership (LLLP). A *limited partnership* for which the *general partners* are also protected from entity liabilities. An LLLP—or "triple LP"—can be formed in about 20 states. In those states, a limited partnership files with the state to adopt LLLP status.

Limited liability partnership (LLP). A form of entity allowed by many of the states, where a general partnership registers with the state as an LLP. Owners are *general partners,* but a *partner* is not liable for any malpractice committed by other partners. The personal assets of the partners are at risk for the entity's contractual liabilities, such as accounts payable. The personal assets of a specific partner are at risk for his or her own professional malpractice and tort liability, and for malpractice and torts committed by those whom he or she supervises.

Limited partner. A *partner* whose liability to third-party creditors of the *partnership* is limited to the amount he or she has invested in the partnership. See also *general partner* and *limited partnership.*

Limited partnership. A *partnership* in which some of the partners are *limited partners.* At least one of the *partners* in a limited partnership must be a *general partner.*

Liquidating distribution. A distribution by a *partnership* or corporation that is in complete liquidation of the entity's trade or business activities. Typically, such distributions generate capital gain or loss to the investors without regard, for instance, to the *earnings and profits* of the corporation or to the partnership's *basis* in the distributed property. They can, however, lead to recognized gain or loss at the corporate level.

Liquidation. See *corporate liquidation.*

Living trust. A revocable trust. Often touted as a means of avoiding some *probate costs.*

Lobbying expenditure. An expenditure made for the purpose of influencing legislation. Such payments can result in the loss of the exempt status and the imposition of Federal income tax on an *exempt organization.*

Long-term capital gain or loss. Results from the sale or other taxable exchange of a *capital asset* that had been held by the seller for more than one year or from other transactions involving statutorily designated assets, including § 1231 property and patents.

Long-term tax-exempt rate. Used in deriving *net operating loss* limitations in the context of an *equity structure shift.* The highest of the Federal long-term interest rates in effect for any of the last three months. § 382.

Low-income housing credit. Beneficial treatment to owners of low-income housing is provided in the form of a tax credit. The calculated credit is claimed in the year the building is placed in service and in the following nine years. § 42. See also *general business credit.*

Lump-sum distribution. Payment of the entire amount due at one time rather than in installments. Such distributions often occur from *qualified pension or profit sharing plans* upon the retirement or death of a covered employee.

M

MACRS. See *accelerated cost recovery system (ACRS).*

Majority. See *legal age.*

Malpractice. Professional misconduct; an unreasonable lack of due diligence in rendering a professional skill.

Marital deduction. A deduction allowed against the *taxable estate* or *taxable gifts* upon the transfer of property from one spouse to another.

Market value. See *fair market value.*

Matching rule. Treatment of an intercompany transaction on a *consolidated return,* when a sold asset remains within the group.

Meaningful reduction test. A decrease in the shareholder's voting control. Used to determine whether a *stock redemption* qualifies for sale or exchange treatment.

Merger. The absorption of one corporation by another with the corporation being absorbed losing its legal identity. Flow Corporation is merged into Jobs Corporation, and the shareholders of Flow receive stock in Jobs in exchange for their stock in Flow. After the merger, Flow ceases to exist as a separate legal entity. If a merger meets certain conditions, it is not currently taxable to the parties involved. § 368(a)(1)(A). See also *corporate acquisition* and *corporate reorganization.*

Minimum credit (AET). A fixed amount, $150,000 for personal service firms and $250,000 for all others, below which the *accumulated earnings credit* cannot be derived. Assures that small and start-up corporations can generate a minimum amount of earnings before being subject to the *accumulated earnings tax* (AET).

Minimum tax. See *alternative minimum tax.*

Minimum tax credit (AMT). When a corporation pays an *alternative minimum tax* (AMT), a minimum tax credit is created on a dollar-for-dollar basis, to be applied against regular tax liabilities incurred in future years. The credit is carried forward indefinitely, but it is not carried back. The effect of the credit for corporate taxpayers alternating between the AMT and regular tax models is to make the AMT liabilities a prepayment of regular taxes. Noncorporate AMT taxpayers are allowed the credit, but only with respect to the elements of the AMT that reflect timing differences between the two tax models.

Minority. See *legal age.*

Mitigate. To make less severe. See also *mitigation of the annual accounting period concept.*

Mitigation of the annual accounting period concept. Various tax provisions that provide relief from the effect of the finality of the *annual accounting period concept.* For example, the *net operating loss* carryover provisions allow the taxpayer to apply the negative taxable income of one year against a corresponding positive amount in another tax accounting period. See also *annual accounting period concept.*

Mortgagee. The party who holds the mortgage; the creditor.

Mortgagor. The party who mortgages the property; the debtor.

Most suitable use value. For *gift* and *estate tax* purposes, property that is transferred normally is valued in accordance with its most suitable or optimal use. Thus, if a farm is worth more as a potential shopping center, the value as a shopping center is used, even though the transferee (the donee or heir) continues to use the property as a farm. For an exception to this rule concerning the valuation of certain kinds of real estate transferred by death, see *special use value.*

Multistate corporation. A corporation that has operations in more than one of the states of the United States. Issues arise relative to the assignment of appropriate amounts of the entity's taxable income to the states in which it has a presence. See also *allocate, apportion, nexus,* and *UDITPA.*

Multistate Tax Commission (MTC). A regulatory body of the states that develops operating rules and regulations for the implementation of the *UDITPA* and other provisions that assign the total taxable income of a *multistate corporation* to specific states.

Multitiered partnerships. See *tiered partnerships.*

N

Necessary. Appropriate and helpful in furthering the taxpayer's business or income-producing activity. §§ 162(a) and 212. See also *ordinary.*

Negligence. Failure to exercise the reasonable or ordinary degree of care of a prudent person in a situation that results in harm or damage to another. Code § 6651 imposes a penalty on taxpayers who show negligence or intentional disregard of rules and Regulations with respect to the underpayment of certain taxes. See also *accuracy-related penalty.*

Net operating loss. To mitigate the effect of the annual accounting period concept, § 172 allows taxpayers to use an excess loss of one year as a deduction for certain past or future years. In this regard, a carryback period of 2 (or more) years and a carryforward period of 20 years currently are allowed. See also *mitigation of the annual accounting period concept.*

Net worth method. An approach used by the IRS to reconstruct the income of a taxpayer who fails to maintain adequate records. The IRS estimates *gross income* for the year as the increase in net worth of the taxpayer (assets in excess of liabilities), with appropriate adjustment for nontaxable receipts and nondeductible expenditures. The net worth method often is used when tax *fraud* is suspected.

Nexus. A *multistate corporation*'s taxable income can be *apportioned* to a specific state only if the entity has established a sufficient presence, or *nexus,* with that state. State law, which often follows the *UDITPA,* specifies various activities that lead to nexus in various states.

Ninety-day letter. See *statutory notice of deficiency.*

Nonacquiescence. Disagreement by the IRS on the result reached by selected tax decisions. Sometimes abbreviated *Nonacq.* or *NA.* See also *acquiescence.*

Nonbusiness bad debt. A bad debt loss that is not incurred in connection with a creditor's *trade or business.* The loss is classified as a short-term capital loss and is allowed only in the year the debt becomes entirely worthless. In addition to family loans, many *investor losses* are nonbusiness bad debts. § 166(d). See also *business bad debts.*

Nonbusiness income. Income generated from investment assets or from the taxable disposition thereof. In some states, the nonbusiness income of a *multistate corporation* is held out of the apportionment procedure and allocated to the state in which the nonbusiness asset is located. See also *allocate* and *apportion.*

Noncontributory qualified pension or profit sharing plan. A plan funded entirely by the employer with no contributions from the covered employees. See also *qualified pension or profit sharing plan.*

Nonliquidating distribution. A payment made by a *partnership* or corporation to the entity's owner is a nonliquidating distribution when the entity's legal existence does not cease thereafter. If the payor is a corporation, such a distribution can result in *dividend* income to the shareholders. If the payor is a partnership, the *partner* usually assigns a *basis* in the distributed property that is equal to the lesser of the partner's basis in the partnership interest or the basis of the distributed asset to the partnership. In this regard, the partner first assigns basis to any cash that is received in the distribution. The partner's remaining basis, if any, is assigned to the noncash assets according to their relative bases to the partnership.

Nonrecourse debt. Debt secured by the property that it is used to purchase. The purchaser of the property is not personally liable for the debt upon default. Rather, the creditor's recourse is to repossess the related property. Nonrecourse debt generally does not increase the purchaser's *at-risk amount.*

Nonresident alien. An individual who is neither a citizen nor a resident of the United States. Citizenship is determined under the immigration and naturalization laws of the United States. Residency is determined under § 7701(b) of the Internal Revenue Code.

Nonseparately stated income. The net income of an *S corporation* that is combined and allocated to the shareholders. Other items, such as *capital gains* and *charitable contributions,* that could be treated differently on the individual tax returns of the shareholders are not included in this amount but are allocated to the shareholders separately.

Not essentially equivalent redemption. See *redemption (not equivalent to a dividend).*

Obligee. The party to whom someone else is obligated under a contract. Thus, if Coop loans money to Dawn, Coop is the obligee and Dawn is the obligor under the loan.

Obligor. See *obligee.*

Offer in compromise. A settlement agreement offered by the IRS in a tax dispute, especially where there is doubt as to the collectibility of the full *deficiency.* Offers in compromise can include installment payment schedules, as well as reductions in the tax and penalties owed by the taxpayer.

Office audit. An *audit* conducted by the IRS in the agent's office. See also *correspondence audit* and *field audit.*

On all fours. A judicial decision exactly in point with another as to result, facts, or both.

Operating agreement. The governing document of a *limited liability company.* This document is similar in structure, function, and purpose to a *partnership agreement.*

Optimal use value. Synonym for *most suitable use value.*

Optional adjustment election. See *Section 754 election.*

Ordinary. Common and accepted in the general industry or type of activity in which the taxpayer is engaged. It comprises one of the tests for the deductibility of expenses incurred or paid in connection with a *trade or business;* for the production or collection of income; for the management, conservation, or maintenance of property held for the production of income; or in connection with the determination, collection, or refund of any tax. §§ 162(a) and 212. See also *necessary.*

Ordinary and necessary. See *necessary* and *ordinary.*

Ordinary gross income (OGI). A concept peculiar to *personal holding companies* and defined in § 543(b)(1). See also *adjusted ordinary gross income.*

Organizational expenditures. Items incurred early in the life of a corporate entity. Can be an immediate $5,000 amortization deduction, otherwise claimed over 180 months. Amortizable expenditures exclude those incurred to obtain capital (underwriting fees) or assets (subject to cost recovery). Typically, eligible expenditures include legal and accounting fees and state incorporation payments. Such items must be incurred by the end of the entity's first tax year. § 248.

Other adjustments account (OAA). Used in the context of a distribution from an *S corporation.* The net accumulation of the entity's exempt income (e.g., municipal bond interest).

Outbound taxation. U.S. tax effects when a U.S. person begins an investment or business activity outside the United States.

Outside basis. A partner's *basis* in his or her *partnership* interest.

Owner shift. Any change in the respective ownership of stock by a 5 percent-or-more shareholder. Change is determined relative to a testing period of the prior three years. If there is a more-than-50 percent change in the ownership of a loss corporation, § 382 limitations apply to the use of *net operating loss* carryovers of the loss corporation.

Ownership change. An event that triggers a *§ 382 limitation* for the acquiring corporation.

P

Parent-subsidiary controlled group. A *controlled* or *affiliated group* of corporations, where at least one corporation is at least 80 percent owned by one or more of the others. The *affiliated group* definition is more difficult to meet.

Partial liquidation. A *stock redemption* where noncorporate shareholders are permitted sale or exchange treatment. In certain cases, an active business must have existed for at least five years. Only a portion of the outstanding stock in the entity is retired.

Partner. See *general partner* and *limited partner.*

Partnership. For income tax purposes, a partnership includes a syndicate, group, pool, or *joint venture,* as well as ordinary partnerships. In an ordinary partnership, two or more parties combine capital and/or services to carry on a business for profit as co-owners. § 7701(a)(2). See also *limited partnership* and *tiered partnerships.*

Partnership agreement. The governing document of a *partnership.* A partnership agreement should describe the rights and obligations of the partners; the allocation of entity income, deductions, and cash flows; initial and future capital contribution requirements; conditions for terminating the partnership; and other matters.

Passive foreign investment company (PFIC). A non-U.S. corporation that generates a substantial amount of *personal holding company income.* Upon receipt of an excess distribution from the entity or the sale of its shares, its *U.S. shareholders* are taxable on their pro rata shares of the tax that has been deferred with respect to the corporation's taxable income, plus an applicable interest charge.

Passive investment company. A means by which a *multistate corporation* can reduce the overall effective tax rate by isolating investment income in a low- or no-tax state.

Passive investment income (PII). Gross receipts from royalties, certain rents, dividends, interest, annuities, and gains from the sale or exchange of stock and securities. When E & P also exist, if the passive investment income of an *S corporation* exceeds 25 percent of the corporation's gross receipts for three consecutive years, S status is lost.

Passive loss. Any loss from (1) activities in which the taxpayer does not materially participate and (2) rental activities. Net passive losses of most taxpayers other than corporations cannot be used to offset income from nonpassive sources. Rather, they are suspended until the taxpayer either generates net passive income (and a deduction of such losses is allowed) or disposes of the underlying property (at which time the loss deductions are allowed in full). Landlords who actively participate in the rental activities can deduct up to $25,000 of passive losses annually. However, this amount is phased out when the landlord's AGI exceeds $100,000. Another exception applies to real estate professionals. See also *portfolio income.*

Payroll factor. The proportion of a *multistate corporation*'s total payroll that is traceable to a specific state. Used in determining the taxable income that is to be apportioned to that state. See also *apportion.*

Pecuniary bequest. A bequest of money to an *heir* by a *decedent.* See also *bequest.*

Percentage depletion. See *depletion.*

Percentage of completion method. A method of reporting gain or loss on certain long-term contracts. Under this method of accounting, the gross contract price is included in income as the contract is completed. Reg. § 1.451–3. See also *completed contract method.*

Permanent differences. Under *ASC 740 (SFAS 109),* tax-related items that appear in the entity's financial statements or its tax return, but not both. For instance, interest income from a municipal bond is a permanent book-tax difference.

Permanently reinvesting. Under *ASC 740-30 (APB 23)* of *Generally Accepted Accounting Principles,* a special rule that relates to the book tax expense of non-U.S. subsidiaries. If a parent corporation documents that it is permanently reinvesting the non-U.S. earning of a non-U.S. subsidiary, the parent does not record as an expense any U.S. income tax that the parent might pay on such earnings, i.e., the book tax expense is deferred until such earnings are (if ever) repatriated to the United States.

Personal and household effects. Items owned by a *decedent* at the time of death. Examples include clothing, furniture, sporting goods, jewelry, stamp and coin collections, silverware, china, crystal, cooking utensils, books, cars, televisions, radios, and sound equipment.

Personal holding company (PHC). A corporation that satisfies the requirements of § 542. Qualification as a personal holding company means a penalty tax may be imposed on the corporation's undistributed *personal holding company income* for the year.

Personal holding company income. Income as defined by § 543. It includes interest, *dividends,* certain rents and royalties, income from the use of corporate property by certain shareholders, income from certain personal service contracts, and distributions from *estates* and *trusts.* Such income is relevant in determining whether a corporation is a *personal holding company* and is therefore subject to the penalty tax on personal holding companies. See also *adjusted ordinary gross income.*

Personal holding company tax. A penalty tax imposed on certain closely held corporations with excessive investment income. Assessed at the top individual tax rate on *personal holding company income,* reduced by *dividends* paid and other adjustments. § 541.

Personal property. Generally, all property other than real estate. It is sometimes referred to as personalty when real estate is termed realty. Personal property also refers to property not used in a taxpayer's trade or business or held for the production or collection of income. When used in this sense, personal property can include both *realty* (e.g., a personal residence) and *personalty* (e.g., personal effects such as clothing and furniture). See also *bequest.*

Personal service corporation (PSC). An entity whose principal activity is the providing of services by owner-employees. Subject to a flat 35 percent tax rate and limited to a calendar tax year.

Personalty. All property that is not attached to real estate (realty) and is movable. Examples of personalty are machinery, automobiles, clothing, household furnishings, inventory, and personal effects. See also *ad valorem tax* and *realty.*

Portfolio income. Income from interest, *dividends,* rentals, royalties, *capital gains,* or other investment sources. Net *passive losses* cannot be used to offset net portfolio income. See also *passive loss* and *investment income.*

Power of appointment. A legal right granted to someone by a will or other document that gives the holder the power to dispose of property or the income from property. When the holder may appoint the property to his or her own benefit, the power usually is called a general power of appointment. If the holder cannot benefit himself or herself but may only appoint to certain other persons, the power is a special power of appointment. Assume Gary places $500,000 worth of securities in *trust* granting Donna the right to determine each year how the trustee is to divide the income between Ann and Babs. Under these circumstances, Donna has a special power of appointment. If Donna had the further right to appoint the income to herself, she probably possesses a general power of appointment. For the *estate tax* and *gift tax* effects of powers of appointment, see §§ 2041 and 2514.

Precontribution gain or loss. *Partnerships* allow for a variety of *special allocations* of gain or loss among the partners, but gain or loss that is "built in" on an asset contributed to the partnership is assigned specifically to the contributing *partner.* § 704(c)(1)(A).

Preferences (AMT). See *alternative minimum tax (AMT)* and *tax preference items.*

Preferred stock bailout. A process where a shareholder used the issuance and sale, or later redemption, of a preferred stock dividend to obtain long-term capital gains, without any loss of voting control over the corporation. In effect, the shareholder received corporate profits without suffering the consequences of *dividend* income treatment. This procedure led Congress to enact § 306, which, if applicable, converts the prior long-term capital gain on the sale or redemption of the tainted stock to dividend income. See also *bailout.*

Present interest. See *future interest.*

Presumption. An inference in favor of a particular fact. If, for example, the IRS issues a notice of *deficiency* against a taxpayer, under certain conditions a presumption of correctness attaches to the assessment. Thus, the taxpayer has the *burden of proof* to show that he or she does not owe the tax listed in the deficiency notice. See also *rebuttable presumption.*

Previously taxed income (PTI). Under prior law, the undistributed taxable income of an *S corporation* was taxed to the shareholders as of the last day of the corporation's tax year and usually could be withdrawn by the shareholders without tax consequences at some later point in time. The role of PTI has been taken over by the *accumulated adjustments account.*

Principal. Property as opposed to income. The term often is used as a synonym for the *corpus* of a *trust.* If, for example, Gil places real estate in trust with income payable to Ann for life and the remainder to Barb upon Ann's death, the real estate is the principal, or corpus, of the trust.

Private foundation. An *exempt organization* subject to additional statutory restrictions on its activities and on contributions made to it. Excise taxes may be levied on certain prohibited transactions, and the Code places more stringent restrictions on the deductibility of contributions to private foundations. § 509.

Pro rata. Proportionately. Assume, for example, a corporation has 10 shareholders, each of whom owns 10 percent of the stock. A pro rata *dividend* distribution of $1,000 means that each shareholder receives $100.

Pro se. The taxpayer represents himself or herself before the court without the benefit of counsel.

Probate. The legal process by which the estate of a *decedent* is administered. Generally, the probate process involves collecting a decedent's assets, liquidating liabilities, paying necessary taxes, and distributing property to heirs.

Probate costs. The costs incurred in administering a *decedent's estate.* See also *probate estate.*

Probate court. The usual designation for the state or local court that supervises the administration (*probate*) of a *decedent's estate.*

Probate estate. The property of a *decedent* that is subject to administration by the *executor* or *administrator* of an estate. See also *administration.*

Profit and loss sharing ratios. Specified in the *partnership* agreement and used to determine each partner's allocation of ordinary taxable income and separately stated items. Profits and losses can be shared in different ratios. The ratios can be changed by amending the *partnership agreement.* § 704(a).

Profits (loss) interest. A *partner's* percentage allocation of *partnership* operating results, determined by the *profit and loss sharing ratios.*

Property. Assets defined in the broadest legal sense. Property includes the *unrealized receivables* of a *cash basis* taxpayer, but not services rendered. § 351.

Property dividend. A *dividend* consisting of in-kind (noncash) assets of the payor, measured by the fair market value of the property on the date of distribution. Distribution of in-kind property causes the distributing *C* or *S corporation* to recognize any underlying realized gain, but not loss.

Property factor. The proportion of a *multistate corporation*'s total property that is traceable to a specific state. Used in determining the taxable income that is to be apportioned to that state. See also *apportion.*

Property tax. An *ad valorem tax,* usually levied by a city or county government, on the value of real or personal property that the taxpayer owns on a specified date. Most states exclude from the tax base intangible property and assets owned by *exempt organizations,* and some exclude inventory, pollution control or manufacturing equipment, and other items to provide relocation or retention incentives for the taxpayer.

Proportionate distribution. A distribution in which each partner in a *partnership* receives a *pro rata* share of *hot assets* being distributed. For example, a distribution of $10,000 of hot assets equally to two 50 percent partners is a proportionate distribution.

Proposed Regulation. A *Regulation* may first be issued in proposed form to give interested parties the opportunity for comment. When and if a Proposed Regulation is finalized, it becomes a *Regulation.*

PTI. See *previously taxed income.*

Public Law 86–272. A congressional limit on the ability of the state to force a *multistate corporation* to assign income to that state. Under P.L. 86–272, where orders for tangible personal property are both filled and delivered outside the state, the entity must establish more than the mere solicitation of such orders before any income can be *apportioned* to the state.

Public policy limitation. A concept precluding an income tax deduction for certain expenses related to activities deemed to be contrary to the public welfare. In this connection, the Code includes specific disallowance provisions covering such items as illegal bribes, kickbacks, and fines and penalties. §§ 162(c) and (f).

Q

Qualified business unit (QBU). A subsidiary, branch, or other business entity that conducts business using a currency other than the U.S. dollar.

Qualified dividends. Distributions made by domestic (and certain non-U.S.) corporations to noncorporate shareholders that are subject to tax at the same rates as those applicable to net long-term *capital gains.* The *dividend* must be paid out of *earnings and profits,* and the shareholders must meet certain holding period requirements as to the stock. Qualified dividend treatment applies to distributions made after 2002 and before 2013. §§ 1(h)(1) and (11).

Qualified nonrecourse debt. Debt issued on realty by a bank, retirement plan, or governmental agency. Included in the *at-risk amount* by the investor. § 465(b)(6).

Qualified pension or profit sharing plan. An employer-sponsored plan that meets the requirements of § 401. If these requirements are met, none of the employer's contributions to the plan are taxed to the employee until distributed (§ 402). The employer is allowed a deduction in the year the contributions are made (§ 404). See also *contributory qualified pension or profit sharing plan, deferred compensation,* and *noncontributory qualified pension or profit sharing plan.*

Qualified production activities income. The base for computing the *domestic production activities deduction.* It comprises qualified production receipts less allocable cost of goods sold and other deductions. § 199.

Qualified small business corporation. A *C corporation* that has aggregate gross assets not exceeding $50 million and that is conducting an active *trade or business.* § 1202.

Qualified small business stock. The shareholder may exclude from gross income 50 percent of the realized gain on the sale of the stock, if he or she held the stock for more than five years. If the stock was acquired from January 1, 2009, through September 27, 2010, the exclusion rate is 75 percent. If the stock was acquired from September 28, 2010, through December 31, 2011, the exclusion rate is 100 percent. Some of the excluded amount may constitute an *AMT preference* item. § 1202.

Qualified terminable interest property (QTIP). Generally, the *marital deduction* (for gift and *estate tax* purposes) is not available if the interest transferred will terminate upon the death of the transferee spouse and pass to someone else. Thus, if Hannah places property in trust, life estate to Will, and remainder to their children upon Will's death, this is a *terminable interest* that will not provide Hannah (or her estate) with a marital deduction. If, however, the transfer in trust is treated as qualified terminable interest property (the QTIP election is made), the terminable interest restriction is waived and the marital deduction becomes available. In exchange for this deduction, the surviving spouse's *gross estate* must include the value of the QTIP election assets, even though he or she has no control over the ultimate disposition of the asset. Terminable interest property qualifies for this election if the donee (or heir) is the only *beneficiary* of the asset during his or her lifetime and receives income distributions relative to the property at least annually. For gifts, the donor spouse is the one who makes the QTIP election. As to property transferred by death, the *executor* of the estate of the deceased spouse has the right to make the election. §§ 2056(b)(7) and 2523(f).

R

RAR. A Revenue Agent's Report, which reflects any adjustments made by the agent as a result of an *audit* of the taxpayer. The RAR is mailed to the taxpayer along with the *30-day letter,* which outlines the appellate procedures available to the taxpayer.

Rate reconciliation. Under *Generally Accepted Accounting Principles,* a footnote to the financial statements often includes a table that accounts for differences in the statutory income tax rate that applies to the entity (say, 35 percent) and the higher or lower *effective tax rate* that the entity realized for the reporting period. The rate reconciliation includes only *permanent differences* between the book tax expense and the entity's *income tax provision*. The rate reconciliation table often is expressed in dollar and/or percentage terms.

Realistic possibility. A preparer penalty is assessed where a tax return includes a position that has no realistic possibility of being sustained by a court.

Realized gain or loss. The difference between the amount realized upon the sale or other disposition of property and the adjusted basis of such property. § 1001. See also *adjusted basis, amount realized, basis,* and *recognized gain or loss.*

Realty. Real estate. See also *personalty.*

Reasonable cause. Relief from taxpayer and preparer penalties often is allowed where there is reasonable cause for the taxpayer's actions. For instance, reasonable cause for the late filing of a tax return might be a flood that damaged the taxpayer's record-keeping systems and made difficult a timely completion of the return.

Reasonable needs of the business. A means of avoiding the penalty tax on an unreasonable accumulation of earnings. In determining base for this tax (*accumulated taxable income*), § 535 allows a deduction for "such part of earnings and profits for the taxable year as are retained for the reasonable needs of the business." § 537.

Rebuttable presumption. A presumption that can be overturned upon the showing of sufficient proof. See also *presumption.*

Recapitalization. An "E" reorganization, constituting a major change in the character and amount of outstanding equity of a corporation. For instance, common stock exchanged for preferred stock can qualify for tax-free "E" reorganization treatment.

Recapture. To recover the tax benefit of a deduction or a credit previously taken. See also *depreciation recapture.*

Recapture potential. A measure with respect to property that, if disposed of in a taxable transaction, would result in the recapture of depreciation (e.g., § 1245), deferred LIFO gain, or deferred *installment method* gain.

Recognized gain or loss. The portion of realized gain or loss subject to income taxation. See also *realized gain or loss.*

Recourse debt. Debt for which the lender may both foreclose on the property and assess a guarantor for any payments due under the loan, even from personal assets. A lender may also make a claim against the assets of any general partner in a partnership to which debt is issued, without regard to whether that partner has guaranteed the debt.

Redemption. See *stock redemption.*

Redemption (complete termination). Sale or exchange treatment is available relative to this type of redemption. The shareholder must retire all of his or her outstanding shares in the corporation (ignoring family attribution rules) and cannot hold an interest, other than that of a creditor, for the 10 years following the redemption. § 302(b)(3).

Redemption (disproportionate). Sale or exchange treatment is available relative to this type of redemption. After the exchange, the shareholder owns less than 80 percent of his or her pre-redemption interest in the corporation and only a minority interest in the entity. § 302(b)(2).

Redemption (not equivalent to a dividend). Sale or exchange treatment is given to this type of redemption. Although various safe-harbor tests are failed, the nature of the redemption is such that *dividend* treatment is avoided, because it represents a meaningful reduction in the shareholder's interest in the corporation. § 302(b)(1).

Redemption to pay death taxes. Sale or exchange treatment is available relative to this type of redemption, to the extent of the proceeds up to the total amount paid by the estate or heir for death taxes and *administration* expenses. The stock value must exceed 35 percent of the value of the decedent's *adjusted gross estate.* In meeting this test, one can combine shareholdings in corporations where the decedent held at least 20 percent of the outstanding shares.

Regular corporation. See *C corporation.*

Regulations. The U.S. Treasury Department Regulations (abbreviated Reg.) represent the position of the IRS as to how the Internal Revenue Code is to be interpreted. Their purpose is to provide taxpayers and IRS personnel with rules of general and specific application to the various provisions of the tax law. Regulations are published in the *Federal Register* and in all tax services.

Related corporations. See *controlled group.*

Related parties. Various Code Sections define related parties and often include a variety of persons within this (usually detrimental) category. Generally, related parties are accorded different tax treatment from that applicable to other taxpayers who enter into similar transactions. For instance, realized losses that are generated between related parties are not recognized in the year of the loss. However, these deferred losses can be used to offset recognized gains that occur upon the subsequent sale of the asset to a nonrelated party. Other uses of a related-party definition include the conversion of gain upon the sale of a depreciable asset into all ordinary income (§ 1239) and the identification of *constructive ownership* of stock relative to corporate distributions, *redemptions,* liquidations, *reorganizations,* and compensation.

Remainder interest. The property that passes to a *beneficiary* after the expiration of an intervening *income interest.* If, for example, Greg places real estate in trust with income to Ann for life and remainder to Bill upon Ann's death, Bill has a remainder interest. See also *life estate* and *reversionary interest.*

Remand. To send back. An appellate court may remand a case to a lower court, usually for additional fact finding. In other words, the appellate court is not in a position to decide the appeal based on the facts determined by the lower court. Remanding is abbreviated *"rem'g."*

Reorganization. See *corporate reorganization.*

Research activities credit. A tax credit whose purpose is to encourage research and development. It consists of three components: the incremental research activities credit, the energy research credit, and the basic research credit. The incremental research activities credit is equal to 20 percent of the excess qualified research expenditures over the base amount. The basic research credit is equal to 20 percent of the excess of basic research payments over the base amount. § 41. The energy research credit is 20 percent of payments to an energy research consortium. See also *general business credit.*

Residential rental property. Buildings for which at least 80 percent of the gross rents are from dwelling units (e.g., an apartment building). This type of building is distinguished from nonresidential (commercial or industrial) buildings in applying the *recapture* of *depreciation* provisions. The term also is relevant in distinguishing between buildings that are eligible for a 27.5-year life versus a 31.5- or 39-year life for *MACRS* purposes.

Residual method. Used to allocate the new stepped-up *basis* of a subsidiary's assets among its property when a § 338 election is in effect. The purchase price that exceeds the aggregate fair market values of the tangible and identifiable *intangible assets* is allocated to *goodwill* or going-concern value. § 1060.

Return of capital. When a taxpayer reacquires financial resources that he or she previously had invested in an entity or venture, the return of his or her capital investment itself does not increase *gross income* for the recovery year. A return of capital may result from an *annuity* or insurance contract, the sale or exchange of any asset, or a distribution from a *partnership* or corporation.

Revenue Agent's Report. See *RAR*.

Revenue neutrality. A change in the tax system that results in the same amount of revenue. Revenue neutral, however, does not mean that any one taxpayer pays the same amount of tax as before. Thus, as a result of a tax law change, corporations could pay more taxes, but the excess revenue will be offset by lower taxes on individuals.

Revenue Procedure. A matter of procedural importance to both taxpayers and the IRS concerning the administration of the tax laws is issued as a Revenue Procedure (abbreviated Rev.Proc.). A Revenue Procedure is published in an *Internal Revenue Bulletin* (I.R.B.).

Revenue Ruling. A Revenue Ruling (abbreviated Rev.Rul.) is issued by the National Office of the IRS to express an official interpretation of the tax law as applied to specific transactions. It is more limited in application than a Regulation. A Revenue Ruling is published in an *Internal Revenue Bulletin* (I.R.B.).

Reversed (Rev'd.). An indication that a decision of one court has been reversed by a higher court in the same case.

Reversing (Rev'g.). An indication that the decision of a higher court is reversing the result reached by a lower court in the same case.

Reversionary interest. The *trust* property that reverts to the *grantor* after the expiration of an intervening *income interest*. Assume Gail places real estate in trust with income to Art for 11 years, and upon the expiration of this term, the property returns to Gail. Under these circumstances, she holds a reversionary interest in the property. A reversionary interest is the same as a *remainder interest*, except that, in the latter case, the property passes to someone other than the original owner (e.g., the grantor of a trust) upon the expiration of the intervening interest. See also *grantor trust*.

Revocable transfer. A transfer of property where the transferor retains the right to recover the property. The creation of a revocable *trust* is an example of a revocable transfer. § 2038. See also *incomplete transfer*.

Rev.Proc. Abbreviation for an IRS *Revenue Procedure*.

Rev.Rul. Abbreviation for an IRS *Revenue Ruling*.

Right of survivorship. See *joint tenants*.

S

S corporation. The designation for a small business corporation. See also *Subchapter S*.

Sales factor. The proportion of a *multistate corporation*'s total sales that is traceable to a specific state. Used in determining the *taxable income* that is to be apportioned to that state. See also *apportion*.

Sales tax. A state- or local-level tax on the retail sale of specified property. Generally, the purchaser pays the tax, but the seller collects it, as an agent for the government. Various taxing jurisdictions allow exemptions for purchases of specific items, including certain food, services, and manufacturing equipment. If the purchaser and seller are in different states, a *use tax* usually applies.

Schedule K-1. A tax information form prepared for each *partner* in a *partnership*, each shareholder of an *S corporation*, and some *beneficiaries* of certain *trusts*. The Schedule K-1 reports the owner's share of the entity's ordinary income or loss from operations, as well as the owner's share of *separately stated items*.

Schedule M-1. On the Form 1120, a reconciliation of book net income with Federal *taxable income*. Accounts for *temporary* and *permanent differences* in the two computations, such as *depreciation* differences, exempt income, and nondeductible items. On Forms 1120S and 1065, the Schedule M-1 reconciles book income with the owners' aggregate ordinary taxable income.

Schedule M-3. An *expanded* reconciliation of book net income with Federal *taxable income* (see *Schedule M-1*). Required of *C* and *S corporations* and *partnerships*/LLCs, with total assets of $10 million or more.

Schedule PH. A tax form required to be filed by *personal holding companies*. The form is filed in addition to *Form 1120* (U.S. Corporation Income Tax Return).

Section 306 stock. Preferred stock issued as a nontaxable stock dividend that, if sold or redeemed, would result in ordinary income recognition. § 306(c). See also *preferred stock bailout*.

Section 306 taint. The ordinary income that would result upon the sale or other taxable disposition of § 306 stock.

Section 338 election. When a corporation acquires at least 80 percent of a subsidiary in a 12-month period, it can elect to treat the acquisition of such stock as an asset purchase. The acquiring corporation's *basis* in the subsidiary's assets then is the cost of the stock. The subsidiary is deemed to have sold its assets for an amount equal to the grossed-up basis in its stock.

Section 382 limitation. When one corporation acquires another, the acquiror's ability to use the loss and credit carryovers of the target may be limited, in an anti-abuse provision specified in the Code. Generally, for instance, the maximum deduction available to the acquiror is the takeover-date value of the target times the tax-exempt interest rate on that date.

Section 754 election. An election that may be made by a *partnership* to adjust the *basis* of partnership assets to reflect a purchasing *partner's* outside basis in interest or to reflect a gain, loss, or basis adjustment of a partner receiving a distribution from a partnership. The intent of the election is to maintain the equivalence between *outside* and *inside basis*. Once the election is made, the partnership must make basis adjustments for all future transactions, unless the IRS consents to revoke the election.

Section 1231 assets. Depreciable assets and real estate used in a *trade or business* and held for the appropriate *holding period*.

Under certain circumstances, the classification also includes timber, coal, domestic iron ore, livestock (held for draft, breeding, dairy, or sporting purposes), and unharvested crops. § 1231(b). See also *Section 1231 gains and losses.*

Section 1231 gains and losses. If the combined gains and losses from the taxable dispositions of *§ 1231 assets* plus the net gain from business *involuntary conversions* (of both § 1231 assets and long-term *capital assets*) is a gain, such gains and losses are treated as long-term *capital gains* and losses. In arriving at § 1231 gains, however, the *depreciation recapture* provisions (e.g., § 1245) are applied first, to produce ordinary income. If the net result of the combination is a loss, the gains and losses from § 1231 assets are treated as ordinary gains and losses. § 1231(a).

Section 1244 stock. Stock issued under § 1244 by qualifying *small business corporations.* If § 1244 stock becomes worthless, the shareholders may claim an ordinary loss rather than the usual capital loss, within statutory limitations.

Section 1245 recapture. Upon a taxable disposition of § 1245 property, all *depreciation* claimed on such property is recaptured as ordinary income (but not to exceed recognized gain from the disposition).

Section 1250 recapture. Upon a taxable disposition of § 1250 property, accelerated *depreciation* or *cost recovery* claimed on the property may be recaptured as ordinary income.

Securities. Generally, stock, debt, and other financial assets. To the extent securities other than the stock of the transferee corporation are received in a § 351 exchange, the new shareholder realizes a gain.

Separate property. In a *community property* jurisdiction, property that belongs entirely to one of the spouses is separate property. Generally, this includes property acquired before marriage or acquired after marriage by *gift* or inheritance.

Separate return limitation year (SRLY). A series of rules limits the amount of an acquired corporation's *net operating loss* carryforwards that can be used by the acquiror. Generally, a *consolidated return* can include the acquiree's NOL carryforward only to the extent of the lesser of the subsidiary's (1) current-year or (2) cumulative positive contribution to consolidated taxable income.

Separately stated item. Any item of a *partnership* or *S corporation* that might be taxed differently to any two owners of the entity. These amounts are not included in ordinary income of the entity, but instead are reported separately to the owners; tax consequences are determined at the owner level.

Sham. A transaction without substance that is disregarded for tax purposes.

Short-term capital gain or loss. Results from the sale or other taxable exchange of a *capital asset* that had been held by the seller for one year or less or from other transactions involving statutorily designated assets, including *nonbusiness bad debts.*

Simple trust. Simple trusts are those that are not complex trusts. Such *trusts* may not have a charitable beneficiary, accumulate income, or distribute corpus. See also *complex trust.*

Small business corporation. A corporation that satisfies the definition of § 1361(b), § 1244(c), or both. Satisfaction of § 1361(b) permits an S election, and satisfaction of § 1244(c) enables the shareholders of the corporation to claim an ordinary loss on the worthlessness of stock.

Small Cases Division of the U.S. Tax Court. Jurisdiction is limited to claims of $50,000 or less. There is no appeal from this court.

Special allocation. Any amount for which an agreement exists among the partners of a *partnership* outlining the method used for assigning the item among the *partners.*

Special power of appointment. See *power of appointment.*

Special use value. Permits the *executor* of an estate to value, for *estate tax* purposes, real estate used in a farming activity or in connection with a closely held business at its *current use value* rather than at its most suitable or *optimal use value.* Under this option, a farm is valued for farming purposes even though, for example, the property might have a higher potential value as a shopping center. For the executor of an estate to elect special use valuation, the conditions of § 2032A must be satisfied. See also *most suitable use value.*

Spin-off. A type of *reorganization* where, for example, Ace Corporation transfers some assets to Bow Corporation in exchange for enough Bow stock to represent control. Ace then distributes the Bow stock to its shareholders.

Split-off. A type of *reorganization* where, for example, Arc Corporation transfers some assets to Bond Corporation in exchange for enough Bond stock to represent control. Arc then distributes the Bond stock to its shareholders in exchange for some of their Arc stock.

Split-up. A type of *reorganization* where, for example, Ally Corporation transfers some assets to Bar Corporation and the remainder to Zip Corporation. In return, Ally receives enough Bar and Zip stock to represent control of each corporation. Ally then distributes the Bar and Zip stock to its shareholders in return for all of their Ally stock. The result of the split-up is that Ally is liquidated, and its shareholders now have control of Bar and Zip.

Sprinkling trust. When a *trustee* has the discretion to either distribute or accumulate the *entity accounting income* of the *trust* and to distribute it among the trust's income *beneficiaries* in varying magnitudes, a sprinkling trust exists. The trustee can "sprinkle" the income of the trust.

Statute of limitations. Provisions of the law that specify the maximum period of time in which action may be taken on a past event. Code §§ 6501–6504 contain the limitation periods applicable to the IRS for additional assessments, and §§ 6511–6515 relate to refund claims by taxpayers.

Statutory depletion. See *depletion.*

Statutory notice of deficiency. Commonly referred to as the 90-day letter, this notice is sent to a taxpayer upon request, upon the expiration of the *30-day letter,* or upon exhaustion by the taxpayer of his or her administrative remedies before the IRS. The notice gives the taxpayer 90 days in which to file a petition with the U.S. *Tax Court.* If such a petition is not filed, the IRS will demand payment of the assessed *deficiency.* §§ 6211–6216.

Step transaction. Disregarding one or more transactions to arrive at the final result. Assume, for example, that the shareholders of Clue Corporation liquidate the corporation and receive cash and operating assets. Immediately after the liquidation, the shareholders transfer the operating assets to newly formed Blue Corporation. Under these circumstances, the IRS may contend that the liquidation of Clue should be disregarded (thereby depriving the shareholders of capital gain treatment). What may really have happened is a *reorganization* of Clue with a distribution of boot (ordinary income) to Clue's shareholders. If so, there will be a carryover of *basis* in the assets transferred from Clue to Blue.

Step-down in basis. A reduction in the tax *basis* of property. See also *step-up in basis.*

Step-up in basis. An increase in the income tax *basis* of property. A step-up in basis occurs when a decedent dies owning appreciated property. Since the *estate* or *heir* acquires a basis in the property equal to the property's *fair market value* on the date of death (or *alternate valuation date* if available and elected), any appreciation is not subject to the income tax. Thus, a step-up in basis is the result, with no income tax consequences.

Stock attribution. See *attribution.*

Stock dividend. A *dividend* consisting of stock of the payor. Not taxable if a *pro rata* distribution of stock or stock rights on common stock. However, some stock dividends are taxable. § 305.

Stock redemption. A corporation buys back its own stock from a specified shareholder. Typically, the corporation recognizes any realized gain on the noncash assets that it uses to effect a redemption, and the shareholder obtains a *capital gain* or loss upon receipt of the purchase price.

Stock rights. Assets that convey to the holder the power to purchase corporate stock at a specified price, often for a limited period of time. Stock rights received may be taxed as a distribution of *earnings and profits.* After the right is exercised, the *basis* of the acquired share includes the investor's purchase price or *gross income,* if any, to obtain the right. Disposition of the right also can be a taxable event.

Subchapter S. Sections 1361–1379 of the Internal Revenue Code. An elective provision permitting certain *small business corporations* (§ 1361) and their shareholders (§ 1362) to elect to be treated for income tax purposes in accordance with the operating rules of §§ 1363–1379. *S corporations* usually avoid the corporate income tax, and corporate losses can be claimed by the shareholders.

Subpart F. The subpart of the Code that identifies the current tax treatment of income earned by a *controlled foreign corporation.* Certain types of income are included in U.S. *gross income* by U.S. shareholders of such an entity as the income is generated, not when it is repatriated.

Substance vs. form concept. A standard used when one must ascertain the true reality of what has occurred. Suppose, for example, a father sells stock to his daughter for $1,000. If the stock is really worth $50,000 at the time of the transfer, the substance of the transaction is probably a *gift* to her of $49,000.

Substantial authority. Taxpayer and tax preparer understatement penalties are waived where substantial authority existed for the disputed position taken on the return.

Substantial economic effect. *Partnerships* are allowed to *allocate* items of income, expense, gain, loss, and credit in any manner that is authorized in the *partnership agreement,* provided that the allocation has an economic effect aside from the corresponding tax results. The necessary substantial economic effect is present, for instance, if the post-contribution appreciation in the value of an asset that was contributed to the partnership by a *partner* was allocated to that partner for *cost recovery* purposes.

Substituted basis. When a taxpayer exchanges one asset for another, many provisions in the tax law allow an assignment of *basis* in the received asset to be that of the traded asset(s) in the hands of its former owner. Thus, no step-up or -down of basis occurs as a result of the exchange. For instance, when an investor contributes an asset to a corporation or *partnership,* the *partner* generally takes a substituted basis in the partnership interest (i.e., the interest has a basis equal to the aggregated bases of the assets contributed by that partner). § 723.

Survivorship. See *joint tenants.*

Syndication costs. Incurred in promoting and marketing *partnership* interests for sale to investors. Examples include legal and accounting fees, printing costs for prospectus and placement documents, and state registration fees. These items are capitalized by the partnership as incurred, with no *amortization* thereof allowed.

T

Tangible property. All property that has form or substance and is not intangible. See also *intangible asset.*

Tax avoidance. A synonym for *tax planning.* Tax minimization through legal means. Tax planning techniques include income deferral, deduction acceleration, and shifting of income to low-tax-rate jurisdictions and/or taxpayers. For example, a *cash basis* taxpayer increases his *charitable contribution* deduction by prepaying next year's church pledge. See also *tax evasion.*

Tax benefit rule. Limits the recognition of income from the recovery of an expense or loss properly deducted in a prior tax year to the amount of the deduction that generated a tax saving. Assume that last year Tom had medical expenses of $3,000 and *adjusted gross income* of $30,000. Because of the 7.5 percent limitation, he could deduct only $750 of these expenses [$3,000 – (7.5% × $30,000)]. If, this year, Tom is reimbursed by his insurance company for the $3,000 of expenses, the tax benefit rule limits the amount of income from the reimbursement to $750 (the amount previously deducted with a tax saving).

Tax Court. The U.S. Tax Court is one of four *trial courts* of original jurisdiction that decide litigation involving Federal income, *estate,* or *gift taxes.* It is the only trial court where the taxpayer must not first pay the *deficiency* assessed by the IRS. The Tax Court does not have jurisdiction over a case unless a *statutory notice of deficiency* (90-day letter) has been issued by the IRS and the taxpayer files the petition for hearing within the time prescribed.

Tax evasion. The reduction of taxes by the use of subterfuge or fraud or other nonlegal means. For example, a *cash basis* taxpayer tries to increase her *charitable contribution* deduction by prepaying next year's church pledge with a pre-dated check issued in the following year. See also *tax avoidance.*

Tax haven. A country in which either locally sourced income or residents of the country are subject to a low rate of taxation.

Tax on unearned income of a child under age 19/24. *Portfolio income,* such as interest and *dividends,* that is recognized by such a child is taxed *to him or her* at the rates that would have applied had the income been incurred by the child's parents, generally to the extent that the income exceeds $1,900. The additional tax is assessed regardless of the source of the income or the income's underlying property. If the child's parents are divorced, the custodial parent's rates are used. The parents' rates reflect any applicable *alternative minimum tax* and the phaseouts of lower tax brackets and other deductions. A special rule applies if the child is a full-time student. § 1(g).

Tax planning. See *tax avoidance.*

Tax preference items. Various items that may result in the imposition of the *alternative minimum tax.* §§ 55–58.

Tax preparer. One who prepares tax returns for compensation. A tax preparer may be qualified to practice before the IRS and represent taxpayers before the agency in tax *audit* actions. The conduct of a tax preparer is regulated under *Circular 230.* Tax preparers also are subject to penalties for inappropriate conduct when working in the tax profession.

Tax treaty. An agreement between the U.S. State Department and another country, designed to alleviate double taxation of income and asset transfers and to share administrative information useful to tax agencies in both countries. The United States has income tax treaties with over 40 countries and transfer tax treaties with about 20.

Tax year. See *accounting period.*

Taxable estate. The *gross estate* of a *decedent* reduced by the deductions allowed by §§ 2053–2057 (e.g., *administration* expenses and marital and charitable deductions). The taxable estate is subject to the *unified transfer tax* at death. See also *adjusted taxable estate* and *gross estate.* § 2051.

Taxable gift. Amount of a *gift* that is subject to the *unified transfer tax.* Thus, a *taxable gift* has been adjusted by the *annual exclusion* and other appropriate deductions (e.g., marital and charitable). § 2503.

Taxable income. The tax base with respect to the prevailing Federal income tax. Taxable income is defined by the *Internal Revenue Code,* Treasury *Regulations,* and pertinent court cases. Currently, taxable income includes *gross income* from all sources except those specifically excluded by the statute. In addition, taxable income is reduced for certain allowable *deductions.* Deductions for business taxpayers must be related to a *trade or business.* Individuals can also deduct certain personal expenses in determining their taxable incomes.

Tax-free exchange. Transfers of property specifically exempted from income tax consequences by the tax law. Examples are a transfer of property to a controlled corporation under § 351(a) and a *like-kind exchange* under § 1031(a).

T.C. An abbreviation for the U.S. *Tax Court* used in citing a Regular Decision of the U.S. Tax Court.

T.C.Memo. An abbreviation used to refer to a Memorandum Decision of the U.S. *Tax Court.*

Technical advice memorandum. An interpretation of the tax law with respect to a disputed item, issued by the IRS, in response to a request from an agent, appellate conferee, or IRS executive. Often used to reconcile perceived differences in the application of the law among taxpayers or to identify an IRS position where no pertinent *Regulations* or rulings exist.

Technical termination of partnership. The entity is treated for tax purposes as though it has terminated, even though it continues in its activities. When there has been a sale or exchange of more than 50 percent of the capital interests of the *partnership* within 12 months, the partnership is deemed to have terminated when the 50 percent threshold is crossed. A new partnership immediately is formed through asset contributions by the partners. These activities can affect the entity's *tax year* and its bases in the assets it holds.

Telescoping. To look through one or more transactions to arrive at the final result. It is also referred to as the *step transaction* approach or the *substance vs. form concept.*

Temporary differences. Under *ASC 740 (SFAS 109),* tax-related items that appear in the entity's financial statements and its tax return, but in different time periods. For instance, doubtful accounts receivable often create a temporary book-tax difference, as a bad debt reserve is used to compute an expense for financial reporting purposes, but a bad debt often is deductible only under the specific write-off rule for tax purposes. The differing amounts observed for the current period create a temporary difference.

Temporary Regulation. The Treasury often issues Temporary Regulations to offer immediate guidance as to elections and other compliance matters after a change in the statute or a court ruling has been issued. Temporary Regulations carry the same precedential value as a final *Regulation,* and they should be followed as such for three years after issuance, after which they expire. Often a Temporary Regulation also is issued as a *Proposed Regulation.*

Tenants by the entirety. Essentially, a joint tenancy between husband and wife. See also *joint tenants* and *tenants in common.*

Tenants in common. A form of ownership where each tenant (owner) holds an undivided interest in property. Unlike a *joint tenancy* or a *tenancy by the entirety,* the interest of a tenant in common does not terminate upon that individual's death (there is no right of survivorship). Assume Brad and Connie acquire real estate as equal tenants in common, each having furnished one-half of the purchase price. Upon Brad's death, his one-half interest in the property passes to his *estate* or heirs, not to Connie.

Tentative minimum tax (TMT). In calculating a taxpayer's *alternative minimum tax (AMT),* the TMT is a subtotal representing the gross amount of tax liability. AMT equals the difference between the TMT and the regular tax liability. If this difference is positive, an AMT is due; if it is zero or negative, the AMT liability is zero. Only a positive AMT creates a *minimum tax credit.*

Term certain. A fixed period of years used to determine the length of an *income interest* (i.e., prior to the termination of a *trust* or *estate*).

Terminable interest. An interest in property that terminates upon the death of the holder or upon the occurrence of some other specified event. The transfer of a terminable interest by one spouse to the other may not qualify for the *marital deduction.* §§ 2056(b) and 2523(b).

Testamentary disposition. The passing of property to another upon the death of the owner.

Thin capitalization. When debt owed by a corporation to the shareholders becomes too large in relation to the corporation's capital structure (i.e., stock and shareholder equity), the IRS may contend that the corporation is thinly capitalized. In effect, some or all of the debt is reclassified as equity. The immediate result is to disallow any interest deduction to the corporation on the reclassified debt. To the extent of the corporation's *earnings and profits,* interest payments and loan repayments are treated as *dividends* to the shareholders.

Thirty-day letter. A letter that accompanies an *RAR* (Revenue Agent's Report) issued as a result of an IRS *audit* of a taxpayer (or the rejection of a taxpayer's claim for refund). The letter outlines the taxpayer's appeal procedure before the IRS. If the taxpayer does not request any such procedure within the 30-day period, the IRS issues a *statutory notice of deficiency.*

Three-factor apportionment formula. A means by which the total taxable income of a *multistate corporation* is assigned to a specific state. Usually, the payroll, property, and sales factors are treated equally, and the average of these factors is used in the apportionment procedure. In some states, however, the *sales factor* may receive a double weight, or it may be the only factor considered. These latter formulas place a greater tax burden on the income of out-of-state corporations. See also *apportion, payroll factor, property factor,* and *UDITPA.*

Throwback rule. If there is no income tax in the state to which a sale otherwise would be *apportioned,* the sale essentially is exempt from state income tax, even though the seller is *domiciled* in a state that levies an income tax. Nonetheless, if the seller's state has adopted a throwback rule, the sale is attributed to the *seller's* state, and the transaction is subjected to a state-level tax.

Tiered partnerships. An ownership arrangement wherein one *partnership* (the parent or first tier) is a partner in one or more partnerships (the subsidiary/subsidiaries or second tier). Frequently, the first tier is a holding partnership, and the second tier is an operating partnership.

Trade or business. Any business or professional activity conducted by a taxpayer. The mere ownership of rental or other investment assets does not constitute a trade or business. Generally, a trade or business generates relatively little *portfolio income.*

Transfer pricing. The process of setting internal prices for transfers of goods and services among related taxpayers. For instance, what price should be used when Subsidiary purchases management services from Parent? Section 482 allows the IRS to adjust transfer prices when it can show that the taxpayers were attempting to avoid tax by, say, shifting losses, deductions, or credits from low-tax to high-tax entities or jurisdictions.

Transfer tax. A tax imposed upon the transfer of property. See also *unified transfer tax.*

Transferee liability. Under certain conditions, if the IRS is unable to collect taxes owed by a transferor of property, it may pursue its claim against the transferee of the property. The transferee's liability for taxes is limited to the extent of the value of the assets transferred. For example, the IRS can force a *donee* to pay the *gift tax* when such tax cannot be paid by the *donor* making the transfer. §§ 6901–6905.

Treasury Regulations. See *Regulations.*

Treaty shopping. An international investor attempts to use the favorable aspects of a *tax treaty* to his or her advantage, often elevating the form of the transaction over its substance (e.g., by establishing only a nominal presence in the country offering the favorable treaty terms).

Trial court. The court of original jurisdiction; the first court to consider litigation. In Federal tax controversies, trial courts include U.S. *District Courts,* the U.S. *Tax Court,* the U.S. *Court of Federal Claims,* and the *Small Cases Division of the U.S. Tax Court.* See also *appellate court.*

Trust. A legal entity created by a *grantor* for the benefit of designated *beneficiaries* under the laws of the state and the valid trust instrument. The trustee holds a *fiduciary* responsibility to manage the trust's *corpus* assets and income for the economic benefit of all of the beneficiaries.

Trustee. An individual or corporation that assumes the *fiduciary* responsibilities under a *trust* agreement.

U

UDITPA. The Uniform Division of Income for Tax Purposes Act has been adopted in some form by many of the states. The Act develops criteria by which the total taxable income of a *multistate corporation* can be assigned to specific states. See also *allocate, apportion, Multistate Tax Commission (MTC),* and *nexus.*

Undistributed personal holding company income. The tax base for the *personal holding company tax.* § 545.

Unearned income. Income received but not yet earned. Normally, such income is taxed when received, even for *accrual basis* taxpayers.

Unified transfer tax. Rates applicable to transfers by *gift* and death made after 1976. § 2001(c).

Unified transfer tax credit. A credit allowed against any *unified transfer tax.* §§ 2010 and 2505.

Uniform Gift to Minors Act. A means of transferring property (usually stocks and bonds) to a minor. The designated custodian of the property can act on behalf of the minor without requiring a *guardianship.* Generally, the custodian possesses the right to change investments (e.g., sell one type of stock and buy another), apply the income from the custodial property to the minor's support, and even terminate the custodianship. During the period of the custodianship, the income from the property is taxed to the minor, although perhaps subject to *kiddie tax* rates. The custodianship terminates when the minor reaches *legal age.*

Unitary state. A state that has adopted the *unitary theory* in its apportionment of the total *taxable income* of a *multistate corporation* to the state.

Unitary theory. Sales, property, and payroll of related corporations are combined for *nexus* and apportionment purposes, and the worldwide income of the unitary entity is *apportioned* to the state. Subsidiaries and other affiliated corporations found to be part of the corporation's unitary business (because they are subject to overlapping ownership, operation, or management) are included in the apportionment procedure. This approach can be limited if a *water's edge election* is in effect.

Unrealized receivables. Amounts earned by a *cash basis* taxpayer but not yet received. Because of the method of accounting used by the taxpayer, these amounts have a zero income tax *basis.* When unrealized receivables are distributed to a *partner,* they generally convert a transaction from nontaxable to taxable or an otherwise *capital gain* to ordinary income.

Unreasonable compensation. A deduction is allowed for "reasonable" salaries or other compensation for personal services actually rendered. To the extent compensation is "excessive" ("unreasonable"), no deduction is allowed. Unreasonable compensation usually is found in *closely held corporations,* where the motivation is to pay out profits in some form that is deductible to the corporation.

Unreasonable position. A *tax preparer* penalty is assessed regarding the understatement of a client's tax liability due to a tax return position that is found to be too aggressive. The penalty is avoided if there is *substantial authority* for the position, or if the position is disclosed adequately on the tax return. The penalty equals the greater of $1,000 or one-half of the tax preparer's fee that is traceable to the aggressive position.

Unrelated business income. Income recognized by an *exempt organization* that is generated from activities not related to the exempt purpose of the entity. For instance, the pharmacy located in a hospital may generate unrelated business income. § 511.

Unrelated business income tax. Levied on the *unrelated business income* of an *exempt organization.*

U.S.-owned foreign corporation. A foreign corporation in which 50 percent or more of the total combined voting power or total value of the stock of the corporation is held directly or indirectly by U.S. persons. A U.S. corporation is treated as a U.S.-owned foreign corporation if the *dividend* or interest income it pays is classified as foreign source under § 861.

U.S. real property interest. Any direct interest in real property situated in the United States and any interest in a *domestic corporation* (other than solely as a creditor) unless the taxpayer can establish that a domestic corporation was not a U.S. real property holding corporation during the five-year period ending on the date of disposition of such interest (the base period). See *FIRPTA.*

U.S. shareholder. For purposes of classification of an entity as a *controlled foreign corporation,* a U.S. person who owns, or is considered to own, 10 percent or more of the total combined voting power of all classes of voting stock of a foreign corporation. Stock owned directly, indirectly, and constructively is counted for this purpose.

U.S.-source income. Generally, income taxed by the United States, regardless of the citizenship or residence of its creator. Examples include income from sales of U.S. real estate and *dividends* from U.S. corporations.

U.S. Tax Court. See *Tax Court.*

U.S. trade or business. A set of activities that is carried on in a regular, continuous, and substantial manner. A non-U.S. taxpayer is subject to U.S. tax on the *taxable income* that is *effectively connected* with a U.S. trade or business.

Use tax. A *sales tax* that is collectible by the seller where the purchaser is domiciled in a different state.

USSC. An abbreviation for the U.S. *Supreme Court,* used in citing court opinions.

USTC. Published by Commerce Clearing House (*CCH*), *U.S. Tax Cases* contain all of the Federal tax decisions issued by the U.S. *District Courts,* U.S. *Court of Federal Claims,* U.S. *Courts of Appeals,* and the U.S. *Supreme Court.*

V

Valuation allowance. Under *ASC 740 (SFAS 109),* a tax-related item is reported for book purposes only when it is more likely than not that the item actually will be realized. When the "more likely than not" test is failed, a contra-asset account is created to offset some or all of the related *deferred tax asset.* For instance, if the entity projects that it will not be able to use all of its *net operating loss* carryforward due to a lack of future taxable income, a valuation allowance is created to reduce the net *deferred tax asset* that corresponds to the carryforward. If income projections later change and it appears that the carryforward will be used, the valuation allowance is reversed or "released." Creation of a valuation allowance usually increases the *current tax expense* and thereby reduces current book income, and its release often increases book income in the later reporting period.

Value. See *fair market value.*

Vested. Absolute and complete. If, for example, a person holds a vested interest in property, such interest cannot be taken away or otherwise defeated.

Voluntary revocation. The owners of a majority of shares in an *S corporation* elect to terminate the S status of the entity, as of a specified date. The day on which the revocation is effective is the first day of the corporation's C tax year.

Voting trust. A *trust* that holds the voting rights to stock in a corporation. It is a useful device when a majority of the shareholders in a corporation cannot agree on corporate policy.

W

W–2 wages. The *domestic production activities deduction (DPAD)* cannot exceed 50 percent of the manufacturer's W–2 wages paid for the year. Several methods can be used to calculate the W–2 wages. The employee's work must be involved in the production process. § 199(b)(2).

Wash sale. A loss from the sale of stock or securities that is disallowed because the taxpayer has, within 30 days before or after the sale, acquired stock or securities substantially identical to those sold. § 1091.

Water's edge election. A limitation on the worldwide scope of the *unitary theory.* If a corporate water's edge election is in effect, the state can consider in the apportionment procedure only the activities that occur within the boundaries of the United States.

WESTLAW. An online database system, produced by the West Group, through which a tax researcher can obtain access to the *Internal Revenue Code, Regulations,* administrative rulings, and court case opinions.

Wherewithal to pay. A concept of tax equity that delays the recognition of gain on a transaction until the taxpayer has received means by which to pay the tax. The *installment method,* whereunder gain is taxed proportionately as installment proceeds are received, embodies the wherewithal to pay concept. See also *involuntary conversion* and *like-kind exchange.*

Whistleblower program. An IRS initiative that offers special rewards to informants who provide evidence regarding tax evasion activities of businesses or high-income individuals. More than $2 million of tax, interest, and penalty must be at stake. The reward can reach 30 percent of the tax recovery that is attributable to the whistleblower's information.

Writ of Certiorari. See *certiorari.*

Appendix D-1

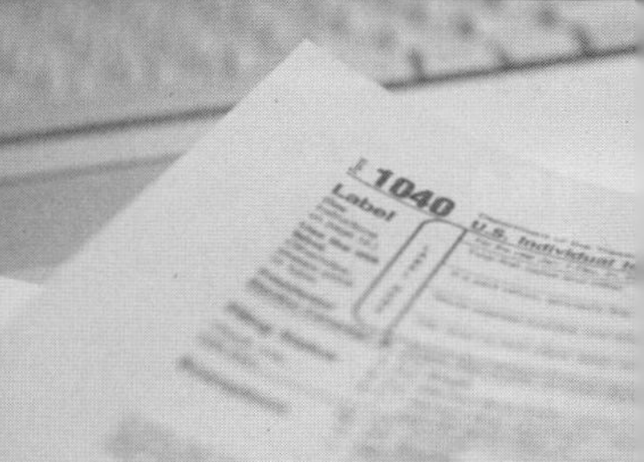

TABLE OF CODE SECTIONS CITED

[See Title 26 U.S.C.A.]

Appendix D-2

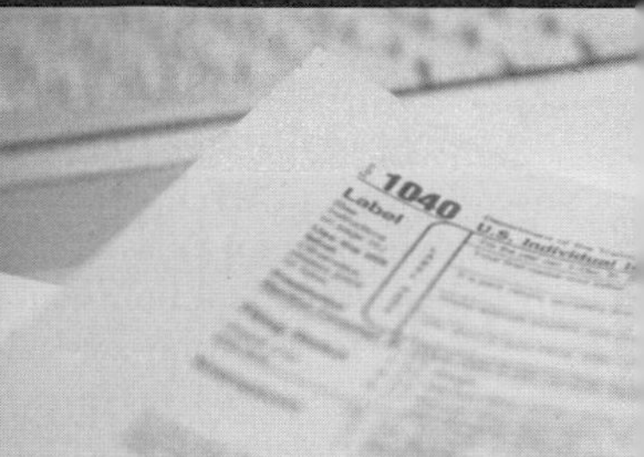

TABLE OF REGULATIONS CITED

Temporary Treasury Regulations

Treasury Regulations

Treasury Regulations

Reg. Sec.	This Work Page
1.355–2	7-25
1.355–2(b)	7-25
1.355–2(b)(4)	7-18
1.362–2(b)	4-18
1.367(a)–3(c)	9-18
1.368–1(b)	7-3, 7-26
1.368–1(c)	7-25, 7-26
1.368–1(d)	7-26
1.368–1(e)(3)	7-26
1.368–1(e)(8)	7-23
1.368–2(c)	7-13, 7-28
1.368–2(d)	7-15
1.368–2(d)(3)	7-17
1.381(c)(2)–1(a)(5)	7-34
1.383–1(d)	7-34
1.453–9(c)	1-50
1.453–9(c)(2)	4-4
1.482–1(a)(3)	9-11
1.509(a)–3(c)	15-13
1.511–2(a)(2)	15-17
1.512(b)–1	15-22
1.513–1(b)	15-16, 15-19
1.513–1(c)	15-22
1.513–1(d)	15-19
1.513–1(d)(4)(ii)	15-19
1.513–1(d)(4)(iii)	15-20
1.513–2(a)	15-18
1.514(a)–1(a)(2)	15-27
1.514(a)–1(a)(3)	15-27
1.514(b)–1(b)(1)(ii)	15-25
1.537–1	3-29
1.537–2(c)	3-29
1.641(a)–0(c)	1-26
1.641(b)–3(a)	20-6
1.642(c)–1(b)	20-16
1.642(c)–3(b)	20-17
1.642(c)–3(c)	20-17
1.642(g)–1	20-16
1.642(g)–2	20-15
1.642(h)–1	20-25
1.642(h)–2	20-25
1.651(a)–1	20-5
1.652(b)–2(b)	20-24
1.662(a)–2	20-21
1.662(a)–3	20-21
1.662(b)–1	20-23
1.663(b)–2	20-25
1.663(c)–1(a)	20-23
1.672(a)–1	20-26
1.675–1(b)	20-27
1.701–2	10-9, 11-37
1.704–1	10-60
1.704–1(b)	10-25
1.704–2	10-60
1.704–3	10-26, 10-32
1.708–1(b)	11-33
1.731 1(c)(3)	10-11

Treasury Regulations

Reg. Sec.	This Work Page
1.736–1(a)(4)	11-20
1.736–1(b)(5)	11-21
1.752–1(a)(4)(ii)	10-29
1.752–1(e)	12-22
1.861–4(b)	9-8
1.861–7(c)	9-8
1.861–8	9-9
1.861–8(e)(7)	9-8
1.861–18	9-9
1.863–3	9-8
1.865–(2)(a)(1)	9-8
1.865–(2)(a)(2)	9-8
1.901–2	9-32
1.903–1	9-32
1.954–3(a)	9-55
1.989(a)–1(b)	9-15
1.1002–1(c)	7-3
1.1032–1(a)	4-15, 7-19
1.1032–1(c)	7-19
1.1239–1(a)	8-30
1.1239–(b)(3)	8-30
1.1244(c)–2(b)(2)	4-23
1.1361–1(l)(2)	12-5
1.1361–1(l)(4)	12-6
1.1362–6(b)(3)(iii)	12-8
1.1367–1(f)	12-21
1.1367–2	12-22
1.1367–2(e)	12-21, 12-23
1.1372–2(b)(1)	12-8
1.1373–1(a)(2)	12-29
1.1377–1(a)(2)(ii)	12-13
1.1501–1	8-4
1.1502–0 through 1.1502–100	8-4
1.1502–1(f)(2)(i)	8-26
1.1502–5(a)(1)	8-14
1.1502–6(a)	8-14
1.1502–6(c)	8-14
1.1502–13	8-30
1.1502–13(a)(1)(i)	8-20
1.1502–13(b)(1)	8-20
1.1502–13(b)(2)	8-20
1.1502–13(c)(7)	8-21
1.1502–13(d)(1)(i)	8-30
1.1502–13(f)(2)	8-21
1.1502–17(a)	8-17
1.1502–19	8-18
1.1502–19(a)	8-21
1.1502–19(a)(1)	8-18
1.1502–19(a)(2)	8-18
1.1502–19(b)(3)	8-18
1.1502–21(c)	8-26
1.1502–21(f)	8-22
1.1502–21(g)	8-27
1.1502–22(g)	8-27
1.1502–24(c)	8-22
1.1502–26(a)(1)(i)	8-28
1.1502–32(a)	8-17

Treasury Regulations

Treasury Regulations

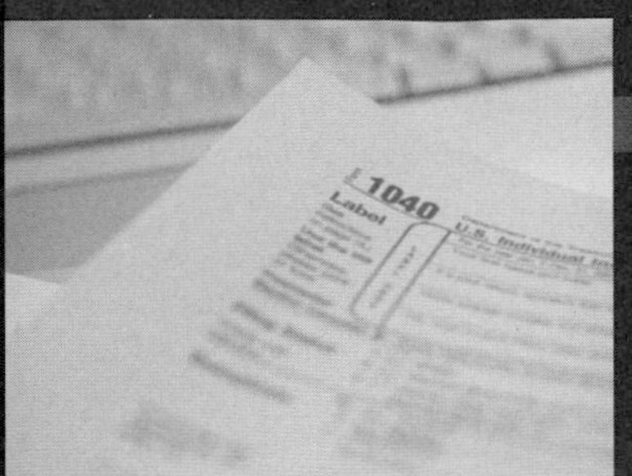

Appendix D-3

TABLE OF REVENUE PROCEDURES AND REVENUE RULINGS CITED

Revenue Procedures

Revenue Rulings

Revenue Rulings

Appendix E

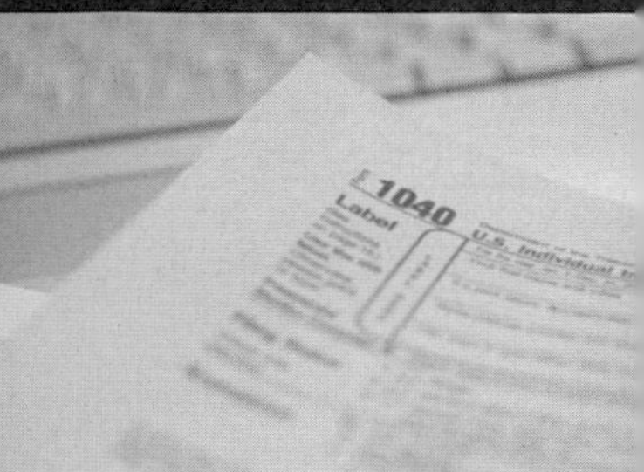

TABLE OF CASES CITED

T

U

V

W

Z

Index

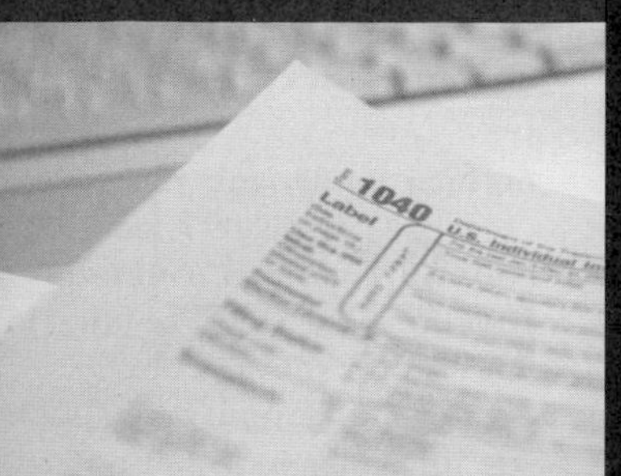

B

C

D

E

F

G

N

O

P

Q

R

S

T

U

V

W